GERMAN-ENGLISH ENGLISH-GERMAN

THE IDEAL COMPANION FOR ALL LEARNERS OF GERMAN

BBC

GERMAN

KU-618-265

WESTMINSTER AES
FRITH STREET CENTRE
19-20 FRITH STREET
LONDON W1V 5TS

LEARNER'S DICTIONARY

ISBN 0-563-40085-4

Published by BBC Books, a division of BBC Worldwide Ltd,
Woodlands, 80 Wood Lane, London W12 0TT
First published 1997

Printed and bound in Great Britain by Mackays of Chatham
Cover printed by Belmont Press Ltd, Northampton

Introduction

The BBC *German Learner's Dictionary* is the result of a collaboration between the BBC and the Larousse Language Reference team. It is aimed at all learners of German and can be used either independently or alongside the BBC's best-selling *Deutsch Plus* course.

Containing over 42,000 translations, the dictionary provides thorough coverage of everyday German and detailed coverage of GCSE word lists. There are also handy cultural notes throughout, giving a useful insight into German-speaking countries and their language and traditions.

Whether you are reading, writing, listening or speaking, the dictionary makes communication simpler as each word is clearly divided, where appropriate, into its different meanings and parts of speech, while there is essential guidance on German pronunciation.

Up-to-date and easy to use, this dictionary is the ideal companion for all learners, whether at school, at home or travelling abroad.

Abbreviations

Abkürzungen

accusative	A	Akkusativ
abbreviation	abk /abbr	Abkürzung
pejorative	abw	abwertend
adjective	adj	Adjektiv
adverb	adv	Adverb
American English	Am	amerikanisches Englisch
administrative, formal	amt	amtssprachlich, formell
anatomy	ANAT	Anatomie
automobile, cars	AUT(O)	Kfz-Technik
auxiliary	aux	Hilfsverb
British English	Br	britisches Englisch
commerce, business	COMM	Handel
comparative	compar	Komparativ
computers	COMPUT	Datenverarbeitung
conjunction	conj	Konjunktion
continuous	cont	Verlaufsform
culinary, cooking	CULIN	Kochkunst
dative	D	Dativ
determiner	det	Determinant
computers	EDV	Datenverarbeitung
	etw	etwas
exclamation	excl	Interjektion
feminine	f	Femininum
informal	fam	umgangssprachlich
figurative	fig	übertragene Bedeutung
finance, financial	FIN	Finanzen
formal	fml	gehoben
inseparable	fus	nicht trennbar

inseparable — shows that a phrasal verb is 'fused', i.e. inseparable, e.g. **look after** where the object cannot come between the verb and the particle, e.g. I *looked after him* but not **I looked him after*

nicht trennbar — zeigt an, daß ein englisches 'phrasal verb', das aus einem Verb und einer Partikel besteht, nicht trennbar ist, d. h. daß kein Objekt zwischen dem Verb und der Partikel stehen kann, z.B. I *looked after him*, aber nicht **I looked him after*

genitive	G	Genitiv
formal	geh	gehoben
generally	gen	generell
grammar	GRAMM	Grammatik
informal	inf	umgangssprachlich
exclamation	interj	Interjektion
invariable	inv	unveränderlich
someone (nominative)	jd	jemand
someone (dative)	jm	jemandem
someone (accusative)	jn	jemanden
someone (genitive)	js	jemandes

V

juridical, legal	JUR	Rechtswesen
comparative	*komp*	Komparativ
conjunction	*konj*	Konjunktion
culinary, cooking	KÜCHE	Kochkunst
mathematics	MATH	Mathematik
medicine	MED	Medizin
military	MIL	Militärwesen
music	MUS	Musik
nautical, maritime	NAVIG	Schiffahrt
northern German	*Norddt*	Norddeutsch
neuter noun (countries and towns) not used with an article	*nt*	Neutrum
numeral	*num*	Zahlwort
oneself	*o.s.*	
East German	*Ostdt*	Ostdeutsch
Austrian German	*Österr*	Österreichisch
pejorative	*pej*	abwertend
plural	*pl*	Plural
politics	POL	Politik
past participle	*pp*	Partizip Perfekt
preposition	*präp*	Präposition
present	*präs*	Präsens
preterite	*prät*	Präteritum
preposition	*prep*	Präposition
pronoun	*pron*	Pronomen
past tense	*pt*	Vergangenheitsform
registered trademark	®	Warenzeichen
reflexive verb	*ref*	reflexives Verb
religion	RELIG	Religion
someone, somebody	*sb*	
subject	*sbj*	Subjekt
school	SCHULE/SCH	Schule
Swiss German	*Schweiz*	Schweizerdeutsch
separable	*sep*	trennbar
– shows that a phrasal verb is separable, e.g. **let in**, **help out** where the object can come between the verb and the particle, e.g. I *let her in, he helped me out*		– zeigt an, daß ein englisches 'phrasal verb', das aus einem Verb und einer Partikel besteht, trennbar ist, d. h. daß ein Objekt zwischen dem Verb und der Partikel stehen kann, z.B. I *let her in, he helped me out*
singular	*sg*	Singular
something	*sthg*	
southern German	*Süddt*	Süddeutsch
superlative	*superl*	Superlativ
technology	TECH	Technik, Technologie
television	TV	Fernsehen

irregular	*unr*	unregelmäßig
verb	*v/vb*	Verb
intransitive verb	*vi*	intransitives Verb
impersonal verb	*vimp/v impers*	unpersönliches Verb
before noun	*vor Subst*	vor Substantiv
– indicates that the translation is always used directly before the noun which it modifies		– zeigt an, daß ein englisches Substantiv in adjektivischer Funktion ein deutsches Adjektiv übersetzt, wobei es unmittelbar vor dem Substantiv steht, das es bestimmt
transitive verb	*vt*	transitives Verb
vulgar	*vulg*	vulgär
cultural equivalent	≃	kulturelle Entsprechung
indicates separable German verb	I	Trennbarkeit des deutschen Verbs

English compounds

A compound is a word or expression which has a single meaning but is made up of more than one word, e.g. **point of view**, **kiss of life**, **virtual reality** and **West Indies.** It is a feature of this dictionary that English compounds appear in the A–Z list in strict alphabetical order. The compound **blood test** will therefore come after **bloodshot** which itself follows **blood pressure**.

Englische Komposita

Als Komposita werden aus mehreren Wörten bestehende Einheiten bezeichnet, die eine eigenständige Bedeutung haben, wie z.B. **point of view**, **kiss of life**, **virtual reality** und **West Indies.** Sie sind daher in diesem Wörterbuch als eigene Einträge alphabetisch eingeordnet; so folgt das Kompositum **blood test** dem Eintrag **bloodshot**, der seinerseits hinter **blood pressure** steht.

Trademarks

Words considered to be trademarks have been designated in this dictionary by the symbol ®. However, neither the presence nor the absence of such designation should be regarded as affecting the legal status of any trademark.

Warenzeichen

Als Warenzeichen geschützte Wörter sind in diesem Wörterbuch durch das Zeichen ® gekennzeichnet. Die Markierung mit diesem Symbol, oder sein Fehlen, hat keinen Einfluß auf die Rechtskräftigkeit eines Warenzeichens.

NOTES ON GERMAN

HINWEISE ZUM DEUTSCHE

Adjectives only used attributively

With German adjectives of this type, the feminine form is shown first, followed by the masculine and neuter endings, e.g. **letzte, -r, -s** (eine letzte Zigarette, ein letzter Kuß, ein letztes Mal).

Attributiv gebrauchte Adjektive

Adjektive dieser Art werden in ihrer femininen Form ange-geben, direkt gefolgt von den Endungen des Maskulinums und des Neutrums; z.B.: **letzte, -r, -s** (eine letzte Zigarette, ein letzter Kuß, ein letztes Mal).

Adjectives used as nouns

Nominalized German adjectives are, like all other nouns, labelled with the definite article. When used with an indefinite article, the ending of this type of noun changes according to the gender, e.g. **Angestellte der**, **die** becomes **ein Angestellter** and **eine Angestellte**.

Gender of compound nouns in translations

When a noun translation is accompanied by an adjective, the adjective ending indicates the gender of the noun. For example, the translation of **first class** is '**erste Klasse**', where the 'e' ending of the adjective shows that '**Klasse**' is feminine.

Substantivierte Adjektive

Die substantivierten Adjektive sind wie alle anderen Substantive mit dem bestimmten Artikel aufgeführt. In Verbin-dung mit einem unbestimmten Artikel verändert sich daher die Endung entsprechend des Genus; z.B.: **Angestellte der**, **die** wird zu **ein Angestellter** und **eine Angestellte**.

Genus der Substantive in zusammengesetzten Aus-drücken (als Übersetzungen)

Wenn das Substantiv von einem Adjektiv begleitet wird, trägt dieses den Genus des Substantives; z.B. zeigt die Übersetzung von **first class**, '**erste Klasse**', durch die feminine Endung des Adjektives an, daß das Wort **Klasse** ein Femininum ist.

Phonetic Transcription

English vowels

[ɑː] barn, car, laugh
[æ] pat, bag, mad
[ɒ] pot, log
[e] pet, tend
[ɜː] burn, learn, bird
[ə] mother, suppose
[iː] bean, weed
[ɪ] pit, big, rid
[ɔː] born, lawn
[uː] loop, loose
[ʌ] run, cut
[ʊ] put, full

English diphthongs

[aɪ] buy, light, aisle
[əʊ] now, shout, town
[eɪ] bay, late, great
[ɔɪ] boy, foil
[əʊ] no, road, blow
[ɪə] peer, fierce, idea
[eə] pair, bear, share
[ʊə] poor, sure, tour

Semi-vowels

| you, spaniel | [j] |
| wet, why, twin | [w] |

Consonants

bottle, bib	[b]
	[ç]
come, kitchen	[k]
dog, did	[d]
jet, fridge	[dʒ]
fib, physical	[f]
gag, great	[g]
how, perhaps	[h]
little, help	[l]
metal, comb	[m]
night, dinner	[n]
sung, parking	[ŋ]

Lautschrift

Deutsche Vokale

[a] Affe, Banane
[ɑː] Arzt, Antrag
[e] Beton
[eː] edel
[ɛ] echt, Händler
[ɛː] Rätsel, Dessert
[ə] Aktie
[iː] Vier
[i] Radio
[ɪ] Winter
[o] Melodie
[oː] apropos
[ɔ] sollen
[ø] Ökologisch
[øː] Öl
[œ] Köchin, Pumps
[u] Kuvert, aktuell
[uː] Kuh
[ʊ] Kunst
[y] Büchse, System
[yː] Tür

Deutsche Diphthonge

[aɪ] Deichsel
[əʊ] Auge
[ɔy] EuroCity

Deutsche Nasal

[ã] Chanson
[ãː] Abonnement
[ɛ̃] Pointe
[ɔ̃] Chanson

Halbvokale

Jubiläum
Hardware

Konsonanten

Baby
Chemie
Achse, Kaviar
Duett, Medien
Gin
Phantasie, Vier
Algerien, gut
Hobby
alphabetisch, Laser
Material, Alarm
November, Angabe
Singen

pop, **pe**o**p**le	[p]	**P**ony, Pa**pp**e
	[pf]	A**pf**el
right, car**r**y	[r]	**R**evue, **r**ot
seal, pea**c**e	[s]	**S**lalom, Sau**c**e
sheep, ma**ch**ine	[ʃ]	**St**adion, **Sch**ule
train, **t**ip	[t]	**T**oast, Vol**t**
	[ts]	Konversa**t**ion
chain, wret**ch**ed	[tʃ]	**Ch**ili
think, fif**th**	[θ]	
this, wi**th**	[ð]	
vine, li**v**id	[v]	**V**ase, **W**agen
	[x]	Ma**ch**t, la**ch**en
zip, hi**s**	[z]	**S**auce, **S**onne
u**s**ual, mea**s**ure	[ʒ]	E**t**age

The symbol ['] indicates that the following syllable carries primary stress and the symbol [,] that the following syllable carries secondary stress.

Der Hauptton eines englischen Wortes ist durch ein vorangestelltes ['] markiert, der Nebenton durch ein vorangestelltes [,].

The symbol [ʳ] in English phonetics indicates that the final 'r' is pronounced only when followed by a word beginning with a vowel. Note that it is nearly always pronounced in American English.

Das Zeichen [ʳ] zeigt in der englischen Phonetik an, daß der Endkonsonant 'r' ausgesprochen wird, wenn das folgende Wort mit einem Vokal beginnt. Im amerikanischen Englisch wird dieses 'r' so gut wie immer mitgesprochen.

German headwords have the stress marked either by a dot for a short stressed vowel (e.g. **Berg**) or by an underscore for a long stressed vowel (e.g. **Magen**).

Die Betonung der deutschen Stichwörter wird mit einem Punkt für einen kurzen betonten Vokal (z.B. **Berg**) und mit einem Strich für einen langen betonten Vokal (z.B. **Magen**) angegeben.

German Verbs

Infinitive	Present	Preterite	Perfect
beginnen	beginnt	begann	hat begonnen
beißen	beißt	biß	hat gebissen
bitten	bittet	bat	hat gebeten
bleiben	bleibt	blieb	ist geblieben
bringen	bringt	brachte	hat gebracht
denken	denkt	dachte	hat gedacht
dürfen	darf	durfte	hat gedurft/dürfen
essen	ißt	aß	hat gegessen
fahren	fährt	fuhr	hat/ist gefahren
finden	findet	fand	hat gefunden
fliegen	fliegt	flog	hat/ist geflogen
fließen	fließt	floß	ist geflossen
geben	gibt	gab	hat gegeben
gehen	geht	ging	ist gegangen
gelten	gilt	galt	hat gegolten
geschehen	geschieht	geschah	ist geschehen
gießen	gießt	goß	hat gegossen
greifen	greift	griff	hat gegriffen
haben	hat	hatte	hat gehabt
halten	hält	hielt	hat gehalten
heben	hebt	hob	hat gehoben
heißen	heißt	hieß	hat geheißen
helfen	hilft	half	hat geholfen
kennen	kennt	kannte	hat gekannt
kommen	kommt	kam	ist gekommen
können	kann	konnte	hat können/gekonnt
lassen	läßt	ließ	hat gelassen/lassen
laufen	läuft	lief	hat/ist gelaufen
leihen	leiht	lieh	hat geliehen
lesen	liest	las	hat gelesen
liegen	liegt	lag	hat gelegen
lügen	lügt	log	hat gelogen
messen	mißt	maß	hat gemessen
mögen	mag	mochte	hat gemocht/mögen
müssen	muß	mußte	hat gemußt/müssen
nehmen	nimmt	nahm	hat genommen
nennen	nennt	nannte	hat genannt
raten	rät	riet	hat geraten
reißen	reißt	riß	hat/ist gerissen
rennen	rennt	rannte	ist gerannt
riechen	riecht	roch	hat gerochen
rufen	ruft	rief	hat gerufen

schieben	schiebt	schob	hat geschoben
schießen	schießt	schoß	hat/ist geschossen
schlafen	schläft	schlief	hat geschlafen
schlagen	schlägt	schlug	hat/ist geschlagen
schließen	schließt	schloß	hat geschlossen
schneiden	schneidet	schnitt	hat geschnitten
schreiben	schreibt	schrieb	hat geschrieben
schreien	schreit	schrie	hat geschrie(e)n
schwimmen	schwimmt	schwamm	hat/ist geschwommen
sehen	sieht	sah	hat gesehen
sein	ist	war	ist gewesen
singen	singt	sang	hat gesungen
sitzen	sitzt	saß	hat gesessen
sprechen	spricht	sprach	hat gesprochen
springen	springt	sprang	hat/ist gesprungen
stehen	steht	stand	hat gestanden
stehlen	stiehlt	stahl	hat gestohlen
sterben	stirbt	starb	ist gestorben
stoßen	stößt	stieß	hat/ist gestoßen
streiten	streitet	stritt	hat gestritten
tragen	trägt	trug	hat getragen
treffen	trifft	traf	hat getroffen
treten	tritt	trat	hat getreten
trinken	trinkt	trank	hat getrunken
tun	tut	tat	hat getan
verlieren	verliert	verlor	hat verloren
waschen	wäscht	wusch	hat gewaschen
werden	wird	wurde	ist geworden/worden
werfen	wirft	warf	hat geworfen
wissen	weiß	wußte	hat gewußt
wollen	will	wollte	hat gewollt/wollen

Numbers

Cardinal numbers are used for counting. The most important ones are:

0 null	12 zwölf	30 dreißig
1 eins	13 dreizehn	40 vierzig
2 zwei	14 vierzehn	50 fünfzig
3 drei	15 fünfzehn	60 sechzig
4 vier	16 sechzehn	70 siebzig
5 fünf	17 siebzehn	80 achtzig
6 sechs	18 achtzehn	90 neunzig
7 sieben	19 neunzehn	100 hundert
8 acht	20 zwanzig	101 hunderteins
9 neun	21 einundzwanzig	102 hundertzwei
10 zehn	22 zweiundzwanzig	150 hundertfünfzig
11 elf	23 dreiundzwanzig	200 zweihundert

1 000	(ein)tausend	1 000 000	eine Million
1 001	tausendeins	2 000 000	zwei Millionen
2 000	zweitausend	1 000 000 000	eine Milliarde
100 000	hunderttausend	2 000 000 000	zwei Milliarden

NOTES:
- both **Million** and **Milliarde** have a plural form (**Millionen, Milliarden**) which is used after a plural number: **drei Millionen Arbeitslose**, **neun Milliarden Mark**.
- if the number **one** is used before a noun it behaves like the indefinite article: **ein Tag**, **eine Woche** (see dictionary entry for **ein**).

Contrary to English usage, German uses a comma to mark the decimal part of a number: **6,5** (**sechs Komma fünf** = 6 point 5). In decimals such as 0.8, German must start with **null** (**null Komma acht**); 0 cannot be omitted as it is in English (point 8).

Numbers of four digits and above (**2.000**, **10.321**) may be written with a full stop before the last three digits, whereas English uses a comma.

Ordinal numbers are used for putting things in order. They are:

1st	erste(r/s)	9th	neunte(r/s)	17th	siebzehnte(r/s)
2nd	zweite(r/s)	10th	zehnte(r/s)	18th	achtzehnte(r/s)
3rd	dritte(r/s)	11th	elfte(r/s)	19th	neunzehnte(r/s)
4th	vierte(r/s)	12th	zwölfte(r/s)	20th	zwanzigste(r/s)
5th	fünfte(r/s)	13th	dreizehnte(r/s)	21st	einundzwanzigste(r/s)
6th	sechste(r/s)	14th	vierzehnte(r/s)	30th	dreißigste(r/s)
7th	siebte(r/s)	15th	fünfzehnte(r/s)	40th	vierzigste(r/s)
8th	achte(r/s)	16th	sechzehnte(r/s)		*etc*

NOTE:
– to form ordinal numbers from 20 upwards, **-ste(r/s)** is added to the cardinal
   number: **hundertste(r/s)**, **tausendste(r/s)**.

Like adjectives, the ordinal numbers agree with the noun they precede (**mein
zweiter Versuch**), unless the number is used with the definite article (**das
erste Mal**, **der fünfte Mann**).

For more information on numbers, look at the entries for **sechs** and **sechste** on
the German-English side of your dictionary, and at the entries for **six** and **sixth**
on the English-German side.

Dates

The most usual ways of asking the date are: **den wievielten haben wir
heute?**, **der wievielte ist heute?** or **welches Datum ist heute?** The reply will
follow the pattern **es ist der sechste Juli** or **wir haben den sechsten Juli**.

To say the year in German: 1997, for example, is **neunzehnhundertsieben-
undneunzig**.

The days of the week are:

Monday	**Montag**
Tuesday	**Dienstag**
Wednesday	**Mittwoch**
Thursday	**Donnerstag**
Friday	**Freitag**
Saturday	**Samstag**
Sunday	**Sonntag**

The months of the year are:

January	**Januar**
February	**Februar**
March	**März**
April	**April**
May	**Mai**
June	**Juni**
July	**Juli**
August	**August**
September	**September**
October	**Oktober**
November	**November**
December	**Dezember**

As in English, the days of the week and the months of the year start with a
capital letter in German, and the ordinal numbers are used to express the
date.

For more information on days and months, look at the entries for **Samstag**
and **September** on the German-English side of your dictionary, and at
Saturday and **September** on the English-German side.

The Time

The most usual ways of asking the time are: **wieviel Uhr ist es?** or **wie spät ist es?** Here are some possible answers:

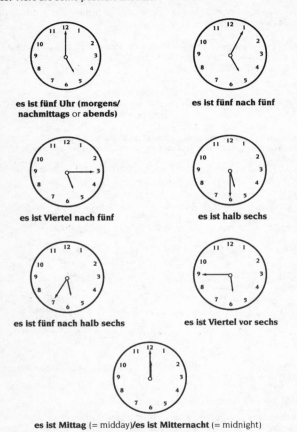

**es ist fünf Uhr (morgens/
nachmittags** or **abends)**

es ist fünf nach fünf

es ist Viertel nach fünf

es ist halb sechs

es ist fünf nach halb sechs

es ist Viertel vor sechs

es ist Mittag (= midday)/**es ist Mitternacht** (= midnight)

Note that in German half past five is expressed as 'half six': **halb sechs**.

In German you may also find times expressed using the 24-hour clock: **der Zug um vierzehn Uhr zwanzig**, for example, would leave at 2.20 p.m.

The Reform of German Spelling

A reform has been introduced to simplify and standardize German spelling by reducing the number of exceptions to rules, increasing the number of general rules and providing alternative spellings. Although the reform has not been incorporated into the dictionary, we have included below a summary of the changes it has brought about.

Some of the new rules you will notice and might want to use:

ss or β

- Short vowels will be followed by **ss**, e.g. Flu**β** → Flu**ss**
- Long vowels and diphthongs will be followed by **β**, e.g. Stra**β**e, Wei**β**
- The conjunction 'da**β**' becomes 'da**ss**', but 'da**s**' remains the same

Written separately

- Adjectives combined with **so-**, **wie-** and **zu-** will be written as two words, e.g. **soviel → so viel**
- Nouns combined with verbs will be written as two words, e.g. **radfahren → Rad fahren**
- Verbs composed of two verbs or an adverb and a verb will be written as two words, e.g. **kennenlernen → kennen lernen**
- Verbs constructed with **einander** will be written as two words, e.g. **auseinandergehen → auseinander gehen**

Small or capital letters

- Languages preceded by a preposition will take a capital, e.g. **auf deutsch → auf Deutsch**
- Nouns combined with a verb will take a capital, e.g. **haltmachen → Halt machen**
- A time of the day combined with **heute**, **gestern** or **morgen** will take a capital, e.g. **gestern abend → gestern Abend**
- Words preceded by an article or a preposition and article will take a capital, e.g. **das letzte → das Letzte** and **im allgemeinen → im Allgemeinen**
- Pronouns and adjectives used as familiar forms of address in correspondence will take a small letter, e.g. **Wie geht es Dir? → Wie geht es dir?**

Some of the new rules you might want to know about:

Word-stems

- Consonants after a short vowel will be doubled, e.g. **numerieren → nummerieren**

Foreign words

- For words of foreign origin two spelling options have been created by allowing certain letters, in certain instances, to replace others. It is possible to replace **gh** with **g**, **ph** with **f**, **th** with **t**, and **t** with **z**, e.g. **Joghurt** or **Jogurt**, **graphisch** or **grafisch**, **Panther** or **Panter**, **Potential** or **Potenzial**.

à *präp* (+A) at; **15 Stück ~ 2,95 DM** 15, at 2.95 marks each.

A (*pl -*) *die* (*abk für Autobahn*) M (Br), I (Am).

ab ♦ *präp* (+D) **1.** (*zeitlich*) from; **~ 8 Uhr** from 8 o'clock; **~ 18** (**Jahren**) over (the age of) 18. **2.** (*räumlich*) from; **~ Dortmund 12.35 Uhr** leaving Dortmund at 12.35. ♦ *adv* (*los, weg*) off; **~ ins Bett!** off you go to bed! ▶ **ab und zu** *adv* now and then.

Abb. *abk* = **Abbildung**.

ab|bestellen *vt* to cancel.

ab|biegen *vi unr ist* (*mit Auto*) to turn off; **nach rechts/links ~** to turn right/left.

Abbiegespur (*pl -en*) *die* filter lane.

ab|bilden *vt* to illustrate.

Abbildung (*pl -en*) *die* illustration.

ab|blenden *vi* to dip one's headlights (Br), to dim one's headlights (Am).

Abblendlicht *das* dipped headlights (Br) (*pl*), dimmed headlights (Am) (*pl*).

ab|brechen ♦ *vt unr hat* to break off. ♦ *vi unr ist* to break off; (*aufhören*) to stop.

ab|buchen *vt* to debit.

ab|dichten *vt* (*gegen kalte Luft*) to insulate; (*gegen Wasser*) to waterproof.

Abdichtung *die* (*gegen kalte Luft*) insulation; (*gegen Wasser*) waterproofing.

abend *adv*: **heute/gestern/morgen ~** this/yesterday/tomorrow evening.

Abend (*pl -e*) *der* evening; **Guten ~!** good evening!; **am ~** in the evening; **zu ~ essen** to have one's evening meal.

Abendbrot *das* evening meal.

Abendessen (*pl -*) *das* evening meal.

Abendgarderobe (*pl -n*) *die* evening dress.

Abendgymnasium (*pl -gymnasien*) *das* adult education college.

Abendkasse (*pl -n*) *die* box office (*open just before performance*).

Abendmahl (*pl -e*) *das* Holy Communion.

abends *adv* in the evening; **spät ~** late in the evening.

Abendschule (*pl -n*) *die* adult education college.

Abenteuer (*pl -*) *das* adventure.

Abenteuerurlaub (*pl -e*) *der* adventure holiday.

aber ♦ *konj* but. ♦ *adv*: **jetzt ist ~ Schluß!** that's enough now!; **das ist ~ nett!** how nice!; **~ gerne!** of course!; **du kommst ~ spät!** you're a bit late, aren't you?; **~ bitte!** go ahead!

Aberglaube *der* superstition.

abergläubisch *adj* superstitious.

ab|fahren ♦ *vi unr ist* to leave; (*von Autobahn*) to turn off. **♦** *vt unr hat* (*Reifen*) to wear down; (*Weg, Strecke*) to drive along.

Abfahrt (*pl* **-en**) *die* (*von Zug, Bus*) departure; (*von Autobahn*) exit; (*von Skifahrer*) descent.

Abfahrtslauf (*pl* **-läufe**) *der* downhill racing.

Abfall (*pl* **Abfälle**) *der* (*Müll*) rubbish (*Br*), garbage (*Am*).

Abfalleimer (*pl* **-**) *der* rubbish bin (*Br*), garbage can (*Am*).

ab|fallen *vi unr ist* (*Straße*) to dip; (*Obst, Blätter*) to fall.

ab|färben *vi* (*Material*) to run.

Abfertigungsschalter (*pl* **-**) *der* check-in desk.

ab|fliegen *vi unr ist* (*Flugzeug*) to depart; (*Person*) to fly.

Abflug (*pl* **-flüge**) *der* departure.

Abflughalle (*pl* **-n**) *die* departure lounge.

Abflugzeit (*pl* **-en**) *die* departure time.

Abfluß (*pl* **-flüsse**) *der* (*im Waschbecken*) plughole.

Abführmittel (*pl* **-**) *das* laxative.

Abgase *pl* exhaust fumes.

ab|geben *vt unr* (*einreichen*) to hand in; (*übergeben*) to hand over; (*an der Garderobe*) to leave; (*verkaufen*) to sell; (*Wärme, Feuchtigkeit*) to give off; (*Erklärung, Urteil*) to make; **jm etw ~** to give sb sthg.

abgebildet *adj*: **wie ~** as illustrated.

abgekocht *adj* boiled.

abgelaufen *adj* (*Paß*) expired; (*Zeit*) up, over.

abgemacht *adj* fixed.

abgenutzt *adj* worn out.

abgepackt *adj* packed.

abgeschlossen ♦ *pp* → **abschließen**. **♦** *adj*: **~e Berufsausbildung** *German vocational qualification obtained after three years' study on a day-release basis.*

ab|gewöhnen *vt*: **sich** (D) **etw ~** to give sthg up.

abgezählt *adj* (*Kleingeld*) correct, exact.

abhaken *vt* to tick off.

Abhang (*pl* **-hänge**) *der* slope.

ab|hängen ♦ *vt* (*Anhänger*) to unhitch; (*Verfolger*) to shake off. **♦** *vi*: **~ von** to depend on; **das hängt davon ab, ob ...** that depends on whether ...

abhängig *adj* (*süchtig*) addicted; **~ sein von** (*von Hilfe*) to be dependent on; (*von Bedingungen*) to depend on.

ab|heben ♦ *vt unr* (*Hörer*) to pick up; (*Geld*) to withdraw. **♦** *vi unr* (*Flugzeug*) to take off.

ab|heften *vt* to file.

ab|holen *vt* to collect.

Abitur *das* = A levels (*Br*), = SATs (*Am*).

ABITUR

The 'Abitur' is the series of exams taken by approximately a third of German pupils at the end of their school career and is a requirement if they wish to go on to university. Pupils select one main subject and a number of optional subjects. Each of the 'Bundesländer' administers its own examinations.

ab|klappern *vt* to search.

Abkommen (*pl* **-**) *das* agreement.

ab|kühlen ♦ *vi ist* to cool down. **♦** *vimp*: **es kühlt ab** (*Wetter*) it's getting cooler.

ab|kürzen *vt* (*Wort*) to abbreviate; **den Weg ~** to take a short cut.

Abkürzung (*pl* **-en**) *die* (*von Strecke*) short cut; (*von Wort*) abbreviation.

ab|legen ♦ *vt* (*Mantel*) to take off; (*Gewohnheit, Charakterzug*) to get rid of; (*Prüfung*) to take; (*Akten*) to file. **♦** *vi* (*Schiff*) to cast off; (*Person*) to take off one's coat/jacket.

ab|lehnen *vt* (*Vorschlag, Bitte*) to reject; (*Geschenk, Einladung*) to refuse; (Person, Ansicht) to disapprove of.

ab|lenken vt to distract.

ab|lesen vt (Temperatur, Kilometerstand) to read; (Text) to read out.

ab|liefern vt to deliver.

ab|lösen vt (Etikett, Pflaster) to peel off; (Person) to take over from. ▶ **sich ablösen** ref (Personen) to take turns; (Tapete, Etikett) to come off.

ab|machen vt (entfernen) to remove; (vereinbaren) to agree on, to fix; **mit jm einen Termin ~** to make an appointment with sb.

ab|melden vt (Telefon) to have disconnected; (Auto) to take off the road; (Person) to cancel the membership of. ▶ **sich abmelden** ref (bei der Polizei) to give notice that one is moving away.

ab|nehmen ◆ vt unr (Bild, Wäsche) to take down; (Brille, Hut) to take off; (Hörer) to pick up; (Fahrzeug, Maschine) to inspect; (amputieren) to amputate; (Blut) to take. ◆ vi unr (Anzahl) to decrease; (an Gewicht) to lose weight; **jm etw ~** (Arbeit, Last) to relieve sb of sthg; (fam: glauben) to buy sthg from sb; (abkaufen) to buy sthg from sb; **fünf Kilo ~** to lose five kilos.

Abonnement (pl -s) das (für Zeitung) subscription; (im Theater) season ticket.

abonnieren vt to subscribe to.

ab|raten vi unr (+D): **(jm) von etw ~** to advise (sb) against sthg.

ab|räumen vt (Tisch) to clear; (Geschirr) to clear away.

ab|reagieren vt (Wut) to take out. ▶ **sich abreagieren** ref: **sich an jm ~** to take it out on sb.

ab|rechnen ◆ vi (mit Rechnung) to settle up; (fam: sich rächen) to get even. ◆ vt (subtrahieren) to deduct.

Abrechnung (pl -en) die: **die ~ machen** to do the accounts.

ab|reiben vt unr (Fläche, Gegenstand) to rub clean; (Schmutz) to rub off.

Abreise die departure.

ab|reisen vi to depart.

ab|reißen ◆ vt unr hat (Pflaster, Zettel) to tear off; (Haus) to tear down. ◆ vi unr ist (Seil) to break; (Verbindung) to end.

ab|richten vt to train (an animal).

ab|runden vt (Zahl) to round down; (Kante, Ecke) to round off.

abrupt ◆ adj abrupt. ◆ adv abruptly.

Abs. abk = **Absender, Absatz**.

ab|sagen vt & vi to cancel; **jm ~** to tell sb one can't come.

Absatz der (vom Schuh) heel; (im Text) paragraph.

ab|schalten vt & vi to switch off.

abscheulich adj disgusting.

ab|schicken vt to post.

ab|schieben vt unr (Flüchtling) to deport.

Abschied (pl -e) der parting.

Abschleppdienst (pl -e) der (vehicle) recovery service.

ab|schleppen vt (Auto) to tow away; (fam: aus Disco, von Party) to pick up.

Abschleppseil (pl -e) das tow-rope.

Abschleppwagen (pl -) der recovery vehicle.

abschließbar adj (Schrank) lockable.

ab|schließen ◆ vt unr (Tür, Wohnung) to lock; (beenden) to complete; (Vertrag) to conclude; (von Außenwelt) to cut off. ◆ vi to lock up.

ab|schmecken vt to season (according to taste).

ab|schminken vt to remove the make-up from. ▶ **sich abschminken** ref to remove one's make-up.

ab|schneiden ◆ vt unr to cut off. ◆ vi unr: **gut/schlecht ~** to do well/badly; **jm/sich (D) etw ~** to cut sthg off for sb/o.s.

Abschnitt (pl -e) der (von Eintrittskarte, Ticket) stub; (im Text; von

Strecke) section; (Zeitraum) period.

ab|schrauben vt to unscrew.

absehbar adj foreseeable; **in ~er Zeit** in the foreseeable future.

abseits adv (SPORT) offside; **~ stehen** (entfernt) to stand a little way away.

Absender (pl -) der (auf Brief) sender's name and address; (Person) sender.

ab|setzen vt (Hut, Brille, Theaterstück) to take off; (Tasche, Glas) to put down; (Mitfahrer) to drop off; (Medikament) to come off; (von der Steuer) to deduct. ► **sich absetzen** ref (Kalk, Schlamm) to be deposited, to build up; (fam: fliehen) to take off.

ab|sichern vt to make safe. ► **sich absichern** ref to cover o.s.

Absicht (pl -en) die intention; **mit ~** intentionally, on purpose.

absichtlich ◆ adj intentional. ◆ adv intentionally, on purpose.

absolut ◆ adj absolute. ◆ adv completely.

ab|sperren ◆ vt (Straße) to block off; (Tür, Wohnung) to lock. ◆ vi to lock up.

Absperrung (pl -en) die barrier.

ab|sprechen vt unr to agree on; **~ mit** to arrange with. ► **sich absprechen** ref to come to an agreement.

Abstand (pl -stände) der (räumlich) distance; (zeitlich) interval; (innere Distanz) reserve; **mit ~** by far; **~ halten** to keep one's distance.

Abstecher (pl -) der detour; **einen ~ machen** to make a detour.

ab|stellen vt (Gerät) to turn off; (Fahrrad, Auto) to put; (Tasche, Tablett) to put down; (Mißstand, Problem) to put an end to.

Abstellraum (pl -räume) der storage room.

Abstieg der (ins Tal) descent; (SPORT) relegation.

ab|stimmen ◆ vi to vote. ◆ vt: **etw auf etw** (+A) **~** to adapt sthg to sthg; **~ über** (+A) to vote on.

Abstimmung (pl -en) die (Wahl) ballot.

abstrakt adj abstract.

ab|streiten vt unr to deny.

ab|stürzen vi ist to crash.

absurd adj absurd.

Abt. (abk für Abteilung) dept.

Abtei (pl -en) die abbey.

Abteil (pl -e) das compartment.

Abteilung (pl -en) die (in Firma, Kaufhaus) department.

Abtreibung (pl -en) die abortion.

ab|trocknen vt to dry; **sich** (D) **die Hände ~** to dry one's hands. ► **sich abtrocknen** ref to dry o.s.

abwärts adv downwards.

Abwasch der washing-up.

ab|waschen ◆ vt unr (Geschirr, Kacheln) to wash; (Schmutz) to wash off. ◆ vi unr to wash up (Br), to wash the dishes (Am).

Abwasser (pl -wässer) das (häuslich) sewage; (industriell) effluent.

ab|wechseln: sich abwechseln ref (Personen) to take turns; (Zustände, Landschaften) to alternate.

abwechselnd adv alternately.

Abwechslung die change.

abweisend adj unfriendly.

ab|werten vt (Person, Idee) to belittle; (Währung) to devalue.

Abwertung (pl -en) die (von Währung) devaluation.

abwesend ◆ adj absent. ◆ adv absently.

ab|wickeln vt (Schnur) to unwind.

ab|wischen vt (Tisch) to wipe; (Schmutz) to wipe off.

Abzeichen (pl -) das badge.

ab|ziehen ◆ vt unr (Hülle) to take off; (Bett) to strip; (Stimme, Anzahl) to take away; (kopieren) to copy; (Foto) to print. ◆ vi unr (Rauch) to clear; (fam: weggehen) to clear off.

Abzug (pl -züge) der (Foto) print.

abzüglich präp (+G) minus; **~ 15% Skonto** less a 15% discount.

Abzweigung (pl -en) die turning.

ach *interj* oh!; **ach ja!** oh, yes!; **ach je!** oh dear!; **ach so!** (oh,) I see!

Achse (*pl* **-n**) *die* (AUTO) axle.

Achsel (*pl* **-n**) *die* armpit.

acht *num* eight, → **sechs**.

achte, -r, -s *adj* eighth, → **sechste**.

Achtel (*pl* **-**) *das* eighth.

achten ♦ *vt* to respect. ♦ *vi*: ~ **auf** (+A) (*sich konzentrieren auf*) to pay attention to; (*aufpassen auf*) to look after.

Achterbahn (*pl* **-en**) *die* roller coaster.

achtlgeben *vi unr* to take care.

Achtung ♦ *die* (*Respekt*) respect. ♦ *interj* look out!; **alle ~!** well done!

achtzehn *num* eighteen, → **sechs**.

achtzig *num* eighty, → **sechs**.

Acker (*pl* **Äcker**) *der* field.

ADAC *der* ≃ AA (Br), ≃ AAA (Am).

Adapter (*pl* **-**) *der* adapter.

addieren *vt & vi* to add.

ade *interj* cheerio!

Ader (*pl* **-n**) *die* vein.

Adler (*pl* **-**) *der* eagle.

adoptieren *vt* to adopt.

Adoptivkind (*pl* **-er**) *das* adopted child.

Adreßbuch (*pl* **-bücher**) *das* (*persönlich*) address book; (*von Stadt*) (local address) directory.

Adresse (*pl* **-n**) *die* address.

Advent *der* Advent.

ADVENT

Advent, the four weeks preceding Christmas, has a special significance in Germany and many traditions are associated with this time of year. Streets and houses are decorated and Christmas fairs are held. In the home it is traditional to hang up Advent wreaths with four candles, one of which is lit each Sunday of Advent, and to bake special Christmas biscuits.

Adventskranz (*pl* **-kränze**) *der* Advent wreath.

Adventszeit *die* Advent.

Aerobic *das* aerobics (*sg*).

Affäre (*pl* **-n**) *die* affair.

Affe (*pl* **-n**) *der* (*klein*) monkey; (*groß*) ape.

Afrika *nt* Africa.

Afrikaner, -in (*mpl* **-**) *der, die* African.

afrikanisch *adj* African.

After (*pl* **-**) *der* anus.

AG (*pl* **-s**) *die* ≃ plc (Br), ≃ corp. (Am).

aggressiv ♦ *adj* aggressive. ♦ *adv* aggressively.

Ägypten *nt* Egypt.

ah *interj* oh!; ~ **so!** (oh,) I see!; ~ **ja!** (oh,) I see!

ähneln *vi* (+D) to be similar to, to be like.

ähnlich ♦ *adj* similar. ♦ *adv* similarly; **jm/etw ~ sein** to be similar to sb/sthg; **jm/etw ~ sehen** to look like sb/sthg.

Ähnlichkeit (*pl* **-en**) *die* similarity.

Ahnung (*pl* **-en**) *die* (*Vorgefühl*) feeling; **keine ~!** no idea!

ahnungslos ♦ *adj* unsuspecting. ♦ *adv* unsuspectingly.

Aids *nt* AIDS.

Aids-Handschuh (*pl* **-e**) *der* surgical glove.

Airbag (*pl* **-s**) *der* airbag.

Akkordeon (*pl* **-s**) *das* accordion.

Akku (*pl* **-s**) *der* (rechargeable) battery.

Akkusativ (*pl* **-e**) *der* accusative (case).

Akne *die* acne.

Akt (*pl* **-e**) *der* (*Handlung, von Drama*) act; (*Bild*) nude; (*Zeremonie*) ceremony.

Akte (*pl* **-n**) *die* file.

Aktenkoffer (*pl* **-**) *der* attaché case.

Aktie (*pl* **-n**) *die* share.

Aktiengesellschaft (*pl* **-en**) *die* public limited company (Br), corporation (Am).

aktiv ♦ *adj* active. ♦ *adv* actively.

Aktivität (*pl* **-en**) *die* activity.

aktuell *adj* (*modisch*) fashionable; (*Thema, Problem*) current; (*Theaterstück, Buch*) topical.

Akustik *die* acoustics (*pl*).

Akzent (*pl* **-e**) *der* accent.

akzeptieren *vt* to accept.

Alarm *der* alarm; **~ schlagen** to raise the alarm.

Alarmanlage (*pl* **-n**) *die* (*von Gebäude*) burglar alarm; (*von Auto*) car alarm.

albern ♦ *adj* silly. ♦ *adv* in a silly way.

alias *adv* alias.

Alkohol *der* alcohol.

alkoholarm *adj* low-alcohol.

alkoholfrei *adj* alcohol-free.

Alkoholiker, -in (*mpl* **-**) *der, die* alcoholic.

alkoholisch *adj* alcoholic.

alkoholkrank *adj* alcoholic.

all *det* all (of); **~ das Warten hat mich müde gemacht** all this waiting has made me tired.

All *das* space.

alle, -r, -s ♦ *det* 1. (*sämtliche*) all; **~ Kleider** all the clothes; **~ beide** both; **~s Gute!** all the best! 2. (*völlig*) all; **in ~r Ruhe** in peace. 3. (*jede*) all; **Getränke ~r Art** all kinds of drinks. 4. (*im Abstand von*) every; **~ 50 Meter** every 50 metres; **~ zwei Wochen** every two weeks. ♦ *pron* all; **das ist ~s** that's all; **~ sind da** everyone's here; **trotz ~m** in spite of everything; **vor ~m** above all. ♦ *adj* (*fam*) **die Butter ist ~** there's no more butter.

Allee (*pl* **-n**) *die* avenue.

allein ♦ *adj* (*ohne andere*) alone; (*einsam*) lonely. ♦ *adv* (*ohne andere*) alone; (*einsam*) alone; (*selbständig*) on one's own; (*nur*) only; **von ~** by oneself/itself etc.

alleinerziehend *adj* single (*parent*).

Alleingang (*pl* **-gänge**) *der* single-handed effort; **im ~** single-handedly.

alleinstehend *adj* (*Person*) single; (*Haus*) detached.

allemal *adv* (*sicher*) definitely.

allenfalls *adv* at most.

allerdings *adv* (*aber*) though; (*ja*) certainly.

allererste, -r, -s *adj* very first.

Allergie (*pl* **-n**) *die* (MED) allergy.

allergisch ♦ *adj* allergic. ♦ *adv* allergically; **~ gegen** (+A) allergic to.

allerhand *pron* all sorts of things.

Allerheiligen *nt* All Saints' Day.

alles *pron* → **alle**.

Alleskleber (*pl* **-**) *der* all-purpose glue.

allgemein ♦ *adj* (*allen gemeinsam, unspezifisch*) general; (*alle betreffend*) universal. ♦ *adv* generally; **im ~en** in general.

alljährlich ♦ *adj* annual. ♦ *adv* annually.

allmählich ♦ *adj* gradual. ♦ *adv* gradually.

Alltag *der* (*Normalität*) everyday life.

alltäglich *adj* everyday.

allzu *adv* far too.

allzusehr *adv* far too much.

allzuviel *adv* far too much.

Allzweckreiniger (*pl* **-**) *der* multi-purpose cleaner.

Alm (*pl* **-en**) *die* mountain pasture.

Alpen *pl*: **die ~** the Alps.

Alpenverein *der* organization which promotes study of the Alps and organizes mountain hikes etc.

Alpenvorland *das* foothills of the Alps.

alphabetisch ♦ *adj* alphabetical. ♦ *adv* alphabetically.

alpin *adj* alpine.

Alptraum (*pl* **-träume**) *der* nightmare.

als *konj* 1. (*zeitlich*) when; (*während*) as; **~ es dunkel wurde** when it got dark; **erst ~** only when. 2. (*vergleichend*) than; **sie ist besser ~ ihr Bruder** she is better than her brother; **der Wein ist besser, ~ ich dachte** the wine is better than I thought it would be; **mehr ~** more than. **3.** (*Angabe von Vermutung*) as if; **~ ob** as if; **es sieht so aus, ~ würde es bald regnen** it looks like it's going to rain soon. **4.** (*Angabe von Urteil, Zweck*) as; **ich verstehe es ~ Kompliment** I take it as a compliment. **5.** (*Angabe von Identität*) as; **~ Kind** as a child.

also ◆ *interj* well. ◆ *konj* (*das heißt*) in other words; (*demnach*) so. ◆ *adv* (*demnach*) so; **~ dann** all right then; **~ nein!** no!

Alsterwasser (*pl* -) *das* shandy.

alt (*komp* **älter,** *superl* **am ältesten**) *adj* old; **wie ~ bist du?** how old are you?; **zwei Jahre älter** two years older; **12 Jahre ~** 12 years old.

Alt¹ (*pl* -) *das* (*Bier*) *type of dark, German beer.*

Alt² (*pl* -e) *der* (MUS) alto.

Altar (*pl* Altäre) *der* altar.

Altbier (*pl* -) *das type of dark, German beer.*

Altenheim (*pl* -e) *das* old people's home.

Alter *das* (*Lebensalter*) age; (*hohes Alter*) old age; **im ~ von** at the age of.

alternativ *adj* alternative.

Alternative (*pl* -n) *die* alternative.

Altersgrenze (*pl* -n) *die* (*allgemein*) age limit; (*für Rente*) retirement age.

Altglas *das* glass for recycling.

Altglascontainer (*pl* -) *der* bottle bank.

Altkleidercontainer (*pl* -) *der recycling bank for old clothes.*

altmodisch *adj* old-fashioned.

Altpapier *das* paper for recycling; **aus ~** made from recycled paper.

Altpapiercontainer (*pl* -) *der* paper bank.

Altstadt *die* old town.

Alufolie *die* tinfoil.

Aluminium *das* aluminium.

am *präp* → **an dem**; **~ besten gehen wir zu Fuß** it would be best if we walked; **das gefällt mir ~ besten** I like

this one best; **wie kommt man ~ besten nach Köln?** what's the best way of getting to Cologne?; **~ Abend** in the evening; **~ Flughafen** at the airport; **~ Freitag** on Friday; **~ Meer** by the sea.

Amateur, -in (*mpl* -e) *der, die* amateur.

Ambulanz (*pl* -en) *die* (*Krankenwagen*) ambulance; (*im Krankenhaus*) outpatients (department).

Ameise (*pl* -n) *die* ant.

amen *interj* amen.

Amerika *nt* America.

Amerikaner, -in (*mpl* -) *der, die* American.

amerikanisch *adj* American.

Amerikanistik *die* American studies (*pl*).

Ampel (*pl* -n) *die* (*im Verkehr*) traffic lights (*pl*).

Amphitheater (*pl* -) *das* amphitheatre.

Amt (*pl* Ämter) *das* (*Behörde*) department; (*Gebäude, Posten*) office.

amtlich *adj* official.

amüsieren *vt* to amuse. ► **sich amüsieren** *ref* to amuse o.s.

Amüsierviertel (*pl* -) *das area with a lot of bars, restaurants etc.*

an ◆ *präp* (+A) **1.** (*räumlich*) to; **sich ~ den Tisch setzen** to sit down at the table; **etw ~ die Wand lehnen** to lean sthg against the wall; **~ Münster 13.45 Uhr** arriving at Münster at 13.45. **2.** (*mit Verb*): **~ jn/etw denken** to think about sb/sthg; **sich ~ jn/etw erinnern** to remember sb/sthg. **3.** (*fast*): **~ die 30 Grad** nearly 30 degrees. ◆ *präp* (+D) **1.** (*räumlich*) at; **am Tisch sitzen** to be sitting at the table; **am See** by the lake; **~ der Wand** on the wall; **~ der Hauptstraße** on the main road; **der Ort, ~ dem wir gepicknickt haben** the place where we had a picnic. **2.** (*zeitlich*) on; **am Freitag** on Friday; **~ diesem Tag** on that day. **3.** (*mit Hilfe von*) with; **am**

Analyse

Stock gehen to walk with a stick; **jn ~ der Stimme erkennen** to recognize sb by their voice. **4.** (*an einer Institution*) at; **Lehrer ~ einem Gymnasium** teacher at a grammar school. **5.** (*von*): **genug ~ Beweisen haben** to have enough proof. ♦ *adv* **1.** (*ein*) on; **Licht ~!** turn the light on!; **~-aus** on-off. **2.** (*ab*): **von jetzt ~** from now on; **von heute ~** from today.

Analyse (*pl* -n) *die* analysis.

analysieren *vt* to analyse.

Ananas (*pl* -) *die* pineapple.

Anbau¹ *der* (*von Pflanzen*) cultivation.

Anbau² (*pl* **-ten**) *der* (*Gebäude*) extension.

an|bauen *vt* (*Pflanzen*) to cultivate, to grow; (*Gebäudeteil*) to build on.

an|bieten *vt unr* to offer; **darf ich Ihnen etwas ~?** may I offer you something to eat/drink?

an|braten *vt unr* to brown.

an|brechen ♦ *vt unr* (*Packung*) to open. ♦ *vi unr* (*Tag*) to dawn; (*Nacht*) to fall.

an|brennen *vi unr* (*Speisen*) to burn; **etw ~ lassen** to burn sthg.

an|bringen *vt unr* (*Schild, Regal*) to fix, to attach; (*fam: mitbringen*) to bring home.

an|dauern *vi* to continue, to go on.

Andenken (*pl* -) *das* (*Souvenir*) souvenir; (*Erinnerung*) memory.

andere, -r, -s ♦ *adj* (*unterschiedlich*) different; (*weitere*) other. ♦ *pron*: **der/die/das ~** the other one; **die ~n** the others; **eine ~/ein ~r** (*Ding*) a different one; (*Person*) someone else; **etwas ~s** something else; **niemand ~s** nobody else; **ich habe noch zwei ~** I have two others; **unter ~m** among other things.

ändern *vt* to change; (*Kleid*) to alter. ▸ **sich ändern** *ref* to change.

anders ♦ *adj* different. ♦ *adv* (*andersartig*) differently; **wer/wo ~?** who/where else?; **~ als** differently from; **irgendwo ~** somewhere else;

jemand ~ someone else.

andersherum *adv* the other way round.

anderswo *adv* (*fam*) somewhere else.

anderthalb *num* one and a half.

Änderung (*pl* -en) *die* change; **~en vorbehalten** subject to alteration.

Änderungsschneiderei (*pl* -en) *die tailor's that does alterations.*

an|deuten *vt* to hint at.

Andorra *nt* Andorra.

aneinander *adv* (*drücken, befestigen*) together; (*grenzen, stoßen*) one another; **~ denken** to think about one another; **sich ~ gewöhnen** to get used to each other.

Anfahrt (*pl* -en) *die* journey there.

Anfang (*pl* -fänge) *der* beginning, start; **am ~** at the beginning; **~ Oktober** at the beginning of October.

an|fangen *vi unr* to begin, to start; **mit etw ~** to start sthg, to begin sthg.

Anfänger, -in (*mpl* -) *der, die* beginner.

Anfängerkurs (*pl* -e) *der* beginner's course.

anfangs *adv* at first.

an|fassen *vt* (*berühren*) to touch.

Anflug (*pl* -flüge) *der* (*von Flugzeug*) descent, approach.

an|fordern *vt* (*Hilfe, Gutachten*) to ask for; (*per Post*) to send off for.

Anforderung (*pl* -en) *die* (*Erwartung*) requirement; **hohe ~en** heavy demands.

Anfrage (*pl* -n) *die* (*amt*) enquiry.

an|fühlen: sich anfühlen *ref*: **sich weich/gut ~** to feel soft/good.

an|führen *vt* (*leiten*) to lead.

Anführungszeichen *pl* inverted commas; **in ~** in inverted commas.

Angabe (*pl* -n) *die* (*Information*) detail; **nähere ~n** further details; **technische ~n** specifications.

an|geben *vt unr* (*Namen, Quellen*) to give; (*Tempo, Ton*) to set.

angeblich ◆ *adj* alleged. ◆ *adv* allegedly.

angeboren *adj* innate.

Angebot (*pl* -e) *das* (*Anbieten*) offer; (*an Waren*) selection; (*Sonderangebot*) special offer; **im ~** on special offer.

an|gehen *vt unr*: **jn nichts ~** to be none of sb's business.

Angehörige (*pl* -n) *der, die* (*in Familie*) relative; (*von Firma, Gruppe*) member.

Angel (*pl* -n) *die* (*zum Fischen*) fishing rod.

Angelegenheit (*pl* -en) *die* matter, affair.

angeln ◆ *vt* (*fischen*) to catch. ◆ *vi* to fish.

Angelschein (*pl* -e) *der* fishing permit.

angenehm ◆ *adj* pleasant. ◆ *adv* pleasantly. ◆ *interj* pleased to meet you!

angesichts *präp* (+G) in view of.

angespannt *adj* (*Aufmerksamkeit*) close; (*konfliktgeladen*) tense.

Angestellte (*pl* -n) *der, die* employee.

angestrengt ◆ *adv* (*nachdenken*) intently. ◆ *adj* (*Gesichtsausdruck*) intent.

angetrunken *adj* slightly drunk.

an|gewöhnen *vt*: **sich** (D) **etw ~** to get into the habit of sthg.

Angewohnheit (*pl* -en) *die* habit.

Anglistik *die* English studies (*pl*).

Angora *nt* angora.

an|greifen *vt & vi unr* to attack.

Angst (*pl* Ängste) *die* fear; **~ haben vor** (+D) to be afraid of; **jm ~ machen** to scare sb.

ängstlich ◆ *adj* (*Mensch, Tier*) easily frightened; (*Verhalten, Blick*) frightened. ◆ *adv* (*blicken, reagieren*) frightenedly.

an|haben *vt unr* (*Hose, Schuhe*) to be wearing; **jm nichts ~ können** to be unable to harm sb.

an|halten ◆ *vi unr* (*stoppen*) to stop; (*andauern*) to last. ◆ *vt unr* to stop.

Anhalter, -in (*mpl* -) *der, die* hitch-hiker; **per ~ fahren** ODER **reisen** to hitchhike.

Anhaltspunkt (*pl* -e) *der* clue.

an|hängen *vt* (*Anhänger*) to hook up; (*hinzufügen*) to add; (*unterschieben*): **jm etw ~** to pin sthg on sb.

Anhänger (*pl* -) *der* (*Wagen*) trailer; (*Schmuck*) pendant; (*von Partei, Ideologie*) supporter.

Anhängerkupplung (*pl* -en) *die* tow hook.

anhänglich *adj* affectionate.

Anhieb *der*: **auf ~** first time, straight off.

an|hören *vt* (*Musikstück, Kassette*) to listen to. ▶ **sich anhören** *ref* to sound; **sich gut/schlecht ~** to sound good/bad.

Anker (*pl* -) *der* anchor.

an|kleben *vt* to stick.

Ankleidekabine (*pl* -n) *die* (changing) cubicle.

an|kommen *vi unr ist* (*Zug, Reisende, Brief*) to arrive; (*gefallen*) to go down well; **~ auf** (+A) to depend on; **das kommt darauf an** it depends.

an|kreuzen *vt* to mark with a cross.

an|kündigen *vt* (*Kursus, Vortrag*) to announce. ▶ **sich ankündigen** *ref* to announce itself; **es hat sich Besuch angekündigt** we're expecting visitors.

Ankunft *die* arrival.

Anlage (*pl* -n) *die* (*Gelände*) park; (TECH) (production) line.

an|lassen *vt unr* (*Motor*) to start up; (*Kleidung, Licht, Apparat*) to leave on.

Anlasser (*pl* -) *der* starter.

Anlauf (*pl* -läufe) *der* (SPORT) run-up; (*Versuch*) attempt.

an|laufen ◆ *vi unr ist* (*Motor, Aktion*) to start; (*Brille, Spiegel*) to mist up. ◆ *vt unr hat* (*Hafen*) to call at.

an|legen ◆ *vt* (*Liste, Register*) to draw up; (*Geld*) to invest; (*Schmuck, Verband*) to put on; (*Garten*) to lay out. ◆ *vi* (*Schiff*) to dock; **es darauf**

anlegen, etw zu tun to intend to do sthg. ▶ **sich anlegen** *ref:* **sich mit jm ~** to pick a fight with sb.

Anlegestelle (*pl* **-n**) *die* mooring.

Anleitung (*pl* **-en**) *die* (*Hinweis*) instruction; (*Text*) instructions (*pl*).

Anlieger, -in (*mpl* **-**) *der, die:* **'~ frei'** 'residents only'.

anlmachen *vt* (*Licht, Gerät*) to turn on; (*fam: Person*) to chat up (*Br*), to hit on (*Am*); (*Salat*) to dress.

anlmelden *vt* (*beim Arzt usw*) to make an appointment for; (*Fernseher, Auto*) to register. ▶ **sich anmelden** *ref* to register; **sich ~ zu** to enrol for.

Anmeldung (*pl* **-en**) *die* (*amtlich*) registration; (*beim Arzt*) appointment; (*Rezeption*) reception.

Anmietung *die* hire (*Br*), rental (*Am*).

anlnähen *vt* to sew on.

annähernd *adv* nearly.

Annahme (*pl* **-n**) *die* (*von Brief, Paket*) receipt; (*Vermutung*) assumption; **'keine ~ von 50 Pfennig-Stücken'** 'this machine does not accept 50 Pfennig coins'.

anlnehmen *vt unr* (*vermuten*) to assume; (*entgegennehmen, akzeptieren*) to accept; (*Form*) to assume; **~, daß** to assume (that).

Annonce (*pl* **-n**) *die* classified advertisement.

Anorak (*pl* **-s**) *der* anorak.

anlpacken *vt* (*berühren*) to seize; (*fam: bewältigen*) to tackle.

anlpassen *vt:* **etw an etw** (A) **~** to adapt sthg to sthg. ▶ **sich anpassen** *ref* to adapt.

Anpassung *die* adaptation.

anlprobieren *vt* to try on.

Anrede *die* form of address.

anlregen ◆ *vt* (*Aktion*) to initiate; (*Verdauung, Phantasie*) to stimulate. ◆ *vi* (*Tee, Kaffee*) to act as a stimulant.

Anregung (*pl* **-en**) *die* (*Hinweis*) suggestion; (*Aktivierung*) stimulation.

anlrichten *vt* (*Salat, Buffet*) to arrange; (*Chaos, Schaden*) to cause.

Anruf (*pl* **-e**) *der* (phone) call.

Anrufbeantworter (*pl* **-**) *der* answerphone.

anlrufen *vt & vi unr* (*per Telefon*) to ring, to call.

Ansage (*pl* **-n**) *die* announcement.

anlschaffen *vt* (*kaufen*) to buy.

anlschauen *vt* to look at; **sich** (D) **etw ~** to look at sthg.

Anschein *der* appearance; **es hat den ~, daß** it appears that.

anscheinend *adv* apparently.

anlschieben *vt unr* to push start.

Anschlag (*pl* **-schläge**) *der* (*Bekanntmachung*) notice; (*Attentat*) assassination attempt.

anlschließen *vt unr* (*Elektrogerät*) to plug in; (*Telefon*) to connect; (*mit Schlüssel*) to lock. ▶ **sich anschließen** *ref unr* (*mit Meinung*) to agree; **sich jm ~** (*Gruppe*) to join sb.

anschließend *adv* afterwards.

Anschluß (*pl* **-schlüsse**) *der* connection; (*Telefonapparat*) extension; (*zu Personen*): **~ finden** to make friends; **im ~ daran** afterwards; **kein ~ unter dieser Nummer!** the number you have dialled has not been recognized; **Sie haben ~ nach Basel, 15.39 Uhr** there is a connection to Basel at 15:39.

Anschlußflug (*pl* **-flüge**) *der* connecting flight.

anlschnallen *vt* to put on. ▶ **sich anschnallen** *ref* to fasten one's seatbelt.

Anschrift (*pl* **-en**) *die* address.

anlschwellen *vi unr ist* (*Körperteil*) to swell; (*Gewässer*) to rise.

Ansehen *das* reputation.

anlsehen *vt unr* to look at; **sich** (D) **etw ~** (*Film, Programm*) to watch sthg; (*Stadt, Gebäude*) to look round sthg; (*prüfend*) to look at sthg.

anlsein *vi unr ist* to be on.

anlsetzen *vt* (*Bowle, Teig*) to prepare; (*Kalk, Grünspan*) to become covered with; (*Termin*) to fix; **Rost ~** to rust.

Ansicht (*pl* **-en**) *die* (*von Stadt*) view; (*Meinung*) opinion; **meiner ~ nach** in my opinion.

Ansichtskarte (*pl* **-n**) *die* postcard.

ansonsten *adv* otherwise.

an|spielen *vi*: **~ auf** (+A) to allude to.

Anspielung (*pl* **-en**) *die* allusion.

Ansprache (*pl* **-n**) *die* speech.

an|springen ♦ *vt unr* (*angreifen*) to pounce on. **♦** *vi unr* (*Motor*) to start; (*fam: auf Vorschlag, Angebot*): **auf etw** (A) **~** to jump at sthg.

Anspruch (*pl* **-sprüche**) *der* (*Recht*) claim; **~ auf etw** (A) **haben** to be entitled to sthg. **► Ansprüche** *pl* (*Forderungen*) demands.

anspruchslos *adj* (*bescheiden*) unpretentious.

anspruchsvoll *adj* demanding.

anstatt *präp* (+G) *& konj* instead of.

an|stecken *vt* (*mit Krankheit*) to infect. **► sich anstecken** *ref*: **sich mit etw ~** to catch sthg.

ansteckend *adj* infectious.

an|stehen *vi unr* (*in Warteschlange*) to queue (Br), to stand in line (Am); (*Termin*) to be set; (*Problem*) to need to be dealt with.

anstelle *präp* (+G) instead of.

an|stellen *vt* (*Gerät*) to turn on; (*Mitarbeiter*) to employ; (*Dummheiten*) to get up to. **► sich anstellen** *ref* (*Wartende*) to queue (Br), to stand in line (Am); **sich dumm bei etw ~** to make a mess of sthg; **sich geschickt bei etw ~** to get the hang of sthg.

an|streichen *vt unr* to paint.

an|strengen *vt* to strain. **► sich anstrengen** *ref* to try (hard).

anstrengend *adj* tiring.

Antarktis *die* Antarctic.

Anteil (*pl* **-e**) *der* share.

Antenne (*pl* **-n**) *die* aerial.

Antibabypille (*pl* **-n**) *die* (contraceptive) pill.

Antibiotikum (*pl* **Antibiotika**) *das* antibiotic.

Antihistamin (*pl* **-e**) *das* antihistamine.

antik *adj* antique.

Antillen *pl* West Indies.

Antiquariat (*pl* **-e**) *das* secondhand bookshop; **modernes ~** remainder bookshop.

Antiquität (*pl* **-en**) *die* antique.

Antiquitätenhändler, -in (*mpl* **-**) *der, die* antique dealer.

Antrag (*pl* **-träge**) *der* application; **einen ~ auf etw** (A) **stellen** to apply for sthg.

an|treffen *vt unr* to find.

an|treiben *vt unr* (*zur Eile*) to urge; (*Maschine*) to drive.

an|treten *vt unr* to start.

Antrieb *der* (*von Maschine*) drive; (*Motivation*) impetus; **aus eigenem ~** on one's own initiative.

Antritt *der* beginning; **vor ~ der Reise** before setting off.

Antwort (*pl* **-en**) *die* answer.

antworten *vi* to answer; **auf etw** (A) **~** to answer sthg; **jm ~** to answer sb.

An- und Verkauf *der*: **'~ von Antiquitäten'** 'antiques bought and sold'.

Anweisung (*pl* **-en**) *die* (*Befehl*) instruction; (*von Geld*) money order.

an|wenden *vt unr* to use.

an|werben *vt unr* to recruit.

Anwerbung *die* recruitment.

anwesend *adj* present.

Anwohner, -in (*mpl* **-**) *der, die* resident.

Anwohnerparkplatz (*pl* **-plätze**) *der* residents' car park.

Anzahl *die* number.

Anzahlung (*pl* **-en**) *die* down payment.

Anzeichen (*pl* **-**) *das* sign.

Anzeige (*pl* **-n**) *die* (*in Zeitung*) advertisement; (*bei Polizei*) report.

an|zeigen *vt* (*Delikt*) to report; (*Temperatur, Zeit*) to show.

an|ziehen *vt unr* (*Kleidung, Schuhe*)

to put on; (anlocken) to attract; (Schraube, Knoten) to tighten. ▶ **sich anziehen** ref unr to get dressed.

Anzug (pl **-züge**) der (Bekleidung) suit.

anzüglich adj offensive.

anzünden vt to light.

anzweifeln vt to doubt.

AOK die compulsory health insurance scheme for German workers, students etc not covered by private insurance policies.

Apartment = **Appartement**.

Apfel (pl **Äpfel**) der apple.

Apfelbaum (pl **-bäume**) der apple tree.

Apfelkorn der apple schnapps.

Apfelkuchen (pl **-**) der apple cake.

Apfelkücherl (pl **-**) das (Süddt) ring-shaped apple fritter, sprinkled with icing sugar.

Apfelmus das apple sauce.

Apfelsaft der apple juice.

Apfelsine (pl **-n**) die orange.

Apfelstreuselkuchen (pl **-**) der = apple crumble.

Apfeltorte (pl **-n**) die apple cake.

Apfelwein der cider.

Apostroph (pl **-e**) der apostrophe.

Apotheke (pl **-n**) die chemist's shop (Br), pharmacy (Am).

apothekenpflichtig adj only available through a chemist.

Apotheker, -in (mpl **-**) der, die pharmacist.

App. abk = **Appartement**.

Apparat (pl **-e**) der (Gerät) appliance; (Telefon) telephone; **am ~!** speaking!

Appartement (pl **-s**) das (Wohnung) flat (Br), apartment (Am); (im Hotel) suite.

Appetit der appetite; **guten ~** enjoy your meal!

appetitlich adj appetizing.

Applaus der applause.

Aprikose (pl **-n**) die apricot.

April der April, → **September**.

Aprilscherz (pl **-e**) der April fool's trick.

apropos adv by the way.

Aquarell (pl **-e**) das watercolour.

Aquarium (pl **Aquarien**) das aquarium.

Äquator der equator.

Arbeit (pl **-en**) die (Tätigkeit, Mühe) work; (Arbeitsstelle, Aufgabe) job; (in Schule) test.

arbeiten vi to work.

Arbeiter, -in (mpl **-**) der, die worker.

Arbeitgeber, -in (mpl **-**) der, die employer.

Arbeitnehmer, -in (mpl **-**) der, die employee.

Arbeitsamt (pl **-ämter**) das job centre.

Arbeitserlaubnis (pl **-se**) die work permit.

Arbeitskraft (pl **-kräfte**) die (Arbeiter) worker. ▶ **Arbeitskräfte** pl labour (sg).

arbeitslos adj unemployed.

Arbeitslose (pl **-n**) der, die unemployed person.

Arbeitsmarkt (pl **-märkte**) der job market.

Arbeitsmöglichkeit (pl **-en**) die job opportunity.

Arbeitsplatz (pl **-plätze**) der (Anstellung) job; (Ort) workplace.

Arbeitstag (pl **-e**) der working day.

Arbeitsteilung die division of labour.

Arbeitszeit (pl **-en**) die working hours (pl).

Arbeitszimmer (pl **-**) das study.

Architekt, -in (mpl **-en**) der, die architect.

Archiv (pl **-e**) das archive.

arg (komp **ärger**, superl **am ärgsten**) adj bad.

Ärger der (Probleme) trouble; (Zorn) anger.

ärgerlich adj (wütend) annoyed; (unangenehm) annoying.

ärgern vt to annoy. ▶ **sich ärgern** ref to get annoyed; **sich ~ über** (+A) to get annoyed at.

Argument (*pl* -e) *das* argument.

Arktis *die* Arctic.

arm *adj* poor.

Arm (*pl* -e) *der* arm.

Armaturenbrett (*pl* -er) *das* dashboard.

Armband (*pl* -bänder) *das* (*Schmuck*) bracelet; (*von Uhr*) strap.

Armbanduhr (*pl* -en) *die* watch.

Armbruch (*pl* -brüche) *der* broken arm.

Armee (*pl* -n) *die* army.

Ärmel (*pl* -) *der* sleeve.

Ärmelkanal *der* (English) Channel.

Armlehne (*pl* -n) *die* armrest.

Aroma (*pl* Aromen) *das* (*Duft*) aroma; (*Geschmacksrichtung*) flavour; (*zum Backen*) flavouring.

arrogant *adj* arrogant.

Arsch (*pl* Ärsche) *der* (*vulg*) arse (Br), ass (Am).

Art (*pl* -en) *die* (*Weise*) way; (*Wesen*) nature; (*Sorte*) sort; (*von Lebewesen*) species; **~ und Weise** way; **auf seine ~** in his own way; **eine ~ (von)** a kind of; **Gulasch nach ~ des Hauses** chef's special goulash.

Arterie (*pl* -n) *die* artery.

artig *adj* good, well-behaved.

Artikel (*pl* -) *der* article.

Artischocke (*pl* -n) *die* artichoke.

Artist, -in (*mpl* -en) *der, die* (circus) performer.

artistisch *adj* acrobatic.

Arznei (*pl* -en) *die* medicine.

Arzt (*pl* Ärzte) *der* doctor; **praktischer ~** general practitioner, GP.

Arztausfahrt (*pl* -en) *der*: 'Arztausfahrt' *sign indicating that driveway should be kept clear as it is used by a doctor.*

Arzthelferin (*pl* -nen) *die* (doctor's) receptionist.

Ärztin (*pl* -nen) *die* doctor.

ärztlich *adj* medical.

Asche *die* ash; 'keine heiße ~ einfüllen' 'no hot ashes'.

Aschenbecher (*pl* -) *der* ashtray.

Aschermittwoch *der* Ash Wednesday.

Asien *nt* Asia.

Aspekt (*pl* -e) *der* aspect.

Asphalt (*pl* -e) *der* asphalt.

Aspirin® *das* aspirin.

aß *prät* → **essen**.

Ast (*pl* Äste) *der* branch.

Asthma *das* (MED) asthma.

Astrologie *die* astrology.

astrologisch *adj* astrological.

Astronomie *die* astronomy.

ASU (*abk für Abgassonderuntersuchung*) test of exhaust emissions.

Asyl (*pl* -e) *das* (*Schutz*) asylum; (*Unterkunft*) hostel, home.

Asylant, -in (*mpl* -en) *der, die* asylum-seeker.

Atem *der* breath; **außer ~** out of breath.

atemlos ◆ *adj* breathless. ◆ *adv* breathlessly.

Atemnot *die* difficulty in breathing.

Athlet, -in (*mpl* -en) *der, die* athlete.

Atlantik *der* Atlantic.

Atlantische Ozean *der* Atlantic Ocean.

atmen *vi & vt* to breathe.

Atom (*pl* -e) *das* atom.

Atomkraft *die* nuclear power.

Atomkraftwerk (*pl* -e) *das* nuclear power station.

Atomwaffe (*pl* -n) *die* nuclear weapon.

Attentat (*pl* -e) *das* (*erfolglos*) assassination attempt; (*erfolgreich*) assassination.

Attest (*pl* -e) *das* doctor's certificate.

Attraktion (*pl* -en) *die* attraction.

attraktiv *adj* attractive.

Attrappe (*pl* -n) *die* dummy.

ätzend *adj* (*Chemikalie*) corrosive; (*fam: unangenehm*) grim, gruesome.

au *interj* (*Ausdruck von Schmerz*) ow!; **~ ja!** great!

Aubergine (*pl* -**en**) *die* aubergine (*Br*), eggplant (*Am*).

auch *adv* (*ebenfalls*) also, too; (*sogar*) even; **wo ~ immer** wherever; **was ~ immer** whatever; **wer ~ immer** whoever; **ich ~** me too; **ich ~ nicht** me neither; **hast du die Tür ~ wirklich zugemacht?** are you sure you closed the door?

audiovisuell *adj* audiovisual.

auf ◆ *präp* (+D) 1. (*räumlich*) on; **~ dem Tisch** on the table; **~ dem Land** in the country; **~ der Post** at the post office. 2. (*während*): **~ der Reise** on the journey; **~ der Hochzeit/Party** at the wedding/party. ◆ *präp* (+A) 1. (*räumlich*) on; **~ den Tisch** on the table; **~s Land** to the country; **~ eine Party gehen** to go to a party. 2. (*Angabe der Art und Weise*): **~ diese Art** in this way; **~ Deutsch** in German. 3. (*Angabe einer Beschäftigung*): **~ Reisen gehen** to go on a tour; **~ die Uni gehen** to go to university. 4. (*Angabe des Anlasses*): **~ js Rat hin** on sb's advice. 5. (*Angabe einer Folge*): **von heute ~ morgen** overnight. 6. (*Angabe eines Wunsches*): **~ Ihr Wohl!** your good health! ◆ *adv* (*offen*) open; **Tür ~!** open the door! ▶ **auf einmal** *adv* (*plötzlich*) suddenly. ▶ **auf und ab** *adv* up and down.

auf|atmen *vi* to breathe a sigh of relief.

Aufbau *der* (*Bauen*) building; (*Struktur*) structure.

auf|bauen *vt* (*Zelt, Gerüst*) to put up; (*Organisation*) to build up.

auf|bewahren *vt* (*Gepäck*) to leave; (*Lebensmittel*) to store.

aufblasbar *adj* inflatable.

auf|bleiben *vi unr ist* (*Person*) to stay up; (*Tür, Fenster*) to stay open.

auf|blenden *vi* to put one's headlights on full beam.

auf|brechen ◆ *vt unr hat* to force open. ◆ *vi unr ist* (*abreisen*) to set off.

auf|bringen *vt unr* (*Geld*) to raise.

Aufbruch *der* departure.

auf|decken *vt* (*Plane, Laken*) to turn back; (*Geheimnis*) to uncover.

auf|drängen *vt*: **jm etw ~** to force sthg on sb.

auf|drehen *vt* (*Wasserhahn*) to turn on.

aufdringlich *adj* pushy.

aufeinander *adv* (*einer auf dem anderen*) one on top of the other; (*nacheinander*) one after the other; (*aufpassen*) one another; **~ eifersüchtig sein** to be jealous of one another.

Aufenthalt (*pl* -**e**) *der* (*von Person*) stay; (*Unterbrechung*) stop; **der Zug hat 10 Minuten ~** the train will stop for 10 minutes; **ständiger ~** place of residence; **schönen ~!** have a nice stay!

Aufenthaltsgenehmigung (*pl* -**en**) *die* residence permit.

Aufenthaltsraum (*pl* -**räume**) *der* common room.

auf|essen *vt unr* to eat up.

auf|fahren *vi unr ist*: **dicht ~** to tailgate.

Auffahrt (*pl* -**en**) *die* (*zu Haus*) drive; (*zu Autobahn*) slip road (*Br*), ramp (*Am*).

Auffahrunfall (*pl* -**unfälle**) *der* rear-end collision.

auf|fallen *vi unr ist* to stand out; **jm ~** to strike sb.

auffallend *adj* striking.

auffällig ◆ *adj* (*Benehmen*) odd; (*Kleidung, Auto*) ostentatious. ◆ *adv* (*sich kleiden*) ostentatiously.

auf|fangen *vt unr* (*Ball*) to catch; (*Funkspruch*) to pick up.

auf|fordern *vt* (*bitten*) to ask; (*befehlen*) to require.

auf|frischen *vt* (*Kenntnisse*) to brush up on; (*Farbe*) to brighten up.

auf|führen *vt* (*auf der Bühne*) to perform; (*auf Liste*) to list.

Aufführung (*pl* -**en**) *die* performance.

Aufgabe (*pl* -**n**) *die* (*Arbeit*) task; (*Verpflichtung*) responsibility; (*bei*

Wettkampf) retirement; (*von Paket*) posting; (*von Koffer*) checking in; (*in der Schule*) exercise.

Aufgang (*pl* -gänge) *der* (*von Treppe*) stairs (*pl*); (*von Sonne*) rising.

au̱f|geben ◆ *vt unr* (*Gewohnheit, Stelle, Geschäft*) to give up; (*Schularbeiten*) to set; (*Paket, Brief*) to post (Br), to mail (Am); (*Koffer*) to check in. ◆ *vi* (*resignieren*) to give up.

au̱f|gehen *vi unr ist* (*Sonne, Mond*) to rise; (*Knoten*) to come undone.

aufgehoben ◆ *pp* → **aufheben**. ◆ *adj*: **gut/schlecht ~ sein** to be/not to be in good hands.

au̱fgelegt *adj*: **gut/schlecht ~ sein** to be in a good/bad mood.

aufgrund *präp* (+G) because of.

au̱f|halten *vt unr* (*Tür*) to hold open; (*Person*) to hold up. ▶ **sich aufhalten** *ref* to stay.

au̱f|hängen *vt* to hang up.

au̱f|heben *vt unr* (*aufbewahren*) to keep; (*vom Boden*) to pick up.

au̱f|hetzen *vt* to incite.

au̱f|holen ◆ *vt* to make up. ◆ *vi* to catch up.

au̱f|horchen *vi* to prick up one's ears.

au̱f|hören *vi* to stop; **~, etw zu machen** to stop doing sthg; **mit etw ~** to stop sthg.

au̱f|klappen *vt* to open.

au̱f|klären *vt* (*Mißverständnis*) to clear up; **jn über etw** (A) **~** to tell sb sthg.

Aufklärung *die* (*von Mißverständnis*) clearing up; (*Information*) information.

Aufkleber (*pl* -) *der* sticker.

au̱f|kommen *vi unr ist* (*entstehen*) to arise; **~ für** (*zahlen*) to pay for.

au̱f|krempeln *vt*: **die Ärmel/Hosenbeine ~** to roll up one's sleeves/trouser legs.

au̱f|kriegen *vt* (*fam*) to get open.

Auflage (*pl* -n) *die* (*von Buch*) edition; (*von Zeitung*) circulation; (*Bedingung*) condition.

au̱f|lassen *vt unr* (*Tür*) to leave open; (*Mütze, Hut*) to keep on.

Auflauf (*pl* -läufe) *der* (*von Menschen*) crowd; (KÜCHE) bake.

au̱f|legen *vt* (*Schallplatte, Tischdecke*) to put on; (*Buch, Zeitschrift*) to publish; (*Telefonhörer*) to hang up.

au̱f|leuchten *vi* to light up.

au̱f|listen *vt* to list.

au̱f|lösen *vt* (*Vertrag*) to cancel; (*Tablette*) to dissolve; (*Knoten*) to undo.

Auflösung (*pl* -en) *die* (*von Rätsel*) solution; (*von Organisation, Verein*) disbanding.

au̱f|machen *vt* to open; **jm ~** to let sb in. ▶ **sich aufmachen** *ref* (*abreisen*) to set off.

au̱fmerksam *adj* attentive; **jn ~ machen auf** (+A) to draw sb's attention to.

Au̱fmerksamkeit (*pl* -en) *die* (*Interesse*) attention; (*Geschenk*) gift.

Aufnahme (*pl* -n) *die* (*Foto*) photograph; (*von Musik*) recording; (*von Protokoll, Aussage*) taking down; (*in Krankenhaus, Verein*) admission.

au̱f|nehmen *vt unr* (*Gast*) to receive; (*Foto*) to take; (*Musik*) to record; (*Protokoll, Aussage*) to take down; **mit jm Kontakt ~** to contact sb.

Aufnehmer (*pl* -) *der* (floor) cloth.

au̱f|passen *vi* to pay attention; **~ auf** (+A) to look after; **paß' auf!** be careful!

au̱f|pumpen *vt* to pump up.

au̱f|räumen ◆ *vt* (*Raum*) to tidy up; (*Gegenstand*) to put away. ◆ *vi* to tidy up.

au̱f|regen *vt* to excite. ▶ **sich aufregen** *ref* to get worked up.

Aufregung (*pl* -en) *die* excitement.

au̱f|rollen *vt* (*Leine, Schnur*) to roll up.

Aufruf *der* call; **letzter ~** last call; **'dringender ~ für Flug LH 404'** 'last call for passengers on flight LH 404'.

au̱f|rufen *vt unr* to call.

au̱f|runden *vt* to round up.

Aufsatz (*pl* -sätze) *der* (SCHULE) essay.

auf|schieben *vt unr* to put off.

Aufschlag (*pl* -schläge) *der* (SPORT) serve; (*auf Preis*) extra charge.

auf|schließen *vt unr* to unlock.

Aufschnitt *der* sliced cold meat and cheese.

auf|schreiben *vt unr* to write down.

Aufsehen *das*: ~ erregen to cause a stir.

auf|sein *vi unr ist* (*fam: offen sein*) to be open; (*Person*) to be up.

Aufsicht *die* (*Person*) supervisor; (*Kontrolle*) supervision.

auf|spannen *vt* (*Regenschirm*) to open.

Aufstand (*pl* -stände) *der* rebellion.

auf|stehen ♦ *vi unr ist* to get up. ♦ *vt unr hat* (*Tür, Fenster*) to be open.

auf|stellen *vt* (*Zelt*) to put up; (*Behauptung*) to put forward.

Aufstellung (*pl* -en) *die* (*von Mannschaft*) line-up; (*von Behauptung*) putting forward.

Aufstieg *der* (*auf Berg*) climb; (*in Sport, Arbeit*) promotion.

auf|stocken *vt* (*erhöhen*) to increase.

Auftakt (*pl* -e) *der* (MUS) upbeat; (*Beginn*) start.

auf|tanken *vi* to fill up.

auf|tauchen *vi ist* (*erscheinen, auftreten*) to appear; (*aus dem Wasser*) to surface.

auf|tauen *vt* (*Gefrorenes*) to thaw.

auf|teilen *vt* to share out.

Auftrag (*pl* -träge) *der* (*Aufgabe*) job; (*Bestellung*) order.

auf|tragen *vt unr* (*Farbe*) to apply; (*befehlen*): jm ~, etw zu tun to tell sb to do sthg.

auf|treten *vi unr ist* (*sich benehmen*) to behave; (*auf Bühne*) to appear; (*Problem*) to come up.

Auftritt (*pl* -e) *der* (*Theater*) entrance.

auf|wachen *vi ist* to wake up.

auf|wachsen *vi unr ist* to grow up.

Aufwand *der* (*Geld*) expenditure; (*Anstrengung*) effort.

auf|wärmen *vt* (*Essen*) to warm up.

aufwärts *adv* upwards.

auf|wecken *vt* to wake (up).

auf|werten *vt* (*Ansehen*) to enhance.

auf|wischen *vt* to wipe up.

auf|zählen *vt* to list.

auf|zeichnen *vt* (*mit Skizze*) to draw; (*Film, Musik*) to record.

auf|ziehen *vt unr* (*Uhr*) to wind up; (*Kind*) to bring up; (*Tier*) to raise.

Aufzug (*pl* -züge) *der* (*Fahrstuhl*) lift (Br), elevator (Am).

Auge (*pl* -n) *das* eye; unter vier ~n in private; ein blaues ~ a black eye; etw im ~ behalten to keep sthg in mind.

Augenblick (*pl* -e) *der* moment; einen ~, bitte! just a moment, please!; im ~ at the moment.

augenblicklich *adv* (*sofort*) immediately.

Augenbraue (*pl* -n) *die* eyebrow.

Augenbrauenstift (*pl* -e) *der* eyebrow pencil.

Augencreme (*pl* -s) *die* eye cream.

Augenfarbe (*pl* -n) *die*: welche ~ hat sie? what colour are her eyes?

Augenoptiker, -in (*mpl* -) *der, die* optician.

Augentropfen *pl* eyedrops.

August *der* August, → September.

Auktion (*pl* -en) *die* auction.

aus ♦ *präp* (+D) **1.** (*zur Angabe der Richtung*) out of; ~ dem Haus gehen to go out of the house. **2.** (*zur Angabe der Herkunft*) from; ~ Amerika from America. **3.** (*zur Angabe des Materials*) made of; ~ Plastik made of plastic. **4.** (*zur Angabe des Grundes*) for; ~ welchem Grund ...? for what reason ...?, why ...?; ~ Spaß for fun; ~ Wut in anger. **5.** (*zur Angabe der Entfernung*) from; ~ 50 m Entfernung from 50 m away. **6.** (*zur Angabe eines Teils*) of; einer ~ der Gruppe a member of the group. ♦ *adv* **1.** (*außer*

Funktion) off; **hier schaltet man die Maschine an und ~** this is where you switch the machine on and off; **Licht ~!** lights out! **2.** (*zu Ende*) over; **~ und vorbei** all over.

Aus *das*: **ins ~ gehen** (SPORT) to go out of play.

aus|arbeiten *vt* (*Entwurf*) to draw up; (*Projekt*) to work on.

aus|baden *vt*: **etw ~ müssen** to take the blame for sthg.

aus|bauen *vt* (*Straße, Haus*) to extend; (*Dach*) to convert; (*Kenntnisse*) to expand; (*Motor, Teil*) to remove.

aus|bessern *vt* to mend.

aus|beulen *vt* to beat out.

Ausbildung (*pl* **-en**) *die* (*schulisch*) education; (*beruflich, fachlich*) training.

aus|brechen *vi unr ist* to break out.

aus|breiten *vt* to spread out. ► **sich ausbreiten** *ref* to spread; (*Landschaft*) to stretch out.

Ausdauer *die* stamina.

ausdauernd *adj* persevering.

aus|denken *vt unr*: **sich** (D) **etw ~** to think sthg up.

Ausdruck¹ (*pl* **-drücke**) *der* expression.

Ausdruck² (*pl* **-e**) *der* (EDV) printout.

aus|drucken *vt* to print out.

aus|drücken *vt* (*sagen*) to express. ► **sich ausdrücken** *ref* to express o.s.

auseinander *adv* apart.

auseinander|gehen *vi unr ist* (*Personen*) to break up; (*Wege*) to fork; (*Vorhang*) to open; (*Meinungen*) to differ.

auseinander|nehmen *vt unr* to dismantle.

Auseinandersetzung (*pl* **-en**) *die* argument.

aus|fahren ◆ *vt unr hat* (*Ware*) to deliver; (*spazierenfahren*) to take for a drive. ◆ *vi unr ist* (*Person*) to go for a drive.

Ausfahrt (*pl* **-en**) *die* exit; **'~ freihalten!'** 'keep clear!'

aus|fallen *vi unr ist* (*Aufführung, Konzert*) to be cancelled; (*Gerät*) to break down; (*Strom*) to be cut off; (*Haare, Zähne*) to fall out; **gut/schlecht ~** to turn out well/badly; **die Schule fällt heute aus** there's no school today.

ausfindig *adv*: **jn/etw ~ machen** to locate sb/sthg.

Ausflug (*pl* **-flüge**) *der* trip.

Ausflugsboot (*pl* **-e**) *das* pleasure boat.

Ausflugslokal (*pl* **-e**) *das* cafe or pub in the countryside, to which you can drive or walk out.

Ausflugsziel (*pl* **-e**) *das* destination (*of a trip*).

Ausfluß (*pl* **-flüsse**) *der* (MED) discharge; (*von Wanne, Becken*) plughole.

aus|fragen *vt* to interrogate.

aus|führen *vt* (*ins Ausland*) to export; (*zum Essen, Tanzen*) to take out; (*Arbeit, Plan, Befehl*) to carry out; (*Hund*) to walk.

ausführlich ◆ *adj* detailed. ◆ *adv* in detail.

aus|füllen *vt* (*Formular*) to fill out; (*Raum*) to fill.

Ausgabe (*pl* **-n**) *die* (*von Geld*) expenditure; (*von Essen*) serving; (*von Buch*) edition. ► **Ausgaben** *pl* expenditure (*sg*).

Ausgang (*pl* **-gänge**) *der* (*von Haus, Raum*) exit; (*von Dorf, Wald*) end.

aus|geben *vt unr* (*Geld*) to spend; (*verteilen*) to give out; **jm etw ~** (*fam*) to buy sb sthg. ► **sich ausgeben** *ref*: **sich als etw ~** to pretend to be sthg.

ausgebucht *adj* fully-booked.

ausgefallen *adj* (*Geschmack, Idee*) unusual.

aus|gehen *vi unr ist* (*Licht, Person*) to go out; (*Heizung*) to go off; (*Motor*) to stop; (*Film, Roman*) to end; **mir ist das Geld ausgegangen** my money has run out; **davon ~, daß** to assume (that).

ausgelastet adj: **voll ~ sein** to have one's hands full; **nicht ~ sein** not to be stretched.

ausgeleiert adj baggy.

ausgenommen konj except.

ausgerechnet adv precisely; **~ du!** you of all people!; **~ heute!** today of all days!

ausgeschaltet adj (switched) off.

ausgeschildert adj signposted.

ausgeschlossen adj (unmöglich): **~ sein** to be impossible.

ausgestellt adj: **auf jn ~** (Scheck) made out to sb; (Paß) issued to sb.

ausgewiesen adj: **~ durch den Reisepaß** passport used as proof of identity.

ausgewogen adj balanced.

ausgezeichnet ♦ adj (sehr gut) excellent; (mit Preis) priced. ♦ adv (sehr gut) extremely well.

ausgiebig adj (Frühstück) large.

ausgießen vt unr (Flüssigkeit) to pour out; (Gefäß) to empty.

ausgleichen vt unr (Differenzen) to even out; (Mangel) to make up for.

Ausguß (pl -güsse) der drain.

aushalten vt unr to stand.

Aushang (pl -hänge) der notice.

aushelfen vi unr to help out.

Aushilfe (pl -n) die (im Büro) temp.

ausholen vi (mit Arm) to move one's arm back.

auskennen: sich auskennen ref unr (in Stadt) to know one's way around; (in Fach) to be an expert.

auskommen vi unr ist: **mit etw ~** to make sthg last; **mit jm gut/schlecht ~** to get on well/badly with sb; **mit jm nicht ~** not to get on with sb.

Auskunft (pl -künfte) die (Information) information; (am Telefon) directory enquiries (pl) (Br), information (Am); (Schalter) information office.

auslachen vt to laugh at.

ausladen vt unr (Gepäck, Fahrzeug) to unload; (Gäste): **jn ~** to tell sb not to come.

Auslage (pl -n) die display. ▶ **Auslagen** pl (Spesen) expenses.

Ausland das: **im ~** abroad; **ins ~** abroad.

Ausländer, -in (mpl -) der, die foreigner.

ausländisch adj foreign.

Auslandsgespräch (pl -e) das international call.

Auslandsschutzbrief (pl -e) der motor insurance document for travel abroad, = green card (Br).

auslassen vt unr (überspringen) to leave out; (Gelegenheit) to miss; **etw an jm ~** (Ärger, Wut) to take sthg out on sb.

Auslauf der: **~ haben/brauchen** to have/need plenty of room (to run about).

auslaufen vi unr ist (Flüssigkeit) to run out; (Gefäß, Tank) to leak.

auslegen vt unr (Ware) to display; (Geld) to lend; **ein Zimmer mit Teppichen ~** to carpet a room.

ausleihen vt unr: **jm etw ~** to lend sb sthg; **sich** (D) **etw ~** to borrow sthg.

Auslese (pl -n) die (Auswahl) selection; (Wein) quality wine made from specially-selected grapes.

auslöschen vt to extinguish.

Auslöser (pl -) der (am Fotoapparat) (shutter release) button.

ausmachen vt (Feuer, Zigarette) to put out; (Licht, Gerät) to turn off; (absprechen) to agree on; (Termin) to make; **mit jm ~, daß etw gemacht wird** to arrange with sb to have sthg done; **das macht mir nichts aus** I don't mind; **macht es Ihnen etwas aus, wenn ich rauche?** do you mind if I smoke?

Ausmaß (pl -e) das extent.

Ausnahme (pl -n) die exception; **eine ~ machen** to make an exception.

au|snahmsweise *adv* just this once.

aus|nutzen *vt* (*Gelegenheit, Zeit*) to use; (*Person*) to exploit.

aus|packen *vt* to unpack.

Auspuff (*pl* -e) *der* exhaust.

aus|rangieren *vt* (*Auto*) to scrap; (*Kleider*) to throw out.

aus|rechnen *vt* to calculate; **sich** (D) **gute Chancen** ~ to fancy one's chances.

Ausrede (*pl* -n) *die* excuse.

aus|reichen *vi* to be enough; **es muß bis März** ~ it has to last until March.

Ausreise *die*: **bei der** ~ on leaving the country.

Ausreisegenehmigung (*pl* -en) *die* exit visa.

aus|reißen ◆ *vi unr ist* to run away. ◆ *vt unr hat* to pull out.

aus|renken *vt*: **sich** (D) **die Schulter** ~ to dislocate one's shoulder.

aus|richten *vt*: **jm etw** ~ to tell sb sthg.

aus|rufen *vt unr* (*über Lautsprecher*) to announce; **jn** ~ **lassen** to page sb.

Ausrufezeichen (*pl* -) *das* exclamation mark.

aus|ruhen: sich ausruhen *ref* to rest.

Ausrüstung (*pl* -en) *die* (*für Sport*) equipment.

aus|rutschen *vi ist* to slip.

aus|sagen *vt* to state.

aus|schalten *vt* to switch off.

Ausschank *der* (*von Getränken*) serving.

Ausschau *die*: ~ **halten nach** to look out for.

aus|schlafen *vi unr* to lie in; **bist du ausgeschlafen?** did you get enough sleep?

Ausschlag (*pl* -schläge) *der* (MED) rash; **den** ~ **geben** to be the decisive factor.

aus|schließen *vt unr* to exclude.

ausschließlich ◆ *adv* exclusively.

◆ *präp* (+G) excluding.

aus|schneiden *vt unr* to cut out.

Ausschnitt (*pl* -e) *der* (*von Kleid, Bluse*) neckline; (*aus Zeitungen*) cutting, clipping; (*aus Film, Programm*) clip.

Ausschreitungen *pl* violent clashes.

aus|schütteln *vt* to shake out.

aus|schütten *vt* (*Gefäß*) to empty; (*Flüssigkeit*) to pour out.

aus|schwenken *vi ist* to swing out.

aus|sehen *vi unr* to look; **gut/ schlecht** ~ (*Person, Gegenstand*) to look nice/horrible; (*Situation*) to look good/bad; **wie sieht es aus?** (*Situation*) how are you getting on?; **es sieht nach Regen aus** it looks like rain.

aus|sein *vi unr ist* (*zu Ende sein*) to be over; (*Gerät, Heizung*) to be off; (*Feuer*) to be out; ~ **auf** (+A) to be after.

außen *adv* outside; **von** ~ from the outside; **nach** ~ outwards.

Außenbordmotor (*pl* -en) *der* outboard motor.

Außenrückspiegel (*pl* -) *der* door mirror.

Außenseite (*pl* -n) *die* outside.

Außenseiter, -in (*mpl* -) *der, die* outsider.

Außenspiegel (*pl* -) *der* door mirror.

Außentemperatur (*pl* -en) *die* outside temperature.

außer ◆ *präp* (+D) (*ausgenommen*) except (for); (*neben*) as well as. ◆ *konj* except; **ich komme,** ~ **es regnet** I'll come, unless it rains; **alle,** ~ **ihm** everyone except (for) him; **nichts,** ~ **...** nothing but ...; ~ **sich sein (vor** (+D)) to be beside o.s. (with); ~ **Betrieb** out of order.

außerdem *adv* also, moreover.

außergewöhnlich ◆ *adj* unusual. ◆ *adv* exceptionally.

außerhalb ◆ *präp* (+G) outside.

♦ adv out of town.

äußerlich ♦ adj external. ♦ adv externally.

äußern vt to express. ► **sich äußern** ref (erkennbar werden) to show (itself); (sprechen) to speak; **sich ~ zu** to comment on.

außerordentlich ♦ adj extraordinary. ♦ adv exceptionally.

außerplanmäßig adj (Zug) extra, special.

äußerst adv extremely.

aus|setzen ♦ vt (Hund, Kind) to abandon; (Preis, Belohnung) to offer. ♦ vi (Herz, Musik) to stop; (bei Spiel) to miss one's turn; **an allem etwas auszusetzen haben** to constantly find fault with everything.

Aussicht (pl -en) die (Blick) view; (Chance) prospect.

aussichtslos adj hopeless.

Aussichtsplattform (pl -en) die viewing platform.

Aussichtspunkt (pl -e) der viewpoint.

Aussichtsterrasse (pl -n) die cafe terrace with a view.

Aussichtsturm (pl -türme) der lookout tower.

Aussiedler, -in (mpl -) der, die person of German origin from Eastern Europe who has resettled in Germany.

aus|spannen vi (sich erholen) to relax.

aus|sperren vt (aus Raum) to lock out.

Aussprache (pl -n) die (von Wörtern) pronunciation; (Gespräch) discussion (to resolve a dispute).

aus|sprechen ♦ vt unr (Wort, Satz) to pronounce; (Gedanke, Verdacht) to express. ♦ vi unr (zu Ende reden) to finish (speaking). ► **sich aussprechen** ref unr to pour one's heart out; **sich mit jm ~** to talk things through with sb.

aus|spucken ♦ vt to spit out. ♦ vi to spit.

aus|spülen vt (Glas, Mund) to rinse

out; (Wunde) to wash; (Haare) to rinse.

Ausstattung (pl -en) die (Ausrüstung) equipment; (von Zimmer) furnishings (pl); (von Auto) fittings (pl).

aus|steigen vi unr ist (aus Fahrzeug) to get out; **'~ bitte Knopf drücken'** 'press to open'.

aus|stellen vt (Gerät) to turn off; (in Museum, Ausstellung) to display; (Paß) to issue; (Quittung) to write out.

Ausstellung (pl -en) die (in Museum) exhibition.

aus|sterben vi unr ist to die out.

aus|strahlen ♦ vt (Programm) to broadcast. ♦ vi (Freude, Ruhe) to radiate.

Ausstrahlung die (von Programm) broadcasting; (von Person) charisma.

aus|strecken vt to stretch out. ► **sich ausstrecken** ref to stretch.

aus|streichen vt unr (Satz) to cross out.

aus|suchen vt to choose; **sich (D) etw ~** to choose sthg.

aus|teilen vt to distribute.

Auster (pl -n) die oyster.

Australien nt Australia.

aus|trinken vt unr (Glas) to empty; (Bier) to finish.

aus|trocknen ♦ vt hat (Erde, Haut) to dry out. ♦ vi ist to dry out.

Ausverkauf der clearance sale.

ausverkauft adj sold out.

Auswahl die selection, choice.

aus|wandern vi ist to emigrate.

auswärts adv: **~ essen** to eat out; **~ spielen** to play away (from home).

aus|wechseln vt (ersetzen) to replace; (Fußballspieler) to substitute.

aus|weichen vi unr ist (+D) (vor Auto, Frage) to avoid.

Ausweis (pl -e) der (Personalausweis) identity card; (für Bibliothek, Studenten) card.

aus|weisen vt unr (aus Land) to expel. ► **sich ausweisen** ref to identify o.s.

Ausweiskontrolle (*pl* -n) *die* identity card check.

Ausweisnummer (*pl* -n) *die* identity card number.

Ausweispapiere *pl* identification (*sg*).

auswendig *adv* by heart.

aus|wringen *vt unr* to wring out.

aus|wuchten *vt* to balance.

aus|zahlen *vt* (*Lohn, Zinsen*) to pay. ▶ **sich auszahlen** *ref* to pay.

Auszahlungsbetrag (*pl* -beträge) *der* total payment.

aus|zeichnen *vt* (*ehren*) to honour; (*mit Preisschild*) to price.

aus|ziehen ♦ *vt unr hat* (*Kleidung, Schuhe*) to take off; (*Antenne, Tisch*) to extend; (*Person*) to undress. ♦ *vi unr ist* (*aus Wohnung*) to move out. ▶ **sich ausziehen** *ref* to undress; **sich die Schuhe ~** to take one's shoes off.

Auszubildende (*pl* -n) *der, die* trainee.

Auto (*pl* -s) *das* car; **mit dem ~ fahren** to go by car, to drive.

Autoatlas (*pl* -atlanten) *der* road atlas.

Autobahn (*pl* -en) *die* motorway (*Br*), freeway (*Am*).

AUTOBAHN

At over 11,000 km, the German motorway network is the second longest in the world after the United States. There is no speed limit on German motorways, although there is a recommended limit of 130 km/h. No toll is charged for using the motorway.

Autobahngebühr (*pl* -en) *die* toll.

Autobahnkreuz (*pl* -e) *das* interchange.

Autobahnmeisterei (*pl* -en) *die* motorway maintenance department.

Autobahnring (*pl* -e) *der* motorway ring road (*Br*), beltway (*Am*).

Autobus (*pl* -se) *der* bus.

Autofähre (*pl* -n) *die* car ferry.

Autofahrer, -in (*mpl* -) *der, die* (car) driver.

Autogramm (*pl* -e) *das* autograph.

Automat (*pl* -en) *der* (*für Zigaretten, Fahrkarten usw.*) vending machine.

Automatik *die* (AUTO) automatic transmission.

Automatikgetriebe (*pl* -) *das* (AUTO) automatic transmission.

Automatikwagen (*pl* -) *der* automatic (car).

automatisch ♦ *adj* automatic. ♦ *adv* automatically.

Autor (*pl* Autoren) *der* author.

Autoradio (*pl* -s) *das* car radio.

Autoreifen (*pl* -) *der* car tyre.

Autoreisezug (*pl* -züge) *der* ≈ motorail train.

Autoreparatur (*pl* -en) *die* car repairs (*pl*).

Autorin (*pl* -nen) *die* author.

Autoschlange (*pl* -n) *die* tailback.

Autostopp *der* hitchhiking; **per ~ fahren** to hitch-hike.

Autounfall (*pl* -unfälle) *der* car accident.

Autovermietung (*pl* -en) *die* (*Firma*) car hire firm (*Br*), car rental firm (*Am*).

Autowaschanlage (*pl* -n) *die* car wash.

Autowäsche (*pl* -n) *die* car wash.

Autowaschstraße (*pl* -n) *die* drive-through car wash.

Autowerkstatt (*pl* -stätten) *die* garage.

Autozubehör *das* car accessories (*pl*).

Avocado (*pl* -s) *die* avocado.

Axt (*pl* Äxte) *die* axe.

B

B (*pl -*) *abk* = **Bundesstraße**.

Baby (*pl -s*) *das* baby.

Babybett (*pl -en*) *das* cot (Br), crib (Am).

Babyfläschchen (*pl -*) *das* baby's bottle.

Babynahrung *die* baby food.

Babysitter, -in (*mpl -*) *der, die* babysitter.

Babysitz (*pl -e*) *der* child seat.

Baby-Wickelraum (*pl -räume*) *der* parent and baby room.

Bach (*pl* Bäche) *der* stream.

Backbord *das* port.

Backe (*pl -n*) *die* (Wange) cheek.

backen *vt & vi unr* to bake.

Bäcker, -in (*mpl -*) *der, die* baker.

Bäckerei (*pl -en*) *die* bakery.

Backmischung (*pl -en*) *die* cake mix.

Backofen (*pl -öfen*) *der* oven.

Backpflaume (*pl -n*) *die* prune.

Backpulver *das* baking powder.

Backstube (*pl -n*) *die* bakery.

bäckt *präs* → **backen**.

Backwaren *pl* bread, cakes and pastries.

Bad (*pl* Bäder) *das* (Badezimmer) bathroom; (Baden) bath; (Kurort) spa; **mit ~ und WC** with en suite bathroom; **ein ~ nehmen** to have a bath.

BAD

When a place name begins with the word 'Bad', as for example in 'Bad Ems' or 'Bad Tölz', this indicates that it is a spa town with a medicinal spring, or a health resort with a beneficial climate. A stay in one of these places may be prescribed by a doctor for people who are ill or convalescing, the costs being covered by the 'Krankenkasse'.

Badeanzug (*pl -anzüge*) *der* swimming costume, swimsuit.

Badegast (*pl -gäste*) *der* (im Badeort) visitor; (im Schwimmbad) bather.

Badehose (*pl -n*) *die* swimming trunks (*pl*).

Badekappe (*pl -n*) *die* swimming cap.

Bademeister, -in (*mpl -*) *der, die* pool attendant.

Bademütze (*pl -n*) *die* swimming cap.

baden ◆ *vi* (in Badewanne) to have a bath; (schwimmen) to swim. ◆ *vt* to bath; **~ gehen** to go for a swim.

Badeort (*pl -e*) *der* (seaside) resort.

Badesachen *pl* swimming things.

Badetuch (*pl -tücher*) *das* bath towel.

Badewanne (*pl -n*) *die* bath (tub).

Badezimmer (*pl -*) *das* bathroom.

Badminton *das* badminton.

baff *adj*: **~ sein** (fam) to be gobsmacked.

BAFöG *das maintenance grant awarded to students and apprentices by the state.*

Bagger (*pl -*) *der* mechanical digger.

Baggersee (*pl -n*) *der artificial lake where people go to have picnics, swim etc.*

Bahn (*pl -en*) *die* (Zug) train; (Straßenbahn) tram (Br), streetcar (Am); (von Rakete, Planet) path; (in Schwimmbad, Stadion) lane; (von Stoff, Tapete) strip; **die ~** (Bundesbahn) German rail company; **drei ~en schwimmen** to swim three lengths; **jn zur ~ bringen** to take sb to the station; **mit der ~** by train, by rail.

Bahnbus (*pl -se*) *der bus run by railway company.*

Bahncard (*pl -s*) *die* railcard.

Bahnfracht *die*: **per ~** by rail (freight).

Bahngesellschaft *die one of the rail*

companies that make up the German Bundesbahn.

Bahnhof (pl -höfe) der (railway) station.

Bahnhofsmission (pl -en) die room at a station where charitable organizations provide care for rail travellers.

Bahnlinie (pl -n) die (Strecke) railway line (Br), railroad line (Am).

Bahnpolizei die railway police (Br), railroad police (Am).

Bahnsteig (pl -e) der platform; **am selben ~ gegenüber** on the opposite side of the platform.

Bahnübergang (pl -übergänge) der level crossing (Br), grade crossing (Am); **unbeschrankter ~** level crossing with no barrier.

Bahnverbindung (pl -en) die (train) connection.

Bakterie (pl -n) die germ.

balancieren vt & vi to balance.

bald adv soon; (fam: fast) almost; **bis ~!** see you soon!

baldmöglichst adv (fml) as soon as possible.

Baldrian der valerian.

Balken (pl -) der beam.

Balkon (pl -e) der balcony.

Ball (pl Bälle) der ball.

Ballett (pl -e) das ballet.

Ballon (pl -s) der balloon.

Ballspiel (pl -e) das ball game.

Ballungsgebiet (pl -e) das conurbation.

banal adj (abw: geistlos) banal; (einfach) everyday.

Banane (pl -n) die banana.

band prät → binden.

Band¹ (pl Bänder) das (Schnur) ribbon; (Tonband) tape.

Band² (pl Bände) der (Buch) volume.

Band³ (pl -s) die (MUS) band.

Bandage (pl -n) die bandage.

bandagieren vt to bandage.

Bandscheibe (pl -n) die disc (in spine).

Bank¹ (pl -en) die bank.

Bank² (pl Bänke) die bench.

Bankangestellte (pl -n) der, die bank employee.

Bankanweisung (pl -en) die banker's order.

Bankett (pl -e) das banquet.

Bankkonto (pl -konten) das bank account.

Bankleitzahl (pl -en) die bank sort code.

Banknote (pl -n) die banknote.

bankrott adj bankrupt.

Bankverbindung (pl -en) die account details (pl).

bar ◆ adv (in) cash. ◆ adj: **~es Geld** cash; **in ~** in cash.

Bar (pl -s) die bar.

Bär (pl -en) der bear.

barfuß ◆ adv barefoot. ◆ adj: **~ sein** to be barefoot.

barg prät → bergen.

Bargeld das cash.

bargeldlos ◆ adj cash-free. ◆ adv without using cash.

Bariton (pl -e) der baritone.

Barkeeper (pl -) der barman.

barock adj baroque.

Barometer (pl -) das barometer.

Barriere (pl -n) die barrier.

barsch adj curt.

Barscheck (pl -s) der uncrossed cheque.

Bart (pl Bärte) der beard.

Barzahlung (pl -en) die payment in cash; **Verkauf nur gegen ~** cash sales only.

Basar (pl -e) der bazaar.

Basel nt Basel, Basle.

Basilikum das basil.

Basis die (Grundlage) basis.

Basketball der basketball.

Baß (pl Bässe) der bass.

basteln ◆ vt to make. ◆ vi: **er bastelt gerne** he likes making things himself.

bat prät → bitten.

Batterie (pl -n) die battery; **wiederaufladbare ~** rechargeable battery.

batteriebetrieben *adj* battery-powered.

Bau¹ (*pl* **-ten**) *der* (*Vorgang, Gebäude*) building; (*Baustelle*) building site.

Bau² (*pl* **-e**) *der* (*von Tier*) hole.

Bauarbeiten *pl* construction work (*sg*); '**wegen ~ gesperrt**' 'road closed due to construction work'.

Bauarbeiter, -in (*mpl* **-**) *der, die* builder.

Bauch (*pl* **Bäuche**) *der* stomach.

Bauchschmerzen *pl* stomachache (*sg*); **~ haben** to have stomachache.

Bauchspeck *der* belly pork.

Bauchspeicheldrüse (*pl* **-n**) *die* pancreas.

Baudenkmal (*pl* **-mäler**) *das* monument.

bauen ♦ *vt* (*Haus, Straße, Auto*) to build; (*Möbel, Maschine*) to make. ♦ *vi* to build; **an etw** (D) **~** to be building sthg; **~ auf** (+A) to rely on.

Bauer (*pl* **-n**) *der* (*Beruf*) farmer; (*Schachfigur*) pawn; (*Spielkarte*) jack.

Bäuerin (*pl* **-nen**) *die* farmer's wife.

Bauernbrot (*pl* **-e**) *das* farmhouse loaf.

Bauernfrühstück (*pl* **-e**) *das* fried potatoes with scrambled egg and pieces of bacon.

Bauernhof (*pl* **-höfe**) *der* farm.

baufällig *adj* dilapidated.

Baum (*pl* **Bäume**) *der* tree.

Baumarkt (*pl* **-märkte**) *der* DIY store.

Baumwolle *die* cotton.

Baustelle (*pl* **-n**) *die* building site; '**Vorsicht ~!**' 'men at work'.

Baustellenausfahrt (*pl* **-en**) *die* works exit.

Bauwerk (*pl* **-e**) *das* building.

Bayern *nt* Bavaria.

Bayreuther Festspiele *pl* Wagner festival held annually in the town of Bayreuth.

BAYREUTHER FESTSPIELE

Every August, a Wagner Festival is held in Bayreuth (Bavaria), commemorating the town's most famous son, Richard Wagner. Events are staged in the 'Festspielhaus' (festival theatre), which was built without an orchestra pit, in accordance with Wagner's wishes. The Bayreuth Festival has become world-famous and attracts thousands of visitors each year.

Bazillus (*pl* **Bazillen**) *der* germ.

Bd. (*abk für* Band) vol.

beabsichtigen *vt* to intend.

beachten *vt* (*Verbot*) to observe; (*Person*) to notice.

Beamte (*pl* **-n**) *der* (*bei Finanzamt, Botschaft*) civil servant; (*Polizist, beim Zoll*) officer.

Beamtin (*pl* **-nen**) *die* (*bei Finanzamt, Botschaft*) civil servant; (*Polizist, beim Zoll*) officer.

beanspruchen *vt* (*strapazieren*) to wear out; (*Zeit, Platz*) to take up; **jn stark ~** to keep sb very busy.

beanstanden *vt* to complain about; **es gibt nichts zu ~** there's no cause for complaint.

Beanstandung (*pl* **-en**) *die* complaint.

beantragen *vt* to apply for.

beantworten *vt* to answer.

bearbeiten *vt* (*Antrag*) to deal with; (*Feld, Stein, Holz*) to work.

Bearbeitungsgebühr (*pl* **-en**) *die* handling charge.

beatmen *vt*: **jn künstlich ~** (MED) to put sb on a respirator.

beaufsichtigen *vt* to supervise.

beauftragen *vt*: **jn mit etw ~** to entrust sthg to sb; **jn ~, etw zu tun** to instruct sb to do sthg.

Becher (*pl* **-**) *der* (*zum Trinken*) cup (*without handles*); (*aus Plastik*) beaker; (*für Eis*) dish; (*für Joghurt*) pot.

Becken (*pl* **-**) *das* (*Waschbecken*) basin; (*Spülbecken*) sink; (*Schwimmbecken*) pool; (*Körperteil*) pelvis; (MUS) cymbal.

Beckenrand *der* edge of the pool;

'Springen vom ~ nicht erlaubt!' 'no diving!'

bedaanken: sich bedanken ref: **sich (bei jm) ~** to say thank you (to sb).

Bedarf der need; **bei ~** if necessary.

Bedarfshaltestelle (pl -n) die request stop.

bedauerlich adj unfortunate.

bedauern ♦ vt (bemitleiden) to feel sorry for; (schade finden) to regret. ♦ vi to be sorry; **bedaure!** I'm sorry!

bedecken vt (Boden, Schultern) to cover.

bedeckt adj overcast.

bedeuten vt (meinen) to mean; **das hat nichts zu ~** that doesn't matter.

bedeutend adj important.

Bedeutung (pl -en) die (Sinn, Inhalt) meaning; (Wichtigkeit) importance.

bedienen ♦ vt (Gast, Kunde) to serve; (Maschine) to operate. ♦ vi (Kellner) to serve. ► **sich bedienen** ref to help o.s.; **~ Sie sich!** help yourself!

Bedienung (pl -en) die (von Gast, Kunde) service; (von Maschine) operation; (Kellner) waiter (waitress); **inklusive ~** including service.

Bedienungsanleitung (pl -en) die operating instructions (pl).

Bedienungshandbuch (pl -bücher) das (operating) manual.

Bedingung (pl -en) die condition; **unter einer ~** on one condition.

bedrohen vt to threaten.

Bedürfnis (pl -se) das need.

beeilen: sich beeilen ref to hurry.

beeindrucken vt to impress.

beeinflussen vt to influence.

beenden vt to end.

Beerdigung (pl -en) die funeral.

Beere (pl -n) die berry.

Beet (pl -e) das (mit Blumen) flower bed; (mit Gemüse) patch.

Beete die: **rote ~** beetroot.

befahl prät → **befehlen**.

befahrbar adj passable.

befahren (präs **befährt**, prät **befuhr**, pp **befahren**) vt to use.

Befehl (pl -e) der order.

befehlen (präs **befiehlt**, prät **befahl**, pp **befohlen**) vt to order.

befestigen vt (anbringen) to fasten; (Straße) to surface.

befiehlt präs → **befehlen**.

befinden: sich befinden (prät **befand**, pp **befunden**) ref to be; **'Sie ~ sich hier'** 'you are here'.

befohlen pp → **befehlen**.

befolgen vt to obey.

befördern vt (mit Auto, Zug) to transport; (beruflich) to promote.

Beförderung (pl -en) die (Transport) transport; (beruflich) promotion.

Beförderungsbedingungen pl (amt) conditions of carriage.

Beförderungsentgelt das (amt) fare.

befragen vt to question.

befreien vt to free. ► **sich befreien** ref to escape.

befreundet adj: **mit jm ~ sein** to be friends with sb.

befriedigend adj (zufriedenstellend) satisfactory.

befristet adj temporary.

Befund (pl -e) der results (pl); **ohne ~** negative.

befürchten vt to fear.

begabt adj talented.

begann prät → **beginnen**.

begegnen vi ist (+D) to meet. ► **sich begegnen** ref to meet.

begehrt adj coveted.

begeistern vt to fill with enthusiasm. ► **sich begeistern** ref: **sich für etw ~** to become enthusiastic about sthg.

begeistert ♦ adj enthusiastic. ♦ adv enthusiastically.

Beginn der beginning; **zu ~** at the beginning.

beginnen (prät **begann**, pp **begonnen**) vt & vi to begin, to start; **~ mit** (+D) to begin with, to start with.

beglaubigen *vt* to certify.

Beglaubigung (*pl* -en) *die* certification.

begleiten *vt* to accompany.

Begleitperson (*pl* -en) *die* escort.

Begleitung *die* company; **in ~ von** accompanied by.

beglückwünschen *vt* to congratulate.

begonnen *pp* → **beginnen**.

Begräbnis (*pl* -se) *das* funeral.

begreifen (*prät* **begriff**, *pp* **begriffen**) *vt & vi* to understand.

Begrenzung (*pl* -en) *die* (*zeitlich*) restriction; (*Grenze*) boundary.

Begriff (*pl* -e) *der* (*Wort*) term.

begründen *vt* to justify; (*gründen*) to establish.

Begründer, -in (*mpl* -) *der, die* founder.

Begründung (*pl* -en) *die* reason; (*Gründung*) establishment.

begrüßen *vt* (*Person*) to greet.

Begrüßung (*pl* -en) *die* greeting.

behalten (*präs* **behält**, *prät* **behielt**, *pp* **behalten**) *vt* (*nicht abgeben*) to keep; (*in Erinnerung*) to remember; **etw für sich ~** (*nicht erzählen*) to keep sthg to o.s.

Behälter (*pl* -) *der* container.

behandeln *vt* to treat; (*Thema*) to deal with; **jn gut/schlecht ~** to treat sb well/badly; **mit Antibiotika ~** to treat with antibiotics.

Behandlung (*pl* -en) *die* treatment.

behaupten *vt* (*versichern*) to claim.
► **sich behaupten** *ref* to assert o.s.

beheimatet *adj* (*geh*): **in Deutschland ~ sein** to come from Germany.

beheizt *adj* heated.

behelfen: sich behelfen (*präs* **behilft**, *prät* **behalf**, *pp* **beholfen**) *ref* to manage.

behelfsmäßig *adj* makeshift.

beherbergen *vt* to put up, to accommodate.

beherrschen *vt* (*bestimmen*) to rule;

(*Sprache*) to have a command of.
► **sich beherrschen** *ref* to control o.s.

behilflich *adj*: **jm ~ sein** to help sb.

behindern *vt* (*Sicht, Verkehr*) to obstruct; (*Person*) to hinder.

behindert *adj* handicapped.

Behinderte (*pl* -n) *der, die* handicapped person.

Behindertenaufzug (*pl* -aufzüge) *der* disabled lift (Br), disabled elevator (Am).

Behinderung (*pl* -en) *die* (*körperlich, geistig*) handicap; (*im Verkehr*) delay; **mit ~en muß gerechnet werden** delays are likely.

Behörde (*pl* -n) *die* authority.

bei *präp* (+D) **1.** (*an einem Ort*) at; **~ der Post** at the post office; **~m Arzt** at the doctor's; **~ meiner Tante** at my aunt's; **~ mir** at my house; **hast du Geld ~ dir?** have you got any money on you?; **sie arbeitet ~ einem Verlag** she works for a publishing company. **2.** (*in der Nähe von*) near; **das Hotel ist gleich ~m Bahnhof** the hotel is right next to the station. **3.** (*Angabe von Umständen*): **~ Regen vorsichtig fahren** drive carefully in the rain; **~ Regen fällt der Ausflug aus** if it rains the trip will be cancelled; **kannst du das Buch ~ Gelegenheit vorbeibringen?** could you bring the book round next time you get the chance?; **~ Tag/Nacht** by day/night. **4.** (*Angabe von Zeit*) at; **~ Beginn** at the beginning; **~ der Arbeit** at work; **~m Sport brach er sich den Arm** he broke his arm (while) playing sport. **5.** (*Angabe von Ursache, Grund*) with; **~ deinem Benehmen muß er ja verärgert sein** it's hardly surprising he's angry, after the way you behaved. **6.** (*trotz*): **~ aller Liebe, aber so nicht!** however much I love you, you can't do that.

beibringen *vt* (*lehren*) to teach.

beichten *vt & vi* to confess.

beide *pron & adj* both; **meine ~n Töchter** both (of) my daughters; **ihr**

~ you two; **jeder der ~n** each of them.

beidseitig ◆ adj (Einverständnis) mutual. ◆ adv (beschrieben) on both sides.

Beifahrer, -in (mpl -) der, die (im PKW) front-seat passenger.

Beifahrersitz (pl -e) der passenger seat.

Beifall der applause; **~ spenden** ODER **klatschen** to applaud.

beige adj beige.

Beilage (pl -n) die: **mit Reis als ~** (served) with rice.

Beileid das condolences (pl); **herzliches** ODER **aufrichtiges ~** my sincere condolences.

beiliegend adj (amt) enclosed.

beim präp = **bei** + **dem**.

Bein (pl -e) das leg.

beinahe adv almost.

Beinbruch (pl -brüche) der broken leg.

beinhalten vt (enthalten) to contain.

Beipackzettel (pl -) der instructions (pl).

Beisammensein das get-together.

Beispiel (pl -e) das example; **zum ~** for example.

beispielsweise adv for example.

beißen (prät **biß**, pp **gebissen**) vt & vi to bite; **in etw** (A) **~** to bite into sthg.

Beitrag (pl -träge) der (Geld, Mitarbeit) contribution; (für Verein) subscription.

bekämpfen vt to fight.

bekannt adj (allgemein) well-known; (individuell) familiar; **jn ~ machen mit** to introduce sb to; **mit jm ~ sein** to know sb.

Bekannte (pl -n) der, die (flüchtig) acquaintance; (Freund) friend.

bekannt|geben vt unr to announce.

bekannt|machen vt to announce; **jn mit jm ~** to introduce sb to sb.

Bekanntschaft (pl -en) die (Kontakt) acquaintance; (Gruppe) acquaintances (pl).

beklagen: sich beklagen ref to complain.

bekleckern vt: **etw mit etw ~** to spill sthg on sthg. ▶ **sich bekleckern** ref: **sich mit etw ~** to spill sthg on o.s.

Bekleidung die clothes (pl).

bekommen (prät **bekam**, pp **bekommen**) ◆ vt hat to get; (Kind, Besuch) to expect; (Zug, Bus) to catch. ◆ vi ist: **jm gut ~** (Klima, Luft) to be good for sb; (Essen) to agree with sb; **jm schlecht ~** to disagree with sb; **etw geschenkt/geliehen ~** to be given/lent sthg; **ich bekomme noch 100 DM von dir** you owe me 100 marks; **was ~ Sie?** what would you like?; **was ~ Sie dafür?** how much is it?; **etw zu essen/trinken ~** to get sthg to eat/drink.

bekömmlich adj easy to digest.

beladen (präs **belädt**, prät **belud**, pp **beladen**) vt to load.

Belag (pl **Beläge**) der (auf Brot) topping; (auf Bremse) lining; (auf Straße) surface.

belangen vt (amt: verklagen) to prosecute.

belasten vt (deprimieren) to put a strain on; (Umwelt, Luft) to pollute; (mit Gewicht) to weigh down.

belästigen vt (sexuell) to harass; (stören) to bother.

Belastung (pl -en) die (psychisch, körperlich) strain; (von Umwelt) pollution; (Last) load.

belaufen: sich belaufen (präs **beläuft**, prät **belief**, pp **belaufen**) ref: **die Rechnung beläuft sich auf 120 DM** the bill comes to 120 marks.

belebt adj busy.

Beleg (pl -e) der (Quittung) receipt.

belegt adj (Sitzplatz) occupied; (Hotel) full; (Telefonanschluß) engaged; (Zunge) furred; (Stimme) hoarse; **~es Brötchen/Brot** open roll/sandwich; **voll ~** no vacancies.

belehren vt to inform.

beleidigen vt to insult.

Beleidigung (pl -en) die (Bemerkung, Handlung) insult.

Beleuchtung die (Scheinwerfer, Lampen) lights (pl).

Belgien nt Belgium.

Belgier, -in (mpl -) der, die Belgian.

belgisch adj Belgian.

belichten vt to expose.

Belichtung (pl -en) die exposure.

Belichtungsmesser (pl -) der light meter.

Belichtungszeit (pl -en) die exposure time.

Belieben das: nach ~ as you like.

beliebig ♦ adj any. ♦ adv: ~ viel as much as you like; in ~er Reihenfolge in any order; zu jeder ~en Zeit whenever you like.

beliebt adj popular.

beliefern vt to supply.

bellen vi to bark.

belohnen vt to reward.

Belohnung (pl -en) die (Geld, Geschenk) reward.

Belüftung die ventilation.

belügen (prät belog, pp belogen) vt to lie to. ▶ sich belügen ref to deceive o.s.

bemerkbar adj noticeable; sich ~ machen (durch Rufen, Klopfen) to attract attention; (sich zeigen) to become apparent.

bemerken vt (wahrnehmen) to notice; (geh: sagen) to remark; nebenbei bemerkt by the way.

Bemerkung (pl -en) die remark; eine ~ machen to make a remark.

bemühen: sich bemühen ref: sich ~, etw zu tun to try to do sthg.

Bemühungen pl efforts.

benachrichtigen vt to inform.

Benachrichtigung (pl -en) die notification.

benehmen: sich benehmen (präs benimmt, prät benahm, pp benommen) ref: sich gut/schlecht ~ to behave well/badly.

beneiden vt to envy.

benötigen vt to need.

benutzen vt to use.

benützen = benutzen.

Benutzer, -in (mpl -) der, die user.

Benzin das petrol (Br), gas (Am); bleifreies ~ unleaded petrol (Br), unleaded gas (Am); ~ tanken to fill up with petrol (Br), to fill up with gas (Am).

Benzingutschein (pl -e) der petrol coupon (Br), gas coupon (Am).

Benzinkanister (pl -) der petrol can (Br), gas can (Am).

Benzin-Öl-Gemisch das petrol-oil mixture (Br), gas-oil mixture (Am).

Benzinpumpe (pl -n) die petrol pump (Br), gas pump (Am).

beobachten vt (betrachten) to observe; (bemerken) to notice; (überwachen) to watch.

Beobachter, -in (mpl -) der, die observer.

bequem ♦ adj (Hose, Sitz, Größe) comfortable; (faul) lazy; (Lösung) easy. ♦ adv comfortably; machen Sie es sich ~! make yourself at home!

Bequemlichkeit die (Komfort) comfort; (Faulheit) laziness.

beraten (präs berät, prät beriet, pp beraten) ♦ vt (Kunde) to advise; (Vorhaben) to discuss. ♦ vi (diskutieren): über etw (A) ~ to discuss sthg. ▶ sich beraten ref: sich über etw (A) ~ to discuss sthg.

Beratungsstelle (pl -n) die advice centre.

berechnen vt (ausrechnen) to calculate; (verlangen) to charge; jm für eine Konsultation 120 DM ~ to charge sb 120 marks for a consultation.

berechtigt adj (Zweifel) justified; ~ sein zu etw to be entitled to sthg.

Bereich (pl -e) der area.

bereisen vt to travel.

bereit adj ready; ~ sein (fertig sein) to be ready; ~ sein, etw zu tun (willens sein) to be willing to do sthg.

bereit|halten *vt unr* to have ready. ▶ **sich bereithalten** *ref* to be ready.

bereit|machen: sich bereitmachen *ref* to get ready.

bereits *adv* already; (*nur, allein*) even; ~ **um 6 Uhr** as early as 6 o'clock.

Bereitschaft *die* readiness.

Bereitschaftsdienst (*pl* **-e**) *der* emergency service.

bereit|stehen *vi unr* to be ready.

bereuen *vt* to regret.

Berg (*pl* **-e**) *der* mountain; (*kleiner*) hill; **in die ~e fahren** to go to the mountains.

bergab *adv* downhill; ~ **fahren/laufen** to drive/run downhill.

bergauf *adv* uphill; ~ **fahren/laufen** to drive/run uphill.

Bergbahn (*pl* **-en**) *die* funicular railway.

Bergbau *der* mining.

bergen (*präs* **birgt**, *prät* **barg**, *pp* **geborgen**) *vt* (*retten*) to rescue.

Bergführer, -in (*mpl* **-**) *der, die* mountain guide.

Berghütte (*pl* **-n**) *die* mountain hut.

bergig *adj* mountainous.

Bergnot *die*: **in ~ geraten** to get into trouble while climbing a mountain.

Bergschuh (*pl* **-e**) *der* climbing boot.

bergsteigen (*pp* **berggestiegen**) *vi* to go (mountain) climbing.

Bergsteigen *das* (mountain) climbing.

Bergsteiger, -in (*mpl* **-**) *der, die* (mountain) climber.

Bergtour (*pl* **-en**) *die* (mountain) hike.

Bergung (*pl* **-en**) *die* rescue.

Bergwacht *die* mountain rescue.

Bergwanderung (*pl* **-en**) *die* hillwalking.

Bergwerk (*pl* **-e**) *das* mine.

Bericht (*pl* **-e**) *der* report.

berichten *vi* to report.

berichtigen *vt* to correct. ▶ **sich**

berichtigen *ref* to correct o.s.

Berichtigung (*pl* **-en**) *die* correction.

Berlin *nt* Berlin.

Berliner (*pl* **-**) *der* (*Gebäck*) doughnut.

Berliner Mauer *die*: **die ~** the Berlin Wall.

DIE BERLINER MAUER

The Berlin Wall, sometimes also known as 'die Mauer' (the Wall), was built on 13 August 1961 in order to stem the growing tide of people leaving East Berlin for the West. It encircled West Berlin, cutting it off from the surrounding GDR, and came to be a potent symbol of the post-war division of Germany. Some 80 people died while attempting to escape over the Wall to West Berlin. The fall of the Wall on 9 November 1989 marked the beginning of the process of German reunification. Today, little of the Wall remains, although a few sections have been left standing as a memorial and others can be found in museums.

Bern *nt* Bern, Berne.

berüchtigt *adj* notorious.

berücksichtigen *vt* (*bei Überlegung*) to take into account; (*Bewerber, Wunsch*) to consider.

Beruf (*pl* **-e**) *der* profession; **Tischler von ~ sein** to be a carpenter; **was sind Sie von ~?** what do you do for a living?

beruflich ◆ *adj* professional. ◆ *adv*: ~ **unterwegs** away on business.

Berufsausbildung (*pl* **-en**) *die* vocational training.

Berufserfahrung *die* job experience.

Berufsschule (*pl* **-n**) *die* vocational school attended part-time by apprentices.

berufstätig *adj* employed.

Berufstätige (*pl* **-n**) *der, die* working person.

Berufsverkehr *der* rush-hour traffic.

beruhigen vt to calm (down).
► **sich beruhigen** ref (Person) to
calm down; (Wetter, See) to become
calm.

Beruhigungsmittel (pl -) das
sedative.

berühmt adj famous; ~ **sein wegen**
ODER **für** to be famous for.

berühren vt & vi to touch; **bitte nicht
~!** please don't touch! ► **sich
berühren** ref to touch.

beschädigen vt to damage.

beschädigt adj damaged.

beschäftigen vt (Angestellte) to
employ; (gedanklich) to occupy.
► **sich beschäftigen** ref: **sich ~ mit**
(mit Person) to devote a lot of attention to; (mit Thema) to deal with; (mit
Gedanken) to think about.

Beschäftigung (pl -en) die (Arbeit)
occupation; (Hobby) activity;
(gedanklich) preoccupation.

Bescheid (pl -e) der (Nachricht)
answer; **jm ~ geben** ODER **sagen** to let
sb know; **~ wissen (über** (+A)) to
know (about).

bescheiden adj modest.

bescheinigen vt (mit Zeugnis) to
certify; (Erhalt von Sendung) to sign
for.

Bescheinigung (pl -en) die certificate.

Bescherung (pl -en) die giving out of
Christmas presents.

beschimpfen vt to swear at.

beschissen adj (vulg) shitty.

Beschlag der: **in ~ nehmen** to
monopolize.

beschlagnahmen vt (Beute) to
confiscate.

beschleunigen ◆ vt (Tempo,
Verfahren, Ablauf) to speed up. ◆ vi
(Auto) to accelerate. ► **sich
beschleunigen** ref to speed up.

Beschleunigung die (von Verfahren)
speeding up; (von Auto) accelera-
tion.

beschließen (prät **beschloß**, pp
beschlossen) vt (entscheiden) to

decide on; (Gesetz) to pass; (beenden)
to end; **~, etw zu tun** to decide to
do sthg.

Beschluß (pl **Beschlüsse**) der decision.

beschränken vt to limit.

Beschränkung (pl -en) die limit.

beschreiben (prät **beschrieb**, pp
beschrieben) vt (schildern) describe;
jm den Weg ~ to tell sb the way.

Beschreibung (pl -en) die description.

beschriften vt to label.

beschuldigen vt to accuse.

Beschuldigung (pl -en) die accusation.

beschützen vt to protect.

Beschwerde (pl -n) die complaint.
► **Beschwerden** pl (Gesundheits-
probleme) trouble (sg).

beschweren: sich beschweren
ref to complain.

beschwipst adj tipsy.

beseitigen vt (Abfall) to get rid of;
(Problem) to deal with.

Besen (pl -) der broom.

besetzt adj: **~ sein** (Telefonanschluß,
Toilette) to be engaged; (Sitzplatz) to
be taken; **das Büro ist zur Zeit nicht ~**
the office is currently closed.

Besetztzeichen das engaged tone
(Br), busy signal (Am).

Besetzung (pl -en) die (am Theater)
cast.

besichtigen vt to look round.

Besichtigung (pl -en) die tour; **'zur
~ freigegeben'** 'open to the public'.

besiegen vt to defeat.

Besitz der (Eigentum) property.

besitzen (prät **besaß**, pp **besessen**) vt
(Eigentum) to own; (Qualität, Ausrüs-
tungsgegenstand) to have.

Besitzer, -in (mpl -) der, die owner.

besoffen adj (fam) sloshed.

besondere, -r, -s adj (speziell) special; (außergewöhnlich) particular.

besonders adv particularly; **nicht ~**
(fam: nicht gut) not very well; **nicht ~**

sein (*fam*: *nicht gut*) to be not very good.

besorgen *vt* (*holen, kaufen*) to get.

besorgt ♦ *adj* worried. ♦ *adv* worriedly.

besprechen (*präs* **bespricht**, *prät* **besprach**, *pp* **besprochen**) *vt* (*diskutieren*) to discuss.

Besprechung (*pl* **-en**) *die* meeting.

besser ♦ *komp* & *adv* better. ♦ *adj* (*sehr gut*) good; (*abw*: *kaum besser*): **das Hotel ist eine ~e Absteige** the hotel is just a glorified dosshouse.

bessern: sich bessern *ref* (*Erkältung*) to get better; (*Chancen, Wetter*) to improve.

Besserung *die*: **gute ~!** get well soon!

beständig *adj* (*Wetter*) settled.

Bestandteil (*pl* **-e**) *der* component, part.

bestätigen *vt* to confirm. ▶ **sich bestätigen** *ref* to prove true.

Bestätigung (*pl* **-en**) *die* confirmation.

beste, -r, -s ♦ *superl* best. ♦ *adj* ideal. ♦ *adv*: **am ~n** best; **ich gehe jetzt am ~n** I'd better go now; **sie spricht am ~n Deutsch von allen** she speaks the best German of everyone.

Beste (*pl* **-n**) *der, die* best.

Bestechung (*pl* **-en**) *die* bribery.

Besteck (*pl* **-e**) *das* (*zum Essen*) cutlery.

bestehen (*prät* **bestand**, *pp* **bestanden**) ♦ *vt* (*Prüfung*) to pass. ♦ *vi* (*existieren*) to exist; (*bei Prüfung*) to pass; **~ auf** (+D) to insist on; **~ aus** to consist of.

besteigen (*prät* **bestieg**, *pp* **bestiegen**) *vt* to climb.

bestellen ♦ *vi* (*im Lokal*) to order. ♦ *vt* (*Ware*) to order; (*Eintrittskarte, Hotelzimmer*) to reserve; (*Nachricht*): **jm schöne Grüße ~** to give sb one's regards.

Bestellformular (*pl* **-e**) *das* order form.

Bestellkarte (*pl* **-n**) *die* order form.

Bestellnummer (*pl* **-n**) *die* order number.

Bestellung (*pl* **-en**) *die* (*von Waren*) ordering; (*von Eintrittskarte, Hotelzimmer*) reservation; (*Ware*) order; **auf ~** to order.

bestens *adv* very well.

bestimmen ♦ *vt* (*ermitteln*) to determine; (*festlegen*) to fix; (*klassifizieren*) to classify. ♦ *vi* (*befehlen*) to decide; **bestimmt sein für** to be meant for.

bestimmt ♦ *adv* (*sehr wahrscheinlich*) no doubt; (*sicher*) certainly; (*wissen*) for certain; (*entschlossen*) decisively. ♦ *adj* (*gewiß*) certain; (*Betrag, Anzahl*) fixed; (*Auftreten*) decisive.

Bestimmung (*pl* **-en**) *die* (*Vorschrift*) regulation; (*ermitteln*) determining.

Bestimmungsland (*pl* **-länder**) *das* (*amt*) (country of) destination.

Bestimmungsort (*pl* **-e**) *der* (*amt*) (place of) destination.

bestmöglich ♦ *adj* best possible. ♦ *adv* as well as possible.

bestrafen *vt* to punish.

bestrahlen *vt* (MED: *Patienten, Haut*) to treat with radiotherapy.

bestreiten (*prät* **bestritt**, *pp* **bestritten**) *vt* (*leugnen*) to deny.

bestürzt *adj*: **~ sein** to be dismayed.

Besuch (*pl* **-e**) *der* visit; (*Gast*) visitor; (*von Schule*) attendance; **bei jm zu ~ sein** to be visiting sb.

besuchen *vt* (*Person, Veranstaltung*) to visit; (*Schule*) to attend.

Besucher, -in (*mpl* **-**) *der, die* visitor; **'nur für ~'** 'visitors only'.

Besuchszeit (*pl* **-en**) *die* visiting hours (*pl*).

besucht *adj*: **gut/schlecht ~ sein** to be well/poorly attended.

betätigen *vt* (*Hebel*) to operate.

betäuben *vt* to anaesthetize.

Betäubung *die*: **unter ~ stehen** to be under anaesthetic.

beteiligen *vt* (*teilnehmen lassen*) to

include; (*finanziell*) to give a share.
▶ **sich beteiligen** *ref*: sich ~ an (+D)
(*teilnehmen*) to take part (in);
(*finanziell*) to have a share (in).
Beteiligung (*pl* -en) *die* (*Teilnahme*)
participation; (*finanziell*) share.

beten *vi* to pray.

Beton *der* concrete.

betonen *vt* to stress.

Betonung (*pl* -en) *die* (*von Wort*)
stress.

betrachten *vt* to look at; **jn als etw
~** to consider sb to be sthg.

Betrachter, -in (*mpl* -) *der, die*
observer.

beträchtlich ◆ *adj* considerable.
◆ *adv* considerably.

Betrag (*pl* **Beträge**) *der* amount;
bitte angezeigten ~ bezahlen please
pay the amount displayed; **~ dank-
end erhalten** (*amt*) received with
thanks.

betragen (*präs* **beträgt**, *prät* **betrug**,
pp **betragen**) *vt* to come to. ▶ **sich
betragen** *ref* (*sich benehmen*) to
behave.

betreffen (*präs* **betrifft**, *prät* **betraf**,
pp **betroffen**) *vt* (*angehen*) to concern;
(*bestürzen*) to affect; **was mich betrifft**
as far as I'm concerned.

betreiben (*prät* **betrieb**, *pp*
betrieben) *vt* (*Handel*) to carry on;
betrieben werden mit to be driven
by.

betreten (*präs* **betritt**, *prät* **betrat**, *pp*
betreten) *vt* to enter; **'Betreten verboten!'** 'no entry!'

betreuen *vt* to look after.

Betreuer, -in (*mpl* -) *der, die* (*von
Patient*) nurse; (*von Kind*) childminder; (*von Touristen*) groupleader.

Betrieb (*pl* -e) *der* (*Firma*) firm;
(*Aktivität, Verkehr*) hustle and bustle;
außer ~ out of order; **in ~** in operation.

betrieben *pp* → **betreiben**.

betriebsbereit *adj* operational.

Betriebsrat (*pl* -räte) *der* works
council.

Betriebswirtschaft *die* business
studies (*pl*).

betrifft *präs* → **betreffen**.

betrinken: sich betrinken (*prät*
betrank, *pp* **betrunken**) *ref* to get
drunk.

betroffen ◆ *pp* → **betreffen**. ◆ *adj*
(*nicht verschont*) affected; (*bestürzt*)
upset. ◆ *adv* (*bestürzt*): **jn ~ ansehen**
to look at sb in consternation.

betrügen (*prät* **betrog**, *pp* **betrogen**)
vt (*finanziell*) to cheat; (*sexuell*) to be
unfaithful to. ▶ **sich betrügen** *ref* to
deceive o.s.

Betrüger, -in (*mpl* -) *der, die* cheat.

betrunken *adj* drunk.

Bett (*pl* -en) *das* (*Möbel*) bed; **das ~
machen** to make the bed; **zu** ODER
ins ~ gehen to go to bed; **französi-
sches ~** double bed.

Bettdecke (*pl* -n) *die* (continental)
quilt.

Bettler, -in (*mpl* -) *der, die* beggar.

Bettsofa (*pl* -s) *das* sofa bed.

Bettuch (*pl* -tücher) *das* sheet.

Bettwäsche *die* bed linen.

Bettzeug *das* bedding.

beugen *vt* (*Kopf, Knie*) to bend;
(*Substantiv, Adjektiv*) to decline; (*Verb*)
to conjugate.

Beule (*pl* -n) *die* (*am Kopf*) swelling;
(*am Auto*) dent.

beunruhigt *adj*: **~ sein** to be worried.

beurteilen *vt* to judge.

Beutel (*pl* -) *der* bag.

Bevölkerung (*pl* -en) *die* population.

bevollmächtigt *adj* authorized.

bevor *konj* before.

bevorzugen *vt* to prefer.

bewacht *adj* guarded.

bewährt *adj* tried and tested.

bewegen *vt* to move. ▶ **sich
bewegen** *ref* to move; (*sportlich*) to
exercise.

Bewegung (*pl* -en) *die* movement; (*Sport*) exercise; (*Rührung*)

emotion; **sich in ~ setzen** to start moving.

Beweis (*pl* -e) *der* (*für Theorie, Annahme*) proof.

beweisen (*prät* **bewies**, *pp* **bewiesen**) *vt* (*Theorie, Annahme*) to prove; (*Mut, Geduld*) to show.

bewerben: sich bewerben (*präs* **bewirbt**, *prät* **bewarb**, *pp* **beworben**) *ref:* **sich ~ (um)** to apply (for).

Bewerbung (*pl* -en) *die* application.

bewilligen *vt* to approve.

Bewohner, -in (*mpl* -) *der, die* inhabitant.

bewohnt *adj* inhabited.

bewölkt *adj* cloudy.

Bewölkung *die* (*Wolken*) cloud; (*Bewölken*) clouding over.

bewundern *vt* to admire.

bewußt ◆ *adj* (*Handlung*) deliberate; (*Entscheidung*) conscious; (*bekannt*) in question. ◆ *adv* (*handeln*) deliberately; (*entscheiden*) consciously; **sich** (D) **einer Sache ~ sein** to be aware of sthg.

bewußtlos *adj* unconscious.

bezahlen ◆ *vt* (*Person*) to pay; (*Ware, Leistung*) to pay for. ◆ *vi* (*für Ware, Leistung*) to pay.

bezahlt *adj* paid.

Bezahlung *die* payment.

Bezeichnung (*pl* -en) *die* (*Wort*) name; **'genaue ~ des Inhalts'** 'exact description of the contents'.

beziehen (*prät* **bezog**, *pp* **bezogen**) *vt* (*Kissen, Sofa*) to cover; (*Haus*) to move into; (*Ware, Zeitung, Einkünfte*) to get; **das Bett frisch ~** to change the bed. ▶ **sich beziehen** *ref* (*Himmel, Wetter*) to cloud over; **sich ~ auf** (+A) to refer to.

Beziehung (*pl* -en) *die* connection; (*erotisch*) relationship. ▶ **Beziehungen** *pl* (*politisch*) relations.

beziehungsweise *konj* (*genauer gesagt*) that is; (*und*) and; (*oder*) or.

Bezirk (*pl* -e) *der* (*amt*) district.

bezweifeln *vt* to doubt.

BH (*pl* -s) *der* (*abk für* Büstenhalter) bra.

Bhf. *abk* = **Bahnhof**.

Bibel (*pl* -n) *die* Bible.

Bibliothek (*pl* -en) *die* library.

biegen (*prät* **bog**, *pp* **gebogen**) ◆ *vt* hat to bend. ◆ *vi ist* (*Auto, Fahrer*): **~ (in** (+A)**)** to turn (into); **nach links ~** to turn left; **um die Ecke ~** to turn the corner. ▶ **sich biegen** *ref* to bend.

Biegung (*pl* -en) *die* bend.

Biene (*pl* -n) *die* bee.

Bienenstich (*pl* -e) *der* (*Insektenstich*) bee sting; (*Kuchen*) *cake coated with sugar and almonds and filled with custard or cream.*

Bier (*pl* -e) *das* beer; **ein Glas ~** a glass of beer; **~ vom Faß** draught beer; **ein großes ~** a half-litre glass of beer; **ein kleines ~** a 30cl glass of beer.

BIER

There are over 1,000 breweries in Germany and each region boasts several different kinds of local beer. The most common kinds are the pale lager beers, either strong, hoppy 'Pils' or the milder 'Export', which in Bavaria is often drunk in a litre glass called a 'Maßkrug'. Another popular beer in Bavaria is 'Weizenbier', a fizzy beer made from wheat which is slightly cloudy because of the yeast sediment that it contains. 'Berliner Weiße' is similar but weaker and is often drunk with a dash of raspberry cordial ('mit Schuß'). In the Rhineland, light 'Kölsch' and dark 'Altbier' are both common. The brewing of beer in Germany is governed by strict laws regulating its purity (the 1516 'Reinheitsgebot').

Biergarten (*pl* -gärten) *der* beer garden.

BIERGARTEN

Beer gardens are a common sight in summer, especially in Bavaria.

Customers sit outdoors at tables with long, wooden benches and drink a 'Maß' (litre measure) of beer. Beer gardens are usually found in parks or outside the major breweries and most of them serve snacks as well as beer, although customers are often allowed to bring their own food with them. Some of the monasteries where beer is brewed, such as 'Andechs' and 'Weihenstephan', have beer gardens which are particularly worth visiting.

Bierglas (*pl* -gläser) *das* beer glass.
Bierzelt (*pl* -e) *das* beer tent.
bieten (*prät* **bot**, *pp* **geboten**) ♦ *vi* (*bei Auktion*) to bid. ♦ *vt* to offer; **einen schönen Anblick ~** to be pretty. ▶ **sich bieten** *ref* (*Chance*) to present itself; **es bietet sich ein wunderbarer Anblick** there is a wonderful view.
Bild (*pl* -er) *das* picture; (*Vorstellung*) idea; (*Abbild*) image.
bilden ♦ *vt* to form; (*unterrichten*) to educate. ♦ *vi* to be educational. ▶ **sich bilden** *ref* (*sich formen*) to form; (*sich informieren*) to educate o.s.
Bilderbuch (*pl* -bücher) *das* picture book.
Bildhauer, -in (*mpl* -) *der*, *die* sculptor (sculptress).
Bildschirm (*pl* -e) *der* screen; '~ berühren!' *sign on information point indicating that the system is operated by touching the screen.*
Bildschirmtext *der* German teletext service offering information, home banking etc via a computer and telephone line.
Bildung *die* (*Wissen*) education; (*Entstehung*) formation.
Billard *das* billiards (*sg*).
billig ♦ *adj* cheap; (*abw: Ausrede*) feeble. ♦ *adv* (*preisgünstig*) cheaply.
bin *präs* → **sein**.
Binde (*pl* -n) *die* (*Monatsbinde*) sanitary towel; (*Verband*) bandage.

Bindehautentzündung (*pl* -en) *die* conjunctivitis (*sg*).
binden (*prät* **band**, *pp* **gebunden**) *vt* to tie; (*Buch*) to bind; (*KÜCHE: Soße*) to thicken.
Bindestrich (*pl* -e) *der* hyphen.
Bindfaden (*pl* -fäden) *der* string.
Bindung (*pl* -en) *die* (*Verpflichtung*) commitment; (*Zuneigung*) attachment; (*für Ski*) binding.
Biokost *die* health food.
Bioladen (*pl* -läden) *der* health food shop.
Biologie *die* biology.
Biotonne (*pl* -n) *die* bin for biodegradable waste.
Biotop (*pl* -e) *der* ODER *das* biotope.
birgt *präs* → **bergen**.
Birne (*pl* -n) *die* (*Obst*) pear; (*Glühbirne*) light bulb; (*fam: Kopf*) nut.
bis ♦ *präp* (+A) **1.** (*zeitlich*) until; **wir bleiben ~ morgen** we're staying until tomorrow; **das muß ~ Mittwoch fertig sein** it must be ready by Wednesday; **von Montag ~ Freitag** from Monday to Friday; **~ auf weiteres** until further notice; **~ bald!** see you soon!; **~ dahin!** until then. **2.** (*örtlich*) to; **es sind noch 200 km ~ Berlin** there are still 200 km to go to Berlin. **3.** (*zwischen*) to; **zwei ~ drei Tage** two to three days. **4.** (*Angabe von Grenze*): **~ zu** up to; **~ zu 20 Personen** up to 20 people. **5.** (*außer*): **~ auf** (+A) except for. ♦ *konj* until.
Bischof (*pl* **Bischöfe**) *der* bishop.
bisher *adv* (*bis jetzt*) until now.
bisherig *adj* previous.
Biskuit (*pl* -s) *das* sponge.
biß *prät* → **beißen**.
Biß (*pl* **Bisse**) *der* bite.
bißchen *pron*: **das ~ Regen macht nichts!** that little bit of rain won't harm you!; **ein ~** a bit, a bit of; **ein ~ Salz** a bit of salt; **kein ~** not at all; **kein ~ Schnee** no snow at all.
bissig *adj* (*Tier*) vicious; **'Vorsicht, ~er Hund'** 'beware of the dog'.

bist *präs* → **sein**.

bitte ◆ *adv* please. ◆ *interj* (*Ausdruck von Zustimmung*) of course!; (*Antwort auf Dank*) you're welcome!; (*Ausdruck von Angebot*) please; **aber ~!** of course!; **ach ~** please; **~ schön** ODER **sehr** you're welcome!; **~?** (*in Geschäft*) can I help you?; **ja ~?** (*am Telefon*) hello?; **wie ~?** sorry?

Bitte (*pl -n*) *die* request; **eine ~ haben** to have a favour to ask.

bitten (*prät* **bat**, *pp* **gebeten**) *vt* (*Person*) to ask; **~ um** to ask for.

bitter *adj & adv* bitter.

Blähung (*pl -en*) *die* wind.

blamieren *vt* to disgrace. ▶ **sich blamieren** *ref* to disgrace o.s.

Blankoscheck (*pl -s*) *der* blank cheque.

Blase (*pl -n*) *die* (*auf der Haut*) blister; (*Harnblase*) bladder; (*Luftblase*) bubble.

blasen (*präs* **bläst**, *prät* **blies**, *pp* **geblasen**) *vi* (*pusten*) to blow.

Blasenentzündung (*pl -en*) *die* cystitis (*sg*).

blaß *adj* (*Haut, Person*) pale.

bläst *prät* → **blasen**.

Blatt (*pl* **Blätter**) *das* (*Papier*) sheet; (*von Pflanze*) leaf; (*Zeitung*) paper; (*bei Kartenspiel*) hand.

Blätterteig *der* puff pastry.

Blattspinat *der* spinach.

blau *adj* blue; **~ sein** (*fam*) to be sloshed.

Blau *das* blue.

Blaubeere (*pl -n*) *die* blueberry.

Blaulicht *das* flashing blue light (*on ambulance etc*).

blaumachen *vi* (*fam*) to skip work.

Blazer (*pl -*) *der* blazer.

Blech (*pl -e*) *das* (*Metall*) tin; (*Kuchenblech*) baking tray.

Blechschaden *der* bodywork damage.

Bleibe *die* place to stay.

bleiben (*prät* **blieb**, *pp* **geblieben**)

◆ *vi ist* to stay; (*als Rest*) to remain. ◆ *vimp ist*: **es bleibt dabei** we'll leave it at that.

bleifrei *adj* unleaded.

Bleistift (*pl -e*) *der* pencil.

Blende (*pl -n*) *die* (FOTO) aperture.

blenden ◆ *vt* (*anstrahlen*) to dazzle. ◆ *vi* (*Licht, Sonne*) to be dazzling.

Blick (*pl -e*) *der* (*Schauen*) look; (*Aussicht*) view; (*Urteil*) eye.

blieb *prät* → **bleiben**.

blind ◆ *adj* blind. ◆ *adv* blindly.

Blinddarmentzündung (*pl -en*) *die* appendicitis (*sg*).

Blinde (*pl -n*) *der, die* blind person.

Blindenschrift *die* braille.

blinken *vi* (*Autofahrer, Auto*) to indicate.

Blinker (*pl -*) *der* indicator.

Blinklicht (*pl -er*) *das* flashing light.

Blitz (*pl -e*) *der* (*bei Gewitter*) (flash of) lightning; (*von Kamera*) flash; **wie der ~** as quick as lightning.

blitzen ◆ *vt* (*Autofahrer*) to photograph with a speed camera. ◆ *vi* (*mit Blitzlicht*) to use a flash. ◆ *vimp*: **es blitzt** there is lightning.

Blitzlicht (*pl -er*) *das* flash.

Blitzlichtwürfel (*pl -*) *der* flashcube.

Block (*pl* **Blöcke**) *der* (*Schreibblock*) pad; (*Gebäude, Stück*) block.

Blockhaus (*pl -häuser*) *das* log cabin.

blockieren ◆ *vt* to block. ◆ *vi* (*Räder*) to lock.

Blockschrift *die* block capitals (*pl*).

blöd ◆ *adj* (*fam*) stupid. ◆ *adv* (*fam*) stupidly.

Blödsinn *der* nonsense.

blond *adj* blond.

bloß *adv* only, just; **~ noch zwei Wochen** only two more weeks left; **was ist ~ los?** so what's wrong, then?; **was hast du ~ wieder angestellt?** what have you gone and done now?; **paß ~ auf!** just watch out!

blühen *vi* (*Pflanze*) to bloom.

Blume (pl -n) die flower.

Blumenkasten (pl -kästen) der window box.

Blumenkohl der cauliflower.

Blumenstand (pl -stände) der flower stall.

Blumenstrauß (pl -sträuße) der bunch of flowers.

Blumentopf (pl -töpfe) der flowerpot.

Blumentopferde die potting compost.

Bluse (pl -n) die blouse.

Blut das blood; ~ **spenden** to give blood.

Blutbild (pl -er) das blood test results (pl).

Blutdruck der blood pressure; **hoher/niedriger** ~ high/low blood pressure.

bluten vi to bleed.

Bluter (pl -) der haemophiliac.

Bluterguß (pl -güsse) der bruise.

Blutgruppe (pl -n) die blood group.

Blutprobe (pl -n) die blood test.

Blutspende (pl -n) die giving blood.

blutstillend adj styptic.

Blutübertragung (pl -en) die blood transfusion.

Blutung (pl -en) die bleeding.

Blutvergiftung (pl -en) die bloodpoisoning.

Blutwurst (pl -würste) die black pudding (Br), blood sausage (Am).

BLZ abk = **Bankleitzahl**.

Bockbier das bock (strong dark beer).

Bocksbeutel (pl -) der wide, round bottle containing 'Frankenwein'.

Bockwurst (pl -würste) die type of pork sausage, usually boiled and eaten in a bread roll with mustard.

Boden (pl Böden) der (im Raum) floor; (Erde) ground; (Speicher) loft; (von Gefäß, Koffer) bottom.

Bodennebel der ground mist.

Bodenpersonal das ground staff.

Bodensee der Lake Constance.

Bodybuilding das bodybuilding.

Böe (pl -n) die gust.

bog prät → **biegen**.

Bogen (pl Bögen) der (Form) curve; (SPORT: Waffe) bow.

Bohne (pl -n) die bean.

bohren vt & vi to drill.

Bohrer (pl -) der drill.

Bohrmaschine (pl -n) die drill.

böig adj gusty.

Boiler (pl -) der boiler.

Boje (pl -n) die buoy.

Bombe (pl -n) die bomb.

Bon (pl -s) der (Kassenzettel) receipt; (Gutschein) voucher.

Bonbon (pl -s) der ODER das sweet.

Bonn nt Bonn.

Boot (pl -e) das boat; ~ **fahren** to go boating.

Bootsverleih der boat hire.

Bord der: **an** ~ on board; **von** ~ **gehen** to disembark.

Bordkarte (pl -n) die boarding card.

Bordstein der kerb.

Bordsteinkante die kerb.

borgen vt: **jm etw** ~ to lend sb sthg; **sich** (D) **etw** ~ to borrow sthg.

Börse (pl -n) die (ECO) stock market; (Gebäude) stock exchange; (Geldbeutel) purse.

Böschung (pl -en) die bank.

böse ◆ adj (bösartig, schlecht) bad; (fam: wütend) angry. ◆ adv (schlimm, bösartig) badly; (wütend) angrily; ~ **sein auf** (+A) to be angry with; **jm** ~ **sein** to be angry with sb.

bot prät → **bieten**.

botanische Garten (pl -Gärten) der botanical gardens (pl).

Botschaft (pl -en) die (diplomatische Vertretung) embassy; (Gebäude) embassy; (Nachricht) message.

Botschafter, -in (mpl -) der, die ambassador.

Boutique (pl -n) die boutique.

Bowle (pl -n) die punch.

Bowling das tenpin bowling.
Box (pl -en) die (Dose, Kiste) box;
(Lautsprecher) speaker.
boxen ♦ vi to box. ♦ vt to punch.
Boykott (pl -s) der boycott.
brach prät → **brechen**.
brachte prät → **bringen**.
Branchenverzeichnis (pl -se) das
= yellow pages (pl).
Brandung die surf.
Brandwunde (pl -n) die burn.
brannte prät → **brennen**.
braten (präs brät, prät briet, pp
gebraten) vt & vi (in der Pfanne) to fry;
(im Ofen) to roast.
Braten (pl -) der roast.
Brathähnchen (pl -) das roast
chicken.
Bratkartoffeln pl fried potatoes.
Bratpfanne (pl -n) die frying pan.
Bratwurst (pl -würste) die (fried)
sausage.
Brauch (pl Bräuche) der custom.
brauchen ♦ vt (benötigen) to need;
(verwenden, verbrauchen) to use. ♦ aux
to need; **du brauchst nur auf den
Knopf zu drücken** all you need (to)
do is press the button; **etw ~ für** to
need sthg for; **etw ~ zu** to need sthg
for.
brauen vt (Bier) to brew.
Brauerei (pl -en) die brewery.
braun adj brown.
Braun das brown.
Bräune die suntan.
bräunen vt (Braten) to brown;
(Haut) to tan. ► **sich bräunen** ref to
sunbathe.
braungebrannt adj tanned.
Bräunungsstudio (pl -s) das tanning studio.
Brause (pl -n) die (Dusche) shower.
brausen vi (duschen) to have a
shower; (sausen) to roar.
Braut (pl Bräute) die bride.
Bräutigam (pl -e) der bridegroom.
brav adj (Kind) good.
bravo interj bravo!

BRD (abk für Bundesrepublik Deutschland) FRG.
brechen (präs bricht, prät brach,
pp gebrochen) ♦ vt hat to break;
(erbrechen) to vomit. ♦ vi ist (zerbrechen)
to break. ♦ vi hat (erbrechen) to vomit;
sich (D) **das Bein ~** to break one's leg.
Brechreiz der nausea.
Brei der (aus Haferflocken) porridge;
(aus Kartoffeln) mashed potatoes (pl).
breit adj wide; (Rücken, Hände)
broad; (allgemein) general.
Breite (pl -n) die width.
Bremsbelag (pl -beläge) der brake
lining.
Bremse (pl -n) die (von Auto, Fahrrad)
brake; (Insekt) horsefly.
bremsen ♦ vt (Auto, Fahrrad) to
brake; (Person, Fortschritt) to slow
down. ♦ vi to brake.
Bremsflüssigkeit die brake fluid.
Bremskraftverstärker der brake
booster.
Bremslicht (pl -er) das brake light.
Bremspedal (pl -e) das brake
pedal.
brennbar adj flammable.
brennen (prät brannte, pp gebrannt)
♦ vi (Feuer, Kerze, Haus) to burn;
(Licht) to be on; (Haut, Augen) to
sting. ♦ vt (Loch) to burn; (Schnaps) to
distil; (Ton, Ziegel) to fire. ♦ vimp: **es
brennt!** fire!
Brennessel (pl -n) die stinging nettle.
Brennholz das firewood.
Brennspiritus der methylated
spirits (sg).
Brennstoff (pl -e) der (zum Heizen)
fuel.
Brett (pl -er) das (aus Holz) plank;
(zum Spielen) board; **schwarzes ~**
noticeboard.
Brettspiel (pl -e) das board game.
Brezel (pl -n) die pretzel.
bricht präs → **brechen**.
Brief (pl -e) der letter;
eingeschriebener ~ = letter sent by
recorded delivery.

Briefdrucksache *die letter compris-ing an order form, questionnaire etc, which costs less to send than an ordinary letter.*

Brieffreund, -in (*mpl -e*) *der, die* penfriend.

Briefkasten (*pl -kästen*) *der* (*öffent-lich*) postbox; (*am Haus*) letterbox.

Briefmarke (*pl -n*) *die* stamp.

Briefmarkenautomat (*pl -en*) *der* stamp machine.

Briefpapier *das* notepaper.

Brieftasche (*pl -n*) *die* wallet.

Briefträger, -in (*mpl -*) *der, die* postman (postwoman).

Briefumschlag (*pl -umschläge*) *der* envelope.

Briefwaage (*pl -n*) *die* letter scales (*pl*).

brief *prät →* **braten**.

Brille (*pl -n*) *die* (*für Augen*) glasses (*pl*).

Brillenetui (*pl -s*) *das* glasses case.

bringen (*prät* **brachte**, *pp* **gebracht**) *vt* (*wegbringen*) to take; (*holen*) to bring; (*Ergebnis*) to cause; (*finanziell*) to make; (*im Fernsehen*) to broadcast; (*in Zeitung*) to publish; **jm etw ~** to bring sb sthg; **jn nach Hause ~** to take sb home.

Brise (*pl -n*) *die* breeze.

Brite (*pl -n*) *der* Briton; **die ~n** the British.

Britin (*pl -nen*) *die* Briton.

britisch *adj* British.

Britischen Inseln *pl*: **die ~** the British Isles.

Broccoli *der* broccoli.

Brombeere (*pl -n*) *die* blackberry.

Bronchitis *die* bronchitis (*sg*).

Bronze *die* bronze.

Brosche (*pl -n*) *die* brooch.

Broschüre (*pl -n*) *die* brochure.

Brot (*pl -e*) *das* bread; (*Brotlaib*) loaf (of bread); (*Brotscheibe*) slice of bread.

BROT

In Germany there are hundreds of different types of bread, the most common being 'Graubrot', which is made from a mixture of rye and wheat flour, although wholemeal and multigrain breads are also popular. At breakfast, instead of sliced bread Germans usually eat bread rolls (known as 'Brötchen' or 'Semmel' depending on the region) and these too come in a wide vari-ety.

Brotaufstrich (*pl -e*) *der* spread.

Brötchen (*pl -*) *das* (bread) roll; **belegtes ~** filled roll.

Brotmesser (*pl -*) *das* bread knife.

Bruch (*pl Brüche*) *der* (*Knochenbruch*) fracture; (*mit Partner, Vergangenheit*) break; (*Leistenbruch*) hernia; (*Bruchteil*) fraction.

Bruchteil (*pl -e*) *der* fraction.

Brücke (*pl -n*) *die* bridge.

Brückenschäden *pl* damaged bridge.

Bruder (*pl Brüder*) *der* brother.

Brüderschaft *die*: **~ trinken** *to agree to use the familiar 'du' form and celebrate with a drink.*

Brühe (*pl -n*) *die* (*Suppe*) broth; (*zum Kochen*) stock.

Brühwürfel (*pl -*) *der* stock cube.

brüllen *vi* to shout.

brummen *vi* (*Tier*) to growl; (*Motor, Maschine*) to drone.

Brunnen (*pl -*) *der* (*zum Wasserholen*) well; (*Springbrunnen*) fountain.

Brüssel *nt* Brussels.

Brust (*pl Brüste*) *die* breast; (*Thorax*) chest.

Brustschwimmen *das* breast-stroke.

Brüstung (*pl -en*) *die* parapet.

brutal *adj* brutal.

brutto *adv* gross.

brutzeln *vt & vi* to fry.

Btx *abk =* **Bildschirmtext**.

Buch (*pl Bücher*) *das* book; **~ führen** to keep a record.

buchen ◆ *vt* (*reservieren*) to book;

(*auf Konto*) to enter. ◆ *vi* (*reservieren*) to book.

Bücherei (*pl* -en) *die* library.

Buchhalter, -in (*mpl* -) *der, die* bookkeeper.

Buchhandlung (*pl* -en) *die* bookshop.

Buchmesse (*pl* -n) *die* book fair.

Büchse (*pl* -n) *die* tin, can.

Büchsenmilch *die* tinned milk.

Büchsenöffner (*pl* -) *der* tin opener, can opener.

Buchstabe (*pl* -n) *der* letter; **kleiner/großer ~** small/capital letter.

buchstabieren *vt* to spell.

Bucht (*pl* -en) *die* bay.

Buchung (*pl* -en) *die* booking.

Buchwesen *das* book trade.

bücken: sich bücken *ref* to bend down.

Bude (*pl* -n) *die* (*Kiosk*) stall; (*fam*: *Wohnung*) place.

Büffet (*pl* -s) *das* buffet; **kaltes ~** cold buffet.

Bügel (*pl* -) *der* (*Kleiderbügel*) (coat) hanger; (*von Brille*) arm.

Bügeleisen (*pl* -) *das* iron.

bügelfrei *adj* non-iron.

bügeln *vt & vi* to iron.

Bügelspray *das* spray used to make *clothes easier to iron.*

Bühne (*pl* -n) *die* stage.

Bulgarien *nt* Bulgaria.

bummeln *vi* ist (*langsam gehen*) to stroll; (*langsam sein*) to dawdle.

Bummelzug (*pl* -züge) *der* slow train.

Bund¹ (*pl* **Bünde**) *der* (*Zusammenschluß*) association; (*fam*: *Bundeswehr*) armed forces (*pl*).

Bund² (*pl* **Bunde**) *das* (*von Gemüse*, *Blumen*) bunch.

Bundesbahn *die* German state railway company.

Bundesbürger, -in (*mpl* -) *der, die* German citizen.

Bundeskanzler, -in (*mpl* -) *der, die* German chancellor.

Bundesland (*pl* -länder) *das* Land (*German state*).

BUNDESLAND

Germany is a federal republic which consists of 16 states known as 'Bundesländer', each with its own parliament and constitution. The states enjoy autonomy from central government in certain areas such as education and culture. Each state is represented in the upper house of the German parliament, the 'Bundesrat', which has the right to reject legislation put forward by the central government.

Bundesliga *die* division of German *football league.*

Bundesregierung (*pl* -en) *die* German government.

Bundesrepublik *die* Federal Republic of Germany.

Bundesstraße (*pl* -n) *die* ≃ A road (Br), ≃ state highway (Am).

Bundestag *der* German parliament.

Bundeswehr *die* German army.

bundesweit ◆ *adj* nationwide (*in Germany*). ◆ *adv* across Germany.

Bündnis (*pl* -se) *das* alliance.

Bungalow (*pl* -s) *der* bungalow.

bunt ◆ *adj* (*vielfarbig*) colourful. ◆ *adv* (*vielfarbig*) colourfully; **~er Abend** social evening.

Buntstift (*pl* -e) *der* coloured pencil.

Burg (*pl* -en) *die* castle.

bürgen *vi*: **für jn/etw ~** to vouch for sb/sthg.

Bürger, -in (*mpl* -) *der, die* (*Einwohner*) citizen; (*aus dem Mittelstand*) middle-class person; **~ zweiter Klasse** second-class citizen.

bürgerlich *adj* (*Küche*) plain; (*Hotel*) respectable.

Bürgermeister, -in (*mpl* -) *der, die* mayor.

Bürgersteig (*pl* -e) *der* pavement (Br), sidewalk (Am).

Büro (*pl* **-s**) *das* office.
Büroklammer (*pl* **-n**) *die* paper clip.
Bürste (*pl* **-n**) *die* brush.
bürsten *vt* to brush.
Bus (*pl* **-se**) *der* bus; **mit dem ~ fahren** to go by bus.
Busbahnhof (*pl* **-bahnhöfe**) *der* bus station.
Busen (*pl* **-**) *der* bosom.
Busfahrer, -in (*mpl* **-**) *der, die* bus driver; '**Fahrscheine beim ~**' 'tickets from the driver'.
Bushaltestelle (*pl* **-n**) *die* bus stop.
Buslinie (*pl* **-n**) *die* bus route.
Busreise (*pl* **-n**) *die* coach trip (Br), bus trip (Am).
Bußgeld (*pl* **-er**) *das* fine.
Bußgeldbescheid (*pl* **-e**) *der* notification of a fine.
Buß- und Bettag *der* Day of Prayer and Repentance, *German public holiday in November.*
Büstenhalter (*pl* **-**) *der* bra.
Busverbindung (*pl* **-en**) *die* bus connection, bus service.
Butangas *das* butane.
Butter *die* butter.
Butterbrot (*pl* **-e**) *das* slice of bread and butter.
Butterfahrt (*pl* **-en**) *die short ferry trip outside German waters to allow passengers to buy duty-free goods.*
Butterkäse (*pl* **-**) *der* full-fat cheese.
Buttermilch *die* buttermilk.
Butterschmalz *das* clarified butter.
bzw. *abk* = **beziehungsweise**.

ca. (*abk für circa*) approx.
Cabaret (*pl* **-s**) *das* cabaret.
Cabrio (*pl* **-s**) *das* convertible.
Café (*pl* **-s**) *das* cafe.

CAFÉ

Most German cafes serve cakes and gâteaux with coffee or tea, although there are also 'Eiscafés' which specialize in ice cream. You normally select your cake at the counter and it is then brought to your table. Two popular types of cake are Black Forest gâteau ('Schwarzwälder Kirschtorte') and a type of cheesecake known as 'Käsekuchen'. Many cafes have a terrace where you can sit outside in summer, but if you do this coffee may only be ordered by the pot.

Cafeteria (*pl* **-ien**) *die* cafeteria.
campen *vi* to camp.
Camping *das* camping.
Campingführer (*pl* **-**) *der* camping guidebook.
Campingplatz (*pl* **-plätze**) *der* campsite.
Campingwagen (*pl* **-**) *der* camper van.
Cashewnuß (*pl* **-nüsse**) *die* cashew nut.
CB-Funker, -in (*mpl* **-**) *der, die* CB ham.
CD (*pl* **-s**) *die* CD.
CD-Spieler (*pl* **-**) *der* CD player.
Cello (*pl* **-s**) *das* cello.
Celsius *nt* celsius; **10 Grad ~** 10 degrees centigrade.
Champagner *der* champagne.
Champignon (*pl* **-s**) *der* mushroom.
Chance (*pl* **-n**) *die* chance, opportunity.

Change der (Geldwechsel) bureau de change.

Chanson (pl -s) das satirical song.

chaotisch adj chaotic.

Charakter (pl -tere) der character.

charakteristisch adj characteristic.

charmant ◆ adj charming. ◆ adv charmingly.

Charterflug (pl -flüge) der charter flight.

Chartermaschine (pl -n) die charter plane.

chartern vt to charter.

chauvinistisch adj chauvinist.

Chef, -in (mpl -s) der, die boss.

Chefarzt (pl -ärzte) der (senior) consultant.

Chefärztin (pl -nen) die (senior) consultant.

Chemie die chemistry.

chemisch adj chemical; ~e Reinigung (Laden) dry cleaner's.

chic adj chic.

Chicoree der, die chicory.

Chiffre (pl -n) die (von Zeitungsanzeige) box number.

Chili der chilli.

China nt China.

Chinarestaurant (pl -s) das Chinese restaurant.

Chinese (pl -n) der Chinese (man); die ~n the Chinese.

Chinesin (pl -nen) die Chinese (woman).

chinesisch adj Chinese.

Chinesisch(e) das Chinese.

Chip (pl -s) der chip.

Chipkarte (pl -n) die (EDV) smart card.

Chips pl (KÜCHE) crisps (Br), chips (Am).

Chirurg, -in (mpl -en) der, die surgeon.

chlorfrei adj chlorine-free; '~ gebleicht' 'produced using chlorine-free bleaching processes'.

Choke (pl -s) der choke.

Cholesterin das cholesterol.

Chor (pl Chöre) der choir.

Choreographie (pl -n) die choreography.

Christ, -in (mpl -en) der, die Christian.

Christi Himmelfahrt nt Ascension Day.

Chronik (pl -en) die chronicle.

chronisch adj chronic.

chronologisch adj chronological.

circa adv approximately.

City (pl Cities) die city centre.

clever adj clever, smart.

Clique (pl -n) die clique.

Clown (pl -s) der clown.

Club (pl -s) der club.

Cluburlaub (pl -e) der club holiday.

Cocktail (pl -s) der cocktail.

Cognac® (pl -s) der cognac.

Cola (pl -s) die ODER das Coke®.

Comic (pl -s) der cartoon.

Computer (pl -) der computer.

Container (pl -) der container.

Cord der corduroy.

Couch (pl -en) die couch.

Cousin (pl -s) der cousin.

Cousine (pl -n) die cousin.

Creme (pl -s) die cream.

Curry (pl -s) das curry.

Currywurst (pl -würste) die sausage with curry sauce.

Cutter, -in (mpl -) der, die editor.

Cybercafé (pl -s) das cybercafe.

Cyberspace der ODER das cyberspace.

D

da ◆ adv 1. (dort) there; ~, wo wir uns das letzte Mal getroffen haben where we met (the) last time; ~ lang along there. 2. (hier) here; ist Herr Müller ~? (am Telefon) is Mr

Müller there?; **sind alle ~** is everyone here?; **~ und dort** here and there. **3.** (*übrig*): **ist noch Butter ~?** is there any butter left? **4.** (*zeitlich*): **gestern, ~ hat es geregnet** it rained yesterday. **5.** (*in diesem Fall*) there; **~ hat er recht** he's right there. **6.** (*plötzlich*): **~ fällt mir ein ...** I've just thought ... ◆ *konj* (*weil*) as, since.

dabei *adv* (*räumlich*) next to it; (*gleichzeitig*) at the same time; (*doch*) and (what is more); **jm ~ helfen, etw zu tun** to help sb do sthg; **ich bin ~, die Koffer zu packen** I'm just packing the cases; **nahe ~** nearby; **nicht ~ sein** to be missing.

dabei|bleiben *vi unr ist* (*an Ort*) to stay on; (*bei Meinung*) to stick with it.

dabei|haben *vt unr* (*Person*) to have with one; (*Gegenstand, Werkzeug*) to have on one.

dabei|sein *vi unr ist* (*anwesend sein*) to be there; **ich bin ~, die Koffer zu packen** I'm just packing the cases.

Dach (*pl* **Dächer**) *das* roof.

Dachboden (*pl* **-böden**) *der* loft.

Dachgepäckträger (*pl* **-**) *der* roofrack.

dachte *prät* → **denken**.

dadurch ◆ *adv* (*räumlich*) through it; (*deshalb*) for that reason. ◆ *konj*: **~, daß ...** because ...

dafür ◆ *adv* (*trotzdem*) nonetheless. ◆ *konj*: **~, daß** considering; **ich habe 200 DM ~ bekommen** I got 200 marks for it; **ich kann nichts ~** it's not my fault.

dafür|können *vt unr*: **sie kann nichts ~** it's not her fault.

dagegen *adv* (*als Gegensatz*) in comparison; **das Auto fuhr ~** the car drove into it; **~ sein** to be against it.

dagegen|haben *vt unr*: **etwas ~, daß** to mind that; **nichts ~, daß** not to mind that.

daheim *adv* at home.

daher *adv* (*Herkunft*) from there; (*deshalb*) that's why.

dahin *adv* (*räumlich*) there; (*zeitlich*): **bis ~** until then.

dahinten *adv* over there.

dahinter *adv* behind it.

dahinter|kommen *vi unr ist* to find out.

dalli *interj* get a move on!

damals *adv* then, in those days.

Dame (*pl* **-n**) *die* (*Person*) lady; (*Spiel*) draughts (*sg*); (*in Schach, Kartenspiel*) queen; **meine ~n und Herren** ladies and gentlemen! ▶ **Damen** *pl* (*Damentoilette*) ladies (*sg*).

Damenbekleidung *die* ladieswear.

Damenbinde (*pl* **-n**) *die* sanitary towel.

Damenschuh (*pl* **-e**) *der* ladies' shoe.

Damentoilette (*pl* **-n**) *die* ladies (toilet).

damit ◆ *konj* so that. ◆ *adv* (*dadurch*) therefore; **ich will ~ spielen** I want to play with it; **was meinst du ~?** what do you mean by that?

Damm (*pl* **Dämme**) *der* (*gegen Überschwemmung*) dam; (*für Straße, Schienen*) embankment.

dämmern *vimp*: **es dämmert** (*morgens*) it's getting light; (*abends*) it's getting dark.

Dämmerung (*pl* **-en**) *die* (*morgens*) dawn; (*abends*) dusk.

dämmrig *adj* dim.

Dampf (*pl* **Dämpfe**) *der* steam. ▶ **Dämpfe** *pl* (*chemisch*) fumes.

Dampfbad (*pl* **-bäder**) *das* Turkish bath.

dampfen *vi* to steam.

dämpfen *vt* (*Licht*) to dim; (*Geräusch*) to muffle; (*Wut*) to calm; (*Begeisterung*) to dampen; (*kochen*) to steam.

Dampfer (*pl* **-**) *der* steamship.

Dampfnudel (*pl* **-n**) *die* (*Süddt*) sweet dumpling made with yeast dough.

danach *adv* (*zeitlich*) afterwards; **sie**

sehnt sich ~ she longs for it; **kurz ~** shortly afterwards.

Däne (*pl* **-n**) *der* Dane.

daneben *adv* (*räumlich*) next to it; (*vergleichend*) in comparison.

Dänemark *nt* Denmark.

Dänin (*pl* **-nen**) *die* Dane.

dänisch *adj* Danish.

Dänisch(e) *das* Danish.

Dank *der* thanks (*pl*); **vielen ~!** thank you!; **besten ~!** thank you!; **herzlichen ~!** thank you!; **schönen ~!** thank you!; **vielen ~ im voraus** thanking you in advance.

dankbar *adj* (*Person*) grateful; **jm für etw ~ sein** to be grateful to sb for sthg.

danke *interj* thanks!; **~, gleichfalls!** thanks, you too!; **~ schön** ODER **sehr!** thanks!

danken *vi* to say thank you; **jm ~** to thank sb; **für etw ~** to say thank you for sthg; **nichts zu ~!** don't mention it!

dann *adv* then; **bis ~!** see you then!; **also ~** all right, then.

daran *adv* (*räumlich*) on/to/against/ next to it; **es liegt ~, daß ...** it is because of the fact that ...

darauf *adv* (*räumlich*) on it; (*zeitlich*) afterwards; **~ warten, daß ...** to wait for ...; **am Tag ~** the next day; **die Tage ~** the next few days.

daraus *adv* (*aus Gefäß, Behälter*) out of it; (*aus Material*) from it; **mach dir nichts ~!** don't let it bother you!

darf *präs* → **dürfen**.

darin *adv* (*räumlich*) in it; **~ liegt ein Widerspruch** that's a contradiction.

Darlehen (*pl* **-**) *das* loan.

Darm (*pl* **Därme**) *der* intestine.

Darmgrippe *die* gastric flu.

Darsteller, -in (*mpl* **-**) *der, die* actor (actress).

Darstellung (*pl* **-en**) *die* representation.

darüber *adv* (*räumlich*) over it; (*sprechen, diskutieren*) about it.

darum *adv* (*deshalb*) that's why; **~ geht es nicht** that's not the point; **es geht ~, zu gewinnen** the main thing is to win.

darunter *adv* (*räumlich*) under it; (*weniger*): **30 Meter oder etwas ~** 30 metres or a little less; **viele Besucher, ~ auch einige aus dem Ausland** many visitors, including some foreigners; **was verstehst du ~?** what do you understand by that?

das ◆ *det* the. ◆ *pron* (*Demonstrativpronomen*) that; (*Relativpronomen*) that, which; **~ Rauchen** smoking; **~ da!** that one there!

dasein *vi unr* ist to be there; **ist noch Bier da?** is there any beer left?

daß *konj* (*im Objektsatz*) that; (*im Subjektsatz*) the fact that; **~ das bloß klappt!** let it work!; **sich so freuen, ~ ...** to be so happy that ...

dasselbe ◆ *det* the same. ◆ *pron* the same one; **~ tun** to do the same (thing).

Datei (*pl* **-en**) *die* file.

Datenschutz *der* data protection.

Dativ *der* dative.

Dattel (*pl* **-n**) *die* date.

Datum (*pl* **Daten**) *das* date.

Dauer *die* duration; **auf (die) ~** in the long term; **für die ~ von vier Jahren** for (a period of) four years.

Dauerauftrag (*pl* **-aufträge**) *der* standing order.

Dauerkarte (*pl* **-n**) *die* season ticket.

Dauerlauf *der* jog.

dauern *vi* to last; **es dauerte drei Wochen, bis ich den Brief bekam** it took three weeks for the letter to reach me.

dauernd ◆ *adj* constant. ◆ *adv* constantly.

Dauerparkplatz (*pl* **-plätze**) *der* long-stay car park.

Dauerwelle (*pl* **-n**) *die* perm.

Daumen (*pl* **-**) *der* thumb; **jm die ~ drücken** to keep one's fingers crossed for sb.

Daunendecke (pl -n) die eider-down.

davon adv (räumlich) from it; (von Thema) about it; (von Menge) of it.

davor adv (räumlich) in front of it; (zeitlich) beforehand; **ich habe Angst ~** I'm scared of it; **kurz ~ sein, etw zu tun** to be on the point of doing sthg.

dazu adv (außerdem) in addition; **es schneit, ~ ist es kalt** it's snowing and it's cold too; **ich habe keine Lust ~** I don't feel like it; **ich bin nicht ~ gekommen** I didn't get round to it.

dazulgeben vt unr to add.

dazulgehören vi (Person) to belong; (Zubehör) to go with it.

dazulkommen vi unr ist (zu Gruppe) to come along; **kommt noch etwas dazu?** would you like anything else?; **es kommt noch Mehrwertsteuer ~** it doesn't include VAT.

dazwischen adv in between.

dazwischenlkommen vi unr ist: **mir ist etwas dazwischengekommen** something has cropped up.

DDR die (abk für Deutsche Demokratische Republik): **die (ehemalige) ~** the (former) GDR.

Deck (pl -s) das deck; **an ~** on deck.

Decke (pl -n) die (von Bett) blanket; (von Tisch) tablecloth; (von Raum) ceiling.

Deckel (pl -) der lid.

decken vt to cover; **etw über jn/etw ~** to cover sb/sthg with sthg.

Deckfarbe (pl -n) die gouache.

Decoder (pl -) der (für Pay-TV) decoder.

defekt adj faulty.

definieren vt to define.

Defizit (pl -e) das deficit.

deftig adj (Speise) substantial.

dehnbar adj elastic.

Deich (pl -e) der dike.

dein, -e det your.

deine, -r, -s ODER **deins** pron yours.

Deklination (pl -en) die declen-sion.

deklinieren vt to decline.

Dekolleté (pl -s) das low neckline.

Dekoration (pl -en) die decoration.

delikat adj (Angelegenheit) delicate; (Speise) delicious.

Delikatesse (pl -n) die delicacy.

Delle (pl -n) die (an Auto) dent.

Delphin (pl -e) der dolphin.

dem ◆ det (to) the. ◆ pron (Demonstrativpronomen: Person) to him; (Sache) to that one; (Relativpronomen: Person) to whom; (Sache) to which.

demnächst adv shortly.

Demokratie (pl -n) die democracy.

demokratisch adj democratic.

demolieren vt to demolish.

Demonstration (pl -en) die demonstration.

demonstrieren vi: **~ gegen/für** to demonstrate against/for.

den ◆ det the. ◆ pron (Demonstrativpronomen: Person) him; (Sache) that (one); (Relativpronomen: Person) whom; (Sache) to which.

denen pron (Demonstrativpronomen) (to) them; (Relativpronomen: Person) to whom; (Sache) to which.

denken (prät **dachte**, pp **gedacht**) vi & vt to think; **~ an** (+A) (planen) to think about; (sich erinnern an, berück-sichtigen) to think of; **denk an den Kaffee!** don't forget the coffee!; **~ über** (+A) to think about; **~ von** to think of; **sich** (D) **etw ~** to imagine sthg; **das hätte ich mir ~ können** I might have known.

Denkmal (pl -mäler) das monu-ment.

Denkmalschutz der: **unter ~ stehen** to be classified as a historical monument.

denn ◆ konj (weil) because. ◆ adv then; **was hast du ~?** so what's wrong?

Deo (pl -s) das deodorant.

Deodorant (pl -s) das deodorant.

Deponie (pl -n) die dump.

deponieren vt (Gepäck, Paket) to deposit.

Depression (*pl* **-en**) *die* depression.

der ♦ *det* (*Nominativ*) the; (*Genitiv*) of the; (*Dativ*) (to) the. ♦ *pron* (*Demonstrativpronomen: Person*) him; (*Sache*) that (one); (*Relativpronomen: Person*) who; (*Sache*) which; **der Hut ~ Frau** the woman's hat; **der Fußball ~ Jungen** the boys' football.

deren ♦ *det* their. ♦ *pron* (*bei Person*) whose; (*bei Sache*) of which.

derselbe ♦ *det* the same. ♦ *pron* the same one.

derzeit *adv* at the moment.

des *det* of the; **der Hut ~ Mannes** the man's hat.

deshalb *adv* therefore.

Desinfektionsmittel (*pl* **-**) *das* disinfectant.

desinfizieren *vt* to disinfect.

dessen ♦ *det* (*bei Person*) his; (*bei Sache*) its. ♦ *pron* (*bei Person*) whose; (*bei Sache*) of which.

Dessert (*pl* **-s**) *das* dessert; **zum ~** for dessert.

desto *konj* → **je**.

deswegen *adv* therefore.

Detail (*pl* **-s**) *das* detail.

Detektiv, -in (*mpl* **-e**) *der, die* detective.

deutlich ♦ *adj* clear. ♦ *adv* clearly; **~ sprechen** to speak clearly.

deutsch ♦ *adj* German. ♦ *adv*: **auf ~** in German.

Deutsch *das* German.

Deutsche¹ (*pl* **-n**) *der, die* (*Person*) German.

Deutsche² *das* (*Sprache*) German.

Deutsche Bundesbahn *die* German state railway company.

Deutsche Bundesbank *die* German federal bank.

Deutsche Bundespost *die* German postal service.

Deutsche Demokratische Republik *die*: **die (ehemalige) ~** the (former) German Democratic Republic.

Deutschland *nt* Germany.

deutschsprachig *adj* German-speaking.

Devisen *pl* foreign currency (*sg*).

Dezember *der* December, → **September**.

d.h. (*abk für das heißt*) i.e.

Dia (*pl* **-s**) *das* slide.

Diabetes *der* diabetes (*sg*).

Diabetiker, -in (*mpl* **-**) *der, die* diabetic; **für ~ geeignet** diabetic (*vor Subst*).

Diafilm (*pl* **-e**) *der* slide film.

Diagnose (*pl* **-n**) *die* (MED) diagnosis.

Dialekt (*pl* **-e**) *der* dialect.

DIALEKT

Although all countries have regional dialects, some of those in the German-speaking world are particularly strong and often even German speakers from other regions are unable to understand them. The main dialects are the following: 'Plattdeutsch', spoken in the north of Germany, 'Kölsch', spoken around Cologne, 'Berlinerisch' in Berlin, 'Sächsisch' in Saxony, 'Bayrisch' in Bavaria and the dialects of Switzerland and Austria. Standard 'high German' is usually used when writing and for official purposes.

Dialog (*pl* **-e**) *der* dialogue.

Diaprojektor (*pl* **-en**) *der* slide projector.

Diarahmen (*pl* **-**) *der* slide frame.

Diät (*pl* **-en**) *die* diet; **eine ~ machen** to go on a diet.

Diavortrag (*pl* **-vorträge**) *der* slide presentation.

dich *pron* you; (*Reflexivpronomen*) yourself.

dicht ♦ *adj* thick; (*gegen Wasser*) watertight; (*gegen Luft*) airtight; (*Dach, Fenster*) weatherproof; (*Verkehr*) heavy. ♦ *adv* tightly; **~ neben etw** (D) **stehen** to stand right next to sthg; **~ davor, etw zu tun** on the verge of doing sthg.

Dichter, -in (*mpl -*) *der, die* (*von Gedichten*) poet; (*von Dramen, Theaterstücken*) writer.

Dichtung (*pl -en*) *die* (*Gedichte*) poetry; (*Literatur*) literature; (*Dichtungsring*) washer.

Dichtungsring (*pl -e*) *der* washer.

dick ◆ *adj* thick; (*Person, Körperteil*) fat; (*geschwollen*) swollen. ◆ *adv* thickly.

Dickmilch *die* sour milk.

die ◆ *det* the. ◆ *pron* (*Demonstrativpronomen: Person*) her, them (*pl*); (*Sache*) that one, those ones (*pl*); (*Relativpronomen: Person*) who; (*Sache*) which.

Dieb, -in (*mpl -e*) *der, die* thief.

Diebstahl (*pl -stähle*) *der* theft; **einen ~ anzeigen** to report a theft.

Diebstahlversicherung (*pl -en*) *die* insurance against theft.

Diele (*pl -n*) *die* (*Flur*) hall.

dienen *vi* (+D) to serve; (*fördern*) to be to the benefit of.

Dienst (*pl -e*) *der* service; **hast du morgen ~?** do you have to go to work tomorrow?; **im ~** on duty; **der öffentliche ~** the civil service.

Dienstag (*pl -e*) *der* Tuesday, → **Samstag**.

dienstags *adv* on Tuesdays.

Dienstbereitschaft *die*: **die Apotheke hat heute nacht ~** the chemist's is open all night tonight.

Dienstfahrt (*pl -en*) *die* business trip.

diensthabend *adj* on duty.

Dienstleistung (*pl -en*) *die* service.

dienstlich ◆ *adj* business (*vor Subst*). ◆ *adv* on business.

Dienstreise (*pl -n*) *die* business trip.

Dienststelle (*pl -n*) *die* (*amt*) office.

Dienstzeit (*pl -en*) *die* working hours (*pl*).

diese, -r, -s ODER **dies** ◆ *det* this, these (*pl*). ◆ *pron* this one, these ones (*pl*).

Diesel (*pl -*) *der* diesel.

dieselbe ◆ *det* the same. ◆ *pron* the same one.

Dieselkraftstoff (*pl -e*) *der* diesel fuel.

Dieselmotor (*pl -en*) *der* diesel engine.

Dieselöl *das* diesel.

dieser *det* → **diese**.

dieses *det* → **diese**.

diesig *adj* misty.

diesmal *adv* this time.

diesseits ◆ *adv* on this side. ◆ *präp* (+G) on this side of.

Differenz (*pl -en*) *die* difference.

Digitalanzeige (*pl -n*) *die* digital display.

Diktat (*pl -e*) *das* (*in Schule*) dictation.

Diktatur (*pl -en*) *die* dictatorship.

diktieren *vt* to dictate.

Dill *der* dill.

DIN (*abk für Deutsche Industrienorm*) ≈ BS (*Br*), ≈ ASA (*Am*).

Ding (*pl -e*) *das* thing.

Dings *der, die, das* (*fam*) thingamajig.

Dingsbums *der, die, das* (*fam*) = **Dings**.

Dingsda *der, die, das* (*fam*) = **Dings**.

DIN-Norm (*pl -en*) *die* (*amt*) German standard.

Dinosaurier (*pl -*) *der* dinosaur.

Diphterie *die* diphtheria.

Diplom (*pl -e*) *das* (*Titel*) degree.

Diplomat, -in (*mpl -en*) *der, die* diplomat.

dir *pron* (to) you.

direkt ◆ *adj* direct. ◆ *adv* directly; (*ohne Zwischenzeit*) straight; **~ neben** right next to.

Direktflug (*pl -flüge*) *der* direct flight.

Direktor (*pl* **Direktoren**) *der* (*von Hotel*) manager; (*von Firma*) director; (*von Schule*) headmaster.

Direktorin (*pl -nen*) *die* (*von Hotel*) manageress; (*von Firma*) director; (*von Schule*) headmistress.

Direktübertragung (*pl* -en) *die* live broadcast.

Dirigent, -in (*mpl* -en) *der, die* conductor.

dirigieren *vt & vi* (MUS) to conduct.

Diskette (*pl* -n) *die* (EDV) (floppy) disk.

Disko (*pl* -s) *die* (*fam*) disco, (night) club; **in die ~ gehen** to go clubbing.

Diskothek (*pl* -en) *die* disco(theque).

diskret ◆ *adj* discreet. ◆ *adv* discretly.

diskriminieren *vt* (*benachteiligen*) to discriminate against.

Diskriminierung (*pl* -en) *die* discrimination.

Diskussion (*pl* -en) *die* discussion.

diskutieren ◆ *vt* to discuss. ◆ *vi* to have a discussion; **~ mit** to have a discussion with; **~ über** (+A) to have a discussion about.

Distanz (*pl* -en) *die* distance.

Distel (*pl* -n) *die* thistle.

diverse *adj* various.

dividieren *vt & vi* to divide.

DLRG *die* German life-savers society.

DM (*abk für* Deutsche Mark) DM.

D-Mark (*pl* -) *die* Deutschmark, German mark.

doch ◆ *interj* yes. ◆ *konj* yet, but. ◆ *adv* (*konzessiv*) anyway; **er wollte erst nicht, aber dann hat er es ~ gemacht** at first he didn't want to, but then he did it anyway; **setzen Sie sich ~!** do sit down!; **nicht ~, so war das nicht gemeint!** okay, okay, I didn't mean it that way; **das kann ~ nicht wahr sein!** but surely that can't be true!; **willst du nicht? – ~, ich will** don't you want to? – yes, I do; **~ noch** after all.

Doktor (*pl* Doktoren) *der* (*fam*: Arzt) doctor; (*Titel*) doctorate.

Doktorin (*pl* -nen) *die* (*fam*: Ärztin) doctor.

Dokument (*pl* -e) *das* (*Urkunde*) document.

Dokumentation (*pl* -en) *die*

(*schriftlich*) documentation; (*filmisch*) documentary.

dolmetschen *vi* to interpret.

Dolmetscher, -in (*mpl* -) *der, die* interpreter.

Dom (*pl* -e) *der* cathedral.

dominieren ◆ *vt* to dominate. ◆ *vi* to predominate.

Domino *das* (Spiel) dominoes (*sg*).

Donau *die*: **die ~** the Danube.

Donner *der* thunder.

donnern *vimp*: **es donnert** it's thundering.

Donnerstag (*pl* -e) *der* Thursday, → **Samstag**.

donnerstags *adv* on Thursdays.

doof ◆ *adj* (*fam*) stupid. ◆ *adv* (*fam*) stupidly.

Doppelbett (*pl* -en) *das* double bed.

Doppeldecker (*pl* -) *der* (Bus) double decker.

Doppelhaus (*pl* -häuser) *das* semi-detached house.

Doppelname (*pl* -n) *der* (Nachname) double-barrelled name.

Doppelpunkt (*pl* -e) *der* colon.

Doppelstecker (*pl* -) *der* two-way adapter.

doppelt ◆ *adj* double. ◆ *adv* twice; **~ so viel** twice as much.

Doppelzimmer (*pl* -) *das* double room.

Dorf (*pl* Dörfer) *das* village.

Dorn (*pl* -en) *der* thorn.

Dörrobst *das* dried fruit.

dort *adv* there; **~ drüben** over there.

dorther *adv* from there.

dorthin *adv* there.

Dose (*pl* -n) *die* (aus Holz, Plastik) box; (aus Porzellan) pot; (Konservendose) tin, can; **Erbsen aus der ~** tinned ODER canned peas.

dösen *vi* to snooze.

Dosenmilch *die* tinned milk, canned milk.

Dosenöffner (*pl* -) *der* tin opener, can opener.

dosieren *vt* to measure out.

Dosierung (*pl* -en) *die* dosage.

Dosierungsanleitung (*pl* -en) *die* directions for use (*pl*).

Dosis (*pl* Dosen) *die* dose.

Dozent, -in (*mpl* -en) *der, die* lecturer.

Dr. (*abk für Doktor*) Dr.

Drachen (*pl* -) *der* (*aus Papier*) kite; (SPORT) hang glider.

Drachenfliegen *das* hang gliding.

Dragee (*pl* -s) *das* (*Medikament*) pill; (*Bonbon*) sweet.

Draht (*pl* Drähte) *der* wire.

Drahtseilbahn (*pl* -en) *die* cable railway.

Drama (*pl* Dramen) *das* drama.

dramatisch *adj* (*spannend*) dramatic.

Dramaturg, -in (*mpl* -en) *der, die* *person who selects and adapts plays for the stage.*

dran *adv* (*fam*) = **daran**; ~ **sein** (*an der Reihe sein*) to be next.

dran|bleiben *vi unr ist* (*am Telefon*) to hold (the line).

drängeln *vi* (*durch Schieben*) to push. ► **sich drängeln** *ref*: **sich nach vorn** ~ to push one's way forward.

drängen *vt* (*schieben*) to push; (*überreden*) to press.

dran|kommen *vi unr ist* (*an die Reihe kommen*) to have one's turn; (*heranreichen*) to reach.

drauf *adv* (*fam*) = **darauf**; **gut/schlecht** ~ **sein** to be in a good/bad mood.

draus *adv* (*fam*) = **daraus**.

draußen *adv* outside; **nach** ~ outside; **von** ~ from outside.

Dreck *der* (*fam: Schmutz*) dirt.

dreckig *adj* (*fam: schmutzig*) dirty; **etw** ~ **machen** to get sthg dirty.

drehen ◆ *vt* (*Kurbel, Schraube*) to turn; (*Film*) to film; (*Zigarette*) to roll. ◆ *vi* (*Fahrzeug, Wind*) to turn; **an etw** (D) ~ to turn sthg; **etw laut/leise** ~ to turn sthg up/down. ► **sich drehen**

ref to turn over; **sich** ~ **um** (*thematisch*) to be about.

Drehtür (*pl* -en) *die* revolving door.

Drehzahlmesser (*pl* -) *der* rev counter.

drei *num* three, → **sechs**.

Dreieck (*pl* -e) *das* triangle.

Dreieckstuch (*pl* -tücher) *das* headscarf.

dreifach *num* triple.

dreihundert *num* three hundred.

Dreikönigstag *der* Epiphany.

dreimal *adv* three times.

dreispurig *adj* three-lane.

dreißig *num* thirty, → **sechs**.

dreiviertel *adv* three quarters; (*Süddt: in Uhrzeit*): **es ist** ~ **acht** it's a quarter to eight (Br), it's a quarter of eight (Am).

dreizehn *num* thirteen, → **sechs**.

dressieren *vt* to train.

Dressing (*pl* -s) *das* dressing.

Dressur (*pl* -en) *die* dressage.

drin *adv* = **darin**; **das ist nicht** ~ that's out.

dringen (*prät* drang, *pp* gedrungen) *vi ist*: **in** ODER **durch etw** (A) ~ to penetrate sthg.

dringend ◆ *adj* urgent. ◆ *adv* urgently.

drinnen *adv* inside.

dritt *num*: **wir sind zu** ~ there are three of us.

dritte, -r, -s *adj* third, → **sechste**.

Drittel (*pl* -) *das* third, → **Sechstel**.

drittens *adv* thirdly.

Dritte Reich *das* Third Reich.

Dritte Welt *die* Third World.

DRK *das* (*abk für Deutsches Rotes Kreuz*) German Red Cross.

Droge (*pl* -n) *die* (*Rauschgift*) drug.

drogenabhängig *adj*: ~ **sein** to be a drug addict.

Drogenberatungsstelle (*pl* -n) *die* drug advice centre.

Drogenhandel *der* drug dealing.

Drogerie (*pl* -n) *die* ≃ chemist's

(shop) (Br), drugstore (Am).

Drogeriemarkt (pl **-märkte**) der discount chemist's (Br), discount drugstore (Am).

drohen vi to threaten.

drosseln vt (Tempo) to reduce.

drüben adv over there.

drüber adv (fam) = **darüber**.

Druck[1] der (Kraft) pressure; (von Finger) touch; (von Hand) shake; (von Büchern) printing.

Druck[2] (pl **-e**) der (Gravur) print.

Druckbuchstabe (pl **-n**) der printed letter; **'bitte in ~n schreiben!'** 'please write in block capitals'.

drucken vt to print.

drücken ◆ vi (pressen) to press; (Schuhe) to pinch. ◆ vt (Knopf, Schalter) to press; **auf etw** (A) **~** to press sthg; **'drücken'** 'push'; **jn ~** (fam: umarmen) to hug sb. ◆ **sich drücken** ref (fam: sich entziehen): **sich ~ vor** (+ D) to get out of.

drückend adj (Hitze) oppressive.

Druckknopf (pl **-knöpfe**) der (an Kleidung) press stud.

Drucksache (pl **-n**) die printed matter.

Druckschrift die block capitals (pl).

drum adv (fam) = **darum**. ▶ **Drum** das: **mit allem Drum und Dran** (fam) with all the trappings.

drunter adv (fam) = **darunter**; **es geht ~ und drüber** (fam) everything's all over the place.

dt. abk = **deutsch**.

du pron you; **~ sagen** to use the 'du' form of address; **mit jm per ~ sein** = to be on first name terms with sb.

Dübel (pl **-**) der Rawlplug®.

Duett (pl **-e**) das duet.

duften ◆ vi to smell nice. ◆ vimp: **es duftet nach ...** there's a smell of ...

dumm (komp **dümmer**, superl **am dümmsten**) ◆ adj stupid. ◆ adv stupidly; **~es Zeug** (abw) rubbish.

Dummkopf (pl **-köpfe**) der idiot.

dumpf adj (Klang) muffled.

Düne (pl **-n**) die dune.

Dünger der fertilizer.

dunkel (komp **dunkler**, superl **am dunkelsten**) ◆ adj dark; (Klang) deep. ◆ adv (färben) dark; **seine Stimme klingt ~** his voice is deep; **es wird ~** it's getting dark.

dunkelblau adj dark blue.

dunkelblond adj light brown.

dunkelhaarig adj dark-haired.

Dunkelheit die (nächtlich) darkness.

dünn ◆ adj thin; (Getränk) weak. ◆ adv thinly; **etw ~ auftragen** to apply sthg sparingly.

dünsten vt to steam.

dunstig adj (Wetter) hazy.

Duo (pl **-s**) das (Musikstück) duet; (zwei Musiker) duo.

Dur das major.

durch ◆ präp (+A) through; (mit Hilfe von) by (means of); (wegen) as a result of. ◆ adv through; **die ganze Nacht ~** throughout the night; **darf ich mal bitte ~?** excuse me please!; **~ und ~** through and through; **~ die Schweiz reisen** to travel across Switzerland.

durch|atmen vi to breathe deeply.

durchaus adv absolutely; **~ nicht** not at all.

Durchblutung die circulation.

durch|brechen ◆ vt unr hat (Stock) to snap. ◆ vi unr ist (Stock, Brett) to snap.

durch|brennen vi unr ist (Sicherung) to blow.

durch|drehen vi ist (Räder) to spin; (fig: Person) to crack up.

durcheinander ◆ adv all over the place. ◆ adj: **~ sein** (Zimmer, Haus) to be in a mess; (Person) to be confused.

Durcheinander das chaos.

durch|fahren vi unr ist (mit Auto) to drive through; (Zug) to go through.

Durchfahrt die: **auf der ~ sein** to be travelling through; **'~ verboten!'** 'no

through road' (Br), 'no outlet' (Am).
Durchfall (pl -fälle) der diarrhoea.
durch|fragen: sich durchfragen
ref to ask the way; **sich zum Bahnhof
~** to ask the way to the station.
durch|führen vt to carry out.
Durchgang (pl -gänge) der (zwischen
Gebäuden) passage; **'kein ~!'** 'keep
out'.
Durchgangsverkehr der through
traffic.
durchgebrannt ◆ pp → **durch-
brennen**. ◆ adj (Sicherung) blown.
durchgebraten adj well-done.
durchgefroren adj frozen.
durch|gehen vi unr ist to go
through; **bitte ~!** (in Bus) please
move to the back of the bus!
durchgehend ◆ adj (Zug) through
(vor Subst). ◆ adv: **'~ geöffnet'** 'open
all day'.
durch|halten ◆ vi unr to hold out.
◆ vt unr to withstand.
durch|kommen vi unr ist to get
through.
durch|lassen vt unr (Person) to let
through; (Wasser) to let in.
durchlässig adj leaky.
Durchlauferhitzer (pl -) der water
heater.
durch|machen vt (ertragen) to go
through; **die Nacht ~** (fam: feiern) to
party all night.
Durchmesser (pl -) der diameter.
Durchreise die: **auf der ~ (sein)** (to
be) travelling through.
Durchreisevisum (pl -visa) das
transit visa.
durch|reißen ◆ vt unr hat to snap.
◆ vi unr ist to snap.
Durchsage (pl -n) die announcement; **Achtung, eine ~!** attention,
please, here is an announcement.
durch|sagen vt to announce.
durchschauen vt to see through.
Durchschlag (pl -schläge) der carbon copy.
durch|schlagen: sich durch-

schlagen ref (zur Grenze) to make it;
(finanziell) to get by.
durch|schneiden vt unr to cut
through.
Durchschnitt der average; **im ~** on
average.
durchschnittlich ◆ adj average.
◆ adv (im Durchschnitt) on average;
(mittelmäßig) averagely.
Durchschnittsgeschwindigkeit
die average speed.
durch|sein vi unr ist (fam: Zug) to
have gone through; (Fleisch) to be
done; (Kleidung, Schuhe) to have
worn through.
durch|setzen vt to push through.
▶ **sich durchsetzen** ref (Person) to
get one's way.
durchsichtig adj (Material) transparent.
durch|stellen vt (an Telefon) to put
through.
durch|streichen vt unr to cross
out.
durchsuchen vt to search.
Durchwahl die extension.
durch|wählen vi to dial direct.
durch|zählen vt to count up.
durch|ziehen vt unr (durch Öffnung)
to pull through; (Plan) to see
through.
Durchzug der (Luftzug) draught.
dürfen (präs **darf**, prät **durfte**, pp
dürfen) ◆ aux 1. (als Erlaubnis): **etw
tun ~** to be allowed to do sthg; **sie ~
gerne hineinkommen** please, come
in! 2. (in Fragen): **darf ich mich setzen?** may I sit down?; **darf ich fragen
...** may I ask ... 3. (als Aufforderung):
das ~ wir nicht vergessen we mustn't
forget that; **so etwas darf einfach
nicht passieren** such a thing simply
should not happen. 4. (als
Annahme): **das dürfte genügen** that
should be enough. ◆ vi (als
Erlaubnis: pp **gedurft**): **sie darf nicht ins
Schwimmbad** she's not allowed to
go swimming. ◆ vt (als Erlaubnis: pp
gedurft): **das darf man nicht!** you're

not allowed to do that; **was darf es sein?** what can I get you?

Durst *der* thirst; **~ auf ein Bier haben** to fancy a beer; **~ haben** to be thirsty.

durstig *adj* thirsty; **~ sein** to be thirsty.

Dusche (*pl* -n) *die* shower.

duschen *vi* to have a shower. ► **sich duschen** *ref* to have a shower.

Duschgel *das* shower gel.

Duschkabine (*pl* -n) *die* shower (cubicle).

Duschvorhang (*pl* -hänge) *der* shower curtain.

Düsenflugzeug (*pl* -e) *das* jet.

düster *adj* (*dunkel*) gloomy.

Dutzend (*pl* -) *das* dozen. ► **Dutzende** *pl* dozens.

duzen *vt* to use the 'du' form of address. ► **sich duzen** *ref* to use the 'du' form of address; **sich ~ mit jm** = to be on first name terms with sb.

Dynamo (*pl* -s) *der* dynamo.

DZ *abk* = **Doppelzimmer**.

D-Zug (*pl* D-Züge) *der* fast train which only stops at major stations.

E

Ebbe (*pl* -n) *die* (*an Meer*) low tide; **~ und Flut** tides (*pl*).

eben ◆ *adj* (*Boden*) flat. ◆ *adv* just. ◆ *interj* (*genau*) exactly!; **~ nicht!** that's not true!; **sie war ~ noch hier** she was just here; **komm mal ~ her!** come here a minute!

Ebene (*pl* -n) *die* (*Flachland*) plain; (*Niveau*) level.

ebenfalls *adv* (*auch*) as well; (*gleichfalls*) you too.

ebenso *adv* just as.

EC (*pl* -s) *abk* = **EuroCity**.

Echo (*pl* -s) *das* echo.

echt ◆ *adj* (*Gold, Leder*) genuine; (*Freund, Gefühl*) real. ◆ *adv* really.

EC-Karte (*pl* -n) *die* Eurocheque card.

Ecke (*pl* -n) *die* corner; **um die ~** round the corner.

eckig *adj* (*quadratisch*) square; (*rechteckig*) rectangular.

Economyklasse *die* economy class.

ECU (*pl* -s) *der* ECU.

Edelstahl *der* stainless steel.

Edelstein (*pl* -e) *der* precious stone.

Edelweiß (*pl* -e) *das* edelweiss.

Edinburg *nt* Edinburgh.

EDV *die* data processing.

Efeu (*pl* -s) *das* ivy.

Effekt (*pl* -e) *der* effect.

EG *die* (*abk für Europäische Gemeinschaft*) EC.

egal *adj* (*gleichgültig*) all the same; **das ist ~** it doesn't matter; **~, wie groß** no matter how big; **~ ob** no matter whether; **es ist mir ~** I don't mind.

EG-Bürger, -in (*mpl* -) *der, die* EC national.

egoistisch *adj* selfish.

ehe *konj* before.

Ehe (*pl* -n) *die* marriage.

Ehefrau (*pl* -en) *die* wife.

Eheleute *pl* married couple (*sg*).

ehemalig *adj* former.

Ehemann (*pl* -männer) *der* husband.

Ehepaar (*pl* -e) *das* married couple.

eher *adv* sooner; **es ist ~ grün als blau** it's more green than blue.

Ehering (*pl* -e) *der* wedding ring.

Ehre (*pl* -n) *die* (*Würde*) honour.

ehren *vt* to honour.

ehrenamtlich *adj* honorary.

Ehrengast (*pl* -gäste) *der* guest of honour.

ehrgeizig adj ambitious.

ehrlich ♦ adj (Person, Antwort) honest. ♦ adv (antworten) honestly.

Ei (pl -er) das egg; **ein weiches/hartgekochtes ~** a soft-boiled/hard-boiled egg.

Eiche (pl -n) die (Baum) oak.

Eichhörnchen (pl -) das squirrel.

Eid (pl -e) der oath.

Eidechse (pl -n) die lizard.

eidesstattlich ♦ adj sworn. ♦ adv solemnly.

Eierbecher (pl -) der egg cup.

Eierstock (pl -stöcke) der ovary.

eifersüchtig adj jealous.

eifrig ♦ adj eager. ♦ adv eagerly.

Eigelb (pl -e) das egg yolk.

eigen adj own.

eigenartig ♦ adj strange. ♦ adv strangely.

Eigenbedarf der: **für den ~** for one's own use.

Eigenschaft (pl -en) die (Charakteristikum) characteristic.

eigentlich ♦ adj (wirklich) actual. ♦ adv (im Grunde) actually; **kennst du ~ meinen Bruder?** do you know my brother?; **wer sind Sie ~?** who might you be?; **was denkst du dir ~?** what on earth do you think you're doing?

Eigentum das property.

Eigentümer, -in (mpl -) der, die owner.

Eigentumswohnung (pl -en) die owner-occupied flat (Br), owner-occupied apartment (Am).

eignen: sich eignen ref to be suitable.

Eilbrief (pl -e) der express letter.

Eile die hurry; **in ~ sein** to be in a hurry.

eilen vi ist to hurry; **eilt!** urgent!

eilig ♦ adj (dringend) urgent; (schnell) hurried. ♦ adv (schnell) hurriedly; **es ~ haben** to be in a hurry.

Eilsendung (pl -en) die express letter/parcel.

Eilzug (pl -züge) der fast stopping train.

Eilzustellung (pl -en) die express delivery.

Eimer (pl -) der bucket.

ein, -e ♦ det a, an (vor Vokal); **~ Hund** a dog; **~e Idee** an idea; **~ Mädchen** a girl; **~es Tages** one day. ♦ adj **1.** (als Zahl) one; **~e einzelne Rose** a single rose; **~ Uhr** one o'clock. **2.** (gleich): **~er Meinung sein** to have the same opinion. ♦ pron **1.** (Teil aus Menge) one; **hier ist noch ~s/ ~e** here's another one. **2.** (fam: man) one; **das kann ~em schon mal passieren** these things can happen to you. ♦ adv: **'~ - aus'** 'on-off'; **~ und aus gehen** to come and go.

einander pron each other.

ein|arbeiten vt (Person): **jn ~ to** show sb the ropes.

ein|atmen vi to breathe in.

Einbahnstraße (pl -n) die one-way street.

ein|bauen vt (Kamin, Bad) to fit.

Einbauküche (pl -n) die fitted kitchen.

ein|behalten vt unr (fml) to retain.

Einbettzimmer (pl -) das single room.

ein|biegen vi unr ist to turn.

ein|bilden vt: **sich** (D) **etw ~** to imagine sthg.

ein|brechen vi unr ist (als Einbrecher) to break in; (in Eis) to fall through.

Einbrecher, -in (mpl -) der, die burglar.

Einbruch (pl -brüche) der (von Einbrecher) break-in; **nach ~ der Dunkelheit** after dark.

Einbürgerung die (von Person) naturalization.

ein|checken vi to check in.

ein|cremen vt to put cream on. ▶ **sich eincremen** ref to put cream on.

eindeutig ♦ adj clear. ♦ adv clearly.

ein|dringen vi unr ist (Wasser) to get in; (Einbrecher) to break in.

Eindruck (pl -drücke) der (von Person) impression; **den ~ haben, daß**

to have the impression that.

eindrucksvoll *adj* impressive.

eine → **ein**.

eineinhalb *num* one and a half.

einerseits *adv*: ~ ... **andererseits** on the one hand ... on the other hand.

einfach ♦ *adj* simple; (*Fahrt, Fahrkarte*) single. ♦ *adv*: ~ **oder hin und zurück?** would you like a single or a return?; ~ **klasse!** just brilliant!

ein|fahren *vi unr ist* (*Zug*) to arrive.

Einfahrt (*pl* -**en**) *die* (*Tor, Weg*) entrance; (*von Zug*) arrival; '~ **freihalten!**' 'keep clear'; ~ **haben** to arrive.

Einfall (*pl* -**fälle**) *der* (*Idee*) idea.

ein|fallen *vi unr ist* (+D): **jm** ~ to occur to sb; **mir fällt gerade ein ...** I've just remembered ...

Einfamilienhaus (*pl* -**häuser**) *das* detached house.

einfarbig *adj* all one colour.

Einfluß (*pl* -**flüsse**) *der* influence; ~ **auf jn/etw haben** (*Effekt*) to influence sb/sthg; (*Macht*) to have influence over sb/sthg.

ein|frieren ♦ *vt unr hat* (*Lebensmittel*) to freeze. ♦ *vi unr ist* to freeze.

Einfuhr (*pl* -**en**) *die* (*von Ware*) importation.

Einfuhrbeschränkung (*pl* -**en**) *die* import tariff.

Einfuhrbestimmungen *pl* import regulations.

ein|führen *vt* (*Waren*) to import; (*Zäpfchen, Sonde*) to insert; (*Neuerung*) to introduce; **jn in etw** (A) ~ to introduce sb to sthg.

Einführung (*pl* -**en**) *die* introduction; (*von Sonde*) insertion.

ein|füllen *vt* to pour in.

Eingang (*pl* -**gänge**) *der* (*von Haus*) entrance; (*von Post*) receipt.

Eingangshalle (*pl* -**n**) *die* entrance hall.

ein|geben *vt unr* (EDV: *Daten*) to input.

eingebildet ♦ *adj* (*arrogant*) arrogant; (*ausgedacht*) imaginary. ♦ *adv*

(*arrogant*) arrogantly.

ein|gehen *vi unr ist* (*Kleidung*) to shrink; (*Pflanze, Tier*) to perish; ~ **auf** (+A) (*auf Vorschlag*) to agree to.

eingeschaltet *adj* (switched) on.

eingeschlossen *pp* → **einschließen**.

eingetragen *adj*: ~**es Warenzeichen** registered trademark.

ein|gewöhnen: sich eingewöhnen *ref* to settle in.

eingezogen *pp* → **einziehen**; '**warten, bis der Geldschein vollständig** ~ **ist**' 'please wait until the note has been accepted by the machine'.

ein|gießen ♦ *vt unr* to pour. ♦ *vi unr*: **darf ich** ~? shall I fill your glass up?

ein|greifen *vi unr* to intervene.

Eingriff (*pl* -**e**) *der* (*Operation*) operation.

ein|hängen *vt* & *vi* to hang up.

einheimisch *adj* local.

Einheit (*pl* -**en**) *die* (*auf Skala*) unit; (*Ganzes*) unity.

einheitlich ♦ *adj* (*Vorschriften*) uniform. ♦ *adv* (*regeln*) uniformly.

einhundert *num* a ODER one hundred.

einig *adj*: **sich** ~ **sein** to agree.

einige, -r, -s *det* & *pron* (*ein paar*) a few; (*reichlich*) quite a few; **nach** ~**r Zeit** after some time; ~ **Probleme** (*ein paar*) a few problems; (*viele*) quite a lot of problems; **nur** ~ **waren da** (*ein paar*) there were only a few people there; ~ **waren da** (*viele*) there were quite a lot of people there.

einigen: sich einigen *ref*: **sich über/auf etw** (A) ~ to agree on sthg.

einigermaßen *adv* (*relativ*) fairly.

Einkauf (*pl* -**käufe**) *der* (*in Laden*) shopping; (ECO) purchase. ► **Einkäufe** *pl* (*Gegenstände*) shopping (*sg*).

ein|kaufen ♦ *vt* (*Ware*) to buy. ♦ *vi* to shop; ~ **gehen** to go shopping.

Einkaufsbummel (*pl* -) *der*: **einen**

~ machen to go round the shops.
Einkaufstasche (*pl* **-n**) *die* shopping bag.
Einkaufstüte (*pl* **-n**) *die* carrier bag.
Einkaufszentrum (*pl* **-zentren**) *das* shopping centre (*Br*), mall (*Am*).
ein|kehren *vi ist* (*in einem Gasthaus*) to stop off.
Einklang *der*: **in ~ mit** in harmony with.
ein|kleiden *vt* (*Kind*) to kit out.
▶ **sich einkleiden** *ref*: **sich neu ~** to buy a whole new wardrobe.
ein|klemmen *vt* to trap.
Einkommen (*pl* **-**) *das* income.
ein|laden *vt unr* (*Gepäck*) to load; (*nach Hause*) to invite; **darf ich Sie zu einem Kaffee ~?** may I buy you a coffee?; **jn in ein Restaurant ~** to take sb out for a meal.
Einladung (*pl* **-en**) *die* invitation.
Einlage (*pl* **-n**) *die* (*in Programm*) interlude; (*in Schuh*) insole; (*in Suppe*) noodles, meat etc in a soup.
Einlaß *der* admission.
ein|laufen *vi unr ist* (*Wasser*) to run in; (*Kleidung*) to shrink.
ein|leben: sich einleben *ref* to settle in.
ein|legen *vt* (*Film*) to put in; (*Gang*) to engage.
Einleitung (*pl* **-en**) *die* (*Text*) introduction.
ein|liefern *vt* (*in Krankenhaus*) to admit.
Einlieferungsschein (*pl* **-e**) *der* proof of delivery.
ein|lösen *vt* (*Scheck*) to cash; (*Gutschein*) to redeem.
einmal *adv* once; (*in der Zukunft*) sometime; **auf ~** (*plötzlich*) all of a sudden; (*gleichzeitig*) at once; **nicht ~** not even; **noch ~** once again, once more.
einmalig *adj* (*einzig*) unique; (*hervorragend*) excellent.
ein|mischen: sich einmischen *ref* to interfere.
Einnahme (*pl* **-n**) *die* (*Geld*) takings

(*pl*); (*von Medikament*) taking.
ein|nehmen *vt unr* to take.
ein|ölen *vt* to rub oil in. ▶ **sich einölen** *ref* to rub oil on o.s.
ein|ordnen *vt* (*in Regal, Kartei*) to put in its place. ▶ **sich einordnen** *ref* (*in Autoschlange*) to get in lane.
ein|packen *vt* (*in Koffer, Tasche*) to pack; (*in Geschenkpapier*) to wrap; **~ oder zum hier essen?** to eat in or take away?
ein|parken *vi & vt* (*Fahrer*) to park.
ein|prägen *vt*: **sich** (D) **etw ~** to memorize sthg.
ein|räumen *vt* (*Bücher, Kleidung*) to put away; (*Schrank, Regal*) to fill up.
ein|reiben *vt unr* (*Salbe, Creme*) to rub in; **jn mit etw ~** to rub sthg into sb; **sich** (D) **das Gesicht mit etw ~** to rub sthg into one's face.
ein|reichen *vt* (*Antrag*) to hand in.
Einreise (*pl* **-n**) *die* entry.
ein|reisen *vi ist* to enter.
Einreisevisum (*pl* **-visa**) *das* entry visa.
ein|richten *vt* (*Wohnung, Zimmer*) to furnish.
Einrichtung (*pl* **-en**) *die* (*Möbel*) furnishings (*pl*); (*Institution*) institution.
eins ◆ *num* one, → **sechs**. ◆ *pron* → **ein**.
einsam ◆ *adj* lonely. ◆ *adv* alone.
ein|sammeln *vt* (*von Boden*) to gather; (*bei Personen*) to collect.
Einsatz (*pl* **-sätze**) *der* (*Verwendung*) use; (*Geld*) stake; (*Engagement*) commitment.
ein|schalten *vt* (*Gerät*) to switch on.
ein|schenken *vt*: **jm etw ~** to pour sb sthg.
ein|schicken *vt* to send in.
ein|schieben *vt unr* to fit in.
ein|schiffen: sich einschiffen *ref* to set sail.
ein|schlafen *vi unr ist* (*Person*) to fall asleep; (*Körperteil*) to go to sleep; (*fig*: *Kontakt*) to drop off.

ein|schließen vt unr (Person, Gegenstand) to lock up; (enthalten) to include.

einschließlich ◆ präp (+G) including, inclusive of. ◆ adv inclusive; **bis Montag ~** up to and including Monday.

ein|schränken vt (Person) to restrict; (Trinken, Rauchen) to cut down on. ▶ **sich einschränken** ref to tighten one's belt.

ein|schreiben: sich einschreiben ref to register.

Einschreiben (pl -) das recorded delivery letter/parcel.

ein|sehen vt unr (Fehler) to recognize.

einseitig adj (Argumentation) one-sided; (Beschriftung) on one side of the page.

ein|senden vt unr to send in.

ein|setzen ◆ vt (Hilfsmittel) to use; (Polizei, Personal) to employ; (Leben) to risk; (Geld) to stake. ◆ vi (beginnen) to begin. ▶ **sich einsetzen** ref: **sich für etw ~** to support sthg.

Einsicht (pl -en) die (Erkenntnis) insight.

ein|sinken vi unr ist to sink.

Einspänner (pl -) der (Österr) glass of black coffee topped with whipped cream.

ein|sparen vt to save.

ein|springen vi unr ist to stand in.

Einspruch (pl -sprüche) der (amt) objection.

einspurig ◆ adj (Straße) single-lane. ◆ adv: **'nur ~ befahrbar'** 'single-lane traffic only'.

einst adv (fml) (früher) once; **die Backstube von ~** the former ODER old bakery.

ein|stecken vt (mitnehmen) to take; (in Briefkasten) to post; (Stecker) to plug in; **vergiß nicht, Geld einzustecken!** don't forget to take some money with you!

ein|steigen vi unr ist (in Auto) to get in; (in Bus, Zug) to get on; **'bitte ~!'**

'please get on, the bus/train is about to depart'.

einstellbar adj adjustable.

ein|stellen vt (regulieren) to adjust; (neu festsetzen) to set; (Programm, Sender) to tune into; (in Firma) to take on; (beenden) to stop; **die Entfernung ~** to focus (the camera). ▶ **sich einstellen** ref: **sich ~ auf** (+A) to prepare o.s. for.

Einstellung (pl -en) die (von Arbeitskräften) appointment; (von Blende) setting; (Meinung) attitude; (von Sender) tuning.

Einstieg der: **'~ nur mit Fahrausweis'** 'do not board without a ticket'; **'~ nur vorne'** 'entry at the front of the vehicle only'.

ein|stürzen vi ist to collapse.

Einsturzgefahr die: **'Vorsicht, ~!'** 'danger, building unsafe!'

eintägig adj one-day.

ein|tauschen vt to exchange.

eintausend num a ODER one thousand, → **sechs**.

ein|teilen vt to divide up.

einteilig adj one-piece.

Einteilung (pl -en) die (von Zeit) organization; (von Geld, Vorrat) management.

Eintopf (pl -töpfe) der stew.

ein|tragen vt unr (in Liste) to put down. ▶ **sich eintragen** ref to register.

ein|treten ◆ vt unr hat (Tür, Eis) to kick down. ◆ vi unr ist (in Raum) to enter; (in Verein): **in etw** (A) **~** to join sthg.

Eintritt (pl -e) der admission; **'~ frei'** 'admission free'; **'~ verboten!'** 'no entry'.

Eintrittsgeld (pl -er) das admission charge.

Eintrittskarte (pl -n) die ticket.

Eintrittspreis (pl -e) der admission charge.

einverstanden ◆ adj agreed. ◆ interj OK!; **mit etw ~ sein** to agree with sthg.

ein|wandern vi ist to immigrate.

einwandfrei ♦ adj perfect. ♦ adv perfectly.

Einwegflasche (pl -n) die disposable bottle.

ein|weichen vt to soak.

Einweihung (pl -en) die (von Gebäude) opening.

Einweihungsparty (pl -s) die housewarming party.

ein|weisen vt unr (in Krankenhaus) to admit.

ein|werfen vt unr (Brief) to post (Br), to mail (Am); (Münze) to insert; (Ball, Bemerkung) to throw in.

ein|wickeln vt (Gegenstand) to wrap up; (fam: Person) to take in.

Einwohner, -in (mpl -) der, die inhabitant.

Einwurf (pl -würfe) der (Frage, Bemerkung) comment; (an Automaten) slot; (SPORT) throw-in.

ein|zahlen vt & vi to pay in.

Einzahlung (pl -en) die (Geld) deposit.

Einzahlungsschein (pl -e) der paying-in slip.

ein|zeichnen vt to mark.

Einzelbett (pl -en) das single bed.

Einzelfahrschein (pl -e) der single (ticket) (Br), one-way ticket (Am).

Einzelgänger, -in (mpl -) der, die loner.

Einzelhandel der retail trade.

Einzelheit (pl -en) die detail.

Einzelkabine (pl -n) die single cabin.

Einzelkind (pl -er) das only child.

einzeln ♦ adj (speziell) individual; (isoliert) single; (ohne Gegenstück) odd. ♦ adv (nacheinander) separately; (extra) individually. ♦ det: ~e Personen/Fragen a few.

einzelne, -r, -s pron (Personen) some people; (Sachen) some things; jeder/jede/jedes ~ (Individuum) every single one.

Einzelperson (pl -en) die single person.

Einzelreisende (pl -n) der, die person travelling alone.

Einzelteil (pl -e) das component.

Einzelticket (pl -s) das single (ticket).

Einzelzimmer (pl -) das single room.

Einzelzimmerzuschlag (pl -zuschläge) der single room supplement.

ein|ziehen ♦ vi unr ist (in Wohnung) to move in; (in Haut) to be absorbed. ♦ vt unr hat (von Konto) to collect; (in Automaten) to take in.

einzig adj & adv only; der/die/das ~e ... the only ...; das ~e, was ... the only thing that ...; ich habe keinen ~en gesehen I didn't see a single one.

Eis das ice; (Speiseeis) ice cream; ~ am Stiel ice lolly (Br), Popsicle® (Am).

Eisbecher (pl -) der sundae.

Eiscafé (pl -s) das ice-cream parlour.

Eiscreme (pl -s) die ice cream.

Eisen das (Metall) iron.

Eisenbahn (pl -en) die (Zug) train; (Institution) railway (Br), railroad (Am).

Eisenbahnbrücke (pl -n) die railway bridge.

Eisenbahnnetz (pl -e) das rail network.

eisgekühlt adj chilled.

Eishockey das ice hockey.

eisig ♦ adj (Wetter, Kälte) freezing. ♦ adv: ~ kalt freezing cold.

Eiskaffee (pl -s) der chilled coffee containing vanilla ice cream and whipped cream.

eiskalt adj (Getränk, Wind) ice-cold; (fig: skrupellos) cold-blooded.

Eiskugel (pl -n) die scoop of ice cream.

Eiskunstlauf der figure skating.

Eismann (pl -männer) der ice cream man.

Eisschokolade (pl -n) die chilled drinking chocolate containing ice cream and whipped cream.

Eiswaffel (*pl* -n) *die* wafer (*in an ice cream*).

Eiswürfel (*pl* -) *der* ice cube.

Eiszapfen (*pl* -) *der* icicle.

eitel (*komp* **eitler**, *superl* **am eitelsten**) *adj* (*Person*) vain.

Eiter *der* pus.

eitern *vi* to fester.

Eiweiß (*pl* -e) *das* (*in Ei*) egg white; (*Protein*) protein.

ekeln: sich ekeln *ref*: **sich ~ (vor** (+ D)) to be disgusted (by).

Ekzem (*pl* -e) *das* eczema.

Elastikbinde (*pl* -n) *die* elastic bandage.

elastisch *adj* (*Material*) elastic.

Elefant (*pl* -en) *der* elephant.

elegant ◆ *adj* elegant. ◆ *adv* elegantly.

Elektriker, -in (*mpl* -) *der, die* electrician.

elektrisch ◆ *adj* electrical. ◆ *adv* electrically.

Elektrizität *die* electricity.

Elektroabteilung (*pl* -en) *die* electrical department.

Elektroartikel *pl* electrical goods.

Elektrogerät (*pl* -e) *das* electrical appliance.

Elektrogeschäft (*pl* -e) *das* electrical goods store.

Elektroherd (*pl* -e) *der* electric oven.

Elektronik *die* (*Fachgebiet*) electronics (*sg*); (*System*) electronics (*pl*).

elektronisch ◆ *adj* electronic. ◆ *adv* electronically.

Element (*pl* -e) *das* element.

Elend *das* misery.

elf *num* eleven, → **sechs**.

elfhundert *num* one thousand one hundred.

Elfmeter (*pl* -) *der* penalty.

elfte *adj* eleventh, → **sechste**.

Ellbogen (*pl* -) *der* (*Gelenk*) elbow.

Eltern *pl* parents.

EM *die* (*abk für Europameisterschaft*) European Championships (*pl*).

Emanzipation *die* emancipation.

emanzipieren: sich emanzipieren *ref* to become emancipated.

emotional *adj* emotional.

empfahl *prät* → **empfehlen**.

empfand *prät* → **empfinden**.

Empfang (*pl* **Empfänge**) *der* reception; (*von Post*) receipt; **etw in ~ nehmen** to receive sthg.

empfangen (*präs* **empfängt**, *prät* **empfing**, *pp* **empfangen**) *vt* to receive.

Empfänger, -in (*mpl* -) *der, die* (*Adressat*) addressee.

Empfängerabschnitt (*pl* -e) *der* (*von Einschreiben*) part of a recorded delivery form given to the addressee.

Empfängnisverhütung *die* contraception.

Empfangsbescheinigung (*pl* -en) *die* proof of receipt.

empfängt *präs* → **empfangen**.

empfehlen (*präs* **empfiehlt**, *prät* **empfahl**, *pp* **empfohlen**) *vt* to recommend; **jm etw ~** to recommend sthg to sb. ▶ **sich empfehlen** *ref* (*ratsam sein*) to be recommended.

empfehlenswert *adj* recommendable.

Empfehlung (*pl* -en) *die* recommendation.

empfiehlt *präs* → **empfehlen**.

empfinden (*prät* **empfand**, *pp* **empfunden**) *vt* to feel.

empfindlich *adj* (*Person, Haut*) sensitive; (*Material*) delicate.

empfing *prät* → **empfangen**.

empfohlen *pp* → **empfehlen**.

empfunden *pp* → **empfinden**.

empört ◆ *adj* indignant. ◆ *adv* indignantly.

Ende (*pl* -n) *das* end; **am ~** at the end; **~ März** at the end of March; **zu ~ sein** to be over.

enden *vi* to end.

endgültig ◆ *adj* final. ◆ *adv* finally.

Endivie (*pl* -n) *die* endive.

endlich *adv* at last.

Endstation (*pl* **-en**) *die* (*von*

Straßenbahn, Bus, U-Bahn) terminus.

Endung (pl -en) die (GRAMM) ending.

Energie (pl -n) die energy.

Energiebedarf der energy requirements (pl).

Energieverbrauch der energy consumption.

energisch adj energetic.

eng ◆ adj (schmal) narrow; (Kleidung) tight; (Kontakt) close. ◆ adv (dichtgedrängt) closely; (anliegen) tightly; (nah) close; ~ befreundet sein to be close friends.

Engagement (pl -s) das (Einsatz) commitment; (Auftrag, Stelle) engagement.

engagieren vt to engage. ► sich **engagieren** ref: sich ~ für to show commitment to.

England nt England.

Engländer, -in (mpl -) der, die Englishman (Englishwoman); die ~ the English.

englisch adj English.

Englisch(e) das English.

Enkel, -in (mpl -) der, die grandson (granddaughter). ► **Enkel** pl grandchildren.

Enkelkind (pl -er) das grandchild.

Enkelsohn (pl -söhne) der grandson.

Enkeltochter (pl -töchter) die granddaughter.

enorm ◆ adj enormous. ◆ adv enormously.

Ensemble (pl -s) das (Musiker) ensemble; (Tänzer) company.

entdecken vt to discover.

Ente (pl -n) die duck.

entfernen vt (Schmutz) to remove.

entfernt ◆ adj distant; (abgelegen) remote. ◆ adv (verwandt) distantly; **50 km von München** ~ 50 km (away) from Munich; **weit** ~ a long way away.

Entfernung (pl -en) die (Distanz) distance; (Beseitigung) removal.

entführen vt (Person) to kidnap; (Flugzeug) to hijack.

Entführung (pl -en) die (von Person) kidnapping; (von Flugzeug) hijacking.

entgegen präp (+D) contrary to.

entgegengesetzt ◆ adj opposite; (Ansichten) opposing. ◆ adv (liegen) opposite.

entgegen|kommen vi unr ist: jm ~ (räumlich) to approach sb; (mit Angebot) to make concessions to sb.

entgegenkommend ◆ adj (Auto) oncoming; (Angebot, Person) accommodating. ◆ adv (sich verhalten) accommodatingly.

entgegnen vt to retort.

Entgelt das remuneration; '~ für Platzreservierung im Zuschlag enthalten' 'seat reservation included in supplement'.

enthaaren vt to remove hair from.

Enthaarungscreme (pl -s) die hair-remover.

enthalten (präs enthält, prät enthielt, pp enthalten) vt (subj: Behälter) to contain; (in Preis) to include. ► **sich enthalten** ref to abstain.

entkommen (prät entkam, pp entkommen) vi ist to escape.

entlang ◆ präp (+A,G) along. ◆ adv: **am Strand** ~ **gehen** to walk along the beach; **die Straße** ~ along the road.

entlang|gehen vt unr ist to walk along.

entlassen (präs entläßt, prät entließ, pp entlassen) vt (Mitarbeiter) to sack; (aus Krankenhaus) to discharge; **aus der Schule** ~ **werden** to leave school.

Entlassung (pl -en) die (Kündigung) dismissal; (aus Krankenhaus) discharge; (aus Schule) leaving.

Entlastungszug (pl -züge) der extra train.

entlaufen (präs entläuft, prät entlief, pp entlaufen) vi ist to escape.

entlegen adj isolated.

Entnahme die (von Wechselgeld, Blut) taking.

entnehmen (präs entnimmt, prät entnahm, pp entnommen) vt (Wechselgeld, Blut) to take.

entrahmt *adj*: ~e **Milch** skimmed milk.

Entschädigung (*pl* -en) *die* (*Geldsumme, Gegenstand*) compensation.

entscheiden (*prät* entschied, *pp* entschieden) *vt* to decide. ▶ **sich entscheiden** *ref* to decide; **sich ~ für/gegen** to decide on/against; **sich ~, etw zu tun** to decide to do sthg.

Entscheidung (*pl* -en) *die* decision.

entschließen: sich entschließen (*prät* entschloß, *pp* entschlossen) *ref* to decide.

entschlossen *pp* → **entschließen**.

Entschluß (*pl* -schlüsse) *der* decision.

entschuldigen *vt* to excuse. ▶ **sich entschuldigen** *ref* to apologize; **sich ~ für** to apologize for; **sich bei jm ~** to apologize to sb; **~ Sie bitte!** excuse me!

Entschuldigung (*pl* -en) ◆ *die* (*Rechtfertigung*) excuse; (*Brief, Worte*) apology. ◆ *interj* sorry!

entsetzlich ◆ *adj* terrible. ◆ *adv* terribly.

entsorgen *vt* (*Müll*) to dispose of.

entspannen *vi & vt* to relax. ▶ **sich entspannen** *ref* to relax.

Entspannung *die* relaxation.

entsprechend ◆ *adj* (*äquivalent*) corresponding; (*geeignet*) appropriate. ◆ *präp* (+D) according to.

entstehen (*prät* entstand, *pp* entstanden) *vi ist* (*sich entwickeln*) to arise; (*Gebäude*) to be built; (*Schaden*) to result.

enttäuschen ◆ *vt* to disappoint. ◆ *vi* to be disappointing.

enttäuscht *adj* disappointed.

Enttäuschung (*pl* -en) *die* disappointment.

entweder *konj*: ~ ... **oder** either ... or.

entwerfen (*präs* entwirft, *prät* entwarf, *pp* entworfen) *vt* (*Zeichnung*) to sketch; (*Gebäude*) to design.

entwerten *vt* (*Fahrkarte*) to validate.

Entwerter (*pl* -) *der* (*für Fahrkarten*) ticket validating machine.

entwickeln *vt* to develop. ▶ **sich entwickeln** *ref* to develop; (*Gase*) to be produced.

Entwicklung (*pl* -en) *die* development; (*von Film*) developing; (*von Gasen*) production.

Entwicklungshilfe *die* development aid.

Entziehungskur (*pl* -en) *die* rehabilitation course.

Entzug *der* (*von Konzession*) withdrawal; (*fam: Entziehungskur*) rehabilitation course.

entzünden *vt* (*Feuer*) to light. ▶ **sich entzünden** *ref* (*Wunde, Blinddarm*) to become inflamed; (*Feuer*) to catch fire.

Entzündung (*pl* -en) *die* (MED) inflammation.

Enzian (*pl* -e) *der* (*Pflanze*) gentian.

Epilepsie (*pl* -n) *die* epilepsy.

er *pron* (*bei Personen*) he; (*bei Sachen*) it.

Erbauer, -in (*mpl* -) *der, die* constructor.

Erbe (*pl* -n) ◆ *der* heir. ◆ *das* inheritance.

erben ◆ *vt* to inherit. ◆ *vi* to come into one's inheritance.

Erbin (*pl* -nen) *die* heiress.

erblich *adj* hereditary.

erbrechen (*präs* erbricht, *prät* erbrach, *pp* erbrochen) ◆ *vt* to bring up. ◆ *vi* to be sick, to vomit. ▶ **sich erbrechen** *ref* to be sick, to vomit.

Erbse (*pl* -n) *die* pea.

Erdbeben (*pl* -) *das* earthquake.

Erdbeere (*pl* -n) *die* strawberry.

Erde (*pl* -n) *die* earth; (*Erdreich*) soil; (TECH: *Draht*) earth (Br), ground (Am).

erden *vt* to earth (Br), to ground (Am).

Erdgas *das* natural gas.

Erdgeschoß (*pl* -geschosse) *das* ground floor.

Erdnuß (*pl* -nüsse) *die* peanut.

Erdöl *das* oil.

Erdteil (*pl* -e) *der* continent.

ereignen: sich ereignen *ref* to happen.

Ereignis (*pl* -se) *das* event.

ereignisreich *adj* eventful.

erfahren (*präs* erfährt, *prät* erfuhr, *pp* erfahren) ◆ *adj* experienced. ◆ *vt* (*aus mündlicher Quelle*) to hear; (*aus schriftlicher Quelle*) to read; etw von jm ~ to learn sthg from sb.

Erfahrung (*pl* -en) *die* experience.

erfinden (*prät* erfand, *pp* erfunden) *vt* to invent.

Erfolg (*pl* -e) *der* success; ~ haben to be successful; viel ~! good luck!

erfolglos ◆ *adj* unsuccessful. ◆ *adv* without success.

erfolgreich ◆ *adj* successful. ◆ *adv* successfully.

erforderlich *adj* necessary.

erforschen *vt* (*Land, Natur*) to explore.

erfreulich ◆ *adj* pleasing. ◆ *adv* pleasingly.

erfrieren (*prät* erfror, *pp* erfroren) *ist* to freeze to death.

erfrischen *vt* to refresh. ▶ **sich erfrischen** *ref* to refresh o.s.

erfrischend *adj* refreshing.

Erfrischung (*pl* -en) *die* refreshment.

erfüllen *vt* to fulfil. ▶ **sich erfüllen** *ref* to come true.

ergänzen *vt* (*vervollständigen*) to complete; (*erweitern*) to expand; (*Bemerkung*) to add.

Ergebnis (*pl* -se) *das* result.

ergebnislos *adj* unsuccessful.

ergiebig *adj* long-lasting.

erhalten (*präs* erhält, *prät* erhielt, *pp* erhalten) *vt* to receive; (*bewahren*) to preserve. ▶ **sich erhalten** *ref* (*sich bewahren*) to endure.

erhältlich *adj* available; hier ~ available here.

erheben (*prät* erhob, *pp* erhoben)
vt: Gebühren ~ to levy a charge.

erheblich ◆ *adj* considerable. ◆ *adv* considerably.

erhitzen *vt* (*Fett, Wasser*) to heat.

erhöhen *vt* (*Zaun, Mauer*) to raise; (*anheben*) to raise, to increase. ▶ **sich erhöhen** *ref* to rise, to increase.

erholen: sich erholen *ref* to rest; sich ~ von to recover from.

erholsam *adj* relaxing.

Erholung *die* recovery; gute ~! have a relaxing time!

erinnern *vt* to remind; jn ~ an (+A) to remind sb of. ▶ **sich erinnern** *ref* to remember; sich ~ an (+A) to remember.

Erinnerung (*pl* -en) *die* (*Gedanke*) memory; (*Souvenir*) memento.

erkälten: sich erkälten *ref* to catch a cold.

erkältet *adj*: ~ sein to have a cold.

Erkältung (*pl* -en) *die* cold.

erkennen (*prät* erkannte, *pp* erkannt) *vt* (*sehen*) to make out; (*Trick, Ursache*) to realize; (*wiedererkennen*) to recognize.

Erker (*pl* -) *der* bay window.

erklären *vt* (*erläutern*) to explain; (*verkünden*) to declare; sich (D) etw ~ to understand sthg; jm etw ~ to explain sthg to sb. ▶ **sich erklären** *ref*: sich zu etw bereit ~ to agree to sthg.

Erklärung (*pl* -en) *die* (*Erläuterung*) explanation.

erkundigen: sich erkundigen *ref*: sich (nach jm/etw) ~ to enquire (about sb/sthg).

erlassen (*präs* erläßt, *prät* erließ, *pp* erlassen) *vt* (*Gebühren*) to waive; (*Schulden*) to write off.

erlauben *vt* (*nicht verbieten*) to allow; jm etw ~ to allow sb sthg; jm ~, etw zu tun to allow sb to do sthg.

Erlaubnis *die* (*Erlauben*) permission; (*Schriftstück*) permit.

Erläuterung (*pl* -en) *die* explanation; '~ siehe Rückseite' 'see reverse for explanation'.

erleben vt (erfahren) to experience.
Erlebnis (pl -se) das (Erfahrung)
experience.
erledigen vt (Arbeit) to see to;
(Auftrag) to fulfil.
erledigt adj: ~ sein (müde sein: (ffam)
to be shattered; (beendet sein) to be
finished; **der Fall ist für mich** ~ as far
as I'm concerned, the matter is
closed.
erleichtert adj relieved.
erlesen adj choice.
erlischt präs → **erlöschen**.
Erlös der proceeds (pl).
erlöschen (präs **erlischt**, prät **erlosch**,
pp **erloschen**) vi ist (Feuer, Licht) to go
out.
ermahnen vt to warn.
ermäßigt adj reduced.
Ermäßigung (pl -en) die reduction.
ermöglichen vt to make possible.
ermorden vt to murder.
ermutigen vt to encourage.
ernähren: sich ernähren ref
(essen) to eat.
Ernährung die (Nahrung) food.
erneuern vt (Fensterscheibe, Schloß) to
replace.
erneut adj renewed.
ernst ♦ adj serious. ♦ adv seriously;
jn/etw ~ nehmen to take sb/sthg
seriously.
Ernst der seriousness.
Ernstfall der emergency.
ernsthaft ♦ adj serious. ♦ adv seriously.
Ernte (pl -n) die harvest.
Erntedankfest (pl -e) das Harvest
Festival.
ernten vt (Heu, Äpfel, Mais) to harvest.
eröffnen vt (Geschäft) to open; **ein
Konto** ~ to open an account.
Eröffnung (pl -en) die opening.
erotisch adj erotic.
Erpressung (pl -en) die blackmail.
erraten (präs **errät**, prät **erriet**, pp
erraten) vt to guess.

Erreger (pl -) der (MED) cause (of illness).
erreichbar adj reachable.
erreichen vt to reach; (Zweck, Ziel)
to achieve.
Ersatz der (Stellvertreter) substitute;
(Entschädigung) replacement.
Ersatzreifen (pl -) der spare tyre.
Ersatzteil (pl -e) das spare part.
erscheinen (prät **erschien**, pp
erschienen) vi ist to appear; (wirken)
to seem, to appear; **gut/wichtig** ~ to
seem good/important.
erschöpft ♦ adj (müde) exhausted.
♦ adv wearily.
Erschöpfung die exhaustion.
erschrecken[1] vt hat to startle.
▶ **sich erschrecken** ref to be startled.
erschrecken[2] (präs **erschrickt**, prät
erschrak, pp **erschrocken**) vi ist to be
startled.
ersetzen vt (auswechseln) to replace;
(Schaden) to make good; jm etw (voll)
~ (Schaden) to compensate sb (fully)
for sthg.
erst adv (relativ spät) not until; (noch
relativ früh, relativ wenig) only; (vor
kurzem) (only) just; (zuerst) first; **der
erste Roman war gut, aber der zweite
~!** the first novel was good, but the
second one was even better; **er
kommt** ~ **um 10 Uhr** he won't be
here until ten o'clock; **sie war** ~
gestern hier she was here only yesterday; ~ **einmal** (nur einmal) only
once.
erstatten vt (Kosten) to refund.
Erstattung die (von Kosten) refund.
Erstaufführung (pl -en) die premiere.
erstaunt adj amazed.
erste, -r, -s adj first; (vorläufig) preliminary; **als** ~s first of all; ~ **Klasse**
first class, sechste.
Erste (pl -n) der, die, das first (one).
Erste Hilfe die first aid; ~ **leisten** to
administer first aid.
erstens adv firstly.

erstklassig *adj* first-class.

erstrecken: sich erstrecken *ref* to stretch.

erteilen *vt (amt)* to give.

Ertrag (*pl* **Erträge**) *der (an Gemüse, Getreide)* yield; *(finanziell)* profits *(pl)*.

ertrinken (*prät* **ertrank**, *pp* **ertrunken**) *vi ist* to drown.

Erw. *abk* = **Erwachsene**.

erwachen *vi ist (Person)* to wake up.

erwachsen *adj* adult, grown-up.

Erwachsene (*pl* **-n**) *der, die* adult; **ein ~r, zwei Kinder, bitte!** one adult and two children, please!

Erwachsenenbildung *die* adult education.

erwähnen *vt* to mention.

erwarten *vt (warten auf)* to wait for; *(rechnen mit)* to expect; **einen Anruf ~** to be expecting a phone call; **ein Kind ~** to be expecting a baby; **erwartet werden** to be expected.

erweitern *vt (Raum)* to extend.
▶ **sich erweitern** *ref* to expand; *(Pupillen)* to dilate.

erwerbstätig *adj* employed.

erwidern *vt (auf Frage)* to reply; *(Besuch)* to return.

erwünscht *adj (willkommen)* welcome.

erzählen *vt* to tell.

Erzählung (*pl* **-en**) *die* story.

erzeugen *vt (produzieren)* to produce.

Erzeugnis (*pl* **-se**) *das (Produkt)* product.

erziehen (*prät* **erzog**, *pp* **erzogen**) *vt* to bring up; *(in Schule)* to educate.

Erzieher, -in (*mpl* **-**) *der, die* teacher.

Erziehung *die (in Schule)* education; *(durch Eltern)* upbringing.

erzogen ◆ *pp* → **erziehen**. ◆ *adj*: **gut/schlecht ~** well/badly brought up.

es *pron* it; *(bei Person: im Nominativ)* he (she); *(bei Person: im Akkusativ)* him (her); **~ freut mich, daß ...** I'm pleased that ...; **~ ist drei Uhr** it's

three o'clock; **~ regnet/schneit** it's raining/snowing; **wer war ~?** who was it?; **~ geht mir gut** I'm fine.

Esel (*pl* **-**) *der* donkey.

Espresso (*pl* **-s**) *der* espresso.

eßbar *adj* edible.

essen (*präs* **ißt**, *prät* **aß**, *pp* **gegessen**) *vt & vi* to eat; **~ gehen** to go out for a meal.

Essen (*pl* **-**) *das (Mahlzeit)* meal; *(fam: Nahrung)* food; **beim ~** while eating; **~ machen/kochen** to make/cook a meal; **vor dem ~** before the meal.

Essig *der* vinegar.

Eßlöffel (*pl* **-**) *der* dessertspoon.

Eßzimmer (*pl* **-**) *das* dining room.

Etage (*pl* **-n**) *die* floor, storey.

Etagenbett (*pl* **-en**) *das* bunk bed.

Etappe (*pl* **-n**) *die* stage.

Etikett (*pl* **-en**) *das* label.

etliche, -r, -s *det & pron* several.

Etui (*pl* **-s**) *das* case.

etwa *adv (ungefähr)* about; *(zum Beispiel)* for example; **ist es ~ schon 10 Uhr?** oh no, is it 10 o'clock already?; **hast du das ~ vergessen?** you haven't gone and forgotten it, have you?

etwas ◆ *pron* something; *(in Fragen)* anything; *(ein wenig)* some. ◆ *det (irgendetwas)* something; *(in Fragen)* anything; *(ein wenig)* a little. ◆ *adv (ein wenig)* rather; **~ anderes** something else; **so ~** such a thing.

euch *pron (im Akkusativ)* you; *(im Dativ)* (to) you; *(Reflexivpronomen)* yourselves.

euer, -e ODER **eure** *det* your.

eure, -r, -s ◆ *pron* yours. ◆ *det* → **euer**.

Eurocard (*pl* **-s**) *die* Eurocard.

Eurocheque (*pl* **-s**) *der* = **Euroscheck**.

EuroCity (*pl* **-s**) *der* international train linking two or more major European cities.

Europa *nt* Europe.

Europäer, -in (*mpl* **-**) *der, die* European.

europäisch *adj* European.

Europaparlament *das* European Parliament.

Euroscheck (*pl* -s) *der* Eurocheque.

ev. *abk* = **evangelisch**.

e.V. *abk* = **eingetragener Verein**.

evangelisch *adj* Protestant.

eventuell ◆ *adv* maybe, perhaps. ◆ *adj* possible; **er übernimmt alle ~en Schäden** he'll pay for any damages.

ewig ◆ *adj* (*nie endend*) eternal; (*fam: ständig*) constant. ◆ *adv* (*nie endend*) eternally; (*fam: ständig*) constantly.

exakt ◆ *adj* exact. ◆ *adv* exactly.

Examen (*pl* -) *das* examination.

Exemplar (*pl* -e) *das* example; (*von Buch*) copy.

Exil *das* exile.

Existenz (*pl* -en) *die* existence.

existieren *vi* to exist.

exklusiv ◆ *adj* exclusive. ◆ *adv* exclusively.

Exkursion (*pl* -en) *die* (*in Schule*) school trip.

exotisch *adj* exotic.

Expedition (*pl* -en) *die* expedition.

experimentell *adj* experimental.

Experte (*pl* -n) *der* expert.

Expertin (*pl* -nen) *die* expert.

explodieren *vi ist* to explode.

Explosion (*pl* -en) *die* explosion.

Export¹ (*pl* -e) *der* (*Ausfuhr, Ware*) export.

Export² (*pl* -) *das* (*Bier*) export.

Exportleiter, -in (*mpl* -) *der, die* export manager.

extra ◆ *adv* (*fam: absichtlich*) on purpose; (*separat*) separately; (*speziell*) specially; (*zusätzlich*) extra. ◆ *adj* (*zusätzlich*) extra.

Extraausgabe (*pl* -n) *die* special edition.

Extrablatt *das* extra.

extrem *adj* extreme.

exzellent *adj* excellent.

EZ *abk* = **Einzelzimmer**.

F

fabelhaft *adj* fantastic.

Fabrik (*pl* -en) *die* factory.

fabrikneu *adj* brand new.

Fach (*pl* **Fächer**) *das* (*in Schrank*) compartment; (*Schulfach, Fachgebiet*) subject.

Facharzt (*pl* -ärzte) *der* specialist.

Fachärztin (*pl* -nen) *die* specialist.

Fachausdruck (*pl* -drücke) *der* specialist term.

Fachgeschäft (*pl* -e) *das* specialist store.

Fachmann (*pl* -leute ODER -männer) *der* expert.

fachmännisch ◆ *adj* expert. ◆ *adv* expertly.

Fachnummer (*pl* -n) *die* locker number.

Fachschule (*pl* -n) *die* technical college.

Fachwerkhaus (*pl* -häuser) *das* timbered building.

fade *adj & adv* bland.

Faden (*pl* **Fäden**) *der* (*zum Nähen*) thread.

fähig *adj* capable; **~ sein, etw zu tun** to be capable of doing sthg.

Fahne (*pl* -n) *die* (*Flagge*) flag; **er hat eine ~** (*fam*) his breath smells of alcohol.

Fahrausweis (*pl* -e) *der* ticket.

Fahrausweisautomat (*pl* -en) *der* ticket machine.

Fahrausweisentwerter (*pl* -) *der* ticket validating machine.

Fahrausweiskontrolle (*pl* -n) *die* ticket inspection.

Fahrausweisverkauf *der* ticket sales (*pl*).

Fahrbahn (*pl* -en) *die* road.

Fahrbahnschäden *pl* damage to road surface.

Fahrbahnverschmutzung die: 'Fahrbahnverschmutzung' sign indicating that there is rubble, oil etc on road ahead.

Fähre (pl -n) die ferry.

fahren (präs **fährt**, prät **fuhr**, pp **gefahren**) ◆ vi ist **1.** (mit Auto) to drive; (mit Fahrrad) to ride; **durch Wien** ~ to drive/ride through Vienna; **langsam** ~ to drive slowly; **zu schnell** ~ to drive too fast; **mit dem Zug/Bus** ~ to go by train/bus; **ins Gebirge** ~ to go to the mountains; **wir** ~ **nach England** we're going to England. **2.** (Fahrzeug) to go. **3.** (abfahren) to leave. ◆ vt hat to drive. ◆ vt ist **1.** (Entfernung, Route) to drive; **120 km/h** ~ to drive at 120 km/h. **2.** (SPORT): **Rollschuh** ~ to rollerskate; **Ski** ~ to ski.

Fahrer, -in (mpl -) der, die driver.

Fahrerflucht die hit-and-run.

Fahrersitz (pl -e) der driver's seat.

Fahrgast (pl -gäste) der passenger.

Fahrgeld das fare.

Fahrgelderstattung die refund (of fare).

Fahrgestell (pl -e) das chassis.

Fahrkarte (pl -n) die ticket.

Fahrkartenausgabe die ticket desk.

Fahrkartenautomat (pl -en) der ticket machine.

Fahrkartenschalter (pl -) der ticket desk.

Fahrkosten pl travelling expenses.

Fahrplan (pl -pläne) der timetable.

Fahrplanauszug (pl -züge) der timetable (for specific route).

Fahrplanhinweise pl details concerning the timetable.

fahrplanmäßig ◆ adj scheduled. ◆ adv on time.

Fahrpreis (pl -e) der fare.

Fahrrad (pl -räder) das bicycle, cycle; **mit dem** ~ by bicycle.

Fahrradflickzeug das bicycle repair kit.

Fahrrad-Mitnahme die possibility of taking bicycles on a railway or underground train.

Fahrradreparatur (pl -en) die cycle repair shop.

Fahrradschlauch (pl -schläuche) der inner tube.

Fahrradschloß (pl -schlösser) das bicycle lock.

Fahrradverleih (pl -e) der cycle hire (Br), cycle rental (Am).

Fahrradweg (pl -e) der cycle path.

Fahrschein (pl -e) der ticket; '~e hier entwerten' 'validate your ticket here'.

Fahrscheinentwerter (pl -) der ticket validating machine.

Fahrschule (pl -n) die driving school.

Fahrspur (pl -en) die lane; **die** ~ **wechseln** to change lane; **die linke/ rechte** ~ the left-hand/right-hand lane.

Fahrstreifen (pl -) der lane; **verengte** ~ road narrows.

Fahrstuhl (pl -stühle) der lift (Br), elevator (Am).

Fahrt (pl -en) die (Reise) journey; (kurzer Ausflug) trip; (in Auto) drive; '**den Fahrer während der** ~ **nicht ansprechen**' 'do not speak to the driver while the vehicle is in motion'; **auf der** ~ **nach Berlin** on the way to Berlin; **nach sechs Stunden** ~ after travelling for six hours; **nun wieder freie** ~ **auf der A3** traffic is moving freely again on the A3; **gute** ~! have a good journey!; **eine** ~ **ins Blaue machen** to go for a drive.

fährt präs → **fahren**.

Fahrtantritt der beginning of the journey; '**Fahrscheine vor** ~ **entwerten**' 'please validate your ticket before beginning your journey'.

Fahrtenschreiber (pl -) der tachograph.

Fahrtrichtung (pl -en) die (im Zug) direction of travel.

fahrtüchtig adj (Person) fit to drive; (Fahrzeug) roadworthy.

Fahrtunterbrechung (pl -en) die stop.

Fahrtziel (pl -e) das destination.

Fahrverbot (pl -e) das (Führerscheinentzug) driving ban; ~ für Traktoren no tractors.

Fahrzeit (pl -en) die journey time.

Fahrzeug (pl -e) das vehicle.

Fahrzeugbrief (pl -e) der registration document.

Fahrzeughalter, -in (mpl -) der, die registered owner.

Fahrzeugpapiere pl vehicle documents.

Fahrzeugschein (pl -e) der vehicle documents (pl).

Fahrziel (pl -e) das destination.

fair adj fair.

Fall (pl Fälle) der case; (Sturz) fall; **auf jeden** ~ in any case; **auf keinen** ~ on no account; **für den** ~, **daß** in case ...; **in diesem** ~ in this case.

fallen (präs **fällt**, prät **fiel**, pp **gefallen**) vi ist to fall; **etw** ~ **lassen** to drop sthg.

fallen‖lassen (pp **fallenlassen** ODER **fallengelassen**) vt (Gegenstand) to drop; (Bemerkung) to let drop.

fällig adj due; **am 1.10.** ~ due on 1 October.

falls konj if.

Fallschirm (pl -e) der parachute.

Fallschirmspringer, -in (mpl -) der, die parachutist.

fällt präs → **fallen**.

falsch ◆ adj (inkorrekt) wrong; (Name, Versprechung, Person) false; (Schmuck) fake; (Paß) forged. ◆ adv (inkorrekt) wrongly; (hinterhältig) falsely; ~ **fahren** to drive in the wrong direction.

fälschen vt to forge.

Falschfahrer, -in (mpl -) der, die person driving on the wrong side of the road.

Falschgeld das forged money.

Fälschung (pl -en) die (Falschgeld, Bild) forgery.

Falte (pl -n) die (Hautfalte) wrinkle; (Knitterfalte) crease; (gebügelt) pleat.

falten vt (Pullover, Papier) to fold.

Familie (pl -n) die family.

Familienbesitz der: **in** ~ family-owned.

Familienname (pl -n) der surname.

Familienstand der marital status.

Fan (pl -s) der fan.

fand prät → **finden**.

fangen (präs **fängt**, prät **fing**, pp **gefangen**) vt to catch. ▶ **Fangen** das: Fangen spielen to play tag.

Farbband (pl -bänder) das typewriter ribbon.

Farbbild (pl -er) das colour photograph; ~**er in 24 Stunden** 24 hour colour photos.

Farbe (pl -n) die (Eigenschaft) colour; (zum Malen, Streichen) paint; **welche** ~ **hat das Auto?** what colour is the car?

farbecht adj colourfast.

färben vt (Stoff, Haare) to dye.

Farbfernseher (pl -) der colour television.

Farbfestiger (pl -) der colour set.

Farbfilm (pl -e) der colour film.

Farbfoto (pl -s) das colour photo.

farbig ◆ adj (mehrfarbig) colourful; (einfarbig, Person) coloured. ◆ adv (mehrfarbig) colourfully.

Farbige (pl -n) der, die coloured person.

Farbposter (pl -) das colour poster.

Farbstoff (pl -e) der colouring; **mit/ohne** ~ with/without colouring.

Fasan (pl -e) der pheasant.

Fasching der (Süddt & Österr) carnival before Lent, → **Karneval**.

Faschismus der fascism.

Faschist, -in (mpl -en) der, die fascist.

faschistisch adj fascist.

Faß (pl Fässer) das barrel; **Bier vom** ~ draught beer.

Faßbier das draught beer.

fassen ◆ vt (mit den Händen) to take,

to hold; (*Verbrecher*) to catch; (*Inhalt*) to hold; (*begreifen*) to grasp. ◆ *vi* (*mit den Händen*): **an etw** (A) **~** to feel sthg; **etw nicht ~ können** to be unable to understand sthg. ▶ **sich fassen** *ref* to pull o.s. together.

Fassung (*pl* **-en**) *die* (*für Glühbirne*) fitting; (*Selbstbeherrschung*) composure.

fast *adv* nearly, almost.

fasten *vi* to fast.

Fastenzeit (*pl* **-en**) *die* (*christlich*) Lent; (*mohammedanisch*) Ramadan.

Fastnacht *die* (*Süddt & Österr*) carnival period before Lent, → **Karneval**.

faszinierend *adj* fascinating.

faul *adj* (*Obst*) rotten; (*Person*) lazy.

faulen *vi hat & ist* to rot.

faulenzen *vi* to laze about.

Faust (*pl* **Fäuste**) *die* fist; **auf eigene ~** off one's own bat.

Fax (*pl* **-e**) *das* fax.

faxen *vt* to fax.

Faxgerät (*pl* **-e**) *das* fax machine.

Faxmodem (*pl* **-s**) *das* fax modem

Faxnummer (*pl* **-n**) *die* fax number.

Faxpapier *das* fax paper.

FCKW *der* CFC.

Februar *der* February, → **September**.

fechten (*präs* **ficht**, *prät* **focht**, *pp* **gefochten**) *vi* to fence.

Feder (*pl* **-n**) *die* (*vom Vogel*) feather; (*aus Metall*) spring; (*zum Schreiben*) nib.

Federball (*pl* **-bälle**) *der* (*Ball*) shuttlecock; (*Spiel*) badminton.

Federbett (*pl* **-en**) *das* quilt.

Federhalter (*pl* **-**) *der* fountain pen.

Federung (*pl* **-en**) *die* (*von Auto*) suspension; (*von Sofa*) springs (*pl*).

Federweiße *der* young, cloudy white wine.

fegen ◆ *vt* (*Boden, Raum*) to sweep. ◆ *vi* (*saubermachen*) to sweep up.

Fehlbetrag (*pl* **-beträge**) *der* shortfall.

fehlen ◆ *vi* to be missing. ◆ *vi*

(+D): **sie fehlt mir** I miss her; **was fehlt Ihnen/dir?** what's the matter?; **im Unterricht ~** to miss school.

Fehler (*pl* **-**) *der* mistake; (*von Charakter*) fault.

Fehlzündung (*pl* **-en**) *die*: **eine ~ haben** to misfire.

Feier (*pl* **-n**) *die* party.

Feierabend (*pl* **-e**) *der*: **~ machen** to finish work.

Feierlichkeiten *pl* celebrations.

feiern *vt & vi* (*Fest*) to celebrate; **jn ~** to fête sb; **eine Party ~** to throw ODER have a party.

Feiertag (*pl* **-e**) *der* holiday; **schöne ~e!** have a good holiday!

feiertags *adv* on public holidays.

feige *adj* (*Person*) cowardly.

Feige (*pl* **-n**) *die* (*Frucht*) fig.

Feile (*pl* **-n**) *die* file.

feilen *vt* to file.

fein ◆ *adj* (*dünn, pulverförmig*) fine; (*vornehm*) refined; (*erfreulich*) great. ◆ *adv* (*dünn, pulverförmig*) finely; (*fam: gut*) well; (*vornehm*) elegantly; (*fam: brav*): **~ hier bleiben!** be a good boy/girl and stay here!; **~ gemacht!** (*fam*) well done! ▶ **Feinste** *der, die, das*: **vom Feinsten** first-class.

Feind, -in (*mpl* **-e**) *der, die* (*von Person*) enemy; **ein ~ des Rauchens sein** to be anti smoking.

feindlich *adj* hostile.

Feinkost *die* delicacies (*pl*).

Feinkostgeschäft (*pl* **-e**) *das* delicatessen.

Feinschmecker, -in (*mpl* **-**) *der, die* gourmet.

Feinwaschmittel (*pl* **-**) *das* mild detergent.

Feld (*pl* **-er**) *das* (*Acker, Thema, im Sport*) field; (*von Brettspiel*) square; (*von Formular*) box.

Feldsalat *der* lamb's lettuce.

Feldweg (*pl* **-e**) *der* footpath.

Felge (*pl* **-n**) *die* wheel rim.

Felgenbremse (*pl* **-n**) *die* wheel rim brake.

Fell (*pl* -e) *das* (*von Tier*) fur; (*verarbeitet*) skin.

Fels (*pl* -en) *der* (*Felsblock*) rock.

Felsen (*pl* -) *der* cliff.

felsig *adj* rocky.

feminin *adj* feminine.

Feminismus *der* feminism.

feministisch *adj* feminist.

Fenchel *der* fennel.

Fenster (*pl* -) *das* window.

Fensterbrett (*pl* -er) *das* windowsill.

Fensterladen (*pl* -läden) *der* shutter.

Fensterplatz (*pl* -plätze) *der* window seat.

Fensterscheibe (*pl* -n) *die* windowpane.

Ferien *pl* holiday (*sg*) (Br), vacation (*sg*) (Am); **~ machen** to go on holiday (Br), to go on vacation (Am); **große ~** summer holidays (Br), summer vacation (Am); **schöne ~!** have a good holiday!; **in ~ sein** to be on holiday (Br), to be on vacation (Am).

Ferienapartment (*pl* -s) *das* holiday flat (Br), holiday apartment (Am).

Ferienbeginn *der* beginning of the school summer holidays.

FERIENBEGINN

In Germany, each state sets its own date for the beginning of the school summer holidays. This is often done years in advance, the only restriction being that they must fall between 15 June and 15 September. The sequence in which the states begin their holidays varies from year to year, with the exception of Bavaria which is always last.

Ferienbungalow (*pl* -s) *der* holiday bungalow.

Feriengast (*pl* -gäste) *der* holidaymaker (Br), vacationer (Am).

Ferienhaus (*pl* -häuser) *das* holiday home.

Ferienhausvermietung (*pl* -en) *die* holiday homes rental.

Ferienlager (*pl* -) *das* holiday camp.

Ferienort (*pl* -e) *der* holiday resort.

Ferienwohnung (*pl* -en) *die* holiday flat (Br), holiday apartment (Am).

fern *adj* (Land) far-off, distant.

Fernbedienung (*pl* -en) *die* remote control.

Ferne *die*: **in der ~** in the distance.

Ferngespräch (*pl* -e) *das* long-distance call.

ferngesteuert ♦ *adj* remote-controlled. ♦ *adv* by remote control.

Fernglas (*pl* -gläser) *das* binoculars (*pl*).

fern|halten *vt unr* to keep away. ▸ **sich fernhalten** *ref* to keep away.

Fernlicht *das* full beam (Br), high beam (Am).

Fernmeldeamt (*pl* -ämter) *das* telephone exchange.

Fernschreiben (*pl* -) *das* telex.

Fernschreiber (*pl* -) *der* teleprinter.

Fernsehapparat (*pl* -e) *der* television (set).

fern|sehen *vi unr* to watch television.

Fernsehen *das* television; **im ~** on television.

Fernseher (*pl* -) *der* television.

Fernsehprogramm (*pl* -e) *das* (Kanal) channel; (Sendung) (television) programme.

Fernsehsendung (*pl* -en) *die* (television) programme.

Fernsehturm (*pl* -türme) *der* television tower.

Fernsehzeitschrift (*pl* -en) *die* TV magazine.

Fernsprechamt (*pl* -ämter) *das* (amt) telephone exchange.

Fernsprechauskunft *die* (amt) directory enquiries (*sg*).

Fernsprecher (*pl* -) *der* (*amt*) telephone; **öffentlicher ~** public telephone.

Fernsteuerung (*pl* -en) *die* remote control.

Fernstraße (*pl* -n) *die* trunk road (*Br*), highway (*Am*).

Fernverkehr *der* long-distance traffic.

Ferse (*pl* -n) *die* heel.

fertig *adj* (*vollendet*) finished; **~ sein** (*vollendet, bereit sein*) to be ready; (*fam: erschöpft sein*) to be worn out; (*fam: niedergeschlagen sein*) to be shattered; **mit etw ~ sein** to have finished sthg.

Fertiggericht (*pl* -e) *das* ready-made meal.

fertig|machen *vt* (*beenden*) to finish; (*bereitmachen*) to get ready; (*fam: zurechtweisen*) to lay into; (*fam: erschöpfen*) to wear out.

fest ◆ *adj* (*Knoten, Verband*) tight; (*Händedruck, Griff*) firm; (*Material, Kleidung*) strong; (*Vertrag, Gehalt, Wohnsitz*) fixed; (*Pläne, Termin*) definite. ◆ *adv* (*straff*) tightly; (*kräftig*) hard; (*verbindlich*) firmly.

Fest (*pl* -e) *das* (*Feier*) party; (*religiös*) festival; **frohes ~!** (*frohe Weihnachten*) happy Christmas!

Festbetrag (*pl* -beträge) *der* fixed amount.

fest|binden *vt unr* to tie up.

Festessen (*pl* -) *das* banquet.

fest|halten *vt unr* (*mit der Hand*) to hold (on to); (*dokumentieren*) to record. ▶ **sich festhalten** *ref*: **sich ~ (an** (+D)) to hold on (to).

Festiger (*pl* -) *der* setting lotion.

Festival (*pl* -s) *das* festival.

Festland *das* mainland.

fest|legen *vt* (*Treffpunkt, Route*) to fix.

festlich *adj* festive.

fest|machen *vt* to fasten; (*Boot*) to moor; (*Termin, Treffpunkt*) to arrange.

fest|nehmen *vt unr* to arrest.

Festpreis (*pl* -e) *der* fixed price.

fest|setzen *vt* (*Termin*) to arrange.

Festspiele *pl* festival (*sg*).

fest|stehen *vi unr* to have been decided.

fest|stellen *vt* (*durch Ermittlung*) to find out; (*beobachten*) to notice.

Feststellung (*pl* -en) *die* (*Anmerkung*) remark.

Festwochen *pl* festival (*sg*).

Fete (*pl* -n) *die* (*fam*) party.

fett *adj* (*Fleisch, Gericht*) fatty; (*abw: Person, Körperteil*) fat.

Fett (*pl* -e) *das* fat.

fettarm *adj* low-fat.

fettig *adj* greasy.

Fettstift (*pl* -e) *der* lip salve.

feucht *adj* damp.

Feuchtigkeitscreme (*pl* -s) *die* moisturizer.

Feuer (*pl* -) *das* fire; (*fig: Temperament*) passion; **(ein) ~ machen** to light a fire; **'~ und offenes Licht verboten!'** 'no naked flames!'; **haben Sie ~, bitte?** have you got a light, please?; **jm ~ geben** to give sb a light.

Feueralarm *der* fire alarm.

feuerfest *adj* fireproof.

feuergefährlich *adj* flammable.

Feuerlöscher (*pl* -) *der* fire extinguisher.

Feuermelder (*pl* -) *der* fire alarm.

Feuertreppe (*pl* -n) *die* fire escape.

Feuerwehr (*pl* -en) *die* fire brigade.

Feuerwehrmann (*pl* -männer) *der* fireman.

Feuerwehr-Zufahrt (*pl* -en) *die* fire lane.

Feuerwerk (*pl* -e) *das* fireworks (*pl*).

Feuerzeug (*pl* -e) *das* lighter.

ficht *präs* → **fechten**.

Fieber *das* (*Körpertemperatur*) temperature; **~ haben** to have a temperature; **bei jm ~ messen** to take sb's temperature.

fiebersenkend *adj*: **~es Mittel** temperature-reducing drug.

Fieberthermometer (pl -) das thermometer.

fiebrig ◆ adj (Erkältung) feverish. ◆ adv (glänzen, sich anfühlen) feverishly.

fiel prät → **fallen**.

Figur (pl -en) die (Körperform, Person) figure; (in Schach) piece; (Plastik) sculpture; **eine gute ~ haben** to have a good figure.

Filet (pl -s) das fillet.

Filetsteak (pl -s) das fillet steak.

Filiale (pl -n) die branch.

Film (pl -e) der film.

filmen vt to film.

Filmkamera (pl -s) die (Camcorder) camcorder.

Filmwissenschaften pl film studies.

Filter (pl -) der filter; **mit ~** filter-tipped; **ohne ~** plain.

Filtertüte (pl -n) die filter.

Filterzigarette (pl -n) die filter-tipped cigarette.

Filzstift (pl -e) der felt-tip pen.

Finale (pl -s) das (in Sport) final.

finanziell ◆ adj financial. ◆ adv financially.

finanzieren vt to finance.

finden (prät fand, pp gefunden) ◆ vi to find one's way. ◆ vt to find; **ich finde, daß ...** I think (that) ...; **ich finde sie nett** I think she's nice; **wie findest du ...?** what do you think of ...?; **wo finde ich die Post, bitte?** where is the post office, please? ▶ **sich finden** ref: **der Schlüssel hat sich gefunden** I/we found the key again.

Finderlohn der reward (for finding something).

fing prät → **fangen**.

Finger (pl -) der finger.

Fingernagel (pl -nägel) der fingernail.

Finne (pl -n) der Finn.

Finnin (pl -nen) die Finn.

finnisch adj Finnish.

Finnisch(e) das Finnish.

Finnland nt Finland.

finster adj (dunkel) dark; (unheimlich) sinister.

Firma (pl Firmen) die firm, company.

Fisch (pl -e) der fish. ▶ **Fische** pl (Sternzeichen) Pisces (sg).

Fischbesteck (pl -e) das fish knife and fork.

fischen ◆ vt (Fische) to fish for. ◆ vi (angeln) to fish.

Fischer (pl -) der fisherman.

Fischerboot (pl -e) das fishing boat.

Fischgericht (pl -e) das fish dish.

Fischhändler, -in (mpl -) der, die fishmonger.

Fischstäbchen (pl -) das fish finger (Br), fish stick (Am).

Fischsuppe (pl -n) die fish soup.

fit adj fit; **sich ~ halten** to keep fit.

Fitnesscenter (pl -) das gym, fitness centre.

fix adj (fam: schnell) quick; (Kosten) fixed; **~ und fertig** (vollendet) finished; (müde) worn-out.

FKK die (abk für Freikörperkultur) nudism.

FKK-Strand (pl -Strände) der nudist beach.

flach adj flat; (Wasser, Teller) shallow.

Fläche (pl -n) die (Oberfläche) surface; (Gebiet) area.

Flagge (pl -n) die flag.

flambiert adj flambé.

Flamme (pl -n) die (von Feuer) flame.

Flanell das flannel.

Flasche (pl -n) die bottle.

Flaschenbier das bottled beer.

Flaschenöffner (pl -) der bottle opener.

Flaschenpfand das deposit (on a bottle).

Flaschenweine pl bottled wines.

Flaute (pl -n) die (Windstille) calm.

flechten (präs flicht, prät flocht, pp geflochten) vt (Haar) to plait (Br), to braid (Am); (Korb) to weave.

Fleck (*pl* **-e**) *der* spot; **blauer ~** bruise.

Fleckentferner (*pl* **-**) *der* stain remover.

Fledermaus (*pl* **-mäuse**) *die* bat.

Fleisch *das* (*Muskel*) flesh; (*Nahrung*) meat.

Fleischbrühe (*pl* **-n**) *die* bouillon.

Fleischer (*pl* **-**) *der* butcher.

Fleischerei (*pl* **-en**) *die* butcher's (shop).

Fleischsalat *der* salad made from strips of meat and vegetables with mayonnaise.

Fleischstand (*pl* **-stände**) *der* meat counter.

Fleisch- und Wurstwaren *pl* meat and sausages.

Fleischvergiftung (*pl* **-en**) *die* food poisoning from meat.

fleißig ♦ *adj* hard-working. ♦ *adv* (*arbeiten*) hard.

flicht *präs* → **flechten**.

flicken *vt* (*Kleidung*) to mend; (*Reifen*) to patch.

Flickzeug *das* (*für Reifen*) puncture repair kit; (*für Kleidung*) sewing kit.

Fliege (*pl* **-n**) *die* (*Insekt*) fly; (*Schleife*) bow tie.

fliegen (*prät* **flog**, *pp* **geflogen**) *vt* & *vi ist* to fly; **nach Paris ~** to fly to Paris; **über Paris ~** to fly via Paris.

fliehen (*prät* **floh**, *pp* **geflohen**) *vi ist* to flee.

Fliese (*pl* **-n**) *die* tile.

Fließband (*pl* **-bänder**) *das* conveyor belt.

fließen (*prät* **floß**, *pp* **geflossen**) *vi ist* to flow.

fließend ♦ *adj* (*Verkehr*) moving. ♦ *adv*: **~ Englisch sprechen** to speak fluent English; **~es Wasser** running water.

Flipper (*pl* **-**) *der* pinball machine.

flippern *vi* to play pinball.

Flirt (*pl* **-s**) *der* flirtation.

flirten *vi* to flirt.

Flitterwochen *pl* honeymoon (*sg*).

flocht *prät* → **flechten**.

flog *prät* → **fliegen**.

floh *prät* → **fliehen**.

Floh (*pl* **Flöhe**) *der* flea.

Flohmarkt (*pl* **-märkte**) *der* flea market.

floß *prät* → **fließen**.

Floß (*pl* **Flöße**) *das* raft.

Flosse (*pl* **-n**) *die* (*Schwimmflosse*) flipper (*Br*), fin (*Am*); (*von Tieren*) fin.

Flöte (*pl* **-n**) *die* (*Blockflöte*) recorder; (*Querflöte*) flute.

fluchen *vi* to swear.

Flucht *die* flight.

flüchten *vi ist* to flee.

Flüchtling (*pl* **-e**) *der* refugee.

Flug (*pl* **Flüge**) *der* (*Flugreise*) flight; **ein ~ nach Berlin** a flight to Berlin; **ein ~ über London** a flight via London; **guten ~!** have a good flight!; **'zu den Flügen'** = 'passengers only beyond this point'.

Flugblatt (*pl* **-blätter**) *das* leaflet.

Flügel (*pl* **-**) *der* wing; (*Instrument*) grand piano.

Fluggast (*pl* **-gäste**) *der* passenger (*on plane*).

Fluggepäck *das* luggage.

Fluggesellschaft (*pl* **-en**) *die* airline.

Flughafen (*pl* **-häfen**) *der* airport.

Fluginformation (*pl* **-en**) *die* flight information.

Flugnummer (*pl* **-n**) *die* flight number.

Flugplan (*pl* **-pläne**) *der* flight schedule.

Flugplatz (*pl* **-plätze**) *der* airfield.

Flugschein (*pl* **-e**) *der* (*Ticket*) plane ticket.

Flugscheinkontrolle (*pl* **-n**) *die* ticket control.

Flugsteig (*pl* **-e**) *der* gate.

Flugstrecke (*pl* **-n**) *die* flight distance.

Flugticket (*pl* **-s**) *das* plane ticket.

Flugverbindung (*pl* **-en**) *die* (flight) connection.

Flugverkehr der air traffic.

Flugzeug (pl -e) das (aero)plane, airplane (Am); **mit dem ~ fliegen** to go by air, to fly.

Flur (pl -e) der (Diele) hall.

Fluß (pl Flüsse) der (Wasserlauf) river.

flüssig ♦ adj (Material) liquid. ♦ adv (sprechen) fluently.

Flüssigkeit (pl -en) die liquid.

flüstern vi & vt to whisper.

Flut (pl -en) die (von Gezeiten) tide; (von Beschwerden, Anträgen) flood. ▶ **Fluten** pl (Wassermassen) floods.

Flutlicht das the floodlight.

focht prät → **fechten**.

Fohlen (pl -) das foal.

Föhn der hot, dry wind typical of the Alps.

Folge (pl -n) die (Konsequenz) result, consequence; (von Fernsehserie) episode; **etw zur ~ haben** to result in sthg.

folgen vi ist (+D) to follow; **~ auf** (+A) to follow; **~ aus** to follow from; **bitte ~!** please follow me!

folgend adj following; (Konsequenz) resulting; **~e Punkte** the following points.

folgendermaßen adv as follows.

Folie (pl -n) die (aus Metall) foil; (aus Kunststoff) film.

Folklore die folklore.

folkloristisch adj folkloric.

Fön® (pl -e) der hairdryer.

Fondue (pl -s) das ODER das fondue.

fönen vt to blow-dry; **sich** (D) **die Haare ~** to dry one's hair.

fordern vt (verlangen) to demand; (Preis) to ask; (beanspruchen) to make demands on.

fördern vt (finanziell) to support; (mit Engagement) to promote.

Forderung (pl -en) die (Verlangen) demand; (finanzieller Anspruch) claim.

Forelle (pl -n) die trout; **~ blau** poached trout; **~ Müllerinnen Art** trout fried in butter and served with lemon juice and parsley.

Form (pl -en) die (räumlich) shape, form; (für Kuchen) baking tin; **in ~ sein** to be in good form; **in ~ von** in the form of.

Formalität (pl -en) die (Regel) formality.

Format (pl -e) das (Größe) format.

Formblatt (pl -blätter) das form.

formen vt (Ton, Teig) to shape.

formlos adj shapeless.

Formular (pl -e) das form; **ein ~ ausfüllen** to fill in a form.

formulieren vt to word.

Forschung (pl -en) die research.

Forst (pl -e) der forest.

fort adv away; **~ sein** to be gone.

fort|bewegen vt to move away. ▶ **sich fortbewegen** ref to move.

fort|fahren ♦ vi unr ist (mit Auto, Zug) to leave; (weitermachen) to continue. ♦ vt unr hat (Auto, Bus) to drive away.

fort|gehen vi unr ist (weggehen) to leave.

Fortgeschrittene (pl -n) der, die advanced student.

Fortschritt (pl -e) der progress; **~e machen** to make progress.

fort|setzen vt to continue.

Fortsetzung (pl -en) die (von Streik, Verhandlungen) continuation; (von Serie) episode.

fort|ziehen vi unr ist to move away.

Foto (pl -s) das photo.

Fotoapparat (pl -e) der camera.

Fotogeschäft (pl -e) das camera shop.

Fotograf, -in (mpl -en) der, die photographer.

Fotografie (pl -n) die (Bild) photograph.

fotografieren ♦ vt to photograph. ♦ vi to take photographs.

Fotokopie (pl -n) die photocopy.

fotokopieren vt & vi to photocopy.

Foyer (pl -s) das foyer.

Fr. (abk für Frau) Mrs.

Fracht (*pl* **-en**) *die* (*mit Zug*) freight; (*mit Schiff*) cargo.

Frachter (*pl* **-**) *der* freighter.

Frack (*pl* **Fräcke**) *der* tails (*pl*).

Frackzwang *der*: **es besteht ~** please wear tails.

Frage (*pl* **-n**) *die* (*Fragesatz*) question; (*Problem*) issue; **eine ~ haben** to have a question; **eine ~ (an jn) stellen** to ask (sb) a question; **die ~ nach** the question of; **noch ~n?** any more questions?; **etw in ~ stellen** to call sthg into question; **nicht in ~ kommen** to be out of the question.

Fragebogen (*pl* **-bögen**) *der* questionnaire.

fragen *vt* & *vi* to ask; **~ nach** to ask about. ▶ **sich fragen** ◆ *ref* to wonder. ◆ *vimp*: **es fragt sich, ob ...** it is debatable whether ...

Fragezeichen (*pl* **-**) *das* question mark.

Fraktion (*pl* **-en**) *die* (POL) (parliamentary) party.

Franken (*pl* **-**) *der*: **(Schweizer) ~** Swiss franc.

Frankenwein (*pl* **-e**) *der* white wine from northern Bavaria.

frankieren *vt* to stamp.

Frankreich *nt* France.

Franzose (*pl* **-n**) *der* Frenchman.

Französin (*pl* **-nen**) *die* Frenchwoman.

französisch *adj* French.

Französisch(e) *das* French.

fraß *prät* → **fressen**.

Frau (*pl* **-en**) *die* (*Erwachsene*) woman; (*Ehefrau*) wife; (*als Anrede*) Mrs (*verheiratet*), Ms (*neutral*).

Frauenarzt (*pl* **-ärzte**) *der* gynaecologist.

Frauenärztin (*pl* **-nen**) *die* gynaecologist.

Frauenberatungsstelle (*pl* **-n**) *die* women's advice centre.

Frauenbewegung *die* women's movement.

Frauenbuchladen (*pl* **-läden**) *der* feminist bookshop.

Frauencafé (*pl* **-s**) *das* café for women only.

frauenfeindlich *adj* misogynistic.

Frauenhaus (*pl* **-häuser**) *das* women's refuge.

Frauenlokal (*pl* **-e**) *das* bar for women only.

Fräulein *das* (*Anrede*) Miss.

frech ◆ *adj* cheeky. ◆ *adv* cheekily.

Frechheit (*pl* **-en**) *die* (*Bemerkung, Handlung*) cheeky thing.

Free-Climbing *das* free climbing.

frei ◆ *adj* free; (*Mitarbeiter*) freelance; (*nackt*) bare. ◆ *adv* freely; (*gratis*) for free; **~ von** free of; **drei Wochen ~ haben** to have three weeks off; **etw ~ Haus liefern** to deliver sthg free; **machen Sie sich bitte ~** please take your clothes off; **im Freien** in the open air.

Freibad (*pl* **-bäder**) *das* open-air swimming pool.

freiberuflich *adj* self-employed.

Freibier *das* free beer.

freigegeben *adv*: '**~ ab 18 Jahren**' indicates that a film can only be watched by people over eighteen.

Freiheit (*pl* **-en**) *die* (*Unabhängigkeit*) freedom; (*Vorrecht*) liberty.

Freikarte (*pl* **-n**) *die* free ticket.

freillassen *vt unr* to set free.

freilich *adv* (*allerdings*) admittedly; (*Süddt: sicher*) of course.

Freilichtbühne (*pl* **-n**) *die* open-air theatre.

freilmachen ◆ *vi* (*fam: Urlaub nehmen*) to take time off. ◆ *vt* (*Brief*) to stamp. ▶ **sich freimachen** *ref* (*Urlaub machen*) to take time off; (*sich ausziehen*) to take one's clothes off.

Freistoß (*pl* **-stöße**) *der* free kick.

Freitag (*pl* **-e**) *der* Friday, → **Samstag**.

freitags *adv* on Fridays.

freiwillig ◆ *adj* voluntary. ◆ *adv* of one's own free will.

Freizeichen (*pl* **-**) *das* ringing tone.

Freizeit *die* free time.

Freizeitbad (pl -bäder) das leisure pool.

Freizeitkleidung die casual clothes (pl).

Freizeitpark (pl -s) der park (with recreational facilities).

fremd adj (ausländisch) foreign; (unbekannt) strange; **~e Angelegenheiten** other people's business; **ich bin hier ~** I'm a stranger here.

Fremde (pl -n) der, die (Unbekannter) stranger.

Fremdenführer, -in (mpl -) der, die tourist guide.

Fremdenverkehrsamt (pl -ämter) das tourist board.

Fremdenverkehrsbüro (pl -s) das tourist information centre.

Fremdenzimmer (pl -) das (guest) room.

Fremdkörper (pl -) der foreign body.

Fremdsprache (pl -n) die foreign language.

Fremdsprachenkenntnisse pl knowledge of foreign languages.

Fremdwort (pl -e) das foreign word.

Frequenz (pl -en) die (von Radiosender) frequency.

fressen (präs frißt, prät fraß, pp gefressen) ◆ vt (Futter) to eat; (Benzin, Strom) to eat up. ◆ vi (Tier) to feed; (abw: Mensch) to stuff o.s.

Freude (pl -n) die pleasure, joy; **jm eine ~ machen** to make sb happy. ► **Freuden** pl pleasures.

freuen vt to please; **freut mich sehr!** pleased to meet you! ► **sich freuen** ref to be pleased; **sich ~ auf** (+A) to look forward to; **sich ~ über** (+A) to be pleased about.

Freund, -in (mpl -e) der, die friend; (Geliebter) boyfriend (girlfriend); **~e und Bekannte** friends and acquaintances.

freundlich ◆ adj (Person) friendly; (Umgebung, Wetter) nice. ◆ adv (grüßen) in a friendly way.

Freundschaft (pl -en) die (vertraute Beziehung) friendship.

Frieden der peace.

Friedhof (pl -höfe) der cemetery.

frieren (prät fror, pp gefroren) ◆ vi hat/ist (Person) to be cold; (Wasser) to freeze. ◆ vimp hat: **es friert** it's freezing.

Frikadelle (pl -n) die rissole.

frisch ◆ adj fresh; (Temperatur) cool; (Farbe) wet. ◆ adv freshly; **sich ~ machen** to freshen up; **'Vorsicht, ~ gestrichen!'** 'wet paint'.

Frischfleisch das fresh meat.

Frischhaltebeutel (pl -) der airtight bag.

Frischhaltefolie (pl -n) die clingfilm (Br), Saranwrap® (Am).

Frischkäse (pl -) der soft cream cheese.

Friseur (pl -e) der hairdresser.

Friseuse (pl -n) die hairdresser.

Frisiercreme (pl -s) die styling cream.

frisieren vt: **jn ~** to do sb's hair. ► **sich frisieren** ref to do one's hair.

frißt präs → **fressen**.

Frist (pl -en) die period; **eine ~ einhalten** to stick to a deadline.

fristgerecht adj within the time allowed.

Frisur (pl -en) die hairstyle.

fritieren vt to deep-fry.

Frl. (abk für Fräulein) Miss.

froh adj happy; **~ sein über** (+A) to be pleased about.

fröhlich ◆ adj cheerful. ◆ adv cheerfully.

Fronleichnam nt Corpus Christi (Catholic festival).

fror prät → **frieren**.

Frost (pl Fröste) der frost.

Frostgefahr die: **es besteht ~** there's a danger of frost.

Frostschutzmittel (pl -) das antifreeze.

Frottee (pl -s) der ODER das towelling.

Frucht (pl Früchte) die fruit.

Fruchteis das fruit-flavoured ice-cream.

Früchtetee (pl -s) der fruit tea.

fruchtig adj fruity.

Fruchtsaft (pl -säfte) der fruit juice.

Fruchtsaftkonzentrat (pl -e) das squash (Br), juice concentrate (Am).

Fruchtsalat (pl -e) der fruit salad.

früh adj & adv early; **~ am Abend** early in the evening; **gestern/heute/morgen ~** yesterday/this/tomorrow morning.

früher ◆ adj (ehemalig) former. ◆ adv formerly.

frühestens adv at the earliest.

Frühjahr (pl -e) das spring.

Frühling (pl -e) der spring; **im ~ in** spring.

Frühlingsrolle (pl -n) die spring roll.

Frühschicht (pl -en) die early shift.

Frühschoppen (pl -) der mid-morning drink with friends in pub.

Frühstück (pl -e) das breakfast; **zum ~** for breakfast.

frühstücken vi to have breakfast.

Frühstücksbuffet (pl -s) das breakfast bar.

Frühstücksraum (pl -räume) der breakfast room.

Fuchs (pl Füchse) der fox.

fühlen vt & vi to feel; **nach etw ~** to feel for sthg. ▶ **sich fühlen** ref to feel.

fuhr prät → **fahren**.

führen ◆ vt (Person, Leben) to lead; (Touristen) to show round; (Geschäft) to run; (Buch, Konto) to keep; (Ware) to stock; (Gespräch) to hold. ◆ vi to lead; **England führt mit 1:0** England are one-nil ahead; **~ zu** (an ein Ziel) to lead to.

Führer (pl -) der (Person, Buch) guide.

Führerin (pl -nen) die guide.

Führerschein (pl -e) der driving licence (Br), driver's license (Am).

Führung (pl -en) die (Besichtigung) (guided) tour; **nächste ~: 12.30 Uhr** the next tour is at 12.30; **in ~ liegen** to be in the lead.

füllen vt (Gefäß) to fill; (Teig, Fleisch) to stuff; (Flüssigkeit) to put.

Füller (pl -) der fountain pen.

Füllung (pl -en) die filling.

Fund (pl -e) der (Vorgang) discovery; (Gegenstand) find.

Fundbüro (pl -s) das lost property office (Br), lost-and-found office (Am).

Fundsachen pl lost property (sg).

fünf num five, → **sechs**.

fünfhundert num five hundred.

fünfmal adv five times.

Fünfmarkstück (pl -e) das five-mark coin.

fünfte adj fifth, → **sechste**.

Fünftel (pl -) das fifth.

fünfzehn num fifteen, → **sechs**.

fünfzig num fifty, → **sechs**.

Fünfzigmarkschein (pl -e) der fifty-mark note.

Funk der radio.

funken vt to radio.

Funkgerät (pl -e) das radio set.

Funktelefon (pl -e) das (Handy) mobile phone; (kabelloses Telefon) cordless phone.

Funktion (pl -en) die function; (Funktionieren) functioning.

funktionieren vi to work.

für präp (+A) for; **Wort ~ Wort** word by word; **Tag ~ Tag** day after day; **was ~ ein Auto hast du?** what kind of car do you have?; **jn ~ dumm halten** to think sb is stupid.

Furcht die fear.

furchtbar ◆ adj terrible. ◆ adv terribly.

fürchten vt to fear. ▶ **sich fürchten** ref to be afraid; **sich ~ vor** (+D) to be afraid of.

fürchterlich ◆ adj terrible. ◆ adv terribly.

füreinander adv for each other.

fürs präp & det = **für das**.

Fuß (pl **Füße**) der foot; (von Möbel) leg; (von Lampe) base; **zu ~** on foot.

Fußball (pl **-bälle**) der (Ball) football (Br), soccer ball (Am); (Sport) football (Br), soccer (Am).

Fußballmannschaft (pl **-en**) die football team (Br), soccer team (Am).

Fußballplatz (pl **-plätze**) der football pitch (Br), soccer pitch (Am).

Fußballspiel (pl **-e**) das football match (Br), soccer match (Am).

Fußballspieler, -in (mpl **-**) der, die footballer (Br), soccer player (Am).

Fußbank (pl **-bänke**) die footstool.

Fußboden (pl **-böden**) der floor.

Fußbremse (pl **-n**) die footbrake.

Fußgänger, -in (mpl **-**) der, die pedestrian.

Fußgängerbrücke (pl **-n**) die footbridge.

Fußgängertunnel (pl **-**) der subway, underpass.

Fußgängerüberweg (pl **-e**) der pedestrian crossing.

Fußgängerzone (pl **-n**) die pedestrian precinct.

Fußgelenk (pl **-e**) das ankle.

Fußnagel (pl **-nägel**) der toenail.

Fußweg (pl **-e**) der footpath.

Futter das (für Tiere) food; (von Mantel, Tasche) lining.

füttern vt to feed; 'bitte nicht ~!' 'please do not feed the animals'.

Futur (pl **-e**) das future (tense).

G

gab prät → **geben**.

Gabel (pl **-n**) die (Besteck) fork.

gabeln: sich gabeln ref to fork.

Gabelung (pl **-en**) die fork.

Gag (pl **-s**) der gag.

gähnen vi to yawn.

Gala (pl **-s**) die (Veranstaltung) gala; (Kleidung) formal dress.

Galerie (pl **-n**) die gallery.

Galle (pl **-n**) die bile.

galoppieren vi ist to gallop.

Galopprennen (pl **-**) das horse racing.

galt prät → **gelten**.

gammeln vi (fam: Essen) to go off; (fam: Person) to loaf around.

Gang (pl **Gänge**) der (Flur) corridor; (in Flugzeug) aisle; (von Menü) course; (von Fahrzeug) gear; (Gangart) gait; (Spaziergang) walk; **etw in ~ setzen** to get sthg going; **im ersten ~** in first gear.

Gangschaltung (pl **-en**) die gears (pl).

Gangway (pl **-s**) die (von Schiff) gangway; (von Flugzeug) steps (pl).

Gans (pl **Gänse**) die goose.

Gänsehaut die goose-pimples (pl).

Gänseleberpastete (pl **-n**) die foie gras, pâté made from goose liver.

ganz ◆ adj (komplett, heil) whole; (alle) all. ◆ adv (sehr) really; (völlig) completely; (ziemlich) quite; **der ~e Kaffee** all the coffee; **~ Paris** the whole of Paris; **~ bleiben** to stay in one piece; **~ bestimmt** quite certainly; **~ und gar** completely; **~ und gar nicht** not at all; **~ gut** quite well/ good.

ganztägig ◆ adj (Beschäftigung) full-time. ◆ adv all day.

ganztags adv all day.

gar ◆ adj (Speise) done. ◆ adv: **es war ~ keiner da** there was no one there at all; **~ nicht** not at all; **~ nichts** nothing at all; **auf ~ keinen Fall** under no circumstances.

Garage (pl **-n**) die garage.

Garagenanlage (pl **-n**) die row of garages.

Garantie (pl **-n**) die guarantee.

garantieren ◆ vt to guarantee. ◆ vi: **~ für** to guarantee.

garantiert adv: **er hat es ~ vergessen** he's bound to have forgotten it.
Garderobe (pl -n) die (Kleidung) coat, scarf, hat, etc; (Raum) cloakroom.
Gardine (pl -n) die curtain.
Garn (pl -e) das thread.
Garten (pl Gärten) der garden.
Gartenabfallcontainer (pl -) der garden waste bin.
Gartenlokal (pl -e) das beer garden.
Gartenstuhl (pl -stühle) der garden chair.
Gärtner, -in (mpl -) der, die gardener.
Gärtnerei (pl -en) die nursery.
Garzeit (pl -en) die cooking time.
Gas (pl -e) das gas; (Gaspedal) accelerator; **~ geben** to accelerate.
Gasflasche (pl -n) die gas cylinder.
Gasheizung (pl -en) die gas heating.
Gaskocher (pl -) der camping stove.
Gaspedal (pl -e) das accelerator.
Gaspistole (pl -n) die pistol that fires gas cartridges.
Gasse (pl -n) die (Straße) lane.
Gast (pl Gäste) der guest; **zu ~ sein bei jm** to be sb's guest.
Gastarbeiter, -in (mpl -) der, die foreign worker.
Gästebett (pl -en) das spare bed.
Gästebuch (pl -bücher) das visitor's book.
Gästehaus (pl -häuser) das guest house.
Gästezimmer (pl -) das guest room.
gastfreundlich adj hospitable.
Gastgeber, -in (mpl -) der, die host.
Gasthaus (pl -häuser) das inn.
Gasthof (pl -höfe) der inn.
Gastland (pl -länder) das foreign country (where someone is staying).

Gastronomie die catering.
Gaststätte (pl -n) die pub (also offering a full menu of local food).
Gaststube (pl -n) die restaurant (in a hotel or inn).
Gastwirt, -in (mpl -e) der, die landlord (landlady).
Gaze die gauze.
geändert adj: **~e Abfahrtszeiten** revised departure times; **~e Öffnungszeiten** new opening hours; **'Vorfahrt ~'** sign indicating altered right of way.
geb. abk = **geboren**.
Gebäck das pastries (pl).
gebacken adj baked.
Gebärmutter die womb.
Gebäude (pl -) das building.
gebeizt adj (Holz) stained.
geben (präs **gibt**, prät **gab**, pp **gegeben**) ◆ vt 1. (reichen, schenken): **jm etw ~** to give sb sthg, to give sthg to sb. 2. (bezahlen) to give; **er hat mir 20 DM dafür gegeben** he gave me 20 marks for it. 3. (sagen, erteilen) to give; **Unterricht ~** to teach. 4. (in Reparatur): **etw in Reparatur ~** to have sthg repaired. 5. (am Telefon): **jm jn ~** to put sb through to sb. ◆ vimp: **es gibt** there is/are; **hier gibt es viele Studenten** there are a lot of students here; **was gibt es?** what's up?; **was gibt es im Fernsehen?** what's on television? ▸ **sich geben** ref to act; **sich cool ~** to act cool.
gebeten pp → **bitten**.
Gebiet (pl -e) das (Gegend) area.
Gebirge (pl -) das mountains (pl).
gebirgig adj mountainous.
Gebiß (pl Gebisse) das (Zähne) teeth (pl); (künstlich) dentures (pl).
gebissen pp beißen.
Gebißreiniger (pl -) der denture tablets (pl).
Gebläse (pl -) das fan.
geblasen pp → **blasen**.
geblieben pp bleiben.
gebogen ◆ pp → **biegen**. ◆ adj bent.

gebohnert *adj* polished; **'frisch ~'** 'slippery floor'.

geboren *adj*: **~e Maier** née Maier.

geborgen *pp* → **bergen**.

geboten *pp* → **bieten**.

gebracht *pp* → **bringen**.

gebrannt *pp* → **brennen**.

gebraten ♦ *pp* → **braten**. ♦ *adj* (*in der Pfanne*) fried; (*im Backofen*) roast.

gebrauchen *vt* to use; **deine Hilfe könnte ich gut ~** I could use your help.

Gebrauchsanweisung (*pl* **-en**) *die* instructions (*pl*).

gebrauchsfertig *adj* ready-to-use.

Gebrauchsgegenstand (*pl* **-stände**) *der* utensil.

gebraucht *adj* used, second-hand.

Gebrauchtwagen (*pl* **-**) *der* used car.

gebrochen ♦ *pp* → **brechen**. ♦ *adj* broken. ♦ *adv*: **~ Englisch sprechen** to speak broken English.

Gebühr (*pl* **-en**) *die* (*für Telefon, Rundfunk*) charge; (*für Arzt, Anwalt*) fee; **'~ bezahlt Empfänger'** 'postage to be paid by the addressee'.

Gebühreneinheit (*pl* **-en**) *die* unit (*on phone*).

gebührenfrei *adj* free of charge.

Gebührenordnung (*pl* **-en**) *die* tariff.

gebührenpflichtig *adj* subject to a charge.

gebunden *pp* → **binden**.

Geburt (*pl* **-en**) *die* birth.

Geburtsdatum *das* date of birth.

Geburtsjahr *das* year of birth.

Geburtsname *der* maiden name.

Geburtsort *der* place of birth.

Geburtstag (*pl* **-e**) *der* birthday; **alles Gute zum ~** happy birthday.

Geburtstagsfeier (*pl* **-n**) *die* birthday party.

Geburtsurkunde (*pl* **-n**) *die* birth certificate.

gedacht *pp* → **denken**.

Gedächtnis (*pl* **-se**) *das* memory.

Gedanke (*pl* **-n**) *der* thought.

Gedeck (*pl* **-e**) *das* place setting.

Gedenkfeier (*pl* **-n**) *die* memorial service.

Gedenkstätte (*pl* **-n**) *die* memorial.

Gedenktafel (*pl* **-n**) *die* (memorial) plaque.

Gedicht (*pl* **-e**) *das* poem.

Geduld *die* patience; **bitte haben Sie etwas ~** (*am Telefon*) please hold the line.

gedulden: sich gedulden *ref* to wait (patiently); **bitte ~ Sie sich einen Augenblick** please wait a moment.

geduldig ♦ *adj* patient. ♦ *adv* patiently.

gedünstet *adj* steamed.

gedurft *pp* → **dürfen**.

geehrt *adj*: **Sehr ~e Frau Müller** Dear Mrs Müller; **Sehr ~er Herr Braun** Dear Mr Braun.

geeignet *adj* suitable; **~ für** suitable for; **er ist zum Lehrer ~** he'd make a good teacher; **nicht ~** unsuitable.

Gefahr (*pl* **-en**) *die* danger; **auf eigene ~** at one's own risk; **'bei ~ Scheibe einschlagen'** 'break the glass in case of emergency'.

gefahren *pp* → **fahren**.

Gefahrenfall *der*: **'nur im ~ benutzen'** 'for emergency use only'.

gefährlich *adj* dangerous.

Gefälle (*pl* **-**) *das* incline.

gefallen *vi*: **es gefällt mir** I like it; **es gefällt ihm** he likes it; **sich** (D) **etw ~ lassen** to put up with sthg; **sich** (D) **nichts ~ lassen** not to put up with any nonsense.

Gefallen (*pl* **-**) *der* favour; **jm einen ~ tun** to do sb a favour; **jm um einen ~ bitten** to ask sb a favour.

gefälligst *adv*: **komm ~ her!** will you please come here!

gefangen *pp* → **fangen**.

Gefängnis (*pl* **-se**) *das* prison.

Gefäß (*pl* **-e**) *das* container, receptacle.

geflochten *pp* → flechten.

geflogen *pp* → fliegen.

geflohen *pp* → fliehen.

geflossen *pp* → fließen.

Geflügel *das* poultry.

gefochten *pp* → fechten.

gefressen *pp* → fressen.

Gefrierbeutel (*pl* -) *der* freezer bag.

gefrieren (*präs* **gefriert**, *prät* **gefror**, *pp* **gefroren**) *vi* ist/hat to freeze.

Gefrierfach (*pl* -fächer) *das* freezer (compartment).

Gefriertruhe (*pl* -n) *die* freezer.

gefroren ◆ *pp* → **frieren**, **gefrieren**. ◆ *adj* frozen.

Gefühl (*pl* -e) *das* feeling.

gefüllt *adj* (*Speisen*) stuffed.

gefunden *pp* → finden.

gegangen *pp* → gehen.

gegeben *pp* → geben.

gegebenenfalls *adv* if necessary.

gegen *präp* (+A) against; (*Angabe eines Vergleiches*) in comparison to; ~ **fünf Uhr** at about five o'clock; ~ **etw sein** to be opposed to sthg; **Leipzig ~ Dresden** Leipzig versus Dresden; **ein Mittel ~ Grippe** a medicine for flu, a flu remedy; **etwas ~ jn haben** to have something against sb; ~ **bar** for cash.

Gegend (*pl* -en) *die* area; **in der ~** nearby; **in der ~ von** near.

gegeneinander *adv* against each other.

Gegenfahrbahn (*pl* -en) *die* opposite carriageway.

Gegenlicht *das*: **bei ~** with the light in one's eyes.

Gegenmittel (*pl* -) *das* antidote.

Gegenrichtung *die* opposite direction.

Gegensatz (*pl* -sätze) *der* contrast; **im ~ zu** in contrast to.

gegenseitig ◆ *adj* mutual. ◆ *adv*: **sich ~ beeinflussen** to influence each other.

Gegensprechanlage (*pl* -n) *die* intercom.

Gegenstand (*pl* -stände) *der* object.

Gegenteil (*pl* -e) *das* opposite; **im ~** on the contrary.

gegenüber *präp* (+D) (*räumlich*) opposite; (*Angabe eines Vergleichs*) in comparison to; (*Angabe einer Beziehung*): **jm ~** towards sb.

Gegenverkehr *der* oncoming traffic.

Gegenwart *die* (GRAMM) present (tense); (*Jetzt*) present; **in ~ von** in the presence of.

Gegenwind *der* headwind.

gegessen *pp* → essen.

geglichen *pp* → gleichen.

geglitten *pp* → gleiten.

Gegner, -in (*mpl* -) *der, die* opponent.

gegolten *pp* → gelten.

gegossen *pp* → gießen.

gegriffen *pp* → greifen.

gegrillt *adj* grilled.

Gehackte *das* mince (Br), mincemeat (Am).

Gehalt (*pl* Gehälter) *das* (*von Angestellten*) salary.

gehbehindert *adj* disabled (*used of people who have difficulty walking*).

geheim *adj* secret.

Geheimnis (*pl* -se) *das* secret.

geheimnisvoll *adj* mysterious.

Geheimnummer (*pl* -n) *die* (*von Scheckkarte*) PIN (number); (*von Telefon*) ex-directory number (Br), unlisted number (Am).

Geheimzahl (*pl* -en) *die* (*von Kreditkarte*) personal identification number.

geheißen *pp* → heißen.

gehen (*präs* **geht**, *prät* **ging**, *pp* **gegangen**) ◆ *vi* ist **1.** (*gen*) to go; **einkaufen ~** to go shopping; **zu Fuß ~** to walk. **2.** (*weggehen, abfahren*) to go; **mein Zug geht um acht Uhr** my train goes at eight o'clock. **3.** (*funktionieren*) to work. **4.** (*erlaubt sein*) to be allowed; **das geht nicht** you can't do that. **5.** (*möglich sein*) to be possible;

heute geht es nicht it's not possible today. **6.** (*reichen*): **~ bis** to come up to, to go as far as. **7.** (*passen*): **in/durch etw ~** to go in/through sthg. **8.** (*berühren*): **an etw** (A) **~** to touch sthg. **9.** (*sich richten*): **es kann nicht immer nach dir ~** you can't always have things your own way. **10.** (*Belastung*): **das geht über unsere Mittel** that's beyond our means. **11.** (*kündigen*) to leave. **12.** (*Teig*) to rise. **13.** (*Post*) to go. ◆ *vimp* **1.** (*sich befinden*): **wie geht's?** how are you?; **wie geht es Ihnen?** how are you?; **es geht mir gut/schlecht** I'm well/not very well; **wie gefällt es dir? – es geht** how do you like it? – it's O.K. **2.** (*sich handeln um*): **es geht um deine Mutter** it's about your mother; **es geht darum, als erster anzukommen** you have to try and arrive first; **worum geht es in diesem Buch?** what's this book about?

gehen‖lassen: sich gehenlassen *ref* to let o.s. go.

Gehirn (*pl* -e) *das* brain.

Gehirnerschütterung (*pl* -en) *die* concussion.

gehoben ◆ *pp* → **heben**. ◆ *adj* (*Position*) senior.

geholfen *pp* → **helfen**.

gehorchen *vi* to obey; **jm ~** to obey sb.

gehören *vi*: **jm ~** to belong to sb; **~ zu** (*als Teil*) to belong to; **~ in** (+A) (*an Platz*) to belong in. ▶ **sich gehören** *ref*: **das gehört sich nicht!** that's not the done thing!

Gehörlose (*pl* -n) *der, die* deaf person.

gehorsam *adj* obedient.

Gehweg (*pl* -e) *der* pavement (*Br*), sidewalk (*Am*).

Geige (*pl* -n) *die* violin.

Geisel (*pl* -n) *die* hostage.

Geist (*pl* -er) *der* (*Verstand*) mind; (*Gespenst*) ghost.

Geisterbahn (*pl* -en) *die* ghost train.

Geisterfahrer, -in (*mpl* -) *der, die* person who drives in the wrong direction on a motorway.

geizig *adj* mean, miserly.

gekannt *pp* → **kennen**.

geklungen *pp* → **klingen**.

gekniffen *pp* → **kneifen**.

gekocht *adj* cooked.

gekommen *pp* → **kommen**.

gekonnt *pp* → **können**.

gekrochen *pp* → **kriechen**.

gekühlt *adj* (*Getränk*) chilled; '**~ mindestens haltbar bis ...**' 'if refrigerated best before ...'

Gel (*pl* -s) *das* gel.

geladen *pp* → **laden**.

gelähmt *adj* paralysed.

Gelände (*pl* -) *das* (*Grundstück*) site; (*Gebiet*) terrain.

Geländer (*pl* -) *das* (*von Treppe*) banister; (*von Brücke*) parapet; (*von Balkon*) railing.

gelang *prät* → **gelingen**.

gelassen *adj* calm, cool.

Gelatine *die* gelatine.

gelaunt *adj*: **gut ~** good-tempered; **schlecht ~** bad-tempered.

gelb *adj* (*Farbe*) yellow; (*Ampel*) amber.

Gelb *das* (*Farbe*) yellow; (*von Ampel*) amber.

Gelbsucht *die* jaundice.

Geld (*pl* -er) *das* money. ▶ **Gelder** *pl* funds.

Geldautomat (*pl* -en) *der* cash dispenser.

Geldbetrag (*pl* -beträge) *der* sum of money.

Geldbörse (*pl* -n) *die* (*Brieftasche*) wallet; (*für Münzen*) purse.

Geldeinwurf *der* coin slot.

Geldrückgabe *die* coin return (button).

Geldschein (*pl* -e) *der* banknote.

Geldstrafe (*pl* -n) *die* fine.

Geldtasche (*pl* -n) *die* money bag.

Geldwechsel *der* exchange; '**kein**

~' 'currency not exchanged here'.

Geldwechselautomat (*pl* -en) *der* change machine.

Gelee (*pl* -s) *das* jelly.

gelegen *pp* → **liegen**.

Gelegenheit (*pl* -en) *die* (*Möglichkeit, Anlaß*) opportunity; (*Angebot*) bargain; **bei ~** when the opportunity arises.

Gelenk (*pl* -e) *das* (*von Knochen*) joint.

Geliebte (*pl* -n) *der, die* lover.

geliehen *pp* → **leihen**.

gelingen *vi unr* ist to be a success; **jm ~** to turn out well for sb; **es ist mir gelungen, ihn zu überreden** I managed to convince him.

gelitten *pp* → **leiden**.

gelockt *adj* curly.

gelogen *pp* → **lügen**.

gelten (*präs* **gilt**, *prät* **galt**, *pp* **gegolten**) ◆ *vt* to be valid for. ◆ *vi* to be valid; **~ bis** to be valid until.

Geltungsbereich (*pl* -e) *der* (*von Fahrkarte*) zone or zones for which a ticket is valid.

Geltungsdauer *die* (*von Fahrkarte, Ausweis*) period for which a ticket, passport etc is valid.

gelungen *pp* → **gelingen**.

gemahlen *adj* (*Kaffee*) ground.

Gemälde (*pl* -) *das* painting.

gemein *adj* (*böse*) nasty, mean.

Gemeinde (*pl* -n) *die* (*Verwaltungseinheit*) municipality; (*Menschen*) community; (*kirchlich*) parish.

gemeinsam ◆ *adj* common. ◆ *adv* together.

Gemeinschaft (*pl* -en) *die* (*Gruppe*) community; (*Zusammensein*) company.

gemeint *adj*: **das war nicht so ~** I didn't mean it like that.

gemieden *pp* → **meiden**.

gemischt *adj* mixed; **~er Salat** mixed salad.

gemocht *pp* → **mögen**.

gemolken *pp* → **melken**.

Gemüse *das* vegetables (*pl*).

Gemüsehändler, -in (*mpl* -) *der, die* greengrocer.

gemußt *pp* → **müssen**.

gemütlich *adj* (*bequem*) cosy; (*Abend*) pleasant; (*langsam*) leisurely; **es sich ~ machen** to make o.s. at home.

genannt *pp* → **nennen**.

genau ◆ *adj* exact. ◆ *adv* (*aufmerksam*) carefully; (*exakt*) precisely, exactly; **~!** (*richtig*) exactly!

genauso *adv* just as; **~ gut/ schlecht/schnell** just as good/bad/ fast.

genehmigen *vt* to authorize.

Genehmigung (*pl* -en) *die* (*Genehmigen*) authorization; (*Schein*) permit.

generalüberholen *vt* to service.

Generation (*pl* -en) *die* generation.

generell *adj* general.

Genf *nt* Geneva.

Genfer See *der* Lake Geneva.

Genick (*pl* -e) *das* (back of the) neck.

genießbar *adj* (*Speise*) edible; **das Fleisch ist nicht mehr ~** the meat has gone off.

genießen (*prät* **genoß**, *pp* **genossen**) *vt* to enjoy.

Genitiv (*pl* -e) *der* genitive.

genommen *pp* → **nehmen**.

genormt *adj* standardized.

genoß *prät* → **genießen**.

genossen *pp* → **genießen**.

genug *adv* enough; **~ haben** (*bei Überdruß*) to have had enough.

genügen *vi* to be enough; **jm ~** to be enough for sb; **das genügt!** that's enough!

Genuß (*pl* **Genüsse**) *der* (*Freude*) pleasure; (*Verzehr, Verbrauch*) consumption.

geöffnet *adj* (*Geschäft, Schalter*) open.

geographisch *adj* geographical.

geordnet *adj* orderly.

Gepäck *das* luggage.

Gepäckabfertigung *die* (luggage) check-in.

Gepäckablage (*pl* -n) *die* luggage rack.

Gepäckannahme *die* (*zur Aufbewahrung*) = **Gepäckaufbewahrung**; (*Abfertigung am Bahnhof*) *office where large items of luggage sent by rail have to be registered.*

Gepäckaufbewahrung *die* left-luggage office (*Br*), baggage room (*Am*).

Gepäckaufgabe *die* (*Abfertigung am Bahnhof*) = **Gepäckannahme**; (*zur Aufbewahrung*) = **Gepäckaufbewahrung**.

Gepäckaufsicht *die* left-luggage office (*Br*), baggage room (*Am*).

Gepäckausgabe *die* (*aus Aufbewahrung*) = **Gepäckaufbewahrung**; (*Abfertigung am Bahnhof*) *office where large items of luggage sent by rail can be collected.*

Gepäckkarren (*pl* -) *der* luggage trolley.

Gepäckkontrolle (*pl* -n) *die* luggage search.

Gepäcknetz (*pl* -e) *das* luggage rack.

Gepäckrückgabe *die* (*aus Aufbewahrung*) = **Gepäckaufbewahrung**; (*Abfertigung am Flughafen*) baggage reclaim.

Gepäckschein (*pl* -e) *der* luggage ticket.

Gepäckschließfach (*pl* -fächer) *das* left-luggage locker (*Br*), baggage locker (*Am*).

Gepäckstück (*pl* -e) *das* item of luggage.

Gepäckträger (*pl* -) *der* (*von Fahrrad*) carrier.

Gepäckversicherung (*pl* -en) *die* luggage insurance.

Gepäckwagen (*pl* -) *der* luggage van (*Br*), luggage car (*Am*).

gepfiffen *pp* → **pfeifen**.

gequollen *pp* → **quellen**.

gerade *adv* just; (*jetzt*) just now; ~ **er** he of all people; ~ **deshalb** precisely for that reason; ~ **erst** only just; ~ **noch** only just; **er wollte** ~ **gehen** he was just about to go; **nicht** ~ not exactly.

geradeaus *adv* straight ahead; **immer** ~ straight ahead.

gerannt *pp* → **rennen**.

geraspelt *adj* grated.

gerät *präs* → **geraten**.

Gerät (*pl* -e) *das* (*Vorrichtung, Maschine*) device; (*Werkzeug*) tool; (*Kochlöffel, Dosenöffner usw.*) utensil; (*Radio, Fernseher*) set.

geraten (*pl* **gerät** *prät* **geriet** *pp* **geraten**) *vi ist* (*gelangen*) to get; **auf die falsche Fahrbahn** ~ to get into the wrong lane; **in Schwierigkeiten** ~ to get into difficulties.

geräuchert *adj* smoked.

geräumig *adj* roomy.

Geräusch (*pl* -e) *das* noise.

gerecht *adj* just, fair.

Gerechtigkeit *die* justice.

Gericht (*pl* -e) *das* (*Institution*) court; (*Speise*) dish.

Gerichtsvollzieher (*pl* -) *der* bailiff.

gerieben ♦ *pp* → **reiben**. ♦ *adj* grated.

geriet *prät* → **geraten**.

gerieten *pp* → **geraten**.

gering *adj* (*Menge, Preis, Temperatur*) low; (*Zeit, Abstand*) short; (*Bedeutung*) minor; (*Chance*) slight; **nicht im ~sten** not in the least.

geringfügig *adj* slight, minor.

gerinnen (*prät* **gerann**, *pp* **geronnen**) *vi ist* (*Milch*) to curdle; (*Blut*) to clot.

gerissen ♦ *pp* → **reißen**. ♦ *adj* (*abw: Person*) cunning.

geritten *pp* → **reiten**.

Germanistik *die* German studies (*pl*).

gern(e) (*komp* **lieber**, *superl* **am liebsten**) *adv:* **jn/etw** ~ **haben** to like sb/sthg; **jn/etw ~ mögen** to like sb/sthg; **etw ~ tun** to like doing sthg; **aber ~!** I'd love to!; **~ geschehen!** don't mention it!; **ich möchte ~ ...** I'd like to ...; **ja ~!** of course!

gerochen pp → **riechen**.

geronnen ◆ pp → **gerinnen, rinnen**. ◆ adj (Milch) curdled.

geröstet adj roasted.

Geruch (pl Gerüche) der smell.

gerufen pp → **rufen**.

gerungen pp → **ringen**.

gesalzen adj (Speise) salted; (fam: Preis) steep.

gesamt adj (Familie, Inhalt) whole; (Einkommen, Kosten) total.

gesamtdeutsch adj united German; **~e** Beziehungen relations between the two Germanys.

Gesamtschule (pl -n) die = comprehensive school.

gesandt pp → **senden**[1].

Geschädigte (pl -n) der, die injured party.

Geschäft (pl -e) das (Laden) shop; (Betrieb) business; (Handel) deal.

Geschäftsbedingungen pl terms.

Geschäftsfrau (pl -en) die businesswoman.

Geschäftsführer, -in (mpl -) der, die manager (< manageress).

Geschäftsleute pl businessmen.

Geschäftsmann (pl -männer) der businessman.

Geschäftsreise (pl -n) die business trip.

Geschäftsschluß der closing time.

Geschäftsstelle (pl -n) die office.

Geschäftsstraße (pl -n) die high street (Br), main street (Am).

Geschäftszeiten pl business hours.

geschah prät → **geschehen**.

geschehen (präs **geschieht**, prät **geschah**, pp **geschehen**) vi ist to happen; **jm ~** to happen to sb; **~ mit** to happen to.

Geschenk (pl -e) das present, gift; **soll ich es als ~ einpacken?** would you like it gift-wrapped?

Geschenkartikel (pl -) der gift.

Geschenkgutschein (pl -e) der gift token.

Geschenkpapier (pl -e) das gift wrap.

Geschichte (pl -n) die (Text) story; (Vergangenheit) history.

geschickt adj skilful.

geschieden ◆ pp → **scheiden**. ◆ adj (Mann, Frau) divorced.

geschieht präs → **geschehen**.

geschienen pp → **scheinen**.

Geschirr das (zum Essen) crockery; (das) **~ spülen** to wash up; **das ~ abtrocknen** to dry up.

Geschirrspülmaschine (pl -n) die dishwasher.

Geschirrspülmittel (pl -) das washing-up liquid.

Geschirrtuch (pl -tücher) das tea towel (Br), dish towel (Am).

geschissen pp → **scheißen**.

Geschlecht das (biologisch) sex; (GRAMM) gender.

Geschlechtskrankheit (pl -en) die sexually transmitted disease.

Geschlechtsverkehr der sexual intercourse.

geschlichen pp → **schleichen**.

geschliffen pp → **schleifen**.

geschlossen ◆ pp → **schließen**. ◆ adj closed; (Ortschaft) built-up.

geschlungen pp → **schlingen**.

Geschmack (pl Geschmäcker) der taste; **guten ~ haben** to have good taste; **schlechten ~ haben** to have bad taste.

geschmacklos adj tasteless.

geschmackvoll adj tasteful.

geschmissen pp → **schmeißen**.

geschmolzen pp → **schmelzen**.

geschmort adj braised.

Geschnetzelte das small pieces of veal

or chicken cooked in a sauce.

geschnitten ◆ *pp* → **schneiden**.
◆ *adj* (*Wurst, Käse*) sliced; **~ oder am Stück?** would you like it sliced or unsliced?

geschoben *pp* → **schieben**.

gescholten *pp* → **schelten**.

geschoren *pp* → **scheren**.

Geschoß (*pl* **Geschosse**) *das* (*Etage*) floor.

geschossen *pp* → **schießen**.

Geschrei *das* shouting.

geschrieben *pp* → **schreiben**.

geschrien *pp* → **schreien**.

geschritten *pp* → **schreiten**.

geschwiegen *pp* → **schweigen**.

Geschwindigkeit (*pl* **-en**) *die* speed.

Geschwindigkeitsbe-schränkung (*pl* **-en**) *die* speed limit.

Geschwindigkeitsübertretung (*pl* **-en**) *die* speeding.

Geschwister *pl* brothers and sisters.

geschwollen ◆ *pp* → **schwellen**.
◆ *adj* (*Finger, Bein*) swollen.

geschwommen *pp* → **schwimmen**.

geschworen *pp* → **schwören**.

geschwungen *pp* → **schwingen**.

Geschwür (*pl* **-e**) *das* ulcer.

gesellig *adj* (*Person*) sociable; (*Abend*) social.

Gesellschaft (*pl* **-en**) *die* (*System*) society; (*Gruppe*) group (of people); (*Touristen*) party; (*Begleitung*) company; **jm ~ leisten** to keep sb company.

Gesellschaftsraum (*pl* **-räume**) *der* function suite.

gesessen *pp* → **sitzen**.

Gesetz (*pl* **-e**) *das* law.

gesetzlich *adj* legal; **~er Feiertag** public holiday.

gesetzwidrig *adj* illegal.

Gesicht (*pl* **-er**) *das* face.

Gesichtscreme (*pl* **-s**) *die* face cream.

Gesichtswasser *das* toner.

gesoffen *pp* → **saufen**.

gesogen *pp* → **saugen**.

gespannt ◆ *adj* (*Atmosphäre*) tense.
◆ *adv* (*warten*) eagerly; **auf etw** (A) **~ sein** (*Person*) to be looking forward to sthg.

gesperrt *adj* (*Straße*) closed off.

gesponnen *pp* → **spinnen**.

Gespräch (*pl* **-e**) *das* (*Konversation*) conversation; (*per Telefon*) call.

Gesprächspartner, -in (*mpl* **-**) *der, die* person one is talking to.

gesprochen *pp* → **sprechen**.

gesprungen ◆ *pp* → **springen**.
◆ *adj* (*Glas*) cracked.

Gestalt (*pl* **-en**) *die* (*Person, Figur*) figure; (*Form*) shape.

gestanden *pp* → **stehen**.

Gestank *der* stench.

gestärkt *adj* (*Wäsche*) starched.

gestatten ◆ *vt* (*geh: erlauben*) to permit, to allow. ◆ *vi* (*geh*): **~: Meier** allow me to introduce myself – my name is Meier; **~ Sie?** may I?; **jm etw ~** to allow sb sthg.

gestattet *adj* (*amt*): **~ sein** to be allowed; **nicht ~** prohibited.

Geste (*pl* **-n**) *die* (*mit Händen, mit Kopf*) gesture.

gestern *adv* yesterday; **~ morgen/ mittag/abend** yesterday morning/ lunchtime/evening; **~ früh** early yesterday.

gestiegen *pp* → **steigen**.

gestochen ◆ *pp* → **stechen**. ◆ *adv*: **~ scharf** sharp.

gestohlen *pp* → **stehlen**; **etw als ~ melden** to report the theft of sthg.

gestorben *pp* → **sterben**.

gestreift *adj* striped, stripy.

gestrichen ◆ *pp* → **streichen**.
◆ *adj* (*Löffel*) level.

gestrig *adj* (*von Vortag*): **die ~e Zeitung** yesterday's paper.

gestritten *pp* → **streiten**.

gestunken *pp* → **stinken**.

gesund

gesund (*komp* **gesünder**, *superl* **am gesündesten**) ♦ *adj* healthy. ♦ *adv* healthily; **wieder ~ werden** to get better.

Gesundheit *die* health; **~!** bless you!

gesundheitsschädlich *adj* (*Inhaltsstoff*) damaging to one's health.

gesungen *pp* → **singen**.

gesunken *pp* → **sinken**.

getan *pp* → **tun**.

Getränk (*pl* -e) *das* drink; **alkoholische ~e** alcoholic beverages; **nichtalkoholische ~e** soft drinks.

Getränkeautomat (*pl* -en) *der* drinks machine.

Getränkekarte (*pl* -n) *die* wine list.

Getränkemarkt (*pl* -märkte) *der* discount drink store.

Getreide *das* cereal, grain.

getrennt ♦ *adj* (*Zimmer*, *Rechnung*) separate. ♦ *adv* separately; **~ leben** to live apart; **~ zahlen** to pay separately.

Getriebe (*pl* -) *das* (*von Auto, in Technik*) gearbox.

getrieben *pp* → **treiben**.

Getriebeschaden (*pl* -schäden) *der* gearbox damage.

getrocknet *adj* dried.

getroffen *pp* → **treffen**.

getrunken *pp* → **trinken**.

gewachsen *pp* → **wachsen**.

Gewähr *die* guarantee; **ohne ~** (*auf Fahrplan*) subject to alteration.

Gewalt *die* (*Brutalität*) violence; (*Kraft*) force; (*Macht*) power.

gewandt *pp* → **wenden**.

gewann *prät* → **gewinnen**.

gewaschen *pp* → **waschen**.

Gewebe (*pl* -) *das* (*Stoff*) fabric; (*Körpergewebe*) tissue.

Gewehr (*pl* -e) *das* gun.

gewellt *adj* (*Haare*) wavy.

Gewerbegebiet (*pl* -e) *das* business park.

gewerblich *adj* (*Nutzung*) commercial.

Gewerkschaft (*pl* -en) *die* trade union.

gewesen *pp* → **sein**.

Gewicht (*pl* -e) *das* weight.

gewiesen *pp* → **weisen**.

Gewinn (*pl* -e) *der* (*Preis*) prize; (*Profit*) profit; (*bei Glücksspiel, beim Wetten*) winnings (*pl*).

gewinnen (*prät* **gewann**, *pp* **gewonnen**) ♦ *vi* to win; (*besser werden*) to gain. ♦ *vt* to win; (*produzieren*) to obtain.

Gewinner, -in (*mpl* -) *der, die* winner.

Gewinnspiel (*pl* -e) *das* game show.

gewiß *adj* certain.

Gewissen *das* conscience.

Gewitter (*pl* -) *das* (*Wetter*) storm.

gewittrig *adj* (*Gewitter ankündigend*) stormy.

gewogen *pp* → **wiegen**.

gewöhnen: **jn an etw** (A) **~** to accustom sb to sthg. ▶ **sich gewöhnen** *ref*: **sich ~ an** (+A) to get used to.

Gewohnheit (*pl* -en) *die* habit.

gewöhnlich ♦ *adj* (*normal*) usual; (*primitiv*) common. ♦ *adv* (*normalerweise*) usually; **wie ~** as usual.

gewohnt *adj* usual; **etw ~ sein** to be used to sthg.

Gewölbe (*pl* -) *das* (*Deckengewölbe*) vault.

gewonnen *pp* → **gewinnen**.

geworben *pp* → **werben**.

geworden *pp* → **werden**.

geworfen *pp* → **werfen**.

Gewürz (*pl* -e) *das* spice.

Gewürzgurke (*pl* -n) *die* pickled gherkin.

gewürzt *adj* seasoned; **scharf ~** hot.

gewußt *pp* → **wissen**.

Gezeiten *pl* tides.

gezogen *pp* → **ziehen**.

gezwungen *pp* → **zwingen**.

gibt *präs* → **geben**.

Gicht *die* gout.

gierig *adj* greedy.

gießen (*prät* **goß**, *pp* **gegossen**) ◆ *vt* (*schütten*) to pour; (*Pflanzen*) to water. ◆ *vimp*: **es gießt** it's pouring (down).

Gießkanne (*pl* **-n**) *die* watering can.

Gift (*pl* **-e**) *das* poison.

giftig *adj* (*Substanz, Pflanze*) poisonous; (*fig: Person, Bemerkung*) venomous.

gilt *präs* → **gelten**.

Gin *der* gin.

ging *prät* → **gehen**.

Gipfel (*pl* **-**) *der* (*von Berg*) summit, peak.

Gips *der* (*Gipspulver*) plaster; (*Gipsverband*) plaster cast.

Gipsbein (*pl* **-e**) *das*: **ein ~ haben** to have one's leg in plaster.

Gipsverband (*pl* **-verbände**) *der* plaster cast.

Giraffe (*pl* **-n**) *die* giraffe.

Girokonto (*pl* **-konten**) *das* current account (Br), checking account (Am).

Gischt *die* spray.

Gitarre (*pl* **-n**) *die* guitar.

Gitter (*pl* **-**) *das* bars (*pl*).

Gitterbett (*pl* **-en**) *das* cot (Br), crib (Am).

glänzen *vi* (*Metall, Wasser*) to shine.

glänzend *adj* (*leuchtend*) shining; (*ausgezeichnet*) brilliant.

Glas (*pl* **Gläser**) *das* glass; (*Einmachglas*) jar; **aus ~** glass; **ein ~ Wein** a glass of wine.

Gläschen (*pl* **-**) *das* little glass.

Glasfenster (*pl* **-**) *das* stained-glass window.

Glasscheibe (*pl* **-n**) *die* pane (of glass).

Glastür (*pl* **-en**) *die* glass door.

glatt ◆ *adj* (*eben*) smooth; (*rutschig*) slippery; (*fam: problemlos*) smooth. ◆ *adv* (*fam: problemlos*) smoothly.

Glätte *die* (*Eisglätte*) (patch of) black ice.

Glatteis *das* black ice.

Glatteisgefahr *die*: **Vorsicht, ~!** watch out for black ice!

Glatze (*pl* **-n**) *die*: **eine ~ haben** to be bald.

glauben ◆ *vt* (*meinen, denken*) to think; (*für wahr halten*) to believe. ◆ *vi* (*meinen, denken*) to think; **~ an** (+A) to believe in; **jm ~** to believe sb.

gleich ◆ *adj* same. ◆ *adv* (*identisch*) equally; (*ähnlich*) the same; (*egal*) no matter; (*sofort, bald*) straight away; (*ebensogut*) just as well; **zwei ~ Tassen** two identical cups; **~ links/rechts** immediately on the left/right; **bis ~!** see you soon!; **~ groß sein** to be the same size; **das ist mir ~** I don't care; **ich komme ~** I'm just coming.

gleichaltrig *adj*: **~ sein** to be the same age.

gleichberechtigt *adj* (*Mann und Frau*): **~ sein** to have equal rights.

gleiche, -r ODER **-s** *pron*: **der/die/das ~** the same (one).

gleichen (*prät* **glich**, *pp* **geglichen**) *vi* (+D) to resemble.

gleichfalls *adv* also, as well; **danke ~!** thanks, you too!

gleichgültig *adj*: **es ist mir ~** it's all the same to me.

gleichmäßig ◆ *adj* (*Tempo*) even. ◆ *adv* (*ziehen*) steadily; (*auftragen*) evenly.

Gleichstrom *der* direct current.

gleichzeitig ◆ *adj* simultaneous. ◆ *adv* at the same time.

Gleis (*pl* **-e**) *das* (*Bahnsteig*) platform.

gleiten (*prät* **glitt**, *pp* **geglitten**) *vi ist* (*rutschen*) to glide.

Gleitschirm (*pl* **-e**) *der* paraglider.

Gleitzeit *die* flexitime.

Gletscher (*pl* **-**) *der* glacier.

glich *prät* → **gleichen**.

Glied (*pl* **-er**) *das* (*Einzelteil*) link; (*Arm, Bein*) limb; (*Penis*) member.

glitschig *adj* slippery.

glitt *prät* → **gleiten**.

glitzern *vi* sparkle.

Glocke (*pl* -n) *die* bell.

Glück *das* (*Ereignis*) luck; (*Gefühl*) happiness; ~ **haben** to be lucky; **viel ~!** good luck!; **zum** ~ luckily.

glücklich ◆ *adj* (*froh*) happy; (*Zufall, Zusammentreffen*) fortunate. ◆ *adv* (*froh*) happily; (*günstig*) fortunately.

glücklicherweise *adv* luckily.

Glücksspiel (*pl* -e) *das* (*um Geld*) game of chance.

Glückwunsch (*pl* -wünsche) *der* congratulations (*pl*); **herzlichen ~!** congratulations!

Glückwunschtelegramm (*pl* -e) *das* telegram sent to congratulate someone.

Glühbirne (*pl* -n) *die* light bulb.

glühen *vi* (*Kohle*) to glow; (*Gesicht, Wangen*) to burn.

Glühwein *der* mulled wine.

Glut *die* (*im Feuer*) embers (*pl*).

Gnagi *das* (*Schweiz*) boiled knuckle of pork.

Gold *das* gold; **aus ~** gold.

golden *adj* (*aus Gold*) gold; (*goldfarben*) golden.

Goldschmied, -in (*mpl* -e) *der, die* goldsmith.

Golf *das* (*Sportart*) golf.

Golfplatz (*pl* -plätze) *der* golf course.

Golfschläger (*pl* -) *der* golf club.

gönnen *vt* (+D): **jm etw ~** not to begrudge sb sthg; **sich** (D) **etw ~** to allow o.s. sthg.

goß *prät* → **gießen**.

gotisch *adj* Gothic.

Gott (*pl* Götter) *der* (*christlich*) God; (*Gottheit*) god; **~ sei Dank!** thank God!; **Grüß ~!** (*Süddt & Österr*) hello!; **um ~es Willen!** for God's sake!

Gottesdienst (*pl* -e) *der* service.

Grab (*pl* Gräber) *das* grave.

graben (*präs* **gräbt**, *prät* **grub**, *pp* **gegraben**) *vt & vi* to dig.

Graben (*pl* Gräben) *der* (*Vertiefung*) ditch.

Grabstein (*pl* -e) *der* gravestone.

gräbt *präs* → **graben**.

Grad (*pl* -e) *der* degree; **drei ~ unter/über Null** three degrees below/above zero; **im höchsten ~** highly.

Graffiti *pl* (*an Haus, U-Bahn*) graffiti.

Grafik (*pl* -en) *die* (*Technik*) graphics (*sg*); (*Bild, Schema*) diagram.

Grafiker, -in (*mpl* -) *der, die* graphic designer.

Gramm (*pl* -) *das* (*Gewichtseinheit*) gram.

Grammatik (*pl* -en) *die* grammar.

Grapefruit (*pl* -s) *die* grapefruit.

Grapefruitsaft (*pl* -säfte) *der* grapefruit juice.

Graphik *die* = **Grafik**.

Gras (*pl* Gräser) *das* grass.

gräßlich ◆ *adj* horrible. ◆ *adv* (*sehr*) terribly; (*schreckenerregend*) terrifyingly.

Gräte (*pl* -n) *die* (fish) bone.

gratis *adv & adj* free.

Gratulation (*pl* -en) *die* (*Glückwunsch*) congratulations (*pl*).

gratulieren *vi*: **jm (zu etw) ~** to congratulate sb (on sthg).

grau *adj* (*Farbe, Haare*) grey; (*trist*) gloomy.

Graubrot (*pl* -e) *das* bread made with mixed wholemeal, rye and wheat flour.

grauhaarig *adj* grey-haired.

Graupelschauer (*pl* -) *der* sleet.

grausam *adj* (*Mensch, Tat*) cruel; (*Schmerzen, Hitze*) terrible.

greifen (*prät* **griff**, *pp* **gegriffen**) ◆ *vt* to take hold of. ◆ *vi* (*Räder*) to grip; **nach etw ~** to reach for sthg.

grell ◆ *adj* (*Licht*) glaring; (*Ton*) harsh; (*Farbe*) loud. ◆ *adv* (*leuchten*) glaringly; (*klingen*) harshly.

Grenzbeamte (*pl* -n) *der* customs and immigration officer.

Grenzbeamtin (*pl* -nen) *die* customs and immigration officer.

Grenze (*pl* -n) *die* (*von Land*) border; (*von Stadt, Grundstück*) boundary;

(begrifflich, ideell) borderline; *(Beschränkung)* limit; **grüne ~** *border area without major road or border patrols.*

grenzen *vi:* **~ an** *(+A) (räumlich)* to border.

Grenzkontrolle *(pl -n) die* border checkpoint.

Grenzübergang *(pl -gänge) der (Ort)* border crossing.

Grenzverkehr *der* cross-border traffic.

Grenzwert *(pl -e) der (für Schadstoffe)* limit.

Griebenschmalz *das* spread made from animal fat, similar to dripping.

Grieche *(pl -n) der* Greek.

Griechenland *nt* Greece.

Griechin *(pl -nen) die* Greek.

griechisch *adj* Greek.

Griechisch(e) *das* Greek.

Grieß *der* semolina.

Griff *(pl -e) der (mit der Hand)* grip; *(zum Halten)* handle.

griff *prät →* **greifen**.

Grill *(pl -e) der* grill.

grillen *vt & vi* to grill.

Grillfest *(pl -e) das* barbecue.

Grillspieß *(pl -e) der (mit Fleisch)* (shish) kebab.

Grillstube *(pl -n) die* grill *(restaurant).*

Grillteller *(pl -) der* mixed grill.

grinsen *vi* to grin.

Grippe *(pl -n) die* flu.

Grippewelle *(pl -n) die* flu epidemic.

grob *(komp* **gröber,** *superl* **am gröbsten)** *adj (Zucker, Salz)* coarse; *(Person, Verhalten)* crude; *(Leder, Stoff)* rough.

Grog *(pl -s) der* hot toddy.

Groschen *(pl -) der (deutsche Münze)* ten pfennig coin; *(österreichische Münze)* one hundredth of an Austrian schilling.

groß *(komp* **größer,** *superl* **am größten)** ◆ *adj (räumlich)* big, large; *(Person)* tall; *(Buchstabe)* capital;

(Gefühl, Lärm, Künstler) great; *(Vermögen)* large; *(Angebot)* wide; *(erwachsen)* grown-up. ◆ *adv (räumlich)* on a large scale; *(glanzvoll)* in style; **es wird ~ geschrieben** it's written with a capital letter; **~ werden** to grow up.

großartig *adj* brilliant.

Großaufnahme *(pl -n) die* close-up.

Großbritannien *nt* Great Britain.

Großbuchstabe *(pl -n) der* capital letter.

Größe *(pl -n) die* size; *(Höhe)* height.

Großeltern *pl* grandparents.

Großhandel *der* wholesale.

Großmarkt *(pl -märkte) der* cash-and-carry.

Großmutter *(pl -mütter) die* grandmother.

Großraum *(pl -räume) der* area; **der ~ Frankfurt** the Frankfurt area.

Großraumwagen *(pl -) der (in Zug)* open carriage *(not divided into compartments).*

Großschreibung *die* capitalization.

Großstadt *(pl -städte) die* city.

Großvater *(pl -väter) der* grandfather.

großzügig ◆ *adj (freigiebig)* generous. ◆ *adv (freigiebig)* generously.

Grotte *(pl -n) die* cave, grotto.

grub *prät →* **graben**.

Gruft *(pl* **Grüfte)** *die* crypt.

grün *adj* green; **~er Pfeil** filter arrow; **~e Versicherungskarte** green card *(Br),* insurance card for travel abroad; **Grüne Punkt** *(auf Verpackungen)* symbol placed on product to indicate that it meets certain recycling standards.

Grün *das* green.

Grünanlage *(pl -n) die* park.

Grund *(pl* **Gründe)** *der (Ursache, Motiv)* reason; *(von Gewässer)* bed; *(Erdboden)* ground; **auf ~ von** *(wegen)* because of; **aus diesem ~** for this reason; **im ~e** basically.

gründen vt (Verein, Betrieb) to found.

Gründer, -in (mpl -) der, die founder.

Grundgebühr (pl -en) die (für Telefon) line rental.

Grundgesetz das German constitution.

Grundkurs (pl -e) der foundation course.

Grundlage (pl -n) die basis; **die ~n der Theorie** the basic principles of the theory.

gründlich ◆ adj thorough. ◆ adv thoroughly.

Grundnahrungsmittel (pl -) das staple (food).

Gründonnerstag (pl -e) der Maundy Thursday.

Grundrecht (pl -e) das basic right.

Grundschule (pl -n) die ≃ primary school (attended by pupils aged 6 to 10).

Grundstück (pl -e) das plot (of land).

Gründung (pl -en) die foundation.

Grüne[1] (pl -n) der, die Green; **die ~n** the Greens.

Grüne[2] das: **im ~n** in the country.

Grünfläche (pl -n) die park.

Grünkohl der kale.

Gruppe (pl -n) die group.

Gruppenermäßigung (pl -en) die group reduction.

Gruppenkarte (pl -n) die group ticket.

Gruppenreise (pl -n) die group tour.

Gruß (pl Grüße) der greeting; **herzliche Grüße an ...** greetings to ...; **mit freundlichen Grüßen** yours sincerely; **viele Grüße!** best wishes!

grüßen ◆ vi to say hello. ◆ vt (begrüßen) to greet; (grüßen lassen) to say hello to; **Michaela läßt dich ~** Michaela says hello; **jn von jm ~** to say hello to sb from sb.

gucken vi to look.

Gulasch (pl -s) der ODER das goulash.

Gulaschkanone (pl -n) die large tureen used to serve hot food at outdoor public events.

gültig adj (Ticket, Vertrag) valid.

Gültigkeit die validity.

Gummi (pl -s) das (Material) rubber; (Gummiring) rubber band.

Gummiband (pl -bänder) das rubber band.

Gummistiefel (pl -) der wellington (boot).

günstig adj (vorteilhaft) favourable; (preisgünstig) cheap; (Moment) convenient.

gurgeln vi to gargle.

Gurke (pl -n) die (Salatgurke) cucumber; saure ~ pickled gherkin.

Gurt (pl -e) der (an Tasche, Sattel) strap; (Sicherheitsgurt) seat belt.

Gürtel (pl -) der (an Hose) belt.

Gürtelreifen (pl -) der radial (tyre).

Gürtelrose die shingles (sg).

Gürteltasche (pl -n) die bumbag (Br), fanny pack (Am).

Gurtpflicht die compulsory wearing of seat belts.

gut (komp besser, superl am besten) ◆ adj good. ◆ adv well; (leicht) easily; **~ befreundet sein** to be good friends; **~ mit jm auskommen** to get on well with sb; **~ gehen** (Geschäft) to go well; **~ schmecken** to taste good; **ihr ist nicht ~** she's not well; **so ~ wie** as good as. ▶ **Gute** das good; **alles Gute!** all the best!

Gutachter, -in (mpl -) der, die expert.

gutbürgerlich adj: **~e Küche** good, plain food.

Güteklasse (pl -n) die grade.

Güterbahnhof (pl -höfe) der goods depot.

Güterzug (pl -züge) der goods train.

gut|gehen ◆ vi unr ist to go well. ◆ vimp unr ist: **es geht ihm gut** he's doing well.

gutgelaunt *adj* in a good mood.
Guthaben (*pl* -) *das* balance (*positive*).
Gutschein (*pl* -e) *der* voucher.
gut|schreiben *vt unr* to credit.
Gutschrift (*pl* -en) *die* (*Quittung*) credit slip.
gut|tun *vi unr* (+D): **jm ~** to do sb good.
Gymnasium (*pl* Gymnasien) *das* ≃ grammar school (Br), *secondary school attended by 10 - 19 year-olds.*
Gymnastik *die* keep-fit.
Gynäkologe (*pl* -n) *der* gynaecologist.
Gynäkologin (*pl* -nen) *die* gynaecologist.
Gyros *das* doner kebab.

Haar (*pl* -e) *das* hair; **sich die ~e schneiden lassen** to have one's hair cut.
Haarbürste (*pl* -n) *die* hairbrush.
Haarfärbemittel (*pl* -) *das* hair dye.
Haarfestiger (*pl* -) *der* setting lotion.
Haargel (*pl* -s) *das* hair gel.
Haarklammer (*pl* -n) *die* hair grip.
Haarkur (*pl* -en) *die* hair treatment cream.
Haarnadel (*pl* -n) *die* hairpin.
Haarnadelkurve (*pl* -n) *die* hairpin bend.
haarscharf *adv* (*sehr nah*) only just; (*fig: sehr genau*) precisely.
Haarschnitt (*pl* -e) *der* haircut.
Haarshampoo (*pl* -s) *das* shampoo.
Haarspange (*pl* -n) *die* hair clip.
Haarspray (*pl* -s) *das* hairspray.

Haartrockner (*pl* -) *der* hairdryer.
Haarwasser (*pl* -wässer) *das* hair tonic.
haben (*präs* hat, *prät* hatte, *pp* gehabt) ♦ *aux* to have; **sie hat gegessen** she has eaten. ♦ *vt* **1.** (*gen*) to have; **sie hat blaue Augen** she has (got) blue eyes; **hast du Geld bei dir?** have you got any money on you? **2.** (*mit Zeitangabe*): **wie spät ~ wir?** what's the time?; **wir ~ zehn Uhr** it's ten o'clock; **heute ~ wir Dienstag** it's Tuesday today. **3.** (*Unterricht, Dienst*) to have; **einen Tag frei ~** to have a day off. **4.** (*Erlebnis*) to have. **5.** (*im Restaurant, Geschäft*): **ich hätte gerne ...** I'd like ... **6.** (*zur Verfügung*) to have; **es eilig ~** to be in a hurry. **7.** (*Krankheit, Problem*) to have; **Kopfschmerzen ~** to have a headache; **was hast du denn?** what's wrong? **8.** (*Gefühl*): **Angst ~** to be afraid; **Durst ~** to be thirsty; **Hunger ~** to be hungry; **~ Sie etwas dagegen, wenn ...?** do you mind if ...? **9.** (*Angabe von Zwang*): **etw zu tun ~** to have to do sthg.
Haben *das* credit.
Hackbraten (*pl* -) *der* meatloaf.
hacken *vt* (*Holz*) to chop.
Hackfleisch *das* mince (Br), mincemeat (Am).
Hafen (*pl* Häfen) *der* (*klein*) harbour; (*groß*) port.
Hafenrundfahrt (*pl* -en) *die* boat trip round the harbour.
Hafenstadt (*pl* -städte) *die* port.
Haferflocken *pl* rolled oats.
Haft *die* custody.
haftbar *adj* liable.
haften *vi* (*für Schaden*) to be liable.
Haftpflichtversicherung (*pl* -en) *die* third party insurance.
Haftpulver *das* (*für Gebiß*) denture fixative.
Haftung *die* liability.
Haftungsbeschränkung (*pl* -en) *die* limited liability.
Hagebuttentee *der* rosehip tea.

Hagel der (Eisregen) hail.

hageln vimp: **es hagelt** it's hailing.

Hahn (pl **Hähne**) der (Tier) cock; (Wasserhahn) tap (Br), faucet (Am).

Hähnchen (pl -) das (Brathähnchen) chicken; **ein halbes ~** half a (roast) chicken.

Hai (pl -e) der shark.

häkeln vt & vi to crochet.

Häkelnadel (pl -n) die crochet hook.

Haken (pl -) der (an der Wand) hook; (Zeichen) tick; **einen ~ haben** (fam) to have a catch.

halb adj & adv half; **ein ~es Kilo** half a kilo; **eine ~e Stunde** half an hour; **die ~e Stadt** half the town; **~ und ~** (fast) more or less; **~ sechs** half past five; **~ so ... wie** half as ... as; **~ durch** (KÜCHE) undercooked.

halbautomatisch adj (Getriebe, Kamera) semi-automatic.

Halbbruder (pl -brüder) der half-brother.

Halbe (pl -n) der, die (Bier) half a litre.

halbfett adj (Margarine, Käse) low-fat.

halbieren vt (teilen) to halve.

Halbinsel (pl -n) die peninsula.

Halbjahr (pl -e) das six months (pl).

Halbmond der half moon.

Halbpension die half board; **ein Zimmer mit ~** a room with half board.

Halbschuh (pl -e) der shoe.

Halbschwester (pl -n) die half-sister.

halbtags adv part-time.

Halbtagsarbeit die part-time work.

halbvoll adj half-full.

halbwegs adv halfway.

Halbzeit (pl -en) die halftime.

half prät → **helfen**.

Hälfte (pl -n) die half; **die ~ (der Flasche)** half (the bottle); **etw zur ~ tun** to half-do sthg; **er hat es erst zur ~ bezahlt** he only paid for half of it.

Halle (pl -n) die hall.

Hallenbad (pl -bäder) das (indoor) swimming pool.

hallo interj hello!

Halogenlampe (pl -n) die halogen lamp.

Hals (pl **Hälse**) der (Körperteil) neck; (Rachen) throat.

Halsausschnitt (pl -e) der neck-line.

Halsband (pl -bänder) das (von Hund) collar.

Halsentzündung (pl -en) die throat infection.

Halskette (pl -n) die necklace.

Hals-Nasen-Ohren-Arzt (pl -Ärzte) der ear, nose and throat specialist.

Hals-Nasen-Ohren-Ärztin (pl -nen) die ear, nose and throat specialist.

Halsschmerzen pl: **~ haben** to have a sore throat.

Halstuch (pl -tücher) das scarf.

halt ◆ interj stop! ◆ adv (Süddt: nun einmal): **so ist das ~** that's just the way it is.

haltbar adj (Lebensmittel): **lange ~ sein** to keep well; **'mindestens ~ bis'** 'best before'.

Haltbarkeitsdatum (pl -daten) das best before date.

halten (präs **hält**, prät **hielt**, pp **gehalten**) ◆ vt 1. (festhalten) to hold; **sie hielt die Tasse in der Hand** she held the cup in her hand. 2. (einhalten, behalten) to keep. 3. (Haustier) to keep. 4. (SPORT) to save. 5. (Vortrag, Rede) to give. 6. (einschätzen, denken): **jn für etw halten** to take sb for sthg; **was hältst du von ihm?** what do you think of him/it?; **ich habe ihn für klüger gehalten** I thought he was cleverer than that; **viel/wenig von jm/etw ~** to think a lot/not much of sb/sthg. ◆ vi 1. (Fahrzeug) to stop. 2. (Beziehung) to last. 3. (Lebensmittel): **~ bis** to keep until. 4. (zur Unterstützung): **zu jm ~** to stand by sb. ▶ **sich halten** ref **1.** (sich festhalten) to hold on. **2.** (Lebensmittel): **sich ~ bis** to keep until. **3.** (Person): **für sein Alter hält er sich gut** he's keeping well for his age. **4.** (in eine Richtung): **sich rechts/links ~** to keep right/left.

Haltepunkt (pl -e) der stop.

Halterung (pl -en) die holder.

Haltestelle (pl -n) die stop.

Halteverbot das (Stelle) no waiting zone, clearway (Br); **hier herrscht ~** there is no waiting here.

Halteverbotsschild (pl -er) das no waiting sign.

halt|machen vi to stop.

Hammelfleisch das mutton.

Hammer (pl Hämmer) der hammer.

hämmern vi to hammer.

Hammerwerfen das (throwing the) hammer.

Hand (pl Hände) die hand; **aus erster/zweiter ~** second-hand (with one/two previous owners); **rechter/linker ~** on the right/left.

Handarbeit (pl -en) die needlework; (Gegenstand) hand-made article.

Handball der handball.

Handbremse (pl -n) die handbrake (Br), parking brake (Am).

Handbuch (pl -bücher) das handbook.

Handel der (An- und Verkauf) trade; (Geschäftsleute, Geschäftswelt) business.

handeln ◆ vi (Handel treiben) to trade; (agieren) to act; (feilschen) to haggle. ◆ vimp: **bei diesem Buch handelt es sich um einen Roman** this book is a novel; **~ von** (von Thema) to be about.

Handelskammer (pl -n) die chamber of commerce.

Handelspartner (pl -) der trading partner.

Handelsschule (pl -n) die business school.

Handfeger (pl -) der brush.

Handfläche (pl -n) die palm.

Handgelenk (pl -e) das wrist.

handgemacht adj handmade.

Handgepäck das hand luggage.

handgeschrieben adj handwritten.

Handgriff (pl -e) der movement (of the hand).

Handkoffer (pl -) der (small) suitcase.

Händler, -in (mpl -) der, die dealer.

handlich adj handy.

Handlung (pl -en) die (von Roman, Film) plot; (Tat, Aktion) act.

Handschlag der: **etw per ~ besiegeln** to shake on sthg.

Handschrift (pl -en) die (Schrift) handwriting; (Text) manuscript.

Handschuh (pl -e) der glove.

Handschuhfach (pl -fächer) das glove compartment.

Handtasche (pl -n) die handbag.

Handtuch (pl -tücher) das towel.

Handwaschbecken (pl -) das handbasin.

Handwerk das craft, trade.

Handwerker, -in (mpl -) der, die craftsman.

Handwerkszeug das tools (pl).

Handy (pl -s) das mobile phone.

Handzeichen (pl -) das hand signal.

Hang (pl Hänge) der (Abhang) slope.

Hängebrücke (pl -n) die suspension bridge.

Hängematte (pl -n) die hammock.

hängen¹ (prät hängte, pp gehängt) vt (anbringen) to hang; **etw an etw** (A) **~** to hang sthg on sthg.

hängen² (prät hing, pp gehangen) vi (angebracht sein) to hang; **~ an** (+D) (örtlich) to hang on; (emotional) to be attached to.

hängen|bleiben vi unr ist: **mit dem Ärmel an der Türklinke ~** to catch one's sleeve on the door handle.

hängen|lassen vt unr (vergessen) to leave behind.

Hannover nt Hanover.

Hansestadt (*pl* **-städte**) *die* town which formerly belonged to the Hanseatic League.

HANSESTADT

The Hanseatic League was originally a guild of merchants which grew into an association of merchant towns, formed to protect trade. It existed from the 12th-17th century and had a major influence on economic and cultural life. Most of the German towns that were members of the League are in the north of the country, on the North Sea and Baltic coasts. They include Lübeck, Hamburg, Bremen and Rostock.

Hantel (*pl* **-n**) *die* dumbbell.

Häppchen (*pl* **-**) *das* (*kleine Speise*) canapé.

Hardware (*pl* **-s**) *die* hardware.

Harke (*pl* **-n**) *die* rake.

harmlos *adj* harmless.

harmonisch *adj* harmonious.

Harn *der* urine.

Harnblase (*pl* **-n**) *die* bladder.

Harpune (*pl* **-n**) *die* harpoon.

hart (*komp* **härter**, *superl* **am härtesten**) ◆ *adj* hard; (*Urteil, Strafe*) harsh. ◆ *adv* (*arbeiten, zuschlagen*) hard; (*urteilen, bestrafen*) harshly; (*sitzen, liegen*) on a hard surface; **~ an** (+D) right next to.

Härte *die* (*von Material*) hardness; (*Strenge*) harshness.

hartgekocht *adj*: **~es Ei** hard-boiled egg.

hartnäckig *adj* stubborn.

Haschisch *das* hashish.

Hase (*pl* **-n**) *der* hare.

Haselnuß (*pl* **-nüsse**) *die* hazelnut.

Haß *der* hatred.

hassen *vt* to hate.

häßlich *adj* (*Aussehen*) ugly.

hast *präs* → **haben**.

hastig *adj* hasty.

hat *präs* → **haben**.

hatte *prät* → **haben**.

Haube (*pl* **-n**) *die* (*von Auto*) bonnet (Br), hood (Am); (*Trockenhaube*) hairdryer.

hauchdünn *adj* wafer-thin.

hauchen *vi* (*blasen*) to breathe.

hauen ◆ *vt* (*Person*) to hit; (*Statue, Figur*) to carve; (*Loch*) to knock. ◆ *vi* (*mit der Hand*) to hit out.

Haufen (*pl* **-**) *der* (*kleiner Berg*) pile; (*fam: größere Menge*): **ein ~ Freunde** loads of friends.

häufig ◆ *adj* frequent. ◆ *adv* often.

Hauptbahnhof (*pl* **-höfe**) *der* main station.

hauptberuflich *adj & adv* full-time.

Haupteingang (*pl* **-gänge**) *der* main entrance.

Hauptfach (*pl* **-fächer**) *das* main subject.

Hauptgericht (*pl* **-e**) *das* main course.

Hauptgeschäftszeit (*pl* **-en**) *die* peak shopping hours (*pl*).

Hauptpost *die* main post office.

Hauptproblem (*pl* **-e**) *das* main problem.

Hauptreisezeit (*pl* **-e**) *die* peak travelling times (*pl*).

Hauptrolle (*pl* **-n**) *die* (*im Film*) main role.

Hauptsache (*pl* **-n**) *die* main thing.

hauptsächlich *adv* principally.

Hauptsaison *die* high season.

Hauptschule (*pl* **-n**) *die* secondary school attended by pupils aged 10 - 15.

Hauptstadt (*pl* **-städte**) *die* capital.

Hauptstraße (*pl* **-n**) *die* main road.

Hauptverkehrsstraße (*pl* **-n**) *die* major road.

Hauptverkehrszeit (*pl* **-en**) *die* rush hour.

Haus (*pl* **Häuser**) *das* house; **nach ~e** home; **zu ~e** at home.

Hausapotheke (*pl* **-n**) *die* medicine cabinet.

Hausarbeit (*pl* **-en**) *die* (*im Haushalt*) housework; (*Hausaufgabe*) homework.

Hausarzt (*pl* -ärzte) *der* family doctor.

Hausärztin (*pl* -nen) *die* family doctor.

Hausbar (*pl* -s) *die* (*Raum*) bar; (*Schrank*) drinks cabinet.

Hausbewohner, -in (*mpl* -) *der, die* occupier.

hauseigen *adj*: **die Firma hat einen ~en Parkplatz** the firm has its own car park.

Hausflur (*pl* -e) *der* hall.

Hausfrau (*pl* -en) *die* housewife.

hausgemacht *adj* home-made.

Haushalt (*pl* -e) *der* (*Hausarbeit*) housework; (*Wohnung*) household; (*Etat*) budget.

Haushälter, -in (*mpl* -) *der, die* housekeeper.

Haushaltsreiniger (*pl* -) *der* household cleaner.

Haushaltswaren *pl* household goods.

Haushaltswarenabteilung (*pl* -en) *die* household goods department.

Hausmannskost *die* plain food.

Hausmarke (*pl* -n) *die* (*Wein*) house wine.

Hausmeister, -in (*mpl* -) *der, die* caretaker (Br), janitor (Am).

Hausnummer (*pl* -n) *die* house number.

Hausordnung (*pl* -en) *die* house rules (*pl*).

Hausschlüssel (*pl* -) *der* house key.

Hausschuh (*pl* -e) *der* slipper.

Haustier (*pl* -e) *das* pet.

Haustür (*pl* -en) *die* front door.

Hausverbot *das*: **~ haben** to be barred.

Hauszelt (*pl* -e) *das* family tent.

Haut (*pl* Häute) *die* skin.

Hautarzt (*pl* -ärzte) *der* dermatologist.

Hautärztin (*pl* -nen) *die* dermatologist.

Hautausschlag (*pl* -schläge) *der* skin rash.

Hautcreme (*pl* -s) *die* skin cream.

hauteng *adj* skintight.

Hautfarbe (*pl* -n) *die* skin colour.

Hbf. *abk* = **Hauptbahnhof.**

Hebamme (*pl* -n) *die* midwife.

Hebel (*pl* -) *der* lever.

heben (*prät* **hob**, *pp* **gehoben**) *vt* (*hochnehmen*) to lift. ▶ **sich heben** *ref* (*Vorhang, Schranke*) to rise.

Heck (*pl* -s) *das* (*von Auto*) rear; (*von Schiff*) stern.

Hecke (*pl* -n) *die* hedge.

Heckklappe (*pl* -n) *die* tailgate.

Heckscheibe (*pl* -n) *die* rear window.

Heckscheibenheizung (*pl* -en) *die* heated rear window.

Hecktür (*pl* -en) *die* tailgate.

Hefe *die* yeast.

Hefeteig *der* dough.

hefetrüb *adj* cloudy.

Heft (*pl* -e) *das* (*Schulheft*) exercise book; (*Zeitschrift*) issue.

Hefter (*pl* -) *der* binder.

heftig ◆ *adj* violent. ◆ *adv* violently.

Heftklammer (*pl* -n) *die* staple.

Heftpflaster (*pl* -) *das* plaster (Br), Bandaid (Am).

Heftzwecke (*pl* -n) *die* drawing pin (Br), thumbtack (Am).

Heide *die* (*Landschaft*) heath, moor.

Heidelbeere (*pl* -n) *die* bilberry.

heikel (*komp* **heikler**, *superl* **am heikelsten**) *adj* (*Problem*) tricky.

heil *adj* intact.

Heilbad (*pl* -bäder) *das* spa.

heilbar *adj* curable.

heilen ◆ *vt* to cure. ◆ *vi* to heal.

heilig *adj* (*Person, Ort*) holy.

Heiligabend *der* Christmas Eve.

Heilkräuter *pl* medicinal herbs.

Heilmittel (*pl* -) *das* treatment.

Heilpflanze (*pl* -n) *die* medicinal plant.

Heilpraktiker, -in (*mpl* -) *der, die*

Heilquelle (*pl* **-n**) *die* medicinal spring.

Heilung (*pl* **-en**) *die* (*durch Arzt*) curing; (*von Wunde*) healing.

Heim (*pl* **-e**) *das* home.

Heimat *die* (*von Person*) home (*town, country*).

Heimatadresse (*pl* **-n**) *die* home address.

Heimathafen (*pl* **-häfen**) *der* home port.

Heimatland (*pl* **-länder**) *das* home country.

Heimatmuseum (*pl* **-museen**) *das* heritage museum.

Heimfahrt *die* return journey, journey home.

heimlich ◆ *adj* secret. ◆ *adv* secretly.

Heimreise *die* return journey, journey home.

Heimspiel (*pl* **-e**) *das* home game.

Heimweg *der* way home.

Heimweh *das* homesickness; **~ haben** to be homesick.

Heimwerker (*pl* **-**) *der* handyman.

Heimwerkermarkt (*pl* **-märkte**) *der* DIY store.

Heirat (*pl* **-en**) *die* marriage.

heiraten *vt & vi* to marry.

heiser ◆ *adj* hoarse. ◆ *adv* hoarsely.

Heiserkeit *die* hoarseness.

heiß ◆ *adj* hot; (*Diskussion*) heated; (*fam: toll*) brilliant. ◆ *adv* (*lieben*) passionately; (*fam: toll*) brilliantly; **~ baden** to have a hot bath; **es ist ~** it's hot; **mir ist ~** I'm hot.

heißen (*prät* **hieß**, *pp* **geheißen**) *vi* (*mit Namen*) to be called; (*bedeuten*) mean; **wie heißt das auf Deutsch?** how do you say that in German?; **wie heißt du?** what's your name?; **das heißt** (*erklärend*) so; (*einschränkend*) that is.

heißIlaufen *vi unr ist* (*Motor*) to overheat.

Heißluftballon (*pl* **-s**) *der* hot air balloon.

Heißwassergerät (*pl* **-e**) *das* water heater.

heiter *adj* (*Person, Stimmung*) cheerful; (*Wetter*) fine.

heizbar *adj* heated.

Heizdecke (*pl* **-n**) *die* electric blanket.

heizen ◆ *vt* (*Raum*) to heat. ◆ *vi* to have the heating on.

Heizgerät (*pl* **-e**) *das* (*elektrisch*) heater.

Heizkissen (*pl* **-**) *das* heated pad (*for back etc*).

Heizkörper (*pl* **-**) *der* radiator.

Heizung (*pl* **-en**) *die* (*Heizungsanlage*) heating; (*Heizkörper*) radiator.

hektisch *adj* hectic.

helfen (*präs* **hilft**, *prät* **half**, *pp* **geholfen**) *vi* to help; **jm ~** to help sb; **jm ~ bei** to help sb with; **sich** (D) **zu ~ wissen** to know what to do.

Helfer, -in (*mpl* **-**) *der, die* helper.

hell ◆ *adj* (*Licht*) bright; (*Farbe*) light; (*Ton*) high. ◆ *adv* (*leuchten*) brightly; **ihre Stimme klingt ~** she has a high-pitched voice; **es wird ~** it's getting light.

hellblau *adj* light blue.

hellblond *adj* very blonde.

Hellseher, -in (*mpl* **-**) *der, die* clairvoyant.

Helm (*pl* **-e**) *der* helmet.

Hemd (*pl* **-en**) *das* (*Oberhemd*) shirt; (*Unterhemd*) vest.

Hendl (*pl* **-n**) *das* (*Süddt & Österr*) roast chicken.

Hengst (*pl* **-e**) *der* stallion.

Henkel (*pl* **-**) *der* handle.

her *adv*: **komm ~!** come here!; **von Norden ~** from the North; **von weit ~** from a long way away; **ich kenne sie von früher ~** I know her from before; **das ist 10 Jahre ~** that was 10 years ago; **von der Größe ~** as far as its size is concerned; **~ damit!** give me that!

herab *adv* down.

herabIsetzen *vt* (*Preis, Tempo*) to reduce.

heran adv: **etwas rechts ~** a bit further to the right.

heran|kommen vi unr ist (sich nähern) to approach.

Heranwachsende (pl **-n**) der, die adolescent.

herauf adv up.

herauf|kommen ◆ vi unr ist (Person, Fahrzeug) to come up. ◆ vt unr ist (Treppe, Berg) to climb (up).

herauf|setzen vt (Preis) to raise.

heraus adv out.

heraus|bekommen vt unr (Geheimnis) to find out; (Lösung) to work out; (Fleck) to get out; (Wechselgeld): **noch 10 Pfennig ~** to get 10 pfennigs change.

heraus|bringen vt unr (Buch, Platte) to bring out.

heraus|finden vt unr (entdecken) to find out.

heraus|fordern vt (provozieren) to provoke.

Herausforderung (pl **-en**) die (Provokation) provocation; (Aufgabe) challenge.

heraus|geben vt unr (Buch, Zeitung) to publish; (Geisel, Beute) to hand over; (Wechselgeld) to give in change; **auf 100 DM ~** to give change for 100 Marks; **jm 2 DM ~** to give sb 2 Marks in change.

Herausgeber, -in (mpl **-**) der, die publisher.

heraus|gehen vi unr ist (nach draußen) to get out.

heraus|halten vt unr to put out. ► **sich heraushalten** ref to stay out of it.

heraus|holen vt (nach draußen) to bring out.

heraus|kommen vi unr ist to come out.

heraus|nehmen vt unr to take out.

heraus|stellen vt (nach draußen) to put out; (hervorheben) to emphasize. ► **sich herausstellen** ref to become clear.

heraus|suchen vt to pick out.

heraus|ziehen vt unr to pull out.

herb ◆ adj (Geschmack) sharp; (Wein) dry; (Enttäuschung) bitter. ◆ adv (bitter) bitterly; (schlimm) badly.

herbei adv: **komm ~!** come here!

Herberge (pl **-n**) die (Jugendherberge) hostel.

her|bringen vt unr to bring.

Herbst (pl **-e**) der autumn (Br), fall (Am); **im ~** in (the) autumn (Br), in (the) fall (Am).

herbstlich adj autumn (vor Subst).

Herd (pl **-e**) der (Küchenherd) cooker.

Herde (pl **-n**) die (von Tieren) herd; (von Schafen) flock.

herein adv in; **~!** come in!

herein|fallen vi unr ist (fallen) to fall in; (getäuscht werden) to be taken in.

herein|holen vt to bring in.

herein|kommen vi unr ist (von draußen) to come in.

herein|lassen vt unr to let in.

herein|legen vt (fam: täuschen) to take for a ride.

Herfahrt die journey here.

her|geben vt unr (geben) to give.

her|gehen vi unr ist: **~ vor/hinter/neben** (+D) to walk in front of/behind/next to.

her|haben vt unr (fam): **wo hast du das her?** where did you get that from?

Hering (pl **-e**) der (Fisch) herring; (am Zelt) tent peg.

Heringstopf (pl **-töpfe**) der salad of marinated herring, onion, mayonnaise and beetroot.

her|kommen vi unr ist to come; **wo kommst du her?** where are you from?

Herkunft die (von Person) origins (pl); (von Sache) origin.

Herkunftsland (pl **-länder**) das country of origin.

Herkunftsort (pl **-e**) der place of origin.

Heroin das heroin.

Herr (pl -en) der (Mann) gentleman; (als Anrede) Mr; **an ~n Müller** to Mr Müller. ▶ **Herren** pl (Herrentoilette): 'Herren' 'gentlemen'.

Herrenbekleidung die menswear.

Herrenfrisör (pl -e) der barber, men's hairdresser.

Herrenschuh (pl -e) der man's shoe.

Herrentoilette (pl -n) die men's toilet.

herrlich ♦ adj wonderful. ♦ adv wonderfully; **es schmeckt ~** it tastes wonderful.

herrschen vi (regieren) to rule; (bestehen) to be.

her|sein vi unr ist (Person, Gegenstand) to come; **es ist erst drei Tage her** it was only three days ago.

her|stellen vt (produzieren) to make, to produce.

Hersteller, -in (mpl -) der, die manufacturer.

Herstellung die (Produktion) production.

herüber adv over.

herum adv round; **um ... ~** around; **um den Tisch ~** around the table; **um die 50 DM ~** around 50 Marks.

herum|drehen vt (auf die andere Seite) to turn over; (Schlüssel, Hebel) to turn. ▶ **sich herumdrehen** ref to turn round.

herum|fahren vi unr ist & vt unr hat to drive around.

herum|führen ♦ vt to show around. ♦ vi to go around.

herum|gehen vi unr ist to walk around.

herum|kommen vi unr ist (reisen) to travel around; **~ um** (fam: sich drücken) to get out of.

herum|liegen vi unr to lie around.

herunter adv down.

herunter|fallen vi unr ist to fall down.

herunter|gehen vi unr ist (Person)

to go down; **mit dem Preis ~** to lower the price.

herunter|handeln vt to beat down.

herunter|holen vt to bring down.

herunter|lassen vt unr (Jalousie) to lower.

herunter|schlucken vt (Essen) to swallow.

hervor adv: **komm ~!** come out!

hervorragend ♦ adj excellent. ♦ adv excellently.

hervor|rufen vt unr (verursachen) to cause.

Herz (pl -en) das heart; (Spielfarbe) hearts (pl); **von ganzem ~en** wholeheartedly.

Herzbeschwerden pl heart trouble (sg).

herzhaft adj (Essen) hearty.

Herzinfarkt (pl -e) der heart attack.

Herzklopfen das: **ich habe ~** my heart is pounding.

herzlich ♦ adj (freundlich) warm; (aufrichtig) sincere. ♦ adv (freundlich) warmly; (aufrichtig) sincerely.

Herzschrittmacher (pl -) der pacemaker.

Herzstillstand (pl -stände) der cardiac arrest.

Hessen nt Hesse.

hetzen vt & vi to rush. ▶ **sich hetzen** ref to rush.

Heu das hay.

heuer adv (Süddt & Österr) this year.

heulen vi to howl.

Heurige (pl -n) der (Österr: Wein) new wine (from most recent harvest); (Lokal) bar, particularly in the region of Vienna, that serves new wine from the local vineyards.

Heuschnupfen der hay fever.

heute adv today; **~ früh** (early) this morning; **~ morgen/mittag/abend** this morning/lunchtime/evening; **~ in einer Woche** a week today.

heutig adj today's.

hielt prät → **halten**.

hier adv here; (zeitlich) now; **das ~**

this one here; **~, nimm!** here, take it!; **~ und da** here and there; **von ~ aus** from here; **~!** here!, present!

hierauf *adv* (*auf diese Sache*) (on) here.

hier|behalten *vt unr* (*fam: Person, Sache*) to keep here.

hier|bleiben *vi unr ist* to stay here.

hierher *adv* here.

hierhin *adv* here.

hiermit *adv* with this.

hier|sein *vi unr ist* to be here.

hiervon *adv* (*von Sache, Menge*) of this.

hiesig *adj* local.

hieß *prät* → **heißen**.

Hilfe (*pl* **-n**) *die* (*Helfen*) help; (*Person*) assistant; **mit ~ von** with the help of; **~!** help!; **um ~ rufen** to call for help.

hilflos ♦ *adj* helpless. ♦ *adv* helplessly.

hilfsbereit *adj* helpful.

hilft *präs* → **helfen**.

Himbeere (*pl* **-n**) *die* (*Frucht*) raspberry.

Himbeergeist *der* raspberry brandy.

Himmel *der* (*Luftraum*) sky; (RELIG) heaven.

Himmelfahrt (*Feiertag*) Ascension Day.

Himmelsrichtung (*pl* **-en**) *die* direction.

hin *adv*: **bis zum Baum ~** up to the tree; **der Weg ~** the way there; **zweimal nach München, ~ und zurück** two returns to Munich; **~ und her** back and forth; **~ und wieder** now and again.

hinab *adv* down.

hinauf *adv* up.

hinauf|gehen *vi & vt unr ist* to go up.

hinauf|steigen *vi & vt unr ist* to climb.

hinaus *adv* (*nach draußen*) out.

hinaus|gehen *vi unr ist* (*nach draußen*) to go out; **zur Straße ~** to look out onto the street.

hinaus|laufen *vi unr ist* (*nach draußen*) to run out.

Hinblick *der*: **in** ODER **im ~ auf** (+A) with regard to.

hindern *vt* to hinder; **jn (daran) ~, etw zu tun** to prevent sb from doing sthg.

Hindernis (*pl* **-se**) *das* obstacle.

hindurch *adv* (*räumlich*) through; (*zeitlich*) throughout.

hinein *adv* (*räumlich*) in.

hinein|gehen *vi unr ist* to go in.

hinein|stecken *vt* to put in.

hin|fahren ♦ *vi unr ist* to go there. ♦ *vt unr hat* (*Passagiere*) to drive there.

Hinfahrt (*pl* **-en**) *die* (*mit Auto*) journey there; (*mit Zug*) outward journey.

hin|fallen *vi unr ist* to fall down.

Hinflug (*pl* **-flüge**) *der* outward flight.

hing *prät* → **hängen**.

hin|gehen *vi unr ist* (*gehen*) to go.

hinken *vi* to limp.

hin|knien: **sich hinknien** *ref* to kneel down.

hin|kommen *vi unr ist* (*ankommen*) to get there; (*hingehören*) to belong; **mit etw ~** to make sthg last.

hin|legen *vt* (*Kind, Besteck, Tasche*) to put down. ▸ **sich hinlegen** *ref* to lie down.

Hinreise (*pl* **-n**) *die* journey there.

hin|setzen *vt* (*Person*) to seat. ▸ **sich hinsetzen** *ref* to sit down.

Hinsicht *die*: **in gewisser ~** in some ways; **in finanzieller ~** financially.

hin|stellen *vt* (*Gegenstand*) to put down. ▸ **sich hinstellen** *ref* to stand.

hinten *adv* (*am Ende*) at the back; (*an der Rückseite*) on the back; (*zur Richtungsangabe*) back; **~ im Buch** at the back of the book; **~ am Radio** on the back of the radio; **~ sitzen** (*im Auto*) to sit in the back; **da** ODER **dort ~** back there; **weit ~** a long way behind; **bitte nach ~ durchgehen!** please move down to the back!

hinter *präp* (+D, A) behind.

Hinterachse (*pl* -n) *die* rear axle.

Hinterausgang (*pl* -ausgänge) *der* rear exit.

hintere, -r, -s *adj* back, rear.

hintereinander *adv* (*räumlich*) one behind the other; (*zeitlich*) one after the other.

Hintereingang (*pl* -eingänge) *der* rear entrance.

Hintergrund (*pl* -gründe) *der* background.

hinterher *adv* (*räumlich*) behind; (*zeitlich*) afterwards.

hinterher|fahren *vi unr ist* to drive behind; **jm ~** to follow sb.

hinterher|gehen *vi unr ist* to walk behind; **jm ~** to follow sb.

hinterlassen (*präs* **hinterläßt**, *prät* **hinterließ**, *pp* **hinterlassen**) *vt* to leave.

hinterlegen *vt* to leave.

Hintern (*pl* -) *der* (*fam*) bottom.

Hinterrad (*pl* -räder) *das* rear wheel.

Hinterradantrieb *der* rear wheel drive.

Hintertür (*pl* -en) *die* back door.

Hinterzimmer (*pl* -) *das* back room.

hinüber *adv* over, across.

Hin- und Rückfahrt *die* round trip.

hinunter *adv* down.

Hinweg (*pl* -e) *der*: **auf dem ~** on the way there.

Hinweis (*pl* -e) *der* (*Tip, Fingerzeig*) tip; (*für Polizei*) lead; (*Anleitung*) instruction; (*Indiz*) sign; **nähere ~e** detailed instructions.

hin|weisen ◆ *vt unr*: **jn auf etw** (A) **~** to point sthg out to sb. ◆ *vi unr* (*zeigen*): **auf jn/etw ~** to point to sb/sthg.

Hinweisschild (*pl* -er) *das* sign.

hin|werfen *vt unr* (*Gegenstand*) to throw down.

hinzu *adv* in addition.

hinzu|fügen *vt* (*Gewürz, Zutat*) to add.

hinzu|kommen *vi unr ist* (*Person*) to arrive; (*Tatsache*): **hinzukommt, daß ...** moreover ...; **kommt noch etwas hinzu?** (*im Geschäft*) would you like anything else?

Hirn (*pl* -e) *das* (*Organ*) brain; (*Gericht*) brains (*pl*).

Hirsch (*pl* -e) *der* (*Tier*) deer; (*Fleisch*) venison.

Hirse *die* millet.

historisch ◆ *adj* (*geschichtlich*) historical. ◆ *adv* (*geschichtlich*) historically.

Hit (*pl* -s) *der* (*Lied*) hit.

Hitparade (*pl* -n) *die* charts (*pl*).

Hitze *die* heat.

hitzebeständig *adj* heat-resistant.

Hitzewelle (*pl* -n) *die* heatwave.

Hitzschlag *der* heatstroke.

HIV-positiv *adj* HIV-positive.

H-Milch *die* long-life milk.

hob *prät* → **heben**.

Hobby (*pl* -s) *das* hobby.

hoch (*komp* **höher**, *superl* **am höchsten**) ◆ *adj* high; (*Baum*) tall; (*Alter, Gewicht*) great; (*Anzahl, Summe*) large. ◆ *adv* high; (*sehr*) highly.

Hoch (*pl* -s) *das* (*Wetterlage*) high.

hochachtungsvoll *adv* Yours faithfully (*nach Dear Sir/Madam*), Yours sincerely (*nach Dear Mr/Mrs X*).

Hochbetrieb *der*: **es herrscht ~** it's the busiest time.

hochdeutsch *adj* standard German.

Hochdruck *der* (*technisch*) high pressure.

Hochdruckgebiet (*pl* -e) *das* area of high pressure.

Hochdruckzone (*pl* -n) *die* area of high pressure.

Hochebene (*pl* -n) *die* plateau.

hocherfreut *adj* delighted.

hoch|fliegen *vi unr ist* to fly up.

Hochgebirge (*pl* -) *das* high mountains (*pl*).

hoch|gehen *vi unr ist* to go up; (*Bombe*) to go off.

hoch|halten *vt unr* (*Gegenstand*) to hold up.

Hochhaus (*pl* -häuser) *das* highrise building.

hoch|heben *vt unr* to lift.

hoch|klappen *vt* to fold up.

hoch|klettern *vi & vt ist* to climb (up).

hoch|kommen *vi & vt unr ist* to come up.

hoch|krempeln *vt* to roll up.

hochnäsig *adj* (*abw*) conceited.

hochprozentig *adj* (*Getränk*) strong.

Hochsaison *die* (*in Ferienort*) high season.

Hochschule (*pl* -n) *die* college; (*Universität*) university.

Hochschulreife *die* *qualification needed for university entrance.*

hochschwanger *adj* heavily pregnant.

Hochsommer (*pl* -) *der* midsummer.

Hochspannung *die* (*Strom*) high voltage; 'Vorsicht, ~: Lebensgefahr!' 'danger, high voltage!'

Hochsprung *der* high jump.

höchste *superl* → **hoch**.

höchstens *adv* (*mit Zahlenangabe*) at (the) most; (*allenfalls*) at best.

Höchstgeschwindigkeit (*pl* -en) *die* (*auf Straße*) speed limit; (*von Auto*) top speed.

Höchstparkdauer *die* maximum stay (*when parking*).

Hochwasser *das*: ~ **haben** to be in spate.

hochwertig *adj* high-quality.

Hochzeit (*pl* -en) *die* wedding.

Hochzeitsfeier (*pl* -n) *die* wedding reception.

Hochzeitskuchen (*pl* -) *der* wedding cake.

Hochzeitsreise (*pl* -n) *die* honeymoon.

Hochzeitstag (*pl* -e) *der* wedding day.

hoch|ziehen *vt unr* (*Strumpf*) to pull up; (*Jalousie*) to raise. ▶ **sich hochziehen** *ref* (*sich nach oben ziehen*) to pull o.s. up.

hocken *vi* (*kauern*) to crouch. ▶ **sich hocken** *ref* (*sich kauern*) to crouch down.

Hocker (*pl* -) *der* stool.

Hockey *das* hockey.

Hof (*pl* Höfe) *der* (*Innenhof, Hinterhof*) yard; (*Bauernhof*) farm.

hoffen *vt* to hope.

hoffentlich *adv* hopefully.

Hoffnung (*pl* -en) *die* (*Wunsch*) hope.

höflich ◆ *adj* polite. ◆ *adv* politely.

Höflichkeit *die* politeness.

Höhe (*pl* -n) *die* height; (*von Summe*) amount; (*von Klang*) pitch; **ein Betrag in ~ von 200 DM** the sum of 200 Marks; **in ~ der ersten Querstraße** level with the first turning.

Höhenlage *die* altitude.

Höhensonne (*pl* -n) *die* (*Gerät*) sunlamp.

Höhepunkt (*pl* -e) *der* (*von Entwicklung, Fest*) high point; (*Orgasmus*) climax.

höher *komp* → **hoch**.

hohl *adj* (*Baum*) hollow; (*abw: Gerede*) empty.

Höhle (*pl* -n) *die* (*im Felsen*) cave; (*von Tieren*) den.

holen *vt* (*heranholen*) to fetch, to collect; (*entnehmen*) to take; (*Polizei, Arzt, Handwerker*) to fetch; (*fam: einkaufen*) to get; **etw ~ kommen** to come for sthg; **sich** (D) **etw ~** (*Gegenstand*) to get sthg; (*Krankheit*) to catch sthg.

Holland *nt* Holland.

Holländer, -in (*mpl* -) *der, die* Dutchman (Dutchwoman).

holländisch *adj* Dutch.

holprig *adj* bumpy.

Holunder (pl -) der (Baum) elder.

Holz (pl **Hölzer**) das wood.

holzig adj (Spargel) woody.

Holzkohle (pl -n) die charcoal.

Home page (pl -s) die home page.

homöopathisch adj homeopathic.

homosexuell adj homosexual.

Homosexuelle (mpl -n) der, die homosexual.

Honig der honey.

Honigmelone (pl -n) die honeydew melon.

Honorar (pl -e) das fee.

Hopfen der hops (pl).

horchen vi (angestrengt hören) to listen.

hören ♦ vt (Laut, Geräusch, Information) to hear; (anhören) to listen to. ♦ vi (als Hörfähigkeit) to hear; (zuhören, gehorchen) to listen; ~ auf (+A) to listen to; **hör mal!** listen!; **schwer ~** to be hard of hearing.

Hörer (pl -) der (von Telefon) receiver; (Person) listener.

Hörerin (pl -nen) die listener.

Hörfunk der radio.

Hörgerät (pl -e) das hearing aid.

hörgeschädigt adj hard of hearing.

Horizont (pl -e) der horizon.

horizontal adj horizontal.

Hormon (pl -e) das hormone.

Horn (pl **Hörner**) das horn.

Hörnchen (pl -) das (Gebäck) croissant.

Hornhaut (pl **-häute**) die (auf Haut) patch of hard skin; (von Augen) cornea.

Hornisse (pl -n) die hornet.

Horoskop (pl -e) das horoscope.

horrend adj horrendous.

Hörspiel (pl -e) das radio play.

Höschenwindel (pl -n) die nappy (Br), diaper (Am).

Hose (pl -n) die (Kleidungsstück) (pair of) trousers (Br), (pair of) pants (Am); (Unterhose) underpants (pl); **kurze ~** shorts (pl).

Hosentasche (pl -n) die trouser pocket.

Hosenträger (pl -) der braces (pl)(Br), suspenders (pl)(Am).

Hospital (pl **Hospitäler**) das hospital.

Hot dog (pl -s) der ODER das hot dog.

Hotel (pl -s) das hotel; **~ Garni** = bed and breakfast.

Hotelbar (pl -s) die hotel bar.

Hotelführer (pl -) der hotel guide.

Hotelhalle (pl -n) die hotel foyer.

Hotelverzeichnis (pl -se) das hotel register.

Hotelzimmer (pl -) das hotel room.

Hr. (abk für Herr) Mr.

Hubraum der (beim Auto) cubic capacity.

hübsch adj (schön) pretty, beautiful.

Hubschrauber (pl -) der helicopter.

huckepack adv (fam): **jn ~ nehmen** to give sb a piggy-back.

Huf (pl -e) der hoof.

Hüfte (pl -n) die hip.

Hügel (pl -) der (kleiner Berg) hill.

hügelig adj hilly.

Huhn (pl **Hühner**) das chicken.

Hühnchen (pl -) das chicken.

Hühnerauge (pl -n) das corn.

Hühnerbrühe (pl -n) die chicken broth.

Hülle (pl -n) die (Schutzhülle) cover; (von Schallplatte) sleeve.

human adj humane.

Hummel (pl -n) die bumblebee.

Hummer (pl -) der lobster.

Humor der humour.

humpeln vi to limp.

Hund (pl -e) der (Tier) dog; **'Vorsicht, bissiger ~'** 'beware of the dog'.

Hundefutter das dog food.

Hundeleine (pl -n) die dog lead.

hundert num a hundred, → **sechs**.

Hunderter (pl -) der (Hundertmarkschein) hundred-mark note.

Hundertmarkschein (pl -e) der hundred-mark note.

Hundertmeterlauf (pl **-läufe**) der hundred metres (sg).

hundertprozentig adj (Alkohol, Lösung) pure; (völlig) complete.

hunderttausend num one hundred thousand.

Hundesteuer (pl -n) die dog licence fee.

Hunger der (nach Nahrung) hunger; ~ **auf** (+A) **haben** to feel like (eating) sthg; ~ **haben** to be hungry.

Hungerstreik (pl -s) der hunger strike.

hungrig adj hungry; ~ **sein** to be hungry.

Hupe (pl -n) die horn.

hupen vi to sound one's horn.

hüpfen vi ist to hop.

Hürdenlauf (pl -läufe) der hurdles (sg).

hurra interj hurray!

husten vi to cough.

Husten der cough; ~ **haben** to have a cough.

Hustenbonbon (pl -s) das cough sweet.

Hustensaft (pl -säfte) der cough mixture.

Hustentee (pl -s) der tea which is good for a cough.

Hut (pl Hüte) der (Kleidungsstück) hat.

Hütte (pl -n) die (kleines Haus) cottage; (Berghütte) hut.

Hüttenkäse der cottage cheese.

hygienisch adj hygienic.

hypnotisieren vt to hypnotize.

I

IC abk = **Intercity**.

ICE abk = **Intercity Express**.

ich pron I; ~ **bin's** it's me.

IC-Zuschlag (pl -Zuschläge) der intercity supplement.

ideal adj ideal.

Idealgewicht das ideal weight.

Idee (pl -n) die idea; (ein bißchen) bit, touch.

identifizieren vt (erkennen) to identify. ▶ **sich identifizieren** ref (sich gleichsetzen): **sich ~ mit** to identify with.

identisch adj identical; ~ **sein** to be exactly the same.

Identität die identity.

Ideologie (pl -n) die ideology.

Idiot (pl -en) der idiot.

idiotisch adj idiotic.

idyllisch ◆ adj idyllic. ◆ adv: ~ **gelegen** in an idyllic location.

Igel (pl -) der hedgehog.

ignorieren vt to ignore.

ihm pron (Dativ von er: Person) (to) him; (: Ding) (to) it.

ihn pron (Akkusativ von er: Person) him; (: Ding) it.

ihnen pron (Dativ Plural von sie) (to) them.

Ihnen pron (Dativ von Sie) (to) you.

ihr¹ pron (Nominativ) you; (Dativ von sie: Person) (to) her; (Ding) (to) it.

ihr², -e det (Singular: von Person) her; (von Ding) its; (Plural) their.

Ihr (pl -e) det your.

ihre, -r, -s pron (Singular: von Person) hers; (: von Ding) its; (Plural) their.

Ihre, -r, -s pron yours.

illegal ◆ adj illegal. ◆ adv illegally.

Illusion (pl -en) die illusion.

Illustrierte (pl -n) die magazine.

im präp = **in** + **dem**.

Image (pl -s) das (von Person) image.

Imbiß (pl Imbisse) der (Mahlzeit) snack; (Imbißbude) snack bar.

Imbißbude (pl -n) die snack bar.

Imbißstube (pl -n) die snack bar.

IMBISSSTUBE

An 'Imbißstube', usually to be found either in city centres or at the side of main roads, is a stall or small snack bar where you can get a drink and something quick and simple to eat, typically a fried sausage in a bread roll ('Bratwurst'), chips, a doner kebab or a pizza. Customers usually eat standing up at tall tables. It is very common for Germans to eat this type of snack between meals.

---

imitieren vt to imitate.

imitiert adj (Material) imitation (vor Subst).

Immatrikulation (pl -en) die matriculation.

immer adv always; ~ schwieriger more and more difficult; ~ stärker stronger and stronger; ~ noch still; ~ wenn whenever; ~ wieder again and again.

immerhin adv (dennoch, trotzdem) nevertheless; (wenigstens) at least; (schließlich) after all, still.

Immigrant, -in (mpl -en) der, die immigrant.

Immobilien pl property (sg).

Immobilienmakler, -in (mpl -) der, die estate agent (Br), realtor (Am).

immun adj (gegen Krankheit) immune.

impfen vt to vaccinate.

Impfschein (pl -e) der vaccination certificate.

Impfstoff (pl -e) der vaccine.

Impfung (pl -en) die vaccination.

Import der (Einfuhr) import.

importieren vt to import.

imprägnieren vt (Kleidung) to waterproof.

imprägniert adj (Holz) water-proofed; (Kleidung) waterproof.

impressionistisch adj (Kunstwerk) Impressionist.

improvisieren vt & vi to improvise.

impulsiv ◆ adj impulsive. ◆ adv impulsively.

imstande adj: ~ sein, etw zu tun to be capable of doing sthg.

in ◆ präp (+A) (räumlich) into; ~s Wasser fallen to fall into the water; ~ die Stadt fahren to go to town; ~ die Schule gehen to go to school. ◆ präp (+D) 1. (räumlich) in; im Bett liegen to be in bed; ~ der Schule at school. 2. (zeitlich) in; ~ dieser Woche this week; im Moment at the moment; wir fahren ~ einer Stunde we're going in an hour; das schaffe ich ~ einer Stunde I can do that in an hour. 3. (zur Angabe von Umständen) in; ~ Betrieb sein to be working. 4. (zur Angabe von Mengen) in. ◆ adj (fam): ~ sein to be in.

inbegriffen adj included.

Inbetriebnahme die (amt: von Anlage) start-up.

indem konj by; er startete die Maschine, ~ er auf den Knopf drückte he started the machine by pressing the button.

Inder, -in (mpl -) der, die Indian.

Indien nt India.

indirekt adj indirect.

indisch adj Indian.

indiskret adj indiscreet.

indiskutabel adj out of the question.

Individualist, -in (mpl -en) der, die individualist.

individuell ◆ adj (persönlich) individual. ◆ adv (persönlich) individually.

Individuum (pl -duen) das (Einzelperson) individual.

Industrie (pl -n) die industry.

Industriegebiet (pl -e) das industrial area.

industriell adj industrial.

Industriepark (pl -s) der industrial estate (Br), industrial park (Am).

Industrie- und Handelskammer (pl -n) die chamber of commerce.

Infarkt (pl -e) der heart attack.

Infektion (pl -en) die infection.

infizieren *vt* to infect. ► **sich infizieren** *ref* to get infected.

Inflation (*pl* **-en**) *die* inflation.

infolge *präp* (+G) (*amt*) owing to.

Information (*pl* **-en**) *die* information; (*Informationstelle*) information desk; **eine ~** a piece of information; **~en über** (+A) information about; **wünschen Sie weitere ~en?** would you like any further information?

Informationsmaterial (*pl* **-ien**) *das* information.

Informationsstand (*pl* **-stände**) *der* information point.

Informationszentrum (*pl* **-zentren**) *das* information centre.

informieren *vt* to inform; **jn ~ über** (+A) to inform sb about. ► **sich informieren** *ref* to find out.

Infusion (*pl* **-en**) *die*: **eine ~ bekommen** to be on a drip.

Ingenieur, -in (*mpl* **-e**) *der, die* engineer.

Inh. *abk* = **Inhaber**.

Inhaber, -in (*mpl* **-**) *der, die* (*Besitzer*) owner; (*von Paß, Genehmigung*) holder.

inhalieren ◆ *vt* (*Rauch*) to inhale. ◆ *vi* (*bei Erkältung*) to use an inhalant.

Inhalt (*pl* **-e**) *der* (*von Behälter*) contents (*pl*); (*von Buch, von Film*) content.

Inhaltsverzeichnis (*pl* **-se**) *das* list of contents.

Initiative (*pl* **-n**) *die* initiative.

Injektion (*pl* **-en**) *die* injection.

inkl. (*abk für inklusive*) incl.

inklusive *präp* (+G) including.

Inklusivpreis (*pl* **-e**) *der* inclusive price.

inkonsequent *adj* inconsistent.

Inland *das*: **im ~** at home.

Inlandsflug (*pl* **-flüge**) *der* domestic flight.

Inlandsgespräch (*pl* **-e**) *das* national call.

innen *adv* inside; **nach ~** inwards.

Innenhof (*pl* **-höfe**) *der* inner courtyard.

Innenpolitik *die* (*Maßnahmen*) domestic policy.

Innenraum (*pl* **-räume**) *der* inner room.

Innenseite (*pl* **-n**) *die* inside.

Innenspiegel (*pl* **-**) *der* rearview mirror.

Innenstadt (*pl* **-städte**) *die* town centre.

innere, -r, -s *adj* (*Schicht, Wand, Gefühl*) inner; (*Verletzung, Organe*) internal; (*Jackentasche*) inside.

innerhalb ◆ *präp* (+G) within. ◆ *adv*: **~ von** within.

innerlich ◆ *adj* (*körperlich*) internal. ◆ *adv* (*psychisch*) inwardly.

Innung (*pl* **-en**) *die* guild.

inoffiziell *adj* unofficial.

ins *präp* = **in** + **das**.

Insassen(unfall)versicherung (*pl* **-en**) *die* passenger insurance.

insbesondere *adv* especially.

Insekt (*pl* **-en**) *das* insect.

Insektenschutzmittel (*pl* **-**) *das* insect repellent.

Insektenstich (*pl* **-e**) *der* insect bite.

Insel (*pl* **-n**) *die* (*geographisch*) island.

Inserat (*pl* **-e**) *das* advertisement.

inserieren *vi* to advertise.

insgesamt *adv* altogether.

Inspektion (*pl* **-en**) *die* (*von Autos*) service.

inspizieren *vt* to inspect.

Installateur, -in (*mpl* **-e**) *der, die* (*für Wasser*) plumber; (*für Strom*) electrician.

installieren *vt* to install.

Instantgetränk (*pl* **-e**) *das* instant drink.

Instinkt (*pl* **-e**) *der* instinct.

Institut (*pl* **-e**) *das* (*Einrichtung*) institute.

Institution (*pl* **-en**) *die* institution.

Instrument (*pl* **-e**) *das* instrument.

Inszenierung (*pl* **-en**) *die* (*am*

Theater) production.
intakt *adj* (*Apparat*) intact.
integrieren *vt* to integrate.
intellektuell *adj* intellectual.
intelligent *adj* intelligent.
Intelligenz *die* intelligence.
Intendant, -in (*mpl* -en) *der, die* director.
intensiv ◆ *adj* (*Schulung, Arbeit*) intensive; (*Geschmack, Gefühl*) strong. ◆ *adv* (*schmecken*) strong; (*sich einarbeiten, vorbereiten*) intensively.
Intensivkurs (*pl* -e) *der* crash course.
Intensivstation (*pl* -en) *die* intensive care unit.
Intercity (*pl* -s) *der* intercity train.
Intercity Express (*pl* -) *der* high-speed train connecting two or more large cities.
Intercity-Zuschlag (*pl* -Zuschläge) *der* intercity supplement.
interessant *adj* interesting.
Interesse (*pl* -n) *das* interest.
interessieren *vt* to interest.
▶ **sich interessieren** *ref*: sich ~ für to be interested in.
Internat (*pl* -e) *das* boarding school.
international *adj* international.
Internet *das*: das ~ the Internet; im ~ surfen to surf the Net.
interpretieren *vt* to interpret.
Interrail-Karte (*pl* -n) *die* interrail ticket.
InterRegio (*pl* -s) *der* train covering medium distances, stopping frequently.
Interview (*pl* -s) *das* interview.
interviewen *vt* to interview.
intim *adj* intimate.
intolerant *adj* intolerant.
intransitiv *adj* intransitive.
intuitiv *adj* intuitive.
Invalide (*pl* -n) *der, die* disabled person.
Inventur (*pl* -en) *die* stocktaking; 'wegen ~ geschlossen' 'closed for stocktaking'.

investieren *vt* (*Geld*) to invest.
inzwischen *adv* (*gleichzeitig*) in the meantime; (*jetzt*) now.
Ire (*pl* -n) *der* Irishman; die ~n the Irish.
irgend *adv*: ~ etwas something; (*beliebige Sache, in Fragen*) anything; ~ jemand someone; (*beliebige Person, in Fragen*) anyone.
irgendein, -e *det* (*unbekannt*) some; (*beliebig, in Fragen*) any.
irgendeine, -r, -s *pron* (*unbekannte Person*) someone; (*beliebige Person, in Fragen*) anyone; (*beliebige Sache*) any.
irgendwann *adv* (*zu unbekannter Zeit*) sometime; (*zu beliebiger Zeit*) any time.
irgendwas *pron* = **irgend etwas**.
irgendwer *pron* = **irgend jemand**.
irgendwie *adv* (*auf unbekannte Weise*) somehow; (*auf beliebige Weise*) anyhow.
irgendwo *adv* (*an unbekanntem Ort*) somewhere; (*an beliebigem Ort*) anywhere.
Irin (*pl* -nen) *die* Irishwoman.
irisch *adj* Irish.
Irland *nt* Ireland.
ironisch *adj* ironic.
irre *adj* (*verrückt*) mad; (*fam*: *gut*) fantastic.
Irre (*pl* -n) *der, die* (*fam*) madman (*f* madwoman).
irren *vi* ist (*herumlaufen*) to wander.
▶ **sich irren** *ref* hat to be wrong.
Irrtum (*pl* -tümer) *der* mistake.
irrtümlich *adj* wrong.
Ischias *der* (*Nerv*) sciatic nerve; (*Schmerz*) sciatica.
Islam *der* Islam.
Isolierband (*pl* -bänder) *das* (*für elektrische Leitungen*) insulating tape.
isolieren ◆ *vt* to insulate; (*Person*) to isolate. ◆ *vi* to insulate. ▶ **sich isolieren** *ref* to isolate o.s.
Isolierung (*pl* -en) *die* insulation; (*von Person*) isolation.

Israel *nt* Israel.

ißt *präs* → **essen**.

ist *präs* → **sein**.

Italien *nt* Italy.

Italiener, -in (*mpl* -) *der, die* Italian.

italienisch *adj* Italian.

Italienisch(e) *das* Italian.

J

ja *interj* yes; (*selbstverständlich*) of course; **das ist ~ toll!** that's really great!; **~, bitte** (*selbstverständlich*) please do; **da bist du ~!** there you are!; **ich komme ~ schon** I'm coming.

Jacht (*pl* -en) *die* yacht.

Jacke (*pl* -n) *die* (*Mantel, Jackett*) jacket; (*Strickjacke*) cardigan.

Jackett (*pl* -s) *das* jacket.

Jagd (*pl* -en) *die* (*auf Tiere*) hunt; **auf die ~ gehen** to go hunting.

jagen *vt* (*Tier*) to hunt.

Jäger, -in (*mpl* -) *der, die* (*Person*) hunter.

Jägerschnitzel (*pl* -) *das* escalope of pork with mushroom sauce.

Jahr (*pl* -e) *das* year; **die 90er ~e** the nineties; **ein gutes Neues ~!** Happy New Year!

jahrelang ◆ *adv* for years. ◆ *adj*: **~es Warten** years of waiting.

Jahresabonnement (*pl* -s) *das* annual subscription.

Jahreseinkommen (*pl* -) *das* annual income.

Jahrestag (*pl* -e) *der* anniversary.

Jahresurlaub *der* annual leave.

Jahreszeit (*pl* -en) *die* season.

Jahrgang (*pl* -gänge) *der* (*von Wein*) year, vintage.

Jahrhundert (*pl* -e) *das* century.

jährlich *adj & adv* yearly.

Jahrmarkt (*pl* -märkte) *der* fair.

Jahrzehnt (*pl* -e) *das* decade.

jähzornig *adj* bad-tempered.

Jalousie (*pl* -n) *die* venetian blind.

jammern *vi* to moan.

Jänner *der* (*Österr*) January, → **September**.

Januar *der* January, September.

Japan *nt* Japan.

Japaner, -in (*mpl* -) *der, die* Japanese.

japanisch *adj* Japanese.

Japanisch(e) *das* Japanese.

jaulen *vi* to howl.

Jause (*pl* -n) *die* (*Österr*) snack.

Jausenstation (*pl* -en) *die* (*Österr*) *mountain refuge where food and drink are served.*

jawohl *interj* (*ja*) yes.

Jazz *der* jazz.

je ◆ *adv* (*jeweils*) each; (*pro*) per; (*jemals*) ever. ◆ *konj*: **~ schneller, desto besser** the quicker the better; **drei Gruppen mit ~ fünf Personen** three groups, each of five people; **30 DM ~ Stunde** 30 Marks per hour; **bist du ~ mit ihm zusammengetroffen?** have you ever met him?; **~ nachdem** it depends; **oh ~!** oh no!

Jeans (*pl* -) *die* (pair of) jeans (*pl*).

jede, -r, -s ◆ *det* every, each. ◆ *pron* (*Person*) everyone; (*Gegenstand*) each (one); **~r dritte** every third one.

jedenfalls *adv* (*wenigstens*) at least; (*auf jeden Fall*) in any case.

jederzeit *adv* at any time.

jedesmal *adv* every time.

jedoch *adv* however.

jemand *pron* (*unbekannte Person*) someone; (*in Fragen*) anyone.

jene, -r, -s ◆ *det* (*geh*) that. ◆ *pron* (*geh*) that one.

jenseits *präp* (+G) (*räumlich*) on the other side of.

jetzig *adj* current.

jetzt *adv* (*momentan*) now; (*heutzutage*) nowadays; (*bald, gleich*) soon;

(*damals*) then; **bis ~** until now; **~ gleich** right now.

jeweils *adv* (*jeder*) each; (*jedesmal*) each time; **~ vier Punkte** four points each; **~ am Monatsersten** on the first of each month.

Jh. (*abk für Jahrhundert*) C.

JH *abk* = **Jugendherberge**.

Job (*pl -s*) *der* job.

jobben *vi* to work.

Jod *das* iodine.

jodeln *vi* to yodel.

joggen *vi ist* to jog.

Jogging *das* jogging.

Jogginganzug (*pl -anzüge*) *der* tracksuit.

Joghurt (*pl -s*) *der* ODER *das* yoghurt.

Johannisbeere (*pl -n*) *die*: **rote ~** redcurrant; **schwarze ~** blackcurrant.

Jolle (*pl -n*) *die* (*Segelboot*) dinghy.

Journal (*pl -e*) *das* magazine.

Journalist, -in (*mpl -en*) *der, die* journalist.

jubeln *vi* to cheer.

Jubiläum (*pl Jubiläen*) *das* jubilee.

jucken *vi* (*Haut*) to itch; (*Material*) to be itchy.

Juckreiz *der* itch.

Jude (*pl -n*) *der* Jew.

Jüdin (*pl -nen*) *die* Jew.

jüdisch *adj* Jewish.

Jugend *die* youth.

jugendfrei *adj*: **nicht ~** not suitable for children.

Jugendherberge (*pl -n*) *die* youth hostel.

Jugendherbergsausweis (*pl -e*) *der* youth hostel card.

Jugendherbergsschlafsack (*pl -säcke*) *der* sheet sleeping bag.

jugendlich ◆ *adj* (*jung*) young; (*jung wirkend*) youthful. ◆ *adv* (*jung wirkend*) youthfully.

Jugendliche (*pl -n*) *der, die* young person.

Jugendstil *der* Art Nouveau.

Jugendzentrum (*pl -zentren*) *das* youth centre.

Jugoslawien *nt* Yugoslavia.

Juli *der* July, → **September**.

jung (*komp* **jünger**, *superl* **am jüngsten**) *adj* young.

Junge (*pl -n*) ◆ *der* (*Knabe*) boy. ◆ *das* (*von Tieren*) young animal; **die ~n** the young; **die Katze hat ~** the cat has got kittens.

Jungfrau *die* (*Sternzeichen*) Virgo; (*Mädchen*) virgin.

Junggeselle (*pl -n*) *der* bachelor.

Juni *der* June, → **September**.

Jura *ohne Artikel* law.

Jurist, -in (*mpl -en*) *der, die* lawyer.

juristisch *adj* legal.

Jury (*pl* **Juries**) *die* jury.

Justiz *die* (*Rechtsbehörden*) judiciary.

Juwelier, -in (*mpl -e*) *der, die* jeweller.

K

Kabarett (*pl -s*) *das* cabaret.

Kabel (*pl -*) *das* (*elektrische Leitung*) cable.

Kabelanschluß (*pl -anschlüsse*) *der*: **~ haben** to have cable television.

Kabelfernsehen *das* cable television.

Kabeljau (*pl -s*) *der* cod.

Kabelkanal (*pl -kanäle*) *der* cable TV channel.

Kabine (*pl -n*) *die* (*Umkleidekabine*) cubicle; (*im Schiff*) cabin.

Kabinenbahn (*pl -en*) *die* cable railway.

Kabinett (*pl -e*) ◆ *das* (*von Ministern*) cabinet. ◆ *der* (*Wein*) *term designating a high-quality German wine*.

Kabrio (*pl -s*) *das* convertible.

Kachel (*pl -n*) *die* tile.

Kachelofen (*pl* **-öfen**) *der tiled wood-burning stove used for heating.*

Käfer (*pl* -) *der beetle.*

Kaffee (*pl* **-s**) *der coffee;* (*Mahlzeit*) *light afternoon meal of coffee and cakes, biscuits etc*; **eine Tasse ~** a cup of coffee; **~ trinken** to drink coffee.

Kaffeebar (*pl* **-s**) *die coffee bar.*

Kaffeefahrt (*pl* **-en**) *die day trip organized by a company on which its products are promoted and sold.*

Kaffeefilter (*pl* -) *der coffee filter.*

Kaffeehaus (*pl* **-häuser**) *das coffee shop.*

KAFFEEHAUS

The 'Kaffeehaus' is one of the most typical sights of the city of Vienna. Customers come here to drink coffee in a friendly atmosphere, to talk, read the newspapers provided on the premises or to play cards and billiards. A wide variety of different types of coffee is available, including 'Brauner' (white coffee), 'Schwarzer' (black coffee), 'Melange' (milky coffee) and 'Einspänner' (mocha topped with cream).

Kaffeekanne (*pl* **-n**) *die coffeepot.*

Kaffeeklatsch (*pl* **-s**) *der = coffee morning.*

Kaffeelöffel (*pl* -) *der teaspoon.*

Kaffeemaschine (*pl* **-n**) *die coffee machine.*

Kaffeepause (*pl* **-n**) *die coffee break.*

Kaffeesahne *die coffee cream.*

Kaffeetasse (*pl* **-n**) *die coffee cup.*

Käfig (*pl* **-e**) *der cage.*

Kahn (*pl* **Kähne**) *der* (*Ruderboot*) rowing boat (Br), rowboat (Am); (*Stechkahn*) punt.

Kai (*pl* **-s**) *der quay.*

Kaiser, -in (*mpl* -) *der, die* emperor, (f empress).

Kaiserschmarrn (*pl* -) *der* (*Süddt &* *Österr*) *pancake cut into thin strips.*

Kajak (*pl* **-s**) *das kayak.*

Kajüte (*pl* **-n**) *die cabin.*

Kakao *der cocoa;* **eine Tasse ~** a cup of cocoa.

Kaktus (*pl* **Kakteen**) *der cactus.*

Kalb (*pl* **Kälber**) *das* (*von Kuh*) calf; (*Fleisch*) veal.

Kalbfleisch *das veal.*

Kalender (*pl* -) *der* (*Wandkalender*) calendar; (*Taschenkalender*) diary.

Kalifornien *nt California.*

Kalk *der* (*im Wasser*) lime.

Kalorie (*pl* **-n**) *die calorie.*

kalorienarm *adj* low-calorie.

kalt (*komp* **kälter**, *superl* **am kältesten**) ♦ *adj* cold. ♦ *adv* (*gefühllos*) coldly; **~ duschen** to have a cold shower; **es ist ~** it's cold; **mir ist ~** I'm cold.

Kälte *die* (*Temperatur*) cold; (*von Person*) coldness.

Kälteeinbruch (*pl* **-einbrüche**) *der cold snap.*

Kaltfront (*pl* **-en**) *die cold front.*

Kaltmiete (*pl* **-n**) *die rent not including bills.*

Kaltstartautomatik *die automatic choke.*

kam *prät* → **kommen**.

Kamel (*pl* **-e**) *das* (*Tier*) camel.

Kamera (*pl* **-s**) *die camera.*

Kamillentee (*pl* **-s**) *der camomile tea.*

Kamin (*pl* **-e**) *der* (*im Raum*) fireplace; (*Schornstein*) chimney.

Kamm (*pl* **Kämme**) *der* (*für Haare*) comb.

kämmen *vt* to comb. ▶ **sich kämmen** *ref* to comb one's hair.

Kammermusik *die* chamber music.

Kampf (*pl* **Kämpfe**) *der* (*Streit*) fight; (*in Sport*) contest; (*politisch, sozial*) struggle; (*im Krieg*) battle.

kämpfen *vi* to fight; (*in Sport*) to compete; **~ für** to fight for; **~ gegen** to fight; **~ um** to fight for; (*in Sport*) to compete for.

Kämpfer, -in (*mpl* -) *der, die fighter.*

Kampfrichter, -in (mpl -) der, die referee.

kampieren vi to camp.

Kanada nt Canada.

Kanal (pl **Kanäle**) der (Wasserweg) canal; (im Radio, Fernsehen) channel; (Abwasserkanal) sewer.

Kanaldeckel (pl -) der manhole cover.

Kanalinseln pl Channel Islands.

Kanalisation (pl -en) die sewers (pl).

Kandidat, -in (mpl -en) der, die (für Amt) candidate.

kandiert adj candied.

Kandiszucker der candy sugar.

Kaninchen (pl -) das rabbit.

Kanister (pl -) der can.

kann präs → **können**.

Kännchen (pl -) das pot; **ein ~ Kaffee** a pot of coffee.

Kanne (pl -n) die (für Kaffee, Tee) pot; (für Milch) jug; (für Öl, zum Gießen) can.

kannte prät → **kennen**.

Kante (pl -n) die edge.

Kantine (pl -n) die canteen.

Kanton (pl -e) der canton.

KANTON

Switzerland is made up of 23 cantons, or states. The cantons have a considerable degree of autonomy from central government, their exact areas of responsibility being enshrined in the constitution.

Kanu (pl -s) das (Paddelboot) canoe.

Kanzel (pl -n) die (in Kirche) pulpit.

Kanzler, -in (mpl -) der, die (Bundeskanzler) chancellor.

Kapelle (pl -n) die (Kirche) chapel; (MUS) band.

Kapern pl capers.

kapieren vt & vi to understand.

Kapital das (Vermögen) capital.

Kapitän (pl -e) der captain.

Kapitel (pl -) das chapter.

kapitulieren vi (resignieren) to give up.

Kaplan (pl **Kapläne**) der chaplain.

Kappe (pl -n) die cap.

Kapsel (pl -n) die (Medikament) capsule.

kaputt adj broken; (fam: erschöpft) exhausted; **~ sein** (fam: erschöpft) to be exhausted; **mein Auto ist ~** my car has broken down.

kaputt|gehen vi unr ist (Gegenstand) to break; (Auto) to break down; **an etw** (D) **~** (Person) to go to pieces because of sthg.

Kapuze (pl -n) die hood.

Kapuziner (pl -) der (Österr) coffee with just a drop of milk.

Karabinerhaken (pl -) der karabiner.

Karaffe (pl -n) die decanter.

Karamelbonbon (pl -s) das toffee.

Karat (pl -) das carat.

Karate das karate.

Kardinal (pl -äle) der cardinal.

Karfreitag (pl -e) der Good Friday.

kariert adj (Hose, Stoff) checked; (Papier) squared.

Karies die tooth decay.

Karikatur (pl -en) die (Bild) caricature.

Karneval der carnival.

KARNEVAL

The biggest 'Karneval' celebrations take place in the Rhineland (Cologne, Düsseldorf and Mainz), although the tradition is also associated with Bavaria (where it is known as 'Fasching') and Swabia (where it is known as 'Fasenacht' or 'Fasnet'). The 'Karneval' period officially begins at eleven minutes past eleven on 11 November and ends on Ash Wednesday. On the Monday before Ash Wednesday ('Rosenmontag'), there are processions with floats carrying figures that caricature social and political life.

Karnevalskostüm (pl -e) das carnival costume.

Karnevalssitzung (*pl* -en) *die evening entertainment at carnival time where satirical sketches are performed.*

Karnevalszug (*pl* -züge) *der* carnival procession.

Kärnten *nt* Corinthia.

Karo *das* (*Spielfarbe*) diamonds (*pl*).

Karosserie (*pl* -n) *die* (AUTO) bodywork.

Karotte (*pl* -n) *die* carrot.

Karpfen (*pl* -) *der* carp.

Karte (*pl* -n) *die* card; (*Eintrittskarte, Fahrkarte*) ticket; (*Postkarte*) postcard; (*Speisekarte*) menu; (*Landkarte*) map; '**folgende ~n werden akzeptiert**' 'the following credit cards are accepted'; '**~ einführen!**' 'please insert your card'; '**~ entnehmen!**' 'please take your card'; '**~ fehlerhaft**' 'this card is faulty'; '**~ ungültig**' 'this card is invalid'; **mit der ~ bezahlen** to pay by credit card; **~n spielen** to play cards.

Kartei (*pl* -en) *die* card index.

Karteikarte (*pl* -n) *die* index card.

Kartenspiel (*pl* -e) *das* (*Karten*) pack of cards (Br), deck of cards (Am); (*Spielen*) card game.

Kartentelefon (*pl* -e) *das* card phone.

Kartenvorverkauf (*pl* -käufe) *der* advance booking.

Kartoffel (*pl* -n) *die* potato.

Kartoffelchips *pl* crisps (Br), chips (Am).

Kartoffelkloß (*pl* -klöße) *der* potato dumpling.

Kartoffelknödel (*pl* -) *der* potato dumpling.

Kartoffelpüree *das* mashed potato.

Kartoffelsalat *der* potato salad.

Karton (*pl* -s) *der* (*Schachtel*) cardboard box.

Karussell (*pl* -s) *das* merry-go-round; **~ fahren** to have a ride on a merry-go-round.

Karwoche (*pl* -n) *die* Holy Week.

Kaschmir *der* (*Material*) cashmere.

Käse *der* cheese; **~ am Stück** unsliced cheese; **~ in Scheiben** sliced cheese.

Käsefondue (*pl* -s) *das* cheese fondue.

Käsekuchen (*pl* -) *der* cheesecake.

Käseplatte (*pl* -n) *die* cheeseboard.

Käse-Sahne-Torte (*pl* -n) *die type of cheesecake made with cream.*

Kasino (*pl* -s) *das* (*Spielkasino*) casino; (*Gemeinschaftsraum*) common room; (*für Offiziere*) mess.

Kaskoversicherung (*pl* -en) *die* fully comprehensive insurance.

Kasperletheater (*pl* -) *das* (*Vorstellung*) Punch and Judy show; (*Gebäude*) Punch and Judy theatre.

Kasse (*pl* -n) *die* (*Apparat*) till; (*in Supermarkt*) checkout; (*in Theater, Kino*) box office; (*in Bank*) counter; '**~ beim Fahrer**' 'please pay the driver'.

Kassenarzt, -ärztin (*mpl* -ärzte) *der, die doctor who treats patients who have health insurance.*

Kassenbereich *der* (*im Supermarkt*) checkout area.

Kassenbon (*pl* -s) *der* receipt; **gegen Vorlage des ~s** on production of a receipt.

Kassenpatient, -in (*mpl* -en) *der, die patient with health insurance policy.*

Kassenzettel (*pl* -) *der* receipt.

Kassette (*pl* -n) *die* (*für Musik, Video*) tape, cassette; (*Behälter*) box.

Kassettenrecorder (*pl* -) *der* tape recorder.

kassieren ◆ *vt* (*Eintrittsgeld, Fahrgeld*) to collect. ◆ *vi* (*Kellner, Busfahrer*) to collect the money.

Kassierer, -in (*mpl* -) *der, die* cashier.

Kastanie (*pl* -n) *die* (*Baum*) chestnut (tree); (*eßbare Frucht*) chestnut; (*nicht eßbare Frucht*) horse chestnut.

Kasten (*pl* Kästen) *der* (*Kiste, Dose*) box; (*Getränkekasten*) crate.

Kat

Kat (pl -s) der catalytic converter.

Katalog (pl -e) der catalogue.

Katalysator (pl Katalysatoren) der (am Auto) catalytic converter.

Katarrh (pl -e) der catarrh.

katastrophal adj disastrous.

Katastrophe (pl -n) die disaster.

Kategorie (pl -n) die category.

Kater (pl -) der (Tier) tomcat; **einen ~ haben** (von Alkohol) to have a hangover.

kath. abk = katholisch.

Kathedrale (pl -n) die cathedral.

Katholik, -in (mpl -en) der, die Catholic.

Katholikentag (pl -e) der biannual congress of German Catholics.

katholisch adj Catholic.

Kat-Motor (pl -en) der engine of a car fitted with a catalytic converter.

Katze (pl -n) die cat.

kauen vt & vi to chew.

Kauf (pl Käufe) der (Handlung) purchase.

kaufen vt to buy; **sich** (D) **etw ~** to buy o.s. sthg.

Käufer, -in (mpl -) der, die buyer.

Kauffrau (pl -en) die businesswoman.

Kaufhaus (pl -häuser) das department store.

Kaufhausdieb, -in (mpl -e) der, die shoplifter (from department stores).

Kaufhausdiebstahl (pl -stähle) der shoplifting (from department stores).

Kaufleute pl (Händler) shopkeepers.

Kaufmann (pl -leute) der (im Betrieb) businessman.

Kaufpreis (pl -e) der purchase price.

Kaufvertrag (pl -träge) der bill of sale.

Kaugummi (pl -s) der ODER das chewing gum.

kaum adv hardly, barely; **es regnet ~ noch** it's almost stopped raining.

Kaution (pl -en) die (für Wohnung) deposit.

Kaviar der caviar.

Kefir der sour-tasting fermented milk.

Kegelbahn (pl -en) die bowling alley.

Kegelklub (pl -s) der bowling club.

kegeln vi to go bowling.

Kehlkopf (pl -köpfe) der larynx.

Kehrblech (pl -e) das dustpan.

kehren vt & vi (fegen) to sweep.

kehrtlmachen vi to turn round.

Keilriemen (pl -) der (AUTO) fan belt.

kein, -e det no; **ich habe ~ Geld/ ~e Zeit** I haven't got any money/time; **~ Mensch** no one; **~e einzige Mark** not a single mark; **~e Stunde** less than an hour.

keine, -r, -s pron (Person) no one; (Gegenstand) none; **~s der Kinder** none of the children; **~r von den beiden** neither of them; **von diesen Gerichten mag ich ~s** I don't like any of these dishes.

keinerlei det: **das hat ~ Wirkung gehabt** it had no effect at all.

keinesfalls adv on no account.

keineswegs adv not at all.

Keks (pl -e) der biscuit (Br), cookie (Am).

Keller (pl -) der cellar.

Kellerei (pl -en) die wine cellars (pl).

Kellergeschoß (pl -geschosse) das basement.

Kellner, -in (mpl -) der, die waiter (waitress).

kennen (prät kannte, pp gekannt) vt to know; **jn/etw gut ~** to know sb/sthg well. ▶ **sich kennen** ref to know each other.

kennenllernen vt to get to know; **freut mich Sie kennenzulernen!** pleased to meet you!

Kenner, -in (mpl -) der, die expert.

Kenntnisse pl knowledge (sg).

Kennwort (pl -e) das (für Sparbuch) password.

Kennzahl (*pl* **-en**) *die* (*für Telefon*) dialling code (*Br*), area code (*Am*).

Kennzeichen (*pl* **-**) *das* (*am Auto*) registration (number) (*Br*), license (number) (*Am*); (*Merkmal*) characteristic; **amtliches ~** registration number (*Br*), license number (*Am*); **'besondere ~'** 'distinguishing features'.

Kennziffer (*pl* **-n**) *die* reference number.

Keramik (*pl* **-en**) *die* (*Gegenstand*) (piece of) pottery.

Kerl (*pl* **-e**) *der* guy.

Kern (*pl* **-e**) *der* (*von Apfel, Birne*) pip; (*von Pfirsich, Aprikose*) stone; (*von Nuß*) kernel.

Kernenergie *die* nuclear power.

Kernforschung *die* nuclear research.

kerngesund *adj* as fit as a fiddle.

Kernkraft *die* nuclear power.

Kernkraftwerk (*pl* **-e**) *das* nuclear power station.

kernlos *adj* (*Weintraube*) seedless.

Kernwaffe (*pl* **-n**) *die* nuclear weapon.

Kerze (*pl* **-n**) *die* (*aus Wachs*) candle; (AUTO: *Zündkerze*) spark plug.

Kerzenlicht *das* candlelight.

Kerzenständer (*pl* **-**) *der* candleholder.

Kessel (*pl* **-**) *der* (*Wasserkessel*) kettle.

Ketchup *der* ODER *das* ketchup.

Kette (*pl* **-n**) *die* chain.

keuchen *vi* to pant.

Keuchhusten *der* whooping cough.

Keule (*pl* **-n**) *die* (*Fleisch*) leg.

Keyboard (*pl* **-s**) *das* keyboard.

Kfz (*pl* **-**) *abk* = **Kraftfahrzeug**.

Kfz-Brief (*pl* **-e**) *der* ≃ logbook (*Br*), *document of ownership of a motor vehicle*.

Kfz-Schein (*pl* **-e**) *der* vehicle registration document.

Kfz-Steuer (*pl* **-n**) *die* road tax.

Kfz-Werkstatt (*pl* **-stätten**) *die* garage.

kichern *vi* to giggle.

Kiefer¹ (*pl* **-**) *der* (*Knochen*) jaw.

Kiefer² (*pl* **-n**) *die* (*Baum*) pine (tree).

Kies *der* (*Steine*) gravel.

Kieselstein (*pl* **-e**) *der* pebble.

Kilo (*pl* **-s** ODER **-**) *das* kilo.

Kilogramm (*pl* **-**) *das* kilogram.

Kilokalorie (*pl* **-n**) *die* kilocalorie.

Kilometer (*pl* **-**) *der* kilometre; **50 ~ pro Stunde** 50 kilometres an hour.

kilometerlang *adj* several kilometres long.

Kilometerstand *der* ≃ mileage.

Kilometerzähler (*pl* **-**) *der* ≃ mileometer.

Kind (*pl* **-er**) *das* child; **ein ~ erwarten** to be expecting (a baby).

Kinderarzt, -ärztin (*mpl* **-ärzte**) *der, die* paediatrician.

Kinderbetreuung *die* child care.

Kinderbett (*pl* **-en**) *das* cot (*Br*), crib (*Am*).

Kinderbuch (*pl* **-bücher**) *das* children's book.

Kinderfahrkarte (*pl* **-n**) *die* child's ticket.

Kinderfrau (*pl* **-en**) *die* nanny.

Kindergarten (*pl* **-gärten**) *der* nursery school.

Kindergärtner, -in (*mpl* **-**) *der, die* nursery school teacher.

Kinderheim (*pl* **-e**) *das* children's home.

Kinderkrankheit (*pl* **-en**) *die* children's illness.

Kinderkrippe (*pl* **-n**) *die* day nursery.

Kinderlähmung *die* polio.

kinderlieb *adj*: **~ sein** to be fond of children.

Kinderlied (*pl* **-er**) *das* nursery rhyme.

Kindernahrung *die* baby food.

Kinderprogramm (*pl* **-e**) *das* (*im Fernsehen*) children's programme.

Kinderschuh (*pl* **-e**) *der* child's shoe.

kindersicher *adj* childproof.

Kindersicherung (pl -en) die (an Tür) childproof lock.

Kindersitz (pl -e) der child seat.

Kinderteller (pl -) der children's portion.

Kindertragesitz (pl -e) der baby sling.

Kinderwagen (pl -) der pram (Br), baby carriage (Am).

Kinderzimmer (pl -) das child's bedroom.

Kindheit die childhood.

kindisch adj childish.

Kinn (pl -e) das chin.

Kino (pl -s) das cinema (Br), movie theater (Am); **ins ~ gehen** to go to the cinema (Br), to go to the movies (Am); **was läuft im ~?** what's on at the cinema? (Br), what's on at the movies? (Am).

Kinobesucher, -in (mpl -) der, die cinemagoer (Br), moviegoer (Am).

Kinoprogramm (pl -e) das (in Zeitung) cinema guide (Br), movie guide (Am).

Kiosk (pl -e) der kiosk.

kippen ♦ vt hat (lehnen) to tip. ♦ vi ist (umfallen) to tip over.

Kirche (pl -n) die church.

Kirchenchor (pl -chöre) der church choir.

Kirchenmusik die church music.

Kirchenschiff (pl -e) das nave.

Kirchentag (pl -e) der German church congress.

Kirchturm (pl -türme) der church steeple.

Kirmes (pl -sen) die fair.

Kirsche (pl -n) die cherry.

Kirschkuchen (pl -) der cherry tart.

Kissen (pl -) das (in Bett) pillow; (auf Stuhl, Sofa) cushion.

Kiste (pl -n) die box; **eine ~ Wein** a case of wine.

kitschig adj kitschy.

Kittel (pl -) der overalls (pl); (für Arzt, Laborant) white coat; (für Hausfrau) housecoat.

kitzelig adj ticklish.

kitzeln vt & vi to tickle.

Kiwi (pl -s) die kiwi fruit.

Klage (pl -n) die (Beschwerde) complaint; (vor Gericht) suit.

klagen vi (jammern) to moan; (vor Gericht) to sue; **~ über** (+A) to complain about.

klamm adj (Finger) numb; (Wäsche) damp.

Klammer (pl -n) die (für Wäsche) clothes peg; (für Zähne) brace; (geschrieben) bracket.

klammern vt (mit Klammer) to peg. ▶ **sich klammern** ref (festhalten): **sich ~ an** (+A) to cling to.

Klamotten pl (fam: Kleider) clothes.

klang prät → **klingen**.

Klang (pl Klänge) der sound.

Klappbett (pl -en) das folding bed.

Klappe (pl -n) die (am Briefkasten) flap; **'~ hochschieben'** (an Verkaufsautomat) 'lift door'.

klappen ♦ vi (gelingen) to work. ♦ vt: **etw nach oben/hinten ~** (Kragen) to turn sthg up/down; **gut ~** to go well.

klappern vi to rattle.

Klapprad (pl -räder) das folding bicycle.

Klappsitz (pl -e) der folding seat.

klar ♦ adj clear. ♦ adv (deutlich) clearly; **mir ist nicht ~, wie das funktioniert** I don't understand how it works; **alles ~?** is everything clear?; **alles ~!** OK!

Kläranlage (pl -n) die sewage works (sg).

Klare (pl -n) der schnapps.

klären vt (Problem, Frage) to settle. ▶ **sich klären** ref (Problem, Frage) to be settled.

Klarinette (pl -n) die clarinet.

klar|kommen vi unr ist (fam): **mit jm ~** to get on well with sb; **mit etw ~** to be able to cope with sthg.

klar|machen vt: **jm etw ~** to explain sthg to sb.

Klarsichtfolie (pl -n) die clingfilm

(Br), Saranwrap® (Am).

Klarsichthülle (pl -n) die clear plastic cover.

klar|stellen vt to make clear; (Mißverständnis) to clear up.

Klärung (pl -en) die (von Problem, Frage) settling.

klar|werden vi unr ist: jm ~ to become clear to sb; sich (D) ~ über etw (A) (erkennen) to realize sthg.

klasse adj (fam) great.

Klasse (pl -n) die class; (Raum) classroom; erster/zweiter ~ (in Zug) first/second class.

Klassenkamerad, -in (mpl -en) der, die classmate.

Klassik die (Epoche) classical period.

klassisch adj (typisch) classic; (Musik) classical.

klatschen vi (Wasser) to splash; (in Hände) to clap; (tratschen) to gossip.

klauen vt (fam) to pinch; jm etw ~ to pinch sthg from sb.

Klavier (pl -e) das piano.

Klavierkonzert (pl -e) das (Komposition) piano concerto.

kleben ◆ vt (reparieren) to stick together; (ankleben) to stick. ◆ vi (klebrig sein) to be sticky; (haften) to stick.

Klebestreifen (pl -) der sticky tape.

klebrig adj sticky.

Klebstoff (pl -e) der glue.

kleckern vi (Person) to make a mess.

Kleid (pl -er) das (für Frauen) dress. ▶ **Kleider** pl (Bekleidung) clothes.

Kleiderbügel (pl -) der (clothes) hanger.

Kleiderschrank (pl -schränke) der wardrobe.

Kleidung die clothes (pl).

Kleidungsstück (pl -e) das garment.

klein ◆ adj small, little; (Pause, Weile) short. ◆ adv: mein ~er Bruder my little brother; ein Wort ~ schreiben to write a word with a small initial letter; ein ~ wenig a little bit; bis ins ~ste to the last detail; haben Sie es ~? do you have the right change?

Kleinanzeige (pl -n) die classified advertisement.

Kleinbus (pl -se) der minibus.

Kleingedruckte das small print.

Kleingeld das change; '~ bitte bereithalten' 'please have the right change ready'.

Kleinigkeit (pl -en) die (Unwichtiges) trifle; (Geschenk) little gift; (Zwischenmahlzeit) snack.

Kleinkind (pl -er) das small child.

Kleinkunstbühne (pl -n) die cabaret.

kleinlich adj petty.

klein|machen vt (fam: Geldschein) to change.

klein|schneiden vt unr to chop finely.

Kleinschreibung die writing with small initial letters.

Kleinstadt (pl -städte) die small town.

Kleister (pl -) der paste.

klemmen vt & vi to jam; sich (D) den Finger in etw ~ to get one's finger caught in sthg.

Klempner, -in (mpl -) der, die plumber.

klettern vi ist (Person) to climb; (Preis, Temperatur) to rise.

Klient, -in (mpl -en) der, die client.

Klima das (Wetter) climate; (Stimmung) atmosphere.

Klimaanlage (pl -n) die air conditioning.

klimatisiert adj air-conditioned.

Klinge (pl -n) die (von Messer) blade.

Klingel (pl -n) die bell.

klingeln ◆ vi to ring; (Radfahrer) to ring one's bell. ◆ vimp: es klingelt there's someone at the door; bitte ~ bei ... please ring at ...

klingen (prät klang, pp geklungen) vi (Person, Äußerung) to sound; (Glocke) to ring.

Klinik (pl -en) die clinic.

Klinke (pl -n) die handle.

Klippe (pl -n) die (am Meer) cliff.

Klischee (pl -s) das stereotype.

Klo (pl -s) das (fam) loo (Br), john (Am); **aufs ~ müssen** to need the loo (Br), to need the john (Am).

Klopapier das (fam) toilet paper.

klopfen ◆ vi (Herz) to beat; (auf Schulter) to tap; (an Tür) to knock. ◆ vimp: **es klopft** (an Tür) there's someone at the door.

Klosett (pl -s) das toilet.

Kloß (pl Klöße) der dumpling.

Kloster (pl Klöster) das (für Mönche) monastery; (für Nonnen) convent.

Klotz (pl Klötze) der (von Baum) log.

Klub (pl -s) der club.

klug adj clever.

knabbern vt & vi to nibble; **an etw** (D) **~** to nibble sthg.

Knäckebrot (pl -e) das crispbread.

knacken ◆ vt (Nuß) to crack; (fam: Auto) to break into; (fam: Schloß) to force. ◆ vi (Holz) to crack.

knackig adj (Obst, Gemüse) crisp; (fam: Körper) sexy.

Knall (pl -e) der bang.

knapp ◆ adj (Vorrat, Angebot) short; (Kleidung) tight; (Mehrheit) narrow. ◆ adv (verlieren, gewinnen) narrowly; (fast) not quite; **~ werden** (Vorrat) to be running short; **~ 10 Meter** not quite 10 metres; **das war ~** that was close.

knarren vi to creak.

Knast (pl Knäste) der (fam) clink, prison.

Knäuel (pl -) das ball (of wool).

knautschen vt to crumple.

kneifen (prät **kniff**, pp **gekniffen**) vt to pinch.

Kneifzange (pl -n) die pincers (pl).

Kneipe (pl -n) die pub.

KNEIPE

Unlike in British pubs, in a German 'Kneipe' light meals are served not only throughout the day but also in the evening. There is usually a waiter or waitress who brings the beer to the tables, and customers pay when they are ready to leave, rather than a round at a time. A feature of many German pubs is the 'Stammtisch' which is a table reserved for regular customers. In Austria, 'Kneipen' are called 'Beisel'.

---

knicken vt (Papier) to fold.

Knie (pl -) das knee.

Kniegelenk (pl -e) das knee(joint).

knien vi to be kneeling. ▶ **sich knien** ref to kneel down.

Kniescheibe (pl -n) die kneecap.

Kniestrumpf (pl -strümpfe) der knee-length sock.

kniff prät → **kneifen**.

knipsen vt (fam: fotografieren) to snap.

knistern vi (Feuer) to crackle; (Papier) to rustle.

knitterfrei adj crease-resistant.

Knoblauch der garlic.

Knöchel (pl -) der (von Fuß) ankle; (von Finger) knuckle.

Knochen (pl -) der bone.

Knochenbruch (pl -brüche) der fracture.

Knödel (pl -) der dumpling.

Knopf (pl Knöpfe) der button; '**~ drücken**' 'press the button'.

Knopfdruck der: **durch ~** by pressing the button.

knöpfen vt to button.

Knopfloch (pl -löcher) das buttonhole.

Knorpel (pl -) der cartilage.

knoten vt to tie.

Knoten (pl -) der knot.

knurren vi (Hund) to growl; (Magen) to rumble.

knusprig adj crusty.

knutschen vi (fam) to neck.

Koalition (pl -en) die coalition.

Koch (pl Köche) der cook, chef.

Kochbeutel (pl -) der (KÜCHE) bag

containing food, for boiling.

kochen ♦ *vi* (*für Mahlzeit*) to cook; (*Wasser*) to boil. ♦ *vt* (*Mahlzeit*) to cook; (*Tee, Kaffee*) to make; (*Eier*) to boil; **jm etw ~** to cook sb sthg.

Kocher (*pl -*) *der* cooker.

Kochgelegenheit (*pl -en*) *die* cooking facilities (*pl*).

Köchin (*pl -nen*) *die* cook.

Kochlöffel (*pl -*) *der* wooden spoon.

Kochrezept (*pl -e*) *das* recipe.

Kochsalz *das* cooking salt.

Kochtopf (*pl -töpfe*) *der* saucepan.

Kochwäsche *die washing that needs to be boiled.*

Koffein *das* caffeine.

koffeinfrei *adj* decaffeinated.

Koffer (*pl -*) *der* suitcase; **die ~ packen** to pack (one's bags).

Kofferkuli (*pl -s*) *der* (luggage) trolley; *'~ nur gegen Pfand' sign indicating that a deposit is required for the use of a luggage trolley.*

Kofferradio (*pl -s*) *das* portable radio.

Kofferraum (*pl -räume*) *der* boot (Br), trunk (Am).

Kognac *der =* **Cognac.**

Kohl *der* cabbage.

Kohle *die* (*Material*) coal; (*fam: Geld*) cash.

Kohlenhydrat (*pl -e*) *das* carbohydrate.

Kohlensäure *die* carbon dioxide; **Mineralwasser mit/ohne ~** sparkling/ still mineral water.

Kohlrabi (*pl -s*) *der* kohlrabi.

Kohlroulade (*pl -n*) *die cabbage leaves stuffed usually with meat.*

Koje (*pl -n*) *die* berth.

Kokosnuß (*pl -nüsse*) *die* coconut.

Kolben (*pl -*) *der* (AUTO) piston; (*von Mais*) cob.

Kolik (*pl -en*) *die* colic.

Kollaps (*pl -e*) *der* (MED) collapse.

Kollege (*pl -n*) *der* colleague.

Kollegin (*pl -nen*) *die* colleague.

Kollision (*pl -en*) *die* collision.

Köln *nt* Cologne.

Kölnisch Wasser *das* eau de Cologne.

Kolonne (*pl -n*) *die* column; (*von Fahrzeugen*) queue.

Kölsch *das strong lager brewed in Cologne.*

Kombi (*pl -s*) *der* (Auto) estate car (Br), station wagon (Am).

Kombination (*pl -en*) *die* combination.

kombinieren *vt* to combine; **etw mit etw ~** to combine sthg with sthg.

Kombi-Ticket (*pl -s*) *das ticket valid for travel on train, bus, metro etc.*

Kombiwagen (*pl -*) *der* estate car (Br), station wagon (Am).

Komfort *der* luxury; **mit allem ~** (*Haus, Hotelzimmer*) with all mod cons.

komfortabel *adj* with all mod cons.

komisch ♦ *adj* funny. ♦ *adv* funnily.

Komma (*pl -ta*) *das* (*in Satz*) comma; (*in Zahl*) decimal point; **null ~ fünf Prozent** nought point five per cent.

kommandieren *vi* to give orders.

kommen (*prät* **kam**, *pp* **gekommen**) ♦ *vi* **1.** (*an einen Ort*) to come; **wie komme ich zum Markt?** how do I get to the market?; **jn/etw ~ lassen** to send for sb/sthg; **nach Hause ~** to get home. **2.** (*aus einem Ort*) to come; **aus Deutschland ~** to come from Germany. **3.** (*erscheinen*) to come; **rechts kommt der Bahnhof** the station's coming up on the right. **4.** (*eintreten*) to come. **5.** (*in Reihenfolge*): **wer kommt zuerst?** who's first? **6.** (*Gefühl, Gedanke*): **mir kam eine Idee** I had an idea; **auf etw** (A) **~** to think of sthg. **7.** (*gehören*) to belong, to go. **8.** (*zum Ziel, Ergebnis*): **zu etw ~** to reach sthg; **hinter etw** (A) **~** (*erraten*) to find sthg out; **an die Macht ~** to come to power. **9.** (*Zeit haben*): **dazu ~, etw zu tun** to get

round to doing sthg. **10.** (um Besitz):
um etw ~ to lose sthg. **11.** (als Folge):
von etw ~ to result from sthg; **das
kommt davon!** see what happens!
12. (zu Bewußtsein): **zu sich ~** to come
round. **13.** (bei Institution): **in die/aus
der Schule ~** to start/leave school;
ins/aus dem Krankenhaus ~ to go
to/leave hospital. **14.** (Film, Programm): **im Fernsehen ~** to be on
(the) television; **im Kino ~** to be on
at the cinema (Br), to be on at the
movies (Am). **15.** (anfangen): **ins
Rutschen/Stocken ~** to slip/falter.
♦ vimp: **es kam zu einem Streit** it
ended in a quarrel.

kommend adj coming.

Kommentar (pl -e) der (in Zeitung,
Fernsehen) commentary; (Bemerkung)
comment.

kommerziell adj commercial.

Kommissar, -in (mpl -e) der, die
police inspector.

Kommode (pl -n) die chest of
drawers.

kommunal adj local.

Kommunikation die communication.

Kommunion (pl -en) die
Communion.

Kommunismus der communism.

Komödie (pl -n) die comedy.

kompakt adj compact.

Komparativ (pl -e) der compara-
tive.

Kompaß (pl Kompasse) der compass.

kompatibel adj compatible; **IBM-
~** IBM-compatible.

kompetent adj competent.

komplett adj complete; **wir sind ~**
we are all here.

Kompliment (pl -e) das compliment.

kompliziert adj complicated.

Komponist, -in (mpl -en) der, die
composer.

Kompott (pl -e) das stewed fruit.

Kompresse (pl -n) die compress.

Kompromiß (pl Kompromisse) der
compromise.

Kondensmilch die condensed
milk.

Kondenswasser das condensation.

Kondition (pl -en) die condition.

Konditionstraining das fitness
training.

Konditor (pl Konditoren) der pastry
cook.

Konditorei (pl -en) die cake shop.

Konditorin (pl -nen) die pastry
cook.

Kondom (pl -e) das condom.

Konfekt das sweets (pl)(Br), candy
(Am).

Konfektionsgröße (pl -n) die size.

Konferenz (pl -en) die conference.

Konferenzraum (pl -räume) der
conference room.

Konfession (pl -en) die denomina-
tion.

Konfetti das confetti.

Konfirmation (pl -en) die confirmation.

Konfitüre (pl -n) die jam.

Konflikt (pl -e) der conflict.

Kongreß (pl Kongresse) der (Treffen)
conference.

Kongreßhalle (pl -n) die conference centre.

Kongreßleitung (pl -en) die conference organizers (pl).

König (pl -e) der king.

Königin (pl -nen) die queen.

Konjugation (pl -en) die (GRAMM)
conjugation.

konjugieren vt (GRAMM) to conjugate.

konkret adj concrete.

Konkurrenz (pl -en) die competition; **jm ~ machen** to compete with
sb.

können (präs **kann**, prät **konnte**, pp
können ODER **gekonnt**) ♦ aux **1.**
(gen)
can; **etw tun ~** to be able to do sthg;
er kann Klavier spielen he can play

the piano; **sie kann nicht kommen** she can't come; **das kann sein** that's quite possible; **wenn ich wollte, könnte ich ein Auto kaufen** I could buy a car if I wanted to; **es kann sein, daß ich mich geirrt habe** I may have been wrong; **man kann nie wissen** you never know. **2.** (*dürfen, sollen*) can; **kann ich noch ein Eis haben?** can I have another ice cream?; **könnte ich mal telefonieren?** could I use the telephone?; **du kannst gehen** you can go. ◆ *vt* (*pp* **gekonnt**) **1.** (*Sprache*) to (be able to) speak; **~ Sie Deutsch?** can ODER do you speak German? **2.** (*fam: auswendig*) to know. **3.** (*Angabe von Verantwortung*): **ich kann nichts dafür** I can't help it; **er kann nichts dafür, daß ...** it's not his fault that ... ◆ *vi* (*pp* **gekonnt**) **1.** (*fähig sein*) can; **fahren, so schnell man kann** to drive as fast as you can; **ich kann nicht mehr** (*fam*) I've had it, I'm exhausted. **2.** (*dürfen*) can; **kann ich ins Kino?** can I go to the cinema?

konnte *prät* → **können.**

konsequent ◆ *adj* consistent. ◆ *adv* consistently.

Konsequenz (*pl* -en) *die* consequence.

konservativ *adj* conservative.

Konserve (*pl* -n) *die* tinned food, canned food.

Konservendose (*pl* -n) *die* tin, can.

Konservierungsmittel (*pl* -) *das* preservative.

Konservierungsstoff (*pl* -e) *der* preservative.

Konsonant (*pl* -en) *der* consonant.

konstruieren *vt* to construct.

Konsulat (*pl* -e) *das* consulate.

Konsum *der* consumption.

Kontakt (*pl* -e) *der* contact; **~ haben zu** ODER **mit** to be in contact with.

Kontaktlinse (*pl* -n) *die* contact lens; **weiche/harte ~** soft/hard contact lens.

Kontinent (*pl* -e) *der* continent.

Konto (*pl* **Konten**) *das* account; **ein ~ eröffnen** to open an account; **ein ~ auflösen** to close an account.

Kontoauszug (*pl* -züge) *der* bank statement.

Kontostand *der* bank balance.

Kontrabaß (*pl* -bässe) *der* double-bass.

Kontrast (*pl* -e) *der* contrast.

Kontrollabschnitt (*pl* -e) *der* stub.

Kontrolle (*pl* -n) *die* (*von Fahrkarte, Gepäck*) inspection, check; (*Aufsicht, Beherrschung*) control; **die ~ über ein Fahrzeug verlieren** to lose control of a vehicle.

Kontrolleuchte (*pl* -n) *die* warning light.

Kontrolleur, -in (*mpl* -e) *der, die* (*in Bus, Straßenbahn*) ticket inspector.

kontrollieren *vt* (*prüfen*) to check.

Kontrolluntersuchung (*pl* -en) *die* check-up.

Konversation (*pl* -en) *die* conversation.

Konzentrationslager (*pl* -) *das* concentration camp.

konzentrieren: sich konzentrieren *ref* to concentrate; **sich ~ auf** (+A) to concentrate on.

konzentriert *adj* concentrated; **~ sein** (*Person*) to be concentrating.

Konzern (*pl* -e) *der* group (of companies).

Konzert (*pl* -e) *das* (*Veranstaltung*) concert.

Konzertsaal (*pl* -säle) *der* concert hall.

kooperativ *adj* cooperative.

koordinieren *vt* to coordinate.

Kopf (*pl* **Köpfe**) *der* head; **den ~ schütteln** to shake one's head; **pro ~** per person.

Kopfhörer (*pl* -) *der* headphone.

Kopfkissen (*pl* -) *das* pillow.

Kopfsalat (*pl* -e) *der* lettuce.

Kopfschmerzen *pl* headache (*sg*); **~ haben** to have a headache.

Kopfsprung (*pl* -sprünge) *der* dive.

Kopfstand (pl -stände) der headstand.

Kopfstütze (pl -n) die headrest.

Kopftuch (pl -tücher) das headscarf.

Kopie (pl -n) die copy.

kopieren vt & vi to copy.

Kopierer (pl -) der photocopier.

Kopiergerät (pl -e) das photocopier.

Korb (pl **Körbe**) der basket; (Material) wicker.

Kordel (pl -n) die cord.

Kordsamt der corduroy.

Korinthe (pl -n) die currant.

Korken (pl -) der cork.

Korkenzieher (pl -) der corkscrew.

Korn[1] (pl **Körner**) das grain; (Getreide) grain, corn.

Korn[2] (pl -) der (Schnaps) schnapps.

Körper (pl -) der body; (Figur) figure.

körperbehindert adj disabled.

Körpergewicht das weight.

Körpergröße (pl -n) die height.

körperlich ◆ adj physical. ◆ adv physically.

Körperlotion (pl -en) die body lotion.

Körperpflege die personal hygiene.

Körperverletzung die physical injury.

korpulent adj corpulent.

korrekt ◆ adj correct. ◆ adv correctly.

Korrektur (pl -en) die correction.

Korridor (pl -e) der corridor.

korrigieren vt to correct. ▶ **sich korrigieren** ref to correct o.s.

Kosmetik die (Pflege) beauty care.

Kosmetika pl cosmetics.

Kosmetikerin (pl -nen) die beautician.

Kosmetiksalon (pl -s) der beauty salon.

Kosmetiktücher pl paper tissues.

Kost die food.

kostbar adj valuable.

kosten ◆ vt to cost; (Wein, Speise) to taste. ◆ vi (Wein, Speise) to have a taste; **was kostet das?** how much does it cost?

Kosten pl costs; **auf js ~** at sb's expense; **~ rückerstatten** to refund expenses.

kostenlos adj & adv free.

kostenpflichtig ◆ adj (amt) liable to pay costs. ◆ adv: **~ abgeschleppt werden** to be towed away at the owner's expense.

Kostenvoranschlag (pl -schläge) der estimate.

köstlich adj (Speise, Getränk) delicious; (amüsant) funny.

Kostprobe (pl -n) die (von Speise, Getränk) taste.

Kostüm (pl -e) das (Damenkleidung) suit; (Verkleidung) costume.

Kot der excrement.

Kotelett (pl -s) das chop, cutlet.

Kotflügel (pl -) der wing.

kotzen vi (vulg) to puke.

Krabbe (pl -n) die (Krebs) crab; (Garnele) shrimp.

krabbeln vi ist to crawl.

Krabbencocktail (pl -s) der prawn cocktail.

Krach (pl **Kräche**) der (Lärm) noise; (fam: Streit) row; **~ haben mit** to row with.

Kräcker (pl -) der cracker.

Kraft (pl **Kräfte**) die (körperlich, psychisch) strength; (physikalisch) force; (Wirkung) power; (Person) worker; **etw außer ~ setzen** to cancel; **in ~** in force.

Kraftbrühe (pl -n) die strong meat broth.

Kraftfahrer, -in (mpl -) der, die driver.

Kraftfahrzeug (pl -e) das motor vehicle.

Kraftfahrzeugbrief (pl -e) der ≃ logbook (Br), document of ownership of a motor vehicle.

Kraftfahrzeugkennzeichen (pl -) das registration number (Br),

license number (Am).
Kraftfahrzeugschein (pl -e) der vehicle registration document.
Kraftfahrzeugsteuer (pl -n) die road tax.
kräftig ◆ adj (Person, Muskeln) strong; (Mahlzeit) nourishing. ◆ adv (stark) hard.
Kraftstoff (pl -e) der fuel.
Kraftstoffverbrauch der fuel consumption.
Kraftwerk (pl -e) das power station.
Kragen (pl -) der collar.
Kralle (pl -n) die claw.
Kram der stuff.
kramen vi (herumsuchen) to rummage about.
Krampf (pl Krämpfe) der (von Muskeln) cramp.
Krampfader (pl -n) die varicose vein.
Kran (pl Kräne) der crane.
krank (komp kränker, superl am kränksten) adj ill, sick; ~ werden to be taken ill.
Kranke (pl -n) der, die sick person; (im Krankenhaus) patient.
Krankenhaus (pl -häuser) das hospital.
Krankenkasse (pl -n) die health insurance association.

KRANKENKASSE

A 'Krankenkasse' is a medical insurance organization that is responsible for national health insurance in Germany. People from different professions belong to different 'Krankenkassen', for example there are ones for miners and seamen, individual firms and guilds, as well as private health insurance schemes. Most people are covered by the 'Allgemeine Ortskrankenkasse' (AOK), which operates at a regional level.

Krankenpfleger (pl -) der (male) nurse.

Krankenschwester (pl -n) die nurse.
Krankenversichertenkarte (pl -n) die smart card which must be shown at the doctor's for health insurance purposes.
Krankenversicherung (pl -en) die health insurance.
Krankenwagen (pl -) der ambulance.
Krankheit (pl -en) die illness; (schwer) disease.
Krapfen (pl -) der doughnut.
Krater (pl -) der crater.
kratzen ◆ vt to scratch; (Reste, Farbe) to scrape. ◆ vi to scratch. ▶ **sich kratzen** ref to scratch o.s.
Kratzer (pl -) der scratch.
kraulen ◆ vi ist (SPORT: schwimmen) to do the crawl. ◆ vt hat (Tier) to tickle.
Kraut (pl Kräuter) das (Heilpflanze, Gewürzpflanze) herb; (Süddt: Kohl) cabbage.
Kräuterbutter die herb butter.
Kräuterlikör (pl -e) der bitter liqueur made from herbs.
Kräutersauce (pl -n) die herb sauce.
Kräutertee (pl -s) der herbal tea.
Krautsalat der œ coleslaw.
Krawatte (pl -n) die tie.
Krawattenzwang der: es besteht ~ ties must be worn.
kreativ adj creative.
Krebs (pl -e) der (Tier) crab; (Krankheit) cancer; (Sternzeichen) Cancer; ~ haben to have cancer.
Kredit (pl -e) der (Darlehen) loan; einen ~ aufnehmen to take out a loan.
Kreditinstitut (pl -e) das bank.
Kreditkarte (pl -n) die credit card; kann ich mit ~ bezahlen? can I pay by credit card?
Kreide (pl -n) die (Tafelkreide) chalk.
Kreis (pl -e) der circle; (Landkreis) district; im ~ in a circle.

Kreislaufstörungen pl circulatory disorder (sg).

Kreisstadt (pl -städte) die district capital.

Kreisverkehr der roundabout (Br), traffic circle (Am).

Krempel der (fam) stuff.

Kren der (Österr) horseradish.

Kresse die cress.

kreuz adv: ~ und quer all over.

Kreuz (pl -e) das cross; (fam: Rücken) small of the back; (Autobahnkreuz) intersection; (Spielfarbe) clubs (pl).

Kreuzfahrt (pl -en) die cruise.

Kreuzgang (pl -gänge) der cloister.

Kreuzigung (pl -en) die crucifixion.

Kreuzschlüssel (pl -) der wheel nut cross brace.

Kreuzung (pl -en) die (Straßenkreuzung) crossroads (sg).

Kreuzworträtsel (pl -) das crossword (puzzle).

kriechen (prät kroch, pp gekrochen) vi ist to crawl.

Kriechspur (pl -en) die crawler lane.

Krieg (pl -e) der war.

kriegen vt (fam: bekommen) to get.

Krimi (pl -s) der (fam) thriller.

Kriminalität die (Handlungen) crime.

Kriminalpolizei die ≃ Criminal Investigation Department (Br), ≃ Federal Bureau of Investigation (Am).

kriminell adj criminal.

Kripo die = **Kriminalpolizei**.

Krise (pl -n) die crisis.

Kritik (pl -en) die (Beurteilung) criticism; (von Buch, Film usw.) review.

kritisch ♦ adj critical. ♦ adv critically.

kritisieren ♦ vt (Person, Verhalten) to criticize; (Buch, Film usw.) to review. ♦ vi (beurteilen) to criticize.

kroch prät → **kriechen**.

Krokant das brittle (crunchy sweet made with nuts).

Krokette (pl -n) die croquette.

Krokodil (pl -e) das crocodile.

Krone (pl -n) die (von König) crown; (von Baum) top.

Kronleuchter (pl -) der chandelier.

Kröte (pl -n) die (Tier) toad.

Krücke (pl -n) die crutch.

Krug (pl Krüge) der jug; (für Bier) stein, mug.

Krümel (pl -) der crumb.

krumm (komp krümmer, superl am krümmsten) adj crooked.

Kruste (pl -n) die (von Brot) crust; (auf Wunde) scab.

Kruzifix (pl -e) das crucifix.

Krypta (pl Krypten) die crypt.

Kt. abk = **Kanton**.

Kto. (abk von Konto) a/c.

Kubikmeter (pl -) der cubic metre.

Küche (pl -n) die kitchen; (Art zu kochen) cooking, cuisine.

Kuchen (pl -) der cake.

Küchenabfall (pl -abfälle) der kitchen waste.

Küchenecke (pl -n) die kitchenette.

Kuchenform (pl -en) die cake tin.

Kuchengabel (pl -n) die cake fork.

Küchenrolle (pl -n) die kitchen roll.

Küchenwaage (pl -n) die kitchen scales (pl).

Kugel (pl -n) die (Gegenstand) ball; (Form) sphere; (Geschoß) bullet.

Kugellager (pl -) das ball bearing.

Kugelschreiber (pl -) der ballpoint pen, Biro®.

Kugelstoßen das shot put.

Kuh (pl Kühe) die cow.

kühl ♦ adj cool. ♦ adv coolly.

kühlen vt to cool.

Kühler (pl -) der (AUTO) radiator.

Kühlerhaube (*pl* **-n**) *die* (AUTO) bonnet (Br), hood (Am).

Kühlschrank (*pl* **-schränke**) *der* fridge.

Kühltasche (*pl* **-n**) *die* cool bag.

Kühltruhe (*pl* **-n**) *die* freezer.

Kühlung (*pl* **-en**) *die* (Kühlen) cooling; (TECH) cooling system.

Kühlwasser *das* (AUTO) radiator water.

Küken (*pl* **-**) *das* (Tier) chick.

kulant *adj* obliging.

Kuli (*pl* **-s**) *der* (fam) Biro®.

kultiviert *adj* cultivated.

Kultur (*pl* **-en**) *die* culture.

Kulturbeutel (*pl* **-**) *der* toilet bag.

kulturell *adj* cultural.

Kümmel *der* (Gewürz) caraway seed.

Kummer *der* (Ärger) trouble; (Leiden) grief, sorrow; **jm ~ machen** to cause sb trouble.

kümmern *vt* (Person) to concern; **jn nicht ~** not to bother sb. ▸ **sich kümmern** *ref*: **sich ~ um** (um Person) to look after; (um Arbeit, Gegenstand) to see to; (um Klatsch, Angelegenheit) to worry about.

Kunde (*pl* **-n**) *der* customer; **'nur für ~n'** 'patrons only'.

Kundendienst *der* customer service.

Kundendienststelle (*pl* **-n**) *die* customer service point.

Kundenkarte (*pl* **-n**) *die* (von Bank) bank card; (von Geschäft) discount card (for regular customers).

Kundennummer (*pl* **-n**) *die* customer number.

Kundenparkplatz (*pl* **-plätze**) *der* customer car park.

Kundenservice *der* customer service.

kündigen ◆ *vt* (Vertrag) to terminate. ◆ *vi* to give notice; **jm ~** to give sb his notice; **die Arbeitsstelle ~** to hand in one's notice; **jm die Wohnung ~** to give sb notice to leave.

Kündigung (*pl* **-en**) *die* (von Vertrag, Kredit) cancellation; (von Wohnung, Arbeitsstelle) notice.

Kündigungsfrist (*pl* **-en**) *die* period of notice.

Kündigungsschutz *der* (für Mieter) protection against wrongful eviction; (für Arbeitnehmer) protection against wrongful dismissal.

Kundin (*pl* **-nen**) *die* customer.

Kunst (*pl* **Künste**) *die* art.

Kunstakademie (*pl* **-n**) *die* art college.

Kunstausstellung (*pl* **-en**) *die* art exhibition.

Kunstfaser (*pl* **-n**) *die* synthetic fibre.

Kunstgalerie (*pl* **-n**) *die* art gallery.

Kunstgewerbe *das* arts and crafts (*pl*).

Kunsthalle (*pl* **-n**) *die* art gallery.

Kunsthandwerk (*pl* **-e**) *das* craft.

Künstler, -in (*mpl* **-**) *der*, *die* artist.

künstlerisch *adj* artistic.

Künstlername (*pl* **-n**) *der* (von Schauspieler, Sänger) stage name.

künstlich *adj* artificial.

Kunstmuseum (*pl* **-museen**) *das* art gallery.

Kunststoff (*pl* **-e**) *der* (Plastik) plastic.

Kunststück (*pl* **-e**) *das* trick.

Kunstwerk (*pl* **-e**) *das* work of art.

Kupfer *das* copper.

Kuppel (*pl* **-n**) *die* dome.

Kupplung (*pl* **-en**) *die* clutch; **die ~ treten** to depress the clutch.

Kupplungspedal (*pl* **-e**) *das* clutch pedal.

Kur (*pl* **-en**) *die* cure (at a health resort); **in** ODER **zur ~ sein** to take a cure (at a health resort).

Kurbel (*pl* **-n**) *die* crank; (an Fenster) winder.

Kürbis (*pl* **-se**) *der* pumpkin.

Kurfestiger (*pl* **-**) *der* setting lotion.

Kurgast (*pl* **-gäste**) *der* visitor at a health resort.

kurieren *vt* (*Krankheit*) to cure.

Kurkonzert (*pl* **-e**) *das* concert at a spa.

Kurort (*pl* **-e**) *der* (*Badeort*) spa; (*in den Bergen*) health resort.

Kurpackung (*pl* **-en**) *die* hair conditioner.

Kurpark (*pl* **-s**) *der* spa gardens (*pl*).

Kurs (*pl* **-e**) *der* (*Unterricht, Richtung*) course; (*von Aktie*) price; (*von Devise*) exchange rate.

Kursbuch (*pl* **-bücher**) *das* timetable.

Kurschatten (*pl* **-**) *der person with whom one has a fling whilst at a health resort.*

Kursus (*pl* **Kurse**) *der* course.

Kurswagen (*pl* **-**) *der* through carriage.

Kurtaxe (*pl* **-n**) *die tax paid by visitors to health resorts, in exchange for which they receive reductions on certain services.*

Kurve (*pl* **-n**) *die* (*Linie*) curve; (*von Straße*) bend; **scharfe ~** sharp bend.

kurvenreich *adj* winding.

Kurverwaltung (*pl* **-en**) *die* spa administration.

kurz (*komp* **kürzer**, *superl* **am kürzesten**) ◆ *adj* short. ◆ *adv* (*zeitlich*) briefly; (*schnell*) quickly; **~ vor/hinter** just in front of/behind; **~ vor dem Konzert** shortly before the concert; **vor ~em** recently; **sich ~ fassen** to be brief; **~ und bündig** concisely.

kurzärmelig *adj* short-sleeved.

kürzen *vt* (*Kleidung*) to shorten; (*Haare, Nägel, Zahlungen*) to cut.

kurzfristig ◆ *adj* (*Absage, Kündigung*) sudden; (*Vertrag*) short-term; (*Entscheidung, Abreise*) quick. ◆ *adv* at short notice.

Kurzgeschichte (*pl* **-n**) *die* short story.

kurzhaarig *adj* short-haired.

kürzlich *adv* recently.

Kurznachrichten *pl* news in brief (*sg*).

Kurzparken *das* short-stay parking.

Kurzparker (*pl* **-**) *der driver who parks for a short period of time.*

Kurzparkzone (*pl* **-n**) *die* short-stay parking zone.

Kurzschluß (*pl* **-schlüsse**) *der* short-circuit.

kurzsichtig *adj* short-sighted.

Kurzstrecke (*pl* **-n**) *die short journey on public transport, within city centre.*

Kurzstreckenkarte (*pl* **-n**) *die ticket valid for a 'Kurzstrecke'.*

Kurzstreckentarif (*pl* **-e**) *der rate for 'Kurzstrecke' tickets.*

Kurzurlaub (*pl* **-e**) *der* short break.

Kurzwelle *die* short wave.

Kurzzeitparken *das* short-stay parking.

Kurzzeitparkplatz (*pl* **-plätze**) *der* short-stay car park.

Kuß (*pl* **Küsse**) *der* kiss.

küssen *vt* to kiss. ▶ **sich küssen** *ref* to kiss.

Küste (*pl* **-n**) *die* coast; **an der ~** at the seaside.

Küstenwache (*pl* **-n**) *die* coastguard.

Kutsche (*pl* **-n**) *die* coach.

Kuvert (*pl* **-s**) *das* envelope.

Kuvertüre (*pl* **-n**) *die* chocolate icing.

L

Labor (*pl* **-s**) *das* laboratory.

Labyrinth (*pl* **-e**) *das* labyrinth.

lächeln *vi* to smile; **~ über** (+A) to smile at.

lachen *vi* to laugh; **~ über** (+A) to laugh at.

lächerlich adj ridiculous.

Lachs (pl -e) der salmon.

Lack (pl -e) der (farbig) paint; (farblos) varnish.

lackieren vt (Holz) to varnish; (Auto) to spray; **sich** (D) **die Nägel ~** to paint one's nails.

Lackierung (pl -en) die (farbig) paint; (farblos) varnish.

Ladefläche (pl -n) die capacity (of lorry).

laden (präs lädt, prät lud, pp geladen) vt to load; **auf sich ~** (Verantwortung) to take on.

Laden (pl Läden) der (Geschäft) shop; (am Fenster) shutter.

Ladendieb, -in (mpl -e) der, die shoplifter.

Ladendiebstahl (pl -stähle) der shoplifting; **'gegen ~ gesichert'** 'security cameras in operation'.

Ladenpreis (pl -e) der shop price.

Ladenschluß der (shop) closing time.

Ladenschlußgesetz das shop closing hours act.

Ladenschlußzeiten pl shop closing times.

LADENSCHLUSSZEITEN

In Germany, shop opening hours are governed by law. Shops can stay open until 8 pm on weekdays and until 4 pm on Saturdays, and some can open on Sundays. The new regulations, which came into effect in 1996, replace the far stricter laws previously in force prohibiting shops from staying open after 6.30 pm on weekdays (except for Thursdays when there was late-night shopping until 8.30 pm) and after 2 pm on Saturdays. Some shops have not changed their opening hours.

---

lädt präs → **laden**.

Ladung (pl -en) die (Fracht) cargo; (Munition) charge.

lag prät → **liegen**.

Lage (pl -n) die situation, position; (Schicht) layer; **in der ~ sein, etw zu tun** to be in a position to do sthg.

Lageplan (pl -pläne) der map.

Lager (pl -) das (für Waren) warehouse; (Camp) camp.

Lagerfeuer (pl -) das campfire.

lagern vt (Lebensmittel, Waren) to store.

Lähmung (pl -en) die (Krankheit) paralysis.

Laib (pl -e) der loaf.

Laie (pl -n) der layman (laywoman).

Laken (pl -) das sheet.

Lakritz (pl -en) die liquorice.

Lamm (pl Lämmer) das lamb.

Lammfleisch das lamb.

Lammkeule (pl -n) die leg of lamb.

Lammrücken (pl -) der saddle of lamb.

Lampe (pl -n) die (in Raum) lamp; (an Fahrrad) light.

Lampenschirm (pl -e) der lampshade.

Lampion (pl -s) der Chinese lantern.

Land (pl Länder) das (Nation, nicht Stadt) country; (Bundesland) state; (Festland) land; **auf dem ~** in the country.

Landbrot (pl -e) das brown rye bread with a hard crust.

Landebahn (pl -en) die runway.

Landeerlaubnis die clearance to land.

landen vi ist to land.

Landeplatz (pl -plätze) der landing strip.

Landesfarben pl national colours.

Landeshauptstadt (pl -städte) die capital (of federal state).

Landesinnere das interior (of a country).

Landesregierung (pl -en) die state government.

Landessprache (pl -n) die national language.

landesüblich adj (Tracht, Gericht)

national, typical of the country.
Landeswährung (*pl* **-en**) *die* national currency.
Landhaus (*pl* **-häuser**) *das* country house.
Landkarte (*pl* **-n**) *die* map.
Landkreis (*pl* **-e**) *der* district.
ländlich *adj* rural.
Landschaft (*pl* **-en**) *die* countryside; (*in Kunst*) landscape.
landschaftlich *adj* (*regional*) regional.
Landschaftsschutzgebiet (*pl* **-e**) *das* nature reserve.
Landsleute *pl* compatriots.
Landstraße (*pl* **-n**) *die* country road.
Landtag (*pl* **-e**) *der* state parliament.
Landung (*pl* **-en**) *die* (*von Flugzeug*) landing.
Landwein (*pl* **-e**) *der* table wine.
Landwirt, -in (*mpl* **-e**) *der, die* farmer.
Landwirtschaft *die* agriculture.
lang (*komp* **länger**, *superl* **am längsten**) ◆ *adj* long; (*Person*) tall. ◆ *adv* (*fam: entlang*) along; (*groß*) tall; **den ganzen Tag ~** all day; **drei Meter ~** three metres long; **es dauerte drei Tage ~** it lasted for three days; **hier/dort ~** this/that way.
langärmelig *adj* long-sleeved.
lange (*komp* **längere**, *superl* **längste**) *adv* (*während langer Zeit*) a long time; (*seit langer Zeit*) for a long time; **es hat ~ gedauert** it lasted a long time; **das Wetter war ~ nicht so gut** the weather hasn't been so good for a long time; **es ist ~ her** it was a long time ago; **wie ~?** how long?
Länge (*pl* **-n**) *die* length; (*von Person*) height; **der ~ nach** lengthways; **von drei km/sechs Stunden ~** three km/six hours long.
Längenmaß (*pl* **-e**) *das* unit of length.
Langeweile *die* boredom.
langfristig ◆ *adj* long-term. ◆ *adv* (*planen*) for the long term.

Langlauf *der* cross-country skiing.
Langlaufski (*pl* **-er**) *der* cross-country ski.
langsam ◆ *adj* slow. ◆ *adv* slowly.
Langschläfer, -in (*mpl* **-**) *der, die* late riser.
längst *adv* for a long time; **~ nicht so gut** nowhere near as good.
Langstreckenlauf *der* long-distance running.
Languste (*pl* **-n**) *die* crayfish.
langweilen *vt* to bore. ▸ **sich langweilen** *ref* to be bored.
langweilig *adj* boring.
Langwelle *die* long wave.
langwierig *adj* lengthy.
Langzeitparker (*pl* **-**) *der* long-stay parker.
Lappen (*pl* **-**) *der* (*zum Wischen*) cloth.
Lärche (*pl* **-n**) *die* (*Baum*) larch.
Lärm *der* noise.
lärmen *vi* to be noisy.
Lärmschutz *der* (*Vorrichtung*) soundproof barrier.
Lärmschutzmauer (*pl* **-n**) *die* soundproof wall.
las *prät* → **lesen**.
Lasche (*pl* **-n**) *die* loop.
Laser (*pl* **-**) *der* laser.
lassen (*präs* **läßt**, *prät* **ließ**, *pp* **gelassen** ODER **lassen**) ◆ *aux* 1. (*veranlassen*): **etw machen** ODER **tun ~** to have sthg done; **jn etw tun ~** to have sb do sthg; **sich** (D) **einen Anzug machen ~** to have a suit made; **sich** (D) **die Haare schneiden ~** to have one's hair cut. 2. (*zulassen*): **jn etw tun ~** to let sb do sthg; **~ wir uns überraschen** we'll see; **es läßt sich machen** it can be done; **es läßt sich trinken** it's drinkable; **etw mit sich machen ~** to put up with sthg; **etw nicht mit sich machen ~** not to stand for sthg. 3. (*geschehen lassen*): **die Milch kochen ~** to leave the milk to boil; **die Vase fallen ~** to drop the vase; **jn warten ~** to keep sb waiting. ◆ *vt* (*pp* **gelassen**) 1. (*unterlassen*) to stop; **das Rauchen sein ~** to stop smoking; **laß**

das! stop it! **2.** (*belassen*) to leave; **laß bitte alles so, wie es ist** leave everything as it is; **jn (in Ruhe) ~** to leave sb alone. **3.** (*gehen lassen*) to let; **jn nicht ins Haus ~** not to let sb in the house. **4.** (*überlassen*): **jm etw ~** to let sb have sthg. **5.** (*zurücklassen*) to leave; **das habe ich zu Hause gelassen** I left it at home. **6.** (*loslassen*) to let go; **laß mich!** let me go! **7.** (*strömen lassen*) to let; **Wasser in die Badewanne ~** to run a bath; **die Luft aus den Reifen ~** to let the tyres down. ◆ *vi* (*pp* **gelassen**) **1.** (*aufgeben*): **von jm/etw ~** (*geh*) to drop sb/sthg; **er ließ schnell von dem Projekt** he quickly dropped the project. **2.** (*seinlassen*): **laß mal, ich mach das schon** leave it, I'll do it; **laß mal, du bist heute eingeladen** no, I'm paying today.

lässig *adj* casual.

läßt *präs* → **lassen**.

Last (*pl* **-en**) *die* (*Traglast*) load; (*psychisch*) burden.

Lastenaufzug (*pl* **-aufzüge**) *der* goods lift (Br), goods elevator (Am).

Laster (*pl* **-**) *der* (*LKW*) lorry.

lästern *vi* to make nasty remarks.

lästig *adj* annoying.

Lastkraftwagen (*pl* **-**) *der* (*amt*) heavy goods vehicle.

Lastschiff (*pl* **-e**) *das* freighter.

Lastschrift (*pl* **-en**) *die* debit.

Lastwagen (*pl* **-**) *der* lorry.

Latein *das* Latin.

Laterne (*pl* **-n**) *die* (*Straßenlaterne*) streetlight; (*Lampion*) Chinese lantern.

Lätzchen (*pl* **-**) *das* bib.

Latzhose (*pl* **-n**) *die* dungarees (*pl*).

lau *adj* (*Wasser*) lukewarm; (*Abend*) mild.

Laub *das* (*auf Baum*) foliage; (*auf Erde*) dead leaves (*pl*).

Lauch *der* leek.

lauern *vi*: **~ auf** (+A) (*im Hinterhalt*) to lie in wait for; (*auf Chance, Vorteil*) to wait for.

Lauf (*pl* **Läufe**) *der* (*Verlauf*) course; (SPORT) race; **im ~e des Tages** in the course of the day; **im ~e der Zeit** in the course of time.

laufen (*präs* **läuft**, *prät* **lief**, *pp* **gelaufen**) ◆ *vi ist* **1.** (*schnell*) to run. **2.** (*gehen*) to walk. **3.** (*Motor, Maschine*) to run. **4.** (*funktionieren*) to work. **5.** (*fließen*) to run; **mir läuft die Nase** my nose is running. **6.** (*andauern*) to go on. **7.** (*Film, Drama*) to run; **der Film läuft schon seit zehn Minuten** the film started ten minutes ago; **was läuft im Kino?** what's on at the cinema? ◆ *vt ist* **1.** (*schnell*) to run; **den Marathon ~** to run the marathon. **2.** (*gehen*) to walk. **3.** (SPORT): **Ski ~** to ski; **Schlittschuh ~** to skate.

laufend ◆ *adj* (*Wechsel*) constant; (*Kosten, Motor, Gerät*) running; (*Monat, Jahr*) current. ◆ *adv* (*ständig*) regularly.

Läufer (*pl* **-**) *der* (*Sportler*) runner; (*Teppich*) rug.

Läuferin (*pl* **-nen**) *die* runner.

Laufmasche (*pl* **-n**) *die* ladder (Br), run (Am).

läuft *präs* → **laufen**.

Laufzeit (*pl* **-en**) *die* (*von Film*) running time.

Lauge (*pl* **-n**) *die* (*zum Waschen*) soapy water.

Laugenbrezel (*pl* **-n**) *die* pretzel.

Laune (*pl* **-n**) *die* (*Stimmung*) mood; **gute/schlechte ~ haben** to be in a good/bad mood.

launisch *adj* moody.

Laus (*pl* **Läuse**) *die* louse.

lauschen *vi* (*konzentriert*) to listen; (*heimlich*) to eavesdrop.

laut ◆ *adj* loud. ◆ *adv* loudly. ◆ *prep* (+G *or* +D) (*amt*) according to.

läuten ◆ *vi* to ring. ◆ *vimp*: **es läutet** the bell is ringing.

lauter *det* nothing but; **aus ~ Dankbarkeit** out of sheer gratitude.

Lautsprecher (*pl* **-**) *der* loudspeaker.

Lautsprecherdurchsage (*pl* **-n**) *die* announcement over the loudspeaker.

Lautstärke *die* volume.
lauwarm *adj* lukewarm.
Lawine (*pl* -n) *die* avalanche.
Lawinengefahr *die* danger of an avalanche.
Leasing (*pl* -s) *das* leasing.
leben *vi* to live; ~ **von** (*Nahrungsmittel*) to live on; (*Tätigkeit*) to make one's living from.
Leben (*pl* -) *das* life; **am ~ sein/bleiben** to be/stay alive; **sich das ~ nehmen** to take one's (own) life; **ums ~ kommen** to die.
lebendig *adj* (*lebhaft*) lively; (*lebend*) alive.
Lebensalter *das* age.
Lebensbedingungen *pl* living conditions.
Lebensgefahr *die*: **'Lebensgefahr!'** 'danger'; **außer ~ sein** to be out of danger; **er ist in ~** his life is at risk.
lebensgefährlich *adj* (*Unternehmen*) very dangerous; (*Krankheit*) critical.
Lebensgefährte, -gefährtin (*mpl* -en) *der, die* companion.
Lebensjahr (*pl* -e) *das*: **im vierten ~** four years old.
lebenslänglich *adj* life (*vor Subst*).
Lebenslauf (*pl* -läufe) *der* curriculum vitae.
lebenslustig *adj* full of life.
Lebensmittel *pl* food (*sg*).
Lebensmittelgeschäft (*pl* -e) *das* grocer's (shop).
Lebensmittelvergiftung (*pl* -en) *die* food poisoning.
lebensnotwendig *adj* essential to life.
Lebensretter, -in (*mpl* -) *der, die* lifesaver.
Lebensunterhalt *der* living, livelihood.
Lebensversicherung (*pl* -en) *die* life assurance.
lebenswichtig *adj* essential.
Lebenszeichen (*pl* -) *das* sign of life.

Leber (*pl* -n) *die* liver.
Leberfleck (*pl* **Leberflecken**) *der* liver spot.
Leberknödel (*pl* -) *der* liver dumpling.
Leberpastete (*pl* -n) *die* liver pâté.
Leberwurst (*pl* -würste) *die* liver sausage.
Lebewesen (*pl* -) *das* living thing.
lebhaft *adj* lively.
Lebkuchen (*pl* -) *der* gingerbread.

LEBKUCHEN

A type of gingerbread, 'Lebkuchen' is made with honey and a mixture of spices including cinnamon, cloves, nutmeg and aniseed. The most famous 'Lebkuchen' is a spongy variety from Nuremberg, which is usually eaten at Christmas. 'Lebkuchen' normally comes in the form of small hearts, stars or round biscuits but, particularly at funfairs, it is also sold as large hearts decorated with icing.

leck *adj* (*Schiff*) leaky.
Leck (*pl* -s) *das* leak.
lecken ◆ *vi* to leak. ◆ *vt* to lick.
lecker *adj* delicious.
Leckerbissen (*pl* -) *der* (*Speise*) delicacy.
Leder *das* leather.
Lederhose (*pl* -n) *die* lederhosen (*pl*), short leather trousers with braces.
Lederwaren *pl* leather goods.
ledig *adj* (*unverheiratet*) single.
lediglich *adv* only.
leer *adj* empty; (*Blatt, Heft*) blank; **etw ~ machen** (*Behälter, Raum*) to empty sthg.
Leergut *das* empties (*pl*).
Leerlauf *der* (*von Auto, Fahrrad*) neutral; **im ~** in neutral.
Leerung (*pl* -en) *die* (*von Briefkästen*) collection; **'nächste ~ 17 Uhr'** 'next collection at 5 pm'.
legal *adj* legal.

legen vt 1. (ablegen) to put; **leg den Schlüssel auf den Tisch** put the key on the table. 2. (waagerecht hinlegen) to lay; **du mußt die Flaschen ins Regal ~, nicht stellen** you should lay the bottles flat in the rack rather than upright. 3. (installieren) to lay. 4. (Termin) to arrange; **den Urlaub auf Juli ~** to arrange one's holidays for July. 5. (Haare) to set; **sich (D) die Haare ~ lassen** to have one's hair set. 6. (Eier) to lay. ▶ **sich legen** ref 1. (sich hinlegen) to lie down. 2. (aufhören) to die down.

Legende (pl -n) die legend.

legitim adj (Forderungen, Interesse) legitimate.

Lehm der clay.

Lehne (pl -n) die (Rückenlehne) back (of chair).

lehnen vt & vi to lean. ▶ **sich lehnen** ref to lean; **sich ~ an** (+A) to lean against.

Lehramt das teaching profession; **~ studieren** to study to be a teacher.

Lehrbuch (pl -bücher) das textbook.

Lehre (pl -n) die (Ausbildung) apprenticeship; (Erfahrung) lesson; (religiös, politisch) doctrine.

lehren vt to teach.

Lehrer, -in (mpl -) der, die teacher.

Lehrgang (pl -gänge) der course.

Lehrling (pl -e) der apprentice.

Leib (pl -er) der body.

Leibgericht (pl -e) das favourite meal.

Leiche (pl -n) die corpse.

leicht ◆ adj light; (Aufgabe, Arbeit) easy; (Erkrankung) slight; (Zigaretten) mild. ◆ adv (einfach, schnell) easily; (regnen, erkältet) slightly; **~ bekleidet** wearing summer clothes.

Leichtathletik die athletics (sg).

leicht|fallen vi unr ist to be easy; **jm ~** to be easy for sb.

leichtsinnig adj careless.

leid adj: **er tut mir ~** I feel sorry for him; **es tut mir ~!** I'm sorry!; **es ~ sein,**

etw zu tun to be tired of doing sthg.

Leid das sorrow.

leiden (prät litt, pp gelitten) vt & vi to suffer; **~ an** (+D) to suffer from; **ich kann ihn/es nicht ~** I can't stand him/it.

leidenschaftlich adj passionate.

leider adv unfortunately.

Leihbücherei (pl -en) die (lending) library.

leihen (prät lieh, pp geliehen) vt (ausleihen) to borrow; **jm etw ~** to lend sb sthg; **sich (D) etw ~** to borrow sthg.

Leihfrist (pl -en) die hire period.

Leihgebühr (pl -en) die hire charge.

Leihwagen (pl -) der hire car.

Leim der glue.

Leine (pl -n) die (Seil) cord; (für Wäsche) (washing) line; (Hundeleine) lead.

Leinen das linen.

Leinsamen der linseed.

Leinwand (pl -wände) die (im Kino) screen; (zum Malen) canvas.

Leipziger Allerlei das mixed vegetables including peas, carrots and green beans.

leise ◆ adj (Geräusch) quiet. ◆ adv quietly.

leisten vt (vollbringen) to achieve; (Beitrag, Zahlung) to make; **sich (D) etw ~** (sich kaufen) to treat o.s. to sthg; **sich (D) etw ~ können** to be able to afford sthg.

Leistung (pl -en) die (Arbeit) performance; (Zahlung) payment.

leistungsfähig adj efficient.

Leistungskurs (pl -e) der (SCHULE) one of the subjects which pupils choose to specialize in for their 'Abitur'.

Leistungssport der competitive sport.

Leitartikel (pl -) der leader.

leiten vt (Team) to lead; (Firma) to run; (Strom) to conduct; (Wasser, Verkehr) to divert.

Leiter[1] (pl -n) die (mit Sprossen) ladder.

Leiter² (pl -) der (von Gruppe) leader; (von Firma) manager.

Leiterin (pl -nen) die (von Gruppe) leader; (von Firma) manager.

Leitfaden (pl -fäden) der introductory guide.

Leitplanke (pl -n) die crash barrier.

Leitung (pl -en) die (von Firma) management; (Telefonleitung) line; (Stromleitung) wire; (Wasserleitung) pipe; **unter der ~ von** (Orchester) conducted by.

Leitungsrohr (pl -e) das (water)pipe.

Leitungswasser das tap water.

Lektion (pl -en) die (Kapitel) lesson.

Lektüre (pl -n) die reading.

lenken vt & vi to steer.

Lenker (pl -) der (Lenkrad) steering wheel; (Lenkstange) handlebars (pl).

Lenkrad (pl -räder) das steering wheel.

Lenkradschloß (pl -schlösser) das steering lock.

Lenkstange (pl -n) die handlebars (pl).

Lenkung (pl -en) die (am Fahrzeug) steering.

lernen ♦ vt to learn; (Beruf) to train as. ♦ vi (für Prüfung) to study; (in Lehre) to train; (aus Erfahrung) to learn.

lesbisch adj lesbian.

Lesebuch (pl -bücher) das reader.

lesen (präs liest, prät las, pp gelesen) vt & vi to read.

Leser, -in (mpl -) der, die reader.

letzte¹ adj last.

letzte², -r, -s det last; **~s Jahr** last year.

Letzte (pl -n) der, die (Person): **der/die ~** the last; **~ werden** to come last.

letztemal adv: **das ~** the last time.

letztenmal adv: **zum ~** for the last time.

letztens adv (vor kurzem) recently.

leuchten vi to shine.

Leuchter (pl -) der (für Kerzen) candlestick.

Leuchtstift (pl -e) der highlighter.

Leuchtstoffröhre (pl -n) die strip light.

Leuchtturm (pl -türme) der lighthouse.

leugnen ♦ vt (Tat, Schuld) to deny. ♦ vi (Angeklagter) to deny everything.

Leukämie die leukaemia.

Leute pl people.

Lexikon (pl Lexika) das (Enzyklopädie) encyclopaedia; (Wörterbuch) dictionary.

liberal adj liberal.

Licht (pl -er) das light; **~ machen** to put the light on; **das ~ ausmachen** to turn the light off; **offenes ~** naked flame.

lichtempfindlich adj (Film) photosensitive.

Lichthupe die: **die ~ betätigen** to flash one's headlights.

Lichtmaschine (pl -n) die alternator.

Lichtschalter (pl -) der light switch.

Lichtschranke (pl -n) die photoelectric beam.

Lichtschutzfaktor (pl -en) der factor (of suntan lotion).

Lichtstrahl (pl -en) der ray of light.

Lichtung (pl -en) die clearing.

Lid (pl -er) das eyelid.

Lidschatten (pl -) der eyeshadow.

lieb adj (nett) kind; (als Anrede) dear; **jn ~ haben** to be fond of sb; **~er Karl-Heinz!** (in Brief) Dear Karl-Heinz.

Liebe die love.

lieben vt to love; (sexuell) to make love to. ► **sich lieben** ref (liebhaben) to be in love; (sexuell) to make love.

liebenswürdig ♦ adj kind. ♦ adv kindly.

lieber ♦ komp rather, → **gern**. ♦ adv (besser) better. ♦ adj (angenehmer): **ein warmes Essen wäre mir ~** I'd prefer a hot meal; **das hättest du ~ nicht sagen sollen** it would have been better if you hadn't said that.

Liebesbrief (*pl* -e) *der* love letter.
Liebespaar (*pl* -e) *das* couple (*of lovers*).
liebevoll *adj* loving.
lieb|haben *vt unr* to love. ▶ **sich liebhaben** *ref* (*sich gern haben*) to be in love; (*erotisch*) to make love.
Liebhaber (*pl* -) *der* lover.
Liebhaberin (*pl* -nen) *die* lover.
lieblich *adj* (*Wein*) sweet.
Liebling (*pl* -e) *der* (*Anrede*) darling.
Lieblingsgericht (*pl* -e) *das* favourite meal.
lieblos *adj* unloving.
Liebste (*pl* -n) *der, die* sweetheart.
liebsten *superl* → **gern**; **am ~** best of all; **das ist mir am ~** I like it best of all.
Liechtenstein *nt* Liechtenstein.
Lied (*pl* -er) *das* song; (RELIG) hymn.
lief *prät* → **laufen**.
Lieferant (*pl* -en) *der* (*Person*) deliveryman; (*Firma*) supplier; '**~en frei**' 'except for loading'.
lieferbar *adj* available.
Lieferfrist (*pl* -en) *die* delivery time.
liefern ◆ *vt* (*Ware*) to deliver; (*Beispiel, Argument*) to provide. ◆ *vi* (*Geschäft*) to deliver; **wir ~ frei Haus** we deliver free to your home.
Lieferung (*pl* -en) *die* delivery.
Lieferwagen (*pl* -) *der* van.
Liege (*pl* -n) *die* camp bed; (*für Garten*) sun lounger.
liegen (*präs* **liegt**, *prät* **lag**, *pp* **gelegen**) *vi* 1. (*Person, Gegenstand*) to lie. 2. (*sich befinden*) to be; **Bonn liegt am Rhein** Bonn is on the Rhine. 3. (*zeitlich*) to be; **das liegt lange zurück** that was a long time ago. 4. (*in Reihenfolge*) to lie; **sie liegt auf dem vierten Platz** she's lying in fourth place. 5. (*Grund, Ursache*): **sein Asthma liegt an der schlechten Luft** his asthma is caused by the poor air; **der Fehler liegt an dir** the mistake is your fault. 6. (*abhängen*): **das liegt bei dir** it's up to you. 7. (*wichtig sein*): **es**

liegt mir viel daran it matters a lot to me. 8. (*begabt sein für*): **Physik liegt mir nicht** physics isn't my subject.
liegen|bleiben *vi unr ist* (*nicht aufstehen*) to stay in bed; (*vergessen werden*) to be left behind; (*Arbeit*) to be left undone; (*fam: mit Auto, Bus*) to break down.
liegen|lassen *vt unr* to leave.
Liegesitz (*pl* -e) *der* reclining seat.
Liegestuhl (*pl* -stühle) *der* (*am Strand*) deck chair; (*im Garten*) sun lounger.
Liegestütz (*pl* -e) *die* press-up.
Liegewagen (*pl* -) *der* couchette car.
Liegewagenplatz (*pl* -plätze) *der* couchette.
Liegewiese (*pl* -n) *die* lawn.
lieh *prät* → **leihen**.
ließ *prät* → **lassen**.
liest *präs* → **lesen**.
Lift (*pl* -e) *der* (*Aufzug*) lift (Br), elevator (Am); (*Skilift*) ski lift.
light *adj* (*Nahrungsmittel*) low-calorie; (*Cola*) diet (*vor Subst*); (*Zigaretten*) mild.
Likör (*pl* -e) *der* liqueur.
lila *adj* light purple, lilac.
Limo (*pl* -s) *die* (*fam*) fizzy drink.
Limonade (*pl* -n) *die* fizzy drink.
Linde (*pl* -n) *die* (*Baum*) lime tree.
lindern *vt* to relieve.
Lineal (*pl* -e) *das* ruler.
Linie (*pl* -n) *die* line; (*Bus, Straßenbahn*) number; **in erster ~** first and foremost.
Linienbus (*pl* -se) *der* regular bus.
Linienflug (*pl* -flüge) *der* scheduled flight.
Linienmaschine (*pl* -n) *die* scheduled plane.
Linienverkehr *der* (*Flugverkehr*) scheduled flights (*pl*).
link *adj* (*abw*) sly.
linke, -r, -s *adj* (*Seite*) left; (*Politik*) left-wing.
links *adv* (*Seitenangabe*) on the left;

(Richtungsangabe) left; (wählen) for the left; ~ **von jm/etw** on sb's/sthg's left; **nach ~** left; **von ~** from the left.

Linksabbieger (pl -) der car turning left.

linksherum adv (nach links) round to the left; (verkehrtherum) the wrong way round.

Linkskurve (pl -n) die left-hand bend.

Linkssteuerung (pl -en) die left-hand drive.

Linksverkehr der driving on the left.

Linse (pl -n) die (Gemüse) lentil; (in Kamera) lens.

Linsensuppe (pl -n) die lentil soup.

Lippe (pl -n) die lip.

Lippenstift (pl -e) der lipstick.

List (pl -en) die (Trick) trick.

Liste (pl -n) die list.

Liter (pl -) der litre.

Literatur (pl -en) die literature.

Literflasche (pl -n) die litre bottle.

Litfaßsäule (pl -n) die advertising column.

litt prät → **leiden**.

Lizenz (pl -en) die (Erlaubnis) licence.

LKW (pl -s) der HGV.

Lob das (von Person) praise.

loben vt to praise.

Loch (pl Löcher) das hole.

lochen vt to punch a hole/holes in.

Locher (pl -) der hole punch.

Locke (pl -n) die curl.

Lockenschere (pl -n) die curling tongs (pl).

Lockenwickler (pl -) der curler.

locker ◆ adj loose; (Haltung) laid-back; (Beziehung) casual. ◆ adv (knoten) loosely; (fam: leicht, einfach) easily.

lockern vt (Knoten) to loosen. ► **sich lockern** ref (Knoten, Schraube) to work itself loose.

lockig adj curly.

Löffel (pl -) der spoon.

Löffelbisquit (pl -s) der sponge finger.

löffeln vt to spoon.

log prät → **lügen**.

Loge (pl -n) die box (at theatre).

logisch adj logical.

Lohn (pl Löhne) der (Bezahlung) wages (pl), pay; (Belohnung) reward.

lohnen: sich lohnen ref to be worth it.

Lohnsteuer die income tax.

Lohnsteuerkarte (pl -n) die form filled in by employer stating annual income and tax paid, = P60 (Br).

Loipe (pl -n) die cross-country ski run.

Lok (pl -s) die = **Lokomotive**.

lokal adj local.

Lokal (pl -e) das pub.

Lokalnachrichten pl local news (sg).

Lokomotive (pl -n) die locomotive.

London nt London.

Los (pl -e) das (von Lotterie) ticket.

los ◆ adj (lose) loose. ◆ interj come on!; **es ist viel/wenig/nichts ~** there is a lot/not much/nothing going on; **jn/etw ~ sein** to have got rid of sb/sthg; **was ist ~?** what's the matter?

löschen vt (Feuer) to put out, to extinguish; (Aufnahme) to erase; (Daten) to delete.

Löschpapier das blotting paper.

lose ◆ adj loose. ◆ adv loosely.

losen vi to draw lots.

lösen vt (Fahrkarte, Eintrittskarte) to buy; (Aufgabe, Rätsel) to solve; (Knoten) to undo; (Bremse) to take off; (auflösen) to dissolve. ► **sich lösen** ref (sich lockern) to become loose; (Problem) to be solved; (sich auflösen) to dissolve.

los|fahren vi unr ist to set off.

los|gehen vi unr ist (Person) to set off; (Veranstaltung) to start.

los|lassen vt unr (Person, Gegenstand) to let go of.

löslich adj (Kaffee) instant.

los|machen vt to untie.

Lösung (pl -en) die solution.

los|werden vt unr ist (Person, Grippe) to get rid of; (Geld) to lose.

Lotion (pl -en) die lotion.

lotsen vt to guide.

Lotterie (pl -n) die lottery.

Lotto das national lottery.

Lottoschein (pl -e) der national lottery ticket.

Löwe (pl -n) der (Tier) lion; (Sternzeichen) Leo.

Löwenzahn der dandelion.

Lücke (pl -n) die gap.

lud prät → **laden**.

Luft die air; frische ~ fresh air.

Luftballon (pl -s) der balloon.

luftdicht adj airtight.

Luftdruck der air pressure.

lüften ◆ vt (Zimmer) to air. ◆ vi (im Zimmer) to let some air in.

Luftfahrtgesellschaft (pl -en) die airline.

Luftfeuchtigkeit die humidity.

Luftfilter (pl -) der air filter.

Luftfracht die air freight.

Luftkissenboot (pl -e) das hovercraft.

Luftkurort (pl -e) der health resort.

Luftlinie die: (es sind) 100 km ~ (it's) 100 km as the crow flies.

Luftmatratze (pl -n) die airbed.

Luftpost die airmail; per ~ (by) airmail.

Luftpumpe (pl -n) die air pump.

Luftröhre (pl -n) die windpipe.

Luftschlange (pl -n) die streamer.

Lüftung (pl -en) die (Gerät) ventilation (system).

Luftverkehr der air traffic.

Luftverschmutzung die air pollution.

Luftzug der draught.

Lüge (pl -n) die lie.

lügen (prät log, pp gelogen) vi to lie.

Lügner, -in (mpl -) der, die liar.

Lunchpaket (pl -e) das packed lunch.

Lunge (pl -n) die lungs (pl).

Lungenentzündung (pl -en) die pneumonia.

Lüngerl das (Süddt) finely-chopped calf's lights boiled in vinegar and usually eaten with 'Semmelknödel'.

Lupe (pl -n) die magnifying glass.

Lust (pl Lüste) die (Bedürfnis) desire; (Freude) pleasure; (sexuell) lust; **(keine) ~ haben auf** (+A) (not) to feel like; **~ haben, etw zu tun** to feel like doing sthg.

lustig adj (komisch) funny; (unterhaltsam) entertaining; **sich ~ machen über** (+A) to make fun of.

lutschen vt to suck.

Lutscher (pl -) der lollipop.

Luxemburg nt Luxembourg.

Luxemburger, -in (mpl -) der, die Luxemburger.

luxemburgisch adj of/from Luxembourg.

luxuriös adj luxurious.

Luxus der luxury.

Luxusgut (pl -güter) das luxury item.

Luzern nt Lucerne.

M

machen ◆ vt 1. (tun) to do; **da kann man nichts ~** there's nothing we can do about it; **mach die Musik leiser** turn the music down; **mach's gut!** take care! 2. (herstellen) to make; (Foto) to take; **jm etw ~** to make sthg for sb; **etw aus etw ~** to make sthg out of sthg; **mach keine Dummheiten!** don't do anything silly! 3. (verändern, bewirken) to make; **jn krank/glücklich ~** to make sb ill/happy; **etw sauber ~** to clean sthg. 4. (Urlaub) to go on; **eine Pause ~** to have a break.

5. (*Reise, Wanderung*) to go on; (*Spaziergang*) to go for; **einen Besuch bei jm ~** to pay sb a visit. **6.** (*Arbeit, Hausaufgaben*) to do; (*Reparatur, Korrektur*) to make. **7.** (*Gefühl*): **jm Angst/Freude ~** to make sb afraid/happy. **8.** (*Kurs, Lehrgang*) to do. **9.** (*Prüfung*) to do, to take. **10.** (*Summe, Ergebnis*) to be; **fünf mal drei macht fünfzehn** five times three is fifteen; **das macht 5 Mark!** that comes to 5 marks. **11.** (*ausmachen*): **die Hitze macht mir nichts** I don't mind the heat; **das macht nichts!** it doesn't matter! **12.** (*mögen*): **sich** (D) **nichts ~ aus** not to be keen on. ◆ *vi*: **mach schnell!** hurry up!; **mach schon!** (*fam*) get a move on! ▸ **sich machen** *ref*: **sich gut ~** (*wirken*) to look good; (*fam: entwickeln*) to make good progress.

Macht (*pl* **Mächte**) *die* power; **an der ~ sein** to be in power.

mächtig *adj* (*König, Land*) powerful.

machtlos *adj* powerless.

Macke (*pl* -n) *die* (*fam: Spleen*) quirk; (*an Tasse, Tisch*) chip.

Mädchen (*pl* -) *das* girl.

Mädchenname (*pl* -n) *der* maiden name.

Made (*pl* -n) *die* maggot.

Madonna (*pl* **Madonnen**) *die* Madonna.

mag *präs* → **mögen**.

Magazin (*pl* -e) *das* magazine; (*Lager*) storeroom.

Magen (*pl* **Mägen**) *der* stomach; **sich** (D) **den ~ verderben** to get an upset stomach.

Magenbeschwerden *pl* stomach trouble (*sg*).

Magenbitter (*pl* -) *der* bitters (*sg*).

Magengeschwür (*pl* -e) *das* stomach ulcer.

Magenschmerzen *pl* stomach-ache (*sg*).

mager *adj* (*Person, Tier*) thin; (*Käse*) low-fat; (*Fleisch*) lean.

Magermilch *die* skimmed milk.

Maggi® *das* type of brown, liquid seasoning.

Magisterarbeit (*pl* -en) *die* ≈ Master of Arts thesis.

Magnet (*pl* -e) *der* (*Metall*) magnet.

mähen *vt* (*Gras, Feld*) to mow.

Mahl (*pl* -e) *das* meal.

mahlen *vt* to grind.

Mahlzeit (*pl* -en) *die* meal; **~!** (*Gruß*) hello! (*said around mealtimes*).

Mähne (*pl* -n) *die* mane.

mahnen *vt* (*erinnern*) to remind.

Mahngebühr (*pl* -en) *die* charge for failure to pay a bill or fine.

Mahnmal (*pl* -e) *das* memorial.

Mahnung (*pl* -en) *die* reminder.

Mai *der* May; **der erste ~** May Day, September.

Maibaum (*pl* -bäume) *der* maypole.

MAIBAUM

The maypole is an old spring tradition. In many areas it is customary to fell a tree, usually a birch, on the day before 1 May. The trunk is decorated with ribbons and erected on the village square. A campfire is then built and the maypole is guarded all night to prevent the young people from neighbouring villages from attempting to steal it. The pole is also used in other festivals throughout the year.

Maifeiertag (*pl* -e) *der* May Day.

Mais *der* (*Körner*) sweetcorn; (*Pflanze*) maize.

Maiskolben (*pl* -) *der* corn on the cob.

Majoran *der* marjoram.

Make-up (*pl* -s) *das* (*Schminke*) make-up; (*Creme*) foundation.

Makkaroni *pl* macaroni (*sg*).

Makler, -in (*mpl* -) *der, die* estate agent.

Makrele (*pl* -n) *die* mackerel.

Makrone (*pl* -n) *die* macaroon.

mal ◆ *adv* (*fam: in Zukunft*) sometime; (in Vergangenheit) once. ◆ konj (zur Multiplikation) times; **bald ~** sometime soon; **komm ~ her** come here; **ich muß dir ~ was sagen** there's something I need to tell you; **hör ~!** (fam) listen; **sag ~!** (fam) tell me; **er redet ~ so, ~ so** (fam) he says one thing one minute and another the next.

Mal (pl -e) das (Zeitpunkt) time; **letztes ~** last time; **nächstes ~** next time; **zum ersten/letzten ~** for the first/last time.

Malaria die malaria.

Malbuch (pl -bücher) das colouring book.

malen vt & vi to paint.

Maler, -in (mpl -) der, die (Künstler) artist; (Anstreicher) painter.

malerisch adj (Ort) picturesque.

Malteser Hilfsdienst der voluntary paramedic service, ≈ St John's Ambulance (Br).

Malventee der mallow tea.

Malzbier das malt beer.

Mama (pl -s) die (fam) mummy.

man pron (jeder, ich) you; (irgendjemand) they; **wie sagt ~ das auf Deutsch?** how do you say that in German?; **dieses Jahr trägt ~ Miniröcke** miniskirts are in this year.

Manager, -in (mpl -) der, die manager.

manche, -r, -s ◆ pron (einige Dinge) some; (einige Leute) some people; (viele, viel) many things. ◆ det (einige) some; (viele) many.

manchmal adv sometimes.

Mandarine (pl -n) die mandarin.

Mandel (pl -n) die almond. ▶ **Mandeln** pl (im Hals) tonsils.

Mandelentzündung (pl -en) die tonsilitis.

Manege (pl -n) die (circus) ring.

Mangel (pl Mängel) der (Zustand) lack; (Fehler) fault; **~ an** (+D) shortage of.

mangelhaft adj (nicht ausreichend) poor; (Schulnote) unsatisfactory, poor.

mangels präp (+G) (amt) owing to lack of.

Mango (pl -s) die mango.

Manieren pl manners.

Maniküre die manicure.

manipulieren vt (Person) to manipulate; (Stimmzettel, Motor) to rig.

Mann (pl Männer) ◆ der (Erwachsener) man; (Ehemann) husband. ◆ interj (fam) my God!

Männchen (pl -) das (Tier) male; (kleiner Mann) little man.

M annequin (pl -s) das model.

männlich adj male; (GRAMM) masculine.

Mannschaft (pl -en) die (beim Sport) team; (von Schiff, Flugzeug) crew.

Manöver (pl -) das manoeuvre.

manövrieren vt (Fahrzeug) to manoeuvre.

Manschettenknopf (pl -knöpfe) der cufflink.

Mantel (pl Mäntel) der (Kleidungsstück) coat; (von Reifen) outer casing.

manuell adj manual.

Manuskript (pl -e) das manuscript.

Mappe (pl -n) die (Hülle) folder; (Tasche) briefcase; (von Schüler) schoolbag.

Maracuja (pl -s) die passion fruit.

Marathon (pl -s) der marathon.

Märchen (pl -) das fairy tale.

Märchenstunde (pl -n) die (children's) story hour.

Margarine die margarine.

Mariä Himmelfahrt nt Assumption.

Marienkäfer (pl -) der ladybird (Br), ladybug (Am).

Marille (pl -n) die (Österr) apricot.

Marillenknödel (pl -n) der (Österr) dessert consisting of a potato dumpling with an apricot in the middle.

Marinade (pl -n) die marinade.

marinieren vt to marinate.

Marionette (*pl* -n) *die* puppet.

Marionettentheater (*pl* -) *das* (*Veranstaltung*) puppet show; (*Gebäude*) puppet theatre.

Mark (*pl* -) *die* (*Währung*) mark; (*Knochenmark*) marrow; (*aus Obst, Gemüse*) purée.

Marke (*pl* -n) *die* (*von Hersteller*) make, brand; (*Briefmarke*) stamp; (*von Polizist*) badge; (*für Garderobe*) (metal) token.

Markenartikel (*pl* -) *der* brand-name article.

Markenzeichen (*pl* -) *das* trademark.

markieren *vt* (*kennzeichnen*) to mark.

Markierung (*pl* -en) *die* marking; '**fehlende ~**' 'no road markings'.

Markise (*pl* -n) *die* awning.

Markklößchen (*pl* -) *das* small dumpling made from marrow and breadcrumbs eaten in soup.

Markstück (*pl* -e) *das* one-mark coin.

Markt (*pl* Märkte) *der* market; (*Marktplatz*) marketplace; **auf den** ODER **zum ~ gehen** to go to (the) market.

Marktforschung *die* market research.

Marktfrau (*pl* -en) *die* market woman.

Markthalle (*pl* -n) *die* covered market.

Marktplatz (*pl* -plätze) *der* market-place.

Marktwirtschaft *die* market economy.

Marmelade (*pl* -n) *die* jam.

Marmor *der* marble.

Marmorkuchen (*pl* -) *der* marble cake, *sponge cake with a pattern made in darker* (*often chocolate*) *sponge on the inside.*

Marone (*pl* -n) *die* (*Kastanie*) chestnut; (*Pilz*) chestnut mushroom.

Marsch[1] (*pl* Märsche) *der* march.

Marsch[2] (*pl* -en) *die* (*an Küste*) marsh (*on coast*).

marschieren *vi ist* to march.

Marschmusik *die* marches (*pl*).

Marxismus *der* Marxism.

März *der* March, → **September**.

Marzipan *das* marzipan.

Maschine (*pl* -n) *die* (*Gerät*) machine; (*fam: Flugzeug*) plane.

maschinell ◆ *adj* machine (*vor Subst*). ◆ *adv* by machine.

maschineschreiben *vi* to type.

Masern *pl* measles (*sg*).

Maske (*pl* -n) *die* mask.

Maskenball (*pl* -bälle) *der* (*Kostümball*) fancy dress party.

maskieren *vt* (*Person*) to disguise. ▶ **sich maskieren** *ref* (*Einbrecher, sich verkleiden*) to disguise o.s.

Maskottchen (*pl* -) *das* mascot.

maskulin *adj* masculine.

maß *prät* → **messen**.

Maß[1] (*pl* -e) *das* (*von Raum, Größe*) measurement; (*Einheit*) measure; **in hohem/geringem ~** to a great/small extent; **nach ~** to measure.

Maß[2] (*pl* -) *die* (*Süddt: Liter*) litre (glass).

Massage (*pl* -n) *die* massage.

Massageöl (*pl* -e) *das* massage oil.

Masse (*pl* -n) *die* (*Brei*) mixture; (*von Personen*) crowd; (*von Dingen*) mass; **in ~n** in great numbers; **die breite ~** the masses (*pl*).

Maßeinheit (*pl* -en) *die* unit of measurement.

massenhaft *adj* great numbers of.

Massenmedien *pl* mass media.

Massentourismus *der* mass tourism.

Masseur, -in (*mpl* -e) *der, die* masseur (masseuse).

maßgeschneidert *adj* (*Kleidung*) made-to-measure.

massieren *vt* to massage.

mäßig ◆ *adj* (*Leistung, Wetter*) average; (*moderat*) moderate. ◆ *adv* (*moderat*) moderately.

massiv *adj* solid; (*Kritik*) strong.

Maßkrug (*pl* -krüge) *der* (*Süddt*) litre beer mug.

Maßnahme (*pl* -n) *die* measure.

Maßstab (*pl* -stäbe) *der* (*auf Landkarten*) scale; (*Richtlinie*) standard; **im ~ 1 : 25 000** to a scale of 1 : 25,000.

Mast (*pl* -en) *der* (*für Segel, Fahne*) mast.

Material (*pl* -ien) *das* material.

materialistisch *adj* (*Person, Einstellung*) materialistic.

materiell *adj* (*Bedürfnis, Schaden*) material; (*Schwierigkeiten*) financial; (*materialistisch*) materialistic.

Mathematik *die* mathematics (*sg*).

Matinee (*pl* -n) *die* matinee.

Matjes (*pl* -) *der* salted herring.

Matratze (*pl* -n) *die* mattress.

Matrose (*pl* -n) *der* sailor.

Matsch *der* (*Schlamm*) mud.

matt *adj* (*glanzlos*) matt; (*müde*) weak.

Matte (*pl* -n) *die* mat.

Mauer (*pl* -n) *die* wall.

Mauerwerk *das* masonry.

Maul (*pl* Mäuler) *das* (*von Tieren*) mouth.

Maulwurf (*pl* -würfe) *der* mole.

Maurer, -in (*mpl* -) *der, die* bricklayer.

Maus (*pl* Mäuse) *die* mouse.

Mausefalle (*pl* -n) *die* mousetrap.

Mautgebühr (*pl* -en) *die* (*Österr*) toll.

Mautstelle (*pl* -n) *die* (*Österr*) tollgate.

Mautstraße (*pl* -n) *die* (*Österr*) toll road.

maximal ◆ *adj* maximum. ◆ *adv* at most.

Maximum (*pl* Maxima) *das* maximum.

Mayo *die* (*fam*) mayonnaise.

Mayonnaise (*pl* -n) *die* mayonnaise.

Mechaniker, -in (*mpl* -) *der, die* mechanic.

mechanisch ◆ *adj* mechanical. ◆ *adv* mechanically.

Mechanismus (*pl* -men) *der* mechanism.

meckern *vi* (*fam: Person*) to moan.

Medaille (*pl* -n) *die* medal.

Medien *pl* media.

Medikament (*pl* -e) *das* medicine; **ein ~ gegen** a medicine for.

Meditation (*pl* -en) *die* meditation.

meditieren *vi* to meditate.

Medizin *die* medicine.

medizinisch *adj* (*Bäder, Anwendungen*) medicinal.

Meer (*pl* -e) *das* sea; **am ~** by the sea; **ans ~ fahren** to go to the seaside.

Meerenge (*pl* -n) *die* straits (*pl*).

Meeresfrüchte *pl* seafood (*sg*).

Meeresspiegel *der* sea level; **50 m über/unter dem ~** 50 m above/below sea level.

Meerrettich *der* horseradish.

Meerschweinchen (*pl* -) *das* guinea pig.

Meerwasser *das* seawater.

Mehl *das* (*aus Getreide*) flour.

Mehlschwitze (*pl* -n) *die* roux.

Mehlspeise (*pl* -n) *die* dish made from flour, eggs and milk, such as pasta, dumplings or pastries.

mehr ◆ *komp* → **viel**. ◆ *det, pron, adv* more; **es ist keiner ~ da** there is no one left there; **vom Käse ist nichts ~ da** there's nothing left of the cheese; **nie ~** never again.

mehrere *adj & vi* several.

mehrfach ◆ *adv* several times. ◆ *adj* multiple.

Mehrfahrten-Ausweis (*pl* -e) *der* multiple journey ticket.

Mehrheit (*pl* -en) *die* majority.

mehrmals *adv* several times.

mehrsprachig *adj* multilingual.

Mehrwegprodukt (*pl* -e) *das* recyclable product.

Mehrwertsteuer *die* VAT (Br), sales tax (Am).

Mehrzahl *die* (GRAMM) plural; (*Mehrheit*) majority.

meiden (*prät* **mied**, *pp* **gemieden**) *vt* to avoid. ▶ **sich meiden** *ref* to avoid each other.

Meile (*pl* **-n**) *die* mile.

mein, -e *det* my.

meine, -r, -s ODER **meines** ♦ *pron* mine. ♦ *det* → **mein**.

meinen *vt* (*denken, glauben*) to think; (*sagen*) to say; (*sich beziehen auf*) to mean; **etw ironisch/wörtlich ~** to mean sthg ironically/literally; **das war nicht so gemeint** it wasn't meant like that.

meinetwegen *adv* (*wegen mir*) because of me; (*von mir aus*) as far as I'm concerned.

Meinung (*pl* **-en**) *die* opinion.

Meinungsumfrage (*pl* **-n**) *die* opinion poll.

Meise (*pl* **-n**) *die* tit.

Meißel (*pl* **-**) *der* chisel.

meist *adv* usually, mostly.

meiste ♦ *superl* → **viel**. ♦ *adj & pron* most; **die ~ n** (**Leute**) most people; **er hat das ~ Geld** he has got the most money.

meistens *adv* usually, mostly.

Meister, -in (*mpl* **-**) *der, die* (*Titel*) master; (SPORT) champion.

Meisterschaft (*pl* **-en**) *die* (SPORT) championship.

Meisterwerk (*pl* **-e**) *das* masterpiece.

Meldefrist (*pl* **-en**) *die* (*für Wettbewerb*) period within which entries must be received.

melden *vt* to report. ▶ **sich melden** *ref* (*sich bemerkbar machen*) to make itself felt; (*am Telefon*) to answer; **es meldet sich niemand** there's no answer.

Meldeschluß *der* closing date.

melken (*prät* **molk**, *pp* **gemolken**) *vt* to milk.

Melodie (*pl* **-n**) *die* melody.

Melone (*pl* **-n**) *die* melon.

Memoiren *pl* memoirs.

Menge (*pl* **-n**) *die* (*Anzahl*) quantity; (*Vielzahl*) lot; (*Menschenmenge*) crowd; **eine (ganze) ~ Geld** (*relativ viel*) (quite) a lot of money; **jede ~** (*fam: sehr viel*) loads of.

Mengenrabatt (*pl* **-e**) *der* bulk discount.

Mensa (*pl* **Mensen**) *die* university canteen.

Mensch (*pl* **-en**) *der* (*Lebewesen*) human (being); (*Person*) person; **kein ~** no one; **Mensch!** (*fam: wütend*) for heaven's sake!; (*begeistert*) wow!

Menschenkenntnis (*pl* **-se**) *die* knowledge of human nature.

menschenleer *adj* deserted.

Menschenmenge (*pl* **-n**) *die* crowd.

Menschenrechte *pl* human rights.

Menschenwürde *die* human dignity.

Menschheit *die* humanity, mankind.

menschlich *adj* (*Körper, Irrtum*) human; (*human*) humane.

Menstruation (*pl* **-en**) *die* menstruation.

Mentalität (*pl* **-en**) *die* mentality.

Menthol *das* menthol.

Menü (*pl* **-s**) *das* (*Essen*) set menu.

Merkblatt (*pl* **-blätter**) *das* leaflet.

merken *vt* (*erkennen*) to realize; **sich** (D) **etw ~** (*sich einprägen*) to remember sthg.

Merkmal (*pl* **-e**) *das* feature.

merkwürdig *adj* strange.

Meßbecher (*pl* **-**) *der* measuring jug.

Messe (*pl* **-n**) *die* (*Gottesdienst*) mass; (*Ausstellung*) (trade) fair.

Messegast (*pl* **-gäste**) *der* visitor at a trade fair.

Messegelände (*pl* **-**) *das* exhibition centre.

messen (*präs* **mißt**, *prät* **maß**, *pp* **gemessen**) *vt* (*Temperatur, Größe*) to measure; (*in Maßangaben*) to be; **sie mißt 1,80m** she's 1.80m tall.

Messer (pl -) das knife.

Messestadt (pl -städte) die town that hosts a major trade fair.

Meßgerät (pl -e) das gauge.

Messing das brass.

Messung (pl -en) die (Handlung) measurement.

Metall (pl -e) das metal.

Meteorologe, -in (mpl -n) der, die weather forecaster.

Meter (pl -) der metre; **ein ~ achtundzwanzig** one metre twenty-eight; **zwei ~ hoch/breit sein** to be two metres high/wide.

Metermaß (pl -e) das tape measure.

Methode (pl -n) die method.

Mettwurst (pl -würste) die soft, smoked pork and beef sausage, usually spread on bread.

Metzger, -in (mpl -n) der, die butcher.

Metzgerei (pl -en) die butcher's (shop).

MEZ (abk für mitteleuropäische Zeit) CET.

Mezzosopran der mezzo-soprano.

MFG abk = **Mitfahrgelegenheit**.

mich pron (Personalpronomen) me; (Reflexivpronomen) myself.

mied prät → **meiden**.

Miederwaren pl corsetry (sg).

Miene (pl -n) die expression.

mies adj (fam) awful; **sich ~ fühlen** to feel awful.

Mietdauer die lease period.

Miete (pl -n) die (für Wohnung) rent; (für Auto) rental.

mieten vt (Wohnung) to rent; (Auto) to hire; **sich** (D) **etw ~** to rent/hire sthg.

Mieter, -in (mpl -) der, die tenant.

Mietfahrzeug (pl -e) das hire car.

Mietkauf (pl -käufe) der hire purchase.

Mietshaus (pl -häuser) das block of flats (Br), apartment building (Am).

Mietvertrag (pl -verträge) der lease.

Mietwagen (pl -) der hire car.

Mietwohnung (pl -en) die rented flat (Br), rented apartment (Am).

Migräne (pl -n) die migraine.

Mikrofon (pl -e) das microphone.

Mikrowellenherd (pl -e) der microwave oven.

Milch die milk; **fettarme ~** skimmed milk.

Milchbrötchen (pl -) das bread roll made with milk.

Milcheis das ice cream (made with milk).

Milchkaffee (pl -s) der milky coffee.

Milchmixgetränk (pl -e) das milk shake.

Milchprodukt (pl -e) das dairy product.

Milchpulver das powdered milk.

Milchreis der rice pudding.

Milchschokolade die milk chocolate.

mild ◆ adj mild. ◆ adv mildly.

Militär das military.

Milliarde (pl -n) die thousand million (Br), billion (Am).

Milligramm (pl -) das milligramme.

Milliliter (pl -) der millilitre.

Millimeter (pl -) der millimetre.

Million (pl -en) die million.

Millionär, -in (mpl -e) der, die millionaire.

Milz (pl -en) die spleen.

Mimik die facial expression.

Minderheit (pl -en) die minority.

minderjährig adj minor, under-age.

Minderjährige (pl -n) der, die minor.

minderwertig adj (Qualität) inferior.

Mindestalter das minimum age.

Mindestbetrag (pl -beträge) der minimum amount.

mindeste adj least.

mindestens *adv (wenigstens)* at least.

Mindesthaltbarkeitsdatum *das* best-before date.

Mindestpreis *(pl -e) der* minimum price.

Mindestumtausch *der minimum amount of money that must be changed when travelling to a particular country.*

Mine *(pl -n) die (von Bleistift)* lead; *(von Kugelschreiber)* refill; *(Bergwerk)* mine.

Mineral *(pl -ien) das* mineral.

Mineralbad *(pl -bäder) das (Kurort)* spa.

Mineralölsteuer *die* tax on oil.

Mineralwasser *(pl -wässer) das* mineral water.

Mini *(pl -s) der (fam: Rock)* miniskirt.

Minigolf *das* crazy golf.

Minigolfanlage *(pl -n) die* crazy golf course.

minimal *adj* minimal.

Minimum *(pl Minima) das* minimum.

Minirock *(pl -röcke) der* miniskirt.

Minister, -in *(mpl -) der, die* minister.

Ministerium *(pl Ministerien) das* ministry.

Ministerpräsident, -in *(mpl -en) der, die (von Bundesland) title given to leader of government in the German federal states; (Premierminister)* prime minister.

minus *konj & adv* minus; **10 Grad ~** minus 10 degrees.

Minus *das (Fehlbetrag)* deficit.

Minute *(pl -n) die* minute.

minutenlang *adv* for minutes.

Minze *(pl -n) die* mint.

Mio. *abk* = **Million**.

mir *pron (Personalpronomen)* me; *(Reflexivpronomen):* **ich habe es ~ so vorgestellt** I imagined it like this.

Mirabelle *(pl -n) die* mirabelle plum.

Mischbrot *(pl -e) das* bread made from a mixture of rye and wheat flour.

mischen *vt (Futtermischung, Salat)* to mix; *(Karten)* to shuffle.

Mischung *(pl -en) die* mixture; *(von Tee, Kaffee)* blend.

mißachten *vt (Vorschrift, Regel)* to disregard.

Mißachtung *die (von Vorschrift)* disregard.

Mißbrauch *(pl -bräuche) der* abuse; **'vor ~ wird gewarnt'** = 'do not exceed the stated dose'.

mißbrauchen *vt* to abuse.

Mißerfolg *(pl -e) der* failure.

Mißgeschick *(pl -e) das* mishap; **mir ist ein kleines ~ passiert** I had a slight mishap.

Mißhandlung *(pl -en) die* mistreatment.

mißlingen *(prät* **mißlang**, *pp* **mißlungen**) *vt* to fail; **das ist mir mißlungen** I failed.

mißt *präs* → **messen**.

mißtrauen *vi (+D)* to mistrust.

Mißtrauen *das* mistrust.

mißtrauisch *adj* mistrustful.

Mißverständnis *(pl -se) das* misunderstanding.

mißverstehen *(prät* **mißverstand**, *pp* **mißverstanden**) *vt* to misunderstand.

Mist *der (Dung)* dung, manure; *(fam: Plunder, Blödsinn)* rubbish.

mit ◆ *präp (+D)* **1.** *(zusammen)* with; **er kommt ~ seiner Frau** he's coming with his wife; **Kaffee ~ Zucker** coffee with sugar. **2.** *(Angabe von Instrument, Mittel)* with; **~ dem Zug/Bus/Flugzeug** by train/bus/plane. **3.** *(Angabe von Umstand):* **~ Verspätung eintreffen** to arrive late; **~ Absicht** intentionally, on purpose. **4.** *(Angabe von Zeitpunkt)* at; **~ 16 Jahren** at the age of 16. **◆** *adv (zusammen mit anderen)* too; **sie war nicht ~ dabei** she wasn't there.

mit|arbeiten *vi* to collaborate.

Mitarbeiter, -in *(mpl -) der, die* colleague.

mit|bekommen *vt unr (verstehen)* to

follow; (*aufschnappen*) to hear.
mit|bestimmen *vi* to have a say.
Mitbestimmung *die* say.
Mitbewohner, -in (*mpl* -) *der, die* flatmate.
mit|bringen *vt unr* to bring; (*von Reise*) to bring back; **jm etw ~** to bring sthg for sb.
Mitbringsel (*pl* -) *das* souvenir.
miteinander *adv* (*zusammen*) with each other.
mit|erleben *vt*: **er hat den Krieg noch miterlebt** he lived through the war.
Mitesser (*pl* -) *der* blackhead.
mit|fahren *vi unr ist* to get a lift.
Mitfahrgelegenheit (*pl* -en) *die* lift.
Mitfahrzentrale (*pl* -n) *die* agency which organizes lifts, passengers contributing to petrol costs.
mit|geben *vt unr* to give; **jm etw ~** to give sb sthg.
Mitgefühl *das* sympathy.
mit|gehen *vi unr ist* (*mitkommen*) to go along.
Mitglied (*pl* -er) *das* member.
Mitgliedsausweis (*pl* -e) *der* membership card.
Mitgliedsbeitrag (*pl* -beiträge) *der* membership fee.
mit|kommen *vi unr ist* (*gemeinsam kommen*) to come along; (*fam: folgen können*) to follow; **kommst du mit?** are you coming?
Mitleid *das* pity.
mit|machen ♦ *vt* (*Kurs, Tätigkeit*) to take part in; (*Schwierigkeiten*) to go through. ♦ *vi* (*sich beteiligen*) to take part.
mit|nehmen *vt unr* to take; **sich** (D) **etw ~** (*kaufen*) to get o.s. sthg; **zum Mitnehmen** to take away (Br), to go (Am).
Mitreisende (*pl* -n) *der, die* fellow traveller.
Mitschüler, -in (*mpl* -) *der, die* classmate.

mit|spielen *vi & vt* to play.
Mitspieler, -in (*mpl* -) *der, die* (*bei Spiel*) player.
mittag *adv*: **heute/gestern/morgen ~** at midday today/yesterday/tomorrow.
Mittag (*pl* -e) *der* (*Tageszeit*) midday; (12 Uhr) noon; **am ~** at midday; **gegen ~** around midday; **zu ~ essen** to have lunch.
Mittagessen (*pl* -) *das* lunch.
mittags *adv* at midday.
Mittagspause (*pl* -n) *die* lunch break.
Mittagstisch *der* lunch.
Mitte (*pl* -n) *die* middle; (*politisch*) centre; **in der ~** in the middle; **nächster Woche** the middle of next week; **~ vierzig sein** to be in one's mid-forties.
mit|teilen *vt*: **jm etw ~** to inform sb of sthg. ▶ **sich mitteilen** *ref* to communicate.
Mitteilung (*pl* -en) *die* announcement.
Mittel (*pl* -) *das* (*Hilfsmittel*) aid; (*zum Reinigen*) agent; (*Medikament*) medicine; **ein ~ gegen Grippe** a flu remedy.
Mittelalter *das* Middle Ages.
mittelalterlich *adj* medieval.
Mittelamerika *nt* Central America.
Mitteleuropa *nt* Central Europe.
Mittelgebirge (*pl* -) *das* low mountain range.
mittelmäßig ♦ *adj* (*Spiel, Wetter*) average. ♦ *adv* (*spielen*) averagely.
Mittelmeer *das*: **das ~** the Mediterranean (Sea).
Mittelohrentzündung (*pl* -en) *die* infection of the middle ear.
Mittelpunkt (*pl* -e) *der* centre; **im ~ stehen** to be the centre of attention.
mittels *präp* (+G) (*amt*) by means of.
Mittelstreifen (*pl* -) *der* (*von Straße*) central reservation (Br), median (Am).

Mittelstufe (*pl* **-n**) *die* (*Niveau*) intermediate level; (*an Gymnasium*) *equivalent to first three years of secondary education*.

Mittelwelle *die* medium wave.

mitten *adv* in the middle; **~ durch** through the middle of; **~ in etw** (A,D) in the middle of sthg; **~ in der Nacht** in the middle of the night.

Mitternacht *die* midnight; **um ~** at midnight.

Mitternachtsgottesdienst (*pl* **-e**) *der* midnight service.

mittlere, -r, -s *adj* (*durchschnittlich*) average; (*in der Mitte*) central.

mittlerweile *adv* (*inzwischen*) in the meantime.

Mittwoch (*pl* **-e**) *der* Wednesday, → **Samstag**.

mittwochs *adv* on Wednesdays.

mixen *vt* (*Cocktail, Salatsoße*) to mix.

Mixer (*pl* **-**) *der* (*Gerät*) food mixer.

Möbel *pl* furniture (*sg*).

Möbelwagen (*pl* **-**) *der* removal van (Br), moving van (Am).

mobil *adj* (*beweglich*) mobile.

Mobiliar *das* furniture.

Mobiltelefon (*pl* **-e**) *das* mobile phone.

möbliert *adj* furnished.

mochte *prät* → **mögen**.

möchte *präs* → **mögen**.

Mode (*pl* **-n**) *die* fashion.

Modehaus (*pl* **-häuser**) *das* fashion house.

Modell (*pl* **-e**) *das* model.

Modenschau (*pl* **-en**) *die* fashion show.

Moderator, -in (*mpl* **-en**) *der, die* presenter.

modern *adj* (*modisch*) fashionable; (*jetzig*) modern.

modernisieren *vt* (*Haus, Betrieb*) to modernize.

Modeschmuck *der* fashion jewellery.

Modezeitschrift (*pl* **-en**) *die* fashion magazine.

modisch *adj* fashionable.

Mofa (*pl* **-s**) *das* moped.

mögen (*präs* **mag**, *prät* **mochte**, *pp* **gemocht** ODER **mögen**) ◆ *vt* (*pp* **gemocht**) 1. (*gern haben*) to like; **jn/ etw gern ~** to like sb/sthg; **jn/etw nicht ~** not to like sb/sthg. 2. (*wollen*): **ich möchte ein Eis** I would like an icecream; **was möchten Sie, bitte?** what would you like? ◆ *vi* (*pp* **mögen**) (*wollen*): **er möchte nach Hause** he wants to go home. ◆ *aux* (*pp* **mögen**) 1. (*wollen*): **möchtest du mitkommen?** would you like to come?; **sie mag nicht ins Kino gehen** she doesn't want to go to the cinema. 2. (*hypothetisch*): **mag sein** that may well be; **mag sein, daß sie noch anruft** she may still call.

möglich *adj & adv* possible; **alles Mögliche** everything possible.

möglicherweise *adv* possibly.

Möglichkeit (*pl* **-en**) *die* possibility; (*Gelegenheit*) opportunity.

möglichst *adv* if possible; **kommt ~ schnell** come as quickly as possible; **~ viel** as much as possible.

Mohammedaner, -in (*mpl* **-**) *der, die* Muslim.

Mohn *der* (*Blume*) poppy; (*Körner*) poppy seeds (*pl*).

Mohnbrötchen (*pl* **-**) *das* poppy seed roll.

Möhre (*pl* **-n**) *die* carrot.

Mohrenkopf (*pl* **-köpfe**) *der* chocolate-covered marshmallow.

Mokka (*pl* **-s**) *der* mocha, *strong coffee drunk in small cups*.

molk *prät* → **melken**.

Molkerei (*pl* **-en**) *die* dairy.

Moll *das* (MUS) minor.

mollig *adj* (*Person*) plump.

Moment (*pl* **-e**) *der* (*Augenblick*) moment; **einen ~, bitte** just a moment, please; **im ~** at the moment; **~ mal!** wait a moment!

momentan ◆ *adj* present. ◆ *adv* at the moment.

Monarchie (*pl* **-en**) *die* monarchy.

Monat (*pl* -e) *der* month; **diesen ~** this month.

monatelang *adj & adv* for several months.

monatlich *adj & adv* monthly.

Monatsbinde (*pl* -n) *die* sanitary towel.

Monatsgehalt (*pl* -gehälter) *das* monthly salary.

Monatskarte (*pl* -n) *die* monthly season ticket.

Monatsrate (*pl* -n) *die* monthly instalment.

Mönch (*pl* -e) *der* monk.

Mond (*pl* -e) *der* moon.

Mondfinsternis (*pl* -se) *die* eclipse of the moon.

Monitor (*pl* -e) *der* (*von Computer*) monitor.

monoton *adj* monotonous.

Montag (*pl* -e) *der* Monday, → **Samstag.**

Montage (*pl* -n) *die* (*von Apparaten*) installation.

montags *adv* on Mondays.

Monteur, -in (*mpl* -e) *der, die* engineer.

montieren *vt* (*anbringen*) to install.

Monument (*pl* -e) *das* monument.

Moor (*pl* -e) *das* bog.

Moos (*pl* -e) *das* (*Pflanze*) moss.

Moped (*pl* -s) *das* moped.

Moral *die* (*Ethik*) morals (*pl*).

moralisch *adj* moral.

Morast *der* quagmire.

Mord (*pl* -e) *der* murder.

Mörder, -in (*mpl* -) *der, die* murderer.

morgen *adv* (*Tag nach heute*) tomorrow; (*vormittag*): **am Dienstag ~ ≃** on Tuesday morning; **bis ~!** see you tomorrow!; **gestern/heute ~** yesterday/this morning; **~ früh** tomorrow morning.

Morgen (*pl* -) *der* (*Tageszeit*) morning; **am ~** in the morning; **guten ~!** good morning!

Morgengrauen *das* dawn.

morgens *adv* in the morning; **früh ~** early in the morning; **von ~ bis abends** from dawn till dusk.

morgig *adj* tomorrow's; **der ~e Tag** tomorrow.

Morphium *das* morphine.

morsch *adj* rotten.

Mosaik (*pl* -en) *das* mosaic.

Moschee (*pl* -n) *die* mosque.

Mosel *die* Moselle.

Moselwein (*pl* -e) *der* white wine from the Moselle valley.

Moskau *nt* Moscow.

Moskito (*pl* -s) *der* mosquito.

Moskitonetz (*pl* -e) *das* mosquito net.

Moslem (*pl* -s) *der* Muslim.

Moslime (*pl* -n) *die* Muslim.

Mostrich *der* (*Norddt*) mustard.

Motel (*pl* -s) *das* motel.

Motiv (*pl* -e) *das* (*von Bild*) subject; (*von Handlung*) motive.

motivieren *vt* (*Person*) to motivate.

Motor (*pl* -en) *der* engine; **~ abstellen!** switch off engine!

Motorboot (*pl* -e) *das* motorboat.

Motorhaube (*pl* -n) *die* bonnet (Br), hood (Am).

Motoröl *das* engine oil.

Motorpanne (*pl* -n) *die* engine failure.

Motorrad (*pl* -räder) *das* motorcycle, motorbike.

Motorradfahrer, -in (*mpl* -) *der, die* motorcyclist.

Motorradhelm (*pl* -e) *der* motorcycle helmet.

Motorradrennen (*pl* -) *das* (*Wettbewerb*) motorcycle race.

Motorroller (*pl* -) *der* (motor)scooter.

Motorschaden (*pl* -schäden) *der* engine trouble.

Motorsport *der* motor sport.

Motoryacht (*pl* -en) *die* motor yacht.

Motte (*pl* -n) *die* moth.

Motto (*pl* -s) *das* motto.

Möwe (*pl* -n) *die* seagull.
Mrd. *abk* = **Milliarde**.
Mücke (*pl* -n) *die* midge.
Mückenstich (*pl* -e) *der* midge bite.
müde *adj* (*schläfrig*) tired.
Müdigkeit *die* tiredness.
Mühe (*pl* -n) *die* effort; **sich** (D) ~ **geben** to make an effort.
Mühle (*pl* -n) *die* (*Gerät*) grinder; (*Gebäude*) mill; (*Spiel*) board game for two players.
mühsam *adj* laborious.
Mull *der* (*Material*) muslin.
Müll *der* rubbish (Br), trash (Am); **etw in den** ~ **werfen** to throw sthg away.
Müllabfuhr *die* (*Institution*) cleansing department.
Mullbinde (*pl* -n) *die* gauze bandage.
Müllcontainer (*pl* -) *der* rubbish skip.
Mülldeponie (*pl* -n) *die* refuse disposal site.
Mülleimer (*pl* -) *der* bin.
Müllplatz (*pl* -plätze) *der* tip.
Müllschlucker (*pl* -) *der* refuse chute.
Mülltonne (*pl* -n) *die* dustbin (Br), garbage can (Am).
Müllwagen (*pl* -) *der* dustbin lorry (Br), garbage truck (Am).
multiplizieren *vt* to multiply.
Mumie (*pl* -n) *die* mummy.
Mumps *der* mumps.
München *nt* Munich.
Mund (*pl* Münder) *der* mouth; **halt den** ~! (*fam*) shut up!
Mundart (*pl* -en) *die* dialect.
münden *vi* (*Fluß*) to flow; **der Rhein mündet in die Nordsee** the Rhine flows into the North Sea.
Mundharmonika (*pl* -s) *die* mouthorgan.
mündlich ◆ *adj* oral. ◆ *adv* orally.
Mündung (*pl* -en) *die* mouth.
Mundwasser *das* mouthwash.

Münster (*pl* -) *das* minster.
munter *adj* (*wach*) wide awake; (*fröhlich*) cheerful.
Münzautomat (*pl* -en) *der* slot machine.
Münze (*pl* -n) *die* coin; **'nur mit ~n zahlen'** 'coins only'.
Münzeinwurf (*pl* -würfe) *der* coin slot.
Münzfernsprecher (*pl* -) *der* payphone.
Münzgeld *das*: **'~ einwerfen'** 'insert coins'.
Münzrückgabe (*pl* -n) *die* coin return; **'keine ~'** 'no change given'.
Münz-Wäscherei (*pl* -en) *die* launderette.
Münzwechsler (*pl* -) *der* change machine.
murmeln *vt & vi* to murmur.
mürrisch *adj* surly.
Mus *das* puree.
Muschel (*pl* -n) *die* (*Schale*) shell; (*Schalentier*) mussel.
Museum (*pl* Museen) *das* museum.
Musical (*pl* -s) *das* musical.
Musik *die* music.
musikalisch *adj* musical.
Musikbox (*pl* -en) *die* (*Automat*) musical box.
Musiker, -in (*mpl* -) *der, die* musician.
Musikinstrument (*pl* -e) *das* musical instrument.
Musikkassette (*pl* -n) *die* cassette, tape.
musizieren *vi* to play an instrument.
Muskat *das* nutmeg.
Muskel (*pl* -n) *der* muscle.
Muskelkater *der* stiff muscles (*pl*).
Muskeltraining *das* body building.
Muskelzerrung (*pl* -en) *die* pulled muscle.
Muskulatur *die* muscles (*pl*).
muskulös *adj* muscular.
Müsli (*pl* -s) *das* muesli.

muß *präs* → **müssen**.

müssen (*präs* **muß**, *prät* **mußte**, *pp* **müssen** ODER **gemußt**) ◆ *aux* (*pp* **müssen**) 1. (*gezwungen sein*) must; **etw tun ~** to have to do sthg; **du mußt aufstehen** you must get up; **sie mußte lachen** she had to laugh; **er hat niesen ~** he had to sneeze. 2. (*nötig sein*): **der Brief muß noch heute weg** the letter has to go today; **das müßte geändert werden** that should be changed, that ought to be changed; **muß das sein?** is that really necessary? 3. (*wahrscheinlich sein*): **sie muß bald hier sein** she should be here soon, she ought to be here soon; **das müßte alles sein** that should be all. ◆ *vi* (*pp* **gemußt**) 1. (*gezwungen sein*) to have to. 2. (*an einen Ort*): **ich muß ins Büro** I have to go to the office. 3. (*fam: zur Toilette*): **ich muß mal** I need to go to the loo.

Muster (*pl* -) *das* (*auf Stoff, auf Teppich, Schema*) pattern; (*Probe*) sample.

Mut *der* (*Furchtlosigkeit*) courage.

mutig *adj* brave.

Mutter[1] (*pl* **Mütter**) *die* (*Person*) mother.

Mutter[2] (*pl* -n) *die* (*für Schrauben*) nut.

Muttersprache (*pl* -n) *die* mother tongue.

Muttertag (*pl* -e) *der* Mother's Day.

Mütze (*pl* -n) *die* cap.

MwSt. (*abk für Mehrwertsteuer*) VAT (Br), sales tax (Am).

mysteriös *adj* mysterious.

Mythologie (*pl* -n) *die* mythology.

Mythos (*pl* **Mythen**) *der* myth.

N

N (*abk für Nord*) N.

na *interj* so; **~ und?** so?; **~ gut!** all right!; **~ also!** finally!; **~ ja,** well then.

Nabe (*pl* -n) *die* hub.

Nabel (*pl* -) *der* navel.

nach *präp* (+D) 1. (*zur Angabe einer Richtung*) to; **~ oben** up; (*in Haus*) upstairs; **~ unten** down; (*in Haus*) downstairs; **~ links/rechts abbiegen** to turn left/right; **~ Frankfurt** to Frankfurt; **~ Süden** south, southwards. 2. (*zeitlich*) after; **~ dem Essen** after the meal; **einer ~ dem anderen** one after another; **~ Ihnen!** after you!; **fünf ~ drei** five past three (Br), five after three (Am). 3. (*entsprechend*) according to; **~ Angaben der Polizei** according to the police. ▶ **nach und nach** *adv* little by little.

Nachbar, -in (*mpl* -n) *der, die* neighbour.

Nachbarschaft *die* neighbourhood.

nachbestellen *vt* (*Ware*) to reorder.

nachdem *konj* after; **je ~** depending on.

nachdenken *vi unr* to think; **~ über** (+A) to think about.

nachdenklich *adj* thoughtful.

nacheinander *adv* one after the other.

nachfolgen *vi ist* (+D) (*folgen*) to follow.

nachforschen *vi* to investigate.

Nachforschungsantrag (*pl* -anträge) *der* lost or damaged mail claim form.

Nachfrage *die* (*Kaufwunsch*) demand.

nachfragen *vi* to ask.

nach|geben vi unr (+D) (bei Streit) to give in.

Nachgebühr (pl **-en**) die excess postage.

nach|gehen vi unr ist (Uhr) to be slow; (folgen) to follow; **etw** (D) ~ (untersuchen) to investigate sthg.

nach|helfen vi unr (helfen) to help.

nachher adv (später) afterwards; **bis ~!** see you later!

Nachhilfe die (SCHULE) extra tuition.

nach|holen vt (Versäumtes) to catch up on.

nach|kommen intr ist to come along later.

nach|lassen vi unr (Qualität) to drop off; (Regen) to ease off; (Schmerz) to ease.

nachlässig ◆ adj careless. ◆ adv carelessly.

nach|lösen vt: **eine Fahrkarte ~** to buy a ticket on the train.

nach|machen vt (nachahmen) to copy.

nachmittag adv: **gestern/heute/ morgen ~** yesterday/this/tomorrow afternoon.

Nachmittag (pl **-e**) der afternoon; **am ~** in the afternoon.

nachmittags adv in the afternoon.

Nachnahme die: **per ~** cash on delivery.

Nachname (pl **-n**) der surname.

Nachporto (pl **-s**) das excess postage.

nach|prüfen vt to check.

nach|rechnen vt to work out.

Nachricht (pl **-en**) die (Mitteilung) message; (Neuigkeit) (piece of) news; **eine ~ hinterlassen** to leave a message. ▶ **Nachrichten** pl news (sg).

nach|sagen vt to repeat.

Nachsaison die: **in der ~** out of season.

nach|schauen vt (prüfen) to check.

nach|schicken vt to forward.

nach|schlagen vt unr (in Wörterbuch) to look up.

Nachschlüssel (pl **-**) der duplicate key.

nach|sehen ◆ vt unr (prüfen) to check. ◆ vi unr (+D) (hinterhersehen) to watch.

Nachsendeantrag (pl **-anträge**) der application for redirection of mail.

nach|senden vt to forward.

nach|sitzen vi unr (SCHULE) to have detention.

Nachspeise (pl **-n**) die dessert.

nächste, -r, -s ◆ superl → **nahe**. ◆ adj next; **der ~, bitte!** next, please!; **~s Mal/Jahr** next time/year; **wie heißt die ~ Haltestelle, bitte?** what's the next stop, please?

nächstens adv soon.

nacht adv: **gestern ~** last night; **heute ~** tonight.

Nacht (pl **Nächte**) die night; **gute ~!** good night!; **über ~** overnight.

Nachtausgang (pl **-gänge**) der night exit.

Nachtbus (pl **-se**) der night bus.

Nachtcreme (pl **-s**) die night cream.

Nachteil (pl **-e**) der disadvantage.

Nachteingang (pl **-gänge**) der night entrance.

Nachtflug (pl **-flüge**) der night flight.

Nachtfrost der overnight frost.

Nachtglocke (pl **-n**) die (bei Apotheke) night bell.

Nachthemd (pl **-en**) das nightshirt.

Nachtisch (pl **-e**) der dessert.

Nachtklub (pl **-s**) der nightclub.

Nachtleben das nightlife.

Nachtportier (pl **-s**) der night porter.

nachtragend adj unforgiving.

nachträglich adv belatedly.

Nachtruhe die sleep.

nachts adv at night.

Nachtschalter (pl **-**) der night desk.

Nachtschicht (*pl* -en) *die* night shift.

Nachttarif (*pl* -e) *der* economy rate.

Nachtzug (*pl* -züge) *der* night train.

Nachwirkung (*pl* -en) *die* after-effect.

nach|zahlen *vt* (*Porto, Fahrgeld*) to pay extra.

nach|zählen *vt* (*Porto, Fahrgeld*) to check.

Nacken (*pl* -) *der* neck.

nackt *adj & adv* naked.

Nacktbadestrand (*pl* -strände) *der* nudist beach.

Nadel (*pl* -n) *die* needle.

Nagel (*pl* Nägel) *der* nail.

Nagelbürste (*pl* -n) *die* nailbrush.

Nagelfeile (*pl* -n) *die* nailfile.

Nagellack (*pl* -e) *der* nail varnish.

Nagellackentferner *der* nail varnish remover.

nageln *vt* (*mit Hammer*) to nail.

Nagelschere (*pl* -n) *die* nail scissors (*pl*).

nah *adj* → **nahe**.

nahe (*komp* **näher**, *superl* **am nächsten**) *adj* near; **~ bei jm/etw** near (to) sb/sthg.

Nähe *die* nearness; **in der ~** nearby; **in der ~ von** near (to); **aus der ~** from close up; **in unserer ~** near us.

naheliegend *adj* (*Frage*) obvious.

nähen *vt* (*Stoff*) to sew; (*Wunde*) to stitch.

Naherholungsgebiet (*pl* -e) *das* area close to a town, with recreational facilities.

näher|kommen *vi unr ist* (+D): **wir sind uns nähergekommen** we've become closer.

nähern: sich nähern *ref* (+D) to approach.

nahe|stehen *vi unr* (+D): **jm ~** to be close to sb.

nahezu *adv* almost.

nahm *prät* → **nehmen**.

Nähmaschine (*pl* -n) *die* sewing machine.

Nähnadel (*pl* -n) *die* (sewing) needle.

Nahrung *die* food.

Nahrungsmittel (*pl* -) *das* food.

Naht (*pl* Nähte) *die* (*in Stoff*) seam; (*Narbe*) scar.

Nahverkehr *der* local traffic; **der öffentliche ~** local public transport.

Nahverkehrszug (*pl* -züge) *der* local train.

Nähzeug *das* sewing kit.

naiv *adj* naive.

Name (*pl* -n) *der* name; **mein ~ ist ...** my name is ...; **wie ist Ihr ~?** what's your name?; **auf den ~n Braun reservieren** to make a reservation in the name of Braun.

Namenstag (*pl* -e) *der* name day.

nämlich *adv* (*weil*) because; (*und zwar*) namely.

nanu *interj* well!

Narbe (*pl* -n) *die* scar.

Narkose (*pl* -n) *die* anaesthetic.

naschen *vt & vi* to nibble.

Nase (*pl* -n) *die* nose; **ich hab' die ~ voll** I've had enough; **meine ~ läuft** my nose is running.

Nasenbluten *das* nosebleed.

Nasenloch (*pl* -löcher) *das* nostril.

Nasentropfen *pl* nose drops.

naß *adj* wet; **~ machen** to wet.

Nässe *die* wet; **überfrierende ~** icy patches; **'80 km/h bei ~'** 'speed limit 80 km/h in wet weather'.

Nation (*pl* -en) *die* nation.

national *adj* national.

Nationalfeiertag (*pl* -e) *der* national day.

Nationalhymne (*pl* -n) *die* national anthem.

Nationalität (*pl* -en) *die* nationality.

Nationalmannschaft (*pl* -en) *die* national team.

Nationalsozialismus *der* national socialism.

NATO *die* NATO.

Natur *die* nature; **in der freien ~** in the countryside.

natürlich ◆ *adv* (*selbstverständlich*) of course; (*nicht künstlich*) naturally. ◆ *adj* natural.

Naturpark (*pl* **-s**) *der* nature reserve.

naturrein *adj* (*Saft*) pure.

Naturschutz *der* conservation; **unter ~ stehen** to be legally protected.

Naturschutzgebiet (*pl* **-e**) *das* nature reserve.

naturtrüb *adj* (*Saft*) naturally cloudy.

n.Chr. (*abk für nach Christus*) AD.

Nebel (*pl* **-**) *der* fog; **dichter ~** dense fog.

Nebelscheinwerfer (*pl* **-**) *der* (AUTO) fog lamp.

Nebelschlußleuchte (*pl* **-n**) *die* (AUTO) rear fog lights (*pl*).

neben ◆ *präp* (+D) (*an der Seite von*) next to; (*außer*) apart from, as well as. ◆ *präp* (+A) (*an die Seite von*) next to.

nebenan *adv* next door.

Nebenausgang (*pl* **-gänge**) *der* side exit.

nebenbei *adv* (*gleichzeitig*) at the same time; **~ gesagt** by the way.

nebendran *adv* (*fam*) next door.

nebeneinander *adv* next to each other.

Nebeneingang (*pl* **-eingänge**) *der* side entrance.

Nebenfach (*pl* **-fächer**) *das* (SCHULE) subsidiary subject.

nebenher *adv* (*arbeiten*) on the side.

Nebenkosten *pl* additional costs (*pl*).

Nebensache (*pl* **-n**) *die* trivial matter.

nebensächlich *adj* trivial.

Nebenstraße (*pl* **-n**) *die* side street.

Nebenwirkung (*pl* **-en**) *die* (MED) side effect.

neblig *adj* foggy.

neblig-trüb *adj* dull and overcast.

Neffe (*pl* **-n**) *der* nephew.

negativ ◆ *adj* negative. ◆ *adv* negatively.

Negativ (*pl* **-e**) *das* (FOTO) negative.

Negerkuß (*pl* **-küsse**) *der* chocolate-covered marshmallow.

nehmen (*präs* **nimmt**, *prät* **nahm**, *pp* **genommen**) *vt* 1. (*greifen, holen*) to take; **sich** (D) **etw ~** to help o.s. to sthg. 2. (*benützen*) to take; **den Bus/ Zug ~** to take the bus/train. 3. (*annehmen*) to take; **sie hat die Stelle genommen** she has taken the job. 4. (*kaufen*) to take; **ich nehme diese Schuhe** I'll take these shoes. 5. (*Medikament, Droge*) to take. 6. (*Gast, Kind*) **jn zu sich ~** (*auf Dauer*) to take sb in; (*für begrenzte Zeit*) to have sb to stay. 7. (*Nahrung*): **etw zu sich ~** to take sthg, to consume sthg. 8. (*einschätzen, auffassen*): **jn/etw ernst ~** to take sb/sthg seriously; **es leicht/ schwer ~** to take it lightly/hard. 9. (*verlangen*): **für etw fünf Mark ~** to charge five marks for sthg.

neidisch *adj* jealous.

nein *adv* no; **~ danke!** no thank you; **zu etw ~ sagen** to say no to sthg.

Nektarine (*pl* **-n**) *die* nectarine.

Nelke (*pl* **-n**) *die* (*Blume*) carnation; (*Gewürz*) cloves (*pl*).

nennen (*prät* **nannte**, *pp* **genannt**) *vt* (*mit Namen*) to call; (*als Beispiel*) to name.

Neonlicht (*pl* **-er**) *das* neon light.

Nepp *der* rip-off.

Nerv (*pl* **-en**) *der* nerve. ▶ **Nerven** *pl* nerves; **jm auf die ~en gehen** to get on sb's nerves.

nervös *adj* nervous.

Nest (*pl* **-er**) *das* (*von Vögeln*) nest.

nett ◆ *adj* nice. ◆ *adv* nicely; **sei so ~ ...** would you mind ...

netto *adv* net.

Netz (*pl* **-e**) *das* net; (*Tasche*) string bag.

Netzanschluß (*pl* **-schlüsse**) *der*

electrical connection.

Netzkarte (*pl* **-n**) *die* (*für Bus, Bahn*) rover ticket.

Netzplan (*pl* **-pläne**) *der* (*von Bus, Bahn*) route map.

neu *adj* new; (*frisch*) fresh; **von ~em** again; **das Neueste** the latest; **was gibt's Neues?** what's new?

Neubau (*pl* **-ten**) *der* new building.

neuerdings *adv* recently.

Neueröffnung (*pl* **-en**) *die* (*Zeremonie*) opening; (*Geschäft*) new business.

Neugier *die* curiosity.

neugierig ♦ *adj* inquisitive. ♦ *adv* inquisitively.

Neuheit (*pl* **-en**) *die* (*Ware*) latest thing.

Neuigkeit (*pl* **-en**) *die* news.

Neujahr *das* New Year; **prost ~!** Happy New Year!

neulich *adv* recently.

Neumond *der* new moon.

neun *num* nine, → **sechs**.

neunte *num* ninth, → **sechste**.

neunzehn *num* nineteen; **~hundertsiebenundneunzig** nineteen ninety seven, sechs.

neunzig *num* ninety, → **sechs**.

neureich *adj* nouveau riche.

neurotisch *adj* neurotic.

Neuseeland *nt* New Zealand.

neutral *adj* neutral.

neuwertig *adj* nearly new.

nicht *adv* not; **ist das ~ schön?** isn't that nice?; **~ nur ..., sondern auch ...** not only ... but also; **du wußtest es schon länger, ~ wahr?** you've known for a while, haven't you?; **es ist wunderbar, ~ wahr?** it's wonderful, isn't it?; **noch ~** not yet; **gar ~** not at all; **warum ~?** why not?

Nichte (*pl* **-n**) *die* niece.

Nichtraucher (*pl* **-**) *der* (*Person*) non-smoker; (*Abteil*) no-smoking compartment.

Nichtraucherzone (*pl* **-n**) *die* no-smoking area.

nichts *pron* nothing; **gar ~** nothing at all; **~ mehr** nothing more; **~ als** nothing but; **das macht ~** that doesn't matter; **~ zu danken** don't mention it.

Nichtschwimmer (*pl* **-**) *der* (*Person*) non-swimmer; (*Becken*) beginners' pool.

Nichtschwimmerbecken (*pl* **-**) *das* beginners' pool.

nichtssagend *adj* meaningless.

Nichtzutreffende *das*: **'~s bitte streichen'** (*amt*) 'delete as applicable'.

nicken *vi* to nod.

Nickerchen (*pl* **-**) *das* nap; **ein ~ machen** to have a nap.

nie *adv* never; **noch ~** never; **~ mehr** ODER **wieder** never again.

Niederlage (*pl* **-n**) *die* defeat.

Niederlande *pl*: **die ~** the Netherlands.

Niederländer, -in (*mpl* **-**) *der, die* Dutchman (Dutchwoman).

niederländisch *adj* Dutch.

Niederländisch(e) *das* Dutch.

Niederlassung (*pl* **-en**) *die* (*Filiale*) branch.

Niedersachsen *nt* Lower Saxony.

Niederschlag (*pl* **-schläge**) *der* precipitation.

niedlich *adj* cute.

niedrig *adj* low.

niemals *adv* never.

niemand *pron* nobody, no one; **das kann ~ als Karl-Heinz gewesen sein** that can only have been Karl-Heinz.

Niere (*pl* **-n**) *die* kidney.

nieseln *vimp* to drizzle.

Nieselregen *der* drizzle.

niesen *vi* to sneeze.

Niete (*pl* **-n**) *die* (*Los*) blank; (*aus Metall*) stud.

Nikolaus *der* Santa Claus (*who brings presents on 6th December*).

NIKOLAUS

Tradition dictates that in Germany, Santa Claus (St Nicholas) visits children on 6 December to reward those who have been good over the past year and to punish the bad ones. If the children have been well-behaved, then the shoes or plates they leave out the night before are filled with sweets and small presents. If they have been bad, they face punishment from Nikolaus' companion 'Knecht Ruprecht' (sometimes also known as 'Krampus'), who will be waiting for them with his stick.

Nikolaustag (pl -e) der 6th of December, when children receive presents from Santa Claus.

Nikotin das nicotine.

nimmt präs → **nehmen**.

nirgends adv nowhere.

nirgendwo adv nowhere.

nirgendwohin adv nowhere.

Nische (pl -n) die (Ecke) corner.

Niveau (pl -s) das level.

nobel adj (kostspielig) luxurious.

Nobelpreis (pl -e) der Nobel Prize.

noch ◆ adv 1. (zum Ausdruck von Dauer) still; **wir haben ~ Zeit** we still have time; **er hat ~ nichts gesagt** he still hasn't said anything; **ich habe ihn ~ letzten Monat besucht** I visited him only last month; **~ nicht** not yet. 2. (vorher): **schafft ihr das ~ bis Freitag?** do you think you'll manage it by Friday?; **das muß ~ heute gemacht werden** it has to be done today at the latest; **er kann ~ kommen** he may yet come, he may still come. 3. (zur Verstärkung) even; **~ schneller** even quicker; **es kann ~ so regnen, ...** however much it rains ... 4. (dazu): **~ einen Kaffee, bitte!** another coffee, please!; **ich muß ~ ein paar Einkäufe machen** I have to buy a few more things; **paßt das ~ in den Kofferraum?** will it fit in the boot?; **wer ~?** who else? 5. (zur Nachfrage) again; **wie war ~ sein Name?** what was his name again? ◆ konj → **weder**. ▶ **noch einmal** adv again.

nochmal adv again.

Nominativ (pl -e) der (GRAMM) nominative.

nonstop adj (Flug) nonstop.

Nord nt north.

Nordamerika nt North America.

Norddeutschland nt Northern Germany.

Norden der north; **im ~** in the north; **nach ~** north.

Nordeuropa nt Northern Europe.

Nordhang (pl -hänge) der north-facing slope.

Nordirland nt Northern Ireland.

nördlich ◆ adj northern. ◆ präp: **~ von** to the north of.

Nordosten der northeast.

Nordrhein-Westfalen nt North Rhine-Westphalia.

Nordsee die: **die ~** the North Sea.

Nordwesten der northwest.

nörgeln vi to moan.

Norm (pl -en) die standard.

normal ◆ adj normal. ◆ adv normally.

Normal das (AUTO) regular.

Normalbenzin das (AUTO) regular petrol (Br), regular gas (Am).

normalerweise adv normally.

Normalnull das: **über/unter ~** above/below sea level.

Norwegen nt Norway.

Norweger, -in (mpl -) der, die Norwegian.

Not die need; **in ~** in need; **zur ~** if needs be.

Notar, -in (mpl -e) der, die notary.

Notarzt, -ärztin (mpl -ärzte) der, die emergency doctor.

Notausgang (pl -gänge) der emergency exit.

Notausstieg (pl -e) der emergency exit.

Notbremse (pl -n) die emergency brake.

Notdienst (pl -e) der: **~ haben** to be on call.

Notdienstapotheke (pl -n) die

emergency chemist's (Br), emergency drugstore (Am).

Note (pl -n) die (MUS) note; (Zensur) mark (Br), grade (Am).

Notfall (pl -fälle) der emergency; **in dringenden Notfällen** in an emergency.

notfalls adv if necessary.

Nothaltebucht (pl -en) die (auf Straße) escape lane.

notieren vt to note down; **sich** (D) **etw ~** to make a note of sthg.

nötig adj necessary; **~ sein** to be necessary; **etw ~ haben** to need sthg; **wenn ~** if needs be.

Notiz (pl -en) die (persönlich) note; (in Zeitung) notice; **sich ~en machen** to take notes; **keine ~ von jm nehmen** to take no notice of sb.

Notizblock (pl -blöcke) der notepad.

Notizbuch (pl -bücher) das notebook.

Notlage (pl -n) die crisis.

Notlandung (pl -en) die emergency landing.

Notruf (pl -e) der emergency call.

Notrufsäule (pl -n) die emergency phone.

Notrutsche (pl -n) die (im Flugzeug) escape chute.

Notsignal (pl -e) das distress signal.

notwendig adj necessary.

Notwendigkeit (pl -en) die necessity.

Nougat der nougat.

November (pl -) der November, → **September**.

Nr. (abk für Nummer) no.

NRW abk = **Nordrhein-Westfalen**.

Nu: im Nu adv in an instant.

nüchtern adj (nicht betrunken) sober; (Magen) empty.

Nudeln pl noodles.

Nudelsalat der pasta salad.

Nudelsuppe (pl -n) die noodle soup.

null num zero, → **sechs**.

Null (pl -en) die zero; **über/unter ~** above/below zero.

numerieren vt to number.

Nummer (pl -n) die number; (Größe) size.

Nummernschild (pl -er) das (AUTO) numberplate (Br), license plate (Am).

NUMMERNSCHILD

German car registration numbers comprise two groups of letters followed by a sequence of numbers. The first group of letters indicates the town in which the car was registered (e.g. M for Munich or B for Berlin), whilst the remaining letters and numbers are the registration number proper. German numberplates also carry a round badge which indicates that the car has been passed as roadworthy.

---

nun adv now; **~, wie steht's?** well, how are things?; **es ist ~ mal so** it's like this; **was ~?** what now?

nur adv only, just; **was meint er ~?** what does he mean?; **der Putz bröckelt ~ so** the plaster is crumbling really badly; **das sagt er ~ so** he's just saying it; **ich habe ~ noch 20 Mark** I've only got 20 marks left.

Nürnberg nt Nuremberg.

Nuß (pl Nüsse) die nut.

Nußknacker (pl -) der nutcracker.

Nutte (pl -n) die (fam) hooker.

nutzen ♦ vt to use. ♦ vi to be of use; **jm ~** to be of use to sb; **nichts ~** to be of no use.

nützen vi = **nutzen**.

nützlich adj useful.

nutzlos adj useless.

Nylonstrumpf (pl -strümpfe) der nylon stocking.

O (abk für Ost) E.

ob konj whether; ~ ..., ~ whether ... or; ~ ... **oder nicht** whether ... or not; **als** ~ as if; **so tun als** ~ to pretend (that); **und ~!** you bet!

OB (pl **-s**) der (abk für Oberbürgermeister) mayor (of large city).

Obazter (pl **Obazten**) der (Süddt) soft camembert, mashed together with onions and pepper.

obdachlos adj homeless.

Obdachlose (pl **-n**) der, die homeless person.

oben adv (räumlich) at the top; (im Text) above; **das fünfte Buch von** ~ the fifth book down; **nach** ~ up; **von** ~ **bis unten** from top to bottom; ~ **ohne** topless.

Ober (pl **-**) der waiter.

obere, -r, -s adj upper.

oberflächlich adj superficial.

oberhalb präp (+G) above.

Oberhemd (pl **-en**) das shirt.

Oberkörper (pl **-**) der upper body.

Oberschenkel (pl **-**) der thigh.

oberste, -r, -s adj top.

Oberstufe die (SCHULE) three final years of secondary education.

Oberteil (pl **-e**) das (von Kleidung) top.

Oberweite (pl **-n**) die bust (measurement).

Objekt (pl **-e**) das object; (Immobilie) property.

objektiv ◆ adj objective. ◆ adv objectively.

Objektiv (pl **-e**) das lens.

obligatorisch adj obligatory.

Oboe (pl **-n**) die oboe.

Obst das fruit.

Obstkuchen (pl **-**) der fruit flan.

Obstsalat (pl **-e**) der fruit salad.

obszön adj obscene.

obwohl konj although.

Ochse (pl **-n**) der ox.

Ochsenschwanzsuppe (pl **-n**) die oxtail soup.

ocker adj ochre.

od. abk = **oder**.

oder konj or; **du kommst doch mit, ~?** you're going to come, aren't you?; ~ **aber** or; ~ **auch** or; ~ **so** or something like that, entweder.

Ofen (pl **Öfen**) der (zum Backen) oven; (zum Heizen) stove.

Ofenheizung die stove heating.

offen ◆ adj open; (Knopf) undone; (Rechnung) outstanding; (Haare) down; (Bein, Haut) grazed. ◆ adv (unverschlossen) open; (erkennbar, sich verhalten) openly; **das Geschäft hat bis 6 Uhr** ~ the shop is open until 6; **~e Weine** wine by the glass/carafe; **auf ~em Meer** on the open sea; ~ **gesagt** quite honestly; **Tag der ~en Tür** open day.

offenbar adv obviously.

offen|bleiben vi unr ist (Fenster) to stay open; (Frage) to remain unresolved.

offen|lassen vt unr to leave open.

offensichtlich adv obviously.

offen|stehen vi unr to be open; **die Welt steht ihm offen** the world's his oyster.

öffentlich ◆ adj public. ◆ adv publicly, in public.

Öffentlichkeit die public.

offiziell adj official.

öffnen vt to open. ▶ **sich öffnen** ref to open.

Öffnungszeiten pl opening hours.

oft (komp **öfter**, superl **am öftesten**) adv often; **wie ~?** how often?

öfters adv from time to time.

ohne präp (+A) & konj without; ~ **mich!** count me out!; ~ **weiteres** without hesitation; ~ **daß** without.

Ohnmacht die (Bewußtlosigkeit) unconsciousness; **in ~ fallen** to faint.

ohnmächtig adj (bewußtlos) unconscious; ~ **werden** to faint.
Ohr (pl -en) das ear.
Ohrclip (pl -s) der clip-on earring.
Ohrentropfen pl ear drops.
ohrfeigen vt: **jn** ~ to slap sb's face.
Ohrring (pl -e) der earring.
okay adv okay, OK.
Ökoladen (pl -läden) der wholefood store.
ökologisch adj ecological.
ökonomisch adj economic.
Oktan das octane.
Oktober (pl -) der October; **der 3. ~** German national holiday commemorating reunification on 3 October 1990, → September.
Oktoberfest (pl -e) das Munich beer festival.

OKTOBERFEST

The world-famous Munich beer festival began in 1811 and is held every year, starting in mid-September and continuing for 16 days. Huge beer tents are erected where the local Munich breweries serve their beers in 1 litre measures along with typical Bavarian food. There are also fairground attractions, such as merry-go-rounds, roller coasters and shooting galleries.

Öl (pl -e) das oil.
ölen vt to oil.
Ölfarbe (pl -n) die oil paint.
ölig adj oily.
Olive (pl -n) die olive.
Olivenöl das olive oil.
Ölstand der oil level; **den ~ prüfen** to check the oil.
Ölverbrauch der oil consumption.
Ölwechsel (pl -) der oil change.
Olympische Spiele pl Olympic Games.
Oma (pl -s) die (fam) grandma.
Omelette (pl -n) die omelette.
Omnibus (pl -se) der (Linienbus) bus; (Reisebus) coach.

Onkel (pl -) der uncle.
OP (pl -s) der operating theatre (Br), OR (Am).
Opa (pl -s) der (fam) grandpa, grandad.
Open-air-Konzert (pl -e) das open-air concert.
Oper (pl -n) die opera; (Gebäude) opera house; **in die ~ gehen** to go to the opera.
Operation (pl -en) die operation.
Operette (pl -n) die operetta.
operieren vt to operate on; **sich ~ lassen** to have an operation.
Opernfestspiele pl opera festival (sg).
Opernhaus (pl -häuser) das opera house.
Opfer (pl -) das sacrifice.
Opposition die opposition.
Optik die optics (sg).
Optiker, -in (mpl -) der, die optician.
optimal ◆ adj optimal, optimum. ◆ °adv optimally.
optimistisch adj optimistic.
orange adj orange.
Orange (pl -n) die (Frucht) orange.
Orangensaft (pl -säfte) der orange juice; **frischgepreßter ~** freshly-squeezed orange juice.
Orchester (pl -) das orchestra.
ordentlich ◆ adj (Raum, Person) tidy; (Leben, Beruf) respectable; (Mahlzeit, Arbeit) proper. ◆ adv (aufräumen) tidily.
ordinär adj (Person, Witz) crude.
ordnen vt to put in order.
Ordner (pl -) der (für Akten) folder; (Person) steward.
Ordnung die order; **in ~!** sure!; **das geht** ODER **ist in ~** that's all right; ~ **machen** to tidy up; **der Fernseher ist nicht in ~** there's something wrong with the television.
Ordnungswidrigkeit (pl -en) die (amt) minor offence.
Oregano der oregano.

Organ (*pl* -e) *das* (*Körperteil*) organ.

Organisation (*pl* -en) *die* organization.

Organisator (*pl* Organisatoren) *der* organizer.

Organisatorin (*pl* -nen) *die* organizer.

organisieren *vt* to organize.

Organismus (*pl* Organismen) *der* organism.

Orgasmus (*pl* Orgasmen) *der* orgasm.

Orgel (*pl* -n) *die* organ.

orientieren: sich orientieren *ref* (*in Richtung*) to orientate o.s.; **sich ~ über** (+A) (*informieren*) to inform o.s. about.

Orientierungssinn *der* sense of direction.

original *adj* original.

Original (*pl* -e) *das* original.

Orkan (*pl* -e) *der* hurricane.

Ort (*pl* -e) *der* place; **an ~ und Stelle** on the spot; **'andere ~e'** 'other routes'.

Orthopäde, Orthopädin (*mpl* -n) *der, die* orthopaedic surgeon.

orthopädisch *adj* orthopaedic.

örtlich *adj* local.

Ortschaft (*pl* -en) *die* village; **geschlossene ~** built-up area.

Ortsgespräch (*pl* -e) *das* local call.

ortskundig *adj*: **ein ~er Führer** a guide with local knowledge.

Ortsmitte *die* centre.

Ortsnetz (*pl* -e) *das* exchange.

Ortstarif (*pl* -e) *der* local rate.

Ortszeit (*pl* -en) *die* local time.

öS *abk* = **österreichischer Schilling**.

Ossi (*pl* -s) *der* (*fam*) East German.

Ost *nt* east.

Ostberlin *nt* East Berlin.

Ostdeutschland *nt* East Germany.

Osten *der* east; **im ~** in the east; **nach ~** east.

Osterei (*pl* -er) *das* Easter egg.

Osterhase (*pl* -n) *der* Easter bunny.

OSTERHASE

At Easter, Germans give each other not only chocolate Easter eggs, but also painted, boiled eggs. Tradition has it that these, together with chocolate rabbits and other sweets, are brought for children by the Easter bunny, who hides them in the garden, the barn, the park or even around the house. On Easter day, the children must then hunt for their eggs.

Ostermontag (*pl* -e) *der* Easter Monday.

Ostern (*pl* -) *nt* Easter; **zu ~** at Easter; **frohe ~!** Happy Easter!

Österreich *nt* Austria.

Österreicher (*pl* -) *der* Austrian.

Österreicherin (*pl* -nen) *die* Austrian.

österreichisch *adj* Austrian.

Ostersonntag (*pl* -e) *der* Easter Sunday.

Osteuropa *nt* Eastern Europe.

Ostküste (*pl* -n) *die* east coast.

östlich ◆ *adj* eastern. ◆ *präp*: **~ von** to the east of.

Ostsee *die*: **die ~** the Baltic (Sea).

oval *adj* oval.

Ozean (*pl* -e) *der* ocean.

Ozon *das* ozone.

Ozonloch *das* hole in the ozone layer.

P

paar *adj* few; **ein ~** a few.

Paar (*pl* -e) *das* (*zwei Personen*) couple; (*zwei Dinge*) pair; **ein ~ Socken** a pair of socks.

paarmal *adv*: **ein ~** a few times.

Pacht (*pl* **-en**) *die* (*Vertrag*) lease; (*Geld*) rent.

Päckchen (*pl* **-**) *das* (*in* Post) small parcel; (*Packung*) pack.

packen *vt* to pack; (*fassen*) to seize.

Packpapier *das* brown paper.

Packung (*pl* **-en**) *die* (*für* Waren) packet; (*Kosmetik*) beauty pack.

Packungsbeilage (*pl* **-n**) *die* (MED) enclosed information; **'lesen Sie die ~'** 'please read the enclosed information'.

Packungsrückseite (*pl* **-n**) *die* back of the packet.

Pädagogik *die* education.

pädagogisch *adj* educational.

Paddel (*pl* **-**) *das* paddle.

Paddelboot (*pl* **-e**) *das* canoe.

paddeln *vi* to paddle.

Paket (*pl* **-e**) *das* (*Postpaket*) parcel; (*Packung*) packet.

Paketannahme (*pl* **-n**) *die* (*Schalter*) *counter dealing with parcels to be sent.*

Paketausgabe (*pl* **-n**) *die* (*Schalter*) *counter from which parcels may be collected.*

Paketkarte (*pl* **-n**) *die* *form showing sender and addressee, to be filled in when sending a parcel.*

Pakistan *nt* Pakistan.

Palast (*pl* **Paläste**) *der* palace.

Palme (*pl* **-n**) *die* palm.

Palmsonntag *der* Palm Sunday.

Pampelmuse (*pl* **-n**) *die* grapefruit.

Paniermehl *das* breadcrumbs (*pl*).

paniert *adj* in breadcrumbs, breaded.

Panik *die* panic.

panisch *adj* (*Reaktion*) panic-stricken; **~e Angst vor etw** (D) **haben** to be terrified of sthg.

Panne (*pl* **-n**) *die* (*mit* Auto) breakdown; (*Fehler*) technical hitch; **ich hatte eine ~ auf der Autobahn** my car broke down on the motorway.

Pannendienst (*pl* **-e**) *der* breakdown service.

Pannenhilfe *die* breakdown service.

Panoramablick (*pl* **-e**) *der* panoramic view.

Pantoffel (*pl* **-n**) *der* slipper.

Pantomime (*pl* **-n**) *die* (*Aufführung*) mime.

Panzer (*pl* **-**) *der* (*Fahrzeug*) tank; (*von* Tier) shell.

Papa (*pl* **-s**) *der* (*fam*) dad.

Papagei (*pl* **-en**) *der* parrot.

Papier (*pl* **-e**) *das* paper. ▶ **Papiere** *pl* (*Ausweise*) papers, documents.

Papiergeld *das* paper money.

Papierkorb (*pl* **-körbe**) *der* wastepaper basket (Br), wastebasket (Am).

Papiertaschentuch (*pl* **-tücher**) *das* paper handkerchief.

Papierwaren *pl* stationery (*sg*).

Pappbecher (*pl* **-**) *der* paper cup.

Pappe (*pl* **-n**) *die* cardboard.

Pappkarton (*pl* **-s**) *der* cardboard box.

Paprika (*pl* **-s**) *der* (*Gemüse*) pepper; (*Gewürz*) paprika.

Papst (*pl* **Päpste**) *der* pope.

Parade (*pl* **-n**) *die* (*Umzug*) parade.

Paradeiser (*pl* **-**) *der* (*Österr*) tomato.

paradiesisch *adj* heavenly.

Paragliding *das* paragliding.

Paragraph (*pl* **-en**) *der* paragraph.

parallel *adj* & *adv* parallel.

Paranuß (*pl* **-nüsse**) *die* brazil nut.

parat *adj* & *adv* ready.

Pärchen (*pl* **-**) *das* (*Liebespaar*) couple.

Pardon *interj* sorry.

Parfüm (*pl* **-s**) *das* perfume.

Parfümerie (*pl* **-n**) *die* perfumery.

parfümfrei *adj* unscented.

Pariser (*pl* **-**) *der* (*fam*: Kondom) rubber.

Park (*pl* **-s**) *der* park.

Parka (*pl* **-s**) *der*, *die* parka.

Park-and-Ride-System *das* park and ride system.

Parkanlage (*pl* -n) *die* park.

Parkdauer *die*: ~ 2 Stunden parking restricted to 2 hours.

Parkdeck (*pl* -s) *das* level (*of multistorey car park*).

parken *vt & vi* to park; **falsch ~** to park wrongly; **'Parken verboten'** 'no parking'.

Parkett (*pl* -s ODER -e) *das* (*Fußboden*) parquet; (*in Zuschauerraum*) stalls (*Br*), parquet (*Am*).

Parkgebühr (*pl* -en) *die* parking fee.

Parkhaus (*pl* -häuser) *das* multistorey car park.

Parkhöchstdauer *die*: ~ 1 Stunde maximum stay 1 hour.

Parklücke (*pl* -n) *die* parking space.

Parkmöglichkeit (*pl* -en) *die* parking space.

Parkplatz (*pl* -plätze) *der* car park (*Br*), parking lot (*Am*).

Parkscheibe (*pl* -n) *die* parking disc.

Parkschein (*pl* -e) *der* parking ticket.

Parkuhr (*pl* -en) *die* parking meter.

Parkverbot (*pl* -e) *das* (*Verbot*) parking ban; (*Stelle*) no-parking zone.

Parlament (*pl* -e) *das* parliament.

Parmesan *der* parmesan (*cheese*).

Partei (*pl* -en) *die* party.

Parterre *das* ground floor; **im ~** on the ground floor.

Partie (*pl* -n) *die* (*Teil*) part; (*Spiel*) game.

Partner, -in (*mpl* -) *der, die* partner.

Partnerschaft (*pl* -en) *die* (*zwischen Personen*) partnership; (*zwischen Städten*) twinning.

Partnerstadt (*pl* -städte) *die* twin town.

Party (*pl* -s) *die* party.

Paß (*pl* Pässe) *der* (*Dokument*) pass-port; (*Straße*) pass.

Passage (*pl* -n) *die* (*Einkaufspassage*) arcade; (*Textabschnitt, Reise*) passage.

Passagier (*pl* -e) *der* passenger; **blinder ~** stowaway.

Passagierschiff (*pl* -e) *das* passenger ship.

Paßamt (*pl* -ämter) *das* passport office.

Passant, -in (*mpl* -en) *der, die* passerby.

Paßbild (*pl* -er) *das* passport photo.

passen *vi* (*Termin*) to be suitable; (*in Größe, Form*) to fit; (*bei Spiel*) to pass; **Freitag paßt mir nicht** Friday doesn't suit me; **~ dir die Schuhe?** do the shoes fit you?; **zu etw ~** to go (well) with sthg; **zu jm ~** to be suited to sb; **das könnte dir so ~!** you'd like that, wouldn't you?

passend *adj* (*Farbe*) matching; **ein ~er Schlüssel** a key that fits; **haben Sie es ~?** do you have the right change?

Paßfoto (*pl* -s) *das* passport photo.

passieren *vi ist* to happen; **mir ist was sehr Unangenehmes passiert** something very unpleasant happened to me; **ist etwas passiert?** (*bei Unfall*) did sb get hurt?; **was ist passiert?** what happened?

Passionsspiele *pl*: **die ~ von Oberammergau** the Oberammergau passion plays.

PASSIONSSPIELE

The Oberammergau passion plays, in which the suffering and death of Christ is performed by amateur actors, are the most famous in the world. They started in 1633, during the plague, and take place every ten years, with over 1,000 locals taking part in the performances.

passiv *adj* passive.

Paßkontrolle (*pl* -n) *die* passport control.

Paste (*pl* -n) *die* (*Masse*) paste.

Pastell (*pl* -e) *das* pastel.

Pastete (*pl* -n) *die* (*aus Teig*) pie; (*Aufstrich*) paste.

Pastor (*pl* **Pastoren**) *der* (*katholisch*) priest; (*evangelisch*) vicar.

Pastorin (*pl* -nen) *die* (*evangelisch*) vicar.

Pate (*pl* -n) *der* (*Patenonkel*) godfather.

Patient, -in (*mpl* -en) *der, die* patient.

Patin (*pl* -nen) *die* godmother.

Patrone (*pl* -n) *die* cartridge.

Pauke (*pl* -n) *die* kettledrum.

pauschal *adj* (*Betrag, Preis*) total; (*Kritik, Urteil*) general.

Pauschale (*pl* -n) *die* flat rate.

Pauschalpreis (*pl* -e) *der* all-inclusive price.

Pauschalreise (*pl* -n) *die* package holiday.

Pauschaltarif (*pl* -e) *der* flat rate.

Pause (*pl* -n) *die* break; (*in Theater, Konzert*) interval.

pausenlos *adj & adv* nonstop.

Pavillon (*pl* -s) *der* (*in Park*) bandstand.

Pazifik *der* Pacific.

Pazifische Ozean *der*: **der ~** the Pacific Ocean.

PC (*pl* -s) *der* PC.

Pech *das* (*Unglück*) bad luck; **~ haben** to be unlucky.

Pedal (*pl* -e) *das* pedal.

pedantisch ♦ *adj* (*Person*) pedantic. **♦** *adv* pedantically.

Peeling (*pl* -s) *das* (*Kosmetikartikel*) face pack.

peinlich *adj* (*unangenehm*) embarrassing; **es war mir ~** I felt embarrassed.

Pellkartoffeln *pl* boiled unpeeled potatoes.

Pelz (*pl* -e) *der* fur.

Pelzmantel (*pl* -mäntel) *der* fur coat.

Pendelverkehr *der* commuter traffic.

Pendler, -in (*mpl* -) *der, die* commuter.

penetrant *adj* (*Person*) insistent; (*Geschmack, Geruch*) penetrating.

Penis (*pl* -se) *der* penis.

Penizillin *das* penicillin.

Pension (*pl* -en) *die* (*Hotel*) guesthouse; (*Rente*) pension; (*Ruhestand*) retirement; **in ~ sein** to be retired.

PENSION

A 'Pension' is a family guesthouse which usually has only a few rooms. Whilst the accommodation is often more basic than in a hotel, guests are normally welcomed into the host family, getting the opportunity to learn about the local culture.

---

pensionieren *vt* to pension off.

Pensionsgast (*pl* -gäste) *der* guest.

Peperoni (*pl* -) *die* chili pepper.

per *präp* (+A) by; (*amt: pro*) per; **~ Luftpost** (by) airmail.

perfekt *adj* perfect.

Pergamentpapier *das* greaseproof paper.

Periode (*pl* -n) *die* period.

Perle (*pl* -n) *die* (*aus Muschel*) pearl; (*aus Holz, Glas*) bead.

Perlenkette (*pl* -n) *die* pearl necklace.

perplex *adj* stunned.

Person (*pl* -en) *die* person; (*in Drama, Roman*) character.

Personal *das* staff.

Personalabteilung (*pl* -en) *die* personnel department.

Personalakte (*pl* -n) *die* personal file.

Personalausweis (*pl* -e) *der* identity card.

Personalausweisnummer (*pl* -n) *die* identity card number.

Personalien *pl* personal details (*pl*).

Personalpronomen (*pl* -pronomina) *das* personal pronoun.

Personenkraftwagen (*pl* -) *der*

(amt) car (Br), automobile (Am).

Personenzug (pl -züge) der (amt) passenger train.

persönlich ◆ adj personal. ◆ adv personally.

Persönlichkeit (pl -en) die personality.

Perspektive (pl -n) die (optisch) perspective; (Möglichkeit) prospect.

Perücke (pl -n) die wig.

pessimistisch adj pessimistic.

Petersilie die parsley.

Petroleum das paraffin (Br), kerosene (Am).

Pf. abk = Pfennig.

Pfad (pl -e) der path.

Pfadfinder, -in (mpl -) der, die boy scout (girl guide).

Pfahl (pl Pfähle) der post.

Pfand das (von Flaschen) deposit.

Pfandflasche (pl -n) die returnable bottle.

Pfandleihhaus (pl -häuser) das pawnbroker's.

Pfandrückgabe die counter for returning bottles.

Pfanne (pl -n) die (zum Braten) frying pan; **beschichtete ~** non-stick frying pan.

Pfannengericht (pl -e) das fried dish.

Pfannkuchen (pl -) der pancake.

Pfarrer (pl -) der (katholisch) priest; (evangelisch) vicar.

Pfarrerin (pl -nen) die (evangelisch) vicar.

Pfeffer der pepper.

Pfefferkuchen (pl -) der gingerbread.

Pfefferminztee der peppermint tea.

pfeffern vt (mit Pfeffer) to season with pepper; (fam: werfen) to fling.

Pfeife (pl -n) die (zum Pfeifen) whistle; (zum Rauchen) pipe; **~ rauchen** to smoke a pipe.

pfeifen (prät pfiff, pp gepfiffen) vi to whistle.

Pfeil (pl -e) der arrow; **'folgen Sie dem gelben ~'** 'follow the yellow arrow'.

Pfeiler (pl -) der pillar.

Pfennig (pl -e) der pfennig.

Pferd (pl -e) das (Tier) horse.

Pferderennen (pl -) das horse race.

Pferdeschwanz (pl -schwänze) der (Frisur) ponytail.

Pferdesport der equestrian sport.

Pferdestärke (pl -n) die (amt) horsepower.

pfiff prät → pfeifen.

Pfiff (pl -e) der (Ton) whistle.

Pfifferling (pl -e) der chanterelle (mushroom).

Pfingsten (pl -) nt Whit.

Pfingstmontag (pl -e) der Whit Monday.

Pfingstsonntag (pl -e) der Whit Sunday.

Pfirsich (pl -e) der peach.

Pflanze (pl -n) die plant.

pflanzen vt to plant.

pflanzlich adj vegetable.

Pflaster (pl -) das (Verband) plaster; (auf Straße) road surface.

Pflaume (pl -n) die plum.

Pflaumenkuchen (pl -) der plum tart.

Pflaumenmus das plum jam.

Pflege die care; (von Kranken) nursing.

pflegeleicht adj (Material) easy-care.

pflegen vt to care for; (Kranke) to nurse; (Garten) to tend. ► **sich pflegen** ref to take care with one's appearance.

Pflegepersonal das nursing staff.

Pfleger, -in (mpl -) der, die (in Krankenhaus) nurse.

Pflicht (pl -en) die (Aufgabe) duty.

pflichtbewußt adj conscientious.

Pflichtversicherung (pl -en) die compulsory insurance.

pflücken vt to pick.

Pforte (*pl* -n) *die* gate.

Pförtner, -in (*mpl* -) *der, die* porter.

Pfote (*pl* -n) *die* paw.

pfui *interj* yuck!

Pfund (*pl* -e) *das* pound; (*Gewichtseinheit*) = 500 g, ≈ pound.

Pfütze (*pl* -n) *die* puddle.

Phantasie (*pl* -n) *die* imagination.

phantastisch ◆ *adj* fantastic. ◆ *adv* (*großartig*) fantastically.

Phase (*pl* -n) *die* phase.

Philharmoniker *pl* (*Orchester*) philharmonic.

Philosoph, -in (*mpl* -en) *der, die* philosopher.

Philosophie (*pl* -n) *die* philosophy.

Photo = **Foto**.

Phrase (*pl* -n) *die* (*abw*) cliché; **leere ~n** empty words.

Physik *die* physics (*sg*).

physikalisch *adj* physical.

Physiker, -in (*mpl* -) *der, die* physicist.

physisch *adj* physical.

Pianist, -in (*mpl* -en) *der, die* pianist.

Pickel (*pl* -) *der* (*auf Haut*) spot; (*Gerät*) pickaxe; (*für Eis*) ice axe.

Picknick (*pl* -s) *das* picnic; **ein ~ machen** to have a picnic.

Pik (*pl* -) *das* spades (*pl*).

pikant *adj & adv* spicy.

Pilger, -in (*mpl* -) *der, die* pilgrim.

Pilgerfahrt (*pl* -en) *die* pilgrimage.

Pille (*pl* -n) *die* pill; **die ~ nehmen** to be on the pill.

Pilot, -in (*mpl* -en) *der, die* pilot.

Pils (*pl* -) *das* Pils (*lager*).

Pilz (*pl* -e) *der* (*eßbar*) mushroom; (*giftig*) toadstool; (*fam: Hautpilz*) fungal infection.

pink *adj* pink.

pinkeln *vi* (*fam*) to pee.

Pinsel (*pl* -) *der* brush.

Pinzette (*pl* -n) *die* tweezers (*pl*).

Pistazie (*pl* -n) *die* pistachio.

Piste (*pl* -n) *die* (*zum Skifahren*) piste, run; (*Landebahn*) runway.

Pistole (*pl* -n) *die* pistol.

Pizza (*pl* -s ODER **Pizzen**) *die* pizza.

Pizzaservice (*pl* -s) *der* pizza delivery service.

Pizzeria (*pl* -s) *die* pizzeria.

Pkw (*pl* -s) *der* = **Personenkraftwagen**.

Plakat (*pl* -e) *das* poster.

Plakette (*pl* -n) *die* sticker.

Plan (*pl* **Pläne**) *der* plan; (*Karte*) map.

Plane (*pl* -n) *die* tarpaulin.

planen *vt* to plan.

Planet (*pl* -en) *der* planet.

Planetarium (*pl* **Planetarien**) *das* planetarium.

planmäßig ◆ *adj* (*Abfahrt*) scheduled. ◆ *adv* (*abfahren*) on time.

Planschbecken (*pl* -) *das* paddling pool (Br), wading pool (Am).

planschen *vi* to splash about.

Planung (*pl* -en) *die* (*Handlung*) planning.

Plastik¹ *das* (*Material*) plastic.

Plastik² (*pl* -en) *die* (*Skulptur*) sculpture.

Plastikgeld *das* (*fam*) plastic money.

Plastiktüte (*pl* -n) *die* plastic bag.

Platin *das* platinum.

platt *adj* flat; **~ sein** (*fam*) to be gobsmacked; **einen Platten haben** (*fam*) to have a flat.

Platt(deutsch) *das* Low German (*dialect spoken in North Germany*).

Platte (*pl* -n) *die* (*zum Servieren*) plate; (*aus Stein*) slab; (*aus Metall, Glas*) sheet; (*Schallplatte*) record; (*von Herd*) ring.

Plattenspieler (*pl* -) *der* record player.

Plattfüße *pl* flat feet.

Platz (*pl* **Plätze**) *der* (*verfügbar*) space, room; (*Stelle, Rang*) place; (*Sitzplatz*) seat; (*angelegt*) square; **jm ~ machen** to make room for sb; **nehmen Sie ~!** sit down!; **viel ~ haben** to have a lot of room; **auf die Plätze, fertig, los!** on your marks, get set, go!

Platzanweiser, -in (mpl -) der, die usher (usherette).

Plätzchen (pl -) das biscuit (Br), cookie (Am).

platzen vi ist (Reifen) to burst; (fam: Termin) to fall through; (Scheck) to bounce.

Platzkarte (pl -n) die (in Zug) seat reservation.

Platzreservierung (pl -en) die seat reservation.

Platzwunde (pl -n) die cut.

plaudern vi (sprechen) to chat.

pleite adj: ~ sein to be broke.

Plombe (pl -n) die (in Zahn) filling.

plombieren vt (Zahn) to fill.

plötzlich ◆ adj sudden. ◆ adv suddenly.

plump adj (schwerfällig) clumsy.

plumpsen vi ist (fam) to crash.

plus konj & adv plus; **fünf Grad ~** plus five degrees.

PLZ abk = **Postleitzahl**.

Po (pl -s) der (fam) bottom.

Podest (pl -e) das pedestal.

Podium (pl Podien) das podium.

Podiumsdiskussion (pl -en) die panel discussion.

Poesie die (Dichtung) poetry.

Pointe (pl -n) die punchline.

Pokal (pl -e) der (SPORT) cup.

Poker der ODER das poker.

pokern vi (Poker spielen) to play poker.

Pol (pl -e) der pole.

Polen nt Poland.

Police (pl -n) die policy.

polieren vt to polish.

Politesse (pl -n) die traffic warden.

Politik die (von Land, Stadt) politics (pl); (Taktik) policy.

Politiker, -in (mpl -) der, die politician.

Politikwissenschaft die political science.

politisch adj political.

Politur (pl -en) die polish.

Polizei die police (pl).

Polizeibeamte (pl -n) der police officer.

Polizeibeamtin (pl -nen) die police officer.

polizeilich adj police; **~es Kennzeichen** registration number (Br), license number (Am).

Polizeirevier (pl -e) das police station.

Polizeistunde (pl -n) die closing time.

Polizeiwache (pl -n) die police station.

Polizist, -in (mpl -en) der, die police officer.

Pollen (pl -) der pollen.

Pollenflug (pl -flüge) der pollen count.

Polo das polo.

Polster (pl -) das (zum Sitzen) cushion; (Schulterpolster) shoulder pad.

Polstermöbel pl upholstered furniture (sg).

Polterabend (pl -e) der celebration usually held on evening before wedding, when crockery is broken to bring good luck.

Pommes pl (fam) chips (Br), french fries (Am).

Pommes frites pl chips (Br), french fries (Am).

Pony (pl -s) ◆ das (Tier) pony. ◆ der (Frisur) fringe (Br), bangs (pl) (Am).

Pool (pl -s) der (Schwimmbecken) pool.

Popmusik die pop music.

populär adj (beliebt) popular.

porös adj porous.

Porree der leek.

Portal (pl -e) das portal.

Portemonnaie (pl -s) das purse.

Portier (pl -s) der porter.

Portion (pl -en) die portion.

Porto (pl -s) das postage.

portofrei adj freepost.

Porträt (pl -s) das portrait.

Portugal nt Portugal.

Portugiese (pl -n) der Portuguese (man); **die ~n** the Portuguese.

Portugiesin (pl -nen) die

Portuguese (woman).
portugiesisch adj Portuguese.
Portugiesisch(e) das Portuguese.
Portwein (pl -e) der port.
Porzellan (pl -e) das china.
Posaune (pl -n) die trombone.
Position (pl -en) die position.
positiv ♦ adj positive. ♦ adv positively.
Post die post; (Institution, Gebäude) post office; **etw mit der ~ schicken** to send sthg by post; **zur ~ gehen** to got to the post office.
Postamt (pl -ämter) das post office.
Postanweisung (pl -en) die postal order (Br), money order (Am).
Postbote (pl -n) der postman (Br), mailman (Am).
Postbotin (pl -nen) die postwoman (Br), mailwoman (Am).
Posten (pl -) der (beruflich) post.
Poster (pl -) das poster.
Postf. abk = Postfach.
Postfach (pl -fächer) das PO box.
Postgiroamt (pl -ämter) das ≈ Girobank.
Postgirokonto (pl -konten) das ≈ Girobank account.
Postkarte (pl -n) die postcard.
postlagernd adj poste restante.
Postleitzahl (pl -en) die post code (Br), zip code (Am).
Postleitzahlenbuch (pl -bücher) das post code directory.
Postschalter (pl -) der post office counter.
Postscheck (pl -s) der giro cheque.
Postscheckamt (pl -ämter) das ≈ Girobank.
Postscheckkonto (pl -konten) das ≈ Girobank account.
Postsparkasse (pl -n) die Post Office Savings Bank.
Poststempel (pl -) der postmark.
Postüberweisung (pl -en) die Giro transfer.
Postvermerk (pl -e) der postmark.
Postweg der: **auf dem ~** by post.

Postwertzeichen (pl -) das (amt) postage stamp.
prächtig adj magnificent.
Prädikat (pl -e) das (GRAMM) predicate; (Note) grade.
prahlen vi to boast.
Praktikant, -in (mpl -en) der, die trainee.
Praktikum (pl Praktika) das work placement; **ein ~ machen** to be on a work placement.
praktisch ♦ adj practical. ♦ adv practically.
Praline (pl -n) die chocolate.
prall adj bulging; **in der ~en Sonne** in the blazing sun.
Prämie (pl -n) die (von Bank, Versicherung) premium; (Belohnung) bonus.
prämieren vt to award.
Präparat (pl -e) das (Medikament) preparation.
Präsens das present (tense).
präsentieren vt to present.
Präservativ (pl -e) das condom.
Präsident, -in (mpl -en) der, die president.
Prater der large park near Vienna.

PRATER

This huge national park is situated near Vienna, between the river Danube and the Danube canal. Besides its wide, open spaces and parkland, it boasts sports facilities such as a golf course, sports stadium and a trotting course for horses. It is also home to the 'Wurstlprater', a permanent funfair which includes the 61 m high Ferris wheel that has become the symbol of Vienna.

Präteritum das imperfect (tense).
Praxis (pl Praxen) die practice; **in der ~** (Wirklichkeit) in practice.
präzise adj precise.
predigen vi to preach.
Preis (pl -e) der price; (Belohnung) prize; **der ~ für** the price of; **im ~**

inbegriffen included in the price.

Preisänderung (pl -en) die price change.

Preisausschreiben (pl -) das competition.

Preiselbeere (pl -n) die cranberry.

Preisermäßigung (pl -en) die reduction in price.

preisgünstig adj cheap.

Preislage (pl -n) die price range.

Preisliste (pl -n) die price list.

Preisschild (pl -er) das price tag.

Preisstufe (pl -n) die (bei Bus) fare stage.

preiswert ◆ adj cheap. ◆ adv cheaply.

prellen vt: die Zeche ~ to leave without paying; sich (D) etw ~ (verletzen) to bruise sthg.

Prellung (pl -en) die bruise.

Premiere (pl -n) die premiere.

Premierminister, -in (mpl -) der, die prime minister.

Presse (pl -n) die press.

pressen vt to press.

prickelnd adj (Wein, Wasser) sparkling.

Priester, -in (mpl -) der, die priest.

prima adj (fam) brilliant.

primitiv adj primitive.

Prinz (pl -en) der prince.

Prinzessin (pl -nen) die princess.

Prinzip (pl -ien) das principle; aus ~ on principle; im ~ in principle.

prinzipiell adj in principle.

Prise (pl -n) die pinch; eine ~ Salz a pinch of salt.

priv. abk = privat.

privat ◆ adj private. ◆ adv privately.

Privatadresse (pl -n) die home address.

Privatbesitz der private ownership.

Privatfernsehen das commercial television.

Privatgespräch (pl -e) das private conversation.

Privatgrundstück (pl -e) das private property.

privatisieren vt to privatize.

Privatpatient, -in (mpl -en) der, die private patient.

Privatquartier (pl -e) das private accommodation.

Privatsender (pl -) der commercial television channel.

Privatunterkunft (pl -künfte) die private accommodation.

Privatversicherung (pl -en) die private insurance.

Privatweg (pl -e) der private footpath.

pro präp (+A) per; ~ Kopf ODER Person per person; zweimal ~ Tag twice a day.

Probe (pl -n) die (probieren, prüfen) test; (Teil) sample; (von Aufführung) rehearsal.

Probefahrt (pl -en) die test drive.

Probezeit (pl -en) die trial period.

probieren vt (Essen, Getränk) to taste; (versuchen) to try.

Problem (pl -e) das problem; kein ~! (fam) no problem!

problematisch adj problematic.

problemlos adj problem-free.

Produkt (pl -e) das product.

Produktion (pl -en) die production.

Produktionsleiter, -in (mpl -) der, die production manager.

Produzent, -in (mpl -en) der, die (von Ware) manufacturer; (von Film) producer.

produzieren vt to produce.
▶ **sich produzieren** ref (abw) to show off.

Prof. abk = Professor.

professionell adj professional.

Professor (pl Professoren) der professor.

Professorin (pl -nen) die professor.

Profi (pl -s) der pro.

Profil (pl -e) das (von Reifen) tread; (von Gesicht) profile.

Profit (pl -e) der profit.

profitieren vi to profit.
Prognose (pl -n) die prognosis.
Programm (pl -e) das programme;
(EDV) program; (von Partei) agenda.
Programmheft (pl -e) das programme.
Programmhinweis (pl -e) der trailer.
programmieren vt (EDV) to program.
Programmierer, -in (mpl -) der, die programmer.
Programmkino (pl -s) das art house cinema.
Programmpunkt (pl -e) der item (on agenda).
Programmübersicht (pl -en) die programme preview.
Programmzeitschrift (pl -en) die TV guide.
progressiv adj progressive.
Projekt (pl -e) das project.
Projektor (pl Projektoren) der projector.
Pro-Kopf-Verbrauch der consumption per head.
Promenade (pl -n) die promenade.
Promille (pl -) das (von Alkohol) alcohol level; **1,5 ~ haben** to have 1.5 grammes of alcohol in one's blood.
prominent adj prominent.
prompt adv promptly.
Propangas das propane.
prophylaktisch adj preventative.
prosit interj cheers!
Prospekt (pl -e) der brochure.
prost interj cheers!
Prostituierte (pl -n) der, die prostitute.
Protest (pl -e) der protest.
Protestant, -in (mpl -en) der, die protestant.
protestantisch adj protestant.
protestieren vi to protest; **~ gegen** to protest against (Br), to protest (Am).
Prothese (pl -n) die artificial limb; (Zahnprothese) dentures (pl).

Protokoll (pl -e) das (Aufzeichnung) record; **etw zu ~ geben** to put sthg on the record.
protokollieren vt to record.
Proviant der provisions (pl).
Provinz (pl -en) die (Landesteil) province; (abw: Hinterland) provinces (pl).
provinziell adj (abw) provincial.
Provision (pl -en) die commission.
provisorisch adj provisional.
provozieren vt to provoke.
Prozent (pl -e) das per cent. ▶ **Prozente** pl (Preisnachlaß) discount (sg).
Prozeß (pl Prozesse) der (vor Gericht) trial; (Vorgang) process.
Prozession (pl -en) die procession.
P+R-Parkplatz (pl -plätze) der park and ride car park.
prüfen vt (Schüler, Qualität) to test; (Rechnung, Maschine) to check.
Prüfung (pl -en) die exam, examination; **eine ~ bestehen** to pass an exam; **eine ~ machen** to sit ODER take an exam.
Prügelei (pl -en) die fight.
prügeln vt to beat. ▶ **sich prügeln** ref to fight.
prunkvoll adj magnificent.
PS das (abk für Pferdestärke) HP; (abk für Postscriptum) PS.
Pseudonym (pl -e) das pseudonym.
Psychiater, -in (mpl -) der, die psychiatrist.
psychisch ◆ adj psychological. ◆ adv psychologically.
Psychologe (pl -n) der psychologist.
Psychologie die psychology.
Psychologin (pl -nen) die psychologist.
Psychotherapie die psychotherapy.
Pubertät die puberty.
Publikum das (von Veranstaltung) audience; (von Restaurant) customers (pl).

Pudding (*pl* **-s**) *der* blancmange.
Puder (*pl* **-**) *der* powder.
Puderdose (*pl* **-n**) *die* (powder) compact.
pudern *vt* to powder. ► **sich pudern** *ref* to powder o.s.
Puderzucker *der* icing sugar.
Pulli (*pl* **-s**) *der* (*fam*) sweater, jumper (Br).
Pullover (*pl* **-**) *der* sweater, jumper (Br).
Puls (*pl* **-e**) *der* pulse.
Pulver (*pl* **-**) *das* powder.
Pulverkaffee *der* instant coffee.
Pulverschnee *der* powder snow.
Pumpe (*pl* **-n**) *die* (*Gerät*) pump.
pumpen *vt* & *vi* to pump; **jm etw ~** (*fam: leihen*) to lend sb sthg; **sich** (D) **etw ~** (*fam*) to borrow sthg.
Pumpernickel *das* pumpernickel (*dark hard bread made from rye flour*).
Pumps (*pl* **-**) *der* court shoe.
Punker, -in (*mpl* **-**) *der, die* punk.
Punkt (*pl* **-e**) *der* the point; (GRAMM) full stop (Br), period (Am); (*auf Stoff*) dot; **~ ein Uhr** one o'clock on the dot.
pünktlich ◆ *adj* punctual. ◆ *adv* punctually.
Punsch (*pl* **-e**) *der* punch.
Puppe (*pl* **-n**) *die* (*Spielzeug*) doll.
pur *adj* pure.
Püree (*pl* **-s**) *das* puree.
Pute (*pl* **-n**) *die* turkey.
Putenschnitzel (*pl* **-**) *das* turkey escalope.
putzen *vt* & *vi* to clean; **sich** (D) **die Nase ~** to blow one's nose; **sich** (D) **die Zähne ~** to clean one's teeth. ► **sich putzen** *ref* (*Tier*) to wash o.s.
Putzfrau (*pl* **-en**) *die* cleaner.
Putzlappen (*pl* **-**) *der* cloth.
Putzmittel (*pl* **-**) *das* cleaning fluid.
Puzzle (*pl* **-s**) *das* jigsaw (puzzle).
Pyramide (*pl* **-n**) *die* pyramid.

Q

Quadrat (*pl* **-e**) *das* (*Form*) square.
quadratisch *adj* square.
Quadratmeter (*pl* **-**) *der* square metre.
quälen *vt* to torture. ► **sich quälen** *ref* to suffer.
Qualifikation (*pl* **-en**) *die* qualification.
Qualität (*pl* **-en**) *die* quality.
Qualle (*pl* **-n**) *die* jellyfish.
Qualm *der* thick smoke.
qualmen *vi* (*Feuer, Schornstein*) to smoke.
Quarantäne (*pl* **-n**) *die* quarantine.
Quark *der* soft cheese.
Quarktasche (*pl* **-n**) *die* pastry filled with soft cheese.
Quarktorte (*pl* **-n**) *die* cheesecake.
Quartett (*pl* **-e**) *das* (MUS) quartet; (*Kartenspiel*) children's card game where players have to collect four of a kind.
Quartier (*pl* **-e**) *das* (*Unterkunft*) accommodation.
Quarzuhr (*pl* **-en**) *die* (*Armband*) quartz watch; (*an Wand*) quartz clock.
quasi *adv* virtually.
Quatsch *der* (*fam*) rubbish.
quatschen *vi* (*fam: reden*) to chat; (*zu viel reden*) to chatter.
Quelle (*pl* **-n**) *die* source; (*von Wasser*) spring.
quellen (*präs* **quillt**, *prät* **quoll**, *pp* **gequollen**) *vi* (*Flüssigkeit*) to stream; (*Reis, Erbsen*) to swell.
quer *adv* (*diagonal*) diagonally; (*rechtwinklig*) at right angles.
querfeldein *adv* cross-country.
Querflöte (*pl* **-n**) *die* flute.
querschnittsgelähmt *adj* paraplegic.

Querstraße (*pl* **-n**) *die*: **die nächste ~ rechts** the next turning on the right.

quetschen *vt* (*zerquetschen*) to crush; (*verletzen*) to squeeze; **ich hab' mir den Finger in der Tür gequetscht** I caught my finger in the door. ► **sich quetschen** *ref* (*sich zwängen*) to squeeze.

Quetschung (*pl* **-en**) *die* bruise.

quietschen *vi* to squeak.

quillt *präs* → **quellen**.

Quitte (*pl* **-n**) *die* quince.

quittieren *vt* (*mit Unterschrift*) to write a receipt for.

Quittung (*pl* **-en**) *die* (*für Zahlung*) receipt; **könnte ich bitte eine ~ bekommen?** could I have a receipt please?

Quiz (*pl* **-**) *das* quiz.

quoll *prät* → **quellen**.

R

Rabatt (*pl* **-e**) *der* discount; **~ bekommen/geben auf** (+A) to get/give a discount on.

rabiat *adj* brutal.

Rache *die* revenge.

rächen *vt* to avenge. ► **sich rächen** *ref* (*Rache nehmen*) to get one's revenge.

Raclette (*pl* **-s**) *das* melted Swiss cheese served with jacket potatoes.

Rad (*pl* **Räder**) *das* wheel; (*Fahrrad*) bike; **mit dem ~ fahren** to cycle.

Radar *der* radar.

Radarkontrolle (*pl* **-n**) *die* speed trap.

radeln *vi ist* to cycle.

rad|fahren *vi unr ist* to cycle.

Radfahrer, -in (*mpl* **-**) *der, die* cyclist.

Radfahrweg (*pl* **-e**) *der* cycle track.

Radi (*pl* **-**) *der* (*Süddt*) radish.

radieren ♦ *vi* (*mit Radiergummi*) to erase. ♦ *vt* (*Bild*) to etch.

Radiergummi (*pl* **-s**) *der* rubber (Br), eraser (Am).

Radieschen (*pl* **-**) *das* radish.

radikal *adj* radical.

Radio (*pl* **-s**) *das* radio.

radioaktiv *adj* radioactive.

Radiologe (*pl* **-n**) *der* radiologist.

Radiologin (*pl* **-nen**) *die* radiologist.

Radiorecorder (*pl* **-**) *der* radio cassette player.

Radiosender (*pl* **-**) *der* radio station.

Radiosendung (*pl* **-en**) *die* radio programme.

Radiowecker (*pl* **-**) *der* radio alarm.

Radler, -in (*mpl* **-**) *der, die* (*fam: Radfahrer*) cyclist.

Radrennen (*pl* **-**) *das* cycle race.

Radsport *der* cycling.

Radtour (*pl* **-en**) *die* cycling tour.

Radwechsel (*pl* **-**) *der* wheel change.

Radweg (*pl* **-e**) *der* cycle path.

raffiniert *adj* (*schlau*) cunning.

Ragout (*pl* **-s**) *das* stew.

Rahm *der* cream.

Rahmen (*pl* **-**) *der* frame; (*von Fahrzeug*) chassis.

Rakete (*pl* **-n**) *die* rocket.

rammen *vt* (*Auto, Bus*) to ram.

Rampe (*pl* **-n**) *die* (*Laderampe*) ramp.

Rand (*pl* **Ränder**) *der* edge; (*von Gefäß*) rim; (*auf Papier*) margin.

randalieren *vi* to rampage.

Randstreifen (*pl* **-**) *der* (*von Straße*) verge (Br), berm (Am); (*von Autobahn*) hard shoulder (Br), shoulder (Am).

randvoll *adj* full to the brim.

rang *prät* → **ringen**.

Rang (*pl* **Ränge**) *der* rank; (*im Theater*) circle; **der erste/zweite ~** dress/upper circle.

rangieren ◆ *vt* (*Fahrzeug*) to shunt. ◆ *vi* (*Sportler*): **an dritter Stelle ~** to be in third place.

ranken *vi ist* (*Pflanze*) to climb. ▶ **sich ranken** *ref* (*Pflanze*) to climb.

rann *prät* → **rinnen**.

rannte *prät* → **rennen**.

ranzig *adj* rancid.

Rappen (*pl* -) *der* (*Münze*) centime (*one hundredth of a Swiss franc*).

Rapsöl *das* rapeseed oil.

Rarität (*pl* -en) *die* (*Gegenstand*) rarity.

rasant *adj* (*Tempo*) rapid.

rasch *adj* quick.

rascheln *vi* (*Blätter*) to rustle.

rasen *vi ist* (*fahren*) to race.

Rasen *der* lawn; (*Gras*) grass.

Rasenfläche (*pl* -n) *die* lawn.

Rasenmäher (*pl* -) *der* lawnmower.

Rasierapparat (*pl* -e) *der* shaver.

Rasiercreme (*pl* -s) *die* shaving cream.

rasieren *vt* to shave. ▶ **sich rasieren** *ref* to shave; **sich naß ~** to have a wet shave.

Rasierer (*pl* -) *der* shaver.

Rasierklinge (*pl* -n) *die* razor blade.

Rasiermesser (*pl* -) *das* razor.

Rasierpinsel (*pl* -) *der* shaving brush.

Rasierschaum *der* shaving foam.

Rasierseife (*pl* -n) *die* shaving soap.

Rasierwasser *das* aftershave.

Rasse (*pl* -n) *die* (*von Menschen*) race; (*von Tieren*) breed.

Rassismus *der* racism.

Rast *die* rest; **~ machen** to have a rest.

rasten *vi* to rest.

Rasthof (*pl* -höfe) *der* (*an Autobahn*) services (*pl*) (*with accommodation*).

Rastplatz (*pl* -plätze) *der* (*an Autobahn*) services (*pl*); (*an Wanderweg*) picnic area; **'~ bitte sauberhalten!'** 'please keep this picnic area tidy'.

Raststätte (*pl* -n) *die* (*an Autobahn*) services (*pl*).

Rasur (*pl* -en) *die* shave.

Rat (*pl* **Räte**) *der* (*Ausschuß*) council; (*Ratschlag*) (piece of) advice; **jm einen ~ geben** to advise sb; **jn um ~ fragen** to ask sb for advice.

rät *präs* → **raten**.

Rate (*pl* -n) *die* (*Zahlung*) instalment; **auf ~n kaufen** to buy on hire purchase.

raten (*präs* **rät**, *prät* **riet**, *pp* **geraten**) *vi & vt* (*erraten*) to guess; **jm ~** (*Rat geben*) to advise sb.

Ratenzahlung (*pl* -en) *die* payment by instalments.

Ratgeber (*pl* -) *der* (*Buch, Heft*) guide.

Rathaus (*pl* -häuser) *das* town hall.

Ration (*pl* -en) *die* ration.

rational *adj* rational.

rationalisieren *vi & vt* to rationalize.

rationell *adj* (*wirksam*) efficient.

ratlos *adj* helpless.

ratsam *adj* advisable.

Ratschlag (*pl* -schläge) *der* piece of advice.

Ratschläge *pl* advice (*sg*).

Rätsel (*pl* -) *das* puzzle.

Ratskeller (*pl* -) *der* cellar bar underneath a town hall.

Ratte (*pl* -n) *die* rat.

Raub *der* robbery.

rauben *vt* (*Geld, Gegenstand*) to steal.

Raubüberfall (*pl* -fälle) *der* robbery.

Rauch *der* smoke.

rauchen *vi & vt* to smoke; **'bitte nicht ~'** 'no smoking please'; **'Rauchen verboten'** 'no smoking'.

Raucher, -in (*mpl* -) *der, die* (*Person*) smoker.

Räucheraal (*pl* -e) *der* smoked eel.

Raucherabteil (*pl* -e) *das* smoking compartment.

Räucherlachs *der* smoked salmon.

räuchern *vt* to smoke.

Rauchfleisch *das* smoked meat.

rauchfrei *adj*: '**~e Zone**' (*in Restaurant*) 'no-smoking area'.

Rauchmelder (*pl* -) *der* smoke alarm.

Rauchverbot *das* ban on smoking.

rauf *adv* (*fam*) = **herauf**.

rauh *adj* rough; (*Klima*) harsh.

Rauhreif *der* frost.

Raum (*pl* **Räume**) *der* room; (*Dimension*) space; (*Region*) area.

räumen *vt* to clear up; (*Straße*) to clear; (*Wohnung, Haus*) to vacate.

Raumfähre (*pl* -n) *die* space shuttle.

Raumfahrt *die* space travel.

Räumlichkeiten *pl* (*Gebäude*) premises.

Raumpfleger, -in (*mpl* -) *der, die* cleaner.

Raumschiff (*pl* -e) *das* spaceship.

Raumtemperatur (*pl* -en) *die* room temperature.

Räumungsarbeiten *pl* clearance work (*sg*).

Räumungsverkauf (*pl* -käufe) *der* clearance sale.

Raupe (*pl* -n) *die* (*Tier*) caterpillar; (*Karussell*) funfair ride shaped like a caterpillar.

raus *adv* (*fam*) = **heraus**; **~ hier!** get out!

Rausch (*pl* **Räusche**) *der* (*von Alkohol*) intoxication; (*Ekstase*) ecstasy.

rauschen ◆ *vi* (*Wasser*) to roar; (*Bäume*) to rustle. ◆ *vimp*: **es rauscht** (*in Telefon*) it's a bad line.

Rauschgift (*pl* -e) *das* drug.

rauschgiftsüchtig *adj* addicted to drugs.

rausfliegen *vi unr ist* (*fam: aus Schule, Lokal*) to be thrown out.

raushalten: sich raushalten *ref* (*fam*) to stay out of it.

rauskriegen *vt unr* (*fam: Geheimnis*) to find out.

räuspern: sich räuspern *ref* to clear one's throat.

rausschmeißen *vt unr* (*fam*) to throw out.

reagieren *vi* to react.

Reaktion (*pl* -en) *die* reaction; **allergische ~** allergic reaction.

real *adj* real.

realisieren *vt* to realize.

realistisch *adj* realistic.

Realität *die* reality.

Realschule (*pl* -n) *die* secondary school for pupils up to the age of 16.

Rebe (*pl* -n) *die* vine.

rebellieren *vi* to rebel.

Rebhuhn (*pl* -hühner) *das* partridge.

Rebsorte (*pl* -n) *die* (type of) vine.

Rebstock (*pl* -stöcke) *der* vine.

rechnen ◆ *vi* (*mit Zahlen*) to calculate. ◆ *vt* (*Aufgabe*) to work out; **~ mit** (*erwarten*) to expect; (*sich verlassen auf*) to count on; **damit ~, etw zu tun** to expect to do sthg.

Rechner (*pl* -) *der* (*Computer*) computer.

Rechnung (*pl* -en) *die* (*Rechenaufgabe*) calculation; (*für Leistung, für Speisen*) bill (*Br*), check (*Am*); **auf js ~** at sb's expense; **die ~, bitte!** could I have the bill please?

Rechnungsbetrag (*pl* -beträge) *der* total amount.

recht ◆ *adj* (*richtig*) right. ◆ *adv* (*ziemlich*) quite; **jm ~ geben** to agree with sb; **ist Ihnen das ~?** is that all right with you?; **~ haben** to be right.

Recht (*pl* -e) *das* right; **zu ~** rightly.

rechte, -r, -s *adj* right; (*politisch*) right-wing.

Rechte¹ *die* (*politisch*) right wing.

Rechte² *das* (*das Richtige*) right thing.

Rechteck (*pl* -e) *das* rectangle.

rechteckig *adj* rectangular.

rechtfertigen *vt* to justify. ► **sich rechtfertigen** *ref* to justify o.s.

Rechtfertigung (*pl* -en) *die* justification.

rechthaberisch adj: er ist immer so ~ he always thinks he's right.

rechtlich adj legal.

rechts adv (Seitenangabe) on the right; (Richtungsangabe) right; ~ sein (politisch) to be right-wing; nach ~ right; ~ von jm/etw to the right of sb/ sthg; von ~ from the right.

Rechtsabbieger (pl -) der car turning right.

Rechtsanwalt, -wältin (mpl -wälte) der, die lawyer.

Rechtschreibung die spelling.

rechtsherum adv to the right.

Rechtskurve (pl -n) die right-hand bend.

Rechtsradikale (pl -n) der, die right-wing extremist.

Rechtsverkehr der driving on the right.

Rechtsweg der (amt) legal action.

rechtswidrig adj illegal.

rechtzeitig ◆ adj timely. ◆ adv on time.

recyceln vt to recycle.

Recycling das recycling.

Recyclingpapier das recycled paper.

Redakteur, -in (mpl -e) der, die editor.

Rede (pl -n) die (Vortrag) talk; eine ~ halten to make a speech; direkte/ indirekte ~ (GRAMM) direct/indirect speech.

reden vt & vi to talk; ~ mit to talk to; ~ über (+A) to talk about.

Redewendung (pl -en) die idiom.

Redner, -in (mpl -) der, die speaker.

reduzieren vt (verringern) to reduce. ▶ sich reduzieren ref to decrease.

reduziert adj: ~e Ware reduced goods.

Reederei (pl -en) die shipping company.

Reeperbahn die street in Hamburg famous for its bars and nightclubs.

reflektieren vt (Licht) to reflect.

Reflex (pl -e) der (Reaktion) reflex.

Reform (pl -en) die reform.

Reformationstag (pl -e) der Reformation Day, 31st October, day on which the Reformation is celebrated.

Reformhaus (pl -häuser) das health food shop.

reformieren vt to reform.

Reformkost die health food.

Regal (pl -e) das shelves (pl).

Regatta (pl Regatten) die regatta.

rege adj (lebhaft) lively.

Regel (pl -n) die rule; (Menstruation) period; in der ~ as a rule.

Regelblutung (pl -en) die period.

regelmäßig ◆ adj regular. ◆ adv regularly; (fam: immer) always.

regeln vt to regulate; (Verhältnisse) to settle; etw vertraglich ~ to stipulate sthg in a contract. ▶ sich regeln ref to sort itself out.

Regelung (pl -en) die (Vorschrift) regulation.

Regen der rain; bei ~ if it rains; im ~ in the rain.

Regenbogen (pl -bögen) der rainbow.

Regenfälle pl rain (sg).

Regenjacke (pl -n) die raincoat.

Regenmantel (*pl* -mäntel) *der* raincoat.

Regenrinne (*pl* -n) *die* gutter.

Regenschauer (*pl* -) *der* shower.

Regenschirm (*pl* -e) *der* umbrella.

Regentropfen (*pl* -) *der* raindrop.

Regenwetter *das* rainy weather.

Regenwurm (*pl* -würmer) *der* earthworm.

Regie *die* direction.

regieren ◆ *vt* (*Land*) to govern. ◆ *vi* (*König*) to rule; (*Partei, Politiker*) to be in power.

Regierung (*pl* -en) *die* government.

Regierungsbezirk (*pl* -e) *der* administrative division of a 'Land'.

Regierungssitz (*pl* -e) *der* seat of government.

Region (*pl* -en) *die* region.

regional ◆ *adj* regional. ◆ *adv*: ~ verschieden different from region to region.

Regionalprogramm (*pl* -e) *das* regional channel.

Regisseur, -in (*mpl* -e) *der, die* director.

registrieren *vt* (*wahrnehmen*) to note; (*eintragen*) to register.

regnen *vimp* to rain; **es regnet** it's raining.

regnerisch *adj* rainy.

regulär *adj* regular; (*fam: normal*) normal.

regulieren *vt* to regulate.

Reh (*pl* -e) *das* (*Tier*) deer; (*Fleisch*) venison.

Rehrücken (*pl* -) *der* saddle of venison.

Reibe (*pl* -n) *die* grater.

Reibekuchen (*pl* -) *der* potato waffle (Br), ≃ hash browns (Am).

reiben (*prät* **rieb**, *pp* **gerieben**) ◆ *vt* to rub; (*Kartoffeln*) to grate. ◆ *vi* (*scheuern*) to rub; **sich** (D) **die Augen/Hände ~** to rub one's eyes/hands.

Reiberdatschi (*pl* -) *der* (*Süddt*) potato waffle (Br), ≃ hash browns (Am).

reibungslos *adj* smooth.

reich *adj* rich; (*Auswahl*) large; **~ sein an** (+D) to be rich in.

Reich (*pl* -e) *das* (*Herrschaftsgebiet*) empire; (*Bereich*) realm.

reichen ◆ *vi* (*genügen*) to be enough; (*räumlich*) to reach. ◆ *vt* (*geh: geben*) to give, to pass; **jm etw ~** to pass sthg to sb; **der Wein reicht nicht** there isn't enough wine; **jetzt reicht's mir!** (*fam*) I've had enough!; **das reicht!** (*fam*) that's enough!

reichhaltig *adj* extensive; **~es Essen** rich food.

reichlich ◆ *adj* (*groß*) large. ◆ *adv* (*viel*) plenty of; (*ziemlich*) pretty.

Reichtum *der* wealth.

reif *adj* (*Obst*) ripe; (*Person*) mature.

Reif *der* (*Rauhreif*) frost.

reifen *vi* ist (*Obst*) to ripen.

Reifen (*pl* -) *der* (*von Auto, Fahrrad*) tyre; (*Ring*) hoop; **den ~ wechseln** to change the tyre.

Reifendruck *der* tyre pressure.

Reifenpanne (*pl* -n) *die* puncture.

Reifenwechsel (*pl* -) *der* tyre change.

Reihe (*pl* -n) *die* (*Linie*) line; (*in Theater, Kino*) row; (*in Fernsehen, Radio*) series; **eine ~ von** (*Menge*) a number of; **in einer ~** in a row; **der ~ nach** in turn; **Sie sind an der ~** it's your turn.

Reihenfolge *die* order.

Reihenhaus (*pl* -häuser) *das* terraced house.

rein ◆ *adj* (*sauber*) clean; (*pur, ungemischt*) pure. ◆ *adv* (*ausnahmslos*) purely; (*fam: überhaupt*) absolutely; (*fam*) = **herein; komm ~!** (*fam*) come in!

rein|fallen *vi unr* ist (*fam: hineinfallen*) to fall in; (*fam: getäuscht werden*) to be taken for a ride; **~ auf** (+A) (*fam*) to fall for.

reinigen *vt* to clean; **chemisch ~** to dry-clean.

Reiniger (*pl* -) *der* cleaner.

Reinigung (*pl* -en) *die* (*Geschäft*) dry cleaner's; (*Handlung*) cleaning.

Reinigungsmilch die cleansing milk.

Reinigungsmittel (pl -) das cleanser.

rein|legen vt (fam: betrügen, ärgern) to take for a ride; (hineinlegen) to put in.

rein|reden vi: jm ~ (ins Wort fallen: (ffam) to interrupt sb; (fam: beeinflussen) to interfere with sb.

Reis der rice.

Reise (pl -n) die journey; (kurz) trip; **eine ~ machen** to go on a journey/trip; **gute ~!** have a good journey/trip!

Reiseandenken (pl -) das souvenir.

Reiseapotheke (pl -n) die first-aid kit.

Reisebegleiter, -in (mpl -) der, die travelling companion.

Reisebüro (pl -s) das travel agency.

Reisebus (pl -se) der coach.

Reiseführer (pl -) der (Buch) guide book; (Person) guide, courier.

Reiseführerin (pl -nen) die guide, courier.

Reisegepäck das luggage.

Reisegesellschaft (pl -en) die (Gruppe) group of tourists; (Firma) tour operator.

Reisegruppe (pl -n) die group of tourists.

reisekrank adj travelsick.

Reiseland (pl -länder) das holiday destination.

Reiseleiter, -in (mpl -) der, die guide, courier.

reiselustig adj fond of travelling.

reisen vi ist to travel; ~ **nach** to go to.

Reisende (pl -n) der, die traveller; ~ **in Richtung Frankfurt** passengers travelling to Frankfurt.

Reisepaß (pl -pässe) der passport.

Reiseproviant der food for the journey.

Reiseroute (pl -n) die route.

Reiseruf (pl -e) der emergency announcement broadcast over the radio.

Reisescheck (pl -s) der traveller's cheque.

Reisetasche (pl -n) die travel bag.

Reiseunternehmen (pl -) das tour operator.

Reiseveranstalter (pl -) der tour operator.

Reiseverkehr der holiday traffic.

Reiseversicherung (pl -en) die travel insurance.

Reisewetterbericht (pl -e) der holiday weather forecast.

Reisezeit (pl -en) die journey time.

Reisezentrum (pl -zentren) das travel centre.

Reiseziel (pl -e) das destination.

reißen (prät riß, pp gerissen) ◆ vi ist (zerreißen) to break. ◆ vi hat (ziehen) to pull. ◆ vt hat (ziehen, wegziehen) to pull; (zerreißen) to tear; **an etw** (D) ~ to pull sthg. ▶ **sich reißen** ref: **sich ~ um** to scramble for.

Reißverschluß (pl -schlüsse) der zip (Br), zipper (Am).

Reißzwecke (pl -n) die drawing pin (Br), thumbtack (Am).

reiten (prät ritt, pp geritten) vi ist & vt hat to ride; **auf einem Pferd** ~ to ride a horse.

Reiter, -in (mpl -) der, die rider.

Reitpferd (pl -e) das horse (for riding).

Reitsport der riding.

Reitstall (pl -ställe) der riding stable.

Reitweg (pl -e) der bridle path.

Reiz (pl -e) der (physikalisch) stimulus; (Schönheit) attraction.

reizen ◆ vt (verlocken) to tempt; (provozieren) to annoy; (Augen, Magen) to irritate. ◆ vi: **es reizt zum Lachen** it makes you want to laugh.

reizend adj charming.

Reizung (pl -en) die (von Schleimhaut, Magen) irritation.

reizvoll adj (schön) attractive.

Reklamation (*pl* -en) *die* complaint.

Reklame *die* advertising.

reklamieren *vt* (*Ware, Service*) to complain about.

Rekord (*pl* -e) *der* record.

relativ ♦ *adj* relative. ♦ *adv* relatively.

relaxen *vi* (*fam*) to relax.

relevant *adj* relevant.

Religion (*pl* -en) *die* religion; (*Schulfach*) religious education.

religiös *adj* religious.

Relikt (*pl* -e) *das* relic.

Reling *die* rail.

remis *adv*: ~ **enden** to end in a draw.

Remoulade (*pl* -n) *die* remoulade, *sauce of eggs, oil and herbs.*

Renaissance *die* Renaissance.

Rendezvous (*pl* -) *das* rendezvous.

Rennbahn (*pl* -en) *die* racetrack.

rennen (*prät* **rannte**, *pp* **gerannt**) *vi* ist (*laufen*) to run; (*fam: gehen*) to go.

Rennen (*pl* -) *das* racing; (*Veranstaltung*) race.

Rennfahrer, -in (*mpl* -) *der, die* racing driver.

Rennrad (*pl* -räder) *das* racing bike.

Rennsport *der* racing.

Rennwagen (*pl* -) *der* racing car.

renommiert *adj* famous.

renovieren *vt* to renovate.

Renovierung (*pl* -en) *die* renovation; '**wegen ~ geschlossen**' 'closed for alterations'.

Rente (*pl* -n) *die* (*Pension*) pension.

Rentner, -in (*mpl* -) *der, die* pensioner.

Reparatur (*pl* -en) *die* repair.

Reparaturdienst (*pl* -e) *der* repair service.

Reparaturkosten *pl* repair costs.

Reparaturwerkstatt (*pl* -stätten) *die* garage.

reparieren *vt* to repair.

Reportage (*pl* -n) *die* report.

Reporter, -in (*mpl* -) *der, die* reporter.

repräsentativ *adj* representative; (*Wagen, Villa*) imposing.

Republik (*pl* -en) *die* republic.

Reserve (*pl* -n) *die* (*Vorrat*) reserve; (SPORT) reserves (*pl*); **etw in ~ haben** to have sthg in reserve.

Reservekanister (*pl* -) *der* spare can.

Reserverad (*pl* -räder) *das* spare wheel.

Reservereifen (*pl* -) *der* spare tyre.

Reservespieler, -in (*mpl* -) *der, die* reserve.

reservieren *vt* to reserve.

reserviert *adj* reserved.

Reservierung (*pl* -en) *die* reservation.

resignieren *vi* to give up.

Respekt *der* (*Achtung*) respect; (*Angst*) fear.

respektieren *vt* to respect.

Rest (*pl* -e) *der* rest.

Restaurant (*pl* -s) *das* restaurant.

Restbetrag (*pl* -träge) *der* balance.

Restgeld *das*: '**kein ~**' 'no change'; '**~ wird erstattet**' 'change given'.

restlich *adj* remaining.

restlos *adv* completely.

Restmülltonne (*pl* -n) *die* bin for *non-recyclable waste.*

Resturlaub *der* remaining holidays (*pl*).

Resultat (*pl* -e) *das* result.

retten *vt* to save; (*aus Gefahr*) to rescue. ▶ **sich retten** *ref* to escape.

Retter, -in (*mpl* -) *der, die* rescuer.

Rettich (*pl* -e) *der* radish.

Rettung (*pl* -en) *die* (*Handlung*) rescue.

Rettungsboot (*pl* -e) *das* lifeboat.

Rettungsdienst (*pl* -e) *der* emergency services (*pl*).

Rettungsring (*pl* -e) *der* life belt.

Rettungswagen (*pl* -) *der* ambulance.

Revier (*pl* -e) *das* (*Bezirk*) district.

Revolution (*pl* -en) *die* revolution.

Revolver (*pl* -) *der* revolver.

Revue (*pl* -n) *die* revue.

Rezept (*pl* -e) *das* (*für Gericht*) recipe; (*für Medikament*) prescription; **nur gegen ~** only on prescription.

rezeptfrei *adj* available without a prescription.

Rezeption (*pl* -en) *die* (*im Hotel*) reception.

rezeptpflichtig *adj* available only on prescription.

R-Gespräch (*pl* -e) *das* reverse charge call (Br), collect call (Am).

Rhabarber *der* rhubarb.

Rhein *der*: **der ~** the Rhine.

rheinisch *adj* Rhenish.

Rheinland *das* Rhineland.

Rheinland-Pfalz *nt* Rhineland-Palatinate.

Rheinufer (*pl* -) *das* bank of the river Rhine.

Rheinwein (*pl* -e) *der* Rhine wine, hock (Br).

rhetorisch *adj* rhetorical.

Rheuma *das* rheumatism.

Rhythmus (*pl* **Rhythmen**) *der* rhythm.

Ribis(e)l (*pl* -(n)) *die* (*Österr: rot*) redcurrant; (*schwarz*) blackcurrant.

richten ◆ *vt* to direct. ◆ *vi* (*urteilen*) to judge. ➤ **sich richten** *ref* (*in Richtung*) to be directed; **sich nach den Vorschriften ~** to go by the rules.

Richter, -in (*mpl* -) *der, die* judge.

Richtgeschwindigkeit *die* recommended speed limit.

richtig ◆ *adj* right; (*echt*) real. ◆ *adv* (*fam: wirklich*) really; (*korrekt*) correctly; **bin ich hier ~?** am I in the right place?; **meine Uhr geht ~** my watch is right.

richtig|stellen *vt* to correct.

Richtlinie (*pl* -n) *die* guideline.

Richtpreis (*pl* -e) *der* recommended price.

Richtung (*pl* -en) *die* direction; **alle ~en** 'all routes'; **in ~ Berlin fahren** to

travel towards Berlin; **in ~ Süden** southwards.

riechen (*prät* **roch**, *pp* **gerochen**) *vt & vi* to smell; **~ nach** to smell of; **es riecht nach …** there is a smell of …; **an etw** (D) **~** to smell sthg.

rief *prät* → **rufen**.

Riegel (*pl* -) *der* (*Verschluß*) bolt; (*Süßigkeit*) bar.

Riemen (*pl* -) *der* (*Band*) strap.

rieseln *vi ist* (*Wasser*) to trickle; (*Schnee*) to float down.

riesengroß *adj* enormous.

Riesenrad (*pl* -räder) *das* big wheel.

Riesenslalom *der* giant slalom.

riesig *adj* (*Person, Gegenstand*) enormous; **ich hab' ~en Hunger** (*fam*) I'm starving.

Riesling (*pl* -e) *der* Riesling (*white wine*).

riet *prät* → **raten**.

Riff (*pl* -e) *das* reef.

Rille (*pl* -n) *die* groove.

Rind (*pl* -er) *das* (*Tier*) cow; (*Fleisch*) beef.

Rinde (*pl* -n) *die* (*von Brot*) crust; (*von Käse*) rind; (*von Bäumen*) bark.

Rinderbraten (*pl* -) *der* (joint of) roast beef.

Rindfleisch *das* beef.

Ring (*pl* -e) *der* ring; (*Straße*) ring road.

Ringbuch (*pl* -bücher) *das* ring binder.

ringen (*prät* **rang**, *pp* **gerungen**) *vi* to wrestle.

Ringer, -in (*mpl* -) *der, die* wrestler.

Ringkampf (*pl* -kämpfe) *der* (*im Sport*) wrestling match.

ringsum: ringsum *präp* all around.

ringsherum *adv* all around.

Ringstraße (*pl* -n) *die* ring road.

ringsum *adv* all around.

rinnen (*prät* **rann**, *pp* **geronnen**) *vi ist* to run.

Rinnstein (*pl* -e) *der* gutter.

Rippchen (*pl* -) *das* slightly smoked pork rib.

Rippe (*pl* -n) *die* (*Knochen*) rib.
Rippenfellentzündung (*pl* -en) *die* pleurisy.
Risiko (*pl* Risiken) *das* risk; **auf eigenes ~** at one's own risk; **'zu Risiken und Nebenwirkungen'** (MED) 'possible risks and side-effects'.
riskant *adj* risky.
riskieren *vt* to risk.
riß *prät* → **reißen**.
Riß (*pl* Risse) *der* (*in Stoff*) tear; (*in Holz, Wand*) crack.
rissig *adj* cracked.
ritt *prät* → **reiten**.
Ritt (*pl* -e) *der* ride.
Ritter (*pl* -) *der* knight.
ritzen *vt* (*gravieren*) to carve.
Rivale (*pl* -n) *der* rival.
Rivalin (*pl* -nen) *die* rival.
Roastbeef (*pl* -s) *das* roast beef.
Roboter (*pl* -) *der* robot.
robust *adj* robust.
roch *prät* → **riechen**.
Rock¹ (*pl* Röcke) *der* (*Kleidungsstück*) skirt.
Rock² *der* (*Musik*) rock.
Rockmusik *die* rock music.
Rodelbahn (*pl* -en) *die* toboggan run.
rodeln *vi ist* to toboggan.
Roggen *der* rye.
Roggenbrot (*pl* -e) *das* rye bread.
roh ◆ *adj* raw; (*Person*) rough. ◆ *adv* (*behandeln*) roughly; **etw ~ essen** to eat sthg raw.
Rohkost *die* raw fruit and vegetables (*pl*).
Rohr (*pl* -e) *das* (*für Wasser, Gas*) pipe; (*Schilfrohr*) reed; (*für Möbel, Körbe*) cane, wicker.
Rohrbruch (*pl* -brüche) *der* burst pipe.
Rohrzucker *der* cane sugar.
Rokoko *das* rococo.
Rolladen (*pl* Rolläden) *der* (*vor Fenster*) shutters (*pl*).
Rollbahn (*pl* -en) *die* runway.
Rollbraten (*pl* -) *der* roast.

Rolle (*pl* -n) *die* roll; (*Funktion, im Film, Theater*) role; (*Rad*) castor; **es spielt keine ~** it doesn't matter.
rollen *vi ist & vt hat* to roll.
Roller (*pl* -) *der* scooter.
Rollerskates *pl* rollerskates.
Rollkragen (*pl* -) *der* polo neck.
Rollkragenpullover (*pl* -) *der* polo neck (jumper).
Rollmops (*pl* -möpse) *der* rollmop, rolled-up pickled herring.
Rollo (*pl* -s) *das* roller blind.
Rollschuh (*pl* -e) *der* roller skate.
Rollschuhfahrer, -in (*mpl* -) *der, die* roller-skater.
Rollsplit *der* loose chippings (*pl*).
Rollstuhl (*pl* -stühle) *der* wheelchair.
Rollstuhlfahrer, -in (*mpl* -) *der, die* wheelchair user.
Rolltreppe (*pl* -n) *die* escalator.
Roman (*pl* -e) *der* novel.
romanisch *adj* (*Bauwerk, Kunst*) Romanesque; (*Sprache*) Romance.
Romantik *die* Romanticism.
romantisch *adj* romantic; (*Kunst*) Romantic.
römisch-katholisch *adj* Roman Catholic.
Rommé *das* rummy.
röntgen *vt* to X-ray.
Röntgenaufnahme (*pl* -n) *die* X-ray.
rosa *adj* pink.
Rose (*pl* -n) *die* rose.
Rosenkohl *der* (Brussels) sprouts (*pl*).
Rosenmontag (*pl* -e) *der* day before Shrove Tuesday.
Roséwein (*pl* -e) *der* rosé (wine).
Rosine (*pl* -n) *die* raisin.
Rost (*pl* -e) *der* (*auf Metall*) rust; (*Gitter*) grating.
Rostbratwurst (*pl* -würste) *die*: **(Thüringer) ~** Thuringian grilled sausage.
rosten *vi hat & ist* to rust.
rösten *vt* to roast; (*Brot*) to toast.
rostfrei *adj* (*Stahl*) stainless.

Rösti pl (Schweiz) fried potato pancake.

rostig adj rusty.

Rostschutzmittel (pl -) das rust-proofing agent.

rot (komp **röter** ODER **roter**, superl **am rötesten** ODER **am rotesten**) adj red; **in den ~en Zahlen sein** to be in the red.

Rot das red; '**bei ~ hier halten**' 'stop here when red light shows'.

Rote Kreuz das Red Cross.

Röteln pl German measles (sg).

rothaarig adj red-haired.

rotieren vi to rotate; (fam: Person) to be in a flap.

Rotkohl der red cabbage.

Rotkraut das red cabbage.

Rotlicht das (rote Lampe) red light.

Rotlichtviertel (pl -) das red-light district.

Rotwein (pl -e) der red wine.

Rouge (pl -s) das blusher.

Roulade (pl -n) die ≃ beef olive.

Roulette (pl -s) das roulette.

Route (pl -n) die route.

Routine die experience; (Gewohnheit) routine.

Rubbellos (pl -e) das scratch card.

rubbeln vi to rub.

Rübe (pl -n) die turnip.

rüber adv (fam) = **herüber**.

Rubin (pl -e) der ruby.

Rubrik (pl -en) die (Spalte) column.

Rückantwort (pl -en) die reply.

Rückbank (pl -bänke) die back seat; **umklappbare ~** folding back seat.

rücken vt hat & vi ist to move; **nach links/rechts ~** to move to the left/right; **rück mal!** move up!

Rücken (pl -) der back; (von Buch) spine.

Rückenlage die: **in ~** (lying) on one's back.

Rückenlehne (pl -n) die back (of chair).

Rückenschmerzen pl backache (sg).

Rückenschwimmen das backstroke.

Rückenwind der tailwind.

Rückerstattung (pl -en) die reimbursement.

Rückfahrkarte (pl -n) die return (ticket) (Br), round-trip (ticket) (Am).

Rückfahrt (pl -en) die return journey.

Rückfall (pl -fälle) der (Krankheit) relapse.

Rückflug (pl -flüge) der return flight.

Rückfrage (pl -n) die question.

Rückgabe die return; **gegen ~** on return.

Rückgabeknopf (pl -knöpfe) der coin return button.

Rückgaberecht das right to return goods if not satisfied.

rückgängig adv: **etw ~ machen** to cancel sthg.

Rückgrat (pl -e) das (Körperteil) spine.

Rückkehr die return.

rückläufig adj declining.

Rücklicht (pl -er) das rear light.

Rückporto das return postage.

Rückreise (pl -n) die return journey.

Rückreiseverkehr der homeward traffic.

Rückruf (pl -e) der (per Telefon) return call.

Rucksack (pl -säcke) der rucksack.

Rucksacktourist, -in (mpl -en) der, die backpacker.

Rückschritt (pl -e) der step backwards.

Rückseite (pl -n) die back.

Rücksicht (pl -en) die consideration; **~ nehmen auf** (+A) to show consideration for.

rücksichtslos adj inconsiderate.

rücksichtsvoll adj considerate.

Rücksitz (pl -e) der back seat.

Rückspiegel (pl -) der rearview mirror.

Rückstand der (SPORT): **sie sind mit 16 Punkten im ~** they are 16 points behind.

Rückstau (pl -s) der tailback.

Rückstrahler (pl -) der reflector.

Rückvergütung (pl -en) die refund.

rückwärts adv backwards.

Rückwärtsgang der reverse (gear).

Rückweg (pl -e) der way back; **auf dem ~** on the way back.

rückwirkend adj retroactive.

Rückzahlung (pl -en) die repayment.

Rückzahlungsbetrag (pl -beträge) der repayment.

rüde adj rude.

Rüde (pl -n) der (male) dog.

Ruder (pl -) das (zum Rudern) oar; (zum Steuern) rudder.

Ruderboot (pl -e) das rowing boat.

Ruderer (pl -) der rower.

Ruderin (pl -nen) die rower.

rudern vi ist (mit Boot) to row.

Rudersport der rowing.

Ruf (pl -e) der (Rufen) call; (Image) reputation.

rufen (prät rief, pp gerufen) vt & vi to call; **um Hilfe ~** to call for help.

Rufname (pl -n) der first name.

Rufnummer (pl -n) die telephone number.

Ruhe die (Stille) silence; (von Person) calm; (eines Ortes) peacefulness; **jn in ~ lassen** to leave sb in peace; **~ bitte!** quiet, please!

ruhen vi to rest.

Ruhestand der retirement.

Ruhestörung (pl -en) die breach of the peace; **nächtliche ~** breach of the peace at night.

Ruhetag (pl -e) der closing day; **'montags ~'** 'closed on Mondays'.

ruhig ◆ adj quiet; (unbewegt) still; (gelassen) calm. ◆ adv quietly; (unbe-weglich) still; (gelassen) calmly; **mach das ~** (fam) do it, by all means.

Rührei (pl -er) das scrambled egg.

rühren ◆ vt (mit Löffel) to stir; (Person) to move. ◆ vi: **~ von** to come from. ▶ **sich rühren** ref (sich bewegen) to move.

Ruhrgebiet nt the Ruhr.

Rührteig (pl -e) der cake mixture.

Ruine (pl -n) die ruin.

ruinieren vt to ruin. ▶ **sich ruinieren** ref to ruin o.s.

rülpsen vi to belch.

rum adv (fam) = **herum**.

Rum der rum.

Rumänien nt Romania.

rum|kriegen vt (fam: Person) to talk round; (Zeit) to pass.

Rummel der (fam: Theater) fuss; (Trubel) bustle.

Rummelplatz (pl -plätze) der fairground.

rumoren vi to rumble.

Rumpf (pl Rümpfe) der (Körperteil) trunk.

Rumpsteak (pl -s) das rump steak.

Rumtopf (pl -töpfe) der fruit soaked for a long time in rum.

rund ◆ adj round; (dick) plump. ◆ adv (ungefähr) about; (im Kreis) around; **~ 500 Leute** about 500 people; **~ um** around; **~ um den Tisch** round the table.

Runde (pl -n) die (Gang) walk; (Rennen) lap; (von Personen) group; **eine ~ ausgeben** to buy a round.

Rundfahrt (pl -en) die tour.

Rundflug (pl -flüge) der sightseeing flight.

Rundfunk der radio.

Rundfunkmeldung (pl -en) die radio report.

Rundfunkprogramm (pl -e) das radio programme.

Rundgang (pl -gänge) der (Spaziergang) walk.

rundherum adv (ringsherum) all around; (ganz) completely.

Rundreise (*pl* -n) *die* tour.
Rundwanderweg (*pl* -e) *der* circular path.
runter *adv* (*fam*) = **herunter**.
Ruß *der* soot.
Russe (*pl* -n) *der* Russian.
Russin (*pl* -nen) *die* Russian.
russisch *adj* Russian.
Russisch(e) *das* Russian.
Rußland *nt* Russia.
rustikal *adj* rustic.
Rüstung (*pl* -en) *die* (*für Militär*) arms (*pl*); (*von Rittern*) armour.
Rutsch *der*: **guten ~!** happy New Year!
Rutschbahn (*pl* -en) *die* slide.
rutschen *vi* ist (*ausrutschen*) to slip; (*gleiten*) to slide; (*fam: zur Seite rücken*) to move over; (*Hose*) to slip down.
rutschfest *adj* non-slip.
rutschig *adj* slippery.
rütteln *vt* to shake.

S

s. *abk* = **siehe**.
S (*abk für* Süd) S.
S. (*abk für* Seite) p.
Saal (*pl* Säle) *der* hall.
Saarland *das* Saarland.
Säbel (*pl* -) *der* sabre.
sabotieren *vt* to sabotage.
Sachbearbeiter, -in (*mpl* -) *der, die* employee in charge of a particular matter.
Sache (*pl* -n) *die* thing; (*Angelegenheit*) matter; **das ist meine ~** that's my business; **bei der ~ bleiben** to keep to the point; **zur ~ kommen** to get to the point. ▶ **Sachen** *pl* (*Kleidung*) things.
Sachertorte (*pl* -n) *die* chocolate cake (*Viennese speciality*).

sachkundig *adj* well-informed.
Sachlage *die* situation.
sachlich ◆ *adj* (*Person, Argument*) objective; (*Gründe*) practical. ◆ *adv* (*argumentieren*) objectively.
sächlich *adj* (GRAMM) neuter.
Sachschaden (*pl* -schäden) *der* material damage.
Sachsen *nt* Saxony.
sacht *adj* (*Berührung*) gentle.
Sachverständige (*pl* -n) *der, die* expert.
Sack (*pl* Säcke) *der* (*Verpackung*) sack.
Sackgasse (*pl* -n) *die* dead end.
Safe (*pl* -s) *der* safe.
Saft (*pl* Säfte) *der* juice.
saftig *adj* juicy.
Säge (*pl* -n) *die* saw.
sagen *vt* to say; (*befehlen*) to tell; (*bedeuten*) to mean; **jm etw ~** to tell sb sthg; **~ zu** to say to; **sag mal!** tell me; **wie gesagt** as I said; **was sagst du dazu?** what do you think about that?; **das kann man wohl ~!** you can say that again!; **sag bloß!** you don't say!
sägen *vt & vi* to saw.
sah *prät* → **sehen**.
Sahne *die* cream.
Sahnequark *der* cream curd cheese.
Sahnetorte (*pl* -n) *die* gâteau.
sahnig *adj* creamy.
Saison (*pl* -s) *die* season.
Sakko (*pl* -s) *das* jacket.
Salami (*pl* -s) *die* salami.
Salat (*pl* -e) *der* (*Pflanze*) lettuce; (*Gericht*) salad; **grüner ~** green salad.
Salatbar (*pl* -s) *die* salad bar.
Salatsoße (*pl* -n) *die* salad dressing.
Salatteller (*pl* -) *der* plate of salad.
Salbe (*pl* -n) *die* ointment.
Salmonellenvergiftung (*pl* -en) *die* salmonella (poisoning).
Salon (*pl* -s) *der* (*Geschäft*) salon.
Salz (*pl* -e) *das* salt.

Salzburger Festspiele *pl music and theatre festival held in Salzburg.*

SALZBURGER FESTSPIELE
The Salzburg Festival was founded in 1920 and takes place every summer. It features a large number of concerts and operas, particularly the works of Mozart, although other composers such as Strauß and Verdi are also included. Another important component is drama, and traditionally every year there is a performance of the play 'Jedermann' by Hugo von Hofmannsthal, who was one of the founders of the Festival.

Salzburger Nockerln *pl* (Österr) *hot dessert made from beaten egg whites and sugar.*

salzen (*pp* **gesalzen**) *vt* to salt.

Salzgurke (*pl* **-n**) *die* pickled gherkin.

salzig *adj* salty.

Salzkartoffeln *pl* boiled potatoes.

Salzstange (*pl* **-n**) *die* pretzel (stick).

Salzstreuer (*pl* **-**) *der* salt cellar.

Salzwasser *das* saltwater; (*zum Kochen*) salted water.

Samen (*pl* **-**) *der* seed.

Sammelfahrschein (*pl* **-e**) *der* = travelcard.

sammeln *vt* to collect; (*Pilze, Kräuter*) to pick. ▶ **sich sammeln** *ref* to gather.

Sammelstelle (*pl* **-n**) *die* collection point.

Sammler, -in (*mpl* **-**) *der, die* collector.

Sammlung (*pl* **-en**) *die* collection.

Samstag (*pl* **-e**) *der* Saturday; **am ~** on Saturday; **~ morgen/abend** Saturday morning/evening; **~ nacht** Saturday night; **langer ~** *first Saturday of the month, when shops stay open till 6 pm.*

samstags *adv* on Saturdays.

samt *präp* (+D) together with.

sämtlich *adj* all; **~e Bücher** all the books.

Sanatorium (*pl* **Sanatorien**) *das* sanatorium.

Sand *der* sand.

Sandale (*pl* **-n**) *die* sandal.

sandig *adj* sandy.

Sandkasten (*pl* **-kästen**) *der* sandpit.

Sandpapier *das* sandpaper.

Sandstrand (*pl* **-strände**) *der* sandy beach.

sandte *prät* → **senden**.

sanft ◆ *adj* gentle; (*Musik*) soft; (*Geburt*) natural; (*Tourismus*) sustainable. ◆ *adv* softly.

sang *prät* → **singen**.

Sänger, -in (*mpl* **-**) *der, die* singer.

sanitär *adj* sanitary; **~e Anlagen** sanitation (*sg*).

Sanitäter, -in (*mpl* **-**) *der, die* paramedic.

sank *prät* → **sinken**.

Sankt Gallen *nt* St. Gallen.

Sardelle (*pl* **-n**) *die* anchovy.

Sardine (*pl* **-n**) *die* sardine.

Sarg (*pl* **Särge**) *der* coffin.

saß *prät* → **sitzen**.

Satellit (*pl* **-en**) *der* satellite.

Satellitenfernsehen *das* satellite television.

Satellitenschüssel (*pl* **-n**) *die* satellite dish.

Satire (*pl* **-n**) *die* satire.

satt *adj* (*nicht hungrig*) full; **bist du ~?** have you had enough?; **jn/etw ~ haben** to be fed up with sb/sthg.

Sattel (*pl* **Sättel**) *der* saddle.

Satz (*pl* **Sätze**) *der* (GRAMM) sentence; (*Sprung*) leap; (SPORT) set; (MUS) movement; (*Tarif*) rate.

Satzzeichen (*pl* **-**) *das* punctuation mark.

sauber *adj* clean; (*gut, korrekt*) neat.

sauber|machen *vt* to clean.

säubern *vt* (*saubermachen*) to clean.

Sauce (pl -n) die sauce; (Bratensoße) gravy.

Saudi-Arabien nt Saudi Arabia.

sauer ◆ adj sour; (ärgerlich) annoyed. ◆ adv: ~ **reagieren** to be annoyed; ~ **sein auf** (+A) to be annoyed with; **saurer Regen** acid rain.

Sauerbraten (pl -) der braised beef marinated in vinegar, sauerbraten.

Sauerkirsche (pl -n) die sour cherry.

Sauerkraut das sauerkraut, pickled cabbage.

Sauerrahm der sour cream.

Sauerstoff der oxygen.

Sauerstoffmaske (pl -n) die oxygen mask.

Sauerteig der sour dough.

saufen (präs **säuft**, prät **soff**, pp **gesoffen**) vi (Tier) to drink; (fam: Person) to booze.

säuft präs → **saufen**.

saugen[1] (prät **sog**, pp **gesogen**) vt & vi to suck.

saugen[2] vt (Teppich) to vacuum.

Säugling (pl -e) der baby.

Säule (pl -n) die (an Bauwerk) column, pillar.

Sauna (pl **Saunen**) die sauna.

Säure (pl -n) die (chemisch) acid.

Saxophon (pl -e) das saxophone.

SB abk → **Selbstbedienung**.

S-Bahn (pl -en) die suburban railway.

S-Bahn-Haltestelle (pl -n) die suburban railway stop.

S-Bahnhof (pl -höfe) der suburban railway station.

S-Bahn-Linie (pl -n) die suburban railway line.

SB-Tankstelle (pl -n) die self-service petrol station (Br), self-service gas station (Am).

Schach das (Spiel) chess.

Schachbrett (pl -er) das chessboard.

Schachfigur (pl -en) die chess piece.

Schachspiel (pl -e) das (Spielen) game of chess; (Brett und Figuren) chess set.

Schachtel (pl -n) die (aus Pappe) box.

schade adj: **es ist** ~ it's a shame; **wie** ~! what a shame!

schaden vi (+D) to damage; (Person) to harm; **es kann nichts** ~ it won't do any harm.

Schaden (pl **Schäden**) der damage; (Nachteil) disadvantage.

Schadenersatz der compensation.

Schadenfreude die malicious pleasure.

schadenfroh adj gloating.

Schadensfall (pl -fälle) der: **im** ~ in the event of damage.

schadhaft adj damaged.

schädlich adj harmful.

Schadstoff (pl -e) der pollutant.

schadstoffarm adj low in pollutants.

Schaf (pl -e) das sheep.

Schäfer, -in (mpl -) der, die shepherd (shepherdess).

Schäferhund (pl -e) der Alsatian.

schaffen[1] ◆ vt 1. (zustande bringen, beenden) to manage; (Prüfung) to get through; **es** ~, **etw zu tun** to manage to do sthg; **er hat nicht einmal das erste Semester geschafft** he didn't even manage to finish the first semester; **geschafft!** that's it! 2. (fam: erschöpfen) to wear out; **geschafft sein** to be worn-out. 3. (transportieren) to take. ◆ vi (Süddt: arbeiten) to work.

schaffen[2] (präs **schafft**, prät **schuf**, pp **geschaffen**) vt (erschaffen) to create.

Schaffner, -in (mpl -) der, die (im Zug) ticket collector; (im Bus) conductor.

Schafskäse der ewe's milk cheese.

schal adj (Getränk) flat.

Schal (pl -s) der scarf.

Schale (pl -n) die (von Obst, Gemüse) skin; (von Apfelsine, Apfel, Kartoffeln) peel; (Schüssel) bowl; (von Nuß, Ei) shell.

schälen *vt* to peel. ▶ **sich schälen** *ref* to peel.

Schalldämpfer (*pl* -) *der* silencer.

Schallplatte (*pl* -n) *die* record.

schalt *prät* → **schelten**.

schalten *vi* (*im Auto*) to change gear; **aufs zweite Programm** ~ to turn to channel two; **in den vierten Gang** ~ to change to fourth gear.

Schalter (*pl* -) *der* (*Knopf*) switch; (*bei Bank, Bahn*) counter.

Schalterbeamte, -beamtin (*mpl* -n) *der, die* counter clerk.

Schalterhalle (*pl* -n) *die* hall (*at post office, station, etc*).

Schalteröffnungszeiten *pl* opening hours.

Schalterschluß *der* closing time.

Schalthebel (*pl* -) *der* (*im Auto*) gear lever.

Schaltknüppel (*pl* -) *der* gear lever.

Schaltung (*pl* -en) *die* (*Gangschaltung*) gear change.

schämen: sich schämen *ref* to be ashamed.

Schanze (*pl* -n) *die* (SPORT) ski-jump.

scharf (*komp* **schärfer**, *superl* **am schärfsten**) ♦ *adj* sharp; (*Gericht*) hot, spicy; (*fam: toll*) great; (*fam: erotisch*) sexy. ♦ *adv* (*bremsen*) hard; (*sehen, analysieren*) closely; ~ **gewürzt** hot, spicy; ~ **sein auf** (+A) (*fam*) to be keen on.

Scharlach *der* (MED) scarlet fever.

Scharnier (*pl* -e) *das* hinge.

Schaschlik (*pl* -s) *das* (shish) kebab.

Schatten (*pl* -) *der* shadow; **im** ~ in the shade.

schattig *adj* shady.

Schatz (*pl* **Schätze**) *der* treasure; (*fam: Liebling*) darling.

schätzen *vt* to estimate; (*glauben, meinen*) to think; (*gern haben*) to value.

schätzungsweise *adv* approximately.

Schau (*pl* -en) *die* show.

schauen *vi* to look; ~ **nach** (*sich kümmern*) to look after; **schau mal!** look!

Schauer (*pl* -) *der* (*Regen*) shower.

Schaufel (*pl* -n) *die* (*zum Graben*) shovel.

Schaufenster (*pl* -) *das* shop window.

Schaufensterbummel (*pl* -) *der* window-shopping trip.

Schaukel (*pl* -n) *die* (*an Seilen*) swing.

schaukeln *vt & vi* to rock.

Schaukelstuhl (*pl* -stühle) *der* rocking chair.

Schaulustige (*pl* -n) *der, die* onlooker.

Schaum *der* foam; (*von Seife*) lather; (*von Bier*) head.

Schaumbad (*pl* -bäder) *das* bubble bath.

Schaumfestiger (*pl* -) *der* (styling) mousse.

Schaumgummi *der* foam rubber.

Schaumkur (*pl* -en) *die* shampoo (*for damaged hair*).

Schaumwein (*pl* -e) *der* sparkling wine.

Schauspiel (*pl* -e) *das* play; (*fam: Spektakel*) spectacle.

Schauspieler, -in (*mpl* -) *der, die* actor (actress).

Schauspielhaus (*pl* -häuser) *das* theatre.

Scheck (*pl* -s) *der* cheque; **einen** ~ **einlösen** to cash a cheque; **mit** ~ **bezahlen** to pay by cheque; '~s **aller Art**' 'all cheques welcome'.

Scheckgebühr (*pl* -en) *die* charge for cheques.

Scheckheft (*pl* -e) *das* cheque-book.

Scheckkarte (*pl* -n) *die* cheque card.

Scheibe (*pl* -n) *die* (*von Brot, Käse*) slice; (*Fensterscheibe*) window pane; (*von Auto*) window.

Scheibenbremse (*pl* -n) *die* disc brake.

Scheibenwischer (*pl* -) *der* windscreen wiper.

Scheide (*pl* -n) *die* (*Vagina*) vagina.

scheiden (*prät* **schied**, *pp* **geschieden**) *vt* (*Ehe*) to dissolve; **sich ~ lassen** to get a divorce.

Scheidung (*pl* -en) *die* divorce.

Schein (*pl* -e) *der* (*Formular*, *Bescheinigung*) certificate; (*Geld*) note; (*Anschein*) appearances (*pl*); (*Licht*) light.

scheinbar ◆ *adj* apparent. ◆ *adv* seemingly.

scheinen (*prät* **schien**, *pp* **geschienen**) ◆ *vi* (*Sonne*) to shine; (*vermutlich*) to seem. ◆ *vimp*: **es scheint** it seems; **es scheint mir ...** it seems to me ...

Scheinwerfer (*pl* -) *der* (AUTO) headlight; (*in Halle, Stadion*) floodlight.

Scheinwerferlicht *das* (AUTO) headlights (*pl*); (*in Halle, Stadion*) floodlight.

Scheiße ◆ *die* (*vulg*) shit. ◆ *interj* (*vulg*) shit!

scheißen (*prät* **schiß**, *pp* **geschissen**) *vi* (*vulg*) to shit.

Scheitel (*pl* -) *der* (*Frisur*) parting (Br), part (Am).

Schelle (*pl* -n) *die* (*an Haustür*) doorbell.

schellen *vi* to ring; **es schellt** the bell is ringing.

schelten (*präs* **schilt**, *prät* **schalt**, *pp* **gescholten**) *vt* (*geh: Kind*) to scold.

Schema (*pl* -ta) *das* (*Vorstellung*) scheme; (*Abbildung*) diagram.

Schemel (*pl* -) *der* (*zum Sitzen*) stool.

Schenkel (*pl* -) *der* thigh.

schenken *vt* to give; **jm etw ~** (*Geschenk*) to give sb sthg (as a present); **sich** (D) **etw ~** (*erlassen*) to give sthg a miss.

Scherbe (*pl* -n) *die* fragment.

Schere (*pl* -n) *die* (*zum Schneiden*) scissors (*pl*).

scheren: sich scheren (*prät* **scherte**, *pp* **geschert**) *ref*: **sich nicht ~**

um (*kümmern*) not to care about.

Scherz (*pl* -e) *der* joke.

scherzhaft *adj* joking.

scheu *adj* shy.

Scheuerlappen (*pl* -) *der* floorcloth.

scheuern ◆ *vt* (*putzen*) to scour. ◆ *vi* (*Sattel, Kleidung*) to rub; **jm eine ~** (*fam: Ohrfeige geben*) to clip sb round the ear.

Scheuerpulver *das* scouring powder.

Scheune (*pl* -n) *die* barn.

scheußlich *adj* terrible.

Schicht (*pl* -en) *die* layer; (*in Gesellschaft*) class; (*Arbeitszeit*) shift.

schick *adj* smart.

schicken *vt* to send; **jm etw ~** to send sb sthg; **~ an** (+A) to send to.

Schicksal (*pl* -e) *das* fate.

Schiebedach (*pl* -dächer) *das* sunroof.

schieben (*prät* **schob**, *pp* **geschoben**) *vt* to push; **die Schuld auf einen anderen ~** to put the blame on sb else. ▶ **sich schieben** *ref* (*Person*) to push (one's way).

Schieber (*pl* -) *der* (*Gerät*) bar, bolt.

Schiebetür (*pl* -en) *die* sliding door.

schied *prät* → **scheiden**.

Schiedsrichter, -in (*mpl* -) *der, die* (*in Fußball*) referee; (*in Tennis*) umpire.

schief *adj* & *adv* crooked.

schief|**gehen** *vi unr ist* (*fam*) to go wrong.

schielen *vi* to squint.

schien *prät* → **scheinen**.

Schienbein (*pl* -e) *das* shin.

Schiene (*pl* -n) *die* (*Gleis*) rail; (MED) splint.

schießen (*prät* **schoß**, *pp* **geschossen**) ◆ *vi hat* & *ist* to shoot. ◆ *vt hat* to shoot; (*Tor*) to score; (*Foto*) to take; (*Ball*) to kick.

Schiff (*pl* -e) *das* ship; (*von Kirche*) nave; **mit dem ~** by ship.

Schiffahrt *die* shipping.

Schiffahrtsgesellschaft (pl -en) die shipping company.

Schiffskarte (pl -n) die (navigation) chart.

Schiffsreise (pl -n) die voyage.

Schiffsverbindung (pl -en) die connecting boat service.

Schiffsverkehr der shipping.

schikanieren vt (abw) to bully.

Schild (pl -er) das sign; (Etikett) label; (Waffe) shield.

Schilddrüse (pl -n) die thyroid gland.

schildern vt to describe.

Schildkröte (pl -n) die (auf dem Land) tortoise; (im Wasser) turtle.

Schilf (pl -e) das (Pflanze) reed.

Schilling (pl -e) der schilling.

schilt präs → **schelten**.

Schimmel (pl -) der (auf Obst, an Wand) mould; (Pferd) grey (horse).

schimmelig adj mouldy.

schimpfen vi to moan; **mit jm ~** to get angry with sb.

Schimpfwort (pl -e) das swearword.

Schinken (pl -) der (Fleisch) ham; **roher/gekochter/geräucherter ~** cured/cooked/smoked ham.

Schinkenspeck der bacon.

Schinkenwurst die ham sausage.

Schirm (pl -e) der (Regenschirm) umbrella.

schiß prät → **scheißen**.

Schlaf der sleep.

Schlafanzug (pl -anzüge) der pyjamas (pl).

schlafen (präs schläft, prät schlief, pp geschlafen) vi to sleep; **~ gehen** to go to bed; **~ mit** to sleep with; **schlaf gut!** sleep well!

Schlafengehen das: **vor dem ~** before going to bed.

Schlafgelegenheit (pl -en) die place to sleep.

Schlaflosigkeit die insomnia.

Schlafmittel (pl -) das sleeping pill.

Schlafsaal (pl -säle) der dormitory.

Schlafsack (pl -säcke) der sleeping bag.

schläft präs → **schlafen**.

Schlaftablette (pl -n) die sleeping pill.

Schlafwagen (pl -) der sleeper.

Schlafwagenkarte (pl -n) die sleeper ticket.

Schlafwagenplatz (pl -plätze) der sleeper berth.

Schlafzimmer (pl -) das bedroom.

Schlag (pl Schläge) der blow; (elektrisch) shock; (von Herz, Puls) beat. ▶ **Schläge** pl (Prügel) beating (sg).

Schlagader (pl -n) die artery.

Schlaganfall (pl -anfälle) der stroke.

schlagen (präs schlägt, prät schlug, pp geschlagen) ◆ vt (verletzen) to hit; (hämmern) to bang; (besiegen, Eiweiß, Sahne) to beat. ◆ vi (mit Hand, Faust) to hit; (Uhr) to strike; (regelmäßig) to beat; **auf etw** (A) **~** (aufprallen) to hit sthg; **jn eins zu null ~** to beat sb one-nil. ▶ **sich schlagen** ref (sich prügeln) to fight.

Schlager (pl -) der (Lied) hit.

Schläger (pl -) der (für Tennis, Badminton) racquet; (für Tischtennis) bat; (für Golf) club; (für Hockey) stick.

Schlagloch (pl -löcher) das pothole.

Schlagobers das (Österr) whipped cream.

Schlagsahne die whipped cream.

schlägt präs → **schlagen**.

Schlagzeile (pl -n) die headline.

Schlagzeug (pl -e) das (in Band) drums (pl); (in Orchester) percussion.

Schlamm der mud.

schlampig adj sloppy.

schlang prät → **schlingen**.

Schlange (pl -n) die (Tier) snake; (von Autos, Personen) queue (Br), line (Am); **~ stehen** to queue (Br), to stand in line (Am).

schlängeln: sich schlängeln ref (Weg, Fluß) to wind.

schlank adj slim; ~ **werden** to slim.

schlapp adj (müde, schwach) tired out.

schlau adj cunning; **man wird nicht ~ aus ihm** I can't make him out.

Schlauch (pl **Schläuche**) der (für Wasser) hose; (im Reifen) tube.

Schlauchboot (pl -e) das rubber dinghy.

schlecht ◆ adj bad; (Lebensmittel) off. ◆ adv badly; (schmecken, riechen) bad; (kaum) hardly; ~ **werden** to go off; **mir wird ~** I feel ill; **das ist nicht ~** that's not bad.

schleichen (prät **schlich**, pp **geschlichen**) vi (Mensch, Tier) to creep; (Verkehr, Auto) to crawl.

Schleife (pl -n) die (Band) bow; (Kurve) bend.

schleifen¹ vt (zerren) to drag.

schleifen² (präs **schleift**, prät **schliff**, pp **geschliffen**) vt (Messer, Schere) to sharpen.

Schleim der (menschlich) mucus; (von Schnecke) slime.

Schleimhaut (pl -häute) die mucous membrane.

Schlemmerlokal (pl -e) das gourmet restaurant.

schlendern vi ist to stroll.

schleppen vt to drag; (Fahrzeug) to tow. ▶ **sich schleppen** ref to drag o.s.

Schlepplift (pl -e) der ski tow.

Schleuder (pl -n) die (für Wäsche) spin-dryer.

Schleudergefahr die: 'Vorsicht ~!' 'slippery road'.

schleudern ◆ vt hat to fling; (Wäsche) to spin-dry. ◆ vt hat (Waschmaschine) to spin. ◆ vi ist (Auto, Fahrer) to skid; **ins Schleudern geraten** ODER **kommen** to go into a skid.

Schleudersitz (pl -e) der ejector seat.

Schleuse (pl -n) die (an Kanal) lock.

schlich prät → **schleichen**.

schlicht adj simple.

schlief prät → **schlafen**.

schließen (prät **schloß**, pp **geschlossen**) ◆ vt to close; (Betrieb, Lokal) to close down; (schlußfolgern) to conclude. ◆ vi to close; (Betrieb, Lokal) to close down. ▶ **sich schließen** ref (Tür, Vorhang) to close.

Schließfach (pl -fächer) das left-luggage locker (Br), baggage locker (Am).

schließlich adv (zuletzt) finally; (nämlich) after all.

schliff prät → **schleifen**.

schlimm ◆ adj bad. ◆ adv badly; **halb so ~** not so bad.

schlingen (prät **schlang**, pp **geschlungen**) vt (Mahlzeit) to gobble down; (Schnur) to tie.

Schlips (pl -e) der tie.

Schlitten (pl -) der (für Kinder) sledge.

Schlittschuh (pl -e) der ice skate; ~ **laufen** to ice-skate.

Schlitz (pl -e) der (Spalt) slit; (für Geld) slot.

schloß prät → **schließen**.

Schloß (pl **Schlösser**) das (Verschluß) lock; (Gebäude) castle.

Schlosser, -in (mpl -) der, die (Metallberuf) metalworker; (Installateur) mechanic.

Schloßpark (pl -s) der castle grounds (pl).

Schlucht (pl -en) die ravine.

schluchzen vi to sob.

Schluck (pl -e) der (Schlucken) gulp, swallow; (Menge) drop.

Schluckauf der hiccups (pl).

schlucken vi & vt to swallow.

Schluckimpfung (pl -en) die oral vaccination.

schlug prät → **schlagen**.

Schlüpfer (pl -) der knickers (pl).

schlurfen vi ist to shuffle.

schlürfen vt to slurp.

Schluß (pl **Schlüsse**) der end; (von Roman, Film) ending; (Folgerung) conclusion; **bis zum ~** to the end; ~ **machen mit** (Person) to break off with; (Sache) to stop.

Schlüssel (*pl* -) *der* (*für Schloß*) key; (*Schraubenschlüssel*) spanner.
Schlüsselbund (*pl* -e) *der* bunch of keys.
Schlüsseldienst (*pl* -e) *der* key-cutting service.
Schlüsselloch (*pl* -löcher) *das* key-hole.
Schlußfolgerung (*pl* -en) *die* conclusion.
Schlußleuchte (*pl* -n) *die* (*Lampe*) rear light.
Schlußverkauf (*pl* -verkäufe) *der* end-of-season sale.
schmal *adj* narrow; (*Person*) thin.
Schmalfilm (*pl* -e) *der* cine-film (Br), movie film (Am).
Schmalz *das* (*zum Kochen*) lard; (*zum Essen*) dripping.
Schmalznudel (*pl* -n) *die* (*Österr*) flat, round cake made from deep-fried dough.
Schmankerl (*pl* -n) *das* (*Süddt & Österr*) delicacy.
schmatzen *vi* to eat noisily.
schmecken *vi* to taste; (*gut schmecken*) to taste good; ~ **nach** to taste of; **das schmeckt mir nicht** I don't like it; **gut/schlecht ~** to taste good/bad; **hat es Ihnen geschmeckt?** did you enjoy your meal?; **laß es dir ~!** enjoy your meal!
schmeißen (*prät* **schmiß**, *pp* **geschmissen**) *vt* (*fam: werfen*) to chuck.
schmelzen (*präs* **schmilzt**, *prät* **schmolz**, *pp* **geschmolzen**) *vi ist & vt hat* to melt.
Schmerz (*pl* -en) *der* pain.
schmerzen *vi* to hurt.
Schmerzensgeld *das* compensation.
schmerzlos *adj* painless.
Schmerzmittel (*pl* -) *das* painkiller.
schmerzstillend *adj* pain-killing.
Schmerztablette (*pl* -n) *die* painkiller.
Schmetterling (*pl* -e) *der* butterfly.
Schmied (*pl* -e) *der* blacksmith.

schmieren *vt* (*Türangel, Maschine*) to oil; (*Butterbrot*) to spread; (*fam: bestechen*) to bribe.
Schmierkäse *der* cheese spread.
Schmiermittel (*pl* -) *das* lubricant.
Schmierseife *die* soft soap.
schmilzt *präs* → **schmelzen**.
Schminke *die* make-up.
schminken *vt* to make up. ▶ **sich schminken** *ref* to put on one's make-up.
Schmirgelpapier *das* sandpaper.
schmiß *prät* → **schmeißen**.
schmollen *vi* to sulk.
schmolz *prät* → **schmelzen**.
Schmorbraten (*pl* -) *der* pot roast.
schmoren *vt* (*Nahrung*) to braise.
Schmuck *der* (*für Person*) jewellery; (*für Raum, Tannenbaum*) decoration.
schmücken *vt* to decorate.
schmuggeln *vt* to smuggle.
schmunzeln *vi* to smile.
schmusen *vi* to cuddle.
Schmutz *der* dirt.
schmutzig *adj* dirty; **sich ~ machen** to get dirty.
Schnalle (*pl* -n) *die* buckle.
schnappen ◆ *vt* to catch; (*fam: packen, nehmen*) to grab. ◆ *vi* (*Tier*) to snap.
Schnappschuß (*pl* -schüsse) *der* snapshot.
Schnaps (*pl* **Schnäpse**) *der* schnapps.
Schnapsglas (*pl* -gläser) *das* shot glass.
schnarchen *vi* to snore.
Schnauze (*pl* -n) *die* (*von Tier*) muzzle; (*vulg: von Mensch*) gob.
Schnecke (*pl* -n) *die* (*Tier*) snail; (*Gebäck*) = Chelsea bun.
Schnee *der* snow; **es liegt ~** there's snow on the ground.
Schneeball (*pl* -bälle) *der* snowball.
schneebedeckt *adj* snow-covered.
Schneebrille (*pl* -n) *die* snow-goggles (*pl*).

Schneefall *der* snowfall.

Schneeflocke (*pl* **-n**) *die* snowflake.

schneefrei *adj* free of snow.

Schneegestöber (*pl* **-**) *das* snowstorm.

Schneeglätte *die* packed snow.

Schneegrenze (*pl* **-n**) *die* snowline.

Schneekette (*pl* **-n**) *die* snow-chain.

Schneemann (*pl* **-männer**) *der* snowman.

Schneepflug (*pl* **-pflüge**) *der* snowplough.

Schneeregen *der* sleet.

Schneeschmelze *die* thaw.

Schneesturm (*pl* **-stürme**) *der* snowstorm.

Schneetreiben (*pl* **-**) *das* driving snow.

Schneewehe (*pl* **-n**) *die* snowdrift.

schneiden (*prät* **schnitt**, *pp* **geschnitten**) ◆ *vt* to cut; (*ignorieren*) to ignore; (*beim Überholen*) to cut in on. ◆ *vi* to cut; **etw in Würfel ~** to cut sthg into cubes; **sich** (D) **in den Finger ~** to cut one's finger. ▶ **sich schneiden** *ref* (*sich verletzen*) to cut o.s.; (*sich kreuzen*) to cross.

Schneider, -in (*mpl* **-**) *der, die* (*Beruf*) tailor.

Schneiderei (*pl* **-en**) *die* (*Geschäft*) tailor's (shop).

schneien *vimp*: **es schneit** it's snowing.

schnell ◆ *adj* quick, fast. ◆ *adv* quickly, fast; **~ machen** to hurry up.

Schnellhefter (*pl* **-**) *der* loose-leaf folder.

Schnelligkeit *die* speed.

Schnellimbiß (*pl* **-imbisse**) *der* snack bar.

Schnellreinigung (*pl* **-en**) *die* express cleaning.

Schnellstraße (*pl* **-n**) *die* expressway.

Schnellzug (*pl* **-züge**) *der* express train.

schnitt *prät* → **schneiden**.

Schnitt (*pl* **-e**) *der* cut; (*Schnittmuster*) pattern.

Schnittblumen *pl* cut flowers.

Schnitte (*pl* **-n**) *die* (*Brotscheibe*) slice; (*belegtes Brot*) open sandwich.

Schnittkäse *der* sliced cheese.

Schnittlauch *der* chives (*pl*).

Schnittwunde (*pl* **-n**) *die* cut.

Schnitzel (*pl* **-**) *das*: **Wiener ~** escalope of veal.

Schnorchel (*pl* **-**) *der* snorkel.

schnorcheln *vi* to snorkel.

Schnuller (*pl* **-**) *der* dummy (Br), pacifier (Am).

Schnulze (*pl* **-n**) *die* (*Lied*) sentimental song.

Schnupfen *der* cold; **~ haben/bekommen** to have/get a cold.

Schnupftabak (*pl* **-e**) *der* snuff.

Schnur (*pl* **Schnüre**) *die* (*zum Binden*) string, cord; (*Kabel*) lead.

Schnurrbart (*pl* **-bärte**) *der* moustache.

Schnürsenkel (*pl* **-**) *der* shoelace.

schob *prät* → **schieben**.

Schock (*pl* **-s**) *der* shock; **unter ~ stehen** to be in shock.

schockieren *vt* to shock.

Schokolade (*pl* **-n**) *die* chocolate; (*Getränk*) hot chocolate.

Scholle (*pl* **-n**) *die* (*Fisch*) plaice.

schon *adv* **1.** (*relativ früh, spät*) already; **wir essen heute ~ um elf Uhr** we're eating earlier today, at eleven o'clock; **es ist ~ lange so** it has been like that for a long time; **~ jetzt** already. **2.** (*bis jetzt*) yet; **warst du ~ bei der Post?** have you been to the post office yet?; **warst du ~ mal in Kanada?** have you ever been to Canada?; **ich war ~ mal im Ausland** I've been abroad before; **ich bereite das ~ mal vor** I'll get that ready now. **3.** (*relativ viel*) already; **~ wieder** again. **4.** (*endlich*): **komm ~!** come on! **5.** (*zur Beruhigung*): **das schaffst du ~** don't worry, I'm sure you'll manage it; **~ gut!** all right! **6.** (*allein*) just; **~ der Gedanke daran macht mich**

nervös just thinking about it makes me nervous.

schön ◆ adj nice; (Frau) beautiful; (Mann) handsome; (beträchtlich) considerable. ◆ adv well; **ganz ~** really; **na ~** all right.

schonen vt (Person) to go easy on; (Gegenstand) to look after. ▶ **sich schonen** ref to take it easy.

Schönheit (pl -en) die beauty.

Schönheitssalon (pl -s) der beauty salon.

Schonkost die light diet.

schön|machen: sich schönmachen ref (fam) to get ready, to do o.s. up.

Schönwetterlage die spell of fine weather.

Schöpfkelle (pl -n) die ladle.

Schoppen (pl -) der large glass of wine.

Schorf der scab.

Schorle (pl -) die (mit Apfelsaft) apple juice with mineral water; (mit Wein) spritzer.

Schornstein (pl -e) der chimney.

schoß prät → **schießen**.

Schoß (pl **Schöße**) der (Körperteil) lap; **bei jm auf dem ~ sitzen** to sit on sb's lap.

Schotte (pl -n) der Scotsman; **die ~n** the Scots.

Schottin (pl -nen) die Scotswoman.

schottisch adj Scottish.

Schottland nt Scotland.

schräg adj (schief) sloping; (Linie) diagonal.

Schramme (pl -n) die scratch.

Schrank (pl **Schränke**) der (mit Fächern) cupboard; (zum aufhängen) wardrobe.

Schranke (pl -n) die (Gegenstand) barrier.

Schrankwand (pl **-wände**) die wall unit.

Schraube (pl -n) die (aus Metall) screw.

schrauben vt to screw.

Schraubenschlüssel (pl -) der spanner (Br), wrench (Am).

Schraubenzieher (pl -) der screwdriver.

Schrebergarten (pl **-gärten**) der allotment.

Schreck der fright; **einen ~ kriegen** to get a fright.

schreckhaft adj easily scared.

schrecklich adj terrible.

Schrei (pl -e) der (Geräusch) shout, cry.

schreiben (prät schrieb, pp geschrieben) ◆ vt 1. (gen) to write; **etw groß/klein ~** to write sthg with/without a capital letter; **wie schreibt man das?** how do you spell that? 2. (Subj: Arzt): **jn krank ~** to give sb a sick note; **jn gesund ~** to give sb a note saying they are fit to work again. ◆ vi to write; **an etw** (D) **~** (Roman) to be writing sthg; **über etw** (A) **~** to write about sthg. ▶ **sich schreiben** ref to be spelt.

Schreiben (pl -) das (amt) letter.

Schreibheft (pl -e) das exercise book.

Schreibmaschine (pl -n) die typewriter.

Schreibpapier das writing paper.

Schreibtisch (pl -e) der desk.

Schreibwaren pl stationery (sg).

Schreibwarengeschäft (pl -e) das stationery shop.

schreien (prät schrie, pp geschrien) vi & vt to shout; **~ nach** to shout at.

Schreiner, -in (mpl -) der, die joiner.

schreiten (prät schritt, pp geschritten) vi ist (geh: gehen) to stride.

schrie prät → **schreien**.

schrieb prät → **schreiben**.

Schrift (pl -en) die (Handschrift) handwriting; (Schriftbild) type; (Aufschrift, Text) writing; (lateinische, arabische) script; **die Heilige ~** the Scriptures (pl).

schriftlich ◆ adj written. ◆ adv in writing.

Schriftsteller, -in (*mpl -*) *der, die* writer.

schritt *prät* → **schreiten**.

Schritt (*pl -e*) *der* step; '~ **fahren**' 'dead slow'.

Schrittempo *das* walking speed.

Schrott *der* (*Metall*) scrap metal; (*fam: Plunder*) rubbish.

Schrottplatz (*pl -plätze*) *der* scrap-yard.

schrubben *vt & vi* to scrub.

Schrubber (*pl -*) *der* scrubbing brush.

Schubkarre (*pl -n*) *die* wheelbarrow.

Schublade (*pl -n*) *die* drawer.

schubsen *vt* to shove.

schüchtern *adj* shy.

schuf *prät* → **schaffen**.

Schüfeli *das* (*Schweiz*) smoked pork.

Schuh (*pl -e*) *der* shoe.

Schuhanzieher (*pl -*) *der* shoehorn.

Schuhbürste (*pl -n*) *die* shoe brush.

Schuhcreme (*pl -s*) *die* shoe polish.

Schuhgeschäft (*pl -e*) *das* shoe shop.

Schuhgröße (*pl -n*) *die* shoe size.

Schuhlöffel (*pl -*) *der* shoehorn.

Schuhmacher, -in (*mpl -*) *der, die* shoemaker.

Schuhputzmittel (*pl -*) *das* shoe polish.

Schuhsohle (*pl -n*) *die* (shoe) sole.

Schulabschluß (*pl -abschlüsse*) *der* school-leaving qualification.

Schulbeginn *der* beginning of term.

schuld *adj*: ~ **sein** ODER **haben an** (+D) to be to blame for; **du bist ~ daran** it's your fault.

Schuld *die* (*Verantwortung*) blame; (*Unrecht*) guilt. ▶ **Schulden** *pl* debts; ~**en haben** to be in debt; ~**en machen** to run up debts.

schuldig *adj* guilty; **jm etw ~ sein** to owe sb sthg.

Schuldschein (*pl -e*) *der* IOU.

Schule (*pl -n*) *die* school; **zur** ODER **in die ~ gehen** to go to school; **in der ~** at school.

schulen *vt* to train.

Schüler, -in (*mpl -*) *der, die* pupil.

Schüleraustausch *der* (student) exchange.

Schülerausweis (*pl -e*) *der* pupil's ID card entitling them to concessions etc.

Schülerkarte (*pl -n*) *die* (*Fahrkarte*) school season ticket.

Schulferien *pl* school holidays.

schulfrei *adj*: **morgen haben wir ~** we don't have to go to school tomorrow.

Schulfreund, -in (*mpl -e*) *der, die* schoolfriend.

Schuljahr (*pl -e*) *das* school year.

Schulklasse (*pl -n*) *die* class.

Schulter (*pl -n*) *die* shoulder.

Schultüte *die* large cone of sweets.

SCHULTÜTE

A 'Schultüte' is a large brightly-coloured paper cone full of sweets and small gifts which parents give to their children on their first day at school to try to make the day a little easier for them. The children may only open the cone once they have arrived at school.

Schulung (*pl -en*) *die* training.

Schulzeit *die* schooldays (*pl*).

Schuppe (*pl -n*) *die* (*von Fisch*) scale. ▶ **Schuppen** *pl* (*auf Kopf*) dandruff (*sg*).

Schürfwunde (*pl -n*) *die* graze.

Schurwolle *die* pure new wool.

Schürze (*pl -n*) *die* apron.

Schuß (*pl Schüsse*) *der* shot; **gut in ~ sein** to be in good shape; **ein ~ Whisky** a dash of whisky.

Schüssel (*pl -n*) *die* bowl.

Schuster, -in (*mpl -*) *der, die* shoemaker.

Schutt *der* rubble; '~ **abladen verboten**' 'no dumping'.

Schüttelfrost *der* shivering fit.

schütteln *vt* to shake; **den Kopf ~** to shake one's head; **vor Gebrauch ~** shake before use. ► **sich schütteln** *ref* to shake.

schütten ◆ *vt* to pour. ◆ *vimp*: **es schüttet** it's pouring (with rain).

Schutz *der* protection; (*vor Regen, Wind*) shelter; **jn in ~ nehmen** to stand up for sb.

Schutzblech (*pl* **-e**) *das* mudguard.

Schutzbrief (*pl* **-e**) *der* travel insurance certificate.

Schutzbrille (*pl* **-n**) *die* goggles (*pl*).

schützen ◆ *vt* to protect. ◆ *vi* (*Dach*) to give shelter; (*Versicherung*) to give cover; **jn vor etw** (D) **~** to protect sb against sthg. ► **sich schützen** *ref* to protect o.s.

Schützenfest (*pl* **-e**) *das* shooting festival.

SCHÜTZENFEST

The 'Schützenfest' is a shooting festival held mainly in rural communities. It is organized by the local rifle club, which is the centre of communal life in many of these rural areas. A competition is held to find the best shot, who is then crowned 'Schützenkönig' (king of the shooting festival). There are also beer tents and fairground attractions, including shooting galleries.

Schutzgebiet (*pl* **-e**) *das* (*von Wasser*) protected area.

Schutzhütte (*pl* **-n**) *die* shelter.

Schutzimpfung (*pl* **-en**) *die* vaccination.

Schutzumschlag (*pl* **-umschläge**) *der* dust jacket.

schwach (*komp* **schwächer**, *superl* **am schwächsten**) *adj* weak; (*schlecht*) poor.

Schwäche (*pl* **-n**) *die* weakness.

schwachsinnig *adj* (*unsinnig*) nonsensical.

Schwachstrom *der* low-voltage current.

Schwager (*pl* **-**) *der* brother-in-law.

Schwägerin (*pl* **-nen**) *die* sister-in-law.

Schwalbe (*pl* **-n**) *die* swallow.

schwamm *prät* → **schwimmen**.

Schwamm (*pl* **Schwämme**) *der* sponge.

Schwammtuch (*pl* **-tücher**) *das* cloth.

Schwan (*pl* **Schwäne**) *der* swan.

schwang *prät* → **schwingen**.

schwanger *adj* pregnant.

Schwangerschaft (*pl* **-en**) *die* pregnancy.

Schwangerschaftstest (*pl* **-s**) *der* pregnancy test.

schwanken *vi* *ist* to sway; (*gedanklich*) to waver; (*Kurs, Preise*) to fluctuate.

Schwanz (*pl* **Schwänze**) *der* tail; (*vulg: von Mann*) cock.

Schwarm (*pl* **Schwärme**) *der* (*von Tieren*) swarm.

schwarz ◆ *adj* black. ◆ *adv* (*illegal*) on the black market; **der ~e Markt** the black market; **in den ~en Zahlen** in the black.

Schwarz *das* black.

Schwarzarbeit *die* moonlighting.

Schwarzbrot (*pl* **-e**) *das* black bread.

Schwarze (*pl* **-n**) *der, die* (*Farbiger*) black; (*Konservativer*) conservative.

schwarz|fahren *vi unr* *ist* to travel without a ticket.

Schwarzfahrer, -in (*mpl* **-**) *der, die* fare dodger.

Schwarzmarkt *der* black market.

Schwarzwald *der* Black Forest.

schwarzweiß *adj* black and white.

Schwarzweißfilm (*pl* **-e**) *der* black and white film.

Schwarzwurzel (*pl* **-n**) *die* oyster plant.

Schwebebahn (*pl* **-en**) *die* cable railway.

schweben *vi* (*fliegen*) to float.

Schwede (pl -n) der Swede.

Schweden nt Sweden.

Schwedin (pl -nen) die Swede.

schwedisch adj Swedish.

Schwedisch(e) das Swedish.

Schwefel der sulphur.

schweigen (prät schwieg, pp geschwiegen) vi (Person) to be silent.

Schweigepflicht die confidentiality.

Schwein (pl -e) das pig; (Fleisch) pork.

Schweinebraten (pl -) der roast pork.

Schweinefleisch das pork.

Schweinerei (pl -en) die (fam: schlimme Sache) scandal; (fam: Schmutz) mess.

Schweinesteak (pl -s) das pork steak.

Schweinshaxe (pl -n) die (Süddt) fried knuckle of pork.

Schweiß der sweat.

schweißen vt to weld.

Schweiz die Switzerland.

Schweizer (pl -) der Swiss.

Schweizerin (pl -nen) die Swiss.

schwellen (präs schwillt, prät schwoll, pp geschwollen) vi (dick werden) to swell.

Schwellung (pl -en) die swelling.

schwer ♦ adj heavy; (stark) serious; (schwierig) difficult. ♦ adv (fam: sehr) really; (verletzt) seriously; (arbeiten) hard; **das ist nur ~ möglich** that won't be easy; **zehn Kilo ~ sein** to weigh ten kilos; **es ~ haben mit** to have a hard time with.

Schwerbehinderte (pl -n) der, die severely handicapped person.

schwerhörig adj hard of hearing.

schwerkrank adj seriously ill.

schwerverletzt adj seriously injured.

Schwester (pl -n) die sister; (Krankenschwester) nurse.

schwieg prät → schweigen.

Schwiegereltern pl parents-in-law.

Schwiegermutter (pl -mütter) die mother-in-law.

Schwiegersohn (pl -söhne) der son-in-law.

Schwiegertochter (pl -töchter) die daughter-in-law.

Schwiegervater (pl -väter) der father-in-law.

schwierig adj difficult.

Schwierigkeit (pl -en) die (Problem) difficulty; **in ~en geraten/stecken** to get into difficulty/be having difficulties.

schwillt präs → schwellen.

Schwimmbad (pl -bäder) das swimming pool.

Schwimmbecken (pl -) das swimming pool.

schwimmen (prät schwamm, pp geschwommen) ♦ vi ist to swim; (Gegenstand) to float. ♦ vt ist (Strecke) to swim.

Schwimmer, -in (mpl -) der, die swimmer.

Schwimmerbecken (pl -) das swimmers' pool.

Schwimmflosse (pl -n) die flipper (Br), fin (Am).

Schwimmflügel (pl -) der armband.

Schwimmhalle (pl -n) die indoor swimming pool.

Schwimmreifen (pl -) der rubber ring.

Schwimmweste (pl -n) die life jacket.

schwindelig adj dizzy; **mir ist/wird ~** I am/am getting dizzy.

schwingen (prät schwang, pp geschwungen) ♦ vi to swing. ♦ vt (Fahne) to wave; (Peitsche) to brandish. ▶ **sich schwingen** ref (aufs Pferd, ins Auto) to jump.

Schwips (pl -e) der (fam): **einen ~ haben** to be tipsy.

schwitzen vi to sweat.

schwoll prät → schwellen.

schwor prät → schwören.

schwören (prät schwor, pp

geschworen) *vt* to swear.

schwul *adj* (*fam*) gay.

schwül *adj* (*Wetter*) muggy, close.

Schwung *der* (*Bewegung*) swing; (*Elan*) zest; **mit ~** with zest.

Schwur (*pl* Schwüre) *der* oath.

sechs *num & pron* six; **fünf vor/nach ~** five to/past six; **~ Uhr fünfundvierzig** six forty-five; **um ~** (*Uhr*) at six (o'clock); **sie ist ~** (*Jahre alt*) she is six (years old); **wir waren ~** there were six of us.

sechshundert *num* six hundred.

sechsmal *adv* six times.

sechsspurig *adj* six-lane.

sechste, -r, -s *adj* sixth; **der ~ Juni** the sixth of June, June the sixth.

Sechstel (*pl* -) *das* sixth.

sechzehn *num* sixteen, → **sechs**.

sechzig *num* sixty, → **sechs**.

See¹ (*pl* -n) *der* (*Teich*) lake.

See² *die* (*Meer*) sea; **an die ~ fahren** to go to the seaside; **an der ~** at the seaside.

Seebad (*pl* -bäder) *das* seaside resort.

Seegang *der*: **leichter/hoher ~** calm/rough seas (*pl*).

Seeigel (*pl* -) *der* sea urchin.

seekrank *adj* seasick.

Seele (*pl* -n) *die* soul.

Seeleute *pl* sailors.

seelisch *adj* mental.

Seelsorger, -in (*mpl* -) *der*, *die* (*Priester*) pastor.

Seeluft *die* sea air.

Seemeile (*pl* -n) *die* nautical mile.

Seenot *die* distress.

Seereise (*pl* -n) *die* voyage.

Seeweg *der*: **auf dem ~** by sea.

Segel (*pl* -) *das* sail.

Segelboot (*pl* -e) *das* sailing boat.

Segelfliegen *das* gliding.

Segelflugzeug (*pl* -e) *das* glider.

segeln *vi* (*mit Boot*) to sail.

Segelschiff (*pl* -e) *das* sailing ship.

sehbehindert *adj* partially sighted.

sehen (*präs* **sieht**, *prät* **sah**, *pp* **gesehen**) *vt & vi* to see; **gut/schlecht ~** to have good/bad eyesight; **jm ähnlich ~** to look like sb; **sieh mal!** look!; **mal ~** we'll see; **siehste** ODER **siehst du!** (*fam*) you see; **nach jm ~** (*aufpassen*) to look after sb. ▶ **sich sehen** *ref* (*sich treffen*) to see each other.

Sehenswürdigkeiten *pl* sights.

Sehne (*pl* -n) *die* (*von Muskeln*) tendon.

sehnen: sich sehnen *ref*: **sich ~ nach** to long for.

Sehnenscheidenentzündung (*pl* -en) *die* tendonitis.

Sehnsucht *die* longing.

sehr *adv* very; **bitte ~!** you're welcome!; **das gefällt mir ~** I like that a lot; **danke ~!** thank you very much; **~ viel Geld** an awful lot of money; **zu ~** too much.

seid *präs* → **sein**.

Seide (*pl* -n) *die* silk.

Seife (*pl* -n) *die* soap.

Seifenlauge (*pl* -n) *die* soap suds (*pl*).

Seil (*pl* -e) *das* rope.

Seilbahn (*pl* -en) *die* cable railway.

sein¹ (*präs* **ist**, *prät* **war**, *pp* **gewesen**) ◆ *aux* 1. (*im Perfekt*) to have; **sie ist gegangen** she has gone. 2. (*im Konjunktiv*): **sie wäre gegangen** she would have gone. ◆ *vi* 1. (*Angabe von Eigenschaft, Zustand, Identität*) to be; **mir ist schlecht/kalt** I'm ill/cold; **Lehrer ~** to be a teacher. 2. (*Angabe von Position*) to be; **das Hemd ist im Koffer** the shirt is in the suitcase. 3. (*Angabe der Zeit*) to be; **das Konzert ist heute** the concert is today. 4. (*Angabe der Herkunft*): **aus Indien/Zürich ~** to be from India/Zürich. 5. (*Angabe der Zusammensetzung*): **aus etw ~** to be made of sthg. 6. (*Angabe der Meinung*): **für etw ~** to be in favour of sthg; **gegen etw ~** to be against sthg. 7. (*Angabe von Zwang*): **mein**

Befehl ist sofort auszuführen my order is to be carried out immediately. **8.** (*Angabe von Möglichkeit*): **das ist nicht zu ändern** there's nothing that can be done about it; **dieses Spiel ist noch zu gewinnen** this game can still be won. **9.** (*Angabe von Tätigkeit*): **dabei ~, etw zu tun** to be doing sthg. **10.** (*Angabe von Teilnahme*): **dabei ~** to be there. **11.** (*fam: Angabe von Reihenfolge*): **ich bin dran** it's my turn; **Sie sind als nächste dran!** you're next! ◆ *vimp*: **es ist zwölf Uhr** it's twelve o'clock; **es ist dunkel** it's dark; **wie wäre es mit ...?** how about ...?; **was ist?** what's up?; **das wär's** that's all; **es sei denn, daß ...** unless ...

sein², **-e** *det* his.

seine, **-r**, **-es** *pron* (*von Person*) his; (*von Tier, Ding*) its.

seinǁlassen *vt unr* (*fam*): **laß das sein!** stop that!

seit *konj & präp* (+D) since; **ich wohne hier ~ drei Jahren** I've lived here for three years; **~ langem** for a long time; **~ wann** since when.

seitdem ◆ *adv* since then. ◆ *konj* since.

Seite (*pl* **-n**) *die* side; (*von Buch, Heft*) page; **auf der rechten/linken ~** on the right-hand/left-hand side; **zur ~ gehen** ODER **treten** to step aside.

Seiteneingang (*pl* **-gänge**) *der* side entrance.

Seitensprung (*pl* **-sprünge**) *der* affair; **einen ~ machen** to have an affair.

Seitenstechen *das* stitch.

Seitenstraße (*pl* **-n**) *die* side street.

Seitenstreifen (*pl* **-**) *der* hard shoulder (Br), shoulder (Am); **'~ nicht befahrbar'** 'soft verges'.

Seitenwind *der*: **'Vorsicht, ~!'** 'caution crosswind'.

seither *adv* since then.

Sekretär (*pl* **-e**) *der* secretary; (*Möbelstück*) bureau.

Sekretärin (*pl* **-nen**) *die* secretary.

Sekt (*pl* **-e**) *der* German sparkling wine similar to champagne.

Sektbar (*pl* **-s**) *die* champagne bar.

Sekte (*pl* **-n**) *die* sect.

Sektglas (*pl* **-gläser**) *das* champagne glass.

Sekunde (*pl* **-n**) *die* second.

Sekundenkleber (*pl* **-**) *der* superglue.

sekundenlang *adj* momentary.

selber *pron* (*fam*) = **selbst**.

selbst ◆ *adv* (*sogar*) even. ◆ *pron* (*er selbst*) himself; (*sie selbst*) herself, themselves (*pl*); (*ich selbst*) myself; (*wir selbst*) ourselves; (*Sie selbst*) yourself, yourselves (*pl*); **von ~** (*automatisch*) automatically, by itself.

selbständig ◆ *adj* independent; (*Unternehmer*) self-employed. ◆ *adv* independently.

Selbstauslöser (*pl* **-**) *der* delayed-action shutter release.

Selbstbedienung *die* self-service.

Selbstbedienungsrestaurant (*pl* **-s**) *das* self-service restaurant.

Selbstbeteiligung *die* excess.

selbstbewußt *adj* self-confident.

Selbstbräuner (*pl* **-**) *der* artificial tanning cream.

selbstgemacht *adj* home-made.

Selbstkostenpreis (*pl* **-e**) *der* cost price.

Selbstmord (*pl* **-e**) *der* suicide.

selbstsicher *adj* self-confident.

Selbstversorger (*pl* **-**) *der* (*im Urlaub*) self-caterer.

selbstverständlich ◆ *adj* natural. ◆ *adv* naturally.

Selbstverteidigung *die* self-defence.

Selbstwählverkehr *der* direct dialling.

Sellerie *der* celery.

selten ◆ *adj* rare. ◆ *adv* rarely.

Selters (*pl* **-**) *die* ODER *das* sparkling mineral water.

seltsam *adj* strange.

Semester (pl -) das semester.
Semesterferien pl (university) vacation (sg).
Semikolon (pl -s) das semicolon.
Seminar (pl -e) das seminar; (Institut) department.
Semmel (pl -n) die (bread) roll.
Semmelknödel (pl -) der bread dumpling.
senden[1] (prät **sandte**, pp **gesandt**) vt (Brief, Glückwünsche) to send; **jm etw ~** to send sb sthg.
senden[2] vt (Film, Konzert) to broadcast.
Sender (pl -) der (Station) station.
Sendung (pl -en) die (in Fernsehen, in Radio) programme; (Brief) letter; (Paket) parcel.
Senf (pl -e) der mustard.
Senior, -in (mpl -en) der, die (in Firma) senior colleague. ▶ **Senioren** pl (Alte) senior citizens; (SPORT) senior team (sg).
Seniorenpaß (pl -pässe) der senior citizen's travel pass.
senken vt to lower.
senkrecht ◆ adj vertical. ◆ adv vertically.
Sensation (pl -en) die sensation.
sensibel adj (Mensch) sensitive.
separat adj separate.
September der September; **am ersten ~** on the first of September; **Anfang/Ende ~** at the beginning/end of September; **Mitte ~** in mid-September; **Berlin, den 12. ~ 1995** Berlin, 12 September 1995; **im ~** in September.
Serie (pl -n) die series; (von Produkten) line.
serienmäßig ◆ adj standard. ◆ adv in series.
seriös adj respectable.
Serpentine (pl -n) die (Straße) steep and winding road.
Service[1] der (von Firma, Hotel) service.
Service[2] (pl -s) das (von Eßgeschirr) (dinner) service.

servieren vt to serve.
Serviette (pl -n) die serviette.
Servolenkung (pl -en) die power steering.
Servus interj (Süddt) hello.
Sesam der sesame.
Sessel (pl -) der armchair.
Sessellift (pl -e) der chairlift.
setzen ◆ vt hat (Person) to sit; (Gegenstand) to put; (festlegen, Text) to set; (Geld) to bet. ◆ vi (bei Wette, Roulette) to bet; **~ auf** (+A) to bet on. ▶ **sich setzen** ref (Person, Tier) to sit (down); **sich ~ zu** to sit with.
Seuche (pl -n) die (Krankheit) epidemic.
seufzen vi to sigh.
Sex der sex.
sexuell adj sexual.
Sfr. (abk für Schweizer Franken) Swiss francs.
Shampoo (pl -s) das shampoo.
Sherry (pl -s) der sherry.
Shorts pl shorts.
Show (pl -s) die show.
Shuttle-Bus (pl -se) der shuttle bus.
sich pron (Reflexivpronomen: unbestimmt) oneself; (Person) himself (herself), themselves (pl); (Ding, Tier) itself, themselves (pl); (bei Höflichkeitsform) yourself, yourselves (pl); **~ freuen auf etw** (A) to look forward to sthg; **~** (D) **etw kaufen** to buy sthg (for o.s.).
sicher ◆ adj (ungefährdet) safe; (zuverlässig) reliable. ◆ adv (ungefährdet) safely; (zuverlässig) reliably; (sicherlich) certainly, definitely; **aber ~!** of course; **bist du ~?** are you sure?; **etw ~ wissen** to know sthg for sure; **sich** (D) **~ sein** to be sure.
Sicherheit (pl -en) die (Schutz) safety; (Zuverlässigkeit) certainty; (Selbstsicherheit) confidence; (finanziell) security.
Sicherheitsdienst (pl -e) der security service.
Sicherheitsgurt (pl -e) der safety belt.

Sicherheitsnadel (*pl* **-n**) *die* safety pin.

Sicherheitsschloß (*pl* **-schlösser**) *das* safety lock.

sicherlich *adv* certainly.

sichern *vt* (*Ort*) to secure.

Sicherung (*pl* **-en**) *die* (*elektrisch*) fuse; (*Schutz*) safeguarding.

Sicht *die* view; **gute ~** good visibility; **in ~ sein** to be in sight.

sichtbar *adj* visible.

Sichtvermerk (*pl* **-e**) *der* visa.

Sichtweite *die* visibility; **außer/in ~** out of/in sight.

sie *pron* (*Singular: Nominativ*) she; (*Akkusativ*) her; (*Tier, Gegenstand*) it; (*Plural: Nominativ*) they; (*Akkusativ*) them.

Sie *pron* (*Singular, Plural*) you.

Sieb (*pl* **-e**) *das* sieve.

sieben ◆ *num* seven, → **sechs**. ◆ *vt* (*Sand, Tee*) to sieve.

siebenhundert *num* seven hundred.

siebenmal *adv* seven times.

siebte, -r, -s *adj* seventh, → **sechste**.

siebzehn *num* seventeen, → **sechs**.

siebzig *num* seventy, → **sechs**.

siedend *adj* boiling.

Siedlung (*pl* **-en**) *die* (*Niederlassung*) settlement; (*am Stadtrand*) (housing) estate.

Sieg (*pl* **-e**) *der* victory.

siegen *vi* to win; **~ gegen** ODER **über** (+A) to beat.

Sieger, -in (*mpl* **-**) *der, die* winner.

Siegerehrung (*pl* **-en**) *die* (SPORT) medals ceremony.

siehe *Imperativ* → **sehen**; **~ oben/unten** see above/below.

sieht *präs* → **sehen**.

siezen *vt*: **jn ~** to use the 'Sie' form of address to sb.

Signal (*pl* **-e**) *das* signal.

Signalton (*pl* **-töne**) *der* tone.

Silbe (*pl* **-n**) *die* syllable.

Silber *das* silver.

Silberhochzeit (*pl* **-en**) *die* silver wedding (anniversary).

Silvester (*pl* **-**) *das* New Year's Eve.

SILVESTER

In Germany, the traditional way of seeing in the New Year is by letting off fireworks when midnight chimes. Another custom associated with New Year's Eve involves pouring molten lead into a bowl of water and trying to tell the future from the shapes into which the lead solidifies.

---

simultan *adj* simultaneous.

sind *präs* → **sein**[1].

Sinfonie (*pl* **-n**) *die* symphony.

Sinfonieorchester (*pl* **-**) *das* symphony orchestra.

singen (*prät* **sang**, *pp* **gesungen**) *vt & vi* to sing.

sinken (*prät* **sank**, *pp* **gesunken**) *vi ist* to sink; (*Preis, Besucherzahlen*) to fall.

Sinn (*pl* **-e**) *der* (*körperlich*) sense; (*Bedeutung*) meaning; (*Zweck*) point; **es hat keinen ~** there's no point.

sinnlos *adj* (*unsinnig*) pointless.

sinnvoll *adj* (*Arbeit*) meaningful; (*vernünftig*) sensible.

Sirene (*pl* **-n**) *die* (*Gerät*) siren.

Sitte (*pl* **-n**) *die* (*Gepflogenheit*) custom. ▶ **Sitten** *pl* (*Benehmen*) manners.

Situation (*pl* **-en**) *die* situation.

Sitz (*pl* **-e**) *der* seat.

sitzen (*prät* **saß**, *pp* **gesessen**) *vi* to sit; **~ auf** (+D) to be sitting on; **gut ~** (*Kleidung*) to be a good fit.

sitzenlassen *vt unr* (*fam: Partner*) to dump; (*bei Verabredung*) to stand up.

Sitzgelegenheit (*pl* **-en**) *die* seating, place to sit.

Sitzplatz (*pl* **-plätze**) *der* seat.

Sitzung (*pl* **-en**) *die* (*Konferenz*) meeting.

Skandal (*pl* **-e**) *der* scandal.

Skat *der* skat, *card game for three players*.

Skateboard (*pl* -s) *das* skateboard.

Skelett (*pl* -e) *das* skeleton.

Ski (*pl* -er) *der* ski; ~ **fahren** ODER **laufen** to ski.

Skianzug (*pl* -züge) *der* ski suit.

Skiausrüstung (*pl* -en) *die* skiing equipment.

Skifahren *das* skiing.

Skigebiet (*pl* -e) *das* skiing area.

Skihose (*pl* -n) *die* ski pants (*pl*).

Skikurs (*pl* -e) *der* skiing course.

Skiläufer, -in (*mpl* -) *der, die* skier.

Skilehrer, -in (*mpl* -) *der, die* ski instructor.

Skilift (*pl* -e) *der* ski lift.

Skipiste (*pl* -n) *die* ski-run.

Skisport *der* skiing.

Skistiefel (*pl* -) *der* ski boot.

Skistock (*pl* -stöcke) *der* ski stick.

Skiurlaub (*pl* -e) *der* skiing holiday.

Skiwachs *das* ski wax.

Skizze (*pl* -n) *die* sketch.

Skorpion (*pl* -e) *der* (*Tier*) scorpion; (*Sternzeichen*) Scorpio.

Skulptur (*pl* -en) *die* sculpture.

S-Kurve (*pl* -n) *die* S-bend.

Slalom (*pl* -s) *der* (*im Sport*) slalom.

Slip (*pl* -s) *der* briefs (*pl*).

Slipeinlage (*pl* -n) *die* panty liner.

Slowakei *die* Slovakia.

Smog *der* smog.

Smoking (*pl* -s) *der* dinner jacket.

so ◆ *adv* **1.** (*auf diese Art*) like this; (*auf jene Art*) like that; ~ **was** (*fam*) something like that; ~ **gut ~!** good! **2.** (*dermaßen*) so; **ich bin ~ froh, daß du gekommen bist** I'm so glad you came; ~ **..., daß** so ... that; ~ **ein** such a; ~ **ein Pech!** what bad luck! **3.** (*fam: circa*) about; **oder ~** or so. **4.** (*mit Geste*) this; **es war ~ groß** it was this big. **5.** (*fam: ohne etwas*) as it is; (*umsonst*) for free; **ich trinke den Tee lieber ~** I'd rather have the tea as it is; **ich bin ~ ins Kino reingekommen** I got into the cinema for free. **6.** (*fam: im allgemeinen*): **was hast du sonst noch ~ gemacht?** what else did you do, then? **7.** (*vergleichend*): ~ **...** **wie** as ... as; **das Loch war ~ breit wie tief** the hole was as wide as it was deep. ◆ *konj* **1.** (*Ausdruck des Vergleichs*) as; **laufen, ~ schnell man kann** to run as fast as one can. **2.** (*Ausdruck der Folge*): ~ **daß** so that. ◆ *interj*: ~, **das war's** so, that's it; ~, **glaubst du das?** so, you believe that, do you? ▶ **so oder so** *adv* anyway.

s.o. *abk* = **siehe oben**.

sobald *konj* as soon as.

Söckchen (*pl* -) *das* ankle sock.

Socke (*pl* -n) *die* sock.

Sodbrennen *das* heartburn.

Sofa (*pl* -s) *das* sofa.

soff *prät* → **saufen**.

sofort *adv* immediately; (*gleich*) in a moment.

Sofortbildkamera (*pl* -s) *die* instant camera.

sog *prät* → **saugen**.

sogar *adv* even.

sogenannt *adj* (*abw: angeblich*) so-called.

Sohle (*pl* -n) *die* sole.

Sohn (*pl* Söhne) *der* son.

Soja *die* soya bean.

solange *konj* as long as.

Solarium (*pl* Solarien) *das* solarium.

solch *det* such; ~ **nette Leute** such nice people.

solche, -r, -s *det* such; **ein ~r Mann** such a man; **das Thema als ~s** the topic as such.

Soldat (*pl* -en) *der* soldier.

solidarisch *adj*: **sich ~ zeigen** to show solidarity.

solide *adj* (*Material*) solid.

Solist, -in (*mpl* -en) *der, die* soloist.

Soll *das* (*Schulden*) debit.

sollen¹ (*pp* **sollen**) *aux* to be supposed to; **ich soll um 10 Uhr dort sein** I'm supposed ODER meant to be there at 10; **wir hätten nicht kommen**

~ we shouldn't have come; **soll ich das Fenster aufmachen?** shall I open the window?; **sollte sie noch kommen, sag ihr ...** if she should turn up, tell her ...

sollen² (*pp* **gesollt**) *vi*: **die Waren ~ nach München** the goods are meant to go to Munich; **was soll das?** (*fam*) what's all this?; **was soll's?** (*fam*) what the hell?

solo *adv* (MUS) solo; (*fam: allein*) alone.

Sommer (*pl* -) *der* summer; **im ~** in (the) summer.

Sommerfahrplan (*pl* -**pläne**) *der* summer timetable.

Sommerferien *pl* summer holidays.

sommerlich *adj* summery.

Sommerpause (*pl* -**n**) *die* summer break.

Sommerreifen (*pl* -) *der* summer tyre.

Sommerschlußverkauf (*pl* -**käufe**) *der* summer sale.

Sommersprosse (*pl* -**n**) *die* freckle.

Sommerzeit *die* summertime.

Sonate (*pl* -**n**) *die* sonata.

Sonderangebot (*pl* -**e**) *das* special offer.

Sonderausstattung (*pl* -**en**) *die*: **ein Auto mit ~** a car with optional extras.

sonderbar *adj* strange.

Sonderfahrplan (*pl* -**pläne**) *der* special timetable.

Sonderfahrt (*pl* -**en**) *die* (*Zugfahrt*) special train; (*Busfahrt*) special bus.

Sondergenehmigung (*pl* -**en**) *die* special permit.

Sonderleistungen *pl* special benefits.

Sondermarke (*pl* -**n**) *die* special issue stamp.

Sondermaschine (*pl* -**n**) *die* special plane.

Sondermüll *der* hazardous waste.

sondern *konj* but.

Sonderpreis (*pl* -**e**) *der* special price.

Sonderschule (*pl* -**n**) *die* special school.

Sondertarif (*pl* -**e**) *der* (*Fahrpreis*) special fare.

Sonderzug (*pl* -**züge**) *der* special train.

Sonnabend (*pl* -**e**) *der* Saturday, → **Samstag**.

sonnabends *adv* on Saturdays.

Sonne *die* sun; **die ~ scheint** the sun is shining; **in der prallen ~** in the blazing sun.

sonnen: sich sonnen *ref* (*in Sonne*) to sun o.s.

Sonnenaufgang (*pl* -**gänge**) *der* sunrise.

Sonnenbad (*pl* -**bäder**) *das*: **ein ~ nehmen** to sunbathe.

Sonnenbank (*pl* -**bänke**) *die* sunbed.

Sonnenblume (*pl* -**n**) *die* sunflower.

Sonnenblumenbrot (*pl* -**e**) *das* sunflower seed bread.

Sonnenblumenkern (*pl* -**e**) *der* sunflower seed.

Sonnenblumenöl *das* sunflower oil.

Sonnenbrand *der* sunburn.

Sonnenbrille (*pl* -**n**) *die* sunglasses (*pl*).

Sonnencreme (*pl* -**s**) *die* sun cream.

Sonnendach (*pl* -**dächer**) *das* (*für Auto*) sunroof.

Sonnendeck (*pl* -**s**) *das* sun deck.

Sonnenmilch *die* suntan lotion.

Sonnenöl (*pl* -**e**) *das* suntan oil.

Sonnenschein *der* sunshine.

Sonnenschirm (*pl* -**e**) *der* sunshade.

Sonnenschutzfaktor *der* protection factor.

Sonnenseite *die* (*von Gebäude*) sunny side.

Sonnenstich der sunstroke.

Sonnenstudio (pl -s) das tanning studio.

Sonnenuntergang (pl -gänge) der sunset.

sonnig adj sunny.

Sonntag (pl -e) der Sunday, → **Samstag**.

sonntags adv on Sundays.

Sonntagsverkauf der Sunday trading.

sonn- und feiertags adv on Sundays and public holidays.

sonst ◆ adv (außerdem) else; (normalerweise) usually; (abgesehen davon) otherwise. ◆ konj (andernfalls) or; ~ habe ich nichts I've got nothing else; ~ nichts nothing else; was ~? (fam) what else?

sonstig adj other.

sooft konj whenever.

Sopran (pl -e) der soprano.

Sorge (pl -n) die worry; sich (D) ~n machen um to worry about; keine ~! (fam) don't worry!

sorgen vi: ~ für (beschaffen) to see to; (sich kümmern um) to look after. ▶ **sich sorgen** ref to worry.

sorgfältig adj careful.

Sorte (pl -n) die (von Dingen) sort, type.

sortieren vt to sort.

Sortiment (pl -e) das assortment.

Soße (pl -n) die sauce.

Souvenir (pl -s) das souvenir.

souverän adj (Person) superior; (Staat) sovereign.

soviel ◆ pron as much. ◆ konj: ~ ich weiß as far as I know; iß, ~ du willst eat as much as you like; doppelt ~ wie twice as much as.

soweit ◆ adv (im allgemeinen) on the whole. ◆ konj as far as. ◆ adj: ~ sein to be ready.

sowie konj (und) as well as, and.

sowieso adv anyway.

sowohl konj: ~ ... als auch ... as well as ...

sozial ◆ adj social. ◆ adv socially.

Sozialarbeiter, -in (mpl -) der, die social worker.

Sozialdemokrat, -in (mpl -en) der, die social democrat.

sozialdemokratisch adj social-democratic.

Sozialhilfe die ≃ income support (Br), ≃ welfare (Am).

sozialistisch adj socialist.

Sozialversicherung (pl -en) die social security.

Sozialwohnung (pl -en) die council flat (Br).

Soziologie die sociology.

sozusagen adv so to speak.

Spachtel (pl -) der spatula.

Spaghetti pl spaghetti (sg).

Spalte (pl -n) die (in Fels, Holz) crack; (von Text) column.

Spanferkel (pl -) das (Fleisch) suckling pig.

Spange (pl -n) die (im Haar) hair slide (Br), barrette (Am).

Spanien nt Spain.

Spanier, -in (mpl -) der, die Spaniard; die ~ the Spanish.

spanisch adj Spanish.

Spanisch(e) das Spanish.

spann prät → **spinnen**.

spannend adj exciting.

Spannung (pl -en) die tension; (elektrisch) voltage. ▶ **Spannungen** pl (Krise) tension (sg).

Sparbuch (pl -bücher) das savings book.

Sparbüchse (pl -n) die piggy bank.

sparen vt & vi to save; ~ für ODER auf (+A) to save up for.

Spargel der asparagus.

Spargelsuppe (pl -n) die asparagus soup.

Sparkasse (pl -n) die savings bank.

Sparkonto (pl -konten) das savings account.

Sparpreis (pl -e) der economy price.

sparsam adj economical.

Sparschwein (*pl* **-e**) *das* piggy bank.

Spaß (*pl* **Späße**) *der* (*Vergnügen*) fun; (*Scherz*) joke; **~ machen** to joke; **Sprachenlernen macht mir ~** I enjoy learning languages; **~ haben** to have fun; **viel ~!** have fun!; **zum ~** for fun; **er versteht keinen ~** he has no sense of humour.

spät *adj & adv* late; **sie kam mal wieder zu ~** she was late again; **wie ~ ist es?** what's the time?

Spaten (*pl* **-**) *der* spade.

später *adv* (*dann*) later; **bis ~!** see you later!

spätestens *adv* at the latest.

Spätlese (*pl* **-n**) *die* (*Wein*) late vintage.

Spätnachmittag (*pl* **-e**) *der* late afternoon.

Spätschicht (*pl* **-en**) *die* late shift.

Spätsommer *der* late summer.

Spätvorstellung (*pl* **-en**) *die* late show.

Spatz (*pl* **-en**) *der* (*Vogel*) sparrow.

Spätzli *pl* (*Schweiz*) *small round noodles, similar to macaroni.*

spazierenǀgehen *vi unr ist* to go for a walk.

Spaziergang (*pl* **-gänge**) *der* walk; **einen ~ machen** to go for a walk.

Speck *der* (*geräuchert*) bacon; (*Fett*) fat.

Spedition (*pl* **-en**) *die* (*für Umzug*) removal firm.

Speiche (*pl* **-n**) *die* (*am Rad*) spoke.

Speichel *der* saliva.

Speicher (*pl* **-**) *der* (*unterm Dach*) loft; (EDV) memory.

speichern *vt* (EDV) to save.

Speise (*pl* **-n**) *die* (*geh: Nahrung*) food; (*Gericht*) meal.

Speiseeis *das* ice cream.

Speisekarte (*pl* **-n**) *die* menu.

Speiseröhre (*pl* **-n**) *die* gullet.

Speisesaal (*pl* **-säle**) *der* dining room.

Speisewagen (*pl* **-**) *der* dining car.

Spende (*pl* **-n**) *die* donation.

spenden *vt* to donate.

spendieren *vt*: **jm etw ~** to buy sb sthg (for a treat).

Sperre (*pl* **-n**) *die* (*auf Straße*) barrier.

sperren *vt* (*Straße*) to close; (*Konto*) to freeze; **jn in ein Zimmer ~** to shut sb in a room.

Sperrgebiet (*pl* **-e**) *das*: **militärisches ~** military range.

Sperrmüll *der* large items of rubbish (*pl*).

Sperrstunde (*pl* **-n**) *die* closing time.

Sperrung (*pl* **-en**) *die* (*von Straße*) closing; (*von Konto*) freezing.

Spesen *pl* expenses.

Spezi® (*pl* **-s**) *das* (*Getränk*) Coke®.

Spezialgebiet (*pl* **-e**) *das* specialist field.

Spezialist, -in (*mpl* **-en**) *der, die* specialist.

Spezialität (*pl* **-en**) *die* speciality.

Spezialitäten-Restaurant (*pl* **-s**) *das* speciality restaurant.

Spiegel (*pl* **-**) *der* mirror.

Spiegelei (*pl* **-er**) *das* fried egg.

spiegelglatt *adj* slippery.

Spiegelreflexkamera (*pl* **-s**) *das* reflex camera.

Spiel (*pl* **-e**) *das* game; (*Karten*) deck, pack.

Spielautomat (*pl* **-en**) *der* fruit machine.

spielen ◆ *vt* to play. ◆ *vi* to play; (*Roman, Film*) to be set; (*um Geld*) to gamble; (*Schauspieler*) to act; **~ gegen** to play against; **~ um** to play for; **Karten ~** to play cards; **Klavier ~** to play the piano; **Tennis ~** to play tennis.

Spieler, -in (*mpl* **-**) *der, die* player.

Spielfilm (*pl* **-e**) *der* (feature) film.

Spielhalle (*pl* **-n**) *die* amusement arcade.

Spielkasino (*pl* **-s**) *das* casino.

Spielplan (*pl* **-pläne**) *der* (*von Theater*) programme.

Spielplatz (pl -plätze) der playground.

Spielregel (pl -n) die rule.

Spielsachen pl toys.

Spielwaren pl toys.

Spielzeug das toy.

Spieß (pl -e) der (für Fleisch) spit; am ~ spit-roasted.

Spießchen (pl -) das skewer.

Spinat der spinach.

Spinne (pl -n) die spider.

spinnen (prät spann, pp gesponnen) ◆ vt (Wolle) to spin. ◆ vi (fam: verrückt sein) to be crazy; **du spinnst!** you're joking!

spionieren vi to spy.

Spirale (pl -n) die spiral; (MED) coil.

Spirituosen pl spirits.

Spiritus der spirit.

Spirituskocher (pl -) der spirit stove.

spitz adj pointed.

Spitze (pl -n) die (von Messer, Nadel) point; (von Berg) peak; (von Kolonne, Gruppe) head.

Spitzer (pl -) der pencil sharpener.

Spitzname (pl -n) der nickname.

Splitter (pl -) der splinter.

spontan adj spontaneous.

Sport der sport; ~ **treiben** to do sport.

Sportabteilung (pl -en) die sports department.

Sportanlage (pl -n) die sports complex.

Sportart (pl -en) die (type of) sport.

Sportartikel (pl -) der piece of sports equipment.

Sportgerät (pl -e) das piece of sports equipment.

Sportgeschäft (pl -e) das sports shop.

Sporthalle (pl -n) die sports hall.

Sporthotel (pl -s) das hotel with sports facilities.

Sportkleidung die sportswear.

Sportler, -in (mpl -) der, die sportsman (sportswoman).

sportlich adj (Leistung) sporting; (Person, Kleidung) sporty.

Sportplatz (pl -plätze) der playing field.

Sportverein (pl -e) der sports club.

Sportwagen (pl -) der sports car.

spotten vi to mock.

sprach prät → **sprechen**.

Sprache (pl -n) die language; **zur ~ kommen** to come up.

Sprachenschule (pl -n) die language school.

Sprachführer (pl -) der phrasebook.

Sprachkenntnisse pl knowledge (sg).

sprachlich adj linguistic.

Sprachreise (pl -n) die journey to a country to learn the language.

Sprachunterricht der language teaching.

sprang prät → **springen**.

Spray (pl -s) das spray.

Sprechanlage (pl -n) die intercom.

sprechen ◆ vi 1. (reden) to talk, to speak; **mit jm ~** to talk to sb; **über jn/etw ~** to talk about sb/sthg; **von jm/etw ~** to talk about sb/sthg. 2. (am Telefon) to speak; **wer spricht da, bitte?** who's speaking? 3. (urteilend): **was spricht dagegen, jetzt Urlaub zu nehmen?** why shouldn't we go on holiday now?; **es spricht für ihn, daß ...** it's in his favour that ... ◆ vt 1. (Sprache) to speak; **Deutsch ~** to speak German. 2. (Person) to speak to. 3. (Gebet) to say. ▶ **sich sprechen** ref to talk.

Sprecher, -in (mpl -) der, die (im Radio, Fernsehen) newsreader; (von Gruppe) spokesperson.

Sprechstunde (pl -n) die (beim Arzt) surgery.

Sprechzeit (pl -en) die (von Ärzten) surgery hours (pl).

Sprechzimmer (pl -) das consulting room.

Sprengarbeiten pl: 'Sprengarbeiten' sign indicating that explosives are *being used for excavation.*

Sprengstoff (*pl* -e) *der* explosive.

spricht *prät* → **sprechen**.

Sprichwort (*pl* -wörter) *das* proverb.

sprießen (*prät* sproß, *pp* gesprossen) *vi ist* (*Blätter*) to shoot.

Springbrunnen (*pl* -) *der* fountain.

springen (*prät* sprang, *pp* gesprungen) *vi* (*Person, Tier*) to jump; (*Glas*) to break.

Springflut (*pl* -en) *die* spring tide.

Sprint (*pl* -s) *der* sprint.

Spritze (*pl* -n) *die* (*Injektion*) injection; (*Nadel, für Sahne*) syringe.

spritzen ♦ *vt* (*Injektion*) to inject; (*Wasser, Gift, Auto*) to spray. ♦ *vi* to splash. ♦ *vimp* (*Fett*) to spit.

spröde *adj* (*Material*) brittle.

Sprudel (*pl* -) *der* (*Mineralwasser*) sparkling mineral water.

Sprudelwasser (*pl* -) *das* (*Mineralwasser*) sparkling mineral water.

sprühen *vt* (*Wasser*) to spray.

Sprühregen *der* drizzle.

Sprung (*pl* Sprünge) *der* (*Springen*) jump; (*Riß*) crack.

Sprungbrett (*pl* -er) *das* springboard.

Sprungschanze (*pl* -n) *die* ski jump.

Spucke *die* (*fam*) spittle.

spucken *vi* (*ausspucken*) to spit.

Spüle (*pl* -n) *die* sink.

spülen ♦ *vt* to rinse. ♦ *vi* (*an Spüle*) to wash up; (*in Toilette*) to flush; Geschirr ~ to wash the dishes.

Spülmaschine (*pl* -n) *die* dishwasher.

Spülmittel (*pl* -) *das* washing-up liquid.

Spülung (*pl* -en) *die* (*von Toilette*) flush.

Spur (*pl* -en) *die* (*von Füßen, Dieb*) track; (*kleine Menge*) touch; (*Fahrspur*) lane; **die ~ wechseln** to change lanes.

spüren *vt* to feel.

Spurrillen *pl* (*auf Straße*): 'Spurrillen' 'temporary road surface'.

Squash *das* squash.

SSV *abk* = **Sommerschlußverkauf**.

St. (*abk für Sankt*) St.

Staat (*pl* -en) *der* state; (*Land*) country.

staatlich ♦ *adj* state. ♦ *adv*: ~ anerkannt government-approved; ~ geprüft government-certified.

Staatsangehörigkeit (*pl* -en) *die* nationality.

Staatsbürger, -in (*mpl* -) *der, die* citizen.

Staatsbürgerschaft (*pl* -en) *die* nationality.

Staatsexamen (*pl* -) *das* final exam taken by law and arts students at university.

Stäbchen (*pl* -) *das* (*zum Essen*) chopstick.

Stabhochsprung *der* pole vault.

stabil *adj* stable; (*Möbel, Bau*) solid.

stach *prät* → **stechen**.

Stachel (*pl* -n) *der* (*von Insekten*) sting; (*von Pflanzen*) thorn.

Stachelbeere (*pl* -n) *die* gooseberry.

Stacheldraht (*pl* -drähte) *der* barbed wire.

Stadion (*pl* Stadien) *das* stadium.

Stadium (*pl* Stadien) *das* stage.

Stadt (*pl* Städte) *die* town; (*sehr groß*) city; (*Verwaltung*) town council; **in die ~ fahren** to go to town.

Stadtautobahn (*pl* -en) *die* urban motorway (Br), freeway (Am).

Stadtbahn (*pl* -en) *die* suburban railway.

Stadtbummel (*pl* -) *der* (*fam*) stroll through town.

Städtepartnerschaft (*pl* -en) *die* town twinning.

Stadtführung (*pl* -en) *die* city sightseeing tour.

Stadtgebiet (*pl* -e) *das* town area.

Stadthalle (*pl* -n) *die* civic hall.

städtisch *adj* (*Kindergarten*, *Verwaltung*) municipal; (*Bevölkerung*) urban.

Stadtkern (*pl* -e) *der* town/city centre.

Stadtmauer (*pl* -n) *die* city wall.

Stadtmitte *die* town/city centre.

Stadtpark (*pl* -s) *der* municipal park.

Stadtplan (*pl* -pläne) *der* street map.

Stadtrand (*pl* -ränder) *der* outskirts (*pl*); **am ~** on the outskirts.

Stadtrat (*pl* -räte) *der* (*Organ*) town council; (*Person*) town councillor.

Stadträtin (*pl* -nen) *die* town councillor.

Stadtrundfahrt (*pl* -en) *die* city tour.

Stadtstaat (*pl* -en) *der* city state.

Stadtteil (*pl* -e) *der* district, quarter.

Stadttor (*pl* -e) *das* city gate.

Stadtviertel (*pl* -) *das* district, quarter.

Stadtzentrum (*pl* -zentren) *das* town/city centre.

stahl *prät* → **stehlen**.

Stahl *der* steel.

Stall (*pl* Ställe) *der* stable.

Stamm (*pl* Stämme) *der* (*von Baum*) trunk; (GRAMM) stem; (*Gruppe*) tribe.

stammen *vi*: **~ aus/von** to come from.

Stammgast (*pl* -gäste) *der* regular.

Stammkunde, -kundin (*mpl* -n) *der, die* regular customer.

Stammtisch (*pl* -e) *der* regulars' table at a pub.

STAMMTISCH

The word 'Stammtisch' can refer both to the table in a pub reserved for the regulars and to the group of regulars who always sit there. The 'Stammtisch' is where the regulars play cards and talk, with politics, especially local politics, being a favourite topic for debate.

---

stand *prät* → **stehen**.

Stand (*pl* Stände) *der* (*auf Markt*, *Messe*) stand; (*in Entwicklung*) state.

Ständer (*pl* -) *der* stand.

ständig ◆ *adj* constant. ◆ *adv* constantly.

Standlicht *das* sidelights (*pl*).

Standort (*pl* -e) *der* (*von Person*) position; (*von Firma*) location.

Standpunkt (*pl* -e) *der* point of view.

Standspur (*pl* -en) *die* hard shoulder.

Stange (*pl* -n) *die* (*aus Holz*) pole; (*aus Metall*) rod, bar; **eine ~ Zigaretten** a carton of 200 cigarettes.

Stangenbrot (*pl* -e) *das* French stick.

stank *prät* → **stinken**.

Stapel (*pl* -) *der* (*Haufen*) pile.

Star¹ (*pl* -e) *der* (*Vogel*) starling.

Star² (*pl* -s) *der* (*Person*) star.

starb *prät* → **sterben**.

stark (*komp* **stärker**, *superl* **am stärksten**) ◆ *adj* strong; (*Verkehr*, *Regen*) heavy; (*Husten*) bad; (*fam*: *toll*) great. ◆ *adv* (*intensiv*) heavily; (*fam*: *toll*) brilliantly.

Stärke (*pl* -n) *die* strength; (*in Nahrung, für Wäsche*) starch; (*Dicke*) thickness.

stärken *vt* (*körperlich*) to strengthen; (*Wäsche*) to starch. ► **sich stärken** *ref* to fortify o.s.

Starkstrom *der* heavy current.

Stärkung (*pl* -en) *die* (*Nahrung*, *Getränk*) refreshment.

starren *vi* (*sehen*): **auf etw** (A) **~** to stare at sthg.

Start (*pl* -s) *der* (*von Flugzeug*) takeoff; (*von Rennen*) start.

Startautomatik *die* automatic choke.

Startbahn (*pl* -en) *die* runway.

starten ◆ *vt* to start. ◆ *vi* (*Läufer*) to start; (*Flugzeug*) to take off.

Starthilfe *die* (*für Auto*) jump start; **jm ~ geben** to give sb a jump start.

Starthilfekabel (*pl* -) *das* jump lead.

Station (*pl* -en) *die* (*von Bus, Zug, U-Bahn*) station; (*von Reise*) stop; (*im Krankenhaus*) ward.

stationär *adj* (*Behandlung*) in-patient (*vor Subst*).

Statistik (*pl* -en) *die* statistics (*sg*).

Stativ (*pl* -e) *das* tripod.

statt *konj & präp* (+G) instead of; **~ dessen** instead.

statt|finden *vi unr* to take place.

Statue (*pl* -n) *die* statue.

Stau (*pl* -s) *der* (*im Verkehr*) traffic jam; **im ~ stehen** to be stuck in a traffic jam; **ein 5 km langer ~** a 5 km tailback.

Staub *der* dust.

stauben ◆ *vi* to be dusty. ◆ *vimp*: **es staubt** it's dusty.

staubig *adj* dusty.

staubsaugen *vi* to vacuum.

Staubsauger (*pl* -) *der* vacuum cleaner.

Staudamm (*pl* -dämme) *der* dam.

Staugefahr *die*: **es besteht ~** delays are possible.

staunen *vi* to be amazed.

Stausee (*pl* -n) *der* reservoir.

Stauwarnung (*pl* -en) *die* traffic report.

Std. (*abk für Stunde*) hr.

Steak (*pl* -s) *das* steak.

Steakhaus (*pl* -häuser) *das* steakhouse.

stechen (*präs* sticht, *prät* stach, *pp* gestochen) *vt* (*mit Nadel, Stachel*) to prick; (*mit Messer*) to stab; (*subj: Insekt*) to sting. ► **sich stechen** *ref* to prick o.s.

Stechmücke (*pl* -n) *die* mosquito.

Steckdose (*pl* -n) *die* socket.

stecken ◆ *vt* (*einstecken*) to put. ◆ *vi* (*Gegenstand*) to be; **wo habt ihr gesteckt?** (*fam*) where were you?

stecken|lassen *vt unr*: **ich habe den Schlüssel ~** I left the key in the lock.

Stecker (*pl* -) *der* plug.

Stecknadel (*pl* -n) *die* pin.

Steg (*pl* -e) *der* (*Brücke*) footbridge.

Steh-Café (*pl* -s) *das* café where customers drink coffee standing at a counter.

stehen (*prät* stand, *pp* gestanden) ◆ *vi* **1.** (*Person, Tier*) to stand. **2.** (*Gegenstand, Pflanze*) to be; **die Vase steht auf dem Tisch** the vase is on the table; **in der Zeitung steht, daß ...** it says in the paper that ... **3.** (*Uhr, Motor*) to have stopped. **4.** (*unterstützend*): **zu jm/etw ~** to stand by sb/sthg. **5.** (*Kleidung, Frisur*): **jm ~** to suit sb; **jm gut/nicht ~** to suit/not to suit sb. **6.** (*fam: mögen*): **auf etw** (A) **~** to be into sthg; **auf jn ~** to fancy sb. ◆ *vimp* **1.** (*im Sport*): **es steht 1 : 0** the score is 1-0. **2.** (*gesundheitlich*): **wie steht es um den Patienten?** how is the patient?; **es steht schlecht um ihn** he is not doing very well.

stehen|bleiben *vi unr ist* to stop.

stehen|lassen *vt unr* to leave.

stehlen (*präs* stiehlt, *prät* stahl, *pp* gestohlen) *vt* to steal.

Stehplatz (*pl* -plätze) *der* standing place.

steif *adj* stiff.

steigen (*prät* stieg, *pp* gestiegen) *vi ist* (*klettern*) to climb; (*in die Luft, ansteigen*) to rise; **in etw** (A) **/aus etw ~** to get on/out of sthg; **auf einen Berg ~** to climb (up) a mountain.

steigern *vt* to raise; (GRAMM) to form the comparative/superlative of.

Steigung (*pl* -en) *die* (*von Straße*) gradient.

steil *adj* steep.

Steilhang (*pl* -hänge) *der* steep slope.

Steilküste (*pl* -n) *die* cliffs (*pl*).

Stein (*pl* -e) *der* stone; (*zum Bauen*) brick; (*zum Spielen*) piece.

Steinbock (*pl* -böcke) *der* (*Tier*) ibex; (*Sternzeichen*) Capricorn.

Steinbutt (*pl* -e) *der* turbot.

Steingut das (Material) earthenware.

Steinpilz (pl -e) der cep, type of large wild mushroom with a rich flavour.

Steinschlag der: 'Achtung ~' 'danger – falling rocks'.

Stelle (pl -n) die (Platz, Rang) place; (Fleck) patch; (Arbeitsplatz) job; (im Text) passage; **an zweiter ~ liegen** to be in second place; **an deiner ~** if I were you; **auf der ~** on the spot.

stellen vt 1. (hinstellen) to put; **eine Vase auf den Tisch ~** to put a vase on the table. 2. (halten): **etw kalt ~** to chill sthg; **etw warm ~** to keep sthg warm. 3. (einstellen) to set; **den Fernseher leiser ~** to turn the television down. 4. (Diagnose, Prognose) to make. 5. (Frage) to ask; (Bedingung) to set. ▶ **sich stellen** ref 1. (sich hinstellen): **sich ans Fenster ~** to walk to the window. 2. (nicht ausweichen): **sich etw (D) ~** to face sthg. 3. (sich verstellen): **sich krank ~** to pretend to be ill; **sich dumm ~** to pretend not to understand.

Stellenangebot (pl -e) das job offer.

stellenweise adv in places.

Stellung (pl -en) die position; **~ zu etw nehmen** to comment on sthg.

Stellvertreter, -in (mpl -) der, die representative.

Stempel (pl -) der stamp.

stempeln vt to stamp.

Steppdecke (pl -n) die quilt.

sterben (präs stirbt, prät starb, pp gestorben) vi ist to die; **~ an** (+D) to die of.

Stereoanlage (pl -n) die stereo system.

steril adj sterile.

sterilisieren vt to sterilize.

Stern (pl -e) der star.

Sternbild (pl -er) das constellation.

Sternschnuppe (pl -n) die shooting star.

Sternwarte (pl -n) die observatory.

Sternzeichen (pl -) das sign of the zodiac.

stets adv (geh) always.

Steuer[1] (pl -n) die (Abgabe) tax.

Steuer[2] (pl -) das (von Auto) steering wheel.

Steuerbord das starboard.

steuerfrei adj tax-free.

steuern vt to steer.

steuerpflichtig adj taxable.

Steuerrad (pl -räder) das steering wheel.

Steuerung (pl -en) die (Gerät) controls (pl).

Steward (pl -s) der steward.

Stewardeß (pl -dessen) die stewardess.

Stich (pl -e) der (Stechen) stab; (von Insekt) sting; (beim Nähen) stitch; (Schmerz) stabbing pain; (Bild) engraving; **jn/etw im ~ lassen** to leave sb/sthg in the lurch.

sticht präs → stechen.

sticken vi to embroider.

Sticker (pl -) der sticker.

Stiefbruder (pl -brüder) der stepbrother.

Stiefel (pl -) der (Schuh) boot.

Stiefmutter (pl -mütter) die stepmother.

Stiefschwester (pl -n) die stepsister.

Stiefvater (pl -väter) der stepfather.

stieg prät → steigen.

Stiel (pl -e) der (von Blumen) stem; (von Besen, Pfanne) handle.

Stier (pl -e) der (Tier) bull; (Sternzeichen) Taurus.

stieß prät → stoßen.

Stift (pl -e) der (zum Schreiben) pencil; (aus Metall) tack.

Stiftung (pl -en) die (Institution) foundation; (Schenkung) donation.

Stil (pl -e) der style.

stilistisch adj stylistic.

still ◆ adj quiet; (bewegungslos) still. ◆ adv (geräuschlos) quietly; (bewegungslos) still; **sei bitte ~!** please be quiet!

stillen vt (Baby) to breast-feed;

(*Schmerz*) to relieve.

stilllhalten vt unr (*sich nicht bewegen*) to keep still.

Stimme (*pl* -n) die (*zum Sprechen*) voice; (*bei Wahl*) vote.

stimmen ◆ vi (*richtig sein*) to be right; (*bei Wahl*) to vote. ◆ vt (*Instrument*) to tune; ~ **für/gegen** to vote for/against; **das stimmt nicht!** that's not true!; **stimmt!** that's right!; **stimmt so!** keep the change!

Stimmrecht das right to vote.

Stimmung (*pl* -en) die (*Laune*) mood; (*Atmosphäre*) atmosphere.

stinken (*prät* **stank**, *pp* **gestunken**) vi (*schlecht riechen*) to stink; **das stinkt mir** I'm fed up with it.

Stipendium (*pl* **Stipendien**) das grant.

stirbt *präs* → **sterben**.

Stirn (*pl* -en) die forehead.

Stock (*pl* **Stöcke**) der (*aus Holz*) stick; (*Etage*) floor, storey; **am ~ gehen** to walk with a stick; **im ersten ~** on the first floor.

Stockung (*pl* -en) die (*im Verkehr*) hold-up.

Stockwerk (*pl* -e) das floor, storey.

Stoff (*pl* -e) der (*Tuch*) material; (*Substanz*) substance.

stöhnen vi to groan.

Stollen (*pl* -) der (*Kuchen*) stollen, *sweet bread made with dried fruit and nuts, eaten at Christmas.*

stolpern vi ist (*beim Gehen*) to stumble.

stolz adj (*Person*) proud.

stop interj stop!

stopfen ◆ vt (*Socken*) to darn; (*hineinstecken*) to stuff. ◆ vi (*fam: Nahrung*) to cause constipation.

Stopp (*pl* -s) der (*Anhalten*) stop.

stoppen vt & vi (*anhalten*) to stop.

Stoppschild (*pl* -er) das stop sign.

Stoppuhr (*pl* -en) die stopwatch.

Stöpsel (*pl* -) der plug.

Storch (*pl* **Störche**) das stork.

stören ◆ vt (*beeinträchtigen*) to dis-

turb; (*mißfallen*) to annoy. ◆ vi (*mißfallen*) to be annoying; **störe ich? am I disturbing you?; 'bitte nicht ~!'** 'do not disturb!'

stornieren vt to cancel.

Stornogebühr (*pl* -en) die cancellation charge.

Störung (*pl* -en) die (*Belästigung*) disturbance; (*im Fernsehen, Radio*) interference; **entschuldigen Sie die ~** sorry to bother you.

Störungsstelle (*pl* -n) die faults service.

Stoß (*pl* **Stöße**) der (*Schlag*) punch; (*Stapel*) pile.

Stoßdämpfer (*pl* -) der shock absorber.

stoßen (*präs* **stößt**, *prät* **stieß**, *pp* **gestoßen**) ◆ vt hat (*schubsen*) to push. ◆ vi ist: ~ **an** (+A) to hit; ~ **auf** (+A) to come across; ~ **gegen** to bump into. ► **sich stoßen** ref to bang o.s.

Stoßstange (*pl* -n) die bumper.

stößt *präs* → **stoßen**.

Stoßzeit (*pl* -en) die rush hour.

stottern vi to stutter.

Str. (*abk für* **Straße**) St.

strafbar adj punishable.

Strafe (*pl* -n) die (*Bestrafung*) punishment; (*Geldbuße*) fine; **zur ~** as a punishment; ~ **zahlen** to pay a fine.

Strafmandat (*pl* -e) das (*Zettel*) ticket.

Straftat (*pl* -en) die criminal offence.

Strafzettel (*pl* -) der (*fam*) ticket.

Strahl (*pl* -en) der (*von Wasser*) jet; (*von Licht*) ray. ► **Strahlen** pl (*von Energie*) rays.

strahlen vi (*Licht*) to shine; (*Person*) to beam; (*radioaktiv*) to radiate.

Strähne (*pl* -n) die strand.

stramm adj (*Band, Seil*) taut.

strampeln vi (*Säugling*) to kick about.

Strand (*pl* **Strände**) der beach.

Strandkorb (*pl* -**körbe**) der wicker beach chair.

Strandpromenade (*pl* -n) *die* promenade.

strapazieren *vt* (*Material*) to wear away; (*Person*) to strain.

Straße (*pl* -n) *die* (*in einer Stadt*) street; **das Zimmer liegt zur ~** the room looks out onto the street.

Straßenarbeiten *pl* roadworks.

Straßenbahn (*pl* -en) *die* tram (Br), streetcar (Am).

Straßenbahnlinie (*pl* -n) *die* tram route.

Straßencafé (*pl* -s) *das* street café.

Straßenfest (*pl* -e) *das* street party.

Straßenglätte *die* slippery road; '**mit ~ muß gerechnet werden**' 'slippery road surface ahead'.

Straßenkarte (*pl* -n) *die* road map.

Straßenlage *die* (*von Auto*) road holding.

Straßenschäden *pl*: '**Achtung ~**' 'uneven road surface'.

Straßenschild (*pl* -er) *das* street sign.

Straßensperre (*pl* -n) *die* roadblock.

Straßenverhältnisse *pl* road conditions.

Straßenverkehr *der* traffic.

Straßenverkehrsordnung *die* Road Traffic Act.

Straßenzustandsbericht (*pl* -e) *der* report on road conditions.

Strategie (*pl* -n) *die* strategy.

Strauch (*pl* Sträucher) *der* bush.

Strauß¹ (*pl* Sträuße) *der* (*Blumen*) bunch of flowers.

Strauß² (*pl* -e) *der* (*Vogel*) ostrich.

Strecke (*pl* -n) *die* (*Entfernung*) distance; (*Weg*) route; **die ~ Düsseldorf/Hamburg** the road between Düsseldorf and Hamburg.

strecken *vt* (*Körperteil*) to stretch. ▶ **sich strecken** *ref* (*sich recken*) to stretch.

Streckennetz (*pl* -e) *das* railway network.

streckenweise *adv* in places.

streicheln *vt* to stroke.

streichen (*prät* strich, *pp* gestrichen) ◆ *vt* (*mit Farbe*) to paint; (*Butter*) to spread; (*durchstreichen*) to cross out; (*annullieren*) to cancel. ◆ *vi* (*mit der Hand*): **jm übers Haar ~** to stroke sb's hair.

Streichholz (*pl* -hölzer) *das* match.

Streichholzschachtel (*pl* -n) *die* matchbox.

Streichkäse *der* cheese spread.

Streifen (*pl* -) *der* (*Muster*) stripe; (*Stück*) strip.

Streifenkarte (*pl* -n) *die* economy ticket for several bus or metro journeys.

Streifenwagen (*pl* -) *der* patrol car.

Streik (*pl* -s) *der* strike.

streiken *vi* (*Arbeiter*) to strike; (*fam*: *Gerät*) to be on the blink.

Streit *der* argument; **~ haben mit** to argue with.

streiten (*prät* stritt, *pp* gestritten) *vi* (*zanken*) to argue; **~ über** (+A) (*sich auseinandersetzen*) to argue about. ▶ **sich streiten** *ref* (*sich zanken*) to argue.

streng ◆ *adj* strict. ◆ *adv* strictly.

Streß *der* stress.

streuen ◆ *vt* (*Salz, Kräuter*) to sprinkle. ◆ *vi* (*gegen Eis*) to grit.

Streuselkuchen (*pl* -) *der* cake with crumble topping.

strich *prät* → **streichen**.

Strich (*pl* -e) *der* (*Linie*) line; (*fam*: *Prostitution*) prostitution.

strichweise *adv*: **~ Regen** patchy rain.

Strick (*pl* -e) *der* rope.

stricken *vt* to knit.

Strickjacke (*pl* -n) *die* cardigan.

Strickleiter (*pl* -n) *die* rope ladder.

Stricknadel (*pl* -n) *die* knitting needle.

Strickwaren *pl* knitwear (*pl*).

Strickzeug *das* knitting.

Striptease *der* striptease.

stritt *prät* → **streiten**.

Stroh *das* straw.

Strohhalm (*pl* -e) *der* straw.

Strom (*pl* **Ströme**) *der* (*elektrisch*) electricity; (*Fluß*) river; (*Menge*) stream; **es regnet in Strömen** it's pouring (with rain).

Stromanschluß (*pl* -anschlüsse) *der* connection to the mains.

Stromausfall (*pl* -ausfälle) *der* power failure.

strömen *vi ist* to stream.

Stromstärke (*pl* -n) *die* strength of electric current.

Strömung (*pl* -en) *die* (*von Fluß, Meer*) current.

Stromverbrauch *der* electricity consumption.

Stromzähler (*pl* -) *der* electricity meter.

Strophe (*pl* -n) *die* verse.

Strudel[1] (*pl* -) *der* (*im Wasser*) whirlpool.

Strudel[2] (*pl* -) *der* (*Gebäck*) strudel.

Struktur (*pl* -en) *die* (*Aufbau*) structure.

Strumpf (*pl* **Strümpfe**) *der* stocking.

Strumpfhose (*pl* -n) *die* tights (*pl*) (Br), pantyhose (*pl*) (Am).

Stube (*pl* -n) *die* (*Raum*) room.

Stück (*pl* -e) *das* (*Teil*) piece; (*von Zucker*) lump; (*Theaterstück*) play; **wieviele Brötchen? – 10 ~, bitte** how many rolls? – 10 please; **am ~** unsliced.

Stückzahl (*pl* -en) *die* number of pieces.

Student, -in (*mpl* -en) *der, die* student.

Studentenausweis (*pl* -e) *der* student card.

Studentenheim = **Studentenwohnheim.**

Studentenwohnheim (*pl* -e) *das* student hostel.

Studienfahrt (*pl* -en) *die* study trip.

Studienreise (*pl* -n) *die* study trip.

studieren *vt & vi* to study.

Studium (*pl* **Studien**) *das* study.

Stufe (*pl* -n) *die* (*von Treppe*) step; **'Vorsicht ~!'** 'mind the step!'

Stuhl (*pl* **Stühle**) *der* (*zum Sitzen*) chair; (*Kot*) stool.

Stuhlgang *der* bowel movement.

stumm *adj* (*behindert*) dumb; (*still*) silent.

stumpf *adj* blunt; (*glanzlos*) dull; (*abgestumpft*) apathetic.

Stumpfsinn *der* (*Monotonie*) monotony.

Stunde (*pl* -n) *die* hour; (*Unterrichtsstunde*) lesson.

Stundenkilometer *pl* kilometres per hour.

stundenlang *adj* for hours.

Stundenlohn (*pl* -löhne) *der* hourly wage.

stündlich *adj & adv* hourly.

Sturm (*pl* **Stürme**) *der* (*Wetter*) storm; (SPORT) forward line; (*Andrang*): **ein ~ auf** a run on.

stürmen ◆ *vt hat* (*überrennen*) to storm. ◆ *vi ist* (*laufen*) to rush. ◆ *vi hat* (SPORT) to attack. ◆ *vimp hat*: **es stürmt** it's blowing a gale.

Sturmflut (*pl* -en) *die* storm tide.

stürmisch *adj* (*Wetter*) stormy; (*Person, Begrüßung*) passionate; **es ist ~** it's blowing a gale.

Sturmwarnung (*pl* -en) *die* gale warning.

Sturz (*pl* **Stürze**) *der* (*Fallen*) fall.

stürzen ◆ *vt hat* (*stoßen*) to push; (*Regierung*) to bring down. ◆ *vi ist* (*fallen*) to fall; (*laufen*) to rush. ▶ **sich stürzen** *ref* (*springen*) to jump.

Sturzhelm (*pl* -e) *der* crash helmet.

Stute (*pl* -n) *die* mare.

Stuten (*pl* -) *der* loaf of white bread with raisins and almonds.

stützen *vt* to support. ▶ **sich stützen** *ref* (*Person*) to lean.

Subjekt (*pl* -e) *das* subject.

subjektiv *adj* subjective.

Substanz (*pl* -en) *die* substance.

subtrahieren *vt* to subtract.

Suche *die* search; **auf der ~ nach** in search of.

suchen ◆ *vt* to look for. ◆ *vi:* **~ nach** to look for.

süchtig *adj* addicted.

Süd *der* south.

Südafrika *nt* South Africa.

Südamerika *nt* South America.

Süddeutschland *nt* South Germany.

Süden *der* south; **im ~** in the south; **nach ~** south.

Südeuropa *nt* Southern Europe.

Südfrucht (*pl* **-früchte**) *die* tropical fruit.

Südhang (*pl* **-hänge**) *der* south-facing slope.

südlich ◆ *adj* (*Gegend*) southern; (*Richtung*) southerly. ◆ *präp:* **~ von** south of.

Südosten *der* (*Gegend*) south-east; (*Richtung*) south-easterly.

Südwesten *der* (*Gegend*) south-west; (*Richtung*) south-westerly.

Sultanine (*pl* **-n**) *die* sultana.

Sülze (*pl* **-n**) *die* brawn (Br), head-cheese (Am).

Summe (*pl* **-n**) *die* sum, total.

Sumpf (*pl* **Sümpfe**) *der* marsh.

super *adj* & *interj* (*fam*) great.

Super *das* (*Benzin*) four-star petrol; **~ verbleit** four-star leaded petrol.

Superlativ (*pl* **-e**) *der* (GRAMM) superlative.

Supermarkt (*pl* **-märkte**) *der* supermarket.

Suppe (*pl* **-n**) *die* soup.

Suppengrün *das* parsley, leeks, celery and carrots, used for making soup.

Suppenlöffel (*pl* **-**) *der* soup spoon.

Suppentasse (*pl* **-n**) *die* soup bowl.

Suppenteller (*pl* **-**) *der* soup plate.

Surfbrett (*pl* **-er**) *das* (*mit Segel*) sail-board; (*ohne Segel*) surfboard.

surfen *vi* ist/hat (*mit Segel*) to wind-surf; (*ohne Segel*) to surf.

Surfer, -in (*mpl* **-**) *der, die* (*mit Segel*)

windsurfer; (*ohne Segel*) surfer.

Surrealismus *der* surrealism.

süß *adj* sweet.

süßen *vt* to sweeten.

Süßigkeit (*pl* **-en**) *die* sweet (Br), candy (Am).

süß-sauer *adj* (*Geschmack*) sweet and sour.

Süßspeise (*pl* **-n**) *die* dessert.

Süßstoff (*pl* **-e**) *der* sweetener.

Süßwaren *pl* sweets (Br), candy (*sg*)(Am).

Süßwasser *das* fresh water.

Süßwasserfisch (*pl* **-e**) *der* fresh-water fish.

Swimmingpool (*pl* **-s**) *der* swim-ming pool.

Sylt *nt* Sylt.

SYLT

The island of Sylt is the largest of the North Frisian Islands and lies off the coast of Schleswig-Holstein and Denmark. It is a very popular holiday and health resort, with beautiful sandy beaches, moorland, cliffs and bird sanctuaries. The exclusive resort of Westerland is the favourite haunt of the rich and famous during the summer months.

Symbol (*pl* **-e**) *das* symbol.

Symmetrie (*pl* **-n**) *die* symmetry.

symmetrisch *adj* symmetrical.

sympatisch ◆ *adj* nice. ◆ *adv:* **er wirkt sehr ~** he seems very nice.

Symphonie (*pl* **-n**) *die* = **Sinfonie**.

Symptom (*pl* **-e**) *das* (*von Krankheit*) symptom.

Synagoge (*pl* **-n**) *die* synagogue.

synthetisch *adj* synthetic.

System (*pl* **-e**) *das* system.

Szene (*pl* **-n**) *die* scene.

T

Tabak (pl -e) der tobacco.

Tabakladen (pl -läden) der tobacconist's.

Tabakwaren pl tobacco (sg).

Tabelle (pl -n) die (Liste) table.

Tablett (pl -s) das tray.

Tablette (pl -n) die tablet.

Tachometer (pl -) der speedometer.

Tafel (pl -n) die (in Schule) blackboard; (geh: Tisch) table; **eine ~ Schokolade** a bar of chocolate.

tafelfertig adj ready to eat.

Tafelwasser (pl -wässer) das mineral water.

Tafelwein (pl -e) der table wine.

Tag (pl -e) der day; **eines ~es** one day; **guten ~!** hello!; **jeden ~** every day; **~ für ~** day after day. ▶ **Tage** pl (Menstruation): **sie hat/bekommt ihre ~e** she's got her period.

Tag der Deutschen Einheit der Day of German Unity.

TAG DER DEUTSCHEN EINHEIT

This day, 3 October, is a public holiday in Germany, commemorating the anniversary of German reunification in 1990, when the GDR officially ceased to exist. It replaces the previous 'Tag der Deutschen Einheit', which before 1990 was celebrated in West Germany on 17 June to mark the crushing of the political uprising in the GDR in 1953 by Soviet troops.

Tagebuch (pl -bücher) das diary.

tagelang adv for days.

Tagesanbruch der dawn.

Tagesausflug (pl -ausflüge) der day trip.

Tagescreme (pl -s) die day cream.

Tagesfahrkarte (pl -n) die day ticket.

Tagesfahrt (pl -en) die day trip.

Tagesgericht (pl -e) das (in Restaurant): **'Tagesgericht'** 'today's special'.

Tageskarte (pl -n) die (Speisekarte) today's menu; (Fahrkarte) day ticket.

Tageslicht das daylight.

Tagesordnung (pl -en) die agenda.

Tagesrückfahrkarte (pl -n) die day return (ticket).

Tagesschau die news.

Tagessuppe (pl -n) die soup of the day.

Tagestour (pl -en) die day trip.

Tageszeit (pl -en) die time of day.

Tageszeitung (pl -en) die daily newspaper.

täglich adj & adv daily; **dreimal ~** three times a day.

tagsüber adv during the day.

Tagung (pl -en) die conference.

Taille (pl -n) die waist.

tailliert adj fitted.

Takt (pl -e) der (musikalische Einheit) bar; (Rhythmus) time; (Feingefühl) tact.

Taktik (pl -en) die tactics (pl).

Tal (pl Täler) das valley.

talentiert adj talented.

Talk-show (pl -s) die talk show.

Talsperre (pl -n) die dam.

Tampon (pl -s) der (für Menstruation) tampon.

Tandem (pl -s) das tandem.

Tang der seaweed.

Tank (pl -s) der tank.

Tankanzeige (pl -n) die fuel gauge.

Tankdeckel (pl -) der petrol cap.

tanken ◆ vi to fill up. ◆ vt: **Benzin ~** to get some petrol (Br), to get some gas (Am).

Tankschloß (pl -schlösser) das petrol cap lock.

Tankstelle (pl -n) die petrol station (Br), gas station (Am).

Tankwart, -in (mpl -e) der, die petrol station attendant (Br), gas station attendant (Am).

Tanne (pl -n) die fir (tree).

Tante (pl -n) die aunt.

Tanz (pl Tänze) der dance.

tanzen vi & vt to dance.

Tänzer, -in (mpl -) der, die dancer.

Tapete (pl -n) die wallpaper.

tapezieren vt to paper.

tapfer adj brave.

Tarif (pl -e) der (Preis) charge; (von Lohn) rate.

Tarifzone (pl -n) die fare zone.

Tasche (pl -n) die (zum Tragen) bag; (in Kleidung) pocket.

Taschenbuch (pl -bücher) das paperback.

Taschendieb, -in (mpl -e) der, die pickpocket; 'vor ~en wird gewarnt' 'beware of pickpockets'.

Taschenformat (pl -e) das pocket size.

Taschenkalender (pl -) der pocket diary.

Taschenlampe (pl -n) die torch (Br), flashlight (Am).

Taschenmesser (pl -) das penknife.

Taschenrechner (pl -) der pocket calculator.

Taschenschirm (pl -e) der collapsible umbrella.

Taschentuch (pl -tücher) das handkerchief.

Taschenuhr (pl -en) die pocket watch.

Tasse (pl -n) die cup.

Tastatur (pl -en) die keyboard.

Taste (pl -n) die key.

tasten vi to feel.

Tastendruck der: auf ~ at the touch of a button.

Tastentelefon (pl -e) das push-button telephone.

tat prät → tun.

Tat (pl -en) die (Handlung) action; (Straftat) crime.

Tatar das steak tartare.

Täter, -in (mpl -) der, die culprit.

Tätigkeit (pl -en) die (beruflich) job; (Aktivität) activity.

Tätowierung (pl -en) die tattoo.

Tatsache (pl -n) die fact.

tatsächlich ♦ adj actual. ♦ adv actually.

Tau¹ der (Niederschlag) dew.

Tau² (pl -e) das (Seil) rope.

taub adj (Person) deaf; (Hände, Gefühl) numb.

Taube (pl -n) ♦ der, die (Person) deaf person. ♦ die (Vogel) pigeon.

taubstumm adj deaf and dumb.

tauchen ♦ vi hat/ist to dive. ♦ vt hat (eintauchen) to dip.

Taucher, -in (mpl -) der, die diver.

Taucherausrüstung (pl -en) die diving equipment.

Taucherbrille (pl -n) die diving goggles (pl).

Tauchkurs (pl -e) der diving course.

Tauchsieder (pl -) der portable water heater.

tauen ♦ vi ist (Eis) to melt. ♦ vimp hat: es taut it's thawing.

taufen vt (Kind, Person) to baptize.

tauschen vt & vi to swap.

täuschen ♦ vt (Person) to deceive. ♦ vi (Eindruck) to be deceptive. ▶ **sich täuschen** ref to be wrong.

tausend num a ODER one thousand.

Tausend (pl - ODER -e) das thousand.

Tausender (pl -) der (Geldschein) thousand mark note.

Tauwetter das thaw.

Taxi (pl -s) das taxi.

Taxifahrer, -in (mpl -) der, die taxi driver.

Taxi-Rufsäule (pl -n) die public telephone exclusively for ordering taxis.

Taxistand (pl -stände) der taxi rank.

Taxizentrale (pl -n) die taxi firm.

Team (pl -s) das team.

Technik (pl -en) die technology; (Methode) technique.

Techniker, -in (*mpl* -) *der, die* engineer; (*im Sport, in Musik*) technician.

technisch ◆ *adj* technological; (*methodisch*) technical. ◆ *adv* technologically; (*methodisch*) technically; **~e Daten** specifications.

Teddy (*pl* -s) *der* teddy bear.

Tee (*pl* -s) *der* tea; **schwarzer ~** (*Getränk*) black tea.

Teebeutel (*pl* -s) *der* tea bag.

Tee-Ei (*pl* -er) *das* tea infuser.

Teekanne (*pl* -n) *die* teapot.

Teelöffel (*pl* -) *der* teaspoon.

Teesieb (*pl* -e) *das* tea strainer.

Teich (*pl* -e) *der* pond.

Teig (*pl* -e) *der* dough.

Teigwaren *pl* pasta (*sg*).

Teil (*pl* -e) ◆ *der* (*Teilmenge, Teilstück*) part; (*Anteil*) share. ◆ *das* (*Einzelteil*) part; **zum ~** partly.

teilen ◆ *vt* to divide; (*übereinstimmen*) to share. ◆ *vi* (*aufteilen*) to share; (*dividieren*) to divide; **sich ~ etw ~** to share sthg. ▶ **sich teilen** *ref* (*Gruppe*) to split up; (*Straße*) to fork.

Teilkaskoversicherung (*pl* -en) *die* third party insurance.

teilmöbliert *adj* partially furnished.

Teilnahme *die* (*an Veranstaltung*) participation.

teilnehmen *vi unr* to take part.

Teilnehmer, -in (*mpl* -) *der, die* participant.

teils ◆ *adv* partly. ◆ *konj*: **~ ... ~** (*sowohl ... als auch*) both ... and ...

Teilstück (*pl* -e) *das* part.

Teilsumme (*pl* -n) *die* subtotal.

teilweise *adv* (*zu gewissen Teilen*) partly; (*zeitweise*) sometimes.

Teilzahlung (*pl* -en) *die* payment by instalments.

Tel. (*abk für Telefon*) tel.

Telefax (*pl* -e) *das* fax.

Telefon (*pl* -e) *das* telephone; **bleiben Sie bitte am ~** please hold the line.

Telefonanruf (*pl* -e) *der* telephone call.

Telefonansage (*pl* -n) *die* telephone information service.

Telefonanschluß (*pl* -anschlüsse) *der* telephone line.

Telefonat (*pl* -e) *das* telephone call.

Telefonbuch (*pl* -bücher) *das* telephone book.

Telefongespräch (*pl* -e) *das* telephone conversation.

telefonieren *vi* to make a telephone call; **mit jm ~** to talk to sb on the telephone; **~ ohne Münzen** to use a phonecard.

telefonisch *adj* (*Abmachung, Verbindung*) telephone (*vor Subst*).

Telefonkarte (*pl* -n) *die* phonecard.

Telefonnummer (*pl* -n) *die* telephone number; **wie ist Ihre ~?** what's your telephone number?

Telefonverbindung (*pl* -en) *die* telephone line.

Telefonzelle (*pl* -n) *die* telephone box.

Telefonzentrale (*pl* -n) *die* switchboard.

telegrafieren *vt* to telegraph.

Telegramm (*pl* -e) *das* telegram.

Telekom *die* German state-owned *telecommunications organization.*

Teleobjektiv (*pl* -e) *das* telephoto lens.

Telex *das* telex.

Teller (*pl* -) *der* plate.

Tellerfleisch *das* (*Süddt*) *roast beef served with horseradish and boiled potatoes.*

Tempel (*pl* -) *der* temple.

Temperament *das* (*Wesen*) temperament; (*Energie*) liveliness.

temperamentvoll *adj* lively.

Temperatur (*pl* -en) *die* temperature; **~ haben** to have a temperature.

Temperaturanzeige (*pl* -n) *die* temperature gauge.

Tempo¹ (*pl* -s) *das* (*fam: Papier-*

taschentuch) tissue.

Tempo² (*pl* **-s**) *das* (*Geschwindigkeit*) speed.

Tempo³ (*pl* **Tempi**) *das* (*von Musik*) tempo.

Tempolimit (*pl* **-s**) *das* speed limit.

Tempotaschentuch® (*pl* **-tücher**) *das* tissue.

Tendenz (*pl* **-en**) *die* tendency.

Tennis *das* tennis.

Tennishalle (*pl* **-n**) *die* tennis centre.

Tenniskleidung *die* tennis clothes (*pl*).

Tennisplatz (*pl* **-plätze**) *der* tennis court.

Tennisschläger (*pl* **-**) *der* tennis racquet.

Tennisschuh (*pl* **-e**) *der* tennis shoe.

Tennisspieler, -in (*mpl* **-**) *der, die* tennis player.

Tenor (*pl* **Tenöre**) *der* tenor.

Teppich (*pl* **-e**) *der* (*Einzelstück*) rug; (*Teppichboden*) carpet.

Teppichboden (*pl* **-böden**) *der* carpet.

Termin (*pl* **-e**) *der* (*Zeitpunkt*) date; (*Vereinbarung*) appointment; **einen ~ haben** to have an appointment.

Terminal (*pl* **-s**) *der* (*Gebäude*) terminal.

Terminkalender (*pl* **-**) *der* diary.

Terpentin *das* turpentine.

Terrasse (*pl* **-n**) *die* (*am Haus*) patio.

Terror *der* terror; (*Terrorismus*) terrorism.

terrorisieren *vt* to terrorize.

Tesafilm® *der* Sellotape® (Br), Scotch® (Am).

Tessin *das* Ticino (*canton in south-east Switzerland*).

Test (*pl* **-s**) *der* test.

Testament (*pl* **-e**) *das* will; **das Alte/Neue ~** the Old/New Testament.

Tetanus *der* tetanus.

teuer ◆ *adj* expensive. ◆ *adv* at a high price; **das haben wir uns ~**

erkauft we paid dearly for it.

Teufel (*pl* **-**) *der* devil.

Text (*pl* **-e**) *der* text.

Textilien *pl* textiles.

Textmarker (*pl* **-**) *der* marker pen.

Textverarbeitung *die* (EDV) word processing.

Theater (*pl* **-**) *das* (*Gebäude*) theatre; (*fam: Ärger*) trouble; (*fam: Vortäuschung*) act; **ins ~ gehen** to go to the theatre.

Theateraufführung (*pl* **-en**) *die* performance.

Theaterkarte (*pl* **-n**) *die* theatre ticket.

Theaterkasse (*pl* **-n**) *die* theatre box office.

Theaterstück (*pl* **-e**) *das* play.

Theatervorstellung (*pl* **-en**) *die* performance.

Theke (*pl* **-n**) *die* (*Bar*) bar; (*im Geschäft*) counter.

Thema (*pl* **Themen**) *das* (*von Text, Gespräch*) subject; (*musikalisch*) theme.

Themse *die*: **die ~** the Thames.

theoretisch *adj* theoretical.

Theorie (*pl* **-n**) *die* theory.

Therapeut, -in (*mpl* **-en**) *der, die* therapist.

Therapie (*pl* **-n**) *die* (*medizinisch*) treatment; (*Psychotherapie*) therapy.

Thermalbad (*pl* **-bäder**) *das* (*Schwimmbad*) thermal bath.

Thermometer (*pl* **-**) *das* thermometer.

Thermosflasche (*pl* **-n**) *die* thermos (flask).

Thermoskanne (*pl* **-n**) *die* thermos (flask).

Thermostat (*pl* **-e**) *das* thermostat.

These (*pl* **-n**) *die* thesis.

Thron (*pl* **-e**) *der* throne.

Thunfisch (*pl* **-e**) *der* tuna.

Thüringen *nt* Thuringia.

Ticket (*pl* **-s**) *das* ticket.

tief ◆ *adj* deep; (*Fall*) long; (*niedrig*) low. ◆ *adv* deep; (*unten*) low; (*atmen*) deeply; ~ **schlafen** to be in a deep sleep.

Tief (pl -s) das (Wetter) depression.

Tiefdruckgebiet (pl -e) das area of low pressure.

Tiefe (pl -n) die depth.

Tiefebene (pl -n) die (lowland) plain.

Tiefgarage (pl -n) die underground car park.

tiefgefroren adj frozen.

tiefgekühlt adj frozen.

Tiefkühlfach (pl -fächer) das freezer compartment.

Tiefkühlkost die frozen food.

Tiefkühltruhe (pl -n) die freezer.

Tier (pl -e) das animal.

Tierart (pl -en) die animal species.

Tierarzt, -ärztin (mpl -ärzte) der, die vet.

Tiergarten (pl -gärten) der zoo.

Tierhandlung (pl -en) die pet shop.

Tierheim (pl -e) das animal home.

tierisch adj (Erzeugnis, Fett) animal (vor Subst); (fam: stark) great.

Tierkreiszeichen (pl -) das sign of the zodiac.

Tiernahrung die animal food.

Tierpark (pl -s) der zoo.

Tierschutz der protection of animals.

Tiger (pl -) der tiger.

Tilsiter (pl -) der strong firm Swiss cheese with holes in it.

Tinktur (pl -en) die tincture.

Tinte (pl -n) die ink.

Tintenfisch (pl -e) der (mit acht Armen) octopus; (Kalmar) squid.

Tip (pl -s) der tip; **jm einen ~ geben** to give sb a tip.

tippen ◆ vt (mit Schreibmaschine) to type. ◆ vi (vorhersagen) to bet; (fam: bei Lotto, Wette) to bet; **an etw** (A) **~ to** tap sthg.

Tirol nt the Tyrol.

Tisch (pl -e) der table; **den ~ decken** to set the table.

Tischdecke (pl -n) die tablecloth.

Tischler, -in (mpl -) der, die carpenter.

Tischtennis das table tennis.

Tischtuch (pl -tücher) das tablecloth.

Titel (pl -) der title.

Toast (pl -s) der (Brotscheibe) (slice of) toast.

Toastbrot (pl -e) das sliced white bread.

toasten vt to toast.

Toaster (pl -) der toaster.

toben ◆ vi hat (Sturm) to rage; (Person) to go crazy. ◆ vi ist (rennen) to charge about.

Tochter (pl Töchter) die (Verwandte) daughter.

Tod (pl -e) der death.

Todesopfer (pl -) das casualty.

todkrank adj terminally ill.

tödlich adj fatal.

todmüde adj (fam) dead tired.

todsicher adj (fam) dead certain.

Tofu der tofu.

Toilette (pl -n) die (Klo) toilet; **zur ~ gehen** to go to the toilet.

Toilettenartikel pl toiletries.

Toilettenpapier das toilet paper.

toi, toi, toi interj (viel Glück): ~! good luck!

tolerant adj tolerant.

toll ◆ adj (fam: wunderbar) brilliant. ◆ adv (fam: wunderbar) brilliantly.

Tollwut die rabies.

Tollwutgebiet (pl -e) das rabies-infected area.

Tomate (pl -n) die tomato.

Tomatenmark das tomato puree.

Tomatensaft (pl -säfte) der tomato juice.

Tombola (pl -s) die tombola.

Ton¹ (pl Töne) der (bei Fernsehen, Radio) sound; (in Tonleiter) note; (Tonfall, von Farbe) tone.

Ton² (pl -e) der (Lehm) clay.

Tonausfall (pl -fälle) der loss of sound.

Tonband (*pl* -**bänder**) *das* (*Band*) tape; (*Gerät*) tape recorder.

tönen *vt* (*Haare*) to tint.

Tonne (*pl* -**n**) *die* (*Behälter*) barrel; (*Gewichtseinheit*) tonne.

Tönung (*pl* -**en**) *die* tint.

Top (*pl* -**s**) *das* top.

Topf (*pl* **Töpfe**) *der* (*Kochtopf*) pan; (*Blumentopf*) pot.

Topfen *der* (*Süddt & Österr*) curd cheese.

Topfenstrudel (*pl* -) *der* (*Süddt & Österr*) curd cheese strudel.

Töpfer, -in (*mpl* -) *der, die* potter.

Töpferei (*pl* -**en**) *die* pottery.

Topfpflanze (*pl* -**n**) *die* potted plant.

Tor (*pl* -**e**) *das* (*Tür*) gate; (*von Scheune, Garage*) door; (*bei Fußball*) goal; **ein ~ schießen** to score a goal.

Toreinfahrt (*pl* -**en**) *die* entrance gate.

Torf *der* peat.

Torte (*pl* -**n**) *die* gâteau.

Tortelett (*pl* -**s**) *das* tartlet.

Torwart (*pl* -**e**) *der* goalkeeper.

tot *adj & adv* dead; **~ umfallen** to drop dead.

total ◆ *adj* total. ◆ *adv* totally.

Totalschaden (*pl* -**schäden**) *der* write-off.

Tote (*pl* -**n**) *der, die* dead person.

töten *vt* to kill.

Totensonntag (*pl* -**e**) *der* day for commemoration of the dead, Sunday before Advent.

totlachen: sich totlachen *ref* (*fam*) to kill o.s. laughing.

Toto *das* football pools (*pl*).

Toupet (*pl* -**s**) *das* toupee.

toupieren *vt* to backcomb.

Tour (*pl* -**en**) *die* (*Ausflug*) trip; (*fam*: *Verhalten*) way.

Tourenski (*pl* -**er**) *der* cross-country ski.

Tourismus *der* tourism.

Tourist, -in (*mpl* -**en**) *der, die* tourist.

Touristeninformation (*pl* -**en**) *die* tourist information office.

Touristenklasse *die* tourist class.

Touristenort (*pl* -**e**) *der* tourist resort.

touristisch *adj* tourist.

Tournee (*pl* -**n**) *die* tour.

traben *vi ist* (*Pferd*) to trot.

Trabrennen (*pl* -) *das* trotting.

Tracht (*pl* -**en**) *die* (*Kleidung*) traditional costume; **eine ~ Prügel** (*fam*: *Schläge*) a beating.

Trachtenfest (*pl* -**e**) *das* event at which traditional costumes are worn.

Trachtenverein (*pl* -**e**) *der* society for the preservation of regional customs.

Tradition (*pl* -**en**) *die* tradition.

traditionell *adj* traditional.

traf *prät* → **treffen**.

Trafik *die* (*Österr*) tobacconist's.

TRAFIK

A 'Trafik' is a small shop found in Austria where all sorts of useful items can be bought, such as stamps, postcards, tickets for local transport services, magazines, cigarettes and tobacco.

Tragbahre (*pl* -**n**) *die* stretcher.

tragbar *adj* (*Gerät*) portable; (*akzeptabel*) acceptable.

träge *adj* (*Person, Bewegung*) lazy.

tragen (*präs* **trägt**, *prät* **trug**, *pp* **getragen**) ◆ *vt* (*transportieren*) to carry; (*Kleidung, Frisur*) to wear; (*abstützen*) to support; (*ertragen, Kosten*) to bear; (*Risiko, Konsequenzen*) to accept. ◆ *vi* (*Eis, Wände*) to hold; (*Tier*) to be pregnant. ▶ **sich tragen** *ref* (*finanziell*) to be self-supporting.

Träger (*pl* -) *der* (*Beruf*) porter; (*Geldgeber*) sponsor; (*von Kleid*) strap; (*Hosenträger*) braces (*pl*) (*Br*), suspenders (*pl*) (*Am*); (*aus Eisen*) girder.

Trägerin (*pl* -**nen**) *die* (*Beruf*) porter; (*Geldgeberin*) sponsor.

Tragetasche (*pl* -**n**) *die* carrier bag.

tragisch *adj* tragic.

Tragödie (*pl* -**n**) *die* tragedy.

trägt *präs* → **tragen**.

Trainer, -in (*mpl* -) *der, die* trainer.

trainieren *vi & vt* to train.

Training (*pl* -s) *das* training.

Trainingsanzug (*pl* -züge) *der* tracksuit.

Traktor (*pl* Traktoren) *der* tractor.

Trambahn (*pl* -en) *die* (*Süddt*) tram (Br), streetcar (Am).

trampen *vi hat/ist* to hitchhike.

Tramper, -in (*mpl* -) *der, die* hitchhiker.

Träne (*pl* -n) *die* tear.

tränen *vi* to water.

Tränengas *das* tear gas.

trank *prät* → **trinken**.

Transfusion (*pl* -en) *die* transfusion.

Transitverkehr *der* transit traffic.

Transitvisum (*pl* -visa) *das* transit visa.

Transport (*pl* -e) *der* transport.

transportabel *adj* (*Fernseher*) portable.

transportieren ◆ *vt* (*befördern*) to transport; (*Film*) to wind on. ◆ *vi* (*Kamera*) to wind on.

Transportmittel (*pl* -) *das* means of transport.

Transportunternehmen (*pl* -) *das* haulier.

Transvestit (*pl* -en) *der* transvestite.

trat *prät* → **treten**.

Traube (*pl* -n) *die* (*Frucht*) grape.

Traubensaft (*pl* -säfte) *der* grape juice.

Traubenzucker *der* glucose.

trauen ◆ *vt* (*Brautpaar*) to marry. ◆ *vi* (+D) (*vertrauen*) to trust. ▶ **sich trauen** *ref* (*wagen*) to dare.

Trauer *die* mourning.

Traum (*pl* Träume) *der* dream.

träumen *vi* to dream; (*abwesend sein*) to daydream.

traumhaft *adj* fantastic.

traurig ◆ *adj* sad. ◆ *adv* sadly.

Trauung (*pl* -en) *die* wedding; kirch-

liche/standesamtliche ~ church/registry office wedding.

Travellerscheck (*pl* -s) *der* traveller's cheque.

treffen (*präs* **trifft**, *prät* **traf**, *pp* **getroffen**) ◆ *vt hat* (*begegnen*) to meet; (*Ziel*) to hit; (*Verabredung, Entscheidung*) to make; (*traurig machen*) to affect. ◆ *vi hat* (*ins Ziel*) to score. ▶ **sich treffen** *ref* to meet; **sich mit jm ~** to meet sb; **wo sollen wir uns ~?** where should we meet?

Treffen (*pl* -) *das* meeting.

Treffer (*pl* -) *der* (SPORT) goal; (*Schuß*) hit.

Treffpunkt (*pl* -e) *der* meeting place.

treiben (*prät* **trieb**, *pp* **getrieben**) ◆ *vt hat* to drive; (*machen, tun*) to do. ◆ *vi ist* (*im Wasser*) to drift; **was treibst du denn so in deiner Freizeit?** what do you do in your spare time?

Treibstoff (*pl* -e) *der* fuel.

Trend (*pl* -s) *der* trend.

trennen *vt* to separate; (*unterscheiden*) to distinguish. ▶ **sich trennen** *ref* to separate.

Trennung (*pl* -en) *die* (*von Beziehung*) separation; (GRAMM) division.

Treppe (*pl* -n) *die* stairs (*pl*); ~ rauf/runter up/down the stairs.

Treppengeländer (*pl* -) *das* banisters (*pl*).

Treppenhaus (*pl* -häuser) *das* stairwell.

Tresen (*pl* -) *der* (*Norddt*) counter.

Tretboot (*pl* -e) *das* paddle boat.

treten (*präs* **tritt**, *prät* **trat**, *pp* **getreten**) ◆ *vt & vi hat* to kick. ◆ *vi ist* (*gehen*) to step; **auf die Bremse ~** to brake.

treu *adj* faithful.

Treuhand *die organization responsible for privatizing state industries of the former GDR.*

Triathlon (*pl* -s) *der* triathlon.

Tribüne (*pl* -n) *die* stand.

Trichter (*pl* -) *der* (*Gerät*) funnel.

Trick (*pl* -s) *der* trick.

Trickfilm (*pl* -e) *der* cartoon.

trieb *prät* → **treiben**.

triefen (*prät* **troff** ODER **triefte**, *pp* **getrieft**) *vi ist & vt* to drip.

trifft *präs* → **treffen**.

Trikot (*pl* -s) *das* jersey.

Trillerpfeife (*pl* -n) *die* whistle.

Trimester (*pl* -) *das* term.

Trimm-Dich-Pfad (*pl* -e) *der* fitness trail.

trinkbar *adj* drinkable.

trinken (*prät* **trank**, *pp* **getrunken**) *vt & vi* to drink; **einen ~ gehen** (*fam*) to go for a drink; **auf jn/etw ~** to drink to sb/sthg.

Trinkgeld (*pl* -er) *das* tip.

Trinkhalle (*pl* -n) *die* drinks stall.

Trinkhalm (*pl* -e) *der* (drinking) straw.

Trinkschokolade (*pl* -n) *die* drinking chocolate.

Trinkwasser *das* drinking water.

Trio (*pl* -s) *das* trio.

tritt *präs* → **treten**.

Tritt (*pl* -e) *der* (*Stoß*) kick; (*Schritt*) step.

triumphieren *vi* to triumph.

trivial *adj* trivial.

trocken *adj* dry; '**~ aufbewahren**' 'keep in a dry place'.

Trockenhaube (*pl* -n) *die* hair dryer.

Trockenheit *die* dryness; (*Wassermangel*) drought.

trocken∥legen *vt* (*Sumpf*) to drain; (*Baby*) to change.

trocknen *vt hat & vi ist* to dry.

Trockner (*pl* -) *der* dryer.

Trödel *der* (*Gegenstände*) junk; (*fam: Trödelmarkt*) flea market.

Trödelmarkt (*pl* -märkte) *der* flea market.

trödeln *vi hat/ist* (*fam: langsam sein*) to dawdle.

troff *prät* → **triefen**.

trog *prät* → **trügen**.

Trommel (*pl* -n) *die* (*Instrument*) drum.

Trommelfell (*pl* -e) *das* eardrum.

Trompete (*pl* -n) *die* trumpet.

Tropen *pl* tropics.

Tropf (*pl* -e) *der* (*Gerät*) drip.

tropfen *vi & vt* to drip.

Tropfen (*pl* -) *der* drop.

tropfnaß *adv*: **~ aufhängen** to drip-dry.

Tropfsteinhöhle (*pl* -n) *die* cave with stalactites and stalagmites.

trösten *vt* to console. ▶ **sich trösten** *ref* to find consolation.

Trostpreis (*pl* -e) *der* consolation prize.

Trottoir (*pl* -e) *das* (*Süddt*) pavement (Br), sidewalk (Am).

trotz *präp* (+G) despite, in spite of.

trotzdem *adv* nevertheless.

trotzig *adj* stubborn.

trüb *adj* (*nicht klar*) cloudy.

Trüffel (*pl* -) *der* truffle.

trug *prät* → **tragen**.

trügen (*prät* **trog**, *pp* **getrogen**) *vi* to be deceptive.

Truhe (*pl* -n) *die* chest.

Trümmer *pl* (*eines Gebäudes*) ruins; (*eines Fahrzeugs*) wreckage (*sg*).

Trumpf (*pl* **Trümpfe**) *der* (*bei Kartenspiel*) trumps (*pl*).

Trunkenheit *die* (*amt*) inebriation.

Truthahn (*pl* -hähne) *der* turkey.

Tschechien *nt* Czech Republic.

tschüs *interj* bye!

Tsd. *abk* = **Tausend**.

T-Shirt (*pl* -s) *das* T-shirt.

Tube (*pl* -n) *die* tube.

Tuberkulose *die* tuberculosis.

Tuch¹ (*pl* **Tücher**) *das* (*Halstuch*) scarf; (*zum Putzen, Abtrocknen*) cloth.

Tuch² (*pl* -e) *das* (*Stoff*) cloth.

tüchtig ♦ *adj* (*geschickt*) competent; (*fam: groß*) big. ♦ *adv* (*fam: viel*): **~ essen** to tuck in.

Tulpe (*pl* -n) *die* tulip.

Tümpel (*pl* -) *der* pond.

tun (*präs* **tut**, *prät* **tat**, *pp* **getan**) ♦ *vt* 1. (*machen*) to do; **was kann ich für Sie ~?** what can I do for you?; **ich**

habe noch nichts für die Prüfung getan I haven't done any work for the exam yet. **2.** (*fam: stellen, legen*) to put. **3.** (*schaden, antun*): **jm/sich etwas ~** to do something to sb/o.s. **4.** (*fam: funktionieren, ausreichen*): **ich danke, das tut es** I think that will do; **das Auto tut es noch/nicht mehr** the car still works/has had it. ◆ *vi* **1.** (*spielen, vortäuschen*): **so ~, als ob** to act as if; **er tut nur so** he's only pretending. **2.** (*Ausdruck von Gefühl, Wirkung*): **der Bettler tut mir leid** I feel sorry for the beggar; **jm gut ~** to do sb good. **3.** (*Ausdruck einer Beziehung*): **zu ~ haben mit** to be linked to; **nichts zu ~ haben mit** to have nothing to do with. ◆ *vimp*: **es tut sich was** something is going on.

tunken *vt* to dunk.

Tunnel (*pl* -) *der* tunnel.

tupfen *vt* to dab.

Tür (*pl* -en) *die* door; **die ~ aufmachen/zumachen** to open/close the door; **~ zu!** shut the door!

Türke (*pl* -n) *der* the Turk.

Türkei *die* Turkey.

Türkin (*pl* -nen) *die* Turk.

türkisch *adj* Turkish.

Türkisch(e) *das* Turkish.

Türklinke (*pl* -n) *die* door handle.

Turm (*pl* **Türme**) *der* (*Gebäude*) tower.

turnen *vi* (SPORT) to do gymnastics.

Turner, -in (*mpl* -) *der, die* gymnast.

Turnhalle (*pl* -n) *die* gym.

Turnhose (*pl* -n) *die* shorts (*pl*).

Turnier (*pl* -e) *das* (SPORT) tournament.

Turnschuh (*pl* -e) *der* gymshoe (Br), sneaker (Am).

Türschloß (*pl* **-schlösser**) *das* lock.

tuscheln *vi* to whisper.

tut *präs* → **tun**.

Tüte (*pl* -n) *die* bag.

TÜV *der* = MOT (Br), *regular official test of car's roadworthiness*.

TV *das* (*abk für Television*) TV.

Typ (*pl* -en) *der* (*Art, Charakter*) type; (*Modell*) model; (*fam: Mann*) guy.

Typhus *der* typhoid.

typisch *adj* typical.

tyrannisieren *vt* to tyrannize.

U

u. *abk* = **und**.

u.a. *abk* = **unter anderem**.

u.a.m. (*abk für und anderes mehr*) etc.

u.A.w.g (*abk für um Antwort wird gebeten*) R.S.V.P.

UB (*pl* -s) *die* (*abk für Universitätsbibliothek*) university library.

U-Bahn (*pl* -en) *die* underground (Br), subway (Am).

U-Bahn-Haltestelle (*pl* -n) *die* underground station (Br), subway station (Am).

U-Bahn-Linie (*pl* -n) *die* underground line (Br), subway line (Am).

U-Bahn-Netz (*pl* -e) *das* underground system (Br), subway system (Am).

übel (*komp* **übler**, *superl* **am übelsten**) *adj* bad; **mir ist/wird ~** I am/feel sick; **nicht ~** (*fam*) not bad.

Übelkeit (*pl* -en) *die* nausea.

übel|nehmen *vt unr* to take badly.

üben *vt & vi* to practise.

über ◆ *präp* (+A) **1.** (*höher als*) over, above; **das Flugzeug flog ~ das Tal** the plane flew over the valley. **2.** (*quer*) over; **~ die Straße gehen** to cross (over) the road. **3.** (*Angabe der Route*) via. **4.** (*Angabe des Themas*) about; **ein Buch ~ Mozart** a book about Mozart. **5.** (*Angabe des Betrages*) for; **eine Rechnung ~ 30 DM** a bill for 30 marks. **6.** (*mehr als*) over; **~ eine Stunde** over an hour; **~ Null** above zero; **Kinder ~ zehn Jahren** children over ten (years of age). **7.** (zeitlich) over; ~ **Nacht** overnight. ◆ präp (+D) **1.** (räumlich: höher) above, over; **die Lampe hängt ~ dem Tisch** the lamp hangs above ODER over the table; **er wohnt ~ uns** he lives above us. **2.** (mehr als) above; ~ **dem Durchschnitt liegen** to be above average. ◆ adv **1.** (zeitlich): **den Sommer ~ bleiben wir hier** we're staying here all summer. **2.** (fam: übrig) left (over). ▶ **über und über** adv all over.

überall adv everywhere.

überallhin adv everywhere.

überanstrengen vt to overstrain. ▶ **sich überanstrengen** ref to overdo it.

überarbeiten vt to revise. ▶ **sich überarbeiten** ref to overwork.

überbacken (präs **überbackt** ODER **überbäckt**, prät **überbackte**, pp **überbacken** en) vt to bake or grill with a cheese topping.

überbelichtet adj overexposed.

Überblick (pl **-e**) der (Übersicht) summary.

überblicken vt (einschätzen) to grasp; (sehen) to overlook.

überbrücken vt (Zeit) to fill in.

überbucht adj overbooked.

überdurchschnittlich adj above average.

übereinander adv on top of each other; ~ **sprechen/denken** to talk/think about each other.

überein|stimmen vi (Personen, Meinungen) to agree.

überfahren (präs **überfährt**, prät **überfuhr**, pp **überfahren**) vt (Tier, Person) to run over.

Überfahrt (pl **-en**) die crossing.

Überfall (pl **-fälle**) der (Angriff) attack.

überfallen (präs **überfällt**, prät **überfiel**, pp **überfallen**) vt (angreifen) to attack.

überfällig adj (Zug) late; (Rechnung) outstanding.

Überfluß der surplus.

überflüssig adj superfluous.

überfordert adj: **damit bin ich ~** that's asking too much of me.

Überführung (pl **-en**) die (Brücke) bridge; (Transport) transfer.

überfüllt adj overcrowded.

Übergabe die (von Dingen) handing over.

Übergang (pl **-gänge**) der (Phase) transition.

übergeben (präs **übergibt**, prät **übergab**, pp **übergeben**) vt (Gegenstand) to hand over. ▶ **sich übergeben** ref to vomit.

übergehen¹ (prät **überging**, pp **übergangen**) vt (ignorieren) to ignore.

über|gehen² vi unr ist (wechseln): **in etw** (A) ~ to change into sthg.

Übergewicht das overweight; ~ **haben** to be overweight.

Übergröße (pl **-n**) die (von Kleidung) outsize.

überhand|nehmen vi unr to get out of hand.

überhaupt adv (Ausdruck von Zweifel) at all; (allgemein, eigentlich) really; **ich habe ~ kein Geld mehr** (gar kein) I've got no money left at all; ~ **nicht** (gar nicht) not at all.

überholen vt to overtake.

Überholspur (pl **-en**) die overtaking lane.

Überholverbot (pl **-e**) das ban on overtaking.

überhören vt (nicht hören) not to hear.

überlassen (präs **überläßt**, prät **überließ**, pp **überlassen**) vt (leihen) to lend.

überlastet adj (Person) overworked.

über|laufen¹ vi unr ist (Topf, Wasser) to overflow.

überlaufen² adj overcrowded.

überleben vt & vi to survive.

überlegen¹ ◆ vt (nachdenken) to consider. ◆ vi (nachdenken) to think; **sich** (D) **etw** ~ to think sthg over.

überlegen² ◆ adj superior. ◆ adv

(*siegen*) convincingly; (*arrogant*) patronizingly.

Überlegung (*pl* -en) *die* consideration.

übermorgen *adv* the day after tomorrow.

übermüdet *adj* overtired.

übernächste, -r, -s *adj* next ... but one; **die ~ Haltestelle** not this stop but the next one; **die ~ Woche** the week after next.

übernachten *vi* to stay (the night).

übernächtigt *adj* worn out.

Übernachtung (*pl* -en) *die* overnight stay; **~ mit Frühstück** bed and breakfast.

Übernachtungsmöglichkeit (*pl* -en) *die* overnight accommodation.

übernehmen (*präs* übernimmt, *prät* übernahm, *pp* übernommen) *vt* (*Kosten*) to pay; (*kopieren*) to adopt; (*Mitarbeiter*) to take on. ▶ **sich übernehmen** *ref* to overdo it.

überprüfen *vt* to check.

überqueren *vt* to cross.

überraschen ◆ *vi* to come as a surprise. ◆ *vt* to surprise; **ich lasse mich ~** I'll wait and see.

Überraschung (*pl* -en) *die* surprise.

überreden *vt* to persuade.

überreichen *vt* to present.

Überrest (*pl* -e) *der* remains (*pl*).

übers *präp* (*fam*) = **über** + **das**.

überschlagen (*präs* überschlägt, *prät* überschlug, *pp* überschlagen) *vt* (*Anzahl, Summe*) to estimate. ▶ **sich überschlagen** *ref* (*Auto*) to turn over; (*Skifahrer*) to crash.

überschneiden: sich überschneiden (*prät* überschnitt, *pp* überschnitten) *ref* (*zeitlich*) to overlap.

Überschrift (*pl* -en) *die* heading.

Überschwemmung (*pl* -en) *die* flood.

Übersee *nt*: **aus ~** from overseas; **nach ~** abroad.

übersehen (*präs* übersieht, *prät* übersah, *pp* übersehen) *vt* (*nicht sehen*) to overlook.

übersetzen[1] *vt* to translate.

über|setzen[2] ◆ *vt hat* (*befördern*) to take across. ◆ *vi ist* (*überqueren*) to cross.

Übersetzer, -in (*mpl* -) *der, die* translator.

Übersetzung (*pl* -en) *die* translation.

Übersicht (*pl* -en) *die* (*Zusammenfassung*) outline.

übersichtlich *adj* (*Gebiet*) open; (*Tabelle*) clear.

Übersichtskarte (*pl* -n) *die* general map.

Übersiedler, -in (*mpl* -) *der, die* emigrant from the former German Democratic Republic.

überspielen *vt* (*kopieren*) to record; (*löschen*) to record over.

Überspielkabel (*pl* -) *das* connecting lead.

überstehen[1] (*prät* überstand, *pp* überstanden) *vt* (*Ereignis*) to survive.

über|stehen[2] *vi unr* (*vorstehen*) to jut out.

Überstunde (*pl* -n) *die* overtime.

übertragbar *adj* (*Fahrkarte*) transferable; (*Krankheit*) infectious.

übertragen (*präs* überträgt, *prät* übertrug, *pp* übertragen) *vt* (*Krankheit*) to pass on; (*Sendung*) to broadcast; (*Blut*) to transfuse; (*anwenden*) to apply. ▶ **sich übertragen** *ref* (*Stimmung*) to be infectious; (*Krankheit*) to be passed on.

Übertragung (*pl* -en) *die* (*von Sendung*) broadcast; (*von Krankheit*) passing on; (*von Blut*) transfusion.

übertreffen (*präs* übertrifft, *prät* übertraf, *pp* übertroffen) *vt* (*besser sein*) to surpass.

übertreiben (*prät* übertrieb, *pp* übertrieben) ◆ *vt* (*bei Darstellung*) to exaggerate; (*Handlung*) to overdo. ◆ *vi* (*darstellen*) to exaggerate.

übertreten (*präs* übertritt, *prät* übertrat, *pp* übertreten) *vt* (*Gesetz*) to break.

übertrieben ◆ *pp* → **über-**

treiben. ◆ adj (Darstellung) exaggerated; (Vorsicht, Eifer) excessive.

überwachen vt to monitor.

überweisen (prät **überwies**, pp **überwiesen**) vt (Geld) to transfer; (Patienten) to refer; **jn ins Krankenhaus ~** to have sb admitted to hospital.

Überweisung (pl -en) die (von Geld) transfer; (von Patienten) referral.

Überweisungsauftrag (pl -träge) der money transfer order.

überwinden (prät **überwand**, pp **überwunden**) vt (Angst, Ekel) to overcome; (Hindernis) to get over. ▶ **sich überwinden** ref to force o.s.

Überzelt (pl -e) das flysheet.

überzeugen vt to convince. ▶ **sich überzeugen** ref to convince o.s.

überzeugt adj convinced; **~ sein von** to be convinced of.

Überzeugung (pl -en) die conviction.

überziehen¹ (prät **überzog**, pp **überzogen**) vt (Konto) to overdraw; **die Betten frisch ~** to put clean sheets on the beds.

über|ziehen² vt unr (Jacke, Pullover) to pull on.

Überziehungskredit (pl -e) der overdraft facility.

üblich adj usual.

übrig adj remaining; **~ sein** to be left over.

übrig|bleiben vi unr ist to be left over.

übrigens adv by the way.

Übung (pl -en) die exercise.

Ufer (pl -) das (von Fluß) bank; (von See) shore; **am ~** (von Fluß) on the bank; (von See) on the shore.

Uferstraße (pl -n) die road which runs alongside a lake or river.

Uhr (pl -en) die (am Arm) watch; (an der Wand) clock; (Zeit): **es ist 3 ~** it's 3 o'clock; **um 3 ~** at 3 o'clock; **um wieviel ~?** what time?; **wieviel ~ ist es?** what time is it?

Uhrzeit (pl -en) die time.

UKW die FM.

Ultraschall der ultrasound.

um ◆ präp (+A) **1.** (räumlich) around; **~ etw herum** around sthg. **2.** (Angabe der Uhrzeit): **~ drei Uhr** at three o'clock. **3.** (Angabe von Ansteigen, Sinken) by; **die Preise steigen ~ 15%** prices are rising by 15%. **4.** (Angabe von Grund) for; **~ etw kämpfen** to fight for sthg; **~ ein Spielzeug streiten** to quarrel over a toy. **5.** (ungefähr) around; **es kostet ~ die 300 DM** it costs around 300 Marks; **so ~ Ostern herum** some time around Easter. ◆ konj: **je schneller, ~ so besser** the quicker the better; **~ so besser** (fam: als Antwort) so much the better; **~ zu** (in order) to. ◆ adv (bei Zeit) up; **die zehn Minuten sind ~** the ten minutes are up.

um|adressieren vt to readdress.

umarmen vt to hug.

Umbau (pl -ten) der renovation.

um|bauen vt to renovate.

um|binden vt unr to tie; **sich** (D) **eine Schürze ~** to put on an apron.

um|blättern vt to turn over.

um|bringen vt unr to kill.

um|buchen vt: **eine Reise ~** to change one's booking for a trip.

um|drehen ◆ vt hat (Schlüssel, Pfannkuchen) to turn. ◆ vi ist/hat (wenden, umkehren) to turn back. ▶ **sich umdrehen** ref (Person) to turn round.

um|fahren¹ vt unr (fam: überfahren) to knock down.

umfahren² (präs **umfährt**, prät **umfuhr**, pp **umfahren**) vt (ausweichen) to avoid.

um|fallen vi unr ist (umkippen) to fall down.

Umfang (pl -fänge) der (von Bauch, Tonne) circumference.

Umfrage (pl -n) die survey.

um|füllen vt to transfer.

Umgangssprache die slang.

Umgebung (*pl* -en) *die* (*Gebiet*) surroundings (*pl*); (*Umfeld*) environment.

um|gehen¹ *vi unr ist* (*Erkältung*) to go around.

umgehen² (*prät* **umging**, *pp* **umgangen**) *vt* (*Problem*) to avoid.

Umgehungsstraße (*pl* -n) *die* bypass.

umgekehrt ◆ *adj* opposite. ◆ *adv* the other way round; **in ~er Richtung** in the opposite direction.

Umhang (*pl* -hänge) *der* cloak.

umher *adv* around.

um|kehren *vi ist* (*zurückgehen, zurückfahren*) to turn back.

um|kippen ◆ *vi ist* (*Person, Vase*) to fall over. ◆ *vt hat* (*Lampe, Vase*) to knock over.

Umkleidekabine (*pl* -n) *die* changing room.

Umkleideraum (*pl* -räume) *der* changing room.

Umkreis *der* (*Gebiet*) surrounding area; **im ~ von 50 km** within a 50 km radius.

Umlaut (*pl* -e) *der* umlaut.

um|leiten *vt* to divert.

Umleitung (*pl* -en) *die* diversion.

umrandet *adj*: **rot ~** circled in red.

um|rechnen *vt* to convert.

Umrechnungskurs (*pl* -e) *der* conversion table.

um|rühren *vt & vi* to stir.

ums *präp* = **um** + **das**.

Umsatz (*pl* -sätze) *der* turnover.

um|schalten ◆ *vt* (*Programm, Fernseher*) to turn over. ◆ *vi* (*auf Programm*) to turn over.

Umschlag (*pl* -schläge) *der* (*für Briefe*) envelope; (*von Buch*) dust jacket; (MED) compress.

um|schlagen ◆ *vi unr ist* (*Wetter, Laune*) to change. ◆ *vt unr hat* (*umdrehen*) to turn over.

um|sehen: sich umsehen *ref unr* to look round; **sich ~ nach** (*suchen*) to look around for.

um|sein *vi unr ist* (*fam*) to be over.

umsonst ◆ *adv* (*erfolglos*) in vain; (*gratis*) for free. ◆ *adj*: **~ sein** (*erfolglos*) to be in vain; (*gratis*) to be free.

umständlich *adj* (*Methode*) laborious; (*Person*) awkward.

Umstandsmoden *pl* maternity wear (*sg*).

Umsteigebahnhof (*pl* -höfe) *der* station where passengers may change to a different line.

um|steigen *vi unr ist* (*beim Reisen*) to change; (*wechseln*) to switch; **in Köln ~** to change in Cologne.

Umstellung (*pl* -en) *die* (*Anpassung*) adjustment; (*Änderung*) switch.

Umtausch *der* exchange; **'vom ~ ausgeschlossen'** 'no refunds or exchanges'.

um|tauschen *vt* (*Ware*) to exchange; (*Geld*) to change; **Mark in Pfund ~** to change marks into pounds.

Umverpackung (*pl* -en) *die* repackaging.

Umweg (*pl* -e) *der* detour.

Umwelt *die* environment.

Umweltbewußtsein *das* environmental awareness.

UMWELTBEWUSSTSEIN

Protection of the environment is a major concern amongst Germans, who see themselves as world leaders in environmental issues and the fight against pollution, having introduced the catalytic converter and large-scale recycling programmes. The need to protect the environment and conserve natural resources is now recognized by all sectors of society.

---

umweltfreundlich *adj* environmentally friendly.

Umweltpapier *das* recycled paper.

umweltschädlich *adj* damaging to the environment.

Umweltschutz *der* environmental protection.

Umweltschützer, -in (*mpl* -) *der, die* environmentalist.

Umweltverschmutzung *die* pollution.

um|werfen *vt unr* (*umstürzen*) to knock over; **sich** (D) **einen Mantel ~** to put a coat around one's shoulders.

um|ziehen ◆ *vi unr ist* to move. ◆ *vt unr hat* to change. ▶ **sich umziehen** *ref* to get changed.

Umzug (*pl* -**züge**) *der* (*Wohnungswechsel*) move; (*Parade*) parade.

unabhängig ◆ *adj* independent. ◆ *adv* independently.

Unabhängigkeit *die* independence.

unabsichtlich ◆ *adj* unintentional. ◆ *adv* unintentionally.

unangenehm ◆ *adj* (*Geschmack, Person*) unpleasant; (*peinlich*) embarrassing. ◆ *adv*: **ich war ~ berührt** I was embarrassed.

unauffällig *adj* inconspicuous.

unbeabsichtigt *adj* unintentional.

unbedingt *adv* (*auf jeden Fall*) really; **du mußt ~ mitkommen!** you really must come!

unbefriedigend ◆ *adj* (*schlecht*) unsatisfactory. ◆ *adv* (*schlecht*) unsatisfactorily.

unbefristet *adj* for an unlimited period.

unbefugt *adj* unauthorized.

Unbefugte (*pl* -**n**) *der, die* unauthorized person; **'für ~ Zutritt verboten!'** 'authorized personnel only'.

unbegrenzt *adj* unlimited.

unbekannt *adj* unknown.

unbeliebt *adj* unpopular.

unbemerkt *adv* unnoticed.

unbenutzt *adj* unused.

unbequem ◆ *adj* (*Stuhl, Kleidung*) uncomfortable. ◆ *adv* (*sitzen, fahren*) uncomfortably.

unberechtigt ◆ *adj* unjustified. ◆ *adv* without authorization; **~ parkende Fahrzeuge** illegally parked vehicles.

unbeständig *adj* (*Wetter*) changeable.

unbeteiligt *adj* (*nicht interessiert*) uninterested; (*nicht verwickelt*) uninvolved.

unbewacht *adj* unattended.

unbewußt ◆ *adj* unconscious. ◆ *adv* unconsciously.

unbrauchbar *adj* useless.

und ◆ *konj* **1.** (*gen*) and; **drei ~ drei ist sechs** three and three makes six; **~ so** (*fam*) and so on; **~ so weiter** and so on; **~ wie!** (*fam*) not half! **2.** (*Ausdruck eines Widerspruchs*): **~ wenn** even if. **3.** (*ironisch*): **ich ~ Motorrad fahren? nie!** me ride a motor bike? Never! ◆ *interj* (*fam*): **na ~!** so what?

undankbar *adj* (*Person*) ungrateful.

undeutlich *adj* unclear.

undicht *adj* leaky.

undurchlässig *adj* impermeable.

uneben *adj* uneven; **'~e Fahrbahn'** 'uneven road surface'.

unecht *adj* (*Schmuck, Stein*) fake.

unendlich *adj* endless.

unentbehrlich *adj* indispensable.

unentgeltlich *adj* free.

unentschieden *adj* (*Ergebnis*) undecided; **das Spiel endete ~** the game was a draw.

unerläßlich *adj* essential.

unerlaubt *adj* unauthorized.

unerträglich *adj* unbearable.

unerwartet *adj* unexpected.

unerwünscht *adj* unwelcome.

unfähig *adj* incapable; **~ sein, etw zu tun** to be incapable of doing sthg.

unfair *adj* unfair.

Unfall (*pl* -**fälle**) *der* accident; **einen ~ haben/verursachen** to have/cause an accident.

Unfallflucht *die* failure to stop after an accident.

Unfallhergang der: **den ~ beschreiben** to give details of the accident.

Unfallschaden der damage.

Unfallstation (pl -en) die casualty (Br), emergency ward (Am).

Unfallstelle (pl -n) die scene of the accident.

Unfallversicherung (pl -en) die accident insurance.

unfreundlich ◆ adj (Person, Verhalten) unfriendly. ◆ adv (sich verhalten) coldly; **~ sein zu** to be unfriendly to.

Unfug der nonsense.

Ungarn nt Hungary.

ungeduldig adj impatient.

ungeeignet adj unsuitable.

ungefähr ◆ adv about, approximately. ◆ adj rough.

ungefährlich adj safe.

ungehorsam adj disobedient.

ungemütlich adj (Raum, Kleidung) uncomfortable.

ungenau ◆ adj inaccurate. ◆ adv inaccurately.

ungenießbar adj inedible; (fam: Person) unbearable.

ungenügend ◆ adj (schlecht) insufficient; (Schulnote) unsatisfactory. ◆ adv (schlecht) badly.

ungerecht adj unjust.

ungern adv reluctantly.

ungeschickt adj (Mensch, Bewegung) clumsy; (Verhalten, Reaktion) undiplomatic.

ungesund ◆ adj unhealthy. ◆ adv: **sie leben sehr ~** they lead a very unhealthy life.

ungewiß adj uncertain.

ungewöhnlich adj unusual.

ungewohnt adj unfamiliar.

Ungeziefer das pests (pl).

unglaublich ◆ adj unbelievable. ◆ adv unbelievably.

Unglück (pl -e) das (Unfall) accident; (Leid) unhappiness; (Pech) bad luck.

unglücklich adj (Person) unhappy; (unklug) unfortunate.

ungültig adj invalid.

unheimlich ◆ adj (gruselig) sinister; (fam: riesig) incredible. ◆ adv (fam: sehr) incredibly.

unhöflich adj impolite.

Uni (pl -s) die (fam) uni.

Uniform (pl -en) die uniform.

Universität (pl -en) die university.

Universitätsstadt (pl -städte) die university town.

UNIVERSITÄTSSTADT

The most famous German university towns include Heidelberg, Marburg, Göttingen and Freiburg. The large, old universities attract large numbers of students, giving the towns a particularly lively atmosphere and cultural life.

Unkosten pl expenses.

Unkostenbeitrag (pl -beiträge) der contribution towards expenses.

Unkraut das weed.

unlogisch adj illogical.

Unmenge (pl -n) die (fam) masses (pl); **eine ~ Leute** masses of people.

unmittelbar ◆ adj immediate. ◆ adv immediately; **in ~er Nähe** in the immediate vicinity.

unmöbliert adj unfurnished.

unmöglich ◆ adj impossible. ◆ adv: **ich kann ~ um 3 Uhr kommen** I can't possibly come at 3 o'clock; **jm ~ sein** (nicht möglich) to be impossible for sb.

unnötig adj unnecessary.

unnütz adj useless.

UNO die: **die ~** the UN.

Unordnung die chaos.

unpassierbar adj impassable.

unpersönlich adj impersonal.

unpraktisch adj (Kleidung, Möbel) impractical; (Person) unpractical.

unpünktlich adj unpunctual; **~ sein** to be late.

Unrecht das wrong; **im ~ sein** to be wrong.

unregelmäßig ◆ adj irregular. ◆ adv irregularly.

unreif adj (Obst) unripe.

Unruhe (pl -n) die (Gefühl) unease; (Bewegung) noise. ▶ **Unruhen** pl riots.

unruhig adj (besorgt) restless.

uns pron (Personalpronomen) us; (Reflexivpronomen) ourselves.

unschädlich adj harmless.

unscharf adj (Aufnahme) blurred.

unschuldig adj innocent.

unselbständig adj dependent.

unser, -e ODER **unsre** det our.

unsere, -r, -s ◆ pron ours. ◆ det → **unser**.

unsicher adj (Person) insecure; (Zukunft) uncertain; (Gegend, Weg) unsafe; **da bin ich mir ~** I'm not sure about that.

Unsinn der nonsense.

Unsumme (pl -n) die enormous amount of money.

unsympathisch adj (Mensch) unpleasant.

unten adv at the bottom; (südlich) down; (in Haus) downstairs; **nach ~** down; **von ~** from below; **siehe ~** see below; **die sind bei uns ~ durch** (fam) we're finished with them.

unter ◆ präp (+D) **1.** (räumlich) under; **~ dem Tisch liegen** to lie under the table. **2.** (weniger als) under; **~ Null** below zero; **Kinder ~ 12 Jahren** children under the age of 12. **3.** (zwischen Dingen, Personen) among; **~ anderem** among other things. **4.** (Angabe von Umständen) under; **~ Streß arbeiten** to work under stress. **5.** (Angabe von Hierarchie) under; **~ der Leitung von ...** under the supervision of ... ◆ präp (+A) **1.** (räumlich) under; **~ den Tisch kriechen** to crawl under the table. **2.** (weniger als) below. **3.** (zwischen): **etw ~ etw mischen** to mix sthg into sthg. **4.** (Angabe von Hierarchie) under.

◆ adj **1.** (räumlich) lower; (Etage) bottom. **2.** (in Rangfolge) lower.

unterbelichtet adj (Foto, Film) underexposed.

Unterbewußtsein das subconscious.

unterbrechen (präs **unterbricht**, prät **unterbrach**, pp **unterbrochen**) vt & vi to interrupt.

Unterbrecherkontakt (pl -e) der contact breaker.

Unterbrechung (pl -en) die interruption.

unter|bringen vt unr (Gäste) to put up; (Gegenstand) to put.

Unterbringung die accommodation.

unterdessen adv (geh) meanwhile.

unterdrücken vt (Person, Volk, Widerstand) to suppress.

untereinander adv (unter sich) among ourselves/themselves; (unter das andere) one under the other.

Unterführung (pl -en) die subway (Br), underpass (Am).

Untergang (pl -gänge) der (von Schiff) sinking; (von Volk, Kultur) decline; (von Sonne, Mond) setting.

unter|gehen vi unr ist (Sonne, Mond) to go down; (Schiff, Person) to sink; (Volk, Kultur) to decline.

Untergeschoß (pl -schosse) das basement.

Untergewicht das: **~ haben** to be underweight.

Untergrund der (Boden) subsoil.

Untergrundbahn (pl -en) die underground (Br), subway (Am).

unterhalb adv & präp (+G) below.

unterhalten (präs **unterhält**, prät **unterhielt**, pp **unterhalten**) vt (amüsieren) to entertain; (Familie) to support. ▶ **sich unterhalten** ref (reden) to talk; (sich amüsieren) to have fun; **sich ~ mit** (sprechen) to talk with.

Unterhaltung (pl -en) die (Gespräch) conversation; (Amüsement) entertainment.

Unterhemd (pl -en) das vest.

Unterhose (*pl* **-n**) *die* underpants (*pl*).

Unterkunft (*pl* **-künfte**) *die* accommodation.

unterlassen (*präs* **unterläßt**, *prät* **unterließ**, *pp* **unterlassen**) *vt* to refrain from.

Unterleib (*pl* **-e**) *der* abdomen.

unternehmen (*präs* **unternimmt**, *prät* **unternahm**, *pp* **unternommen**) *vt* (*Ausflug, Reise*) to make; **etwas/nichts ~** to do something/nothing.

Unternehmer, -in (*mpl* **-**) *der, die* entrepreneur.

unternehmungslustig *adj* enterprising.

Unterricht *der* lessons (*pl*); **jm ~ geben** to teach sb.

unterrichten *vt* (*Schüler, Schulfach*) to teach; (*mitteilen*) to inform.

Unterrock (*pl* **-röcke**) *der* slip.

untersagt *adj* prohibited.

unterscheiden (*prät* **unterschied**, *pp* **unterschieden**) ◆ *vt* to distinguish. ◆ *vi*: **~ zwischen** to differentiate between; **etw ~ von** to distinguish sthg from. ▶ **sich unterscheiden** *ref* to be different.

Unterschied (*pl* **-e**) *der* difference.

unterschiedlich *adj* different.

unterschreiben (*prät* **unterschrieb**, *pp* **unterschrieben**) *vt & vi* to sign; **hier ~** sign here.

Unterschrift (*pl* **-en**) *die* signature; **Datum und ~** date and signature.

Unterseeboot (*pl* **-e**) *das* submarine.

Untersetzer (*pl* **-**) *der* coaster.

unter|stellen¹ *vt* to store. ▶ **sich unterstellen** *ref* to shelter.

unterstellen² *vt* (*Boshaftigkeit, Gemeinheit*) to imply.

unterstreichen (*prät* **unterstrich**, *pp* **unterstrichen**) *vt* (*mit Strich*) to underline.

unterstützen *vt* to support.

Unterstützung *die* support.

untersuchen *vt* to examine; (*absuchen*) to investigate.

Untersuchung (*pl* **-en**) *die* examination; (*von Justiz, Polizei*) investigation.

Untertasse (*pl* **-n**) *die* saucer.

Unterteil (*pl* **-e**) *das* bottom half.

Untertitel (*pl* **-**) *der* subtitle.

Unterwäsche *die* underwear.

unterwegs ◆ *adv* on the way. ◆ *adj*: **~ sein** to be on the way; **~ nach ...** **sein** to be on the way to ...

unterzeichnen *vt* to sign.

unüberlegt ◆ *adj* rash. ◆ *adv* rashly.

ununterbrochen ◆ *adj* uninterrupted. ◆ *adv* nonstop.

unverbindlich *adj* (*ohne Verpflichtung*) not binding.

unverbleit *adj* lead-free.

unverheiratet *adj* unmarried.

unverkäuflich *adj* not for sale.

unvermeidlich *adj* unavoidable.

unvernünftig *adj* irresponsible.

unverschämt *adj* (*taktlos*) impertinent.

unverständlich *adj* incomprehensible.

unverträglich *adj* (*Nahrung*) indigestible.

unvollständig *adj* incomplete.

unvorsichtig *adj* careless.

unwahrscheinlich *adj* (*Geschichte*) improbable; (*fam: Glück*) incredible.

Unwetter (*pl* **-**) *das* storm.

unwichtig *adj* unimportant.

unwiderstehlich *adj* irresistible.

unwohl *adj* unwell; **sich ~ fühlen** (*körperlich*) to feel unwell; (*psychisch*) to feel uneasy.

unzerbrechlich *adj* unbreakable.

unzufrieden *adj* dissatisfied; **~ mit** dissatisfied with.

unzugänglich *adv*: **'für Kinder ~ aufbewahren'** 'keep out of reach of children'.

unzulässig *adj* (*nicht erlaubt*) forbidden.

üppig *adj* (*Essen*) sumptuous; (*Person*) curvaceous.

uralt *adj* ancient.
Uraufführung (*pl* -en) *die* premiere.
Urenkel, -in (*mpl* -) *der, die* great-grandchild.
Urgroßeltern *pl* great-grandparents.
Urin *der* urine.
Urkunde (*pl* -n) *die* certificate.
Urlaub (*pl* -e) *der* holiday (Br), vacation (Am); **im ~ sein** to be on holiday (Br), to be on vacation (Am); **in ~ fahren** to go on holiday (Br), to go on vacation (Am); **~ machen** to have a holiday (Br), to vacation (Am).
Urlauber, -in (*mpl* -) *der, die* holidaymaker (Br), vacationer (Am).
Urlaubsanschrift (*pl* -en) *die* holiday address.
Urlaubsgeld *das* holiday pay.
Urlaubsland (*pl* -länder) *das* holiday destination.
Urlaubsort (*pl* -e) *der* holiday resort.
Urlaubszeit (*pl* -en) *die* holiday season (Br), vacation season (Am).
Ursache (*pl* -n) *die* cause; **keine ~!** don't mention it!
Ursprung (*pl* -sprünge) *der* origin.
ursprünglich *adj* (*Idee, Meinung*) original.
Ursprungsland (*pl* -länder) *das* country of origin.
Urteil (*pl* -e) *das* (*vor Gericht*) verdict; (*Bewertung*) judgement.
Urwald (*pl* -wälder) *der* jungle.
usw. (*abk für und so weiter*) etc.
Utensilien *pl* utensils.
Utopie (*pl* -n) *die* utopia.

V

vage *adj* vague.
Vagina (*pl* Vaginen) *die* vagina.
vakuumverpackt *adj* vacuum-packed.
Vanille *die* vanilla.
Vanilleeis *das* vanilla ice-cream.
Vanillezucker *der* vanilla sugar.
Varieté (*pl* -s) *das* variety show.
variieren *vt & vi* to vary.
Vase (*pl* -n) *die* vase.
Vaseline *die* Vaseline®.
Vater (*pl* Väter) *der* father.
Vatertag (*pl* -e) *der* Father's Day.
V-Ausschnitt (*pl* -e) *der* V-neck.
v. Chr. (*abk für vor Christus*) BC.
Vegetarier, -in (*mpl* -) *der, die* vegetarian.
vegetarisch *adj* vegetarian.
Vene (*pl* -n) *die* vein.
Ventil (*pl* -e) *das* (TECH) valve.
Ventilator (*pl* Ventilatoren) *der* fan.
verabreden *vt* to arrange. ▶ **sich verabreden** *ref* to arrange to meet; **sich mit jm ~** to arrange to meet sb.
verabredet *adj*: **sie ist mit Karla ~** she has arranged to meet Karla; **ich bin schon ~** I have something else on.
Verabredung (*pl* -en) *die* (*Treffen*) appointment; (*mit Freund*) date.
verabscheuen *vt* to detest.
verabschieden *vt* (*Gast*) to say goodbye to. ▶ **sich verabschieden** *ref* to say goodbye.
Veranda (*pl* Veranden) *die* veranda.
verändern *vt* to change. ▶ **sich verändern** *ref* (*anders werden*) to change.
Veränderung (*pl* -en) *die* change.
veranlassen *vt*: **jn ~, etw zu tun** to cause sb to do sthg; **etw ~** to arrange for sthg.

veranstalten vt (organisieren) to organize.

Veranstalter, -in (mpl -) der, die organizer.

Veranstaltung (pl -en) die (Ereignis) event; (Organisation) organization.

Veranstaltungskalender (pl -) der calendar of events.

Veranstaltungsprogramm (pl -e) das programme of events.

verantwortlich adj responsible.

Verantwortung die responsibility.

verarbeiten vt (Material) to process; (fig: Ereignis) to come to terms with.

Verb (pl -en) das verb; **starkes/schwaches ~** strong/weak verb.

Verband (pl -bände) der (Organisation) association; (für Wunde) bandage; **einen ~ anlegen** to apply a bandage.

Verbandskasten (pl -kästen) der first-aid box.

Verbandszeug das first-aid kit.

verbergen (präs verbirgt, prät verbarg, pp verborgen) vt to hide. ▶ **sich verbergen** ref to hide.

verbessern vt (besser machen) to improve; (Fehler) to correct. ▶ **sich verbessern** ref (besser werden) to improve; (sich korrigieren) to correct o.s.

Verbesserung (pl -en) die (von Fehlern, Text) correction; (von Anlage, Angebot) improvement.

verbieten (prät verbat, pp verboten) vt to forbid.

verbilligt adj reduced.

verbinden (prät verband, pp verbunden) ◆ vt to connect; (Wunde) to bandage; (am Telefon) to put through. ◆ vi (am Telefon): **einen Moment, ich verbinde** one moment please, I'll put you through; **falsch verbunden!** wrong number!

Verbindung (pl -en) die connection; (chemisch) compound; **sich in ~ setzen mit** to contact.

verbleit adj (Benzin) leaded; **Super ~** super leaded.

verborgen pp → verbergen.

Verbot (pl -e) das ban.

verboten ◆ pp → verbieten. ◆ adj forbidden; **streng ~!** strictly forbidden!

Verbotsschild (pl -er) das sign indicating a restriction, eg no parking, no entry, etc.

verbrannt ◆ pp → verbrennen. ◆ adj burnt.

Verbrauch der consumption.

verbrauchen vt to consume.

Verbraucher, -in (mpl -) der, die consumer.

Verbraucherberatung (pl -en) die (Institution) consumer advice agency.

Verbrechen (pl -) das crime.

Verbrecher, -in (mpl -) der, die criminal.

verbreiten vt to spread. ▶ **sich verbreiten** ref to spread.

verbrennen (prät verbrannte, pp verbrannt) vt hat & vi ist to burn. ▶ **sich verbrennen** ref: **er hat sich verbrannt** he burned himself; **er hat sich (D) die Finger verbrannt** he burnt his fingers.

Verbrennung (pl -en) die (Verletzung) burn; (Verbrennen) burning.

verbringen (prät verbrachte, pp verbracht) vt to spend.

verbrühen: sich verbrühen ref to scald o.s.

Verdacht der suspicion.

verdammt adj & adv (fam) damn.

verdarb prät → verderben.

verdaulich adj: **leicht/schwer ~** easy/difficult to digest.

Verdauung die digestion.

Verdeck (pl -e) das (von Auto) soft top; (von Kinderwagen) hood.

verderben (präs verdirbt, prät verdarb, pp verdorben) ◆ vt hat to ruin. ◆ vi ist (Nahrung) to go off.

verderblich adj perishable.

verdienen vt to earn.

Verdienst (pl -e) ◆ der (Gehalt) salary. ◆ das (Leistung) achievement.

verdirbt *präs* → **verderben**.
verdoppeln *vt* to double. ▶ **sich**
verdoppeln *ref* to double.
verdorben ◆ *pp* → **verderben**.
◆ *adj* (*Lebensmittel*) off.
verdünnen *vt* to dilute.
verehren *vt* (*anbeten*) to worship.
Verehrer, -in (*mpl -*) *der, die*
(*Bewunderer*) admirer.
Verein (*pl -e*) *der* association, society; **eingetragener ~** registered society; **wohltätiger ~** charity.

VEREIN

More than half the population of
Germany belongs to one of the
country's 300,000 clubs and societies, making them one of the most
popular ways in which people spend
their leisure time. The most popular
types of club are sports clubs, bowling clubs, rifle clubs, music societies
and pet breeding clubs.

---

vereinbaren *vt* (*Termin, Treffen*) to
arrange.
Vereinbarung (*pl -en*) *die* arrangement; **nach ~** by appointment.
vereinen *vt* to unite. ▶ **sich ver-**
einen *ref* to unite.
vereinheitlichen *vt* to standardize.
Vereinigte Staaten *pl* United
States.
Vereinigung (*pl -en*) *die* (*Gruppe*)
organization; (*Vorgang*) unification.
Vereinte Nationen *pl* United
Nations.
vereist *adj* (*Straße*) icy.
Verf. *abk* = **Verfasser**.
verfahren (*präs* **verfährt**, *prät*
verfuhr, *pp* **verfahren**) ◆ *vi* (*um-*
gehen, handeln) to proceed. ◆ *vt hat*
(*Benzin*) to use up. ▶ **sich ver-**
fahren *ref* to get lost.
verfallen (*präs* **verfällt**, *prät* **verfiel**,
pp **verfallen**) *vi ist* (*Fahrkarte, Garantie*)
to expire; (*Gutschein*) to be no longer
valid; (*Haus*) to decay.

Verfallsdatum (*pl -daten*) *das* (*von*
Lebensmittel) sell-by date.
verfärben: sich verfärben *ref* to
change colour; **der Himmer verfärbte**
sich rot the sky turned red.
Verfasser, -in (*mpl -*) *der, die* author.
Verfassung (*pl -en*) *die* (*Gesetz*) constitution; (*Zustand*) condition.
verfaulen *vi ist* to rot.
verfeinern *vt* to refine.
Verfilmung (*pl -en*) *die* film version.
verfolgen *vt* (*jagen*) to pursue;
(*beobachten*) to follow; (*unterdrücken*)
to persecute.
verfügen *vi*: **~ über** (+A) (*besitzen*)
to have; (*benutzen*) to make use of;
(*bestimmen*) to be in charge of.
Verfügung (*pl -en*) *die* (*Gebrauch,*
Bestimmung): **etw zur ~ haben** to have
sthg at one's disposal; **zur ~ stehen**
to be available.
verführerisch *adj* (*anziehend*)
attractive; (*erotisch*) seductive.
vergangen *adj* (*letzte*) last; **~e**
Woche last week.
Vergangenheit *die* past; (GRAMM)
past tense.
Vergaser (*pl -*) *der* carburettor.
vergaß *prät* → **vergessen**.
vergeben (*präs* **vergibt**, *prät*
vergab, *pp* **vergeben**) *vt* (*verzeihen*)
to forgive; (*Zimmer*) to allocate; (*Preis*)
to award.
vergeblich *adj* in vain.
vergessen (*präs* **vergißt**, *prät*
vergaß, *pp* **vergessen**) *vt* to forget.
vergeßlich *adj* forgetful.
vergewaltigen *vt* to rape.
Vergewaltigung (*pl -en*) *die* rape.
vergiften *vt* to poison.
Vergiftung (*pl -en*) *die* poisoning.
vergißt *präs* → **vergessen**.
Vergleich (*pl -e*) *der* comparison;
im ~ zu compared to.
vergleichen (*prät* **verglich**, *pp* **ver-**
glichen) *vt* to compare; **verglichen mit**
compared with.

Vergnügen das pleasure; **mit ~** with pleasure; **viel ~!** have fun!

Vergnügungsdampfer (pl -) der pleasure steamer.

Vergnügungspark (pl -s) der fun fair.

Vergnügungsviertel (pl -) das area of a town where most bars, nightclubs, cinemas, etc are situated.

vergoldet adj gilded.

vergriffen adj (Buch) out of print.

vergrößern ◆ vt to enlarge. ◆ vi (Mikroskop) to magnify. ▶ **sich vergrößern** ref to expand.

Vergrößerung (pl -en) die enlargement.

Vergünstigung (pl -en) die reduction.

vergüten vt (bezahlen) to pay.

verhaften vt to arrest.

verhalten: sich verhalten (präs verhält, prät verhielt, pp verhalten) ref (sich benehmen) to behave.

Verhalten das behaviour.

Verhältnis (pl -se) das relationship; (von Größe, Anzahl) ratio.

verhältnismäßig adv relatively.

verhandeln ◆ vi to negotiate. ◆ vt (vor Gericht) to hear; **~ über etw** (A) to negotiate sthg.

Verhandlung (pl -en) die (Beratung) negotiation; (vor Gericht) hearing.

verheilen vi ist to heal.

verheimlichen vt to keep secret.

verheiratet adj married.

verhindern vt to prevent.

Verhör (pl -e) das interrogation.

verhüten ◆ vi (beim Sex) to take precautions. ◆ vt to prevent.

Verhütungsmittel (pl -) das contraceptive.

verirren: sich verirren ref to get lost.

verk. abk = **verkaufen.**

Verkauf der sale.

verkaufen vt & vi to sell; **etw an jn ~** to sell sb sthg, to sell sthg to sb; **zu ~** for sale.

Verkäufer, -in (mpl -) der, die (in Geschäft) sales assistant (Br), sales clerk (Am); (juristisch) trader.

verkäuflich adj (zum Verkauf bestimmt) for sale.

verkaufsoffen adj: **~er Samstag** first Saturday in the month, on which shops are open till 6pm instead of closing at midday.

Verkaufsstelle (pl -n) die point of sale.

Verkaufsveranstaltung (pl -en) die event organized to sell a product.

verkauft adj sold.

Verkehr der (Straßenverkehr) traffic; (amt: Sex) intercourse.

verkehren vi (amt: Zug, Bus) to run; **in einem Lokal ~** to frequent a bar; '**verkehrt nicht täglich**' 'does not run daily'.

Verkehrsampel (pl -n) die traffic light.

Verkehrsaufkommen das: **hohes/dichtes ~** heavy traffic.

Verkehrsberuhigung die traffic calming.

Verkehrsführung (pl -en) die: '**~ beachten**' 'follow road signs'.

Verkehrsfunk der traffic bulletin service.

Verkehrsmeldung (pl -en) die traffic bulletin.

Verkehrsmittel (pl -) das means of transport; **öffentliche ~** public transport.

Verkehrsnachrichten pl traffic news.

Verkehrspolizist, -in (mpl -en) der, die traffic policeman (traffic policewoman).

Verkehrsregel (pl -n) die traffic regulation.

Verkehrsschild (pl -er) das road sign.

Verkehrsunfall (pl -unfälle) der road accident.

Verkehrsverbindung (pl -en) die connection.

Verkehrsverein (*pl -e*) *der* tourist information office.

Verkehrszeichen (*pl -*) *das* road sign.

verkehrt ◆ *adj* wrong. ◆ *adv* wrongly; **~ herum** inside out.

verklagen *vt* to prosecute.

verkleiden *vt* (*Wand, Fassade*) to cover. ► **sich verkleiden** *ref*: **sich (als etw) ~** (*zum Spaß*) to dress up (as sthg); (*zur Tarnung*) to disguise o.s. (as sthg).

Verkleidung (*pl -en*) *die* (*Kostüm*) costume; (*von Wand, Fassade*) covering.

Verkleinerung (*pl -en*) *die* reduction.

verkommen (*prät* **verkam**, *pp* **verkommen**) ◆ *vi ist* (*Lebensmittel*) to go off; (*Haus, Wohnung*) to become run-down. ◆ *adj* (*Haus, Wohnung*) run-down.

verkraften *vt* to cope with.

verkratzt *adj* scratched.

verkürzen *vt* to shorten.

verladen (*präs* **verlädt**, *prät* **verlud**, *pp* **verladen**) *vt* to load.

Verlag (*pl -e*) *der* publishing house.

verlangen *vt* (*fordern*) to demand; (*im Geschäft, Lokal*) to ask for; (*erfordern*) to call for; **jn am Telefon ~** to ask to speak to sb on the phone.

Verlangen *das* (*Wunsch*) desire; (*Forderung*) request; **auf ~** on demand.

verlängern *vt* to extend; (*Rock*) to lengthen; (*Paß, Erlaubnis*) to renew. ► **sich verlängern** *ref* (*Frist; Vertrag*) to be extended.

Verlängerung (*pl -en*) *die* extension; (*von Rock*) lengthening; (*von Paß, Erlaubnis*) renewal; (SPORT) extra time.

Verlängerungskabel (*pl -*) *das* extension lead.

verlassen (*präs* **verläßt**, *prät* **verließ**, *pp* **verlassen**) *vt* to leave. ► **sich verlassen** *ref*: **sich ~ auf** (+A) to rely on.

verlaufen (*präs* **verläuft**, *prät* **verlief**, *pp* **verlaufen**) *vi ist* (*Weg, Strecke,* *Farbe*) to run; (*Operation, Prüfung*) to go. ► **sich verlaufen** *ref* (*sich verirren*) to get lost.

verlegen ◆ *vt* (*Brille, Portemonnaie*) to mislay; (*Veranstaltung, Besuch*) to postpone; (*Standort*) to move; (*Kabel, Teppichboden*) to lay; (*Buch*) to publish. ◆ *adj* embarrassed.

Verleger, -in (*mpl -*) *der, die* publisher.

Verleih (*pl -e*) *der* rental shop.

verleihen (*prät* **verlieh**, *pp* **verliehen**) *vt* (*leihen*) to lend; (*vermieten*) to hire (Br), to rent; (*Preis, Auszeichnung*) to award.

verlernen *vt* to forget.

verletzen *vt* to injure; (*Gefühl*) to hurt. ► **sich verletzen** *ref* to hurt o.s.

verletzt *adj* injured; (*psychisch*) hurt.

Verletzte (*pl -n*) *der, die* injured person.

Verletzung (*pl -en*) *die* injury.

verlieben: sich verlieben *ref* to fall in love.

verlieren (*prät* **verlor**, *pp* **verloren**) *vt & vi* to lose. ► **sich verlieren** *ref* (*Personen*) to lose each other.

Verlierer, -in (*mpl -*) *der, die* loser.

verlobt *adj* engaged.

Verlobung (*pl -en*) *die* engagement.

verlor *prät* → **verlieren**.

verloren ◆ *pp* → **verlieren**. ◆ *adj* lost.

verloren|gehen *vi unr ist* (*Kind, Brille*) to go missing; (*Geschmack, Qualität*) to disappear.

Verlosung (*pl -en*) *die* prize draw.

Verlust (*pl -e*) *der* loss; **einen ~ melden** to report a loss.

verm. *abk* = **vermieten**.

vermeiden (*prät* **vermied**, *pp* **vermieden**) *vt* to avoid.

Vermerk (*pl -e*) *der* note.

vermerken *vt* to make a note of.

vermieten *vt & vi* to rent out; **'zu ~!** 'for rent'.

Vermieter, -in (mpl -) der, die landlord (landlady).

vermischen vt (Farben, Zutaten) to mix.

vermissen vt to miss; **er vermißt seine Uhr** his watch is missing.

vermißt adj missing.

vermitteln ◆ vt (Ehe, Treffen) to arrange; (Wissen, Erfahrung) to impart. ◆ vi (bei Streit, Verhandlung) to arbitrate; **jm eine Arbeitsstelle/einen Babysitter ~** to find a job/babysitter for sb.

Vermittlung (pl -en) die (Telefonzentrale) telephone exchange; (von Arbeit, Mitarbeitern) finding; (von Ehe, Treffen) arranging; (bei Streit, Verhandlung) arbitration; (von Erfahrung, Kenntnissen) imparting; (Büro) agency.

Vermittlungsgebühr (pl -en) die commission.

Vermögen (pl -) das (Besitz) fortune.

vermuten vt to suspect.

vermutlich adv probably.

vernehmen (präs **vernimmt**, prät **vernahm**, pp **vernommen**) vt (befragen) to question.

verneinen vt: **eine Frage ~** to say no (to a question).

vernichten vt to destroy.

Vernissage (pl -n) die preview.

Vernunft die reason.

vernünftig adj (klug) sensible.

veröffentlichen vt to publish.

verordnen vt (Medikament) to prescribe.

Verordnung (pl -en) die (medizinisch) prescription; (amtlich) decree.

verpacken vt (Produkt) to pack; (Geschenk) to wrap up.

Verpackung (pl -en) die packaging.

verpassen vt (Person, Film, Chance) to miss; (fam: geben) to give; **den Bus/Zug ~** to miss the bus/train.

Verpflegung die (Essen) food.

verpflichtet adj & adv obliged.

verprügeln vt to beat up.

verraten (präs **verrät**, prät **verriet**, pp **verraten**) vt (Geheimnis, Land) to betray; (sagen) to let slip. ► **sich verraten** ref to give o.s. away.

verrechnen vt to offset. ► **sich verrechnen** ref (falsch rechnen) to miscalculate; **sich um 3 Mark ~** to be 3 marks out.

Verrechnung die miscalculation.

Verrechnungsscheck (pl -s) der crossed cheque.

verregnet adj: **~ sein** to be a washout.

verreisen vi ist to go away.

Verrenkung (pl -en) die dislocation.

verrosten vi ist to rust.

verrückt adj (geistesgestört) mad; (ausgefallen) crazy; **~ sein nach** to be mad about; **wie ~** like mad.

versagen vi to fail; '**bei Versagen Knopf drücken**' 'in the event of failure, press button'.

versalzen ◆ vt (Essen) to put too much salt in. ◆ adj (Essen) too salty.

versammeln vt to assemble. ► **sich versammeln** ref to assemble.

Versammlung (pl -en) die meeting.

Versand der (Schicken) dispatch; (Abteilung) dispatch department.

Versandhaus (pl -häuser) das mail order firm.

versäumen vt (verpassen) to miss.

verschaffen vt (besorgen) to get.

verschenken vt (Geschenk) to give away; **zu ~** to give away.

verscheuchen vt (Hund, Wespe) to shoo away.

verschicken vt (per Post) to send out.

verschieben (prät **verschob**, pp **verschoben**) vt (Termin, Urlaub) to postpone; (Bett, Kommode) to move. ► **sich verschieben** ref to be postponed.

verschieden ◆ *adj* different. ◆ *adv* differently; **~ groß** of different sizes.

verschiedene *adj* (*einige*) several.

verschimmelt *adj* mouldy.

verschlafen (*präs* **verschläft**, *prät* **verschlief**, *pp* **verschlafen**) ◆ *vi* to oversleep. ◆ *vt* (*Morgen*) to sleep through. ▸ **sich verschlafen** *ref* to oversleep.

verschlechtern *vt* to make worse. ▸ **sich verschlechtern** *ref* to deteriorate.

Verschlechterung (*pl* **-en**) *die* (*von Zustand*) deterioration.

Verschleiß *der* (*von Material*) wear.

verschleißen (*prät* **verschliß**, *pp* **verschlissen**) *vi ist* to become worn.

verschließen (*prät* **verschloß**, *pp* **verschlossen**) *vt* (*Haus, Tür, Schrank*) to lock; (*Dose, Flasche*) to seal. ▸ **sich verschließen** *ref* (*Person*) to shut o.s. off.

verschlimmern *vt* to make worse. ▸ **sich verschlimmern** *ref* to get worse.

verschlingen (*prät* **verschlang**, *pp* **verschlungen**) *vt* (*Mahlzeit*) to wolf down.

verschlossen ◆ *pp* → **verschließen**. ◆ *adj* (*Person*) reticent; (*Tür, Safe*) locked; (*Dose, Briefumschlag*) sealed.

verschlucken *vt* (*schlucken*) to swallow. ▸ **sich verschlucken** *ref* to choke.

Verschluß (*pl* **Verschlüsse**) *der* (*von Kette, Tasche*) fastener; (*von Flaschen*) top.

Verschmutzung (*pl* **-en**) *die* pollution.

verschneit *adj* snow-covered.

verschreiben (*prät* **verschrieb**, *pp* **verschrieben**) *vt* (*Medikamente*) to prescribe. ▸ **sich verschreiben** *ref* (*falsch schreiben*): **ich habe mich verschrieben** I've written it down wrongly.

verschreibungspflichtig *adj* available on prescription only.

verschrotten *vt* to scrap.

verschulden *vt* (*Unfall, Verlust*) to be to blame for.

verschweigen (*prät* **verschwieg**, *pp* **verschwiegen**) *vt* to hide.

verschwenden *vt* to waste.

verschwinden (*prät* **verschwand**, *pp* **verschwunden**) *vi ist* to disappear.

Versehen (*pl* **-**) *das* oversight; **aus ~** accidentally.

versehentlich *adv* accidentally.

versenden (*prät* **versandte**, *pp* **versendet**) *vt* to send.

versichern *vt* (*bei Versicherung*) to insure; (*sagen*) to assure. ▸ **sich versichern** *ref* (*bei Versicherung*) to insure o.s.; (*prüfen*) to assure o.s.

versichert *adj* insured.

Versicherte (*pl* **-n**) *der, die* insured party.

Versicherung (*pl* **-en**) *die* (*Firma*) insurance company; (*Vertrag*) insurance.

Versicherungsbedingungen *pl* terms of insurance.

Versicherungskarte (*pl* **-n**) *die* insurance card; **grüne ~** green card (Br), insurance card required if taking a vehicle abroad.

versilbert *adj* silver-plated.

versöhnen *vt* to reconcile. ▸ **sich versöhnen** *ref* to make up.

versorgen *vt* (*mit Lebensmitteln, Nachrichten*) to supply; (*Patienten, Tier*) to look after.

Versorgung *die* (*mit Lebensmitteln, Nachrichten*) supply; (*von Patienten, Tier*) care.

verspäten: sich verspäten *ref* to be late.

Verspätung (*pl* **-en**) *die* delay; **mit ~** late; **~ haben** to be delayed; **5 Minuten ~ haben** to be 5 minutes late.

versprechen (*präs* **verspricht**, *prät* **versprach**, *pp* **versprochen**) *vt* to promise; **jm etw ~** to promise sb sthg. ▸ **sich versprechen** *ref* to make a mistake.

Versprechen (pl -) das promise.

verstaatlichen vt to nationalize.

Verstand der (Denkvermögen) reason.

verständigen vt (informieren) to notify. ▶ **sich verständigen** ref (kommunizieren) to make o.s. understood.

Verständigung die (Kommunikation) communication; (Information) notification.

verständlich adj (Stimme) audible; (Text) comprehensible; (Handlung, Reaktion) understandable; **sich ~ machen** to make o.s. understood.

Verständnis das understanding.

verständnisvoll adj understanding.

Verstärker (pl -) der amplifier.

verstauchen vt: **sich** (D) **etw ~** to sprain sthg.

Verstauchung (pl -en) die sprain.

Versteck (pl -e) das hiding place; **~ spielen** to play hide-and-seek.

verstecken vt to hide. ▶ **sich verstecken** ref to hide.

verstehen (prät verstand, pp verstanden) vt to understand; **etwas/nichts ~ von** to know a bit/nothing about. ▶ **sich verstehen** ref (Personen) to get on; **sich gut ~ mit** to get on well with; **es versteht sich von selbst** it goes without saying.

Versteigerung (pl -en) die auction.

verstellbar adj adjustable.

verstellen vt (Hebel, Wecker) to reset; (Weg, Tür) to block; (Stimme) to disguise. ▶ **sich verstellen** ref (Person) to disguise o.s.

Verstopfung die constipation.

Verstoß (pl Verstöße) der breach.

Versuch (pl -e) der (Handlung) attempt; (wissenschaftlich) experiment.

versuchen vt & vi to try.

vertauschen vt to mix up.

verteidigen vt to defend. ▶ **sich verteidigen** ref to defend o.s.

verteilen vt to distribute. ▶ **sich**

verteilen ref (sich ausbreiten) to spread out.

Vertrag (pl Verträge) der contract.

vertragen (präs verträgt, prät vertrug, pp vertragen) vt (Hitze, Kaffee) to stand, to bear. ▶ **sich vertragen** ref (Personen) to get on.

Vertragshändler (pl -) der authorized dealer.

Vertragswerkstatt (pl -werkstätten) die authorized workshop.

vertrauen vi (+D) to trust.

Vertrauen das confidence, trust; **~ haben zu** to have confidence in.

vertreten (präs vertritt, prät vertrat, pp vertreten) ♦ vt (bei Urlaub, Krankheit) to stand in for; (Interessen) to represent. ♦ adj represented; **sich** (D) **den Fuß ~** to trip and hurt one's foot.

Vertreter, -in (mpl -) der, die (bei Urlaub, Krankheit) stand-in; (Repräsentant) representative; (Beruf) rep.

Vertretung (pl -en) die (Lehrer) supply teacher; (Arzt) locum; (Delegation) representatives (pl); (bei Urlaub, Krankheit): **die ~ für jn übernehmen** to stand in for sb.

vertrocknen vi ist to dry out.

vertun (prät vertat, pp vertan) vt (verschwenden) to waste. ▶ **sich vertun** ref (fam: sich irren) to get it wrong.

verunglücken vi ist (bei Unfall) to have a nasty accident.

verursachen vt to cause.

Verurteilung (pl -en) die (vor Gericht) sentence.

verwackelt adj blurred.

verwählen: sich verwählen ref to dial the wrong number.

verwahren vt (aufbewahren) to put away.

verwalten vt to administrate.

Verwalter, -in (mpl -) der, die administrator.

Verwaltung (pl -en) die administration.

verwandt ♦ pp → **verwenden**.

♦ *adj* (*Personen*) related; ~ **sein mit** to be related to.

Verwandte (*pl* -n) *der, die* relative.

Verwandtschaft (*pl* -en) *die* family.

Verwarnung (*pl* -en) *die* caution; **gebührenpflichtige** ~ fine.

verwechseln *vt* to mix up; **jn mit jm** ~ to mistake sb for sb.

verweigern *vt* to refuse.

verwendbar *adj* usable.

verwenden (*prät* **verwandte** ODER **verwendete**, *pp* **verwandt** ODER **verwendet**) *vt* to use.

Verwendung *die* use.

verwirklichen *vt* to realize. ▶ **sich verwirklichen** *ref* (*Person*) to develop.

verwirrt *adj* confused.

verwitwet *adj* widowed.

verwöhnen *vt* to spoil.

Verwundete (*pl* -n) *der, die* wounded person.

verzählen: sich verzählen *ref* to miscount.

Verzehr *der* (*geh*) consumption.

verzehren *vt* (*geh: essen*) to consume.

Verzeichnis (*pl* -se) *das* catalogue; **alphabetisches** ~ index.

verzeihen (*prät* **verzieh**, *pp* **verziehen**) *vt* to forgive; ~ **Sie bitte!** excuse me please!

Verzeihung *die* forgiveness; ~! sorry!

verzichten *vi*: ~ **auf** (+A) to do without.

verzögern *vt* (*verschieben*) to delay. ▶ **sich verzögern** *ref* (*sich verspäten*) to be delayed.

Verzögerung (*pl* -en) *die* (*Verspätung*) delay.

verzollen *vt* to declare; **haben Sie etwas zu ~?** have you anything to declare?

verzweifeln *vi ist* to despair.

verzweifelt *adj* desperate.

Vesper (*pl* -n) *die* (*Süddt: Mahlzeit*) afternoon snack.

Veterinär, -in (*mpl* -e) *der, die* (*amt*) veterinary surgeon.

Vetter (*pl* -n) *der* cousin.

vgl. (*abk für vergleiche*) cf.

vibrieren *vi* to vibrate.

Video (*pl* -s) *das* video.

Videofilm (*pl* -e) *der* video.

Videogerät (*pl* -e) *das* video (Br), VCR (Am).

Videokamera (*pl* -s) *die* video camera.

Videokassette (*pl* -n) *die* video (tape).

Videorecorder (*pl* -) *der* video (recorder) (Br), VCR (Am).

Videospiel (*pl* -e) *das* video game.

Videothek (*pl* -en) *die* video store.

Vieh *das* (*Tiere*) cattle.

viel (*kompar* **mehr**, *superl* **am meisten**) ♦ *det* 1. (*Menge, Anzahl*) a lot of; ~ **Tee** a lot of tea; ~**e Bücher** a lot of books; ~**e Leute** many people. 2. (*in Floskeln*): ~**en Dank!** thank you very much!; ~ **Spaß!** have fun! ♦ *adv* 1. (*intensiv, oft*) a lot; ~ **arbeiten** to work a lot. 2. (*zum Ausdruck der Verstärkung*) much; ~ **mehr** much more; ~ **zu ...** much too ...; **es dauert** ~ **zu lange** it's far too long; **zu** ~ too much; ~ **zu** ~ much too much. ♦ *pron* a lot. ♦ *adj*: **das** ~**e Geld** all the money; **das Kleid mit den** ~**en Knöpfen** the dress with all the buttons.

viele ♦ *det* → **viel**. ♦ *pron* lots.

vielfach *adj* multiple.

Vielfalt *die* variety.

vielleicht *adv* perhaps; (*fam: etwa, sehr*) really.

vielmals *adv*: **danke** ~ thank you very much.

vielseitig *adj* (*Person*) versatile.

vier *num* four, → **sechs**.

Viereck (*pl* -e) *das* rectangle.

viereckig *adj* rectangular.

vierhundert *num* four hundred.

viermal *adv* four times.

vierspurig *adj* four-lane.

vierte, -r, -s *adj* fourth, → **sechste**.

Viertel (*pl* -) *das* quarter; ~ **vor sechs** a quarter to six; ~ **nach sechs** a quarter past six (Br), a quarter after six (Am).

Viertelstunde (*pl* -n) *die* quarter of an hour.

Vierwaldstätter See *der* Lake Lucerne.

vierzehn *num* fourteen; ~ **Tage** a fortnight, → **sechs**.

vierzig *num* forty, → **sechs**.

Villa (*pl* Villen) *die* villa.

violett *adj* purple.

Violine (*pl* -n) *die* violin.

Virus (*pl* Viren) *der* virus.

Virusinfektion (*pl* -en) *die* viral infection.

Visite (*pl* -n) *die* (MED) rounds (*pl*).

Visitenkarte (*pl* -n) *die* visiting card.

Visum (*pl* Visa) *das* visa.

Vitamin (*pl* -e) *das* vitamin.

Vogel (*pl* Vögel) *der* bird.

Vokabel (*pl* -n) *die* vocabulary.

Vokal (*pl* -e) *der* vowel.

Volk (*pl* Völker) *das* people.

Völkerkunde *die* anthropology.

Volksfest (*pl* -e) *das* festival.

Volkshochschule (*pl* -n) *die* ≃ college of adult education.

Volkslied (*pl* -er) *das* folk song.

Volkstanz (*pl* -tänze) *der* folk dance.

Volkswagen® (*pl* -) *der* Volkswagen®.

Volkswirtschaft *die* (Wissenschaft) economics (*sg*).

voll ◆ *adj* full. ◆ *adv* (ganz) fully ; (fam: total, absolut) totally; ~ **mit** ODER **von** full of; **halb** ~ half full; ~ **sein** (fam: betrunken) to be plastered.

vollendet ◆ *adj* (perfekt) perfect; (fertig) completed. ◆ *adv* (perfekt) perfectly; **mit ~em 18. Lebensjahr** at 18 years of age.

Volleyball (*pl* -bälle) *der* volleyball.

Vollgas *das* full throttle.

völlig ◆ *adj* total. ◆ *adv* totally.

volljährig *adj* of age.

Vollkaskoversicherung (*pl* -en) *die* comprehensive insurance.

vollklimatisiert *adj* fully air-conditioned.

vollkommen ◆ *adj* (perfekt) perfect; (vollständig, total) total. ◆ *adv* (perfekt) perfectly; (vollständig) totally.

Vollkornbrot (*pl* -e) *das* wholemeal bread.

voll|machen *vt* (Behälter) to fill up. ▶ **sich vollmachen** *ref* (fam: sich beschmutzen) to get dirty.

Vollmacht (*pl* -en) *die* (Befugnis) authority; (Dokument) authorization.

Vollmilch *die* full-fat milk.

Vollmilchschokolade *die* milk chocolate.

Vollmond *der* full moon.

Vollpension *die* full board.

vollständig *adj* (Sammlung) complete.

voll|tanken *vi* to fill up.

Vollwaschmittel (*pl* -) *das* detergent.

vollwertig *adj* (Ernährung) wholefood; (gleichwertig) equal.

Vollwertkost *die* wholefood.

vollzählig *adj* entire.

Volontär, -in (*mpl* -e) *der, die* trainee.

Volt (*pl* -) *das* volt.

Volumen (*pl* -) *das* volume.

vom *präp* = **von dem**.

von *präp* (+D) **1.** (räumlich) from; ~ **hier an** from here; ~ **hier aus** from here; ~ **Köln bis Paris** from Cologne to Paris; ~ **der Straße her** from the street; ~ ... **nach** from ... to. **2.** (zeitlich) of; **die Zeitung** ~ **gestern** yesterday's paper; ~ **heute an** from today; ~ **Montag bis Freitag** from Monday to Friday. **3.** (in Passivsätzen) by; ~ **einem Hund gebissen werden** to be bitten by a dog; **das war dumm** ~ **dir** that was stupid of you. **4.** (Angabe von Besitz): **ist das Buch** ~ **dir?** is the book yours? **5.** (*Angabe von Zusammengehörigkeit*) of; **der Bürgermeister ~ Frankfurt** the mayor of Frankfurt; **ein Verwandter ~ mir** a relation of mine. **6.** (*Angabe der Herkunft*) from; **ich bin ~ hier** (*fam*) I'm from round here; **ein Brief ~ meiner Schwester** a letter from my sister. **7.** (*Angabe der Ursache*) from; **~ mir aus** (*fam*) as far as I'm concerned; **~ wegen!** (*fam*) no way! **8.** (*Angabe des Maßes*) of; **ein Sack ~ 25 kg** a 25 kg bag.

voneinander *adv* from each other.

vor ♦ *präp* (+D) **1.** (*räumlich*) in front of; **~ dem Haus stehen** to stand in front of the house. **2.** (*zeitlich*) before; **fünf ~ zwölf** five to twelve (Br), five before twelve (Am); **fünf ~ halb neun** twenty-five past eight (Br), twenty-five after eight (Am); **~ kurzem** recently; **~ (fünf) Jahren** (five) years ago. **3.** (*Angabe des Grunds*) with; **~ Freude in die Luft springen** to jump for joy; **~ allem** (*hauptsächlich*) above all. ♦ *präp* (+A) in front of. ♦ *adv* forwards.

voran *adv* (*vorne*) at the front; **mach ~!** (*fam*) hurry up!

voraus *adv*: **im ~** in advance.

vorausgesetzt *adj* provided (that).

Voraussetzung (*pl* -en) *die* (*Bedingung*) condition; (*Annahme*) assumption.

voraussichtlich ♦ *adj* expected. ♦ *adv* probably.

vorbei *adj*: **~ sein** (*zeitlich*) to be over; (*räumlich*) to be past.

vorbei|fahren *vi unr ist* (*an Stadt, Haus*) to drive past; (*fam: bei Person*) to drop in.

vorbei|gehen *vi unr ist* to pass; (*fam: Besuch*) to drop in.

vorbei|kommen *vi unr ist* (*an Stadt, Haus*) to go past; (*fam: bei Person*) to call round; (*an Hindernis*) to get past.

vorbei|lassen *vt unr* to let past.

vor|bereiten *vt* to prepare. ▶ **sich vorbereiten** *ref* to prepare o.s.; **sich ~ auf** (+A) to prepare for.

Vorbereitung *die* preparation.

vor|bestellen *vt* to order in advance.

Vorbestellung (*pl* -en) *die* advance booking.

vor|beugen *vi* (+D) to prevent. ▶ **sich vorbeugen** *ref* to lean forwards.

Vorbild (*pl* -er) *das* (*Idol*) example.

Vorderachse (*pl* -n) *die* front axle.

vordere *adj* front.

Vordergrund *der* foreground.

Vorderrad (*pl* -räder) *das* front wheel.

Vorderradantrieb (*pl* -e) *der* front-wheel drive.

Vorderseite (*pl* -n) *die* front.

Vordersitz (*pl* -e) *der* front seat.

vor|drängen: sich vordrängen *ref* (*räumlich*) to push one's way forward.

Vordruck (*pl* -e) *der* form.

vor|fahren *vi unr ist* (*nach vorn*) to drive up.

Vorfahrt *die* right of way; **'~ gewähren'** 'give way'; **'~ geändert'** 'altered right of way'.

Vorfahrtsstraße (*pl* -n) *die* major road.

Vorfall (*pl* -fälle) *der* (*Ereignis*) occurrence.

Vorführung (*pl* -en) *die* (*im Theater, Kino*) performance; (*von Auto, Maschine*) demonstration.

Vorgänger, -in (*mpl* -) *der, die* predecessor.

vor|gehen *vi unr ist* (*passieren*) to go on; (*handeln*) to proceed; (*Uhr*) to be fast; (*nach vorn*) to go forward; (*fam: voraus*) to go on ahead.

vorgekocht *adj* precooked.

vorgesehen *adj* intended.

Vorgesetzte (*pl* -n) *der, die* superior.

vorgestern *adv* (*vor zwei Tagen*) the

day before yesterday.

vor|haben vt unr: etw ~ to have sthg planned.

vorhanden adj available.

Vorhang (pl -hänge) der curtain.

Vorhängeschloß (pl -schlösser) das padlock.

vorher adv beforehand.

Vorhersage (pl -n) die (für Wetter) forecast.

vorhin adv just now.

vorige adj last.

Vorkenntnisse pl prior knowledge (sg).

vor|kommen ◆ vi unr ist (passieren) to occur; (existieren) to exist. ◆ vi (+D) (scheinen) to seem; (fam: nach vorne) to come forwards.

Vorkommnis (pl -se) das (amt) incident.

vor|lassen vt unr (fam): jn ~ to let sb go first.

vorläufig ◆ adj provisional. ◆ adv provisionally.

vor|lesen vt unr to read out.

Vorlesung (pl -en) die lecture.

vorletzte, -r, -s adj last but one.

vorm. (abk für vormittags) am.

vor|machen vt (vortäuschen) to fool; (zeigen): jm etw ~ to show sb how to do sthg.

vor|merken vt (Termin) to pencil in.

vormittag adv morning; heute/ gestern/morgen ~ this/yesterday/ tomorrow morning.

Vormittag (pl -e) der morning.

vormittags adv in the morning.

vorn adv at the front; da ~ over there; nach ~ (zeitlich) forwards; von ~ from the beginning.

Vorname (pl -n) der first name.

vorne adv = vorn.

vornehm adj elegant.

vor|nehmen vt (ausführen) to undertake; sich (D) etw ~ (planen) to plan to do sthg.

Vorort (pl -e) der suburb.

vorrangig adj principal.

Vorrat (pl Vorräte) der store; auf ~ in stock; solange der ~ reicht while stocks last.

vorrätig adj in stock.

Vorsaison die pre-season.

Vorsatz (pl -sätze) der resolution.

Vorschau (pl -en) die preview.

Vorschlag (pl Vorschläge) der suggestion.

vor|schlagen vt unr to suggest; jm etw ~ to suggest sthg to sb.

vor|schreiben vt unr (befehlen) to dictate.

Vorschrift (pl -en) die regulation.

Vorschuß (pl Vorschüsse) der advance.

Vorsicht die care; ~! look out!

vorsichtig ◆ adj careful. ◆ adv carefully.

Vorsilbe (pl -n) die prefix.

Vorsorge die provision; ~ treffen für etw to make provision for sthg.

Vorspeise (pl -n) die starter.

Vorsprung (pl Vorsprünge) der (Abstand) lead; (an Mauer) projection.

vor|stellen vt (Person, Projekt) to introduce; (Uhr) to put forward; sich (D) etw ~ (ausdenken) to imagine sthg. ▶ sich vorstellen ref (bekannt machen) to introduce o.s.

Vorstellung (pl -en) die (in Kino, Theater) performance; (von Bekannten) introduction; (Idee) idea; (bei Firma) interview.

Vorstellungsgespräch (pl -e) das job interview.

vor|strecken vt (Geld) to advance.

Vorteil (pl -e) der advantage.

Vortrag (pl Vorträge) der (Rede) talk; einen ~ halten to give a talk.

vorüber adj: ~ sein to be over.

vorüber|gehen vi unr ist (vorbeigehen) to pass by; (zu Ende gehen) to come to an end.

vorübergehend ◆ adj temporary. ◆ adv temporarily; ~ geschlossen temporarily closed.

Vor- und Zuname (pl -n) der first name and surname.

Vorurteil (pl -e) das prejudice.

Vorverkauf der advance booking.

Vorverkaufskasse (pl -n) die advance booking desk.

Vorverkaufsstelle (pl -n) die advance booking office.

Vorwahl (pl -en) die (Telefonnummer) dialling code (Br), area code (Am).

Vorwahlnummer (pl -n) die dialling code (Br), area code (Am).

vorwärts adv (nach vorn) forwards.

vorwärts|kommen vi unr ist to make progress.

vor|werfen vt unr (Fehler): jm etw ~ to accuse sb of sthg.

Vorwort (pl -e) das preface.

Vorwurf (pl -würfe) der accusation.

vor|zeigen vt to show.

vor|ziehen vt unr (lieber mögen) to prefer; (Vorhang) to draw; (nach vorn ziehen) to pull up.

vorzüglich adj excellent.

Vorzugspreis (pl -e) der special price.

vulgär adj vulgar.

Vulkan (pl -e) volcano.

W

W (abk für West) W.

Waadt die Vaud (Swiss canton).

Waage (pl -n) die (Gerät) scales (pl); (Sternzeichen) Libra.

waagerecht adj horizontal.

wach adj (nicht schlafend): ~ sein to be awake; ~ werden to wake up.

Wache (pl -n) die (Wächter) guard; (Polizeidienststelle) police station.

Wacholder der (Gewürz) juniper.

Wachs das wax.

wachsen¹ (präs wächst, prät wuchs, pp gewachsen) vi ist to grow.

wachsen² vt (Skier) to wax.

Wachsfigurenkabinett (pl -e) das waxworks (pl).

Wachsmalstift (pl -e) der wax crayon.

wächst präs → **wachsen**.

Wachstum das growth.

Wachtel (pl -n) die quail.

Wächter, -in (mpl -) der, die guard.

wackelig adj (Möbel) wobbly.

Wackelkontakt (pl -e) der loose contact.

wackeln vi (Möbel) to be wobbly; (bewegen) to shake.

Wackelpeter der jelly.

Wade (pl -n) die calf.

Waffe (pl -n) die weapon.

Waffel (pl -n) die waffle.

Waffeleisen (pl -) das waffle iron.

wagen vt (riskieren) to risk. ▶ **sich wagen** ref (sich trauen) to dare.

Wagen (pl -) der (Auto) car; (von Zug, U-Bahn) carriage (Br), car (Am); (Pferdewagen) carriage; '~ hält' 'bus stopping'.

Wagenheber (pl -) der jack.

Wagenpapiere pl vehicle documents.

Wagentyp (pl -en) der make of car.

Wagenwäsche (pl -n) die car wash.

Waggon (pl -s) der carriage (Br), car (Am).

Wahl (pl -en) die (Auswahl) choice; (Abstimmung) election; **erste** ~ top quality.

wählen ◆ vt (aussuchen) to choose; (Telefonnummer) to dial; (Kandidaten) to elect. ◆ vi (aussuchen) to choose; (am Telefon) to dial; (abstimmen) to vote.

Wählscheibe (pl -n) die dial.

wahlweise adv: ~ in Rot, Grün oder Blau in either red, green or blue; ~ mit Reis oder Gemüse with a choice of

rice or **vegetables**.
Wahnsinn der madness; ~! brilliant!
wahnsinnig ◆ adj (unvernünftig) mad. ◆ adv (fam: groß, stark) incredibly.
wahr adj true.
während ◆ konj (zeitlich) while. ◆ präp (+G) during.
währenddessen adv in the meantime.
Wahrheit (pl -en) die truth; **in ~** in reality.
wahrlnehmen vt unr (bemerken) to notice.
Wahrsager, -in (mpl -) der, die fortune-teller.
wahrscheinlich ◆ adj probable. ◆ adv probably.
Währung (pl -en) die currency.
Wahrzeichen (pl -) das symbol.
Waise (pl -n) die orphan.
Wald (pl **Wälder**) der wood; (groß) forest.
Waldbrand (pl -**brände**) der forest fire.
Wäldchen (pl -) das copse.
Waldgebiet (pl -e) das wooded area.
waldig adj wooded.
Waldlauf (pl -**läufe**) der cross-country run.
Waldlehrpfad (pl -e) der nature trail.
Waldmeister der (Pflanze) woodruff.
Waldorfsalat (pl -e) der Waldorf salad.
Waldpilz (pl -e) der wild mushroom.
Waldsterben das forest dieback.

WALDSTERBEN

This is the German term used to refer to the damage caused to trees by environmental pollution. It was in Germany that public attention was first drawn to this phenomenon during the 1970s. The characteristic

symptoms whereby needles, leaves and entire treetops turn yellow and die initially affected only coniferous trees, but have now spread to deciduous trees as well. Forest dieback is attributed to acid rain, the hole in the ozone layer and general chemical pollution, and two-thirds of German forests now suffer from its effects.

Waldweg (pl -e) der forest track.
Wales nt Wales.
Walise (pl -n) der Welshman; **die ~n** the Welsh.
Waliserin (pl -nen) die Welshwoman.
walisisch adj Welsh.
Walkie-Talkie (pl -s) das walkie-talkie.
Walkman® (pl -men) der Walkman®.
Wallfahrt (pl -en) die pilgrimage.
Wallfahrtsort (pl -e) der place of pilgrimage.
Wallis das Valais (Swiss canton).
Walnuß (pl -nüsse) die walnut.
Walzer (pl -) der waltz.
wand prät → **winden**.
Wand (pl **Wände**) die (von Häusern, Räumen) wall.
wandeln: sich wandeln ref to change.
Wanderer (pl -) der rambler.
Wanderkarte (pl -n) die walking map.
wandern vi ist to go walking.
Wanderschuh (pl -e) der walking boot.
Wanderweg (pl -e) der trail.
Wandmalerei (pl -en) die mural.
Wandschrank (pl -schränke) der built-in cupboard.
wandte prät → **wenden**.
Wandteppich (pl -e) er tapestry.
Wange (pl -n) die (geh) cheek.
wann adv when; **bis ~?** till when?; **seit ~ lebst du schon hier?** how long

have you been living here?

Wanne (pl -n) die (Badewanne) bath; (Gefäß) tank.

Wappen (pl -) das coat of arms.

war prät → **sein**.

warb prät → **werben**.

Ware (pl -n) die product; **~n** goods.

Warenhaus (pl -häuser) das department store.

Warenlager (pl -) das warehouse.

Warenmuster (pl -) das sample.

Warensendung (pl -en) die sample sent by post.

Warenzeichen (pl -) das trademark.

warf prät → **werfen**.

warm (komp **wärmer**, superl am **wärmsten**) ◆ adj warm. ◆ adv warmly; **~ essen** to have a hot meal; **sich ~ anziehen** to put on warm clothes; **es ist ~** it's warm; **ist dir nicht zu ~?** aren't you too hot?; **~e Getränke** hot drinks.

Wärme die warmth.

wärmen vt to warm. ▶ **sich wärmen** ref to warm o.s.

Wärmflasche (pl -n) die hot-water bottle.

Warmfront (pl -en) die warm front.

warm‖laufen vi unr ist (Motor) to warm up. ▶ **sich warmlaufen** ref (Person) to warm up.

Warmmiete (pl -n) die rent including heating bills.

Warmwasser das hot water.

Warnblinkanlage (pl -n) die hazard lights (pl).

Warndreieck (pl -e) das warning triangle.

warnen vt to warn; **'vor ... wird gewarnt'** 'beware of ...'

Warnschild (pl -er) das warning sign.

Warnung (pl -en) die warning.

Warteliste (pl -n) die waiting list.

warten ◆ vi to wait. ◆ vt (TECH) to service; **~ auf** (+A) to wait for; **'hier ~'** 'wait here'.

Wartenummer (pl -n) die number assigned to someone to indicate their position in a waiting system.

Wärter, -in (mpl -) der, die attendant.

Wartesaal (pl -säle) der waiting room.

Wartezimmer (pl -) das waiting room.

Wartung (pl -en) die servicing.

warum adv why; **~ nicht?** why not?

Warze (pl -n) die wart.

was pron what; (Relativpronomen) which; (fam: etwas) something; (fam: nicht wahr): **da freust du dich, ~** you're pleased, aren't you?; **~ für** what kind of; **na so ~!** well!

Waschanlage (pl -n) die car wash.

waschbar adj washable.

Waschbecken (pl -) das washbasin.

Wäsche (pl -n) die washing; (Unterwäsche) underwear; **schmutzige ~** dirty washing.

waschecht adj (Kleidung) colourfast.

Wäscheklammer (pl -n) die clothes peg (Br), clothespin (Am).

Wäscheleine (pl -n) die washing line.

waschen (präs **wäscht**, prät **wusch**, pp **gewaschen**) vt to wash. ▶ **sich waschen** ref to have a wash; **sich** (D) **die Hände ~** to wash one's hands; **Waschen und Legen** shampoo and set.

Wäscherei (pl -en) die laundrette.

Wäscheschleuder (pl -n) die spin-dryer.

Wäscheständer (pl -) der clotheshorse.

Wäschestärke die starch.

Wäschetrockner (pl -) der (Maschine) tumble-dryer.

Waschgelegenheit (pl -en) die washing facilities.

Waschlappen (pl -) der (zum Waschen) face cloth.

Waschmaschine (*pl* **-n**) *die* washing machine.

Waschmittel (*pl* **-**) *das* detergent.

Waschpulver (*pl* **-**) *das* washing powder.

Waschraum (*pl* **-räume**) *der* washroom.

Waschsalon (*pl* **-s**) *der* laundrette.

Waschstraße (*pl* **-n**) *die* car wash.

wäscht *präs* → **waschen**.

Wasser (*pl* **Wässer** ODER **Wasser**) *das* water; **am ~** next to the water; **im ~** in the water; **destilliertes ~** distilled water.

Wasseranschluß (*pl* **-anschlüsse**) *der* water mains.

wasserdicht *adj* waterproof.

Wasserfall (*pl* **-fälle**) *der* waterfall.

Wasserfarbe (*pl* **-n**) *die* watercolour.

Wassergraben (*pl* **-gräben**) *der* ditch.

Wasserhahn (*pl* **-hähne**) *der* tap (*Br*), faucet (*Am*).

Wasserleitung (*pl* **-en**) *die* (*Rohr*) water pipe; (*Anlage*) plumbing.

wasserlöslich *adj* soluble (*in water*).

Wassermangel *der* drought.

Wassermann *der* (*Sternzeichen*) Aquarius.

Wassermelone (*pl* **-n**) *die* watermelon.

wasserscheu *adj* scared of water.

Wasserschutzpolizei *die* river police.

Wasserski (*pl* **-er**) ◆ *der* (*Gerät*) water ski. ◆ *das* (*Sportart*) water skiing.

Wasserspiegel (*pl* **-**) *der* (*Wasserstand*) water level.

Wassersport *der* water sport.

Wasserspülung (*pl* **-en**) *die* flush.

Wasserstand (*pl* **-stände**) *der* water level.

wasserundurchlässig *adj* waterproof.

Wasserversorgung *die* water supply.

Wasserwerk (*pl* **-e**) *das* waterworks (*sg*).

Watt¹ (*pl* **-en**) *das* (*Küstengebiet*) mudflats (*pl*).

Watt² (*pl* **-**) *das* (*Maßeinheit*) watt.

Watte *die* cotton wool.

Wattenmeer (*pl* **-e**) *das* mudflats (*pl*).

WATTENMEER

This is the name given to an area of mudflats on the North Sea coast, characterized by 'Prielen' (occasionally very deep water channels). At high tide the area is covered by the sea, but at low tide a unique natural landscape is revealed, making it a very popular place for visitors to go on walks.

Wattestäbchen (*pl* **-**) *das* cotton bud.

wattiert *adj* padded.

WC (*pl* **-s**) *das* WC.

WC-Reiniger (*pl* **-**) *der* lavatory cleaner.

weben (*prät* **webte** ODER **wob**, *pp* **gewebt** ODER **gewoben**) *vt* (*Teppich Stoff*) to weave.

Web-Seite (*pl* **-n**) *die* Web site

Wechsel (*pl* **-**) *der* (*Austausch, Änderung*) change; (*von Devisen*) exchange.

Wechselbad (*pl* **-bäder**) *das* (*in Wasser*) bath in alternating hot and then cold water.

Wechselgeld *das* change.

wechselhaft *adj* changeable.

Wechseljahre *pl* menopause (*sg*).

Wechselkurs (*pl* **-e**) *der* exchange rate.

wechseln *vt & vi* to change; **Mark in Pfund ~** to change marks into pounds.

Wechselrahmen (*pl* **-**) *der* clip frame.

Wechselstrom *der* alternating current.

Wechselstube (pl -n) die bureau de change.

Weckdienst (pl -e) der morning call.

wecken vt (Person, Tier) to wake.

Wecker (pl -) der alarm clock.

weder konj neither; ~ ... **noch** neither ... nor.

weg adv away; **weit ~** far away; **Frau Miller ist schon ~** Frau Miller has already gone.

Weg (pl -e) der (Pfad) path; (Strecke, Methode) way; **der ~ nach** the way to; **dem ausgeschilderten ~ folgen** follow the signposted path; **im ~ sein** to be in the way.

weg|bringen vt unr to take away.

wegen präp (+G or D) because of.

weg|fahren ◆ vi unr ist to leave. ◆ vt unr hat to drive away.

weg|gehen vi unr ist (Person) to go away; (Fleck) to come off.

weg|kommen vi unr ist (fam: fortgehen können) to get away; (verschwinden) to disappear.

weg|lassen vt unr (fam: Textstelle) to leave out; (Gäste) to let go.

weg|laufen vi unr ist to run away.

weg|legen vt to put down.

weg|machen vt (fam) to get off.

weg|müssen vi unr (fam) to have to go.

weg|nehmen vt unr to take away.

weg|räumen vt to clear away.

weg|schicken vt (Brief, Packet) to send; (Person) to send away.

weg|sehen vi unr (nicht hinsehen) to look away.

weg|tun vt unr (fam: weglegen) to put away; (wegwerfen) to throw away.

Wegweiser (pl -) der signpost.

weg|werfen vt unr to throw away.

weg|wischen vt to wipe away.

weh adj: ~ **tun** (schmerzen) to hurt; **jm ~ tun** (verletzen) to hurt sb.

Wehe (pl -n) die contraction.

wehen vi (Wind) to blow.

Wehrdienst der military service.

wehren: sich wehren ref to defend o.s.

weiblich adj female; (GRAMM) feminine.

weich ◆ adj soft. ◆ adv (sitzen, liegen) comfortably.

weichgekocht adj soft-boiled.

Weichkäse der soft cheese.

Weichspüler (pl -) der fabric conditioner.

Weide (pl -n) die (mit Gras) meadow.

weigern: sich weigern ref to refuse.

Weigerung (pl -en) die refusal.

Weihnachten (pl -) Christmas; **frohe ~!** Merry Christmas!

WEIHNACHTEN

German Christmas traditions differ somewhat from those in the English-speaking world. Presents are exchanged on Christmas Eve rather than on Christmas Day and before going to Midnight Mass it is customary to light the candles with which the Christmas tree is decorated. 'Weihnachtsplätzchen' are plates of typical Christmas biscuits and cakes such as 'Lebkuchen', and mulled wine is the traditional drink. In addition to Christmas Day, 26 December is also a public holiday.

Weihnachtsabend (pl -e) der Christmas Eve.

Weihnachtsbaum (pl -bäume) der Christmas tree.

Weihnachtsferien pl Christmas holidays (Br), Christmas vacation (sg)(Am).

Weihnachtsgeld das Christmas bonus.

Weihnachtsgeschäft das Christmas trade.

Weihnachtsgeschenk (pl -e) das Christmas present.

Weihnachtskarte (pl -n) die Christmas card.

Wei̲hnachtslied (*pl* **-er**) *das*
Christmas carol.
Wei̲hnachtsmann (*pl* **-männer**)
der Father Christmas.
Wei̲hnachtsmarkt (*pl* **-märkte**)
der Christmas market.

WEIHNACHTSMARKT

During the Christmas period, many
German towns have a 'Weihnachtsmarkt' or Christmas market, usually
on the main square, where you can
buy Christmas decorations, hand-
made goods, gift items, Christmas
biscuits and cakes etc. There are
also several stalls selling mulled
wine and the local culinary speciali-
ties. The Nuremberg 'Christkindl-
markt' and the Dresden Christmas
market are the best-known.

Wei̲hnachtstag (*pl* **-e**) *der*
Christmas Day; **erster ~** Christmas
Day; **zweiter ~** Boxing Day.
Wei̲hnachtszeit *die* Christmas.
wei̲l *konj* because.
Wei̲n (*pl* **-e**) *der* (*Getränk*) wine;
(*Pflanze*) vine.

WEIN

Almost 90% of the wine produced in
Germany is white wine. The main
wine-producing areas are the
Rhineland, the Mosel-Saar-Ruwer
region, Nahe, Baden, Württemberg,
Franconia, the Elbe valley and
Saale-Unstrut. Franconian wine is
bottled in characteristic wide, round
bottles called 'Bocksbeutel'. After
the grape harvest, many areas hold
wine festivals where the local wines
may be sampled. 'Federweißer' is a
young, cloudy, sweet wine which is
especially popular in the autumn,
whilst on special occasions Germans drink 'Sekt', a champagne-
style wine that must contain a specific percentage of German grapes.

Wei̲nanbaugebiet (*pl* **-e**) *das*
wine-growing area.

Wei̲nberg (*pl* **-e**) *der* vineyard.
Wei̲nbergschnecke (*pl* **-n**) *die*
snail.
Wei̲nbrand (*pl* **-brände**) *der*
brandy.
wei̲nen *vi* to cry.
Wei̲nflasche (*pl* **-n**) *die* wine bot-
tle.
Wei̲nglas (*pl* **-gläser**) *das* wine
glass.
Wei̲nkarte (*pl* **-n**) *die* wine list.
Wei̲nkeller (*pl* **-**) *der* wine cellar.
Wei̲nlese (*pl* **-n**) *die* grape harvest.
Wei̲nlokal (*pl* **-e**) *das* wine bar.
Wei̲nprobe (*pl* **-n**) *die* wine tasting.
Wei̲nstube (*pl* **-n**) *die* wine bar.
Wei̲ntraube (*pl* **-n**) *die* grape.
wei̲sen (*prät* **wie̲s**, *pp* **gewie̲sen**)
♦ *vt* (*zeigen*) to show. ♦ *vi* (*zeigen*) to
point.
Wei̲sheit *die* (*Klugheit*) wisdom.
wei̲ß ♦ *präs* → **wissen**. ♦ *adj* white.
Wei̲ß *das* white.
Wei̲ßbier (*pl* **-e**) *das* *fizzy lager beer
made from wheat.*
Wei̲ßbrot (*pl* **-e**) *das* white bread.
Wei̲ße[1] (*pl* **-n**) *der, die* (*Mensch*) white
person.
Wei̲ße[2] (*pl* **-**) *die* (*fam*) = **Weißbier**;
Berliner ~ *type of fizzy lager often drunk
with raspberry syrup.*
Wei̲ßkohl *der* white cabbage.
Wei̲ßwein (*pl* **-e**) *der* white wine.
Wei̲ßwurst (*pl* **Wei̲ßwürste**) *die*
white sausage.
wei̲t ♦ *adj* wide; (*Reise, Fahrt*) long.
♦ *adv* (*wesentlich*) far; (*gehen, fahren,
fallen*) a long way; **bei ~em** by far; **von
~em** from a distance; **~ weg** far
away; **wie ~ ist es bis ...?** how far is it
to ...?; **so ~ sein** (*fam*) to be ready;
zu ~ gehen to go too far.
wei̲ter *adv* (*fortgesetzt*) further;
(*sonst*) else; **immer ~** on and on; **nicht
~** (*nicht weiter fort*) no further; **nichts ~**
nothing more; **und so ~** and so on.
wei̲ter|arbeiten *vi* to carry on
working.

weitere *adj* further; **ohne ~s** (*problemlos*) with no problem at all.

weiter|empfehlen *vt unr* to recommend.

weiter|fahren *vi unr ist* to drive on.

Weiterfahrt *die*: **zur ~ in Richtung Hausen bitte hier umsteigen** passengers for Hausen, please change here.

weiter|geben *vt unr* to pass on.

weiter|gehen *vi unr ist* to go on.

weiter|helfen *vi unr* (+D) to help.

weiter|machen *vi* to carry on.

weitsichtig *adj* farsighted; (MED) longsighted (Br), farsighted (Am).

Weitsprung *der* long jump.

Weitwinkelobjektiv (*pl* **-e**) *das* wide-angle lens.

Weizen *der* wheat.

Weizenbier (*pl* **-e**) *das fizzy lager beer made from wheat.*

welche, -r, -s ◆ *det* (*zur Einleitung einer Frage*) which. ◆ *pron* (*Relativpronomen*) which, that; (*Indefinitpronomen*) any; (*Interrogativpronomen*) which (one); **hast du ~?** have you got any?

welk *adj* wilted.

Welle (*pl* **-n**) *die* wave.

Wellenbad (*pl* **-bäder**) *das swimming pool with wave machine.*

Wellengang *der* swell.

Wellenreiten *das* surfing.

wellig *adj* (*Haar*) wavy; (*Landschaft*) undulating.

Welt (*pl* **-en**) *die* world; **auf der ~ in** the world.

Weltall *das* universe.

weltberühmt *adj* world-famous.

Weltkrieg (*pl* **-e**) *der*: **der Erste/Zweite ~** the First/Second World War.

Weltmeister, -in (*mpl* **-**) *der, die* world champion.

Weltmeisterschaft (*pl* **-en**) *die* world championship.

Weltreise (*pl* **-n**) *die* round-the-world trip.

Weltrekord (*pl* **-e**) *der* world record.

Weltstadt (*pl* **-städte**) *die* cosmopolitan city.

weltweit *adj & adv* worldwide.

wem *pron* (to) who.

wen *pron* who.

Wende (*pl* **-n**) *die* (*Veränderung*) change; (*im Sport*) turn; **die ~** (the) reunification (of Germany).

Wendefläche (*pl* **-n**) *die* turning area.

Wendekreis (*pl* **-e**) *der* (*von Fahrzeug*) turning circle.

Wendemöglichkeit (*pl* **-en**) *die* turning; **keine ~** no turning.

wenden¹ *vt & vi* to turn.

wenden² ▸ **sich wenden** (*prät* **wandte**, *pp* **gewandt**) *ref*: **sich an jn ~** to consult sb.

wenig ◆ *det* (*Geld, Interesse*) little; (*Tage, Leute*) a few. ◆ *pron* (*Geld, Kaffee*) a little; (*Leute*) a few. ◆ *adv* a little; **ein ~** a little; **zu ~** too little.

weniger *adv* (*minus*) minus.

wenigste, -r, -s *adj* least; **am ~n** least.

wenigstens *adv* at least.

wenn *konj* (*zeitlich*) when; (*falls*) if.

wer *pron* who.

Werbefernsehen *das* television advertising.

Werbegeschenk (*pl* **-e**) *das* free sample.

werben (*präs* **wirbt**, *prät* **warb**, *pp* **geworben**) ◆ *vi* (*Firma, Produzent*) to advertise. ◆ *vt* (*Mitglieder*) to recruit; (*Kunden*) to attract.

Werbung *die* (*in Zeitung, Fernsehen*) advertising.

werden (*präs* **wird**, *prät* **wurde**, *pp* **ist geworden** ODER **worden**) ◆ *aux* 1. (*im Futur*) will; **sie wird kommen** she will come; **sie wird nicht kommen** she won't come. 2. (*im Konjunktiv*) would; **würden Sie das machen?** would you do this?; **ich würde gern gehen** I would like to go; **ich würde**

lieber noch bleiben I would prefer to stay a bit longer. **3.** (*im Passiv: pp* **worden**) to be; **sie wurde kritisiert** she was criticized. **4.** (*Ausdruck der Möglichkeit*): **sie wird es wohl vergessen haben** she has probably forgotten. ◆ *vi* (*pp* **geworden**) to become; **Vater ~** to become a father; **er will Lehrer ~** he wants to be a teacher; **ich werde morgen 25** I'll be 25 tomorrow; **das Kind wird groß** the child's getting bigger; **alt ~** to grow old, to get old; **rot ~** to go red, to turn red; **zu Stein ~** to turn to stone; **schlecht ~** to go off; **mir wird schlecht** I feel sick. ◆ *vimp* (*pp* **geworden**): **es wird langsam spät** it's getting late; **es wird bald Sommer** it will soon be summer.

werfen (*präs* **wirft**, *prät* **warf**, *pp* **geworfen**) *vt & vi* to throw.

Werft (*pl* **-en**) *die* shipyard.

Werk (*pl* **-e**) *das* (*Arbeit*) work; (*Fabrik*) works (*pl*).

Werkstatt (*pl* **-stätten**) *die* workshop.

Werktag (*pl* **-e**) *der* working day.

werktags *adv* on working days.

Werkzeug (*pl* **-e**) *das* tool.

Werkzeugkasten (*pl* **-kästen**) *der* tool box.

Wermut (*pl* **-s**) *der* (*Getränk*) vermouth.

wert *adj*: **~ sein** to be worth.

Wert (*pl* **-e**) *der* value; **im ~ von** to the value of; **im ~ steigen/fallen** to increase/decrease in value; **~ legen auf** (+ A) to attach importance to.

Wertangabe (*pl* **-n**) *die* registered value; **Sendung mit ~** registered mail.

Wertbrief (*pl* **-e**) *der* registered letter.

Wertgegenstand (*pl* **-gegenstände**) *der* valuable object.

wertlos *adj* worthless.

Wertmarke (*pl* **-n**) *die* token.

Wertpapier (*pl* **-e**) *das* bond.

Wertsachen *pl* valuables; **'bitte**

achten Sie auf Ihre ~!' 'please take care of your valuables'.

wertvoll *adj* valuable.

Wertzeichen (*pl* **-**) *das* stamp.

Wesen (*pl* **-**) *das* (*Charakter*) nature; (*Lebewesen*) creature.

wesentlich ◆ *adj* (*wichtig*) essential. ◆ *adv* (*viel*) considerably.

weshalb *adv* why.

Wespe (*pl* **-n**) *die* wasp.

wessen *pron* whose.

Wessi (*pl* **-s**) *der* (*fam*) West German.

West *der* West.

Westberlin *nt* West Berlin.

Westdeutschland *das* (*westliche Teil*) western Germany; (*frühere BRD*) West Germany.

Weste (*pl* **-n**) *die* waistcoat.

Westen *der* west; **im ~** in the west; **nach ~** (*Richtung*) west.

Westeuropa *nt* Western Europe.

Westküste (*pl* **-n**) *die* west coast.

westlich ◆ *adj* western. ◆ *präp*: **~ von** west of.

weswegen *adv* why.

Wettbewerb (*pl* **-e**) *der* (*Veranstaltung*) competition.

Wettbüro (*pl* **-s**) *das* betting office.

Wette (*pl* **-n**) *die* bet.

wetten *vi & vt* to bet; **ich wette mit dir um 10 DM** I bet you 10 marks.

Wetter *das* weather; **bei gutem/ schlechtem ~** if the weather is good/ bad.

Wetteraussichten *pl* weather prospects.

Wetterbericht (*pl* **-e**) *der* weather report.

wetterfest *adj* weatherproof.

Wetterkarte (*pl* **-n**) *die* weather map.

Wetterlage (*pl* **-n**) *die* general weather situation.

Wettervorhersage (*pl* **-n**) *die* weather forecast.

Wettkampf (*pl* **-kämpfe**) *der* contest.

Wettlauf (*pl* **-läufe**) *der* race.

Wettrennen (*pl* **-**) *das* race.

WG *abk* = **Wohngemeinschaft**.

Whg. *abk* = **Wohnung**.

Whiskey (*pl* **-s**) *der* whisky.

wichtig *adj* & *adv* important.

wickeln *vt* (*Schnur, Papier*) to wind; (*Baby*): **ein Kind ~** to change a child's nappy (*Br*), to change a child's diaper (*Am*).

Wickelraum (*pl* **-räume**) *der* baby changing room.

Widder *der* (*Sternzeichen*) Aries.

widerlich *adj* disgusting.

widerrechtlich ◆ *adj* illegal. ◆ *adv*: **~ abgestellte Fahrzeuge** illegally parked cars.

Widerruf (*pl* **-e**) *der* retraction.

widerrufen *vt* (*Aussage*) to retract.

widersprechen (*präs* **widerspricht**, *prät* **widersprach**, *pp* **widersprochen**) *vi* (+D) to contradict; **sich** (D) **~** to contradict o.s.

Widerspruch (*pl* **-sprüche**) *der* contradiction; (*Protest*) objection.

Widerstand (*pl* **-stände**) *der* (*Abwehr*) resistance.

widerstandsfähig *adj* resilient.

Widmung (*pl* **-en**) *die* dedication.

wie ◆ *adv* **1.** (*in Fragesätzen*) how; **~ heißen Sie?** what's your name?; **~ war das Wetter?** what was the weather like?; **~ spät ist es?** what is the time?; **~ bitte?** sorry?; **~ oft?** how often?; **~ wäre es, wenn ...?** how about if ...?; **sie fragte ihn, ~ alt er sei** she asked him how old he was. **2.** (*als Ausruf*) how; **~ nett von dir!** how kind of you! ◆ *konj* **1.** (*zum Vergleich*) like; **so ... ~ as ... as**; **~ ich schon sagte** as I was saying. **2.** (*Maßangabe, Qualitätsangabe*) as; **soviel, ~ du willst** as much as you like; **und ~!** not half!

wieder *adv* again; **immer ~** again and again; **nie ~** never again.

wiederbekommen *vt unr* to get back.

wiedererkennen *vt unr* to recognize.

wiederfinden *vt unr* to find.

wiedergeben *vt unr* (*zurückgeben*) to give back.

wiederhaben *vt unr* (*fam*) to have back.

wiederholen *vt* (*noch einmal*) to repeat; (*lernen*) to revise. ▸ **sich wiederholen** *ref* (*Person*) to repeat o.s.; (*Ereignis*) to recur; **~ Sie bitte!** could you repeat that please?

Wiederholung (*pl* **-en**) *die* (*von Lernstoff*) revision; (*von Test, Klasse*) repeat; (*von Satz*) repetition.

Wiederhören *das*: **auf ~!** (*am Telefon*) bye!

wiederkommen *vi unr ist* (*zurückkommen*) to come back; (*noch einmal kommen*) to come again.

Wiedersehen (*pl* **-**) *das* reunion; **auf ~!** goodbye!

wiedertreffen *vt unr* to meet up again.

Wiedervereinigung (*pl* **-en**) *die* reunification.

Wiederverwendung *die* reuse.

wiegen (*prät* **wog**, *pp* **gewogen**) *vi* to weigh. ▸ **sich wiegen** *ref* (*auf Waage*) to weigh o.s.

Wien *nt* Vienna.

Wiener Schnitzel (*pl* **-**) *das* Wiener schnitzel (*escalope of veal coated with breadcrumbs*).

wies *prät* → **weisen**.

Wiese (*pl* **-n**) *die* meadow.

wieso *pron* why.

wieviel *pron* how much; **~ Uhr ist es?** what time is it?

wievielte, -r, -s *adj*: **das ~ Glas ist das?** how many glasses is that?; **der Wievielte ist heute?** what's today's date?

wild ◆ *adj* wild; (*heftig*) frenzied. ◆ *adv* (*unkultiviert*) wild; (*heftig*) furiously; (*parken, zelten*) illegally.

Wild *das* game.

Wildbret *das* game.

Wildleder *das* suede.

Wildpark (*pl* **-s**) *der* game reserve.

Wildschwein (pl -e) das wild boar.

Wildwasser (pl -) das white water.

will präs → **wollen**.

Wille der (Absicht) wishes (pl); (Fähigkeit) will; **seinen eigenen ~n haben** to have a mind of one's own.

willkommen adj welcome; **herzlich ~!** welcome!

Willkommen das welcome.

Wimper (pl -n) die eyelash.

Wimperntusche (pl -n) die mascara.

Wind (pl -e) der wind; **starker/ schwacher/böiger ~** strong/mild/ gusty wind.

Windbeutel (pl -) der = éclair.

Windel (pl -n) die nappy (Br), diaper (Am).

winden: sich winden (prät wand, pp gewunden) ref (Weg, Linie) to wind.

windgeschützt adj sheltered.

windig adj (Tag, Wetter) windy; **es ist ~** it's windy.

Windjacke (pl -n) die windcheater.

Windmühle (pl -n) die windmill.

Windpocken pl chickenpox (sg).

Windrichtung (pl -en) die wind direction.

Windschutzscheibe (pl -n) die windscreen (Br), windshield (Am).

Windstärke (pl -n) die force (of wind).

windstill adj still.

Windsurfen das windsurfing.

Winkel (pl -) der (von Linien) angle; (Platz) corner.

winken (pp **gewinkt** ODER **gewunken**) vi (+D) to wave; **jm ~** to wave to sb.

Winter (pl -) der winter; **im ~** in winter.

Winterausrüstung (pl -en) die (zum Skifahren) skiing equipment.

Winterfahrplan (pl -fahrpläne) der winter timetable.

Wintermantel (pl -mäntel) der winter coat.

Winterreifen (pl -) der winter tyre.

Winterschlußverkauf (pl -verkäufe) der January sale.

Wintersport der winter sport.

Winzer, -in (mpl -) der, die wine grower.

winzig adj tiny.

wir pron we.

Wirbel (pl -) der (Knochen) vertebra; (in Wasser) whirlpool.

Wirbelsäule (pl -n) die spine.

wirbt präs → **werben**.

wird präs → **werden**.

wirft präs → **werfen**.

wirken vi (erscheinen) to seem; (Mittel) to have an effect; **~ gegen** to counteract.

wirklich ◆ adj real. ◆ adv really.

Wirklichkeit die reality.

wirksam adj effective.

Wirkstoff (pl -e) der active substance.

Wirkung (pl -en) die (von Mittel) effect.

Wirsing der savoy cabbage.

Wirt, -in (mpl -e) der, die (Gastwirt) landlord (landlady).

Wirtschaft (pl -en) die (Ökonomie) economy; (Lokal) pub.

wirtschaftlich adj (ökonomisch) economic.

Wirtschaftspolitik die economic policy.

Wirtshaus (pl -häuser) das pub, often with accommodation.

Wirtsleute pl (von Lokal) landlord and landlady.

Wirtsstube (pl -n) die bar.

Wischblatt (pl -blätter) das wiper blade.

wischen ◆ vt (Boden, Mund) to wipe; (Schmutz) to wipe away. ◆ vi (putzen) to clean.

wissen (präs **weiß**, prät **wußte**, pp **gewußt**) ◆ vt to know. ◆ vi: **von etw ~** to know about sthg; **etw ~ über** (+A) to know sthg about; **ich weiß!** I know!; **weißt du was?** you know what?

Wissenschaft (*pl* -en) *die* science.

Wissenschaftler, -in (*mpl* -) *der, die* scientist.

wissenswert *adj* worth knowing.

Witterung *die* (*Wetter*) weather.

Witwe (*pl* -n) *die* widow.

Witwer (*pl* -) *der* widower.

Witz (*pl* -e) *der* joke.

WM *abk* = **Weltmeisterschaft**.

wo *adv & pron* where; **von ~ kam das Geräusch?** where did that noise come from?

woanders *adv* somewhere else.

woandershin *adv* somewhere else.

wob *prät* → **weben**.

wobei *pron* (*als Frage*): **~ ist er erwischt worden?** what was he caught doing?

Woche (*pl* -n) *die* week; **diese/ letzte/nächste ~** this/last/next week; **dreimal die ~** three times a week.

Wochenende (*pl* -n) *das* weekend; **schönes ~!** have a good weekend!

Wochenendtarif (*pl* -e) *der* week-end rate.

Wochenkarte (*pl* -n) *die* weekly season ticket.

wochenlang *adj & adv* for weeks.

Wochenmarkt (*pl* -märkte) *der* weekly market.

Wochentag (*pl* -e) *der* weekday.

wochentags *adv* on weekdays.

wöchentlich *adj & adv* weekly.

Wodka (*pl* -s) *der* vodka.

wodurch *pron* (*als Frage*): **~ unterscheiden sich die beiden?** what is the difference between the two?

wofür *pron* (*als Frage*) for what; **~ hast du das Geld ausgegeben?** what did you spend the money on?; **~ brauchst du das?** what do you need that for?

wog *prät* → **wiegen**.

Woge (*pl* -n) *die* (*im Wasser*) breaker.

wogegen *pron* (*als Frage*) against what.

woher *pron* from where; **~ kommen Sie?** where do you come from?

wohin *pron* where.

wohl (*komp* **wohler** ODER **besser**, *superl* **am wohlsten** ODER **am besten**) *adv* well; (*wahrscheinlich*) probably; **sich ~ fühlen** (*gesund*) to feel well; (*angenehm*) to feel at home.

Wohl *das*: **auf Ihr ~!** your good health!; **zum ~!** cheers!

Wohlstand *der* affluence.

wohltuend *adj* pleasant.

Wohnanlage (*pl* -n) *die* housing estate.

Wohnblock (*pl* -blöcke) *der* block of flats (Br), apartment house (Am).

wohnen *vi* (*dauerhaft*) to live; (*vorübergehend*) to stay; **wo ~ Sie?** (*dauerhaft*) where do you live?; (*vorübergehend*) where are you staying?

Wohngemeinschaft (*pl* -en) *die*: **in einer ~ leben** to share a flat/house.

wohnhaft *adj* (*amt*): **~ in ...** resident at ...

Wohnhaus (*pl* -häuser) *das* house.

Wohnmobil (*pl* -e) *das* camper (van) (Br), RV (Am).

Wohnort (*pl* -e) *der* place of residence.

Wohnsitz (*pl* -e) *der* (*amt*) place of residence.

Wohnung (*pl* -en) *die* flat (Br), apartment (Am).

Wohnwagen (*pl* -) *der* caravan (Br), trailer (Am).

Wohnzimmer (*pl* -) *das* living room.

Wolf (*pl* **Wölfe**) *der* (*Tier*) wolf.

Wolke (*pl* -n) *die* cloud.

Wolkenbruch (*pl* -brüche) *der* cloudburst.

Wolkenkratzer (*pl* -) *der* skyscraper.

wolkenlos *adj* cloudless.

wolkig *adj* cloudy.

Wolldecke (*pl* -n) *die* blanket.

Wolle *die* wool.

wollen (*präs* **will**, *prät* **wollte**, *pp* **gewollt** ODER **wollen**) ◆ *aux* (*pp* **wollen**) (*Ausdruck einer Absicht*): **er will anrufen** he wants to make a call; **ich wollte gerade gehen** I was just about to go; **ich wollte, das wäre schon vorbei!** I wish it was over!; **diese Entscheidung will überlegt sein** this decision needs to be thought about. ◆ *vi* (*pp* **gewollt**) **1.** (*Ausdruck einer Absicht*): **wie du willst!** as you like!; **das Kind will nicht** the child doesn't want to. **2.** (*an einen Ort*) to want to go; **sie will nach Hause** she wants to go home. ◆ *vt* (*pp* **gewollt**) (*haben wollen*) to want; **ich will ein Eis** I want an ice-cream; **ich will, daß du gehst** I want you to go.

Wollstoff (*pl* -e) *der* wool.

Wollwaschmittel (*pl* -) *das* detergent for woollens.

womit *pron* (*als Frage*) with what; **~ habe ich das verdient?** what did I do to deserve that?

wonach *pron* (*als Frage*) for what; **~ suchst du?** what are you looking for?

woran *pron* (*als Frage*) on what; **~ denkst du?** what are you thinking about?

worauf *pron* (*als Frage*) on what; **~ wartest du?** what are you waiting for?

woraus *pron* (*als Frage*) from what; **~ ist das?** what is it made of?

worin *pron* (*als Frage*) in what; **~ besteht der Unterschied?** what's the difference?

Workshop (*pl* -s) *der* workshop.

World Wide Web *das*: **das ~** the World Wide Web.

Wort¹ (*pl* **Wörter**) *das* (*sprachliche Einheit*) word.

Wort² (*pl* -e) *das* (*Äußerung, Zusage*) word.

Wörterbuch (*pl* -bücher) *das* dictionary.

wörtlich *adj* (*Wiederholung*) word-for-word; **~e Rede** direct speech.

wortlos *adj* silent.

worüber *pron* (*als Frage*) about what; **~ lachst du?** what are you laughing about?

worum *pron* (*als Frage*) about what; **~ geht es?** what's it about?

worunter *pron* (*als Frage*) under what; **~ hast du es eingeordnet?** what did you file it under?

wovon *pron* (*als Frage*) from what; **~ hast du geträumt?** what did you dream about?

wovor *pron* (*als Frage*) of what; **~ hast du Angst?** what are you frightened of?

wozu *pron* (*als Frage*) why.

WSV *abk* = **Winterschlußverkauf**.

Wucherpreis (*pl* -e) *der* extortionate price.

wuchs *prät* → **wachsen**.

wühlen *vi* to rummage.

Wühltisch (*pl* -e) *der* bargain counter.

wund *adj* sore.

Wunde (*pl* -n) *die* wound.

wunderbar *adj* wonderful.

wundern *vt* to amaze; **es wundert mich** I'm amazed. ▶ **sich wundern** *ref* to be amazed.

wunderschön *adj* beautiful.

Wundstarrkrampf *der* tetanus.

Wunsch (*pl* **Wünsche**) *der* wish; **auf ~** on request; **nach ~** as desired; **(sonst) noch einen ~?** anything else? ▶ **Wünsche** *pl* wishes; **mit den besten Wünschen von** with best wishes from.

wünschen *vt* to wish; **jm etw ~** to wish sb sthg; **sich** (D) **etw ~** to want sthg; **was ~ Sie?** can I help you?

wünschenswert *adj* desirable.

wurde *prät* → **werden**.

Wurf (*pl* **Würfe**) *der* (*Werfen*) throw.

Würfel (*pl* -) *der* (*zum Spielen*) dice; (*Form*) cube.

würfeln ◆ *vt* (*Fleisch, Brot*) to dice; (*Zahl*) to throw. ◆ *vi* (*beim Spielen*) to throw the dice.

Würfelspiel (*pl* **-e**) *das* dice game.
Würfelzucker *der* sugar cubes (*pl*).
Wurm (*pl* **Würmer**) *der* (Tier) worm.
Wurst (*pl* **Würste**) *die* sausage.

WURST

Sausages are extremely popular in Germany and there is a wide variety, with every region having its own speciality. Some sausages are always eaten hot - they may be fried, grilled or boiled. These include 'Bratwurst', 'Bockwurst', 'Wiener' and 'Frankfurter'. Others, such as 'Leberwurst' (liver sausage) and 'Blutwurst' (black pudding), can be served hot or cold. Cold meats such as salami are also popular and are eaten with bread for supper or even for breakfast.

Wurstbraterei (*pl* **-en**) *die* hot dog stand.
Würstchen (*pl* **-**) *das* sausage.
Wurstwaren *pl* sausages and cold meats.
Würze (*pl* **-n**) *die* (Gewürz) spice.
Wurzel (*pl* **-n**) *die* root.
würzen *vt* (Speisen) to season.
würzig *adj* spicy.
Würzmischung (*pl* **-en**) *die* spice mix.
wusch *prät* → **waschen**.
wußte *prät* → **wissen**.
wüst *adj* (chaotisch) chaotic; (wild) wild.
Wüste (*pl* **-n**) *die* desert.
Wut *die* rage.
wütend *adj* (Person) furious; **~ sein auf** (+A) to be furious with; **~ sein über** (+A) to be furious about.

x-beliebig *adj* (fam) any (old).
x-mal *adv* (fam) countless times.

Yacht (*pl* **-en**) *die* yacht.
Yachthafen (*pl* **-häfen**) *der* marina.
Yoga *das* yoga.

zäh ◆ *adj* tough. ◆ *adv*: **~ fließender Verkehr** slow-moving traffic.
Zahl (*pl* **-en**) *die* number; (Ziffer) figure; **in den roten/schwarzen ~en sein** to be in the red/black.
zahlbar *adj* payable.
zahlen *vt* & *vi* to pay; **ich zahle den Wein** I'll pay for the wine; **~, bitte!** the bill please! (Br), the check please! (Am).
zählen *vt* & *vi* to count; **~ zu** (gehören) to be among.
Zähler (*pl* **-**) *der* (Gerät) meter.
Zahlgrenze (*pl* **-n**) *die* fare stage.
Zahlkarte (*pl* **-n**) *die* money transfer form.
zahlreich *adj* numerous.
Zahlschein (*pl* **-e**) *der* payment slip.

Zahlung (*pl* -en) *die* payment.

Zählung (*pl* -en) *die* census.

Zahlungsanweisung (*pl* -en) *die* money transfer order.

zahm *adj* (Tier) tame.

Zahn (*pl* **Zähne**) *der* tooth; **sich** (D) **die Zähne putzen** to clean one's teeth; **die dritten Zähne** (Gebiß) false teeth.

Zahnarzt, -ärztin (*mpl* -ärzte) *der, die* dentist.

Zahnbürste (*pl* -n) *die* toothbrush.

Zahncreme (*pl* -s) *die* toothpaste.

Zahnersatz *der* false teeth (*pl*).

Zahnfleisch *das* gums (*pl*).

Zahnfleischbluten *das* bleeding gums (*pl*).

Zahnfüllung (*pl* -en) *die* filling.

Zahnklammer (*pl* -n) *die* brace.

Zahnpasta (*pl* -pasten) *die* toothpaste.

Zahnradbahn (*pl* -en) *die* cog railway.

Zahnschmerzen *pl* toothache (*sg*).

Zahnseide (*pl* -n) *die* dental floss.

Zahnspange (*pl* -n) *die* brace.

Zahnstocher (*pl* -) *der* toothpick.

Zange (*pl* -n) *die* (Werkzeug) pliers (*pl*).

zanken *vi* (fam) to quarrel. ▶ **sich zanken** *ref* (fam) to have a row.

Zäpfchen (*pl* -) *das* (Medikament) suppository.

zapfen *vt* to draw.

Zapfsäule (*pl* -n) *die* petrol pump.

zart *adj* (Fleisch, Gemüse) tender; (Haut) smooth.

zartbitter *adj* (Schokolade) dark.

zärtlich *adj* (Berührung) affectionate.

Zauberer (*pl* -) *der* (Zauberkünstler) magician.

zauberhaft ◆ *adj* (sehr schön) enchanting. ◆ *adv* enchantingly.

Zauberin (*pl* -nen) *die* (Zauberkünstlerin) magician.

Zauberkünstler, -in (*mpl* -) *der, die* magician.

zaubern *vi* (Zauberer) to do magic.

Zaun (*pl* **Zäune**) *der* fence.

z.B. (abk für zum Beispiel) e.g.

Zebrastreifen (*pl* -) *der* zebra crossing (Br), crosswalk (Am).

Zeche (*pl* -n) *die* (Bergwerk) pit; (fam: Rechnung) tab.

Zechtour (*pl* -en) *die* (fam) pub crawl.

Zecke (*pl* -n) *die* tick.

Zeh (*pl* -en) *der* toe.

Zehe (*pl* -n) *die* (Zeh) toe; (von Knoblauch) clove.

Zehennagel (*pl* -nägel) *der* toe nail.

zehn *num* ten, → **sechs**.

Zehner (*pl* -) *der* (fam: Geldschein) ten mark note.

Zehnerkarte (*pl* -n) *die* book of ten tickets.

zehnmal *adv* ten times.

Zehnmarkschein (*pl* -e) *der* ten mark note.

zehntausend *num* ten thousand.

zehnte, -r, -s *adj* tenth, → **sechste**.

Zehntel (*pl* -) *das* tenth.

Zehntelsekunde (*pl* -n) *die* tenth of a second.

Zeichen (*pl* -) *das* sign; **jm ein ~ geben** to give sb a signal.

Zeichenblock (*pl* -blöcke) *der* drawing pad.

Zeichenerklärung (*pl* -en) *die* key.

Zeichensetzung *die* punctuation.

Zeichensprache (*pl* -n) *die* sign language.

Zeichentrickfilm (*pl* -e) *der* cartoon.

zeichnen *vt & vi* to draw.

Zeichnung (*pl* -en) *die* (Bild) drawing.

zeigen ◆ *vt* to show; (vorführen) to demonstrate. ◆ *vi*: ~ **auf** (+A) to point at; **jm etw ~** to show sb sthg. ▶ **sich zeigen** *ref* (sich herausstellen) to emerge; (erscheinen) to show o.s.

Zeiger (pl -) der hand.

Zeile (pl -n) die (von Text) line.

Zeit (pl -en) die time; (GRAMM) tense; sich (D) ~ lassen to take one's time; ~ haben to be free; zur ~ at the moment; von ~ zu ~ from time to time.

Zeitansage (pl -n) die speaking clock.

Zeitarbeit die temporary work.

Zeitersparnis die time-saving.

Zeitgeist der spirit of the times.

zeitig adj & adv early.

zeitlich adj (Reihenfolge) chronological.

Zeitlupe die slow motion.

Zeitplan (pl -pläne) der timetable.

Zeitpunkt (pl -e) der point in time.

Zeitraum (pl -räume) der period.

Zeitschrift (pl -en) die (illustrierte) magazine; (literaturwissenschaftliche) periodical.

Zeitung (pl -en) die newspaper.

Zeitungsannonce (pl -n) die newspaper advertisement.

Zeitungsartikel (pl -) der newspaper article.

Zeitungskiosk (pl -e) der newspaper kiosk.

Zeitunterschied (pl -e) der time difference.

Zeitverschiebung (pl -en) die (Unterschied) time difference.

zeitweise adv (gelegentlich) occasionally; (vorübergehend) temporarily.

Zeitzone (pl -n) die time zone.

Zelle (pl -n) die (biologisch) cell.

Zellophan das cellophane®.

Zellstoff der cellulose.

Zelt (pl -e) das tent.

zelten vi to camp.

Zeltlager (pl -) das campsite.

Zeltplane (pl -n) die tarpaulin.

Zeltplatz (pl -plätze) der campsite.

Zeltstange (pl -n) die tent pole.

Zentimeter (pl -) der centimetre.

Zentimetermaß (pl -e) das tape measure.

Zentner (pl -) der unit of measurement, equivalent to 50 kg in Germany and 100 kg in Austria and Switzerland.

zentral adj central.

Zentrale (pl -n) die (Telefonzentrale) switchboard; (übergeordnete Stelle) headquarters (pl).

Zentralheizung (pl -en) die central heating.

Zentralverriegelung (pl -en) die central locking.

Zentrum (pl Zentren) das centre.

zerbrechen (präs zerbricht, prät zerbrach, pp zerbrochen) vi ist & vt hat to smash.

zerbrechlich adj (Gegenstand) fragile.

Zeremonie (pl -en) die ceremony.

zerkleinern vt to cut up.

zerknautscht adj scrunched up.

zerkratzen vt to scratch.

zerlassen adj (Butter) to melt.

zerlegen vt (Möbel) to take apart; (Braten) to carve.

zerreißen (prät zerriß, pp zerrissen) ◆ vt hat (Brief, Stoff) to tear up. ◆ vi ist to tear.

zerren vt (ziehen) to drag.

Zerrung (pl -en) die pulled muscle.

zerschneiden (prät zerschnitt, pp zerschnitten) vt (in Stücke) to cut up.

Zerstäuber (pl -) der atomizer.

zerstechen (präs zersticht, prät zerstach, pp zerstochen) vt (Luftballon, Reifen) to puncture; (Sbj: Mücken) to to bite.

zerstören vt to destroy.

Zerstörung (pl -en) die destruction.

zerstreut adj distracted.

zerteilen vt to cut up.

Zertifikat (pl -e) das certificate.

Zettel (pl -) der note.

Zeug das (fam: Sachen) stuff; (Kleidung) gear; dummes ~ (fam) rubbish.

Zeuge (pl -n) der witness.

Zeugin (*pl* **-nen**) *die* witness.

Zeugnis (*pl* **-se**) *das* (*von Schüler*) report; (*von Prüfung*) certificate; (*von Arbeitgeber*) reference.

Zickzack *der*: im ~ fahren to zigzag.

Ziege (*pl* **-n**) *die* (*Tier*) goat.

Ziegenkäse *der* goat's cheese.

Ziegenleder *das* goatskin.

ziehen (*prät* **zog**, *pp* **gezogen**) ◆ *vt* hat (*bewegen, betätigen*) to pull; (*herausziehen*) to pull out; (*auslosen*) to draw. ◆ *vi ist* (*umziehen*) to move. ◆ *vi* hat (*bewegen*) to pull; (*Tee*) to brew. ◆ *vimp*: es zieht there's a draught; ~ an (+D) (*bewegen*) to pull. ▶ **sich ziehen** *ref* (*fam*: *zeitlich*) to drag on.

Ziehung (*pl* **-en**) *die* draw.

Ziel (*pl* **-e**) *das* destination; (SPORT) finish; (*Zweck*) goal.

Zielbahnhof (*pl* **-bahnhöfe**) *der* destination.

zielen *vi* (*mit Waffe, Ball*) to aim.

Zielscheibe (*pl* **-n**) *die* target.

ziemlich *adv* (*relativ*) quite; (*fast*) almost; ~ viel quite a lot.

zierlich *adj* (*Person*) petite.

Ziffer (*pl* **-n**) *die* (*Zahlensymbol*) figure.

Zifferblatt (*pl* **-blätter**) *das* face.

zig *num* (*fam*) umpteen.

Zigarette (*pl* **-n**) *die* cigarette.

Zigarettenautomat (*pl* **-en**) *der* cigarette machine.

Zigarettenpapier *das* cigarette paper.

Zigarettenschachtel (*pl* **-n**) *die* cigarette packet.

Zigarettentabak (*pl* **-e**) *der* tobacco.

Zigarillo (*pl* **-s**) *der* cigarillo.

Zigarre (*pl* **-n**) *die* cigar.

Zigeuner, -in (*mpl* **-**) *der, die* gypsy.

Zimmer (*pl* **-**) *das* room; '~ frei' 'vacancies'; ~ mit Bad room with en suite bathroom; ~ mit Frühstück bed and breakfast.

Zimmerkellner (*pl* **-**) *der* room-service waiter.

Zimmermädchen (*pl* **-**) *das* chambermaid.

Zimmernachweis (*pl* **-e**) *der* accommodation service.

Zimmerpflanze (*pl* **-n**) *die* house plant.

Zimmerschlüssel (*pl* **-**) *der* room key.

Zimmerservice *der* room service.

Zimt *der* cinnamon.

Zinn *das* (*Metall*) tin.

Zins (*pl* **-en**) *der* interest.

zinslos *adj* interest-free.

Zinssatz (*pl* **-sätze**) *der* interest rate.

zirka *adv* circa.

Zirkel (*pl* **-**) *der* (*Gerät*) compasses (*pl*).

Zirkus (*pl* **-se**) *der* (*Betrieb*) circus; (*fam*: *Aufregung*) palaver.

zischen *vi* (*Geräusch*) to hiss.

Zitat (*pl* **-e**) *das* quote.

zitieren *vt & vi* to quote.

Zitronat *das* candied lemon peel.

Zitrone (*pl* **-n**) *die* lemon.

Zitronensaft (*pl* **-säfte**) *der* lemon juice.

Zitruspresse (*pl* **-n**) *die* lemon squeezer.

zittern *vi* (*vibrieren*) to tremble.

zivil *adj* (*nicht militärisch*) civil.

Zivildienst *der* community work undertaken by men who choose not to do military service.

Zivilisation (*pl* **-en**) *die* civilization.

ZOB (*abk für Zentraler Omnibusbahnhof*) *central bus station*.

zog *prät* → **ziehen**.

zögern *vi* to hesitate.

Zoll (*pl* **Zölle**) *der* (*Abgabe*) duty; (*Behörde*) customs (*pl*).

Zollabfertigung *die* customs clearance.

Zollamt (*pl* **-ämter**) *das* customs office.

Zollbeamte (*pl* **-n**) *der* customs officer.

Zollbeamtin (*pl* -nen) *die* customs officer.

Zollerklärung (*pl* -en) *die* customs declaration.

zollfrei *adj* duty-free.

Zollgebühren *pl* duty (*sg*).

Zollkontrolle (*pl* -n) *die* customs check.

Zöllner, -in (*mpl* -) *der, die* customs officer.

zollpflichtig *adj* liable for duty.

Zollschranke (*pl* -n) *die* customs barrier.

Zollstock (*pl* -stöcke) *der* ruler.

Zone (*pl* -n) *die* (*Gebiet*) zone.

Zoo (*pl* -s) *der* zoo.

zoologische Garten (*pl* Gärten) *der* zoo.

Zopf (*pl* Zöpfe) *der* plait (Br), braid (Am).

Zopfspange (*pl* -n) *die* hair slide (Br), barrette (Am).

Zorn *der* anger.

zornig ♦ *adj* angry. ♦ *adv* angrily.

zu ♦ *präp* (+D) **1.** (*an einen Ort*) to; **~r Post gehen** to go to the post office; **~m Frisör gehen** to go to the hairdresser's; **~ Hause** (to) home. **2.** (*Angabe des Mittels*): **~ Fuß** on foot; **~ Fuß gehen** to walk. **3.** (*zeitlich*) at; **~ Ostern/Weihnachten** at Easter/Christmas. **4.** (*mit*) with; **weiße Socken ~m Anzug tragen** to wear white socks with a suit. **5.** (*Angabe des Grunds*) for; **~m Spaß** for fun; **alles Gute ~m Geburtstag!** best wishes on your birthday! **6.** (*Mengenangabe*): **Säcke ~ 50 kg** 50 kg bags. **7.** (*Angabe des Produkts*) into; **~ Eis werden** to turn into ice. **8.** (SPORT): **eins ~ null** one-nil. ♦ *adv* **1.** (*mit Adjektiv*) too; **~ viel** too many. **2.** (*fam: zumachen*): **Tür ~!** shut the door! ♦ *konj* (*mit Infinitiv*) to; **es fängt an ~ schneien** it's starting to snow; **~ verkaufen** for sale.

Zubehör (*pl* -e) *das* accessories (*pl*).

zu|bereiten *vt* to prepare.

Zubereitung (*pl* -en) *die* preparation.

zu|binden *vt unr* to fasten.

Zubringer (*pl* -) *der* (*Straße*) slip road (Br), ramp (Am).

Zucchini (*pl* -s) *die* courgette (Br), zucchini (Am).

züchten *vt* to breed.

Züchter, -in (*mpl* -) *der, die* breeder.

zucken *vi* (*Person, Muskel*) to twitch.

Zucker *der* sugar.

Zuckerdose (*pl* -n) *die* sugar bowl.

zuckerkrank *adj* diabetic.

zuckern *vt* to sweeten.

Zuckerwatte *die* candyfloss.

Zuckerzusatz *der*: **ohne ~** no added sugar.

zu|decken *vt* (*Person*) to cover up; (*Gegenstand*) to cover. ▶ **sich zudecken** *ref* to cover o.s. up.

zu|drehen *vt* (*Wasserhahn*) to turn off.

zueinander *adv* (*sprechen*) to each other; **sie passen gut ~** they go well together.

zuerst *adv* (*als erster*) first; (*am Anfang*) at first.

Zufahrt (*pl* -en) *die* access.

Zufahrtsstraße (*pl* -n) *die* access road.

Zufall (*pl* Zufälle) *der* coincidence.

zufällig ♦ *adj* chance. ♦ *adv* by chance.

zufrieden *adj* satisfied; **~ sein mit** to be satisfied with.

zufriedenstellend *adj* satisfactory.

Zug (*pl* Züge) *der* (*Eisenbahn*) train; (*Menschenmenge*) procession; (*Zugluft*) draught; (*mit Spielfigur*) move; (*Geste*) gesture; **mit dem ~ fahren** to go by train.

Zugabe (*pl* -n) *die* (*bei Konzert*) encore.

Zugabteil (*pl* -e) *das* compartment.

Zugang (*pl* -gänge) *der* access.

Zugauskunft (*pl* -auskünfte) *die* train information.

Zugbegleiter (pl -) der (Fahrplan-auszug) timetable.

Zugbrücke (pl -n) die drawbridge.

zu|geben vt unr (gestehen) to admit; (hinzutun) to add.

zu|gehen vi unr ist (sich schließen) to close; ~ **auf** (+A) (gehen) to approach.

Zügel (pl -) der reins (pl).

Zuger Kirschtorte (pl -n) die (Schweiz) buttercream cake with a middle layer of sponge soaked in kirsch and a top and bottom layer of nut meringue.

Zugführer, -in (mpl -) der, die senior conductor.

zugig adj draughty.

zügig ◆ adj rapid. ◆ adv rapidly.

Zugluft die draught.

Zugpersonal das train crew.

zu|greifen vi unr: **greifen Sie zu!** help yourself!

Zugrestaurant (pl -s) das restaurant car.

zugrunde adv: ~ **gehen** to perish.

Zugschaffner, -in (mpl -) der, die ticket inspector.

Zugunglück (pl -e) das train crash.

zugunsten präp (+G) in favour of.

Zugverbindung (pl -en) die (train) connection.

zu|haben vi unr (fam) to be shut.

Zuhause das home.

zu|hören vi (+D) to listen; **jm** ~ to listen to sb.

Zuhörer, -in (mpl -) der, die listener.

zu|kleben vt (Loch) to glue; (Brief) to seal.

zu|kommen vi unr ist: ~ **auf** (+A) (Person, Fahrzeug) to approach.

zu|kriegen vt (fam): **ich krieg' die Tür nicht zu** the door won't shut.

Zukunft die future.

zu|lassen vt unr (erlauben) to allow; (Auto) to license; (fam: nicht öffnen): **laß das Paket bis Weihnachten zu!** don't open the parcel till Christmas!

zulässig adj permissible; **~e**

Höchstgeschwindigkeit maximum speed limit; **~es Gesamtgewicht** maximum weight limit.

Zulassung (pl -en) die authorization.

zu|laufen vi unr ist (Tier): **der Hund ist uns zugelaufen** the dog adopted us; ~ **auf** (+A) (Person) to run towards.

zuletzt adv (als letzter) lastly; (am Ende) in the end, finally; (fam: das letzte Mal): ~ **war ich vor 3 Jahren hier** I was last here three years ago.

zuliebe präp (+D): **ihr** ~ for her sake.

zum präp = zu + dem.

zu|machen vt & vi to close.

zu|muten vt: **jm etw** ~ to expect sthg of sb.

zunächst adv (als erster) first; (am Anfang) at first.

Zuname (pl -n) der surname.

zünden vi (Motor) to fire.

Zündholz (pl -hölzer) das match.

Zündkerze (pl -n) die spark plug.

Zündschloß (pl -schlösser) das ignition.

Zündschlüssel (pl -) der ignition key.

Zündung (pl -en) die (AUTO) ignition.

zunehmen vi unr to increase; (dicker werden) to put on weight.

Zunge (pl -n) die tongue.

zupfen ◆ vi (ziehen) to tug. ◆ vt (herausziehen) to pick; (Augenbrauen) to pluck.

zur präp = zu + der.

zurecht|kommen vi unr ist to get on.

Zürich nt Zürich.

zurück adv back.

zurück|bekommen vt unr to get back.

zurück|bringen vt unr to bring back.

zurück|erstatten vt to refund.

zurück|fahren vi unr ist & vt unr hat

(an Ausgangspunkt) to drive back; (rückwärts) to back away.

zurück|führen ◆ vt (begründen) to attribute. ◆ vi (Weg, Straße) to lead back.

zurück|geben vt unr to give back; **jm etw ~** to give sb sthg back.

zurück|gehen vi unr ist (zum Ausgangspunkt) to go back; (rückwärts) to retreat; (Anzahl, Häufigkeit) to fall.

zurück|halten vt unr (festhalten) to hold back. ▶ **sich zurückhalten** ref to restrain o.s.

zurück|holen vt to bring back.

zurück|kehren vi ist (fml) to return.

zurück|kommen vi unr ist to come back.

zurück|lassen vt unr to leave behind.

zurück|legen vt (wieder hinlegen) to put back; (reservieren) to put aside; (Strecke) to cover; (Kopf) to lay back; **etw ~ lassen** (reservieren) to have sthg put aside. ▶ **sich zurücklegen** ref to lie back.

zurück|nehmen vt unr to take back.

zurück|rufen vt unr & vi to call back.

zurück|schicken vt to send back.

zurück|stellen vt to put back.

zurück|treten vi unr ist (rückwärts) to step back; (Präsident, Vorstand) to resign; **bitte ~!** stand back, please!

zurück|verlangen vt to demand back.

zurück|zahlen vt (Geld) to pay back.

Zusage (pl -n) die (auf Einladung, Bewerbung) acceptance.

zu|sagen vt (bei Einladung) to accept.

zusammen adv together; (insgesamt) altogether.

Zusammenarbeit die collaboration.

zusammen|brechen vi unr ist (Person) to collapse; (psychisch,

Verkehr) to break down.

zusammen|fassen vt (Text) to summarize.

Zusammenfassung (pl -en) die summary.

zusammen|gehören vt to belong together.

zusammen|halten vi unr (Personen) to stick together.

Zusammenhang (pl -hänge) der context.

zusammenhängend adj (Text) coherent.

zusammenhanglos adj incoherent.

zusammenklappbar adj collapsible.

zusammen|knüllen vt to scrunch up.

Zusammenkunft (pl -künfte) die gathering.

zusammen|legen ◆ vt (Gruppen, Termine) to group together; (falten) to fold up. ◆ vi (bezahlen) to club together.

zusammen|nehmen: sich zusammennehmen ref unr to pull o.s. together.

zusammen|passen vi (Personen) to be well suited; (Einzelteile) to fit together.

zusammen|rechnen vt to add up.

Zusammensetzung (pl -en) die composition.

Zusammenstoß (pl -stöße) der crash.

zusammen|stoßen vi unr ist (Fahrzeuge) to crash.

zusammen|wachsen vi unr ist to grow together; (Knochen) to knit.

zusammen|zählen vt to add up.

zusammen|ziehen ◆ vt unr hat (addieren) to add up. ◆ vi unr ist (in Wohnung) to move in together.

zusammen|zucken vi ist to jump.

Zusatz (pl Zusätze) der (Substanz) additive.

Zusatzgerät (pl -e) das attachment.

zusätzlich ♦ *adj* extra. ♦ *adv* in addition.

Zusatzzahl (*pl* **-en**) *die* bonus number.

zu|schauen *vi* to watch.

Zuschauer, -in (*mpl* **-**) *der, die* (*von Fernsehen*) viewer; (*von Sport*) spectator.

Zuschauertribüne (*pl* **-n**) *die* stands (*pl*).

zu|schicken *vt* to send.

Zuschlag (*pl* **Zuschläge**) *der* supplement; **~ erforderlich** supplement required.

zuschlagpflichtig *adj* subject to a supplement.

zu|schließen *vt unr* to lock.

Zuschuß (*pl* **Zuschüsse**) *der* grant.

zu|sehen *vi unr* (*zuschauen*) to watch.

zu|sein *vi unr ist* to be closed.

zu|sichern *vt* to assure.

Zustand (*pl* **Zustände**) *der* state, condition. ▶ **Zustände** *pl* situation (*sg*).

zuständig *adj* responsible; **~ sein für** to be responsible for.

zu|steigen *vi unr ist* to get on; **noch jemand zugestiegen?** tickets, please.

Zustellung (*pl* **-en**) *die* (*von Post*) delivery.

zu|stimmen *vi* (+D) to agree; **er stimmte dem Plan zu** he agreed to the plan.

Zustimmung *die* agreement.

zu|stoßen *vi unr ist*: **was ist ihm zugestoßen?** what happened to him?

Zutat (*pl* **-en**) *die* ingredient.

zu|teilen *vt* (*Ration*) to allocate.

zu|trauen *vt*: **jm etw ~** to think sb capable of sthg.

zu|treffen *vi unr* to apply; **'Zutreffendes bitte ankreuzen'** 'tick as applicable'.

Zutritt *der* entry.

zuverlässig *adj* reliable.

zuviel *pron* too much.

Zuwachs *der* growth.

zu|weisen *vt unr* to allocate.

zuwenig *pron* too little.

zu|winken *vi* (+D): **jm ~** to wave to sb.

zu|zahlen *vt*: **5 Mark ~** to pay another 5 marks.

zuzüglich *präp* (+G or D) plus.

zwang *prät* → **zwingen**.

Zwang (*pl* **Zwänge**) *der* force.

zwanglos *adj* relaxed.

zwanzig *num* twenty, → **sechs**.

Zwanziger (*pl* **-**) *der* (*Person*) someone in their twenties; (*Geld*) twenty mark note.

Zwanzigmarkschein (*pl* **-e**) *der* twenty mark note.

zwanzigste, -r, -s *adj* twentieth; **das ~ Jahrhundert** the twentieth century.

zwar *adv*: **und ~** (*genauer*) to be exact; **das ist ~ schön, aber viel zu teuer** it is nice but far too expensive.

Zweck (*pl* **-e**) *der* purpose; **es hat keinen ~** there's no point.

zwecklos *adj* pointless.

zweckmäßig *adj* practical.

zwei *num* two, → **sechs**.

Zweibettabteil (*pl* **-e**) *das* compartment with two beds.

Zweibettkabine (*pl* **-n**) *die* cabin with two beds.

Zweibettzimmer (*pl* **-**) *das* twin room.

zweifach *adj* twice.

Zweifel (*pl* **-**) *der* doubt; **ohne ~** without doubt; **~ haben an** (+D) to doubt.

zweifellos *adv* doubtless.

zweifeln *vi* to doubt; **an etw** (D) **~** to doubt sthg.

Zweig (*pl* **-e**) *der* branch.

Zweigstelle (*pl* **-n**) *die* branch.

zweihundert *num* two hundred.

Zweihundertmarkschein (*pl* **-e**) *der* two hundred mark note.

zweimal *adv* twice.

Zweimarkstück (*pl* **-stücke**) *das* two mark coin.

Zweirad (*pl* **-räder**) *das* two-wheeled vehicle.

zweisprachig *adj* bilingual.

zweispurig *adj* two-lane.

zweit *adv*: **sie waren nur zu ~** there were only two of them.

Zweitakter (*pl* -) *der* two-stroke engine.

Zweitakter-Gemisch *das* two-stroke mixture.

zweitbeste, -r, -s *adj* second best.

zweite, -r, -s *adj* second, → **sechs**.

zweiteilig *adj* two-part.

zweitens *adv* secondly.

Zwerchfell (*pl* -e) *das* diaphragm.

Zwerg (*pl* -e) *der* dwarf.

Zwetschge (*pl* -n) *die* (*Frucht*) plum.

Zwetschgendatschi (*pl* -) *der* (*Süddt*) plum slice.

Zwieback (*pl* **Zwiebäcke**) *der* rusk.

Zwiebel (*pl* -n) *die* (*Gemüse*) onion.

Zwiebelsuppe (*pl* -n) *die* onion soup.

Zwilling (*pl* -e) *der* (*Geschwister*) twin; (*Sternzeichen*) Gemini.

zwingen (*prät* **zwang**, *pp* **gezwungen**) *vt* to force. ▶ **sich zwingen** *ref* to force o.s.

zwinkern *vi* to wink.

Zwirn *der* thread.

zwischen *präp* (+A,D) between; (*in Menge*) among.

zwischendurch *adv* (*zeitlich*) every now and then.

Zwischenfall (*pl* **-fälle**) *der* incident.

Zwischenlandung (*pl* **-en**) *die* short stopover.

Zwischenraum (*pl* **-räume**) *der* gap.

Zwischenstecker (*pl* -) *der* adapter.

Zwischenstop (*pl* **-s**) *der* stop.

Zwischensumme (*pl* **-n**) *die* subtotal.

Zwischenzeit *die*: **in der ~** in the meantime.

zwölf *num* twelve, → **sechs**.

zynisch *adj* cynical.

a [stressed eɪ, unstressed ə] indefinite article **1.** (gen) ein (eine); **a woman** eine Frau; **a restaurant** ein Restaurant; **a friend** ein Freund (eine Freundin); **an apple** ein Apfel; **I'm a doctor** ich bin Arzt. **2.** (instead of the number one) ein (eine); **a hundred** hundert; **a hundred and twenty** einhundertzwanzig; **for a week** eine Woche lang. **3.** (in prices, ratios) pro; **£2 a kilo** 2 Pfund pro Kilo.

AA n (Br: abbr of Automobile Association) ≃ ADAC der.

aback [ə'bæk] adv: **to be taken ~** verblüfft sein.

abandon [ə'bændən] vt (plan) aufgeben; (place, person) verlassen.

abattoir ['æbətwɑːʳ] n Schlachthof der.

abbey ['æbɪ] n Abtei die.

abbreviation [ə,briːvɪ'eɪʃn] n Abkürzung die.

abdomen ['æbdəmən] n Unterleib der.

abide [ə'baɪd] vt: **I can't ~ him** ich kann ihn nicht ausstehen. ▶ **abide by** vt fus (rule, law) befolgen.

ability [ə'bɪlətɪ] n Fähigkeit die.

able ['eɪbl] adj fähig; **to be ~ to do sthg** etw tun können.

abnormal [æb'nɔːml] adj anormal.

aboard [ə'bɔːd] adv & prep an Bord (+G).

abode [ə'bəud] n (fml) Wohnsitz der.

abolish [ə'bɒlɪʃ] vt ab|schaffen.

aborigine [,æbə'rɪdʒənɪ] n Ureinwohner der.

abort [ə'bɔːt] vt (give up) ab|brechen.

abortion [ə'bɔːʃn] n Abtreibung die.

about [ə'baut] ◆ adv **1.** (approximately) ungefähr, etwa; **~ 50** ungefähr 50; **at ~ six o'clock** gegen sechs Uhr. **2.** (referring to place) herum; **to walk ~** herum|laufen. **3.** (on the point of): **to be ~ to do sthg** im Begriff sein, etw zu tun. ◆ prep **1.** (concerning) um, über; **a book ~ Scotland** ein Buch über Schottland; **what's it ~?** worum geht's?; **what ~ a drink?** wie wär's mit etwas zu trinken? **2.** (referring to place) herum; **there are lots of hotels ~ the town** es gibt viele Hotels in der Stadt.

above [ə'bʌv] ◆ prep (higher than) über (+A,D); (more than) über (+A). ◆ adv oben; **children aged ten and ~** Kinder ab zehn Jahren; **~ all** vor allem.

abroad [ə'brɔːd] adv im Ausland; **to go ~** ins Ausland fahren.

abrupt [ə'brʌpt] adj (sudden) abrupt.

abscess ['æbses] n Abszeß der.

absence ['æbsəns] n Abwesenheit die.

absent ['æbsənt] adj abwesend.

absent-minded [-'maɪndɪd] *adj* zerstreut.

absolute ['æbsəluːt] *adj* absolut.

absolutely [*adv* 'æbsəluːtlɪ, *excl* ˌæbsə'luːtlɪ] ◆ *adv* absolut. ◆ *excl* genau!

absorb [əb'sɔːb] *vt* (*liquid*) auflsaugen.

absorbed [əb'sɔːbd] *adj*: **to be ~ in sthg** in etw vertieft sein.

absorbent [əb'sɔːbənt] *adj* saugfähig.

abstain [əb'steɪn] *vi*: **to ~ (from)** sich enthalten (+G).

absurd [əb'sɜːd] *adj* absurd.

ABTA ['æbtə] *n Verband britischer Reisebüros.*

abuse [*n* ə'bjuːs, *vb* ə'bjuːz] ◆ *n* (*insults*) Beschimpfungen *pl*; (*misuse, maltreatment*) Mißbrauch *der*. ◆ *vt* (*insult*) beschimpfen; (*misuse, maltreat*) mißbrauchen.

abusive [ə'bjuːsɪv] *adj* beleidigend.

AC *abbr* = **alternating current**.

academic [ˌækə'demɪk] ◆ *adj* akademisch. ◆ *n* Akademiker *der* (-in *die*).

academy [ə'kædəmɪ] *n* Akademie *die*.

accelerate [ək'seləreɪt] *vi* beschleunigen.

accelerator [ək'seləreɪtər] *n* Gaspedal *das*.

accent ['æksent] *n* Akzent *der*.

accept [ək'sept] *vt* (*offer, gift, invitation*) anlnehmen; (*blame*) auf sich nehmen; (*fact, truth*) akzeptieren; (*story*) glauben; (*responsibility*) übernehmen.

acceptable [ək'septəbl] *adj* akzeptabel.

access ['ækses] *n* Zugang *der*.

accessible [ək'sesəbl] *adj* (*place*) erreichbar.

accessories [ək'sesərɪz] *npl* (*extras*) Zubehör *das*; (*fashion items*) Accessoires *pl*.

access road *n* Zufahrtsstraße *die*.

accident ['æksɪdənt] *n* Unfall *der*; (*chance*) Zufall *der*; **by ~** zufällig.

accidental [ˌæksɪ'dentl] *adj* zufällig.

accident insurance *n* Unfallversicherung *die*.

accident-prone *adj*: **to be ~** ein Pechvogel sein.

acclimatize [ə'klaɪmətaɪz] *vi* sich akklimatisieren.

accommodate [ə'kɒmədeɪt] *vt* unterlbringen.

accommodation [əˌkɒmə'deɪʃn] *n* Unterkunft *die*.

accommodations [əˌkɒmə'deɪʃnz] *npl* (*Am*) = **accommodation**.

accompany [ə'kʌmpənɪ] *vt* begleiten.

accomplish [ə'kʌmplɪʃ] *vt* erreichen.

accord [ə'kɔːd] *n*: **of one's own ~** aus eigenem Antrieb.

accordance [ə'kɔːdəns] *n*: **in ~ with** gemäß (+D).

according to [ə'kɔːdɪŋ-] *prep* laut (+G or D).

accordion [ə'kɔːdɪən] *n* Akkordeon *das*.

account [ə'kaʊnt] *n* (*at bank, shop*) Konto *das*; (*report*) Bericht *der*; **to take into ~** berücksichtigen; **on no ~** auf keinen Fall; **on ~ of** wegen. ▶ **account for** *vt fus* (*explain*) erklären; (*constitute*) auslmachen.

accountant [ə'kaʊntənt] *n* Buchhalter *der* (-in *die*).

account number *n* Kontonummer *die*.

accumulate [ə'kjuːmjʊleɪt] *vt* sammeln.

accurate ['ækjʊrət] *adj* genau.

accuse [ə'kjuːz] *vt*: **to ~ sb of sthg** jn einer Sache beschuldigen.

accused [ə'kjuːzd] *n*: **the ~** der/die Angeklagte.

ace [eɪs] *n* As *das*.

ache [eɪk] ◆ *vi* weh tun. ◆ *n* Schmerzen *pl*.

achieve [ə'tʃiːv] *vt* erreichen.

acid ['æsɪd] ◆ adj sauer. ◆ n Säure die; (inf: drug) Acid das.

acid rain n saurer Regen.

acknowledge [ək'nɒlɪdʒ] vt (accept) an|erkennen; (admit) zulgeben; (letter) den Empfang (+G) bestätigen.

acne ['æknɪ] n Akne die.

acorn ['eɪkɔːn] n Eichel die.

acoustic [ə'kuːstɪk] adj akustisch.

acquaintance [ə'kweɪntəns] n (person) Bekannte der die.

acquire [ə'kwaɪər] vt erwerben.

acre ['eɪkər] n = 4046,9 m², ≃ 40 Ar.

acrobat ['ækrəbæt] n Akrobat der (-in die).

across [ə'krɒs] ◆ prep über (+A,D). ◆ adv hinüber, herüber; (in crossword) waagrecht; ~ **the street** auf der anderen Straßenseite; **10 miles** ~ 10 Meilen breit; ~ **from** gegenüber von.

acrylic [ə'krɪlɪk] n Acryl das.

act [ækt] ◆ vi (do something) handeln; (behave) sich benehmen; (in play, film) spielen. ◆ n (action) Handlung die; (POL) Gesetz das; (of play) Akt der; (performance) Nummer die; **to** ~ **as** (serve as) dienen als.

action ['ækʃn] n Handlung die; **to take** ~ Maßnahmen ergreifen; **to put sthg into** ~ etw in die Tat um|setzen; **out of** ~ (machine) außer Betrieb; (person) außer Gefecht.

active ['æktɪv] adj aktiv.

activity [æk'tɪvətɪ] n Aktivität die. ► **activities** npl (leisure events) Veranstaltungen pl.

activity holiday n Aktivurlaub der.

act of God n höhere Gewalt.

actor ['æktər] n Schauspieler der.

actress ['æktrɪs] n Schauspielerin die.

actual ['æktʃʊəl] adj eigentlich.

actually ['æktʃʊəlɪ] adv (really) wirklich; (in fact) eigentlich; (by the way) übrigens.

acupuncture ['ækjʊpʌŋktʃər] n Akupunktur die.

acute [ə'kjuːt] adj (pain) heftig; (angle) spitz; ~ **accent** Akut der.

ad [æd] n (inf: in newspaper) Annonce die; (on TV) Werbespot der.

AD (abbr of Anno Domini) n. Chr.

adapt [ə'dæpt] ◆ vt an|passen. ◆ vi sich an|passen.

adapter [ə'dæptər] n (for foreign plug) Adapter der; (for several plugs) Mehrfachsteckdose die.

add [æd] vt (put, say in addition) hinzu|fügen; (numbers) addieren. ► **add up** vt sep addieren. ► **add up to** vt fus (total) machen.

adder ['ædər] n Kreuzotter die.

addict ['ædɪkt] n Süchtige der die.

addicted [ə'dɪktɪd] adj: **to be** ~ **to** sthg nach etw süchtig sein.

addiction [ə'dɪkʃn] n Sucht die.

addition [ə'dɪʃn] n (added thing) Ergänzung die; (in maths) Addition die; **in** ~ außerdem; **in** ~ **to** zusätzlich zu.

additional [ə'dɪʃənl] adj zusätzlich.

additive ['ædɪtɪv] n Zusatz der.

address [ə'dres] ◆ n Adresse die. ◆ vt (speak to) an|sprechen; (letter) adressieren.

address book n Adreßbuch das.

addressee [,ædre'siː] n Empfänger der (-in die).

adequate ['ædɪkwət] adj (sufficient) ausreichend; (satisfactory) angemessen.

adhere [əd'hɪər] vi: **to** ~ **to** (stick to) kleben an (+D); (obey) ein|halten.

adhesive [əd'hiːsɪv] ◆ adj klebrig. ◆ n Klebstoff der.

adjacent [ə'dʒeɪsənt] adj angrenzend.

adjective ['ædʒɪktɪv] n Adjektiv das.

adjoining [ə'dʒɔɪnɪŋ] adj angrenzend.

adjust [ə'dʒʌst] ◆ vt (machine) ein|stellen. ◆ vi: **to** ~ **to** sich an|passen an (+A).

adjustable [ə'dʒʌstəbl] adj verstellbar.

adjustment [ə'dʒʌstmənt] n (of machine) Einstellung die.

administration [əd,mɪnɪ'streɪʃn] n (organizing) Verwaltung die; (Am: government) Regierung die.

administrator [əd'mɪnɪstreɪtə^r] n Verwalter der (-in die).

admiral ['ædmərəl] n Admiral der.

admire [əd'maɪə^r] vt bewundern.

admission [əd'mɪʃn] n (permission to enter) Zutritt der; (entrance cost) Eintritt der.

admission charge n Eintrittspreis der.

admit [əd'mɪt] vt (confess) zulgeben; (allow to enter) hereinllassen; **to ~ to** sthg etw zulgeben; **'~s one'** (on ticket) 'gültig für eine Person'.

adolescent [,ædə'lesnt] n Jugendliche der die.

adopt [ə'dɒpt] vt (child) adoptieren; (attitude) anlnehmen; (plan) übernehmen.

adopted [ə'dɒptɪd] adj adoptiert.

adorable [ə'dɔ:rəbl] adj entzückend.

adore [ə'dɔ:^r] vt über alles lieben.

adult ['ædʌlt] ♦ n Erwachsene der die. ♦ adj (entertainment, films) für Erwachsene; (animal) ausgewachsen.

adult education n Erwachsenenbildung die.

adultery [ə'dʌltərɪ] n Ehebruch der.

advance [əd'vɑ:ns] ♦ n (money) Vorschuß der; (movement) Vorrücken das; (progress) Fortschritt der. ♦ vt (money) vorlschießen; (bring forward) vorlverlegen. ♦ vi (move forward) vorlrücken; (improve) voranlkommen. ♦ adj: ~ **warning** Vorwarnung die.

advance booking n Vorbestellung die.

advanced [əd'vɑ:nst] adj (student, level) fortgeschritten.

advantage [əd'vɑ:ntɪdʒ] n Vorteil der; **to take ~ of** auslnutzen.

Advent ['ædvənt] n (RELIG) Advent der.

adventure [əd'ventʃə^r] n Abenteuer das.

adventurous [əd'ventʃərəs] adj (person) abenteuerlustig.

adverb ['ædvɜ:b] n Adverb das.

adverse ['ædvɜ:s] adj ungünstig.

advert ['ædvɜ:t] = **advertisement**.

advertise ['ædvətaɪz] vt (product) werben für; (event) bekanntlmachen.

advertisement [əd'vɜ:tɪsmənt] n (in newspaper) Anzeige die; (on TV) Werbespot der.

advice [əd'vaɪs] n Rat der; **a piece of ~** ein Ratschlag.

advisable [əd'vaɪzəbl] adj ratsam.

advise [əd'vaɪz] vt raten (+D); **to ~ sb to do sthg** jm raten, etw zu tun; **to ~ sb against doing sthg** jm von etw ablraten.

advocate [n 'ædvəkət, vb 'ædvəkeɪt] ♦ n (JUR) Anwalt der (Anwältin die). ♦ vt befürworten.

aerial ['eərɪəl] n Antenne die.

aerobics [eə'rəʊbɪks] n Aerobic das.

aerodynamic [,eərəʊdaɪ'næmɪk] adj aerodynamisch.

aeroplane ['eərəpleɪn] n Flugzeug das.

aerosol ['eərəsɒl] n Spray der.

affair [ə'feə^r] n (event) Angelegenheit die; (love affair) Verhältnis das.

affect [ə'fekt] vt (influence) beeinflussen.

affection [ə'fekʃn] n Zuneigung die.

affectionate [ə'fekʃnət] adj zärtlich.

affluent ['æfluənt] adj wohlhabend.

afford [ə'fɔ:d] vt: **to be able to ~ sthg** sich (D) etw leisten können; **I can't ~ the time** ich habe keine Zeit; **I can't ~ it** das kann ich mir nicht leisten.

affordable [ə'fɔ:dəbl] adj erschwinglich.

afloat [ə'fləʊt] adj über Wasser.

afraid [ə'freɪd] adj: **to be ~ (of)** Angst haben (vor (+D)); **I'm ~ so/not** leider ja/nicht.

Africa ['æfrɪkə] *n* Afrika *nt*.
African ['æfrɪkən] ◆ *adj* afrikanisch.
◆ *n* Afrikaner *der* (-in *die*).
after ['ɑːftəʳ] ◆ *prep* nach. ◆ *conj* nachdem. ◆ *adv* danach; ~ **we had eaten** nachdem wir gegessen hatten; **a quarter ~ ten** (Am) Viertel nach zehn; **to be ~ sb/sthg** (*in search of*) jn/etw suchen; ~ **all** (*in spite of everything*) doch; (*it should be remembered*) schließlich. ► **afters** *npl* Nachtisch *der*.
aftercare ['ɑːftəkeəʳ] *n* Nachbehandlung *die*.
aftereffects ['ɑːftərɪ,fekts] *npl* Nachwirkung *die*.
afternoon [,ɑːftə'nuːn] *n* Nachmittag *der*; **good ~!** guten Tag!
afternoon tea *n* Nachmittagstee *der*.
aftershave ['ɑːftəʃeɪv] *n* Rasierwasser *das*.
aftersun ['ɑːftəsʌn] *n* Aftersunlotion *die*.
afterwards ['ɑːftəwədz] *adv* danach.
again [ə'gen] *adv* wieder; ~ **and** ~ immer wieder; **never ... ~** nie ... wieder.
against [ə'genst] *prep* gegen; **he was leaning ~ the wall** er stand an die Wand gelehnt; ~ **the law** rechtswidrig.
age [eɪdʒ] *n* Alter *das*; (*in history*) Zeitalter *das*; **under ~** minderjährig; **I haven't seen him for ~s** (*inf*) ich hab' ihn schon ewig nicht mehr gesehen.
aged [eɪdʒd] *adj*: **to be ~ eight** acht Jahre alt sein; **children ~ eight** Kinder von acht Jahren.
age group *n* Altersgruppe *die*.
age limit *n* Altersgrenze *die*.
agency ['eɪdʒənsɪ] *n* Agentur *die*.
agenda [ə'dʒendə] *n* Tagesordnung *die*.
agent ['eɪdʒənt] *n* (*representative*) Vertreter *der* (-in *die*).
aggression [ə'greʃn] *n* Aggression *die*.

aggressive [ə'gresɪv] *adj* aggressiv.
agile [Br 'ædʒaɪl, Am 'ædʒəl] *adj* beweglich.
agility [ə'dʒɪlətɪ] *n* Beweglichkeit *die*.
agitated ['ædʒɪteɪtɪd] *adj* erregt.
ago [ə'gəʊ] *adv*: **a month ~** vor einem Monat; **how long ~ was it?** wie lange ist das her?
agonizing ['ægənaɪzɪŋ] *adj* qualvoll.
agony ['ægənɪ] *n* Qual *die*.
agree [ə'griː] *vi* (*be in agreement, correspond*) überein|stimmen; (*consent*) ein|willigen; **it doesn't ~ with me** (*food*) das bekommt mir nicht; **to ~ to sthg** mit etw einverstanden sein; **to ~ to do sthg** bereit sein, etw zu tun. ► **agree on** *vt fus* (*time, price*) sich einigen auf (+A).
agreed [ə'griːd] *adj* vereinbart.
agreement [ə'griːmənt] *n* Zustimmung *die*; (*contract*) Vertrag *der*; **in ~ with** in Übereinstimmung mit.
agriculture ['ægrɪkʌltʃəʳ] *n* Landwirtschaft *die*.
ahead [ə'hed] *adv*: **the road ~** die Straße vor mir/uns etc; **straight ~** geradeaus; **the weeks ~** die kommenden Wochen; **to be ~** (*winning*) Vorsprung haben; ~ **of** (*in front of*) vor (+D); ~ **of the other team** der anderen Mannschaft voraus; ~ **of schedule** früher als geplant.
aid [eɪd] ◆ *n* Hilfe *die*. ◆ *vt* helfen (+D); **in ~ of** zugunsten (+G); **with the ~ of** mit Hilfe (+G).
AIDS [eɪdz] *n* Aids *das*.
ailment ['eɪlmənt] *n* (*fml*) Leiden *das*.
aim [eɪm] ◆ *n* (*purpose*) Ziel *das*. ◆ *vt* (*gun, camera, hose*) richten. ◆ *vi*: **to ~ (at)** zielen (auf (+A)); **to ~ to do sthg** beabsichtigen, etw zu tun.
air [eəʳ] ◆ *n* Luft *die*. ◆ *vt* (*room*) lüften. ◆ *adj* (*terminal, travel*) Flug-; **by ~** (*travel*) mit dem Flugzeug; (*send*) mit Luftpost.

airbed ['eəbed] n Luftmatratze die.

airborne ['eəbɔːn] adj (plane): **whilst we are ~** während des Fluges.

air-conditioned [-kən'dɪʃnd] adj klimatisiert.

air-conditioning [-kən'dɪʃnɪŋ] n Klimaanlage die.

aircraft ['eəkrɑːft] (pl inv) n Flugzeug das.

aircraft carrier [-ˌkærɪəʳ] n Flugzeugträger der.

airfield ['eəfiːld] n Flugplatz der.

airforce ['eəfɔːs] n Luftwaffe die.

air freshener [-ˌfreʃnəʳ] n Raumspray das.

airhostess ['eəˌhəʊstɪs] n Stewardeß die.

airing cupboard ['eərɪŋ-] n Trockenschrank zum Wäschetrocknen.

airletter ['eəˌletəʳ] n Luftpostbrief der.

airline ['eəlaɪn] n Fluggesellschaft die.

airliner ['eəˌlaɪnəʳ] n Verkehrsflugzeug das.

airmail ['eəmeɪl] n Luftpost die; **by ~** mit Luftpost.

airplane ['eəpleɪn] n (Am) Flugzeug das.

airport ['eəpɔːt] n Flughafen der.

air raid n Luftangriff der.

airsick ['eəsɪk] adj luftkrank.

air steward n Steward der.

air stewardess n Stewardeß die.

air traffic control n (people) die Fluglotsen pl.

airy ['eərɪ] adj luftig.

aisle [aɪl] n (in church) Seitenschiff das; (in plane, cinema, supermarket) Gang der.

aisle seat n Sitz der am Gang.

ajar [ə'dʒɑːʳ] adj angelehnt.

alarm [ə'lɑːm] ◆ n (device) Alarmanlage die. ◆ vt beunruhigen.

alarm clock n Wecker der.

alarmed [ə'lɑːmd] adj (door, car) alarmgesichert.

alarming [ə'lɑːmɪŋ] adj alarmierend.

Albert Hall ['ælbət-] n: **the ~** Londoner Konzerthalle.

album ['ælbəm] n Album das.

alcohol ['ælkəhɒl] n Alkohol der.

alcohol-free adj alkoholfrei.

alcoholic [ˌælkə'hɒlɪk] ◆ adj (drink) alkoholisch. ◆ n Alkoholiker der (-in die).

alcoholism ['ælkəhɒlɪzm] n Alkoholismus der.

alcopop ['ælkəʊpɒp] n limonadeartiges, kohlensäurehaltiges Getränk mit Alkohol.

alcove ['ælkəʊv] n Nische die.

ale [eɪl] n Ale das.

alert [ə'lɜːt] ◆ adj wachsam. ◆ vt (police, authorities) alarmieren.

A level n (Br) einzelne Prüfung des englischen Schulabschlusses.

algebra ['ældʒɪbrə] n Algebra die.

Algeria [æl'dʒɪərɪə] n Algerien nt.

alias ['eɪlɪəs] adv alias.

alibi ['ælɪbaɪ] n Alibi das.

alien ['eɪlɪən] n (foreigner) Ausländer der (-in die); (from outer space) Außerirdische der die.

alight [ə'laɪt] ◆ vi (fml: from train, bus) auslsteigen (aus). ◆ adj: **to be ~** brennen.

align [ə'laɪn] vt auslrichten.

alike [ə'laɪk] ◆ adj gleich. ◆ adv ähnlich; **to look ~** gleich auslsehen.

alive [ə'laɪv] adj (living) lebendig.

all [ɔːl] ◆ adj 1. (with singular noun) ganze; **~ the money** das ganze Geld; **~ the time** immer, die ganze Zeit. 2. (with plural noun) alle(-r)(-s); **~ the people** alle Menschen, alle Leute; **~ trains stop at Tonbridge** alle Züge halten in Tonbridge. ◆ adv 1. (completely) ganz; **~ alone** ganz allein. 2. (in scores) beide; **it's two ~** es steht zwei beide. 3. (in phrases): **~ but empty** fast leer; **~ over** (finished) zu Ende. ◆ pron 1. (everything): **~ of the cake** der ganze Kuchen; **is that ~?** (in shop) ist das alles?; **the best of ~** der/die/das

Allerbeste; **the biggest of** ~ der/die/
das Allergrößte. **2.** (*everybody*) alle; ~
of us went wir sind alle gegangen.
3. (*in phrases*): **in** ~ (*in total*) zusammen; (*in summary*) alles in allem.

Allah [ˈælə] *n* Allah *der*.

allege [əˈledʒ] *vt* behaupten.

allergic [əˈlɜːdʒɪk] *adj*: **to be** ~ **to**
allergisch sein auf (+A).

allergy [ˈælədʒɪ] *n* Allergie *die*.

alleviate [əˈliːvɪeɪt] *vt* lindern.

alley [ˈælɪ] *n* Gasse *die*.

alligator [ˈælɪɡeɪtəʳ] *n* Alligator *der*.

all-in *adj* (Br: *inclusive*) Pauschal-.

all-night *adj* (*bar, petrol station*)
nachts durchgehend geöffnet.

allocate [ˈæləkeɪt] *vt* zu|teilen.

allotment [əˈlɒtmənt] *n* (Br: *for vegetables*) Schrebergarten *der*.

allow [əˈlaʊ] *vt* (*permit*) erlauben;
(*time, money*) rechnen; **to** ~ **sb to do**
sthg jm erlauben, etw zu tun; **to be**
~**ed to do sthg** etw tun dürfen.
▶ **allow for** *vt fus* ein|kalkulieren.

allowance [əˈlaʊəns] *n* (*state benefit*)
Unterstützung *die*; (*for expenses*)
Spesen *pl*; (Am: *pocket money*)
Taschengeld *das*.

all right ◆ *adj* (*satisfactory, acceptable*)
in Ordnung. **◆** *adv* (*satisfactorily*) ganz
gut; (*yes, okay*) okay; (*safely*) gut; **how**
are you? – I'm ~ wie geht's dir? – mir
geht's gut.

ally [ˈælaɪ] *n* Verbündete *der die*;
(MIL) Alliierte *der die*.

almond [ˈɑːmənd] *n* Mandel *die*.

almost [ˈɔːlməʊst] *adv* fast.

alone [əˈləʊn] *adj & adv* allein; **to**
leave sb ~ jn in Ruhe lassen; **to leave**
sthg ~ etw in Ruhe lassen.

along [əˈlɒŋ] **◆** *adv* (*forward*) weiter.
◆ *prep* entlang; **to walk** ~
entlang|gehen; **to bring sthg** ~ etw
mit|bringen; **all** ~ die ganze Zeit; ~
with zusammen mit.

alongside [əˌlɒŋˈsaɪd] **◆** *prep*
neben. **◆** *adv*: **to come** ~ (*boat*) längs-
seits kommen.

aloof [əˈluːf] *adj* distanziert.

aloud [əˈlaʊd] *adv* laut.

alphabet [ˈælfəbet] *n* Alphabet *das*.

Alps [ælps] *npl*: **the** ~ die Alpen.

already [ɔːlˈredɪ] *adv* schon.

also [ˈɔːlsəʊ] *adv* auch.

altar [ˈɔːltəʳ] *n* Altar *der*.

alter [ˈɔːltəʳ] *vt* ändern.

alteration [ˌɔːltəˈreɪʃn] *n* Änderung
die; (*to house*) Umbau *der*.

alternate [Br ɔːlˈtɜːnət, Am
ˈɔːltərnət] *adj* abwechselnd; **on** ~
days jeden zweiten Tag.

alternating current [ˈɔːltəneɪtɪŋ-]
n Wechselstrom *der*.

alternative [ɔːlˈtɜːnətɪv] **◆** *adj*
andere(-r)(-s); (*lifestyle, medicine*)
alternativ. **◆** *n* Alternative *die*.

alternatively [ɔːlˈtɜːnətɪvlɪ] *adv*
oder aber.

alternator [ˈɔːltəneɪtəʳ] *n*
Wechselstromgenerator *der*.

although [ɔːlˈðəʊ] *conj* obwohl.

altitude [ˈæltɪtjuːd] *n* Höhe *die*.

altogether [ˌɔːltəˈɡeðəʳ] *adv* (*completely*) ganz; (*in total*) insgesamt.

aluminium [ˌæljʊˈmɪnɪəm] *n* (Br)
Aluminium *das*.

aluminum [əˈluːmɪnəm] (Am) =
aluminium.

always [ˈɔːlweɪz] *adv* immer.

am [æm] → **be**.

a.m. (*abbr of ante meridiem*): **at 2** ~ um
2 Uhr morgens.

amateur [ˈæmətəʳ] *n* Amateur *der*.

amazed [əˈmeɪzd] *adj* erstaunt.

amazing [əˈmeɪzɪŋ] *adj* erstaunlich.

Amazon [ˈæməzn] *n* (*river*): **the** ~
der Amazonas.

ambassador [æmˈbæsədəʳ] *n*
Botschafter *der* (-in *die*).

amber [ˈæmbəʳ] *adj* (*traffic lights*)
gelb; (*jewellery*) Bernstein-.

ambiguous [æmˈbɪɡjʊəs] *adj* zwei-
deutig.

ambition [æmˈbɪʃn] *n* (*desire*)
Ehrgeiz *der*; (*thing desired*) Wunsch *der*.

ambitious [æmˈbɪʃəs] *adj* ehrgeizig.

ambulance [ˈæmbjʊləns] *n*

Krankenwagen der.

ambush ['æmbʊʃ] n Hinterhalt der.

amenities [ə'miːnətɪz] npl Annehmlichkeiten pl.

America [ə'merɪkə] n Amerika nt.

American [ə'merɪkən] ◆ adj amerikanisch. ◆ n Amerikaner der (-in die).

amiable ['eɪmɪəbl] adj freundlich.

ammunition [ˌæmjʊ'nɪʃn] n Munition die.

amnesia [æm'niːzɪə] n Gedächtnisschwund der.

among(st) [ə'mʌŋ(st)] prep unter (+D).

amount [ə'maʊnt] n (money) Betrag der; (quantity) Menge die. ▶ **amount to** vt fus (total) sich belaufen auf (+A).

amp [æmp] n Ampere das; **a 13-~ plug** ein Stecker für 13 Ampere.

ample ['æmpl] adj reichlich.

amplifier ['æmplɪfaɪər] n Verstärker der.

amputate ['æmpjʊteɪt] vt amputieren.

Amtrak ['æmtræk] n amerikanische Eisenbahngesellschaft.

amuse [ə'mjuːz] vt (make laugh) belustigen; (entertain) unterhalten.

amusement arcade [ə-'mjuːzmənt-] n Spielhalle die.

amusement park [ə'mjuːzmənt-] n Vergnügungspark der.

amusements [ə'mjuːzmənts] npl Vergnügungsmöglichkeiten pl.

amusing [ə'mjuːzɪŋ] adj lustig.

an [stressed æn, unstressed ən] → **a**.

anaemic [ə'niːmɪk] adj (Br) blutarm.

anaesthetic [ˌænɪs'θetɪk] n (Br) Narkose die.

analgesic [ˌænæl'dʒiːzɪk] n Schmerzmittel das.

analyse ['ænəlaɪz] vt analysieren.

analyst ['ænəlɪst] n Analytiker der (-in die).

analyze ['ænəlaɪz] (Am) = **analyse**.

anarchy ['ænəkɪ] n Anarchie die.

anatomy [ə'nætəmɪ] n (science) Anatomie die; (of person, animal) Körperbau der.

ancestor ['ænsestər] n Vorfahr der (-in die).

anchor ['æŋkər] n Anker der.

anchovy ['æntʃəvɪ] n Sardelle die.

ancient ['eɪnʃənt] adj alt.

and [strong form ænd, weak form ənd, ən] conj und; **~ you?** und du/Sie?; **a hundred ~ one** hunderteins; **to try ~ do sthg** versuchen, etw zu tun; **more ~ more** immer mehr.

Andes ['ændiːz] npl: **the ~** die Anden.

anecdote ['ænɪkdəʊt] n Anekdote die.

anemic [ə'niːmɪk] (Am) = **anaemic**.

anesthetic [ˌænɪs'θetɪk] (Am) = **anaesthetic**.

angel ['eɪndʒl] n Engel der.

anger ['æŋgər] n Ärger der.

angina [æn'dʒaɪnə] n Angina die.

angle ['æŋgl] n Winkel der; **at an ~** schräg.

angler ['æŋglər] n Angler der (-in die).

angling ['æŋglɪŋ] n Angeln das.

angry ['æŋgrɪ] adj böse; **to get ~ (with sb)** sich (über jn) ärgern.

animal ['ænɪml] n Tier das.

aniseed ['ænɪsiːd] n Anis der.

ankle ['æŋkl] n Knöchel der.

annex ['æneks] n (building) Anbau der.

annihilate [ə'naɪəleɪt] vt vernichten.

anniversary [ˌænɪ'vɜːsərɪ] n Jahrestag der.

announce [ə'naʊns] vt (declare) bekanntgeben; (delay, departure) durchsagen.

announcement [ə'naʊnsmənt] n Bekanntmachung die; (at airport, station) Durchsage die.

announcer [ə'naʊnsər] n (on TV, radio) Ansager der (-in die).

annoy [ə'nɔɪ] vt ärgern.

annoyed [ə'nɔɪd] *adj* ärgerlich; **to get ~ (with)** sich ärgern (über (+A)).

annoying [ə'nɔɪɪŋ] *adj* ärgerlich.

annual ['ænjʊəl] *adj* jährlich.

anonymous [ə'nɒnɪməs] *adj* anonym.

anorak ['ænəræk] *n* Anorak *der*.

another [ə'nʌðə^r] ◆ *adj* (*additional*) noch ein/eine; (*different*) ein anderer/ eine andere/ein anderes. ◆ *pron* (*one more*) noch einer/eine/eins; (*different one*) ein anderer/eine andere/ ein anderes; **in ~ two weeks** in weiteren zwei Wochen; **~ one** noch einer/eine/eins; **one ~ einander; one after ~** einer nach dem anderen/ eine nach der anderen/eins nach dem anderen.

answer ['ɑːnsə^r] ◆ *n* Antwort *die*. ◆ *vt* (*person*) antworten (+D); (*question, letter*) beantworten. ◆ *vi* antworten; **to ~ the door** an die Tür gehen; **to ~ the phone** ans Telefon gehen. ▶ **answer back** *vi* (*child*) eine freche Antwort geben.

answering machine ['ɑːnsərɪŋ-] = **answerphone**.

answerphone ['ɑːnsəfəʊn] *n* Anrufbeantworter *der*.

ant [ænt] *n* Ameise *die*.

Antarctic [æn'tɑːktɪk] *n*: **the ~** die Antarktis.

antenna [æn'tenə] *n* (*Am: aerial*) Antenne *die*.

anthem ['ænθəm] *n* Hymne *die*.

antibiotics [ˌæntɪbaɪ'ɒtɪks] *npl* Antibiotika *pl*.

anticipate [æn'tɪsɪpeɪt] *vt* erwarten.

anticlimax [ˌæntɪ'klaɪmæks] *n* Enttäuschung *die*.

anticlockwise [ˌæntɪ'klɒkwaɪz] *adv* (Br) gegen den Uhrzeigersinn.

antidote ['æntɪdəʊt] *n* Gegenmittel *das*.

antifreeze ['æntɪfriːz] *n* Frostschutzmittel *das*.

antihistamine [ˌæntɪ'hɪstəmɪn] *n* Antihistamin *das*.

antiperspirant [ˌæntɪ'pɜːspərənt]

n Antitranspirant *das*.

antiquarian bookshop [ˌæntɪ'kweərɪən-] *n* Antiquariat *das*.

antique [æn'tiːk] *n* Antiquität *die*.

antique shop *n* Antiquitätenladen *der*.

antiseptic [ˌæntɪ'septɪk] *n* Antiseptikum *das*.

antisocial [ˌæntɪ'səʊʃl] *adj* (*person*) ungesellig; (*behaviour*) asozial.

antlers ['æntləz] *npl* Geweih *das*.

anxiety [æŋ'zaɪətɪ] *n* (*worry*) Sorge *die*.

anxious ['æŋkʃəs] *adj* (*worried*) besorgt; (*eager*) sehnlich.

any ['enɪ] ◆ *adj* 1. (*in questions*): **have you got ~ money?** hast du Geld?; **have you got ~ postcards?** haben Sie Postkarten? 2. (*in negatives*): **I haven't got ~ money** ich habe kein Geld; **we don't have ~ rooms** wir haben keine Zimmer frei. 3. (*no matter which*) irgendein(-e); **take ~ one you like** nimm, welches du willst. ◆ *pron* 1. (*in questions*) welche; **I'm looking for a hotel – are there ~ nearby?** ich suche ein Hotel – gibt es hier welche in der Nähe? 2. (*in negatives*): **I don't want ~ (of them)** ich möchte keinen/keine/keines (von denen). 3. (*no matter which one*) jede(-r)(-s); **you can sit at ~ of the tables** Sie können sich an jeden beliebigen Tisch setzen. ◆ *adv* 1. (*in questions*): **is there ~ more ice cream?** ist noch Eis da?; **is that ~ better?** ist das besser? 2. (*in negatives*): **we can't wait ~ longer** wir können nicht mehr länger warten.

anybody ['enɪˌbɒdɪ] = **anyone**.

anyhow ['enɪhaʊ] *adv* (*carelessly*) irgendwie; (*in any case*) jedenfalls; (*in spite of that*) trotzdem.

anyone ['enɪwʌn] *pron* (*any person*) jeder; (*in questions*) irgend jemand; **there wasn't ~ in** niemand war zu Hause.

anything ['enɪθɪŋ] *pron* (*no matter what*) alles; (*in questions*) irgend etwas; **he didn't tell me ~** er hat mir nichts gesagt.

anyway ['enɪweɪ] adv (in any case) sowieso; (in spite of that) trotzdem; (in conversation) jedenfalls.

anywhere ['enɪweə^r] adv (any place) überall; (in questions) irgendwo; **I can't find it ~** ich kann es nirgends finden.

apart [ə'pɑːt] adv auseinander; **to come ~** auseinanderlgehen; **to live ~** getrennt leben; **~ from** (except for) abgesehen von; (as well as) außer (+D).

apartheid [ə'pɑːtheɪt] n Apartheid die.

apartment [ə'pɑːtmənt] n (Am) Wohnung die.

apathetic [ˌæpə'θetɪk] adj apathisch.

ape [eɪp] n Affe der.

aperitif [əˌperə'tiːf] n Aperitif der.

aperture ['æpətʃə^r] n (of camera) Blende die.

Apex n (plane ticket) reduziertes Flugticket, das im voraus reserviert werden muß; (Br: train ticket) reduzierte Fahrkarte für Fernstrecken, die nur für bestimmte Züge gilt und im voraus reserviert werden muß.

apiece [ə'piːs] adv je; **they cost £5 ~** sie kosten je 5 Pfund.

apologetic [əˌpɒlə'dʒetɪk] adj entschuldigend; **to be ~** sich entschuldigen.

apologize [ə'pɒlədʒaɪz] vi: **to ~ (to sb for sthg)** sich (bei jm für etw) entschuldigen.

apology [ə'pɒlədʒɪ] n Entschuldigung die.

apostrophe [ə'pɒstrəfɪ] n Apostroph der.

appal [ə'pɔːl] vt (Br) entsetzen.

appall [ə'pɔːl] (Am) = **appal**.

appalling [ə'pɔːlɪŋ] adj entsetzlich.

apparatus [ˌæpə'reɪtəs] n (device) Gerät das.

apparently [ə'pærəntlɪ] adv (it seems) scheinbar; (evidently) anscheinend.

appeal [ə'piːl] ◆ n (JUR) Berufung die; (for money, help) Aufruf der. ◆ vi (JUR) Berufung einllegen; **to ~ to sb (for sthg)** jn (um etw) bitten; **it doesn't ~ to me** das gefällt mir nicht.

appear [ə'pɪə^r] vi erscheinen; (seem) scheinen; (in play) aufltreten; **it ~s that** es scheint, daß.

appearance [ə'pɪərəns] n Erscheinen das; (of performer) Auftritt der; (look) Aussehen das.

appendices [ə'pendɪsiːz] pl → **appendix**.

appendicitis [əˌpendɪ'saɪtɪs] n Blinddarmentzündung die.

appendix [ə'pendɪks] (pl -dices) n (ANAT) Blinddarm der; (of book) Anhang der.

appetite ['æpɪtaɪt] n Appetit der.

appetizer ['æpɪtaɪzə^r] n Appetithappen der.

appetizing ['æpɪtaɪzɪŋ] adj appetitlich.

applaud [ə'plɔːd] vt & vi Beifall klatschen (+D).

applause [ə'plɔːz] n Beifall der.

apple ['æpl] n Apfel der.

apple charlotte [-'ʃɑːlət] n Apfelauflauf, der in einer mit Brot ausgelegten und bedeckten Form gebacken wird.

apple crumble n mit Streuseln bestreuter Apfelauflauf.

apple juice n Apfelsaft der.

apple pie n Art gedeckter Apfelkuchen mit dünnen Teigwänden.

apple sauce n Apfelmus das.

apple tart n Apfelkuchen der.

apple turnover [-'tɜːn,əʊvə^r] n Apfeltasche die.

appliance [ə'plaɪəns] n Gerät das; **electrical ~** Elektrogerät das; **domestic ~** Haushaltsgerät das.

applicable [ə'plɪkəbl] adj: **to be ~ (to)** zultreffen (auf (+A); **if ~** falls zutreffend.

applicant ['æplɪkənt] n Bewerber der (-in die).

application [ˌæplɪ'keɪʃn] n (for job)

Bewerbung *die*; (*for membership*) Antrag *der*.

application form *n* (*for job*) Bewerbungsformular *das*; (*for membership*) Antragsformular *das*.

apply [ə'plaɪ] ♦ *vt* (*lotion, paint*) auf|tragen; (*brakes*) betätigen. ♦ *vi*: **to ~ (to sb for sthg)** (*make request*) sich (bei jm um etw) bewerben; **to ~ (to sb)** (*be applicable*) zu|treffen (auf jn).

appointment [ə'pɔɪntmənt] *n* (*with doctor, hairdresser*) Termin *der*; **to have an ~ (with)** einen Termin haben (bei); **to make an ~ (with)** einen Termin vereinbaren (mit); **by ~** nach Vereinbarung.

appreciable [ə'priːʃəbl] *adj* merklich.

appreciate [ə'priːʃɪeɪt] *vt* schätzen; (*understand*) verstehen.

apprehensive [ˌæprɪ'hensɪv] *adj* ängstlich.

apprentice [ə'prentɪs] *n* Lehrling *der*.

apprenticeship [ə'prentɪsʃɪp] *n* Lehre *die*.

approach [ə'prəʊtʃ] ♦ *n* (*road*) Zufahrt *die*; (*to problem, situation*) Ansatz *der*. ♦ *vt* sich nähern (+D); (*problem, situation*) an|gehen. ♦ *vi* näher|kommen.

appropriate [ə'prəʊprɪət] *adj* passend.

approval [ə'pruːvl] *n* Zustimmung *die*.

approve [ə'pruːv] *vi*: **to ~ (of sb/sthg)** (mit jm/etw) einverstanden sein.

approximate [ə'prɒksɪmət] *adj* ungefähr.

approximately [ə'prɒksɪmətlɪ] *adv* ungefähr.

Apr. *abbr* = **April**.

apricot ['eɪprɪkɒt] *n* Aprikose *die*, Marille *die* (Österr).

April ['eɪprəl] *n* April *der*, → **September**.

April Fools' Day *n* der erste April.

apron ['eɪprən] *n* Schürze *die*.

apt [æpt] *adj* (*appropriate*) passend; **to be ~ to do sthg** dazu neigen, etw zu tun.

aquarium [ə'kweərɪəm] (*pl* **-ria** [-rɪə]) *n* Aquarium *das*.

Aquarius [ə'kweərɪəs] *n* Wassermann *der*.

aqueduct ['ækwɪdʌkt] *n* Aquädukt *der*.

Arab ['ærəb] ♦ *adj* arabisch. ♦ *n* Araber *der* (-in *die*).

Arabic ['ærəbɪk] ♦ *adj* arabisch. ♦ *n* Arabisch *das*.

arbitrary ['ɑːbɪtrərɪ] *adj* willkürlich.

arc [ɑːk] *n* Bogen *der*.

arcade [ɑː'keɪd] *n* (*for shopping*) Passage *die*; (*of video games*) Spielhalle *die*.

arch [ɑːtʃ] *n* Bogen *der*.

archaeology [ˌɑːkɪ'ɒlədʒɪ] *n* Archäologie *die*.

archbishop [ˌɑːtʃ'bɪʃəp] *n* Erzbischof *der*.

archery ['ɑːtʃərɪ] *n* Bogenschießen *das*.

archipelago [ˌɑːkɪ'pelɪgəʊ] *n* Archipel *der*.

architect ['ɑːkɪtekt] *n* Architekt *der* (-in *die*).

architecture ['ɑːkɪtektʃər] *n* Architektur *die*.

archives ['ɑːkaɪvz] *npl* Archiv *das*.

Arctic ['ɑːktɪk] *n*: **the ~** die Arktis.

are [*weak form* ər, *strong form* ɑːr] → **be**.

area ['eərɪə] *n* (*region*) Gegend *die*; (*space, zone*) Bereich *der*; (*surface size*) Fläche *die*.

area code *n* (Am) Vorwahl *die*.

arena [ə'riːnə] *n* (*at circus*) Manege *die*; (*at sportsground*) Stadion *das*.

aren't [ɑːnt] = **are not**.

Argentina [ˌɑːdʒən'tiːnə] *n* Argentinien *nt*.

argue ['ɑːgjuː] *vi*: **to ~ (with sb about sthg)** sich (mit jm über etw) streiten; **to ~ (that)** ... die Meinung vertreten, daß ...

argument ['ɑːgjʊmənt] n (quarrel) Streit der; (reason) Argument das.

arid ['ærɪd] adj trocken.

Aries ['eəriːz] n Widder der.

arise [ə'raɪz] (pt **arose**, pp **arisen** [ə'rɪzn]) vi: **to ~ (from)** sich ergeben (aus).

aristocracy [ˌærɪ'stɒkrəsɪ] n Adel der.

arithmetic [ə'rɪθmətɪk] n Rechnen das.

arm [ɑːm] n Arm der; (of chair) Armlehne die; (of garment) Ärmel der.

arm bands npl (for swimming) Schwimmflügel pl.

armchair ['ɑːmtʃeər] n Sessel der.

armed [ɑːmd] adj bewaffnet.

armed forces npl: **the ~** die Streitkräfte.

armor ['ɑːmər] (Am) = **armour**.

armour ['ɑːmər] n (Br) Rüstung die.

armpit ['ɑːmpɪt] n Achselhöhle die.

arms [ɑːmz] npl Waffen pl.

army ['ɑːmɪ] n Armee die.

A-road n (Br) = Bundesstraße die.

aroma [ə'rəumə] n Aroma das.

aromatic [ˌærə'mætɪk] adj aromatisch.

arose [ə'rəuz] pt → **arise**.

around [ə'raund] ◆ prep um; (near) rings herum; (approximately) ungefähr. ◆ adv herum; (present): **is she ~?** ist sie da?; **~ here** (in the area) hier in der Gegend; **to travel ~** herum|reisen; **to turn ~** sich um|drehen; **to look ~** sich um|sehen.

arouse [ə'rauz] vt (suspicion, interest) erregen.

arrange [ə'reɪndʒ] vt (objects) ordnen; (flowers) arrangieren; (meeting) vereinbaren; (event) planen; **to ~ to do sthg (with sb)** (mit jm) vereinbaren, etw zu tun.

arrangement [ə'reɪndʒmənt] n (agreement) Vereinbarung die; (layout) Anordnung die; **by ~** nach Vereinbarung; **to make ~s (to do sthg)** Vorkehrungen treffen (, etw zu tun).

arrest [ə'rest] ◆ n Verhaftung die. ◆ vt verhaften; **under ~** verhaftet.

arrival [ə'raɪvl] n Ankunft die; **on ~** bei der Ankunft; **new ~** Neuankömmling der.

arrive [ə'raɪv] vi an|kommen.

arrogant ['ærəgənt] adj arrogant.

arrow ['ærəu] n Pfeil der.

arson ['ɑːsn] n Brandstiftung die.

art [ɑːt] n Kunst die; (paintings, sculptures etc) Kunstwerk das. ▶ **arts** npl (humanities) Geisteswissenschaften pl; **the ~s** (fine arts) die schönen Künste pl.

art college n Kunstakademie die.

artefact ['ɑːtɪfækt] n Artefakt das.

artery ['ɑːtərɪ] n Arterie die.

art gallery n Kunstgalerie die.

arthritis [ɑː'θraɪtɪs] n Arthritis die.

artichoke ['ɑːtɪtʃəuk] n Artischocke die.

article ['ɑːtɪkl] n (object) Gegenstand der; (in newspaper, grammar) Artikel der.

articulate [ɑː'tɪkjʊlət] adj: **to be ~** sich gut ausdrücken können.

artificial [ˌɑːtɪ'fɪʃl] adj künstlich.

artist ['ɑːtɪst] n Künstler der (-in die).

artistic [ɑː'tɪstɪk] adj künstlerisch.

arts centre n = Kulturtreff der.

arty ['ɑːtɪ] adj (pej) pseudokünstlerisch.

as [unstressed əz, stressed æz] ◆ adv (in comparisons): **~ ... ~** so ... wie; **he's ~ tall ~ I am** er ist so groß wie ich; **~ many ~** so viele wie; **~ much ~** so viel wie. ◆ conj 1. (referring to time) als; **~ the plane was coming in to land** als das Flugzeug beim Landeanflug war. 2. (referring to manner) wie; **~ expected, ...** wie erwartet ... 3. (introducing a statement) wie; **~ I told you ...** wie ich dir bereits gesagt habe ... 4. (because) weil, da. 5. (in phrases): **~ for me** was mich betrifft; **~ from Monday** ab Montag; **~ if** als ob. ◆ prep (referring to function, job) als.

asap (abbr of as soon as possible) baldmöglichst.

ascent [ə'sent] n Aufstieg der.

ascribe [ə'skraɪb] vt: **to ~ sthg to sb/ sthg** jm/einer Sache etw zu|schreiben.

ash [æʃ] n (from cigarette, fire) Asche die; (tree) Esche die.

ashore [ə'ʃɔːʳ] adv an Land.

ashtray ['æʃtreɪ] n Aschenbecher der.

Asia [Br 'eɪʃə, Am 'eɪʒə] n Asien nt.

Asian [Br 'eɪʃn, Am 'eɪʒn] ◆ adj asiatisch. ◆ n Asiat der (-in die).

aside [ə'saɪd] adv beiseite; **to move ~** beiseite treten.

ask [ɑːsk] ◆ vt fragen; (a question) stellen; (permission) bitten um; (advice) fragen um; (invite) einladen. ◆ vi: **to ~ after** sich erkundigen nach; **to ~ about sthg** nach etw fragen; **to ~ sb about sthg** jm Fragen über etw stellen; **to ~ sb to do sthg** jn bitten, etw zu tun; **to ~ sb for sthg** jn um etw bitten. ▶ **ask for** vt fus (ask to talk to) verlangen; (request) bitten um.

asleep [ə'sliːp] adj: **to be ~** schlafen; **to fall ~** ein|schlafen.

asparagus [ə'spærəgəs] n Spargel der.

asparagus tips npl Spargelspitzen pl.

aspect ['æspekt] n Aspekt der.

aspirin ['æsprɪn] n Aspirin das.

ass [æs] n (animal) Esel der.

assassinate [ə'sæsɪneɪt] vt ermorden.

assault [ə'sɔːlt] ◆ n Angriff der. ◆ vt an|greifen.

assemble [ə'sembl] ◆ vt (build) zusammen|bauen. ◆ vi sich versammeln.

assembly [ə'semblɪ] n (at school) Morgenandacht die.

assembly hall n (at school) Aula die.

assembly point n Treffpunkt der.

assert [ə'sɜːt] vt behaupten; **to ~ o.s.** sich durch|setzen.

assess [ə'ses] vt (person, situation, effect) bewerten; (value, damage) schätzen.

assessment [ə'sesmənt] n (of situation, person, effect) Bewertung die; (of value, damage, cost) Schätzung die.

asset ['æset] n (thing) Vorteil der; (person) Stütze die.

assign [ə'saɪn] vt: **to ~ sthg to sb** jm etw zu|teilen; **to ~ sb to sthg** jm etw zu|teilen.

assignment [ə'saɪnmənt] n (task) Aufgabe die; (SCH) Projekt das.

assist [ə'sɪst] vt helfen (+D).

assistance [ə'sɪstəns] n Hilfe die; **to be of ~ (to sb)** (jm) helfen.

assistant [ə'sɪstənt] n Assistent der (-in die).

associate [n ə'səʊʃɪət, vb ə'səʊʃɪeɪt] ◆ n Partner der (-in die). ◆ vt: **to ~ sb/ sthg with** jn/etw in Verbindung bringen mit.

association [ə,səʊsɪ'eɪʃn] n (group) Verband der.

assorted [ə'sɔːtɪd] adj gemischt.

assortment [ə'sɔːtmənt] n Auswahl die.

assume [ə'sjuːm] vt (suppose) an|nehmen; (control, responsibility) übernehmen.

assurance [ə'ʃʊərəns] n Versicherung die.

assure [ə'ʃʊəʳ] vt versichern; **to ~ sb (that) ...** jm versichern, daß ...

asterisk ['æstərɪsk] n Sternchen das.

asthma ['æsmə] n Asthma das.

asthmatic [æs'mætɪk] adj asthmatisch.

astonished [ə'stɒnɪʃt] adj erstaunt.

astonishing [ə'stɒnɪʃɪŋ] adj erstaunlich.

astound [ə'staʊnd] vt überraschen.

astray [ə'streɪ] adv: **to go ~** (person) sich verlaufen; (thing) verloren|gehen.

astrology [ə'strɒlədʒɪ] n Astrologie die.

astronomy [ə'strɒnəmɪ] n Astronomie die.

asylum [ə'saɪləm] n (mental hospital) psychiatrische Klinik die.

asylum seeker [-siːkəʳ] n Asylant der (-in die).

at [unstressed ət, stressed æt] prep 1. (indicating place, position) in (+D); ~ the end of am Ende (+G); ~ school in der Schule; ~ the hotel (inside) im Hotel; (outside) beim Hotel; ~ my mother's bei meiner Mutter; ~ home zu Hause. 2. (indicating direction) an (+A); to look ~ sb/sthg jn/etw anlschauen; to smile ~ sb jn anllächeln. 3. (indicating time) um; ~ nine o'clock um neun Uhr; ~ Christmas an Weihnachten; ~ night nachts. 4. (indicating rate, level, speed) mit; it works out ~ £5 each es kommt für jeden auf 5 Pfund; ~ 60 km/h mit 60 km/h. 5. (indicating activity): to be ~ lunch beim Mittagessen sein; to be good/bad ~ sthg in einer Sache gut/ schlecht sein. 6. (indicating cause) über (+D); to be pleased ~ sthg über etw (D) erfreut sein.

ate [Br et, Am eɪt] pt → eat.

atheist ['eɪθɪɪst] n Atheist der (-in die).

athlete ['æθliːt] n Athlet der (-in die).

athletics [æθ'letɪks] n Leicht- athletik die.

Atlantic [ət'læntɪk] n: the ~ (Ocean) der Atlantik.

atlas ['ætləs] n Atlas der.

atmosphere ['ætməsfɪəʳ] n Atmosphäre die.

atom ['ætəm] n Atom das.

A to Z n Stadtplan der (im Buchformat).

atrocious [ə'trəʊʃəs] adj grauen- haft.

attach [ə'tætʃ] vt befestigen; to ~ sthg to sthg etw an etw (D) befesti- gen.

attachment [ə'tætʃmənt] n (device) Zusatzgerät das.

attack [ə'tæk] ◆ n Angriff der; (of coughing, asthma etc) Anfall der. ◆ vt angreifen.

attacker [ə'tækəʳ] n Angreifer der (-in die).

attain [ə'teɪn] vt (fml) erreichen.

attempt [ə'tempt] ◆ n Versuch der. ◆ vt versuchen; to ~ to do sthg ver- suchen, etw zu tun.

attend [ə'tend] vt (meeting) teillnehmen an (+D); (Mass, school) besuchen. ▶ attend to vt fus (deal with) sich kümmern um.

attendance [ə'tendəns] n Besuch der; (number of people) Besucherzahl die.

attendant [ə'tendənt] n (in museum) Wärter der (-in die); (in car park) Wächter der (-in die).

attention [ə'tenʃn] n Aufmerk- samkeit die; to pay ~ aufmerksam sein; to pay ~ to sthg etw beachten.

attic ['ætɪk] n Dachboden der.

attitude ['ætɪtjuːd] n (mental) Einstellung die; (behaviour) Haltung die.

attorney [ə'tɜːnɪ] n (Am) Anwalt der (Anwältin die).

attract [ə'trækt] vt anlziehen; (atten- tion) erwecken.

attraction [ə'trækʃn] n (liking) Anziehung die; (attractive feature) Reiz der; (of town, resort) Attraktion die.

attractive [ə'træktɪv] adj (person) attraktiv; (idea, offer) reizvoll.

attribute [ə'trɪbjuːt] vt: to ~ sthg to etw zurücklführen auf (+A).

aubergine ['əʊbəʒiːn] n (Br) Aubergine die.

auburn ['ɔːbən] adj rotbraun.

auction ['ɔːkʃn] n Auktion die.

audience ['ɔːdɪəns] n (of play, concert, film) Publikum das; (of TV) Zuschauer pl; (of radio) Zuhörer pl.

audio ['ɔːdɪəʊ] adj Ton-.

audio-visual [-'vɪzʊəl] adj audiovi- suell.

auditorium [ˌɔːdɪ'tɔːrɪəm] n Zuschauerraum der.

Aug. abbr = August.

August ['ɔːgəst] n August der, → September.

aunt [ɑːnt] n Tante die.

au pair [ˌəʊ'peəʳ] n Au-pair-Mädchen das.

aural ['ɔːrəl] adj: an ~ exam ein Hörverständnistest.

Australia [ɒ'streɪliə] n Australien nt.

Australian [ɒ'streɪliən] ◆ adj australisch. ◆ n Australier der (-in die).

Austria ['ɒstriə] n Österreich nt.

Austrian ['ɒstriən] ◆ adj österreichisch. ◆ n Österreicher der (-in die).

authentic [ɔː'θentɪk] adj echt.

author ['ɔːθəʳ] n (of book, article) Autor der (-in die); (by profession) Schriftsteller der (-in die).

authority [ɔː'θɒrɪtɪ] n (power) Autorität die; (official organization) Behörde die; **the authorities** die Behörden.

authorization [ˌɔːθəraɪ'zeɪʃn] n Genehmigung die.

authorize ['ɔːθəraɪz] vt genehmigen; **to ~ sb to do sthg** jn ermächtigen, etw zu tun.

autobiography [ˌɔːtəbaɪ'ɒɡrəfɪ] n Autobiographie die.

autograph ['ɔːtəɡrɑːf] n Autogramm das.

automatic [ˌɔːtə'mætɪk] ◆ adj automatisch. ◆ n (car) Wagen der mit Automatikgetriebe.

automatically [ˌɔːtə'mætɪklɪ] adv automatisch.

automobile ['ɔːtəməbiːl] n (Am) Auto das.

autumn ['ɔːtəm] n Herbst der; **in (the) ~** im Herbst.

auxiliary (verb) [ɔːɡ'zɪljərɪ-] n Hilfsverb das.

available [ə'veɪləbl] adj verfügbar; (product) lieferbar; **to be ~** (person) zur Verfügung stehen.

avalanche ['ævəlɑːnʃ] n Lawine die.

Ave. abbr = **avenue**.

avenue ['ævənjuː] n (road) Allee die.

average ['ævərɪdʒ] ◆ adj durchschnittlich. ◆ n Durchschnitt der; **on ~** im Durchschnitt.

aversion [ə'vɜːʃn] n Abneigung die.

aviation [ˌeɪvɪ'eɪʃn] n Luftfahrt die.

avid ['ævɪd] adj begeistert.

avocado (pear) [ˌævə'kɑːdəʊ-] n Avocado die.

avoid [ə'vɔɪd] vt vermeiden; (person, place) meiden; **to ~ doing sthg** vermeiden, etw zu tun.

await [ə'weɪt] vt erwarten.

awake [ə'weɪk] (pt awoke, pp awoken) ◆ adj wach. ◆ vi erwachen.

award [ə'wɔːd] ◆ n (prize) Auszeichnung die. ◆ vt: **to ~ sb sthg** (prize) jm etw verleihen; (damages, compensation) jm etw zulsprechen.

aware [ə'weəʳ] adj: **to be ~ of sthg** sich (D) einer Sache (G) bewußt sein.

away [ə'weɪ] adv weg; (not at home, in office) nicht da; **to take sthg ~ (from sb)** (jm) etw weglnehmen; **far ~** weit entfernt; **10 miles ~ (from here)** 10 Meilen (von hier) entfernt; **two weeks ~** in zwei Wochen.

awesome ['ɔːsəm] adj überwältigend; (inf: excellent) toll.

awful ['ɔːfəl] adj furchtbar.

awfully ['ɔːflɪ] adv (very) furchtbar.

awkward ['ɔːkwəd] adj (position, shape, situation) ungünstig; (movement) ungeschickt; (question, task) schwierig.

awning ['ɔːnɪŋ] n (on house) Markise die; (of tent) Vordach das.

awoke [ə'wəʊk] pt → **awake**.

awoken [ə'wəʊkən] pp → **awake**.

axe [æks] n Axt die.

axle ['æksl] n Achse die.

B

BA (abbr of Bachelor of Arts) Bakkalaureus der Geisteswissenschaften.

babble ['bæbl] vi plappern.

baby ['beɪbɪ] n Baby das; **to have a ~** ein Kind bekommen; **~ sweetcorn**

Maiskölbchen pl.

baby carriage n (Am) Kinderwagen der.

baby food n Babynahrung die.

baby-sit vi babysitten.

baby wipe n Babyöltuch das.

bachelor ['bætʃələr] n Junggeselle der.

back [bæk] ◆ adv zurück. ◆ n (of person, hand, book) Rücken der; (of chair) Lehne die; (inside car) Rücksitz der; (of room) hintere Teil der; (of bank note) Rückseite die. ◆ adj (wheels) Hinter-. ◆ vi (car, driver) zurücksetzen. ◆ vt (support) unterstützen; **at the ~ of** hinter (+D); **in ~ of** (Am) hinter (+D); **~ to front** verkehrt herum. ▶ **back up** vt sep (support) unterstützen; (confirm) bestätigen. ◆ vi (car, driver) zurücksetzen.

backache ['bækeɪk] n Rückenschmerzen pl.

backbone ['bækbəʊn] n Wirbelsäule die.

back door n Hintertür die.

backfire [,bæk'faɪər] vi (car) fehlzünden.

background ['bækgraʊnd] n Hintergrund der; (of person) Herkunft die.

backlog ['bæklɒg] n Rückstand der.

backpack ['bækpæk] n Rucksack der.

backpacker ['bækpækər] n Rucksacktourist der (-in die).

back seat n Rücksitz der.

backside [,bæk'saɪd] n (inf) Hintern der.

back street n Seitenstraße die.

backstroke ['bækstrəʊk] n Rückenschwimmen das.

backwards ['bækwədz] adv rückwärts; (look) nach hinten.

bacon ['beɪkən] n Speck der; **~ and eggs** Eier pl mit Speck.

bacteria [bæk'tɪərɪə] npl Bakterien pl.

bad [bæd] (compar **worse**, superl **worst**) adj schlecht; (serious) schwer;

(eyesight, excuse) schwach; (naughty) ungezogen; (injured) schlimm; (rotten, off) verdorben; **not ~** nicht schlecht.

badge [bædʒ] n Abzeichen das.

badger ['bædʒər] n Dachs der.

badly ['bædlɪ] (compar **worse**, superl **worst**) adv schlecht; (seriously) schwer; (very much) sehr; **to need sthg ~** etw dringend brauchen.

badly paid [-peɪd] adj schlecht bezahlt.

badminton ['bædmɪntən] n Federball der; (SPORT) Badminton das.

bad-tempered [-'tempəd] adj schlechtgelaunt.

bag [bæg] n (of paper, plastic) Tüte die; (handbag) Tasche die; (suitcase) Reisetasche die; **a ~ of crisps** eine Tüte Chips.

bagel ['beɪgəl] n ringförmiges Brötchen das.

baggage ['bægɪdʒ] n Gepäck das.

baggage allowance n Freigepäck das.

baggage reclaim n Gepäckausgabe die.

baggy ['bægɪ] adj weit; (too baggy) ausgeleiert.

bagpipes ['bægpaɪps] npl Dudelsack der.

bail [beɪl] n Kaution die.

bailiff ['beɪlɪf] n Gerichtsvollzieher der.

bait [beɪt] n Köder der.

bake [beɪk] ◆ vt backen. ◆ n Auflauf der.

baked [beɪkt] adj überbacken.

baked Alaska [-ə'læskə] n Dessert aus Eiskrem auf Biskuit, das mit Baiser überzogen ist und kurz überbacken wird.

baked beans npl Bohnen pl (in Tomatensoße).

baked potato n (in der Schale) gebackene Kartoffel.

baker ['beɪkər] n Bäcker der (-in die); **~'s** (shop) Bäckerei die.

Bakewell tart ['beɪkwel-] n Torte, die mit einer Schicht Marmelade zwischen *zwei Schichten Mandelmasse gefüllt ist und mit einer wellenförmigen Glasur überzogen ist.*

balance ['bæləns] ◆ n (of person) Gleichgewicht das; (of bank account) Kontostand der; (remainder) Rest der. ◆ vt (object) balancieren.

balcony ['bælkənɪ] n Balkon der.

bald [bɔːld] adj kahlköpfig.

bale [beɪl] n Ballen der.

ball [bɔːl] n Ball der; (in snooker) Kugel die; (of wool, string, paper) Knäuel das; **on the ~** (fig) auf Draht.

ballad ['bæləd] n Ballade die.

ballerina [,bælə'riːnə] n Ballerina die.

ballet ['bæleɪ] n Ballett das.

ballet dancer n Ballettänzer der (-in die).

balloon [bə'luːn] n Luftballon der.

ballot ['bælət] n Wahl die.

ballpoint pen ['bɔːlpɔɪnt-] n Kugelschreiber der.

ballroom ['bɔːlrʊm] n Tanzsaal der.

ballroom dancing n Gesellschaftstanz der.

balti ['bɔːltɪ] n (pan) in der indischen Küche verwendete Metallpfanne; (food) in einer Balti-Pfanne zubereitetes, stark gewürztes indisches Gericht.

bamboo [bæm'buː] n Bambus der.

bamboo shoots npl Bambussprossen pl.

ban [bæn] ◆ n Verbot das. ◆ vt verbieten; **to ~ sb from doing sthg** jm verbieten, etw zu tun.

banana [bə'nɑːnə] n Banane die.

banana split n Bananensplit das.

band [bænd] n (musical group) Band die; (strip of paper, rubber) Band das.

bandage ['bændɪdʒ] ◆ n Verband der. ◆ vt verbinden.

B and B abbr = **bed and breakfast**.

bandstand ['bændstænd] n Musikpavillon der.

bang [bæŋ] ◆ n (noise) Knall der. ◆ vt knallen; (door) zuknallen; **to ~ one's head** sich (D) den Kopf stoßen.

banger ['bæŋər] n (Br: inf: sausage) Würstchen das; **~s and mash** Würstchen mit Kartoffelbrei.

bangle ['bæŋgl] n Armreif der.

bangs [bæŋz] npl (Am) Pony der.

banister ['bænɪstər] n Treppengeländer das.

banjo ['bændʒəʊ] n Banjo das.

bank [bæŋk] n (for money) Bank die; (of river, lake) Ufer das; (slope) Böschung die.

bank account n Bankkonto das.

bank book n Sparbuch das.

bank charges npl Bankgebühren pl.

bank clerk n Bankangestellte der/die.

bank draft n Banküberweisung die.

banker ['bæŋkər] n Banker der.

banker's card n Scheckkarte die.

bank holiday n (Br) öffentlicher Feiertag.

bank manager n Zweigstellenleiter der (-in die).

bank note n Geldschein der.

bankrupt ['bæŋkrʌpt] adj bankrott.

bank statement n Kontoauszug der.

banner ['bænər] n Spruchband das.

bannister ['bænɪstər] = **banister**.

banquet ['bæŋkwɪt] n (formal dinner) Bankett das; (at Indian restaurant etc) Menü für eine bestimmte Anzahl Personen.

bap [bæp] n (Br) Brötchen das.

baptize [Br bæp'taɪz, Am 'bæptaɪz] vt taufen.

bar [bɑːr] ◆ n (pub, in hotel) Bar die; (counter in pub) Theke die; (of metal, wood) Stange die; (of soap) Stück das; (of chocolate) Riegel der. ◆ vt (obstruct) versperren.

barbecue ['bɑːbɪkjuː] ◆ n (apparatus) Grill der; (party) Grillfest das. ◆ vt grillen.

barbecue sauce n Barbecuesoße die.

barbed wire [baːbd-] n Stacheldraht der.

barber ['baːbər] n Herrenfriseur der; **~'s** (shop) Herrenfriseur der.

bar code n Strichkode der.

bare [beər] adj bloß; (room, cupboard) leer.

barefoot [ˌbeəˈfʊt] adv barfuß.

barely ['beəlɪ] adv kaum.

bargain ['baːgɪn] ♦ n (agreement) Abmachung die; (cheap buy) gutes Geschäft. ♦ vi (haggle) handeln. ▶ **bargain for** vt fus rechnen mit.

bargain basement n Tiefgeschoß im Kaufhaus mit Sonderangeboten.

barge [baːdʒ] n Kahn der. ▶ **barge in** vi: **to ~ in** (on sb) hereinplatzen (bei jm).

bark [baːk] ♦ n (of tree) Rinde die. ♦ vi (dog) bellen.

barley ['baːlɪ] n Gerste die.

barmaid ['baːmeɪd] n Bardame die.

barman ['baːmən] (pl **-men** [-mən]) n Barkeeper der.

bar meal n einfaches Essen in einer Kneipe.

barn [baːn] n Scheune die.

barometer [bəˈrɒmɪtər] n Barometer das.

baron ['bærən] n Baron der.

baroque [bəˈrɒk] adj barock.

barracks ['bærəks] npl Kaserne die.

barrel ['bærəl] n (of beer, wine, oil) Faß das; (of gun) Lauf der.

barren ['bærən] adj (land, soil) unfruchtbar.

barricade [ˌbærɪˈkeɪd] n Barrikade die.

barrier ['bærɪər] n (fence, wall etc) Absperrung die; (problem) Barriere die.

barrister ['bærɪstər] n (Br) Barrister der, ≈ Rechtsanwalt der (-anwältin die).

bartender ['baːtendər] n (Am) Barkeeper der.

barter ['baːtər] vi tauschen.

base [beɪs] ♦ n (of lamp, pillar, mountain) Fuß der; (MIL) Stützpunkt der. ♦ vt: **to ~ sthg on sthg** etw auf etw (D) aufbauen.

baseball ['beɪsbɔːl] n Baseball der.

baseball cap n Baseballkappe die.

basement ['beɪsmənt] n (in house) Kellergeschoß das; (in store) Tiefgeschoß das.

bases ['beɪsiːz] pl → **basis**.

bash [bæʃ] vt (inf): **to ~ one's head** sich (D) den Kopf anlhauen.

basic ['beɪsɪk] adj grundlegend; (accommodation, meal) einfach. ▶ **basics** npl: **the ~s** die Grundlagen.

basically ['beɪsɪklɪ] adv grundsätzlich.

basil ['bæzl] n Basilikum das.

basin ['beɪsn] n (washbasin) Becken das; (bowl) Schüssel die.

basis ['beɪsɪs] (pl **-ses**) n Grundlage die; **on a weekly ~** wöchentlich; **on the ~ of** auf der Grundlage von.

basket ['baːskɪt] n Korb der.

basketball ['baːskɪtbɔːl] n Basketball der.

basmati rice [bəzˈmæti-] n Basmatireis der.

bass¹ [beɪs] ♦ n (singer, instrument) Baß der. ♦ adj: **a ~ guitar** eine Baßgitarre.

bass² [bæs] n (fish) Barsch der.

bassoon [bəˈsuːn] n Fagott das.

bastard ['baːstəd] n (vulg) Scheißkerl der.

bat [bæt] n (in cricket, baseball) Schlagholz das; (in table tennis) Schläger der; (animal) Fledermaus die.

batch [bætʃ] n (of letters, books) Stapel der; (of people) Gruppe die.

bath [baːθ] ♦ n Bad das; (tub) Badewanne die. ♦ vt baden; **to have a ~** ein Bad nehmen. ▶ **baths** npl (Br: public swimming pool) Schwimmbad das.

bathe [beɪð] *vi* (Br: *swim*) baden; (Am: *have bath*) ein Bad nehmen.

bathing ['beɪðɪŋ] *n* (Br) Baden *das*.

bathrobe ['bɑːθrəʊb] *n* Bademantel *der*.

bathroom ['bɑːθrʊm] *n* Badezimmer *das*; (Am: *toilet*) Toilette *die*.

bathroom cabinet *n* Badezimmerschrank *der*.

bathtub ['bɑːθtʌb] *n* Badewanne *die*.

baton ['bætən] *n* (*of conductor*) Taktstock *der*; (*truncheon*) Schlagstock *der*.

batter ['bætər] ◆ *n* (CULIN) Teig *der*. ◆ *vt* (*wife, child*) schlagen.

battered ['bætəd] *adj* (CULIN) im Teigmantel.

battery ['bætərɪ] *n* Batterie *die*.

battery charger [-,tʃɑːdʒər] *n* Batterieladegerät *das*.

battle ['bætl] *n* Schlacht *die*; (*fig: struggle*) Kampf *der*.

battlefield ['bætlfiːld] *n* Schlachtfeld *das*.

battlements ['bætlmənts] *npl* Zinnen *pl*.

battleship ['bætlʃɪp] *n* Schlachtschiff *das*.

Bavaria [bə'veərɪə] *n* Bayern *nt*.

bay [beɪ] *n* Bucht *die*.

bay leaf *n* Lorbeerblatt *das*.

bay window *n* Erkerfenster *das*.

B & B *abbr* = **bed and breakfast**.

BC (*abbr of before Christ*) v. Chr.

be [biː] (*pt* was,were, *pp* been) ◆ *vi* 1. (*exist*) sein; **there is/are** es ist/sind ... da, es gibt; **are there any shops near here?** gibt es hier in der Nähe irgendwelche Geschäfte? 2. (*referring to location*) sein; **the hotel is near the airport** das Hotel ist in der Nähe des Flughafens. 3. (*referring to movement*) sein; **have you ever been to Ireland?** warst du/waren Sie schon mal in Irland?; **I'll ~ there in ten minutes** ich komme in zehn Minuten. 4. (*occur*) sein; **my birthday is in June**

mein Geburtstag ist im Juni. 5. (*identifying, describing*) sein; **he's a doctor** er ist Arzt; **I'm British** ich bin Brite; **I'm hot/cold** mir ist heiß/kalt. 6. (*referring to health*): **how are you?** wie geht es dir/Ihnen?; **I'm fine** mir geht es gut; **she's ill** sie ist krank. 7. (*referring to age*): **how old are you?** wie alt bist du/sind Sie?; **I'm 14 (years old)** ich bin 14 (Jahre alt). 8. (*referring to cost*) kosten; **how much is it?** wieviel kostet es?; **it's £10** es kostet 10 Pfund. 9. (*referring to time, dates*) sein; **what time is it?** wieviel Uhr ist es?; **it's ten o'clock** es ist zehn Uhr. 10. (*referring to measurement*) sein; **it's 10 metres long/high** es ist 10 Meter lang/hoch; **I'm 8 stone** ich wiege 50 Kilo. 11. (*referring to weather*) sein; **it's hot/cold** es ist heiß/kalt. ◆ *aux vb* 1. (*forming continuous tense*): **I'm learning German** ich lerne deutsch; **we've been visiting the museum** wir waren im Museum. 2. (*forming passive*) werden; **they were defeated** sie wurden geschlagen; **the flight was delayed** das Flugzeug hatte Verspätung. 3. (*with infinitive to express order*): **all rooms are to ~ vacated by 10.00 am** alle Zimmer müssen bis 10 Uhr geräumt sein. 4. (*with infinitive to express future tense*): **the race is to start at noon** das Rennen ist für 12 Uhr angesetzt. 5. (*in tag questions*): **it's cold, isn't it?** es ist kalt, nicht wahr?

beach [biːtʃ] *n* Strand *der*.

bead [biːd] *n* (*of glass, wood etc*) Perle *die*.

beak [biːk] *n* Schnabel *der*.

beaker ['biːkər] *n* Becher *der*.

beam [biːm] ◆ *n* (*of light*) Strahl *der*; (*of wood, concrete*) Balken *der*. ◆ *vi* strahlen.

bean [biːn] *n* Bohne *die*.

bean curd [-kɜːd] *n* Tofu *der*.

beansprouts ['biːnsprəʊts] *npl* Sojabohnensprossen *pl*.

bear [beər] (*pt* bore, *pp* borne) ◆ *n* (*animal*) Bär *der*. ◆ *vt* (*support*) tragen;

(endure) ertragen. ♦ *vi*: **to ~ left/right** sich links/rechts halten.

bearable ['beərəbl] *adj* erträglich.

beard [bɪəd] *n* Bart *der*.

bearer ['beərər] *n* *(of cheque, passport)* Inhaber *der* (-in *die*).

bearing ['beərɪŋ] *n* *(relevance)* Auswirkung *die*; **to get one's ~s** sich orientieren.

beast [biːst] *n* *(animal)* Tier *das*.

beat [biːt] *(pt inv, pp* **beaten** [biːtn]*)* ♦ *n* *(of heart, pulse)* Herzschlag *der*; *(MUS)* Takt *der*. ♦ *vt* schlagen. ► **beat down** *vt sep* herunter|handeln. ♦ *vi* *(sun)* herunter|brennen; *(rain)* herunter|prasseln. ► **beat up** *vt sep* verprügeln.

beautiful ['bjuːtɪful] *adj* schön.

beauty ['bjuːtɪ] *n* Schönheit *die*.

beauty parlour *n* Schönheits-salon *der*.

beauty spot *n* *(place)* Ausflugsort *der*.

beaver ['biːvər] *n* Biber *der*.

became [bɪ'keɪm] *pt* → **become**.

because [bɪ'kɒz] *conj* weil; **~ of** wegen (+G *or* D).

beckon ['bekən] *vi*: **to ~ to** zu|winken (+D).

become [bɪ'kʌm] *(pt* **became**, *pp inv)* *vi* werden; **what became of him?** was ist aus ihm geworden?

bed [bed] *n* Bett *das*; *(of sea)* Meeresboden *der*; *(CULIN)*: **served on a ~ of ...** angerichtet auf (+D) ...; **in ~** im Bett; **to get out of ~** auf|stehen; **to go to ~** ins Bett gehen; **to go to ~ with sb** mit jm ins Bett gehen; **to make the ~** das Bett machen.

bed and breakfast *n* (Br) ≃ Zimmer *das* mit Frühstück.

bedclothes ['bedkləʊðz] *npl* Bettwäsche *die*.

bedding ['bedɪŋ] *n* Bettzeug *das*.

bed linen *n* Bettwäsche *die*.

bedroom ['bedrʊm] *n* Schlafzimmer *das*.

bedside table ['bedsaɪd-] *n* Nachttisch *der*.

bedsit ['bed,sɪt] *n* (Br) ≃ möbliertes Zimmer.

bedspread ['bedspred] *n* Tages-decke *die*.

bedtime ['bedtaɪm] *n* Schlafenszeit *die*.

bee [biː] *n* Biene *die*.

beech [biːtʃ] *n* Buche *die*.

beef [biːf] *n* Rindfleisch *das*; **~ Wellington** Filet *das* Wellington.

beefburger ['biːf,bɜːgər] *n* Hamburger *der*.

beehive ['biːhaɪv] *n* Bienenstock *der*.

been [biːn] *pp* → **be**.

beer [bɪər] *n* Bier *das*.

beer garden *n* Biergarten *der*.

beer mat *n* Bierdeckel *der*.

beetle ['biːtl] *n* Käfer *der*.

beetroot ['biːtruːt] *n* rote Bete *die*.

before [bɪ'fɔːr] ♦ *adv* schon einmal. ♦ *prep* vor (+D). ♦ *conj* bevor; **~ you leave** bevor du gehst; **the day ~** der Tag zuvor; **the week ~ last** vorletzte Woche.

beforehand [bɪ'fɔːhænd] *adv* vorher.

befriend [bɪ'frend] *vt* sich an|freun-den mit.

beg [beg] ♦ *vi* betteln. ♦ *vt*: **to ~ sb to do sthg** jn bitten, etw zu tun; **to ~ for** *(for money, food)* betteln um.

began [bɪ'gæn] *pt* → **begin**.

beggar ['begər] *n* Bettler *der* (-in *die*).

begin [bɪ'gɪn] *(pt* **began**, *pp* **begun**) *vt & vi* an|fangen, beginnen; **to ~ doing** OR **to do sthg** an|fangen, etw zu tun; **to ~ by doing sthg** etw als erstes tun; **to ~ with** zunächst.

beginner [bɪ'gɪnər] *n* Anfänger *der* (-in *die*); **beginner's course** Anfänger-kurs *der*.

beginning [bɪ'gɪnɪŋ] *n* Anfang *der*.

begun [bɪ'gʌn] *pp* → **begin**.

behalf [bɪ'hɑːf] *n*: **on ~ of** im Auftrag (+G).

behave [bɪ'heɪv] *vi* sich verhalten;

to ~ (o.s.) (be good) sich benehmen.
behavior [bɪ'heɪvjər] (Am) =
behaviour.
behaviour [bɪ'heɪvjər] n Verhalten
das; **good/bad ~** gutes/schlechtes
Benehmen.
behind [bɪ'haɪnd] ◆ prep hinter
(+A,D). ◆ n (inf) Hintern der. ◆ adv
hinten; (late): **to be ~** im Verzug sein;
to leave sthg ~ etw zurückllassen; **to
stay ~** dalbleiben.
beige [beɪʒ] adj beige.
being ['biːɪŋ] n Wesen das; **to come
into ~** entstehen.
belated [bɪ'leɪtɪd] adj verspätet.
belch [beltʃ] vi rülpsen.
Belgian ['beldʒən] ◆ adj belgisch.
◆ n Belgier der (-in die).
Belgium ['beldʒəm] n Belgien nt.
belief [bɪ'liːf] n Glaube der; **it is my ~
that** ich bin davon überzeugt, daß.
believe [bɪ'liːv] ◆ vt (story, think)
glauben; (person) glauben (+D). ◆ vi:
to ~ in sthg glauben an etw (A); **to ~
in doing sthg** viel von etw halten.
believer [bɪ'liːvər] n Gläubige der die.
bell [bel] n Glocke die; (of phone, door)
Klingel die.
bellboy ['belbɔɪ] n Page der.
bellow ['beləʊ] vi brüllen.
belly ['belɪ] n (inf) Bauch der.
belly button n (inf) Bauchnabel
der.
belong [bɪ'lɒŋ] vi gehören; **to ~ to**
(property) gehören (+D); (to club,
party) anlgehören (+D).
belongings [bɪ'lɒŋɪŋz] npl Sachen
pl.
below [bɪ'ləʊ] ◆ adv unten. ◆ prep
unter (+A,D).
belt [belt] n (for clothes) Gürtel der;
(TECH) Riemen der.
beltway ['beltweɪ] n (Am) Ringautobahn die.
bench [bentʃ] n Bank die.
bend [bend] (pt & pp bent) ◆ n
(in road) Kurve die; (in river, pipe)
Biegung die. ◆ vt (leg, knees) beugen;
(pipe, wire) biegen. ◆ vi (road, river,

pipe) sich biegen. ▶ **bend down** vi
sich bücken. ▶ **bend over** vi sich
nach vorn beugen.
beneath [bɪ'niːθ] ◆ adv unten.
◆ prep unter (+A,D).
beneficial [ˌbenɪ'fɪʃl] adj nützlich.
benefit ['benɪfɪt] ◆ n (advantage)
Vorteil der; (usefulness) Nutzen der;
(money) Unterstützung die. ◆ vt
nützen (+D). ◆ vi: **to ~ from sthg** von
etw profitieren; **for the ~ of** für.
benign [bɪ'naɪn] adj (MED) gutartig.
bent [bent] pt & pp → **bend**.
bereaved [bɪ'riːvd] n: **the ~** der/die
Hinterbliebene.
beret ['bereɪ] n Baskenmütze die.
Berlin [bɜː'lɪn] n Berlin nt.
Bermuda shorts [bə'mjuːdə-] npl
Bermudashorts pl.
Bern [bɜːn] n Bern nt.
berry ['berɪ] n Beere die.
berserk [bə'zɜːk] adj: **to go ~** vor
Wut außer sich geraten.
berth [bɜːθ] n (for ship) Liegeplatz
der; (in ship) Koje die; (in train) Bett
das.
beside [bɪ'saɪd] prep neben (+A,D);
~ the sea/river am Meer/Fluß; **to be ~
the point** nichts damit zu tun haben.
besides [bɪ'saɪdz] ◆ adv außerdem.
◆ prep außer (+D).
best [best] ◆ adj beste(-r)(-s). ◆ adv
am besten. ◆ n: **the ~** der/die/das
Beste; **a pint of ~** (beer) ein großes
Glas 'bitter'-Bier; **the ~ thing to do is**
... am besten wäre es, ...; **to make
the ~ of sthg** das Beste aus einer
Sache machen; **to do one's ~** sein
Bestes tun; **'~ before ...'** 'mindestens haltbar bis ...'; **at ~** besten-
falls; **all the ~!** alles Gute!
best man n Trauzeuge der (des
Bräutigams).
best-seller [-'selər] n (book)
Bestseller der.
bet [bet] (pt & pp inv) ◆ n Wette die.
◆ vt wetten. ◆ vi: **to ~ on sthg** auf etw
(A) setzen; **I ~ (that) you can't do it**
ich wette, du kannst das nicht.

betray [bɪ'treɪ] vt verraten.

better ['betər] adj & adv besser; **I'm much ~ now** es geht mir jetzt viel besser; **you had ~ ...** du solltest lieber ...; **to get ~** (in health) gesund werden; (improve) sich verbessern.

betting ['betɪŋ] n Wetten das.

betting shop n (Br) Wettbüro das.

between [bɪ'twi:n] ◆ prep zwischen (+D); (in space) zwischen (+A,D); (share) unter (+A,D). ◆ adv dazwischen; **in ~** (in space) zwischen (+A,D); (in time) zwischen (+D), dazwischen.

beverage ['bevərɪdʒ] n (fml) Getränk das.

beware [bɪ'weər] vi: **to ~ of** sich in acht nehmen vor (+D); **'~ of the dog'** 'Vorsicht, bissiger Hund'.

bewildered [bɪ'wɪldəd] adj verwirrt.

beyond [bɪ'jɒnd] ◆ prep über ... (+A) hinaus; (responsibility) außerhalb (+G); (doubt, reach) außer (+D). ◆ adv darüber hinaus.

biased ['baɪəst] adj parteiisch.

bib [bɪb] n (for baby) Lätzchen das.

bible ['baɪbl] n Bibel die.

biceps ['baɪseps] n Bizeps der.

bicycle ['baɪsɪkl] n Fahrrad das.

bicycle path n Radweg der.

bicycle pump n Luftpumpe die.

bid [bɪd] (pt & pp inv) ◆ n (at auction) Gebot das; (attempt) Versuch der. ◆ vt (money) bieten. ◆ vi: **to ~ (for)** bieten (auf (+A).

bidet ['bi:deɪ] n Bidet das.

big [bɪg] adj groß; **my ~ brother** mein großer Bruder; **how ~ is it?** wie groß ist es?

bike [baɪk] n (inf: bicycle) Rad das; (motorcycle) Maschine die.

biking ['baɪkɪŋ] n: **to go ~** eine Radtour machen.

bikini [bɪ'ki:nɪ] n Bikini der.

bikini bottom n Bikinihose die.

bikini top n Bikinioberteil das.

bilingual [baɪ'lɪŋgwəl] adj zweisprachig.

bill [bɪl] n (for meal, hotel room) Rechnung die; (Am: bank note) Geldschein der; (at cinema, theatre) Programm das; (POL) Gesetzentwurf der; **can I have the ~, please?** die Rechnung, bitte.

billboard ['bɪlbɔːd] n Anschlagtafel die.

billfold ['bɪlfəʊld] n (Am) Brieftasche die.

billiards ['bɪljədz] n Billard das.

billion ['bɪljən] n (thousand million) Milliarde die; (Br: million million) Billion die.

bin [bɪn] n (rubbish bin) Mülleimer der; (wastepaper bin) Papierkorb der; (for bread, flour) Kasten der; (on plane) Ablage die.

bind [baɪnd] (pt & pp **bound**) vt (tie up) festlbinden.

binding ['baɪndɪŋ] n (of book) Einband der; (for ski) Bindung die.

bingo ['bɪŋgəʊ] n Bingo das.

binoculars [bɪ'nɒkjʊləz] npl Fernglas das.

biodegradable [,baɪəʊdɪ'greɪdəbl] adj biologisch abbaubar.

biography [baɪ'ɒgrəfɪ] n Biographie die.

biological [,baɪə'lɒdʒɪkl] adj biologisch.

biology [baɪ'ɒlədʒɪ] n Biologie die.

birch [bɜːtʃ] n Birke die.

bird [bɜːd] n Vogel der; (Br: inf: woman) Mieze die.

bird-watching [-,wɒtʃɪŋ] n: **to go ~** Vögel beobachten gehen.

Biro® ['baɪərəʊ] n Kugelschreiber der.

birth [bɜːθ] n Geburt die; **by ~** von Geburt; **to give ~ to** zur Welt bringen.

birth certificate n Geburtsurkunde die.

birth control n Geburtenregelung die.

birthday ['bɜːθdeɪ] n Geburtstag der; **happy ~!** herzlichen Glückwunsch zum Geburtstag!

birthday card n Geburtstagskarte die.

birthday party n Geburtstagsfeier die.

birthplace ['bɜːθpleɪs] n Geburtsort der.

biscuit ['bɪskɪt] n (Br) Plätzchen das; (Am: scone) Hefebrötchen, das üblicherweise mit Bratensaft gegessen wird.

bishop ['bɪʃəp] n (RELIG) Bischof der (Bischöfin die); (in chess) Läufer der.

bistro ['biːstrəʊ] n Bistro das.

bit [bɪt] ♦ pt → **bite**. ♦ n (piece) Stück das; (of drill) Bohrer der (Metallstift); (of bridle) Gebiß das; **a ~** ein bißchen; **a ~ of cheese** ein bißchen Käse; **not a ~** überhaupt nicht; **~ by ~** allmählich.

bitch [bɪtʃ] n (vulg: woman) Kuh die; (dog) Hündin die.

bite [baɪt] (pt **bit**, pp **bitten** ['bɪtn]) ♦ n (of food) Happen der; (from insect) Stich der; (from snake) Biß der. ♦ vt beißen; (subj: insect) stechen; **to have a ~ to eat** eine Kleinigkeit essen.

bitter ['bɪtər] ♦ adj bitter. ♦ n (Br: beer) dem Altbier ähnliches Bier.

bitter lemon n Bitter Lemon das.

bizarre [bɪ'zɑːr] adj bizarr.

black [blæk] ♦ adj schwarz. ♦ n (colour) Schwarz das; (person) Schwarze der die. ▶ **black out** vi ohnmächtig werden.

black and white adj (film, photo) schwarzweiß.

blackberry ['blækbrɪ] n Brombeere die.

blackbird ['blækbɜːd] n Amsel die.

blackboard ['blækbɔːd] n Tafel die.

black cherry n schwarze Kirsche.

blackcurrant [,blæk'kʌrənt] n schwarze Johannisbeere.

black eye n blaues Auge.

Black Forest n Schwarzwald der.

Black Forest gâteau n Schwarzwälder Kirschtorte die.

black ice n Glatteis das.

blackmail ['blækmeɪl] ♦ n Erpressung die. ♦ vt erpressen.

blackout ['blækaʊt] n (power cut) Stromausfall der.

black pepper n schwarzer Pfeffer.

black pudding n (Br) Blutwurst die (in Scheiben geschnitten und gebraten).

blacksmith ['blæksmɪθ] n Schmied der.

bladder ['blædər] n Blase die.

blade [bleɪd] n (of knife, razor) Klinge die; (of saw, propeller, oar) Blatt das; (of grass) Halm der.

blame [bleɪm] ♦ n Schuld die. ♦ vt beschuldigen; **to ~ sb (for sthg)** jm die Schuld (an etw (D) geben; **to ~ sthg on sb** die Schuld an etw (D) auf jn schieben.

bland [blænd] adj fade.

blank [blæŋk] ♦ adj leer. ♦ n (empty space) Lücke die.

blank cheque n Blankoscheck der.

blanket ['blæŋkɪt] n Decke die.

blast [blɑːst] ♦ n (explosion) Explosion die; (of air, wind) Windstoß der. ♦ excl (inf) Mist!; **at full ~** mit Volldampf.

blaze [bleɪz] ♦ n (fire) Feuer das. ♦ vi (fire) brennen; (sun, light) leuchten.

blazer ['bleɪzər] n Blazer der.

bleach [bliːtʃ] ♦ n Bleichmittel das. ♦ vt bleichen.

bleak [bliːk] adj trostlos.

bleed [bliːd] (pt & pp **bled** [bled]) vi bluten.

blend [blend] ♦ n (of coffee, whisky) Mischung die. ♦ vt mischen.

blender ['blendər] n Mixer der.

bless [bles] vt segnen; **~ you!** (said after sneeze) Gesundheit!

blessing ['blesɪŋ] n Segen der.

blew [bluː] pt → **blow**.

blind [blaɪnd] ♦ adj blind. ♦ n (for window) Rouleau das. ♦ npl: **the ~** die Blinden.

blind corner n unübersichtliche Kurve.

blindfold ['blaɪndfəʊld] ♦ n

Augenbinde die. ◆ vt: **to ~ sb** jm die Augen verbinden.

blind spot n (AUT) toter Winkel.

blink [blɪŋk] vi zwinkern.

blinkers ['blɪŋkəz] npl (Br) Scheuklappen pl.

bliss [blɪs] n vollkommenes Glück.

blister ['blɪstər] n Blase die.

blizzard ['blɪzəd] n Schneesturm der.

bloated ['bləʊtɪd] adj (after eating) übersatt.

blob [blɒb] n (of paint) Klecks der; (of cream) Klacks der.

block [blɒk] ◆ n Block der. ◆ vt (obstruct) blockieren; **to have a ~ed (up) nose** eine verstopfte Nase haben. ▶ **block up** vt sep (pipe) verstopfen.

blockage ['blɒkɪdʒ] n Verstopfung die.

block capitals npl Druckbuchstaben pl.

block of flats n Wohnblock der.

bloke [bləʊk] n (Br: inf) Typ der.

blond [blɒnd] ◆ adj blond. ◆ n Blonde die.

blonde [blɒnd] ◆ adj blond. ◆ n Blondine die.

blood [blʌd] n Blut das.

blood donor n Blutspender der (-in die).

blood group n Blutgruppe die.

blood poisoning n Blutvergiftung die.

blood pressure n Blutdruck der.

bloodshot ['blʌdʃɒt] adj blutunterlaufen.

blood test n Blutprobe die.

blood transfusion n Bluttransfusion die.

bloody ['blʌdɪ] ◆ adj blutig; (Br: vulg: damn) verdammt. ◆ adv (Br: vulg) verdammt.

Bloody Mary [-'meərɪ] n Bloody Mary der (Cocktail aus Wodka und Tomatensaft).

bloom [bluːm] ◆ n Blüte die. ◆ vi

blühen; **to be in ~** in Blüte stehen.

blossom ['blɒsəm] n Blüte die.

blot [blɒt] n (of ink) (Tinten)klecks der.

blotch [blɒtʃ] n Fleck der.

blotting paper ['blɒtɪŋ-] n Löschpapier das.

blouse [blaʊz] n Bluse die.

blow [bləʊ] (pt blew, pp blown) ◆ vt blasen; (subj: wind) wehen. ◆ vi (wind) wehen; (person) blasen; (fuse) durchlbrennen. ◆ n Schlag der; **to ~ one's nose** sich (D) die Nase putzen. ▶ **blow up** vt sep (cause to explode) sprengen; (inflate) auflblasen. ◆ vi (explode) explodieren.

blow-dry ◆ n Fönen das. ◆ vt fönen.

blown [bləʊn] pp → **blow**.

BLT n (sandwich) Sandwich mit Speck, grünem Salat und Tomaten.

blue [bluː] ◆ adj blau; (film) Porno-. ◆ n Blau das. ▶ **blues** n (MUS) Blues der.

bluebell ['bluːbel] n Glockenblume die.

blueberry ['bluːbərɪ] n Blaubeere die.

bluebottle ['bluːˌbɒtl] n Schmeißfliege die.

blue cheese n Blauschimmelkäse der.

bluff [blʌf] ◆ n (cliff) Steilhang der. ◆ vi bluffen.

blunder ['blʌndər] n Schnitzer der.

blunt [blʌnt] adj (knife, pencil) stumpf; (fig: person) unverblümt.

blurred [blɜːd] adj unscharf.

blush [blʌʃ] vi erröten.

blusher ['blʌʃər] n Rouge das.

blustery ['blʌstərɪ] adj stürmisch.

board [bɔːd] ◆ n (plank, for games) Brett das; (notice board) Schwarzes Brett; (blackboard) Tafel die; (of company) Vorstand der; (hardboard) Preßspan der. ◆ vt (plane, ship) an Bord (+G) gehen; (bus) einlsteigen in (+A); **~ and lodging** Unterkunft die und Verpflegung; **full ~** Vollpension die; **half ~** Halbpension *die*; **on ~** an Bord; (*plane, ship*) an Bord (+G); (*bus*) in (+D).

board game *n* Brettspiel *das*.

boarding ['bɔːdɪŋ] *n* (*of plane*) Einsteigen *das*.

boarding card *n* Bordkarte *die*.

boardinghouse ['bɔːdɪŋhaus, *pl* -hauzɪz] *n* Pension *die*.

boarding school *n* Internat *das*.

board of directors *n* Vorstand *der*.

boast [bəust] *vi*: **to ~ (about sthg)** anǀgeben (mit etw).

boat [bəut] *n* Boot *das*; (*large*) Schiff *das*; **to go by ~** mit dem Schiff fahren.

bob [bɒb] *n* (*hairstyle*) Bubikopf *der*.

bobby pin ['bɒbɪ-] *n* (Am) Haarspange *die*.

bodice ['bɒdɪs] *n* Oberteil *das*.

body ['bɒdɪ] *n* Körper *der*; (*corpse*) Leiche *die*; (*of car*) Karosserie *die*; (*organization*) Organisation *die*.

body building *n* Bodybuilding *das*.

bodyguard ['bɒdɪgaːd] *n* Leibwächter *der*.

bodywork ['bɒdɪwɜːk] *n* Karosserie *die*.

bog [bɒg] *n* Sumpf *der*.

bogus ['bəugəs] *adj* (*name*) falsch.

boil [bɔɪl] ◆ *vt & vi* kochen. ◆ *n* (*on skin*) Furunkel *der*; **to ~ the kettle** Wasser aufǀsetzen.

boiled egg [bɔɪld-] *n* gekochtes Ei.

boiled potatoes [bɔɪld-] *npl* Salzkartoffeln *pl*.

boiler ['bɔɪlər] *n* Boiler *der*.

boiling (hot) ['bɔɪlɪŋ-] *adj* (*inf: water*) kochendheiß; (*weather*) wahnsinnig heiß; **I'm ~** mir ist fürchterlich heiß.

bold [bəuld] *adj* (*brave*) mutig.

bollard ['bɒlaːd] *n* (Br: *on road*) Poller *der*.

bolt [bəult] ◆ *n* (*on door, window*) Riegel *der*; (*screw*) Bolzen *der*. ◆ *vt* (*door, window*) verriegeln.

bomb [bɒm] ◆ *n* Bombe *die*. ◆ *vt* bombardieren.

bombard [bɒm'baːd] *vt* bombardieren.

bomb scare *n* Bombenalarm *der*.

bomb shelter *n* Luftschutzkeller *der*.

bond [bɒnd] *n* (*tie, connection*) Verbindung *die*.

bone [bəun] *n* Knochen *der*; (*of fish*) Gräte *die*.

boned [bəund] *adj* (*chicken*) ohne Knochen; (*fish*) entgrätet.

boneless ['bəunləs] *adj* (*chicken, pork*) ohne Knochen.

bonfire ['bɒn,faɪər] *n* Feuer *das* (*draußen*).

bonnet ['bɒnɪt] *n* (Br: *of car*) Motorhaube *die*.

bonus ['bəunəs] (*pl* **-es**) *n* (*extra money*) Prämie *die*; (*additional advantage*) Bonus *der*.

bony ['bəunɪ] *adj* (*fish*) grätig; (*chicken*) mit viel Knochen.

boo [buː] *vi* buhen.

boogie ['buːgɪ] *vi* (*inf*) schwofen.

book [buk] ◆ *n* Buch *das*; (*of stamps, matches, tickets*) Heft *das*. ◆ *vt* (*reserve*) buchen. ▸ **book in** *vi* (*at hotel*) sich anǀmelden.

bookable ['bukəbl] *adj* (*seats, flight*) im Vorverkauf erhältlich.

bookcase ['bukkeɪs] *n* Bücherschrank *der*.

booking ['bukɪŋ] *n* (*reservation*) Buchung *die*.

booking office *n* (*in theatre, cinema*) Kasse *die*; (*at train station*) Fahrkartenschalter *der*.

bookkeeping ['buk,kiːpɪŋ] *n* Buchhaltung *die*.

booklet ['buklɪt] *n* Broschüre *die*.

bookmaker's ['buk,meɪkəz] *n* Wettbüro *das*.

bookmark ['bukmaːk] *n* Lesezeichen *das*.

bookshelf ['bukʃelf] (*pl* **-shelves** [-ʃelvz]) *n* (*shelf*) Bücherregal *das*; (*bookcase*) Bücherschrank *der*.

bookshop ['bukʃɒp] *n* Buchhandlung *die*.

bookstall ['bʊkstɔːl] n Bücher-stand der.

bookstore ['bʊkstɔːʳ] = **book-shop**.

book token n Büchergutschein der.

boom [buːm] ◆ n (sudden growth) Boom der. ◆ vi dröhnen.

boost [buːst] vt (profits, production) steigern; (confidence) stärken.

booster ['buːstəʳ] n (injection) Nachimpfung die.

boot [buːt] n (shoe) Stiefel der; (Br: of car) Kofferraum der.

booth [buːð] n (for telephone) Telefonzelle die; (at fairground) Bude die.

booze [buːz] ◆ n (inf) Alkohol der. ◆ vi (inf) saufen.

bop [bɒp] n (inf: dance): **to have a ~** schwofen.

border ['bɔːdəʳ] n (of country) Grenze die; (edge) Rand der; **the Borders** an England grenzender südlicher Teil Schottlands.

bore [bɔːʳ] ◆ pt → **bear**. ◆ n (inf: boring person) langweiliger Mensch; (boring thing) langweilige Sache. ◆ vt (person) langweilen; (hole) bohren.

bored [bɔːd] adj: **to be ~** sich lang-weilen.

boredom ['bɔːdəm] n Langeweile die.

boring ['bɔːrɪŋ] adj langweilig.

born [bɔːn] adj: **to be ~** geboren werden; **I was ~ in 1975** ich bin 1975 geboren.

borne [bɔːn] pp → **bear**.

borough ['bʌrə] n Regierungsbezirk, der entweder eine Stadt oder einen Stadtteil umfaßt.

borrow ['bɒrəʊ] vt sich (D) borgen, (sich (D) leihen.

bosom ['bʊzəm] n Busen der.

boss [bɒs] n Chef der (-in die). ▶ **boss around** vt sep herum|kom-mandieren.

bossy ['bɒsɪ] adj herrisch.

botanical garden [bə'tænɪkl-] n botanischer Garten.

both [bəʊθ] ◆ adj & pron beide. ◆ adv: **~ ... and ...** sowohl ... als auch ...; **~ of them speak German** sie sprechen beide Deutsch; **~ of us** wir beide.

bother ['bɒðəʳ] ◆ vt stören. ◆ n (trouble) Mühe die. ◆ vi: **don't ~!** das ist nicht nötig!; **he didn't even ~ to say thank you** er hat sich noch nicht mal bedankt; **you needn't have ~ed** das wäre nicht nötig gewesen; **I can't be ~ed** ich habe keine Lust; **it's no ~!** kein Problem!

bottle ['bɒtl] n Flasche die.

bottle bank n Altglascontainer der.

bottled ['bɒtld] adj in Flaschen; **~ beer** Flaschenbier das; **~ water** Wasser das in der Flasche.

bottle opener [-ˌəʊpnəʳ] n Flaschenöffner der.

bottom ['bɒtəm] ◆ adj (lowest) unter-ste(-r)(-s); (last, worst) schlech-teste(-r)(-s). ◆ n (of hill, page, stairs) Fuß der; (of glass, bin, box) Boden der; (of sea, river) Grund der; (buttocks) Hintern der; **he's ~ of the class** er ist der Schlechteste in der Klasse; **in ~ gear** im ersten Gang; **at the ~ of** (bag, box) unten in (A,D); (page) unten auf (A,D); (street, garden) am Ende (+G).

bought [bɔːt] pt & pp → **buy**.

boulder ['bəʊldəʳ] n Felsblock der.

bounce [baʊns] vi (rebound) ab|prallen; (jump) springen; (cheque) nicht gedeckt sein.

bouncer ['baʊnsəʳ] n (inf) Raus-schmeißer der.

bouncy ['baʊnsɪ] adj (person) munter.

bound [baʊnd] ◆ pt & pp → **bind**. ◆ vi (leap) springen. ◆ adj: **to be ~ to do sthg** etw ganz bestimmt tun; **it's ~ to rain** es wird ganz bestimmt reg-nen; **to be ~ for** auf dem Weg sein nach/zu; **this room is out of ~s** dieses Zimmer darf nicht betreten werden.

boundary ['baʊndrɪ] n Grenze die.
bouquet [bʊ'keɪ] n (of flowers) Strauß der; (of wine) Bukett das.
bourbon ['bɜːbən] n Bourbon der.
bout [baʊt] n (of illness) Anfall der; (of activity) Drang der.
boutique [buː'tiːk] n Boutique die.
bow¹ [baʊ] ◆ n (of head) Verbeugung die; (of ship) Bug der. ◆ vi sich verbeugen.
bow² [bəʊ] n (knot) Schleife die; (weapon, for instrument) Bogen der.
bowels ['baʊəlz] npl Darm der.
bowl [bəʊl] n Schüssel die; (shallower) Schale die; (for soup) Teller der.
▶ **bowls** npl Art Bocciaspiel, bei dem Kugeln über den Rasen gerollt werden.
bowling alley ['bəʊlɪŋ-] n Bowlingbahn die.
bowling green ['bəʊlɪŋ-] n Rasenfläche zum 'Bowls'-Spielen.
bow tie [,bəʊ-] n Fliege die.
box [bɒks] ◆ n (container) Kiste die; (smaller) Schachtel die; (of cardboard) Karton der; (on form) Kästchen das; (in theatre) Loge die. ◆ vi boxen; **a ~ of chocolates** eine Schachtel Pralinen.
boxer ['bɒksər] n Boxer der.
boxer shorts npl Boxershorts pl.
boxing ['bɒksɪŋ] n Boxen das.
Boxing Day n zweiter Weihnachtsfeiertag.
boxing gloves npl Boxhandschuhe pl.
boxing ring n Boxring der.
box office n Kasse die.
boy [bɔɪ] ◆ n Junge der. ◆ excl (inf): **(oh) ~!** Mensch!
boycott ['bɔɪkɒt] vt boykottieren.
boyfriend ['bɔɪfrend] n Freund der.
boy scout n Pfadfinder der.
BR abbr = **British Rail**.
bra [brɑː] n BH der.
brace [breɪs] n (for teeth) Spange die.
▶ **braces** npl (Br) Hosenträger pl.
bracelet ['breɪslɪt] n Armband das.
bracken ['brækn] n Farnkraut das.
bracket ['brækɪt] n (written symbol)

Klammer die; (support) Konsole die.
brag [bræg] vi prahlen.
braid [breɪd] n (hairstyle) Zopf der; (on clothes) Zopfmuster das.
brain [breɪn] n Gehirn das.
brainy ['breɪnɪ] adj (inf) clever.
braised [breɪzd] adj geschmort.
brake [breɪk] ◆ n Bremse die. ◆ vi bremsen.
brake block n Bremsklotz der.
brake fluid n Bremsflüssigkeit die.
brake light n Bremslicht das.
brake pad n Bremsbelag der.
brake pedal n Bremspedal das.
bran [bræn] n Kleie die.
branch [brɑːntʃ] n (of tree) Ast der; (of bank, company) Filiale die; (of subject) Zweig der. ▶ **branch off** vi abzweigen.
branch line n Nebenlinie die.
brand [brænd] ◆ n (of product) Marke die. ◆ vt: **to ~ sb (as)** jn abstempeln (als).
brand-new adj nagelneu.
brandy ['brændɪ] n Weinbrand der.
brash [bræʃ] adj (pej) dreist.
brass [brɑːs] n Messing das.
brass band n Blaskapelle die.
brasserie ['bræsərɪ] n Brasserie die.
brassiere [Br 'bræsɪər, Am brə'zɪr] n Büstenhalter der.
brat [bræt] n (inf) Balg der or das.
brave [breɪv] adj mutig.
bravery ['breɪvərɪ] n Mut der.
bravo [,brɑː'vəʊ] excl bravo!
brawl [brɔːl] n Rauferei die.
Brazil [brə'zɪl] n Brasilien nt.
brazil nut n Paranuß die.
breach [briːtʃ] vt (contract, confidence) brechen.
bread [bred] n Brot das; **~ and butter** Butterbrot das.
bread bin n (Br) Brotkasten der.
breadboard ['bredbɔːd] n Brotbrett das.
bread box (Am) = **bread bin**.
breadcrumbs ['bredkrʌmz] npl Brotkrumen pl.

breaded ['bredɪd] *adj* paniert.

bread knife *n* Brotmesser *das.*

bread roll *n* Brötchen *das,* Semmel *die* (Süddt, Österr).

breadth [bretθ] *n* Breite *die.*

break [breɪk] (*pt* **broke,** *pp* **broken**) ◆ *n* (*interruption*) Unterbrechung *die;* (*rest, playtime*) Pause *die.* ◆ *vt* (*damage*) kaputtlmachen; (*smash*) zerbrechen; (*law, promise, record*) brechen; (*journey*) unterbrechen. ◆ *vi* (*object, machine*) kaputtlgehen; (*glass*) zerbrechen; (*dawn*) dämmern; (*voice*) im Stimmbruch sein; **to ~ the news** melden, daß; **without a ~** ohne Pause; **a lucky ~** ein Glückstreffer; **to ~ one's leg** sich (D) das Bein brechen. ► **break down** *vi* (*car*) eine Panne haben; (*machine*) versagen. ◆ *vt sep* (*door*) auflbrechen; (*barrier*) niederlreißen. ► **break in** *vi* einlbrechen. ► **break off** *vt sep* & *vi* ablbrechen. ► **break out** *vi* auslbrechen; **to ~ out in a rash** einen Ausschlag bekommen. ► **break up** *vi* (*with spouse, partner*) sich trennen; (*meeting*) zu Ende gehen; (*marriage*) in die Brüche gehen; **school ~s up on Friday** am Freitag fangen die Ferien an.

breakage ['breɪkɪdʒ] *n* Bruchschaden *der.*

breakdown ['breɪkdaun] *n* (*of car*) Panne *die;* (*in communications, negotiations*) Scheitern *das;* (*mental*) Nervenzusammenbruch *der.*

breakdown truck *n* Abschleppwagen *der.*

breakfast ['brekfəst] *n* Frühstück *das;* **to have ~** frühstücken; **to have sthg for ~** etw zum Frühstück essen.

breakfast cereal *n* Frühstücksflocken *pl.*

break-in *n* Einbruch *der.*

breakwater ['breɪk,wɔːtər] *n* Wellenbrecher *der.*

breast [brest] *n* Brust *die.*

breastbone ['brestbəun] *n* Brustbein *das.*

breast-feed *vt* stillen.

breaststroke ['breststrəuk] *n* Brustschwimmen *das.*

breath [breθ] *n* Atem *der;* **out of ~** außer Atem; **to go for a ~ of fresh air** frische Luft schnappen gehen.

Breathalyser® ['breθəlaɪzər] *n* (Br) Alcotest *der.*

Breathalyzer® ['breθəlaɪzər] (Am) = **Breathalyser®.**

breathe [briːð] *vi* atmen. ► **breathe in** *vi* einlatmen. ► **breathe out** *vi* auslatmen.

breathtaking ['breθ,teɪkɪŋ] *adj* atemberaubend.

breed [briːd] (*pt* & *pp* **bred** [bred]) ◆ *n* (*of animal*) Rasse *die;* (*of plant*) Art *die.* ◆ *vt* züchten. ◆ *vi* sich vermehren.

breeze [briːz] *n* Brise *die.*

breezy ['briːzɪ] *adj* (*weather, day*) windig.

brew [bruː] ◆ *vt* (*beer*) brauen; (*tea, coffee*) auflbrühen. ◆ *vi* (*tea*) ziehen; (*coffee*) sich setzen.

brewery ['bruərɪ] *n* Brauerei *die.*

bribe [braɪb] ◆ *n* Bestechungsgeld *das.* ◆ *vt* bestechen.

bric-a-brac ['brɪkəbræk] *n* Nippes *pl.*

brick [brɪk] *n* Backstein *der.*

bricklayer ['brɪk,leɪər] *n* Maurer *der* (-in *die*).

brickwork ['brɪkwɜːk] *n* Mauerwerk *das.*

bride [braɪd] *n* Braut *die.*

bridegroom ['braɪdgrum] *n* Bräutigam *der.*

bridesmaid ['braɪdzmeɪd] *n* Brautjungfer *die.*

bridge [brɪdʒ] *n* Brücke *die;* (*card game*) Bridge *das.*

bridle ['braɪdl] *n* Zaumzeug *das.*

bridle path *n* Reitweg *der.*

brief [briːf] ◆ *adj* kurz. ◆ *vt* einlweisen; **in ~** kurz gesagt. ► **briefs** *npl* (*for men*) Slip *der;* (*for women*) Schlüpfer *der.*

briefcase ['briːfkeɪs] n Aktenkoffer der.

briefly ['briːflɪ] adv kurz.

brigade [brɪ'geɪd] n Brigade die.

bright [braɪt] adj hell; (colour) leuchtend; (clever) aufgeweckt; (lively, cheerful) fröhlich.

brilliant ['brɪljənt] adj (colour, light, sunshine) leuchtend; (idea, person) großartig; (inf: wonderful) toll.

brim [brɪm] n (of hat) Krempe die; **full to the ~** bis an den Rand voll.

brine [braɪn] n Salzlake die.

bring [brɪŋ] (pt & pp **brought**) vt (take along) mitlbringen; (move) bringen; (cause) führen zu. ▶ **bring along** vt sep mitlbringen. ▶ **bring back** vt sep (return) zurücklbringen; (shopping, gift) mitlbringen. ▶ **bring in** vt sep (introduce) einlführen; (earn) einlbringen. ▶ **bring out** vt sep (new product) herauslbringen. ▶ **bring up** vt sep (child) erziehen; (subject) zur Sprache bringen; (food) erbrechen.

brink [brɪŋk] n: **on the ~ of** am Rande (+G).

brisk [brɪsk] adj zügig; (wind) frisch.

bristle ['brɪsl] n (of brush) Borste die; (on chin) Bartstoppel die.

Britain ['brɪtn] n Großbritannien nt.

British ['brɪtɪʃ] ◆ adj britisch. ◆ npl: **the ~** die Briten.

British Rail n die britische Eisenbahn.

British Telecom [-'telɪkɒm] n die britische Telekom.

Briton ['brɪtn] n Brite der (Britin die).

brittle ['brɪtl] adj zerbrechlich.

broad [brɔːd] adj breit; (wide-ranging) weit; (description, outline) allgemein; (accent) stark.

B road n (Br) ≈ Landstraße die.

broad bean n dicke Bohne die.

broadcast ['brɔːdkɑːst] (pt & pp inv) ◆ n Sendung die. ◆ vt senden.

broadly ['brɔːdlɪ] adv im großen und ganzen; **~ speaking** allgemein gesagt.

broccoli ['brɒkəlɪ] n Brokkoli der or pl.

brochure ['brəʊʃər] n Broschüre die.

broiled [brɔɪld] adj (Am) gegrillt.

broke [brəʊk] ◆ pt → **break**. ◆ adj (inf) pleite.

broken ['brəʊkn] ◆ pp → **break**. ◆ adj (machine) kaputt; (window, glass) zerbrochen; (English, German) gebrochen; **to have a ~ leg** ein gebrochenes Bein haben.

bronchitis [brɒŋ'kaɪtɪs] n Bronchitis die.

bronze [brɒnz] n Bronze die.

brooch [brəʊtʃ] n Brosche die.

brook [brʊk] n Bach der.

broom [bruːm] n Besen der.

broomstick ['bruːmstɪk] n Besenstiel der.

broth [brɒθ] n (soup) Eintopf der.

brother ['brʌðər] n Bruder der.

brother-in-law n Schwager der.

brought [brɔːt] pt & pp → **bring**.

brow [braʊ] n (forehead) Stirn die; (eyebrow) Braue die.

brown [braʊn] ◆ adj braun. ◆ n Braun das.

brown bread n Mischbrot das.

brownie ['braʊnɪ] n (CULIN) kleiner Schokoladenkuchen mit Nüssen.

Brownie ['braʊnɪ] n Pfadfinderin die (bis 10 Jahren).

brown rice n Naturreis der.

brown sauce n (Br) aus Gemüseextrakten hergestellte ketchupähnliche Soße.

brown sugar n brauner Zucker.

browse [braʊz] vi (in shop) sich umlsehen; **to ~ through sthg** in etw (D) blättern.

browser ['braʊzər] n: **'~s welcome'** 'Bitte sehen Sie sich um'.

bruise [bruːz] n blauer Fleck.

brunch [brʌntʃ] n Brunch der.

brunette [bruː'net] n Brünette die.

brush [brʌʃ] ◆ n Bürste die; (for painting) Pinsel der. ◆ vt (floor) fegen; (clothes) bürsten; **to ~ one's hair** sich (D) die Haare bürsten; **to ~ one's teeth** sich (D) die Zähne putzen.

brussels sprouts [ˌbrʌslz-] npl
Rosenkohl der.
brutal [ˈbruːtl] adj brutal.
BSc n (abbr of Bachelor of Science)
Bakkalaureus der Naturwissenschaften.
BT abbr = **British Telecom**.
bubble [ˈbʌbl] n Blase die.
bubble bath n Badeschaum der.
bubble gum n Kaugummi der.
bubbly [ˈbʌblɪ] n (inf) Schampus
der.
buck [bʌk] n (Am: inf: dollar) Dollar
der; (male animal) Bock der.
bucket [ˈbʌkɪt] n Eimer der.
Buckingham Palace [ˈbʌkɪŋəm-]
n Buckinghampalast der (Residenz der
britischen Königin in London).
buckle [ˈbʌkl] ◆ n Schnalle die. ◆ vt
(fasten) zuschnallen. ◆ vi (warp) sich
verbiegen.
Buck's Fizz n Champagner mit
Orangensaft.
bud [bʌd] ◆ n Knospe die. ◆ vi
knospen.
Buddhist [ˈbudɪst] n Buddhist der
(-in die).
buddy [ˈbʌdɪ] n (inf) Kumpel der.
budge [bʌdʒ] vi sich rühren.
budgerigar [ˈbʌdʒərɪgɑːʳ] n
Wellensittich der.
budget [ˈbʌdʒɪt] ◆ adj (holiday, travel)
Billig-. ◆ n Budget das; **the Budget**
(Br) der Haushaltsplan. ▶ **budget**
for vt fus einplanen.
budgie [ˈbʌdʒɪ] n (Inf) Wellensittich
der.
buff [bʌf] n (inf) Kenner der (-in die).
buffalo [ˈbʌfələʊ] (pl **-s** OR **-es**) n
Büffel der.
buffalo wings npl (Am) fritierte und
gewürzte Hähnchenflügel.
buffer [ˈbʌfəʳ] n Puffer der.
buffet [Br ˈbufeɪ, Am bəˈfeɪ] n (meal)
kalte Büfett das; (cafeteria) Imbißstube die.
buffet car [ˈbufeɪ-] n Speisewagen
der.
bug [bʌg] ◆ vt (inf: annoy) nerven.

◆ n (insect) Ungeziefer das; (inf: mild
illness): **to catch a** ~ sich (D) was
holen.
buggy [ˈbʌgɪ] n (pushchair)
Sportwagen der; (Am: pram)
Kinderwagen der.
bugle [ˈbjuːgl] n Bügelhorn das.
build [bɪld] (pt & pp **built**) ◆ n
Körperbau der. ◆ vt bauen. ▶ **build**
up vt sep aufbauen. ◆ vi zunehmen;
to ~ **up speed** sich verbessern.
builder [ˈbɪldəʳ] n Bauunternehmer
der (-in die).
building [ˈbɪldɪŋ] n Gebäude das.
building site n Baustelle die.
building society n (Br) Bausparkasse die.
built [bɪlt] pt & pp → **build**.
built-in adj eingebaut.
built-up area n bebautes Gebiet
das.
bulb [bʌlb] n (for lamp) Glühbirne
die; (of plant) Zwiebel die.
Bulgaria [bʌlˈgeərɪə] n Bulgarien nt.
bulge [bʌldʒ] vi (suitcase, box) prall
gefüllt sein.
bulk [bʌlk] n: **the** ~ **of** der Hauptteil
(+G); **in** ~ en gros.
bulky [ˈbʌlkɪ] adj sperrig.
bull [bul] n Bulle der.
bulldog [ˈbuldɒg] n Bulldogge die.
bulldozer [ˈbuldəʊzəʳ] n Bulldozer
der.
bullet [ˈbulɪt] n Kugel die.
bulletin [ˈbulətɪn] n (on radio, TV)
Kurzmeldung die; (publication)
Bulletin das.
bullfight [ˈbulfaɪt] n Stierkampf der.
bull's-eye n Schwarze das.
bully [ˈbulɪ] ◆ n Schüler, der
Schwächere schikaniert. ◆ vt schikanieren.
bum [bʌm] n (inf: bottom) Po der; (Am:
inf: tramp) Penner der.
bum bag n (Br) Gürteltasche die.
bumblebee [ˈbʌmblbiː] n Hummel
die.
bump [bʌmp] ◆ n (on surface)
Unebenheit die; (on head, leg) Beule

die; (*sound*) Bums der; (*minor accident*) Zusammenstoß der. ◆ *vt*: **to ~ one's head** sich (D) den Kopf stoßen. ► **bump into** *vt fus* (*hit*) stoßen gegen; (*meet*) zufällig treffen.

bumper ['bʌmpər] *n* (*on car*) Stoßstange die; (Am: *on train*) Puffer der.

bumpy ['bʌmpɪ] *adj* (*road*) uneben; (*flight*) unruhig; (*journey*) holprig.

bun [bʌn] *n* (*cake*) süßes Brötchen; (*bread roll*) Brötchen das, Semmel die (Süddt, Österr); (*hairstyle*) Knoten der.

bunch [bʌntʃ] *n* (*of people*) Haufen der; (*of flowers*) Strauß der; (*of grapes*) Traube die; (*of bananas*) Staude die; (*of keys*) Bund der.

bundle ['bʌndl] *n* Bündel das.

bung [bʌŋ] *n* Pfropfen der.

bungalow ['bʌŋgələu] *n* Bungalow der.

bunion ['bʌnjən] *n* Ballen der.

bunk [bʌŋk] *n* Koje die.

bunk beds *npl* Etagenbett das.

bunker ['bʌŋkər] *n* Bunker der.

bunny ['bʌnɪ] *n* Häschen das.

buoy [Br bɔɪ, Am 'buːɪ] *n* Boje die.

buoyant ['bɔɪənt] *adj* schwimmend.

BUPA ['buːpə] *n* private britische Krankenkasse.

burden ['bɜːdn] *n* Last die.

bureaucracy [bjuə'rɒkrəsɪ] *n* Bürokratie die.

bureau de change [,bjuərəudə-'ʃɒndʒ] *n* Wechselstube die.

burger ['bɜːgər] *n* Hamburger der; (*made with nuts, vegetables etc*) Bratling der.

burglar ['bɜːglər] *n* Einbrecher der (-in die).

burglar alarm *n* Alarmanlage die.

burglarize ['bɜːgləraɪz] (Am) = **burgle**.

burglary ['bɜːglərɪ] *n* Einbruch der.

burgle ['bɜːgl] *vt* einǀbrechen in (+A).

burial ['berɪəl] *n* Beerdigung die.

burn [bɜːn] (*pt & pp* **burnt** OR **burned**) ◆ *n* Verbrennung die; (*on material*) Brandstelle die. ◆ *vt* verbrennen; (*food*) anǀbrennen; (*hand, skin, clothes*) sich (D) verbrennen. ◆ *vi* brennen. ► **burn down** *vt sep & vi* abǀbrennen.

burning (**hot**) ['bɜːnɪŋ-] *adj* glühend heiß.

Burns' Night [bɜːnz-] *n* Tag zur Feier des Geburtstags vom schottischen Dichter Robert Burns.

burnt [bɜːnt] *pt & pp* → **burn**.

burp [bɜːp] *vi* (*inf*) rülpsen.

burrow ['bʌrəu] *n* Bau der.

burst [bɜːst] (*pt & pp inv*) ◆ *n* (*of gunfire*) Hagel der; (*of applause*) Sturm der. ◆ *vt* platzen lassen. ◆ *vi* platzen; **he ~ into the room** er stürzte ins Zimmer; **to ~ into tears** in Tränen ausǀbrechen; **to ~ open** aufǀspringen.

bury ['berɪ] *vt* (*person*) beerdigen; (*hide underground*) vergraben.

bus [bʌs] *n* Bus der; **by ~** mit dem Bus.

bus conductor [-,kən'dʌktər] *n* Busschaffner der (-in die).

bus driver *n* Busfahrer der (-in die).

bush [buʃ] *n* Busch der.

business ['bɪznɪs] *n* Geschäft das; (*firm*) Betrieb der; (*things to do*) Angelegenheiten *pl*; (*affair*) Sache die; **mind your own ~!** kümmer' dich um deine eigenen Angelegenheiten!; '**~ as usual**' 'Wir haben offen'.

business card *n* Visitenkarte die.

business class *n* Business Class die.

business hours *npl* Geschäftszeit die.

businessman ['bɪznɪsmæn] (*pl* -**men** [-men]) *n* Geschäftsmann der.

business studies *npl* Betriebswirtschaft die.

business trip *n* Dienstreise die.

businesswoman ['bɪznɪs,wumən] (*pl* -**women** [-,wɪmɪn]) *n* Geschäftsfrau die.

busker ['bʌskər] *n* (Br) Straßenmusikant der (-in die).

bus lane n Busspur die.

bus pass n Zeitkarte die.

bus shelter n Wartehäuschen das.

bus station n Busbahnhof der.

bus stop n Bushaltestelle die.

bust [bʌst] ◆ n (of woman) Busen der. ◆ adj: **to go ~** (inf) pleite machen.

bustle ['bʌsl] n Betrieb der.

bus tour n Busreise die; (sightseeing) Busrundfahrt die.

busy ['bɪzɪ] adj (person) beschäftigt; (day, schedule) hektisch; (street, office) belebt; (telephone, line) besetzt; **to be ~ doing sthg** mit etw beschäftigt sein.

busy signal n (Am) Besetztzeichen das.

but [bʌt] ◆ conj aber. ◆ prep (except) außer; **the last ~ one** der/die/das vorletzte; **~ for** außer.

butcher ['butʃər] n Fleischer der, Metzger der (Südt); **~'s** (shop) Fleischerei die, Metzgerei die (Südt).

butt [bʌt] n (of rifle) Kolben der; (of cigarette) Stummel der.

butter ['bʌtər] ◆ n Butter die. ◆ vt buttern.

butter bean n weiße Bohne die.

buttercup ['bʌtəkʌp] n Butterblume die.

butterfly ['bʌtəflaɪ] n Schmetterling der.

butterscotch ['bʌtəskɒtʃ] n Karamelbonbon der or das.

buttocks ['bʌtəks] npl Hintern der.

button ['bʌtn] n Knopf der; (Am: badge) Button der.

buttonhole ['bʌtnhəʊl] n Knopfloch das.

button mushroom n Champignon der.

buttress ['bʌtrɪs] n Pfeiler der.

buy [baɪ] (pt & pp **bought**) ◆ vt kaufen. ◆ n: **a good ~** ein guter Kauf; **to ~ sthg for sb, to ~ sb sthg** jm etw kaufen.

buzz [bʌz] ◆ vi summen. ◆ n (inf: phone call): **to give sb a ~** jn an|rufen.

buzzer ['bʌzər] n Summer der.

by [baɪ] ◆ prep 1. (expressing cause, agent) von; **he was hit ~ a car** er ist von einem Auto angefahren worden; **composed ~ Mozart** von Mozart komponiert. 2. (expressing method, means) mit; **~ car/train** mit dem Auto/Zug; **to pay ~ credit card** mit Kreditkarte bezahlen. 3. (near to, beside) an (+D); **~ the sea** am Meer. 4. (past) an (+D) ... vorbei; **a car went ~ the house** ein Auto fuhr am Haus vorbei. 5. (via) durch; **exit ~ the door on the left** Ausgang durch die Tür auf der linken Seite. 6. (with time): **it will be ready ~ tomorrow** bis morgen wird es fertig sein; **be there ~ nine** sei um neun da; **~ day** tagsüber; **~ now** inzwischen. 7. (expressing quantity): **sold ~ the dozen** im Dutzend verkauft; **prices fell ~ 20%** die Preise fielen um 20%; **we charge ~ the hour** wir berechnen nach Stunde. 8. (expressing meaning): **what do you mean ~ that?** was meinst du/meinen Sie damit? 9. (in division) durch; (in multiplication) mit; **two metres ~ five** zwei mal fünf Meter. 10. (according to) nach; **~ law** nach dem Gesetz; **it's fine ~ me** ich bin damit einverstanden. 11. (expressing gradual process): **one ~ one** eins nach dem anderen; **day ~ day** Tag für Tag. 12. (in phrases): **~ mistake** versehentlich; **~ oneself** allein; **~ profession** von Beruf. ◆ adv (past) vorbei; **to go ~** (walk) vorbei|gehen; (drive) vorbei|fahren.

bye(-bye) [baɪ(baɪ)] excl (inf) tschüs.

bypass ['baɪpɑːs] n Umgehungsstraße die.

C

C (abbr of Celsius, centigrade) C.

cab [kæb] n (taxi) Taxi das; (of lorry) Führerhaus das.

cabaret ['kæbərei] n Kabarett das.

cabbage ['kæbidʒ] n Kohl der.

cabin ['kæbin] n Kabine die; (wooden house) Hütte die.

cabin crew n Flugpersonal das.

cabinet ['kæbinit] n (cupboard) Schrank der; (POL) Kabinett das.

cable ['keibl] n (rope) Tau das; (electrical) Kabel das.

cable car n Seilbahn die.

cable television n Kabelfernsehen das.

cactus ['kæktəs] (pl -tuses OR -ti [-tai]) n Kaktus der.

Caesar salad [,si:zə-] n grüner Salat mit Sardellen, Oliven, Parmesan und Croûtons.

cafe ['kæfei] n Café das.

cafeteria [,kæfi'tiəriə] n Cafeteria die.

cafetière [kæf't jeər] n Kolbenfilter-Kaffeemaschine die.

caffeine ['kæfi:n] n Kaffein das.

cage [keidʒ] n Käfig der.

cagoule [kə'gu:l] n (Br) Regenjacke die.

Cajun ['keidʒən] adj cajun.

cake [keik] n Kuchen der; (of soap) Stück das; **fish ~** Fischfrikadelle die.

calculate ['kælkjuleit] vt berechnen; (risks, effect) kalkulieren.

calculator ['kælkjuleitər] n Taschenrechner der.

calendar ['kælindər] n Kalender der.

calf [ka:f] (pl **calves**) n (of cow) Kalb das; (part of leg) Wade die.

call [kɔ:l] ◆ n (visit) Besuch der; (phone call) Anruf der; (of bird) Ruf der; (at airport) Aufruf der. ◆ vt rufen; (name, describe) nennen; (telephone) an|rufen; (meeting) ein|berufen; (election) aus|schreiben; (flight) auf|rufen. ◆ vi (visit) vorbei|kommen; (phone) an|rufen; **to be ~ed** sich nennen; **what is he ~ed?** wie heißt er?; **to be on ~** (nurse, doctor) Bereitschaftsdienst haben; **to pay sb a ~** bei jm vorbei|gehen; **this train ~s at ...** dieser Zug hält in ...; **who's ~ing?** wer spricht da, bitte? ▶ **call back** vt sep zurück|rufen. ◆ vi (phone again) zurück|rufen; (visit again) zurück|kommen. ▶ **call for** vt fus (come to fetch) ab|holen; (demand) verlangen; (require) erfordern. ▶ **call on** vt fus (visit) vorbei|gehen bei; **to ~ on sb to do sthg** jn bitten, etw zu tun. ▶ **call out** vt sep aus|rufen; (doctor, fire brigade) rufen. ◆ vi rufen. ▶ **call up** vt sep (MIL) ein|berufen; (telephone) an|rufen.

call box n Telefonzelle die.

caller ['kɔ:lər] n (visitor) Besucher der (-in die); (on phone) Anrufer der (-in die).

calm [ka:m] ◆ adj ruhig. ◆ vt beruhigen. ▶ **calm down** vt sep beruhigen. ◆ vi sich beruhigen.

Calor gas® ['kælə-] n Butangas das.

calorie ['kæləri] n Kalorie die.

calves [ka:vz] pl → **calf**.

camcorder ['kæm,kɔ:dər] n Camcorder der.

came [keim] pt → **come**.

camel ['kæml] n Kamel das.

camembert ['kæməmbeər] n Camembert der.

camera ['kæmərə] n Fotoapparat der; (for filming) Kamera die.

cameraman ['kæmərəmæn] (pl -men [-men]) n Kameramann der.

camera shop n Fotogeschäft das.

camisole ['kæmisəul] n Mieder das.

camp [kæmp] ◆ n Lager das. ◆ vi zelten.

campaign [kæm'pein] ◆ n

Kampagne die. ♦ vi: **to ~ (for/against)** kämpfen (für/gegen).

camp bed n Campingliege die.

camper ['kæmpər] n Camper der (-in die); (van) Wohnmobil das.

camping ['kæmpɪŋ] n: **to go ~** zelten gehen.

camping stove n Kocher der.

campsite ['kæmpsaɪt] n Campingplatz der.

campus ['kæmpəs] (pl -es) n Universitätsgelände das.

can¹ [kæn] n (of food, drink, paint) Dose die; (of oil) Kanister der.

can² [weak form kən, strong form kæn] (pt & conditional **could**) aux vb 1. (be able to) können; **~ you help me?** können Sie mir helfen?; **I ~ see** you ich kann dich sehen. 2. (know how to) können; **~ you drive?** können Sie/kannst du Auto fahren?; **I ~ speak German** ich spreche Deutsch. 3. (be allowed to) können, dürfen; **you can't smoke here** Sie können OR dürfen hier nicht rauchen. 4. (in polite requests) können; **~ you tell me the time?** können Sie mir sagen, wieviel Uhr es ist? 5. (expressing occasional occurrence) können; **it ~ get cold at night** es kann nachts kalt werden. 6. (expressing possibility) können; **they could be lost** sie könnten sich verlaufen haben.

Canada ['kænədə] n Kanada nt.

Canadian [kə'neɪdɪən] ♦ adj kanadisch. ♦ n Kanadier der (-in die).

canal [kə'næl] n Kanal der.

canapé ['kænəpeɪ] n Canapé das.

cancel ['kænsl] vt (meeting, visit) ablsagen; (booking) rückgängig machen; (flight, train) streichen; (cheque) ungültig machen.

cancellation [ˌkænsə'leɪʃn] n Streichung die; (booking) Stornierung die; (cancelled visit) Absage die.

cancer ['kænsər] n Krebs der.

Cancer ['kænsər] n Krebs der.

candidate ['kændɪdət] n (for parliament, job) Bewerber der; (in exam) Prüfling der.

candle ['kændl] n Kerze die.

candlelit dinner ['kændllɪt-] n Essen das bei Kerzenlicht.

candy ['kændɪ] n (Am: confectionery) Süßigkeiten pl; (sweet) Bonbon der or das.

candyfloss ['kændɪflɒs] n (Br) Zuckerwatte die.

cane [keɪn] n Stock der; (for furniture, baskets) Rohr das.

canister ['kænɪstər] n (for tea) Dose die; (for gas) Gasflasche die.

cannabis ['kænəbɪs] n Cannabis der.

canned [kænd] adj (food, drink) in der Dose.

cannon ['kænən] n Kanone die.

cannot ['kænɒt] = **can not**.

canoe [kə'nu:] n Paddelboot das; (SPORT) Kanu das.

canoeing [kə'nu:ɪŋ] n Paddeln das; (SPORT) Kanusport der.

canopy ['kænəpɪ] n Baldachin der.

can't [kɑːnt] = **cannot**.

cantaloup(e) ['kæntəluːp] n Kantalupmelone die.

canteen [kæn'tiːn] n (at work) Kantine die; (at school) Speisesaal der.

canvas ['kænvəs] n (for tent, bag) Segeltuch das.

cap [kæp] n Mütze die; (of pen, bottle) Kappe die; (contraceptive) Spirale die.

capable ['keɪpəbl] adj fähig; **to be ~ of doing sthg** fähig sein, etw zu tun.

capacity [kə'pæsɪtɪ] n (ability) Fähigkeit die; (of stadium, theatre) Fassungsvermögen das.

cape [keɪp] n (of land) Kap das; (cloak) Cape das.

capers ['keɪpəz] npl Kapern pl.

capital ['kæpɪtl] n (of country) Hauptstadt die; (money) Kapital das; (letter) Großbuchstabe der.

capital punishment n Todesstrafe die.

cappuccino [ˌkæpu'tʃiːnəʊ] n Cappuccino der.

Capricorn [ˈkæprɪkɔːn] *n* Steinbock *der*.

capsicum [ˈkæpsɪkəm] *n* Paprika *der*.

capsize [kæpˈsaɪz] *vi* kentern.

capsule [ˈkæpsjuːl] *n* Kapsel *die*.

captain [ˈkæptɪn] *n* Kapitän *der*; (MIL) Hauptmann *der*.

caption [ˈkæpʃn] *n* (*under picture*) Unterschrift *die*; (*above picture*) Überschrift *die*.

capture [ˈkæptʃər] *vt* fangen; (*town, castle*) erobern.

car [kaːr] *n* Auto *das*, Wagen *der*; (*railway wagon*) Wagen *der*.

carafe [kəˈræf] *n* Karaffe *die*.

caramel [ˈkærəmel] *n* (*sweet*) Karamelbonbon *der* or *das*; (*burnt sugar*) Karamel *der*.

carat [ˈkærət] *n* Karat *das*; **24- ~ gold** 24-karätiges Gold.

caravan [ˈkærəvæn] *n* (Br) Wohnwagen *der*.

caravanning [ˈkærəvænɪŋ] *n* (Br): **to go ~** Urlaub im Wohnwagen machen.

caravan site *n* (Br) Campingplatz *der* für Wohnwagen.

carbohydrate [ˌkaːbəʊˈhaɪdreɪt] *n* (*in foods*) Kohlenhydrat *das*.

carbon [ˈkaːbən] *n* Kohlenstoff *der*.

carbon copy *n* Durchschlag *der*.

carbon dioxide [-daɪˈɒksaɪd] *n* Kohlendioxid *das*.

carbon monoxide [-mɒˈnɒksaɪd] *n* Kohlenmonoxid *das*.

car boot sale *n* (Br) Basar, bei dem die Waren im Kofferraum ausgelegt werden.

carburetor [ˌkaːbəˈretər] (Am) = **carburettor**.

carburettor [ˌkaːbəˈretər] *n* (Br) Vergaser *der*.

car crash *n* Autounfall *der*.

card [kaːd] *n* Karte *die*; (*cardboard*) Pappe *die*, Karton *der*; **~s** (*game*) Karten *pl*.

cardboard [ˈkaːdbɔːd] *n* Pappe *die*, Karton *der*.

car deck *n* Fahrzeugdeck *das*.

cardiac arrest [ˌkaːdɪæk-] *n* Herzstillstand *der*.

cardigan [ˈkaːdɪgən] *n* Strickjacke *die*.

care [keər] ◆ *n* (*attention*) Sorgfalt *die*. ◆ *vi* (*mind*): **I don't ~** eś ist mir egal; **to take ~ of** sich kümmern um; **would you ~ to ...?** (*fml*) würden Sie gerne ...?; **to take ~ to do sthg** auflpassen, daβ man etw tut; **medical ~** ärztliche Betreuung; **take ~!** (*goodbye*) mach's gut!; **with ~** aufmerksam, sorgfältig; **to ~ about sthg** (*think important*) etw wichtig finden; **to ~ about sb** jn mögen.

career [kəˈrɪər] *n* (*type of job*) Beruf *der*; (*professional life*) Laufbahn *die*.

carefree [ˈkeəfriː] *adj* sorglos.

careful [ˈkeəfʊl] *adj* (*cautious*) vorsichtig; (*thorough*) sorgfältig; **be ~!** Vorsicht!

carefully [ˈkeəflɪ] *adv* (*cautiously*) vorsichtig; (*thoroughly*) sorgfältig.

careless [ˈkeələs] *adj* (*inattentive*) unaufmerksam; (*unconcerned*) sorglos.

caretaker [ˈkeəˌteɪkər] *n* (Br: *of school, flats*) Hausmeister *der* (-in *die*).

car ferry *n* Autofähre *die*.

cargo [ˈkaːgəʊ] (*pl* **-es** OR **-s**) *n* Ladung *die*.

car hire *n* (Br) Autovermietung *die*.

Caribbean [Br ˌkærɪˈbiːən, Am kəˈrɪbɪən] *n*: **the ~** die Karibik.

caring [ˈkeərɪŋ] *adj* fürsorglich.

carnation [kaːˈneɪʃn] *n* Nelke *die*.

carnival [ˈkaːnɪvl] *n* Karneval *der*.

carousel [ˌkærəˈsel] *n* (*for luggage*) Gepäckförderband *das*; (Am: *merry-go-round*) Karussell *das*.

carp [kaːp] *n* Karpfen *der*.

car park *n* (Br) Parkplatz *der*; (*building*) Parkhaus *das*; (*underground*) Tiefgarage *die*.

carpenter [ˈkaːpəntər] *n* Zimmermann *der*; (*for furniture*) Tischler *der* (-in *die*).

carpentry ['kɑːpəntrɪ] n Zimmerhandwerk das; (furniture making) Tischlerei die.

carpet ['kɑːpɪt] n Teppich der.

car rental n (Am) Autovermietung die.

carriage ['kærɪdʒ] n (Br: of train) Abteil das; (horse-drawn) Kutsche die.

carriageway ['kærɪdʒweɪ] n (Br) Fahrbahn die.

carrier (bag) ['kærɪər-] n Tragetasche die.

carrot ['kærət] n Karotte die, Möhre die.

carrot cake n Möhrenkuchen der, Rüblitorte die (Schweiz).

carry ['kærɪ] ◆ vt tragen; (transport) befördern; (disease) übertragen; (cash, passport, map) bei sich haben. ◆ vi (voice, sound) tragen, reichen. ▶ **carry on** vi (continue) weiterlmachen. ◆ vt fus (continue) fortlsetzen; to ~ on doing sthg weiterhin etw tun. ▶ **carry out** vt sep (repairs, order) auslführen; (plan) durchlführen; (promise) erfüllen.

carrycot ['kærɪkɒt] n (Br) Babytragetasche die.

carryout ['kærɪaʊt] n (Am & Scot) Essen das zum Mitnehmen.

carsick ['kɑːsɪk] adj: I get ~ mir wird beim Autofahren schlecht.

cart [kɑːt] n Karren der; (Am: in supermarket) Einkaufswagen der; (inf: video game cartridge) Videospiel das.

carton ['kɑːtn] n Tüte die.

cartoon [kɑːˈtuːn] n (drawing) Cartoon der; (film) Zeichentrickfilm der.

cartridge ['kɑːtrɪdʒ] n Patrone die; (for film) Kassette die.

carve [kɑːv] vt (wood) schnitzen; (stone) meißeln; (meat) auflschneiden.

carvery ['kɑːvərɪ] n Büfett mit verschiedenen Fleischgerichten und Bedienung.

car wash n Autowaschanlage die.

case [keɪs] n (Br: suitcase) Koffer der; (container) Etui das; (for jewellery) Schatulle die; (instance) Fall der; (JUR: trial) Fall der; (patient) Fall der; **in any ~** sowieso; **in ~ falls; in ~ of** im Fall (+G); **just in ~** für alle Fälle; **in that ~** in dem Fall.

cash [kæʃ] ◆ n (coins, notes) Bargeld das; (money in general) Geld das. ◆ vt: **to ~ a cheque** einen Scheck einllösen; **to pay ~** bar bezahlen.

cash desk n Kasse die.

cash dispenser [-,dɪˈspensər] n Geldautomat der.

cashew (nut) ['kæʃuː-] n Cashewnuß die.

cashier [kæˈʃɪər] n Kassierer der (-in die).

cashmere [kæʃˈmɪər] n Kaschmir der.

cashpoint ['kæʃpɔɪnt] n (Br) Geldautomat der.

cash register n Kasse die.

casino [kəˈsiːnəʊ] (pl -s) n Kasino das.

cask [kɑːsk] n Faß das.

cask-conditioned [-,kənˈdɪʃnd] adj (beer) bezeichnet 'real ale'-Bier, das in Fässern gebraut wird.

casserole ['kæsərəʊl] n (stew) Schmorgericht aus Fleisch und Gemüse; ~ **(dish)** Schmortopf der.

cassette [kæˈset] n Kassette die.

cassette recorder n Kassettenrecorder der.

cast [kɑːst] (pt & pp inv) ◆ n (actors) Besetzung die; (for broken bone) Gipsverband der. ◆ vt werfen; **to ~ a vote** wählen; **to ~ doubt on** in Zweifel ziehen. ▶ **cast off** vi (boat, ship) abllegen.

caster ['kɑːstər] n (wheel) Rolle die.

caster sugar n (Br) Streuzucker der.

castle ['kɑːsl] n Schloß das; (fortified) Burg die; (in chess) Turm der.

casual ['kæʒʊəl] adj (relaxed) ungezwungen, lässig; (remark) beiläufig; (clothes) leger; ~ **work** Gelegenheitsarbeit die.

casualty ['kæʒjʊəltɪ] n (injured) Verletzte der die; (dead) Tote der die; ~ (ward) Unfallstation die.

cat [kæt] n Katze die.

catalog ['kætəlɒg] (Am) = **catalogue**.

catalogue ['kætəlɒg] n Katalog der.

catapult ['kætəpʌlt] n Katapult das.

cataract ['kætərækt] n (in eye) grauer Star.

catarrh [kə'tɑːr] n Katarrh der.

catastrophe [kə'tæstrəfɪ] n Katastrophe die.

catch [kætʃ] (pt & pp caught) ◆ vt fangen; (bus, train, plane, taxi) nehmen; (surprise) erwischen; (illness) bekommen; (hear) verstehen; (attention) erregen. ◆ vi (become hooked) sich verfangen. ◆ n (of window, door) Schnappschloß das; (snag) Haken der. ▶ **catch up** vt sep & vi einlholen, auflholen.

catching ['kætʃɪŋ] adj (inf) ansteckend.

category ['kætəgərɪ] n Kategorie die.

cater ['keɪtər]: **cater for** vt fus (Br) eingestellt sein auf (+A).

caterpillar ['kætəpɪlər] n Raupe die.

cathedral [kə'θiːdrəl] n Kathedrale die.

Catholic ['kæθlɪk] ◆ adj katholisch. ◆ n Katholik der (-in die).

Catseyes® ['kætsaɪz] npl (Br) Reflektoren pl (auf der Straße).

cattle ['kætl] npl Vieh das.

cattle grid n Gitter auf Landstraßen, um Vieh am Überqueren zu hindern.

caught [kɔːt] pt & pp → **catch**.

cauliflower ['kɒlɪˌflaʊər] n Blumenkohl der, Karfiol der (Österr).

cauliflower cheese n Blumenkohlauflauf der.

cause [kɔːz] ◆ n Ursache die, Grund der; (principle, aim) Sache die. ◆ vt verursachen; **to ~ sb to do sthg** jn veranlassen, etw zu tun.

causeway ['kɔːzweɪ] n Damm der.

caustic soda [ˌkɔːstɪk-] n Ätznatron das.

caution ['kɔːʃn] n Vorsicht die; (warning) Verwarnung die.

cautious ['kɔːʃəs] adj vorsichtig.

cave [keɪv] n Höhle die. ▶ **cave in** vi einlstürzen.

caviar(e) ['kævɪɑːr] n Kaviar der.

cavity ['kævətɪ] n (in tooth) Loch das.

CD n (abbr of compact disc) CD die.

CDI n (abbr of compact disc interactive) CD-Wechsler.

CD player n CD-Player der.

CDW n (abbr of collision damage waiver) Vollkaskoversicherung die.

cease [siːs] ◆ vt (fml) auflhören mit. ◆ vi (fml) auflhören.

ceasefire ['siːsˌfaɪər] n Waffenstillstand der.

ceilidh ['keɪlɪ] n traditionelle Tanzveranstaltung in Schottland und Irland.

ceiling ['siːlɪŋ] n Decke die.

celebrate ['selɪbreɪt] vt & vi feiern.

celebration [ˌselɪ'breɪʃn] n (event) Feier die. ▶ **celebrations** npl (festivities) Festlichkeiten pl.

celebrity [sɪ'lebrətɪ] n (person) Prominente die der.

celeriac [sɪ'lerɪæk] n Knollensellerie der.

celery ['selərɪ] n Sellerie der.

cell [sel] n Zelle die.

cellar ['selər] n Keller der.

cello ['tʃeləʊ] (pl -s) n Cello das.

Cellophane® ['seləfeɪn] n (Br) Cellophan® das.

Celsius ['selsɪəs] adj Celsius.

cement [sɪ'ment] n Zement der.

cement mixer n Zementmischer der.

cemetery ['semɪtrɪ] n Friedhof der.

cent [sent] n (Am) Cent der.

center ['sentər] (Am) = **centre**.

centigrade ['sentɪgreɪd] adj Celsius.

centimetre ['sentɪˌmiːtər] n Zentimeter der.

centipede ['sentɪpiːd] n Tausendfüßler der.

central ['sentrəl] adj zentral.

central heating n Zentralheizung die.

central locking [-'lɒkɪŋ] n Zentralverriegelung die.

central reservation n (Br) Mittelstreifen der.

centre ['sentə^r] ◆ n (Br) Mitte die; (building) Zentrum das. ◆ adj (Br) mittlere(-r)(-s); **to be the ~ of attention** im Mittelpunkt stehen.

century ['sentʃʊrɪ] n Jahrhundert das.

ceramic [sɪ'ræmɪk] adj Keramik-. ► **ceramics** npl Keramik die.

cereal ['sɪərɪəl] n (breakfast food) Frühstücksflocken pl.

ceremony ['serɪmənɪ] n Zeremonie die.

certain ['sɜːtn] adj sicher; (particular) bestimmt, gewiß; **to be ~ to do sthg** etw bestimmt tun; **to be ~ of sthg** sich (D) einer Sache (G) sicher sein; **to make ~ (that)** sich vergewissern, daß.

certainly ['sɜːtnlɪ] adv bestimmt; (of course) natürlich, sicher.

certificate [sə'tɪfɪkət] n Bescheinigung die; (from school) Zeugnis das.

certify ['sɜːtɪfaɪ] vt bescheinigen.

chain [tʃeɪn] ◆ n Kette die. ◆ vt: **to ~ sthg to sthg** etw an etw (+A) anlketten.

chain store n zu einer Ladenkette gehörendes Geschäft.

chair [tʃeə^r] n Stuhl der; (armchair) Sessel der.

chair lift n Sessellift der.

chairman ['tʃeəmən] (pl -men [-mən]) n Vorsitzende der.

chairperson ['tʃeə,pɜːsn] n Vorsitzende der die.

chairwoman ['tʃeə,wʊmən] (pl -women [-,wɪmɪn]) n Vorsitzende die.

chalet ['ʃæleɪ] n Chalet das; (at holiday camp) Ferienhaus das.

chalk [tʃɔːk] n Kreide die; **a piece of ~** ein Stück Kreide.

chalkboard ['tʃɔːkbɔːd] n (Am) Tafel die.

challenge ['tʃælɪndʒ] ◆ n Herausforderung die. ◆ vt (question) in Frage stellen; **to ~ sb (to sthg)** jn herauslfordern (zu etw).

chamber ['tʃeɪmbə^r] n Kammer die.

chambermaid ['tʃeɪmbəmeɪd] n Zimmermädchen das.

champagne [,ʃæm'peɪn] n Champagner der.

champion ['tʃæmpjən] n Meister der (-in die).

championship ['tʃæmpjənʃɪp] n Meisterschaft die.

chance [tʃɑːns] ◆ n (luck) Glück das; (possibility) Chance die, Möglichkeit die; (opportunity) Gelegenheit die. ◆ vt: **to ~ it** (inf) es riskieren; **to take a ~** es darauf anlkommen lassen; **by ~** zufällig; **on the off ~** auf gut Glück.

Chancellor of the Exchequer [,tʃɑːnsələrəvðəɪks'tʃekə^r] n (Br) Schatzkanzler der.

chandelier [,ʃændə'lɪə^r] n Kronleuchter der.

change [tʃeɪndʒ] ◆ n Veränderung die; (alteration) Änderung die; (money received back) Wechselgeld das; (coins) Kleingeld das. ◆ vt ändern; (switch) wechseln; (exchange) umltauschen; (clothes, bedding) wechseln. ◆ vi verändern; (on bus, train) umlsteigen; (change clothes) sich umlziehen; **a ~ of clothes** Kleidung zum Wechseln; **do you have ~ for a pound?** können Sie mir ein Pfund wechseln?; **for a ~** zur Abwechslung; **to get ~d** sich umlziehen; **to ~ money** Geld wechseln; **to ~ a nappy** eine Windel wechseln; **to ~ a wheel** ein Rad wechseln; **to ~ trains/planes** umlsteigen; **all ~!** (on train) alles aussteigen!

changeable ['tʃeɪndʒəbl] adj (weather) veränderlich.

change machine n Wechselgeldautomat der.

changing room ['tʃeɪndʒɪŋ-] n (for

sport) Umkleideraum *der*; (*in shop*) Umkleidekabine *die*.

channel ['tʃænl] *n* Kanal *der*; (*on radio*) Sender *der*; (*in sea*) Fahrrinne *die*; **the (English) Channel** der Ärmelkanal.

Channel Islands *npl*: **the ~** die Kanalinseln.

Channel Tunnel *n*: **the ~** der Euro-Tunnel.

chant [tʃɑːnt] *vt* (RELIG) singen; (*words, slogan*) Sprechchöre an|stimmen.

chaos ['keɪɒs] *n* Chaos *das*.

chaotic [keɪ'ɒtɪk] *adj* chaotisch.

chap [tʃæp] *n* (Br: *inf*) Kerl *der*.

chapel ['tʃæpl] *n* Kapelle *die*.

chapped [tʃæpt] *adj* aufgesprungen.

chapter ['tʃæptər] *n* Kapitel *das*.

character ['kærəktər] *n* Charakter *der*; (*of person*) Persönlichkeit *die*; (*in film, book, play*) Gestalt *die*; (*letter*) Schriftzeichen *das*.

characteristic [,kærəktə'rɪstɪk] ♦ *adj* charakteristisch. ♦ *n* Kennzeichen *das*.

charcoal ['tʃɑːkəʊl] *n* (*for barbecue*) Grillkohle *die*.

charge [tʃɑːdʒ] ♦ *n* (*price*) Gebühr *die*; (JUR) Anklage *die*. ♦ *vt* (*money*) berechnen; (JUR) an|klagen; (*battery*) auf|laden. ♦ *vi* (*ask money*) in Rechnung stellen; (*rush*) stürmen; **to be in ~ (of)** verantwortlich sein (für); **to take ~ of sthg** die Leitung für etw übernehmen; **free of ~** gratis; **there is no ~ for service** es gibt keinen Bedienungszuschlag.

char-grilled ['tʃɑːgrɪld] *adj* vom Holzkohlengrill.

charity ['tʃærətɪ] *n* (*organization*) Wohltätigkeitsverein *der*; **to give to ~** für wohltätige Zwecke spenden.

charity shop *n* Gebrauchtwarenladen, *dessen Erlös zugunsten wohltätiger Zwecke geht.*

charm [tʃɑːm] ♦ *n* (*attractiveness*) Reiz *der*. ♦ *vt* bezaubern.

charming ['tʃɑːmɪŋ] *adj* reizend.

chart [tʃɑːt] *n* (*diagram*) Diagramm *das*; (*map*) Karte *die*; **the ~s** die Hitparade.

chartered accountant [,tʃɑːtəd-] *n* Wirtschaftsprüfer *der* (-in *die*).

charter flight ['tʃɑːtə-] *n* Charterflug *der*.

chase [tʃeɪs] ♦ *n* Verfolgungsjagd *die*. ♦ *vt* verfolgen, jagen.

chat [tʃæt] ♦ *n* Plauderei *die*. ♦ *vi* plaudern; **to have a ~ (with sb)** plaudern (mit jm). ► **chat up** *vt sep* (Br: *inf*) an|machen.

chat show *n* (Br) Talk-Show *die*.

chatty ['tʃætɪ] *adj* (*person*) gesprächig; (*letter*) unterhaltsam.

chauffeur ['ʃəʊfər] *n* Chauffeur *der*.

cheap [tʃiːp] *adj* billig.

cheap day return *n* (Br) *reduzierte Rückfahrkarte für bestimmte Züge.*

cheaply ['tʃiːplɪ] *adv* billig.

cheat [tʃiːt] ♦ *n* Betrüger *der* (-in *die*); (*in games*) Mogler *der* (-in *die*). ♦ *vi* betrügen; (*in games*) mogeln. ♦ *vt*: **to ~ sb (out of sthg)** jn betrügen (um etw).

check [tʃek] ♦ *n* (*inspection*) Kontrolle *die*; (Am: *bill*) Rechnung *die*; (Am: *tick*) Haken *der*; (Am) = **cheque**. ♦ *vt* kontrollieren. ♦ *vi* überprüfen; **to ~ for sthg** auf etw prüfen. ► **check in** *vt sep & vi* ein|checken. ► **check off** *vt sep* ab|haken. ► **check out** *vi* ab|reisen, aus|checken. ► **check up** *vi*: **to ~ up (on)** überprüfen.

checked [tʃekt] *adj* kariert.

checkers ['tʃekəz] *n* (Am) Damespiel *das*.

check-in desk *n* (*at airport*) Abfertigungsschalter *der*; (*at hotel*) Rezeption *die*.

checkout ['tʃekaʊt] *n* Kasse *die*.

checkpoint ['tʃekpɔɪnt] *n* Kontrollpunkt *der*.

checkroom ['tʃekrʊm] *n* (Am) Gepäckaufbewahrung *die*.

checkup ['tʃekʌp] *n* Untersuchung *die*.

cheddar (cheese) ['tʃedər-] n Cheddarkäse der.

cheek [tʃiːk] n Backe die; **what a ~!** so eine Frechheit!

cheeky ['tʃiːkɪ] adj frech.

cheer [tʃɪər] ◆ n Beifallsruf der. ◆ vi jubeln, applaudieren.

cheerful ['tʃɪəful] adj fröhlich.

cheerio [,tʃɪərɪ'əu] excl (Br: inf) tschüs!

cheers [tʃɪəz] excl (when drinking) prost!; (Br: inf: thank you) danke!

cheese [tʃiːz] n Käse der.

cheeseboard ['tʃiːzbɔːd] n Käseplatte die.

cheeseburger ['tʃiːz,bɜːgər] n Cheeseburger der.

cheesecake ['tʃiːzkeɪk] n Käsekuchen der.

chef [ʃef] n Koch der.

chef's special n Tagesgericht das.

chemical ['kemɪkl] ◆ adj chemisch. ◆ n Chemikalie die.

chemist ['kemɪst] n (Br: pharmacist) Apotheker der (-in die); (scientist) Chemiker der (-in die); **~'s** (Br: shop) Drogerie die; (dispensing) Apotheke die.

chemistry ['kemɪstrɪ] n Chemie die.

cheque [tʃek] n (Br) Scheck der; **to pay by ~** mit Scheck bezahlen.

chequebook ['tʃekbuk] n Scheckbuch das.

cheque card n Scheckkarte die.

cherry ['tʃerɪ] n Kirsche die.

chess [tʃes] n Schach das.

chest [tʃest] n (of body) Brust die; (box) Truhe die.

chestnut ['tʃesnʌt] ◆ n Kastanie die. ◆ adj (colour) kastanienbraun.

chest of drawers n Kommode die.

chew [tʃuː] ◆ vt kauen. ◆ n (sweet) Kaubonbon der or das.

chewing gum ['tʃuːɪŋ-] n Kaugummi der.

chic [ʃiːk] adj schick.

chicken ['tʃɪkɪn] n Huhn das; (grilled, roasted) Hähnchen das.

chicken breast n Hühnerbrust die.

chicken Kiev [-'kiːev] n mit Knoblauchbutter gefülltes paniertes Hähnchenfilet.

chickenpox ['tʃɪkɪnpɒks] n Windpocken pl.

chickpea ['tʃɪkpiː] n Kichererbse die.

chicory ['tʃɪkərɪ] n Chicorée der.

chief [tʃiːf] ◆ adj (highest-ranking) leitend, Ober-; (main) Haupt-. ◆ n Leiter der (-in die), Chef der (-in die); (of tribe) Häuptling der.

chiefly ['tʃiːflɪ] adv (mainly) hauptsächlich; (especially) vor allem.

child [tʃaɪld] (pl children) n Kind das.

child abuse n Kindesmißhandlung die.

child benefit n (Br) Kindergeld das.

childhood ['tʃaɪldhud] n Kindheit die.

childish ['tʃaɪldɪʃ] adj (pej: immature) kindisch.

childminder ['tʃaɪld,maɪndər] n (Br) Tagesmutter die.

children ['tʃɪldrən] pl → **child**.

childrenswear ['tʃɪldrənzweər] n Kinderkleidung die.

child seat n Kindersitz der.

Chile ['tʃɪlɪ] n Chile nt.

chill [tʃɪl] ◆ n (illness) Erkältung die. ◆ vt kühlen; **there's a ~ in the air** es ist kühl draußen.

chilled [tʃɪld] adj gekühlt; **'serve ~'** 'gekühlt servieren'.

chilli ['tʃɪlɪ] (pl -ies) n Chili der.

chilli con carne ['tʃɪlɪkɒn'kɑːnɪ] n Chili con carne das.

chilly ['tʃɪlɪ] adj kühl.

chimney ['tʃɪmnɪ] n Schornstein der.

chimneypot ['tʃɪmnɪpɒt] n Schornsteinaufsatz der.

chimpanzee [,tʃɪmpən'ziː] n Schimpanse der.

chin [tʃɪn] n Kinn das.

china [ˈtʃaɪnə] n (material) Porzellan das.

China [ˈtʃaɪnə] n China nt.

Chinese [ˌtʃaɪˈniːz] ◆ adj chinesisch. ◆ n (language) Chinesisch das. ◆ npl: **the ~** die Chinesen; **a ~ restaurant** ein China-Restaurant.

chip [tʃɪp] ◆ n (small piece) Stückchen das; (mark) angeschlagene Stelle; (for gambling, in computer) Chip der. ◆ vt an|schlagen. ▶ **chips** npl (Br: French fries) Pommes frites pl; (Am: crisps) Chips pl.

chiropodist [kɪˈrɒpədɪst] n Fußpfleger der (-in die).

chisel [ˈtʃɪzl] n Meißel der; (for wood) Stemmeisen das.

chives [tʃaɪvz] npl Schnittlauch der.

chlorine [ˈklɔːriːn] n Chlor das.

choc-ice [ˈtʃɒkaɪs] n (Br) Eiscremeriegel mit Schokoladenüberzug.

chocolate [ˈtʃɒkələt] ◆ n Schokolade die; (sweet) Praline die. ◆ adj Schokoladen-.

chocolate biscuit n Schokoladenkeks der.

choice [tʃɔɪs] ◆ n Wahl die; (variety) Auswahl die. ◆ adj (meat, ingredients) Qualitäts-; **with the topping of your ~** mit der Garnitur Ihrer Wahl.

choir [ˈkwaɪər] n Chor der.

choke [tʃəʊk] ◆ n (AUT) Choke der. ◆ vt verstopfen. ◆ vi (on fishbone etc) sich verschlucken; (to death) ersticken.

cholera [ˈkɒlərə] n Cholera die.

choose [tʃuːz] (pt chose, pp chosen) ◆ vt wählen, sich (D) aus|suchen. ◆ vi wählen; **to ~ to do sthg** (decide) beschließen, etw zu tun.

chop [tʃɒp] ◆ n (of meat) Kotelett das. ◆ vt hacken. ▶ **chop down** vt sep fällen, um|hauen. ▶ **chop up** vt sep klein|hacken.

chopper [ˈtʃɒpər] n (inf: helicopter) Hubschrauber der.

chopping board [ˈtʃɒpɪŋ-] n Hackbrett das.

choppy [ˈtʃɒpɪ] adj kabbelig.

chopsticks [ˈtʃɒpstɪks] npl Stäbchen pl.

chop suey [ˌtʃɒpˈsuːɪ] n Chop-suey das.

chord [kɔːd] n Akkord der.

chore [tʃɔːr] n lästige Pflicht; **household ~s** Hausarbeit die.

chorus [ˈkɔːrəs] n (of song) Refrain der; (singers, dancers) Chor der.

chose [tʃəʊz] pt → **choose**.

chosen [ˈtʃəʊzn] pp → **choose**.

choux pastry [ʃuː-] n Brandteig der.

chowder [ˈtʃaʊdər] n Suppe mit Fisch oder Meeresfrüchten.

chow mein [ˌtʃaʊˈmeɪn] n chinesisches Gericht mit gebratenen Nudeln.

Christ [kraɪst] n Christus (ohne Artikel).

christen [ˈkrɪsn] vt taufen.

Christian [ˈkrɪstʃən] ◆ adj christlich. ◆ n Christ der (-in die).

Christian name n Vorname der.

Christmas [ˈkrɪsməs] n Weihnachten das; **Happy ~!** Fröhliche Weihnachten!

Christmas card n Weihnachtskarte die.

Christmas carol [-ˈkærəl] n Weihnachtslied das.

Christmas Day n erster Weihnachtsfeiertag.

Christmas Eve n Heiligabend der.

Christmas pudding n Plumpudding der.

Christmas tree n Weihnachtsbaum der.

chrome [krəʊm] n Chrom das.

chuck [tʃʌk] vt (inf: throw) schmeißen; (boyfriend, girlfriend) Schluß machen mit. ▶ **chuck away** vt sep (inf) weg|schmeißen.

chunk [tʃʌŋk] n (of meat, cake etc) Stück das.

church [tʃɜːtʃ] n Kirche die; **to go to ~** in die Kirche gehen.

churchyard [ˈtʃɜːtʃjɑːd] n Friedhof der.

chute [ʃuːt] n Rutsche die.

chutney ['tʃʌtnɪ] n Chutney das (Sauce aus Früchten und Gewürzen).

cider ['saɪdər] n = Apfelwein der.

cigar [sɪ'gɑːr] n Zigarre die.

cigarette [ˌsɪgə'ret] n Zigarette die.

cigarette lighter n Feuerzeug das.

cinema ['sɪnəmə] n Kino das.

cinnamon ['sɪnəmən] n Zimt der.

circle ['sɜːkl] ◆ n Kreis der; (in theatre) Rang der. ◆ vt (draw circle around) ein|kreisen; (move round) um|kreisen. ◆ vi (plane) kreisen.

circuit ['sɜːkɪt] n (track) Rennbahn die; (lap) Runde die.

circular ['sɜːkjʊlər] ◆ adj rund. ◆ n Rundschreiben das.

circulation [ˌsɜːkjʊ'leɪʃn] n (of blood) Kreislauf der; (of newspaper, magazine) Auflage die.

circumstances ['sɜːkəmstənsɪz] npl Umstände pl; **in** OR **under the ~** unter diesen Umständen.

circus ['sɜːkəs] n Zirkus der.

cistern ['sɪstən] n (of toilet) Wasserbehälter der.

citizen ['sɪtɪzn] n Bürger der (-in die).

city ['sɪtɪ] n größere Stadt; **the City** Banken- und Börsenviertel in London.

city centre n Stadtzentrum das.

city hall n (Am) Rathaus das.

civilian [sɪ'vɪljən] n Zivilist der (-in die).

civilized ['sɪvɪlaɪzd] adj (society) zivilisiert; (person, evening) charmant.

civil rights [ˌsɪvl-] npl Bürgerrechte pl.

civil servant [ˌsɪvl-] n Beamte der (Beamtin die) (im Staatsdienst).

civil service [ˌsɪvl-] n Staatsdienst der.

civil war [ˌsɪvl-] n Bürgerkrieg der.

cl (abbr of centilitre) cl.

claim [kleɪm] ◆ n (assertion) Anspruch der; (demand) Forderung die; (for insurance) Schadenersatzanspruch der. ◆ vt (allege) behaupten; (demand) fordern; (credit) Anspruch erheben auf (+A). ◆ vi (on insurance) Schadenersatz fordern.

claimant ['kleɪmənt] n Antragsteller der (-in die).

claim form n Antragsformular das.

clam [klæm] n Klaffmuschel die.

clamp [klæmp] ◆ n (for car) Parkkralle die. ◆ vt (car) eine Parkkralle an|legen.

clap [klæp] vi klatschen.

claret ['klærət] n roter Bordeaux.

clarinet [ˌklærə'net] n Klarinette die.

clash [klæʃ] ◆ n (noise) Geklirr das; (confrontation) Konflikt der. ◆ vi (colours) sich beißen; (event, date) sich überschneiden.

clasp [klɑːsp] ◆ n (fastener) Schnalle die. ◆ vt fest|halten.

class [klɑːs] ◆ n Klasse die; (teaching period) Stunde die; (type) Art die. ◆ vt: **to ~ sb/sthg as sthg** jn/etw als etw ein|stufen.

classic ['klæsɪk] ◆ adj klassisch. ◆ n Klassiker der.

classical ['klæsɪkl] adj klassisch.

classical music n klassische Musik.

classification [ˌklæsɪfɪ'keɪʃn] n Klassifizierung die; (category) Kategorie die.

classified ads [ˌklæsɪfaɪd-] npl Annoncen pl.

classroom ['klɑːsrʊm] n Klassenzimmer das.

claustrophobic [ˌklɔːstrə'fəʊbɪk] adj: **to feel ~** Platzangst haben.

claw [klɔː] n Kralle die; (of crab, lobster) Schere die.

clay [kleɪ] n Ton der.

clean [kliːn] ◆ adj sauber. ◆ vt sauber|machen; (floor) putzen; **to ~ one's teeth** sich (D) die Zähne putzen.

cleaner ['kliːnər] n (person) Putzfrau die (Putzer der); (substance) Putzmittel das.

cleanse [klenz] vt reinigen.

cleanser ['klenzər] n (for skin)

Reinigungsmilch die; (detergent) Reinigungsmittel das.

clear [klɪərˈ] ♦ adj klar; (image, sound) deutlich; (obvious) eindeutig; (road, view) frei. ♦ vt (road, path) räumen; (jump over) überspringen; (declare not guilty) freilsprechen; (authorize) genehmigen; (cheque) verrechnen. ♦ vi (weather, fog) sich auflklären; **to be ~ (about sthg)** sich (D) im klaren sein (über etw (A); **to be ~ of sthg** (not touching) etw nicht berühren; **to ~ one's throat** sich räuspern; **to ~ the table** den Tisch ablräumen. ▶ **clear up** vt sep (room, toys) auflräumen; (problem, confusion) klären. ♦ vi (weather) sich auflklären; (tidy up) auflräumen.

clearance ['klɪərəns] n (authorization) Genehmigung die; (free distance) Entfernung die; (for takeoff) Starterlaubnis die.

clearance sale n Ausverkauf der.

clearing ['klɪərɪŋ] n Lichtung die.

clearly ['klɪəlɪ] adv (see, speak) deutlich; (marked, defined) klar, deutlich; (obviously) eindeutig.

clearway ['klɪəweɪ] n (Br) Straße mit Halteverbot.

clementine ['kleməntaɪn] n Klementine die.

clerk [Br klɑːk, Am klɜːrk] n Büroangestellte der die; (Am: in shop) Verkäufer der (-in die).

clever ['klevər] adj (person) klug; (idea, device) clever.

click [klɪk] ♦ n Klicken das. ♦ vi klicken.

client ['klaɪənt] n Kunde der (Kundin die).

cliff [klɪf] n Klippe die.

climate ['klaɪmɪt] n Klima das.

climax ['klaɪmæks] n Höhepunkt der.

climb [klaɪm] ♦ vt (hill, mountain) besteigen; (ladder) hinauflsteigen; (tree) hochlklettern. ♦ vi klettern; (plane) steigen. ▶ **climb down** vt fus herunterlklettern. ♦ vi klein

beilgeben. ▶ **climb up** vt fus hochlklettern.

climber ['klaɪmər] n Bergsteiger der (-in die).

climbing ['klaɪmɪŋ] n (mountaineering) Bergsteigen das; (rock climbing) Bergklettern das; **to go ~** Bergsteigen/Bergklettern gehen.

climbing frame n (Br) Klettergerüst das.

clingfilm ['klɪŋfɪlm] n (Br) Klarsichtfolie die.

clinic ['klɪnɪk] n Klinik die.

clip [klɪp] ♦ n (fastener) Klammer die; (of film, programme) Ausschnitt der. ♦ vt (fasten) zusammenlheften; (cut) schneiden.

cloak [kləʊk] n Umhang der.

cloakroom ['kləʊkrʊm] n (for coats) Garderobe die; (Br: toilets) Toilette die.

clock [klɒk] n Uhr die; (mileometer) Kilometerzähler der; **round the ~** rund um die Uhr.

clockwise ['klɒkwaɪz] adv im Uhrzeigersinn.

clog [klɒg] ♦ n Clog der. ♦ vt verstopfen.

close¹ [kləʊs] ♦ adj nahe; (friend, contact, link) eng; (resemblance) stark; (examination) genau; (race, contest) knapp. ♦ adv nah; **~ behind** dicht dahinter; **~ by** in der Nähe; **~ to** nahe an (+A,D), dicht bei.

close² [kləʊz] ♦ vt schließen. ♦ vi (door, eyes) sich schließen; (shop, office) schließen; (deadline, offer) enden. ▶ **close down** vt sep & vi schließen.

closed [kləʊzd] adj geschlossen.

closely ['kləʊslɪ] adv (related, involved) eng; (follow) dicht; (examine) genau.

closet ['klɒzɪt] n (Am) Schrank der.

close-up ['kləʊs-] n Nahaufnahme die.

closing time ['kləʊzɪŋ-] n Ladenschlußzeit die.

clot [klɒt] n (of blood) Gerinnsel das.

cloth [klɒθ] n (fabric) Stoff der; (piece of cloth) Tuch das.

clothes [kləʊðz] *npl* Kleider *pl.*

clothesline ['kləʊðzlaɪn] *n* Wäscheleine *die.*

clothes peg *n* (Br) Wäscheklammer *die.*

clothespin ['kləʊðzpɪn] (Am) =
clothes peg.

clothes shop *n* Bekleidungs-
geschäft *das.*

clothing ['kləʊðɪŋ] *n* Kleidung *die.*

clotted cream [,klɒtɪd-] *n* sehr dicke
Sahne, Spezialität Südwestenglands.

cloud [klaʊd] *n* Wolke *die.*

cloudy ['klaʊdɪ] *adj* bewölkt; (liquid)
trüb.

clove [kləʊv] *n* (of garlic) Zehe *die.*
► **cloves** *npl* (spice) Gewürznelken
pl.

clown [klaʊn] *n* Clown *der.*

club [klʌb] *n* Klub *der*; (nightclub)
Nachtklub *der*; (stick) Knüppel *der.*
► **clubs** *npl* (in cards) Kreuz *das.*

clubbing ['klʌbɪŋ] *n*: **to go ~** (inf)
tanzen gehen.

club class *n* Club Class *die.*

club sandwich *n* (Am) Club-
Sandwich *das.*

club soda *n* (Am) Sodawasser *das.*

clue [kluː] *n* Hinweis *der*; (in crossword) Frage *die*; **I haven't got a ~** ich
habe keine Ahnung.

clumsy ['klʌmzɪ] *adj* (person)
ungeschickt.

clutch [klʌtʃ] ♦ *n* Kupplung *die.* ♦ *vt*
(hold tightly) umklammern.

cm (abbr of centimetre) cm.

c/o (abbr of care of) bei, c/o.

Co. (abbr of company) Co.

coach [kəʊtʃ] *n* (bus) Bus *der*; (of
train) Wagen *der*; (SPORT) Trainer *der*
(-in *die*).

coach party *n* (Br) Busreisende *pl.*

coach station *n* Busbahnhof *der.*

coach trip *n* (Br) Busausflug *der.*

coal [kəʊl] *n* Kohle *die.*

coal mine *n* Kohlenbergwerk *das.*

coarse [kɔːs] *adj* (rough) grob; (vulgar) vulgär.

coast [kəʊst] *n* Küste *die.*

coaster ['kəʊstər] *n* (for glass)
Untersetzer *der.*

coastguard ['kəʊstgɑːd] *n* (person)
Küstenwächter *der* (-in *die*); (organization) Küstenwache *die.*

coastline ['kəʊstlaɪn] *n* Küste *die.*

coat [kəʊt] ♦ *n* Mantel *der*; (of animal) Fell *das.* ♦ *vt*: **to ~ sthg (with)** etw
überziehen (mit).

coat hanger *n* Kleiderbügel *der.*

coating ['kəʊtɪŋ] *n* (on surface) Be-
schichtung *die*; (on food) Überzug
der.

cobbled street ['kɒbld-] *n* Straße
die mit Kopfsteinpflaster.

cobbles ['kɒblz] *npl* Kopfsteinpflaster *das.*

cobweb ['kɒbweb] *n* Spinnennetz
das.

Coca-Cola® [,kəʊkə'kəʊlə] *n* Coca-
Cola® *die or das.*

cocaine [kəʊ'keɪn] *n* Kokain *das.*

cock [kɒk] *n* Hahn *der.*

cock-a-leekie [,kɒkə'liːkɪ] *n*
Hühnersuppe mit Lauch.

cockerel ['kɒkrəl] *n* junger Hahn.

cockles ['kɒklz] *npl* Herzmuscheln
die.

cockpit ['kɒkpɪt] *n* (of plane) Cockpit
das.

cockroach ['kɒkrəʊtʃ] *n* Küchen-
schabe *die.*

cocktail ['kɒkteɪl] *n* Cocktail *der.*

cocktail party *n* Cocktailparty *die.*

cock-up *n* (Br: vulg): **to make a ~**
Scheiße bauen.

cocoa ['kəʊkəʊ] *n* Kakao *der.*

coconut ['kəʊkənʌt] *n* Kokosnuß *die.*

cod [kɒd] (pl inv) *n* Kabeljau *der.*

code [kəʊd] *n* Kode *der*; (dialling code)
Vorwahl *die.*

cod-liver oil *n* Lebertran *der.*

coeducational [,kəʊedjuː'keɪʃənl]
adj koedukativ.

coffee ['kɒfɪ] *n* Kaffee *der*; **black ~**
schwarzer Kaffee; **white ~** Kaffee mit
Milch; **ground ~** gemahlener Kaffee;

instant ~ Instantkaffee.
coffee bar n (Br) Café das.
coffee break n Kaffeepause die.
coffeepot ['kɒfɪpɒt] n Kaffeekanne die.
coffee shop n (cafe) Café das.
coffee table n Couchtisch der.
coffin ['kɒfɪn] n Sarg der.
cog(wheel) ['kɒg(wi:l)] n Zahnrad das.
coil [kɔɪl] ◆ n Rolle die; (Br: contraceptive) Spirale die. ◆ vt auflrollen.
coin [kɔɪn] n Münze die.
coinbox ['kɔɪnbɒks] n (Br) Münztelefon das.
coincide [ˌkəʊɪn'saɪd] vi: **to ~ (with)** zusammenlfallen (mit).
coincidence [kəʊ'ɪnsɪdəns] n Zufall der.
Coke® [kəʊk] n Cola® die or das.
colander ['kʌləndər] n Sieb das.
cold [kəʊld] ◆ adj kalt; (unfriendly) kühl. ◆ n (illness) Erkältung die, Schnupfen der; (temperature) Kälte die; **to get ~** kalt werden; **to catch (a) ~** sich erkälten.
cold cuts (Am) = **cold meats**.
cold meats npl Aufschnitt der.
coleslaw ['kəʊlslɔ:] n Krautsalat der.
colic ['kɒlɪk] n Kolik die.
collaborate [kə'læbəreɪt] vi zusammenlarbeiten.
collapse [kə'læps] vi (building, tent) einlstürzen; (person) zusammenlbrechen.
collar ['kɒlər] n Kragen der; (of dog, cat) Halsband das.
collarbone ['kɒləbəʊn] n Schlüsselbein das.
colleague ['kɒli:g] n Kollege der (Kollegin die).
collect [kə'lekt] ◆ vt sammeln; (go and get) ablholen. ◆ vi sich sammeln. ◆ adv (Am): **to call (sb) ~** ein R-Gespräch (mit jm) führen.
collection [kə'lekʃn] n Sammlung die; (of mail) Leerung die.

collector [kə'lektər] n Sammler der (-in die).
college ['kɒlɪdʒ] n (school) Schule die; (Br: of university) College das; (Am: university) Universität die.
collide [kə'laɪd] vi: **to ~ (with)** zusammenlstoßen (mit).
collision [kə'lɪʒn] n Zusammenstoß der.
cologne [kə'ləʊn] n Kölnischwasser das.
Cologne [kə'ləʊn] n Köln nt.
colon ['kəʊlən] n (GRAMM) Doppelpunkt der.
colonel ['kɜ:nl] n Oberst der.
colony ['kɒlənɪ] n Kolonie die.
color ['kʌlər] (Am) = **colour**.
colour ['kʌlər] ◆ n Farbe die. ◆ adj (photograph, film) Farb-. ◆ vt färben.
▶ **colour in** vt sep auslmalen.
colour-blind adj farbenblind.
colourful ['kʌləfʊl] adj bunt; (fig: person, place) schillernd.
colouring ['kʌlərɪŋ] n (of food) Farbstoff der; (complexion) Hautfarbe die.
colouring book n Malbuch das.
colour supplement n Farbbeilage die.
colour television n Farbfernsehen das.
column ['kɒləm] n Säule die; (of figures) Kolumne die; (of writing) Spalte die.
coma ['kəʊmə] n Koma das.
comb [kəʊm] ◆ n Kamm der. ◆ vt: **to ~ one's hair** sich (D) die Haare kämmen.
combination [ˌkɒmbɪ'neɪʃn] n (mixture) Mischung die; (of lock) Kombination die.
combine [kəm'baɪn] vt: **to ~ sthg (with)** etw verbinden (mit).
combine harvester ['kɒmbaɪn-'hɑ:vɪstər] n Mähdrescher der.
come [kʌm] (pt came, pp inv) vi 1. (move) kommen; **we came by taxi** wir sind mit dem Taxi gekommen; **~ and see!** komm und schau!; **~ here!**

komm her! **2.** (*arrive*) kommen; **to ~ home** nach Hause kommen; **'coming soon'** 'demnächst'. **3.** (*in competition*): **to ~ first** Erster werden; **to ~ last** Letzter werden. **4.** (*reach*): **to ~ up/down** to gehen bis. **5.** (*become*) werden; **to ~ true** wahr werden; **to ~ undone** auf|gehen. **6.** (*be sold*): **they ~ in packs of six** es gibt sie im Sechserpack. ▶ **come across** *vt fus* stoßen auf (+A). ▶ **come along** *vi* (*progress*) voran|kommen; (*arrive*) kommen; **~ along!** (*as encouragement*) komm!; (*hurry up*) komm schon! ▶ **come apart** *vi* kaputt|gehen. ▶ **come back** *vi* zurück|kommen. ▶ **come down** *vi* (*price*) fallen. ▶ **come down with** *vt fus* (*illness*) bekommen. ▶ **come from** *vt fus* stammen aus (+D), kommen aus (+D). ▶ **come in** *vi* herein|kommen; (*train*) ein|fahren; **~ in!** herein! ▶ **come off** *vi* (*button, top*) ab|gehen; (*succeed*) klappen. ▶ **come on** *vi* (*progress*) voran|kommen; **~ on!** (*as encouragement*) komm!; (*hurry up*) komm schon! ▶ **come out** *vi* heraus|kommen; (*stain*) heraus|gehen; **only two photos came out** nur zwei Bilder sind was geworden. ▶ **come over** *vi* (*visit*) vorbei|kommen. ▶ **come round** *vi* (*visit*) vorbei|kommen; (*regain consciousness*) zu sich kommen. ▶ **come to** *vt fus*: **the bill ~s to £20** das macht 20 Pfund. ▶ **come up** *vi* (*go upstairs*) hoch|kommen; (*be mentioned*) erwähnt werden; (*happen*) passieren; (*sun, moon*) auf|gehen. ▶ **come up with** *vt fus* (*idea*) sich aus|denken.

comedian [kə'miːdjən] *n* Komiker *der*.

comedy ['kɒmədɪ] *n* Komödie *die*; (*humour*) Komik *die*.

comfort ['kʌmfət] ◆ *n* Bequemlichkeit *die*; (*consolation*) Trost *der*. ◆ *vt* trösten.

comfortable ['kʌmftəbl] *adj* bequem; (*hotel*) komfortabel; (*financially*) ohne Sorgen; **she is ~** (*after*

operation) es geht ihr gut.

comic ['kɒmɪk] ◆ *adj* komisch. ◆ *n* (*person*) Komiker *der*; (*magazine*) Comicheft *das*.

comical ['kɒmɪkl] *adj* ulkig.

comic strip *n* Comic *der*.

comma ['kɒmə] *n* Komma *das*.

command [kə'mɑːnd] ◆ *n* Befehl *der*; (*mastery*) Beherrschung *die*. ◆ *vt* befehlen (+D); (*be in charge of*) befehligen.

commander [kə'mɑːndə^r] *n* Kommandant *der*.

commemorate [kə'meməreɪt] *vt* gedenken (+G).

commence [kə'mens] *vi* (*fml*) beginnen.

comment ['kɒment] ◆ *n* Kommentar *der*. ◆ *vi* bemerken.

commentary ['kɒməntrɪ] *n* (*on TV, radio*) Reportage *die*.

commentator ['kɒmənteɪtə^r] *n* (*on TV, radio*) Reporter *der* (-in *die*).

commerce ['kɒmɜːs] *n* Handel *der*.

commercial [kə'mɜːʃl] ◆ *adj* kommerziell. ◆ *n* Werbespot *der*.

commercial break *n* Werbepause *die*.

commission [kə'mɪʃn] *n* (*money*) Provision *die*; (*committee*) Kommission *die*.

commit [kə'mɪt] *vt* (*crime, sin, suicide*) begehen; **to ~ o.s.** (**to sthg**) sich (zu etw) verpflichten.

committee [kə'mɪtɪ] *n* Ausschuß *der*.

commodity [kə'mɒdətɪ] *n* Produkt *das*.

common ['kɒmən] ◆ *adj* (*usual, widespread*) häufig; (*shared*) gemeinsam; (*pej: vulgar*) gewöhnlich. ◆ *n* (*Br: land*) Gemeindewiese *die*; **in ~** gemeinsam.

commonly ['kɒmənlɪ] *adv* (*generally*) allgemein.

Common Market *n* Gemeinsamer Markt.

common room *n* Gemeinschaftsraum *der*.

common sense n gesunder Menschenverstand.

Commonwealth ['kɒmənwelθ] n Commonwealth das.

communal ['kɒmjʊnl] adj (bathroom, kitchen) Gemeinschafts-.

communicate [kə'mju:nɪkeɪt] vi: **to ~ (with)** sich verständigen (mit).

communication [kə,mju:nɪ'keɪʃn] n Verständigung die.

communication cord n (Br) Notbremse die.

communist ['kɒmjʊnɪst] n Kommunist der (-in die).

community [kə'mju:nətɪ] n Gemeinschaft die; **(local)** ~ Gemeinde die.

community centre n Gemeindezentrum das.

commute [kə'mju:t] vi pendeln.

commuter [kə'mju:tər] n Pendler der (-in die).

compact [adj kəm'pækt, n 'kɒmpækt] ◆ adj kompakt. ◆ n (for make-up) Puderdose die; (Am: car) Kleinwagen der.

compact disc [,kɒmpækt-] n Compact Disc die.

compact disc player n CD-Player der.

company ['kʌmpənɪ] n Gesellschaft die; (firm) Firma die; (guests) Besuch der; **to keep sb ~** jm Gesellschaft leisten.

company car n Firmenwagen der.

comparatively [kəm'pærətɪvlɪ] adv (relatively) relativ.

compare [kəm'peər] vt: **to ~ sthg (with)** etw vergleichen (mit).

comparison [kəm'pærɪsn] n Vergleich der; **in ~ with** im Vergleich zu.

compartment [kəm'pɑ:tmənt] n (of train) Abteil das; (section) Fach das.

compass ['kʌmpəs] n Kompaß der; **(a pair of) ~es** ein Zirkel.

compatible [kəm'pætəbl] adj: **to be ~** zusammenpassen.

compensate ['kɒmpenseɪt] ◆ vt entschädigen. ◆ vi: **to ~ for sthg** etw auslgleichen; **to ~ sb for sthg** jn für etw entschädigen.

compensation [,kɒmpen'seɪʃn] n (money) Abfindung die.

compete [kəm'pi:t] vi (take part) teillnehmen; **to ~ with sb for sthg** mit jm um etw konkurrieren.

competent ['kɒmpɪtənt] adj fähig.

competition [,kɒmpɪ'tɪʃn] n (race, contest) Wettbewerb der; (rivalry, rivals) Konkurrenz die.

competitive [kəm'petətɪv] adj (price) konkurrenzfähig; (person) wetteifernd.

competitor [kəm'petɪtər] n (in race, contest) Teilnehmer der (-in die); (COMM) Konkurrent der (-in die).

complain [kəm'pleɪn] vi: **to ~ (about)** sich beschweren (über (+A).

complaint [kəm'pleɪnt] n Beschwerde die; (illness) Beschwerden pl.

complement ['kɒmplɪ,ment] vt ergänzen.

complete [kəm'pli:t] ◆ adj (whole) vollständig; (finished) fertig; (utter) völlig. ◆ vt (finish) fertiglstellen; (a form) auslfüllen; (make whole) vervollständigen; **~ with** komplett mit.

completely [kəm'pli:tlɪ] adv ganz.

complex ['kɒmpleks] ◆ adj kompliziert. ◆ n Komplex der.

complexion [kəm'plekʃn] n (of skin) Teint der.

complicated ['kɒmplɪkeɪtɪd] adj kompliziert.

compliment [n 'kɒmplɪmənt, vb 'kɒmplɪment] ◆ n Kompliment das. ◆ vt: **to ~ sb** jm ein Kompliment machen.

complimentary [,kɒmplɪ'mentərɪ] adj (seat, ticket) Frei-, gratis; (words, person) schmeichelhaft.

compose [kəm'pəuz] vt (music) komponieren; (letter, poem) verfassen; **to be ~d of** bestehen aus.

composed [kəm'pəuzd] adj gefaßt.

composer [kəm'pəuzər] n Komponist der (-in die).

composition [ˌkɒmpə'zɪʃn] n (essay) Aufsatz der.

compound ['kɒmpaund] n (substance) Verbindung die; (word) Kompositum das.

comprehensive [ˌkɒmprɪ'hensɪv] adj umfassend.

comprehensive (school) n (Br) Gesamtschule die.

compressed air [kəm'prest-] n Preßluft die.

comprise [kəm'praɪz] vt bestehen aus.

compromise ['kɒmprəmaɪz] n Kompromiß der.

compulsory [kəm'pʌlsərɪ] adj: **to be ~** Pflicht sein.

computer [kəm'pju:tər] n Computer der.

computer game n Computerspiel das.

computerized [kəm'pju:təraɪzd] adj computerisiert.

computer operator n Anwender der (-in die).

computer programmer [-'prəugræmər] n Programmierer der (-in die).

computing [kəm'pju:tɪŋ] n Computertechnik die.

con [kɒn] n (inf: trick) Schwindel der; **all mod ~s** alle modernen Haushaltsgeräte.

conceal [kən'si:l] vt verbergen.

conceited [kən'si:tɪd] adj (pej) eingebildet.

concentrate ['kɒnsəntreɪt] ◆ vt konzentrieren. ◆ vi: **to ~ (on sthg)** sich (auf etw (A) konzentrieren.

concentrated ['kɒnsəntreɪtɪd] adj konzentriert.

concentration [ˌkɒnsən'treɪʃn] n Konzentration die.

concern [kən'sɜːn] ◆ n (worry) Sorge die; (affair) Angelegenheit die; (COMM) Unternehmen das. ◆ vt (be about) betreffen; (worry) beunruhigen;

(involve) anlgehen; **it's no ~ of mine** das geht mich nichts an; **to be ~ed about** besorgt sein um; **to be ~ed with** handeln von; **to ~ o.s. with sthg** sich um etw kümmern; **as far as I'm ~ed** was mich betrifft.

concerned [kən'sɜːnd] adj besorgt.

concerning [kən'sɜːnɪŋ] prep betreffend.

concert ['kɒnsət] n Konzert das.

concession [kən'seʃn] n (reduced price) Ermäßigung die.

concise [kən'saɪs] adj prägnant.

conclude [kən'klu:d] ◆ vt (deduce) folgern; (fml: end) ablschließen. ◆ vi (fml: end) schließen.

conclusion [kən'klu:ʒn] n Schluß der.

concrete ['kɒŋkri:t] ◆ adj (building, path) Beton-; (idea, plan) konkret. ◆ n Beton der.

concussion [kən'kʌʃn] n Gehirnerschütterung die.

condensation [ˌkɒnden'seɪʃn] n Kondensation die.

condensed milk [kən'denst-] n Kondensmilch die.

condition [kən'dɪʃn] n (state) Zustand der; (proviso) Bedingung die; (illness) Leiden das; **to be out of ~** keine Kondition haben; **on ~ that** unter der Bedingung, daß. ► **conditions** npl (circumstances) Verhältnisse pl.

conditioner [kən'dɪʃnər] n (for hair) Spülung die; (for clothes) Weichspüler der.

condo ['kɒndəu] (Am: inf) = **condominium**.

condom ['kɒndəm] n Kondom das.

condominium [ˌkɒndə'mɪnɪəm] n (Am: apartment) Eigentumswohnung die; (building) Appartmenthaus das (mit Eigentumswohnungen).

conduct [vb kən'dʌkt, n 'kɒndʌkt] ◆ vt durchlführen; (MUS) dirigieren. ◆ n (fml: behaviour) Benehmen das; **to ~ o.s.** (fml) sich verhalten.

conductor [kən'dʌktər] n (MUS)

Dirigent der (-in die); (on bus, train) Schaffner der (-in die).

cone [kəʊn] n (shape) Kegel der; (for ice cream) Waffeltüte die; (on roads) Leitkegel der.

confectioner's [kən'fekʃnəz] n (shop) Süßwarenladen der.

confectionery [kən'fekʃnərı] n Süßigkeiten pl.

conference ['kɒnfərəns] n Konferenz die.

confess [kən'fes] vi: **to ~ (to)** gestehen.

confession [kən'feʃn] n Geständnis das; (RELIG) Beichte die.

confidence ['kɒnfɪdəns] n (self-assurance) Selbstvertrauen das; (trust) Vertrauen das; **to have ~ in** Vertrauen haben zu.

confident ['kɒnfɪdənt] adj (self-assured) selbstbewußt; (certain) zuversichtlich.

confined [kən'faınd] adj begrenzt.

confirm [kən'fɜːm] vt bestätigen.

confirmation [ˌkɒnfə'meıʃn] n Bestätigung die; (of Catholic) Firmung die; (of Protestant) Konfirmation die.

conflict [n 'kɒnflıkt, vb kən'flıkt] ♦ n Konflikt der; (war) Kämpfe pl. ♦ vi: **to ~ (with)** im Widerspruch stehen (zu).

conform [kən'fɔːm] vi: **to ~ (to)** sich an|passen (an (+A).

confuse [kən'fjuːz] vt verwirren; **to ~ sthg with sthg** eine Sache mit etw verwechseln.

confused [kən'fjuːzd] adj verwirrt; (situation) wirr.

confusing [kən'fjuːzıŋ] adj verwirrend.

confusion [kən'fjuːʒn] n Verwirrung die; (disorder) Durcheinander das; (mix-up) Verwechslung die.

congested [kən'dʒestıd] adj (street) verstopft.

congestion [kən'dʒestʃn] n (traffic) Stau der.

congratulate [kən'grætʃʊleıt] vt: **to ~ sb (on sthg)** jm (zu etw) gratulieren.

congratulations [kənˌgrætʃʊ-'leıʃənz] excl herzlichen Glückwunsch.

congregate ['kɒŋgrıgeıt] vi sich versammeln.

Congress ['kɒŋgres] n (Am) der Kongreß.

conifer ['kɒnıfəʳ] n Nadelbaum der.

conjunction [kən'dʒʌŋkʃn] n (GRAMM) Konjunktion die.

conjurer ['kʌndʒərəʳ] n Zauberer der (Zauberin die).

connect [kə'nekt] ♦ vt verbinden; (telephone, machine) an|schließen. ♦ vi: **to ~ with** (train, plane) Anschluß haben an (+A).

connecting flight [kə'nektıŋ-] n Anschlußflug der.

connection [kə'nekʃn] n (link) Zusammenhang der; (train, plane) Anschluß der; **a bad ~** (on phone) eine schlechte Verbindung; **a loose ~** (in machine) ein Wackelkontakt; **in ~ with** in Zusammenhang mit.

conquer ['kɒŋkəʳ] vt erobern.

conscience ['kɒnʃəns] n Gewissen das.

conscientious [ˌkɒnʃı'enʃəs] adj gewissenhaft.

conscious ['kɒnʃəs] adj bewußt; **to be ~** (awake) bei Bewußtsein sein.

consent [kən'sent] n Zustimmung die.

consequence ['kɒnsıkwəns] n (result) Folge die.

consequently ['kɒnsıkwəntlı] adv folglich.

conservation [ˌkɒnsə'veıʃn] n Erhaltung die.

conservative [kən'sɜːvətıv] adj konservativ. ▶ **Conservative** adj konservativ. ♦ n Konservative der die.

conservatory [kən'sɜːvətrı] n Wintergarten die.

consider [kən'sıdəʳ] vt (think about) sich (D) überlegen; (take into account) berücksichtigen; (judge) halten für.

considerable [kən'sıdrəbl] adj beträchtlich.

consideration [kən͵sɪdə'reɪʃn] *n* (*careful thought*) Überlegung *die*; (*factor*) Faktor *der*; **to take sthg into ~** etw berücksichtigen.

considering [kən'sɪdərɪŋ] *prep* in Anbetracht (+G).

consist [kən'sɪst]: **consist in** *vt fus* bestehen in (+D). ▶ **consist of** *vt fus* bestehen aus.

consistent [kən'sɪstənt] *adj* (*coherent*) übereinstimmend; (*worker, performance*) konsequent.

consolation [͵kɒnsə'leɪʃn] *n* Trost *der*.

console ['kɒnsəʊl] *n* (*for machine*) Steuerpult *das*; (*for computer game*) Spielkonsole *die*.

consonant ['kɒnsənənt] *n* Konsonant *der*.

conspicuous [kən'spɪkjʊəs] *adj* auffällig.

constable ['kʌnstəbl] *n* (Br) Wachtmeister *der* (-in *die*).

constant ['kɒnstənt] *adj* (*unchanging*) gleichmäßig; (*continuous*) ständig.

constantly ['kɒnstəntlɪ] *adv* (*all the time*) ständig.

constipated ['kɒnstɪpeɪtɪd] *adj* verstopft.

constitution [͵kɒnstɪ'tjuːʃn] *n* (*health*) Konstitution *die*.

construct [kən'strʌkt] *vt* bauen.

construction [kən'strʌkʃn] *n* Bau *der*; **under ~** im Bau.

consul ['kɒnsəl] *n* Konsul *der* (-in *die*).

consulate ['kɒnsjʊlət] *n* Konsulat *das*.

consult [kən'sʌlt] *vt* (*person*) um Rat fragen; (*doctor*) konsultieren; (*dictionary, map*) nachlschauen.

consultant [kən'sʌltənt] *n* (Br: *doctor*) Facharzt *der* (-ärztin *die*).

consume [kən'sjuːm] *vt* (*food*) essen; (*fuel, energy*) verbrauchen.

consumer [kən'sjuːməʳ] *n* Verbraucher *der* (-in *die*).

contact ['kɒntækt] ◆ *n* (*communication, person*) Kontakt *der*. ◆ *vt* sich in Verbindung setzen mit; **in ~ with** (*touching*) in Berührung mit; (*in communication with*) in Verbindung mit.

contact lens *n* Kontaktlinse *die*.

contagious [kən'teɪdʒəs] *adj* ansteckend.

contain [kən'teɪn] *vt* enthalten; (*control*) zurücklhalten.

container [kən'teɪnəʳ] *n* Behälter *der*.

contaminate [kən'tæmɪneɪt] *vt* verunreinigen.

contemporary [kən'tempərərɪ] ◆ *adj* zeitgenössisch. ◆ *n* Zeitgenosse *der* (-genossin *die*).

contend [kən'tend]: **contend with** *vt fus* fertiglwerden mit.

content [*adj* kən'tent, *n* 'kɒntent] ◆ *adj* zufrieden. ◆ *n* (*of vitamins, fibre etc*) Anteil *der*. ▶ **contents** *npl* Inhalt *der*.

contest [*n* 'kɒntest, *vb* kən'test] ◆ *n* (*competition*) Wettbewerb *der*; (*struggle*) Kampf *der*. ◆ *vt* (*election, seat*) kandidieren; (*decision, will*) anlfechten.

context ['kɒntekst] *n* Zusammenhang *der*.

continent ['kɒntɪnənt] *n* Kontinent *der*; **the Continent** (Br) Europa.

continental [͵kɒntɪ'nentl] *adj* (Br: *European*) europäisch.

continental breakfast *n* Frühstück mit Kaffee oder Tee, Brötchen und Marmelade.

continental quilt *n* (Br) Federbett *das*.

continual [kən'tɪnjʊəl] *adj* ständig.

continually [kən'tɪnjʊəlɪ] *adv* ständig.

continue [kən'tɪnjuː] ◆ *vt* fortlsetzen. ◆ *vi* weiterlgehen; (*start again*) weiterlmachen; (*carry on speaking*) fortlfahren; (*keep driving*) weiterlfahren; **to ~ doing sthg** etw weiterhin tun; **to ~ with sthg** mit etw fortlfahren.

continuous [kən'tɪnjʊəs] *adj* (*constant*) gleichmäßig; (*unbroken*) ununterbrochen.

continuously [kən'tɪnjʊəslɪ] *adv* ununterbrochen.

contraception [ˌkɒntrə'sepʃn] *n* Empfängnisverhütung *die*.

contraceptive [ˌkɒntrə'septɪv] *n* Verhütungsmittel *das*.

contract [*n* 'kɒntrækt, *vb* kən'trækt] ◆ *n* Vertrag *der*. ◆ *vt* (*fml: illness*) sich (D) zuⵏziehen.

contradict [ˌkɒntrə'dɪkt] *vt* widersprechen (+D).

contraflow ['kɒntrəfləʊ] *n* (Br) Umleitung auf die Gegenfahrbahn.

contrary ['kɒntrərɪ] *n*: **on the ~** im Gegenteil.

contrast [*n* 'kɒntrɑːst, *vb* kən'trɑːst] ◆ *n* Kontrast *der*. ◆ *vt* vergleichen; **in ~ to** im Gegensatz zu.

contribute [kən'trɪbjuːt] *vt & vi* beiⵏtragen; **to ~ to** beiⵏtragen zu.

contribution [ˌkɒntrɪ'bjuːʃn] *n* Beitrag *der*.

control [kən'trəʊl] ◆ *n* (*power*) Macht *die*; (*over emotions*) Kontrolle *die*; (*operating device*) Steuerung *die*. ◆ *vt* (*have power over*) beherrschen; (*car, machine*) steuern; (*restrict*) beschränken; **to be in ~** Macht haben; **out of ~** außer Kontrolle; **under ~** unter Kontrolle. ▶ **controls** *npl* (*for TV, video*) Fernbedienung *die*; (*of aeroplane*) Steuerung *die*.

control tower *n* Kontrollturm *der*.

controversial [ˌkɒntrə'vɜːʃl] *adj* umstritten.

convenience [kən'viːnjəns] *n* Bequemlichkeit *die*; **at your ~** wann es Ihnen paßt.

convenient [kən'viːnjənt] *adj* günstig; (*well-situated*) in Reichweite; **to be ~ for sb** jm passen.

convent ['kɒnvənt] *n* Kloster *das*.

conventional [kən'venʃənl] *adj* konventionell.

conversation [ˌkɒnvə'seɪʃn] *n* Gespräch *das*.

conversion [kən'vɜːʃn] *n* Umwandlung *die*; (*to building*) Umbau *der*.

convert [kən'vɜːt] *vt* umⵏwandeln; (RELIG) bekehren; **to ~ sthg into** etw umⵏwandeln in (+A).

converted [kən'vɜːtɪd] *adj* (*building, loft*) ausgebaut.

convertible [kən'vɜːtəbl] *n* Kabrio *das*.

convey [kən'veɪ] *vt* (*fml: transport*) befördern; (*idea, impression*) vermitteln.

convict [*n* 'kɒnvɪkt, *vb* kən'vɪkt] ◆ *n* Strafgefangene *der die*. ◆ *vt*: **to ~ sb (of)** jn verurteilen (wegen).

convince [kən'vɪns] *vt*: **to ~ sb (of sthg)** jn (von etw) überzeugen; **to ~ sb to do sthg** jn überreden, etw zu tun.

convoy ['kɒnvɔɪ] *n* Konvoi *der*.

cook [kʊk] ◆ *n* Koch *der* (Köchin *die*). ◆ *vt & vi* kochen.

cookbook ['kʊk,bʊk] = **cookery book**.

cooker ['kʊkər] *n* Herd *der*.

cookery ['kʊkərɪ] *n* Kochen *das*.

cookery book *n* Kochbuch *das*.

cookie ['kʊkɪ] *n* (Am) Keks *der*.

cooking ['kʊkɪŋ] *n* Kochen *das*; (*food*) Küche *die*.

cooking apple *n* Kochapfel *der*.

cooking oil *n* Öl zum Kochen.

cool [kuːl] ◆ *adj* kühl; (*inf: great*) toll. ◆ *vt* kühlen. ▶ **cool down** *vi* abⵏkühlen; (*become calmer*) sich beruhigen.

cooperate [kəʊ'ɒpəreɪt] *vi* zusammenⵏarbeiten.

cooperation [kəʊ,ɒpə'reɪʃn] *n* Zusammenarbeit *die*.

cooperative [kəʊ'ɒpərətɪv] *adj* hilfsbereit.

coordinates [kəʊ'ɔːdɪnəts] *npl* (*clothes*) Kleidung zum Kombinieren.

cope [kəʊp] *vi*: **to ~ (with)** zurechtⵏkommen (mit).

copilot ['kəʊ,paɪlət] *n* Kopilot *der* (-in *die*).

copper ['kɒpər] *n* Kupfer *das*; (Br: *inf: coin*) Penny *der*.

copy ['kɒpɪ] ◆ n Kopie die; (of newspaper, book) Exemplar das. ◆ vt kopieren.

cord(uroy) ['kɔːd(ərɔɪ)] n Kord(samt) der.

core [kɔːʳ] n (of fruit) Kerngehäuse das.

coriander [ˌkɒrɪˈændəʳ] n Koriander der.

cork [kɔːk] n (in bottle) Korken der.

corkscrew ['kɔːkskruː] n Korkenzieher der.

corn [kɔːn] n (Br: crop) Getreide das; (Am: maize) Mais der; (on foot) Hühnerauge das.

corned beef [ˌkɔːnd-] n Corned beef das.

corner ['kɔːnəʳ] n Ecke die; (bend in road) Kurve die; **it's just around the ~** es ist gleich um die Ecke.

corner shop n (Br) Tante-Emma-Laden der.

cornet ['kɔːnɪt] n (Br: ice-cream cone) Waffeltüte die.

cornflakes ['kɔːnfleɪks] npl Cornflakes pl.

corn-on-the-cob n (gekochter) Maiskolben der.

corporal ['kɔːpərəl] n Unteroffizier der.

corpse [kɔːps] n Leiche die.

correct [kəˈrekt] ◆ adj richtig. ◆ vt verbessern.

correction [kəˈrekʃn] n Verbesserung die.

correspond [ˌkɒrɪˈspɒnd] vi: **to ~ (to)** (match) entsprechen (+D); **to ~ (with)** (exchange letters) korrespondieren (mit).

corresponding [ˌkɒrɪˈspɒndɪŋ] adj entsprechend.

corridor ['kɒrɪdɔːʳ] n Korridor der.

corrugated iron ['kɒrəgeɪtɪd-] n Wellblech das.

corrupt [kəˈrʌpt] adj korrupt.

cosmetics [kɒzˈmetɪks] npl Kosmetik die.

cost [kɒst] (pt & pp inv) ◆ n Kosten pl; (fig: loss) Preis der. ◆ vt kosten;

how much does it ~? wieviel kostet es?

costly ['kɒstlɪ] adj teuer.

costume ['kɒstjuːm] n Kostüm das; (of country, region) Tracht die.

cosy ['kəʊzɪ] adj (Br: room, house) gemütlich.

cot [kɒt] n (Br: for baby) Kinderbett das; (Am: camp bed) Feldbett das.

cottage ['kɒtɪdʒ] n Cottage das, Häuschen das.

cottage cheese n Hüttenkäse der.

cottage pie n (Br) Hackfleischauflauf bedeckt mit einer Schicht Kartoffelbrei.

cotton ['kɒtn] ◆ adj (dress, shirt) Baumwoll-. ◆ n Baumwolle die; (thread) Nähgarn das.

cotton candy n (Am) Zuckerwatte die.

cotton wool n Watte die.

couch [kaʊtʃ] n Couch die; (at doctor's) Liege die.

couchette [kuːˈʃet] n (on train) Liegeplatz der; (seat on ship) Liegesessel das.

cough [kɒf] ◆ n Husten der. ◆ vi husten; **to have a ~** Husten haben.

cough mixture n Hustenmittel das.

could [kʊd] pt → **can**.

couldn't ['kʊdnt] = **could not**.

could've ['kʊdəv] = **could have**.

council ['kaʊnsl] n (Br: of town) Stadtrat der; (Br: of county) Gemeinderat der; (organization) Rat der.

council house n (Br) ≃ Sozialwohnung die.

councillor ['kaʊnsələʳ] n (Br: of town) Stadtrat der (-rätin die); (of county) Gemeinderat der (-rätin die).

council tax n (Br) ≃ Gemeindesteuer die.

count [kaʊnt] ◆ vt & vi zählen. ◆ n (nobleman) Graf der. ▶ **count on** vt fus (rely on) sich verlassen auf (+A); (expect) rechnen auf (+A).

counter ['kaʊntəʳ] n (in shop) Ladentisch der; (in bank) Schalter der; (in board game) Spielmarke die.

counterclockwise [,kaʊntə-ˈklɒkwaɪz] adv (Am) **gegen den Uhrzeigersinn.**

counterfoil [ˈkaʊntəfɔɪl] n Beleg der.

countess [ˈkaʊntɪs] n Gräfin die.

country [ˈkʌntrɪ] ◆ n Land das; (scenery) Landschaft die; (population) Volk das. ◆ adj Land-.

country and western n Country-music die.

country house n Landhaus das.

country road n Landstraße die.

countryside [ˈkʌntrɪsaɪd] n (place) Land das; (scenery) Landschaft die.

county [ˈkaʊntɪ] n (in Britain) Grafschaft die; (in US) Verwaltungsbezirk der.

couple [ˈkʌpl] n Paar das; **a ~ (of)** (two) zwei; (a few) ein paar.

coupon [ˈkuːpɒn] n (for discount etc) Gutschein der; (for orders, enquiries) Coupon der.

courage [ˈkʌrɪdʒ] n Mut der.

courgette [kɔːˈʒet] n (Br) Zucchini die.

courier [ˈkʊrɪəʳ] n (for holidaymakers) Reiseleiter der (-in die); (for delivering letters) Bote der.

course [kɔːs] n (of meal) Gang der; (at university, college) Studiengang der; (of evening classes etc) Kurs der; (of treatment, injections) Kur die; (of ship, plane) Kurs der; (of river) Lauf der; (for golf) Platz der; **of ~** natürlich; **of ~ not** natürlich nicht; **in the ~ of** im Laufe (+G).

court [kɔːt] n (JUR: building) Gericht das; (JUR: room) Gerichtssaal der; (SPORT) Platz der; (of king, queen) Hof der.

courtesy coach [ˈkɜːtɪsɪ-] n kostenloser Zubringerbus.

court shoes npl Pumps pl.

courtyard [ˈkɔːtjɑːd] n Hof der.

cousin [ˈkʌzn] n Vetter der (Kusine die).

cover [ˈkʌvəʳ] ◆ n (covering) Abdeckung die; (of cushion) Bezug der; (lid) Deckel der; (of book) Einband der; (of magazine) Umschlag der; (blanket) Decke die; (insurance) Versicherung die. ◆ vt bedecken; (travel) zurückllegen; (apply to) gelten für; (discuss) behandeln; (report) berichten über (+A); (be enough for) decken; (subj: insurance) versichern; **to be ~ed in sthg** voller etw sein; **to be ~ed in dust** völlig verstaubt sein; **to ~ sthg with sthg** etw mit etw abldecken; **to take ~** Schutz suchen. ▶ **cover up** vt sep zuldecken; (facts, truth) vertuschen.

cover charge n Gedeck das.

cover note n (Br) Deckungskarte die.

cow [kaʊ] n Kuh die.

coward [ˈkaʊəd] n Feigling der.

cowboy [ˈkaʊbɔɪ] n Cowboy der.

crab [kræb] n Krabbe die.

crack [kræk] ◆ n (in cup, glass) Sprung der; (in wood) Riß der; (gap) Spalt der. ◆ vt (cup, glass) anlschlagen; (wood) anlknacksen; (nut) knacken; (egg) auflschlagen; (whip) knallen. ◆ vi (cup, glass) einen Sprung bekommen; (wood) einen Riß bekommen; **to ~ a joke** (inf) einen Witz reißen.

cracker [ˈkrækəʳ] n (biscuit) Cracker der; (for Christmas) Knallbonbon der or das.

cradle [ˈkreɪdl] n Wiege die.

craft [krɑːft] n (skill) Geschick das; (trade) Handwerk das; (boat: pl inv) Boot das.

craftsman [ˈkrɑːftsmən] (pl -men [-mən]) n Handwerker der.

cram [kræm] vt: **to ~ sthg into** etw stopfen in (+A); **to be crammed with** vollgestopft sein mit.

cramp [kræmp] n Krampf der; **stomach ~s** Magenkrämpfe.

cranberry [ˈkrænbərɪ] n Preiselbeere die.

cranberry sauce n Preiselbeersoße die.

crane [kreɪn] n (*machine*) Kran der.

crap [kræp] ◆ adj (*vulg*) Scheiß-. ◆ n (*vulg: excrement*) Scheiße die.

crash [kræʃ] ◆ n (*accident*) Unfall der; (*noise*) Krachen das. ◆ vt (*car*) einen Unfall haben mit. ◆ vi (*car, train*) einen Unfall haben; (*plane*) ablstürzen. ► **crash into** vt fus krachen gegen.

crash helmet n Sturzhelm der.

crash landing n Bruchlandung die.

crate [kreɪt] n Kiste die.

crawl [krɔːl] ◆ vi kriechen; (*baby*) krabbeln. ◆ n (*swimming stroke*) Kraulen das.

crawler lane ['krɔːlər-] n (Br) Kriechspur die.

crayfish ['kreɪfɪʃ] (*pl inv*) n Languste die.

crayon ['kreɪɒn] n (*of wax*) Wachsmalstift der; (*pencil*) Buntstift der.

craze [kreɪz] n Mode die.

crazy ['kreɪzɪ] adj verrückt; **to be ~ about** verrückt sein nach.

crazy golf n Minigolf das.

cream [kriːm] ◆ n (*food*) Sahne die; (*for face, burns*) Creme die. ◆ adj (*in colour*) cremefarben.

cream cake n (Br) Sahnetörtchen das.

cream cheese n Frischkäse der.

cream sherry n Cream Sherry der.

cream tea n (Br) Tee mit Gebäck und Sahne.

creamy ['kriːmɪ] adj (*food*) sahnig; (*drink*) cremig.

crease [kriːs] n Falte die.

creased [kriːst] adj zerknittert.

create [kriːˈeɪt] vt schaffen; (*impression*) machen; (*interest*) verursachen.

creative [kriːˈeɪtɪv] adj kreativ.

creature ['kriːtʃər] n Geschöpf das.

crèche [kreʃ] n (Br) Kinderkrippe die.

credit ['kredɪt] n (*praise*) Anerkennung die; (*money*) Guthaben das; (*at school, university*) Aus-

zeichnung die; **to be in ~** im Haben sein. ► **credits** npl (*of film*) Nachspann der.

credit card n Kreditkarte die; **'all major ~s accepted'** 'alle wichtigen Kreditkarten werden angenommen'.

creek [kriːk] n (*inlet*) Bucht die; (Am: *river*) Bach der.

creep [kriːp] (*pt & pp* **crept**) ◆ vi kriechen. ◆ n (*inf: groveller*) Schleimer der.

cremate [krɪˈmeɪt] vt einläschern.

crematorium [ˌkreməˈtɔːrɪəm] n Krematorium das.

crepe [kreɪp] n (*thin pancake*) dünner Eierkuchen.

crept [krept] pt & pp → **creep**.

cress [kres] n Kresse die.

crest [krest] n Kamm der; (*emblem*) Wappen das.

Creutzfeldt-Jakob disease [ˌkrɔɪtsfeltˈjækɒb-] n Creutzfeldt-Jakob-Krankheit die.

crew [kruː] n Besatzung die.

crew neck n runder Halsausschnitt.

crib [krɪb] n (Am: *cot*) Kinderbett das.

cricket ['krɪkɪt] n (*game*) Kricket das; (*insect*) Grille die.

crime [kraɪm] n Verbrechen das.

criminal ['krɪmɪnl] ◆ adj kriminell. ◆ n Kriminelle der die.

cripple ['krɪpl] ◆ n Krüppel der. ◆ vt zum Krüppel machen.

crisis ['kraɪsɪs] (*pl* **crises** ['kraɪsiːz]) n Krise die.

crisp [krɪsp] adj (*bacon, pastry*) knusprig; (*apple*) knackig. ► **crisps** npl (Br) Chips pl.

crispy ['krɪspɪ] adj knusprig.

critic ['krɪtɪk] n Kritiker der (-in die).

critical ['krɪtɪkl] adj kritisch; (*very important*) entscheidend.

criticize ['krɪtɪsaɪz] vt kritisieren.

crockery ['krɒkərɪ] n Geschirr das.

crocodile ['krɒkədaɪl] n Krokodil das.

crocus ['krəʊkəs] (pl **-es**) n Krokus der.

crooked ['krʊkɪd] adj (bent) krumm.

crop [krɒp] n (kind of plant) Feldfrucht die; (harvest) Ernte die. ► **crop up** vi auf|tauchen.

cross [krɒs] ♦ adj verärgert. ♦ n Kreuz das. ♦ vt (road, river, ocean) überqueren. ♦ vi (intersect) sich kreuzen; **to ~ one's arms** die Arme verschränken; **to ~ one's legs** die Beine übereinander|schlagen; **to ~ a cheque** (Br) einen Scheck zur Verrechnung aus|stellen. ► **cross out** vt sep aus|streichen. ► **cross over** vt fus (road) überqueren.

crossbar ['krɒsbɑːr] n (of goal) Querlatte die; (of bicycle) Stange die.

cross-Channel ferry n Fähre die über den Ärmelkanal.

cross-country (running) n Querfeldeinlauf der.

crossing ['krɒsɪŋ] n (on road) Überweg der; (sea, journey) Überfahrt die.

crossroads ['krɒsrəʊdz] (pl inv) n Kreuzung die.

crosswalk ['krɒswɔːk] n (Am) Fußgängerüberweg der.

crossword (puzzle) ['krɒswɜːd-] n Kreuzworträtsel das.

crotch [krɒtʃ] n Schritt der.

crouton ['kruːtɒn] n Croûton der.

crow [krəʊ] n Krähe die.

crowbar ['krəʊbɑːr] n Brechstange die.

crowd [kraʊd] n Menge die (von Personen).

crowded ['kraʊdɪd] adj überfüllt.

crown [kraʊn] n Krone die; (of head) Scheitel der.

Crown Jewels npl Kronjuwelen pl.

crucial ['kruːʃl] adj entscheidend.

crude [kruːd] adj (rough) grob; (rude) ungeschliffen.

cruel [krʊəl] adj grausam.

cruelty ['krʊəltɪ] n Grausamkeit die.

cruet (set) ['kruːɪt-] n Menage die.

cruise [kruːz] ♦ n Kreuzfahrt die. ♦ vi (plane) fliegen; (ship) kreuzen.

cruiser ['kruːzər] n (pleasure boat) Kajütboot das.

crumb [krʌm] n Krümel der.

crumble ['krʌmbl] ♦ n mit Streuseln überbackenes Obstdessert. ♦ vi (building) ein|stürzen; (cliff) bröckeln.

crumpet ['krʌmpɪt] n Teigküchlein zum Toasten.

crunchy ['krʌntʃɪ] adj knusprig.

crush [krʌʃ] ♦ n (drink) Saftgetränk das. ♦ vt (flatten) quetschen; (garlic, ice) zerstoßen.

crust [krʌst] n Kruste die.

crusty ['krʌstɪ] adj knusprig.

crutch [krʌtʃ] n (stick) Krücke die; (between legs) = **crotch**.

cry [kraɪ] ♦ n Schrei der. ♦ vi (weep) weinen; (shout) schreien. ► **cry out** vi auf|schreien.

crystal ['krɪstl] n Kristall der; (glass) Kristallglas das.

cub [kʌb] n (animal) Junge das.

Cub [kʌb] n Wölfling der (junger Pfadfinder).

cube [kjuːb] n Würfel der.

cubicle ['kjuːbɪkl] n Kabine die.

Cub Scout = **Cub**.

cuckoo ['kʊkuː] n Kuckuck der.

cucumber ['kjuːkʌmbər] n Salatgurke die.

cuddle ['kʌdl] n Liebkosung die.

cuddly toy ['kʌdlɪ-] n Plüschtier das.

cue [kjuː] n (in snooker, pool) Queue das.

cuff [kʌf] n (of sleeve) Manschette die; (Am: of trousers) Aufschlag der.

cuff links npl Manschettenknöpfe pl.

cuisine [kwɪˈziːn] n Küche die.

cul-de-sac ['kʌldəsæk] n Sackgasse die.

cult [kʌlt] n Kult der.

cultivate ['kʌltɪveɪt] vt (grow) züchten.

cultivated ['kʌltɪveɪtɪd] adj (person) kultiviert.

cultural ['kʌltʃərəl] adj kulturell.

culture ['kʌltʃər] n Kultur die.

cumbersome ['kʌmbəsəm] adj sperrig.

cumin ['kju:mɪn] n Kreuzkümmel der.

cunning ['kʌnɪŋ] adj schlau.

cup [kʌp] n Tasse die; (trophy, competition) Pokal der; (of bra) Körbchen das.

cupboard ['kʌbəd] n Schrank der.

curator [ˌkjʊə'reɪtər] n Direktor der (-in die).

curb [kɜ:b] (Am) = **kerb**.

curd cheese [ˌkɜ:d-] n = Quark der.

cure [kjʊər] ◆ n Heilmittel das. ◆ vt (illness, person) heilen; (with salt) pökeln; (with smoke) räuchern; (by drying) trocknen.

curious ['kjʊərɪəs] adj (inquisitive) neugierig; (strange) seltsam.

curl [kɜ:l] ◆ n Locke die. ◆ vt locken.

curler ['kɜ:lər] n Lockenwickler der.

curly ['kɜ:lɪ] adj lockig.

currant ['kʌrənt] n Korinthe die.

currency ['kʌrənsɪ] n (money) Währung die.

current ['kʌrənt] ◆ adj aktuell. ◆ n Strömung die; (electricity) Strom der.

current account n (Br) Girokonto das.

current affairs npl aktuelle Fragen pl.

currently ['kʌrəntlɪ] adv zur Zeit.

curriculum [kə'rɪkjələm] n Lehrplan der.

curriculum vitae [-'vi:taɪ] n (Br) Lebenslauf der.

curried ['kʌrɪd] adj Curry-.

curry ['kʌrɪ] n Currygericht das.

curse [kɜ:s] vi fluchen.

cursor ['kɜ:sər] n Cursor der.

curtain ['kɜ:tn] n Vorhang der.

curve [kɜ:v] ◆ n (shape) Rundung die; (in road, river) Biegung die. ◆ vi einen Bogen machen.

curved [kɜ:vd] adj gebogen.

cushion ['kʊʃn] n Kissen das.

custard ['kʌstəd] n Vanillesoße die.

custom ['kʌstəm] n (tradition) Brauch der; **'thank you for your ~'** 'wir danken Ihnen für Ihre Kundschaft'.

customary ['kʌstəmrɪ] adj üblich.

customer ['kʌstəmər] n Kunde der (Kundin die).

customer services n (department) Kundendienst der.

customs ['kʌstəmz] n (place) Zoll der; **to go through ~** durch den Zoll gehen.

customs duty n Zoll der.

customs officer n Zollbeamte der (-beamtin die).

cut [kʌt] (pt & pp inv) ◆ n Schnitt der; (in skin) Schnittwunde die; (reduction) Kürzung die; (in price) Senkung die; (piece of meat) Stück das. ◆ vi schneiden. ◆ vt schneiden; (reduce) kürzen; (price) senken; **to ~ one's finger** sich (D) in den Finger schneiden; **~ and blow-dry** schneiden und fönen; **to ~ o.s.** sich schneiden; **to have one's hair ~** sich die Haare schneiden lassen; **to ~ the grass** den Rasen mähen; **to ~ sthg open** etw auf|schneiden. ► **cut back** vi: **to ~ back on sthg** etw ein|schränken. ► **cut down** vt sep (tree) fällen. ► **cut down on** vt fus ein|schränken. ► **cut off** vt sep ab|schneiden; (disconnect) ab|stellen; **I've been ~ off** (on phone) ich wurde unterbrochen; **to be ~ off** (isolated) abgeschnitten sein. ► **cut out** vt sep aus|schneiden. ◆ vi (engine) aus|setzen; **to ~ out smoking** mit dem Rauchen auf|hören; **~ it out!** (inf) laß das! ► **cut up** vt sep zerschneiden.

cute [kju:t] adj niedlich.

cut-glass adj Kristall-.

cutlery ['kʌtlərɪ] n Besteck das.

cutlet ['kʌtlɪt] n Kotelett das; (of nuts, vegetables) Bratling der.

cut-price adj herabgesetzt.

cutting ['kʌtɪŋ] n (from newspaper) Ausschnitt der.

CV n (Br: abbr of curriculum vitae) Lebenslauf der.

cwt *abbr* = **hundredweight**.

cybercafe ['saɪbə,kæfeɪ] *n* Cyber-café *das*.

cyberspace ['saɪbəspeɪs] *n* Cyber-space *der or das*.

cycle ['saɪkl] ◆ *n* Zyklus *der*; (*bicycle*) Rad *das*. ◆ *vi* mit dem Rad fahren.

cycle hire *n* Fahrradverleih *der*.

cycle lane *n* Fahrradspur *die*.

cycle path *n* Radweg *der*.

cycling ['saɪklɪŋ] *n* Radfahren *das*; **to go ~** radfahren gehen.

cycling shorts *npl* Radlerhose *die*.

cycling tour *n* Radtour *die*.

cyclist ['saɪklɪst] *n* Radfahrer *der* (-in *die*).

cylinder ['sɪlɪndər] *n* Zylinder *der*; (*for gas*) Flasche *die*.

cynical ['sɪnɪkl] *adj* zynisch.

Czech [tʃek] ◆ *adj* tschechisch. ◆ *n* (*person*) Tscheche *der* (Tschechin *die*); (*language*) Tschechisch *das*.

Czechoslovakia [,tʃekəslə-'vækɪə] *n* die Tschechoslowakei.

Czech Republic *n*: **the ~** die Tschechische Republik.

D

dab [dæb] *vt* (*ointment*, *cream*) auf|tupfen.

dad [dæd] *n* (*inf*) Papi *der*.

daddy ['dædɪ] *n* (*inf*) Papi *der*.

daddy longlegs [-'lɒŋlegz] (*pl* -) *n* Schnake *die*.

daffodil ['dæfədɪl] *n* Osterglocke *die*.

daft [dɑːft] *adj* (Br: *inf*) doof.

daily ['deɪlɪ] ◆ *adj & adv* täglich. ◆ *n*: **a ~ (newspaper)** eine Tageszeitung.

dairy ['deərɪ] *n* (*on farm*) Molkerei *die*; (*shop*) Milchladen *der*.

dairy product *n* Milchprodukt *das*.

daisy ['deɪzɪ] *n* Gänseblümchen *das*.

dam [dæm] *n* Damm *der*.

damage ['dæmɪdʒ] ◆ *n* Schaden *der*; (*to property*) Beschädigung *die*; (*fig: to reputation*) Schädigung *die*; (*fig: to chances*) Beeinträchtigung *die*. ◆ *vt* beschädigen; (*fig: reputation*) schädigen; (*fig: chances*) beeinträchtigen.

damn [dæm] ◆ *excl & adj* (*inf*) verdammt. ◆ *n* (*inf*): **I don't give a ~** ist mir total egal.

damp [dæmp] ◆ *adj* feucht. ◆ *n* Feuchtigkeit *die*.

damson ['dæmzn] *n* Haferpflaume *die*.

dance [dɑːns] ◆ *n* Tanz *der*; (*social event*) Tanzveranstaltung *die*. ◆ *vi* tanzen; **to have a ~** tanzen.

dance floor *n* Tanzfläche *die*.

dancer ['dɑːnsər] *n* Tänzer *der* (-in *die*).

dancing ['dɑːnsɪŋ] *n* Tanzen *das*; **to go ~** tanzen gehen.

dandelion ['dændɪlaɪən] *n* Löwenzahn *der*.

dandruff ['dændrʌf] *n* Schuppen *pl*.

Dane [deɪn] *n* Däne *der* (Dänin *die*).

danger ['deɪndʒər] *n* Gefahr *die*.

dangerous ['deɪndʒərəs] *adj* gefährlich.

Danish ['deɪnɪʃ] ◆ *adj* dänisch. ◆ *n* Dänisch *das*.

Danish pastry *n* Plundergebäck *das*.

Danube ['dænjuːb] *n*: **the ~** die Donau.

dare [deər] *vt*: **to ~ to do sthg** wagen, etw zu tun; **to ~ sb to do sthg** jn her-aus|fordern, etw zu tun; **how ~ you!** was fällt dir ein!

daring ['deərɪŋ] *adj* kühn.

dark [dɑːk] ◆ *adj* dunkel; (*person with dark hair*) dunkelhaarig. ◆ *n*: **after ~** nach Einbruch der Dunkelheit; **in the ~** im Dunkeln.

dark chocolate n bittere Schokolade.

dark glasses npl Sonnenbrille die.

darkness ['dɑːknɪs] n Dunkelheit die.

darling ['dɑːlɪŋ] n Liebling der.

dart [dɑːt] n Pfeil der. ► **darts** n (game) Darts das.

dartboard ['dɑːtbɔːd] n Dartscheibe die.

dash [dæʃ] ◆ n (of liquid) Schuß der; (in writing) Gedankenstrich der. ◆ vi flitzen.

dashboard ['dæʃbɔːd] n Armaturenbrett das.

data ['deɪtə] n Daten pl.

database ['deɪtəbeɪs] n Datenbank die.

date [deɪt] ◆ n Datum das; (meeting) Verabredung die; (Am: person) Freund der (-in die); (fruit) Dattel die. ◆ vt (cheque, letter) datieren; (person) gehen mit. ◆ vi aus der Mode kommen; **what's the ~?** der Wievielte ist heute?; **to have a ~ with sb** eine Verabredung mit jm haben.

date of birth n Geburtsdatum das.

daughter ['dɔːtər] n Tochter die.

daughter-in-law n Schwiegertochter die.

dawn [dɔːn] n Morgendämmerung die.

day [deɪ] n Tag der; **what ~ is it today?** welcher Tag ist heute?; **what a lovely ~!** so ein schöner Tag!; **to have a ~ off** einen Tag frei haben; **to have a ~ out** einen Ausflug machen; **by ~** tagsüber; **the ~ after tomorrow** übermorgen; **the ~ before** am Tag davor; **the ~ before yesterday** vorgestern; **the following ~** am nächsten Tag; **have a nice ~!** viel Spaß!

daylight ['deɪlaɪt] n Tageslicht das.

day return n (Br) Tagesrückfahrkarte die.

dayshift ['deɪʃɪft] n Tagschicht die.

daytime ['deɪtaɪm] n Tag der.

day-to-day adj (everyday) tagtäglich.

day trip n Tagesausflug der.

dazzle ['dæzl] vt blenden.

DC (abbr of direct current) GS.

dead [ded] ◆ adj tot; (battery) leer. ◆ adv (precisely) genau; (inf: very) total; **it's ~ ahead** es ist genau geradeaus; **'~ slow'** 'Schrittgeschwindigkeit'.

dead end n (street) Sackgasse die.

deadline ['dedlaɪn] n Termin der.

deaf [def] ◆ adj taub. ◆ npl: **the ~** die Tauben pl.

deal [diːl] (pt & pp dealt) ◆ n (agreement) Geschäft das. ◆ vt (cards) geben; **a good/bad ~** ein gutes/schlechtes Geschäft; **a great ~ of** viel; **it's a ~!** abgemacht! ► **deal in** vt fus handeln mit. ► **deal with** vt fus: **to ~ with sthg** (handle) sich um etw kümmern; (be about) sich mit etw befassen.

dealer ['diːlər] n Händler der (-in die); (in drugs) Dealer der.

dealt [delt] pt & pp → **deal**.

dear [dɪər] ◆ adj lieb; (expensive) teuer. ◆ n: **my ~** Schatz; **Dear Sir** Sehr geehrter Herr; **Dear Madam** Sehr geehrte gnädige Frau; **Dear John** Lieber John; **oh ~!** ach du liebe Güte!

death [deθ] n Tod der.

debate [dɪ'beɪt] ◆ n Debatte die. ◆ vt (wonder) sich fragen.

debit ['debɪt] ◆ n Soll das. ◆ vt (account) belasten.

debt [det] n (money owed) Schulden pl; **to be in ~** Schulden haben.

Dec. (abbr of December) Dez.

decaff ['diːkæf] n (inf) entkoffeinierter Kaffee.

decaffeinated [dɪ'kæfɪneɪtɪd] adj koffeinfrei.

decanter [dɪ'kæntər] n Karaffe die.

decay [dɪ'keɪ] ◆ n (of building) Zerfall der; (of wood) Verrotten das; (of tooth) Fäule die. ◆ vi (rot) verfaulen.

deceive [dɪ'siːv] vt betrügen.

decelerate [ˌdiː'seləreɪt] vi langsamer werden.

December [dɪ'sembər] n Dezember

59 **delay**

der, → **September**.

decent ['diːsnt] *adj* anständig; (*kind*) nett.

decide [dɪ'saɪd] ◆ *vt* entscheiden. ◆ *vi* sich entscheiden; **to ~ to do sthg** sich entschließen, etw zu tun. ▶ **decide on** *vt fus* sich entscheiden für.

decimal ['desɪml] *adj* Dezimal-.

decimal point *n* Komma *das*.

decision [dɪ'sɪʒn] *n* Entscheidung *die*; **to make a ~** eine Entscheidung treffen.

decisive [dɪ'saɪsɪv] *adj* (*person*) entschlußfreudig; (*event, factor*) entscheidend.

deck [dek] *n* Deck *das*; (*of cards*) Spiel *das*.

deckchair ['dektʃeəʳ] *n* Liegestuhl *der*.

declare [dɪ'kleəʳ] *vt* erklären; **'goods to ~'** 'Waren zu verzollen'; **'nothing to ~'** 'nichts zu verzollen'.

decline [dɪ'klaɪn] ◆ *n* Rückgang *der*. ◆ *vi* (*get worse*) nachlassen; (*refuse*) ablehnen.

decorate ['dekəreɪt] *vt* (*with wallpaper*) tapezieren; (*with paint*) streichen; (*make attractive*) schmücken.

decoration [ˌdekə'reɪʃn] *n* (*of room*) Innenausstattung *die*; (*decorative object*) Schmuck *der*.

decorator ['dekəreɪtəʳ] *n* Maler und Tapezierer *der*.

decrease [*n* 'diːkriːs, *vb* diː'kriːs] ◆ *n* Abnahme *die*. ◆ *vi* abnehmen.

dedicated ['dedɪkeɪtɪd] *adj* (*committed*) engagiert.

deduce [dɪ'djuːs] *vt* folgern.

deduct [dɪ'dʌkt] *vt* abziehen.

deduction [dɪ'dʌkʃn] *n* (*reduction*) Abzug *der*; (*conclusion*) Folgerung *die*.

deep [diːp] *adj* & *adv* tief.

deep end *n* (*of swimming pool*) tiefer Teil.

deep freeze *n* Tiefkühltruhe *die*.

deep-fried ['-fraɪd] *adj* fritiert.

deep-pan *adj*: **~ pizza** Pfannenpizza *die*.

deer [dɪəʳ] (*pl inv*) *n* (*male*) Hirsch *der*; (*female*) Reh *das*.

defeat [dɪ'fiːt] ◆ *n* Niederlage *die*. ◆ *vt* schlagen.

defect ['diːfekt] *n* Fehler *der*.

defective [dɪ'fektɪv] *adj* fehlerhaft.

defence [dɪ'fens] *n* Verteidigung *die*; (Br: *protection*) Schutz *der*.

defend [dɪ'fend] *vt* verteidigen.

defense [dɪ'fens] (Am) = **defence**.

deficiency [dɪ'fɪʃnsɪ] *n* (*lack*) Mangel *der*.

deficit ['defɪsɪt] *n* Defizit *das*.

define [dɪ'faɪn] *vt* definieren.

definite ['defɪnɪt] *adj* (*clear*) klar; (*certain*) sicher.

definite article *n* bestimmter Artikel.

definitely ['defɪnɪtlɪ] *adv* eindeutig; **I'm ~ coming** ich komme ganz bestimmt.

definition [defɪ'nɪʃn] *n* Definition *die*.

deflate [dɪ'fleɪt] *vt* (*tyre*) die Luft abllassen aus.

deflect [dɪ'flekt] *vt* (*ball*) ablfälschen.

defogger [ˌdiː'fɒgəʳ] *n* (Am) Defroster *der*.

deformed [dɪ'fɔːmd] *adj* entstellt.

defrost [ˌdiː'frɒst] *vt* (*food*) aufltauen; (Am: *demist*) freimachen; (*fridge*) abltauen.

degree [dɪ'griː] *n* Grad *der*; (*amount*) Maß *das*; (*qualification*) akademischer Grad; **to have a ~ in sthg** einen Hochschulabschluß in etw (D) haben.

dehydrated [ˌdiːhaɪ'dreɪtɪd] *adj* (*food*) Trocken-; (*person*) ausgetrocknet.

de-ice [diː'aɪs] *vt* enteisen.

de-icer [diː'aɪsəʳ] *n* Defroster *der*.

dejected [dɪ'dʒektɪd] *adj* niedergeschlagen.

delay [dɪ'leɪ] ◆ *n* Verspätung *die*. ◆ *vt* aufhalten. ◆ *vi* zögern; **without ~** ohne Verzögerung.

delayed [dɪ'leɪd] *adj* (*train, flight*) verspätet.

delegate [*n* 'delɪgət, *vb* 'delɪgeɪt] ◆ *n* Vertreter *der* (-in *die*). ◆ *vt* delegieren.

delete [dɪ'liːt] *vt* streichen.

deli ['delɪ] *n* (*inf*) (*abbr of delicatessen*) Feinkostgeschäft *das.*

deliberate [dɪ'lɪbərət] *adj* absichtlich.

deliberately [dɪ'lɪbərətlɪ] *adv* absichtlich.

delicacy ['delɪkəsɪ] *n* (*food*) Delikatesse *die.*

delicate ['delɪkət] *adj* (*situation, question*) heikel; (*object, china*) zerbrechlich; (*health, person*) zart; (*taste, smell*) fein.

delicatessen [ˌdelɪkə'tesn] *n* Feinkostgeschäft *das.*

delicious [dɪ'lɪʃəs] *adj* köstlich.

delight [dɪ'laɪt] ◆ *n* Freude *die.* ◆ *vt* erfreuen; **to take (a) ~ in doing sthg** Freude daran haben, etw zu tun.

delighted [dɪ'laɪtɪd] *adj* hocherfreut.

delightful [dɪ'laɪtfʊl] *adj* reizend.

deliver [dɪ'lɪvəʳ] *vt* (*goods*) liefern; (*letters, newspapers*) zulstellen; (*speech, lecture*) halten; (*baby*) entbinden.

delivery [dɪ'lɪvərɪ] *n* (*of goods*) Lieferung *die;* (*of letters*) Zustellung *die;* (*birth*) Entbindung *die.*

delude [dɪ'luːd] *vt* täuschen.

de luxe [də'lʌks] *adj* Luxus-.

demand [dɪ'mɑːnd] ◆ *n* Forderung *die;* (*COMM*) Nachfrage *die;* (*requirement*) Anforderung *die.* ◆ *vt* verlangen; (*require*) erfordern; **to ~ to do sthg** verlangen, etw zu tun; **to be in ~** gefragt sein.

demanding [dɪ'mɑːndɪŋ] *adj* anspruchsvoll.

demerara sugar [deməˈreərə-] *n* brauner Zucker.

demist [ˌdiːˈmɪst] *vt* (Br) freilmachen.

demister [ˌdiːˈmɪstəʳ] *n* (Br) Defroster *der.*

democracy [dɪ'mɒkrəsɪ] *n* Demokratie *die.*

Democrat ['deməkræt] *n* (Am) Demokrat *der* (-in *die*).

democratic [deməˈkrætɪk] *adj* demokratisch.

demolish [dɪ'mɒlɪʃ] *vt* ablreißen.

demonstrate ['demənstreɪt] ◆ *vt* (*prove*) beweisen; (*machine, skill*) vorlführen. ◆ *vi* demonstrieren.

demonstration [demənˈstreɪʃn] *n* (*protest*) Demonstration *die;* (*proof*) Beweis *der;* (*of machine, skill*) Vorführung *die.*

denial [dɪ'naɪəl] *n* Leugnen *das.*

denim ['denɪm] *n* Jeansstoff *der.* ▶ **denims** *npl* Jeans *pl.*

denim jacket *n* Jeansjacke *die.*

Denmark ['denmɑːk] *n* Dänemark *nt.*

dense [dens] *adj* dicht.

dent [dent] *n* Delle *die.*

dental ['dentl] *adj* Zahn-.

dental floss [-flɒs] *n* Zahnseide *die.*

dental surgeon *n* Zahnarzt *der* (-ärztin *die*).

dental surgery *n* (*place*) Zahnarztpraxis *die.*

dentist ['dentɪst] *n* Zahnarzt *der* (-ärztin *die*); **to go to the ~'s** zum Zahnarzt gehen.

dentures ['dentʃəz] *npl* Zahnprothese *die.*

deny [dɪ'naɪ] *vt* (*declare untrue*) bestreiten; (*refuse*) verweigern.

deodorant [diːˈəʊdərənt] *n* Deodorant *das.*

depart [dɪ'pɑːt] *vi* (*person*) ablreisen; (*train, bus*) ablfahren; (*plane*) ablfliegen.

department [dɪ'pɑːtmənt] *n* (*of business, shop*) Abteilung *die;* (*of government*) Ministerium *das;* (*of school*) Fachbereich *der;* (*of university*) Seminar *das.*

department store *n* Kaufhaus *das.*

departure [dɪ'pɑːtʃəʳ] *n* (*of person*)

Abreise die; (of train, bus) Abfahrt die; (of plane) Abflug der; '**~s**' (at airport) 'Abflug'.

departure lounge n Abflughalle die.

depend [dɪ'pend] vi: **it ~s** es kommt darauf an. ▶ **depend on** vt fus abhängen von; (rely on) sich verlassen auf (+A); **~ing on** je nachdem; **~ing on the weather** je nachdem, wie das Wetter wird.

dependable [dɪ'pendəbl] adj zuverlässig.

deplorable [dɪ'plɔːrəbl] adj beklagenswert.

deport [dɪ'pɔːt] vt aus|reisen.

deposit [dɪ'pɒzɪt] ◆ n (in bank) Guthaben das; (part-payment) Anzahlung die; (against damage) Kaution die; (on bottle) Pfand das; (substance) Ablagerung die. ◆ vt (put down) ab|legen; (money in bank) ein|zahlen.

deposit account n (Br) Sparkonto das.

depot ['diːpəʊ] n (Am: for buses, trains) Bahnhof der.

depressed [dɪ'prest] adj deprimiert.

depressing [dɪ'presɪŋ] adj deprimierend.

depression [dɪ'preʃn] n Depression die.

deprive [dɪ'praɪv] vt: **to ~ sb of sthg** jm etw entziehen.

depth [depθ] n Tiefe die; **to be out of one's ~** (when swimming) nicht mehr stehen können; (fig) überfordert sein; **~ of field** Schärfentiefe.

deputy ['depjʊtɪ] adj stellvertretend.

derailleur [də'reɪljər] n Kettenschaltung die.

derailment [dɪ'reɪlmənt] n Entgleisen das.

derelict ['derəlɪkt] adj verfallen.

derv [dɜːv] n (Br) Diesel der.

descend [dɪ'send] vt & vi (subj: person) herunter|gehen; (subj: car) herunter|fahren.

descendant [dɪ'sendənt] n Nachkomme der.

descent [dɪ'sent] n Abstieg der; (slope) Abfall der.

describe [dɪ'skraɪb] vt beschreiben.

description [dɪ'skrɪpʃn] n Beschreibung die.

desert [n 'dezət, vb dɪ'zɜːt] ◆ n Wüste die. ◆ vt verlassen.

deserted [dɪ'zɜːtɪd] adj verlassen.

deserve [dɪ'zɜːv] vt verdienen.

design [dɪ'zaɪn] ◆ n (pattern) Muster das; (art) Design das; (of machine, building) Konstruktion die. ◆ vt (machine, building) konstruieren; (dress) entwerfen; **to be ~ed for** vorgesehen sein für.

designer [dɪ'zaɪnər] ◆ n (of clothes) Designer der (-in die); (of machine) Konstrukteur der (-in die). ◆ adj (clothes, sunglasses) Designer-.

desirable [dɪ'zaɪərəbl] adj wünschenswert.

desire [dɪ'zaɪər] ◆ n Wunsch der. ◆ vt wünschen; **it leaves a lot to be ~d** es läßt viel zu wünschen übrig.

desk [desk] n (in home, office) Schreibtisch der; (in school) Pult das; (at airport, station) Schalter der; (at hotel) Empfang der.

desktop publishing ['desk,tɒp-] n Desktop Publishing das.

despair [dɪ'speər] n Verzweiflung die.

despatch [dɪ'spætʃ] = **dispatch**.

desperate ['despərət] adj verzweifelt; **to be ~ for sthg** etw dringend brauchen.

despicable [dɪ'spɪkəbl] adj verachtenswert.

despise [dɪ'spaɪz] vt verachten.

despite [dɪ'spaɪt] prep trotz (+G).

dessert [dɪ'zɜːt] n Nachtisch der.

dessertspoon [dɪ'zɜːtspuːn] n Dessertlöffel der.

destination [,destɪ'neɪʃn] n (of person) Reiseziel das; (of goods) Bestimmungsort der.

destroy [dɪ'strɔɪ] vt zerstören.

destruction [dɪ'strʌkʃn] n Zerstörung die.

detach [dɪ'tætʃ] vt ablnehmen; (tear off) abltrennen.

detached house [dɪ'tætʃt-] n Einzelhaus das.

detail ['diːteɪl] n Einzelheit die; **in ~** im Detail. ► **details** npl (facts) Angaben pl.

detailed ['diːteɪld] adj detailliert.

detect [dɪ'tekt] vt entdecken.

detective [dɪ'tektɪv] n (policeman) Kriminalbeamte der (-beamtin die); (private) Detektiv der (-in die); **a ~ story** ein Krimi.

detention [dɪ'tenʃn] n (SCH) Nachsitzen das.

detergent [dɪ'tɜːdʒənt] n (for clothes) Waschmittel das; (for dishes) Spülmittel das.

deteriorate [dɪ'tɪərɪəreɪt] vi sich verschlechtern.

determination [dɪˌtɜːmɪ'neɪʃn] n Entschlossenheit die.

determine [dɪ'tɜːmɪn] vt bestimmen.

determined [dɪ'tɜːmɪnd] adj entschlossen; **to be ~ to do sthg** fest entschlossen sein, etw zu tun.

deterrent [dɪ'terənt] n Abschreckungsmittel das.

detest [dɪ'test] vt verabscheuen.

detour ['diːˌtʊər] n Umweg der.

detrain [ˌdiː'treɪn] vi (fml) aus dem Zug steigen.

deuce [djuːs] n (in tennis) Einstand der.

devastate ['devəsteɪt] vt (country, town) verwüsten.

develop [dɪ'veləp] ► vt entwickeln; (land) erschließen; (illness) bekommen; (habit) anlnehmen. ► vi sich entwickeln.

developing country [dɪ'veləpɪŋ-] n Entwicklungsland das.

development [dɪ'veləpmənt] n Entwicklung die; **a housing ~** eine Neubausiedlung.

device [dɪ'vaɪs] n Gerät das.

devil ['devl] n Teufel der; **what the ~ ...?** (inf) was zum Teufel ...?

devise [dɪ'vaɪz] vt entwerfen.

devoted [dɪ'vəʊtɪd] adj treu; **to be ~ to sb** jn innig lieben.

dew [djuː] n Tau der.

diabetes [ˌdaɪə'biːtiːz] n Zuckerkrankheit die.

diabetic [ˌdaɪə'betɪk] ► adj zuckerkrank; (chocolate) Diabetiker-. ► n Diabetiker der (-in die).

diagnosis [ˌdaɪəg'nəʊsɪs] (pl -oses [-əʊsiːz]) n Diagnose die.

diagonal [daɪ'ægənl] adj diagonal.

diagram ['daɪəgræm] n schematische Darstellung.

dial ['daɪəl] ► n (of telephone) Wählscheibe die; (of clock) Zifferblatt das; (on radio) Skala die. ► vt wählen.

dialling code ['daɪəlɪŋ-] n (Br) Vorwahl die.

dialling tone ['daɪəlɪŋ-] n (Br) Freizeichen das.

dial tone (Am) = **dialling tone**.

diameter [daɪ'æmɪtər] n Durchmesser der.

diamond ['daɪəmənd] n Diamant der. ► **diamonds** npl (in cards) Karo das.

diaper ['daɪpər] n (Am) Windel die.

diarrhoea [ˌdaɪə'rɪə] n Durchfall der.

diary ['daɪərɪ] n (for appointments) Terminkalender der; (journal) Tagebuch das.

dice [daɪs] (pl inv) n Würfel der.

diced [daɪst] adj in Würfel geschnitten.

dictate [dɪk'teɪt] vt diktieren.

dictation [dɪk'teɪʃn] n Diktat das.

dictator [dɪk'teɪtər] n Diktator der (-in die).

dictionary ['dɪkʃənrɪ] n Wörterbuch das.

did [dɪd] pt → **do**.

die [daɪ] (pt & pp died, cont dying ['daɪɪŋ]) vi sterben; (animal, plant) einlgehen; **to be dying for sthg** (inf) etw unbedingt brauchen; **to be dying to do sthg** (*inf*) darauf brennen, etw zu tun. ▶ **die away** *vi* schwächer werden. ▶ **die out** *vi* aus|sterben.

diesel ['diːzl] *n* Diesel *der*.

diet ['daɪət] ◆ *n* Diät *die*; (*food eaten*) Kost *die*. ◆ *vi* eine Diät machen. ◆ *adj* Diät-.

diet Coke® *n* Colalight® *die*.

differ ['dɪfər] *vi* sich unterscheiden; (*disagree*) anderer Meinung sein.

difference ['dɪfrəns] *n* Unterschied *der*; **it makes no ~** es ist egal; **a ~ of opinion** eine Meinungsverschiedenheit.

different ['dɪfrənt] *adj* (*not the same*) verschieden; (*separate*) andere(-r) (-s); **to be ~ (from)** anders sein (als).

differently ['dɪfrəntlɪ] *adv* anders.

difficult ['dɪfɪkəlt] *adj* schwierig.

difficulty ['dɪfɪkəltɪ] *n* Schwierigkeit *die*; **with ~** mühsam.

dig [dɪg] (*pt & pp* **dug**) ◆ *vt* graben; (*garden, land*) um|graben. ◆ *vi* graben. ▶ **dig out** *vt sep* (*rescue*) bergen; (*find*) aus|graben. ▶ **dig up** *vt sep* aus|graben.

digest [dɪ'dʒest] *vt* verdauen.

digestion [dɪ'dʒestʃn] *n* Verdauung *die*.

digestive (biscuit) [dɪ'dʒestɪv-] *n* (Br) Vollkornkeks *der*.

digit ['dɪdʒɪt] *n* (*number*) Ziffer *die*; (*finger*) Finger *der*; (*toe*) Zehe *die*.

digital ['dɪdʒɪtl] *adj* Digital-.

dill [dɪl] *n* Dill *der*.

dilute [daɪ'luːt] *vt* verdünnen.

dim [dɪm] ◆ *adj* (*light*) trüb; (*room*) dämmrig; (*inf: stupid*) beschränkt. ◆ *vt* (*light*) dämpfen.

dime [daɪm] *n* (Am) Zehncentstück *das*.

dimensions [dɪ'menʃnz] *npl* (*measurements*) Abmessungen *pl*; (*aspect*) Dimension *die*.

din [dɪn] *n* Lärm *der*.

dine [daɪn] *vi* speisen. ▶ **dine out** *vi* auswärts essen.

diner ['daɪnər] *n* (Am: *restaurant*) Lokal *das*; (*person*) Gast *der*.

dinghy ['dɪŋgɪ] *n* (*with sail*) Dingi *das*; (*with oars*) Schlauchboot *das*.

dingy ['dɪndʒɪ] *adj* (*room*) düster.

dining car ['daɪnɪŋ-] *n* Speisewagen *der*.

dining hall ['daɪnɪŋ-] *n* (SCH) Speisesaal *der*.

dining room ['daɪnɪŋ-] *n* Eßzimmer *das*; (*in hotel*) Speisesaal *der*.

dinner ['dɪnər] *n* (*at lunchtime*) Mittagessen *das*; (*in evening*) Abendessen *das*; **to have ~** (*at lunchtime*) zu Mittag essen; (*in evening*) zu Abend essen.

dinner jacket *n* Smoking *der*.

dinner party *n* Abendgesellschaft *die*.

dinner set *n* Tafelgeschirr *das*.

dinner suit *n* Smoking *der*.

dinnertime ['dɪnətaɪm] *n* Essenszeit *die*.

dinosaur ['daɪnəsɔːr] *n* Dinosaurier *der*.

dip [dɪp] ◆ *n* (*in road, land*) Mulde *die*; (*food*) Dip *der*. ◆ *vt* (*into liquid*) tauchen. ◆ *vi* sich senken; **to have a ~** (*swim*) kurz schwimmen gehen; **to ~ one's headlights** (Br) ab|blenden.

diploma [dɪ'pləʊmə] *n* Diplom *das*.

dipstick ['dɪpstɪk] *n* Ölmeßstab *der*.

direct [dɪ'rekt] ◆ *adj & adv* direkt. ◆ *vt* (*aim*) richten; (*traffic*) regeln; (*control*) leiten; (*film, play*) Regie führen bei; (*give directions to*): **to ~ sb** jm den Weg beschreiben.

direct current *n* Gleichstrom *der*.

direction [dɪ'rekʃn] *n* Richtung *die*; **to ask for ~s** nach dem Weg fragen. ▶ **directions** *npl* (*instructions*) Gebrauchsanweisung *die*.

directly [dɪ'rektlɪ] *adv* direkt; (*soon*) sofort.

director [dɪ'rektər] *n* (*of company*) Direktor *der* (-in *die*); (*of film, play*) Regisseur *der* (-in *die*); (*organizer*) Leiter *der* (-in *die*).

directory [dɪ'rektərɪ] n Telefonbuch das.

directory enquiries n (Br) Fernsprechauskunft die.

dirt [dɜ:t] n Schmutz der; (earth) Erde die.

dirty ['dɜ:tɪ] adj schmutzig; (joke) unanständig.

disability [‚dɪsə'bɪlətɪ] n Behinderung die.

disabled [dɪs'eɪbld] ◆ adj behindert. ◆ npl: the ~ die Behinderten pl; '~ toilet' 'Behindertentoilette'.

disadvantage [‚dɪsəd'vɑ:ntɪdʒ] n Nachteil der.

disagree [‚dɪsə'gri:] vi (people) anderer Meinung sein; to ~ with sb (about sthg) mit jm (über etw (+A) nicht überein)stimmen; those mussels ~d with me diese Muscheln sind mir nicht bekommen.

disagreement [‚dɪsə'gri:mənt] n (argument) Meinungsverschiedenheit die; (dissimilarity) Diskrepanz die.

disappear [‚dɪsə'pɪər] vi verschwinden.

disappearance [‚dɪsə'pɪərəns] n Verschwinden das.

disappoint [‚dɪsə'pɔɪnt] vt enttäuschen.

disappointed [‚dɪsə'pɔɪntɪd] adj enttäuscht.

disappointing [‚dɪsə'pɔɪntɪŋ] adj enttäuschend.

disappointment [‚dɪsə'pɔɪntmənt] n Enttäuschung die.

disapprove [‚dɪsə'pru:v] vi: to ~ of mißbilligen.

disarmament [dɪs'ɑ:məmənt] n Abrüstung die.

disaster [dɪ'zɑ:stər] n Katastrophe die.

disastrous [dɪ'zɑ:strəs] adj katastrophal.

disc [dɪsk] n (Br) Scheibe die; (CD) Compact Disc die; (record) Schallplatte die; to slip a ~ einen Bandscheibenvorfall erleiden.

discard [dɪ'skɑ:d] vt weg|werfen.

discharge [dɪs'tʃɑ:dʒ] vt (patient, prisoner) entlassen; (liquid, smoke) ab|lassen.

discipline ['dɪsɪplɪn] n Disziplin die.

disc jockey n Diskjockey der.

disco ['dɪskəʊ] n Disko die.

discoloured [dɪs'kʌləd] adj verfärbt.

discomfort [dɪs'kʌmfət] n (pain) Beschwerden pl.

disconnect [‚dɪskə'nekt] vt (unplug) den Stecker heraus|ziehen (von); (telephone, gas supply) ab|stellen; (pipe) trennen.

discontinued [‚dɪskən'tɪnju:d] adj (product) auslaufend.

discotheque ['dɪskəʊtek] n Diskothek die.

discount ['dɪskaʊnt] n Rabatt der.

discover [dɪ'skʌvər] vt entdecken.

discovery [dɪ'skʌvərɪ] n Entdeckung die.

discreet [dɪ'skri:t] adj taktvoll.

discrepancy [dɪ'skrepənsɪ] n Diskrepanz die.

discriminate [dɪ'skrɪmɪneɪt] vi: to ~ against sb jn diskriminieren.

discrimination [dɪ‚skrɪmɪ'neɪʃn] n (unfair) Diskriminierung die.

discuss [dɪ'skʌs] vt besprechen.

discussion [dɪ'skʌʃn] n Gespräch das.

disease [dɪ'zi:z] n Krankheit die.

disembark [‚dɪsɪm'bɑ:k] vi von Bord gehen.

disgrace [dɪs'greɪs] n Schande die.

disgraceful [dɪs'greɪsfʊl] adj erbärmlich.

disguise [dɪs'gaɪz] ◆ n Verkleidung die. ◆ vt verkleiden; in ~ verkleidet.

disgust [dɪs'gʌst] ◆ n Abscheu der. ◆ vt an|widern.

disgusting [dɪs'gʌstɪŋ] adj widerlich.

dish [dɪʃ] n (container) Schüssel die; (shallow) Schale die; (food) Gericht das; (Am: plate) Teller der; to do the ~es ab|waschen; '~ of the day' 'Tagesgericht'. ► **dish up** vt sep auf|tragen.

dishcloth ['dɪʃklɒθ] n Spültuch das.

disheveled [dɪ'ʃevəld] (Am) = **dishevelled**.

dishevelled [dɪ'ʃevəld] adj (Br) zerzaust.

dishonest [dɪs'ɒnɪst] adj unehrlich.

dish towel n (Am) Geschirrtuch das.

dishwasher ['dɪʃ,wɒʃər] n (machine) Geschirrspülmaschine die.

disinfectant [,dɪsɪn'fektənt] n Desinfektionsmittel das.

disintegrate [dɪs'ɪntɪgreɪt] vi zer-fallen.

disk [dɪsk] n (Am) = **disc**; (COMPUT) Diskette die.

disk drive n Disketten-Laufwerk das.

dislike [dɪs'laɪk] ◆ n Abneigung die. ◆ vt nicht mögen; **to take a ~ to** eine Abneigung empfinden gegen.

dislocate ['dɪsləkeɪt] vt (shoulder, hip) aus|renken.

dismal ['dɪzml] adj (weather, place) trostlos; (terrible) kläglich.

dismantle [dɪs'mæntl] vt auseinan-der|nehmen.

dismay [dɪs'meɪ] n Bestürzung die.

dismiss [dɪs'mɪs] vt (idea, suggestion) ab|tun; (from job, classroom) ent-lassen.

disobedient [,dɪsə'biːdjənt] adj ungehorsam.

disobey [,dɪsə'beɪ] vt nicht gehorchen (+D).

disorder [dɪs'ɔːrdər] n (confusion) Unordnung die; (violence) Unruhen pl; (illness) Störung die.

disorganized [dɪs'ɔːgənaɪzd] adj chaotisch.

dispatch [dɪ'spætʃ] vt schicken.

dispense [dɪ'spens]: **dispense with** vt fus verzichten auf (+A).

dispenser [dɪ'spensər] n (device) Automat der.

dispensing chemist [dɪ'spensɪŋ-] n (Br) Apotheker der (-in die).

disperse [dɪ'spɜːs] ◆ vt zerstreuen. ◆ vi sich zerstreuen.

display [dɪ'spleɪ] ◆ n (of goods) Auslage die; (exhibition) Ausstellung die; (readout) Anzeige die. ◆ vt (goods) aus|stellen; (feeling, quality) zeigen; (information) aus|hängen; **to be on ~** ausgestellt werden.

displeased [dɪs'pliːzd] adj verär-gert.

disposable [dɪ'spəʊzəbl] adj (nappy) Wegwerf-; (lighter) Einweg-.

dispute [dɪ'spjuːt] ◆ n Streit der; (industrial) Auseinandersetzung die. ◆ vt bestreiten.

disqualify [,dɪs'kwɒlɪfaɪ] vt dis-qualifizieren; **to be disqualified from driving** (Br) den Führerschein ent-zogen haben.

disregard [,dɪsrɪ'gɑːd] vt igno-rieren.

disrupt [dɪs'rʌpt] vt unterbrechen.

disruption [dɪs'rʌpʃn] n Unter-brechung die.

dissatisfied [,dɪs'sætɪsfaɪd] adj unzufrieden.

dissolve [dɪ'zɒlv] ◆ vt auf|lösen. ◆ vi sich auf|lösen.

dissuade [dɪ'sweɪd] vt: **to ~ sb from doing sthg** jn davon ab|bringen, etw zu tun.

distance ['dɪstəns] n Entfernung die; **from a ~** aus der Entfernung; **in the ~** in der Ferne.

distant ['dɪstənt] adj weit entfernt; (in time) fern; (reserved) distanziert.

distilled water [dɪ'stɪld-] n destil-liertes Wasser.

distillery [dɪ'stɪlərɪ] n Brennerei die.

distinct [dɪ'stɪŋkt] adj (separate) ver-schieden; (noticeable) deutlich.

distinction [dɪ'stɪŋkʃn] n Unterschied der; (mark for work) Auszeichnung die.

distinctive [dɪ'stɪŋktɪv] adj unver-wechselbar.

distinguish [dɪ'stɪŋgwɪʃ] vt (perceive)

erkennen; **to ~ sthg from sthg** etw von etw unterscheiden.

distorted [dɪ'stɔːtɪd] *adj* verzerrt.

distract [dɪ'strækt] *vt* abllenken.

distraction [dɪ'strækʃn] *n* Ablenkung *die*.

distress [dɪ'stres] *n* (*pain*) Leiden *das*; (*anxiety*) Kummer *der*.

distressing [dɪ'stresɪŋ] *adj* schmerzlich.

distribute [dɪ'strɪbjuːt] *vt* verteilen.

distributor [dɪ'strɪbjutəʳ] *n* (COMM) Vertreiber *der* (-in *die*); (AUT) Verteiler *der*.

district ['dɪstrɪkt] *n* (*region*) Gebiet *das*; (*of town*) Bezirk *der*.

district attorney *n* (Am) Bezirksstaatsanwalt *der* (-anwältin *die*).

disturb [dɪ'stɜːb] *vt* stören; (*worry*) beunruhigen; (*move*) durcheinanlderlbringen; **'do not ~'** 'bitte nicht stören'.

disturbance [dɪ'stɜːbəns] *n* (*violence*) Unruhe *die*.

ditch [dɪtʃ] *n* Graben *der*.

ditto ['dɪtəʊ] *adv* ebenso.

divan [dɪ'væn] *n* Liege *die*.

dive [daɪv] (*pt* Am **-d** OR **dove**, *pt* Br **-d**) ◆ *n* (*of swimmer*) Kopfsprung *der*. ◆ *vi* einen Kopfsprung machen; (*under sea*) tauchen; (*bird, plane*) einen Sturzflug machen.

diver ['daɪvəʳ] *n* (*from divingboard, rock*) Springer *der* (-in *die*); (*under sea*) Taucher *der* (-in *die*).

diversion [daɪ'vɜːʃn] *n* (*of traffic*) Umleitung *die*; (*amusement*) Ablenkung *die*.

divert [daɪ'vɜːt] *vt* umlleiten; (*attention*) abllenken.

divide [dɪ'vaɪd] *vt* teilen; (*share out*) verteilen; (*into two parts*) zerteilen. ▸ **divide up** *vt sep* auflteilen.

diving ['daɪvɪŋ] *n* (*from divingboard, rock*) Springen *das*; (*under sea*) Tauchen *das*; **to go ~** Tauchen gehen.

divingboard ['daɪvɪŋbɔːd] *n* Sprungbrett *das*.

division [dɪ'vɪʒn] *n* (SPORT) Liga *die*; (COMM) Abteilung *die*; (*in maths*) Division *die*; (*disagreement*) Uneinigkeit *die*.

divorce [dɪ'vɔːs] ◆ *n* Scheidung *die*. ◆ *vt* sich scheiden lassen von.

divorced [dɪ'vɔːst] *adj* geschieden.

DIY *abbr* = **do-it-yourself**.

dizzy ['dɪzɪ] *adj* schwindlig.

DJ *abbr* = **disc jockey**.

do [duː] (*pt* **did**, *pp* **done**, *pl* **dos**) ◆ *aux vb* **1.** (*in negatives*): **don't ~ that!** tu das nicht!; **she didn't** listen sie hat nicht zugehört. **2.** (*in questions*): **did he like it?** hat es ihm gefallen?; **how ~ you do it?** wie machen Sie/machst du das? **3.** (*referring to previous verb*): **I eat more than you ~** ich esse mehr als du; **no I didn't!** nein, habe ich nicht!; **so ~ I** ich auch. **4.** (*in question tags*): **so, you like Scotland, ~ you?** Sie mögen Schottland also, nicht wahr?; **you come from Ireland, don't you?** Sie kommen aus Irland, oder? **5.** (*for emphasis*): **I ~ like this bedroom** das Schlafzimmer gefällt mir wirklich; **~ come in!** kommen Sie doch herein! ◆ *vt* **1.** (*perform*) machen, tun; **I've a lot to ~** ich habe viel zu tun; **to ~ one's homework** seine Hausaufgaben machen; **what is she doing?** was macht sie?; **what can I ~ for you?** was kann ich für Sie tun? **2.** (*clean, brush etc*): **to ~ one's make-up** sich schminken; **to ~ one's teeth** (D) die Zähne putzen. **3.** (*cause*): **to ~ damage** Schaden zulfügen; **to ~ sb good** jm gutltun. **4.** (*have as job*): **what do you ~?** was machen Sie beruflich? **5.** (*provide, offer*) anlbieten; **we ~ pizzas for under £4** wir bieten Pizzas für weniger als 4 Pfund an. **6.** (*study*) studieren, machen. **7.** (*subj: vehicle*) fahren. **8.** (*inf: visit*): **we're doing Switzerland next week** wir fahren nächste Woche nach der Schweiz. ◆ *vi* **1.** (*behave, act*) tun; **~ as I say** tu, was ich sage. **2.** (*progress, get on*): **to ~ badly** schlecht voranlkommen; (*in exam*) schlecht ablschneiden; **to ~**

well gut voran|kommen; (*in exam*) gut ab|schneiden. **3.** (*be sufficient*) reichen, genügen; **will £5 ~?** sind 5 Pfund genug? **4.** (*in phrases*): **how do you ~?** Guten Tag!; **how are you doing?** wie geht's?; **what has that got to ~ with it?** was hat das damit zu tun? ◆ *n* (*party*) Party *die*; **the ~s and don'ts** was man tun und lassen sollte. ► **do out of** *vt sep* (*inf*): **to ~ sb out of £10** jn um 10 Pfund betrügen. ► **do up** *vt sep* (*fasten*) zu|machen; (*decorate*) renovieren; (*wrap up*) ein|packen. ► **do with** *vt fus* (*need*): **I could ~ with a drink** ich könnte einen Drink gebrauchen. ► **do without** *vt fus*: **to ~ without sthg** ohne etw aus|kommen.

dock [dɒk] ◆ *n* (*for ships*) Dock *das*; (*JUR*) Anklagebank *die*. ◆ *vi* an|legen.

doctor ['dɒktəʳ] *n* Arzt *der* (Ärztin *die*); (*academic*) Doktor *der* (-in *die*); **to go to the ~'s** zum Arzt gehen.

document ['dɒkjumənt] *n* Dokument *das*.

documentary [,dɒkju'mentərɪ] *n* Dokumentarfilm *der*.

Dodgems® ['dɒdʒəmz] *npl* (Br) Autoskooter *pl*.

dodgy ['dɒdʒɪ] *adj* ([Br]: *inf*: *plan*) gewagt; (*car, machine*) unzuverlässig.

does [*weak form* dəz, *strong form* dʌz] → **do**.

doesn't ['dʌznt] = **does not**.

dog [dɒg] *n* Hund *der*.

dog food *n* Hundefutter *das*.

doggy bag ['dɒgɪ-] *n* Tüte, in der aus einem Restaurant Essensreste mit nach Hause genommen werden.

do-it-yourself *n* Do-it-yourself *das*.

dole [dəʊl] *n*: **to be on the ~** (Br) stempeln gehen.

doll [dɒl] *n* Puppe *die*.

dollar ['dɒləʳ] *n* Dollar *der*.

dolphin ['dɒlfɪn] *n* Delphin *der*.

dome [dəʊm] *n* Kuppel *die*.

domestic [də'mestɪk] *adj* (*of house*) Haushalts-; (*of family*) familiär; (*of country*) Innen-.

domestic appliance *n* Haushaltsgerät *das*.

domestic flight *n* Inlandflug *der*.

domestic science *n* Hauswirtschaftslehre *die*.

dominate ['dɒmɪneɪt] *vt* beherrschen.

dominoes ['dɒmɪnəʊz] *n* Domino *das*.

donate [də'neɪt] *vt* spenden.

donation [də'neɪʃn] *n* Spende *die*.

done [dʌn] ◆ *pp* → **do**. ◆ *adj* (*finished*) fertig; (*cooked*) gar.

donkey ['dɒŋkɪ] *n* Esel *der*.

don't [dəʊnt] = **do not**.

door [dɔːʳ] *n* Tür *die*.

doorbell ['dɔːbel] *n* Türklingel *die*.

doorknob ['dɔːnɒb] *n* Türknauf *der*.

doorman ['dɔːmən] (*pl* **-men**) *n* Portier *der*.

doormat ['dɔːmæt] *n* Fußabstreifer *der*.

doormen ['dɔːmən] *pl* → **doorman**.

doorstep ['dɔːstep] *n* Türstufe *die*; (Br: *piece of bread*) dicke Scheibe Brot.

doorway ['dɔːweɪ] *n* Eingang *der*.

dope [dəʊp] *n* (*inf*: *drug*) Stoff *der*.

dormitory ['dɔːmətrɪ] *n* Schlafsaal *der*.

Dormobile® ['dɔːmə,biːl] *n* Camper *der*.

dosage ['dəʊsɪdʒ] *n* Dosis *die*.

dose [dəʊs] *n* Dosis *die*; (*of illness*) Anfall *der*.

dot [dɒt] *n* Punkt *der*; **on the ~** (*fig*) pünktlich.

dotted line ['dɒtɪd-] *n* gepunktete Linie.

double ['dʌbl] ◆ *adj* doppelt, Doppel-. ◆ *adv* doppelt. ◆ *n* (*twice the amount*) Doppelte *das*; (*alcohol*) Doppelte *der*. ◆ *vt* verdoppeln. ◆ *vi* sich verdoppeln; **it's ~ the size** es ist doppelt so groß; **to bend sthg ~** etw zusammen|falten; **a ~ whisky** ein doppelter Whisky; **~ seven** sieben

sieben. ► **doubles** *n* (SPORT) Doppel *das*.

double bed *n* Doppelbett *das*.

double-breasted [-'brestɪd] *adj* zweireihig.

double cream *n* (Br) *Sahne mit hohem Fettgehalt.*

double-decker (bus) [-'dekər↓] *n* Doppeldeckerbus *der*.

double doors *npl* Flügeltür *die*.

double-glazing [-'gleɪzɪŋ] *n* Doppelverglasung *die*.

double room *n* Doppelzimmer *das*.

doubt [daut] ◆ *n* Zweifel *der*. ◆ *vt* zweifeln an (+D); **I ~ it** das bezweifle ich; **I ~ she'll come** ich bezweifle, daß sie kommt; **in ~** zweifelhaft; **no ~** zweifellos.

doubtful ['dautful] *adj* (*person*) skeptisch; (*result*) zweifelhaft; **it's ~ that ...** (*unlikely*) es ist fraglich, ob ...

dough [dəu] *n* Teig *der*.

doughnut ['dəunʌt] *n* Berliner *der*, Krapfen *der* (*Süddt, Österr*).

dove¹ [dʌv] *n* (*bird*) Taube *die*.

dove² [dəuv] *pt* (*Am*) → **dive**.

Dover ['dəuvər] *n* Dover *nt*.

Dover sole *n* Seezunge *die*.

down¹ [daun] ◆ *adv* **1.** (*towards the bottom*) nach unten, hinunter/herunter; **~ here** hier unten; **~ there** dort unten; **to fall ~** (*person*) hinfallen; (*thing*) herunter|fallen. **2.** (*along*): **I'm going ~ to the shops** ich gehe zum Einkaufen. **3.** (*downstairs*) herunter, nach unten; **I'll come ~ later** ich komme später herunter. **4.** (*southwards*) hinunter/herunter; **we're going ~ to London** wir fahren hinunter nach London; **they're coming ~ from Manchester** sie kommen von Manchester herunter. **5.** (*in writing*): **to write sthg ~** etw auf|schreiben. ◆ *prep* **1.** (*towards the bottom of*): **they ran ~ the hill** sie liefen den Hügel herunter; **to fall ~ the stairs** die Treppe hinunter|fallen. **2.** (*along*) entlang; **I was walking ~ the street** ich

lief gerade die Straße entlang. ◆ *adj* (*inf: depressed*) down. ◆ *n* (*feathers*) Daunen *pl*. ► **downs** *npl* (Br) Hügelland *das*.

downhill [ˌdaun'hɪl] *adv* bergab.

downhill racing *n* Abfahrtslauf *der*.

Downing Street ['daunɪŋ-] *n* Downing Street *die Straße, in der sich der offizielle Wohnsitz des britischen Premierministers und Schatzkanzlers befindet.*

downpour ['daunpɔːr] *n* Regenguß *der*.

downstairs [ˌdaun'steəz] *adv* unten; **to go ~** nach unten gehen.

downtown [ˌdaun'taun] *adj & adv* in der Innenstadt; **to go ~** in die Stadt gehen; **~ New York** die Innenstadt von New York.

down under *adv* (Br: *inf*) in Australien.

downwards ['daunwədz] *adv* nach unten.

doz. *abbr* = **dozen**.

doze [dəuz] *vi* dösen.

dozen ['dʌzn] *n* Dutzend *das*; **a ~ eggs** zwölf Eier.

Dr (*abbr of Doctor*) Dr.

drab [dræb] *adj* trist.

draft [drɑːft] *n* (*early version*) Entwurf *der*; (*money order*) Überweisung *die*; (*Am*) = **draught**.

drag [dræg] ◆ *vt* schleppen. ◆ *vi* (*along ground*) schleifen; **what a ~!** (*inf*) ist das langweilig! ► **drag on** *vi* sich in die Länge ziehen.

dragonfly ['drægnflaɪ] *n* Libelle *die*.

drain [dreɪn] ◆ *n* (*sewer*) Abflußrohr *das*; (*grating in street*) Gully *der*. ◆ *vt* (*tank, radiator*) Wasser ab|lassen von. ◆ *vi* (*vegetables, washing-up*) ab|tropfen.

draining board ['dreɪnɪŋ-] *n* Abtropffläche *die*.

drainpipe ['dreɪnpaɪp] *n* (*for rain water*) Regenrohr *das*; (*for waste water*) Abwasserleitung *die*.

drama ['drɑːmə] *n* Drama *das*; (*art*) Dramatik *die*.

dramatic [drə'mætɪk] *adj* dramatisch.

drank [dræŋk] *pt* → **drink**.

drapes [dreɪps] *npl* (Am) Vorhänge *pl*.

drastic ['dræstɪk] *adj* drastisch.

drastically ['dræstɪklɪ] *adv* drastisch.

draught [drɑːft] *n* (Br: *of air*) Luftzug *der*.

draught beer *n* Faßbier *das*.

draughts [drɑːfts] *n* (Br) Damespiel *das*.

draughty ['drɑːftɪ] *adj* zugig.

draw [drɔː] (*pt* **drew**, *pp* **drawn**) ◆ *vt* ziehen; (*picture, map*) zeichnen; (*attract*) anlziehen. ◆ *vi* (*with pen, pencil*) zeichnen; (SPORT) unentschieden spielen. ◆ *n* (SPORT: *result*) Unentschieden *das*; (*lottery*) Ziehung *die*; **to ~ the curtains** (*open*) die Vorhänge auflziehen; (*close*) die Vorhänge zulziehen. ▶ **draw out** *vt sep* (*money*) ablheben. ▶ **draw up** *vt sep* (*list*) auflstellen; (*plan*) entwerfen. ◆ *vi* (*car, bus*) anlhalten.

drawback ['drɔːbæk] *n* Nachteil *der*.

drawer [drɔːr] *n* Schublade *die*.

drawing ['drɔːɪŋ] *n* (*picture*) Zeichnung *die*; (*activity*) Zeichnen *das*.

drawing pin *n* (Br) Reißzwecke *die*.

drawing room *n* Wohnzimmer *das*.

drawn [drɔːn] *pp* → **draw**.

dreadful ['dredfʊl] *adj* schrecklich.

dream [driːm] ◆ *n* Traum *der*. ◆ *vt* & *vi* träumen; **a ~ house** ein Traumhaus.

dress [dres] ◆ *n* Kleid *das*; (*clothes*) Kleidung *die*. ◆ *vt* anlziehen; (*wound*) verbinden; (*salad*) anlmachen. ◆ *vi* sich anlziehen; **he was ~ed in a black suit** er trug einen schwarzen Anzug; **to get ~ed** sich anlziehen. ▶ **dress up** *vi* (*in smart clothes*) sich feinlmachen; (*in costume*) sich verkleiden.

dress circle *n* erster Rang.

dresser ['dresər] *n* (Br: *for crockery*) Büffet *das*; (Am: *chest of drawers*) Kommode *die*.

dressing ['dresɪŋ] *n* (*for salad*) Soße *die*; (*for wound*) Verband *der*.

dressing gown *n* Morgenrock *der*.

dressing room *n* (*for actors*) Künstlergarderobe *die*; (*for players*) Umkleidekabine *die*.

dressing table *n* Frisierkommode *die*.

dressmaker ['dres,meɪkər] *n* Damenschneider *der* (-in *die*).

dress rehearsal *n* Generalprobe *die*.

drew [druː] *pt* → **draw**.

dribble ['drɪbl] *vi* (*liquid*) tropfen; (*baby*) sabbern.

drier ['draɪər] = **dryer**.

drift [drɪft] ◆ *n* (*of snow*) Schneewehe *die*. ◆ *vi* treiben.

drill [drɪl] ◆ *n* Bohrer *der*. ◆ *vt* (*hole*) bohren.

drink [drɪŋk] (*pt* **drank**, *pp* **drunk**) ◆ *n* Getränk *das*; (*alcoholic*) Drink *der*. ◆ *vt* & *vi* trinken; **to have a ~** (*alcoholic*) einen trinken; **to ~ to sb/sthg** auf jn/etw trinken.

drinkable ['drɪŋkəbl] *adj* trinkbar.

drinking water ['drɪŋkɪŋ-] *n* Trinkwasser *das*.

drip [drɪp] ◆ *n* Tropfen *der*. ◆ *vi* tropfen; **to be on a ~** eine Infusion bekommen.

drip-dry *adj* bügelfrei.

dripping (wet) ['drɪpɪŋ-] *adj* tropfnaß.

drive [draɪv] (*pt* **drove**, *pp* **driven**) ◆ *n* Fahrt *die*; (*in front of house*) Einfahrt *die*. ◆ *vt* fahren; (*operate, power*) anltreiben. ◆ *vi* fahren; **to ~ sb to do sthg** jn dazu bringen, etw zu tun; **to go for a ~** spazierenlfahren; **to ~ sb mad** jn verrückt machen.

drivel ['drɪvl] *n* Blödsinn *der*.

driven ['drɪvn] *pp* → **drive**.

driver ['draɪvər] *n* Fahrer *der* (-in *die*); (*of train*) Führer *der* (-in *die*).

driver's license (Am) = **driving licence**.

driveshaft ['draɪvʃɑːft] n Antriebswelle die.

driveway ['draɪvweɪ] n Zufahrt die.

driving lesson ['draɪvɪŋ-] n Fahrstunde die.

driving licence ['draɪvɪŋ-] n (Br) Führerschein der.

driving test ['draɪvɪŋ-] n Fahrprüfung die.

drizzle ['drɪzl] n Sprühregen der.

drop [drɒp] ♦ n (of liquid) Tropfen der; (distance down) Höhenunterschied der; (decrease) Rückgang der; (in value, wages) Minderung die. ♦ vt fallen lassen; (reduce) senken; (from vehicle) ablsetzen; (omit) wegllassen. ♦ vi fallen; (decrease) sinken; **to ~ a hint** eine Anspielung machen; **to ~ sb a line** jm ein paar Zeilen schreiben. ► **drop in** vi (inf) vorbeilkommen. ► **drop off** vt sep (from vehicle) ablsetzen. ♦ vi (fall asleep) einlnicken; (fall off) ablfallen. ► **drop out** vi (of college, race) ablbrechen.

drought [draʊt] n Dürre die.

drove [drəʊv] pt → **drive**.

drown [draʊn] vi ertrinken.

drug [drʌg] ♦ n (MED) Medikament das; (stimulant) Droge die. ♦ vt betäuben.

drug addict n Drogenabhängige der die.

druggist ['drʌgɪst] n (Am) Drogist der (-in die).

drum [drʌm] n Trommel die.

drummer ['drʌmər] n Schlagzeuger der (-in die).

drumstick ['drʌmstɪk] n (of chicken) Keule die.

drunk [drʌŋk] ♦ pp → **drink**. ♦ adj betrunken. ♦ n Betrunkene der die; **to get ~** sich betrinken.

dry [draɪ] ♦ adj trocken. ♦ vt (hands, washing-up) abltrocknen; (clothes) trocknen. ♦ vi trocknen; **to ~ o.s.** sich abltrocknen; **to ~ one's hair** sich

(D) die Haare trocknen. ► **dry up** vi auslltrocknen; (dry the dishes) abltrocknen.

dry-clean vt chemisch reinigen.

dry cleaner's n chemische Reinigung.

dryer ['draɪər] n (for clothes) Wäschetrockner der; (for hair) Fön® der.

dry-roasted peanuts [-'rəʊstɪd] npl ohne Fett geröstete Erdnüsse pl.

DSS n (Br) Amt für Sozialwesen.

DTP n (abbr of desktop publishing) DTP das.

dual carriageway ['djuːəl-] n (Br) vierspurige Straße.

dubbed [dʌbd] adj (film) synchronisiert.

dubious ['djuːbjəs] adj zweifelhaft.

duchess ['dʌtʃɪs] n Herzogin die.

duck [dʌk] ♦ n Ente die. ♦ vi sich ducken.

due [djuː] adj fällig; (owed) geschuldet; **in ~ course** zu gegebener Zeit; **~ to** aufgrund (+G); **to be ~** (train) planmäßig ankommen.

duet [djuː'et] n Duett das.

duffel bag ['dʌfl-] n Seesack der.

duffel coat ['dʌfl-] n Dufflecoat der.

dug [dʌg] pt & pp → **dig**.

duke [djuːk] n Herzog der.

dull [dʌl] adj (boring) langweilig; (colour) fahl; (weather) trüb; (pain) dumpf.

dumb [dʌm] adj (inf: stupid) doof; (unable to speak) stumm.

dummy ['dʌmi] n (Br: for baby) Schnuller der; (for clothes) Schaufensterpuppe die.

dump [dʌmp] ♦ n (for rubbish) Müllkippe die; (inf: place) Schweinestall der. ♦ vt (drop carelessly) fallen lassen; (get rid of) loslwerden.

dumpling ['dʌmplɪŋ] n Knödel der.

dune [djuːn] n Düne die.

dungarees [,dʌŋgə'riːz] npl Latzhose die; (Am: jeans) Arbeitsjeans pl.

dungeon ['dʌndʒən] *n* Kerker *der*.

duplicate ['dju:plɪkət] *n* Duplikat *das*.

during ['djʊərɪŋ] *prep* während (+G).

dusk [dʌsk] *n* Abenddämmerung *die*.

dust [dʌst] ◆ *n* Staub *der*. ◆ *vt* ab|stauben.

dustbin ['dʌstbɪn] *n* (Br) Mülltonne *die*.

dustcart ['dʌstkɑ:t] *n* (Br) Müllwagen *der*.

duster ['dʌstər] *n* Staubtuch *das*.

dustman ['dʌstmən] (*pl* -men [-mən]) *n* (Br) Müllmann *der*.

dustpan ['dʌstpæn] *n* Kehrschaufel *die*.

dusty ['dʌstɪ] *adj* staubig.

Dutch [dʌtʃ] ◆ *adj* holländisch. ◆ *n* Holländisch *das*. ◆ *npl*: **the** ~ die Holländer *pl*.

Dutchman ['dʌtʃmən] (*pl* -men [-mən]) *n* Holländer *der*.

Dutchwoman ['dʌtʃˌwʊmən] (*pl* -women [-ˌwɪmɪn]) *n* Holländerin *die*.

duty ['dju:tɪ] *n* Pflicht *die*; (*tax*) Zoll *der*; **to be on** ~ Dienst haben; **to be off** ~ keinen Dienst haben. ▶ **duties** *npl* (*job*) Aufgaben *pl*.

duty chemist's *n* Apotheke *die* mit Notdienst.

duty-free ◆ *adj* zollfrei. ◆ *n* (*shop*) Duty-free-Shop *der*; (*goods*) zollfreie Waren *pl*.

duty-free shop *n* Duty-free-Shop *der*.

duvet ['du:veɪ] *n* Bettdecke *die*.

dwarf [dwɔ:f] (*pl* **dwarves** [dwɔ:vz]) *n* Zwerg *der*.

dwelling ['dwelɪŋ] *n* (*fml*) Wohnung *die*.

dye [daɪ] ◆ *n* Farbe *die*. ◆ *vt* färben.

dynamite ['daɪnəmaɪt] *n* Dynamit *das*.

dynamo ['daɪnəməʊ] (*pl* -s) *n* (*on bike*) Dynamo *der*.

dyslexic [dɪs'leksɪk] *adj*: **to be** ~ Legastheniker sein.

E (*abbr of east*) O.

E111 *n* E111 Formular *das*.

each [i:tʃ] ◆ *adj* jede(-r)(-s). ◆ *pron*: ~ **(one)** jede(-r)(-s); ~ **other** einander; **there's one** ~ es ist für jeden eins da; **I'd like one of** ~ ich möchte von jedem/jeder eins; **they cost £10** ~ sie kosten je 10 Pfund.

eager ['i:gər] *adj* eifrig; **to be** ~ **to do sthg** unbedingt etw tun wollen.

eagle ['i:gl] *n* Adler *der*.

ear [ɪər] *n* Ohr *das*; (*of corn*) Ähre *die*.

earache ['ɪəreɪk] *n*: **to have** ~ Ohrenschmerzen haben.

earl [ɜ:l] *n* Graf *der*.

early ['ɜ:lɪ] *adj & adv* früh; **at the earliest** frühestens; ~ **on** schon früh; **to have an** ~ **night** früh zu Bett gehen.

earn [ɜ:n] *vt* verdienen; **to** ~ **a living** seinen Lebensunterhalt verdienen.

earnings ['ɜ:nɪŋz] *npl* Einkommen *das*.

earphones ['ɪəfəʊnz] *npl* Kopfhörer *pl*.

earplugs ['ɪəplʌgz] *npl* Ohropax® *pl*.

earrings ['ɪərɪŋz] *npl* Ohrringe *pl*.

earth [ɜ:θ] ◆ *n* Erde *die*. ◆ *vt* (Br: *appliance*) erden; **how on** ~ ...? wie in aller Welt ...?

earthenware ['ɜ:θnweər] *adj* aus Steingut.

earthquake ['ɜ:θkweɪk] *n* Erdbeben *das*.

ease [i:z] ◆ *n* Leichtigkeit *die*. ◆ *vt* (*pain*) lindern; (*problem*) verringern; **at** ~ unbefangen. ▶ **ease off** *vi* (*pain, rain*) nach|lassen.

easily ['i:zɪlɪ] *adv* leicht.

east [iːst] ◆ n Osten der. ◆ adv nach Osten; (be situated) im Osten; **in the ~ of England** im Osten Englands; **the East** (Asia) der Osten.

eastbound ['iːstbaʊnd] adj (in) Richtung Osten.

Easter ['iːstər] n Ostern das.

eastern ['iːstən] adj östlich, Ost-; **Eastern** (Asian) östlich, Ost-.

Eastern Europe n Osteuropa nt.

East Germany n Ostdeutschland nt.

eastwards ['iːstwədz] adv ostwärts.

easy ['iːzɪ] adj leicht, einfach; **to take it ~** sich schonen.

easygoing [ˌiːzɪ'gəʊɪŋ] adj gelassen.

eat [iːt] (pt **ate**, pp **eaten** ['iːtn]) vt & vi essen; (subj: animal) fressen. ► **eat out** vi essen gehen.

eating apple ['iːtɪŋ-] n Eßapfel der.

ebony ['ebənɪ] n Ebenholz das.

EC n (abbr of European Community) EG die.

eccentric [ɪk'sentrɪk] adj exzentrisch.

echo ['ekəʊ] (pl -es) ◆ n Echo das. ◆ vi widerǀhallen.

ecology [ɪ'kɒlədʒɪ] n Ökologie die.

economic [ˌiːkə'nɒmɪk] adj wirtschaftlich. ► **economics** n Wirtschaftswissenschaften pl.

economical [ˌiːkə'nɒmɪkl] adj wirtschaftlich; (person) sparsam.

economize [ɪ'kɒnəmaɪz] vi sparsam sein.

economy [ɪ'kɒnəmɪ] n (of country) Wirtschaft die; (saving) Sparsamkeit die.

economy class n Touristenklasse die.

economy size adj Spar-.

ecstasy ['ekstəsɪ] n Ekstase die; (drug) Ecstasy das.

ECU ['ekjuː] n Ecu der.

eczema ['eksɪmə] n Ekzem das.

edge [edʒ] n Rand der; (of knife) Schneide die.

edible ['edɪbl] adj eßbar.

Edinburgh ['edɪnbrə] n Edinburg nt.

Edinburgh Festival n: **the ~** großes Musik- und Theaterfestival in Edinburg.

edition [ɪ'dɪʃn] n Ausgabe die.

editor ['edɪtər] n (of newspaper, magazine) Chefredakteur der (-in die); (of book) Redakteur der (-in die); (of film, TV programme) Cutter der (-in die).

editorial [ˌedɪ'tɔːrɪəl] n Leitartikel der.

educate ['edʒʊkeɪt] vt erziehen.

education [ˌedʒʊ'keɪʃn] n (field) Ausbildung die; (process) Erziehung die; (result) Bildung die.

EEC n EWG die.

eel [iːl] n Aal der.

effect [ɪ'fekt] n Wirkung die; **to put sthg into ~** etw in Kraft setzen; **to take ~** in Kraft treten.

effective [ɪ'fektɪv] adj wirksam.

effectively [ɪ'fektɪvlɪ] adv wirksam; (in fact) effektiv.

efficient [ɪ'fɪʃənt] adj tüchtig; (machine, organization) leistungsfähig.

effort ['efət] n (exertion) Anstrengung die; (attempt) Versuch der; **to make an ~ to do sthg** sich bemühen, etw zu tun; **it's not worth the ~** es ist nicht der Mühe wert.

e.g. adv z.B.

egg [eg] n Ei das.

egg cup n Eierbecher der.

egg mayonnaise n Brotaufstrich aus gehacktem Ei und Mayonnaise.

eggplant ['egplɑːnt] n (Am) Aubergine die.

egg white n Eiweiß das.

egg yolk n Eigelb das.

Egypt ['iːdʒɪpt] n Ägypten nt.

eiderdown ['aɪdədaʊn] n Daunendecke die.

eight [eɪt] num acht, → **six**.

eighteen [ˌeɪ'tiːn] num achtzehn, → **six**.

eighteenth [ˌeɪ'tiːnθ] num achtzehnte(-r)(-s), → **sixth**.

eighth [eɪtθ] *num* achte(-r)(-s), → sixth.

eightieth ['eɪtɪɪθ] *num* achtzigste(-r) (-s), → sixth.

eighty ['eɪtɪ] *num* achtzig, → six.

Eire ['eərə] *n* Irland *nt*.

Eisteddfod [aɪ'stedfəd] *n* walisisches Kulturfestival.

either ['aɪðəʳ, 'iːðəʳ] ♦ *adj*: ~ book will do beide Bücher sind okay. ♦ *pron*: I'll take ~ (of them) ich nehme einen/eine/eins (von beiden); I don't like ~ (of them) ich mag keinen/keine/keins (von beiden). ♦ *adv*: I can't ~ ich auch nicht; ~ ... or entweder ... oder; I don't like ~ him or her ich mag weder ihn noch sie; on ~ side auf beiden Seiten.

eject [ɪ'dʒekt] *vt (cassette)* auslwerfen.

elaborate [ɪ'læbrət] *adj* kunstvoll.

elastic [ɪ'læstɪk] *n* Gummi *der* or *das*.

elastic band *n* (Br) Gummiband *das*.

elbow ['elbəʊ] *n* Ellbogen *der*.

elder ['eldəʳ] *adj* ältere(-r) (-s).

elderly ['eldəlɪ] ♦ *adj* ältere(-r) (-s). ♦ *npl*: the ~ die ältere Generation.

eldest ['eldɪst] *adj* älteste(-r) (-s).

elect [ɪ'lekt] *vt* wählen; to ~ to do sthg *(fml: choose)* sich entscheiden, etw zu tun.

election [ɪ'lekʃn] *n* Wahl *die*.

electric [ɪ'lektrɪk] *adj* elektrisch.

electrical goods [ɪ'lektrɪkl-] *npl* Elektrowaren *pl*.

electric blanket *n* Heizdecke *die*.

electric drill *n* Bohrmaschine *die*.

electric fence *n* Elektrozaun *der*.

electrician [ˌɪlek'trɪʃn] *n* Elektriker *der* (-in *die*).

electricity [ˌɪlek'trɪsətɪ] *n (supply)* Strom *der*; *(in physics)* Elektrizität *die*.

electric shock *n* elektrischer Schlag.

electrocute [ɪ'lektrəkjuːt] *vt* durch einen elektrischen Schlag töten.

electronic [ˌɪlek'trɒnɪk] *adj* elektronisch.

elegant ['elɪgənt] *adj* elegant.

element ['elɪmənt] *n* Element *das*; *(degree)* Spur *die*; *(of fire, kettle)* Heizelement *das*; the ~s *(weather)* die Elemente.

elementary [ˌelɪ'mentərɪ] *adj* elementar.

elephant ['elɪfənt] *n* Elefant *der*.

elevator ['elɪveɪtəʳ] *n* (Am) Aufzug *der*.

eleven [ɪ'levn] *num* elf, → six.

eleventh [ɪ'levnθ] *num* elfte(-r) (-s), → sixth.

eligible ['elɪdʒəbl] *adj (qualified)* berechtigt.

eliminate [ɪ'lɪmɪneɪt] *vt* auslschalten.

Elizabethan [ɪˌlɪzə'biːθn] *adj* elisabethanisch *(zweite Hälfte des 16. Jh)*.

elm [elm] *n* Ulme *die*.

else [els] *adv*: I don't want anything ~ ich will nichts mehr; anything ~? sonst noch etwas?; *(in shop)* kommt noch etwas dazu?; everyone ~ alle anderen; nobody ~ niemand anders; nothing ~ sonst nichts; somebody ~ *(additional person)* noch jemand anders; *(different person)* jemand anders; something ~ *(additional thing)* noch etwas; *(different thing)* etwas anders; somewhere ~ woanders; to go somewhere ~ woandershin gehen; what ~? was sonst?; who ~? wer sonst?; or ~ sonst.

elsewhere [els'weəʳ] *adv* woanders; *(go, move)* woandershin.

embankment [ɪm'bæŋkmənt] *n (next to river, railway)* Damm *der*; *(next to road)* Böschung *die*.

embark [ɪm'bɑːk] *vi (board ship)* an Bord gehen.

embarkation card [ˌembɑː'keɪʃn-] *n* Bordkarte *die*.

embarrass [ɪm'bærəs] *vt* in Verlegenheit bringen.

embarrassed [ɪm'bærəst] *adj* verlegen.

embarrassing [ɪm'bærəsɪŋ] *adj* peinlich.

embarrassment [ɪmˈbærəsmənt] n Verlegenheit die.

embassy [ˈembəsɪ] n Botschaft die.

emblem [ˈembləm] n Emblem das.

embrace [ɪmˈbreɪs] vt umarmen.

embroidered [ɪmˈbrɔɪdəd] adj bestickt.

embroidery [ɪmˈbrɔɪdərɪ] n Stickerei die.

emerald [ˈemərəld] n Smaragd der.

emerge [ɪˈmɜːdʒ] vi herauskommen; (fact, truth) sich herausstellen.

emergency [ɪˈmɜːdʒənsɪ] ◆ n Notfall der. ◆ adj Not-; **in an ~** im Notfall.

emergency exit n Notausgang der.

emergency landing n Notlandung die.

emergency services npl Notdienst der.

emigrate [ˈemɪɡreɪt] vi auswandern.

emit [ɪˈmɪt] vt (light) ausstrahlen; (gas) ausströmen.

emotion [ɪˈməʊʃn] n Gefühl das.

emotional [ɪˈməʊʃənl] adj (situation) emotionsgeladen; (person) gefühlsbetont.

emphasis [ˈemfəsɪs] (pl -ases [-əsiːz]) n Betonung die.

emphasize [ˈemfəsaɪz] vt betonen.

empire [ˈempaɪəʳ] n Reich das.

employ [ɪmˈplɔɪ] vt (subj: company) beschäftigen; (fml: use) benutzen.

employed [ɪmˈplɔɪd] adj angestellt.

employee [ɪmˈplɔɪiː] n Angestellte der, die.

employer [ɪmˈplɔɪəʳ] n Arbeitgeber der (-in die).

employment [ɪmˈplɔɪmənt] n Arbeit die.

employment agency n Stellenvermittlung die.

empty [ˈemptɪ] ◆ adj leer. ◆ vt leeren.

EMU n EWU die.

emulsion (paint) [ɪˈmʌlʃn-] n Emulsionsfarbe die.

enable [ɪˈneɪbl] vt: **to ~ sb to do sthg** jm ermöglichen, etw zu tun.

enamel [ɪˈnæml] n (decorative) Email das; (on tooth) Zahnschmelz der.

enclose [ɪnˈkləʊz] vt (surround) umgeben; (with letter) beilegen.

enclosed [ɪnˈkləʊzd] adj (space) abgeschlossen.

encounter [ɪnˈkaʊntəʳ] vt (experience) stoßen auf (+A); (fml: meet) begegnen (+D).

encourage [ɪnˈkʌrɪdʒ] vt ermutigen; **to ~ sb to do sthg** jm Mut machen, etw zu tun.

encouragement [ɪnˈkʌrɪdʒmənt] n Ermutigung die.

encyclopedia [ɪnˌsaɪkləˈpiːdjə] n Lexikon das.

end [end] ◆ n Ende das; (of finger, knife) Spitze die; (purpose) Ziel das. ◆ vt beenden. ◆ vi enden; **at the ~ of April** Ende April; **to come to an ~** zu Ende gehen; **to put an ~ to sthg** etw beenden; **for days on ~** tagelang; **in the ~** schließlich; **to make ~s meet** gerade auskommen. ▶ **end up** vi landen; **to ~ up doing sthg** schließlich etw tun.

endangered species [ɪnˈdeɪndʒəd-] n (vom Aussterben) bedrohte Art.

ending [ˈendɪŋ] n Schluß der, Ende das; (GRAMM) Endung die.

endive [ˈendaɪv] n (curly) Endivie die; (chicory) Chicorée der.

endless [ˈendlɪs] adj endlos.

endorsement [ɪnˈdɔːsmənt] n (of driving licence) Strafvermerk der.

endurance [ɪnˈdjʊərəns] n Ausdauer die.

endure [ɪnˈdjʊəʳ] vt ertragen.

enemy [ˈenɪmɪ] n Feind der.

energy [ˈenədʒɪ] n Energie die.

enforce [ɪnˈfɔːs] vt durchsetzen.

engaged [ɪnˈɡeɪdʒd] adj (to be married) verlobt; (Br: phone, toilet) besetzt; **to get ~** sich verloben.

engaged tone n (Br) Besetztzeichen das.

engagement [ɪnˈgeɪdʒmənt] n (to marry) Verlobung die; (appointment) Verabredung die.

engagement ring n Verlobungsring der.

engine [ˈendʒɪn] n Motor der; (of train) Lokomotive die.

engineer [ˌendʒɪˈnɪər] n Ingenieur der (-in die).

engineering [ˌendʒɪˈnɪərɪŋ] n Technik die.

engineering works npl (on railway line) technische Bauarbeiten pl.

England [ˈɪŋglənd] n England nt.

English [ˈɪŋglɪʃ] ◆ adj englisch. ◆ n Englisch das. ◆ npl: **the ~** die Engländer pl.

English breakfast n englisches Frühstück (mit gebratenem Speck, Würstchen, Eiern, Toast und Kaffee oder Tee).

English Channel n: **the ~** der Ärmelkanal.

Englishman [ˈɪŋglɪʃmən] (pl -men [-mən]) n Engländer der.

Englishwoman [ˈɪŋglɪʃˌwumən] (pl -women [-ˌwɪmɪn]) n Engländerin die.

engrave [ɪnˈgreɪv] vt gravieren.

engraving [ɪnˈgreɪvɪŋ] n Stich der.

enjoy [ɪnˈdʒɔɪ] vt genießen; (film, music, hobby) mögen; **to ~ doing sthg** etw gerne tun; **to ~ o.s.** sich amüsieren; **~ your meal!** guten Appetit!

enjoyable [ɪnˈdʒɔɪəbl] adj nett.

enjoyment [ɪnˈdʒɔɪmənt] n Vergnügen das.

enlargement [ɪnˈlɑːdʒmənt] n Vergrößerung die.

enormous [ɪˈnɔːməs] adj riesig.

enough [ɪˈnʌf] adj, pron & adv genug; **~ time** Zeit genug; **is that ~?** reicht das?; **to have had ~ (of sthg)** genug (von etw) haben.

enquire [ɪnˈkwaɪər] vi: **to ~ (about)** sich erkundigen (nach).

enquiry [ɪnˈkwaɪərɪ] n (question)

Anfrage die; (investigation) Untersuchung die; **'Enquiries'** 'Information', 'Auskunft'.

enquiry desk n Informationsschalter der.

enrol [ɪnˈrəul] vi (Br) sich einlschreiben.

enroll [ɪnˈrəul] (Am) = **enrol**.

en suite bathroom [ɒnˈswiːt-] n Zimmer das mit Bad.

ensure [ɪnˈʃuər] vt sicherlstellen; **to ~ (that)** ... dafür sorgen, daß ...

entail [ɪnˈteɪl] vt (involve) mit sich bringen.

enter [ˈentər] ◆ vt gehen in (+A); (plane, bus) einlsteigen in (+A); (college, army) einltreten in (+A); (competition) teillnehmen an (+D); (on form) einltragen. ◆ vi hereinlkommen; (in competition) teillnehmen.

enterprise [ˈentəpraɪz] n Unternehmen das.

entertain [ˌentəˈteɪn] vt unterhalten.

entertainer [ˌentəˈteɪnər] n Entertainer der.

entertaining [ˌentəˈteɪnɪŋ] adj unterhaltsam.

entertainment [ˌentəˈteɪnmənt] n Unterhaltung die.

enthusiasm [ɪnˈθjuːzɪæzm] n Begeisterung die.

enthusiast [ɪnˈθjuːzɪæst] n Enthusiast der (-in die).

enthusiastic [ɪnˌθjuːzɪˈæstɪk] adj enthusiastisch.

entire [ɪnˈtaɪər] adj ganze(-r)(-s).

entirely [ɪnˈtaɪəlɪ] adv völlig.

entitle [ɪnˈtaɪtl] vt: **to ~ sb to sthg** jn zu etw berechtigen; **to ~ sb to do sthg** jn berechtigen, etw zu tun.

entrance [ˈentrəns] n Eingang der; (admission) Zutritt der.

entrance fee n Eintrittspreis der.

entry [ˈentrɪ] n Eingang der; (admission) Zutritt der; (in dictionary) Eintrag der; (in competition) Einsendung die; **'no ~'** 'Eintritt verboten'.

envelope [ˈenvələup] n

Briefumschlag *der*.

envious ['enviəs] *adj* neidisch.

environment [in'vaiərənmənt] *n* Umwelt *die*.

environmental [in,vaiərən'mentl] *adj* Umwelt-.

environmentalist [in,vaiərən-'mentəlist] *n* Umweltschützer *der* (-in *die*).

environmentally friendly [in-,vaiərən'mentəli-] *adj* umweltfreundlich.

envy ['envi] *vt* beneiden.

epic ['epik] *n* Epos *das*.

epidemic [,epi'demik] *n* Epidemie *die*.

epileptic [,epi'leptik] *adj* epileptisch.

episode ['episəud] *n* Episode *die*; (*of* TV *programme*) Folge *die*.

equal ['iːkwəl] ◆ *adj* gleich. ◆ *vt* gleich sein; **to be ~ to** gleich sein.

equality [ɪ'kwɒləti] *n* (*equal rights*) Gleichberechtigung *die*.

equalize ['iːkwəlaiz] *vi* (SPORT) ausgleichen.

equally ['iːkwəli] *adv* gleich; (*share*) gleichmäßig; (*at the same time*) ebenso.

equation [ɪ'kweiʒn] *n* Gleichung *die*.

equator [ɪ'kweitə^r] *n*: **the ~** der Äquator.

equip [ɪ'kwip] *vt*: **to ~ sb/sthg with** jn/etw ausIrüsten mit.

equipment [ɪ'kwipmənt] *n* AusIrüstung *die*.

equipped [ɪ'kwipt] *adj*: **to be ~ with** ausgerüstet sein mit.

equivalent [ɪ'kwivələnt] ◆ *adj* gleichwertig. ◆ *n* Äquivalent *das*.

erase [ɪ'reiz] *vt* (*letter*, *word*) ausIradieren.

eraser [ɪ'reizə^r] *n* Radiergummi *der*.

erect [ɪ'rekt] ◆ *adj* (*person*, *posture*) aufrecht. ◆ *vt* aufIstellen.

ERM *n* Wechselkursmechanismus *der*.

erotic [ɪ'rɒtik] *adj* erotisch.

errand ['erənd] *n* Besorgung *die*.

erratic [ɪ'rætik] *adj* unregelmäßig.

error ['erə^r] *n* Fehler *der*.

escalator ['eskəleitə^r] *n* Rolltreppe *die*.

escalope ['eskələp] *n* Schnitzel *das*.

escape [ɪ'skeip] ◆ *n* Flucht *die*; (*of gas*) Ausströmen *das*. ◆ *vi*: **to ~ (from)** entkommen (aus); (*gas*) ausIströmen (aus); (*water*) ausIlaufen (aus).

escort [*n* 'eskɔːt, *vb* ɪ'skɔːt] ◆ *n* (*guard*) Eskorte *die*. ◆ *vt* begleiten.

espadrilles ['espə,drilz] *npl* Espadrilles *pl*.

especially [ɪ'speʃəli] *adv* besonders.

esplanade [,esplə'neid] *n* Esplanade *die*.

essay ['esei] *n* (*at school, university*) Aufsatz *die*.

essential [ɪ'senʃl] *adj* wesentlich. ▸ **essentials** *npl* Wesentliche *das*; **the bare ~s** das Nötigste.

essentially [ɪ'senʃəli] *adv* im Grunde.

establish [ɪ'stæbliʃ] *vt* (*set up, create*) gründen; (*fact, truth*) herausIfinden.

establishment [ɪ'stæbliʃmənt] *n* (*business*) Unternehmen *das*.

estate [ɪ'steit] *n* (*land in country*) Landsitz *der*; (*for housing*) Wohnsiedlung *die*; (Br: *car*) = **estate car**.

estate agent *n* (Br) Immobilienmakler *der*.

estate car *n* (Br) Kombiwagen *der*.

estimate [*n* 'estimət, *vb* 'estimeit] ◆ *n* Schätzung *die*; (*of cost*) Kostenvoranschlag *der*. ◆ *vt* schätzen.

estuary ['estjuəri] *n* Mündung *die*.

ethnic minority ['eθnik-] *n* ethnische Minderheit.

EU *n* (*abbr of* European Union) EU *die*.

Eurocheque ['juərəu,tʃek] *n* Euroscheck *der*.

Eurocheque card *n* Euroscheckkarte *die*.

Europe ['jʊərəp] n Europa nt.

European [,jʊərə'pɪən] ♦ adj europäisch. ♦ n Europäer der (-in die).

European Community n Europäische Gemeinschaft die.

evacuate [ɪ'vækjʊeɪt] vt evakuieren.

evade [ɪ'veɪd] vt vermeiden.

evaporated milk [ɪ'væpəreɪtɪd-] n Kondensmilch die.

eve [iːv] n: **on the ~ of** am Vorabend (+G).

even ['iːvn] ♦ adj (rate, speed) gleichmäßig; (level, flat) eben; (teams) gleich stark; (number) gerade. ♦ adv sogar; **to break ~** die Kosten decken; **~ so** trotzdem; **~ though** obwohl; **not ~** nicht einmal.

evening ['iːvnɪŋ] n Abend der; **good ~!** guten Abend!; **in the ~** am Abend, abends.

evening classes npl Abendkursus der.

evening dress n (formal clothes) Gesellschaftskleidung die; (woman's garment) Abendkleid das.

evening meal n Abendessen das, Abendbrot das.

event [ɪ'vent] n Ereignis das; (SPORT) Wettkampf der; **in the ~ of** (fml) im Falle (+G).

eventual [ɪ'ventʃʊəl] adj: **the ~ decision was ...** schließlich wurde entschieden, daß ...

eventually [ɪ'ventʃʊəlɪ] adv schließlich.

ever ['evər] adv (at any time) je, jemals; **he was ~ so angry** er war sehr verärgert; **for ~** (eternally) für immer; (for a long time) seit Ewigkeiten; **hardly ~** fast nie; **~ since** seitdem, seit.

every ['evrɪ] adj jede(-r) (-s); **~ other day** jeden zweiten Tag; **~ few days** alle paar Tage; **one in ~ ten** einen/ eine/eins von zehn; **we make ~ effort ...** wir geben uns alle Mühe ...; **~ so often** dann und wann.

everybody ['evrɪ,bɒdɪ] = **everyone**.

everyday ['evrɪdeɪ] adj alltäglich.

everyone ['evrɪwʌn] pron alle; (each person) jeder.

everyplace ['evrɪ,pleɪs] (Am) = **everywhere**.

everything ['evrɪθɪŋ] pron alles.

everywhere ['evrɪweər] adv überall; (go) überallhin.

evidence ['evɪdəns] n (proof) Beweis der; (of witness) Aussage die.

evident ['evɪdənt] adj klar.

evidently ['evɪdəntlɪ] adv offensichtlich.

evil ['iːvl] ♦ adj böse. ♦ n Böse das.

ex [eks] n (inf) Verflossene der die.

exact [ɪg'zækt] adj genau; **'~ fare ready please'** 'Bitte das genaue Fahrgeld bereithalten'.

exactly [ɪg'zæktlɪ] adv & excl genau.

exaggerate [ɪg'zædʒəreɪt] vt & vi übertreiben.

exaggeration [ɪg,zædʒə'reɪʃn] n Übertreibung die.

exam [ɪg'zæm] n Prüfung die; **to take an ~** eine Prüfung abllegen.

examination [ɪg,zæmɪ'neɪʃn] n (at school) Prüfung die; (at university) Examen das; (MED) Untersuchung die.

examine [ɪg'zæmɪn] vt untersuchen.

example [ɪg'zɑːmpl] n Beispiel das; **for ~** zum Beispiel.

exceed [ɪk'siːd] vt übersteigen.

excellent ['eksələnt] adj ausgezeichnet.

except [ɪk'sept] prep & conj außer; **~ for** abgesehen von; **'~ for access'** 'frei für Anliegerverkehr'; **'~ for loading'** 'Be- und Entladen gestattet'.

exception [ɪk'sepʃn] n Ausnahme die.

exceptional [ɪk'sepʃnəl] adj außergewöhnlich.

excerpt ['eksɜːpt] n Auszug der.

excess [ɪk'ses, before noun 'ekses] ♦ adj Über-. ♦ n Übermaß das.

excess baggage n Übergewicht das.

excess fare n (Br) Nachlösegebühr die.

excessive [ɪk'sesɪv] adj übermäßig; (price) übermäßig hoch.

exchange [ɪks'tʃeɪndʒ] ◆ n (of telephones) Fernamt das; (of students) Austausch der. ◆ vt um|tauschen; to ~ sthg for sthg etw gegen etw ein|tauschen; to be on an ~ Austauschschüler sein.

exchange rate n Wechselkurs der.

excited [ɪk'saɪtɪd] adj aufgeregt.

excitement [ɪk'saɪtmənt] n Aufregung die.

exciting [ɪk'saɪtɪŋ] adj aufregend.

exclamation mark [,eksklə-'meɪʃn-] n (Br) Ausrufezeichen das.

exclamation point [,eksklə-'meɪʃn-] (Am) = **exclamation mark**.

exclude [ɪk'skluːd] vt aus|schließen.

excluding [ɪk'skluːdɪŋ] prep ausgenommen (+D).

exclusive [ɪk'skluːsɪv] ◆ adj (highclass) exklusiv; (sole) ausschließlich. ◆ n Exklusivbericht der; ~ of ausschließlich (+G).

excursion [ɪk'skɜːʃn] n Ausflug der.

excuse [n ɪk'skjuːs, vb ɪk'skjuːz] ◆ n Entschuldigung die. ◆ vt entschuldigen; ~ me! entschuldigen Sie, bitte!; (as apology) Entschuldigung!

ex-directory adj (Br): to be ~ nicht im Telefonbuch stehen.

execute ['eksɪkjuːt] vt (kill) hin|richten.

executive [ɪg'zekjutɪv] n (person) leitende Angestellte der die.

exempt [ɪg'zempt] adj: ~ (from) befreit (von).

exemption [ɪg'zempʃn] n Befreiung die.

exercise ['eksəsaɪz] ◆ n (physical) Bewegung die; (piece of work) Übung die. ◆ vi sich bewegen; to do ~s Gymnastik treiben.

exercise book n Heft das.

exert [ɪg'zɜːt] vt aus|üben.

exhaust [ɪg'zɔːst] ◆ vt erschöpfen. ◆ n: ~ (pipe) Auspuff der.

exhausted [ɪg'zɔːstɪd] adj erschöpft.

exhibit [ɪg'zɪbɪt] ◆ n (in museum, gallery) Ausstellungsstück das. ◆ vt (in exhibition) aus|stellen.

exhibition [,eksɪ'bɪʃn] n (of art) Ausstellung die.

exist [ɪg'zɪst] vi existieren.

existence [ɪg'zɪstəns] n Existenz die; to be in ~ existieren.

existing [ɪg'zɪstɪŋ] adj bestehend.

exit ['eksɪt] ◆ n (door) Ausgang der; (from motorway) Ausfahrt die; (act of leaving) Abgang der. ◆ vi hinaus|gehen.

exotic [ɪg'zɒtɪk] adj exotisch.

expand [ɪk'spænd] vi sich aus|dehnen; (in number) sich vermehren.

expect [ɪk'spekt] vt erwarten; to ~ to do sthg voraussichtlich etw tun; to ~ sb to do sthg erwarten, daß jd etw macht; to be ~ing (be pregnant) in anderen Umständen sein.

expedition [,ekspɪ'dɪʃn] n Expedition die; (short outing) Tour die.

expel [ɪk'spel] vt (from school) von der Schule verweisen.

expense [ɪk'spens] n Ausgaben pl; at the ~ of auf Kosten (+G). ▶ **expenses** npl (of businessman) Spesen pl.

expensive [ɪk'spensɪv] adj teuer.

experience [ɪk'spɪərɪəns] ◆ n Erfahrung die. ◆ vt erfahren.

experienced [ɪk'spɪərɪənst] adj erfahren.

experiment [ɪk'sperɪmənt] ◆ n Experiment das. ◆ vi experimentieren.

experimental [ɪk,sperɪ'mentl] adj experimentell.

expert ['ekspɜːt] ◆ adj (advice, treat-

ment) fachmännisch. ♦ *n* Experte *der* (Expertin *die*).

expire [ɪk'spaɪəʳ] *vi* ab|laufen.

expiry date [ɪk'spaɪɪ-] *n*: ~: 15/4/95 gültig bis 15/4/95.

explain [ɪk'spleɪn] *vt* erklären.

explanation [ˌekspləˈneɪʃn] *n* Erklärung *die*.

explode [ɪk'spləʊd] *vi* explodieren.

exploit [ɪk'splɔɪt] *vt* aus|beuten.

explore [ɪk'splɔ:ʳ] *vt* (*place*) erforschen.

explosion [ɪk'spləʊʒn] *n* (*of bomb etc*) Explosion *die*.

explosive [ɪk'spləʊsɪv] *n* Sprengstoff *der*.

export [*n* 'ekspɔ:t, *vb* ɪk'spɔ:t] ♦ *n* Export *der*, Ausfuhr *die*. ♦ *vt* exportieren.

exposed [ɪk'spəʊzd] *adj* (*place*) ungeschützt.

exposure [ɪk'spəʊʒəʳ] *n* (*photograph*) Aufnahme *die*; (MED) Unterkühlung *die*; (*to heat, radiation*) Aussetzung *die*.

express [ɪk'spres] ♦ *adj* (*letter, delivery*) Eil-. ♦ *n* (*train*) = D-Zug *der*. ♦ *vt* (*opinion, idea*) aus|drücken. ♦ *adv* (*send*) per Eilboten.

expression [ɪk'spreʃn] *n* Ausdruck *der*.

expresso [ɪk'spresəʊ] *n* Espresso *der*.

expressway [ɪk'spreswei] *n* (Am) Schnellstraße *die*.

extend [ɪk'stend] ♦ *vt* (*visa, permit*) verlängern; (*road, building*) aus|bauen; (*hand*) aus|strecken. ♦ *vi* (*stretch*) sich erstrecken.

extension [ɪk'stenʃn] *n* (*of building*) Anbau *der*; (*for phone*) Nebenanschluß *der*; (*of deadline*) Verlängerung *die*; ~ **1263** Apparat 1263.

extension lead *n* Verlängerungskabel *das*.

extensive [ɪk'stensɪv] *adj* umfangreich; (*damage*) beträchtlich.

extent [ɪk'stent] *n* (*of knowledge*) Umfang *der*; (*of damage*) Ausmaß *das*;

to a certain ~ in gewissem Maße; **to what** ~ ...? inwieweit ...?

exterior [ɪk'stɪərɪəʳ] ♦ *adj* äußere(-r) (-s). ♦ *n* (*of car, building*) Außenseite *die*.

external [ɪk'stɜ:nl] *adj* äußere(-r) (-s).

extinct [ɪk'stɪŋkt] *adj* (*species*) ausgestorben; (*volcano*) erloschen.

extinction [ɪk'stɪŋkʃn] *n* Aussterben *das*.

extinguish [ɪk'stɪŋgwɪʃ] *vt* (*fire*) löschen; (*cigarette*) aus|machen.

extinguisher [ɪk'stɪŋgwɪʃəʳ] *n* Feuerlöscher *der*.

extortionate [ɪk'stɔ:ʃnət] *adj* (*price*) Wucher-.

extra ['ekstrə] ♦ *adj* zusätzlich. ♦ *n* (*bonus*) Sonderleistung *die*; (*optional thing*) Extra *das*. ♦ *adv* (*large, hard*) extra; ~ **charge** Zuschlag *der*; ~ **large** übergroß. ► **extras** *npl* (*in price*) zusätzliche Kosten *pl*.

extract [*n* 'ekstrækt, *vb* ɪk'strækt] ♦ *n* Auszug *der*. ♦ *vt* (*tooth*) ziehen.

extractor fan [ɪk'stræktə-] *n* (Br) Ventilator *der*.

extraordinary [ɪk'strɔ:dnrɪ] *adj* (*wonderful*) außerordentlich; (*strange*) ungewöhnlich.

extravagant [ɪk'strævəgənt] *adj* veschwenderisch.

extreme [ɪk'stri:m] ♦ *adj* äußerste(-r) (-s); (*radical*) extrem. ♦ *n* Extrem *das*.

extremely [ɪk'stri:mlɪ] *adv* äußerst.

extrovert ['ekstrəvɜ:t] *n* extravertierter Mensch.

eye [aɪ] ♦ *n* Auge *das*; (*of needle*) Öhr *das*. ♦ *vt* an|sehen; **to keep an** ~ **on** auf|passen auf (+A).

eyebrow ['aɪbraʊ] *n* Augenbraue *die*.

eye drops *npl* Augentropfen *pl*.

eyeglasses ['aɪglɑ:sɪz] *npl* (Am) Brille *die*.

eyelash ['aɪlæʃ] *n* Wimper *die*.

eyelid ['aɪlɪd] *n* Augenlid *das*.

eyeliner ['aɪˌlaɪnəʳ] *n* Eyeliner *der*.

eye shadow n Lidschatten der.
eyesight ['aɪsaɪt] n: **to have good/ bad ~** gute/schlechte Augen haben.
eye test n Sehtest der.
eyewitness [,aɪ'wɪtnɪs] n Augenzeuge der (-zeugin die).

F

F (abbr of Fahrenheit) F.
fabric ['fæbrɪk] n (cloth) Stoff der.
fabulous ['fæbjʊləs] adj sagenhaft.
facade [fə'sɑːd] n Fassade die.
face [feɪs] ◆ n Gesicht das; (of cliff, mountain) Wand die; (of clock, watch) Zifferblatt das. ◆ vt: **to face sb/sthg** jm/etw (D) gegenüber|stehen; **to ~ facts** sich den Tatsachen stellen; **the hotel ~s the harbour** das Hotel geht zum Hafen hinaus; **to be ~d with sthg** (problem) etw (D) gegenüber|stehen. ▶ **face up to** vt fus ins Auge sehen (+D).
facecloth ['feɪsklɒθ] n (Br) Waschlappen der.
facial ['feɪʃl] n Gesichtsmassage die.
facilitate [fə'sɪlɪteɪt] vt (fml) erleichtern.
facilities [fə'sɪlɪtiːz] npl Einrichtungen pl.
facsimile [fæk'sɪmɪlɪ] n Faksimile das.
fact [fækt] n Tatsache die; **in ~** (in reality) tatsächlich; (moreover) sogar.
factor ['fæktər] n Faktor der; **~ ten suntan lotion** Sonnenschutzmittel das mit Schutzfaktor zehn.
factory ['fæktərɪ] n Fabrik die.
faculty ['fækltɪ] n (at university) Fakultät die.
FA Cup n Pokalwettbewerb des britischen Fußballbundes.

fade [feɪd] vi (sound) ab|klingen; (flower) verwelken; (jeans, wallpaper) verbleichen.
faded ['feɪdɪd] adj (jeans) ausgewaschen.
fag [fæg] n (Br: inf: cigarette) Kippe die.
Fahrenheit ['færənhaɪt] adj Fahrenheit.
fail [feɪl] ◆ vt (exam) nicht bestehen. ◆ vi (not succeed) scheitern; (in exam) durch|fallen; (engine) aus|fallen; **to ~ to do sthg** (not do) etw nicht tun.
failing ['feɪlɪŋ] ◆ n Fehler der. ◆ prep: **~ that** andernfalls.
failure ['feɪljər] n Mißerfolg der; (person) Versager der.
faint [feɪnt] ◆ adj schwach. ◆ vi ohnmächtig werden; **I haven't the ~est idea** ich habe keinen blassen Schimmer.
fair [feər] ◆ adj (just) fair, gerecht; (quite large) ziemlich groß; (quite good) ziemlich gut; (SCH) befriedigend; (skin) hell; (hair, person) blond; (weather) gut. ◆ n (funfair) Jahrmarkt der; (trade fair) Messe die; **~ enough!** na gut!; **a ~ number of times** ziemlich oft.
fairground ['feəgraʊnd] n Jahrmarkt der.
fair-haired [-'heəd] adj blond.
fairly ['feəlɪ] adv (quite) ziemlich.
fairy ['feərɪ] n Fee die.
fairy tale n Märchen das.
faith [feɪθ] n Glaube der; (confidence) Vertrauen das; **to have ~ in sb** Vertrauen zu jm haben.
faithfully ['feɪθfʊlɪ] adv: **Yours ~** Hochachtungsvoll.
fake [feɪk] ◆ n (false thing) Fälschung die. ◆ vt fälschen.
fall [fɔːl] (pt fell, pp fallen ['fɔːln]) ◆ vi fallen. ◆ n (accident) Sturz der; (decrease) Sinken das; (of snow) Schneefall der; (Am: autumn) Herbst der; **to ~ asleep** ein|schlafen; **to ~ ill** krank werden; **to ~ in love** sich verlieben. ▶ **falls** npl (waterfall) Fälle pl.

▶ **fall behind** vi (with work, rent) in Rückstand geraten. ▶ **fall down** vi hin|fallen. ▶ **fall off** vi herunter|fallen; (handle) ab|fallen; (branch) ab|brechen. ▶ **fall out** vi (hair, teeth) aus|fallen; (argue) sich streiten. ▶ **fall over** vi hin|fallen. ▶ **fall through** vi ins Wasser fallen.

false [fɔːls] adj falsch.

false alarm n falscher Alarm.

false teeth npl Gebiß das.

fame [feɪm] n Ruhm der.

familiar [fəˈmɪljəʳ] adj bekannt; (informal) vertraulich; **to be ~ with** (know) sich aus|kennen mit.

family [ˈfæmlɪ] ◆ n Familie die. ◆ adj (pack, size) Familien-; (film, holiday) für die ganze Familie.

family planning clinic [-ˈplænɪŋ-] n ≃ Pro Familia-Beratungsstelle die.

family room n (at hotel) Doppelzimmer mit Kinderbett; (at pub, airport) Raum für Familien mit kleinen Kindern.

famine [ˈfæmɪn] n Hungersnot die.

famished [ˈfæmɪʃt] adj (inf) ausgehungert.

famous [ˈfeɪməs] adj berühmt.

fan [fæn] n (electric) Ventilator der; (held in hand) Fächer der; (enthusiast, supporter) Fan der.

fan belt n Keilriemen der.

fancy [ˈfænsɪ] ◆ vt (inf: feel like) Lust haben auf (+A); (be attracted to) scharf sein auf (+A). ◆ adj (elaborate) ausgefallen; **~ (that)!** also so was!

fancy dress n Verkleidung die (Kostüm).

fan heater n Heizlüfter der.

fanlight [ˈfænlaɪt] n (Br) Oberlicht das.

fantastic [fænˈtæstɪk] adj phantastisch.

fantasy [ˈfæntəsɪ] n Phantasie die.

fantasy football n Spiel, bei dem sich jeder Teilnehmer eine virtuelle Mannschaft aus echten Fußballspielern zusammenstellt und Punkte gewinnt, wenn diese in echten Spielen Tore erzielen.

far [fɑːʳ] (compar **further** OR **farther**, superl **furthest** OR **farthest**) ◆ adv weit. ◆ adj: **at the ~ end** am anderen Ende; **have you come ~?** sind Sie von weit her gekommen?; **how ~ is it (to London)?** wie weit ist es (bis London)?; **as ~ as** (town, country) bis nach; (station, school) bis zu (+D); **as ~ as I'm concerned** was mich betrifft; **as ~ as I know** soweit ich weiß; **~ better** weitaus besser; **by ~** bei weitem; **so ~** (until now) bisher.

farce [fɑːs] n Farce die.

fare [feəʳ] ◆ n Fahrpreis der; (for plane) Flugpreis der; (fml: food) Kost die. ◆ vi: **she ~d well/badly** es ist ihr gut/schlecht ergangen.

Far East n: **the ~** der Ferne Osten.

fare stage n (Br) Teilstrecke die.

farm [fɑːm] n Bauernhof der.

farmer [ˈfɑːməʳ] n Bauer der (Bäuerin die).

farmhouse [ˈfɑːmhaʊs, pl -haʊzɪz] n Bauernhaus das.

farming [ˈfɑːmɪŋ] n Landwirtschaft die.

farmland [ˈfɑːmlænd] n Ackerland das.

farmyard [ˈfɑːmjɑːd] n Hof der.

farther [ˈfɑːðəʳ] compar → **far**.

farthest [ˈfɑːðəst] superl → **far**.

fascinating [ˈfæsɪneɪtɪŋ] adj faszinierend.

fascination [ˌfæsɪˈneɪʃn] n Faszination die.

fashion [ˈfæʃn] n Mode die; (manner) Art die; **to be in ~** in Mode sein; **to be out of ~** aus der Mode sein.

fashionable [ˈfæʃnəbl] adj modisch.

fashion show n Modenschau die.

fast [fɑːst] ◆ adv schnell; (securely) fest. ◆ adj schnell; (clock, watch): **to be ~** vor|gehen; **to be ~ asleep** fest schlafen; **a ~ train** ein Schnellzug.

fasten [ˈfɑːsn] vt (coat, door, window) zu|machen; (seatbelt) sich an|schnallen; (two things) fest|machen.

fastener ['fɑːsnər] n Verschluß der.

fast food n Fast food der.

fat [fæt] ◆ adj dick; (meat) fett. ◆ n Fett das.

fatal ['feɪtl] adj tödlich.

father ['fɑːðər] n Vater der.

Father Christmas n (Br) Weihnachtsmann der.

father-in-law n Schwiegervater der.

fattening ['fætnɪŋ] adj: **to be ~** dick machen.

fatty ['fætɪ] adj fettreich.

faucet ['fɔːsɪt] n (Am) Hahn der.

fault ['fɔːlt] n (responsibility) Schuld die; (error) Fehler der; **it's your ~** du hast Schuld.

faulty ['fɔːltɪ] adj fehlerhaft.

favor ['feɪvər] (Am) = **favour**.

favour ['feɪvər] ◆ n (Br: kind act) Gefallen der. ◆ vt (Br: prefer) vorziehen; **to be in ~ of sthg** für etw sein; **to do sb a ~** jm einen Gefallen tun.

favourable ['feɪvrəbl] adj günstig.

favourite ['feɪvrɪt] ◆ adj Lieblings-. ◆ n (in sport) Favorit der (-in die).

fawn [fɔːn] adj hellbraun.

fax [fæks] ◆ n Fax das. ◆ vt faxen.

fax modem n Faxmodem das.

fear [fɪər] ◆ n Angst die. ◆ vt fürchten; **for ~ of doing sthg** aus Angst, etw zu tun.

feast [fiːst] n Festessen das.

feather ['feðər] n Feder die.

feature ['fiːtʃər] ◆ n (characteristic) Merkmal das; (of face) Gesichtszug der; (in newspaper, on radio, TV) Feature das. ◆ vt (subj: film): **this film ~s Marlon Brando** Marlon Brando spielt die Hauptrolle in diesem Film.

feature film n Spielfilm der.

Feb. (abbr of February) Febr.

February ['februərɪ] n Februar der, → **September**.

fed [fed] pt & pp → **feed**.

fed up adj: **to be ~ (with)** die Nase voll haben (von).

fee [fiː] n Gebühr die.

feeble ['fiːbəl] adj schwach.

feed [fiːd] (pt & pp **fed**) vt füttern; (coins) ein|werfen.

feel [fiːl] (pt & pp **felt**) ◆ vt fühlen; (think) glauben. ◆ vi sein; (ill, old, young) sich fühlen; (seem) sich an|fühlen. ◆ n (of material): **it has a soft ~** es fühlt sich weich an; **I ~ cold** mir ist kalt; **I ~ ill** ich fühle mich nicht gut; **to ~ like sthg** (fancy) Lust haben auf etw (A); **to ~ up to doing sthg** sich einer Sache gewachsen fühlen.

feeling ['fiːlɪŋ] n Gefühl das.

feet [fiːt] pl → **foot**.

fell [fel] ◆ pt → **fall**. ◆ vt (tree) fällen.

fellow ['feləʊ] ◆ adj Mit-. ◆ n (man) Mann der.

felt [felt] ◆ pt & pp → **feel**. ◆ n Filz der.

felt-tip pen n Filzstift der.

female ['fiːmeɪl] ◆ adj weiblich. ◆ n (animal) Weibchen das.

feminine ['femɪnɪn] adj feminin.

feminist ['femɪnɪst] n Feministin die.

fence [fens] n Zaun der.

fencing ['fensɪŋ] n (SPORT) Fechten das.

fend [fend] vi: **to ~ for o.s.** allein zurecht|kommen.

fender ['fendər] n (for fireplace) Kamingitter das; (Am: on car) Kotflügel der.

fennel ['fenl] n Fenchel der.

fern [fɜːn] n Farn der.

ferocious [fə'rəʊʃəs] adj wild.

ferry ['ferɪ] n Fähre die.

fertile ['fɜːtaɪl] adj (land) fruchtbar.

fertilizer ['fɜːtɪlaɪzər] n Dünger der.

festival ['festəvl] n (of music, arts etc) Festspiele pl; (holiday) Feiertag der.

feta cheese ['fetə-] n griechischer Schafskäse.

fetch [fetʃ] vt holen; (be sold for) ein|bringen.

fete [feɪt] n Wohltätigkeitsbazar der.

fever ['fiːvəʳ] n Fieber das; **to have a ~** Fieber haben.

feverish ['fiːvərɪʃ] adj fiebrig.

few [fjuː] adj & pron wenige; **the first ~ times** die ersten paar Male; **a ~** ein paar; **quite a ~** eine ganze Menge.

fewer ['fjuːəʳ] adj & pron weniger.

fiancé [frˈɒnseɪ] n Verlobte der.

fiancée [frˈɒnseɪ] n Verlobte die.

fib [fɪb] n (inf): **to tell a ~** flunkern.

fiber ['faɪbər] (Am) = **fibre**.

fibre ['faɪbəʳ] n ([Br]) Faser die; (in food) Ballaststoffe pl.

fibreglass ['faɪbəglɑːs] n Glasfiber die.

fickle ['fɪkl] adj wankelmütig.

fiction ['fɪkʃn] n Belletristik die.

fiddle ['fɪdl] ◆ n (violin) Geige die. ◆ vi: **to ~ with sthg** an etw (D) fummeln.

fidget ['fɪdʒɪt] vi zappeln.

field [fiːld] n Feld das; (subject) Gebiet das.

field glasses npl Feldstecher der.

fierce [fɪəs] adj (animal) wild; (person, storm) heftig; (heat) brütend.

fifteen [fɪfˈtiːn] num fünfzehn, → **six**.

fifteenth [ˌfɪfˈtiːnθ] num fünfzehnte(-r)(-s), → **sixth**.

fifth [fɪfθ] num fünfte(-r)(-s), → **sixth**.

fiftieth ['fɪftɪəθ] num fünfzigste(-r)(-s), → **sixth**.

fifty ['fɪftɪ] num fünfzig, → **six**.

fig [fɪg] n Feige die.

fight [faɪt] (pt & pp **fought**) ◆ n Kampf der; (brawl) Prügelei die; (argument) Streit der. ◆ vt kämpfen gegen; (combat) bekämpfen. ◆ vi kämpfen; (brawl) sich schlagen; (quarrel) sich streiten; **to have a ~ with sb** sich mit jm schlagen. ► **fight back** vi zurück|schlagen. ► **fight off** vt sep ab|wehren.

fighting ['faɪtɪŋ] n Prügelei die; (military) Kämpfe pl.

figure [Br 'fɪgəʳ, Am 'fɪgjər] n Zahl die; (shape of body) Figur die; (outline of person) Gestalt die; (diagram) Abbildung die. ► **figure out** vt sep heraus|finden.

file [faɪl] ◆ n Akte die; (COMPUT) Datei die; (tool) Feile die. ◆ vt (complaint, petition) ein|reichen; **to ~ one's nails** sich (D) die Nägel feilen; **in single ~** im Gänsemarsch.

filing cabinet ['faɪlɪŋ-] n Aktenschrank der.

fill [fɪl] vt füllen; (role) aus|füllen. ► **fill in** vt sep (form) aus|füllen. ► **fill out** vt sep = **fill in**. ► **fill up** vt sep füllen; **~ her up!** (with petrol) volltanken, bitte!

filled roll ['fɪld-] n belegtes Brötchen.

fillet ['fɪlɪt] n Filet das.

fillet steak n Filetsteak das.

filling ['fɪlɪŋ] ◆ n Füllung die. ◆ adj sättigend.

filling station n Tankstelle die.

film [fɪlm] ◆ n Film der. ◆ vt filmen.

film star n Filmstar der.

filter ['fɪltəʳ] n Filter der.

filthy ['fɪlθɪ] adj dreckig.

fin [fɪn] n Flosse die; (Am: of swimmer) Schwimmflosse die.

final ['faɪnl] ◆ adj letzte(-r)(-s); (decision) endgültig. ◆ n Finale das.

finalist ['faɪnəlɪst] n (SPORT) Finalist der (-in die).

finally ['faɪnəlɪ] adv schließlich.

finance [n 'faɪnæns, vb faɪˈnæns] ◆ n Geldmittel pl; (management of money) Finanzwesen das. ◆ vt finanzieren. ► **finances** npl Finanzen pl.

financial [frˈnænʃl] adj finanziell.

find [faɪnd] (pt & pp **found**) ◆ vt finden; (find out) heraus|finden. ◆ n Fund der; **to ~ the time to do sthg** die Zeit finden, etw zu tun. ► **find out** vt sep heraus|finden. ◆ vi: **to ~ out (about)** heraus|finden (über (+A).

fine [faɪn] ◆ adj (good) herrlich; (satisfactory) gut, in Ordnung; (thin) fein. ◆ adv (thinly) fein; (well) gut. ◆ n Geldstrafe die. ◆ vt zu einer

Geldstrafe verurteilen; **I'm ~** mir geht es gut.

fine art n schöne Künste pl.

finger ['fɪŋgəʳ] n Finger der.

fingernail ['fɪŋgəneɪl] n Fingernagel der.

fingertip ['fɪŋgətɪp] n Fingerspitze die.

finish ['fɪnɪʃ] ♦ n Schluß der; (SPORT) Finish das; (on furniture) Oberfläche die, Aspekt der. ♦ vt beenden; (food, meal) auflessen; (drink) ausltrinken. ♦ vi (end) zu Ende gehen; (in race) durchs Ziel gehen; **to ~ doing sthg** etw zu Ende machen. ▶ **finish off** vt sep (complete) zu Ende machen; (food, meal) auflessen; (drink) ausltrinken. ▶ **finish up** vi hinlgelangen; **to ~ up doing sthg** zum Schluß etw tun.

Finland ['fɪnlənd] n Finnland nt.

Finn [fɪn] n Finne der (Finnin die).

Finnan haddock ['fɪnən-] n schottischer geräucherter Schellfisch.

Finnish ['fɪnɪʃ] ♦ adj finnisch. ♦ n Finnisch das.

fir [fɜːʳ] n Tanne die.

fire ['faɪəʳ] ♦ n Feuer das; (device) Ofen der. ♦ vt (gun) ablfeuern; (from job) feuern; **to be on ~** brennen; **to catch ~** Feuer fangen.

fire alarm n Feuermelder der.

fire brigade n (Br) Feuerwehr die.

fire department (Am) = **fire brigade**.

fire engine n Feuerwehrauto das.

fire escape n (staircase) Feuertreppe die; (ladder) Feuerleiter die.

fire exit n Notausgang der.

fire extinguisher n Feuerlöscher der.

fire hazard n: **to be a ~** feuergefährlich sein.

fireman ['faɪəmən] (pl -men [-mən]) n Feuerwehrmann der.

fireplace ['faɪəpleɪs] n Kamin der.

fire regulations npl feuerpolizeiliche Vorschriften pl.

fire station n Feuerwache die.

firewood ['faɪəwʊd] n Brennholz das.

firework display ['faɪəwɜːk-] n Feuerwerk das.

fireworks ['faɪəwɜːks] npl Feuerwerkskörper pl.

firm [fɜːm] ♦ adj fest; (mattress) hart. ♦ n Firma die.

first [fɜːst] ♦ adj erste(-r)(-s). ♦ adv zuerst; (in order) als erste; (for the first time) zum ersten Mal. ♦ pron erste der die das. ♦ n (event) erstmaliges Ereignis; **~ (gear)** erster Gang; **~ thing (in the morning)** gleich morgens früh; **for the ~ time** zum ersten Mal; **the ~ of January** der erste Januar; **at ~** zuerst; **~ of all** zu allererst.

first aid n Erste Hilfe.

first-aid kit n Verbandkasten der.

first class n erste Klasse; (mail) Post, die schneller befördert werden soll oder in die EU geht.

first-class adj (stamp) für Briefe, die schneller befördert werden sollen oder in die EU gehen; (ticket) erster Klasse; (very good) erstklassig.

first floor n (Br) erster Stock; (Am: ground floor) Erdgeschoß das.

firstly ['fɜːstlɪ] adv zuerst.

First World War n: **the ~** der Erste Weltkrieg.

fish [fɪʃ] (pl inv) ♦ n Fisch der. ♦ vi (with net) fischen; (with rod) angeln.

fish and chips n ausgebackener Fisch mit Pommes frites.

fishcake ['fɪʃkeɪk] n Fischfrikadelle die.

fisherman ['fɪʃəmən] (pl -men [-mən]) n Fischer der.

fish farm n Fischzucht die.

fish fingers npl (Br) Fischstäbchen pl.

fishing ['fɪʃɪŋ] n (hobby) Angeln das; (business) Fischerei die; **to go ~** angeln gehen.

fishing boat n Fischerboot das.

fishing rod n Angel die.

fishmonger's ['fɪʃˌmʌŋgəz] n (shop) Fischgeschäft das.

fish sticks (Am) = **fish fingers**.

fish supper n (Scot) ausgebackener Fisch mit Pommes frites.

fist [fɪst] n Faust die.

fit [fɪt] ♦ adj (healthy) fit. ♦ vt passen (+D); (install) einlbauen; (insert) einlstecken. ♦ vi passen. ♦ n (epileptic, of coughing, anger) Anfall der; (of clothes, shoes): **to be a good ~** gut passen; **to be ~ for sthg** (suitable) für etw geeignet sein; **~ to eat** eßbar; **it doesn't ~** es paßt nicht; **to get ~** fit werden; **to keep ~** sich fit halten. ► **fit in** vt sep (find time for) einlschieben. ♦ vi (belong) sich einlfügen.

fitness ['fɪtnɪs] n (health) Fitneß die.

fitted carpet [ˌfɪtəd-] n Teppichboden der.

fitted sheet [ˌfɪtəd-] n Spannbettlaken das.

fitting room ['fɪtɪŋ-] n Umkleideraum der.

five [faɪv] num fünf, → **six**.

fiver ['faɪvər] n (Br: inf: £5) fünf Pfund pl; (£5 note) Fünfpfundschein der.

fix [fɪks] vt (attach) anlbringen; (mend) reparieren; (decide on, arrange) festllegen; **to ~ sb a drink/meal** jm einen Drink/etwas zu essen machen. ► **fix up** vt sep: **to ~ sb up with sthg** jm etw besorgen.

fixture ['fɪkstʃər] n (SPORT) Spiel das; **~s and fittings** zu einer Wohnung gehörende Ausstattung und Installationen.

fizzy ['fɪzɪ] adj kohlensäurehaltig.

flag [flæg] n Fahne die.

flake [fleɪk] ♦ n Flocke die. ♦ vi ablblättern.

flame [fleɪm] n Flamme die.

flammable ['flæməbl] adj leicht entflammbar.

flan [flæn] n (sweet) Torte die; (savoury) Pastete die.

flannel ['flænl] n (material) Flanell der; (Br: for washing face) Waschlappen der. ► **flannels** npl Flanellhose die.

flap [flæp] ♦ n Klappe die. ♦ vt

(wings) schlagen mit.

flapjack ['flæpdʒæk] n (Br) Haferflockenplätzchen das.

flare [fleər] n (signal) Leuchtrakete die.

flared [fleəd] adj (trousers, skirt) ausgestellt.

flash [flæʃ] ♦ n Blitz der. ♦ vi (light) blinken; **a ~ of lightning** ein Blitz; **to ~ one's headlights** die Lichthupe benutzen.

flashlight ['flæʃlaɪt] n Taschenlampe die.

flask [flɑːsk] n (Thermos) Thermosflasche die; (hip flask) Taschenflasche die.

flat [flæt] ♦ adj flach; (battery) leer; (drink) abgestanden; (rate, fee) Pauschal-. ♦ adv flach. ♦ n (Br: apartment) Wohnung die; **a ~ (tyre)** eine Reifenpanne; **~ out** (run, work) mit Volldampf.

flatter ['flætər] vt schmeicheln (+D).

flavor ['fleɪvər] (Am) = **flavour**.

flavour ['fleɪvər] n (Br) Geschmack der.

flavoured ['fleɪvəd] adj mit Geschmacksstoffen.

flavouring ['fleɪvərɪŋ] n Geschmacksstoff der.

flaw [flɔː] n Fehler der.

flea [fliː] n Floh der.

flea market n Flohmarkt der.

fleece [fliːs] n (downy material) Fleece der.

fleet [fliːt] n Flotte die.

Flemish ['flemɪʃ] ♦ adj flämisch. ♦ n Flämisch das.

flesh [fleʃ] n Fleisch das.

flew [fluː] pt → **fly**.

flex [fleks] n Schnur die.

flexible ['fleksəbl] adj (bendable) biegsam; (adaptable) flexibel.

flexitime ['fleksɪtaɪm] n Gleitzeit die.

flick [flɪk] vt knipsen. ► **flick through** vt fus durchlblättern.

flies [flaɪz] npl (of trousers) Hosenschlitz der.

flight [flaɪt] n Flug der; **a ~ (of stairs)** eine Treppe.

flight attendant n Flugbegleiter der (-in die).

flimsy ['flɪmzɪ] adj leicht.

fling [flɪŋ] (pt & pp **flung**) vt schleudern.

flint [flɪnt] n (of lighter) Feuerstein der.

flip-flop [flɪp-] n (Br) Plastiksandale die.

flipper ['flɪpər] n (Br: of swimmer) Schwimmflosse die.

flirt [flɜːt] vi: **to ~ (with sb)** (mit jm) flirten.

float [fləʊt] ◆ n (for swimming) Schwimmkork der; (for fishing) Schwimmer der; (in procession) Festwagen der; (drink) Limonade mit einer Kugel Speiseeis. ◆ vi treiben.

flock [flɒk] ◆ n (of birds) Schwarm der; (of sheep) Herde die. ◆ vi (people) strömen.

flood [flʌd] ◆ n Überschwemmung die. ◆ vt überschwemmen. ◆ vi (river) über die Ufer treten.

floodlight ['flʌdlaɪt] n Flutlicht das.

floor [flɔːr] n Boden der; (storey) Stock der; (of nightclub) Tanzfläche die.

floorboard ['flɔːbɔːd] n Diele die.

floor show n Revue die.

flop [flɒp] n (inf: failure) Flop der.

floppy disk ['flɒpɪ-] n Diskette die.

floral ['flɔːrəl] adj (pattern) Blumen-, geblümt.

Florida Keys ['flɒrɪdə-] npl Inselkette vor der Küste Floridas.

florist's ['flɒrɪsts] n (shop) Blumenladen der.

flour ['flaʊər] n Mehl das.

flow [fləʊ] ◆ n Fluß der. ◆ vi fließen.

flower ['flaʊər] n Blume die.

flowerbed ['flaʊəbed] n Blumenbeet das.

flowerpot ['flaʊəpɒt] n Blumentopf der.

flown [fləʊn] pp → **fly**.

fl oz abbr = **fluid ounce**.

flu [fluː] n Grippe die.

fluent ['fluːənt] adj fließend; **she speaks ~ German** sie spricht fließend Deutsch.

fluff [flʌf] n (on clothes) Fussel die.

fluid ounce ['fluːɪd-] n = 0,0284 Liter.

flume [fluːm] n Wasserbahn die.

flung [flʌŋ] pt & pp → **fling**.

flunk [flʌŋk] vt (Am: inf: exam) verhauen.

fluorescent [flʊəˈresənt] adj fluoreszierend.

flush [flʌʃ] ◆ vt spülen. ◆ vi: **the toilet won't ~** die Spülung funktioniert nicht.

flute [fluːt] n Querflöte die.

fly [flaɪ] (pt **flew**, pp **flown**) ◆ n (insect) Fliege die; (of trousers) Hosenschlitz der. ◆ vt fliegen; (airline) fliegen mit. ◆ vi fliegen; (flag) wehen.

fly-drive n Fly-drive Urlaub der.

flying ['flaɪɪŋ] n Fliegen das.

flyover ['flaɪˌəʊvər] n (Br) Fly-over der, Straßenüberführung die.

flypaper ['flaɪˌpeɪpər] n Fliegenfänger der.

flysheet ['flaɪʃiːt] n Überzelt das.

FM n = UKW.

foal [fəʊl] n Fohlen das.

foam [fəʊm] n Schaum der; (foam rubber) Schaumstoff der.

focus ['fəʊkəs] ◆ n Brennpunkt der. ◆ vi: **to ~ on sthg** (with camera) die Kamera scharf auf etw (A) einlstellen; **in ~** scharf; **out of ~** unscharf.

fog [fɒg] n Nebel der.

fogbound ['fɒgbaʊnd] adj (airport) wegen Nebel geschlossen.

foggy ['fɒgɪ] adj neblig.

fog lamp n Nebelscheinwerfer der.

foil [fɔɪl] n (thin metal) Folie die.

fold [fəʊld] ◆ n Falte die. ◆ vt falten; (wrap) einlwickeln; **to ~ one's arms** die Arme verschränken. ▶ **fold up**

vi (*chair, bed, bicycle*) sich zusammenklappen lassen.

folder ['fəʊldər] *n* Mappe *die*.

foliage ['fəʊlɪdʒ] *n* Laub *das*.

folk [fəʊk] ◆ *npl* (*people*) Leute *pl*. ◆ *n*: ~ (**music**) (*popular*) Folk *der*; (*traditional*) Volksmusik *die*. ▶ **folks** *npl* (*inf: relatives*) Leute *pl*.

follow ['fɒləʊ] ◆ *vt* folgen (+D); (*with eyes*) mit den Augen folgen (+D); (*news, fashion*) verfolgen. ◆ *vi* folgen; **~ed by** gefolgt von; **as ~s** wie folgt. ▶ **follow on** *vi* (*come later*) später folgen.

following ['fɒləʊɪŋ] ◆ *adj* folgend. ◆ *prep* nach.

follow on call *n* in Telefonzelle, weiterer Anruf, um die eingeworfene Münze zu verbrauchen.

fond [fɒnd] *adj*: **to be ~ of** gern haben.

fondue ['fɒnduː] *n* Fondue *das*.

food [fuːd] *n* Essen *das*; (*for animals*) Futter *das*.

food poisoning [-ˌpɔɪznɪŋ] *n* Lebensmittelvergiftung *die*.

food processor [-ˌprəʊsesər] *n* Küchenmaschine *die*.

foodstuffs ['fuːdstʌfs] *npl* Nahrungsmittel *pl*.

fool [fuːl] ◆ *n* (*idiot*) Dummkopf *der*; (*pudding*) Cremespeise aus Sahne und Obst. ◆ *vt* irrelführen.

foolish ['fuːlɪʃ] *adj* dumm.

foot [fʊt] (*pl* **feet**) *n* Fuß *der*; **by ~** zu Fuß; **on ~** zu Fuß.

football ['fʊtbɔːl] *n* (Br) Fußball *der*; (Am: *American football*) Football *der*; (Am: *in American football*) Ball *der*.

footballer ['fʊtbɔːlər] *n* (Br) Fußballer *der* (-in *die*).

football pitch *n* (Br) Fußballfeld *das*.

footbridge ['fʊtbrɪdʒ] *n* Fußgängerbrücke *die*.

footpath ['fʊtpɑːθ, *pl* -pɑːðz] *n* Fußweg *der*.

footprint ['fʊtprɪnt] *n* Fußabdruck *der*.

footstep ['fʊtstep] *n* Schritt *der*.

footwear ['fʊtweər] *n* Schuhwerk *das*.

for [fɔːr] *prep* **1.** (*expressing purpose, reason, destination*) für; **this book is ~ you** dieses Buch ist für dich/Sie; **a ticket ~ Manchester** eine Fahrkarte nach Manchester; **a town famous ~ its wine** eine Stadt, die für ihren Wein bekannt ist; **~ this reason** aus diesem Grund; **a cure ~ sore throats** ein Mittel gegen Halsschmerzen; **what did you do that ~?** wozu hast du das getan?; **what's it ~?** wofür ist das?; **to go ~ a walk** spazierenlgehen; **'~ sale'** 'zu verkaufen'. **2.** (*during*) seit; **I've lived here ~ ten years** ich lebe seit zehn Jahren hier; **we talked ~ hours** wir redeten stundenlang. **3.** (*by, before*) für; **be there ~ 8 p.m.** sei um 8 Uhr abends da; **I'll do it ~ tomorrow** ich mache es bis morgen. **4.** (*on the occasion of*) zu; **I got socks ~ Christmas** ich habe Socken zu Weihnachten bekommen; **what's ~ dinner?** was gibt's zum Abendessen? **5.** (*on behalf of*) für; **to do sthg ~ sb** etw für jn tun. **6.** (*with time and space*) für; **there's no room ~ it** dafür ist kein Platz; **to have time ~ sthg** für etw Zeit haben. **7.** (*expressing distance*): **we drove ~ miles** wir fuhren meilenweit; **road works ~ 20 miles** Straßenarbeiten auf 20 Meilen. **8.** (*expressing price*) für; **I bought it ~ £5** ich kaufte es für 5 Pfund. **9.** (*expressing meaning*): **what's the German ~ 'boy'?** wie heißt 'Junge' auf Deutsch? **10.** (*with regard to*) für; **it's warm ~ November** es ist warm für November; **it's easy ~ you** es ist leicht für dich; **it's too far ~ us to walk** zum Gehen ist es für uns zu weit.

forbid [fəˈbɪd] (*pt* **-bade** [-ˈbeɪd], *pp* **-bidden**) *vt* verbieten; **to ~ sb to do sthg** jm verbieten, etw zu tun.

forbidden [fəˈbɪdn] *adj* verboten.

force [fɔːs] ◆ *n* Kraft *die*; (*violence*) Gewalt *die*. ◆ *vt* (*physically*) zwingen; (*lock, door*) auflbrechen; **to ~ sb to do**

sthg jn zwingen, etw zu tun; **to ~ one's way through** sich gewaltsam einen Weg bahnen; **the ~s** die Streitkräfte.

ford [fɔːd] n Furt die.

forecast ['fɔːkɑːst] n Vorhersage die.

forecourt ['fɔːkɔːt] n Vorhof der.

forefinger ['fɔːˌfɪŋgər] n Zeigefinger der.

foreground ['fɔːgraʊnd] n Vordergrund der.

forehead ['fɔːhed] n Stirn die.

foreign ['fɒrən] adj ausländisch, Auslands-; **~ country** Ausland das; **~ language** Fremdsprache die.

foreign currency n Devisen pl.

foreigner ['fɒrənər] n Ausländer der (-in die).

foreign exchange n Devisen pl.

Foreign Secretary n (Br) Außenminister der (-in die).

foreman ['fɔːmən] (pl **-men** [-mən]) n Vorarbeiter der.

forename ['fɔːneɪm] n (fml) Vorname der.

foresee [fɔːˈsiː] (pt **-saw** [-ˈsɔː], pp **-seen** [-ˈsiːn]) vt vorausǀsehen.

forest ['fɒrɪst] n Wald der.

forever [fəˈrevər] adv ewig; (continually) ständig.

forgave [fəˈgeɪv] pt → **forgive**.

forge [fɔːdʒ] vt (copy) fälschen.

forgery ['fɔːdʒərɪ] n Fälschung die.

forget [fəˈget] (pt **-got**, pp **-gotten**) vt & vi vergessen; **to ~ about sthg** etw vergessen; **to ~ how to do sthg** etw verlernen; **to ~ to do sthg** vergessen, etw zu tun; **~ it!** vergiß es!

forgetful [fəˈgetful] adj vergeßlich.

forgive [fəˈgɪv] (pt **-gave**, pp **-given** [-ˈgɪvn]) vt vergeben; **to ~ sb for sthg** jm etw vergeben.

forgot [fəˈgɒt] pt → **forget**.

forgotten [fəˈgɒtn] pp → **forget**.

fork [fɔːk] n Gabel die; (of road, path) Gabelung die. ▶ **forks** npl (of bike, motorbike) Gabel die.

form [fɔːm] ◆ n (type, shape) Form die; (piece of paper) Formular das; (SCH) Klasse die. ◆ vt bilden. ◆ vi sich bilden; **off ~** nicht in Form; **on ~** in Form; **to ~ part of** einen Teil bilden von.

formal ['fɔːml] adj förmlich; (occasion, clothes) festlich.

formality [fɔːˈmælətɪ] n Formalität die; **it's just a ~** das ist eine reine Formalität.

format ['fɔːmæt] n Format das.

former ['fɔːmər] ◆ adj ehemalig; (first) früher. ◆ pron: **the ~** der/die/das erstere.

formerly ['fɔːməlɪ] adv früher.

formula ['fɔːmjʊlə] (pl **-as** OR **-ae** [-iː]) n Formel die.

fort [fɔːt] n Fort das.

forthcoming [fɔːθˈkʌmɪŋ] adj (future) bevorstehend.

fortieth ['fɔːtɪɪθ] num vierzigste(-r) (-s), → **sixth**.

fortnight ['fɔːtnaɪt] n (Br) vierzehn Tage pl.

fortunate ['fɔːtʃnət] adj glücklich; **to be ~** Glück haben.

fortunately ['fɔːtʃnətlɪ] adv glücklicherweise.

fortune ['fɔːtʃuːn] n (money) Vermögen das; (luck) Glück das; **it costs a ~** (inf) es kostet ein Vermögen.

forty ['fɔːtɪ] num vierzig, → **six**.

forward ['fɔːwəd] ◆ adv (move, lean) nach vorn. ◆ n (SPORT) Stürmer der. ◆ vt (letter, goods) nachǀsenden; **to look ~ to** sich freuen auf (+A).

forwarding address ['fɔːwədɪŋ-] n Nachsendeadresse die.

fought [fɔːt] pt & pp → **fight**.

foul [faʊl] ◆ adj (unpleasant) ekelhaft. ◆ n Foul das.

found [faʊnd] ◆ pt & pp → **find**. ◆ vt gründen.

foundation (cream) [faʊnˈdeɪʃn-] n Make-up das.

foundations [faʊnˈdeɪʃnz] npl Fundament das.

fountain ['faʊntɪn] n Brunnen der.

fountain pen n Füllfederhalter der.

four [fɔːʳ] num vier, → **six**.

four-star (petrol) n Super das.

fourteen [ˌfɔːˈtiːn] num vierzehn, → **six**.

fourteenth [ˌfɔːˈtiːnθ] num vierzehnte(-r)(-s), → **sixth**.

fourth [fɔːθ] num vierte(-r)(-s), → **sixth**.

four-wheel drive n (car) Geländewagen der.

fowl [faʊl] (pl inv) n Geflügel das.

fox [fɒks] n Fuchs der.

foyer ['fɔɪeɪ] n Foyer das.

fraction ['frækʃn] n (small amount) Bruchteil der; (in maths) Bruch der.

fracture ['fræktʃəʳ] ◆ n Bruch der. ◆ vt brechen.

fragile ['frædʒaɪl] adj zerbrechlich.

fragment ['frægmənt] n Bruchstück das.

fragrance ['freɪgrəns] n Duft der.

frail [freɪl] adj gebrechlich.

frame [freɪm] ◆ n Rahmen der; (of glasses) Gestell das. ◆ vt einlrahmen.

France [frɑːns] n Frankreich nt.

frank [fræŋk] adj offen.

frankfurter ['fræŋkfɜːtəʳ] n Frankfurter die.

frankly ['fræŋklɪ] adv (to be honest) ehrlich gesagt.

frantic ['fræntɪk] adj (person) außer sich; (activity, pace) hektisch.

fraud [frɔːd] n (crime) Betrug der.

freak [friːk] ◆ adj anormal. ◆ n (inf: fanatic) Freak der.

freckles ['freklz] npl Sommersprossen pl.

free [friː] ◆ adj frei. ◆ vt (prisoner) befreien. ◆ adv (without paying) umsonst, gratis; **for ~** umsonst, gratis; **~ of charge** umsonst, gratis; **to be ~ to do sthg** etw tun können.

freedom ['friːdəm] n Freiheit die.

freefone ['friːfəʊn] adj (Br): **a ~ number** eine gebührenfreie Telefonnummer.

free gift n Werbegeschenk das.

free house n (Br) brauereiunabhängiges Wirtshaus.

free kick n Freistoß der.

freelance ['friːlɑːns] adj freiberuflich.

freely ['friːlɪ] adv frei.

free period n (SCH) Freistunde die.

freepost ['friːpəʊst] n gebührenfreie Sendung; **'freepost'** 'Gebühr zahlt Empfänger'.

free-range adj (eggs) von Hühnern aus Bodenhaltung.

free time n Freizeit die.

freeway ['friːweɪ] n (Am) Autobahn die.

freeze [friːz] (pt **froze**, pp **frozen**) ◆ vt einlfrieren. ◆ vi gefrieren. ◆ v impers: **it's freezing** es friert.

freezer ['friːzəʳ] n (deep freeze) Tiefkühltruhe die, Gefrierschrank der; (part of fridge) Gefrierfach das.

freezing ['friːzɪŋ] adj eiskalt.

freezing point n Gefrierpunkt der.

freight [freɪt] n (goods) Fracht die.

French [frentʃ] ◆ adj französisch. ◆ n (language) Französisch das. ◆ npl: **the ~** die Franzosen pl.

French bean n grüne Bohne.

French bread n Baguette die.

French dressing n (in UK) Vinaigrette die; (in US) French Dressing das.

French fries npl Pommes frites pl.

Frenchman ['frentʃmən] (pl -men [-mən]) n Franzose der.

French toast n arme Ritter pl.

French windows npl Verandatür die.

Frenchwoman ['frentʃˌwʊmən] (pl -women [-ˌwɪmɪn]) n Französin die.

frequency ['friːkwənsɪ] n Frequenz die.

frequent ['friːkwənt] adj häufig.

frequently ['friːkwəntlɪ] adv häufig.

fresh [freʃ] adj frisch; (new, recent) neu; **~ water** Süßwasser das; **to get**

some ~ **air** an die frische Luft gehen.
fresh cream n Sahne die.
freshen ['freʃn]: **freshen up** vi sich frisch machen.
freshly ['freʃlɪ] adv frisch.
fresh orange (juice) n frischer Orangensaft.
Fri (abbr of Friday) Fr.
Friday ['fraɪdɪ] n Freitag der, → **Saturday**.
fridge [frɪdʒ] n Kühlschrank der.
fried egg [fraɪd-] n Spiegelei das.
fried rice [fraɪd-] n gebratener Reis.
friend [frend] n Freund der (-in die); **to be ~s with sb** mit jm befreundet sein; **to make ~s with sb** mit jm Freundschaft schließen.
friendly ['frendlɪ] adj freundlich; **to be ~ with sb** mit jm befreundet sein.
friendship ['frendʃɪp] n Freundschaft die.
fries [fraɪz] = **French fries**.
fright [fraɪt] n Furcht die; **to give sb a ~** jn erschrecken.
frighten ['fraɪtn] vt Angst machen (+D), erschrecken.
frightened ['fraɪtnd] adj: **to be ~ (of)** Angst haben (vor (+D).
frightening ['fraɪtnɪŋ] adj beängstigend.
frightful ['fraɪtfʊl] adj fürchterlich.
frilly ['frɪlɪ] adj gerüscht.
fringe [frɪndʒ] n (Br: of hair) Pony der; (of clothes, curtain etc) Fransen pl.
frisk [frɪsk] vt durchsuchen.
fritter ['frɪtə'] n Ausgebackene das, in Pfannkuchenteig getauchtes fritiertes Obst oder Gemüse.
fro [frəʊ] adv → **to**.
frog [frɒg] n Frosch der.
from [frɒm] prep **1.** (expressing origin, source) von; **where did you get that ~?** woher hast du das?; **I'm ~ England** ich bin aus England; **I bought it ~ a supermarket** ich habe es in einem Supermarkt gekauft; **the train ~ Manchester** der Zug aus Manchester.

2. (expressing removal, deduction) von; **away ~ home** weg von zu Hause; **to take sthg (away) ~ sb** jm etw wegInehmen; **10% will be deducted ~ the total** es wird 10% von der Gesamtsumme abgezogen. **3.** (expressing distance) von; **five miles ~ London** fünf Meilen von London entfernt; **it's not far ~ here** es ist nicht weit von hier. **4.** (expressing position) von; **~ here you can see the valley** von hier aus kann man das Tal sehen. **5.** (expressing starting time) von ... an; **open ~ nine to five** von neun bis fünf geöffnet; **~ next year** ab nächstem Jahr. **6.** (expressing change) von; **the price has gone up ~ £1 to £2** der Preis ist von 1 auf 2 Pfund gestiegen. **7.** (expressing range): **tickets cost ~ £10** Karten gibt es ab 10 Pfund; **it could take ~ two to six months** es könnte zwischen zwei und sechs Monaten dauern. **8.** (as a result of) von; **I'm tired ~ walking** ich bin vom Gehen müde; **to suffer ~ asthma** an Asthma leiden. **9.** (expressing protection) von; **sheltered ~ the wind** vor dem Wind geschützt. **10.** (in comparisons): **different ~** anders als.
fromage frais [ˌfrɒmɑːˈʒfreɪ] n Sahnequark der.
front [frʌnt] ◆ adj Vorder-, vordere (-r)(-s). ◆ n Vorderteil das; (of weather) Front die; (by the sea) Promenade die; **in ~** vorne; **in ~ of** vor (+D).
front door n (of house) Haustür die; (of flat) Wohnungstür die.
frontier [frʌnˈtɪə'] n Grenze die.
front page n Titelseite die.
front seat n Vordersitz der.
frost [frɒst] n (on ground) Reif der; (cold weather) Frost der.
frosty ['frɒstɪ] adj frostig.
froth [frɒθ] n Schaum der.
frown [fraʊn] ◆ n Stirnrunzeln das. ◆ vi die Stirn runzeln.
froze [frəʊz] pt → **freeze**.
frozen ['frəʊzn] ◆ pp → **freeze**. ◆ adj gefroren; (food) tiefgekühlt,

Gefrier-; **I'm ~** mir ist eiskalt.

fruit [fruːt] n Obst das; (variety of fruit) Frucht die; **~s of the forest** Waldbeeren pl.

fruit cake n englischer Kuchen.

fruiterer ['fruːtərər] n (Br) Obsthändler der.

fruit juice n Fruchtsaft der.

fruit machine n (Br) Spielautomat der.

fruit salad n Obstsalat der.

frustrating [frʌ'streitɪŋ] adj frustrierend.

frustration [frʌ'streiʃn] n Frustration die.

fry [frai] vt braten.

frying pan ['fraiɪŋ-] n Bratpfanne die.

ft abbr = **foot, feet**.

fudge [fʌdʒ] n weiches Bonbon aus Milch, Zucker und Butter.

fuel [fjʊəl] n Kraftstoff der.

fuel pump n Zapfsäule die.

fulfil [fʊl'fɪl] vt (Br) erfüllen; (role) ausˈfüllen.

fulfill [fʊl'fɪl] (Am) = **fulfil**.

full [fʊl] adj & adv voll; **I'm ~ (up)** ich bin satt; **~ of** voll von, voller; **in ~** vollständig.

full board n Vollpension die.

full-cream milk n Vollmilch die.

full-length adj (skirt, dress) lang.

full moon n Vollmond der.

full stop n Punkt der.

full-time ◆ adj ganztägig, Ganztags-. ◆ adv ganztags.

fully ['fʊlɪ] adv ganz.

fully-licensed adj mit Schankerlaubnis.

fumble ['fʌmbl] vi wühlen.

fun [fʌn] n Spaß der; **it's good ~** es macht Spaß; **for ~** aus Spaß; **to have ~** sich amüsieren; **to make ~ of** sich lustig machen über (+A).

function ['fʌŋkʃn] ◆ n Funktion die; (formal event) Veranstaltung die. ◆ vi funktionieren.

fund [fʌnd] ◆ n (of money) Fonds der.

◆ vt finanzieren. ▶ **funds** npl Geldmittel pl.

fundamental [,fʌndə'mentl] adj Grund-, grundlegend.

funeral ['fjuːnərəl] n Beerdigung die.

funfair ['fʌnfeər] n Jahrmarkt der.

funky ['fʌŋkɪ] adj (inf: music) funky.

funnel ['fʌnl] n (for pouring) Trichter der; (on ship) Schornstein der.

funny ['fʌnɪ] adj komisch; **I feel ~** (ill) mir ist (ganz) komisch.

fur [fɜːr] n Pelz der.

fur coat n Pelzmantel der.

furious ['fjʊərɪəs] adj wütend.

furnished ['fɜːnɪʃt] adj möbliert.

furnishings ['fɜːnɪʃɪŋz] npl Einrichtungsgegenstände pl.

furniture ['fɜːnɪtʃər] n Möbel pl; **a piece of ~** ein Möbelstück.

furry ['fɜːrɪ] adj (animal) mit dichtem Fell; (toy, material) Plüsch-.

further ['fɜːðər] ◆ compar → **far**. ◆ adv weiter. ◆ adj weitere(-r)(-s); **until ~ notice** bis auf weiteres; **would you like anything ~?** sonst noch etwas?

furthermore [,fɜːðə'mɔːr] adv außerdem.

furthest ['fɜːðɪst] ◆ superl → **far**. ◆ adj am weitesten entfernt. ◆ adv am weitesten.

fuse [fjuːz] ◆ n (of plug) Sicherung die; (on bomb) Zündschnur die. ◆ vi (plug, device) durchˈbrennen.

fuse box n Sicherungskasten der.

fuss [fʌs] n Theater das.

fussy ['fʌsɪ] adj (person) pingelig.

future ['fjuːtʃər] ◆ n Zukunft die. ◆ adj künftig; **in ~** in Zukunft.

G

g (*abbr of gram*) g.
gable ['geɪbl] *n* Giebel *der.*
gadget ['gædʒɪt] *n* Gerät *das.*
Gaelic ['geɪlɪk] *n* Gälisch *das.*
gag [gæg] *n* (*inf: joke*) Gag *der.*
gain [geɪn] ◆ *vt* (*get more of*) gewinnen; (*achieve*) erzielen; (*victory*) erringen; (*subj: clock, watch*) vor|gehen. ◆ *vi* (*get benefit*) profitieren. ◆ *n* Gewinn *der;* **to ~ weight** zu|nehmen.
gale [geɪl] *n* Sturm *der.*
gallery ['gælərɪ] *n* (*for art etc*) Galerie *die;* (*at theatre*) dritter Rang.
gallon ['gælən] *n* (*in UK*) = 4,546 l, Gallone *die;* (*in US*) = 3,78 l, Gallone.
gallop ['gæləp] *vi* galoppieren.
gamble ['gæmbl] ◆ *n* Risiko *das.* ◆ *vi* (*bet money*) (um Geld) spielen.
gambling ['gæmblɪŋ] *n* Glücksspiel *das.*
game [geɪm] *n* Spiel *das;* (*wild animals, meat*) Wild *das.* ▶ **games** *n* (SCH) Sport *der.* ◆ *npl* (*sporting event*) Spiele *pl.*
gammon ['gæmən] *n* geräucherter Schinken.
gang [gæŋ] *n* (*of criminals*) Bande *die;* (*of friends*) Clique *die.*
gangster ['gæŋstər] *n* Gangster *der.*
gangway ['gæŋweɪ] *n* (*for ship*) Gangway *die;* (*Br: in aeroplane, theatre*) Gang *der.*
gaol [dʒeɪl] (*Br*) = **jail.**
gap [gæp] *n* Lücke *die;* (*of time*) Pause *die;* (*difference*) Unterschied *der.*
garage ['gærɑːʒ, 'gærɪdʒ] *n* (*for keeping car*) Garage *die;* (*Br: for petrol*) Tankstelle *die;* (*for repairs*) Autowerkstatt *die;* (*Br: for selling cars*) Autohandlung *die.*
garbage ['gɑːbɪdʒ] *n* (*Am*) Müll *der.*
garbage can *n* (*Am*) Mülleimer *der.*

garbage truck *n* (*Am*) Müllwagen *der.*
garden ['gɑːdn] ◆ *n* Garten *der.* ◆ *vi* im Garten arbeiten. ▶ **gardens** *npl* (*public park*) Anlagen *pl.*
garden centre *n* Gärtnerei *die.*
gardener ['gɑːdnər] *n* Gärtner *der* (-in *die*).
gardening ['gɑːdnɪŋ] *n* Gartenarbeit *die.*
garden peas *npl* Erbsen *pl.*
garlic ['gɑːlɪk] *n* Knoblauch *der.*
garlic bread *n* Knoblauchbaguette *das.*
garlic butter *n* Knoblauchbutter *die.*
garment ['gɑːmənt] *n* Kleidungsstück *das.*
garnish ['gɑːnɪʃ] ◆ *n* (*herbs, vegetables*) Garnierung *die;* (*sauce*) Soße *die.* ◆ *vt* garnieren.
gas [gæs] *n* Gas *das;* (*Am: petrol*) Benzin *das.*
gas cooker *n* (*Br*) Gasherd *der.*
gas cylinder *n* Gasflasche *die.*
gas fire *n* (*Br*) Gasofen *der.*
gasket ['gæskɪt] *n* Dichtung *die.*
gas mask *n* Gasmaske *die.*
gasoline ['gæsəliːn] *n* (*Am*) Benzin *das.*
gasp [gɑːsp] *vi* (*in shock, surprise*) nach Luft schnappen.
gas pedal *n* (*Am*) Gaspedal *das.*
gas station *n* (*Am*) Tankstelle *die.*
gas stove (*Br*) = **gas cooker.**
gas tank *n* (*Am*) Benzintank *der.*
gasworks ['gæswɜːks] (*pl inv*) *n* Gaswerk *das.*
gate [geɪt] *n* Tor *das;* (*at airport*) Flugsteig *der.*
gâteau ['gætəu] (*pl* -**x** [-z]) *n* (*Br*) Sahnetorte *die.*
gateway ['geɪtweɪ] *n* (*entrance*) Tor *das.*
gather ['gæðər] ◆ *vt* sammeln; (*understand*) an|nehmen. ◆ *vi* (*come together*) sich versammeln; **to ~ speed** schneller werden.

gaudy ['gɔːdɪ] adj grell.

gauge [geɪdʒ] ◆ n (for measuring) Meßgerät das; (of railway track) Spurweite die. ◆ vt (calculate) ablschätzen.

gauze [gɔːz] n Gaze die.

gave [geɪv] pt → **give**.

gay [geɪ] adj (homosexual) schwul.

gaze [geɪz] vi: **to ~ at** blicken auf (+A).

GB (abbr of Great Britain) GB.

GCSE n Abschlußprüfung in der Schule, die meist mit 16 Jahren abgelegt wird.

gear [gɪəʳ] n (wheel) Gangschaltung die; (speed) Gang der; (equipment, clothes) Sachen pl; **is the car in ~?** ist der Gang eingelegt?; **to change ~** schalten.

gearbox ['gɪəbɒks] n Getriebe das.

gear lever n Schaltknüppel der.

gear shift (Am) = **gear lever**.

gear stick (Br) = **gear lever**.

geese [giːs] pl → **goose**.

gel [dʒel] n Gel das.

gelatine [,dʒelə'tiːn] n Gelatine die.

gem [dʒem] n Juwel das.

Gemini ['dʒemɪnaɪ] n Zwillinge pl.

gender ['dʒendəʳ] n Geschlecht das.

general ['dʒenərəl] ◆ adj allgemein. ◆ n General der; **in ~** im allgemeinen.

general anaesthetic n Vollnarkose die.

general election n allgemeine Wahlen.

generally ['dʒenərəlɪ] adv (usually) normalerweise; (by most people) allgemein.

general practitioner [-præk'tɪʃənəʳ] n praktischer Arzt (praktische Ärztin).

general store n Lebensmittelgeschäft das.

generate ['dʒenəreɪt] vt erzeugen.

generation [,dʒenə'reɪʃn] n Generation die.

generator ['dʒenəreɪtəʳ] n Generator der.

generosity [,dʒenə'rɒsətɪ] n Großzügigkeit die.

generous ['dʒenərəs] adj großzügig.

Geneva [dʒɪ'niːvə] n Genf nt.

genitals ['dʒenɪtlz] npl Geschlechtsteile pl.

genius ['dʒiːnjəs] n Genie das.

gentle ['dʒentl] adj sanft.

gentleman ['dʒentlmən] (pl -men [-mən]) n (man) Herr der; (well-behaved man) Kavalier der; '**gentlemen**' 'Herren'.

gently ['dʒentlɪ] adv sanft.

gents [dʒents] n (Br) Herrentoilette die.

genuine ['dʒenjuɪn] adj echt.

geographical [dʒɪə'græfɪkl] adj geographisch.

geography [dʒɪ'ɒgrəfɪ] n Geographie die; (terrain) geographische Gegebenheiten pl.

geology [dʒɪ'ɒlədʒɪ] n Geologie die.

geometry [dʒɪ'ɒmətrɪ] n Geometrie die.

Georgian ['dʒɔːdʒən] adj (architecture etc) georgianisch (1714-1830).

geranium [dʒɪ'reɪnjəm] n Geranie die.

German ['dʒɜːmən] ◆ adj deutsch. ◆ n (person) Deutsche der die; (language) Deutsch das; **in ~** auf deutsch.

German measles n Röteln pl.

German studies n Germanistik die.

Germany ['dʒɜːmənɪ] n Deutschland nt.

germs [dʒɜːmz] npl Bazillen pl.

gesture ['dʒestʃəʳ] n Geste die.

get [get] (pt & pp **got**, Am pp **gotten**) ◆ vt 1. (obtain) bekommen; (buy) kaufen; **she got a job** sie hat eine Stelle gefunden. 2. (receive) bekommen; **I got a book for Christmas** ich habe zu Weihnachten ein Buch bekommen. 3. (train, plane, bus etc) nehmen; **let's ~ a taxi** laß uns ein Taxi nehmen. 4. (fetch) holen; **could you ~ me the manager?** (in shop) könnten Sie mir den Geschäftsführer holen?; (*on phone*) könnten Sie mir den Geschäftsführer geben? **5.** (*illness*) bekommen; **I've got a cold** ich habe eine Erkältung. **6.** (*cause to become*): **to ~ sthg done** etw machen lassen; **can I ~ my car repaired here?** kann ich mein Auto hier reparieren lassen? **7.** (*ask, tell*): **to ~ sb to do sthg** jn bitten, etw zu tun. **8.** (*move*): **I can't ~ it through the door** ich bekomme es nicht durch die Tür. **9.** (*understand*) verstehen. **10.** (*time, chance*) haben; **we didn't ~ the chance to see everything** wir hatten nicht die Gelegenheit, uns alles anzuschauen. **11.** (*idea, feeling*) haben; **I ~ a lot of enjoyment from it** ich habe viel Spaß daran. **12.** (*phone*): **could you ~ the phone?** könntest du ans Telefon gehen? **13.** (*in phrases*): **you ~ a lot of rain here in winter** hier regnet es viel im Winter, → **have.** ◆ *vi* **1.** (*become*) werden; **it's getting late** es wird spät; **to ~ lost** sich verirren; **to ~ ready** fertig|werden; **~ lost!** (*inf*) hau ab!, verschwinde! **2.** (*into particular state, position*): **to ~ into trouble** in Schwierigkeiten geraten; **how do you ~ to Luton from here?** wie kommt man von hier nach Luton?; **to ~ into the car** ins Auto ein|steigen. **3.** (*arrive*) an|kommen; **when does the train ~ here?** wann kommt der Zug hier an? **4.** (*in phrases*): **to ~ to do sthg** die Gelegenheit haben, etw zu tun. ◆ *aux vb* werden; **to ~ delayed** aufgehalten werden; **to ~ killed** getötet werden. ▶ **get back** *vi* (*return*) zurück|kommen. ▶ **get in** *vi* (*arrive*) an|kommen; (*into car, bus*) ein|steigen. ▶ **get off** *vi* (*leave train, bus*) aus|steigen; (*leave*) los|gehen; (*in car*) los|fahren. ▶ **get on** *vi* (*enter train, bus*) ein|steigen; (*in relationship*) sich verstehen; (*cope*) zurecht|kommen; (*progress*): **how are you getting on?** wie kommst du voran? ▶ **get out** *vi* (*of car, bus, train*) aus|steigen. ▶ **get through** *vi* (*on phone*)

durch|kommen. ▶ **get up** *vi* auf|stehen.

get-together *n* (*inf*) Treffen *das*.

ghastly ['gɑːstlɪ] *adj* (*inf*) schrecklich.

gherkin ['gɜːkɪn] *n* Gewürzgurke *die*.

ghetto blaster ['getəʊ,blɑːstər] *n* (*inf*) Radiorecorder *der*.

ghost [gəʊst] *n* Geist *der*.

giant ['dʒaɪənt] ◆ *adj* riesig. ◆ *n* Riese *der*.

giblets ['dʒɪblɪts] *npl* Innereien *pl*.

giddy ['gɪdɪ] *adj* schwindlig.

gift [gɪft] *n* (*present*) Geschenk *das*; (*talent*) Begabung *die*.

gifted ['gɪftɪd] *adj* begabt.

gift shop *n* Geschenkeladen *der*.

gift voucher *n* (Br) Geschenkgutschein *der*.

gig [gɪg] *n* (*inf: concert*) Gig *der*.

gigantic [dʒaɪˈgæntɪk] *adj* riesig.

giggle ['gɪgl] *vi* kichern.

gill [dʒɪl] *n* (*measurement*) = 0,142 l.

gimmick ['gɪmɪk] *n* Gimmick *der*.

gin [dʒɪn] *n* Gin *der*; **~ and tonic** Gin Tonic *der*.

ginger ['dʒɪndʒər] ◆ *n* Ingwer *der*. ◆ *adj* (*colour*) rotblond.

ginger ale *n* Ginger-ale *das*.

ginger beer *n* Ginger-beer *das*.

gingerbread ['dʒɪndʒəbred] *n* Pfefferkuchen *der*.

gipsy ['dʒɪpsɪ] *n* Zigeuner *der* (-in *die*).

giraffe [dʒɪˈrɑːf] *n* Giraffe *die*.

girdle ['gɜːdl] *n* Hüfthalter *der*.

girl [gɜːl] *n* Mädchen *das*.

girlfriend ['gɜːlfrend] *n* Freundin *die*.

girl guide *n* (Br) Pfadfinderin *die*.

girl scout (Am) = **girl guide**.

giro ['dʒaɪrəʊ] *n* (*system*) Giro *das*.

give [gɪv] (*pt* gave, *pp* given ['gɪvn]) *vt* geben; (*speech*) halten; (*attention, time*) widmen; **to ~ sb sthg** jm etw geben; (*as present*) jm etw schenken; **to ~ sb a look** jm an|sehen; **to ~ sb a**

push jm einen Schubs geben; **to ~ sb a kiss** jm einen Kuß geben; **~ or take** mehr oder weniger; **'~ way'** 'Vorfahrt beachten'. ► **give away** vt sep (get rid of) weg|geben; (reveal) verraten. ► **give back** vt sep zurück|geben. ► **give in** vi nach|geben. ► **give off** vt fus ab|geben. ► **give out** vt sep (distribute) aus|teilen. ► **give up** vt sep & vi auf|geben.

glacier ['glæsjər] n Gletscher der.

glad [glæd] adj froh; **to be ~ to do sthg** sich freuen, etw zu tun.

gladly ['glædlɪ] adv (willingly) gern.

glamorous ['glæmərəs] adj glamourös.

glance [glɑːns] ◆ n Blick der. ◆ vi: **to ~ at** einen Blick werfen auf (+A).

gland [glænd] n Drüse die.

glandular fever ['glændjʊlə-] n Drüsenfieber das.

glare [gleər] vi (sun, light) blenden; (person): **to ~ at** böse ansehen.

glass [glɑːs] ◆ n Glas das. ◆ adj Glas-. ► **glasses** npl Brille die.

glassware ['glɑːsweər] n Glaswaren pl.

glen [glen] n (Scot) enges Tal.

glider ['glaɪdər] n Segelflugzeug das.

glimpse [glɪmps] vt flüchtig sehen.

glitter ['glɪtər] vi glitzern.

global warming [,gləʊbl'wɔːmɪŋ] n die Erwärmung der Erdatmosphäre.

globe [gləʊb] n Globus der.

gloomy ['gluːmɪ] adj düster.

glorious ['glɔːrɪəs] adj (weather, sight) großartig; (victory, history) glorreich.

glory ['glɔːrɪ] n Ruhm der.

gloss [glɒs] n (shine) Glanz der; **~ (paint)** Lackfarbe die.

glossary ['glɒsərɪ] n Glossar das.

glossy ['glɒsɪ] adj (magazine) Hochglanz-; (photo) Glanz-.

glove [glʌv] n Handschuh der.

glove compartment n Handschuhfach das.

glow [gləʊ] ◆ n Glühen das. ◆ vi glühen.

glucose ['gluːkəʊs] n Glukose die.

glue [gluː] ◆ n Klebstoff der. ◆ vt kleben.

gnat [næt] n Mücke die.

gnaw [nɔː] vt nagen an (+D).

go [gəʊ] (pt went, pp gone, pl goes) ◆ vi 1. (move) gehen; (travel) fahren; **to ~ for a walk** spazieren|gehen; **I'll ~ and collect the cases** ich gehe die Koffer abholen; **to ~ home** nach Hause gehen; **to ~ to Austria** nach Österreich fahren; **to ~ by bus** mit dem Bus fahren; **to ~ shopping** einkaufen gehen. 2. (leave) gehen; (in vehicle) fahren; **when does the bus ~?** wann fährt der Bus ab?; **~ away!** geh weg! 3. (become) werden; **she went pale** sie wurde bleich; **the milk has gone sour** die Milch ist sauer geworden. 4. (expressing future tense): **to be going to do sthg** etw tun werden; **it's going to rain tomorrow** morgen wird es regnen; **we're going to go to Switzerland** wir fahren in die Schweiz. 5. (function) laufen; (watch) gehen; **the car won't ~** das Auto springt nicht an. 6. (stop working) kaputt|gehen; **the fuse has gone** die Sicherung ist herausgesprungen. 7. (time) vergehen. 8. (progress) gehen, laufen; **to ~ well** gut|gehen. 9. (alarm) los|gehen. 10. (match) zusammen|passen; **to ~ with** passen zu; **red wine doesn't ~ with fish** Rotwein paßt nicht zu Fisch. 11. (be sold) verkauft werden; **'everything must ~'** 'alles muß weg'. 12. (fit) passen, gehen. 13. (lead) führen; **where does this path ~?** wohin führt dieser Weg? 14. (belong) gehören. 15. (in phrases): **to let ~ of sthg** (drop) etw los|lassen; **to ~** (Am: to take away) zum Mitnehmen; **how long is there to ~ until Christmas?** wie lange ist es noch bis Weihnachten? ◆ n 1. (turn): **it's your ~** du bist an der Reihe. 2. (attempt) Versuch der; **to have a ~ at sthg** etw versuchen, etw probieren; '50p a ~' (for game) 'jede Runde 50p'. ▶ **go ahead** vi (begin) anｌfangen, beginnen; (take place) stattｌfinden; ~ **ahead!** bitte! ▶ **go back** vi (return) zurückｌgehen. ▶ **go down** vi (decrease) sinken; (sun) unterｌgehen; (tyre) platt werden. ▶ **go down with** vt fus (inf: illness) bekommen. ▶ **go in** vi hineinｌgehen. ▶ **go off** vi (alarm) losｌgehen; (go bad) schlecht werden; (light, heating) ausｌgehen. ▶ **go on** vi (happen) los sein; (light, heating) anｌgehen; (continue): **to ~ on doing sthg** etw weiter tun; ~ **on!** los! ▶ **go out** vi ausｌgehen; (have relationship): **to ~ out with sb** mit jm gehen; **to ~ out for a meal** essen gehen; **to ~ out for a walk** einen Spaziergang machen. ▶ **go over** vt fus (check) überprüfen. ▶ **go round** vi (revolve) sich drehen. ▶ **go through** vt fus (experience) durchｌmachen; (spend) ausｌgeben; (search) durchsuchen. ▶ **go up** vi (increase) steigen. ▶ **go without** vt fus: **to ~ without sthg** ohne etw ausｌkommen.

goal [gəʊl] n (SPORT) Tor das; (aim) Ziel das.

goalkeeper ['gəʊlˌkiːpər] n Torwart der.

goalpost ['gəʊlpəʊst] n Torpfosten der.

goat [gəʊt] n Ziege die.

gob [gɒb] n (Br: inf: mouth) Maul das.

god [gɒd] n Gott der (Göttin die). ▶ **God** n Gott.

goddaughter ['gɒdˌdɔːtər] n Patentochter die.

godfather ['gɒdˌfɑːðər] n Pate der.

godmother ['gɒdˌmʌðər] n Patin die.

gods [gɒdz] npl: **the ~** (in theatre: (Br: inf) der Olymp.

godson ['gɒdsʌn] n Patensohn der.

goes [gəʊz] → **go**.

goggles ['gɒglz] npl (for swimming) Taucherbrille die; (for skiing) Skibrille die.

going ['gəʊɪŋ] adj (available) erhältlich; **the ~ rate** der übliche Betrag.

go-kart [-kɑːt] n Go-Kart der.

gold [gəʊld] ◆ n Gold das. ◆ adj (bracelet, watch) golden.

goldfish ['gəʊldfɪʃ] (pl inv) n Goldfisch der.

gold-plated [-'pleɪtɪd] adj vergoldet.

golf [gɒlf] n Golf das.

golf ball n Golfball der.

golf club n (place) Golfklub der; (equipment) Golfschläger der.

golf course n Golfplatz der.

golfer ['gɒlfər] n Golfspieler der (-in die).

gone [gɒn] ◆ pp → **go**. ◆ prep (Br: past) nach.

good [gʊd] (compar **better**, superl **best**) ◆ adj gut; (well-behaved) artig, brav; (thorough) gründlich. ◆ n (moral correctness) Gute das; **to have a ~ time** sich gut amüsieren; **to be ~ at sthg** etw gut können; **a ~ ten minutes** gute zehn Minuten; **in ~ time** beizeiten; **to make ~ sthg** (damage, loss) etw wieder gutｌmachen; **for ~** für immer; **for the ~ of** zum Wohle (+G); **it's no ~** (there's no point) es hat keinen Zweck; **that's very ~ of you** das ist sehr nett von Ihnen; ~ **afternoon!** guten Tag!; ~ **evening!** guten Abend!; ~ **morning!** guten Morgen!; ~ **night!** gute Nacht! ▶ **goods** npl Waren pl.

goodbye [ˌgʊd'baɪ] excl auf Wiedersehen!

Good Friday n Karfreitag der.

good-looking [-'lʊkɪŋ] adj gutaussehend.

goods train [gʊdz-] n Güterzug der.

goose [guːs] (pl geese) n Gans die.

gooseberry ['gʊzbəri] n Stachelbeere die.

gorge [gɔːdʒ] n Schlucht die.

gorgeous ['gɔːdʒəs] adj (day, meal, countryside) wunderschön; (inf: good-looking): **to be ~** eine Wucht sein.

gorilla [gə'rɪlə] n Gorilla der.

gossip ['gɒsɪp] ◆ n Klatsch der. ◆ vi klatschen.

gossip column n Klatschspalte die.

got [gɒt] pt & pp → **get**.

gotten ['gɒtn] pp (Am) → **get**.

goujons ['guːdʒɒnz] npl panierte und fritierte Fisch- oder Fleischstreifen.

goulash ['guːlæʃ] n Gulasch das.

gourmet ['guəmeɪ] ◆ n Feinschmecker der (-in die). ◆ adj (food, restaurant) Feinschmecker-.

govern ['gʌvən] vt regieren.

government ['gʌvnmənt] n Regierung die.

gown [gaʊn] n (dress) Kleid das.

GP abbr = **general practitioner**.

grab [græb] vt (take hold of) greifen.

graceful ['greɪsfʊl] adj (elegant) graziös.

grade [greɪd] n (quality) Klasse die; (in exam) Note die; (Am: year at school) Klasse die.

gradient ['greɪdjənt] n (upward) Steigung die; (downward) Gefälle das.

gradual ['grædʒʊəl] adj allmählich.

gradually ['grædʒʊəlɪ] adv allmählich.

graduate [n 'grædʒʊət, vb 'grædʒʊeɪt] ◆ n Akademiker der (-in die); (Am: from high school) Schulabgänger der (-in die). ◆ vi die Universität ab⎮schließen; (Am: from high school) die Schule ab⎮schließen.

graduation [ˌgrædʒʊ'eɪʃn] n (ceremony) Abschlußfeier einer Universität.

graffiti [grə'fiːtɪ] n Graffiti das.

grain [greɪn] n (seed) Korn das; (crop) Getreide das; (of sand, salt) Körnchen das.

gram [græm] n Gramm das.

grammar ['græmər] n Grammatik die.

grammar school n (in UK) = Gymnasium das.

gramme [græm] = **gram**.

gramophone ['græməfəʊn] n Plattenspieler der.

gran [græn] n (Br: inf) Oma die.

grand [grænd] ◆ adj (impressive) großartig. ◆ n (inf: thousand pounds) tausend Pfund pl; (thousand dollars) tausend Dollar pl.

grandchild ['græntʃaɪld] (pl -children [-ˌtʃɪldrən]) n Enkelkind das.

granddad ['grændæd] n (inf) Opa der.

granddaughter ['grænˌdɔːtər] n Enkelin die.

grandfather ['grændˌfɑːðər] n Großvater der.

grandma ['grænmɑː] n (inf) Oma die.

grandmother ['grænˌmʌðər] n Großmutter die.

grandpa ['grænpɑː] n (inf) Opa der.

grandparents ['grænˌpeərənts] npl Großeltern pl.

grandson ['grænsʌn] n Enkel der.

granite ['grænɪt] n Granit der.

granny ['grænɪ] n (inf) Oma die.

grant [grɑːnt] ◆ n (POL) Zuschuß der; (for university) Stipendium das. ◆ vt (fml: give) gewähren; **to take sthg for ~ed** etw als selbstverständlich an⎮sehen; **he takes his wife for ~ed** er weiß nicht zu schätzen, was seine Frau für ihn tut.

grape [greɪp] n Traube die.

grapefruit ['greɪpfruːt] n Grapefruit die, Pampelmuse die.

grapefruit juice n Grapefruitsaft der.

graph [grɑːf] n Kurvendiagramm das.

graphic designer ['græfɪk-] n Grafiker der (-in die).

graph paper n Millimeterpapier das.

grasp [grɑːsp] vt fest⎮halten; (understand) verstehen.

grass [grɑːs] n Gras das; (lawn) Rasen der; **'keep off the ~'** 'den Rasen nicht betreten'.

grasshopper ['grɑːsˌhɒpər] n Heuschrecke die.

grate [greɪt] n (of fire) Rost der.

grated ['greɪtɪd] adj gerieben.

grateful ['greɪtful] adj dankbar.

grater ['greɪtər] n Reibe die.

gratitude ['grætɪtjuːd] n Dankbarkeit die.

gratuity [grə'tjuːɪtɪ] n (fml) Trinkgeld das.

grave¹ [greɪv] ♦ adj (mistake) schwer; (news) schlimm; (situation) ernst. ♦ n Grab das.

grave² [grɑːv] adj (accent) grave.

gravel ['grævl] n Kies der.

graveyard ['greɪvjɑːd] n Friedhof der.

gravity ['grævɪtɪ] n Schwerkraft die.

gravy ['greɪvɪ] n Soße die.

gray [greɪ] (Am) = grey.

graze [greɪz] vt (injure) auf|schürfen.

grease [griːs] n (for machine, tool) Schmiere die; (animal fat) Fett das.

greaseproof paper ['griːspruːf-] n (Br) Pergamentpapier das.

greasy ['griːsɪ] adj (tools, clothes) schmierig; (food, skin, hair) fettig.

great [greɪt] adj (large, famous, important) groß; (very good) großartig; (that's) ~! (das ist) toll!

Great Britain n Großbritannien nt.

great-grandfather n Urgroßvater der.

great-grandmother n Urgroßmutter die.

greatly ['greɪtlɪ] adv sehr.

Greece [griːs] n Griechenland nt.

greed [griːd] n Gier die.

greedy ['griːdɪ] adj gierig.

Greek [griːk] ♦ adj griechisch. ♦ n (person) Grieche der (Griechin die); (language) Griechisch das.

Greek salad n griechischer Salat.

green [griːn] ♦ adj grün. ♦ n (colour) Grün das; (in village) Gemeindewiese die; (on golf course) Green der. ▶ **greens** npl (vegetables) Grüngemüse das.

green beans npl grüne Bohnen pl.

green card n (Br: for car) grüne Karte; (Am: work permit) Arbeitserlaubnis die.

green channel n Ausgang 'nichts zu verzollen' am Flughafen.

greengage ['griːngeɪdʒ] n Reineclaude die.

greengrocer's ['griːn,grəʊsəz] n (shop) Obst- und Gemüsegeschäft das.

greenhouse ['griːnhaʊs, pl -haʊzɪz] n Gewächshaus das.

greenhouse effect n Treibhauseffekt der.

green light n grünes Licht.

green pepper n grüner Paprika.

Greens [griːnz] npl: **the ~** die Grünen.

green salad n grüner Salat.

greet [griːt] vt grüßen.

greeting ['griːtɪŋ] n Gruß der.

grenade [grə'neɪd] n Granate die.

grew [gruː] pt → grow.

grey [greɪ] ♦ adj grau. ♦ n Grau das; **to go ~** grau werden.

greyhound ['greɪhaʊnd] n Windhund der.

grid [grɪd] n Gitter das; (on map etc) Gitternetz das.

grief [griːf] n Trauer die; **to come to ~** scheitern.

grieve [griːv] vi trauern.

grill [grɪl] ♦ n Grill der. ♦ vt grillen.

grille [grɪl] n (AUT) Kühlergrill der.

grilled [grɪld] adj gegrillt.

grim [grɪm] adj (place, news, reality) düster; (determined) grimmig.

grimace ['grɪməs] n Grimasse die.

grimy ['graɪmɪ] adj verschmutzt.

grin [grɪn] ♦ n Grinsen das. ♦ vi grinsen.

grind [graɪnd] (pt & pp ground) vt (pepper, coffee) mahlen.

grip [grɪp] ♦ n Griff der; (of tyres) Profil das; (bag) Reisetasche die. ♦ vt (hold) fest|halten.

gristle ['grɪsl] n Knorpel der.

groan [grəʊn] ♦ n Stöhnen das. ♦ vi stöhnen; (complain) sich beklagen.

groceries ['grəʊsəriz] npl
Lebensmittel pl.

grocer's ['grəʊsəz] n (shop)
Lebensmittelgeschäft das.

grocery ['grəʊsəri] n (shop)
Lebensmittelgeschäft das.

groin [grɔin] n Leiste die.

groove [gru:v] n Rille die.

grope [grəʊp] vi (search) tasten.

gross [grəʊs] adj (weight, income)
brutto.

grossly ['grəʊsli] adv (extremely)
äußerst.

grotty ['grɒti] adj (Br: inf) mies.

ground [graʊnd] ◆ pt & pp → **grind**.
◆ n Boden der; (SPORT) Platz der. ◆ adj
(coffee) gemahlen. ◆ vt: **to be ~ed**
(plane) keine Starterlaubnis erhalten; (Am: ELEC) geerdet sein.
▶ **grounds** npl (of building) Anlagen
pl; (of coffee) Satz der; (reason) Grund
der.

ground floor n Erdgeschoß das.

groundsheet ['graʊndʃi:t] n
Bodenplane die.

group [gru:p] n Gruppe die.

grouse [graʊs] (pl inv) n (bird)
Moorschneehuhn das.

grovel ['grɒvl] vi (be humble)
kriechen.

grow [grəʊ] (pt grew, pp grown) ◆ vi
wachsen; (become) werden. ◆ vt
(plant, crop) anlbauen; (beard) sich (D)
wachsen lassen. ▶ **grow up** vi
auflwachsen; (mentally) erwachsen
werden.

growl [graʊl] vi (dog) knurren.

grown [grəʊn] pp → **grow**.

grown-up ◆ adj erwachsen. ◆ n
Erwachsene der die.

growth [grəʊθ] n Wachstum das;
(MED) Geschwulst die.

grub [grʌb] n (inf: food) Futter das.

grubby ['grʌbi] adj (inf) schmudd-
lig.

grudge [grʌdʒ] ◆ n Abneigung die.
◆ vt: **to ~ sb sthg** jm etw neiden; **to
have a ~ against sb** etw gegen jn
haben.

grueling ['gruəliŋ] (Am) = **gruelling**.

gruelling ['gruəliŋ] adj (Br) anstrengend.

gruesome ['gru:səm] adj grausig.

grumble ['grʌmbl] vi (complain) sich
beschweren.

grumpy ['grʌmpi] adj (inf) grantig.

grunt [grʌnt] vi grunzen.

guarantee [ˌgærən'ti:] ◆ n
Garantie die. ◆ vt garantieren; (product) Garantie geben.

guard [gɑːd] ◆ n (of prisoner etc)
Wärter der (-in die); (Br: on train)
Schaffner der (-in die); (protective cover)
Schutz der. ◆ vt bewachen; **to be on
one's ~** auf der Hut sein.

guess [ges] ◆ n Vermutung die. ◆ vt
erraten. ◆ vi raten; **I ~ (so)** ich denke
(schon).

guest [gest] n Gast der.

guesthouse ['gesthaʊs, pl -haʊziz] n
Pension die.

guestroom ['gestrʊm] n Gästezimmer das.

guidance ['gaidəns] n Beratung die.

guide [gaid] ◆ n (for tourists)
Fremdenführer der (-in die); (guide-
book) Reiseführer der. ◆ vt führen.
▶ **Guide** n (Br) Pfadfinderin die.

guidebook ['gaidbʊk] n Reiseführer der.

guide dog n Blindenhund der.

guided tour ['gaidid-] n Führung
die.

guidelines ['gaidlainz] npl Richt-
linien pl.

guilt [gilt] n Schuld die.

guilty ['gilti] adj schuldig; (remorse-
ful) schuldbewußt; **to be ~ of sthg**
etw (G) schuldig sein; **to feel ~** ein
schlechtes Gewissen haben.

guinea pig ['gini-] n Meerschweinchen das.

guitar [gi'tɑːr] n Gitarre die.

guitarist [gi'tɑːrist] n Gitarrist der
(-in die).

gulf [gʌlf] n (of sea) Golf der.

Gulf War *n*: **the ~** der Golfkrieg.
gull [gʌl] *n* Möwe *die*.
gullible ['gʌləbl] *adj* leichtgläubig.
gulp [gʌlp] *n* (*of drink*) Schluck *der*.
gum [gʌm] *n* (*chewing gum, bubble gum*) Kaugummi *der*; (*adhesive*) Klebstoff *der*. ▶ **gums** *npl* (*in mouth*) Zahnfleisch *das*.
gun [gʌn] *n* (*pistol*) Pistole *die*; (*rifle*) Gewehr *das*; (*cannon*) Kanone *die*.
gunfire ['gʌnfaɪəʳ] *n* Geschützfeuer *das*.
gunshot ['gʌnʃɒt] *n* Schuß *der*.
gust [gʌst] *n* Windstoß *der*.
gut [gʌt] *n* (*inf: stomach*) Bauch *der*. ▶ **guts** *npl* (*inf: intestines*) Eingeweide *pl*; (*courage*) Mut *der*.
gutter ['gʌtəʳ] *n* (*beside road*) Rinnstein *der*; (*of house*) Regenrinne *die*.
guy [gaɪ] *n* (*inf: man*) Typ *der*. ▶ **guys** *npl* (Am: *inf: people*): **you ~s** ihr.
Guy Fawkes Night [-'fɔːks-] *n* Nacht des 5. November, in der mit Feuerwerk an den Versuch Guy Fawkes', das Parlament in die Luft zu sprengen, erinnert wird.
guy rope *n* Zeltschnur *die*.
gym [dʒɪm] *n* (SCH: *building*) Turnhalle *die*; (*health club*) Fitneßcenter *das*; (*in health club, hotel*) Fitneßraum *der*; (SCH: *lesson*) Turnen *das*.
gymnast ['dʒɪmnæst] *n* Turner *der* (-in *die*).
gymnastics [dʒɪm'næstɪks] *n* Turnen *das*.
gym shoes *npl* Turnschuhe *pl*.
gynaecologist [ˌgaɪnə'kɒlədʒɪst] *n* Frauenarzt *der* (-ärztin *die*).
gypsy ['dʒɪpsɪ] = **gipsy**.

H

H *abbr* = **hot, hospital**.
habit ['hæbɪt] *n* Gewohnheit *die*.
hacksaw ['hæksɔː] *n* Metallsäge *die*.
had [hæd] *pt & pp* → **have**.
haddock ['hædək] (*pl inv*) *n* Schellfisch *der*.
hadn't ['hædnt] = **had not**.
haggis ['hægɪs] *n schottische Spezialität, bestehend aus mit Schafsinnereien gefülltem Schafsmagen, üblicherweise serviert mit Kartoffel- und Kohlrabipüree*.
haggle ['hægl] *vi* feilschen.
hail [heɪl] ◆ *n* Hagel *der*. ◆ *v impers* hageln.
hailstone ['heɪlstəʊn] *n* Hagelkorn *das*.
hair [heəʳ] *n* Haare *pl*; (*individual hair*) Haar *das*; **to have one's ~ cut** sich (D) die Haare schneiden lassen.
hairband ['heəbænd] *n* Haarband *das*.
hairbrush ['heəbrʌʃ] *n* Haarbürste *die*.
hairclip ['heəklɪp] *n* Haarklip *der*.
haircut ['heəkʌt] *n* (*style*) Haarschnitt *der*; **to have a ~** sich (D) die Haare schneiden lassen.
hairdo ['heəduː] (*pl -s*) *n* Frisur *die*.
hairdresser ['heəˌdresəʳ] *n* Friseur *der* (Friseuse *die*); **~'s** (*salon*) Friseursalon *der*; **to go to the ~'s** zum Friseur gehen.
hairdryer ['heəˌdraɪəʳ] *n* Fön® *der*.
hair gel *n* Haargel *das*.
hairgrip ['heəgrɪp] *n* (Br) Haarklammer *die*.
hairnet ['heənet] *n* Haarnetz *das*.
hairpin bend ['heəpɪn-] *n* Haarnadelkurve *die*.
hair remover [-rɪˌmuːvəʳ] *n*

handle

Enthaarungsmittel *das*.

hair rollers [-'rəʊləz] *npl* Lockenwickler *pl*.

hair slide *n* Haarspange *die*.

hairspray ['heəspreɪ] *n* Haarspray *das*.

hairstyle ['heəstaɪl] *n* Frisur *die*.

hairy ['heərɪ] *adj* haarig.

half [Br hɑːf, Am hæf] (*pl* **halves**) ◆ *n* Hälfte *die*; (*of match*) Spielhälfte *die*; (*half pint*) halbes Pint, ≈ kleines Bier; (*child's ticket*) Kinderfahrkarte *die*. ◆ *adj & adv* halb; **~ of it** die Hälfte davon; **four and a ~** viereinhalb; **~ past seven** halb acht; **~ as big as** halb so groß wie; **an hour and a ~** anderthalb Stunden; **an hour** eine halbe Stunde; **~ a dozen** ein halbes Dutzend.

half board *n* Halbpension *die*.

half-day *n* halber Tag.

half fare *n* halber Fahrpreis.

half portion *n* halbe Portion.

half-price *adj* zum halben Preis.

half term *n* (Br) Ferien in der Mitte des Trimesters.

half time *n* Halbzeit *die*.

halfway [hɑːf'weɪ] *adv* auf halbem Wege; **~ through the holiday** mitten im Urlaub.

halibut ['hælɪbət] (*pl inv*) *n* Heilbutt *der*.

hall [hɔːl] *n* (*of house*) Diele *die*, Flur *der*; (*large room*) Saal *der*; (*building*) Halle *die*; (*country house*) Landsitz *der*.

hallmark ['hɔːlmɑːk] *n* (*on silver, gold*) Stempel *der*.

hallo [hə'ləʊ] = **hello**.

hall of residence *n* Studentenwohnheim *das*.

Halloween [ˌhæləʊ'iːn] *n* Abend vor Allerheiligen, an dem sich Kinder oft als Gespenster verkleiden.

halt [hɔːlt] ◆ *vi* anlhalten. ◆ *n*: **to come to a ~** zum Stillstand kommen.

halve [Br hɑːv, Am hæv] *vt* halbieren.

halves [Br hɑːvz, Am hævz] *pl* → **half**.

ham [hæm] *n* Schinken *der*.

hamburger ['hæmbɜːgəʳ] *n* Hamburger *der*; (Am: *mince*) Hackfleisch *das*.

hamlet ['hæmlɪt] *n* kleines Dorf.

hammer ['hæməʳ] ◆ *n* Hammer *der*. ◆ *vt* (*nail*) einlschlagen.

hammock ['hæmək] *n* Hängematte *die*.

hamper ['hæmpəʳ] *n* Picknickkorb *der*.

hamster ['hæmstəʳ] *n* Hamster *der*.

hamstring ['hæmstrɪŋ] *n* Kniesehne *die*.

hand [hænd] *n* Hand *die*; (*of clock, watch, dial*) Zeiger *der*; **to give sb a ~** jm helfen; **to get out of ~** außer Kontrolle geraten; **written by ~** handgeschrieben; **to arrive with an hour in ~** eine Stunde zu früh ankommen; **on the one ~** einerseits; **on the other ~** andererseits. ▶ **hand in** *vt sep* einlreichen, ablgeben. ▶ **hand out** *vt sep* auslteilen. ▶ **hand over** *vt sep* (*give*) übergeben.

handbag ['hændbæg] *n* Handtasche *die*.

handbasin ['hændbeɪsn] *n* Waschbecken *das*.

handbook ['hændbʊk] *n* Handbuch *das*.

handbrake ['hændbreɪk] *n* Handbremse *die*.

hand cream *n* Handcreme *die*.

handcuffs ['hændkʌfs] *npl* Handschellen *pl*.

handful ['hændfʊl] *n* (*amount*) Handvoll *die*.

handicap ['hændɪkæp] *n* Behinderung *die*; (*disadvantage*) Handikap *das*.

handicapped ['hændɪkæpt] ◆ *adj* behindert. ◆ *npl*: **the ~** die Behinderten *pl*.

handkerchief ['hæŋkətʃɪf] (*pl* -**chiefs** OR -**chieves** [-tʃiːvz]) *n* Taschentuch *das*.

handle ['hændl] ◆ *n* Griff *der*. ◆ *vt*

(touch) an|fassen; (situation) bewälti-
gen; '**~ with care**' 'mit Vorsicht
behandeln'.

handlebars ['hændlbɑːz] npl
Lenkstange die.

hand luggage n Handgepäck das.

handmade [,hænd'meɪd] adj
handgearbeitet.

handout ['hændaʊt] n (leaflet)
Handout das.

handrail ['hændreɪl] n Geländer
das.

handset ['hændset] n Hörer der;
'**please replace the ~**' 'bitte den
Hörer auflegen'.

handshake ['hændʃeɪk] n Händedruck der.

handsome ['hænsəm] adj (man)
gutaussehend.

handstand ['hændstænd] n Handstand der.

handwriting ['hænd,raɪtɪŋ] n
Handschrift die.

handy ['hændɪ] adj praktisch; (person) geschickt; **to come in ~** (inf)
nützlich sein; **to have sthg ~** (near)
etw zur Hand haben.

hang [hæŋ] (pt & pp hung) ◆ vt
auf|hängen; (execute: pt & pp **hanged**)
hängen. ◆ vi hängen. ◆ n: **to get the ~**
of sthg etw kapieren. ▶ **hang about**
vi (Br: inf) rum|hängen. ▶ **hang**
around (inf) = **hang about**.
▶ **hang down** vi herunter|hängen.
▶ **hang on** vi (inf: wait) warten.
▶ **hang out** vt sep (washing) auf|hän-
gen. ◆ vi (inf: spend time) sich
herum|treiben. ▶ **hang up** vi (on
phone) auf|legen, ein|hängen.

hangar ['hæŋər] n Hangar der.

hanger ['hæŋər] n Kleiderbügel der.

hang gliding n Drachenfliegen
das.

hangover ['hæŋ,əʊvər] n Kater der.

hankie ['hæŋkɪ] n (inf) Taschentuch
das.

happen ['hæpən] vi passieren,
geschehen; **to ~ to do sthg** etw zufällig tun.

happily ['hæpɪlɪ] adv (luckily) glücklicherweise.

happiness ['hæpɪnɪs] n Glück das.

happy ['hæpɪ] adj glücklich; **to be ~**
about sthg mit etw zufrieden sein; **to**
be ~ to do sthg (willing) etw gern tun;
to be ~ with sthg mit etw zufrieden
sein; **Happy Birthday!** Herzlichen
Glückwunsch zum Geburtstag!;
Happy Christmas! Fröhliche Weihnachten!; **Happy New Year!** ein
gutes neues Jahr!

happy hour n (inf) Zeit am frühen
Abend, zu der in Bars usw. alkoholische
Getränke billiger verkauft werden.

harassment ['hærəsmənt] n
Belästigung die.

harbor ['hɑːbər] (Am) = **harbour**.

harbour ['hɑːbər] n (Br) Hafen
der.

hard [hɑːd] ◆ adj hart; (difficult, stren-
uous) schwer. ◆ adv (work) hart; (listen)
gut; (hit) schwer; (rain) heftig; **to try ~**
sich (D) Mühe geben.

hardback ['hɑːdbæk] n Hardcover
das.

hardboard ['hɑːdbɔːd] n Hart-
faserplatte die.

hard-boiled egg [-bɔɪld-] n hart-
gekochtes Ei.

hard disk n Festplatte die.

hardly ['hɑːdlɪ] adv kaum; **~ ever**
fast nie.

hardship ['hɑːdʃɪp] n Härte die.

hard shoulder n (Br) Seitenstreifen der.

hard up adj (inf): **to be ~** knapp bei
Kasse sein.

hardware ['hɑːdweər] n (tools,
equipment) Haushaltsgeräte pl; (COM-
PUT) Hardware die.

hardwearing [,hɑːd'weərɪŋ] adj
(Br) strapazierfähig.

hardworking [,hɑːd'wɜːkɪŋ] adj
fleißig.

hare [heər] n Hase der.

harm [hɑːm] ◆ n Schaden der. ◆ vt
schaden (+D); (person) verletzen.

harmful ['hɑːmfʊl] adj schädlich.

harmless ['hɑːmlɪs] *adj* unschädlich.

harmonica [hɑːˈmɒnɪkə] *n* Mundharmonika *die*.

harmony ['hɑːmənɪ] *n* Harmonie *die*.

harness ['hɑːnɪs] *n* (*for horse*) Geschirr *das*; (*for child*) Laufgeschirr *das*.

harp [hɑːp] *n* Harfe *die*.

harsh [hɑːʃ] *adj* rauh; (*cruel*) hart.

harvest ['hɑːvɪst] *n* Ernte *die*.

has [*weak form* həz, *strong form* hæz] → **have**.

hash browns [hæʃ-] *npl* amerikanische Kartoffelpuffer.

hasn't ['hæznt] = **has not**.

hassle ['hæsl] *n* (*inf*) Ärger *der*.

hastily ['heɪstɪlɪ] *adv* (*rashly*) vorschnell.

hasty ['heɪstɪ] *adj* (*hurried*) eilig; (*rash*) vorschnell.

hat [hæt] *n* Hut *der*.

hatch [hætʃ] ◆ *n* (*for serving food*) Durchreiche *die*. ◆ *vi* (*chick*) aus|schlüpfen.

hatchback ['hætʃˌbæk] *n* Auto *das* mit Hecktür.

hatchet ['hætʃɪt] *n* Beil *das*.

hate [heɪt] ◆ *n* Haß *der*. ◆ *vt* hassen; **to ~ doing sthg** etw ungern tun.

hatred ['heɪtrɪd] *n* Haß *der*.

haul [hɔːl] ◆ *vt* ziehen. ◆ *n*: **a long ~** eine weite Strecke.

haunted ['hɔːntɪd] *adj*: **this house is ~** in diesem Haus spukt es.

have [hæv] (*pt & pp* **had**) ◆ *aux vb* **1.** (*to form perfect tenses*) haben/sein; **~ you seen the film?** hast du den Film gesehen?; **I ~ finished** ich bin fertig; **~ you been there? - no, I haven't** warst du schon mal dort? – nein, noch nie; **we had already left** wir waren schon gegangen. **2.** (*must*): **to ~ (got) to do sthg** etw tun müssen; **do you ~ to pay?** muß man bezahlen? ◆ *vt* **1.** (*possess*): **to ~ (got)** haben; **do you ~** OR **~ you got a double room?** haben Sie ein Doppelzimmer?; **she has (got) brown hair** sie hat braunes Haar. **2.** (*experience*) haben; **to ~ a cold** eine Erkältung haben; **to ~ a great time** sich großartig amüsieren. **3.** (*replacing other verbs*): **to ~ a bath** ein Bad nehmen; **to ~ breakfast** frühstücken; **to ~ a cigarette** eine Zigarette rauchen; **to ~ a drink** etwas trinken; **to ~ lunch** zu Mittag essen; **to ~ a shower** duschen; **to ~ a swim** schwimmen; **to ~ a walk** spazieren|gehen. **4.** (*feel*) haben; **I ~ no doubt about it** ich habe keine Zweifel daran. **5.** (*cause to be*): **to ~ sthg done** etw machen lassen; **to ~ one's hair cut** sich die Haare schneiden lassen. **6.** (*be treated in a certain way*): **I've had my wallet stolen** mir ist mein Geldbeutel gestohlen worden.

haversack ['hævəsæk] *n* Rucksack *der*.

havoc ['hævək] *n* Verwüstung *die*.

hawk [hɔːk] *n* Falke *der*.

hawker ['hɔːkəʳ] *n* Hausierer *der* (-in *die*).

hay [heɪ] *n* Heu *das*.

hay fever *n* Heuschnupfen *der*.

haystack ['heɪˌstæk] *n* Heuhaufen *der*.

hazard ['hæzəd] *n* Risiko *das*.

hazardous ['hæzədəs] *adj* gefährlich.

hazard warning lights *npl* (Br) Warnblinkanlage *die*.

haze [heɪz] *n* Dunst *der*.

hazel ['heɪzl] *adj* nußbraun.

hazelnut ['heɪzlˌnʌt] *n* Haselnuß *die*.

hazy ['heɪzɪ] *adj* (*misty*) dunstig.

he [hiː] *pron* er; **~'s tall** er ist groß.

head [hed] ◆ *n* Kopf *der*; (*of table, bed*) Kopfende *das*; (*of company, department*) Leiter *der* (-in *die*); (*of school*) Schulleiter *der* (-in *die*); (*of beer*) Schaumkrone *die*. ◆ *vt* (*list, procession*) an|führen; (*organization*) leiten. ◆ *vi* gehen; (*in vehicle*) fahren; **£10 a ~** 10 Pfund pro Kopf; **~s or tails?** Kopf oder Zahl? ▶ **head for** vt fus (place) zulsteuern auf (+A).

headache ['hedeɪk] n Kopfschmerzen pl; **to have a ~** Kopfschmerzen haben.

heading ['hedɪŋ] n Überschrift die.

headlamp ['hedlæmp] (Br) = **headlight**.

headlight ['hedlaɪt] n Scheinwerfer der.

headline ['hedlaɪn] n Schlagzeile die.

headmaster [,hed'mɑːstər] n Schulleiter der.

headmistress [,hed'mɪstrɪs] n Schulleiterin die.

head of state n Staatsoberhaupt das.

headphones ['hedfəʊnz] npl Kopfhörer pl.

headquarters [,hed'kwɔːtəz] npl Hauptquartier das.

headrest ['hedrest] n Kopfstütze die.

headroom ['hedrʊm] n (under bridge) Höhe die.

headscarf ['hedskɑːf] (pl -scarves [-skɑːvz]) n Kopftuch das.

head start n Vorsprung der.

head teacher n Schulleiter der (-in die).

head waiter n Oberkellner der.

heal [hiːl] vt & vi heilen.

health [helθ] n Gesundheit die; **to be in good ~** guter Gesundheit sein; **to be in poor ~** kränklich sein; **your (very) good ~!** auf dein/Ihr Wohl!

health centre n Ärztezentrum das.

health food n Biokost die.

health food shop n Bioladen der.

health insurance n Krankenversicherung die.

healthy ['helθɪ] adj gesund.

heap [hiːp] n Haufen der; **~s of money** (inf) ein Haufen Geld.

hear [hɪər] (pt & pp **heard** [hɜːd]) vt & vi hören; **to ~ about sthg** von etw hören; **to ~ from sb** von jm hören; **to**

have heard of schon mal gehört haben von.

hearing ['hɪərɪŋ] n (sense) Gehör das; (at court) Verhandlung die; **to be hard of ~** schwerhörig sein.

hearing aid n Hörgerät das.

heart [hɑːt] n Herz das; **to know sthg (off) by ~** etw auswendig können; **to lose ~** den Mut verlieren. ▶ **hearts** npl (in cards) Herz das.

heart attack n Herzinfarkt der.

heartbeat ['hɑːtbiːt] n Herzschlag der.

heartburn ['hɑːtbɜːn] n Sodbrennen das.

heart condition n: **to have a ~** herzkrank sein.

hearth [hɑːθ] n Kamin der.

hearty ['hɑːtɪ] adj (meal) herzhaft.

heat [hiːt] n Hitze die; (pleasant) Wärme die; (of oven) Temperatur die. ▶ **heat up** vt sep auflwärmen.

heater ['hiːtər] n Heizgerät das.

heath [hiːθ] n Heide die.

heather ['heðər] n Heidekraut das.

heating ['hiːtɪŋ] n Heizung die.

heat wave n Hitzewelle die.

heave [hiːv] vt wuchten.

Heaven ['hevn] n der Himmel.

heavily ['hevɪlɪ] adv stark.

heavy ['hevɪ] adj schwer; (rain, traffic) stark; **how ~ is it?** wie schwer ist es?; **to be a ~ smoker** ein starker Raucher sein.

heavy cream n (Am) Schlagsahne die, Schlagobers das (Österr).

heavy goods vehicle n (Br) Lastkraftwagen der.

heavy industry n Schwerindustrie die.

heavy metal n Heavy metal das.

heckle ['hekl] vt unterbrechen.

hectic ['hektɪk] adj hektisch.

hedge [hedʒ] n Hecke die.

hedgehog ['hedʒhɒg] n Igel der.

heel [hiːl] n (of person) Ferse die; (of shoe) Absatz der.

hefty ['heftɪ] adj (person) stämmig; (fine) saftig.

height [haɪt] n Höhe die; (of person) Körpergröße die; (peak period) Höhepunkt der; **what ~ is it?** wie hoch ist es?

heir [eəʳ] n Erbe der.

heiress ['eərɪs] n Erbin die.

held [held] pt & pp → **hold**.

helicopter ['helɪkɒptəʳ] n Hubschrauber der.

he'll [hiːl] = **he will**.

Hell [hel] n die Hölle.

hello [hə'ləʊ] excl hallo!; (on phone) guten Tag!

helmet ['helmɪt] n Helm der.

help [help] ◆ n Hilfe die. ◆ vt helfen (+D). ◆ vi helfen. ◆ excl Hilfe!; **I can't ~** ich kann nichts dafür; **to ~ sb (to) do sthg** jm helfen, etw zu tun; **to ~ to do sthg** (contribute) dazu beitragen, etw zu tun; **to ~ o.s. to sthg** sich (D) etw nehmen; **can I ~ you?** (in shop) kann ich Ihnen behilflich sein? ► **help out** vi auslhelfen.

helper ['helpəʳ] n Helfer der (-in die); (Am: cleaner) Hausangestellte der die.

helpful ['helpfʊl] adj (person) hilfsbereit; (useful) nützlich.

helping ['helpɪŋ] n Portion die.

helpless ['helplɪs] adj hilflos.

hem [hem] n Saum der.

hemophiliac [ˌhiːmə'fɪlɪæk] n Bluter der.

hemorrhage ['hemərɪdʒ] n Blutung die.

hen [hen] n Henne die.

hepatitis [ˌhepə'taɪtɪs] n Hepatitis die.

her [hɜːʳ] ◆ adj ihr. ◆ pron (accusative) sie; (dative) ihr; **I know ~** ich kenne sie; **it's ~** sie ist es; **send it to ~** schick es ihr; **tell ~** sag ihr; **he's worse than ~** er ist schlimmer als sie.

herb [hɜːb] n Kraut das.

herbal tea ['hɜːbl-] n Kräutertee der.

herd [hɜːd] n Herde die.

here [hɪəʳ] adv hier; **come ~!** komm her!; **~ you are** hier.

heritage ['herɪtɪdʒ] n Erbe das.

heritage centre n Museum an einem Ort mit historischer Bedeutung.

hernia ['hɜːnjə] n Bruch der.

hero ['hɪərəʊ] (pl -es) n Held der.

heroin ['herəʊɪn] n Heroin das.

heroine ['herəʊɪn] n Heldin die.

heron ['herən] n Reiher der.

herring ['herɪŋ] n Hering der.

hers [hɜːz] pron ihre(-r)(-s), ihre (pl); **a friend of ~** ein Freund von ihr; **these shoes are ~** diese Schuhe gehören ihr.

herself [hɜː'self] pron sich; (after prep) sich selbst; **she did it ~** sie hat es selbst getan.

hesitant ['hezɪtənt] adj zögernd.

hesitate ['hezɪteɪt] vi zögern.

hesitation [ˌhezɪ'teɪʃn] n Zögern das.

heterosexual [ˌhetərəʊ'sekʃʊəl] ◆ adj heterosexuell. ◆ n Heterosexuelle der die.

hey [heɪ] excl (inf) he!

HGV n (abbr of heavy goods vehicle) Lkw der.

hi [haɪ] excl (inf) hallo!

hiccup ['hɪkʌp] n: **to have (the) ~s** (einen) Schluckauf haben.

hide [haɪd] (pt hid [hɪd], pp hidden ['hɪdn]) ◆ vt verstecken; (truth) verschweigen; (feelings) verbergen. ◆ vi sich verstecken. ◆ n (of animal) Haut die, Fell das; **to be hidden** (obscured) sich verbergen.

hideous ['hɪdɪəs] adj scheußlich.

hi-fi ['haɪfaɪ] n Hi-Fi-Anlage die.

high [haɪ] ◆ adj hohe(-r)(-s); (inf: from drugs) high. ◆ n (weather front) Hoch das. ◆ adv hoch; **to be ~** (tall) hoch sein; **how ~ is it?** wie hoch ist es?; **it's 10 metres ~** es ist 10 Meter hoch.

high chair n Kinderhochstuhl der.

high-class adj (good-quality) erstklassig.

Higher ['haɪəʳ] n (Scot) schottischer Schulabschluß.

higher education n Hochschulbildung die.

high heels npl hochhackige Schuhe pl.

high jump n Hochsprung der.

Highland Games ['haɪlənd-] npl typisches schottisches Sport- und Musikfestival.

Highlands ['haɪləndz] npl: **the ~** das (schottische) Hochland.

highlight ['haɪlaɪt] ♦ n (best part) Höhepunkt der. ♦ vt hervor|heben. ▶ **highlights** npl (of football match etc) Highlights pl; (in hair) Strähnchen pl.

highly ['haɪlɪ] adv höchst; **to think ~ of** viel halten von; **~ paid** hochbezahlt.

high-pitched [-'pɪtʃt] adj hohe(-r) (-s).

high-rise n (building) Hochhaus das.

high school n (in UK) Schule für elf- bis achtzehnjährige; (in US) Schule für fünfzehn- bis achtzehnjährige.

high season n Hochsaison die.

high-speed train n Hochgeschwindigkeitszug der.

high street n (Br) Hauptgeschäftsstraße die.

high tide n Flut die.

highway ['haɪweɪ] n (Am) Highway der; (Br: any main road) Straße die.

Highway Code n (Br) Straßenverkehrsordnung die.

hijack ['haɪdʒæk] vt entführen.

hijacker ['haɪdʒækər] n Entführer der.

hike [haɪk] ♦ n Wanderung die. ♦ vi wandern.

hiking ['haɪkɪŋ] n: **to go ~** auf eine Wanderung gehen.

hilarious [hɪ'leərɪəs] adj lustig.

hill [hɪl] n Hügel der.

hillwalking ['hɪlwɔːkɪŋ] n Bergwandern das.

hilly ['hɪlɪ] adj hügelig.

him [hɪm] pron (accusative) ihn; (dative) ihm; **I know ~** ich kenne ihn; **it's ~** er ist es; **send it to ~** schick es

ihm; **tell ~** sag ihm; **she's worse than ~** sie ist schlimmer als er.

himself [hɪm'self] pron sich; (after prep) sich selbst; **he did it ~** er hat es selbst getan.

hinder ['hɪndər] vt (prevent) behindern; (delay) verzögern.

Hindu ['hɪnduː] (pl -s) ♦ adj Hindu-. ♦ n Hindu der.

hinge [hɪndʒ] n Scharnier das.

hint [hɪnt] ♦ n Andeutung die; (piece of advice) Hinweis der; (slight amount) Spur die. ♦ vi: **to ~ at sthg** etw an|deuten.

hip [hɪp] n Hüfte die.

hippopotamus [ˌhɪpə'pɒtəməs] n Nilpferd das.

hippy ['hɪpɪ] n Hippie der.

hire ['haɪər] vt (car, bicycle, television) mieten; **'for ~'** (taxi) 'frei'. ▶ **hire out** vt sep vermieten.

hire car n (Br) Mietwagen der.

hire purchase n (Br) Ratenkauf der.

his [hɪz] ♦ adj sein. ♦ pron seine(-r) (-s), seine (pl); **a friend of ~** ein Freund von ihm; **these shoes are ~** diese Schuhe gehören ihm.

historical [hɪ'stɒrɪkəl] adj historisch.

history ['hɪstərɪ] n Geschichte die.

hit [hɪt] (pt & pp inv) ♦ vt schlagen; (collide with) treffen; (vehicle) prallen gegen. ♦ n (record, play, film) Hit der; **to ~ one's head** sich (D) den Kopf an|schlagen; **to ~ the target** das Ziel treffen.

hit-and-run adj: **a ~ accident** ein Unfall mit Fahrerflucht.

hitch [hɪtʃ] ♦ n (problem) Haken der. ♦ vi per Anhalter fahren, trampen. ♦ vt: **to ~ a lift** per Anhalter fahren.

hitchhike ['hɪtʃhaɪk] vi per Anhalter fahren, trampen.

hitchhiker ['hɪtʃhaɪkər] n Anhalter der (-in die).

hive [haɪv] n Bienenstock der.

HIV-positive adj HIV-positiv.

hoarding ['hɔːdɪŋ] n (Br: for adverts) Plakatwand die.

hoarse [hɔːs] *adj* heiser.

hoax [həʊks] *n* Schwindel *der*.

hob [hɒb] *n* Kochplatte *die*.

hobby ['hɒbɪ] *n* Hobby *das*.

hock [hɒk] *n* (*wine*) Rheinwein *der*.

hockey ['hɒkɪ] *n* Hockey *das*; (*Am*: *ice hockey*) Eishockey *das*.

hoe [həʊ] *n* Hacke *die*.

hold [həʊld] (*pt & pp* **held**) ◆ *vt* halten; (*meeting, election*) abIhalten; (*contain*) fassen; (*possess*) haben. ◆ *vi* (*offer*) gelten; (*weather*) sich halten; (*on telephone*) warten. ◆ *n* (*grip*) Halt *der*, Griff *der*; (*of ship, aircraft*) Laderaum *der*; **to ~ sb prisoner** jn gefangenIhalten; **~ the line, please** warten Sie, bitte. ► **hold back** *vt sep* zurückIhalten; (*keep secret*) vorIenthalten. ► **hold on** *vi* (*wait*) warten; **to ~ on to sthg** (*grip*) etw festIhalten. ► **hold out** *vt sep* (*extend*) ausIstrecken. ► **hold up** *vt sep* (*delay*) aufIhalten.

holdall ['həʊldɔːl] *n* (*Br*) Reisetasche *die*.

holder ['həʊldəʳ] *n* (*of passport, licence*) Inhaber *der* (-in *die*); (*container*) Halter *der*.

holdup ['həʊldʌp] *n* (*delay*) Verzögerung *die*.

hole [həʊl] *n* Loch *das*.

holiday ['hɒlɪdeɪ] ◆ *n* (*period of time*) Urlaub *der*, Ferien *pl*; (*day off*) freier Tag; (*public*) Feiertag *der*. ◆ *vi* (*Br*) Ferien machen, urlauben; **to be on ~** im Urlaub sein, in Ferien sein; **to go on ~** in Urlaub fahren, in die Ferien fahren.

holidaymaker ['hɒlɪdɪˌmeɪkəʳ] *n* (*Br*) Urlauber *der* (-in *die*).

holiday pay *n* (*Br*) Urlaubsgeld *das*.

Holland ['hɒlənd] *n* Holland *nt*.

hollow ['hɒləʊ] *adj* hohl.

holly ['hɒlɪ] *n* Stechpalme *die*.

Hollywood ['hɒlɪwʊd] *n* Hollywood *nt*.

holy ['həʊlɪ] *adj* heilig.

home [həʊm] ◆ *n* Zuhause *das*; (*own country*) Heimat *die*; (*one's family*) Elternhaus *das*; (*for old people*) Altersheim *das*. ◆ *adj* (*not foreign*) einheimisch. ◆ *adv*: **to be ~** zu Hause sein; **to go ~** nach Hause gehen; **at ~** zu Hause; **to make o.s. at ~** es sich (D) bequem machen; **~ address** Heimatanschrift *die*; **~ number** private Telefonnummer.

home economics *n* Hauswirtschaftslehre *die*.

home help *n* (*Br*) Haushaltshilfe *die* (*meist Sozialarbeiterin*).

homeless ['həʊmlɪs] *npl*: **the ~** die Obdachlosen *pl*.

homemade [ˌhəʊm'meɪd] *adj* selbstgemacht.

homeopathic [ˌhəʊmɪəʊ'pæθɪk] *adj* homöopathisch.

home page *n* (*on Internet*) Home page *die*.

Home Secretary *n* (*Br*) Innenminister *der*.

homesick ['həʊmsɪk] *adj*: **to be ~** Heimweh haben.

homework ['həʊmwɜːk] *n* Hausaufgaben *pl*.

homosexual [ˌhɒmə'sekʃʊəl] ◆ *adj* homosexuell. ◆ *n* Homosexuelle *der* *die*.

honest ['ɒnɪst] *adj* ehrlich.

honestly ['ɒnɪstlɪ] *adv* ehrlich.

honey ['hʌnɪ] *n* Honig *der*.

honeymoon ['hʌnɪmuːn] *n* Flitterwochen *pl*.

honor ['ɒnər] (*Am*) = **honour**.

honour ['ɒnəʳ] *n* (*Br*) Ehre *die*.

honourable ['ɒnrəbl] *adj* ehrenwert; (*deed*) ehrenvoll.

hood [hʊd] *n* Kapuze *die*; (*on convertible car*) Verdeck *das*; (*Am*: *car bonnet*) Kühlerhaube *die*.

hoof [huːf] *n* Huf *der*.

hook [hʊk] *n* Haken *der*; **off the ~** (*telephone*) ausgehängt.

hooligan ['huːlɪgən] *n* Hooligan *der*.

hoop [huːp] *n* Reifen *der*.

hoot [huːt] *vi* (*driver*) hupen.

Hoover® ['huːvəʳ] n (Br) Staubsauger der.

hop [hɒp] vi hüpfen.

hope [həʊp] ♦ n Hoffnung die. ♦ vt hoffen; **to ~ for sthg** auf etw (A) hoffen; **to ~ to do sthg** hoffen, etw zu tun; **I ~ so** ich hoffe es.

hopeful ['həʊpfʊl] adj hoffnungsvoll.

hopefully ['həʊpfəlɪ] adv hoffentlich.

hopeless ['həʊplɪs] adj (inf: useless) miserabel; (without any hope) hoffnungslos.

hops [hɒps] npl Hopfen der.

horizon [həˈraɪzn] n Horizont der.

horizontal [ˌhɒrɪˈzɒntl] adj horizontal.

horn [hɔːn] n (of car) Hupe die; (on animal) Horn das.

horoscope ['hɒrəskəʊp] n Horoskop das.

horrible ['hɒrəbl] adj furchtbar.

horrid ['hɒrɪd] adj schrecklich.

horrific [hɒˈrɪfɪk] adj entsetzlich.

hors d'oeuvre [ɔːˈdɜːvrə] n Hors d'oeuvre das.

horse [hɔːs] n Pferd das.

horseback ['hɔːsbæk] n: **on ~** zu Pferd.

horse chestnut n Roßkastanie die.

horse-drawn carriage n Pferdedroschke die.

horsepower ['hɔːsˌpaʊəʳ] n Pferdestärke die.

horse racing n Pferderennen das.

horseradish (sauce) ['hɔːsˌrædɪʃ-] n Meerrettich der (traditionell zu Roastbeef gegessen).

horse riding n Reiten das.

horseshoe ['hɔːsʃuː] n Hufeisen das.

hose [həʊz] n Schlauch der.

hosepipe ['həʊzpaɪp] n Schlauch der.

hosiery ['həʊzɪərɪ] n Strumpfwaren pl.

hospitable [hɒˈspɪtəbl] adj gastfreundlich.

hospital ['hɒspɪtl] n Krankenhaus das; **in ~** im Krankenhaus.

hospitality [ˌhɒspɪˈtælətɪ] n Gastfreundschaft die.

host [həʊst] n Gastgeber der; (of show, TV programme) Moderator der (-in die).

hostage ['hɒstɪdʒ] n Geisel die.

hostel ['hɒstl] n (youth hostel) Jugendherberge die.

hostess ['həʊstes] n (on aeroplane) Stewardeß die; (of party, event) Gastgeberin die.

hostile [Br 'hɒstaɪl, Am 'hɒstl] adj feindselig.

hostility [hɒˈstɪlətɪ] n Feindseligkeit die.

hot [hɒt] adj heiß; (water, drink, food) warm; (spicy) scharf; **I'm ~** mir ist heiß.

hot chocolate n heiße Schokolade.

hot-cross bun n rundes Rosinenbrötchen mit Gewürzen, das vor allem zu Ostern gegessen wird.

hot dog n Hot dog der or das.

hotel [həʊˈtel] n Hotel das.

hot line n heißer Draht.

hotplate ['hɒtpleɪt] n Kochplatte die.

hotpot ['hɒtpɒt] n Fleischauflauf, bedeckt mit einer Schicht Kartoffelscheiben.

hot-water bottle n Wärmflasche die.

hour ['aʊəʳ] n Stunde die; **I've been waiting for ~s** ich warte schon seit Stunden.

hourly ['aʊəlɪ] adj & adv stündlich.

house [n haʊs, pl 'haʊzɪz, vb haʊz] ♦ n Haus das; (SCH) traditionelle Schülergemeinschaften innerhalb einer Schule, die untereinander Wettbewerbe veranstalten. ♦ vt unterbringen.

household ['haʊshəʊld] n Haushalt der.

housekeeping ['haʊsˌkiːpɪŋ] n Haushaltung die.

House of Commons n (Br) britisches Unterhaus.

House of Lords n (Br) britisches Oberhaus.

Houses of Parliament *npl* (Br) Houses of Parliament *pl*, Sitz *des britischen Parlaments*.

housewife ['haʊswaɪf] (*pl* **-wives** [-waɪvz]) *n* Hausfrau *die*.

house wine *n* Hauswein *der*.

housework ['haʊswɜːk] *n* Hausarbeit *die*.

housing ['haʊzɪŋ] *n* (*houses*) Wohnungen *pl*.

housing estate *n* (Br) Wohnsiedlung *die*.

housing project (Am) = **housing estate**.

hovercraft ['hɒvəkrɑːft] *n* Luftkissenboot *das*.

hoverport ['hɒvəpɔːt] *n* Hafen für Luftkissenfahrzeuge.

how [haʊ] *adv* **1.** (*asking about way or manner*) wie; ~ **do you get there?** wie kommt man dahin?; **tell me ~ to do it** sag mir, wie man das macht. **2.** (*asking about health, quality*) wie; ~ **are you?** wie geht's dir?, wie geht es Ihnen?; ~ **are you doing?** wie geht's dir?, wie geht es Ihnen?; ~ **are things?** wie geht's?; ~ **do you do?** Guten Tag!; ~ **is your room?** wie ist Ihr/dein Zimmer? **3.** (*asking about degree, amount*) wie; ~ **far?** wie weit?; ~ **long?** wie lang?; ~ **many?** wie viele?; ~ **much?** wieviel?; ~ **much is it?** wieviel kostet es?; ~ **old are you?** wie alt bist du/sind Sie? **4.** (*in phrases*): ~ **about a drink?** wie wäre es mit etwas zu trinken/einem Drink?; ~ **lovely!** wie hübsch!, wie nett!

however [haʊ'evər] *adv* jedoch, aber; ~ **long it takes** egal, wie lange es dauert.

howl [haʊl] *vi* heulen.

HP *abbr* (Br) = **hire purchase**.

HQ *abbr* = **headquarters**.

hub airport [hʌb-] *n* zentraler Flughafen.

hubcap ['hʌbkæp] *n* Radkappe *die*.

hug [hʌg] ◆ *vt* umarmen. ◆ *n*: **to give sb a ~** jn umarmen.

huge [hjuːdʒ] *adj* riesig.

hull [hʌl] *n* Schiffsrumpf *der*.

hum [hʌm] *vi* summen.

human ['hjuːmən] ◆ *adj* menschlich. ◆ *n*: ~ **(being)** Mensch *der*.

humanities [hjuː'mænətɪz] *npl* Geisteswissenschaften *pl*.

human rights *npl* Menschenrechte *pl*.

humble ['hʌmbl] *adj* (*not proud*) demütig; (*of low status*) niedrig.

humid ['hjuːmɪd] *adj* feucht.

humidity [hjuː'mɪdətɪ] *n* Feuchtigkeit *die*.

humiliating [hjuː'mɪlɪeɪtɪŋ] *adj* erniedrigend.

humiliation [hjuːˌmɪlɪ'eɪʃn] *n* Erniedrigung *die*.

hummus ['hʊməs] *n* Paste aus pürierten Kichererbsen und Knoblauch.

humor ['hjuːmər] (Am) = **humour**.

humorous ['hjuːmərəs] *adj* lustig.

humour ['hjuːmər] *n* Humor *der*; **a sense of ~** Sinn für Humor.

hump [hʌmp] *n* Buckel *der*; (*of camel*) Höcker *der*.

humpbacked bridge ['hʌmpbækt-] *n* gewölbte Brücke.

hunch [hʌntʃ] *n* Gefühl *das*.

hundred ['hʌndrəd] *num* hundert, → **six**; **a** OR **one ~** einhundert.

hundredth ['hʌndrətθ] *num* hundertste(-r)(-s), → **sixth**.

hundredweight ['hʌndrədweɪt] *n* (*in UK*) = 50,8 kg, ≈ Zentner *der*; (*in US*) = 45,36 kg, ≈ Zentner *der*.

hung [hʌŋ] *pt* & *pp* → **hang**.

Hungarian [hʌŋ'geərɪən] ◆ *adj* ungarisch. ◆ *n* (*person*) Ungar *der* (-in *die*); (*language*) Ungarisch *das*.

Hungary ['hʌŋgərɪ] *n* Ungarn *nt*.

hunger ['hʌŋgər] *n* Hunger *der*.

hungry ['hʌŋgrɪ] *adj* hungrig; **to be ~** Hunger haben.

hunt [hʌnt] ◆ *n* (Br: *for foxes*) Fuchsjagd *die*. ◆ *vt* & *vi* jagen; **to ~ (for)** (*search*) suchen.

hunting ['hʌntɪŋ] *n* Jagd *die*; (Br: *for foxes*) Fuchsjagd *die*.

hurdle ['hɜːdl] n Hürde die.

hurl [hɜːl] vt schleudern.

hurricane ['hʌrɪkən] n Orkan der.

hurry ['hʌrɪ] ◆ vt (person) hetzen. ◆ vi sich beeilen. ◆ n: **to be in a ~** es eilig haben; **to do sthg in a ~** etw hastig tun. ▶ **hurry up** vi sich beeilen.

hurt [hɜːt] (pt & pp inv) ◆ vt verletzen. ◆ vi (be painful) weh tun; **to ~ o.s.** sich (D) weh tun; **to ~ one's head** sich (D) den Kopf verletzen.

husband ['hʌzbənd] n Ehemann der.

hustle ['hʌsl] n: **~ and bustle** geschäftiges Treiben.

hut [hʌt] n Hütte die.

hyacinth ['haɪəsɪnθ] n Hyazinthe die.

hydrofoil ['haɪdrəfɔɪl] n Tragflächenboot das.

hygiene ['haɪdʒiːn] n Hygiene die.

hygienic [haɪ'dʒiːnɪk] adj hygienisch.

hymn [hɪm] n Hymne die.

hypermarket ['haɪpəˌmɑːkɪt] n Großmarkt der.

hyphen ['haɪfn] n Bindestrich der.

hypocrite ['hɪpəkrɪt] n Heuchler der (-in die).

hypodermic needle [ˌhaɪpə-'dɜːmɪk-] n Kanüle die.

hysterical [hɪs'terɪkl] adj hysterisch; (inf: very funny) lustig.

I

I [aɪ] pron ich; **I'm tall** ich bin groß.

ice [aɪs] n Eis das.

iceberg ['aɪsbɜːg] n Eisberg der.

iceberg lettuce n Eisbergsalat der.

icebox ['aɪsbɒks] n (Am) Kühlschrank der.

ice-cold adj eiskalt.

ice cream n Eis das.

ice cube n Eiswürfel der.

ice hockey n Eishockey das.

Iceland ['aɪslənd] n Island nt.

ice lolly n (Br) Eis das am Stil.

ice rink n Eisbahn die.

ice skates npl Schlittschuhe pl.

ice-skating n Schlittschuhlaufen das, Eislaufen das; **to go ~** Schlittschuh laufen gehen.

icicle ['aɪsɪkl] n Eiszapfen der.

icing ['aɪsɪŋ] n Zuckerguß der.

icing sugar n Puderzucker der.

icy ['aɪsɪ] adj (road, pavement) vereist; (weather) eisig.

I'd [aɪd] = **I would, I had**.

ID abbr = **identification**.

ID card n Personalausweis der.

IDD code n internationale Vorwahlkennziffer.

idea [aɪ'dɪə] n Idee die; (opinion) Vorstellung die; (understanding) Begriff der; **I've no ~** ich habe keine Ahnung.

ideal [aɪ'dɪəl] ◆ adj ideal. ◆ n Ideal das.

ideally [aɪ'dɪəlɪ] adv (situated, suited) ideal; (preferably) idealerweise.

identical [aɪ'dentɪkl] adj identisch.

identification [aɪˌdentɪfɪ'keɪʃn] n (proof of identity) Ausweis der.

identify [aɪ'dentɪfaɪ] vt erkennen.

identity [aɪ'dentətɪ] n Identität die.

idiom ['ɪdɪəm] n Redewendung die.

idiot ['ɪdɪət] n Idiot der.

idle ['aɪdl] ◆ adj faul; (machine) stillstehend. ◆ vi (engine) leer laufen.

idol ['aɪdl] n (person) Idol das.

idyllic [ɪ'dɪlɪk] adj idyllisch.

i.e. (abbr of id est) d.h.

if [ɪf] conj wenn, falls; (in indirect questions, after 'know', 'wonder') ob; **~ I were you** wenn ich du wäre; **~ not** (otherwise) wenn nicht, falls nicht.

ignition [ɪg'nɪʃn] n (AUT) Zündung die.

ignorant ['ɪgnərənt] *adj* unwissend; (*pej: stupid*) beschränkt.

ignore [ɪg'nɔːʳ] *vt* ignorieren.

ill [ɪl] *adj* krank; (*treatment*) schlecht; ~ **luck** Pech *das*.

I'll [aɪl] = **I will, I shall**.

illegal [ɪ'liːgl] *adj* illegal.

illegible [ɪ'ledʒəbl] *adj* unleserlich.

illegitimate [ˌɪlɪ'dʒɪtɪmət] *adj* (*child*) unehelich.

illiterate [ɪ'lɪtərət] *adj*: **to be ~** Analphabet sein.

illness ['ɪlnɪs] *n* Krankheit *die*.

illuminate [ɪ'luːmɪneɪt] *vt* beleuchten.

illusion [ɪ'luːʒn] *n* Illusion *die*.

illustration [ˌɪlə'streɪʃn] *n* (*picture*) Illustration *die*; (*example*) Beispiel *das*.

I'm [aɪm] = **I am**.

image ['ɪmɪdʒ] *n* Bild *das*; (*of company, person*) Image *das*.

imaginary [ɪ'mædʒɪnrɪ] *adj* eingebildet.

imagination [ɪˌmædʒɪ'neɪʃn] *n* (*ability*) Phantasie *die*; (*mind*) Einbildung *die*.

imagine [ɪ'mædʒɪn] *vt* sich (D) vor|stellen.

imitate ['ɪmɪteɪt] *vt* nach|ahmen.

imitation [ˌɪmɪ'teɪʃn] ◆ *n* Nachahmung *die*. ◆ *adj*: ~ **leather** Lederimitation *die*.

immaculate [ɪ'mækjʊlət] *adj* makellos.

immature [ˌɪmə'tjʊəʳ] *adj* unreif.

immediate [ɪ'miːdjət] *adj* (*without delay*) unmittelbar.

immediately [ɪ'miːdjətlɪ] ◆ *adv* (*at once*) sofort. ◆ *conj* (Br) sobald; ~ **on the left/right** gleich links/rechts.

immense [ɪ'mens] *adj* enorm.

immersion heater [ɪ'mɜːʃn-] *n* Heißwasserbereiter *der*.

immigrant ['ɪmɪgrənt] *n* Einwanderer *der* (Einwanderin *die*).

immigration [ˌɪmɪ'greɪʃn] *n* Einwanderung *die*; (*section of airport, port*) Einwanderungskontrolle *die*.

imminent ['ɪmɪnənt] *adj* nahe bevorstehend.

immune [ɪ'mjuːn] *adj*: **to be ~ to sthg** immun sein gegen etw.

immunity [ɪ'mjuːnətɪ] *n* Immunität *die*.

immunize ['ɪmjuːnaɪz] *vt* immunisieren.

impact ['ɪmpækt] *n* (*effect*) Auswirkung *die*; (*hitting*) Aufprall *der*.

impair [ɪm'peəʳ] *vt* beeinträchtigen.

impatient [ɪm'peɪʃnt] *adj* ungeduldig; **to be ~ to do sthg** es nicht erwarten können, etw zu tun.

imperative [ɪm'perətɪv] *n* (GRAMM) Imperativ *der*.

imperfect [ɪm'pɜːfɪkt] *n* (GRAMM) Imperfekt *das*.

impersonate [ɪm'pɜːsəneɪt] *vt* (*for amusement*) nachlahmen.

impertinent [ɪm'pɜːtɪnənt] *adj* frech.

implement [*n* 'ɪmplɪmənt, *vb* 'ɪmplɪment] ◆ *n* Gerät *das*. ◆ *vt* durch|führen.

implication [ˌɪmplɪ'keɪʃn] *n* (*consequence*) Konsequenz *die*.

imply [ɪm'plaɪ] *vt* an|deuten.

impolite [ˌɪmpə'laɪt] *adj* unhöflich.

import [*n* 'ɪmpɔːt, *vb* ɪm'pɔːt] ◆ *n* Import *der*. ◆ *vt* importieren.

importance [ɪm'pɔːtns] *n* Wichtigkeit *die*.

important [ɪm'pɔːtnt] *adj* wichtig; (*person*) einflußreich.

impose [ɪm'pəʊz] ◆ *vt* auferlegen. ◆ *vi* zur Last fallen; **to ~ sthg on** etw auferlegen (+D).

impossible [ɪm'pɒsəbl] *adj* unmöglich.

impractical [ɪm'præktɪkl] *adj* unpraktisch.

impress [ɪm'pres] *vt* (*person*) beeindrucken.

impression [ɪm'preʃn] *n* (*opinion*) Eindruck *der*.

impressive [ɪm'presɪv] *adj* eindrucksvoll.

improbable [ɪm'prɒbəbl] *adj* unwahrscheinlich.

improper [ɪm'prɒpər] *adj* (*incorrect*) inkorrekt; (*illegal*) unlauter; (*rude*) unanständig.

improve [ɪm'pruːv] ◆ *vt* verbessern. ◆ *vi* besser werden. ▶ **improve on** *vt fus* übertreffen.

improvement [ɪm'pruːvmənt] *n* Besserung *die*; (*to home, to machine*) Verbesserung *die*.

improvise ['ɪmprəvaɪz] *vi* improvisieren.

impulse ['ɪmpʌls] *n* Impuls *der*; **on ~** spontan.

impulsive [ɪm'pʌlsɪv] *adj* impulsiv.

in [ɪn] ◆ *prep* **1.** (*expressing place, position*) in (+A,D); **to put sthg ~ sthg** etw in etw (A) tun; **it comes ~ a box** man bekommt es in einer Schachtel; **~ the bedroom** im Schlafzimmer; **~ the street** auf der Straße; **~ California** in Kalifornien; **~ Sheffield** in Sheffield; **~ here/there** hier/dort drinnen. **2.** (*participating in*) in (+D); **who's ~ the play?** wer spielt in dem Stück? **3.** (*expressing arrangement*) in (+D); **~ a circle** in einem Kreis; **they come ~ packs of three** es gibt sie in Dreierpacks. **4.** (*during*) in (+D); **~ April** im April; **~ the afternoon** am Nachmittag; **~ the morning** am Morgen; **ten o'clock ~ the morning** zehn Uhr morgens; **~ 1994** 1994. **5.** (*within, after*) in (+D); **it'll be ready ~ an hour** es ist in einer Stunde fertig. **6.** (*expressing means*): **write ~ ink** mit Tinte schreiben; **~ writing** schriftlich; **they were talking ~ English** sie sprachen Englisch. **7.** (*wearing*) in (+D). **8.** (*state*) in (+D); **~ a hurry** in Eile; **to be ~ pain** Schmerzen haben; **~ ruins** in Trümmern. **9.** (*with regard to*): **a rise ~ prices** ein Preisanstieg; **to be 50 metres ~ length** 50 Meter lang sein. **10.** (*with numbers*): **one ~ ten** jeder Zehnte. **11.** (*expressing age*): **she's ~ her twenties** sie ist in den Zwanzigern. **12.** (*with colours*): **it comes ~ green or blue** es gibt es in grün oder blau. **13.** (*with superlatives*) in (+D); **the best ~ the world** der/die/das Beste in der Welt. ◆ *adv* **1.** (*inside*) herein/hinein; **you can go ~ now** Sie können/du kannst jetzt hineingehen. **2.** (*at home, work*) da; **she's not ~** sie ist nicht da; **to stay ~** zu Hause bleiben. **3.** (*train, bus, plane*): **to get ~** ankommen; **to ~ in** zu Hause bleiben; **the train's not ~ yet** der Zug is noch nicht angekommen. **4.** (*tide*): **the tide is ~** es ist Flut. ◆ *adj* (*inf: fashionable*) in.

inability [ˌɪnə'bɪlətɪ] *n*: **~ (to do sthg)** Unfähigkeit *die* (, etw zu tun).

inaccessible [ˌɪnək'sesəbl] *adj* unzugänglich.

inaccurate [ɪn'ækjʊrət] *adj* ungenau.

inadequate [ɪn'ædɪkwət] *adj* ungenügend.

inappropriate [ˌɪnə'prəʊprɪət] *adj* unpassend.

inauguration [ɪˌnɔːgjʊ'reɪʃn] *n* Amtseinführung *die*.

incapable [ɪn'keɪpəbl] *adj*: **to be ~ of doing sthg** nicht fähig sein, etw zu tun.

incense ['ɪnsens] *n* Weihrauch *der*.

incentive [ɪn'sentɪv] *n* Anreiz *der*.

inch [ɪntʃ] *n* = 2,54 cm, Inch *der*.

incident ['ɪnsɪdənt] *n* Vorfall *der*.

incidentally [ˌɪnsɪ'dentəlɪ] *adv* übrigens.

incline ['ɪnklaɪn] *n* Abhang *der*.

inclined [ɪn'klaɪnd] *adj* (*sloping*) abschüssig; **to be ~ to do sthg** (*have tendency*) dazu neigen, etw zu tun.

include [ɪn'kluːd] *vt* ein|schließen; (*contain*) enthalten.

included [ɪn'kluːdɪd] *adj* (*in price*) inbegriffen; **to be ~ in sthg** in etw (D) eingeschlossen sein.

including [ɪn'kluːdɪŋ] *prep* einschließlich (+G).

inclusive [ɪn'kluːsɪv] *adj*: **from the 8th to the 16th ~** vom 8. bis einschließlich 16.; ~ **of VAT** inklusive MwSt.

income ['ɪŋkʌm] n Einkommen das.

income support n (Br) zusätzliche staatliche Unterstützung zum Lebensunterhalt.

income tax n Einkommensteuer die.

incoming ['ɪn,kʌmɪŋ] adj (train) einfahrend; (plane) landend; (phone call) eingehend.

incompetent [ɪn'kɒmpɪtənt] adj unfähig.

incomplete [,ɪnkəm'pli:t] adj unvollständig.

inconsiderate [,ɪnkən'sɪdərət] adj rücksichtslos.

inconsistent [,ɪnkən'sɪstənt] adj (person) unbeständig; (statement) widersprüchlich.

incontinent [ɪn'kɒntɪnənt] adj inkontinent.

inconvenient [,ɪnkən'vi:njənt] adj ungünstig.

incorporate [ɪn'kɔːpəreɪt] vt auf|nehmen.

incorrect [,ɪnkə'rekt] adj unrichtig.

increase [n 'ɪnkri:s, vb ɪn'kri:s] ◆ n Anstieg der; (in wages) Erhöhung die. ◆ vt erhöhen. ◆ vi steigen; **an ~ in unemployment** eine Zunahme der Arbeitslosigkeit.

increasingly [ɪn'kri:sɪŋlɪ] adv zunehmend.

incredible [ɪn'kredəbl] adj unglaublich.

incredibly [ɪn'kredəblɪ] adv unglaublich.

incur [ɪn'kɜːr] vt sich (D) zu|ziehen.

indecisive [,ɪndɪ'saɪsɪv] adj unentschlossen.

indeed [ɪn'di:d] adv wirklich, tatsächlich; (certainly) natürlich; **very big ~** wirklich sehr groß.

indefinite [ɪn'defɪnɪt] adj unbestimmt; (answer, opinion) unklar.

indefinitely [ɪn'defɪnətlɪ] adv (closed, delayed) bis auf weiteres.

independence [,ɪndɪ'pendəns] n

Unabhängigkeit die.

independent [,ɪndɪ'pendənt] adj unabhängig.

independently [,ɪndɪ'pendəntlɪ] adv unabhängig.

independent school n (Br) nichtstaatliche Schule.

index ['ɪndeks] n Verzeichnis das, Register das.

index finger n Zeigefinger der.

India ['ɪndjə] n Indien nt.

Indian ['ɪndjən] ◆ adj indisch. ◆ n Inder der (-in die); ~ **restaurant** indisches Restaurant.

Indian Ocean n Indischer Ozean.

indicate ['ɪndɪkeɪt] ◆ vi (AUT) blinken. ◆ vt (point to) zeigen auf (+A); (show) an|deuten.

indicator ['ɪndɪkeɪtər] n (AUT) Blinker der.

indifferent [ɪn'dɪfrənt] adj gleichgültig.

indigestion [,ɪndɪ'dʒestʃn] n Magenverstimmung die.

indigo ['ɪndɪgəʊ] adj indigoblau.

indirect [,ɪndɪ'rekt] adj indirekt; **an ~ route** ein Umweg.

individual [,ɪndɪ'vɪdʒʊəl] ◆ adj einzeln; (tuition) Einzel-. ◆ n Einzelne der die.

individually [,ɪndɪ'vɪdʒʊəlɪ] adv einzeln.

Indonesia [,ɪndə'ni:zjə] n Indonesien nt.

indoor ['ɪndɔ:r] adj (swimming pool, sports) Hallen-.

indoors [,ɪn'dɔ:z] adv drinnen, im Haus.

indulge [ɪn'dʌldʒ] vi: **to ~ in** sich (D) gönnen.

industrial [ɪn'dʌstrɪəl] adj industriell; (country, town) Industrie-.

industrial estate n (Br) Industriesiedlung die.

industry ['ɪndəstrɪ] n Industrie die.

inedible [ɪn'edɪbl] adj ungenießbar.

inefficient [,ɪnɪ'fɪʃnt] adj nicht leistungsfähig.

inequality [ˌɪnɪˈkwɒlətɪ] n Ungleichheit die.

inevitable [ɪnˈevɪtəbl] adj unvermeidlich.

inevitably [ɪnˈevɪtəblɪ] adv zwangsläufig.

inexpensive [ˌɪnɪkˈspensɪv] adj preiswert.

infamous [ˈɪnfəməs] adj berüchtigt.

infant [ˈɪnfənt] n (baby) Säugling der; (young child) Kind das.

infant school n (Br) Vorschule die (für 5- bis 7jährige).

infatuated [ɪnˈfætjʊeɪtɪd] adj: **to be ~ with** vernarrt sein in (+A).

infected [ɪnˈfektɪd] adj infiziert.

infectious [ɪnˈfekʃəs] adj ansteckend.

inferior [ɪnˈfɪərɪər] adj (person) untergeordnet; (goods, quality) minderwertig.

infinite [ˈɪnfɪnət] adj unendlich.

infinitely [ˈɪnfɪnətlɪ] adv unendlich.

infinitive [ɪnˈfɪnɪtɪv] n Infinitiv der.

infinity [ɪnˈfɪnətɪ] n Unendlichkeit die.

infirmary [ɪnˈfɜːmərɪ] n Krankenhaus das.

inflamed [ɪnˈfleɪmd] adj entzündet.

inflammation [ˌɪnfləˈmeɪʃn] n Entzündung die.

inflatable [ɪnˈfleɪtəbl] adj aufblasbar.

inflate [ɪnˈfleɪt] vt aufpumpen.

inflation [ɪnˈfleɪʃn] n (of prices) Inflation die.

inflict [ɪnˈflɪkt] vt (suffering) aufbürden; (wound) beibringen.

in-flight adj während des Fluges.

influence [ˈɪnflʊəns] ◆ vt beeinflussen. ◆ n: ~ (on) Einfluß der (auf (+A).

inform [ɪnˈfɔːm] vt informieren.

informal [ɪnˈfɔːml] adj zwanglos.

information [ˌɪnfəˈmeɪʃn] n Information die; **a piece of ~** eine Information.

information desk n Auskunftsschalter der.

information office n Auskunftsbüro das.

informative [ɪnˈfɔːmətɪv] adj informativ.

infuriating [ɪnˈfjʊərɪeɪtɪŋ] adj ärgerlich.

ingenious [ɪnˈdʒiːnjəs] adj raffiniert.

ingredient [ɪnˈgriːdjənt] n (CULIN) Zutat die.

inhabit [ɪnˈhæbɪt] vt bewohnen.

inhabitant [ɪnˈhæbɪtənt] n Einwohner der (-in die).

inhale [ɪnˈheɪl] vi einatmen.

inhaler [ɪnˈheɪlər] n Inhaliergerät das.

inherit [ɪnˈherɪt] vt erben.

inhibition [ˌɪnhɪˈbɪʃn] n Hemmung die.

initial [ɪˈnɪʃl] ◆ adj Anfangs-. ◆ vt mit Initialen unterschreiben. ▶ **initials** npl Initialen pl.

initially [ɪˈnɪʃəlɪ] adv anfangs.

initiative [ɪˈnɪʃətɪv] n Initiative die.

injection [ɪnˈdʒekʃn] n (MED) Spritze die.

injure [ˈɪndʒər] vt verletzen; **to ~ one's arm** sich (D) den Arm verletzen; **to ~ o.s.** sich verletzen.

injured [ˈɪndʒəd] adj verletzt.

injury [ˈɪndʒərɪ] n Verletzung die.

ink [ɪŋk] n Tinte die.

inland [adj ˈɪnlənd, adv ɪnˈlænd] ◆ adj Binnen-. ◆ adv landeinwärts.

inn [ɪn] n Gasthaus das.

inner [ˈɪnər] adj innere(-r)(-s).

inner city n Viertel in der Nähe der Innenstadt, in denen es oft soziale Probleme gibt.

inner tube n Schlauch der.

innocence [ˈɪnəsəns] n Unschuld die.

innocent [ˈɪnəsənt] adj unschuldig.

inoculate [ɪˈnɒkjʊleɪt] vt: **to ~ sb (against sthg)** jn (gegen etw) impfen.

inoculation [ɪˌnɒkjʊˈleɪʃn] n Impfung die.

input [ˈɪnpʊt] vt (COMPUT) einlgeben.

inquire [ɪn'kwaɪər] = **enquire**.

inquiry [ɪn'kwaɪərɪ] = **enquiry**.

insane [ɪn'seɪn] adj verrückt.

insect ['ɪnsekt] n Insekt das.

insect repellent [-rə'pelənt] n Insektenvertreibungsmittel das.

insensitive [ɪn'sensətɪv] adj (unkind) gefühllos.

insert [ɪn'sɜːt] vt (coin) ein|werfen; (ticket) ein|führen; (key) ein|stecken.

inside [ɪn'saɪd] ◆ prep (be) in (+D); (go, move) in (+A). ◆ adv innen. ◆ adj (internal) Innen-. ◆ n: **the ~** das Innere; (AUT: in UK) die linke Fahrspur; (AUT: in Europe, US) die rechte Fahrspur; **~ out** (clothes) links (herum); **to be ~** drinnen sein; **to go ~** hinein|gehen.

inside lane n (AUT: in UK) linke Fahrspur; (in Europe, US) rechte Fahrspur.

inside leg n Schrittlänge die.

insight ['ɪnsaɪt] n Einblick der.

insignificant [,ɪnsɪg'nɪfɪkənt] adj unbedeutend.

insinuate [ɪn'sɪnjʊeɪt] vt an|deuten.

insist [ɪn'sɪst] vi darauf bestehen; **to ~ on doing sthg** darauf bestehen, etw zu tun.

insole ['ɪnsəʊl] n Einlegesohle die.

insolent ['ɪnsələnt] adj unverschämt.

insomnia [ɪn'sɒmnɪə] n Schlaflosigkeit die.

inspect [ɪn'spekt] vt (ticket, passport) kontrollieren; (look at closely) genau betrachten.

inspection [ɪn'spekʃn] n (of ticket, passport) Kontrolle die.

inspector [ɪn'spektər] n (on bus, train) Kontrolleur der (-in die); (in police force) Kommissar der (-in die).

inspiration [,ɪnspə'reɪʃn] n Inspiration die.

instal [ɪn'stɔːl] (Am) = **install**.

install [ɪn'stɔːl] vt (Br) installieren.

installment [ɪn'stɔːlmənt] (Am) = **instalment**.

instalment [ɪn'stɔːlmənt] n (payment) Rate die; (episode) Folge die.

instance ['ɪnstəns] n Fall der; **for ~** zum Beispiel.

instant ['ɪnstənt] ◆ adj sofortig; (food) Instant-. ◆ n Moment der, Augenblick der.

instant coffee n Instantkaffee der, Pulverkaffee der.

instead [ɪn'sted] adv statt dessen; **~ of** statt (+G), anstelle (+G).

instep ['ɪnstep] n Spann der.

instinct ['ɪnstɪŋkt] n Instinkt der.

institute ['ɪnstɪtjuːt] n Institut das.

institution [,ɪnstɪ'tjuːʃn] n Institution die.

instructions [ɪn'strʌkʃnz] npl (for use) Anleitung die.

instructor [ɪn'strʌktər] n Lehrer der (-in die).

instrument ['ɪnstrʊmənt] n (musical) Instrument das; (tool) Gerät das.

insufficient [,ɪnsə'fɪʃnt] adj nicht genügend.

insulating tape ['ɪnsjʊleɪtɪŋ-] n Isolierband das.

insulation [,ɪnsjʊ'leɪʃn] n (material) Isoliermaterial das.

insulin ['ɪnsjʊlɪn] n Insulin das.

insult [n 'ɪnsʌlt, vb ɪn'sʌlt] ◆ n Beleidigung die. ◆ vt beleidigen.

insurance [ɪn'ʃʊərəns] n Versicherung die.

insurance certificate n Versicherungsschein der.

insurance company n Versicherungsgesellschaft die.

insurance policy n Versicherungspolice die.

insure [ɪn'ʃʊər] vt versichern.

insured [ɪn'ʃʊəd] adj: **to be ~** versichert sein.

intact [ɪn'tækt] adj unbeschädigt.

intellectual [,ɪntə'lektjʊəl] ◆ adj intellektuell. ◆ n Intellektuelle der, die.

intelligence [ɪn'telɪdʒəns] n Intelligenz die.

intelligent [ɪn'telɪdʒənt] adj intelligent.

intend [ɪn'tend] vt meinen; **to ~ to do sthg** vor|haben, etw zu tun.

intense [ɪn'tens] adj stark.

intensity [ɪn'tensətɪ] n Intensität die.

intensive [ɪn'tensɪv] adj intensiv.

intensive care n Intensivstation die.

intent [ɪn'tent] adj: **to be ~ on doing sthg** etw unbedingt tun wollen.

intention [ɪn'tenʃn] n Absicht die.

intentional [ɪn'tenʃənl] adj absichtlich.

intentionally [ɪn'tenʃənəlɪ] adv absichtlich.

interchange ['ɪntətʃeɪndʒ] n (on motorway) Autobahnkreuz das.

Intercity® [,ɪntə'sɪtɪ] n (Br) Intercity der.

intercom ['ɪntəkɒm] n Sprechanlage die.

interest ['ɪntrəst] ♦ n Interesse das; (on money) Zinsen pl. ♦ vt interessieren; **to take an ~ in sthg** sich für etw interessieren.

interested ['ɪntrəstɪd] adj interessiert; **to be ~ in sthg** an etw (D) interessiert sein.

interesting ['ɪntrəstɪŋ] adj interessant.

interest rate n Zinssatz der.

interfere [,ɪntə'fɪər] vi (meddle) sich ein|mischen; **to ~ with sthg** (damage) etw beeinträchtigen.

interference [,ɪntə'fɪərəns] n (on TV, radio) Störung die.

interior [ɪn'tɪərɪər] ♦ adj Innen-. ♦ n Innere das.

intermediate [,ɪntə'miːdjət] adj (stage, level) Zwischen-.

intermission [,ɪntə'mɪʃn] n Pause die.

internal [ɪn'tɜːnl] adj (not foreign) inländisch; (on the inside) innere(-r) (-s).

internal flight n Inlandflug der.

international [,ɪntə'næʃənl] adj international.

international flight n Auslandsflug der.

Internet ['ɪntənet] n: **the ~** das Internet.

interpret [ɪn'tɜːprɪt] vi dolmetschen.

interpreter [ɪn'tɜːprɪtər] n Dolmetscher der (-in die).

interrogate [ɪn'terəgeɪt] vt verhören.

interrupt [,ɪntə'rʌpt] vt unterbrechen.

intersection [,ɪntə'sekʃn] n (of roads) Kreuzung die.

interval ['ɪntəvl] n Zeitraum der; (Br: at cinema, theatre) Pause die.

intervene [,ɪntə'viːn] vi (person) ein|greifen; (event) dazwischen|kommen.

interview ['ɪntəvjuː] ♦ n (on TV, in magazine) Interview das; (for job) Vorstellungsgespräch das. ♦ vt (on TV, in magazine) interviewen; (for job) ein Vorstellungsgespräch führen mit.

interviewer ['ɪntəvjuːər] n Interviewer der (-in die).

intestine [ɪn'testɪn] n Darm der.

intimate ['ɪntɪmət] adj (friends, relationship) eng; (secrets, thoughts) intim; (cosy) gemütlich.

intimidate [ɪn'tɪmɪdeɪt] vt ein|schüchtern.

into ['ɪntʊ] prep in (+A); (crash) gegen; (research, investigation) über (+A); **4 ~ 20 goes 5 (times)** 20 (geteilt) durch 4 ist 5; **to translate ~ German** ins Deutsche übersetzen; **to change ~ sthg** (clothes) sich (D) etw an|ziehen; (become) zu etw werden; **to be ~ sthg** (inf: like) auf etw (A) stehen.

intolerable [ɪn'tɒlrəbl] adj unerträglich.

intransitive [ɪn'trænzətɪv] adj intransitiv.

intricate ['ɪntrɪkət] adj kompliziert.

intriguing [ɪn'triːgɪŋ] *adj* faszinierend.

introduce [ˌɪntrə'djuːs] *vt* (*person*) vorlstellen; (*new measure*) einlführen; (*TV programme*) anlkündigen; **I'd like to ~ you to Fred** ich möchte Ihnen/dir Fred vorstellen.

introduction [ˌɪntrə'dʌkʃn] *n* Einführung *die*; (*to book*) Einleitung *die*; (*to person*) Vorstellung *die*.

introverted ['ɪntrə,vɜːtɪd] *adj* introvertiert.

intruder [ɪn'truːdə^r] *n* Eindringling *der*.

intuition [ˌɪntjuː'ɪʃn] *n* Intuition *die*.

invade [ɪn'veɪd] *vt* einlfallen in.

invalid [*adj* ɪn'vælɪd, *n* 'ɪnvəlɪd] ◆ *adj* (*ticket, cheque*) ungültig. ◆ *n* Kranke *der, die*.

invaluable [ɪn'væljʊəbl] *adj* unschätzbar.

invariably [ɪn'veərɪəblɪ] *adv* immer.

invasion [ɪn'veɪʒn] *n* Invasion *die*.

invent [ɪn'vent] *vt* erfinden.

invention [ɪn'venʃn] *n* Erfindung *die*.

inventory ['ɪnventrɪ] *n* (*list*) Bestandsaufnahme *die*; (*Am: stock*) Lagerbestand *der*.

inverted commas [ɪn'vɜːtɪd-] *npl* Anführungszeichen *pl*.

invest [ɪn'vest] ◆ *vt* investieren. ◆ *vi*: **to ~ in sthg** in etw (A) investieren.

investigate [ɪn'vestɪgeɪt] *vt* untersuchen.

investigation [ɪnˌvestɪ'geɪʃn] *n* Untersuchung *die*.

investment [ɪn'vestmənt] *n* Anlage *die*.

invisible [ɪn'vɪzɪbl] *adj* unsichtbar.

invitation [ˌɪnvɪ'teɪʃn] *n* Einladung *die*.

invite [ɪn'vaɪt] *vt* einlladen; **to ~ sb to do sthg** (*ask*) jn einladen, etw zu tun; **to ~ sb round** jn zu sich einladen.

invoice ['ɪnvɔɪs] *n* Rechnung *die*.

involve [ɪn'vɒlv] *vt* (*entail*) mit sich bringen; **what does it ~?** was ist erforderlich?; **to be ~d in sthg** (*scheme, activity*) an etw (D) beteiligt sein; (*accident*) in etw (A) verwickelt sein.

involved [ɪn'vɒlvd] *adj*: **what's ~?** was ist erforderlich?

inwards ['ɪnwədz] *adv* nach innen.

IOU *n* Schuldschein *der*.

IQ *n* IQ *der*.

Iran [ɪ'rɑːn] *n* Iran *der*.

Iraq [ɪ'rɑːk] *n* Irak *der*.

Ireland ['aɪələnd] *n* Irland *nt*.

iris ['aɪərɪs] (*pl* **-es**) *n* (*flower*) Iris *die*.

Irish ['aɪrɪʃ] ◆ *adj* irisch. ◆ *n* (*language*) Irische *das*. ◆ *npl*: **the ~** die Iren *pl*.

Irish coffee *n* Irish coffee *der* (*Kaffee mit Whisky und Schlagsahne*).

Irishman ['aɪrɪʃmən] (*pl* **-men** [-mən]) *n* Ire *der*.

Irish stew *n* Irish-Stew *das* (*Gericht aus Fleisch, Kartoffeln und Zwiebeln*).

Irishwoman ['aɪrɪʃ,wʊmən] (*pl* **-women** [-,wɪmɪn]) *n* Irin *die*.

iron ['aɪən] ◆ *n* Eisen *das*; (*for clothes*) Bügeleisen *das*. ◆ *vt* bügeln.

ironic [aɪ'rɒnɪk] *adj* ironisch.

ironing board ['aɪənɪŋ-] *n* Bügelbrett *das*.

ironmonger's ['aɪən,mʌŋgəz] *n* (*Br*) Eisenwarengeschäft *das*.

irrelevant [ɪ'reləvənt] *adj* belanglos.

irresistible [ˌɪrɪ'zɪstəbl] *adj* unwiderstehlich.

irrespective [ˌɪrɪ'spektɪv]: **irrespective of** *prep* ungeachtet (+G).

irresponsible [ˌɪrɪ'spɒnsəbl] *adj* unverantwortlich.

irrigation [ˌɪrɪ'geɪʃn] *n* Bewässerung *die*.

irritable ['ɪrɪtəbl] *adj* reizbar.

irritate ['ɪrɪteɪt] *vt* (*annoy*) ärgern; (*skin, eyes*) reizen.

irritating ['ɪrɪteɪtɪŋ] *adj* (*annoying*) ärgerlich.

IRS *n* (*Am*) *amerikanisches Finanzamt.*

is [ɪz] → **be**.

Islam ['ɪzlɑːm] n Islam der.

island ['aɪlənd] n Insel die; (in road) Verkehrsinsel die.

isle [aɪl] n Insel die.

isolated ['aɪsəleɪtɪd] adj (place) isoliert; (case, error) vereinzelt.

Israel ['ɪzreɪəl] n Israel nt.

issue ['ɪʃuː] ◆ n (problem, subject) Thema das; (of newspaper, magazine) Ausgabe die. ◆ vt (statement) veröffentlichen; (passport, document) auslstellen; (stamps, bank notes) herauslgeben.

it [ɪt] pron 1. (referring to specific thing: subject) er/sie/es; (direct object) den/sie/es; **~'s big** er/sie/es ist groß; **she hit ~** sie hat den/sie/es getroffen; **a free book came with ~** es war ein kostenloses Buch dabei. 2. (nonspecific) es; **~'s easy** es ist einfach; **~'s a difficult question** das ist eine schwierige Frage; **tell me about ~!** erzähl mir davon!; **~'s me** ich bin's; **who is ~?** wer ist da? 3. (used impersonally) es; **~'s hot** es ist heiß; **~'s six o'clock** es ist sechs Uhr; **~'s Sunday** es ist Sonntag.

Italian [ɪ'tæljən] ◆ adj italienisch. ◆ n (person) Italiener der (-in die); (language) Italienisch das; **an ~ restaurant** ein italienisches Restaurant.

Italy ['ɪtəlɪ] n Italien nt.

itch [ɪtʃ] vi jucken.

item ['aɪtəm] n (object) Gegenstand der; (on agenda) Punkt der; (of news) Meldung die.

itemized bill ['aɪtəmaɪzd-] n spezifizierte Rechnung.

its [ɪts] adj (masculine or neuter subject) sein; (feminine subject) ihr.

it's [ɪts] = **it is, it has**.

itself [ɪt'self] pron (reflexive) sich; (after prep) sich selbst; **the house ~ is fine** das Haus selbst ist in Ordnung.

I've [aɪv] = **I have**.

ivory ['aɪvərɪ] n Elfenbein das.

ivy ['aɪvɪ] n Efeu der.

J

jab [dʒæb] n (Br: inf: injection) Spritze die.

jack [dʒæk] n (for car) Wagenheber der; (playing card) Bube der.

jacket ['dʒækɪt] n (garment) Jacke die; (of book) Umschlag der; (Am: of record) Plattenhülle die; (of potato) Schale die.

jacket potato n in der Schale gebackene Kartoffel.

jack-knife vi Klappmesser das.

Jacuzzi® [dʒə'kuːzɪ] n Whirlpool der.

jade [dʒeɪd] n Jade die.

jail [dʒeɪl] n Gefängnis das.

jam [dʒæm] ◆ n (food) Konfitüre die; (of traffic) Stau der; (inf: difficult situation) Klemme die. ◆ vt (pack tightly) hineinlquetschen. ◆ vi (get stuck) klemmen; **the roads are jammed** die Straßen sind verstopft.

jam-packed [-'pækt] adj (inf) gestopft voll.

Jan. [dʒæn] (abbr of January) Jan.

janitor ['dʒænɪtər] n (Am & Scot) Hausmeister der.

January ['dʒænjʊərɪ] n Januar der, → **September**.

Japan [dʒə'pæn] n Japan nt.

Japanese [ˌdʒæpə'niːz] ◆ adj japanisch. ◆ n (language) Japanisch das. ◆ npl: **the ~** die Japaner pl.

jar [dʒɑːr] n Glas das.

javelin ['dʒævlɪn] n Speer der.

jaw [dʒɔː] n Kiefer der.

jazz [dʒæz] n Jazz der.

jealous ['dʒeləs] adj (envious) neidisch; (possessive) eifersüchtig.

jeans [dʒiːnz] npl Jeans pl.

Jeep® [dʒiːp] n Jeep® der.

Jello® ['dʒeləʊ] n (Am) Wackelpudding der.

jelly ['dʒelɪ] n (dessert) Wackelpudding der; (Am: jam) Gelee das.

jellyfish ['dʒelɪfɪʃ] (*pl inv*) *n* Qualle *die*.

jeopardize ['dʒepədaɪz] *vt* gefährden.

jerk [dʒɜːk] *n* (*movement*) Ruck *der*; (*inf*: *idiot*) Blödmann *der*.

jersey ['dʒɜːzɪ] (*pl* -s) *n* (*garment*) Pullover *der*.

jet [dʒet] *n* (*aircraft*) Jet *der*; (*of liquid, gas*) Strahl *der*; (*outlet*) Düse *die*.

jetfoil ['dʒetfɔɪl] *n* Tragflächenboot *das*.

jet lag *n* Jet-lag *das*.

jet-ski *n* Jetski *der*.

jetty ['dʒetɪ] *n* Bootsanlegestelle *die*.

Jew [dʒuː] *n* Jude *der* (Jüdin *die*).

jewel ['dʒuːəl] *n* Edelstein *der*. ▶ **jewels** *npl* (*jewellery*) Juwelen *pl*.

jeweler's ['dʒuːələz] (Am) = **jeweller's**.

jeweller's ['dʒuːələz] *n* (Br) Juweliergeschäft *das*.

jewellery ['dʒuːəlrɪ] *n* (Br) Schmuck *der*.

jewelry ['dʒuːəlrɪ] (Am) = **jewellery**.

Jewish ['dʒuːɪʃ] *adj* jüdisch.

jigsaw (**puzzle**) ['dʒɪgsɔ:-] *n* Puzzlespiel *das*.

jingle ['dʒɪŋgl] *n* (*of advert*) Jingle *der*.

job [dʒɒb] *n* (*regular work*) Stelle *die*, Job *der*; (*task*) Arbeit *die*; (*function*) Aufgabe *die*; **to lose one's ~** entlassen werden.

job centre *n* (Br) Arbeitsvermittlungsstelle *die*.

job market *n* Arbeitsmarkt *der*.

jockey ['dʒɒkɪ] (*pl* -s) *n* Jockei *der*.

jog [dʒɒg] ◆ *vt* (*bump*) an|stoßen. ◆ *vi* joggen. ◆ *n*: **to go for a ~** joggen gehen.

jogging ['dʒɒgɪŋ] *n* Jogging *das*; **to go ~** joggen gehen.

join [dʒɔɪn] *vt* (*club, organization*) beitreten (+D); (*fasten together, link*) verbinden; (*other people*) sich an|schließen (+D); (*participate in*) teill|nehmen an (+D). ▶ **join in** *vt fus*

mit|machen an (+D). ◆ *vi* mit|machen.

joint [dʒɔɪnt] ◆ *adj* gemeinsam. ◆ *n* (*of body*) Gelenk *das*; (Br: *of meat*) Braten *der*; (*in structure*) Verbindungsstelle *die*.

joke [dʒəʊk] ◆ *n* Witz *der*. ◆ *vi* scherzen.

joker ['dʒəʊkə'] *n* (*playing card*) Joker *der*.

jolly ['dʒɒlɪ] ◆ *adj* (*cheerful*) lustig, fröhlich. ◆ *adv* (Br: *inf*: *very*) sehr.

jolt [dʒəʊlt] *n* Ruck *der*.

jot [dʒɒt]: **jot down** *vt sep* notieren.

journal ['dʒɜːnl] *n* (*professional magazine*) Zeitschrift *die*; (*diary*) Tagebuch *das*.

journalist ['dʒɜːnəlɪst] *n* Journalist *der* (-in *die*).

journey ['dʒɜːnɪ] (*pl* -s) *n* Reise *die*.

joy [dʒɔɪ] *n* Freude *die*.

joypad ['dʒɔɪpæd] *n* (*of video game*) Joypad *der*.

joyrider ['dʒɔɪraɪdə'] *n* Autodieb, der mit gestohlenen Autos Spritztouren unternimmt.

joystick ['dʒɔɪstɪk] *n* (*of video game*) Joystick *der*.

judge [dʒʌdʒ] ◆ *n* (JUR) Richter *der* (-in *die*); (*of competition*) Preisrichter *der* (-in *die*); (SPORT) Schiedsrichter *der* (-in *die*). ◆ *vt* (*competition*) beurteilen; (*evaluate*) ein|schätzen.

judg(e)ment ['dʒʌdʒmənt] *n* (JUR) Urteil *das*; (*opinion*) Beurteilung *die*; (*capacity to judge*) Urteilsvermögen *das*.

judo ['dʒuːdəʊ] *n* Judo *das*.

jug [dʒʌg] *n* Krug *der*.

juggernaut ['dʒʌgənɔːt] *n* (Br) Schwerlastzug *der*.

juggle ['dʒʌgl] *vi* jonglieren.

juice [dʒuːs] *n* (*from fruit, vegetables*) Saft *der*; (*from meat*) Bratensaft *der*.

juicy ['dʒuːsɪ] *adj* (*food*) saftig.

jukebox ['dʒuːkbɒks] *n* Jukebox *die*.

July [dʒuːˈlaɪ] *n* Juli *der*, → **September**.

jumble sale [ˈdʒʌmbl-] n (Br) Wohltätigkeitsbasar der.

jumbo [ˈdʒʌmbəʊ] adj (inf: big) Riesen-.

jumbo jet n Jumbo-Jet der.

jump [dʒʌmp] ◆ n Sprung der. ◆ vi springen; (with fright) zusammen|fahren; (increase) rapide an|steigen. ◆ vt (Am: train, bus) schwarz|fahren in (+D); **to ~ the queue** (Br) sich vor|drängen.

jumper [ˈdʒʌmpər] n (Br: pullover) Pullover der; (Am: dress) ärmelloses Kleid.

jump leads npl Starthilfekabel pl.

junction [ˈdʒʌŋkʃn] n (of roads) Kreuzung die; (of railway lines) Knotenpunkt der.

June [dʒuːn] n Juni der, → **September**.

jungle [ˈdʒʌŋgl] n Dschungel der.

junior [ˈdʒuːnjər] ◆ adj (of lower rank) untergeordnet; (Am: after name) junior. ◆ n (younger person) Junior der.

junior school n (Br) Grundschule die (für 7- bis 11jährige).

junk [dʒʌŋk] n (inf: unwanted things) Trödel der.

junk food n (inf) ungesundes Essen wie z.B. Fast Food, Chips, Süßigkeiten.

junkie [ˈdʒʌŋkɪ] n (inf) Junkie der.

junk shop n Trödelladen der.

jury [ˈdʒʊərɪ] n Geschworenen pl; (in competition) Jury die.

just [dʒʌst] ◆ adv (recently) gerade; (exactly) genau; (only) nur; (simply) einfach. ◆ adj gerecht; **~ a bit more** etwas mehr; **~ over an hour** etwas mehr als eine Stunde; **it's ~ as good** es ist genauso gut; **to be ~ about to do sthg** dabei sein, etw zu tun; **to have ~ done sthg** gerade etw getan haben; **~ about** (almost) fast; **(only) ~** (almost not) gerade (noch); **~ a minute!** einen Moment!

justice [ˈdʒʌstɪs] n Gerechtigkeit die.

justify [ˈdʒʌstɪfaɪ] vt rechtfertigen.

jut [dʒʌt]: **jut out** vi vor|stehen.

juvenile [ˈdʒuːvənaɪl] adj (young) jugendlich; (childish) kindisch.

K

kangaroo [ˌkæŋgəˈruː] n Känguruh das.

karate [kəˈrɑːtɪ] n Karate das.

kebab [kɪˈbæb] n: **doner ~** Gyros der; **shish ~** Kebab der.

keel [kiːl] n Kiel der.

keen [kiːn] adj (enthusiastic) begeistert; (eyesight, hearing) scharf; **to be ~ on** mögen; **to be ~ to do sthg** etw unbedingt tun wollen.

keep [kiːp] (pt & pp **kept**) ◆ vt (retain) behalten; (store) auf|bewahren; (maintain) halten; (promise, appointment) ein|halten; (secret) für sich behalten; (delay) auf|halten; (record, diary) führen. ◆ vi (food) sich halten; (remain) bleiben; **to ~ (on) doing sthg** (do continuously) etw weiter tun; (do repeatedly) etw dauernd tun; **to ~ sb from doing sthg** jn davon ab|halten, etw zu tun; **~ back!** bleib zurück!; **to ~ clear (of)** (etw) frei|halten; **'~ in lane!'** Schild, das anzeigt, daß es verboten ist, die Spur zu wechseln; **'~ left'** 'Links fahren'; **'~ off the grass!'** 'Den Rasen nicht betreten!'; **'~ out!'** 'Betreten verboten!'; **'~ your distance!'** 'Abstand halten!' ▸ **keep up** vt sep aufrecht|erhalten. ◆ vi mit|halten.

keep-fit n (Br) Fitneßübungen pl.

kennel [ˈkenl] n Hundehütte die.

kept [kept] pt & pp → **keep**.

kerb [kɜːb] n (Br) Randstein der.

kerosene [ˈkerəsiːn] n (Am) Petroleum das.

ketchup [ˈketʃəp] n Ketchup der.

kettle [ˈketl] n Wasserkessel der; **to put the ~ on** Wasser auf|setzen.

key [kiː] ◆ n Schlüssel der; (of piano, typewriter) Taste die. ◆ adj Schlüssel-.

keyboard [ˈkiːbɔːd] n (of typewriter,

piano) Tastatur die; (*musical instrument*) Keyboard das.

keyhole ['ki:həʊl] n Schlüsselloch das.

keypad ['ki:pæd] n Tastenfeld das.

key ring n Schlüsselring der.

kg (*abbr of kilogram*) kg.

kick [kɪk] ◆ n (*of foot*) Tritt der. ◆ vt treten.

kickoff ['kɪkɒf] n Spielbeginn der.

kid [kɪd] ◆ n (*inf: child*) Kind das. ◆ vi (*joke*) scherzen.

kidnap ['kɪdnæp] vt entführen, kidnappen.

kidnaper ['kɪdnæpər] (*Am*) = **kidnapper**.

kidnapper ['kɪdnæpər] n (*Br*) Entführer der, Kidnapper der.

kidney ['kɪdnɪ] (*pl* -s) n Niere die.

kidney bean n Kidneybohne die.

kill [kɪl] vt töten; (*time*) tot|schlagen; **my feet are ~ing me!** meine Füße bringen mich um!

killer ['kɪlər] n Mörder der (-in die).

kilo ['ki:ləʊ] (*pl* -s) n Kilo das.

kilogram ['kɪlə,græm] n Kilogramm das.

kilometre ['kɪlə,mi:tər] n Kilometer der.

kilt [kɪlt] n Kilt der, Schottenrock der.

kind [kaɪnd] ◆ adj nett. ◆ n Art die; (*of cheese, wine etc*) Sorte die; **what ~ of music do you like?** welche Musik magst du?; **what ~ of car do you drive?** was für ein Auto hast du?; **~ of** (*Am: inf*) irgendwie.

kindergarten ['kɪndə,ɡɑːtn] n Kindergarten der.

kindly ['kaɪndlɪ] adv: **would you ~ wait here?** wären Sie so nett, hier zu warten?

kindness ['kaɪndnɪs] n Freundlichkeit die.

king [kɪŋ] n König der.

kingfisher ['kɪŋ,fɪʃər] n Eisvogel der.

king prawn n Riesengarnele die.

king-size bed n King-size-Bett das.

kiosk ['ki:ɒsk] n (*for newspapers etc*) Kiosk der; (*Br: phone box*) öffentlicher Fernsprecher.

kipper ['kɪpər] n Räucherhering der.

kiss [kɪs] ◆ n Kuß der. ◆ vt küssen.

kiss of life n Mund-zu-Mund-Beatmung die.

kit [kɪt] n (*set*) Ausrüstung die; (*clothes*) Bekleidung die; (*for assembly*) Bausatz der.

kitchen ['kɪtʃɪn] n Küche die.

kitchen unit n Einbauküchenelement das.

kite [kaɪt] n (*toy*) Drachen der.

kitten ['kɪtn] n Kätzchen das.

kitty ['kɪtɪ] n (*money*) Gemeinschaftskasse die.

kiwi fruit ['ki:wi:-] n Kiwi die.

Kleenex® ['kli:neks] n Papiertaschentuch das.

km (*abbr of kilometre*) km.

km/h (*abbr of kilometres per hour*) km/h.

knack [næk] n: **to get the ~ of doing sthg** den Dreh heraus|kriegen, wie man etw macht.

knackered ['nækəd] adj (*Br: inf*) erledigt.

knapsack ['næpsæk] n Rucksack der.

knee [ni:] n Knie das.

kneecap ['ni:kæp] n Kniescheibe die.

kneel [ni:l] (*pt & pp* knelt [nelt]) vi knien; (*go down on one's knees*) sich hin|knien.

knew [nju:] pt → **know**.

knickers ['nɪkəz] npl (*Br*) Schlüpfer der.

knife [naɪf] (*pl* knives) n Messer das.

knight [naɪt] n (*in history*) Ritter der; (*in chess*) Springer der.

knit [nɪt] vt stricken.

knitted ['nɪtɪd] adj gestrickt.

knitting ['nɪtɪŋ] n (*thing being knitted*) Strickzeug das; (*activity*) Stricken das.

knitting needle n Stricknadel die.

knitwear ['nɪtweəʳ] n Strickwaren pl.

knives [naɪvz] pl → **knife**.

knob [nɒb] n (on door etc) Knauf der; (on machine) Knopf der.

knock [nɒk] ◆ n (at door) Klopfen das. ◆ vt (hit) stoßen. ◆ vi (at door etc) klopfen. ► **knock down** vt sep (pedestrian) an|fahren; (building) ab|reißen; (price) reduzieren. ► **knock out** vt sep bewußtlos schlagen; (of competition): **to be ~ed out** aus|scheiden. ► **knock over** vt sep um|stoßen; (pedestrian) um|fahren.

knocker ['nɒkəʳ] n (on door) Türklopfer der.

knot [nɒt] n Knoten der.

know [nəʊ] (pt knew, pp known) vt wissen; (person, place) kennen; (language) können; **to get to ~ sb** jn kennen|lernen; **to ~ about sthg** (understand) sich mit etw aus|kennen; (have heard) etw wissen; **to ~ how to do sthg** etw tun können; **to ~ of** kennen; **to be ~n as** bekannt sein als; **to let sb ~ sthg** jm über etw (A) Bescheid sagen; **you ~** (for emphasis) weißt du.

knowledge ['nɒlɪdʒ] n (facts known) Kenntnisse pl; (awareness) Wissen das; **to my ~** soweit ich weiß.

known [nəʊn] pp → **know**.

knuckle ['nʌkl] n Knöchel der; (of pork) Haxe die.

Koran [kɒ'rɑːn] n: **the ~** der Koran.

L

l (abbr of litre) l.

L (abbr of large) L; (abbr of learner) in Großbritannien Schild am Auto, um anzuzeigen, daß der Fahrer noch keinen Führerschein hat und nur in Begleitung fahren darf.

lab [læb] n (inf) Labor das.

label ['leɪbl] n Etikett das.

labor ['leɪbər] (Am) = **labour**.

laboratory [Br lə'bɒrətrɪ, Am 'læbrə,tɔːrɪ] n Labor das.

labour ['leɪbəʳ] n Arbeit die; **to be in ~** (MED) in den Wehen liegen.

labourer ['leɪbərəʳ] n Arbeiter der (-in die).

Labour Party n (Br) links ausgerichtete Partei in Großbritannien.

labour-saving adj arbeitssparend.

lace [leɪs] n (material) Spitze die; (for shoe) Schnürsenkel der.

lace-ups npl Schnürschuhe pl.

lack [læk] ◆ n Mangel der. ◆ vt mangeln an (+D). ◆ vi: **to be ~ing** fehlen.

lacquer ['lækəʳ] n (paint) Lackfarbe die; (for hair) Haarspray der.

lad [læd] n (inf: boy) Junge der.

ladder ['lædəʳ] n Leiter die; (Br: in tights) Laufmasche die.

ladies ['leɪdɪz] n (Br: toilet) Damen pl.

ladies room (Am) = **ladies**.

ladieswear ['leɪdɪz,weəʳ] n Damenbekleidung die.

ladle ['leɪdl] n Kelle die.

lady ['leɪdɪ] n Dame die; **Lady Diana** Lady Diana.

ladybird ['leɪdɪbɜːd] n Marienkäfer der.

lag [læg] vi: **to ~ (behind)** zurück|bleiben.

lager ['lɑːgəʳ] n helles Bier, Lagerbier das.

lagoon [lə'guːn] n Lagune die.

laid [leɪd] pt & pp → **lay**.

lain [leɪn] pp → **lie**.

lake [leɪk] n See der.

Lake District n: **the ~** der Lake District (Seenlandschaft in Nordwestengland).

lamb [læm] n (animal) Lamm das; (meat) Lammfleisch das.

lamb chop n Lammkotelett das.

lame [leɪm] adj lahm.

lamp [læmp] n Lampe die.

lamppost ['læmppəust] n Laternenpfahl der.

lampshade ['læmpʃeid] n Lampenschirm der.

land [lænd] ◆ n Land das. ◆ vi landen.

landing ['lændɪŋ] n (of plane) Landung die; (at top of stairs) Gang der; (between stairs) Treppenabsatz der.

landlady ['lænd,leɪdɪ] n (of house) Vermieterin die; (of pub) Gastwirtin die.

landlord ['lændlɔːd] n (of house) Vermieter der; (of pub) Gastwirt der.

landmark ['lændmɑːk] n Orientierungspunkt der.

landscape ['lændskeɪp] n Landschaft die.

landslide ['lændslaɪd] n Erdrutsch der.

lane [leɪn] n (in country) kleine Landstraße; (in town) Gasse die; (on road, motorway) Fahrspur die; 'get in ~' 'Einordnen'.

language ['læŋgwɪdʒ] n Sprache die; (words) Ausdrucksweise die; bad ~ Kraftausdrücke pl.

lap [læp] n (of person) Schoß der; (of race) Runde die.

lapel [lə'pel] n Aufschlag der.

lapse [læps] vi (passport, membership) abllaufen.

lard [lɑːd] n Schmalz das.

larder ['lɑːdər] n Vorratskammer die.

large [lɑːdʒ] adj groß.

largely ['lɑːdʒlɪ] adv größtenteils.

large-scale adj Groß-.

lark [lɑːk] n Lerche die.

laryngitis [,lærɪn'dʒaɪtɪs] n Kehlkopfentzündung die.

lasagne [lə'zænjə] n Lasagne die.

laser ['leɪzər] n Laser der.

lass [læs] n (inf: girl) Mädel das.

last [lɑːst] ◆ adj letzte(-r)(-s). ◆ adv zuletzt. ◆ vi dauern; (weather) bleiben; (money, supply) auslreichen. ◆ pron: the ~ to come als letzte(-r)(-s) kommen; the ~ but one der/die/das Vorletzte; the day before ~ vorgestern; ~ year letztes Jahr; the ~ year das letzte Jahr; at ~ endlich.

lastly ['lɑːstlɪ] adv zuletzt.

last-minute adj in letzter Minute.

latch [lætʃ] n Riegel der; to be on the ~ nicht abgeschlossen sein.

late [leɪt] ◆ adj spät; (train, flight) verspätet; (dead) verstorben. ◆ adv spät; (not on time) zu spät; two hours ~ zwei Stunden Verspätung.

lately ['leɪtlɪ] adv in letzter Zeit.

late-night adj (chemist) Nacht-; (shop) länger geöffnet.

later ['leɪtər] ◆ adj später. ◆ adv: ~ (on) (afterwards) später; at a ~ date zu einem späteren Zeitpunkt.

latest ['leɪtɪst] adj: the ~ fashion die neueste Mode; the ~ das Neueste; at the ~ spätestens.

lather ['lɑːðər] n Schaum der.

Latin ['lætɪn] n Latein das.

Latin America n Lateinamerika nt.

Latin American ◆ adj lateinamerikanisch. ◆ n Lateinamerikaner der (-in die).

latitude ['lætɪtjuːd] n Breite die.

latter ['lætər] n: the ~ der/die/das Letztere.

laugh [lɑːf] ◆ n Lachen das. ◆ vi lachen; to have a ~ (Br: inf: have fun) sich amüsieren. ► **laugh at** vt fus (mock) sich lustig machen über (+A).

laughter ['lɑːftər] n Gelächter das.

launch [lɔːntʃ] vt (boat) vom Stapel lassen; (new product) auf den Markt bringen.

laund(e)rette [lɔːn'dret] n Waschsalon der.

laundry ['lɔːndrɪ] n (washing) Wäsche die; (place) Wäscherei die.

lavatory ['lævətrɪ] n Toilette die.

lavender ['lævəndər] n Lavendel der.

lavish ['lævɪʃ] *adj* üppig.

law [lɔː] *n* (*rule*) Gesetz *das*; (*system*) Recht *das*; (*study*) Jura *pl*; **to be against the ~** gesetzeswidrig sein.

lawn [lɔːn] *n* Rasen *der*.

lawnmower ['lɔːn,məʊəʳ] *n* Rasenmäher *der*.

lawyer ['lɔːjəʳ] *n* Rechtsanwalt *der* (-anwältin *die*).

laxative ['læksətɪv] *n* Abführmittel *das*.

lay [leɪ] (*pt & pp* laid) ◆ *pt* → lie. ◆ *vt* legen; **to ~ the table** den Tisch decken. ▶ **lay off** *vt sep* (*worker*) Feierschichten machen lassen. ▶ **lay on** *vt sep* (*food, etc*) sorgen für; (*transport*) ein|setzen. ▶ **lay out** *vt sep* aus|legen.

lay-by (*pl* lay-bys) *n* Parkbucht *die*.

layer ['leɪəʳ] *n* Schicht *die*.

layman ['leɪmən] (*pl* -men [-mən]) *n* Laie *der* (Laiin *die*).

layout ['leɪaʊt] *n* Plan *der*.

lazy ['leɪzɪ] *adj* faul.

lb (*abbr of pound*) Pfd.

lead¹ [liːd] (*pt & pp* led) ◆ *vt* führen; (*be in front of*) an|führen. ◆ *vi* führen. ◆ *n* (*for dog*) Leine *die*; (*cable*) Schnur *die*; **to ~ sb to do sthg** jn dazu bringen, etw zu tun; **to ~ to** führen zu (+D); **to ~ the way** voran|gehen; **to be in the ~** (*in race, match*) führen.

lead² [led] ◆ *n* (*metal*) Blei *das*; (*for pencil*) Mine *die*. ◆ *adj* Blei-.

leaded petrol ['ledɪd-] *n* bleihaltiges Benzin.

leader ['liːdəʳ] *n* (*person in charge*) Leiter *der* (-in *die*); (*in race*) **to be the ~** führen.

leadership ['liːdəʃɪp] *n* Leitung *die*.

lead-free [led-] *adj* bleifrei.

leading ['liːdɪŋ] *adj* leitend.

lead singer [liːd-] *n* Leadsänger *der* (-in *die*).

leaf [liːf] (*pl* leaves) *n* Blatt *das*.

leaflet ['liːflɪt] *n* Reklameblatt *das*.

league [liːg] *n* Liga *die*.

leak [liːk] ◆ *n* (*hole*) undichte Stelle die; (*of water*) Leck *das*; (*of gas*) Gasausfluß *der*. ◆ *vi* undicht sein.

lean [liːn] (*pt & pp* leant [lent] OR -ed) ◆ *adj* (*meat, person*) mager. ◆ *vi* sich lehnen. ◆ *vt*: **to ~ sthg against sthg** etw gegen etw lehnen; **to ~ on** sich lehnen an (+A). ▶ **lean forward** *vi* sich nach vorne lehnen. ▶ **lean over** *vi* sich nach vorne beugen.

leap [liːp] (*pt & pp* leapt [lept] OR -ed) *vi* springen.

leap year *n* Schaltjahr *das*.

learn [lɜːn] (*pt & pp* learnt OR -ed) *vt* lernen; **to ~ (how) to do sthg** lernen, etw zu tun; **to ~ about sthg** (*hear about*) etw erfahren; (*study*) etw lernen.

learner (driver) ['lɜːnəʳ-] *n* Fahrschüler *der* (-in *die*).

learnt [lɜːnt] *pt & pp* → learn.

lease [liːs] ◆ *n* Pacht *die*; (*contract*) Mietvertrag *der*. ◆ *vt* pachten; **to ~ sthg from sb** etw von jm pachten; **to ~ sthg to sb** jm etw verpachten.

leash [liːʃ] *n* Leine *die*.

least [liːst] ◆ *adv* am wenigsten. ◆ *adj* wenigste(-r)(-s). ◆ *pron*: **(the) ~** das wenigste; **it's the ~ I can do** das ist das Mindeste, was ich tun kann; **at ~** wenigstens.

leather ['leðəʳ] *n* Leder *das*. ▶ **leathers** *npl* (*of motorcyclist*) Lederanzug *der*.

leave [liːv] (*pt & pp* left) ◆ *vt* verlassen; (*not take away*) lassen; (*not use, not eat*) übrig|lassen; (*a mark, scar, in will*) hinter|lassen; (*space, gap*) lassen. ◆ *vi* gehen, fahren; (*train, bus*) ab|fahren. ◆ *n* (*time off work*) Urlaub *der*, → left; **to ~ a message** eine Nachricht hinter|lassen. ▶ **leave behind** *vt sep* lassen. ▶ **leave out** *vt sep* aus|lassen.

leaves [liːvz] *pl* → leaf.

Lebanon ['lebənən] *n* Libanon *der*.

lecture ['lektʃəʳ] *n* (*at university, conference*) Vorlesung *die*.

lecturer ['lektʃərəʳ] *n* Dozent *der* (-in *die*).

lecture theatre n Vorlesungssaal der.

led [led] pt & pp → **lead¹**.

ledge [ledʒ] n Sims der.

leek [liːk] n Lauch der.

left [left] ♦ pt & pp → **leave**. ♦ adj linke(-r)(-s). ♦ adv links. ♦ n linke Seite, Linke die; **on the ~** links; **to be ~** übrig sein; **there are none ~** sie sind alle.

left-hand adj linke(-r)(-s).

left-hand drive n Linkssteuerung die.

left-handed [-'hændɪd] adj (implement) für Linkshänder; **to be ~** Linkshänder(-in) sein.

left-luggage locker n (Br) Schließfach das.

left-luggage office n (Br) Gepäckaufbewahrung die.

left-wing adj linke(-r)(-s).

leg [leg] n Bein das; **~ of lamb** Lammkeule die.

legal ['liːgl] adj (concerning the law) rechtlich, Rechts-; (lawful) gesetzlich.

legal aid n Prozeßkostenhilfe die.

legalize ['liːgəlaɪz] vt legalisieren.

legal system n Rechtswesen das.

legend ['ledʒənd] n Legende die.

leggings ['legɪnz] npl Leggings pl.

legible ['ledʒɪbl] adj leserlich.

legislation [,ledʒɪs'leɪʃn] n Gesetze pl.

legitimate [lɪ'dʒɪtɪmət] adj legitim.

leisure [Br 'leʒər, Am 'liːʒər] n Freizeit die.

leisure centre n Freizeitzentrum das.

leisure pool n Freizeitbad das.

lemon ['lemən] n Zitrone die.

lemonade [,lemə'neɪd] n Limonade die.

lemon curd [-kɜːd] n (Br) Brotaufstrich aus Zitronensaft, Eiern und Butter.

lemon juice n Zitronensaft der.

lemon sole n Seezunge die.

lemon tea n Zitronentee der.

lend [lend] (pt & pp lent) vt leihen; **to ~ sb sthg** jm etw leihen.

length [leŋθ] n Länge die; (of swimming pool) Bahn die.

lengthen ['leŋθən] vt verlängern.

lens [lenz] n (of camera) Objektiv das; (of glasses) Brillenglas das; (contact lens) Kontaktlinse die.

lent [lent] pt & pp → **lend**.

Lent [lent] n Fastenzeit die.

lentils ['lentlz] npl Linsen pl.

Leo ['liːəʊ] n Löwe der.

leopard ['lepəd] n Leopard der.

leopard-skin adj Leopardenfell-.

leotard ['liːətɑːd] n Trikot das.

leper ['lepər] n Leprakranke der, die.

lesbian ['lezbɪən] ♦ adj lesbisch. ♦ n Lesbierin die.

less [les] adj, adv & pron weniger; **~ than 20** weniger als 20.

lesson ['lesn] n (class) Stunde die.

let [let] (pt & pp inv) vt lassen; (rent out) vermieten; **to ~ sb do sthg** jn etw tun lassen; **to ~ go of sthg** etw loslassen; **to ~ sb have sthg** jm etw überlassen; **to ~ sb know sthg** jn etw wissen lassen; **~'s go!** gehen wir!; **'to ~'** (for rent) 'zu vermieten'. ► **let in** vt sep hereinllassen. ► **let off** vt sep (excuse) davonkommen lassen; **can you ~ me off at the station?** kannst du mich am Bahnhof auslsteigen lassen? ► **let out** vt sep hinausllassen.

letdown ['letdaʊn] n (inf) Enttäuschung die.

lethargic [lə'θɑːdʒɪk] adj lethargisch.

letter ['letər] n (written message) Brief der; (of alphabet) Buchstabe der.

letterbox ['letəbɒks] n (Br) Briefkasten der.

lettuce ['letɪs] n Kopfsalat der.

leuk(a)emia [luːˈkiːmɪə] n Leukämie die.

level ['levl] ♦ adj (flat) eben; (horizontal) waagerecht; (at same height) auf gleicher Höhe. ◆ n (*height*) Höhe die; (*storey*) Etage die; (*standard*) Niveau das; **to be ~ with** (*in height*) sich auf gleicher Höhe befinden wie; (*in standard*) auf dem gleichen Niveau sein wie.

level crossing n (Br) Bahn-übergang der.

lever [Br 'li:vər, Am 'levər] n Hebel der.

liability [ˌlaɪəˈbɪlətɪ] n Haftung die.

liable ['laɪəbl] adj: **to be ~ to do sthg** (*likely*) etw leicht tun können; **to be ~ for sthg** (*responsible*) für etw haften.

liaise [lɪˈeɪz] vi: **to ~ with** in ständigem Kontakt stehen mit.

liar ['laɪər] n Lügner der (-in die).

liberal ['lɪbərəl] adj (*tolerant*) tolerant; (*generous*) großzügig.

Liberal Democrat Party n britische liberale Partei.

liberate ['lɪbəreɪt] vt befreien.

liberty ['lɪbətɪ] n Freiheit die.

Libra ['li:brə] n Waage die.

librarian [laɪˈbreərɪən] n Bibliothekar der (-in die).

library ['laɪbrərɪ] n Bibliothek die.

Libya ['lɪbɪə] n Libyen nt.

lice [laɪs] npl Läuse pl.

licence ['laɪsəns] ◆ n (Br) Genehmigung die; (*for driving*) Führerschein der; (*for TV*) Fernsehgenehmigung die. ◆ vt (Am) = **license**.

license ['laɪsəns] ◆ vt (Br) genehmigen. ◆ n (Am) = **licence**.

licensed ['laɪsənst] adj (*restaurant, bar*) mit Schankkonzession.

licensing hours ['laɪsənsɪŋ-] npl (Br) Ausschankzeiten pl.

lick [lɪk] vt lecken.

lid [lɪd] n Deckel der.

lie [laɪ] (*pt* lay, *pp* lain, *cont* lying) ◆ n Lüge die. ◆ vi (*tell lie*) lügen; (*be horizontal, be situated*) liegen; (*lie down*) sich legen; **to ~ to sb** jn anlügen; **to tell ~s** lügen; **to ~ about sthg** etw nicht richtig anlgeben. ▶ **lie down** vi sich hinllegen.

lieutenant [Br lefˈtenənt, Am lu:-ˈtenənt] n Leutnant der.

life [laɪf] (*pl* lives) n Leben das.

life assurance n Lebensversicherung die.

life belt n Rettungsring der.

lifeboat ['laɪfbəʊt] n Rettungsboot das.

lifeguard ['laɪfɡɑːd] n (*at swimming pool*) Bademeister der (-in die); (*at beach*) Rettungsschwimmer der (-in die).

life jacket n Schwimmweste die.

lifelike ['laɪflaɪk] adj naturgetreu.

life preserver [-prɪˈzɜːvər] n (Am: *life belt*) Rettungsring der; (*life jacket*) Schwimmweste die.

life-size adj lebensgroß.

lifespan ['laɪfspæn] n Lebensdauer die.

lifestyle ['laɪfstaɪl] n Lebensstil der.

lift [lɪft] ◆ n (Br: *elevator*) Aufzug der. ◆ vt heben. ◆ vi (*fog*) sich lichten; **to give sb a ~** jn mitlnehmen. ▶ **lift up** vt sep hochlheben.

light [laɪt] (*pt & pp* lit OR -ed) ◆ adj (*not dark*) hell; (*not heavy*) leicht. ◆ n Licht das; (*for cigarette*) Feuer das. ◆ vt (*fire, cigarette*) anlzünden; (*room, stage*) beleuchten; **have you got a ~?** haben Sie Feuer?; **to set ~ to sthg** etw anlzünden. ▶ **lights** (*traffic lights*) Ampel die. ▶ **light up** vt sep (*house, road*) erleuchten. ◆ vi (*inf*: *light a cigarette*) sich (D) eine anlstecken.

light bulb n Glühbirne die.

lighter ['laɪtər] n Feuerzeug das.

light-hearted [-ˈhɑːtɪd] adj unbekümmert, leicht.

lighthouse ['laɪthaʊs, pl -haʊzɪz] n Leuchtturm der.

lighting ['laɪtɪŋ] n Beleuchtung die.

light meter n Belichtungsmesser der.

lightning ['laɪtnɪŋ] n Blitz der.

lightweight ['laɪtweɪt] adj leicht.

like [laɪk] ◆ prep wie; (*typical of*) typisch für. ◆ vt mögen; **~ this/that** so;

to ~ doing sthg etw gern tun; **do you ~ it?** gefällt es dir?; **what's it ~?** wie ist es?; **to look ~ sthg** jm/etw ähnlich sehen; **I'd ~ to sit down** ich würde mich gern hinsetzen; **I'd ~ a drink** ich würde gern etwas trinken.

likelihood ['laɪklɪhʊd] n Wahrscheinlichkeit die.

likely ['laɪklɪ] adj wahrscheinlich.

likeness ['laɪknɪs] n Ähnlichkeit die.

likewise ['laɪkwaɪz] adv ebenso.

lilac ['laɪlək] adj lila.

Lilo® ['laɪləʊ] (pl -s) n (Br) Luftmatratze die.

lily ['lɪlɪ] n Lilie die.

lily of the valley n Maiglöckchen das.

limb [lɪm] n Glied das.

lime [laɪm] n (fruit) Limone die; ~ (juice) Limonensaft der.

limestone ['laɪmstəʊn] n Kalkstein der.

limit ['lɪmɪt] ◆ n Grenze die. ◆ vt begrenzen; **the city ~s** die Stadtgrenze.

limited ['lɪmɪtɪd] adj begrenzt; (in company name) = GmbH.

limp [lɪmp] ◆ adj schlapp. ◆ vi hinken.

line [laɪn] ◆ n Linie die; (row) Reihe die; (Am: queue) Schlange die; (of writing, poem, song) Zeile die; (rope, for fishing) Leine die; (for telephone) Leitung die; (railway track) Gleis das; (of business, work) Branche die. ◆ vt (coat) füttern; (drawers) auslkleiden; **in ~** (aligned) in einer Linie; **in ~ with** parallel zu; **it's a bad ~** (on phone) die Verbindung ist schlecht; **the ~ is engaged** (on phone) der Anschluß ist besetzt; **to drop sb a ~** (inf) jm schreiben; **to stand in ~** (Am) Schlange stehen. ▶ **line up** vt sep (arrange) auflstellen. ◆ vi sich auflstellen.

lined [laɪnd] adj (paper) liniert.

linen ['lɪnɪn] n (cloth) Leinen das; (tablecloths, sheets) Wäsche die.

liner ['laɪnər] n Passagierschiff das.

linesman ['laɪnzmən] (pl -men [-mən]) n Linienrichter der.

linger ['lɪŋgər] vi verweilen.

lingerie ['lænʒərɪ] n Unterwäsche die.

lining ['laɪnɪŋ] n (of coat, jacket) Futter das; (of brake) Bremsbelag der.

link [lɪŋk] ◆ n (connection) Verbindung die. ◆ vt verbinden; **rail ~** Zugverbindung die; **road ~** Straßenverbindung die.

lino ['laɪnəʊ] n (Br) Linoleum das.

lion ['laɪən] n Löwe der.

lioness ['laɪənes] n Löwin die.

lip [lɪp] n Lippe die.

lip salve [-sælv] n Lippenpomade die.

lipstick ['lɪpstɪk] n Lippenstift der.

liqueur [lɪ'kjʊər] n Likör der.

liquid ['lɪkwɪd] n Flüssigkeit die.

liquor ['lɪkər] n (Am) Spirituosen pl.

liquorice ['lɪkərɪs] n Lakritze die.

lisp [lɪsp] n: **to have a ~** lispeln.

list [lɪst] ◆ n Liste die. ◆ vt auflisten.

listen ['lɪsn] vi: **to ~ (to)** (to person, sound) zulhören (+D); (to advice) beherzigen (+A); **to ~ to the radio** Radio hören.

listener ['lɪsnər] n Hörer der (-in die).

lit [lɪt] pt & pp → **light**.

liter ['liːtər] (Am) = **litre**.

literally ['lɪtərəlɪ] adv (actually) buchstäblich.

literary ['lɪtərərɪ] adj gehoben.

literature ['lɪtrətʃər] n Literatur die; (printed information) Informationsmaterial das.

litre ['liːtər] n (Br) Liter der.

litter ['lɪtər] n Abfall der.

litterbin ['lɪtəbɪn] n (Br) Abfalleimer der.

little ['lɪtl] ◆ adj klein; (distance, time) kurz; (not much) wenig. ◆ pron & adv wenig; **as ~ as possible** so wenig wie möglich; **~ by ~** nach und nach; **a ~** (not much) ein bißchen.

little finger n kleiner Finger.

live¹ [lɪv] vi (have home) wohnen; (be

alive) leben; (*survive*) überleben; **to ~ with sb** mit jm zusammen|wohnen. ▶ **live together** *vi* zusammen|wohnen.

live² [laɪv] ◆ *adj* (*alive*) lebendig; (*programme, performance*) Live-; (*wire*) geladen. ◆ *adv* live.

lively ['laɪvlɪ] *adj* lebhaft.

liver ['lɪvər] *n* Leber *die*.

lives [laɪvz] *pl* → **life**.

living ['lɪvɪŋ] ◆ *adj* lebend. ◆ *n*: **to earn a ~** seinen Lebensunterhalt verdienen; **what do you do for a ~?** was sind Sie von Beruf?

living room *n* Wohnzimmer *das*.

lizard ['lɪzəd] *n* Echse *die*.

load [ləʊd] ◆ *n* Ladung *die*. ◆ *vt* laden; **~s of** (*inf*) ein Haufen.

loaf [ləʊf] (*pl* **loaves**) *n*: **~ (of bread)** Brot *das*.

loan [ləʊn] ◆ *n* (*of money*) Kredit *der*. ◆ *vt* leihen.

loathe [ləʊð] *vt* verabscheuen.

loaves [ləʊvz] *pl* → **loaf**.

lobby ['lɒbɪ] *n* (*hall*) Hotelhalle *die*.

lobster ['lɒbstər] *n* Hummer *der*.

local ['ləʊkl] ◆ *adj* hiesig. ◆ *n* (*inf: local person*) Einheimische *der die*; (Br: *pub*) Stammkneipe *die*; (Am: *train*) Nahverkehrszug *der*; (Am: *bus*) Nahverkehrsbus *der*.

local anaesthetic *n* örtliche Betäubung.

local call *n* Ortsgespräch *das*.

local government *n* Kommunalverwaltung *die*.

locate [Br ləʊ'keɪt, Am 'ləʊkeɪt] *vt* (*find*) finden; **to be ~d** sich befinden.

location [ləʊ'keɪʃn] *n* Lage *die*.

loch [lɒk] *n* (Scot) Loch *der*.

lock [lɒk] ◆ *n* Schloß *das*; (*on canal*) Schleuse *die*. ◆ *vt* (*door, house, bicycle*) ab|schließen; (*valuable object*) ein|schließen. ◆ *vi* (*door, case*) sich ab|schließen lassen; (*wheels*) blockieren. ▶ **lock in** *vt sep* ein|sperren. ▶ **lock out** *vt sep* aus|sperren. ▶ **lock up** *vt sep* (*imprison*) ein|sperren. ◆ *vi* ab|schließen.

locker ['lɒkər] *n* Schließfach *das*.

locker room *n* (Am) Umkleideraum *der*.

locket ['lɒkɪt] *n* Medaillon *das*.

locomotive [,ləʊkə'məʊtɪv] *n* Lokomotive *die*.

locum ['ləʊkəm] *n* (*doctor*) Vertretung *die*.

locust ['ləʊkəst] *n* Heuschrecke *die*.

lodge [lɒdʒ] ◆ *n* (*for hunters, skiers*) Hütte *die*. ◆ *vi* (*stay*) wohnen; (*get stuck*) stecken|bleiben.

lodger ['lɒdʒər] *n* Untermieter *der* (-in *die*).

lodgings ['lɒdʒɪŋz] *npl* möbliertes Zimmer.

loft [lɒft] *n* Dachboden *der*.

log [lɒg] *n* Holzscheit *der*.

logic ['lɒdʒɪk] *n* Logik *die*.

logical ['lɒdʒɪkl] *adj* logisch.

logo ['ləʊgəʊ] (*pl* **-s**) *n* Logo *das*.

loin [lɔɪn] *n* Lendenstück *das*.

loiter ['lɔɪtər] *vi* herum|lungern.

lollipop ['lɒlɪpɒp] *n* Lutscher *der*.

lolly ['lɒlɪ] *n* (*inf: lollipop*) Lutscher *der*; (Br: *ice lolly*) Eis *das* am Stiel.

London ['lʌndən] *n* London *nt*.

Londoner ['lʌndənər] *n* Londoner *der* (-in *die*).

lonely ['ləʊnlɪ] *adj* einsam.

long [lɒŋ] ◆ *adj* lang. ◆ *adv* lange; **it's 2 metres ~** es ist 2 Meter lang; **it's two hours ~** es dauert zwei Stunden; **how ~ is it?** (*in distance*) wie lang ist es?; (*in time*) wie lange dauert es?; **a ~ time** lange; **all day ~** den ganzen Tag; **as ~ as** solange; **for ~** lange; **no ~er** nicht mehr; **so ~!** (*inf*) tschüs! ▶ **long for** *vt fus* sich sehnen nach.

long-distance *adj* (*phone call*) Fern-.

long drink *n* Longdrink *der*.

long-haul *adj* Langstrecken-.

longitude ['lɒndʒɪtjuːd] *n* Länge *die*.

long jump *n* Weitsprung *der*.

long-life *adj* (*fruit juice*) haltbar gemacht; (*battery*) mit langer Lebensdauer; **~ milk** H-Milch *die*.

longsighted [ˌlɒŋˈsaɪtɪd] adj weitsichtig.

long-term adj langfristig.

long wave n Langwelle die.

longwearing [ˌlɒŋˈweərɪŋ] adj (Am) dauerhaft.

loo [luː] (pl -s) n (Br: inf) Klo das.

look [lʊk] ◆ n Blick der; (appearance) Aussehen das. ◆ vi sehen, schauen; (search) suchen; (seem) auslsehen; **to ~ onto** (building, room) gehen auf (+A); **to have a ~** nachlsehen; (search) suchen; **to have a ~ at sthg** sich (D) etw anlsehen; **(good) ~s** gutes Aussehen; **I'm just ~ing** (in shop) ich wollte mich nur umsehen. ▶ **look after** vt fus sich kümmern um. ▶ **look at** vt fus anlsehen. ▶ **look for** vt fus suchen. ▶ **look forward to** vt fus sich freuen auf (+A). ▶ **look out** vi Vorsicht!; **~ out!** Vorsicht! ▶ **look out for** vt fus achten auf (+A). ▶ **look round** vt fus (city, museum) besichtigen. ◆ vi sich umlsehen; **to ~ round the shops** einen Einkaufsbummel machen. ▶ **look up** vt sep (in dictionary) nachlschlagen; (in phone book) herauslsuchen.

loony [ˈluːnɪ] n (inf) Spinner der.

loop [luːp] n (shape) Schleife die.

loose [luːs] adj lose; **to let sb/sthg ~** jn/etw loslassen.

loosen [ˈluːsn] vt lockern.

lop-sided [-ˈsaɪdɪd] adj schief.

lord [lɔːd] n Lord der.

lorry [ˈlɒrɪ] n (Br) Lastwagen der, LKW der.

lorry driver n (Br) Lastwagenfahrer der (-in die).

lose [luːz] (pt & pp lost) ◆ vt verlieren; (subj: watch, clock) nachlgehen. ◆ vi verlieren; **to ~ weight** ablnehmen.

loser [ˈluːzər] n (in contest) Verlierer der (-in die).

loss [lɒs] n Verlust der.

lost [lɒst] ◆ pt & pp → **lose**. ◆ adj (person): **to be ~** sich verlaufen

haben; **to get ~** (lose way) sich verlaufen.

lost-and-found office (Am) = **lost property office**.

lost property office n (Br) Fundbüro das.

lot [lɒt] n (at auction) Posten der; (Am: car park) Parkplatz der; (group): **two ~s of books** zwei Stapel Bücher; **two ~s of people** zwei Gruppen; **a ~ (of)** viel, viele pl; **a ~** nicer viel netter; **the ~** (everything) alles; **~s (of)** eine Menge.

lotion [ˈləʊʃn] n Lotion die.

lottery [ˈlɒtərɪ] n Lotterie die.

loud [laʊd] adj laut; (colour) grell; (pattern) aufdringlich.

loudspeaker [ˌlaʊdˈspiːkər] n Lautsprecher der.

lounge [laʊndʒ] n Salon der; (at airport) Halle die.

lounge bar n (Br) besser ausgestatteter Teil einer Gaststätte.

lousy [ˈlaʊzɪ] adj (inf: poor-quality) lausig.

lout [laʊt] n Flegel der.

love [lʌv] ◆ n Liebe die; (in tennis) null. ◆ vt lieben; **I would ~ to go to Berlin** ich würde gerne nach Berlin fahren; **I would ~ a drink** ich hätte gern etwas zu trinken; **to ~ doing sthg** etw sehr gerne tun; **to be in ~ (with)** verliebt sein (in (+A)); **(with) ~ from** (in letter) alles Liebe.

love affair n Verhältnis das.

lovely [ˈlʌvlɪ] adj (very beautiful) sehr hübsch; (very nice) nett.

lover [ˈlʌvər] n Liebhaber der (-in die).

loving [ˈlʌvɪŋ] adj liebevoll.

low [ləʊ] ◆ adj niedrig; (standard, quality, opinion) schlecht; (level, sound, note) tief; (voice) leise; (depressed) niedergeschlagen. ◆ n (area of low pressure) Tief das; **we're ~ on petrol** wir haben nicht mehr viel Benzin.

low-alcohol adj alkoholarm.

low-calorie adj kalorienarm.

low-cut adj tief ausgeschnitten.

lower [ˈləʊər] ◆ adj untere(-r)(-s).

♦ vt herunterllassen; (reduce) senken.

lower sixth n (Br) ≃ elfte Klasse die.

low-fat adj fettarm.

low tide n Ebbe die.

loyal ['lɔɪəl] adj treu.

loyalty ['lɔɪəltɪ] n Loyalität die.

lozenge ['lɒzɪndʒ] n (sweet) Lutschbonbon der or das.

LP n LP die.

L-plate n (Br) Fahrschule-Schild das, L-Schild, das den Fahrschüler in einem Privatwagen kennzeichnet.

Ltd (abbr of limited) GmbH.

lubricate ['luːbrɪkeɪt] vt schmieren.

luck [lʌk] n Glück das; **bad ~** Pech das; **good ~!** viel Glück!; **with ~** hoffentlich.

luckily ['lʌkɪlɪ] adv glücklicherweise.

lucky ['lʌkɪ] adj glücklich; (number, colour) Glücks-; **to be ~** Glück haben.

ludicrous ['luːdɪkrəs] adj lächerlich.

lug [lʌg] vt (inf) schleppen.

luggage ['lʌgɪdʒ] n Gepäck das.

luggage compartment n Gepäckraum der.

luggage locker n Schließfach das.

luggage rack n Gepäckablage die.

lukewarm ['luːkwɔːm] adj lauwarm.

lull [lʌl] n Pause die.

lullaby ['lʌləbaɪ] n Schlaflied das.

lumbago [lʌmˈbeɪgəʊ] n Hexenschuß der.

lumber ['lʌmbər] n (Am: timber) Bauholz das.

luminous ['luːmɪnəs] adj leuchtend, Leucht-.

lump [lʌmp] n (of mud, butter) Klumpen der; (of coal) Stück das; (of sugar) Würfel der; (on body) Beule die.

lump sum n einmaliger Betrag.

lumpy ['lʌmpɪ] adj klumpig.

lunatic ['luːnətɪk] n (pej) Spinner der.

lunch [lʌntʃ] n Mittagessen das; **to**

have ~ zu Mittag essen.

luncheon ['lʌntʃən] n (fml) Mittagessen das.

luncheon meat n Frühstücksfleisch das.

lunch hour n Mittagspause die.

lunchtime ['lʌntʃtaɪm] n Mittagszeit die.

lung [lʌŋ] n Lunge die.

lunge [lʌndʒ] vi: **to ~ at sb** sich auf jn stürzen.

lurch [lɜːtʃ] vi torkeln.

lure [ljʊər] vt locken.

lurk [lɜːk] vi lauern.

lush [lʌʃ] adj (grass, field) üppig.

lust [lʌst] n (sexual desire) Verlangen das.

Luxembourg ['lʌksəmbɜːg] n Luxemburg nt.

luxurious [lʌgˈʒʊərɪəs] adj luxuriös.

luxury ['lʌkʃərɪ] ♦ adj Luxus-. ♦ n Luxus der.

lying ['laɪɪŋ] cont → lie.

lyrics ['lɪrɪks] npl Liedertext der.

M

m ♦ (abbr of metre) m. ♦ abbr = **mile**.

M (Br: abbr of motorway) A; (abbr of medium) M.

MA n (abbr of Master of Arts) britischer Hochschulabschluß in einem Geisteswissenschaftlichen Fach.

mac [mæk] n (Br: inf) Regenmantel der.

macaroni [ˌmækəˈrəʊnɪ] n Makkaroni pl.

macaroni cheese n Auflauf aus Makkaroni und Käsesauce.

machine [məˈʃiːn] n Maschine die.

machinegun [məˈʃiːngʌn] n Maschinengewehr das.

machinery [məˈʃiːnərɪ] n Maschinen pl.

machine-washable adj waschmaschinenfest.

mackerel [ˈmækrəl] (pl inv) n Makrele die.

mackintosh [ˈmækɪntɒʃ] n (Br) Regenmantel der.

mad [mæd] adj verrückt; (angry) wütend; **to be ~ about** (inf: like a lot) verrückt sein auf (+A); **like ~** wie verrückt.

Madam [ˈmædəm] n (form of address) gnädige Frau.

made [meɪd] pt & pp → **make**.

madeira [məˈdɪərə] n Madeira der.

made-to-measure adj maßgeschneidert.

madman [ˈmædmən] (pl -men [-mən]) n Irre der.

madness [ˈmædnɪs] n Wahnsinn der.

magazine [ˌmægəˈziːn] n Zeitschrift die.

maggot [ˈmægət] n Made die.

magic [ˈmædʒɪk] n (supernatural force) Magie die; (conjuring) Zauberei die; (special quality) Zauber der.

magician [məˈdʒɪʃn] n Zauberer der (Zauberin die).

magistrate [ˈmædʒɪstreɪt] n Friedensrichter der (-in die).

magnet [ˈmægnɪt] n Magnet der.

magnetic [mægˈnetɪk] adj magnetisch.

magnificent [mægˈnɪfɪsənt] adj herrlich.

magnifying glass [ˈmægnɪfaɪɪŋ-] n Lupe die.

mahogany [məˈhɒgənɪ] n Mahagoni das.

maid [meɪd] n Dienstmädchen das.

maiden name [ˈmeɪdn-] n Mädchenname der.

mail [meɪl] ◆ n Post die. ◆ vt (Am) schicken.

mailbox [ˈmeɪlbɒks] n (Am) Briefkasten der.

mailman [ˈmeɪlmən] (pl -men [-mən]) n (Am) Briefträger der, Postbote der.

mail order n Versandhandel der.

main [meɪn] adj Haupt-.

main course n Hauptgericht das.

main deck n Hauptdeck das.

mainland [ˈmeɪnlənd] n: **the ~** das Festland.

main line n Hauptstrecke die.

mainly [ˈmeɪnlɪ] adv hauptsächlich.

main road n Hauptstraße die.

mains [meɪnz] npl: **the ~** die Hauptleitung.

main street n (Am) Hauptstraße die.

maintain [meɪnˈteɪn] vt aufrecht|erhalten; (keep in good condition) instand halten.

maintenance [ˈmeɪntənəns] n (of car, machine) Instandhaltung die; (money) Unterhalt der.

maisonette [ˌmeɪzəˈnet] n (Br) Maisonette die.

maize [meɪz] n Mais der.

major [ˈmeɪdʒəʳ] ◆ adj (important) groß; (most important) Haupt-. ◆ n (MIL) Major der. ◆ vi (Am): **to ~ in sthg** etw als Hauptfach studieren.

majority [məˈdʒɒrətɪ] n Mehrheit die.

major road n Hauptstraße die.

make [meɪk] (pt & pp **made**) ◆ vt 1. (produce) machen; (manufacture) her|stellen; **to be made of sthg** aus etw gemacht sein; **to ~ lunch/supper** Mittagessen/Abendessen machen; **made in Japan** in Japan hergestellt. 2. (perform, do) machen; **to ~ a decision** eine Entscheidung treffen; **to ~ a mistake** einen Fehler machen; **to ~ a phone call** telephonieren; **to ~ a speech** eine Rede halten. 3. (cause to be) machen; **to ~ sb happy** jn glücklich machen. 4. (cause to do, force): **it made her laugh** das brachte sie zum Lachen; **to ~ sb do sthg** jn etw tun lassen; (force) jn zwingen etw zu tun. 5. (amount to, total) machen; **that ~s £5** das macht 5 Pfund. 6. (calculate): **I**

~ **it £4** ich komme auf 4 Pfund; **I ~ it seven o'clock** nach meiner Uhr ist es sieben Uhr. **7.** (*earn*) verdienen. **8.** ((*inf: arrive in time for*): **we didn't ~ the 10 o'clock train** wir haben den 10 Uhr-Zug nicht geschafft. **9.** (*friend, enemy*) machen. **10.** (*have qualities for*) ablgeben; **this would ~ a lovely bedroom** das wäre ein hübsches Schlafzimmer. **11.** (*bed*) machen. **12.** (*in phrases*): **to ~ do with** auslkommen mit; **to ~ good** (*damage*) wiederlgutlmachen; **to ~ it** es schaffen. ◆ *n* (*of product*) Marke *die*. ▶ **make out** *vt sep* (*cheque, receipt*) auslstellen; (*see*) auslmachen; (*hear*) verstehen. ▶ **make up** *vt sep* (*invent*) erfinden, sich (D) ausldenken; (*comprise*) bilden; (*difference*) auslgleichen; **to be made up of** bestehen aus. ▶ **make up for** *vt fus* wettlmachen.

makeshift ['meɪkʃɪft] *adj* behelfsmäßig.

make-up *n* (*cosmetics*) Make-up *das*.

malaria [mə'leərɪə] *n* Malaria *die*.

Malaysia [mə'leɪzɪə] *n* Malaysia *nt*.

male [meɪl] ◆ *adj* männlich. ◆ *n* (*animal*) Männchen *das*.

malfunction [mæl'fʌŋkʃn] *vi* (*fml*) nicht richtig funktionieren.

malignant [mə'lɪgnənt] *adj* bösartig.

mall [mɔːl] *n* (*shopping centre*) Einkaufszentrum *das*.

mallet ['mælɪt] *n* Holzhammer *der*.

malt [mɔːlt] *n* Malz *das*.

maltreat [,mæl'triːt] *vt* mißhandeln.

malt whisky *n* Malt-Whisky *der*.

mammal ['mæml] *n* Säugetier *das*.

man [mæn] (*pl* **men**) ◆ *n* Mann *der*; (*human being, mankind*) Mensch *der*. ◆ *vt* (*phones, office*) besetzen.

manage ['mænɪdʒ] ◆ *vt* (*company, business*) leiten; (*job*) bewältigen; (*food*) schaffen. ◆ *vi* (*cope*) zurechtlkommen; **can you ~ Friday?** paßt dir/Ihnen Freitag?; **to ~ to do sthg** es schaffen, etw zu tun.

management ['mænɪdʒmənt] *n* Geschäftsführung *die*.

manager ['mænɪdʒər] *n* (*of business, bank*) Direktor *der*; (*of shop*) Geschäftsführer *der*; (*of sports team*) Trainer *der* (-in *die*); (*of department*) Leiter *der* (-in *die*); **export ~** Exportleiter *der* (-in *die*).

manageress [,mænɪdʒə'res] *n* (*of business, bank*) Direktorin *die*; (*of shop*) Geschäftsführerin *die*.

managing director ['mænɪdʒɪŋ-] *n* leitender Direktor (leitende Direktorin).

mandarin ['mændərɪn] *n* Mandarine *die*.

mane [meɪn] *n* Mähne *die*.

maneuver [mə'nuːvər] (Am) = **manoeuvre**.

mangetout [,mɒnʒ'tuː] *n* Zuckererbse *die*.

mangle ['mæŋgl] *vt* zerquetschen.

mango ['mæŋgəʊ] (*pl* **-es** OR **-s**) *n* Mango *die*.

Manhattan [mæn'hætən] *n* Manhattan *nt*.

manhole ['mænhəʊl] *n* Kanalschacht *der*.

maniac ['meɪnɪæk] *n* (*inf*) Wilde *der*, *die*.

manicure ['mænɪkjʊər] *n* Maniküre *die*.

manifold ['mænɪfəʊld] *n* (AUT: *exhaust*) Auspuffrohr *das*.

manipulate [mə'nɪpjʊləɪt] *vt* (*person*) manipulieren; (*machine, controls*) handhaben.

mankind [,mæn'kaɪnd] *n* Menschheit *die*.

manly ['mænlɪ] *adj* männlich.

man-made *adj* künstlich.

manner ['mænər] *n* (*way*) Art *die*. ▶ **manners** *npl* Manieren *pl*.

manoeuvre [mə'nuːvər] ◆ *n* (Br) Manöver *das*. ◆ *vt* (Br) manövrieren.

manor ['mænər] *n* Gut *das*.

mansion ['mænʃn] *n* Villa *die*.

manslaughter ['mæn,slɔːtər] *n* Totschlag *der*.

mantelpiece ['mæntlpi:s] n Kamin-sims der.

manual ['mænjʊəl] ◆ adj (work) Hand-; (operated by hand) handbe-trieben. ◆ n (book) Handbuch das.

manufacture [,mænjʊ'fæktʃər] ◆ n Herstellung die. ◆ vt herlstellen.

manufacturer [,mænjʊ'fæktʃərər] n Hersteller der.

manure [mə'njʊər] n Mist der.

many ['menɪ] (compar **more**, superl **most**) adj & pron viele.

map [mæp] n Karte die.

Mar. (abbr of March) Mrz.

marathon ['mærəθn] n Marathon der.

marble ['mɑːbl] n (stone) Marmor der; (glass ball) Murmel die.

march [mɑːtʃ] ◆ n Marsch der. ◆ vi marschieren.

March [mɑːtʃ] n März der, → **September**.

mare [meər] n Stute die.

margarine [,mɑːdʒə'riːn] n Marga-rine die.

margin ['mɑːdʒɪn] n (of page) Rand der; (difference) Abstand der.

marina [mə'riːnə] n Jachthafen der.

marinated ['mærɪneɪtɪd] adj mari-niert.

marital status ['mærɪtl-] n Fami-lienstand der.

mark [mɑːk] ◆ n (spot) Fleck der; (trace) Spur die; (on skin) Mal das; (sym-bol) Zeichen das; (SCH) Note die. ◆ vt (blemish) beschädigen; (put symbol on) kennzeichnen; (SCH) benoten; (on map) markieren; (gas) ~ **five** Stufe fünf.

marker pen ['mɑːkə-] n Marker der.

market ['mɑːkɪt] n Markt der.

marketing ['mɑːkɪtɪŋ] n Marketing das.

marketplace ['mɑːkɪtpleɪs] n Marktplatz der.

markings ['mɑːkɪŋz] npl (on road) Markierungen pl.

marmalade ['mɑːməleɪd] n Mar-melade die.

marquee [mɑː'kiː] n Festzelt das.

marriage ['mærɪdʒ] n (event) Hochzeit die; (time married) Ehe die.

married ['mærɪd] adj verheiratet; **to get** ~ heiraten.

marrow ['mærəʊ] n (vegetable) Kürbis der.

marry ['mærɪ] vt & vi heiraten.

marsh [mɑːʃ] n Sumpf der.

martial arts [,mɑːʃl-] npl Kampfsport der.

marvellous ['mɑːvələs] adj (Br) wunderbar.

marvelous ['mɑːvələs] (Am) = **marvellous**.

marzipan ['mɑːzɪpæn] n Marzipan das.

mascara [mæs'kɑːrə] n Wim-perntusche die, Mascara das.

masculine ['mæskjʊlɪn] adj (typically male) männlich; (woman, in grammar) maskulin.

mashed potatoes [mæʃt-] npl Kartoffelbrei der.

mask [mɑːsk] n Maske die.

masonry ['meɪsnrɪ] n Mauerwerk das.

mass [mæs] n Masse die; (RELIG) Messe die; ~**es of** (inf: lots) ein Haufen.

massacre ['mæsəkər] n Massaker das.

massage [Br 'mæsɑːʒ, Am mə'sɑːʒ] ◆ n Massage die. ◆ vt massieren.

masseur [mæ'sɜːr] n Masseur der.

masseuse [mæ'sɜːz] n Masseuse die.

massive ['mæsɪv] adj riesig.

mast [mɑːst] n Mast der.

master ['mɑːstər] ◆ n (at school) Lehrer der; (of servant) Herr der; (of dog) Herrchen das. ◆ vt (skill, language) beherrschen.

masterpiece ['mɑːstəpiːs] n Mei-sterwerk das.

mat [mæt] n Matte die; (on table) Untersetzer der.

match [mætʃ] ◆ n (for lighting)

Streichholz *das*; *(game)* Spiel *das*. ◆ *vt* *(in colour, design)* passen zu; *(be the same as)* entsprechen (+G); *(be as good as)* gleich|kommen (+D). ◆ *vi* *(in colour, design)* zusammen|passen.

matchbox ['mætʃbɒks] *n* Streichholzschachtel *die*.

matching ['mætʃɪŋ] *adj* passend.

mate [meɪt] ◆ *n* *(inf: friend)* Kumpel *der*; *(Br: inf: form of address)* alter Freund. ◆ *vi* sich paaren.

material [mə'tɪərɪəl] *n* Stoff *der*, Material *das*. ▶ **materials** *npl* Sachen *pl*.

maternity leave [mə'tɜːnətɪ-] *n* Mutterschaftsurlaub *der*.

maternity ward [mə'tɜːnətɪ-] *n* Entbindungsstation *die*.

math [mæθ] (*Am*) = **maths**.

mathematics [,mæθə'mætɪks] *n* Mathematik *die*.

maths [mæθs] *n* (*Br*) Mathe *die*.

matinée ['mætɪneɪ] *n* Nachmittagsvorstellung *die*.

matt [mæt] *adj* matt.

matter ['mætər] ◆ *n* *(issue, situation)* Angelegenheit *die*; *(physical material)* Materie *die*. ◆ *vi* wichtig sein; **it doesn't ~** das macht nichts; **no ~ what happens** egal was passiert; **there's something the ~ with my car** mit meinem Auto stimmt etwas nicht; **what's the ~?** was ist los?; **as a ~ of course** selbstverständlich; **as a ~ of fact** eigentlich.

mattress ['mætrɪs] *n* Matratze *die*.

mature [mə'tjʊər] *adj* reif.

mauve [məʊv] *adj* lila.

max. [mæks] (*abbr of maximum*) max.

maximum ['mæksɪməm] ◆ *adj* maximal. ◆ *n* Maximum *das*.

may [meɪ] *aux vb* **1.** *(expressing possibility)* können; **it ~ be done as follows** man kann wie folgt vorgehen; **it ~ rain** es könnte regnen; **they ~ have got lost** sie haben sich vielleicht verirrt. **2.** *(expressing permission)* können; **~ I smoke?** darf ich rauchen?; **you ~ sit, if you wish** Sie können sich

hinsetzen, wenn Sie wollen. **3.** *(when conceding a point)*: **it ~ be a long walk, but it's worth it** es ist vielleicht ein weiter Weg, aber es lohnt sich.

May [meɪ] *n* Mai *der*, → **September**.

maybe ['meɪbiː] *adv* vielleicht.

mayonnaise [,meɪə'neɪz] *n* Mayonnaise *die*.

mayor [meər] *n* Bürgermeister *der*.

mayoress ['meərɪs] *n* *(female mayor)* Bürgermeisterin *die*; *(mayor's wife)* Frau *die* des Bürgermeisters.

maze [meɪz] *n* Irrgarten *der*.

me [miː] *pron (direct object)* mich; *(indirect object)* mir; *(after prep: accusative)* mich; *(after prep: dative)* mir; **she knows ~** sie kennt mich; **it's ~** ich bin's; **send it to ~** schick' es mir; **tell ~** sagen Sie mal, sag' mal; **he's worse than ~** er ist schlechter als ich.

meadow ['medəʊ] *n* Wiese *die*.

meal [miːl] *n* Mahlzeit *die*.

mealtime ['miːltaɪm] *n* Essenszeit *die*.

mean [miːn] (*pt & pp* **meant**) ◆ *adj* *(miserly)* geizig; *(unkind)* gemein. ◆ *vt* bedeuten; *(intend)* beabsichtigen; **to ~ to do sthg** vorhaben, etw zu tun; **the bus was meant to leave at eight** der Bus hätte eigentlich um acht Uhr abfahren sollen; **it's meant to be good** das soll gut sein; **I didn't ~ it** ich habe es nicht so gemeint.

meaning ['miːnɪŋ] *n* Bedeutung *die*.

meaningless ['miːnɪŋlɪs] *adj* bedeutungslos.

means [miːnz] (*pl inv*) ◆ *n* *(method)* Mittel *das*. ◆ *npl* *(money)* Mittel *pl*; **by all ~!** auf jeden Fall!; **by ~ of** mit Hilfe (+G).

meant [ment] *pt & pp* → **mean**.

meantime ['miːn,taɪm]: **in the meantime** *adv* in der Zwischenzeit.

meanwhile ['miːn,waɪl] *adv* inzwischen.

measles ['miːzlz] *n* Masern *pl*.

measure ['meʒər] ◆ *vt* messen. ◆ *n*

(*step, action*) Maßnahme *die*; (*of alcohol*) Dosis *die*; **the room ~s 10 m²** das Zimmer mißt 10 m².

measurement ['meʒəmənt] *n* Maß *das*.

meat [miːt] *n* Fleisch *das*; **red ~** Lamm- *und* Rindfleisch; **white ~** Kalbfleisch *und* Huhn.

meatball ['miːtbɔːl] *n* Fleischklößchen *das*.

mechanic [mɪ'kænɪk] *n* Mechaniker *der* (*-in die*).

mechanical [mɪ'kænɪkl] *adj* mechanisch.

mechanism ['mekənɪzm] *n* Mechanismus *der*.

medal ['medl] *n* Medaille *die*.

media ['miːdjə] *n or npl*: **the ~** die Medien *pl*.

medical ['medɪkl] ◆ *adj* medizinisch; (*treatment*) ärztlich. ◆ *n* Untersuchung *die*.

medication [,medɪ'keɪʃn] *n* Medikament *das*.

medicine ['medsɪn] *n* Medikament *das*; (*science*) Medizin *die*.

medicine cabinet *n* Medizinschrank *der*.

medieval [,medɪ'iːvl] *adj* mittelalterlich.

mediocre [,miːdɪ'əʊkər] *adj* mittelmäßig.

Mediterranean [,medɪtə'reɪnjən] *n*: **the ~** (*region*) der Mittelmeerraum; **the ~ (Sea)** das Mittelmeer.

medium ['miːdjəm] *adj* mittelgroß; (*wine*) halbtrocken.

medium-dry *adj* halbtrocken.

medium-sized [-saɪzd] *adj* mittelgroß.

meet [miːt] (*pt & pp* **met**) ◆ *vt* (*by arrangement*) sich treffen mit; (*by chance*) treffen; (*get to know*) kennenllernen; (*go to collect*) ablholen; (*need, requirement*) erfüllen; (*cost, expenses*) begleichen. ◆ *vi* (*by arrangement, by chance*) sich treffen; (*get to know each other*) sich kennenllernen; (*intersect*) aufeinan-

derltreffen. ▶ **meet up** *vi* sich treffen. ▶ **meet with** *vt fus* (*problems, resistance*) stoßen auf (+A); (*Am: by arrangement*) sich treffen mit.

meeting ['miːtɪŋ] *n* (*for business*) Besprechung *die*.

meeting point *n* Treffpunkt *der*.

melody ['melədɪ] *n* Melodie *die*.

melon ['melən] *n* Melone *die*.

melt [melt] *vi* schmelzen.

member ['membər] *n* Mitglied *das*.

Member of Congress [-'kɒŋgres] *n* Abgeordneter *des amerikanischen Kongresses*.

Member of Parliament *n* Abgeordneter *des britischen Parlaments*.

membership ['membəʃɪp] *n* Mitgliedschaft *die*; (*members*) Mitgliederzahl *die*.

memorial [mɪ'mɔːrɪəl] *n* Denkmal *das*.

memorize ['meməraɪz] *vt* sich (D) einlprägen.

memory ['memərɪ] *n* Erinnerung *die*; (*of computer*) Speicher *der*.

men [men] *pl* → **man**.

menacing ['menəsɪŋ] *adj* drohend.

mend [mend] *vt* reparieren.

menopause ['menəpɔːz] *n* Wechseljahre *pl*.

men's room *n* (*Am*) Herrentoilette *die*.

menstruate ['menstrʊeɪt] *vi* menstruieren.

menswear ['menzweər] *n* Herrenbekleidung *die*.

mental ['mentl] *adj* geistig; (MED) Geistes-.

mental hospital *n* psychiatrische Klinik.

mentally handicapped ['mentəlɪ-] ◆ *adj* geistig behindert. ◆ *npl*: **the ~** die geistig Behinderten *pl*.

mentally ill ['mentəlɪ-] *adj* geisteskrank.

mention ['menʃn] *vt* erwähnen; **don't ~ it!** bitte!

menu ['menjuː] *n* Speisekarte *die*;

(COMPUT) Menü *das*; **children's ~** Kinderspeisekarte *die*.

merchandise ['mɜːtʃəndaɪz] *n* Ware *die*.

merchant marine [ˌmɜːtʃəntməˈriːn] (Am) = **merchant navy**.

merchant navy [ˌmɜːtʃənt-] *n* (Br) Handelsmarine *die*.

mercury ['mɜːkjʊrɪ] *n* Quecksilber *das*.

mercy ['mɜːsɪ] *n* Gnade *die*.

mere [mɪəʳ] *adj* bloß.

merely ['mɪəlɪ] *adv* bloß.

merge [mɜːdʒ] *vi* (*combine*) sich zusammen|schließen; **'merge'** (Am) Schild an Autobahnauffahrten, das dazu auffordert, sich in die rechte Spur der Autobahn einzuordnen.

merger ['mɜːdʒəʳ] *n* Fusion *die*.

meringue [məˈræŋ] *n* Baiser *das*.

merit ['merɪt] *n* (*worthiness*) Verdienst *der*; (*good quality*) Vorzug *der*; (*in exam*) Auszeichnung *die*.

merry ['merɪ] *adj* fröhlich; (*inf: tipsy*) angeheitert; **Merry Christmas!** Fröhliche Weihnachten!

merry-go-round *n* Karussell *das*.

mess [mes] *n* Durcheinander *das*; (*difficult situation*) Schwierigkeiten *pl*; **in a ~** (*untidy*) unordentlich. ▸ **mess about** *vi* (*inf*) herum|albern; **to ~ about with sthg** (*interfere*) mit etw herum|spielen. ▸ **mess up** *vt sep* (*inf: plans*) durcheinander|bringen; (*clothes*) schmutzig machen.

message ['mesɪdʒ] *n* Nachricht *die*.

messenger ['mesɪndʒəʳ] *n* Bote *der* (Botin *die*).

messy ['mesɪ] *adj* unordentlich.

met [met] *pt & pp* → **meet**.

metal ['metl] ◆ *adj* Metall-. ◆ *n* Metall *das*.

metalwork ['metəlwɜːk] *n* (*craft*) Metallbearbeitung *die*.

meter ['miːtəʳ] *n* (*device*) Zähler *der*; (Am) = **metre**.

method ['meθəd] *n* Methode *die*.

methodical [mɪˈθɒdɪkl] *adj* methodisch.

meticulous [mɪˈtɪkjʊləs] *adj* sorgfältig.

metre ['miːtəʳ] *n* (Br) Meter *der*.

metric ['metrɪk] *adj* metrisch.

mews [mjuːz] (*pl inv*) *n* (Br) kleine Seitenstraße mit früheren Stallungen, die oft zu eleganten Wohnungen umgebaut wurden.

Mexican ['meksɪkn] ◆ *adj* mexikanisch. ◆ *n* Mexikaner *der* (-in *die*).

Mexico ['meksɪkəʊ] *n* Mexiko *nt*.

mg (*abbr of milligram*) mg.

miaow [miːˈaʊ] *vi* (Br) miauen.

mice [maɪs] *pl* → **mouse**.

microchip ['maɪkrəʊtʃɪp] *n* Mikrochip *der*.

microphone ['maɪkrəfəʊn] *n* Mikrofon *das*.

microscope ['maɪkrəskəʊp] *n* Mikroskop *das*.

microwave (oven) ['maɪkrəweɪv-] *n* Mikrowellenherd *der*.

midday [ˌmɪdˈdeɪ] *n* Mittag *der*.

middle ['mɪdl] ◆ *n* Mitte *die*. ◆ *adj* (*central*) mittlere(-r)(-s); **in the ~ of the road** in der Straßenmitte; **in the ~ of April** Mitte April; **to be in the ~ of doing sthg** gerade dabei sein, etw zu tun.

middle-aged *adj* mittleren Alters; **a ~ woman** eine Frau mittleren Alters.

middle-class *adj* (*suburb*) bürgerlich; **a ~ family** eine Familie der Mittelschicht.

Middle East *n*: **the ~** der Nahe Osten.

middle name *n* zweiter Vorname.

middle school *n* (*in UK*) staatliche Schule für 9- bis 13jährige.

midge [mɪdʒ] *n* Mücke *die*.

midget ['mɪdʒɪt] *n* Zwerg *der* (-in *die*).

Midlands ['mɪdləndz] *npl*: **the ~** Mittelengland *nt*.

midnight ['mɪdnaɪt] *n* Mitternacht *die*.

midsummer ['mɪdˈsʌməʳ] *n* Hochsommer *der*.

midway [ˌmɪdˈweɪ] *adv* mitten.

midweek [*adj* ˈmɪdwiːk, *adv* mɪdˈwiːk] *adj & adv* in der Wochenmitte.

midwife [ˈmɪdwaɪf] (*pl* **-wives** [-waɪvz]) *n* Hebamme *die*.

midwinter [ˈmɪdˈwɪntəʳ] *n* Mittwinter *der*.

might [maɪt] *aux vb* **1.** (*expressing possibility*) können; **they ~ still come** sie könnten noch kommen; **they ~ have been killed** sie sind vielleicht umgekommen. **2.** (*fml: expressing permission*) können; **~ I have a few words?** könnte ich Sie mal sprechen? **3.** (*when conceding a point*): **it ~ be expensive, but it's good quality** es ist zwar teuer, aber es ist eine gute Qualität. **4.** (*would*): **I'd hoped you ~ come too** ich hatte gehofft, du würdest auch mitkommen.

migraine [ˈmiːgreɪn, ˈmaɪgreɪn] *n* Migräne *die*.

mild [maɪld] ◆ *adj* mild; (*illness, surprise*) leicht. ◆ *n* (*Br: beer*) Bier, *das schwächer und dunkler ist als* ʻbitter'.

mile [maɪl] *n* Meile *die*; **it's ~s away** das ist meilenweit entfernt.

mileage [ˈmaɪlɪdʒ] *n* Entfernung *die* in Meilen.

mileometer [maɪˈlɒmɪtəʳ] *n* ≃ Kilometerzähler *der*.

military [ˈmɪlɪtrɪ] *adj* Militär-, militärisch.

milk [mɪlk] ◆ *n* Milch *die*. ◆ *vt* melken.

milk chocolate *n* Milchschokolade *die*.

milkman [ˈmɪlkmən] (*pl* **-men** [-mən]) *n* Milchmann *der*.

milk shake *n* Milchmixgetränk *das*.

milky [ˈmɪlkɪ] *adj* (*drink*) milchig.

mill [mɪl] *n* Mühle *die*; (*factory*) Fabrik *die*.

milligram [ˈmɪlɪgræm] *n* Milligramm *das*.

millilitre [ˈmɪlɪˌliːtəʳ] *n* Milliliter *der*.

millimetre [ˈmɪlɪˌmiːtəʳ] *n* Millimeter *der*.

million [ˈmɪljən] *n* Million *die*; **~s of** (*fig*) Tausende von.

millionaire [ˌmɪljəˈneəʳ] *n* Millionär *der* (**-in** *die*).

mime [maɪm] *vi* sich ohne Worte ausdrücken.

min. [mɪn] (*abbr of minute, minimum*) Min.

mince [mɪns] *n* (*Br*) Hackfleisch *das*.

mincemeat [ˈmɪnsmiːt] *n* (*sweet filling*) süße Füllung aus Zitronat, Orangeat, Rosinen, Gewürzen u.a.; (*Am: mince*) Hackfleisch *das*.

mince pie *n* mit Zitronat, Orangeat, Rosinen, Gewürzen u.a. gefülltes Weihnachtsgebäck.

mind [maɪnd] ◆ *n* Verstand *der*; (*memory*) Gedächtnis *das*. ◆ *vt* aufpassen auf (+A); (*be bothered by*) sich stören an (+D). ◆ *vi*: **I don't ~** es ist mir egal; **it slipped my ~** es ist mir entfallen; **to my ~** was mich betrifft; **to bear sthg in ~** etw nicht vergessen; **to change one's ~** seine Meinung ändern; **to have sthg in ~** etw vorhaben; **to have sthg on one's ~** sich mit etw beschäftigen; **to make one's ~ up** sich entscheiden; **do you ~ if ...?** stört es, wenn ...; **I wouldn't ~ a drink** ich würde eigentlich gerne etwas trinken; **ʻ~ the gap!'** (*on underground*) ʻVorsicht beim Einsteigen und Aussteigen'; **never ~!** (*don't worry*) macht nichts!

mine¹ [maɪn] *pron* meine(-r)(-s), meine *pl*; **it's ~** es gehört mir; **a friend of ~** ein Freund von mir.

mine² [maɪn] *n* (*for coal etc*) Bergwerk *das*; (*bomb*) Mine *die*.

miner [ˈmaɪnəʳ] *n* Bergmann *der*.

mineral [ˈmɪnərəl] *n* Mineral *das*.

mineral water *n* Mineralwasser *das*.

minestrone [ˌmɪnɪˈstrəʊnɪ] *n* Minestrone *die*.

mingle [ˈmɪŋgl] *vi* sich mischen; (*with other people*) Konversation machen.

miniature ['mɪnətʃər] ◆ adj Miniatur-. ◆ n (of alcohol) Miniflasche die.

minibar ['mɪnɪbɑːr] n Hausbar die.

minibus ['mɪnɪbʌs] (pl -es) n Kleinbus der.

minicab ['mɪnɪkæb] n (Br) Mietauto das.

minimal ['mɪnɪml] adj minimal.

minimum ['mɪnɪməm] ◆ adj Mindest-. ◆ n Minimum das.

miniskirt ['mɪnɪskɜːt] n Minirock der.

minister ['mɪnɪstər] n (in government) Minister der (-in die); (in church) Geistliche der die.

ministry ['mɪnɪstrɪ] n (of government) Ministerium das.

minor ['maɪnər] ◆ adj kleiner. ◆ n (fml) Minderjährige der die.

minority [maɪ'nɒrətɪ] n Minderheit die.

minor road n Nebenstraße die.

mint [mɪnt] n (sweet) Pfefferminz das; (plant) Minze die.

minus ['maɪnəs] prep minus; it's ~ 10 (degrees C) es ist minus 10 (Grad Celsius).

minuscule ['mɪnəskjuːl] adj winzig.

minute[1] ['mɪnɪt] n Minute die; any ~ jeden Moment; just a ~! Moment, bitte!

minute[2] [maɪ'njuːt] adj winzig.

minute steak [ˌmɪnɪt-] n kurzgebratenes Steak.

miracle ['mɪrəkl] n Wunder das.

miraculous [mɪ'rækjʊləs] adj wunderbar.

mirror ['mɪrər] n Spiegel der.

misbehave [ˌmɪsbɪ'heɪv] vi sich schlecht benehmen.

miscarriage [ˌmɪs'kærɪdʒ] n Fehlgeburt die.

miscellaneous [ˌmɪsə'leɪnjəs] adj verschieden.

mischievous ['mɪstʃɪvəs] adj ungezogen.

misconduct [ˌmɪs'kɒndʌkt] n unkorrektes Verhalten.

miser ['maɪzər] n Geizhals der.

miserable ['mɪzrəbl] adj erbärmlich; (weather) fürchterlich.

misery ['mɪzərɪ] n (unhappiness) Kummer der; (poor conditions) Elend das.

misfire [ˌmɪs'faɪər] vi (car) fehlⅼzünden.

misfortune [mɪs'fɔːtʃuːn] n (bad luck) Pech das.

mishap ['mɪshæp] n Zwischenfall der.

misjudge [ˌmɪs'dʒʌdʒ] vt falsch einⅼschätzen.

mislay [ˌmɪs'leɪ] (pt & pp -laid) vt verlegen.

mislead [ˌmɪs'liːd] (pt & pp -led) vt irreⅼführen.

miss [mɪs] ◆ vt (plane, train, appointment, opportunity) verpassen; (not notice) übersehen; (target) verfehlen; (regret absence of) vermissen. ◆ vi (fail to hit) nicht treffen. ▶ **miss out** vt sep ausⅼlassen. ◆ vi: **to ~ out on sthg** sich (D) etw entgehen lassen.

Miss [mɪs] n Fräulein das.

missile [Br 'mɪsaɪl, Am 'mɪsl] n (weapon) Rakete die; (thing thrown) Geschoß das.

missing ['mɪsɪŋ] adj verschwunden; **to be ~** (not there) fehlen.

missing person n Vermißte der die.

mission ['mɪʃn] n Mission die.

missionary ['mɪʃənrɪ] n Missionar der (-in die).

mist [mɪst] n Nebel der.

mistake [mɪ'steɪk] (pt -took, pp -taken) ◆ n Fehler der. ◆ vt (misunderstand) mißverstehen; **by ~** aus Versehen; **to make a ~** sich irren; **to ~ sb/sthg for** jn/etw verwechseln mit.

Mister ['mɪstər] n Herr der.

mistook [mɪ'stʊk] pt → **mistake**.

mistress ['mɪstrɪs] n (lover) Geliebte die; (Br: teacher) Lehrerin die.

mistrust [,mɪs'trʌst] vt mißtrauen (+D).

misty ['mɪstɪ] adj nebelig.

misunderstanding [,mɪsʌndə-'stændɪŋ] n Mißverständnis das.

misuse [,mɪs'juːs] n Mißbrauch der.

mitten ['mɪtn] n Fausthandschuh der.

mix [mɪks] ◆ vt mischen; (drink) mixen. ◆ n (for cake, sauce) Mischung die; **to ~ sthg with sthg** etw mit etw vermischen. ▶ **mix up** vt sep durcheinander|bringen.

mixed [mɪkst] adj gemischt.

mixed grill n Grillteller der.

mixed salad n gemischter Salat.

mixed vegetables npl Mischgemüse das.

mixer ['mɪksər] n (for food) Mixer der; (drink) Mixgetränk das.

mixture ['mɪkstʃər] n Mischung die.

mix-up n (inf) Irrtum der.

ml (abbr of millilitre) ml.

mm (abbr of millimetre) mm.

moan [məʊn] vi stöhnen.

moat [məʊt] n Burggraben der.

mobile ['məʊbaɪl] adj mobil.

mobile phone n Mobilfunk-Telefon das.

mock [mɒk] ◆ adj Schein-. ◆ vt verspotten. ◆ n (Br: exam) Vorprüfung die.

mode [məʊd] n Art die.

model ['mɒdl] n Modell das; (fashion model) Mannequin das.

moderate ['mɒdərət] adj (size, speed, amount) mittlere(-r)(-s); (views, politician) gemäßigt; (drinker, smoker) mäßig.

modern ['mɒdən] adj modern.

modernized ['mɒdənaɪzd] adj modernisiert.

modern languages npl Fremdsprachen pl.

modest ['mɒdɪst] adj bescheiden.

modify ['mɒdɪfaɪ] vt abländern.

mohair ['məʊheər] n Mohair der.

moist [mɔɪst] adj feucht.

moisture ['mɔɪstʃər] n Feuchtigkeit die.

moisturizer ['mɔɪstʃəraɪzər] n Feuchtigkeitscreme die.

molar ['məʊlər] n Backenzahn der.

mold [məʊld] (Am) = **mould**.

mole [məʊl] n (animal) Maulwurf der; (spot) Leberfleck der.

molest [mə'lest] vt (child, woman) belästigen.

mom [mɒm] n (Am: inf) Mutti die.

moment ['məʊmənt] n Moment der; **at the ~** im Moment; **for the ~** momentan.

Mon. (abbr of Monday) Mo.

monarchy ['mɒnəkɪ] n: **the ~** die Monarchie.

monastery ['mɒnəstrɪ] n Kloster das.

Monday ['mʌndɪ] n Montag der, → **Saturday**.

money ['mʌnɪ] n Geld das.

money belt n Geldgürtel der.

money order n Zahlungsanweisung die.

mongrel ['mʌŋgrəl] n Promenadenmischung die.

monitor ['mɒnɪtər] ◆ n (computer screen) Monitor der. ◆ vt überwachen.

monk [mʌŋk] n Mönch der.

monkey ['mʌŋkɪ] (pl **monkeys**) n Affe der.

monkfish ['mʌŋkfɪʃ] n Seeteufel der.

monopoly [mə'nɒpəlɪ] n Monopol das.

monorail ['mɒnəʊreɪl] n Einschienenbahn die.

monotonous [mə'nɒtənəs] adj monoton.

monsoon [mɒn'suːn] n Monsun der.

monster ['mɒnstər] n Monster das.

month [mʌnθ] n Monat der; **in a ~'s time** in einem Monat.

monthly ['mʌnθlɪ] adj & adv monatlich.

monument ['mɒnjʊmənt] n Denkmal das.

mood 140

mood [muːd] *n* Laune *die*, Stimmung *die*; **to be in a (bad)** ~ schlechte Laune haben; **to be in a good** ~ gute Laune haben.

moody ['muːdɪ] *adj* launisch.

moon [muːn] *n* Mond *der*.

moonlight ['muːnlaɪt] *n* Mondlicht *das*.

moor [mɔːr] ◆ *n* Moor *das*. ◆ *vt* festlmachen.

moose [muːs] (*pl inv*) *n* Elch *der*.

mop [mɒp] ◆ *n* (*for floor*) Mop *der*. ◆ *vt* (*floor*) moppen. ➤ **mop up** *vt sep* auflwischen.

moped ['məʊped] *n* Moped *das*.

moral ['mɒrəl] ◆ *adj* moralisch. ◆ *n* Moral *die*.

morality [mə'rælɪtɪ] *n* Moral *die*.

more [mɔːr] ◆ *adj* **1.** (*a larger amount of*) mehr; **there are ~ tourists than usual** es sind mehr Touristen als gewöhnlich da. **2.** (*additional*) noch mehr; **are there any ~ cakes?** ist noch mehr Kuchen da?; **I'd like two ~ bottles** ich möchte zwei Flaschen mehr; **there's no ~ wine** es ist kein Wein mehr da. **3.** (*in phrases*): ~ **and more** mehr und mehr. ◆ *adv* **1.** (*in comparatives*): **it's ~ difficult than before** es ist schwieriger als vorher; **speak ~ clearly** sprich/sprechen Sie deutlicher. **2.** (*to a greater degree*) mehr; **we ought to go to the cinema ~** wir sollten öfters ins Kino gehen. **3.** (*in phrases*): **I don't go there any ~** ich gehe da nicht mehr hin; **once ~** noch einmal; ~ **or less** mehr oder weniger; **we'd be ~ than happy to help** wir würden sehr gerne helfen. ◆ *pron* **1.** (*a larger amount*) mehr; **I've got ~ than you** ich habe mehr als du; ~ **than 20 types of pizza** mehr als 20 Pizzasorten. **2.** (*an additional amount*) noch mehr; **is there any ~?** ist noch mehr da?; **there's no ~** es ist nichts mehr da.

moreover [mɔː'rəʊvər] *adv* (*fml*) außerdem.

morning ['mɔːnɪŋ] *n* Morgen *der*; **two o'clock in the ~** zwei Uhr morgens; **good ~!** guten Morgen!; **in the ~** (*early in the day*) morgens, am Morgen; (*tomorrow morning*) morgen früh.

morning-after pill *n* Pille *die* danach.

morning sickness *n* Schwangerschaftserbrechen *das*.

Morocco [mə'rɒkəʊ] *n* Marokko *nt*.

moron ['mɔːrɒn] *n* (*inf*) Blödian *der*.

Morse (code) [mɔːs-] *n* Morsealphabet *das*.

mortgage ['mɔːgɪdʒ] *n* Hypothek *die*.

mosaic [mə'zeɪɪk] *n* Mosaik *das*.

Moslem ['mɒzləm] = **Muslim**.

mosque [mɒsk] *n* Moschee *die*.

mosquito [mə'skiːtəʊ] (*pl* -es) *n* Mücke *die*; (*tropical*) Moskito *der*.

mosquito net *n* Moskitonetz *das*.

moss [mɒs] *n* Moos *das*.

most [məʊst] ◆ *adj* **1.** (*the majority of*) die meisten; ~ **people agree** die meisten Leute sind dieser Meinung. **2.** (*the largest amount of*) der/die/das meiste; **I drank (the) ~ beer** ich habe das meiste Bier getrunken. ◆ *adv* **1.** (*in superlatives*): **she spoke (the) ~ clearly** sie sprach am deutlichsten; **the ~ expensive hotel in town** das teuerste Hotel in der Stadt. **2.** (*to the greatest degree*) am meisten; **I like this one ~** mir gefällt dieses am besten. **3.** (*fml: very*) äußerst, höchst; **it was a ~ pleasant evening** es war ein äußerst angenehmer Abend. ◆ *pron* **1.** (*the majority*) die meisten; ~ **of the villages** die meisten Dörfer; ~ **of the time** die meiste Zeit. **2.** (*the largest amount*) das meiste; **she earns (the) ~** sie verdient am meisten. **3.** (*in phrases*): **at ~** höchstens; **to make the ~ of sthg** das Beste aus etw machen.

mostly ['məʊstlɪ] *adv* hauptsächlich.

MOT *n* (Br: *test*) TÜV *der*.

motel [məʊ'tel] *n* Motel *das*.

moth [mɒθ] *n* Nachtfalter *der*; (*in clothes*) Motte *die*.

mother ['mʌðər] n Mutter die.

mother-in-law n Schwiegermutter die.

mother-of-pearl n Perlmutt das.

motif [məʊ'tiːf] n Motiv das.

motion ['məʊʃn] ◆ n Bewegung die. ◆ vi: **to ~ to sb** jm ein Zeichen geben.

motionless ['məʊʃənlɪs] adj unbeweglich.

motivate ['məʊtɪveɪt] vt motivieren.

motive ['məʊtɪv] n Motiv das.

motor ['məʊtər] n Motor der.

Motorail® ['məʊtəreɪl] n Autoreisezug der.

motorbike ['məʊtəbaɪk] n Motorrad das.

motorboat ['məʊtəbəʊt] n Motorboot das.

motorcar ['məʊtəkɑːr] n Kraftfahrzeug das.

motorcycle ['məʊtə,saɪkl] n Motorrad das.

motorcycle racing n Motorradrennen das.

motorcyclist ['məʊtə,saɪklɪst] n Motorradfahrer der (-in die).

motorist ['məʊtərɪst] n Autofahrer der (-in die).

motor racing n Autorennen das.

motorway ['məʊtəweɪ] n (Br) Autobahn die.

motto ['mɒtəʊ] (pl -s) n Motto das.

mould [məʊld] ◆ n ([Br]: shape) Form die; (substance) Schimmel der. ◆ vt (Br: shape) formen.

mouldy ['məʊldɪ] adj (Br) schimmelig.

mound [maʊnd] n (hill) Hügel der; (pile) Haufen der.

mount [maʊnt] ◆ n (for photo) Passepartout das; (mountain) Berg der. ◆ vt (horse) besteigen; (photo) auflziehen. ◆ vi (increase) steigen.

mountain ['maʊntɪn] n Berg der.

mountain bike n Mountainbike das.

mountaineer [,maʊntɪ'nɪər] n Bergsteiger der (-in die).

mountaineering [,maʊntɪ'nɪərɪŋ] n: **to go ~** Bergsteigen gehen.

mountainous ['maʊntɪnəs] adj bergig.

Mount Rushmore [-'rʌʃmɔːr] n Mount Rushmore.

mourning ['mɔːnɪŋ] n: **to be in ~** in Trauer sein.

mouse [maʊs] (pl mice) n Maus die.

moussaka [muː'sɑːkə] n Moussaka die.

mousse [muːs] n Mousse die.

moustache [mə'stɑːʃ] n (Br) Schnurrbart der.

mouth [maʊθ] n Mund der; (of cave, tunnel) Öffnung die; (of river) Mündung die.

mouthful ['maʊθfʊl] n (of food) Happen der; (of drink) Schluck der.

mouthorgan ['maʊθ,ɔːgən] n Mundharmonika die.

mouthpiece ['maʊθpiːs] n (of telephone) Sprechmuschel die; (of musical instrument) Mundstück das.

mouthwash ['maʊθwɒʃ] n Mundwasser das.

move [muːv] ◆ n (change of house) Umzug der; (movement) Bewegung die; (in games) Zug der; (course of action) Schritt der. ◆ vt bewegen; (furniture) rücken; (car) weglfahren; (emotionally) rühren. ◆ vi sich bewegen; (vehicle) fahren; **to ~ (house)** umlziehen; **to make a ~** (leave) auflbrechen. ▶ **move along** vi weiterlgehen. ▶ **move away** vi fortlziehen. ▶ **move in** vi (to house) einlziehen. ▶ **move off** vi (train, car) sich in Bewegung setzen. ▶ **move on** vi (on foot) weiterlgehen; (car, bus etc) weiterlfahren. ▶ **move out** vi (from house) auslziehen. ▶ **move over** vi zur Seite rücken. ▶ **move up** vi (on seat) rücken.

movement ['muːvmənt] n Bewegung die.

movie ['muːvɪ] n Film der.

movie theater n (Am) Kino das.

moving ['muːvɪŋ] adj bewegend.

mow [məʊ] vt: **to ~ the lawn** den Rasen mähen.

mozzarella [ˌmɒtsəˈrelə] n Mozzarella der.

MP abbr = **Member of Parliament**.

mph (abbr of miles per hour) Meilen pro Stunde.

Mr ['mɪstər] abbr Hr.

Mrs ['mɪsɪz] abbr Fr.

Ms [mɪz] abbr Anrede für Frauen, mit der man die Unterscheidung zwischen 'Frau' (verheiratet) und 'Fräulein' (unverheiratet) vermeidet.

MSc n (abbr of Master of Science) britischer Hochschulabschluß in einem naturwissenschaftlichen Fach.

much [mʌtʃ] (compar **more**, superl **most**) ◆ adj viel; **I haven't got ~ money** ich habe nicht viel Geld; **as ~ food as you can eat** soviel du essen kannst/Sie essen können; **how ~ time is left?** wieviel Zeit bleibt noch?; **we have too ~ work** wir haben zuviel Arbeit. ◆ adv 1. (to a great extent) viel; **it's ~ better** es ist viel besser; **I like it very ~** es gefällt mir sehr gut; **it's not ~ good** (inf) es ist nicht besonders; **thank you very ~** vielen Dank. 2. (often) oft; **we don't go there ~** wir gehen da nicht oft hin. ◆ pron viel; **I haven't got ~** ich habe nicht viel; **as ~ as you like** so viel Sie wollen/du willst; **how ~ is it?** wieviel kostet es?; **you've got too ~** du hast zuviel.

muck [mʌk] n Dreck der. ▶ **muck about** vi (Br: inf) herumlalbern. ▶ **muck up** vt sep (Br: inf) vermasseln.

mud [mʌd] n Schlamm der.

muddle ['mʌdl] n: **to be in a ~** durcheinander sein.

muddy ['mʌdɪ] adj schlammig.

mudguard ['mʌdgɑːd] n Schutzblech das.

muesli ['mjuːzlɪ] n Müsli das.

muffin ['mʌfɪn] n (roll) Muffin das; (cake) Kleingebäck aus Mürbeteig.

muffler ['mʌflər] n (Am: silencer) Schalldämpfer der.

mug [mʌg] ◆ n (cup) Becher der. ◆ vt (attack) überfallen.

mugging ['mʌgɪŋ] n Überfall der.

muggy ['mʌgɪ] adj schwül.

mule [mjuːl] n Maultier das.

multicoloured [ˌmʌltɪˌkʌləd] adj bunt.

multigym ['mʌltɪdʒɪm] n Gerät das zum Krafttraining.

multiple ['mʌltɪpl] adj mehrfach.

multiplex cinema ['mʌltɪpleks-] n Cinemax das.

multiplication [ˌmʌltɪplɪˈkeɪʃn] n Multiplikation die.

multiply ['mʌltɪplaɪ] ◆ vt multiplizieren. ◆ vi sich vermehren.

multistorey (car park) [ˌmʌltɪˈstɔːrɪ-] n Parkhaus das.

mum [mʌm] n (Br: inf) Mutti die.

mummy ['mʌmɪ] n (Br: inf: mother) Mami die.

mumps [mʌmps] n Mumps der.

munch [mʌntʃ] vt kauen.

Munich ['mjuːnɪk] n München nt.

municipal [mjuːˈnɪsɪpl] adj städtisch, Stadt-.

mural ['mjuːərəl] n Wandgemälde das.

murder ['mɜːdər] ◆ n Mord der. ◆ vt ermorden.

murderer ['mɜːdərər] n Mörder der (-in die).

muscle ['mʌsl] n Muskel der.

museum [mjuːˈziːəm] n Museum das.

mushroom ['mʌʃrʊm] n Pilz der; (CULIN) Champignon der.

music ['mjuːzɪk] n Musik die.

musical ['mjuːzɪkl] ◆ adj musikalisch. ◆ n Musical das.

musical instrument n Musikinstrument das.

musician [mjuːˈzɪʃn] n Musiker der (-in die).

Muslim ['mʊzlɪm] ◆ adj moslemisch. ◆ n Moslem der (Moslime die).

mussels ['mʌslz] npl Miesmuscheln pl.

must [mʌst] ◆ aux vb müssen; (with negative) dürfen. ◆ n: **it's a ~** (inf) das ist ein Muß; **I ~ go** ich muß gehen; **you ~n't be late** du darfst nicht zu spät kommen; **the room ~ be vacated by ten** das Zimmer ist bis zehn Uhr zu räumen; **you ~ have seen it** du mußt es doch gesehen haben; **you ~ see that film** du mußt dir diesen Film ansehen; **you ~ be joking!** das kann doch nicht dein Ernst sein!

mustache ['mʌstæʃ] (Am) = **moustache**.

mustard ['mʌstəd] n Senf der.

mustn't ['mʌsənt] = **must not**.

mutter ['mʌtər] vt murmeln.

mutton ['mʌtn] n Hammelfleisch das.

mutual ['mjuːtʃʊəl] adj (feeling) gegenseitig; (friend, interest) gemeinsam.

muzzle ['mʌzl] n Maulkorb der.

my [maɪ] adj mein.

myself [maɪ'self] pron (reflexive: accusative) mich; (reflexive: dative) mir; (after prep: accusative) mich selbst; (after prep: dative) mir selbst; **I did it ~** ich habe es selbst gemacht.

mysterious [mɪ'stɪərɪəs] adj rätselhaft.

mystery ['mɪstərɪ] n Rätsel das.

myth [mɪθ] n (ancient story) Mythos der; (false idea) Märchen das.

mythology [mɪ'θɒlədʒɪ] n Mythologie die.

N

N (abbr of North) N.

nag [næg] vt herumlnörgeln an (+D).

nail [neɪl] ◆ n Nagel der. ◆ vt anlnageln.

nailbrush ['neɪlbrʌʃ] n Nagelbürste die.

nail file n Nagelfeile die.

nail scissors npl Nagelschere die.

nail varnish n Nagellack der.

nail varnish remover [-rə-'muːvər] n Nagellackentferner der.

naive [naɪ'iːv] adj naiv.

naked ['neɪkɪd] adj nackt.

name [neɪm] ◆ n Name der; (reputation) Ruf der. ◆ vt nennen; (place) benennen; **first ~** Vorname der; **last ~** Nachname der; **what's your ~?** wie heißen Sie/heißt du?; **my ~ is ...** ich heiße ...

namely ['neɪmlɪ] adv nämlich.

nan bread [næn-] n indisches Fladenbrot, das heiß gegessen wird.

nanny ['nænɪ] n (childminder) Kindermädchen das; (inf: grandmother) Oma die.

nap [næp] n: **to have a ~** ein Nickerchen machen.

napkin ['næpkɪn] n Serviette die.

nappy ['næpɪ] n Windel die.

nappy liner n Windeleinlage die.

narcotic [nɑː'kɒtik] n Rauschgift das.

narrow ['nærəʊ] ◆ adj schmal, eng. ◆ vi sich verengen.

narrow-minded [-'maɪndɪd] adj engstirnig.

nasty ['nɑːstɪ] adj (spiteful) gemein; (accident, fall) schlimm; (smell, taste, weather) scheußlich.

nation ['neɪʃn] n Nation die.

national ['næʃənl] ◆ adj national. ◆ n Staatsbürger der (-in die).

national anthem n Nationalhymne die.

National Health Service n staatlicher britischer Gesundheitsdienst.

National Insurance n (Br) Sozialversicherung die.

nationality [ˌnæʃə'nælətɪ] n Nationalität die.

national park n Nationalpark der.

nationwide ['neɪʃənwaɪd] adj landesweit.

native ['neɪtɪv] ◆ adj (customs, population) einheimisch. ◆ n Einheimische der die; ~ **country** Heimatland das; **he is a ~ speaker of English** Englisch ist seine Muttersprache.

NATO ['neɪtəʊ] n NATO die.

natural ['nætʃrəl] adj natürlich; (swimmer, actor) geboren.

natural gas n Erdgas das.

naturally ['nætʃrəlɪ] adv natürlich.

natural yoghurt n Biojoghurt der.

nature ['neɪtʃər] n Natur die; (quality, character) Wesen das.

nature reserve n Naturschutzgebiet das.

naughty ['nɔːtɪ] adj (child) ungezogen.

nausea ['nɔːzɪə] n Übelkeit die.

navigate ['nævɪgeɪt] vi navigieren; (in car) lotsen.

navy ['neɪvɪ] ◆ n (ships) Marine die. ◆ adj: ~ **(blue)** marineblau.

NB (abbr of nota bene) NB.

near [nɪər] ◆ adj & adv nahe. ◆ prep: ~ **(to)** nahe an (+D); **in the ~ future** demnächst.

nearby [nɪə'baɪ] ◆ adv in der Nähe. ◆ adj nahe gelegen.

nearly ['nɪəlɪ] adv fast.

nearside ['nɪəsaɪd] n (AUT) (in UK) linke Seite; (in US, Europe) rechte Seite.

neat [niːt] adj ordentlich; (writing) sauber; (whisky, vodka etc) pur.

neatly ['niːtlɪ] adv ordentlich; (written) sauber.

necessarily [ˌnesə'serɪlɪ, 'nesəsrəlɪ] adv: **not ~** nicht unbedingt.

necessary ['nesəsrɪ] adj nötig, notwendig.

necessity [nɪ'sesətɪ] n Notwendigkeit die. ▶ **necessities** npl Lebensnotwendige das.

neck [nek] n Hals der; (of jumper, dress, shirt) Kragen der.

necklace ['neklɪs] n Halskette die.

neckline ['neklaɪn] n Ausschnitt der.

nectarine ['nektərɪn] n Nektarine die.

need [niːd] ◆ n Bedürfnis das. ◆ vt brauchen; **to ~ to do sthg** etw tun müssen.

needle ['niːdl] n Nadel die.

needlework ['niːdlwɜːk] n (SCH) Handarbeit die.

needn't ['niːdənt] = **need not**.

needy ['niːdɪ] adj notleidend.

negative ['negətɪv] ◆ adj negativ; (person) ablehnend. ◆ n (in photography) Negativ das; (GRAMM) Verneinung die.

neglect [nɪ'glekt] vt vernachlässigen.

negligence ['neglɪdʒəns] n Nachlässigkeit die.

negotiations [nɪˌgəʊʃɪ'eɪʃnz] npl Verhandlungen pl.

negro ['niːgrəʊ] (pl -es) n Neger der (-in die).

neighbour ['neɪbər] n Nachbar der (-in die).

neighbourhood ['neɪbəhʊd] n Nachbarschaft die.

neighbouring ['neɪbərɪŋ] adj benachbart.

neither ['naɪðər] ◆ adj: ~ **bag is big enough** keine der beiden Taschen ist groß genug. ◆ pron: ~ **of us** keiner von uns beiden. ◆ conj: ~ **do I** ich auch nicht; ~ ... **nor** ... weder ... noch ...

neon light ['niːɒn-] n Neonlicht das.

nephew ['nefjuː] n Neffe der.

nerve [nɜːv] n Nerv der; (courage) Mut der; **what a ~!** so eine Frechheit!

nervous ['nɜːvəs] adj nervös.

nervous breakdown n Nervenzusammenbruch der.

nest [nest] n Nest das.

Net [net] n: **the ~** das Internet; **to surf the ~** im Internet surfen.

net [net] ◆ n Netz das. ◆ adj (profit, result, weight) netto.

netball ['netbɔːl] n Sportart, die meist von Frauen gespielt wird und dem Basketball ähnelt.

Netherlands ['neðələndz] npl: **the ~** die Niederlande.

nettle ['netl] n Nessel die.

network ['netwɜːk] n Netz das.

neurotic [ˌnjuəˈrɒtɪk] adj neurotisch.

neutral ['njuːtrəl] ◆ adj neutral. ◆ n (AUT): **in ~** im Leerlauf.

never ['nevər] adv nie; (simple negative) nicht; **she's ~ late** sie kommt nie zu spät; **~ mind!** macht nichts!

nevertheless [ˌnevəðəˈles] adv trotzdem.

new [njuː] adj neu.

newly ['njuːlɪ] adv frisch.

new potatoes npl neue Kartoffeln.

news [njuːz] n (information) Nachricht die; (on TV, radio) Nachrichten pl; **a piece of ~** eine Neuigkeit.

newsagent ['njuːzeɪdʒənt] n (shop) Zeitungshändler der.

newspaper ['njuːzˌpeɪpər] n Zeitung die.

New Year n Neujahr das.

New Year's Day n Neujahrstag der.

New Year's Eve n Silvester der.

New York [-ˈjɔːk] n New York nt.

New Zealand [-ˈziːlənd] n Neuseeland nt.

next [nekst] ◆ adj nächste(-r)(-s). ◆ adv (afterwards) als nächstes, danach; (on next occasion) das nächste Mal; **when does the ~ bus leave?** wann fährt der nächste Bus ab?; **~ to** neben; **the week after ~** übernächste Woche.

next door adv nebenan.

next of kin [-kɪn] n nächster Angehörige (nächste Angehörige).

NHS abbr = **National Health Service**.

nib [nɪb] n Feder die.

nibble ['nɪbl] vt knabbern.

nice [naɪs] adj (meal, feeling, taste) gut; (clothes, house, car, weather) schön; (kind) nett; **to have a ~ time** Spaß haben; **~ to see you!** schön, dich wiederzusehen!

nickel ['nɪkl] n (metal) Nickel das; (Am: coin) Fünfcentstück das.

nickname ['nɪkneɪm] n Spitzname der.

niece [niːs] n Nichte die.

night [naɪt] n Nacht die; (evening) Abend der; **at ~** nachts; (in evening) abends; **by ~** nachts.

nightclub ['naɪtklʌb] n Nachtklub der.

nightdress ['naɪtdres] n Nachthemd das.

nightie ['naɪtɪ] n (inf) Nachthemd das.

nightlife ['naɪtlaɪf] n Nachtleben das.

nightly ['naɪtlɪ] adv nächtlich.

nightmare ['naɪtmeər] n Alptraum der.

night safe n Nachttresor der.

night school n Abendschule die.

nightshift ['naɪtʃɪft] n Nachtschicht die.

nil [nɪl] n (SPORT) null.

Nile [naɪl] n: **the ~** der Nil.

nine [naɪn] num neun, → **six**.

nineteen [ˌnaɪnˈtiːn] num neunzehn, → **six**; **~ ninety-five** neunzehnhundertfünfundneunzig.

nineteenth [ˌnaɪnˈtiːnθ] num neunzehnte(-r)(-s), → **sixth**.

ninetieth ['naɪntɪəθ] num neunzigste(-r)(-s), → **sixth**.

ninety ['naɪntɪ] *num* neunzig, → **six**.

ninth [naɪnθ] *num* neunte(-r)(-s), → **sixth**.

nip [nɪp] *vt* (*pinch*) zwicken.

nipple ['nɪpl] *n* (*of breast*) Brustwarze *die*; (*of bottle*) Sauger *der*.

nitrogen ['naɪtrədʒən] *n* Stickstoff *der*.

no [nəʊ] ◆ *adv* nein. ◆ *adj* (*not any*) kein. ◆ *n* Nein *das*; **I've got ~ money left** ich habe kein Geld übrig.

noble ['nəʊbl] *adj* (*character*) edel; (*aristocratic*) adlig.

nobody ['nəʊbədɪ] *pron* niemand.

nod [nɒd] *vi* nicken.

noise [nɔɪz] *n* Lärm *der*.

noisy ['nɔɪzɪ] *adj* laut.

nominate ['nɒmɪneɪt] *vt* nennen.

nonalcoholic [ˌnɒnælkə'hɒlɪk] *adj* alkoholfrei.

none [nʌn] *pron* keine(-r)(-s); **~ of us** keiner von uns; **~ of the money** nichts von dem Geld.

nonetheless [ˌnʌnðə'les] *adv* nichtsdestoweniger.

nonfiction [ˌnɒn'fɪkʃn] *n* Sachliteratur *die*.

non-iron *adj* bügelfrei.

nonsense ['nɒnsəns] *n* Unsinn *der*.

non-smoker *n* (*person*) Nichtraucher *der* (-in *die*); (*railway carriage*) Nichtraucherabteil *das*.

nonstick [ˌnɒn'stɪk] *adj* mit Antihaftbeschichtung.

nonstop [ˌnɒn'stɒp] ◆ *adj* (*flight*) Nonstop-. ◆ *adv* (*fly, run, rain*) ohne Unterbrechung, nonstop.

noodles ['nuːdlz] *npl* Nudeln *pl*.

noon [nuːn] *n* Mittag *der*.

no one = **nobody**.

nor [nɔːʳ] *conj* auch nicht; **~ do I** ich auch nicht; → **neither**.

normal ['nɔːml] *adj* normal.

normally ['nɔːməlɪ] *adv* (*usually*) normalerweise; (*properly*) normal.

north [nɔːθ] ◆ *n* Norden *der*. ◆ *adv* nach Norden; **in the ~ of England** in Nordengland.

North America *n* Nordamerika *nt*.

northbound ['nɔːθbaʊnd] *adj* in Richtung Norden.

northeast [ˌnɔːθ'iːst] *n* Nordosten *der*.

northern ['nɔːðən] *adj* nördlich.

Northern Ireland *n* Nordirland *nt*.

North Pole *n* Nordpol *der*.

North Sea *n* Nordsee *die*.

northwards ['nɔːθwədz] *adv* nach Norden.

northwest [ˌnɔːθ'west] *n* Nordwesten *der*.

Norway ['nɔːweɪ] *n* Norwegen *nt*.

Norwegian [nɔː'wiːdʒən] ◆ *adj* norwegisch. ◆ *n* (*person*) Norweger *der* (-in *die*); (*language*) Norwegisch *das*.

nose [nəʊz] *n* Nase *die*; (*of animal*) Schnauze *die*.

nosebleed ['nəʊzbliːd] *n* Nasenbluten *das*.

no smoking area *n* Nichtraucherecke *die*.

nostril ['nɒstrəl] *n* Nasenloch *das*; (*of animal*) Nüster *die*.

nosy ['nəʊzɪ] *adj* neugierig.

not [nɒt] *adv* nicht; **she's ~ there** sie ist nicht da; **~ yet** noch nicht; **~ at all** (*pleased, interested*) überhaupt nicht; (*in reply to thanks*) gern geschehen.

notably ['nəʊtəblɪ] *adv* besonders.

note [nəʊt] ◆ *n* (*message*) Nachricht *die*; (MUS) Note *die*; (*comment*) Anmerkung *die*; (*bank note*) Geldschein *der*. ◆ *vt* (*notice*) bemerken; (*write down*) notieren; **to take ~s** Notizen machen.

notebook ['nəʊtbʊk] *n* Notizbuch *das*.

noted ['nəʊtɪd] *adj* bekannt.

notepaper ['nəʊtpeɪpəʳ] *n* Briefpapier *das*.

nothing ['nʌθɪŋ] *pron* nichts; **~ new/ interesting** nichts Neues/Interessantes; **for ~** (*for free*) umsonst; (*in vain*) vergeblich.

notice ['nəʊtɪs] ◆ vt bemerken. ◆ n (in newspaper) Anzeige die; (on board) Aushang der; (warning) Ankündigung die; **to take ~ of** zur Kenntnis nehmen; **to hand in one's ~** kündigen.

noticeable ['nəʊtɪsəbl] adj bemerkenswert.

notice board n Anschlagtafel die.

notion ['nəʊʃn] n Vorstellung die.

notorious [nəʊˈtɔːrɪəs] adj berüchtigt.

nougat ['nuːgɑː] n Nougat das.

nought [nɔːt] n Null die.

noun [naʊn] n Substantiv das.

nourishment ['nʌrɪʃmənt] n Nahrung die.

Nov. (abbr of November) Nov.

novel ['nɒvl] ◆ n Roman der. ◆ adj neu.

novelist ['nɒvəlɪst] n Romanautor der (-in die).

November [nəˈvembər] n November der, → **September**.

now [naʊ] ◆ adv jetzt. ◆ conj: **~ (that)** jetzt, wo ...; **just ~** gerade eben; **right ~** (at the moment) im Moment; (immediately) sofort; **by ~** inzwischen; **from ~ on** von jetzt an.

nowadays ['naʊədeɪz] adv heutzutage.

nowhere ['nəʊweər] adv nirgends.

nozzle ['nɒzl] n Düse die.

nuclear ['njuːklɪər] adj Atom-.

nude [njuːd] adj nackt.

nudge [nʌdʒ] vt anstoßen.

nuisance ['njuːsns] n: **it's a real ~!** es ist wirklich ärgerlich!; **he's such a ~!** er ist wirklich lästig!

numb [nʌm] adj gefühllos.

number ['nʌmbər] ◆ n Nummer die; (quantity) Anzahl die. ◆ vt numerieren.

numberplate ['nʌmbəpleɪt] n Nummernschild das.

numeral ['njuːmərəl] n Ziffer die.

numerous ['njuːmərəs] adj zahlreich.

nun [nʌn] n Nonne die.

nurse [nɜːs] ◆ n Krankenschwester die. ◆ vt pflegen; **male ~** Krankenpfleger der.

nursery ['nɜːsəri] n (in house) Kinderzimmer das; (for plants) Gärtnerei die.

nursery (school) n Kindergarten der.

nursery slope n Idiotenhügel der.

nursing ['nɜːsɪŋ] n (profession) Krankenpflege die.

nut [nʌt] n (to eat) Nuß die; (of metal) Mutter die.

nutcrackers ['nʌtˌkrækəz] npl Nußknacker der.

nutmeg ['nʌtmeg] n Muskatnuß die.

nylon ['naɪlɒn] ◆ n Nylon das. ◆ adj aus Nylon.

o' [ə] abbr = **of**.

O n (zero) Null die.

oak [əʊk] ◆ n Eiche die. ◆ adj Eichen-.

OAP abbr = **old age pensioner**.

oar [ɔːr] n Ruder das.

oatcake ['əʊtkeɪk] n Haferkeks der.

oath [əʊθ] n (promise) Eid der.

oatmeal ['əʊtmiːl] n Hafermehl das.

oats [əʊts] npl Haferflocken pl.

obedient [əˈbiːdjənt] adj gehorsam.

obey [əˈbeɪ] vt gehorchen (+D).

object [n ˈɒbdʒɪkt, vb ɒbˈdʒekt] ◆ n Objekt das; (purpose) Zweck der. ◆ vi: **to ~ (to)** Einspruch erheben (gegen).

objection [əbˈdʒekʃn] n Einwand der.

objective [əbˈdʒektɪv] n Ziel das.

obligation [ˌɒblɪˈgeɪʃn] n Verpflichtung die.

obligatory [ə'blɪgətrɪ] adj obligatorisch.

oblige [ə'blaɪdʒ] vt: **to ~ sb to do sthg** jn zwingen, etw zu tun.

oblique [ə'bliːk] adj schief.

oblong ['ɒblɒŋ] ◆ adj rechteckig. ◆ n Rechteck das.

obnoxious [əb'nɒkʃəs] adj unausstehlich.

oboe ['əubəu] n Oboe die.

obscene [əb'siːn] adj obszön.

obscure [əb'skjuər] adj unklar; (not well-known) unbekannt.

observant [əb'zɜːvnt] adj aufmerksam.

observation [ˌɒbzə'veɪʃn] n (watching) Beobachtung die; (comment) Bemerkung die.

observatory [əb'zɜːvətrɪ] n Sternwarte die.

observe [əb'zɜːv] vt (watch, see) beobachten.

obsessed [əb'sest] adj besessen.

obsession [əb'seʃn] n fixe Idee.

obsolete ['ɒbsəliːt] adj veraltet.

obstacle ['ɒbstəkl] n Hindernis das.

obstinate ['ɒbstənət] adj starrsinnig.

obstruct [əb'strʌkt] vt versperren.

obstruction [əb'strʌkʃn] n Blockierung die.

obtain [əb'teɪn] vt erhalten.

obtainable [əb'teɪnəbl] adj erhältlich.

obvious ['ɒbvɪəs] adj eindeutig.

obviously ['ɒbvɪəslɪ] adv offensichtlich.

occasion [ə'keɪʒn] n Gelegenheit die.

occasional [ə'keɪʒənl] adj gelegentlich.

occasionally [ə'keɪʒnəlɪ] adv gelegentlich.

occupant ['ɒkjupənt] n (of house) Bewohner der (-in die); (of car, plane) Insasse der (Insassin die).

occupation [ˌɒkju'peɪʃn] n (job) Beruf der; (pastime) Beschäftigung die.

occupied ['ɒkjupaɪd] adj (toilet) besetzt.

occupy ['ɒkjupaɪ] vt (building) bewohnen; (seat, country) besetzen; (keep busy) beschäftigen.

occur [ə'kɜːr] vi vorkommen.

occurrence [ə'kʌrəns] n Ereignis das; (existence) Auftreten das.

ocean ['əuʃn] n Ozean der; **the ~** (Am: sea) das Meer.

o'clock [ə'klɒk] adv: **(at) one ~** (um) ein Uhr.

Oct. (abbr of October) Okt.

October [ɒk'təubər] n Oktober der, → **September**.

octopus ['ɒktəpəs] n Krake der.

odd [ɒd] adj (strange) seltsam; (number) ungerade; (not matching) einzeln; (occasional) gelegentlich; **60 ~ miles** ungefähr 60 Meilen; **some ~ bits of paper** irgendwelches Papier; **~ jobs** Gelegenheitsarbeiten pl.

odds [ɒdz] npl Chancen pl; **~ and ends** Kram der.

odor ['əudər] (Am) = **odour**.

odour ['əudər] n (Br) Geruch der.

of [ɒv] prep 1. (gen) von, use the genitive case; **the colour ~ the car** die Farbe des Autos; **a map ~ Britain** eine Karte von Großbritannien; **a group ~ people** eine Gruppe Menschen; **a glass ~ beer** ein Glas Bier; **the handle ~ the door** der Türgriff. 2. (expressing amount): **a pound ~ sweets** ein Pfund Bonbons; **a piece ~ cake** ein Stück Kuchen; **a fall ~ 20%** ein Sinken um 20%; **a town ~ 50,000 people** eine Stadt mit 50.000 Einwohnern; **a girl ~ six** ein sechsjähriges Mädchen. 3. (made from) aus; **a house ~ stone** ein Haus aus Stein; **it's made ~ wood** es ist aus Holz. 4. (referring to time): **the summer ~ 1969** der Sommer 1969; **the 26th ~ August** der 26. August. 5. (on the part of) von; **that was very kind ~ you** das war sehr nett von Ihnen/dir. 6. (Am: in telling the time) vor; **it's ten ~ four** es ist zehn vor vier.

off [ɒf] ◆ adv 1. (away) weg; **to get ~** (from bus, train, plane) auslsteigen; **we're ~ to Austria next week** wir fahren nächste Woche nach Österreich. 2. (expressing removal) ab; **to take sthg ~** (clothes, shoes) etw auslziehen; (lid, wrapper) etw ablnehmen. 3. (so as to stop working): **to turn sthg ~** (TV, radio, engine) etw auslschalten; (tap) etw zuldrehen. 4. (expressing distance or time away): **it's 10 miles ~** es sind noch 10 Meilen bis dahin; **it's two months ~ yet** es sind noch zwei Monate bis dahin; **it's a long way ~** (in distance) es ist noch ein weiter Weg bis dahin; (in time) bis dahin ist es noch lange hin. 5. (not at work): **I'm taking a week ~** ich nehme mir eine Woche frei. ◆ prep 1. (away from) von; **to get ~ sthg** auslsteigen aus etw; **~ the coast** vor der Küste; **it's just ~ the main road** es ist gleich in der Nähe der Hauptstraße. 2. (indicating removal) von ...ab; **take the lid ~ the jar** mach den Deckel von dem Glas ab; **they've taken £20 ~ the price** sie haben es um 20 Pfund billiger gemacht. 3. (absent from): **to be ~ work** frei haben. 4. (inf: from) von; **I bought it ~ her** ich habe es von ihr gekauft. 5. (inf: no longer liking): **I'm ~ my food** ich mag mein Essen nicht mehr. ◆ adj 1. (meat, cheese, milk, beer) schlecht. 2. (not working) aus; (tap) zu. 3. (cancelled) abgesagt. 4. (not available): **the soup's ~** es ist keine Suppe mehr da.

offence [ə'fens] n ([Br]: crime) Straftat die; (upset) Beleidigung die.

offend [ə'fend] vt (upset) beleidigen.

offender [ə'fendər] n Täter der (-in die).

offense [ə'fens] (Am) = **offence**.

offensive [ə'fensɪv] adj (insulting) beleidigend.

offer ['ɒfər] ◆ n Angebot das. ◆ vt anlbieten; (provide) bieten; **on ~** im Angebot; **to ~ to do sthg** anlbieten,

etw zu tun; **to ~ sb sthg** (gift) jm etw schenken; (food, job, seat, money) jm etw anlbieten.

office ['ɒfɪs] n (room) Büro das.

office block n Bürogebäude das.

officer ['ɒfɪsər] n (MIL) Offizier der; (policeman) Beamte der (Beamtin die).

official [ə'fɪʃl] ◆ adj offiziell. ◆ n Repräsentant der (-in die).

officially [ə'fɪʃəlɪ] adv offiziell.

off-licence n (Br) Wein- und Spirituosenhandlung die.

off-peak adj (train, traffic) außerhalb der Hauptverkehrszeiten; (ticket) zum Spartarif.

off sales npl (Br) Verkauf von Alkohol in Geschäften oder Pubs zum Mitnehmen.

off-season n Nebensaison die.

offshore ['ɒfʃɔːr] adj (breeze) vom Land her; (island) küstennah.

off side n (AUT) Fahrerseite die.

off-the-peg adj von der Stange.

often ['ɒfn, 'ɒftn] adv oft; **how ~ do the buses run?** wie oft fährt der Bus?; **every so ~** gelegentlich.

oh [əʊ] excl oh!

oil [ɔɪl] n Öl das.

oilcan ['ɔɪlkæn] n Ölkanister der.

oil filter n Ölfilter der.

oil paint n Ölfarbe die.

oil rig n Bohrinsel die.

oily ['ɔɪlɪ] adj ölig; (food) fettig.

ointment ['ɔɪntmənt] n Salbe die.

OK [,əʊ'keɪ] ◆ adj (inf) in Ordnung, okay. ◆ adv (inf: expressing agreement) in Ordnung, okay; (satisfactorily, well) gut.

okay [,əʊ'keɪ] = **OK**.

old [əʊld] adj alt; **how ~ are you?** wie alt bist du?; **I'm 36 years ~** ich bin 36 (Jahre alt); **to get ~** alt werden.

old age n Alter das.

old age pensioner n Senior der (-in die).

O level n ehemaliger britischer Schulabschluß, ersetzt durch das 'GCSE'.

olive ['ɒlɪv] n Olive die.

olive oil n Olivenöl das.

Olympic Games [ə'lɪmpɪk-] *npl* Olympische Spiele *pl.*

omelette ['ɒmlɪt] *n* Omelett *das;* **mushroom ~** Omelett mit Pilzen.

ominous ['ɒmɪnəs] *adj* unheilvoll.

omit [ə'mɪt] *vt* ausllassen.

on [ɒn] ◆ *prep* **1.** (*expressing position, location*) auf (+D,A); **it's ~ the table** es ist auf dem Tisch; **put it ~ the table** leg es auf den Tisch; **a picture ~ the wall** ein Bild an der Wand; **the exhaust ~ the car** der Auspuff am Auto; **~ my left** zu meiner Linken; **~ the right** auf der rechten Seite; **we stayed ~ a farm** wir übernachteten auf einem Bauernhof; **~ the Rhine** am Rhein; **~ the main road** an der Hauptstraße. **2.** (*with forms of transport*): **~ the train/plane** (*inside*) im Zug/Flugzeug; (*travel*) mit dem Zug/Flugzeug; **to get ~ a bus** in einen Bus einlsteigen. **3.** (*expressing means, method*) auf (+D); **~ foot** zu Fuß; **~ TV/the radio** im Radio/Fernsehen; **~ tape** auf Band. **4.** (*using*): **it runs ~ unleaded petrol** es fährt mit bleifreiem Benzin; **to be ~ medication** Medikamente nehmen. **5.** (*about*) über (+A); **a book ~ Germany** ein Buch über Deutschland. **6.** (*expressing time*) an (+D); **~ arrival** bei Ankunft; **~ Tuesday** am Dienstag; **~ 25th August** am 25. August. **7.** (*with regard to*) auf (+D); **a tax ~ imports** eine Steuer auf Importe; **the effect ~ Britain** die Auswirkungen auf Großbritannien. **8.** (*describing activity, state*): **to be ~ fire** brennen; **~ holiday** in Ferien, im Urlaub; **~ offer** im Angebot. **9.** (*in phrases*): **do you have any money ~ you?** (*inf*) hast du Geld bei dir?; **the drinks are ~ me** die Drinks gehen auf mich. ◆ *adv* **1.** (*in place, covering*): **to have sthg ~** (*clothes, hat*) etw anlhaben; **put the lid ~** mach den Deckel drauf; **to put one's clothes ~** sich (D) seine Kleider anlziehen. **2.** (*film, play, programme*): **the news is ~** die Nachrichten laufen; **what's ~ at**

the cinema? was läuft im Kino? **3.** (*with transport*): **to get ~** einlsteigen. **4.** (*functioning*) an; **to turn sthg ~** (*TV, radio, engine*) etw einlschalten; (*tap*) etw auldrehen. **5.** (*taking place*): **how long is the festival ~?** wie lange geht das Festival? **6.** (*further forward*) weiter; **to drive ~** weiterlfahren. **7.** (*in phrases*): **to have sthg ~** etw vorlhaben. ◆ *adj* (*TV, engine, light*) an; (*tap*) auf.

once [wʌns] ◆ *adv* einmal; (*previously*) einst. ◆ *conj* wenn; **at ~** (*immediately*) sofort; (*at the same time*) gleichzeitig; **for ~** ausnahmsweise; **~ more** (*one more time*) noch einmal; (*again*) wieder.

oncoming ['ɒn,kʌmɪŋ] *adj* (*traffic*) Gegen-.

one [wʌn] ◆ *num* (*the number 1*) eins; (*with noun*) ein/eine/ein. ◆ *adj* (*only*) einzige(-r)(-s). ◆ *pron* eine/einer/eines; (*fml: you*) man; **this ~** diese/dieser/dieses; **thirty-~** einunddreißig; **~ fifth** ein Fünftel; **I like that ~** ich mag den/die/das (da); **which ~?** welche/welcher/welches?; **the ~ I told you about** der/die/das, von dem/der/dem ich dir erzählt habe; **~ of my friends** einer meiner Freunde; **~ day** (*in past, future*) eines Tages.

one-piece (swimsuit) *n* Einteiler *der.*

oneself [wʌn'self] *pron* (*reflexive*) sich; (*after prep*) sich selbst.

one-way *adj* (*street*) Einbahn-; (*ticket*) einfach.

onion ['ʌnjən] *n* Zwiebel die.

onion bhaji [-'bɑːdʒɪ] *n* indische Vorspeise aus ausgebackenen Teigbällchen mit gehackten Zwiebeln.

onion rings *npl* fritierte Zwiebelringe *pl.*

only ['əʊnlɪ] ◆ *adj* einzige(-r)(-s). ◆ *adv* nur; **an ~ child** ein Einzelkind; **I ~ want one** ich möchte nur einen/eine/eines; **we've ~ just arrived** wir sind gerade erst angekommen; **there's ~ just enough** es ist gerade noch genug da; **'members ~'** 'nur für Mitglieder'; **not ~** nicht nur.

onto ['ɒntuː] *prep* auf (+A); **to get ~ sb** (*telephone*) jn an|rufen.

onward ['ɒnwəd] ◆ *adj* (*journey*) Weiter-. ◆ *adv* = **onwards**.

onwards ['ɒnwədz] *adv* (*forwards*) vorwärts; **from now ~** von jetzt an; **from October ~** ab Oktober.

opal ['əupl] *n* Opal *der*.

opaque [əu'peɪk] *adj* undurchsichtig.

open ['əupn] ◆ *adj* offen. ◆ *vt* öffnen; (*door, window, mouth*) öffnen, auf|machen; (*bank account, meeting, new building*) eröffnen. ◆ *vi* (*door, window, lock*) sich öffnen; (*shop, office, bank*) öffnen, auf|machen; (*start*) beginnen, an|fangen; **are you ~ at the weekend?** haben Sie am Wochenende geöffnet?; **wide ~** weit offen; **in the ~** (**air**) im Freien.
▶ **open onto** *vt fus* führen auf (+A).
▶ **open up** *vi* (*unlock the door*) auf|schließen; (*shop, cinema, etc*) öffnen.

open-air *adj* (*swimming pool*) Frei-; (*theatre, concert*) Freilicht-.

opening ['əupnɪŋ] *n* (*gap*) Öffnung *die*; (*beginning*) Eröffnung *die*; (*opportunity*) Möglichkeit *die*.

opening hours *npl* Öffnungszeiten *pl*.

open-minded [-'maɪndɪd] *adj* aufgeschlossen.

open-plan *adj* Großraum-.

open sandwich *n* belegtes Brot.

opera ['ɒpərə] *n* Oper *die*.

opera house *n* Opernhaus *das*.

operate ['ɒpəreɪt] ◆ *vt* (*machine*) bedienen. ◆ *vi* (*work*) funktionieren; **to ~ on sb** jn operieren.

operating room ['ɒpəreɪtɪŋ-] (Am) = **operating theatre**.

operating theatre ['ɒpəreɪtɪŋ-] *n* (Br) Operationssaal *der*.

operation [,ɒpə'reɪʃn] *n* (*in hospital*) Operation *die*; (*task*) Aktion *die*; **to be in ~** (*law, system*) in Kraft sein; **to have**

an ~ sich operieren lassen.

operator ['ɒpəreɪtə'] *n* (*on phone*) Vermittlung *die*.

opinion [ə'pɪnjən] *n* Meinung *die*; **in my ~** meiner Meinung nach.

opponent [ə'pəunənt] *n* Gegner *der* (-in *die*).

opportunity [,ɒpə'tjuːnətɪ] *n* Gelegenheit *die*.

oppose [ə'pəuz] *vt* sich wenden gegen; (*argue against*) sprechen gegen.

opposed [ə'pəuzd] *adj*: **to be ~ to sthg** gegen etw sein.

opposite ['ɒpəzɪt] ◆ *adj* gegenüberliegend; (*totally different*) entgegengesetzt. ◆ *prep* gegenüber (+D). ◆ *n*: **the ~** (**of**) das Gegenteil (von).

opposition [,ɒpə'zɪʃn] *n* (*objections*) Opposition *die*; (SPORT) Gegner *der*; **the Opposition** (POL) die Opposition.

opt [ɒpt] *vt*: **to ~ to do sthg** sich entscheiden, etw zu tun.

optician's [ɒp'tɪʃns] *n* (*shop*) Optiker *der*.

optimist ['ɒptɪmɪst] *n* Optimist *der* (-in *die*).

optimistic [,ɒptɪ'mɪstɪk] *adj* optimistisch.

option ['ɒpʃn] *n* (*alternative*) Möglichkeit *die*; (*optional extra*) Extra *das*.

optional ['ɒpʃənl] *adj* freiwillig; (*subject*) wahlfrei.

or [ɔː'] *conj* oder; (*after negative*) noch.

oral ['ɔːrəl] ◆ *adj* (*spoken*) mündlich; (*hygiene*) Mund-. ◆ *n* (*exam*) mündliche Prüfung.

orange ['ɒrɪndʒ] ◆ *adj* orange. ◆ *n* (*fruit*) Orange *die*, Apfelsine *die*; (*colour*) Orange *das*.

orange juice *n* Orangensaft *der*.

orange squash *n* (Br) Orangensaftkonzentrat *das*.

orbit ['ɔːbɪt] *n* Umlaufbahn *die*.

orbital (**motorway**) ['ɔːbɪtl-] *n* (Br) Ringautobahn *die*.

orchard ['ɔːtʃəd] *n* Obstgarten *der*.

orchestra [ˈɔːkɪstrə] n Orchester das.

ordeal [ɔːˈdiːl] n Tortur die.

order [ˈɔːdəʳ] ◆ n (sequence) Reihenfolge die; (command) Befehl der; (in restaurant) Bestellung die; (neatness, discipline) Ordnung die; (COMM) Auftrag der, Bestellung die. ◆ vt (command) befehlen (+D); (food, taxi, product) bestellen. ◆ vi (in restaurant) bestellen; in ~ to do sthg um etw zu tun; out of ~ außer Betrieb; in working ~ in Betrieb; to ~ sb to do sthg jm befehlen, etw zu tun.

order form n Bestellschein der.

ordinary [ˈɔːdənrɪ] adj gewöhnlich.

ore [ɔːʳ] n Erz das.

oregano [ˌɒrɪˈɡɑːnəʊ] n Oregano der.

organ [ˈɔːɡən] n (MUS) Orgel die; (in body) Organ das.

organic [ɔːˈɡænɪk] adj biodynamisch angebaut.

organization [ˌɔːɡənaɪˈzeɪʃn] n Organisation die.

organize [ˈɔːɡənaɪz] vt organisieren.

organizer [ˈɔːɡənaɪzəʳ] n Organisator der (-in die); (diary) Zeitplanbuch das.

oriental [ˌɔːrɪˈentl] adj orientalisch.

orientate [ˈɔːrɪenteɪt] vt: to ~ o.s. sich orientieren.

origin [ˈɒrɪdʒɪn] n Ursprung der.

original [əˈrɪdʒənl] adj (first) ursprünglich; (novel) originell.

originally [əˈrɪdʒənəlɪ] adv ursprünglich.

originate [əˈrɪdʒəneɪt] vi: to ~ (from) stammen (aus +D).

ornament [ˈɔːnəmənt] n (object) Schmuckgegenstand der.

ornamental [ˌɔːnəˈmentl] adj Zier-.

ornate [ɔːˈneɪt] adj reich verziert.

orphan [ˈɔːfn] n Waise die.

orthodox [ˈɔːθədɒks] adj orthodox.

ostentatious [ˌɒstənˈteɪʃəs] adj pompös.

ostrich [ˈɒstrɪtʃ] n Strauß der.

other [ˈʌðəʳ] ◆ adj & pron andere(-r) (-s). ◆ adv: ~ than außer; the ~ (one) der/die/das andere; the ~ day neulich; one after the ~ hintereinander.

otherwise [ˈʌðəwaɪz] adv sonst; (differently) anders.

otter [ˈɒtəʳ] n Otter der.

ought [ɔːt] aux vb: I ~ to go now ich sollte jetzt gehen; you ~ not to have said that du hättest das nicht sagen sollen; you ~ to see a doctor du solltest zum Arzt gehen; the car ~ to be ready by Friday das Auto sollte Freitag fertig sein.

ounce [aʊns] n (unit of measurement) = 28,35 g, Unze die.

our [ˈaʊəʳ] adj unser.

ours [ˈaʊəz] pron unsere(-r)(-s); this suitcase is ~ der Koffer gehört uns; a friend of ~ ein Freund von uns.

ourselves [aʊəˈselvz] pron (reflexive, after prep) uns; we did it ~ wir haben es selbst gemacht.

out [aʊt] ◆ adj (light, cigarette) aus. ◆ adv 1. (outside) draußen; to come ~ (of) herauskommen (aus); to get ~ (of) aussteigen (aus); to go ~ (of) hinausgehen (aus); it's cold ~ today es ist kalt draußen heute. 2. (not at home, work): she's ~ sie ist nicht da; to go ~ ausgehen. 3. (so as to be extinguished) aus; put your cigarette ~! mach deine Zigarette aus! 4. (expressing removal): to take sthg ~ (of) etw herausnehmen (aus); (money) etw abheben (von). 5. (outwards): to stick ~ herausstehen. 6. (expressing distribution): to hand sthg ~ etw austeilen. 7. (wrong): the bill's £10 ~ die Rechnung stimmt um 10 Pfund nicht. 8. (in phrases): stay ~ of the sun bleib aus der Sonne; made ~ of wood aus Holz (gemacht); five ~ of ten women fünf von zehn Frauen; I'm ~ of cigarettes ich habe keine Zigaretten mehr.

outback [ˈaʊtbæk] n: the ~ das Hinterland (in Australien).

outboard (motor) [ˈautbɔːd-] n
Außenbordmotor der.

outbreak [ˈautbreɪk] n Ausbruch
der.

outburst [ˈautbɜːst] n Ausbruch der.

outcome [ˈautkʌm] n Ergebnis das.

outcrop [ˈautkrɒp] n Felsvorsprung
der.

outdated [ˌautˈdeɪtɪd] adj veraltet.

outdo [ˌautˈduː] vt übertreffen.

outdoor [ˈautdɔːr] adj (swimming
pool) Frei-; (activities) im Freien.

outdoors [autˈdɔːz] adv draußen; **to
go ~** nach draußen gehen.

outer [ˈautər] adj äußere(-r)(-s).

outer space n Weltraum der.

outfit [ˈautfɪt] n (clothes) Kleider pl.

outing [ˈautɪŋ] n Ausflug der.

outlet [ˈautlet] n (pipe) Abfluß der;
'no ~' (Am) 'Sackgasse'.

outline [ˈautlaɪn] n (shape) Umriß der;
(description) kurze Beschreibung.

outlook [ˈautluk] n (for future, of
weather) Aussichten pl; (attitude)
Einstellung die.

out-of-date adj (old-fashioned) veraltet; (passport, licence) abgelaufen.

outpatients' (department) [-
ˈautˌpeɪʃnts-] n Poliklinik die.

output [ˈautput] n Output der.

outrage [ˈautreɪdʒ] n (cruel act)
Greueltat die.

outrageous [autˈreɪdʒəs] adj em-
pörend.

outright [ˌautˈraɪt] adv (tell, deny)
unumwunden; (own) ganz.

outside [adv ˌautˈsaɪd, adj, prep &
ˈautsaɪd] ◆ adv draußen. ◆ prep
außerhalb (+G); (in front of) vor
(+A,D). ◆ adj (exterior) Außen-; (help,
advice) von außen. ◆ n: **the ~** (of building, car, container) die Außenseite;
(AUT: in UK) rechts; (AUT: in Europe,
US) links; **an ~ line** eine Außenlinie;
to go ~ nach draußen gehen; **~ the
door** vor der Tür; **~ of** ([ɑm]: on the
outside of) außerhalb (+G); (apart
from) außer (+D).

outside lane n (AUT) (in UK)

rechter Fahrstreifen; (in Europe, US)
linker Fahrstreifen.

outsize [ˈautsaɪz] adj übergroß.

outskirts [ˈautskɜːts] npl Außen-
bezirke pl.

outstanding [ˌautˈstændɪŋ] adj
(remarkable) hervorragend; (problem)
ungeklärt; (debt) ausstehend.

outward [ˈautwəd] adj (external)
Außen-; **~ journey** Hinreise die.

outwards [ˈautwədz] adv nach
außen.

oval [ˈəuvl] adj oval.

ovation [əuˈveɪʃn] n Applaus der.

oven [ˈʌvn] n Ofen der.

oven glove n Topflappen der.

ovenproof [ˈʌvnpruːf] adj feuerfest.

oven-ready adj bratfertig.

over [ˈəuvər] ◆ prep 1. (above) über
(+D); **a bridge ~ the road** eine
Brücke über die Straße. 2. (across)
über (+A); **to walk ~ sthg** über etw
laufen; **it's just ~ the road** es ist
gerade gegenüber; **with a view ~ the
gardens** mit Aussicht auf die
Gärten. 3. (covering) über (+D,A); **put
a plaster ~ the wound** klebe ein
Pflaster auf die Wunde. 4. (more
than) über (+A); **it cost ~ £1,000** es
hat über 1.000 Pfund gekostet.
5. (during): **~ New Year** über
Neujahr; **~ the weekend** am
Wochenende; **~ the past two years** in
den letzten zwei Jahren. 6. (with
regard to) über (+A); **an argument ~
the price** ein Streit über den Preis.
◆ adv 1. (downwards): **to fall ~** um|fal-
len; **to lean ~** sich vornüber lehnen.
2. (referring to position, movement)
herüber/hinüber; **to drive ~**
herüber|fahren; **~ here** hier drüben;
~ there da drüben. 3. (round to other
side): **to turn sthg ~** etw um|drehen.
4. (more): **children aged 12 and ~**
Kinder ab 12. 5. (remaining) übrig; **to
be (left) ~** übrig bleiben. 6. (to one's
house): **to invite sb ~ for dinner** jn zu
sich zum Essen ein|laden. 7. (in

phrases): **all ~** (*finished*) zu Ende; **all ~ the world** in der ganzen Welt. ◆ *adj* (*finished*): **to be ~** fertig sein, zu Ende sein.

overall [*adv* ,əuvər'ɔ:l, *n* 'əuvərɔ:l] ◆ *adv* (*in general*) im allgemeinen. ◆ *n* (Br: *coat*) Kittel *der*; (Am: *boiler suit*) Overall *der*; **how much does it cost ~?** wieviel kostet das insgesamt? ▶ **overalls** *npl* (Br: *boiler suit*) Overall *der*; (Am: *dungarees*) Latzhose *die*.

overboard [ˈəuvəbɔ:d] *adv* über Bord.

overbooked [,əuvə'bukt] *adj* überbucht.

overcame [,əuvə'keɪm] *pt* → **overcome**.

overcast [,əuvə'kɑ:st] *adj* bedeckt.

overcharge [,əuvə'tʃɑ:dʒ] *vt*: **to ~ sb** jm zu viel berechnen.

overcoat [ˈəuvəkəut] *n* Wintermantel *der*.

overcome [,əuvə'kʌm] (*pt* **-came**, *pp* **-come**) *vt* überwältigen.

overcooked [,əuvə'kukt] *adj* verkocht.

overcrowded [,əuvə'krɑudɪd] *adj* überfüllt.

overdo [,əuvə'du:] (*pt* **-did**, *pp* **-done**) *vt* (*exaggerate*) übertreiben; **to ~ it** es übertreiben; (*work too hard*) sich übernehmen.

overdone [,əuvə'dʌn] ◆ *pp* → **overdo**. ◆ *adj* (*food*) verkocht.

overdose [ˈəuvədəus] *n* Überdosis *die*.

overdraft [ˈəuvədrɑ:ft] *n* Kontoüberziehung *die*; **to have an ~** sein Konto überzogen haben.

overdue [,əuvə'dju:] *adj* überfällig.

over easy *adj* (Am: *eggs*) auf beiden Seiten gebraten.

overexposed [,əuvərɪk'spəuzd] *adj* (*photograph*) überbelichtet.

overflow [*vb* ,əuvə'fləu, *n* 'əuvəfləu] ◆ *vi* (*container, bath*) überǁlaufen; (*river*) überschwemmen. ◆ *n* (*pipe*) Überlaufrohr *das*.

overgrown [,əuvə'grəun] *adj* überwachsen.

overhaul [,əuvə'hɔ:l] *n* Überholung *die*.

overhead [*adj* 'əuvəhed, *adv* ,əuvə-'hed] ◆ *adj* Ober-; (*in ceiling*) Decken-. ◆ *adv* oben.

overhead locker *n* (*on plane*) Gepäckfach *das*.

overhear [,əuvə'hɪər] (*pt & pp* **-heard**) *vt* zufällig (mitǁ)hören.

overheat [,əuvə'hi:t] *vi* sich überhitzen.

overland [ˈəuvəlænd] *adv* auf dem Landweg.

overlap [,əuvə'læp] *vi* sich überlappen.

overleaf [,əuvə'li:f] *adv* umseitig.

overload [,əuvə'ləud] *vt* überladen.

overlook [*vb* ,əuvə'luk, *n* 'əuvəluk] ◆ *vt* (*subj: building, room*) überblicken; (*miss*) übersehen. ◆ *n*: **(scenic) ~** (Am) Aussichtspunkt *der*.

overnight [*adv* ,əuvə'naɪt *adj* 'əuvənaɪt] ◆ *adv* über Nacht. ◆ *adj* (*train, journey*) Nacht-.

overnight bag *n* Reisetasche *die*.

overpass [ˈəuvəpɑ:s] *n* Überführung *die*.

overpowering [,əuvə'pɑuərɪŋ] *adj* überwältigend.

oversaw [,əuvə'sɔ:] *pt* → **oversee**.

overseas [*adv* ,əuvə'si:z, *adj* 'əuvəsi:z] ◆ *adj* Übersee-. ◆ *adv* in Übersee; **to go ~** nach Übersee gehen.

oversee [,əuvə'si:] (*pt* **-saw**, *pp* **-seen**) *vt* (*supervise*) beaufsichtigen.

overshoot [,əuvə'ʃu:t] (*pt & pp* **-shot**) *vt* (*turning, motorway exit*) vorbeifahren an (+D).

oversight [ˈəuvəsaɪt] *n* Versehen *das*.

oversleep [,əuvə'sli:p] (*pt & pp* **-slept**) *vi* verschlafen.

overtake [,əuvə'teɪk] (*pt* **-took**, *pp* **-taken**) *vt & vi* überholen; **'no overtaking'** 'Überholverbot'.

overtime [ˈəuvətaɪm] *n* Überstunden *pl*.

overtook [ˌəʊvəˈtʊk] *pt* → **overtake**.

overture [ˈəʊvəˌtjʊəʳ] *n* Ouvertüre *die*.

overturn [ˌəʊvəˈtɜːn] *vi* (*boat*) kentern; (*car*) sich überschlagen.

overweight [ˌəʊvəˈweɪt] *adj* übergewichtig.

overwhelm [ˌəʊvəˈwelm] *vt* überwältigen.

owe [əʊ] *vt* schulden; **to ~ sb sthg** jm etw schulden; **owing to** wegen (+G).

owl [aʊl] *n* Eule *die*.

own [əʊn] ◆ *adj* & *pron* eigen. ◆ *vt* besitzen; **I have my ~ bedroom** ich habe ein eigenes Zimmer; **on my ~** allein; **to get one's ~ back** sich revanchieren. ▶ **own up** *vi*: **to ~ up (to sthg)** (etw (A) zugeben).

owner [ˈəʊnəʳ] *n* Eigentümer *der* (-in *die*).

ownership [ˈəʊnəʃɪp] *n* Besitz *der*.

ox [ɒks] (*pl* **oxen** [ˈɒksən]) *n* Ochse *der*.

oxtail soup [ˈɒksteɪl-] *n* Ochsenschwanzsuppe *die*.

oxygen [ˈɒksɪdʒən] *n* Sauerstoff *der*.

oyster [ˈɔɪstəʳ] *n* Auster *die*.

oz *abbr* = **ounce**.

ozone-friendly [ˈəʊzəʊn-] *adj* ohne FCKW, treibmittelfrei.

P

p ◆ (*abbr of page*) S. ◆ *abbr* = **penny**, **pence**.

pace [peɪs] *n* Schritt *der*.

pacemaker [ˈpeɪsˌmeɪkəʳ] *n* (*for heart*) Schrittmacher *der*.

Pacific [pəˈsɪfɪk] *n*: **the ~ (Ocean)** der Pazifik.

pacifier [ˈpæsɪfaɪəʳ] *n* (Am: *for baby*) Schnuller *der*.

pacifist [ˈpæsɪfɪst] *n* Pazifist *der* (-in *die*).

pack [pæk] ◆ *n* (*packet*) Packung *die*; (*of crisps*) Tüte *die*; (Br: *of cards*) Kartenspiel *das*; (*rucksack*) Rucksack *der*. ◆ *vt* (*suitcase, bag*) packen; (*clothes, camera etc*) einpacken; (*product*) verpacken. ◆ *vi* (*for journey*) packen; **a ~ of lies** ein Haufen Lügen; **to ~ sthg into sthg** etw in etw (A) einpacken; **to ~ one's bags** sein Bündel schnüren. ▶ **pack up** *vi* (*pack suitcase*) packen; (*tidy up*) wegräumen; (Br: *inf: machine, car*) den Geist aufgeben.

package [ˈpækɪdʒ] ◆ *n* (*parcel*) Päckchen *das*; (COMPUT) Paket *das*. ◆ *vt* verpacken.

package holiday *n* Pauschalreise *die*.

package tour *n* Pauschalreise *die*.

packaging [ˈpækɪdʒɪŋ] *n* (*material*) Verpackung *die*.

packed [pækt] *adj* (*crowded*) voll.

packed lunch *n* Lunchpaket *das*.

packet [ˈpækɪt] *n* Päckchen *das*; **it cost a ~** (Br: *inf*) es hat ein Heidengeld gekostet.

packing [ˈpækɪŋ] *n* (*for journey*) Packen *das*; (*material*) Verpackung *die*.

pad [pæd] *n* (*of paper*) Block *der*; (*of cloth, cotton wool*) Bausch *der*; (*for protection*) Polster *das*.

padded [ˈpædɪd] *adj* (*jacket, seat*) gepolstert.

padded envelope *n* gefütterter Briefumschlag.

paddle [ˈpædl] ◆ *n* (*pole*) Paddel *das*. ◆ *vi* paddeln.

paddling pool [ˈpædlɪŋ-] *n* Planschbecken *das*.

paddock [ˈpædək] *n* (*at racecourse*) Sattelplatz *der*.

padlock [ˈpædlɒk] *n* Vorhängeschloß *das*.

page [peɪdʒ] ◆ *n* Seite *die*. ◆ *vt* (*call*) ausrufen; **'paging Mr Hill'** 'Herr Hill, bitte'.

paid [peɪd] ◆ *pt & pp* → **pay**. ◆ *adj* (*holiday, work*) bezahlt.

pain [peɪn] *n* Schmerz *der*; **to be in ~** (*physical*) Schmerzen haben; **he's such a ~!** (*inf*) er nervt! ▶ **pains** *npl* (*trouble*) Mühe *die*.

painful ['peɪnfʊl] *adj* schmerzhaft.

painkiller ['peɪn,kɪlər] *n* Schmerzmittel *das*.

paint [peɪnt] ◆ *n* Farbe *die*. ◆ *vt* (*wall, room, furniture*) streichen; (*picture*) malen. ◆ *vi* malen; **to ~ one's nails** sich (D) die Nägel lackieren. ▶ **paints** *npl* (*tubes, pots etc*) Farbe *die*.

paintbrush ['peɪntbrʌʃ] *n* Pinsel *der*.

painter ['peɪntər] *n* Maler *der* (-in *die*).

painting ['peɪntɪŋ] *n* (*picture*) Gemälde *das*; (*activity*) Malerei *die*; (*by decorator*) Malerarbeiten *pl*.

pair [peər] *n* Paar *das*; **in ~s** paarweise; **a ~ of pliers** eine Zange; **a ~ of scissors** eine Schere; **a ~ of shorts** Shorts *pl*; **a ~ of tights** eine Strumpfhose; **a ~ of trousers** eine Hose.

pajamas [pə'dʒɑːməz] (*Am*) = **pyjamas**.

Pakistan [Br ,pɑːkɪ'stɑːn, Am ,pækɪ'stæn] *n* Pakistan *nt*.

Pakistani [Br ,pɑːkɪ'stɑːnɪ, Am ,pækɪ'stænɪ] ◆ *adj* pakistanisch. ◆ *n* Pakistani *der die*.

pakora [pə'kɔːrə] *npl* indische Vorspeise aus scharfgewürzten, fritierten Gemüsestückchen.

pal [pæl] *n* (*inf*) Kumpel *der*.

palace ['pælɪs] *n* Palast *der*.

palatable ['pælətəbl] *adj* schmackhaft.

palate ['pælət] *n* (*of mouth*) Gaumen *der*; (*ability to taste*) Geschmack *der*.

pale [peɪl] *adj* blaß.

pale ale *n* Pale Ale *das* (*helles englisches Dunkelbier*).

palm [pɑːm] *n* (*of hand*) Handfläche *die*; **~ (tree)** Palme *die*.

palpitations [,pælpɪ'teɪʃnz] *npl* Herzklopfen *pl*.

pamphlet ['pæmflɪt] *n* Broschüre *die*.

pan [pæn] *n* Pfanne *die*; (*saucepan*) Topf *der*.

pancake ['pænkeɪk] *n* Eierkuchen *der*, Pfannkuchen *der*.

pancake roll *n* Frühlingsrolle *die*.

panda ['pændə] *n* Panda *der*.

panda car *n* (*Br*) Streifenwagen *der*.

pane [peɪn] *n* Scheibe *die*.

panel ['pænl] *n* (*of wood*) Tafel *die*; (*group of experts*) Gremium *das*; (*on TV, radio*) Diskussionsrunde *die*.

paneling ['pænəlɪŋ] (*Am*) = **panelling**.

panelling ['pænəlɪŋ] *n* (*Br*) Täfelung *die*.

panic ['pænɪk] (*pt & pp* -**ked**, *cont* -**king**) ◆ *n* Panik *die*. ◆ *vi* in Panik geraten.

panniers ['pænɪəz] *npl* (*for bicycle*) Satteltaschen *pl*.

panoramic [,pænə'ræmɪk] *adj* Panorama-.

pant [pænt] *vi* keuchen.

panties ['pæntɪz] *npl* (*inf*) Schlüpfer *der*.

pantomime ['pæntəmaɪm] *n* (*Br: show*) meist um die Weihnachtszeit aufgeführtes Märchenspiel.

pantry ['pæntrɪ] *n* Speisekammer *die*.

pants [pænts] *npl* (*Br: for men*) Unterhose *die*; (*Br: for women*) Schlüpfer *der*; (*Am: trousers*) Hose *die*.

panty hose ['pæntɪ-] *npl* (*Am*) Strumpfhose *die*.

papadum ['pæpədəm] *n* sehr dünnes, knuspriges indisches Brot.

paper ['peɪpər] ◆ *n* Papier *das*; (*newspaper*) Zeitung *die*; (*exam*) Prüfung *die*. ◆ *adj* (*cup, plate, hat*) Papp-. ◆ *vt* tapezieren; **a piece of ~** (*sheet*) ein Blatt Papier; (*scrap*) ein Papierfetzen. ▶ **papers** *npl* (*documents*) Papiere *pl*.

paperback ['peɪpəbæk] *n* Taschenbuch *das*.

paper bag n Papiertüte die.
paperboy ['peɪpəbɔɪ] n Zeitungsjunge der.
paper clip n Büroklammer die.
papergirl ['peɪpəgɜːl] n Zeitungsmädchen das.
paper handkerchief n Papiertaschentuch das.
paper shop n Zeitungshändler der.
paperweight ['peɪpəweɪt] n Briefbeschwerer der.
paprika ['pæprɪkə] n Paprika der.
par [pɑːr] n (in golf) Par das.
paracetamol [,pærə'siːtəmɒl] n fiebersenkende Schmerztablette.
parachute ['pærəʃuːt] n Fallschirm der.
parade [pə'reɪd] n (procession) Umzug der; (of shops) Ladenzeile die.
paradise ['pærədaɪs] n Paradies das.
paraffin ['pærəfɪn] n Paraffinöl das.
paragraph ['pærəgrɑːf] n Absatz der.
parallel ['pærəlel] adj: ~ (to) parallel (zu).
paralysed ['pærəlaɪzd] adj (Br) gelähmt.
paralyzed ['pærəlaɪzd] (Am) = **paralysed**.
paramedic [,pærə'medɪk] n Rettungssanitäter der (-in die).
paranoid ['pærənɔɪd] adj mißtrauisch.
parasite ['pærəsaɪt] n Schmarotzer der.
parasol ['pærəsɒl] n Sonnenschirm der.
parcel ['pɑːsl] n Paket das.
parcel post n Paketpost die.
pardon ['pɑːdn] excl: ~? bitte?; ~ (me)! Entschuldigung!; I beg your ~! (apologizing) Entschuldigung!; I beg your ~? (asking for repetition) bitte?
parent ['peərənt] n (father) Vater der; (mother) Mutter die; ~s Eltern pl.
parish ['pærɪʃ] n Gemeinde die.

park [pɑːk] ◆ n Park der. ◆ vt & vi parken.
park and ride n Park-and-ride-System das.
parking ['pɑːkɪŋ] n Parken das.
parking brake n (Am) Handbremse die.
parking lot n (Am) Parkplatz der.
parking meter n Parkuhr die.
parking space n Parkplatz der.
parking ticket n Strafzettel der.
parkway ['pɑːkweɪ] n (Am) breite Straße, deren Mittelstreifen mit Bäumen, Blumen usw bepflanzt ist.
parliament ['pɑːləmənt] n Parlament das.
Parmesan (cheese) [pɑːmɪ'zæn-] n Parmesan der.
parrot ['pærət] n Papagei der.
parsley ['pɑːslɪ] n Petersilie die.
parsnip ['pɑːsnɪp] n Pastinake die.
parson ['pɑːsn] n Pfarrer der.
part [pɑːt] ◆ n Teil der; (in play, film) Rolle die; (Am: in hair) Scheitel der. ◆ adv (partly) teils. ◆ vi (couple) sich trennen; **in this ~ of Germany** in dieser Gegend Deutschlands; **to form ~ of** Teil sein von; **to play a ~ in** eine Rolle spielen in (+D); **to take ~ in** teilnehmen an (+D); **for my ~** was mich betrifft; **for the most ~** größtenteils; **in these ~s** in dieser Gegend.
partial ['pɑːʃl] adj teilweise; **to be ~ to sthg** eine Schwäche für etw haben.
participant [pɑː'tɪsɪpənt] n Teilnehmer der (-in die).
participate [pɑː'tɪsɪpeɪt] vi: **to ~ (in)** teillnehmen (an (+D).
particular [pə'tɪkjʊlər] adj besondere(-r)(-s); (fussy) eigen; **in ~** besonders; **nothing in ~** nichts Besonderes. ▸ **particulars** npl (details) Einzelheiten pl.
particularly [pə'tɪkjʊləlɪ] adv insbesondere; (especially) besonders.
parting ['pɑːtɪŋ] n (Br: in hair) Scheitel der.

partition [pɑːˈtɪʃn] n (*wall*) Trennwand *die*.

partly [ˈpɑːtlɪ] adv teilweise.

partner [ˈpɑːtnəʳ] n Partner *der* (-in *die*).

partnership [ˈpɑːtnəʃɪp] n Partnerschaft *die*.

partridge [ˈpɑːtrɪdʒ] n Rebhuhn *das*.

part-time ◆ adj Teilzeit-. ◆ adv halbtags.

party [ˈpɑːtɪ] n (*for fun*) Party *die*; (POL) Partei *die*; (*group of people*) Gruppe *die*; **to have a ~** eine Party geben.

pass [pɑːs] ◆ vt (*walk past*) vorbeigehen an (+D); (*drive past*) vorbeifahren an (+D); (*hand over*) reichen; (*test, exam*) bestehen; (*time, life*) verbringen; (*overtake*) überholen; (*law*) verabschieden. ◆ vi (*walk past*) vorbeigehen; (*drive past*) vorbeifahren; (*road, river, path, pipe*) führen; (*overtake*) überholen; (*in test, exam*) bestehen; (*time, holiday*) vergehen. ◆ n (*document*) Ausweis *der*; (*in mountain*) Paß *der*; (SPORT) Paß *der*; **to ~ sb sthg** jm etw reichen. ▶ **pass by** vt fus (*walk past*) vorbeigehen an (+D); (*drive past*) vorbeifahren an (+D). ◆ vi (*walk past*) vorbeigehen; (*drive past*) vorbeifahren. ▶ **pass on** vt sep (*message*) weiter⎪geben. ▶ **pass out** vi (*faint*) ohnmächtig werden. ▶ **pass up** vt sep (*opportunity*) vorübergehen lassen.

passable [ˈpɑːsəbl] adj (*road*) befahrbar; (*satisfactory*) passabel.

passage [ˈpæsɪdʒ] n (*corridor*) Gang *der*; (*in book*) Passage *die*; (*sea journey*) Überfahrt *die*.

passageway [ˈpæsɪdʒweɪ] n Gang *der*.

passenger [ˈpæsɪndʒəʳ] n Passagier *der* (-in *die*).

passerby [ˌpɑːsəˈbaɪ] n Passant *der* (-in *die*).

passing place [ˈpɑːsɪŋ-] n Ausweichstelle *die*.

passion [ˈpæʃn] n Leidenschaft *die*.

passionate [ˈpæʃənət] adj leidenschaftlich.

passive [ˈpæsɪv] n Passiv *das*.

passport [ˈpɑːspɔːt] n Reisepaß *der*.

passport control n Paßkontrolle *die*.

passport photo n Paßfoto *das*.

password [ˈpɑːswɜːd] n Paßwort *das*.

past [pɑːst] ◆ adj (*earlier*) vergangene(-r)(-s); (*finished*) vorbei; (*last*) letzte(-r)(-s); (*former*) ehemalig. ◆ prep (*in times*) nach; (*in front of*) an (+D) ... vorbei. ◆ adv vorbei. ◆ n (*former time*) Vergangenheit *die*; **~ (tense)** (GRAMM) Vergangenheit *die*; **the ~ month** der letzte Monat; **he drove ~ the house** er fuhr am Haus vorbei; **twenty ~ four** zwanzig nach vier; **in the ~** früher.

pasta [ˈpæstə] n Nudeln *pl*.

paste [peɪst] n (*spread*) Paste *die*; (*glue*) Kleister *der*.

pastel [ˈpæstl] n (*for drawing*) Pastellstift *der*; (*colour*) Pastellfarbe *die*.

pasteurized [ˈpɑːstʃəraɪzd] adj pasteurisiert.

pastille [ˈpæstɪl] n Pastille *die*.

pastime [ˈpɑːstaɪm] n Hobby *das*.

pastry [ˈpeɪstrɪ] n (*for pie*) Teig *der*; (*cake*) Gebäck *das*.

pasture [ˈpɑːstʃəʳ] n Weide *die*.

pasty [ˈpæstɪ] n (Br) Pastete *die* (*Gebäck*).

pat [pæt] vt klopfen.

patch [pætʃ] n (*for clothes*) Flicken *der*; (*of colour, damp*) Fleck *der*; (*for skin*) Pflaster *das*; (*for eye*) Augenklappe *die*; **a bad ~** (*fig*) eine Pechsträhne.

pâté [ˈpæteɪ] n Pastete *die* (*Leberwurst usw.*).

patent [Br ˈpeɪtənt, Am ˈpætənt] n Patent *das*.

path [pɑːθ] n Weg *der*, Pfad *der*.

pathetic [pəˈθetɪk] adj (*pej: useless*) kläglich.

patience [ˈpeɪʃns] n Geduld *die*; (Br:

card game) Patience *die*.

patient ['peɪʃnt] ◆ *adj* geduldig. ◆ *n* Patient *der* (-in *die*).

patio ['pætɪəʊ] *n* Terrasse *die*.

patriotic [Br ˌpætrɪ'ɒtɪk, Am ˌpeɪtrɪ-'ɒtɪk] *adj* patriotisch.

patrol [pə'trəʊl] ◆ *vt* (*subj: police*) seine Runden machen in (+D); (MIL) ab|patrouillieren. ◆ *n* Patrouille *die*.

patrol car *n* Streifenwagen *der*.

patron ['peɪtrən] *n* (*fml: customer*) Kunde *der* (Kundin *die*); **'~s only**' 'nur für Gäste'.

patronizing ['pætrənaɪzɪŋ] *adj* herablassend.

pattern ['pætn] *n* (*of shapes, colours*) Muster *das*; (*for sewing*) Schnitt *der*.

patterned ['pætənd] *adj* gemustert.

pause [pɔːz] ◆ *n* Pause *die*. ◆ *vi* inne|halten.

pavement ['peɪvmənt] *n* (*Br: beside road*) Bürgersteig *der*; (*Am: roadway*) Straßenbelag *der*.

pavilion [pə'vɪljən] *n* Klubhaus *das*.

paving stone ['peɪvɪŋ-] *n* Pflasterstein *der*.

pavlova *n* Nachtisch *aus zwei Baiserstücken, die mit Sahne und Früchten gefüllt sind*.

paw [pɔː] *n* Pfote *die*.

pawn [pɔːn] ◆ *vt* verpfänden. ◆ *n* (*in chess*) Bauer *der*.

pay [peɪ] (*pt & pp* **paid**) ◆ *vt* (*money*) zahlen; (*person, bill, fine*) bezahlen. ◆ *vi* zahlen; (*be profitable*) sich lohnen. ◆ *n* (*salary*) Gehalt *das*; **to ~ sb for sthg** jn für etw bezahlen; **to ~ money into an account** Geld auf ein Konto ein|zahlen; **to ~ attention (to)** achten (auf (+A); **to ~ sb a visit** jn besuchen; **to ~ by credit card** mit Kreditkarte zahlen. ▶ **pay back** *vt sep* (*money*) zurück|zahlen; **to ~ sb back** jm Geld zurück|zahlen. ▶ **pay for** *vt fus* (*purchase*) bezahlen. ▶ **pay in** *vt sep* (*cheque, money*) ein|zahlen. ▶ **pay out** *vt sep* (*money*) aus|geben. ▶ **pay up** *vi* zahlen.

payable ['peɪəbl] *adj* zahlbar; **to**

make a cheque ~ to sb einen Scheck aus|stellen auf jn.

payment ['peɪmənt] *n* Bezahlung *die*; (*amount*) Zahlung *die*.

payphone ['peɪfəʊn] *n* Münzfernsprecher *der*.

PC ◆ *n* (*abbr of personal computer*) PC *der*. ◆ *abbr* (Br) = **police constable**.

PE *abbr* = **physical education**.

pea [piː] *n* Erbse *die*.

peace [piːs] *n* (*no anxiety*) Ruhe *die*; (*no war*) Frieden *der*; **to leave sb in ~** jn in Ruhe lassen; **~ and quiet** Ruhe und Frieden.

peaceful ['piːsfʊl] *adj* friedlich.

peach [piːtʃ] *n* Pfirsich *der*.

peach melba [-'melbə] *n* Pfirsich Melba *das*.

peacock ['piːkɒk] *n* Pfau *der*.

peak [piːk] *n* (*of mountain*) Gipfel *der*; (*of hat*) Schirm *der*; (*fig: highest point*) Höhepunkt *der*.

peak hours *npl* (*for electricity*) Hauptbelastungszeit *die*; (*for traffic*) Stoßzeit *die*.

peak rate *n* Höchsttarif *der*.

peanut ['piːnʌt] *n* Erdnuß *die*.

peanut butter *n* Erdnußbutter *die*.

pear [peəʳ] *n* Birne *die*.

pearl [pɜːl] *n* Perle *die*.

peasant ['peznt] *n* Bauer *der* (Bäuerin *die*).

pebble ['pebl] *n* Kieselstein *der*.

pecan pie ['piːkæn-] *n* Pekannußkuchen *der*.

peck [pek] *vi* picken.

peculiar [pɪ'kjuːljəʳ] *adj* (*strange*) seltsam; **to be ~ to** (*exclusive*) eigentümlich sein für; **to be ~ to a country** nur in einem Land vor|kommen.

peculiarity [pɪˌkjuːlɪ'ærətɪ] *n* (*special feature*) Besonderheit *die*.

pedal ['pedl] ◆ *n* Pedal *das*. ◆ *vi* in die Pedale treten.

pedal bin *n* Treteimer *der*.

pedalo ['pedələʊ] *n* Tretboot *das*.

pedestrian [pɪ'destrɪən] *n* Fußgänger *der* (-in *die*).

pedestrian crossing n Fußgängerüberweg der.

pedestrianized [pɪ'destrɪənaɪzd] adj zur Fußgängerzone gemacht.

pedestrian precinct n (Br) Fußgängerzone die.

pedestrian zone (Am) = **pedestrian precinct**.

pee [piː] ◆ vi (inf) pinkeln. ◆ n: **to have a ~** (inf) pinkeln.

peel [piːl] ◆ n Schale die. ◆ vt (fruit, vegetables) schälen. ◆ vi (paint) ab|blättern; (skin) sich schälen.

peep [piːp] n: **to have a ~** gucken.

peer [pɪər] vi angestrengt schauen.

peg [peg] n (for tent) Hering der; (hook) Haken der; (for washing) Klammer die.

pelican crossing ['pelɪkən-] n (Br) Ampelübergang der.

pelvis ['pelvɪs] n Becken das.

pen [pen] n (ballpoint pen) Kugelschreiber der; (fountain pen) Füller der; (for animals) Pferch der.

penalty ['penltɪ] n (fine) Geldstrafe die; (in football) Elfmeter der.

pence [pens] npl Pence pl; **it costs 20 ~** es kostet 20 Pence.

pencil ['pensl] n Bleistift der.

pencil case n Federmäppchen das.

pencil sharpener n Spitzer der.

pendant ['pendənt] n (on necklace) Anhänger der.

pending ['pendɪŋ] prep (fml) bis zu.

penetrate ['penɪtreɪt] vt durchdringen.

penfriend ['penfrend] n Brieffreund der (-in die).

penguin ['peŋgwɪn] n Pinguin der.

penicillin [ˌpenɪ'sɪlɪn] n Penizillin das.

peninsula [pə'nɪnsjʊlə] n Halbinsel die.

penis ['piːnɪs] n Penis der.

penknife ['pennaɪf] (pl **-knives** [-naɪvz]) n Taschenmesser das.

penny ['penɪ] (pl **pennies**) n (in UK)

Penny der; (in US) Cent der.

pension ['penʃn] n Rente die.

pensioner ['penʃənər] n Rentner der (-in die).

penthouse ['penthaʊs, pl -haʊzɪz] n Penthouse das.

penultimate [pe'nʌltɪmət] adj vorletzte(-r)(-s).

people ['piːpl] ◆ npl Leute pl. ◆ n (nation) Volk das; **the ~** (citizens) die Bevölkerung; **lots of ~** viele Menschen; **German ~** die Deutschen pl.

pepper ['pepər] n (spice) Pfeffer der; (vegetable) Paprika der.

peppercorn ['pepəkɔːn] n Pfefferkorn das.

peppermint ['pepəmɪnt] ◆ adj Pfefferminz-. ◆ n (sweet) Pfefferminzbonbon der or das.

pepper pot n Pfefferstreuer der.

pepper steak n Pfeffersteak das.

Pepsi® ['pepsɪ] n Pepsi® das.

per [pɜːr] prep pro; **~ person** pro Person; **~ week** pro Woche; **£20 ~ night** 20 Pfund pro Nacht.

perceive [pə'siːv] vt wahr|nehmen.

per cent adv Prozent.

percentage [pə'sentɪdʒ] n Prozentsatz der.

perch [pɜːtʃ] n (for bird) Stange die.

percolator ['pɜːkəleɪtər] n Kaffeemaschine die.

perfect [adj & n 'pɜːfɪkt, vb pə'fekt] ◆ adj perfekt. ◆ vt perfektionieren. ◆ n: **the ~** (tense) das Perfekt.

perfection [pə'fekʃn] n: **to do sthg to ~** etw perfekt machen.

perfectly ['pɜːfɪktlɪ] adv perfekt.

perform [pə'fɔːm] ◆ vt (task, operation) aus|führen; (play, concert) auf|führen. ◆ vi (actor) spielen; (singer) singen.

performance [pə'fɔːməns] n (of play, concert, film) Aufführung die; (by actor, musician) Vorstellung die; (of car) Leistung die.

performer [pə'fɔːmər] n Künstler der (-in die).

perfume ['pɜːfjuːm] n Parfüm das.

perhaps [pə'hæps] adv vielleicht.

perimeter [pərɪmɪtəʳ] n Grenze die.

period ['pɪərɪəd] ◆ n (of time, history) Periode die, Zeit die; (SCH) Stunde die; (menstruation) Periode die; (Am: full stop) Punkt der. ◆ adj (costume) zeitgenössisch; (furniture) antik.

periodic [,pɪərɪ'ɒdɪk] adj regelmäßig.

period pains npl Menstruationsschmerzen pl.

periphery [pə'rɪfərɪ] n Rand der.

perishable ['perɪʃəbl] adj (food) leicht verderblich.

perk [pɜːk] n Vergünstigung die.

perm [pɜːm] ◆ n Dauerwelle die. ◆ vt: **to have one's hair ~ed** sich (D) eine Dauerwelle machen lassen.

permanent ['pɜːmənənt] adj (lasting) bleibend; (present all the time) ständig; (job) fest.

permanent address n fester Wohnsitz.

permanently ['pɜːmənəntlɪ] adv ständig.

permissible [pə'mɪsəbl] adj (fml) zulässig.

permission [pə'mɪʃn] n Erlaubnis die; (official) Genehmigung die.

permit [vb pə'mɪt, n 'pɜːmɪt] ◆ vt (allow) erlauben. ◆ n Genehmigung die; **to ~ sb to do sthg** jm erlauben, etw zu tun; **'~ holders only'** 'nur für Anleger'.

perpendicular [,pɜːpən'dɪkjʊləʳ] adj senkrecht.

persevere [,pɜːsɪ'vɪəʳ] vi durchlhalten.

persist [pə'sɪst] vi (continue to exist) anlhalten; **to ~ in doing sthg** etw weiterhin tun.

persistent [pə'sɪstənt] adj hartnäckig.

person ['pɜːsn] (pl people) n Mensch der; (GRAMM) Person die; **in ~** persönlich.

personal ['pɜːsənl] adj persönlich.

personal assistant n (of manager) Assistentin die.

personal belongings npl persönlicher Besitz.

personal computer n Personalcomputer der.

personality [,pɜːsə'nælətɪ] n Persönlichkeit die.

personally ['pɜːsnəlɪ] adv persönlich.

personal property n persönliches Eigentum.

personal stereo n Walkman® der.

personnel [,pɜːsə'nel] npl Personal das.

personnel department n Personalabteilung die.

perspective [pə'spektɪv] n Perspektive die.

Perspex® ['pɜːspeks] n (Br) = Plexiglas® das.

perspiration [,pɜːspə'reɪʃn] n Schweiß der.

persuade [pə'sweɪd] vt: **to ~ sb (to do sthg)** jn überreden (, etw zu tun); **to ~ sb that ...** jn davon überzeugen, daß ...

persuasive [pə'sweɪsɪv] adj überzeugend.

pervert ['pɜːvɜːt] n Perverse der, die.

pessimist ['pesɪmɪst] n Pessimist der (-in die).

pessimistic [,pesɪ'mɪstɪk] adj pessimistisch.

pest [pest] n (insect, animal) Schädling der; (inf: person) Nervensäge die.

pester ['pestəʳ] vt nerven.

pesticide ['pestɪsaɪd] n Schädlingsbekämpfungsmittel das.

pet [pet] n Haustier das; **the teacher's ~** der Liebling des Lehrers.

petal ['petl] n Blütenblatt das.

pet food n Tierfutter das.

petition [pɪ'tɪʃn] n (letter) Petition die.

petits pois [,pətɪ'pwɑ] npl feine Erbsen pl.

petrified ['petrɪfaɪd] adj (frightened) starr vor Schrecken.

petrol ['petrəl] *n* (Br) Benzin *das*.

petrol can *n* (Br) Benzinkanister *der*.

petrol cap *n* (Br) Tankverschluß *der*.

petrol gauge *n* (Br) Kraftstoffanzeiger *der*.

petrol pump *n* (Br) Benzinpumpe *die*.

petrol station *n* (Br) Tankstelle *die*.

petrol tank *n* (Br) Benzintank *der*.

pet shop *n* Tierhandlung *die*.

petticoat ['petɪkəut] *n* Unterrock *der*.

petty ['petɪ] *adj* (*pej: person, rule*) kleinlich.

petty cash *n* Portokasse *die*.

pew [pju:] *n* Bank *die*.

pewter ['pju:tər] *adj* Zinn-.

PG (*abbr of parental guidance*) ≃ bedingt jugendfrei.

pharmacist ['fɑ:məsɪst] *n* Apotheker *der* (-in *die*).

pharmacy ['fɑ:məsɪ] *n* (*shop*) Apotheke *die*.

phase [feɪz] *n* Phase *die*.

PhD *n* Dr.phil.

pheasant ['feznt] *n* Fasan *der*.

phenomena [fɪ'nɒmɪnə] *pl* → **phenomenon**.

phenomenal [fɪ'nɒmɪnl] *adj* phänomenal.

phenomenon [fɪ'nɒmɪnən] (*pl* -**mena**) *n* Phänomen *das*.

Philippines ['fɪlɪpi:nz] *npl*: **the ~** die Philippinen *pl*.

philosophy [fɪ'lɒsəfɪ] *n* Philosophie *die*.

phlegm [flem] *n* Schleim *der*.

phone [fəun] ◆ *n* Telefon *das*. ◆ *vt* (Br) an|rufen. ◆ *vi* (Br) telefonieren; **to be on the ~** (*talking*) telefonieren; (*connected*) das Telefon haben. ▶ **phone up** *vt sep & vi* an|rufen.

phone book *n* Telefonbuch *das*.

phone booth *n* Telefonzelle *die*.

phone box *n* (Br) Telefonzelle *die*.

phone call *n* Telefonanruf *der*.

phonecard ['fəunkɑ:d] *n* Telefonkarte *die*.

phone number *n* Telefonnummer *die*.

photo ['fəutəu] *n* Foto *das*; **to take a ~ of** ein Foto machen von.

photo album *n* Fotoalbum *das*.

photocopier [,fəutəu'kɒpɪər] *n* Fotokopiergerät *das*.

photocopy ['fəutəu,kɒpɪ] ◆ *n* Fotokopie *die*. ◆ *vt* fotokopieren.

photograph ['fəutəgrɑ:f] ◆ *n* Foto *das*. ◆ *vt* fotografieren.

photographer [fə'tɒgrəfər] *n* Fotograf *der* (-in *die*).

photography [fə'tɒgrəfɪ] *n* Fotografie *die*.

phrase [freɪz] *n* (*expression*) Ausdruck *der*.

phrasebook ['freɪzbuk] *n* Sprachführer *der*.

physical ['fɪzɪkl] ◆ *adj* körperlich. ◆ *n* Vorsorgeuntersuchung *die*.

physical education *n* Sportunterricht *der*.

physically handicapped ['fɪzɪklɪ-] *adj* körperbehindert.

physics ['fɪzɪks] *n* Physik *die*.

physiotherapy [,fɪzɪəu'θerəpɪ] *n* Physiotherapie *die*.

pianist ['pɪənɪst] *n* Pianist *der* (-in *die*).

piano [pɪ'ænəu] (*pl* -**s**) *n* Klavier *das*.

pick [pɪk] ◆ *vt* (*select*) aus|suchen; (*fruit, flowers*) pflücken. ◆ *n* (*pickaxe*) Spitzhacke *die*; **to ~ a fight** einen Streit an|fangen; **to ~ one's nose** in der Nase bohren; **to take one's ~** aus|suchen. ▶ **pick on** *vt fus* herum|hacken auf (+D). ▶ **pick out** *vt sep* (*select*) aus|suchen; (*see*) entdecken. ▶ **pick up** *vt sep* (*lift up*) hoch|nehmen; (*after dropping*) auf|heben; (*collect*) ab|holen; (*acquire*) erwerben; (*skill, language*) lernen; (*hitchhiker*) mit|nehmen; (*inf: woman, man*) ab|schleppen. ◆ *vi* (*improve*) sich bessern.

pickaxe ['pɪkæks] n Spitzhacke die.

pickle ['pɪkl] n (Br: food) Mixed Pickles pl; (Am: pickled cucumber) Essiggurke die.

pickled onion ['pɪkld-] n eingelegte Zwiebel.

pickpocket ['pɪkˌpɒkɪt] n Taschendieb der (-in die).

pick-up (truck) n Lieferwagen der.

picnic ['pɪknɪk] n Picknick das.

picnic area n Picknickplatz der.

picture ['pɪktʃər] n Bild das; (film) Film der. ▶ **pictures** npl: **the ~s** (Br) das Kino.

picture frame n Bilderrahmen der.

picturesque [ˌpɪktʃə'resk] adj malerisch.

pie [paɪ] n (savoury) Pastete die; (sweet) Kuchen der.

piece [piːs] n Stück das; (component) Teil das; (in chess) Figur die; **a 20p ~** ein 20-Pence-Stück; **a ~ of advice** ein Rat; **a ~ of furniture** ein Möbelstück; **to fall to ~s** zerbrechen; **in one ~** (intact) unbeschädigt; (unharmed) heil.

pier [pɪər] n Pier der or die.

pierce [pɪəs] vt durch|bohren; **to have one's ears ~d** sich (D) die Ohrläppchen durchstechen lassen.

pig [pɪg] n Schwein das; (inf: greedy person) Vielfraß der.

pigeon ['pɪdʒɪn] n Taube die.

pigeonhole ['pɪdʒɪnhəʊl] n Fach das.

pigskin ['pɪgskɪn] adj Schweinsleder-.

pigtail ['pɪgteɪl] n Zopf der.

pike [paɪk] n (fish) Hecht der.

pilau rice ['pɪlaʊ-] n Pilaureis der, mit Gewürzen gekochter Reis, der dadurch eine bestimmte Farbe annimmt.

pilchard ['pɪltʃəd] n Sardine die.

pile [paɪl] ◆ n (heap) Haufen der; (neat stack) Stapel der. ◆ vt stapeln; **~s of money** (inf: a lot) haufenweise Geld. ▶ **pile up** vt sep an|häufen; (neatly) auf|stapeln. ◆ vi (accumulate) sich an|sammeln.

piles [paɪlz] npl (MED) Hämorrhoiden pl.

pileup ['paɪlʌp] n Massenkarambolage die.

pill [pɪl] n Tablette die; **the ~** (contraceptive) die Pille.

pillar ['pɪlər] n Säule die.

pillar box n (Br) Briefkasten der.

pillion ['pɪljən] n: **to ride ~** auf dem Soziussitz mit|fahren.

pillow ['pɪləʊ] n Kissen das.

pillowcase ['pɪləʊkeɪs] n Kopfkissenbezug der.

pilot ['paɪlət] n Pilot der (-in die); (of ship) Lotse der.

pilot light n Zündflamme die.

pimple ['pɪmpl] n Pickel der.

pin [pɪn] ◆ n (for sewing) Stecknadel die; (drawing pin) Reißnagel der; (safety pin) Sicherheitsnadel die; (Am: brooch) Brosche die; (Am: badge) Anstecknadel die. ◆ vt (fasten) stecken; **a two-~ plug** ein zweipoliger Stecker; **I've got ~s and needles in my leg** mein Bein ist eingeschlafen.

pinafore ['pɪnəfɔːr] n (apron) Schürze die; (Br: dress) Trägerkleid das.

pinball ['pɪnbɔːl] n Flippern das.

pincers ['pɪnsəz] npl (tool) Beißzange die.

pinch [pɪntʃ] ◆ vt (squeeze) kneifen; (Br: inf: steal) klauen. ◆ n (of salt) Prise die.

pine [paɪn] ◆ n Kiefer die. ◆ adj Kiefern-.

pineapple ['paɪnæpl] n Ananas die.

pink [pɪŋk] ◆ adj rosa. ◆ n Rosa das.

pinkie ['pɪŋkɪ] n (Am) kleiner Finger.

PIN number ['pɪn-] n persönliche Kodenummer.

pint [paɪnt] n (in UK) = 0,57 Liter, Pint das; (in US) = 0,47 Liter, Pint das; **a ~ (of beer)** (Br) = ein (großes) Bier.

pip [pɪp] n Kern der.

pipe [paɪp] n (for smoking) Pfeife die; (for gas, water) Rohr das.

pipe cleaner n Pfeifenreiniger der.

pipeline ['paɪplaɪn] n Pipeline die.

pipe tobacco n Pfeifentabak der.

pirate ['paɪrət] n Pirat der.

Pisces ['paɪsiːz] n Fische pl.

piss [pɪs] ◆ vi (vulg) pissen. ◆ n: **to have a ~** (vulg) pissen gehen; **it's ~ing down** (vulg) es schifft.

pissed [pɪst] adj (Br: vulg: drunk) besoffen; (Am: vulg: angry) stocksauer.

pissed off adj (vulg) stocksauer.

pistachio [pɪˈstɑːʃɪəʊ] ◆ n Pistazie die. ◆ adj (flavour) Pistazien-.

pistol ['pɪstl] n Pistole die.

piston ['pɪstən] n Kolben der.

pit [pɪt] n (hole, coalmine) Grube die; (for orchestra) Orchestergraben der; (Am: in fruit) Stein der.

pitch [pɪtʃ] ◆ n (Br: SPORT) Spielfeld das. ◆ vt (throw) werfen; **to ~ a tent** ein Zelt auflschlagen.

pitcher ['pɪtʃər] n Krug der.

pitfall ['pɪtfɔːl] n Falle die.

pith [pɪθ] n (of orange) weiße Haut.

pitta (bread) ['pɪtə-] n Pittabrot das.

pitted ['pɪtɪd] adj (olives) entsteint.

pity ['pɪtɪ] n (compassion) Mitleid das; **to have ~ on sb** Mitleid mit jm haben; **it's a ~ (that)** ... schade, daß ...; **what a ~!** wie schade!

pivot ['pɪvət] n Zapfen der.

pizza ['piːtsə] n Pizza die.

pizzeria [ˌpiːtsəˈriːə] n Pizzeria die.

Pl. (abbr of Place) Platz (als Straßenname).

placard ['plækɑːd] n Plakat das.

place [pleɪs] ◆ n (location) Ort der; (spot) Stelle die; (house, flat) Haus das; (seat, position, in race, list) Platz der. ◆ vt (put) setzen; (put flat) legen; (put upright) stellen; (an order) auflgeben; **do you want to come round to my ~?** möchtest du zu mir kommen?; **to lay six ~s** (at table) für sechs decken; **in the first ~** (firstly) erstens; **to take ~**

stattlfinden; **to take sb's ~** (replace) js Platz einlnehmen; **all over the ~** überall; **in ~ of** statt (+G); **to ~ a bet on** Geld setzen auf (+A).

place mat n Platzdeckchen das.

placement ['pleɪsmənt] n (work experience) Praktikum das.

place of birth n Geburtsort der.

plague [pleɪg] n Pest die.

plaice [pleɪs] n Scholle die.

plain [pleɪn] ◆ adj (not decorated) schlicht; (simple) einfach; (yoghurt) Natur-; (clear) klar; (paper) unliniert; (pej: not attractive) nicht sehr attraktiv. ◆ n Ebene die.

plain chocolate n Zartbitterschokolade die.

plainly ['pleɪnlɪ] adv deutlich.

plait [plæt] ◆ n Zopf der. ◆ vt flechten.

plan [plæn] ◆ n Plan der. ◆ vt planen; **have you any ~s for tonight?** hast du heute abend etwas vor?; **according to ~** planmäßig; **to ~ to do sthg, to ~ on doing sthg** vorlhaben, etw zu tun.

plane [pleɪn] n (aeroplane) Flugzeug das; (tool) Hobel der.

planet ['plænɪt] n Planet der.

plank [plæŋk] n Brett das.

plant [plɑːnt] ◆ n Pflanze die; (factory) Werk das. ◆ vt pflanzen; (land) bepflanzen; **'heavy ~ crossing'** 'Baustellenverkehr'.

plantation [plænˈteɪʃn] n Plantage die.

plaque [plɑːk] n (plate) Gedenktafel die; (on teeth) Zahnstein der.

plaster ['plɑːstər] n (Br: for cut) Pflaster das; (for walls) Verputz der; **in ~** (arm, leg) in Gips.

plaster cast n Gipsverband der.

plastic ['plæstɪk] ◆ n Plastik das. ◆ adj Plastik-, Kunststoff-.

plastic bag n Plastiktüte die.

Plasticine® ['plæstɪsiːn] n (Br) Plastilin das.

plate [pleɪt] n Teller der; (of metal, glass) Platte die.

plateau ['plætəʊ] n Hochebene die.
plate-glass adj Flachglas-.
platform ['plætfɔːm] n (at railway station) Bahnsteig der; (raised structure) Podium das; **~ 12** Gleis 12.
platinum ['plætɪnəm] n Platin das.
platter ['plætər] n (of food) Platte die.
play [pleɪ] ♦ vt spielen; (opponent) spielen gegen. ♦ vi spielen. ♦ n (in theatre) Theaterstück das; (on TV) Fernsehspiel das; (button on CD, tape recorder) Playtaste die; **to ~ the piano** Klavier spielen. ► **play back** vt sep ab|spielen. ► **play up** vi (machine, car) Schwierigkeiten machen.
player ['pleɪər] n Spieler der (-in die).
playful ['pleɪfʊl] adj verspielt.
playground ['pleɪgraʊnd] n (in school) Schulhof der; (in park etc) Spielplatz der.
playgroup ['pleɪgruːp] n Krabbelgruppe die.
playing card ['pleɪɪŋ-] n Spielkarte die.
playing field ['pleɪɪŋ-] n Sportplatz der.
playroom ['pleɪrʊm] n Spielzimmer das.
playschool ['pleɪskuːl] = **playgroup**.
playtime ['pleɪtaɪm] n Pause die.
playwright ['pleɪraɪt] n Bühnenautor der (-in die).
plc (Br: abbr of public limited company) ≈ GmbH.
pleasant ['pleznt] adj angenehm.
please [pliːz] ♦ adv bitte. ♦ vt (give enjoyment to) gefallen (+D); **yes ~!** ja, bitte!; **whatever you ~** (ganz) wie Sie wollen.
pleased [pliːzd] adj (happy) erfreut; (satisfied) zufrieden; **to be ~ with** sich freuen über (+A); **~ to meet you!** angenehm!
pleasure ['pleʒər] n Freude die; **with ~** gerne; **it's a ~!** gern geschehen!
pleat [pliːt] n Falte die.
pleated ['pliːtɪd] adj Falten-.

plentiful ['plentɪfʊl] adj reichlich.
plenty ['plentɪ] pron: **there are ~** es gibt viele; **~ of** viele.
pliers ['plaɪəz] npl Zange die.
plimsoll ['plɪmsəl] n (Br) Turnschuh der.
plonk [plɒŋk] n (Br: inf: wine) billiger Wein.
plot [plɒt] n (scheme) Komplott das; (of story, film, play) Handlung die; (of land) Stück das Land.
plough [plaʊ] ♦ n (Br) Pflug der. ♦ vt (Br) pflügen.
ploughman's (lunch) [-'plaʊmənz-] n (Br) beliebte Pubmahlzeit aus Brot, Käse, Salat und Mixed Pickles.
plow [plaʊ] (Am) = **plough**.
ploy [plɔɪ] n Taktik die.
pluck [plʌk] vt (eyebrows) zupfen; (chicken) rupfen.
plug [plʌg] n (electrical) Stecker der; (socket) Steckdose die; (for bath, sink) Stöpsel der. ► **plug in** vt sep an|schließen.
plughole ['plʌghəʊl] n Abfluß der.
plum [plʌm] n Pflaume die, Zwetschge die.
plumber ['plʌmər] n Installateur der.
plumbing ['plʌmɪŋ] n (pipes) Wasserleitungen pl.
plump [plʌmp] adj rundlich.
plunge [plʌndʒ] vi stürzen; (dive) tauchen.
plunge pool n Swimmingpool der.
plunger ['plʌndʒər] n (for unblocking pipe) Sauger der.
pluperfect (tense) [ˌpluːˈpɜːfɪkt-] n: **the ~** das Plusquamperfekt.
plural ['plʊərəl] n Plural der; **in the ~** im Plural.
plus [plʌs] ♦ prep plus; (and) und. ♦ adj: **30 ~** über 30.
plush [plʌʃ] adj feudal.
plywood ['plaɪwʊd] n Sperrholz das.
p.m. (abbr of post meridiem) nachmittags.

PMT n (abbr of premenstrual tension) PMS das.

pneumatic drill [nju:'mætɪk-] n Preßluftbohrer der.

pneumonia [nju:'məʊnjə] n Lungenentzündung die.

poached egg [pəʊtʃt-] n pochiertes Ei, verlorenes Ei.

poached salmon [pəʊtʃt-] n Lachs der blau.

poacher ['pəʊtʃər] n Wilderer der.

PO Box n (abbr of Post Office Box) Postfach das.

pocket ['pɒkɪt] ◆ n Tasche die; (on car door) Seitentasche die. ◆ adj (camera) Pocket-; (calculator) Taschen-.

pocketbook ['pɒkɪtbʊk] n (notebook) Notizbuch das; (Am: handbag) Handtasche die.

pocket money n (Br) Taschengeld das.

podiatrist [pə'daɪətrɪst] n (Am) Fußpfleger der (-in die).

poem ['pəʊɪm] n Gedicht das.

poet ['pəʊɪt] n Dichter der (-in die).

poetry ['pəʊɪtrɪ] n Dichtung die.

point [pɔɪnt] ◆ n Punkt der; (tip) Spitze die; (most important thing) Sinn der, Zweck der; (Br: electric socket) Steckdose die. ◆ vi: **to ~ to** (with finger) zeigen auf (+A); (arrow, sign) zeigen nach; **five ~ seven** fünf Komma sieben; **strong ~** Stärke die; **weak ~** Schwäche die; **what's the ~?** wozu?; **there's no ~** es hat keinen Sinn; **to be on the ~ of doing sthg** im Begriff sein, etw zu tun; **to come to the ~** zur Sache kommen. ▶ **points** npl (Br: on railway) Weichen pl. ▶ **point out** vt sep hinlweisen auf (+A).

pointed ['pɔɪntɪd] adj (in shape) spitz.

pointless ['pɔɪntlɪs] adj sinnlos.

point of view n Standpunkt der.

poison ['pɔɪzn] ◆ n Gift das. ◆ vt vergiften.

poisoning ['pɔɪznɪŋ] n Vergiftung die.

poisonous ['pɔɪznəs] adj giftig, Gift-.

poke [pəʊk] vt (with finger, stick, elbow) stoßen.

poker ['pəʊkər] n (card game) Poker das.

Poland ['pəʊlənd] n Polen nt.

polar bear ['pəʊlə-] n Eisbär der.

Polaroid® ['pəʊlərɔɪd] n (photograph) Polaroidbild das; (camera) Polaroidkamera® die.

pole [pəʊl] n (of wood) Stange die.

Pole [pəʊl] n (person) Pole der (Polin die).

police [pə'li:s] npl: **the ~** die Polizei.

police car n Polizeiwagen der.

police force n Polizei die.

policeman [pə'li:smən] (pl -men [-mən]) n Polizist der.

police officer n Polizeibeamte der (-beamtin die).

police station n Polizeiwache die.

policewoman [pə'li:s,wʊmən] (pl -women [-,wɪmɪn]) n Polizistin die.

policy ['pɒləsɪ] n (approach) Handlungsweise die; (for insurance) Police die; (in politics) Politik die.

policy-holder n Versicherte der die.

polio ['pəʊlɪəʊ] n Kinderlähmung die.

polish ['pɒlɪʃ] ◆ n (for cleaning) Politur die. ◆ vt polieren.

Polish ['pəʊlɪʃ] ◆ adj polnisch. ◆ n (language) Polnisch das. ◆ npl: **the ~** die Polen pl.

polite [pə'laɪt] adj höflich.

political [pə'lɪtɪkl] adj politisch.

politician [,pɒlɪ'tɪʃn] n Politiker der (-in die).

politics ['pɒlətɪks] n Politik die.

poll [pəʊl] n (survey) Umfrage die; **the ~s** (election) die Wahlen pl.

pollen ['pɒlən] n Pollen der.

Poll Tax n (Br) ≃ Gemeindesteuer die.

pollute [pə'lu:t] vt verschmutzen.

pollution [pə'lu:ʃn] n Verschmutzung *die*; (*substances*) Schmutz *der*.

polo neck ['pəuləu-] *n* (Br) Rollkragen *der*.

polyester [,pɒlɪ'estər] *n* Polyester *der*.

polystyrene [,pɒlɪ'staɪriːn] *n* Styropor® *das*.

polytechnic [,pɒlɪ'teknɪk] *n* Hochschule in Großbritannien; seit 1993 haben die meisten Universitätsstatus.

polythene ['pɒlɪθiːn] *n* Polyäthylen *das*.

pomegranate ['pɒmɪ,grænɪt] *n* Granatapfel *der*.

pompous ['pɒmpəs] *adj* aufgeblasen.

pond [pɒnd] *n* Teich *der*.

pontoon [pɒn'tuːn] *n* (Br: *card game*) Siebzehnundvier *das*.

pony ['pəunɪ] *n* Pony *das*.

ponytail ['pəunɪteɪl] *n* Pferdeschwanz *der*.

pony-trekking [-,trekɪŋ] *n* (Br) Ponyreiten *das*.

poodle ['puːdl] *n* Pudel *der*.

pool [puːl] *n* (*for swimming*) Schwimmbecken *das*; (*of water, blood, milk*) Lache *die*; (*small pond*) Teich *der*; (*game*) Poolbillard *das*. ► **pools** *npl* (Br): **the ~s** = das Toto.

poor [pɔːr] ◆ *adj* arm; (*bad*) schlecht. ◆ *npl*: **the ~** die Armen *pl*.

poorly ['pɔːlɪ] ◆ *adv* schlecht. ◆ *adj* (Br: *ill*): **he's ~** es geht ihm schlecht.

pop [pɒp] ◆ *n* (*music*) Pop *der*. ◆ *vt* (*inf*: *put*) stecken. ◆ *vi* (*balloon*) knallen; **my ears popped** ich hab' Druck auf den Ohren. ► **pop in** *vi* (Br: *visit*) vorbeischauen.

popcorn ['pɒpkɔːn] *n* Popcorn *das*.

Pope [pəup] *n*: **the ~** der Papst.

pop group *n* Popgruppe *die*.

poplar (tree) ['pɒplər-] *n* Pappel *die*.

pop music *n* Popmusik *die*.

popper ['pɒpər] *n* (Br) Druckknopf *der*.

poppy ['pɒpɪ] *n* Klatschmohn *der*.

Popsicle® ['pɒpsɪkl] *n* (Am) Eis *das* am Stiel.

pop socks *npl* Kniestrümpfe *pl*.

pop star *n* Popstar *der*.

popular ['pɒpjulər] *adj* beliebt; (*opinion, ideas*) weitverbreitet.

popularity [,pɒpju'lærətɪ] *n* Beliebtheit *die*.

populated ['pɒpjuleɪtɪd] *adj* bevölkert.

population [,pɒpju'leɪʃn] *n* Bevölkerung *die*.

porcelain ['pɔːsəlɪn] *n* Porzellan *das*.

porch [pɔːtʃ] *n* (*entrance*) Windfang *der*; (Am: *outside house*) Veranda *die*.

pork [pɔːk] *n* Schweinefleisch *das*.

pork chop *n* Schweinekotelett *das*.

pork pie *n* Schweinepastete *die*.

pornographic [,pɔːnə'græfɪk] *adj* pornographisch.

porridge ['pɒrɪdʒ] *n* Haferbrei *der*.

port [pɔːt] *n* (*town*) Hafenstadt *die*; (*harbour area*) Hafen *der*; (*drink*) Portwein *der*.

portable ['pɔːtəbl] *adj* tragbar.

porter ['pɔːtər] *n* (*at hotel, museum*) Portier *der*; (*at station, airport*) Gepäckträger *der*.

porthole ['pɔːthəul] *n* Bullauge *das*.

portion ['pɔːʃn] *n* (*part*) Teil *das*; (*of food*) Portion *die*.

portrait ['pɔːtreɪt] *n* Porträt *das*.

Portugal ['pɔːtʃugl] *n* Portugal *nt*.

Portuguese [,pɔːtʃu'giːz] ◆ *adj* portugiesisch. ◆ *n* (*language*) Portugiesisch *das*. ◆ *npl*: **the ~** die Portugiesen *pl*.

pose [pəuz] ◆ *vt* (*problem, threat*) darlstellen. ◆ *vi* (*for photo*) sitzen.

posh [pɒʃ] *adj* (*inf*) piekfein.

position [pə'zɪʃn] *n* (*place, situation*) Lage *die*; (*of plane, ship*) Position *die*; (*of body*) Haltung *die*; (*setting, rank*) Stellung *die*; (*in race, contest*) Platz *der*; (*fml*: *job*) Stelle *die*; **'~ closed'** (*in bank, post office etc*) 'Schalter geschlossen'.

positive ['pɒzətɪv] *adj* positiv; *(certain, sure)* sicher.

possess [pə'zes] *vt* besitzen.

possession [pə'zeʃn] *n* Besitz *der*.

possessive [pə'zesɪv] *adj* (*pej: person*) besitzergreifend; (GRAMM) Possessiv-.

possibility [,pɒsə'bɪlətɪ] *n* Möglichkeit *die*.

possible ['pɒsəbl] *adj* möglich; **it's ~ that we may be late** es kann sein, daß wir zu spät kommen; **would it be ~ for me to ...?** könnte ich vielleicht ...?; **as much as ~** so viel wie möglich; **if ~** wenn möglich.

possibly ['pɒsəblɪ] *adv* (*perhaps*) möglicherweise.

post [pəust] ♦ *n* (*system, letters, delivery*) Post *die*; (*pole*) Pfahl *der*; (*fml: job*) Stelle *die*. ♦ *vt* (*letter, parcel*) ab|schicken; **by ~** per Post.

postage ['pəustɪdʒ] *n* Porto *das*; **~ and packing** Porto und Verpackung; **~ paid** Porto zahlt Empfänger.

postage stamp *n* (*fml*) Briefmarke *die*.

postal order ['pəustl-] *n* Postanweisung *die*.

postbox ['pəustbɒks] *n* (Br) Briefkasten *der*.

postcard ['pəustkɑːd] *n* Postkarte *die*.

postcode ['pəustkəud] *n* (Br) Postleitzahl *die*.

poster ['pəustəʳ] *n* (*for advertisement*) Plakat *das*; (*decoration*) Poster *das*.

poste restante [,pəustres'tɑːnt] *n* (Br) Schalter *der* für postlagernde Sendungen.

post-free *adv* portofrei.

postgraduate [,pəust'grædʒuət] *n* Student, *der* auf einen höheren Studienabschluß hinarbeitet.

postman ['pəustmən] (*pl* **-men** [-mən]) *n* Briefträger *der*.

postmark ['pəustmɑːk] *n* Poststempel *der*.

post office *n* (*building*) Post *die*; **the Post Office** die Post.

postpone [,pəust'pəun] *vt* verschieben.

posture ['pɒstʃəʳ] *n* Haltung *die*.

postwoman ['pəust,wumən] (*pl* **-women** [-,wɪmɪn]) *n* Briefträgerin *die*.

pot [pɒt] *n* (*for cooking*) Topf *der*; (*for jam*) Glas *das*; (*for paint*) Dose *die*; (*for coffee, tea*) Kanne *die*; (*inf: cannabis*) Pot *das*; **a ~ of tea** ein Kännchen Tee.

potato [pə'teɪtəu] (*pl* **-es**) *n* Kartoffel *die*.

potato salad *n* Kartoffelsalat *der*.

potential [pə'tenʃl] ♦ *adj* potentiell. ♦ *n* Potential *das*.

pothole ['pɒthəul] *n* (*in road*) Schlagloch *das*.

pot plant *n* Topfpflanze *die*.

pot scrubber [-'skrʌbəʳ] *n* Topfreiniger *der*.

potted ['pɒtɪd] *adj* (*meat, fish*) Dosen-; (*plant*) Topf-.

pottery ['pɒtərɪ] *n* (*clay objects*) Töpferwaren *pl*; (*craft*) Töpferei *die*.

potty ['pɒtɪ] *n* Töpfchen *das*.

pouch [pautʃ] *n* (*for money*) Beutel *der*.

poultry ['pəultrɪ] *n* OR *npl* Geflügel *das*.

pound [paund] ♦ *n* (*unit of money*) Pfund *das*; (*unit of weight*) = 0,45 Kg, Pfund. ♦ *vi* (*heart*) pochen; (*head*) dröhnen.

pour [pɔːʳ] ♦ *vt* gießen; (*sugar, sand*) schütten; (*drink*) ein|gießen. ♦ *vi* (*flow*) fließen; **it's ~ing (with rain)** es gießt. ► **pour out** *vt sep* (*drink*) ein|gießen.

poverty ['pɒvətɪ] *n* Armut *die*.

powder ['paudəʳ] *n* Pulver *das*.

power ['pauəʳ] ♦ *n* Macht *die*; (*strength, force*) Kraft *die*; (*energy*) Energie *die*; (*electricity*) Strom *der*. ♦ *vt* an|treiben; **to be in ~** an der Macht sein.

power cut *n* Stromsperre *die*.

power failure *n* Stromausfall *der*.

powerful ['pauəful] *adj* stark; (*leader*) mächtig; (*voice*) kräftig.

power point *n* (Br) Steckdose *die*.

power station n Kraftwerk das.
power steering n Servolenkung die.
practical ['præktɪkl] adj praktisch.
practically ['præktɪklɪ] adv praktisch.
practice ['præktɪs] ◆ n (training) Übung die; (training session) Training das; (of doctor, lawyer) Praxis die; (regular activity) Gewohnheit die; (custom) Brauch der. ◆ vt (Am) = **practise**; **out of ~** außer Übung.
practise ['præktɪs] ◆ n (Am) = **practice**. ◆ vt & vi üben; **to ~ as a doctor** als Arzt tätig sein.
praise [preɪz] ◆ n Lob das. ◆ vt loben.
pram [præm] n (Br) Kinderwagen der.
prank [præŋk] n Streich der.
prawn [prɔ:n] n Garnele die.
prawn cocktail n Krabbencocktail der.
prawn cracker n chinesischer Chip mit Krabbengeschmack.
pray [preɪ] vi beten; **to ~ for sthg** um etw beten.
prayer [preəʳ] n Gebet das.
precarious [prɪ'keərɪəs] adj unsicher.
precaution [prɪ'kɔ:ʃn] n Vorsichtsmaßnahme die.
precede [prɪ'si:d] vt (fml) voranlgehen (+D).
preceding [prɪ'si:dɪŋ] adj vorhergehend.
precinct ['pri:sɪŋkt] n (Br: for shopping) Einkaufsviertel das; (Am: area of town) Bezirk der.
precious ['preʃəs] adj kostbar; (metal, jewel) Edel-.
precious stone n Edelstein der.
precipice ['presɪpɪs] n Steilabhang der.
precise [prɪ'saɪs] adj genau.
precisely [prɪ'saɪslɪ] adv genau.
predecessor ['pri:dɪsesəʳ] n Vorgänger der (-in die).

predicament [prɪ'dɪkəmənt] n Dilemma das.
predict [prɪ'dɪkt] vt vorherlsagen.
predictable [prɪ'dɪktəbl] adj (foreseeable) vorhersehbar; (pej: unoriginal) berechenbar.
prediction [prɪ'dɪkʃn] n Voraussage die.
preface ['prefɪs] n Vorwort das.
prefect ['pri:fekt] n (Br: at school) älterer Schüler in britischen Schulen, der den Lehrern bei der Aufsicht hilft.
prefer [prɪ'fɜ:ʳ] vt vorlziehen; **to ~ to do sthg** etw lieber tun.
preferable ['prefrəbl] adj: **to be ~ (to)** vorzuziehen sein (+D).
preferably ['prefrəblɪ] adv vorzugsweise.
preference ['prefərəns] n Vorzug der; **to have a ~ for sthg** etw bevorzugen.
prefix ['pri:fɪks] n Vorsilbe die.
pregnancy ['pregnənsɪ] n Schwangerschaft die.
pregnant ['pregnənt] adj schwanger.
prejudice ['predʒʊdɪs] n Voreingenommenheit die; **to have a ~ against sb/sthg** ein Vorurteil gegen jn/etw haben.
prejudiced ['predʒʊdɪst] adj voreingenommen.
preliminary [prɪ'lɪmɪnərɪ] adj Vor-.
premature ['premə,tjʊəʳ] adj vorzeitig; **a ~ baby** eine Frühgeburt.
premier ['premjəʳ] ◆ adj bedeutendste(-r)(-s). ◆ n Premier der.
premiere ['premɪeəʳ] n Premiere die.
premises ['premɪsɪz] npl (grounds) Gelände das; (shop, restaurant) Räumlichkeiten pl.
premium ['pri:mjəm] n (for insurance) Prämie die.
premium-quality adj (meat) Qualitäts-.
preoccupied [pri:'ɒkjʊpaɪd] adj beschäftigt.
prepacked [,pri:'pækt] adj abgepackt.

prepaid ['pri:peɪd] adj (envelope) frankiert.

preparation [,prepə'reɪʃn] n Vorbereitung die.

preparatory school [prɪ'pærətrɪ-] n (in UK) private Grundschule; (in US) private Oberschule.

prepare [prɪ'peəʳ] ◆ vt vorlbereiten; (food) kochen. ◆ vi sich vorlbereiten.

prepared [prɪ'peəd] adj vorbereitet; **to be ~ to do sthg** bereit sein, etw zu tun.

preposition [,prepə'zɪʃn] n Präposition die.

prep school [prep-] = **preparatory school**.

prescribe [prɪ'skraɪb] vt (medicine, treatment) verschreiben.

prescription [prɪ'skrɪpʃn] n (paper) Rezept das; (medicine) Medikament das.

presence ['prezns] n (being present) Anwesenheit die; **in his ~** in seiner Gegenwart.

present [adj & n 'preznt, vb prɪ'zent] ◆ adj (in attendance) anwesend; (current) gegenwärtig. ◆ vt (hand over) überreichen; (represent) darlstellen; (TV, radio programme) moderieren; (play) auflführen. ◆ n (gift) Geschenk das; (current time): **the ~** die Gegenwart; **the ~ (tense)** (GRAMM) das Präsens; **at ~** zur Zeit; **to ~ sb with sthg** jm etw überreichen; **to ~ sb to sb** jn einer Person vorlstellen.

presentable [prɪ'zentəbl] adj präsentabel.

presentation [,prezn'teɪʃn] n (way of presenting) Präsentation die; (ceremony) Verleihung die.

presenter [prɪ'zentəʳ] n (of TV, radio programme) Moderator der (-in die).

presently ['prezntlɪ] adv (soon) bald; (now) zur Zeit.

preservation [,prezə'veɪʃn] n Erhaltung die.

preservative [prɪ'zɜːvətɪv] n Konservierungsstoff der.

preserve [prɪ'zɜːv] ◆ n (jam) Konfitüre die. ◆ vt erhalten; (food) konservieren.

president ['prezɪdənt] n Präsident der (-in die); (of company) Vorsitzende der die.

press [pres] ◆ vt drücken; (button) drücken auf (+A); (iron) plätten. ◆ n: **the ~** (media) die Presse; **to ~ sb to do sthg** jn drängen, etw zu tun.

press conference n Pressekonferenz die.

press-stud n Druckknopf der.

press-up n Liegestütz der.

pressure ['preʃəʳ] n Druck der.

pressure cooker n Schnellkochtopf der.

prestigious [pre'stɪdʒəs] adj renommiert.

presumably [prɪ'zjuːməblɪ] adv vermutlich.

presume [prɪ'zjuːm] vt anlnehmen.

pretend [prɪ'tend] vt: **to ~ to do sthg** vorlgeben, etw zu tun.

pretentious [prɪ'tenʃəs] adj hochgestochen.

pretty ['prɪtɪ] ◆ adj hübsch. ◆ adv (inf: quite) ziemlich.

prevent [prɪ'vent] vt verhindern; **to ~ sb from doing sthg** jn daran hindern, etw zu tun.

prevention [prɪ'venʃn] n Vorbeugung die.

preview ['priːvjuː] n Vorschau die.

previous ['priːvjəs] adj (earlier) früher; (preceding) vorig.

previously ['priːvjəslɪ] adv vorher.

price [praɪs] ◆ n Preis der. ◆ vt auslzeichnen.

priceless ['praɪslɪs] adj unbezahlbar.

price list n Preisliste die.

pricey ['praɪsɪ] adj (inf) teuer.

prick [prɪk] vt stechen.

prickly ['prɪklɪ] adj stachelig.

prickly heat n Hitzepickel pl.

pride [praɪd] ◆ n Stolz der. ◆ vt: **to ~ o.s. on sthg** stolz sein auf etw (A).

priest [priːst] *n* Priester *der*.
primarily ['praɪmərɪlɪ] *adv* hauptsächlich.
primary school ['praɪmərɪ-] *n* Grundschule *die*.
prime [praɪm] *adj* (*chief*) Haupt-; (*quality, beef, cut*) erstklassig.
prime minister *n* Premierminister *der* (-in *die*).
primitive ['prɪmɪtɪv] *adj* primitiv.
primrose ['prɪmrəʊz] *n* Himmelschlüssel *der*.
prince [prɪns] *n* Prinz *der*.
Prince of Wales *n* Prinz *der* von Wales.
princess [prɪn'ses] *n* Prinzessin *die*.
principal ['prɪnsəpl] ◆ *adj* Haupt-. ◆ *n* (*of school, university*) Rektor *der* (-in *die*).
principle ['prɪnsəpl] *n* Prinzip *das*; **in ~** im Prinzip.
print [prɪnt] ◆ *n* Druck *der*; (*photo*) Abzug *der*; (*mark*) Abdruck *der*. ◆ *vt* drucken; (*write*) in Druckschrift schreiben; (*photo*) ablziehen; **out of ~** vergriffen. ▶ **print out** *vt sep* ausldrucken.
printed matter ['prɪntɪd-] *n* Drucksache *die*.
printer ['prɪntər] *n* Drucker *der*.
printout ['prɪntaʊt] *n* Ausdruck *der*.
prior ['praɪər] *adj* (*previous*) frühere(-r)(-s); **~ to sthg** (*fml*) vor etw (D).
priority [praɪ'ɒrətɪ] *n* Priorität *die*; **to have ~ over** Vorrang haben vor (+D).
prison ['prɪzn] *n* Gefängnis *das*.
prisoner ['prɪznər] *n* Häftling *der*.
prisoner of war *n* Kriegsgefangene *der die*.
prison officer *n* Gefängniswärter *der* (-in *die*).
privacy ['prɪvəsɪ] *n* Privatleben *das*.
private ['praɪvɪt] ◆ *adj* Privat-; (*confidential*) vertraulich; (*quiet*) ruhig. ◆ *n* (MIL) Gefreite *der*; **in ~** privat.
private health care *n* private Krankenpflege *die*.

private property *n* Privatgrundstück *das*.
private school *n* Privatschule *die*.
privilege ['prɪvɪlɪdʒ] *n* Privileg *das*; **it's a ~!** es ist mir eine Ehre!
prize [praɪz] *n* Preis *der*.
prize-giving [-ˌgɪvɪŋ] *n* Preisverleihung *die*.
pro [prəʊ] (*pl* **-s**) *n* (*inf: professional*) Profi *der*. ▶ **pros** *npl*: **~s and cons** Pro und Kontra *das*.
probability [ˌprɒbə'bɪlətɪ] *n* Wahrscheinlichkeit *die*.
probable ['prɒbəbl] *adj* wahrscheinlich.
probably ['prɒbəblɪ] *adv* wahrscheinlich.
probation officer [prə'beɪʃn-] *n* Bewährungshelfer *der* (-in *die*).
problem ['prɒbləm] *n* Problem *das*; **no ~!** (*inf*) kein Problem!
procedure [prə'siːdʒər] *n* Verfahren *das*.
proceed [prə'siːd] *vi* (*fml: continue*) fortlfahren; (*act*) vorlgehen; (*walk*) gehen; (*drive*) fahren; **'~ with caution'** 'Vorsichtig fahren'.
proceeds ['prəʊsiːdz] *npl* Erlös *der*.
process ['prəʊses] *n* Prozeß *der*; **to be in the ~ of doing sthg** dabei sein, etw zu tun.
processed cheese ['prəʊsest-] *n* Schmelzkäse *der*.
procession [prə'seʃn] *n* Prozession *die*.
prod [prɒd] *vt* (*poke*) stupsen.
produce [prə'djuːs] ◆ *vt* (*make, manufacture*) herlstellen; (*work of art*) schaffen; (*cause*) hervorlrufen; (*create naturally*) erzeugen; (*passport, identification*) vorlzeigen; (*proof*) liefern; (*play*) inszenieren; (*film*) produzieren. ◆ *n* Erzeugnisse *pl*.
producer [prə'djuːsər] *n* (*manufacturer*) Produzent *der* (-in *die*); (*of film*) Produzent *der* (-in *die*); (*of play*) Regisseur *der* (-in *die*).
product ['prɒdʌkt] *n* Produkt *das*.
production [prə'dʌkʃn] *n* (*manufac-*

ture) Produktion *die*; (*of film, play*) Produktion *die*; (*play*) Aufführung *die*.

productivity [ˌprɒdʌkˈtɪvətɪ] *n* Produktivität *die*.

profession [prəˈfeʃn] *n* Beruf *der*.

professional [prəˈfeʃənl] ◆ *adj* (*relating to work*) Berufs-; (*expert*) fachmännisch. ◆ *n* (*not amateur*) Fachmann *der*; (SPORT) Profi *der*.

professor [prəˈfesər] *n* (*in UK*) Professor *der* (-in *die*); (*in US*) Dozent *der* (-in *die*).

profile [ˈprəʊfaɪl] *n* Profil *das*; (*description*) Kurzdarstellung *die*.

profit [ˈprɒfɪt] ◆ *n* Profit *der*, Gewinn *der*. ◆ *vi*: **to ~ (from)** profitieren (von).

profitable [ˈprɒfɪtəbl] *adj* gewinnbringend.

profiteroles [prəˈfɪtərəʊlz] *npl* Profiterolen *pl*.

profound [prəˈfaʊnd] *adj* tief.

program [ˈprəʊɡræm] ◆ *n* (COMPUT) Programm *das*; (*Am*) = **programme**. ◆ *vt* (COMPUT) programmieren.

programme [ˈprəʊɡræm] *n* (*Br*) Programm *das*; (*on TV, radio*) Sendung *die*.

progress [*n* ˈprəʊɡres, *vb* prəˈɡres] ◆ *n* (*improvement*) Fortschritt *der*; (*forward movement*) Vorankommen *das*. ◆ *vi* voranǀkommen; (*day, meeting*) vergehen; **to make ~** (*improve*) Fortschritte machen; (*in journey*) voranǀkommen; **in ~** im Gange.

progressive [prəˈɡresɪv] *adj* (*forward-looking*) fortschrittlich.

prohibit [prəˈhɪbɪt] *vt* verbieten; **'smoking strictly ~ed'** 'Rauchen streng verboten'.

project [ˈprɒdʒekt] *n* Projekt *das*; (*at school*) Arbeit *die*.

projector [prəˈdʒektər] *n* Projektor *der*.

prolong [prəˈlɒŋ] *vt* verlängern.

prom [prɒm] *n* (*Am: dance*) Studentenball *der*.

promenade [ˌprɒməˈnɑːd] *n* (*Br: by the sea*) Strandpromenade *die*.

prominent [ˈprɒmɪnənt] *adj* (*person*) prominent; (*noticeable*) auffallend.

promise [ˈprɒmɪs] ◆ *n* Versprechen *das*. ◆ *vt & vi* versprechen; **to show ~** (*work, person*) vielversprechend sein; **I ~ (that) I'll come** ich verspreche, daß ich komme; **to ~ sb sthg** jm etw versprechen; **to ~ to do sthg** versprechen, etw zu tun.

promising [ˈprɒmɪsɪŋ] *adj* vielversprechend.

promote [prəˈməʊt] *vt* befördern.

promotion [prəˈməʊʃn] *n* Beförderung *die*; (*of product*) Sonderangebot *das*.

prompt [prɒmpt] ◆ *adj* (*quick*) prompt. ◆ *adv*: **at six o'clock ~** um Punkt sechs Uhr.

prone [prəʊn] *adj*: **to be ~ to sthg** zu etw neigen; **to be ~ to do sthg** dazu neigen, etw zu tun.

prong [prɒŋ] *n* Zinke *die*.

pronoun [ˈprəʊnaʊn] *n* Pronomen *das*.

pronounce [prəˈnaʊns] *vt* (*word*) ausǀsprechen.

pronunciation [prəˌnʌnsɪˈeɪʃn] *n* Aussprache *die*.

proof [pruːf] *n* (*evidence*) Beweis *der*; **12% ~** 12% vol.

prop [prɒp]: **prop up** *vt sep* stützen.

propeller [prəˈpelər] *n* Propeller *der*.

proper [ˈprɒpər] *adj* richtig; (*behaviour*) anständig.

properly [ˈprɒpəlɪ] *adv* richtig.

property [ˈprɒpətɪ] *n* (*possessions*) Eigentum *das*; (*land*) Besitz *der*; (*fml: building*) Immobilien *pl*; (*quality*) Eigenschaft *die*.

proportion [prəˈpɔːʃn] *n* (*part, amount*) Teil *der*; (*ratio*) Verhältnis *das*; (*in art*) Proportion *die*.

proposal [prəˈpəʊzl] *n* Vorschlag *der*.

propose [prəˈpəʊz] ◆ *vt* vorǀschlagen. ◆ *vi*: **to ~ (to sb)** (jm) einen Heiratsantrag machen.

proposition [ˌprɒpəˈzɪʃn] *n* Vorschlag *der*.

proprietor [prə'praɪətər] n (fml) Eigentümer der (-in die).

prose [prəʊz] n (not poetry) Prosa die; (SCH) Übersetzung die (in die Fremdsprache).

prosecution [ˌprɒsɪ'kjuːʃn] n (JUR: charge) Anklage die.

prospect ['prɒspekt] n Aussicht die.

prospectus [prə'spektəs] (pl -es) n Broschüre die.

prosperous ['prɒspərəs] adj wohlhabend.

prostitute ['prɒstɪtjuːt] n Prostituierte die.

protect [prə'tekt] vt schützen; **to ~ sb/sthg from** jn/etw schützen vor (+D); **to ~ sb/sthg against** jn/etw schützen vor (+D).

protection [prə'tekʃn] n Schutz der.

protection factor n (of suntan lotion) Schutzfaktor der.

protective [prə'tektɪv] adj (person) beschützend; (clothes) Schutz-.

protein ['prəʊtiːn] n Protein das.

protest [n 'prəʊtest, vb prə'test] ◆ n (complaint) Protest der; (demonstration) Protestmarsch der. ◆ vt (Am: protest against) protestieren gegen. ◆ vi: **to ~ (against)** protestieren (gegen).

Protestant ['prɒtɪstənt] n Protestant der (-in die).

protester [prə'testər] n Demonstrant der (-in die).

protractor [prə'træktər] n Winkelmaß das.

protrude [prə'truːd] vi vor|stehen.

proud [praʊd] adj stolz; **to be ~ of** stolz sein auf (+A).

prove [pruːv] (pp -d OR proven [pruːvn]) vt beweisen; (turn out to be) sich erweisen als.

proverb ['prɒvɜːb] n Sprichwort das.

provide [prə'vaɪd] vt (supply) liefern; **to ~ sb with sthg** jn mit etw versorgen. ▶ **provide for** vt fus: **to ~ for sb** für js Lebensunterhalt sorgen.

provided (that) [prə'vaɪdɪd-] conj vorausgesetzt (, daß).

providing (that) [prə'vaɪdɪŋ-] = **provided (that)**.

province ['prɒvɪns] n Provinz die.

provision [prə'vɪʒn] n Vorsorge die; **to make ~ for** Vorsorge für etw treffen.

provisional [prə'vɪʒənl] adj provisorisch.

provisions [prə'vɪʒnz] npl Proviant der.

provocative [prə'vɒkətɪv] adj provozierend.

provoke [prə'vəʊk] vt (cause) hervor|rufen; (annoy) provozieren.

prowl [praʊl] vi herum|streichen.

prune [pruːn] ◆ n Dörrpflaume die. ◆ vt (tree, bush) beschneiden.

PS (abbr of postscript) PS.

psychiatrist [saɪ'kaɪətrɪst] n Psychiater der (-in die).

psychic ['saɪkɪk] adj: **to be ~** übernatürliche Kräfte haben.

psychological [ˌsaɪkə'lɒdʒɪkl] adj psychologisch.

psychologist [saɪ'kɒlədʒɪst] n Psychologe der (Psychologin die).

psychology [saɪ'kɒlədʒɪ] n Psychologie die.

psychotherapist [ˌsaɪkəʊ'θerəpɪst] n Psychotherapeut der (-in die).

pt abbr = **pint**.

PTO (abbr of please turn over) b.w.

pub [pʌb] n Pub der, Kneipe die.

puberty ['pjuːbətɪ] n Pubertät die.

public ['pʌblɪk] ◆ adj öffentlich. ◆ n: **the ~** die Öffentlichkeit; **in ~** öffentlich.

publican ['pʌblɪkən] n (Br) Gastwirt der (-in die).

publication [ˌpʌblɪ'keɪʃn] n Veröffentlichung die.

public bar n (Br) Raum in einem Pub, der weniger bequem ausgestattet ist als die 'lounge bar' oder 'saloon bar'.

public convenience n (Br) öffentliche Toilette die.

public footpath n (Br) öffentlicher Fußweg.

public holiday n gesetzlicher Feiertag.

public house n (Br: (fml)) Pub der, Wirtshaus das.

publicity [pʌb'lɪsɪtɪ] n Publicity die.

public school n (in UK) Privatschule die; (in US) staatliche Schule.

public telephone n öffentlicher Fernsprecher.

public transport n öffentliche Verkehrsmittel pl.

publish ['pʌblɪʃ] vt veröffentlichen.

publisher ['pʌblɪʃə^r] n (person) Verleger der; (company) Verlag der.

publishing ['pʌblɪʃɪŋ] n (industry) Verlagswesen das.

pub lunch n meist einfaches Mittagessen in einem Pub.

pudding ['pʊdɪŋ] n (sweet dish) Pudding der; (Br: course) Nachtisch der.

puddle ['pʌdl] n Pfütze die.

puff [pʌf] ◆ vi (breathe heavily) keuchen. ◆ n (of air) Stoß der; (of smoke) Wolke die; **to ~ at** (cigarette, pipe) ziehen an (+D).

puff pastry n Blätterteig der.

pull [pʊl] ◆ vt ziehen an (+D); (tow) ziehen. ◆ vi ziehen. ◆ n: **to give sthg a ~** an etw (D) ziehen; **to ~ a face** eine Grimasse schneiden; **to ~ a muscle** sich (D) einen Muskel zerren; **to ~ the trigger** ab|drücken; **'pull'** (on door) 'Ziehen'. ▶ **pull apart** vt sep (book) auseinander|reißen; (machine) auseinander|nehmen. ▶ **pull down** vt sep (lower) herunter|ziehen; (demolish) ab|reißen. ▶ **pull in** vi (train) ein|fahren; (car) an|halten. ▶ **pull out** vt sep heraus|ziehen. ◆ vi (train) ab|fahren; (car) aus|scheren; (withdraw) sich zurück|ziehen. ▶ **pull over** vi (car) an den Straßenrand fahren. ▶ **pull up** vt sep (socks, trousers, sleeve) hoch|ziehen. ◆ vi (stop) an|halten.

pulley ['pʊlɪ] (pl **pulleys**) n Flaschenzug der.

pull-out n (Am: beside road) Parkbucht die.

pullover ['pʊl,əʊvə^r] n Pullover der.

pulpit ['pʊlpɪt] n Kanzel die.

pulse [pʌls] n (MED) Puls der.

pump [pʌmp] n Pumpe die. ▶ **pumps** npl (sports shoes) Freizeitschuhe pl. ▶ **pump up** vt sep auf|pumpen.

pumpkin ['pʌmpkɪn] n Kürbis der.

pun [pʌn] n Wortspiel das.

punch [pʌntʃ] ◆ n (blow) Faustschlag der; (drink) Punsch der. ◆ vt (hit) boxen; (ticket) lochen.

Punch and Judy show [-'dʒuːdɪ-] n Kasperltheater das.

punctual ['pʌŋktʃʊəl] adj pünktlich.

punctuation [,pʌŋktʃʊ'eɪʃn] n Interpunktion die.

puncture ['pʌŋktʃə^r] ◆ n (of car tyre) Reifenpanne die; (of bicycle tyre) Platten der. ◆ vt stechen in (+A).

punish ['pʌnɪʃ] vt: **to ~ sb (for sthg)** jn (für etw) bestrafen.

punishment ['pʌnɪʃmənt] n Strafe die.

punk [pʌŋk] n (person) Punker der (-in die); (music) Punk der.

punnet ['pʌnɪt] n (Br) Körbchen das.

pupil ['pjuːpl] n (student) Schüler der (-in die); (of eye) Pupille die.

puppet ['pʌpɪt] n Puppe die.

puppy ['pʌpɪ] n junger Hund.

purchase ['pɜːtʃəs] ◆ vt (fml) kaufen. ◆ n (fml) Kauf der.

pure [pjʊə^r] adj rein.

puree ['pjʊəreɪ] n Püree das.

purely ['pjʊəlɪ] adv rein.

purity ['pjʊərətɪ] n Reinheit die.

purple ['pɜːpl] adj violett.

purpose ['pɜːpəs] n Zweck der; **on ~** absichtlich.

purr [pɜː^r] vi (cat) schnurren.

purse [pɜːs] n (Br: for money) Portemonnaie das; (Am: handbag) Handtasche die.

pursue [pə'sjuː] vt (follow) verfolgen;

(*study, inquiry, matter*) nach|gehen (+D).

pus [pʌs] *n* Eiter *der.*

push [pʊʃ] ◆ *vt* schieben; (*button*) drücken auf (+A); (*product*) puschen. ◆ *vi* schubsen. ◆ *n*: **to give sb/sthg a ~** jm/einer Sache einen Schubs geben; **to ~ sb into doing sthg** jn drängen, etw zu tun; **'push'** (*on door*) 'Drücken'. ► **push in** *vi* (*in queue*) sich vor|drängen. ► **push off** *vi* (*inf: go away*) ab|hauen.

push-button telephone *n* Drucktastentelefon *das.*

pushchair ['pʊʃtʃeər] *n* (Br) Sportwagen *der* (*für Kinder*).

pushed [pʊʃt] *adj* (*inf*): **to be ~ (for time)** in Eile sein.

push-ups *npl* Liegestütze *pl.*

put [pʊt] (*pt & pp inv*) *vt* (*place*) tun; (*place upright*) stellen; (*lay flat*) legen; (*express*) sagen; (*write*) schreiben; (*a question*) stellen; (*estimate*): **to ~ sthg at** etw schätzen auf (+A); **to ~ a child to bed** ein Kind ins Bett bringen; **to ~ money into sthg** Geld in etw (A) investieren; **to ~ sb under pressure** jn unter Druck setzen; **to ~ the blame on sb** jm die Schuld geben. ► **put aside** *vt sep* (*money*) zur Seite legen. ► **put away** *vt sep* (*tidy up*) weg|räumen. ► **put back** *vt sep* (*replace*) zurück|legen; (*postpone*) verschieben; (*clock, watch*) zurück|stellen. ► **put down** *vt sep* (*place*) setzen; (*place upright*) (hin|)stellen; (*lay flat*) (hin|)legen; (*passenger*) ab|setzen; (Br: *animal*) ein|schläfern; (*deposit*) an|zahlen. ► **put forward** *vt sep* (*clock, watch*) vor|stellen; (*suggest*) vor|schlagen. ► **put in** *vt sep* (*insert*) hinein|stecken; (*install*) ein|bauen. ► **put off** *vt sep* (*postpone*) verschieben; (*distract*) ab|lenken; (*repel*) ab|stoßen; (*passenger*) ab|setzen. ► **put on** *vt sep* (*clothes*) an|ziehen; (*glasses*) auf|setzen; (*make-up*) auf|legen; (*television, light, radio*) an|schalten; (*CD, record*) auf|legen; (*tape*) ein|legen; (*play, show*)

auf|führen; **to ~ on weight** zu|nehmen; **to ~ the kettle on** Wasser auf|setzen. ► **put out** *vt sep* (*cigarette, fire, light*) aus|machen; (*publish*) veröffentlichen; (*hand, arm, leg*) aus|strecken; **to ~ sb out** jm Umstände machen; **to ~ one's back out** sich (D) den Rücken verrenken. ► **put together** *vt sep* (*assemble*) zusammen|setzen; (*combine*) zusammen|stellen. ► **put up** *vt sep* (*tent, statue, building*) errichten; (*umbrella*) auf|spannen; (*a notice*) an|schlagen; (*sign*) an|bringen; (*price, rate*) hoch|treiben; (*visitor*) unter|bringen. ◆ *vi* (Br: *in hotel*) unter|kommen. ► **put up with** *vt fus* dulden.

putter ['pʌtər] *n* (*club*) Putter *der.*

putting green ['pʌtɪŋ-] *n* Platz *der* zum Putten.

putty ['pʌtɪ] *n* Kitt *der.*

puzzle ['pʌzl] ◆ *n* Rätsel *das*; (*jigsaw*) Puzzle *das.* ◆ *vt* verblüffen.

puzzling ['pʌzlɪŋ] *adj* verblüffend.

pyjamas [pəˈdʒɑːməz] *npl* (Br) Schlafanzug *der.*

pylon ['paɪlən] *n* Mast *der.*

pyramid ['pɪrəmɪd] *n* Pyramide *die.*

Pyrenees [ˌpɪrəˈniːz] *npl*: **the ~** die Pyrenäen *pl.*

Pyrex® ['paɪreks] *n* ≈ Jenaer Glas® *das.*

quail [kweɪl] *n* Wachtel *die.*

quail's eggs *npl* Wachteleier *pl.*

quaint [kweɪnt] *adj* (*village, cottage*) malerisch.

qualification [ˌkwɒlɪfɪˈkeɪʃn] *n* (*diploma*) Zeugnis *das*; (*ability*) Qualifikation *die.*

qualified ['kwɒlɪfaɪd] *adj* qualifiziert.

qualify ['kwɒlɪfaɪ] *vi* sich qualifizieren.

quality ['kwɒlətɪ] ♦ *n* Qualität *die*; (*feature*) Eigenschaft *die*. ♦ *adj* (*product*) Qualitäts-; (*newspaper*) seriös.

quarantine ['kwɒrəntiːn] *n* Quarantäne *die*.

quarrel ['kwɒrəl] ♦ *n* Streit *der*. ♦ *vi* sich streiten.

quarry ['kwɒrɪ] *n* (*for stone, sand*) Steinbruch *der*.

quart [kwɔːt] *n* = 0,14 Liter, Quart *das*.

quarter ['kwɔːtər] *n* Viertel *das*; (*Am: coin*) Vierteldollar *der*; (*4 ounces*) = 0,1134 kg, Viertelpfund *das*; (*three months*) Quartal *das*; (a) ~ **of an hour** eine Viertelstunde; (a) ~ **to five** (Br) Viertel vor fünf; (a) ~ **of five** (Am) Viertel vor fünf; (a) ~ **past five** (Br) Viertel nach fünf; (a) ~ **after five** (Am) Viertel nach fünf.

quarterpounder [ˌkwɔːtəˈpaʊndər] *n* Viertelpfünder *der* (*großer Hamburger*).

quartet [kwɔːˈtet] *n* Quartett *das*.

quartz [kwɔːts] *adj* (*watch*) Quarz-.

quay [kiː] *n* Kai *der*.

queasy ['kwiːzɪ] *adj* (*inf*) unwohl.

queen [kwiːn] *n* Königin *die*; (*in chess, cards*) Dame *die*.

queer [kwɪər] *adj* (*strange*) seltsam; (*inf: ill*) unwohl; (*inf: homosexual*) schwul.

quench [kwentʃ] *vt*: **to ~ one's thirst** seinen Durst löschen.

query ['kwɪərɪ] *n* Frage *die*.

question ['kwestʃn] ♦ *n* Frage *die*. ♦ *vt* (*person*) auslfragen; (*subj: police*) verhören; **it's out of the ~** das kommt nicht in Frage.

question mark *n* Fragezeichen *das*.

questionnaire [ˌkwestʃəˈneər] *n* Fragebogen *der*.

queue [kjuː] ♦ *n* (Br) Schlange *die*. ♦ *vi* (Br) Schlange stehen. ▶ **queue up** *vi* (Br) Schlange stehen.

quiche [kiːʃ] *n* Quiche *die*.

quick [kwɪk] *adj* & *adv* schnell.

quickly ['kwɪklɪ] *adv* schnell.

quid [kwɪd] (*pl inv*) *n* (Br: inf: *pound*) Pfund *das*.

quiet ['kwaɪət] ♦ *adj* ruhig; (*voice, car*) leise. ♦ *n* Ruhe *die*; **keep ~!** Ruhe!; **to keep ~** still sein; **to keep ~ about sthg** etw verschweigen.

quieten ['kwaɪətn]: **quieten down** *vi* sich beruhigen.

quietly ['kwaɪətlɪ] *adv* ruhig; (*speak*) leise.

quilt [kwɪlt] *n* (*duvet*) Steppdecke *die*; (*eiderdown*) Patchworkdecke *die*.

quince [kwɪns] *n* Quitte *die*.

quirk [kwɜːk] *n* Schrulle *die*.

quit [kwɪt] (*pt & pp inv*) ♦ *vi* (*resign*) kündigen; (*give up*) auflhören. ♦ *vt* (*Am: school, job*) auflgeben; **to ~ doing sthg** auflhören, etw zu tun.

quite [kwaɪt] *adv* (*fairly*) ziemlich; (*completely*) ganz; **not ~** nicht ganz; ~ **a lot (of)** ziemlich viel.

quiz [kwɪz] (*pl* -**zes**) *n* Quiz *das*.

quota ['kwəʊtə] *n* Quote *die*.

quotation [kwəʊˈteɪʃn] *n* (*phrase*) Zitat *das*; (*estimate*) Kostenvoranschlag *der*.

quotation marks *npl* Anführungszeichen *pl*.

quote [kwəʊt] ♦ *vt* (*phrase, writer*) zitieren; (*price*) nennen. ♦ *n* (*phrase*) Zitat *das*; (*estimate*) Kostenvoranschlag *der*.

R

rabbit ['ræbɪt] *n* Kaninchen *das*.

rabies ['reɪbiːz] *n* Tollwut *die*.

RAC *n* = ADAC *der*.

race [reɪs] ♦ *n* (*competition*) Rennen *das*; (*ethnic group*) Rasse *die*. ♦ *vi* (*compete*) um die Wette laufen/fahren etc; (go fast) **rennen**; (engine) **durch|drehen.** ◆ vt um die Wette laufen/fahren etc mit.

racecourse ['reɪskɔːs] n Rennbahn die.

racehorse ['reɪshɔːs] n Rennpferd das.

racetrack ['reɪstræk] n (for horses) Pferderennbahn die.

racial ['reɪʃl] adj Rassen-.

racing ['reɪsɪŋ] n: **(horse)** ~ Pferderennen das.

racing car n Rennwagen der.

racism ['reɪsɪzm] n Rassismus der.

racist ['reɪsɪst] n Rassist der (-in die).

rack [ræk] n (for coats, hats) Ständer der; (for plates, bottles) Gestell das; **(luggage)** ~ Gepäckablage die; ~ **of lamb** Lammrücken der.

racket ['rækɪt] n Schläger der; (noise) Lärm der.

racquet ['rækɪt] n Schläger der.

radar ['reɪdɑːr] n Radar der.

radiation [,reɪdɪ'eɪʃn] n Strahlung die.

radiator ['reɪdɪeɪtər] n (in building) Heizkörper der; (of vehicle) Kühler der.

radical ['rædɪkl] adj radikal.

radii ['reɪdɪaɪ] pl → **radius**.

radio ['reɪdɪəʊ] (pl -s) ◆ n (device) Radio das; (system) Rundfunk der. ◆ vt (person) an|funken; **on the** ~ im Radio.

radioactive [,reɪdɪəʊ'æktɪv] adj radioaktiv.

radio alarm n Radiowecker der.

radish ['rædɪʃ] n Radieschen das.

radius ['reɪdɪəs] (pl radii) n Radius der.

raffle ['ræfl] n Tombola die.

raft [rɑːft] n (of wood) Floß das; (inflatable) Schlauchboot das.

rafter ['rɑːftər] n Sparren der.

rag [ræg] n (old cloth) Lumpen der.

rage [reɪdʒ] n Wut die.

raid [reɪd] ◆ n (attack) Angriff der; (by police) Razzia die; (robbery) Überfall der. ◆ vt (subj: police) eine Razzia machen in (+D); (subj: thieves) überfallen.

rail [reɪl] ◆ n (bar) Stange die; (on stairs) Geländer das; (for train, tram) Schiene die. ◆ adj (travel, transport, network) Bahn-; **by** ~ mit der Bahn.

railcard ['reɪlkɑːd] n (Br) Berechtigungsausweis für verbilligte Bahnfahrten.

railings ['reɪlɪŋz] npl Gitter das.

railroad ['reɪlrəʊd] (Am) = **railway**.

railway ['reɪlweɪ] n (system) Eisenbahn die; (track) Eisenbahnstrecke die; (rails) Gleis das.

railway line n (route) Bahn die; (track) Eisenbahnstrecke die; (rails) Gleis das.

railway station n Bahnhof der.

rain [reɪn] ◆ n Regen der. ◆ v impers regnen; **it's ~ing** es regnet.

rainbow ['reɪnbəʊ] n Regenbogen der.

raincoat ['reɪnkəʊt] n Regenmantel der.

raindrop ['reɪndrɒp] n Regentropfen der.

rainfall ['reɪnfɔːl] n Niederschlag der.

rainy ['reɪnɪ] adj regnerisch.

raise [reɪz] ◆ vt (lift) heben; (increase) erhöhen; (money) beschaffen; (child) großziehen; (cattle, sheep etc) auf|ziehen; (question, subject) auf|werfen. ◆ n (Am: pay increase) Gehaltserhöhung die.

raisin ['reɪzn] n Rosine die.

rake [reɪk] n Harke die.

rally ['rælɪ] n (public meeting) Kundgebung die; (motor race) Rallye die; (in tennis, badminton, squash) Ballwechsel der.

ram [ræm] ◆ n (sheep) Widder der. ◆ vt (bang into) rammen.

Ramadan [,ræmə'dæn] n Ramadan der.

ramble ['ræmbl] n Wanderung die.

ramp [ræmp] n Rampe die; **'ramp'**

(Am: *to freeway*) Auffahrt *die*; (Br: *bump*) Schild an Baustellen, *das auf Straßenschäden hinweist.*

ramparts ['ræmpɑːts] *npl* Wall *der.*

ran [ræn] *pt* → **run.**

ranch [rɑːntʃ] *n* Ranch *die.*

ranch dressing *n* (Am) cremige, würzige Soße.

rancid ['rænsɪd] *adj* ranzig.

random ['rændəm] ◆ *adj* willkürlich. ◆ *n*: **at ~** wahllos.

rang [ræŋ] *pt* → **ring.**

range [reɪndʒ] ◆ *n* (of radio, aircraft) Reichweite *die*; (of prices, temperatures, ages) Reihe *die*; (selection of products) Auswahl *die*; (of hills, mountains) Kette *die*; (for shooting) Schießstand *der*; (cooker) Kochherd *der.* ◆ *vi* (vary): **to ~ from X to Y** zwischen X und Y liegen.

ranger ['reɪndʒər] *n* (of park, forest) Förster *der* (-in *die*).

rank [ræŋk] ◆ *n* Rang *der.* ◆ *adj* (smell, taste) übel.

ransom ['rænsəm] *n* Lösegeld *das.*

rap [ræp] *n* (music) Rap *der.*

rape [reɪp] ◆ *n* Vergewaltigung *die.* ◆ *vt* vergewaltigen.

rapid ['ræpɪd] *adj* schnell. ▶ **rapids** *npl* Stromschnellen *pl.*

rapidly ['ræpɪdlɪ] *adv* schnell.

rapist ['reɪpɪst] *n* Vergewaltiger *der.*

rare [reər] *adj* selten; (meat) englisch gebraten.

rarely ['reəlɪ] *adv* selten.

rash [ræʃ] ◆ *n* Ausschlag *der.* ◆ *adj* unbedacht.

rasher ['ræʃər] *n* Streifen *der.*

raspberry ['rɑːzbərɪ] *n* Himbeere *die.*

rat [ræt] *n* Ratte *die.*

ratatouille [rætə'tuːɪ] *n* Ratatouille *die.*

rate [reɪt] ◆ *n* (level) Rate *die*; (charge) Satz *der*; (speed) Tempo *das.* ◆ *vt* (consider) einlschätzen; (deserve) verdienen; **~ of exchange** Wechselkurs *der*; **at any ~** auf jeden Fall; **at this ~** auf diese Weise.

rather ['rɑːðər] *adv* (quite) ziemlich; (expressing preference) lieber; **I'd ~ not** lieber nicht; **would you ~ ...?** möchtest du lieber ...?; **~ than** statt.

ratio ['reɪʃɪəʊ] (pl **-s**) *n* Verhältnis *das.*

ration ['ræʃn] *n* Ration *die.* ▶ **rations** *npl* (food) Ration *die.*

rational ['ræʃnl] *adj* rational.

rattle ['rætl] ◆ *n* (of baby) Rassel *die.* ◆ *vi* klappern.

rave [reɪv] *n* (party) Rave *der.*

raven ['reɪvn] *n* Rabe *der.*

ravioli [rævɪ'əʊlɪ] *n* Ravioli *pl.*

raw [rɔː] *adj* roh.

raw material *n* Rohstoff *der.*

ray [reɪ] *n* Strahl *der.*

razor ['reɪzər] *n* Rasierapparat *der.*

razor blade *n* Rasierklinge *die.*

Rd (abbr of Road) Str.

re [riː] *prep* betreffs (+G).

RE *n* (abbr of religious education) Religionsunterricht *der.*

reach [riːtʃ] ◆ *vt* erreichen; (town, country) anlkommen in (+D); (manage to touch) kommen an (+A); (extend up to) reichen bis; (agreement, decision) kommen zu. ◆ *n*: **out of ~** außer Reichweite; **within ~ of the beach** im Strandbereich. ▶ **reach out** *vi*: **to ~ out (for)** die Hand auslstrecken (nach).

react [rɪ'ækt] *vi* reagieren.

reaction [rɪ'ækʃn] *n* Reaktion *die.*

read [riːd] (pt & pp inv [red]) ◆ *vt* lesen; (say aloud) vorllesen; (subj: sign, note) besagen; (subj: meter, gauge) anlzeigen. ◆ *vi* lesen; **to ~ about sthg** von etw lesen. ▶ **read out** *vt sep* laut vorllesen.

reader ['riːdər] *n* Leser *der* (-in *die*).

readily ['redɪlɪ] *adv* (willingly) gern; (easily) leicht.

reading ['riːdɪŋ] *n* Lesen *das*; (of meter, gauge) Stand *der.*

reading matter *n* Lesestoff *der.*

ready ['redɪ] *adj* (prepared) fertig; **to be ~ for sthg** (prepared) für etw fertig sein; **to be ~ to do sthg** (*willing*) bereit sein, etw zu tun; (*likely*) im Begriff sein, etw zu tun; **to get ~** sich fertig|machen; **to get sthg ~** etw fertig|machen.

ready cash *n* Bargeld *das*.

ready-cooked [-kʊkt] *adj* vorgekocht.

ready-to-wear *adj* von der Stange.

real ['rɪəl] ◆ *adj* (*actual*) wirklich; (*genuine, for emphasis*) echt. ◆ *adv* (*Am*) echt, wirklich.

real ale *n* dunkles, nach traditionellem Rezept gebrautes britisches Bier.

real estate *n* Immobilien *pl*.

realistic [,rɪə'lɪstɪk] *adj* realistisch.

reality [rɪ'ælətɪ] *n* Realität *die*; **in ~** in Wirklichkeit.

realize ['rɪəlaɪz] *vt* (*become aware of*) erkennen; (*know*) wissen; (*ambition, goal*) verwirklichen.

really ['rɪəlɪ] *adv* wirklich; **not ~** eigentlich nicht; **~?** (*expressing surprise*) wirklich?

realtor ['rɪəltər] *n* (*Am*) Immobilienhändler *der* (-in *die*).

rear [rɪər] ◆ *adj* hintere(-r)(-s); (*window*) Heck-, Hinter-. ◆ *n* (*back*) Rückseite *die*.

rearrange [,riːə'reɪndʒ] *vt* (*room, furniture*) um|stellen; (*meeting*) verlegen.

rearview mirror ['rɪəvjuː-] *n* Rückspiegel *der*.

rear-wheel drive *n* Auto *das* mit Hinterradantrieb.

reason ['riːzn] *n* Grund *der*; **for some ~** aus irgendeinem Grund.

reasonable ['riːznəbl] *adj* (*fair*) angemessen; (*not too expensive*) preiswert; (*sensible*) vernünftig; (*quite big*) annehmbar.

reasonably ['riːznəblɪ] *adv* (*quite*) ziemlich.

reasoning ['riːznɪŋ] *n* Denken *das*.

reassure [,riːə'ʃɔːr] *vt* versichern (+D).

reassuring [,riːə'ʃɔːrɪŋ] *adj* beruhigend.

rebate ['riːbeɪt] *n* Rückzahlung *die*.

rebel [rɪ'bel] ◆ *n* Rebell *der* (-in *die*). ◆ *vi* rebellieren.

rebound [rɪ'baʊnd] *vi* ab|prallen.

rebuild [,riː'bɪld] (*pt & pp* **rebuilt** [,riː-'bɪlt]) *vt* wieder auf|bauen.

rebuke [rɪ'bjuːk] *vt* tadeln.

recall [rɪ'kɔːl] *vt* (*remember*) sich erinnern an (+A).

receipt [rɪ'siːt] *n* (*for goods, money*) Quittung *die*; **on ~ of** bei Erhalt von.

receive [rɪ'siːv] *vt* erhalten; (*guest*) empfangen.

receiver [rɪ'siːvər] *n* (*of phone*) Hörer *der*.

recent ['riːsnt] *adj* kürzlich, erfolgte(-r)(-s).

recently ['riːsntlɪ] *adv* kürzlich.

receptacle [rɪ'septəkl] *n* (*fml*) Behälter *der*.

reception [rɪ'sepʃn] *n* Empfang *der*; (*in hotel*) Rezeption *die*; (*in hospital*) Aufnahme *die*.

reception desk *n* (*in hotel*) Rezeption *die*.

receptionist [rɪ'sepʃənɪst] *n* (*in hotel*) Empfangsdame *die*; (*man*) Empfangschef *der*; (*at doctor's*) Sprechstundenhilfe *die*.

recess ['riːses] *n* (*in wall*) Nische *die*; (*Am: SCH*) Pause *die*.

recession [rɪ'seʃn] *n* Rezession *die*.

recipe ['resɪpɪ] *n* Rezept *das*.

recite [rɪ'saɪt] *vt* (*poem*) auf|sagen; (*list*) auf|zählen.

reckless ['reklɪs] *adj* leichtsinnig.

reckon ['rekn] *vt* (*inf: think*) denken. ► **reckon on** *vt fus* rechnen mit. ► **reckon with** *vt fus* (*expect*) rechnen mit.

reclaim [rɪ'kleɪm] *vt* (*baggage*) ab|holen.

reclining seat [rɪ'klaɪnɪŋ-] *n* Liegesitz *der*.

recognition [,rekəg'nɪʃn] *n* (*recognizing*) Erkennen *das*; (*acceptance*) Anerkennung *die*.

recognize ['rekəgnaız] vt erkennen; (accept) an|erkennen.

recollect [,rekə'lekt] vt sich erinnern an (+A).

recommend [,rekə'mend] vt empfehlen; **to ~ sb to do sthg** jm empfehlen, etw zu tun.

recommendation [,rekəmen-'deıʃn] n Empfehlung die.

reconsider [,ri:kən'sıdər] vt sich (D) nochmals überlegen.

reconstruct [,ri:kən'strʌkt] vt wieder auf|bauen.

record [n 'rekɔ:d, vb rı'kɔ:d] ◆ n (MUS) Schallplatte die; (best performance, highest level) Rekord der; (account) Aufzeichnung die. ◆ vt (keep account of) auf|zeichnen; (on tape) auf|nehmen.

recorded delivery [rı'kɔ:dıd-] n (Br) Einschreiben das.

recorder [rı'kɔ:dər] n (tape recorder) Kassettenrecorder der; (instrument) Blockflöte die.

recording [rı'kɔ:dıŋ] n (tape, record) Aufnahme die.

record player n Plattenspieler der.

record shop n Schallplattengeschäft das.

recover [rı'kʌvər] ◆ vt (get back) sicher|stellen. ◆ vi (from illness, shock) sich erholen.

recovery [rı'kʌvərı] n (from illness) Erholung die.

recovery vehicle n (Br) Abschleppwagen der.

recreation [,rekrı'eıʃn] n Erholung die.

recreation ground n Spielplatz der.

recruit [rı'kru:t] ◆ n (to army) Rekrut der. ◆ vt (staff) an|werben.

recruitment [rı'kru:tmənt] n Anwerbung die.

rectangle ['rek,tæŋgl] n Rechteck das.

rectangular [rek'tæŋgjʊlər] adj rechteckig.

recycle [,ri:'saıkl] vt recyceln.

red [red] ◆ adj rot. ◆ n Rot das; **in the ~** in den roten Zahlen.

red cabbage n Rotkohl der, Blaukraut das (Österr).

Red Cross n Rotes Kreuz.

redcurrant ['redkʌrənt] n rote Johannisbeere.

redecorate [,ri:'dekəreıt] vt neu tapezieren/streichen.

redhead ['redhed] n Rothaarige der, die.

red-hot adj (metal) rotglühend.

redial [ri:'daıəl] vi wieder wählen.

redirect [,ri:dı'rekt] vt (letter) nach|senden; (traffic, plane) um|leiten.

red pepper n rote Paprikaschote.

reduce [rı'dju:s] ◆ vt reduzieren. ◆ vi (Am: slim) ab|nehmen.

reduced price [rı'dju:st-] n reduzierter Preis.

reduction [rı'dʌkʃn] n (in size) Verkleinerung die; (in price) Reduzierung die.

redundancy [rı'dʌndənsı] n (Br) Entlassung die.

redundant [rı'dʌndənt] adj (Br): **to be made ~** entlassen werden.

red wine n Rotwein der.

reed [ri:d] n (plant) Schilf das.

reef [ri:f] n Riff das.

reek [ri:k] vi stinken.

reel [ri:l] n (of thread) Spule die; (on fishing rod) Rolle die.

refectory [rı'fektərı] n Speisesaal der.

refer [rı'fɜ:r]: **refer to** vt fus (speak about) sich beziehen auf (+A); (relate to) betreffen; (dictionary, book) nach|schlagen in (+D).

referee [,refə'ri:] n (SPORT) Schiedsrichter der (-in die).

reference ['refrəns] ◆ n (mention) Erwähnung die; (letter for job) Referenz die. ◆ adj (book, library) Nachschlage-; **with ~ to** bezüglich (+G).

referendum [,refə'rendəm] n Volksabstimmung die.

refill [n 'riːfɪl, vb ˌriːˈfɪl] ◆ vt nach|füllen. ◆ n (for ballpoint pen) Mine die; (for fountain pen) Patrone die; (inf: drink): **would you like a ~?** darf ich dir nachschenken?

refinery [rɪˈfaɪnərɪ] n Raffinerie die.

reflect [rɪˈflekt] ◆ vt (light, heat, image) reflektieren. ◆ vi (think) nach|denken.

reflection [rɪˈflekʃn] n (image) Spiegelbild das.

reflector [rɪˈflektər] n (on bicycle, car) Rückstrahler der.

reflex ['riːfleks] n Reflex der.

reflexive [rɪˈfleksɪv] adj reflexiv.

reform [rɪˈfɔːm] ◆ n Reform die. ◆ vt reformieren.

refresh [rɪˈfreʃ] vt erfrischen.

refreshing [rɪˈfreʃɪŋ] adj erfrischend.

refreshments [rɪˈfreʃmənts] npl Erfrischungen pl.

refrigerator [rɪˈfrɪdʒəreɪtər] n Kühlschrank der.

refugee [ˌrefjʊˈdʒiː] n Flüchtling der.

refund [n 'riːfʌnd, vb rɪˈfʌnd] ◆ n Rückerstattung die. ◆ vt zurück|erstatten.

refundable [rɪˈfʌndəbl] adj rückerstattbar.

refusal [rɪˈfjuːzl] n Weigerung die.

refuse¹ [rɪˈfjuːz] ◆ vt (not accept) ab|lehnen; (not allow) verweigern. ◆ vi ab|lehnen; **to ~ to do sthg** sich weigern, etw zu tun.

refuse² ['refjuːs] n (fml) Abfall der.

refuse collection ['refjuːs-] n (fml) Müllabfuhr die.

regard [rɪˈgɑːd] ◆ vt (consider) an|sehen. ◆ n: **with ~ to** in bezug auf (+A); **as ~s** in bezug auf (+A). ▶ **regards** npl (in greetings) Grüße pl; **give them my ~s** grüße sie von mir.

regarding [rɪˈgɑːdɪŋ] prep bezüglich (+G).

regardless [rɪˈgɑːdlɪs] adv trotzdem; **~ of** ohne Rücksicht auf (+A).

reggae ['regeɪ] n Reggae der.

regiment ['redʒɪmənt] n Regiment das.

region ['riːdʒən] n Gebiet das; **in the ~ of** im Bereich von.

regional ['riːdʒənl] adj regional.

register ['redʒɪstər] ◆ n Register das. ◆ vt registrieren; (subj: machine, gauge) an|zeigen. ◆ vi sich registrieren lassen; (at hotel) sich ein|tragen.

registered ['redʒɪstəd] adj (letter, parcel) eingeschrieben.

registration [ˌredʒɪˈstreɪʃn] n (for course) Einschreibung die; (at conference) Anmeldung die.

registration (number) n polizeiliches Kennzeichen.

registry office ['redʒɪstrɪ-] n Standesamt das.

regret [rɪˈgret] ◆ n Bedauern das. ◆ vt bedauern; **to ~ doing sthg** etw leider tun müssen; **we ~ any inconvenience caused** wir bedauern etwa entstandene Unannehmlichkeiten.

regrettable [rɪˈgretəbl] adj bedauerlich.

regular ['regjʊlər] ◆ adj regelmäßig; (intervals) gleichmäßig; (time) üblich; (Coke, fries) normal. ◆ n (customer) Stammkunde der (-kundin die).

regularly ['regjʊləlɪ] adv regelmäßig; (spaced, distributed) gleichmäßig.

regulate ['regjʊleɪt] vt regulieren.

regulation [ˌregjʊˈleɪʃn] n (rule) Regelung die.

rehearsal [rɪˈhɜːsl] n Probe die.

rehearse [rɪˈhɜːs] vt proben.

reign [reɪn] ◆ n Herrschaft die. ◆ vi (monarch) regieren.

reimburse [ˌriːɪmˈbɜːs] vt (fml) zurück|erstatten.

reindeer ['reɪnˌdɪər] (pl inv) n Rentier das.

reinforce [ˌriːɪnˈfɔːs] vt verstärken; (argument, opinion) bestärken.

reinforcements [ˌriːɪnˈfɔːsmənts] *npl* Verstärkung *die*.

reins [reɪnz] *npl* (*for horse*) Zügel *der*; (*for child*) Leine *die*.

reject [rɪˈdʒekt] *vt* abllehnen; (*subj: machine*) nicht anlnehmen.

rejection [rɪˈdʒekʃn] *n* Ablehnung *die*.

rejoin [ˌriːˈdʒɔɪn] *vt* (*motorway*) wieder kommen auf (+A).

relapse [rɪˈlæps] *n* Rückfall *der*.

relate [rɪˈleɪt] ◆ *vt* (*connect*) in Zusammenhang bringen. ◆ *vi*: **to ~ to** (*be connected with*) in Zusammenhang stehen mit; (*concern*) sich beziehen auf (+A).

related [rɪˈleɪtɪd] *adj* verwandt.

relation [rɪˈleɪʃn] *n* (*member of family*) Verwandte *der, die*; (*connection*) Beziehung *die*; **in ~ to** in bezug auf (+A). ► **relations** *npl* (*between countries, people*) Beziehungen *pl*.

relationship [rɪˈleɪʃnʃɪp] *n* Beziehung *die*.

relative [ˈrelətɪv] ◆ *adj* relativ; (GRAMM) Relativ-. ◆ *n* Verwandte *der, die*.

relatively [ˈrelətɪvlɪ] *adv* relativ.

relax [rɪˈlæks] *vi* sich entspannen.

relaxation [ˌriːlækˈseɪʃn] *n* Entspannung *die*.

relaxed [rɪˈlækst] *adj* entspannt.

relaxing [rɪˈlæksɪŋ] *adj* entspannend.

relay [ˈriːleɪ] *n* (*race*) Staffel *die*.

release [rɪˈliːs] ◆ *vt* (*set free*) freillassen; (*let go of*) losllassen; (*record, film*) herauslbringen; (*brake, catch*) lösen. ◆ *n*: **a new ~** (*film*) ein neuer Film; (*record*) eine neue Platte.

relegate [ˈrelɪgeɪt] *vt*: **to be ~d** (SPORT) ablsteigen.

relevant [ˈreləvənt] *adj* relevant; (*appropriate*) entsprechend.

reliable [rɪˈlaɪəbl] *adj* (*person, machine*) zuverlässig.

relic [ˈrelɪk] *n* (*vestige*) Relikt *das*.

relief [rɪˈliːf] *n* (*gladness*) Er-leichterung *die*; (*aid*) Hilfe *die*.

relief road *n* Entlastungsstraße *die*.

relieve [rɪˈliːv] *vt* (*pain, headache*) lindern.

relieved [rɪˈliːvd] *adj* erleichtert.

religion [rɪˈlɪdʒn] *n* Religion *die*.

religious [rɪˈlɪdʒəs] *adj* (*of religion*) Religions-; (*devout*) gläubig.

relish [ˈrelɪʃ] *n* (*sauce*) dickflüssige Soße.

reluctant [rɪˈlʌktənt] *adj* widerwillig.

rely [rɪˈlaɪ]: **rely on** *vt fus* (*trust*) sich verlassen auf (+A); (*depend on*) abhängig sein von.

remain [rɪˈmeɪn] *vi* bleiben; (*be left over*) übriglbleiben. ► **remains** *npl* Überreste *pl*.

remainder [rɪˈmeɪndər] *n* Rest *der*.

remaining [rɪˈmeɪnɪŋ] *adj* restlich.

remark [rɪˈmɑːk] ◆ *n* Bemerkung *die*. ◆ *vt* bemerken.

remarkable [rɪˈmɑːkəbl] *adj* bemerkenswert.

remedy [ˈremədɪ] *n* (*medicine*) Heilmittel *das*; (*solution*) Lösung *die*.

remember [rɪˈmembər] ◆ *vt* sich erinnern an (+A); (*not forget*) denken an (+A). ◆ *vi* sich erinnern; **to ~ doing sthg** sich daran erinnern, etw getan zu haben; **to ~ to do sthg** daran denken, etw zu tun.

remind [rɪˈmaɪnd] *vt*: **to ~ sb of sthg** jn an etw (A) erinnern; **to ~ sb to do sthg** jn daran erinnern, etw zu tun.

reminder [rɪˈmaɪndər] *n* (*for bill, library book*) Mahnung *die*.

remittance [rɪˈmɪtns] *n* (*money*) Überweisung *die*.

remnant [ˈremnənt] *n* Rest *der*.

remote [rɪˈməut] *adj* entfernt.

remote control *n* (*device*) Fernbedienung *die*.

removal [rɪˈmuːvl] *n* Entfernung *die*; (*of furniture*) Umzug *der*.

removal van *n* Möbelwagen *der*.

remove [rɪˈmuːv] *vt* entfernen; (*clothes*) auslziehen.

renew [rɪ'njuː] vt (licence, membership) verlängern.

renovate ['renəveɪt] vt renovieren.

renowned [rɪ'naʊnd] adj berühmt.

rent [rent] ◆ n Miete die. ◆ vt mieten.

rental ['rentl] n (money) Leihgebühr die.

repaid [riː'peɪd] pt & pp → **repay**.

repair [rɪ'peəʳ] ◆ vt reparieren. ◆ n: **in good ~** in gutem Zustand. ▶ **repairs** npl Reparatur die.

repair kit n (for bicycle) Flickzeug das.

repay [riː'peɪ] (pt & pp **repaid**) vt (money) zurücklzahlen; (favour, kindness) sich revanchieren für.

repayment [riː'peɪmənt] n Rückzahlung die.

repeat [rɪ'piːt] ◆ vt wiederholen. ◆ n (on TV, radio) Wiederholung die.

repetition [ˌrepɪ'tɪʃn] n Wiederholung die.

repetitive [rɪ'petɪtɪv] adj eintönig.

replace [rɪ'pleɪs] vt ersetzen; (put back) zurücklsetzen.

replacement [rɪ'pleɪsmənt] n Ersatz der.

replay ['riːpleɪ] n (rematch) Wiederholungsspiel das; (on TV) Wiederholung die.

reply [rɪ'plaɪ] ◆ n Antwort die. ◆ vt & vi antworten (+D).

report [rɪ'pɔːt] ◆ n Bericht der; (Br: SCH) Zeugnis das. ◆ vt (announce) berichten; (theft, disappearance, person) melden. ◆ vi: **to ~ (on)** berichten (über (+A); **to ~ to sb** (go to) sich bei jm melden.

report card n Zeugnis das.

reporter [rɪ'pɔːtəʳ] n Reporter der (-in die).

represent [ˌreprɪ'zent] vt (act on behalf of) vertreten; (symbolize) darstellen.

representative [ˌreprɪ'zentətɪv] n Vertreter der (-in die).

repress [rɪ'pres] vt unterdrücken.

reprieve [rɪ'priːv] n (delay) Aufschub der.

reprimand ['reprɪmɑːnd] vt tadeln.

reproach [rɪ'prəʊtʃ] vt Vorwürfe machen (+D).

reproduction [ˌriːprə'dʌkʃn] n (of painting, furniture) Reproduktion die.

reptile ['reptaɪl] n Reptil das.

republic [rɪ'pʌblɪk] n Republik die.

Republican [rɪ'pʌblɪkən] ◆ n (in US) Republikaner der (-in die). ◆ adj (in US) republikanisch.

repulsive [rɪ'pʌlsɪv] adj abstoßend.

reputable ['repjʊtəbl] adj angesehen.

reputation [ˌrepjʊ'teɪʃn] n Ruf der, Ansehen das.

reputedly [rɪ'pjuːtɪdlɪ] adv angeblich.

request [rɪ'kwest] ◆ n Bitte die. ◆ vt bitten um; **to ~ sb to do sthg** jn bitten, etw zu tun; **available on ~** auf Anfrage erhältlich.

request stop n (Br) Bedarfshaltestelle die.

require [rɪ'kwaɪəʳ] vt (need) brauchen; **to be ~d to do sthg** etw tun müssen.

requirement [rɪ'kwaɪəmənt] n (condition) Erfordernis das; (need) Bedarf der.

resat [ˌriː'sæt] pt & pp → **resit**.

rescue ['reskjuː] vt retten.

research [rɪ's3ːtʃ] n Forschung die.

resemblance [rɪ'zembləns] n Ähnlichkeit die.

resemble [rɪ'zembl] vt ähneln (+D).

resent [rɪ'zent] vt übellnehmen.

reservation [ˌrezə'veɪʃn] n (booking) Reservierung die; (doubt) Zweifel der; **to make a ~** reservieren.

reserve [rɪ'zɜːv] ◆ n (SPORT) Reservespieler der (-in die); (for wildlife) Reservat das. ◆ vt reservieren.

reserved [rɪ'zɜːvd] adj (booked) reserviert; (shy) verschlossen.

reservoir ['rezəvwɑːʳ] n Reservoir das.

reset [ˌriː'set] (*pt* & *pp inv*) *vt* (*watch, meter, device*) neu stellen.

reside [rɪ'zaɪd] *vi* (*fml: live*) wohnhaft sein.

residence ['rezɪdəns] *n* (*fml: house*) Wohnsitz *der*; **place of ~** Wohnsitz *der*.

residence permit *n* Aufenthaltserlaubnis *die*.

resident ['rezɪdənt] *n* (*of country*) Bewohner *der* (-in *die*); (*of hotel*) Gast *der*; (*of area*) Anwohner *der* (-in *die*); (*of house*) Hausbewohner *der* (-in *die*); **'~s only'** (*for parking*) 'Parken nur für Anlieger'.

residential [ˌrezɪ'denʃl] *adj* (*area*) Wohn-.

residue ['rezɪdjuː] *n* Rest *der*.

resign [rɪ'zaɪn] ◆ *vi* (*from job*) kündigen. ◆ *vt*: **to ~ o.s. to sthg** sich mit etw ablfinden.

resignation [ˌrezɪg'neɪʃn] *n* (*from job*) Kündigung *die*.

resilient [rɪ'zɪlɪənt] *adj* unverwüstlich.

resist [rɪ'zɪst] *vt* (*temptation*) widerstehen (+D); (*fight against*) sich widersetzen (+D); **I can't ~ cream cakes** ich kann Sahnetorte nicht widerstehen; **to ~ doing sthg** etw nicht tun.

resistance [rɪ'zɪstəns] *n* Widerstand *der*.

resit [ˌriː'sɪt] (*pt* & *pp* **resat**) *vt* wiederholen.

resolution [ˌrezə'luːʃn] *n* (*promise*) Vorsatz *der*.

resolve [rɪ'zɒlv] *vt* (*solve*) lösen.

resort [rɪ'zɔːt] *n* (*for holidays*) Urlaubsort *der*; **as a last ~** als letzter Ausweg. ▶ **resort to** *vt fus* zurücklgreifen auf (+A); **to ~ doing sthg** darauf zurücklgreifen, etw zu tun.

resourceful [rɪ'sɔːsfʊl] *adj* erfinderisch.

resources [rɪ'sɔːsɪz] *npl* Ressourcen *pl*.

respect [rɪ'spekt] ◆ *n* Respekt *der*; (*aspect*) Aspekt *der*. ◆ *vt* respek-

tieren; **in some ~s** in mancher Hinsicht; **with ~ to** in bezug auf (+A).

respectable [rɪ'spektəbl] *adj* (*person, job etc*) anständig; (*acceptable*) ansehnlich.

respective [rɪ'spektɪv] *adj* jeweilig.

respond [rɪ'spɒnd] *vi* (*reply*) antworten; (*react*) reagieren.

response [rɪ'spɒns] *n* (*reply*) Antwort *die*; (*reaction*) Reaktion *die*.

responsibility [rɪˌspɒnsə'bɪlətɪ] *n* Verantwortung *die*.

responsible [rɪ'spɒnsəbl] *adj* (*in charge*) verantwortlich; (*sensible*) verantwortungsbewußt; **to be ~ (for)** (*in charge, to blame*) verantwortlich sein (für).

rest [rest] ◆ *n* (*break*) Ruhepause *die*; (*support*) Stütze *die*. ◆ *vi* (*relax*) sich auslruhen; **the ~** (*remainder*) der Rest; **to have a ~** sich auslruhen; **to ~ against** lehnen an (+A).

restaurant ['restərɒnt] *n* Restaurant *das*.

restaurant car *n* (*Br*) Speisewagen *der*.

restful ['restfʊl] *adj* erholsam.

restless ['restlɪs] *adj* (*bored, impatient*) ruhelos; (*fidgety*) unruhig.

restore [rɪ'stɔːr] *vt* (*reintroduce*) wiederlherlstellen; (*renovate*) renovieren.

restrain [rɪ'streɪn] *vt* zurücklhalten.

restrict [rɪ'strɪkt] *vt* beschränken.

restricted [rɪ'strɪktɪd] *adj* beschränkt.

restriction [rɪ'strɪkʃn] *n* Beschränkung *die*.

rest room *n* (*Am*) Toilette *die*.

result [rɪ'zʌlt] ◆ *n* (*outcome*) Ergebnis *das*; (*consequence*) Folge *die*. ◆ *vi*: **to ~ in** zur Folge haben; **as a ~** infolgedessen. ▶ **results** *npl* (*of test, exam*) Ergebnisse *pl*.

resume [rɪ'zjuːm] *vi* wieder beginnen.

résumé ['rezjuːmeɪ] *n* (*summary*) Zusammenfassung *die*; (*Am: curriculum vitae*) Lebenslauf *der*.

retail ['ri:teɪl] ♦ n Einzelhandel der. ♦ vt (sell) im Einzelhandel verkaufen. ♦ vi: **to ~ at** (im Einzelhandel) kosten.

retailer ['ri:teɪlər] n Einzelhändler der (-in die).

retail price n Einzelhandelspreis der.

retain [rɪ'teɪn] vt (fml: keep) bewahren.

retaliate [rɪ'tælɪeɪt] vi sich rächen.

retire [rɪ'taɪər] vi (stop working) in den Ruhestand treten.

retired [rɪ'taɪəd] adj pensioniert.

retirement [rɪ'taɪəmənt] n (leaving job) Pensionierung die; (period after retiring) Ruhestand der.

retreat [rɪ'tri:t] ♦ vi sich zurück-ziehen. ♦ n (place) Zufluchtsort der.

retrieve [rɪ'tri:v] vt (get back) zurück|holen.

return [rɪ'tɜ:n] ♦ n (arrival back) Rückkehr die; (Br: ticket) Rück-fahrkarte die; (Br: for plane) Rück-flugschein der. ♦ vt (put back) zurück|stellen; (give back) zurück|geben; (ball, serve) zurück|schlagen. ♦ vi (come back) zurück|kommen; (go back) zurück|gehen; (drive back) zurück|fahren; (happen again) wieder|auf|treten. ♦ adj (journey) Rück-; **to ~ sthg (to sb)** (give back) (jm) etw zurück|geben; **by ~ of post** (Br) postwendend; **many happy ~s!** herzlichen Glückwunsch zum Geburtstag!; **in ~ (for)** als Gegenleistung (für).

return flight n Rückflug der.

return ticket n (Br: for train, bus) Rückfahrkarte die; (for plane) Rückflugschein der.

reunification [,ri:ju:nɪfɪ'keɪʃn] n Wiedervereinigung die.

reunite [,ri:ju:'naɪt] vt wieder ver-einigen.

reveal [rɪ'vi:l] vt enthüllen.

revelation [,revə'leɪʃn] n Ent-hüllung die.

revenge [rɪ'vendʒ] n Rache die.

reverse [rɪ'vɜ:s] ♦ adj umgekehrt. ♦ n (AUT) Rückwärtsgang der; (of coin, document) Rückseite die. ♦ vt (car) rückwärts fahren; (decision) rück-gängig machen. ♦ vi (car, driver) rück-wärts fahren; **the ~** (opposite) das Gegenteil; **in ~ order** in umgekehrter Reihenfolge; **to ~ the charges** (Br) ein R-Gespräch führen.

reverse-charge call n (Br) R-Gespräch das.

review [rɪ'vju:] ♦ n (of book, record, film) Kritik die; (examination) Prüfung die. ♦ vt (Am: for exam) wiederholen.

revise [rɪ'vaɪz] ♦ vt (reconsider) revi-dieren. ♦ vi (Br: for exam) wieder-holen.

revision [rɪ'vɪʒn] n (Br: for exam) Wiederholung die.

revive [rɪ'vaɪv] vt (person) wieder beleben; (economy, custom) wieder aufleben lassen.

revolt [rɪ'vəʊlt] n Revolte die.

revolting [rɪ'vəʊltɪŋ] adj scheuß-lich.

revolution [,revə'lu:ʃn] n Revo-lution die.

revolutionary [revə'lu:ʃnərɪ] adj revolutionär.

revolver [rɪ'vɒlvər] n Revolver der.

revolving door [rɪ'vɒlvɪŋ-] n Drehtür die.

revue [rɪ'vju:] n Revue die.

reward [rɪ'wɔ:d] ♦ n Belohnung die. ♦ vt belohnen.

rewind [,ri:'waɪnd] (pt & pp rewound [,ri:'waʊnd]) vt zurück|spulen.

rheumatism ['ru:mətɪzm] n Rheuma das.

Rhine [raɪn] n: **the ~** der Rhein.

rhinoceros [raɪ'nɒsərəs] (pl inv OR -es) n Nashorn das.

rhubarb ['ru:bɑ:b] n Rhabarber der.

rhyme [raɪm] ♦ n Reim der. ♦ vi sich reimen.

rhythm ['rɪðm] n Rhythmus der.

rib [rɪb] n Rippe die.

ribbon ['rɪbən] n Band das; (for type-writer) Farbband das.

rice [raɪs] n Reis der.

rice pudding n Milchreis der.

rich [rɪtʃ] ◆ adj reich; (food) schwer. ◆ npl: **the** ~ die Reichen pl; **to be** ~ **in** sthg reich an etw (D) sein.

ricotta cheese [rɪ'kɒtə-] n Ricottakäse der.

rid [rɪd] vt: **to get** ~ **of** los|werden.

ridden ['rɪdn] pp → ride.

riddle ['rɪdl] n Rätsel das.

ride [raɪd] (pt rode, pp ridden) ◆ n (on horse) Ritt der; (on bike, in vehicle) Fahrt die. ◆ vt (horse) reiten; (bike) fahren mit. ◆ vi (on horse) reiten; (on bike) rad|fahren; (in vehicle) fahren; **to go for a** ~ (in car) eine Spritztour machen.

rider ['raɪdər] n (on horse) Reiter der (-in die); (on bike) Fahrer der (-in die).

ridge [rɪdʒ] n (of mountain) Kamm der; (raised surface) Erhebung die.

ridiculous [rɪ'dɪkjʊləs] adj lächer-lich.

riding ['raɪdɪŋ] n Reiten das.

riding school n Reitschule die.

rifle ['raɪfl] n Gewehr das.

rig [rɪg] ◆ n (offshore) Bohrinsel die. ◆ vt (fix) manipulieren.

right [raɪt] ◆ adj **1.** (correct) richtig; **to be** ~ (person) recht haben; **you were** ~ **to tell me** es war richtig von dir, mir das zu erzählen; **have you got the** ~ **time?** haben Sie/hast du die richtige Uhrzeit?; **that's** ~! das stimmt! das ist richtig! **2.** (fair) richtig, gerecht; **that's not** ~! das ist nicht richtig! **3.** (on the right) rechte(-r)(-s); **the** ~ **side of the road** die rechte Straßenseite. ◆ n **1.** (side): **the** ~ die rechte Seite. **2.** (entitlement) Recht das; **to have the** ~ **to do sthg** das Recht haben, etw zu tun. ◆ adv **1.** (towards the right) rechts; **turn** ~ **at the post office** biegen Sie am Postamt nach rechts ab. **2.** (correctly) richtig; **am I pronouncing it** ~? spreche ich es richtig aus? **3.** (for emphasis) genau; ~ **here** genau hier; **I'll be** ~ **back** ich bin gleich zurück; ~ **away** sofort.

right angle n rechter Winkel.

right-hand adj rechte(-r)(-s).

right-hand drive n Auto das mit Rechtssteuerung.

right-handed [-'hændɪd] adj (person) rechtshändig; (implement) für Rechtshänder.

rightly ['raɪtlɪ] adv (correctly) richtig; (justly) zu Recht.

right of way n (AUT) Vorfahrt die; (path) öffentlicher Weg.

right-wing adj rechte(-r)(-s).

rigid ['rɪdʒɪd] adj starr.

rim [rɪm] n Rand der.

rind [raɪnd] n (of fruit) Schale die; (of bacon) Schwarte die; (of cheese) Rinde die.

ring [rɪŋ] (pt rang, pp rung) ◆ n Ring der; (of people) Kreis der; (sound) Klingeln das; (on cooker) Kochplatte die; (in circus) Manege die. ◆ vt (Br: make phone call to) an|rufen; (bell) läuten. ◆ vi (bell, telephone) klingeln; (Br: make phone call) telefonieren; **to give sb a** ~ (phone call) jn an|rufen; **to** ~ **the bell** (of house, office) klingeln, läuten. ► **ring back** vt sep & vi (Br) zurück|rufen. ► **ring off** vi (Br) auf|legen. ► **ring up** vt sep & vi (Br) an|rufen.

ringing tone ['rɪŋɪŋ-] n Frei-zeichen das.

ring road n Ringstraße die.

rink [rɪŋk] n Eisbahn die.

rinse [rɪns] vt (clothes, hair) aus|spülen; (hands) ab|spülen. ► **rinse out** vt sep (clothes, mouth) aus|spülen.

riot ['raɪət] n Aufruhr der; ~**s** Unruhen pl.

rip [rɪp] ◆ n Riß der. ◆ vt & vi zerreißen. ► **rip up** vt sep zerreißen.

ripe [raɪp] adj reif.

ripen ['raɪpn] vi reifen.

rip-off n (inf) Betrug der.

rise [raɪz] (pt rose, pp risen ['rɪzn])

◆ vi steigen; (sun, moon) auflgehen; (stand up) auflstehen. ◆ n (increase) Anstieg der; (Br: pay increase) Gehaltserhöhung die; (slope) Anhöhe die.

risk [rɪsk] ◆ n Risiko das. ◆ vt riskieren; **to take a ~** ein Risiko einlgehen; **at your own ~** auf eigenes Risiko; **to ~ doing sthg** riskieren, etw zu tun; **to ~ it** es riskieren.

risky ['rɪskɪ] adj riskant.

risotto [rɪ'zɒtəʊ] (pl -s) n Risotto das.

ritual ['rɪtʃʊəl] n Ritual das.

rival ['raɪvl] ◆ adj gegnerisch. ◆ n Rivale der (Rivalin die).

river ['rɪvər] n Fluß der.

river bank n Flußufer das.

riverside ['rɪvəsaɪd] n Flußufer das.

Riviera [ˌrɪvɪ'eərə] n: **the (French) ~** die (französische) Riviera.

roach [rəʊtʃ] n (Am: cockroach) Kakerlake die.

road [rəʊd] n Straße die; **by ~** mit dem Auto.

road book n Straßenatlas der.

road map n Straßenkarte die.

road rage n Wutanfall eines Autofahrers, der zu Gewalttaten gegenüber anderen Fahrern ausarten kann.

road safety n Straßensicherheit die.

roadside ['rəʊdsaɪd] n: **the ~** der Straßenrand.

road sign n Straßenschild das.

road tax n Kraftfahrzeugsteuer die.

roadway ['rəʊdweɪ] n Fahrbahn die.

road works npl Straßenarbeiten pl.

roam [rəʊm] vi herumlstreifen.

roar [rɔːr] ◆ n (of crowd) Gebrüll das; (of aeroplane) Dröhnen das. ◆ vi (lion, crowd) brüllen; (traffic) donnern.

roast [rəʊst] ◆ n Braten der. ◆ vt (meat) braten. ◆ adj: **~ beef** Rinderbraten der; **~ chicken** Brathähnchen das, Broiler der (Österr)

(Ostdt); **~ lamb** Lammbraten der; **~ pork** Schweinebraten der; **~ potatoes** Bratkartoffeln pl.

rob [rɒb] vt (house, bank) auslrauben; (person) berauben; **to ~ sb of sthg** jm etw stehlen.

robber ['rɒbər] n Räuber der (-in die).

robbery ['rɒbərɪ] n Raub der.

robe [rəʊb] n (Am: bathrobe) Bademantel der.

robin ['rɒbɪn] n Rotkehlchen das.

robot ['rəʊbɒt] n Roboter der.

rock [rɒk] ◆ n (boulder) Felsen der; (Am: stone) Stein der; (substance) Stein der; (music) Rock der; (Br: sweet) Zuckerstange die. ◆ vt schaukeln; **on the ~s** (drink) on the rocks.

rock climbing n Klettern das; **to go ~ climbing** klettern gehen.

rocket ['rɒkɪt] n Rakete die.

rocking chair ['rɒkɪŋ-] n Schaukelstuhl der.

rock 'n' roll [ˌrɒkən'rəʊl] n Rock'n'Roll der.

rocky ['rɒkɪ] adj felsig.

rod [rɒd] n (pole) Stange die; (for fishing) Angelrute die.

rode [rəʊd] pt → ride.

roe [rəʊ] n Fischrogen der.

role [rəʊl] n Rolle die.

roll [rəʊl] ◆ n (of bread) Brötchen das, Semmel die (Süddt) (Österr); (of film, paper) Rolle die. ◆ vi rollen; (ship) schlingern. ◆ vt rollen; **to ~ the dice** würfeln. ▶ **roll over** vi (person, animal) sich drehen; (car) sich überschlagen. ▶ **roll up** vt sep (map, carpet) auflrollen; (sleeves, trousers) hochlkrempeln.

roller coaster ['rəʊləˌkəʊstər] n Achterbahn die.

roller skate ['rəʊlə-] n Rollschuh der.

roller-skating ['rəʊlə-] n Rollschuhlaufen das.

rolling pin ['rəʊlɪŋ-] n Nudelholz das.

Roman ['rəʊmən] ◆ adj römisch.

◆ *n* Römer *der* (-in *die*).

Roman Catholic *n* Katholik *der* (-in *die*).

romance [rəʊ'mæns] *n* (*love*) Romantik *die*; (*love affair*) Romanze *die*; (*novel*) Liebesroman *der*.

Romania [ruː'meɪnjə] *n* Rumänien *nt*.

romantic [rəʊ'mæntɪk] *adj* romantisch.

romper suit ['rɒmpə-] *n* Strampelanzug *der*.

roof [ruːf] *n* Dach *das*.

roof rack *n* Dachgepäckträger *der*.

room [ruːm, rʊm] *n* Zimmer *das*; (*space*) Platz *der*.

room number *n* Zimmernummer *die*.

room service *n* Zimmerservice *der*.

room temperature *n* Zimmertemperatur *die*.

roomy ['ruːmɪ] *adj* geräumig.

root [ruːt] *n* Wurzel *die*.

rope [rəʊp] ◆ *n* Seil *das*. ◆ *vt* fest|binden.

rose [rəʊz] ◆ *pt* → **rise**. ◆ *n* Rose *die*.

rosé ['rəʊzeɪ] *n* Roséwein *der*.

rosemary ['rəʊzmərɪ] *n* Rosmarin *der*.

rot [rɒt] *vi* verfaulen.

rota ['rəʊtə] *n* Dienstplan *der*.

rotate [rəʊ'teɪt] *vi* rotieren.

rotten ['rɒtn] *adj* (*food, wood*) verfault; (*inf: not good*) mies; **I feel ~ (ill)** ich fühle mich lausig.

rouge [ruːʒ] *n* Rouge *das*.

rough [rʌf] ◆ *adj* (*road, ground*) uneben; (*surface, skin, cloth, conditions*) rauh; (*sea, crossing*) stürmisch; (*person, estimate*) grob; (*area, town*) unsicher; (*wine*) sauer. ◆ *n* (*on golf course*) Rough *das*; **at a ~ guess** grob geschätzt; **to have a ~ time** es schwer haben.

roughly ['rʌflɪ] *adv* (*approximately*) ungefähr; (*push, handle*) grob.

roulade [ruː'lɑːd] *n* (*savoury*)

Roulade *die*; (*sweet*) Rolle *die*.

roulette [ruː'let] *n* Roulette *das*.

round [raʊnd] ◆ *adj* rund. ◆ *n* **1.** (*gen*) Runde *die*. **2.** (*of sandwiches*) belegtes Brot mit zwei Scheiben Brot. **3.** (*of toast*) Scheibe *die*. ◆ *adv* **1.** (*in a circle*): **to go ~** sich drehen; **to spin ~** sich im Kreis drehen. **2.** (*surrounding*) herum; **it had a fence all (the way) ~** es hatte einen Zaun rundherum. **3.** (*near*): **~ about** in der Nähe. **4.** (*to someone's house*): **why don't you come ~?** warum kommst du nicht vorbei?; **to ask some friends ~** ein paar Freunde zu sich ein|laden. **5.** (*continuously*): **all year ~** das ganze Jahr über. ◆ *prep* **1.** (*surrounding, circling*) um … herum; **to go ~ the corner** um die Ecke gehen; **we walked ~ the lake** wir gingen um den See herum. **2.** (*visiting*): **to go ~ a museum** ein Museum besuchen; **to go ~ a town** sich eine Stadt ansehen; **to show sb ~ sthg** jn in etw (D) herum|führen. **3.** (*approximately*) rund; **~ (about) 100** rund 100; **~ ten o'clock** gegen zehn Uhr. **4.** (*near*): **~ here** hier in der Nähe. **5.** (*in phrases*): **it's just ~ the corner** (*nearby*) es ist gerade um die Ecke; **~ the clock** rund um die Uhr. ▶ **round off** *vt sep* (*meal, day, visit*) ab|runden.

roundabout ['raʊndəbaʊt] *n* (Br: *in road*) Kreisverkehr *der*; (*at fairground, in playground*) Karussell *das*.

rounders ['raʊndəz] *n* dem Baseball ähnliches britisches Ballspiel.

round trip *n* Hin- und Rückfahrt *die*.

route [ruːt] ◆ *n* Route *die*; (*of bus*) Linie *die*. ◆ *vt* (*flight, plane*) die Route fest|legen für.

routine [ruː'tiːn] ◆ *n* Routine *die*; (*pej: drudgery*) Trott *der*. ◆ *adj* Routine-.

row¹ [rəʊ] ◆ *n* (*line*) Reihe *die*. ◆ *vt & vi* rudern; **in a ~** (*in succession*) nacheinander.

row² [raʊ] *n* (*argument*) Streit *der*; (*inf: noise*) Krach *der*; **to have a ~** sich streiten.

rowboat ['rəʊbəʊt] (Am) = **rowing boat**.

rowdy ['raʊdɪ] adj rowdyhaft.

rowing ['rəʊɪŋ] n Rudern das.

rowing boat n (Br) Ruderboot das.

royal ['rɔɪəl] adj königlich.

royal family n königliche Familie.

royalty ['rɔɪəltɪ] n Mitglieder pl der königlichen Familie.

RRP (abbr of recommended retail price) unverbindliche Preisempfehlung.

RSVP (abbr of répondez s'il vous plaît) u.A.w.g.

rub [rʌb] ◆ vt reiben; (polish) polieren. ◆ vi (with hand, cloth) reiben; (shoes) scheuern. ▶ **rub in** vt sep (lotion, oil) ein|reiben. ▶ **rub out** vt sep (erase) aus|radieren.

rubber ['rʌbər] ◆ adj Gummi-. ◆ n Gummi das; (Br: eraser) Radiergummi der; (Am: inf: condom) Gummi der.

rubber band n Gummiband das.

rubber gloves npl Gummihandschuhe pl.

rubber ring n Gummiring der.

rubbish ['rʌbɪʃ] n (refuse) Müll der; (inf: worthless thing) Schund der; (inf: nonsense) Quatsch der.

rubbish bin n (Br) Mülleimer der.

rubbish dump n (Br) Müllhalde die.

rubble ['rʌbl] n Schutt der.

ruby ['ruːbɪ] n Rubin der.

rucksack ['rʌksæk] n Rucksack der.

rudder ['rʌdər] n Ruder das.

rude [ruːd] adj unhöflich; (joke, picture) unanständig.

rug [rʌg] n Läufer der; (large) Teppich der; (Br: blanket) Wolldecke die.

rugby ['rʌgbɪ] n Rugby das.

ruin ['ruːɪn] vt ruinieren. ▶ **ruins** npl Ruinen pl.

ruined ['ruːɪnd] adj (building) zerstört; (clothes, meal, holiday) ruiniert.

rule [ruːl] ◆ n Regel die. ◆ vt (country) regieren; **against the ~s** gegen die Regeln; **as a ~** in der Regel. ▶ **rule out** vt sep aus|schließen.

ruler ['ruːlər] n (of country) Herrscher der (-in die); (for measuring) Lineal das.

rum [rʌm] n Rum der.

rumor ['ruːmər] (Am) = **rumour**.

rumour ['ruːmər] n (Br) Gerücht das.

rump steak [,rʌmp-] n Rumpsteak das.

run [rʌn] (pt ran, pp inv) ◆ vi 1. (on foot) rennen, laufen; **we had to ~ for the bus** wir mußten rennen, um den Bus zu erwischen. 2. (train, bus) fahren; **the bus ~s every hour** der Bus fährt jede Stunde; **the train is running an hour late** der Zug hat eine Stunde Verspätung. 3. (operate) laufen; **to ~ on unleaded petrol** mit bleifreiem Benzin fahren. 4. (tears, liquid) laufen. 5. (road, track) führen, verlaufen; (river) fließen; **the path ~s along the coast** der Weg verläuft entlang der Küste. 6. (play, event) laufen; **'now running at the Palladium'** 'jetzt im Palladium'. 7. (tap) laufen. 8. (nose) laufen; (eyes) tränen; **my nose is running** mir läuft die Nase. 9. (colour) aus|laufen; (clothes) ab|färben. 10. (remain valid) gültig sein, laufen; **the offer ~s until July** das Angebot gilt bis Juli. ◆ vt 1. (on foot) rennen, laufen. 2. (compete in): **to ~ a race** ein Rennen laufen. 3. (business, hotel) führen; (course) leiten. 4. (bus, train): **we're running a special bus to the airport** wir betreiben einen Sonderbus zum Flughafen. 5. (take in car) fahren; **I'll ~ you home** ich fahre dich nach Hause. 6. (bath): **to ~ a bath** ein Bad ein|lassen. ◆ n 1. (on foot) Lauf der; **to go for a ~** laufen gehen. 2. (in car) Fahrt die; **to go for a ~** eine Fahrt machen. 3. (of play, show) Laufzeit die. 4. (for skiing) Piste die. 5. (Am: in tights) Laufmasche die. 6. (in phrases): **in the long ~** auf lange Sicht (gesehen). ▶ **run away** vi weg|rennen, weg|laufen. ▶ **run down** vt sep (run over) über|fahren; (criticize) herunter|machen. ◆ vi (battery) leer werden. ▶ **run into** vt fus (meet) zufällig treffen; (subj: car) laufen gegen, fahren gegen; (problem, difficulty) stoßen auf (A). ▶ **run out** vi (supply) aus|gehen. ▶ **run out of** vt fus: **we've ~ out of petrol/money** wir haben kein Benzin/Geld mehr. ▶ **run over** vt sep (hit) über|fahren.

runaway ['rʌnəweɪ] n Ausreißer der (-in die).

rung [rʌŋ] ◆ pp → **ring**. ◆ n (of ladder) Sprosse die.

runner ['rʌnər] n (person) Läufer der (-in die); (for door, drawer) Laufschiene die; (of sledge) Kufe die.

runner bean n Stangenbohne die.

runner-up (pl **runners-up**) n Zweite der die.

running ['rʌnɪŋ] ◆ n (SPORT) Laufen das; (management) Leitung die. ◆ adj: **three days ~** drei Tage hintereinander; **to go ~** Joggen gehen.

running water n fließendes Wasser.

runny ['rʌnɪ] adj (sauce, egg, omelette) dünnflüssig; (eye) tränend; (nose) laufend.

runway ['rʌnweɪ] n Landebahn die.

rural ['rʊərəl] adj ländlich.

rush [rʌʃ] ◆ n Eile die; (of crowd) Andrang der. ◆ vi (move quickly) rasen; (hurry) sich beeilen. ◆ vt (food) hastig essen; (work) hastig erledigen; (transport quickly) schnell transportieren; **to be in a ~** in Eile sein; **there's no ~!** keine Eile!; **don't ~ me!** hetz mich nicht!

rush hour n Hauptverkehrszeit die, Stoßzeit die.

Russia ['rʌʃə] n Rußland nt.

Russian ['rʌʃn] ◆ adj russisch. ◆ n (person) Russe der (Russin die); (language) Russisch das.

rust [rʌst] ◆ n Rost der. ◆ vi rosten.

rustic ['rʌstɪk] adj rustikal.

rustle ['rʌsl] vi rascheln.

rustproof ['rʌstpruːf] adj rostfrei.

rusty ['rʌstɪ] adj rostig; (fig: language, person) eingerostet.

RV n (Am: abbr of recreational vehicle) Wohnmobil das.

rye [raɪ] n Roggen der.

rye bread n Roggenbrot das.

S

S (abbr of south, small) S.

saccharin ['sækərɪn] n Saccharin das.

sachet ['sæʃeɪ] n (of shampoo, cream) Einzelpackung die; (of sugar, coffee) Portionspackung die.

sack [sæk] ◆ n (bag) Sack der. ◆ vt entlassen; **to get the ~** entlassen werden.

sacrifice ['sækrɪfaɪs] n (fig) Opfer das.

sad [sæd] adj traurig; (unfortunate) bedauerlich.

saddle ['sædl] n Sattel der.

saddlebag ['sædlbæg] n Satteltasche die.

sadly ['sædlɪ] adv (unfortunately) leider; (unhappily) traurig.

sadness ['sædnɪs] n Traurigkeit die.

s.a.e. n (Br: abbr of stamped addressed envelope) adressierter Freiumschlag.

safari park [sə'fɑːrɪ-] n Safaripark der.

safe [seɪf] ◆ adj sicher; (out of harm) in Sicherheit. ◆ n Safe der; **a ~ place** ein sicherer Platz; **(have a) ~ journey!** gute Fahrt!; **~ and sound** gesund und wohlbehalten.

safe-deposit box n Tresorfach das.

safely ['seɪflɪ] adv sicher; (arrive) gut.

safety ['seɪftɪ] n Sicherheit die.

safety belt n Sicherheitsgurt der.

safety pin n Sicherheitsnadel die.

sag [sæg] vi (hang down) durch|hängen; (sink) sich senken.

sage [seɪdʒ] n (herb) Salbei der.

Sagittarius [,sædʒɪ'teərɪəs] n Schütze der.

said [sed] pt & pp → **say**.

sail [seɪl] ◆ n Segel das. ◆ vi segeln; (ship) fahren; (depart) aus|laufen. ◆ vt: to ~ a boat segeln; to set ~ aus|laufen.

sailboat ['seɪlbəʊt] (Am) = **sailing boat**.

sailing ['seɪlɪŋ] n Segeln das; (departure) Abfahrt die; **to go ~** segeln gehen.

sailing boat n Segelboot das.

sailor ['seɪlər] n (on ferry, cargo ship etc) Seemann der; (in navy) Matrose der.

saint [seɪnt] n Heilige der die.

sake [seɪk] n: **for my/their ~** um meinetwillen/ihretwillen; **for God's ~!** um Gottes willen!

salad ['sæləd] n Salat der.

salad bar n Salatbar die.

salad bowl n Salatschüssel die.

salad cream n (Br) Salatmayonnaise die.

salad dressing n Salatsoße die.

salami [sə'lɑːmɪ] n Salami die.

salary ['sælərɪ] n Gehalt das.

sale [seɪl] n Verkauf der; (at reduced prices) Ausverkauf der; '**for ~**' 'zu verkaufen'; **on ~** im Handel; **on ~ at** erhältlich bei. ▶ **sales** npl (COMM) Absatz der; **the ~s** (at reduced prices) der Ausverkauf.

sales assistant ['seɪlz-] n Verkäufer der (-in die).

salesclerk ['seɪlzklɜːrk] (Am) = **sales assistant**.

salesman ['seɪlzmən] (pl -men [-mən]) n (in shop) Verkäufer der; (rep) Vertreter der.

sales rep(resentative) n Vertreter der (-in die).

saleswoman ['seɪlz,wʊmən] (pl -women [-,wɪmɪn]) n Verkäuferin die.

saliva [sə'laɪvə] n Speichel der.

salmon ['sæmən] (pl inv) n Lachs der.

salon ['sælɒn] n (hairdresser's) Salon der.

saloon [sə'luːn] n (Br: car) Limousine die; (Am: bar) Saloon der; **~ (bar)** (Br) Nebenraum eines Pubs mit mehr Komfort.

salopettes [,sælə'pets] npl Skihose die.

salt [sɔːlt, sɒlt] n Salz das.

saltcellar ['sɔːlt,selər] n (Br) Salzstreuer der.

salted peanuts ['sɔːltɪd-] npl gesalzene Erdnüsse pl.

salt shaker [-,ʃeɪkər] (Am) = **saltcellar**.

salty ['sɔːltɪ] adj salzig.

salute [sə'luːt] ◆ n Salut der. ◆ vi salutieren.

same [seɪm] ◆ adj: **the ~** (unchanged) der/die/das gleiche, die gleichen (pl); (identical) derselbe/dieselbe/dasselbe, dieselben (pl). ◆ pron: **the ~** derselbe/dieselbe/dasselbe, dieselben (pl); **they look the ~** sie sehen gleich aus; **I'll have the ~ as her** ich möchte das gleiche wie sie; **you've got the ~ book as me** du hast das gleiche Buch wie ich; **it's all the ~ to me** es ist mir gleich; **all the ~** trotzdem; **the ~** to you gleichfalls.

samosa [sə'məʊsə] n gefüllte und fritierte dreieckige indische Teigtasche.

sample ['sɑːmpl] ◆ n (of work, product) Muster das; (of blood, urine) Probe die. ◆ vt (food, drink) probieren.

sanctions ['sæŋkʃnz] npl Sanktionen pl.

sanctuary ['sæŋktʃʊərɪ] n (for birds, animals) Tierschutzgebiet das.

sand [sænd] ◆ n Sand der. ◆ vt (wood) ab|schmirgeln. ▶ **sands** npl (beach) Strand der.

sandal ['sændl] n Sandale die.

sandcastle ['sænd,kɑːsl] n Sandburg die.

sandpaper ['sænd,peɪpəʳ] n Sand-papier das.

sandwich ['sænwɪdʒ] n Sandwich das.

sandwich bar n = Imbißbar die.

sandy ['sændɪ] adj (beach) sandig; (hair) dunkelblond.

sang [sæŋ] pt → sing.

sanitary ['sænɪtrɪ] adj (conditions, measures) sanitär; (hygienic) Hygiene-.

sanitary napkin (Am) = sanitary towel.

sanitary towel n (Br) Monats-binde die.

sank [sæŋk] pt → sink.

sapphire ['sæfaɪəʳ] n Saphir der.

sarcastic [sɑː'kæstɪk] adj sarka-stisch.

sardine [sɑː'diːn] n Sardine die.

SASE n (Am: abbr of self-addressed stamped envelope) adressierter Freium-schlag.

sat [sæt] pt & pp → sit.

Sat. (abbr of Saturday) Sa.

satchel ['sætʃəl] n Ranzen der.

satellite ['sætəlaɪt] n (in space) Satellit der; (at airport) Satelliten-terminal der.

satellite dish n Parabolantenne die.

satellite TV n Satellitenfernsehen das.

satin ['sætɪn] n Satin der.

satisfaction [,sætɪs'fækʃn] n (plea-sure) Befriedigung die.

satisfactory [,sætɪs'fæktərɪ] adj befriedigend.

satisfied ['sætɪsfaɪd] adj zufrieden.

satisfy ['sætɪsfaɪ] vt (please) zufrieden|stellen; (need, requirement, conditions) erfüllen.

satsuma [,sæt'suːmə] n (Br) Satsuma die.

saturate ['sætʃəreɪt] vt (with liquid) tränken.

Saturday ['sætədɪ] n Samstag der, Sonnabend der; it's ~ es ist Samstag; ~ morning Samstagmorgen; on ~ am

Samstag; on ~s samstags; last ~ letzten Samstag; this ~ diesen Samstag; next ~ nächsten Samstag; ~ week, a week on ~ Samstag in einer Woche.

sauce [sɔːs] n Soße die.

saucepan ['sɔːspən] n Kochtopf der.

saucer ['sɔːsəʳ] n Untertasse die.

Saudi Arabia [,saʊdɪə'reɪbjə] n Saudi-Arabien nt.

sauna ['sɔːnə] n Sauna die.

sausage ['sɒsɪdʒ] n Wurst die.

sausage roll n Blätterteig mit Wurstfüllung.

sauté [Br 'səʊteɪ, Am səʊ'teɪ] adj sautiert.

savage ['sævɪdʒ] adj brutal.

save [seɪv] ◆ vt (rescue) retten; (money, time, space) sparen; (reserve) auf|heben; (SPORT) ab|wehren; (COM-PUT) speichern. ◆ n (SPORT) Parade die; **to ~ a seat for sb** jm einen Platz frei|halten. ▶ **save up** vi: **to ~ up (for sthg)** (auf etw (A) sparen).

saver ['seɪvəʳ] n (Br: ticket) verbil-ligte Fahrkarte.

savings ['seɪvɪŋz] npl Ersparnisse pl.

savings and loan association n (Am) Bausparkasse die.

savings bank n Sparkasse die.

savory ['seɪvərɪ] (Am) = savoury.

savoury ['seɪvərɪ] adj (Br: not sweet) pikant.

saw [sɔː] (Br pt -ed, pp sawn, Am & pt & pp -ed) ◆ pt → see. ◆ n (tool) Säge die. ◆ vt sägen.

sawdust ['sɔːdʌst] n Sägemehl das.

sawn [sɔːn] pp → saw.

Saxony ['sæksənɪ] n Sachsen nt.

saxophone ['sæksəfəʊn] n Saxo-phon das.

say [seɪ] (pt & pp said) ◆ vt sagen; (subj: clock, meter) an|zeigen; (subj: sign) besagen. ◆ n: **to have a ~ in sthg** etw zu sagen haben bei etw; **could you ~ that again?** könntest du das nochmal sagen?; **~ we met at nine?** könnten wir uns um neun treffen?; **that is to ~** das heißt; **what did you ~?** was hast du gesagt?; **the letter ~s ...** in dem Brief steht ...

saying ['seɪɪŋ] n Redensart die.

scab [skæb] n Schorf der.

scaffolding ['skæfəldɪŋ] n Gerüst das.

scald [skɔːld] vt verbrühen.

scale [skeɪl] n (for measurement) Skala die; (of map, drawing, model) Maßstab der; (extent) Umfang der; (MUS) Tonleiter die; (of fish, snake) Schuppe die; (in kettle) Kalk der. ▶ **scales** npl (for weighing) Waage die.

scallion ['skæljən] n (Am) Schalotte die.

scallop ['skɒləp] n Jakobsmuschel die.

scalp [skælp] n Kopfhaut die.

scampi ['skæmpɪ] n Scampi pl.

scan [skæn] ◆ vt (consult quickly) überfliegen. ◆ n (MED) Szintigramm das.

scandal ['skændl] n (disgrace) Skandal der; (gossip) Klatsch der.

Scandinavia [ˌskændɪ'neɪvjə] n Skandinavien nt.

scar [skɑːʳ] n Narbe die.

scarce ['skeəs] adj knapp.

scarcely ['skeəslɪ] adv (hardly) kaum.

scare [skeəʳ] vt erschrecken.

scarecrow ['skeəkrəʊ] n Vogelscheuche die.

scared ['skeəd] adj: **to be ~ (of)** Angst haben (vor (+D).

scarf [skɑːf] (pl **scarves**) n (woollen) Schal der; (for women) Tuch das.

scarlet ['skɑːlət] adj scharlachrot.

scarves [skɑːvz] pl → **scarf**.

scary ['skeərɪ] adj (inf) unheimlich.

scatter ['skætəʳ] ◆ vt verstreuen. ◆ vi sich zerstreuen.

scene [siːn] n (in play, film, book) Szene die; (of crime, accident) Schauplatz der; (view) Anblick der; **the music ~** die Musikszene; **to make a ~** eine Szene machen.

scenery ['siːnərɪ] n (countryside) Landschaft die; (in theatre) Bühnenbild das.

scenic ['siːnɪk] adj malerisch.

scent [sent] n (smell) Duft der; (of animal) Fährte die; (perfume) Parfüm das.

sceptical ['skeptɪkl] adj (Br) skeptisch.

schedule [Br 'ʃedjuːl, Am 'skedʒʊl] ◆ n (of things to do) Programm das; (of work) Arbeitsplan der; (timetable) Fahrplan der; (list) Tabelle die. ◆ vt (plan) planen; **according to ~** planmäßig; **behind ~** im Verzug; **on ~** planmäßig; **to arrive on ~** pünktlich ankommen.

scheduled flight [Br 'ʃedjuːld-, Am 'skedʒʊld-] n Linienflug der.

scheme [skiːm] n (plan) Programm das; (pej: dishonest plan) Komplott das.

scholarship ['skɒləʃɪp] n (award) Stipendium das.

school [skuːl] ◆ n Schule die; (university department) Fakultät die; (Am: university) Hochschule die. ◆ adj (age, holiday, report) Schul-; **at ~** in der Schule; **to go to ~** in die Schule gehen.

schoolbag ['skuːlbæg] n Schultasche die.

schoolbook ['skuːlbʊk] n Schulbuch das.

schoolboy ['skuːlbɔɪ] n Schuljunge der.

school bus n Schulbus der.

schoolchild ['skuːltʃaɪld] (pl **-children** [-tʃɪldrən]) n Schulkind das.

schoolgirl ['skuːlgɜːl] n Schulmädchen das.

schoolmaster ['skuːlˌmɑːstəʳ] n (Br) Schullehrer der.

schoolmistress ['skuːlˌmɪstrɪs] n (Br) Schullehrerin die.

schoolteacher ['skuːlˌtiːtʃəʳ] n Lehrer der (-in die).

school uniform n Schuluniform die.

science ['saɪəns] n Wissenschaft die; (SCH) Physik, Chemie und Biologie die.

science fiction n Science-fiction die.

scientific [ˌsaɪən'tɪfɪk] adj wissenschaftlich.

scientist ['saɪəntɪst] n Wissenschaftler der (-in die).

scissors ['sɪzəz] npl: **(pair of)** ~ Schere die.

scold [skəʊld] vt aus|schimpfen.

scone [skɒn] n britisches Teegebäck.

scoop [skuːp] n (for ice cream) Portionierer der; (of ice cream) Kugel die; (in media) Exklusivmeldung die.

scooter ['skuːtər] n (motor vehicle) Roller der.

scope [skəʊp] n (possibility) Spielraum der; (range) Rahmen der.

scorch [skɔːtʃ] vt (clothes) versengen.

score [skɔːr] ◆ n (total, final result) Ergebnis das; (current position) Stand der. ◆ vt (goal) schießen; (point, try, in test) erzielen. ◆ vi (get goal) ein Tor schießen; (get point) einen Punkt erzielen.

scorn [skɔːn] n Verachtung die.

Scorpio ['skɔːpɪəʊ] n Skorpion der.

scorpion ['skɔːpjən] n Skorpion der.

Scot [skɒt] n Schotte der (Schottin die).

scotch [skɒtʃ] n Scotch der.

Scotch broth n Eintopf aus Fleischbrühe, Gemüse und Graupen.

Scotch tape® n (Am) Tesafilm® der.

Scotland ['skɒtlənd] n Schottland nt.

Scotsman ['skɒtsmən] (pl -men [-mən]) n Schotte der.

Scotswoman ['skɒtswʊmən] (pl -women [-ˌwɪmɪn]) n Schottin die.

Scottish ['skɒtɪʃ] adj schottisch.

scout [skaʊt] n (boy scout) Pfadfinder der.

scowl [skaʊl] vi ein böses Gesicht machen.

scrambled eggs [ˌskræmbld-] npl Rührei das.

scrap [skræp] n (of paper, cloth) Fetzen der; (old metal) Schrott der.

scrapbook ['skræpbʊk] n Sammelbuch das.

scrape [skreɪp] vt (rub) reiben; (scratch) kratzen.

scrap paper n (Br) Schmierzettel der.

scratch [skrætʃ] ◆ n Kratzer der. ◆ vt kratzen; (mark) zerkratzen; **to be up to** ~ gut genug sein; **to start from** ~ von vorne an|fangen.

scratch card n Rubbellos das.

scratch paper (Am) = **scrap paper**.

scream [skriːm] ◆ n Schrei der. ◆ vi schreien.

screen [skriːn] ◆ n (of TV, computer) Bildschirm der; (for cinema film) Leinwand die; (hall in cinema) Kinosaal der; (panel) Trennwand die. ◆ vt (film, programme) vor|führen.

screening ['skriːnɪŋ] n (of film) Vorführung die.

screen wash n Scheibenwaschmittel das.

screw [skruː] ◆ n Schraube die. ◆ vt (fasten) an|schrauben; (twist) schrauben.

screwdriver ['skruːˌdraɪvər] n Schraubenzieher der.

scribble ['skrɪbl] vi kritzeln.

script [skrɪpt] n (of play, film) Drehbuch das.

scrub [skrʌb] vt schrubben.

scruffy ['skrʌfɪ] adj vergammelt.

scrumpy ['skrʌmpɪ] n stark alkoholischer Apfelwein aus dem Südwesten Englands.

scuba diving ['skuːbə-] n Sporttauchen das.

sculptor ['skʌlptər] n Bildhauer der (-in die).

sculpture ['skʌlptʃər] n (statue) Skulptur die.

sea [siː] n Meer das, See die; **by** ~ auf dem Seeweg; **by the** ~ am Meer.

seafood ['siːfuːd] n Meeresfrüchte pl.

seafront ['si:frʌnt] n Uferpromenade die (am Meer gelegene Straße eines Küstenortes).

seagull ['si:gʌl] n Seemöwe die.

seal [si:l] ◆ n (animal) Seehund der; (on bottle, container) Verschluß der; (official mark) Siegel das. ◆ vt versiegeln.

seam [si:m] n (in clothes) Saum der.

search [sɜ:tʃ] ◆ n Suche die. ◆ vt durchsuchen. ◆ vi: **to ~ for** suchen nach.

seashell ['si:ʃel] n Muschel die.

seashore ['si:ʃɔ:r] n Meeresküste die.

seasick ['si:sɪk] adj seekrank.

seaside ['si:saɪd] n: **the ~** die Küste.

seaside resort n Urlaubsort der an der Küste.

season ['si:zn] ◆ n (of year) Jahreszeit die; (period) Saison, Zeit die. ◆ vt (food) würzen; **in ~** (holiday) in der Hochsaison; **out of ~** (holiday) in der Nebensaison; **strawberries are in/out of ~** es ist die Zeit/nicht die Zeit für Erdbeeren.

seasoning ['si:znɪŋ] n Gewürz das.

season ticket n (for train) Dauerkarte die; (for theatre) Abonnement das.

seat [si:t] ◆ n (place) Platz der; (chair) (Sitz)platz der; (in parliament) Sitz der. ◆ vt (subj: building, vehicle) Sitzplatz haben für; **'please wait to be ~ed'** 'bitte warten Sie hier, bis Sie zu Ihrem Platz geleitet werden'.

seat belt n Sicherheitsgurt der.

seaweed ['si:wi:d] n Seetang der.

secluded [sɪ'klu:dɪd] adj abgeschieden.

second ['sekənd] ◆ n Sekunde die. ◆ num zweite(-r)(-s); **~ gear** zweiter Gang, → **sixth**. ► **seconds** npl (goods) Waren pl zweiter Wahl; (inf: of food) zweite Portion.

secondary school ['sekəndrɪ-] n höhere Schule.

second-class adj (ticket) zweiter

Klasse; (inferior) zweitklassig; **~ stamp** billigere Briefmarke für Post, die weniger schnell befördert wird.

second-hand adj gebraucht.

Second World War n: **the ~** der zweite Weltkrieg.

secret ['si:krɪt] ◆ adj geheim. ◆ n Geheimnis das.

secretary [Br 'sekrətrɪ, Am 'sekrə,terɪ] n Sekretär der (-in die).

Secretary of State n (Am: foreign minister) Außenminister der (-in die); (Br: government minister) Minister der (-in die).

section ['sekʃn] n (part) Teil der.

sector ['sektər] n Sektor der.

secure [sɪ'kjuər] ◆ adj sicher; (firmly fixed) fest. ◆ vt (fix) sichern; (fml: obtain) sich (D) sichern.

security [sɪ'kjuərətɪ] n Sicherheit die.

security guard n Sicherheitsbeamter der (-beamtin die).

sedative ['sedətɪv] n Beruhigungsmittel das.

seduce [sɪ'dju:s] vt verführen.

see [si:] (pt **saw**, pp **seen**) ◆ vt sehen; (visit) besuchen; (doctor, solicitor) gehen zu; (understand) einsehen; (accompany) begleiten. ◆ vi sehen; **I ~** (understand) ich verstehe; **to ~ if one can do sthg** sehen, ob man etw tun kann; **to ~ to sthg** (deal with) sich um etw kümmern; (repair) etw reparieren; **~ you!** tschüs!; **~ you later!** bis bald!; **~ you soon!** bis bald!; **~ p 14** siehe S. 14. ► **see off** vt sep (say goodbye to) verabschieden.

seed [si:d] n Samen der.

seedy ['si:dɪ] adj heruntergekommen.

seeing (as) ['si:ɪŋ-] conj in Anbetracht dessen, daß.

seek [si:k] (pt & pp **sought**) vt (fml) (look for) suchen; (request) erbitten.

seem [si:m] ◆ vi scheinen. ◆ v impers: **it ~ (that)** ... anscheinend.

seen [si:n] pp → **see**.

seesaw ['si:sɔ:] *n* Wippe *die.*

segment ['segmənt] *n* (*of fruit*) Scheibe *die,* Schnitt *der* (*Süddt*).

seize [si:z] *vt* (*grab*) ergreifen; (*drugs, arms*) beschlagnahmen. ▶ **seize up** *vi* (*machine*) sich fest|fressen; (*leg, back*) sich versteifen.

seldom ['seldəm] *adv* selten.

select [sɪ'lekt] ♦ *vt* aus|wählen. ♦ *adj* (*exclusive*) ausgesucht.

selection [sɪ'lekʃn] *n* (*selecting*) Wahl *die;* (*range*) Auswahl *die.*

self-assured [,selfə'ʃʊəd] *adj* selbstsicher.

self-catering [,self'keɪtərɪŋ] *adj* mit Selbstversorgung.

self-confident [,self-] *adj* selbstbewußt.

self-conscious [,self-] *adj* gehemmt.

self-contained [,selfkən'teɪnd] *adj* (*flat*) abgeschlossen.

self-defence [,self-] *n* Selbstverteidigung *die.*

self-employed [,self-] *adj* selbständig.

selfish ['selfɪʃ] *adj* egoistisch.

self-raising flour [,self'reɪzɪŋ-] *n* (Br) Mehl *das* mit Backpulverzusatz.

self-rising flour [,self'raɪzɪŋ-] (Am) = **self-raising flour**.

self-service [,self-] *adj* mit Selbstbedienung.

sell [sel] (*pt & pp* **sold**) *vt & vi* verkaufen; **to ~ for £20** 20 Pfund kosten; **to ~ sb sthg** jm etw verkaufen.

sell-by date *n* Mindesthaltbarkeitsdatum *das.*

seller ['selər] *n* Verkäufer *der* (-in *die*).

Sellotape® ['seləteɪp] *n* (Br) ≈ Tesafilm® *der.*

semester [sɪ'mestər] *n* Semester *das.*

semicircle ['semɪ,sɜ:kl] *n* Halbkreis *der.*

semicolon [,semɪ'kəʊlən] *n* Strichpunkt *der.*

semidetached [,semɪdɪ'tætʃt] *adj:* **a ~ house** eine Doppelhaushälfte.

semifinal [,semɪ'faɪnl] *n* Halbfinale *das.*

seminar ['semɪnɑ:r] *n* Seminar *das.*

semolina [,semə'li:nə] *n* Grieß *der.*

send [send] (*pt & pp* **sent**) *vt* schicken; (*TV or radio signal*) senden; **to ~ sthg to sb** jm etw schicken. ▶ **send back** *vt sep* zurück|schicken. ▶ **send off** *vt sep* (*letter, parcel*) ab|schicken; (SPORT) vom Platz stellen. ♦ *vi:* **to ~ off for sthg** sich (D) etw schicken lassen.

sender ['sendər] *n* Absender *der.*

senile ['si:naɪl] *adj* senil.

senior ['si:njər] ♦ *adj* (*high-ranking*) leitend; (*higher-ranking*) höher. ♦ *n* (Br: SCH) *Schüler der höheren Klassen;* (Am: SCH) *amerikanischer Student im letzten Studienjahr.*

senior citizen *n* Senior *der* (-in *die*).

sensation [sen'seɪʃn] *n* Gefühl *das;* (*cause of excitement*) Sensation *die.*

sensational [sen'seɪʃənl] *adj* (*very good*) sensationell.

sense [sens] ♦ *n* Sinn *der;* (*common sense*) Verstand *der;* (*of word, expression*) Bedeutung *die.* ♦ *vt* spüren; **to make ~** Sinn ergeben; **~ of direction** Orientierungssinn *der;* **~ of humour** Sinn für Humor.

sensible ['sensəbl] *adj* (*person*) vernünftig; (*clothes, shoes*) praktisch.

sensitive ['sensɪtɪv] *adj* empfindlich; (*emotionally*) sensibel; (*subject, issue*) heikel.

sent [sent] *pt & pp* → **send**.

sentence ['sentəns] ♦ *n* (GRAMM) Satz *der;* (*for crime*) Strafe *die.* ♦ *vt* verurteilen.

sentimental [,sentɪ'mentl] *adj* sentimental.

Sep. (*abbr of September*) Sept.

separate [*adj* 'seprət, *vb* 'sepəreɪt] ♦ *adj* getrennt; (*different*) verschieden. ♦ *vt* trennen. ♦ *vi* sich trennen. ▶ **separates** *npl* (Br) Separates *pl.*

separately ['seprətlı] adv (individually) einzeln; (alone) getrennt.

separation [,sepə'reıʃn] n Trennung die.

September [sep'tembər] n September der; **at the beginning of ~** Anfang September; **at the end of ~** Ende September; **during ~** im September; **every ~** jeden September; **in ~** im September; **last ~** letzten September; **next ~** nächsten September; **this ~** diesen September; **2 ~ 1994** (in letters etc) 2. September 1994.

septic ['septɪk] adj vereitert.

septic tank n Klärgrube die.

sequel ['si:kwəl] n Fortsetzung die.

sequence ['si:kwəns] n (series) Reihe die; (order) Reihenfolge die.

sequin ['si:kwɪn] n Paillette die.

sergeant ['sɑːdʒənt] n (in police force) Wachtmeister der; (in army) Feldwebel der.

serial ['sɪərɪəl] n Serie die.

series ['sɪərɪːz] (pl inv) n (sequence) Reihe die; (on TV, radio) Serie die.

serious ['sɪərɪəs] adj ernst; (injury, problem) schwer; **are you ~?** ist das dein Ernst?; **to be ~ about sthg** etw ernst nehmen.

seriously ['sɪərɪəslı] adv ernsthaft.

sermon ['sɜːmən] n Predigt die.

servant ['sɜːvənt] n Diener der (-in die).

serve [sɜːv] ◆ vt (food) servieren; (drink) aus|schenken; (customer) bedienen. ◆ vi (SPORT) auf|schlagen; (work) dienen. ◆ n (SPORT) Aufschlag der; **to ~ as** (be used for) dienen als; **the town is ~d by two airports** die Stadt hat zwei Flughäfen; **'~s two'** (on packaging, menu) 'für zwei Personen'; **it ~s you right** geschieht dir recht!

service ['sɜːvɪs] ◆ n (in shop, restaurant etc) Bedienung die; (job, organization) Dienst der; (at church) Gottesdienst der; (SPORT) Aufschlag der; (of car) Wartung die. ◆ vt (car) warten; **'out of ~'** 'außer Betrieb'; **'~ included'** 'Bedienung inbegriffen'; **'~ not included'** 'Bedienung nicht inbegriffen'; **to be of ~ to sb** (fml) jm behilflich sein. ► **services** npl (on motorway) Raststätte die; (of person) Dienste pl.

service area n Tankstelle die und Raststätte.

service charge n Bedienungszuschlag der.

service department n Kundendienst der.

service station n Tankstelle die.

serviette [,sɜːvɪ'et] n Serviette die.

serving ['sɜːvɪŋ] n (helping) Portion die.

serving spoon n Servierlöffel der.

sesame seeds ['sesəmɪ-] npl Sesam der.

session ['seʃn] n (of activity) Runde die; (formal meeting) Sitzung die.

set [set] (pt & pp inv) ◆ adj 1. (fixed) fest; (date) festgesetzt; **a ~ lunch** ein Mittagsmenü. 2. (text, book) Pflicht-. ◆ n 1. (collection) Satz der; **a chess ~** ein Schachspiel. 2. (TV): **a (TV) ~** ein Fernsehgerät. 3. (in tennis) Satz der. 4. (SCH) Gruppe von Schülern mit gleichem Niveau innerhalb eines Faches. 5. (of play) Bühnenbild das. 6. (at hairdresser's): **a shampoo and ~** Waschen und Legen. ◆ vt 1. (put) setzen; (put upright) stellen; (put flat) legen. 2. (cause to be): **to ~ a machine going** eine Maschine in Gang bringen; **to ~ fire to sthg** etw in Brand setzen. 3. (controls) ein|stellen; (clock) stellen; **~ the alarm for 7 a.m.** stell den Wecker für 7 Uhr früh. 4. (price, time) festlegen. 5. (the table) decken. 6. (a record) auf|stellen. 7. (broken bone) richten. 8. (homework, essay) auf|geben; (exam) zusammen|stellen. 9. (play, film, story): **to be ~** spielen. ◆ vi 1. (sun) unter|gehen. 2. (glue, jelly) fest werden. ► **set down** vt sep (Br: passengers) ab|setzen. ► **set off** vt sep (alarm) aus|lösen. ◆ vi (on journey) auf|brechen. ► **set out** vt sep (*arrange*) her|richten. ◆ *vi* (*on journey*) auf|brechen. ► **set up** *vt sep* (*barrier*) auf|stellen; (*equipment*) auf|bauen; (*meeting, interview*) organisieren.

set meal *n* Menü *das*.

set menu *n* Menü *das*.

settee [se'ti:] *n* Sofa *das*.

setting ['setɪŋ] *n* (*on machine*) Einstellung *die*; (*surroundings*) Lage *die*.

settle ['setl] ◆ *vt* (*argument*) bei|legen; (*bill*) bezahlen; (*stomach, nerves*) beruhigen; (*arrange, decide on*) entscheiden. ◆ *vi* (*start to live*) sich nieder|lassen; (*come to rest*) sich hin|setzen; (*sediment, dust*) sich setzen. ► **settle down** *vi* (*calm down*) sich beruhigen; (*sit comfortably*) sich gemütlich hin|setzen. ► **settle up** *vi* (*pay bill*) bezahlen.

settlement ['setlmənt] *n* (*agreement*) Einigung *die*; (*place*) Siedlung *die*.

seven ['sevn] *num* sieben, → **six**.

seventeen [,sevn'ti:n] *num* siebzehn, → **six**.

seventeenth [,sevn'ti:nθ] *num* siebzehnte(-r)(-s), → **sixth**.

seventh ['sevnθ] *num* siebte(-r)(-s), → **sixth**.

seventieth ['sevntjəθ] *num* siebzigste(-r)(-s), → **sixth**.

seventy ['sevntɪ] *num* siebzig, → **six**.

several ['sevrəl] *adj & pron* mehrere, einige.

severe [sɪ'vɪər] *adj* (*conditions, illness*) schwer; (*criticism, person, punishment*) hart; (*pain*) heftig.

sew [səʊ] (*pp* sewn) *vt & vi* nähen.

sewage ['su:ɪdʒ] *n* Abwasser *das*.

sewing ['səʊɪŋ] *n* (*activity*) Nähen *das*; (*things sewn*) Nähzeug *das*.

sewing machine *n* Nähmaschine *die*.

sewn [səʊn] *pp* → **sew**.

sex [seks] *n* (*gender*) Geschlecht *das*; (*sexual intercourse*) Sex *der*; **to have ~ (with)** Sex haben (mit).

sexist ['seksɪst] *n* Sexist *der*.

sexual ['seksʊəl] *adj* sexuell.

sexy ['seksɪ] *adj* sexy.

shabby ['ʃæbɪ] *adj* (*clothes, room*) schäbig; (*person*) heruntergekommen.

shade [ʃeɪd] ◆ *n* (*shadow*) Schatten *der*; (*lampshade*) Schirm *der*; (*of colour*) Ton *der*. ◆ *vt* (*protect*) schützen. ► **shades** *npl* (*inf: sunglasses*) Sonnenbrille *die*.

shadow ['ʃædəʊ] *n* Schatten *der*.

shady ['ʃeɪdɪ] *adj* schattig; (*inf: person, deal*) zwielichtig.

shaft [ʃɑ:ft] *n* (*of machine*) Welle *die*; (*of lift*) Schacht *der*.

shake [ʃeɪk] (*pt* shook, *pp* shaken [-'ʃeɪkn]) ◆ *vt* schütteln; (*shock*) erschüttern. ◆ *vi* (*person*) zittern; (*building, earth*) beben; **to ~ hands with sb** jm die Hand geben; **to ~ one's head** den Kopf schütteln.

shall [*weak form* ʃəl, *strong form* ʃæl] *aux vb* **1.** (*expressing future*) werden; **I ~ be late tomorrow** morgen werde ich später kommen; **I ~ be ready soon** ich bin bald fertig. **2.** (*in questions*) sollen; **~ I buy some wine?** soll ich Wein kaufen?; **where ~ we go?** wo sollen wir hingehen? **3.** (*fml: expressing order*): **payment ~ be made within a week** die Zahlung muß innerhalb einer Woche erfolgen.

shallot [ʃə'lɒt] *n* Schalotte *die*.

shallow ['ʃæləʊ] *adj* (*pond, water*) seicht.

shallow end *n* (*of swimming pool*) flaches Ende.

shambles ['ʃæmblz] *n* wildes Durcheinander.

shame [ʃeɪm] *n* (*remorse*) Scham *die*; (*disgrace*) Schande *die*; **it's a ~ that** schade, daß; **what a ~!** wie schade!

shampoo [ʃæm'pu:] (*pl* -s) *n* (*liquid*) Shampoo *das*; (*wash*) Shampoonieren *das*.

shandy ['ʃændɪ] *n* Radler *der*.

shape [ʃeɪp] *n* Form *die*; (*person*) Gestalt *die*; **to be in good/bad ~** in guter/schlechter Form sein.

share [ʃeəʳ] ♦ n (part) Anteil der; (in company) Aktie die. ♦ vt (room, work, cost, responsibility) teilen; (divide) aufiteilen. ▶ **share out** vt sep aufiteilen.

shark [ʃɑːk] n Hai der.

sharp [ʃɑːp] ♦ adj scharf; (pencil, needle, teeth) spitz; (rise, change, bend) steil; (quick, intelligent) aufgeweckt; (painful) stechend; (food, taste) säuerlich. ♦ adv (exactly): **at one o'clock ~** Punkt eins.

sharpen [ʃɑːpn] vt (knife) schärfen; (pencil) spitzen.

shatter [ʃætəʳ] ♦ vt (break) zerschmettern. ♦ vi zerbrechen.

shattered [ʃætəd] adj (Br: inf: tired) erschlagen.

shave [ʃeɪv] ♦ vt rasieren. ♦ vi sich rasieren. ♦ n: **to have a ~** sich rasieren; **to ~ one's legs** sich (D) die Beine rasieren.

shaver [ʃeɪvəʳ] n Rasierapparat der.

shaver point n Steckdose für einen Rasierapparat.

shaving brush [ʃeɪvɪŋ-] n Rasierpinsel der.

shaving cream [ʃeɪvɪŋ-] n Rasiercreme die.

shaving foam [ʃeɪvɪŋ-] n Rasierschaum der.

shawl [ʃɔːl] n Schultertuch das.

she [ʃiː] pron sie; **~'s tall** sie ist groß.

sheaf [ʃiːf] (pl sheaves) n (of paper, notes) Bündel das.

shears [ʃɪəz] npl Gartenschere die.

sheaves [ʃiːvz] pl → sheaf.

shed [ʃed] (pt & pp inv) ♦ n Schuppen der. ♦ vt (tears, blood) vergießen.

she'd [weak form ʃɪd, strong form ʃiːd] = **she had, she would**.

sheep [ʃiːp] (pl inv) n Schaf das.

sheepdog [ʃiːpdɒg] n Schäferhund der.

sheepskin [ʃiːpskɪn] adj Schaffell das.

sheer [ʃɪəʳ] adj (pure, utter) rein; (cliff) steil; (stockings) hauchdünn.

sheet [ʃiːt] n (for bed) Laken das; (of paper) Blatt das; (of glass, metal, wood) Platte die.

shelf [ʃelf] (pl shelves) n Regal das.

shell [ʃel] n (of egg, nut) Schale die; (on beach) Muschel die; (of tortoise) Panzer der; (of snail) Haus das; (bomb) Granate die.

she'll [ʃiːl] = **she will, she shall**.

shellfish [ʃelfɪʃ] n (food) Meeresfrüchte pl.

shell suit n (Br) Freizeitanzug der (aus Polyamid Außenmaterial und Baumwollfutter).

shelter [ʃeltəʳ] ♦ n Schutz der; (structure) Schutzdach das. ♦ vt (protect) schützen. ♦ vi sich unteristellen; **to take ~** sich unteristellen.

sheltered [ʃeltəd] adj (place) geschützt.

shelves [ʃelvz] pl → shelf.

shepherd [ʃepəd] n Schafhirte der (-hirtin die).

shepherd's pie [ʃepədz-] n Auflauf aus Hackfleisch, bedeckt mit einer Schicht Kartoffelbrei.

sheriff [ʃerɪf] n (in US) Sheriff der.

sherry [ʃerɪ] n Sherry der.

she's [ʃiːz] = **she is, she has**.

shield [ʃiːld] ♦ n Schild der. ♦ vt schützen.

shift [ʃɪft] ♦ n (change) Veränderung die; (period of work) Schicht die. ♦ vt (move) rücken; (rearrange) umistellen. ♦ vi (move) sich verschieben; (change) sich verändern.

shin [ʃɪn] n Schienbein das.

shine [ʃaɪn] (pt & pp shone) ♦ vi scheinen; (surface, glass) glänzen. ♦ vt (shoes) polieren; (torch) leuchten.

shiny [ʃaɪnɪ] adj glänzend.

ship [ʃɪp] n Schiff das; **by ~** mit dem Schiff.

shipwreck [ʃɪprek] n (accident) Schiffbruch der; (wrecked ship) Wrack das.

shirt [ʃɜːt] n Hemd das.

shit [ʃɪt] n (vulg) Scheiße die.

shiver [ˈʃɪvər] vi zittern.

shock [ʃɒk] ◆ n (surprise) Schock der; (force) Wucht die. ◆ vt (surprise) einen Schock versetzen (+D); (horrify) schockieren; **to be in ~** (MED) unter Schock stehen.

shock absorber [-əb,zɔːbər] n Stoßdämpfer der.

shocking [ˈʃɒkɪŋ] adj (very bad) entsetzlich.

shoe [ʃuː] n Schuh der.

shoelace [ˈʃuːleɪs] n Schnürsenkel der.

shoe polish n Schuhcreme die.

shoe repairer's [-rɪ,peərəz] n Schuhmacher der.

shoe shop n Schuhgeschäft das.

shone [ʃɒn] pt & pp → **shine**.

shook [ʃʊk] pt → **shake**.

shoot [ʃuːt] (pt & pp shot) ◆ vt (kill) erlschießen; (injure) anlschießen; (gun, arrow) schießen; (film) drehen. ◆ vi schießen. ◆ n (of plant) Trieb der.

shop [ʃɒp] ◆ n Geschäft das, Laden der. ◆ vi einlkaufen.

shop assistant n (Br) Verkäufer der (-in die).

shop floor n Produktion die.

shopkeeper [ˈʃɒp,kiːpər] n Geschäftsinhaber der (-in die).

shoplifter [ˈʃɒp,lɪftər] n Ladendieb der (-in die).

shopper [ˈʃɒpər] n Käufer der (-in die).

shopping [ˈʃɒpɪŋ] n (things bought) Einkäufe pl; (activity) Einkaufen das; **to do the ~** den Einkauf erledigen; **to go ~** einkaufen gehen.

shopping bag n Einkaufstüte die.

shopping basket n Einkaufskorb der.

shopping centre n Einkaufszentrum das.

shopping list n Einkaufsliste die.

shopping mall n Einkaufszentrum das.

shop steward n gewerkschaftlicher Vertrauensmann.

shop window n Schaufenster das.

shore [ʃɔːr] n (of sea, river, lake) Ufer das; **on ~** (on land) an Land.

short [ʃɔːt] ◆ adj kurz; (not tall) klein. ◆ adv (cut) kurz. ◆ n (Br: drink) Kurze der; (film) Kurzfilm der; **to be ~ of sthg** (time, money) zuwenig von etw haben; **to be ~ of breath** außer Atem sein; **in ~** kurz (gesagt). ▶ **shorts** npl (short trousers) Shorts pl; (Am: underpants) Unterhose die.

shortage [ˈʃɔːtɪdʒ] n Mangel der.

shortbread [ˈʃɔːtbred] n Buttergebäck das.

short-circuit vi einen Kurzschluß haben.

shortcrust pastry [ˈʃɔːtkrʌst-] n Mürbeteig der.

short cut n Abkürzung die.

shorten [ˈʃɔːtn] vt (in time) verkürzen; (in length) kürzen.

shorthand [ˈʃɔːthænd] n Stenografie die.

shortly [ˈʃɔːtlɪ] adv (soon) in Kürze; **~ before** kurz bevor.

shortsighted [ˌʃɔːtˈsaɪtɪd] adj kurzsichtig.

short-sleeved [-ˌsliːvd] adj kurzärmelig.

short-stay car park n Parkplatz der für Kurzparker.

short story n Kurzgeschichte die.

short wave n Kurzwelle die.

shot [ʃɒt] ◆ pt & pp → **shoot**. ◆ n (of gun, in football) Schuß der; (in tennis, golf) Schlag der; (photo) Aufnahme die; (in film) Einstellung die; (inf: attempt) Versuch der; (of alcohol) Schuß der.

shotgun [ˈʃɒtgʌn] n Schrotflinte die.

should [ʃʊd] aux vb 1. (expressing desirability): **we ~ leave now** wir sollten jetzt gehen. 2. (asking for advice): **~ I go too?** soll ich auch gehen? 3. (expressing probability): **she ~ be home soon** sie müßte bald zu Hause sein. 4. (ought to): **they ~ have won the match** sie hätten das Spiel

sideways

gewinnen sollen. **5.** (*fml: in conditionals*): ~ **you need anything, call reception** sollten Sie irgendetwas brauchen, rufen Sie die Rezeption an. **6.** (*fml: expressing wish*): **I ~ like to come with you** ich würde gerne mit dir mitkommen.

shoulder ['ʃəʊldəʳ] *n* Schulter *die*; (*of meat*) Schulterstück *das*; (*Am: of road*) Seitenstreifen *der*.

shoulder pad *n* Schulterpolster *das*.

shouldn't ['ʃʊdnt] = **should not**.

should've ['ʃʊdəv] = **should have**.

shout [ʃaʊt] ◆ *n* Schrei *der.* ◆ *vt & vi* schreien. ► **shout out** *vt sep* herauslschreien.

shove [ʃʌv] *vt* stoßen; (*put carelessly*) stopfen.

shovel ['ʃʌvl] *n* Schaufel *die.*

show [ʃəʊ] (*pp* -**ed** OR **shown**) ◆ *n* (*at theatre, on TV, radio*) Show *die*; (*exhibition*) Schau *die.* ◆ *vt* zeigen; (*accompany*) begleiten. ◆ *vi* (*be visible*) sichtbar sein; (*film*) laufen; **to ~ sthg to sb** jm etw zeigen; **to ~ sb how to do sthg** jm zeigen, wie man etw tut. ► **show off** *vi* anlgeben. ► **show up** *vi* (*come along*) kommen; (*be visible*) zu sehen sein.

shower ['ʃaʊəʳ] ◆ *n* (*for washing*) Dusche *die*; (*of rain*) Guß *der.* ◆ *vi* (*wash*) duschen; **to have a ~** duschen.

shower gel *n* Duschgel *das.*

shower unit *n* Dusche *die.*

showing ['ʃəʊɪŋ] *n* (*of film*) Vorführung *die.*

shown [ʃəʊn] *pp* → **show**.

showroom ['ʃəʊrʊm] *n* Ausstellungsraum *der.*

shrank [ʃræŋk] *pt* → **shrink**.

shrimp [ʃrɪmp] *n* Krabbe *die.*

shrine [ʃraɪn] *n* Schrein *der.*

shrink [ʃrɪŋk] (*pt* **shrank**, *pp* **shrunk**) ◆ *n* (*inf: psychoanalyst*) Psychiater *der.* ◆ *vi* (*become smaller*) schrumpfen; (*clothes*) einllaufen; (*diminish*) abl-nehmen.

shrub [ʃrʌb] *n* Strauch *der.*

shrug [ʃrʌg] ◆ *n* Achselzucken *das.* ◆ *vi* die Achseln zucken.

shrunk [ʃrʌŋk] *pp* → **shrink**.

shuffle ['ʃʌfl] ◆ *vt* (*cards*) mischen. ◆ *vi* schlurfen.

shut [ʃʌt] (*pt & pp inv*) ◆ *adj* zu, geschlossen. ◆ *vt* schließen, zulmachen. ◆ *vi* (*door, mouth, eyes*) schließen; (*shop, restaurant*) schließen, zulmachen. ► **shut down** *vt sep* schließen. ► **shut up** *vi* (*inf: stop talking*) den Mund halten.

shutter ['ʃʌtəʳ] *n* (*on window*) Fensterladen *der*; (*on camera*) Verschluß *der.*

shuttle ['ʃʌtl] *n* (*plane*) Pendelmaschine *die*; (*bus*) Pendelbus *der.*

shuttlecock ['ʃʌtlkɒk] *n* Federball *der.*

shy [ʃaɪ] *adj* schüchtern.

sick [sɪk] *adj* (*ill*) krank; **to be ~** (*vomit*) sich übergeben; **I feel ~** mir ist schlecht; **to be ~ of** (*fed up with*) die Nase voll haben von.

sick bag *n* Tüte, *die Passagiere in Flugzeugen benutzen können, wenn ihnen schlecht wird.*

sickness ['sɪknɪs] *n* Krankheit *die.*

sick pay *n* Krankengeld *das.*

side [saɪd] ◆ *n* Seite *die*; (*Br: TV channel*) Kanal *der.* ◆ *adj* (*door, pocket*) Seiten-; **at the ~ of** neben (+D); **on the other ~** auf der anderen Seite; **on this ~** auf dieser Seite; **~ by ~** Seite an Seite.

sideboard ['saɪdbɔ:d] *n* Anrichte *die.*

sidecar ['saɪdkɑ:ʳ] *n* Beiwagen *der.*

side dish *n* Beilage *die.*

side effect *n* Nebenwirkung *die.*

sidelight ['saɪdlaɪt] *n* (*Br: of car*) Begrenzungsleuchte *die.*

side order *n* Beilage *die.*

side salad *n* Salatbeilage *die.*

side street *n* Seitenstraße *die.*

sidewalk ['saɪdwɔ:k] *n* (*Am*) Bürgersteig *der.*

sideways ['saɪdweɪz] *adv* seitwärts.

sieve [sɪv] n Sieb das.

sigh [saɪ] ◆ n Seufzer der. ◆ vi seufzen.

sight [saɪt] n (eyesight) Sehvermögen das; (thing seen) Anblick der; **at first ~** auf den ersten Blick; **to catch ~ of** erblicken; **in ~** in Sicht; **to lose ~ of** aus den Augen verlieren; **out of ~** außer Sicht. ▶ **sights** npl (of city, country) Sehenswürdigkeiten pl.

sightseeing ['saɪtˌsiːɪŋ] n: **to go ~** Sehenswürdigkeiten besichtigen.

sign [saɪn] ◆ n Zeichen das; (next to road, in shop, station) Schild das. ◆ vt & vi unterschreiben; **there's no ~ of her** von ihr ist nichts zu sehen. ▶ **sign in** vi (at hotel, club) sich einltragen.

signal ['sɪgnl] ◆ n Signal das; (Am: traffic lights) Ampel die. ◆ vi (in car, on bike) die Fahrtrichtung anlzeigen.

signature ['sɪgnətʃəʳ] n Unterschrift die.

significant [sɪg'nɪfɪkənt] adj (large) beträchtlich; (important) bedeutend.

signpost ['saɪnpəʊst] n Wegweiser der.

Sikh [siːk] n Sikh der die.

silence ['saɪləns] n Stille die.

silencer ['saɪlənsəʳ] n (Br: AUT) Auspufftopf der.

silent ['saɪlənt] adj still.

silk [sɪlk] n Seide die.

sill [sɪl] n Sims der.

silly ['sɪlɪ] adj albern.

silver ['sɪlvəʳ] ◆ n Silber das; (coins) Silbergeld das. ◆ adj (made of silver) Silber-.

silver foil n Alu-folie die.

silver-plated [-'pleɪtɪd] adj versilbert.

similar ['sɪmɪləʳ] adj ähnlich; **to be ~ to** ähnlich sein (+D).

similarity [ˌsɪmɪ'lærətɪ] n Ähnlichkeit die.

simmer ['sɪməʳ] vi leicht kochen.

simple ['sɪmpl] adj einfach.

simplify ['sɪmplɪfaɪ] vt vereinfachen.

simply ['sɪmplɪ] adv einfach.

simulate ['sɪmjʊleɪt] vt simulieren.

simultaneous [Br ˌsɪməl'teɪnjəs, Am ˌsaɪməl'teɪnjəs] adj gleichzeitig.

simultaneously [Br ˌsɪməl'teɪnjəslɪ, Am ˌsaɪməl'teɪnjəslɪ] adv gleichzeitig.

sin [sɪn] ◆ n Sünde die. ◆ vi sündigen.

since [sɪns] ◆ adv seitdem. ◆ prep seit. ◆ conj (in time) seit; (as) da; **I've been here ~ six o'clock** ich bin hier seit sechs Uhr; **ever ~** seitdem, seit.

sincere [sɪn'sɪəʳ] adj aufrichtig.

sincerely [sɪn'sɪəlɪ] adv aufrichtig; **Yours ~** mit freundlichen Grüßen.

sing [sɪŋ] (pt **sang**, pp **sung**) vt & vi singen.

singer ['sɪŋəʳ] n Sänger der (-in die).

single ['sɪŋgl] ◆ adj (just one) einzig; (not married) ledig. ◆ n (Br: ticket) einfache Fahrkarte; (record) Single die; **every ~** jede(-r)(-s) einzelne. ▶ **singles** n (SPORT) Einzel das. ◆ adj Singles-.

single bed n Einzelbett das.

single cream n (Br) Sahne mit niedrigem Fettgehalt.

single parent n Alleinerziehende der die.

single room n Einzelzimmer das.

single track road n einspurige Straße.

singular ['sɪŋgjʊləʳ] n Singular der; **in the ~** im Singular.

sinister ['sɪnɪstəʳ] adj finster.

sink [sɪŋk] (pt **sank**, pp **sunk**) ◆ n (in kitchen) Spülbecken das; (washbasin) Waschbecken das. ◆ vi sinken.

sink unit n Spüle die.

sinuses ['saɪnəsɪz] npl Nebenhöhlen pl.

sip [sɪp] ◆ n Schlückchen das. ◆ vt in kleinen Schlucken trinken.

siphon ['saɪfn] ◆ n (tube) Saugheber der. ◆ vt (liquid) ablsaugen.

sir [sɜːʳ] n mein Herr; **Dear Sir/Sirs** Sehr geehrte Herren; **Sir Richard**

Blair Sir Richard Blair.

siren ['saɪərən] *n* Sirene *die*.

sirloin steak [,sɜːlɔɪn-] *n* Lenden-steak *das*.

sister ['sɪstər] *n* Schwester *die*.

sister-in-law *n* Schwägerin *die*.

sit [sɪt] (*pt & pp* **sat**) ◆ *vi* (*be seated*) sitzen; (*sit down*) sich setzen; (*be situated*) liegen. ◆ *vt* (*place*) setzen; (*Br: exam*) machen; **to be sitting** sitzen. ► **sit down** *vi* sich hinsetzen; **to be sitting down** sitzen. ► **sit up** *vi* (*after lying down*) sich auflsetzen; (*stay up late*) auflbleiben.

site [saɪt] *n* Stelle *die*; (*building site*) Baustelle *die*.

sitting room ['sɪtɪŋ-] *n* Wohnzimmer *das*.

situated ['sɪtjʊeɪtɪd] *adj*: **to be ~** liegen.

situation [,sɪtjʊ'eɪʃn] *n* Lage *die*; **'~s vacant'** 'Stellenangebote'.

six [sɪks] ◆ *num adj* sechs. ◆ *num n* Sechs *die*; **to be ~ (years old)** sechs (Jahre alt) sein; **it's ~ (o'clock)** es ist sechs Uhr; **a hundred and ~** hundertsechs; **~ Hill St** Hill St sechs; **it's minus ~ (degrees)** es ist minus sechs (Grad).

sixteen [sɪks'tiːn] *num* sechzehn, → **six**.

sixteenth [sɪks'tiːnθ] *num* sechzehnte(-r)(-s), → **sixth**.

sixth [sɪksθ] ◆ *num adj & adv* sechste(-r)(-s). ◆ *num pron* Sechste *der, die*. ◆ *num n* (*fraction*) Sechstel *das*; **the ~ (of September)** der sechste (September).

sixth form *n* (*Br*) die letzten beiden Klassen vor den 'A-level'-Prüfungen.

sixth-form college *n* (*Br*) College für Schüler, die ihre 'A-level'-Prüfungen machen.

sixtieth ['sɪkstɪəθ] *num* sechzigste(-r)(-s), → **sixth**.

sixty ['sɪkstɪ] *num* sechzig, → **six**.

size [saɪz] *n* Größe *die*; **what ~ do you take?** welche Größe haben Sie?; **what ~ is this?** welche Größe ist das?

sizeable ['saɪzəbl] *adj* beträchtlich.

skate [skeɪt] ◆ *n* (*ice skate*) Schlittschuh *der*; (*roller skate*) Rollschuh *der*; (*fish*) Rochen *der*. ◆ *vi* (*ice-skate*) Schlittschuh laufen; (*roller-skate*) Rollschuh laufen.

skateboard ['skeɪtbɔːd] *n* Skateboard *das*.

skater ['skeɪtər] *n* (*ice-skater*) Schlittschuhläufer *der* (-in *die*); (*roller-skater*) Rollschuhläufer *der* (-in *die*).

skating ['skeɪtɪŋ] *n*: **to go ~** (*ice-skating*) Schlittschuhlaufen gehen; (*roller-skating*) Rollschuhlaufen gehen.

skeleton ['skelɪtn] *n* Skelett *das*.

skeptical ['skeptɪkl] (*Am*) = **sceptical**.

sketch [sketʃ] ◆ *n* (*drawing*) Skizze *die*; (*humorous*) Sketch *der*. ◆ *vt* skizzieren.

skewer ['skjʊər] *n* Spieß *der*.

ski [skiː] (*pt & pp* **skied**, *cont* **skiing**) ◆ *n* Ski *der*. ◆ *vi* Ski laufen.

ski boots *npl* Skistiefel *pl*.

skid [skɪd] ◆ *n* Schleudern *das*. ◆ *vi* schleudern.

skier ['skiːər] *n* Skiläufer *der* (-in *die*).

skiing ['skiːɪŋ] *n* Skilaufen *das*, Skifahren *das*; **to go ~** Skilaufen gehen; **a ~ holiday** ein Skiurlaub.

skilful ['skɪlfʊl] *adj* (*Br*) geschickt.

ski lift *n* Skilift *der*.

skill [skɪl] *n* (*ability*) Geschick *das*; (*technique*) Fertigkeit *die*.

skilled [skɪld] *adj* (*worker, job*) qualifiziert, Fach-; (*driver, chef*) erfahren.

skillful ['skɪlfʊl] (*Am*) = **skilful**.

skimmed milk ['skɪmd-] *n* entrahmte Milch.

skin [skɪn] *n* Haut *die*; (*on fruit, vegetable*) Schale *die*; (*from animal*) Fell *das*.

skin freshener [-,freʃnər] *n* Gesichtswasser *das*.

skinny ['skɪnɪ] *adj* mager.

skip [skɪp] ◆ *vi* (*with rope*) seillspringen; (*jump*) hüpfen. ◆ *vt* (*omit*) aus|lassen. ◆ n (container) Container der.

ski pants npl Skihose die.

ski pass n Skipaß der.

ski pole n Skistock der.

skipping rope ['skɪpɪŋ-] n Sprungseil das.

skirt [skɜːt] n Rock der.

ski slope n Skipiste die.

ski tow n Schlepplift der.

skittles ['skɪtlz] n (game) Kegeln das.

skull [skʌl] n Schädel der.

sky [skaɪ] n Himmel der.

skylight ['skaɪlaɪt] n Dachfenster das.

skyscraper ['skaɪˌskreɪpər] n Wolkenkratzer der.

slab [slæb] n Platte die.

slack [slæk] adj (rope) locker; (careless) nachlässig; (not busy) ruhig.

slacks [slæks] npl Hose die.

slam [slæm] vt zu|schlagen.

slander ['slɑːndər] n Verleumdung die.

slang [slæŋ] n Slang der.

slant [slɑːnt] ◆ n (slope) Schräge die. ◆ vi sich neigen.

slap [slæp] ◆ n (smack) Schlag der. ◆ vt schlagen.

slash [slæʃ] ◆ vt (cut) auf|schlitzen; (fig: prices) reduzieren. ◆ n (written symbol) Schrägstrich der.

slate [sleɪt] n (rock) Schiefer der; (on roof) Schieferplatte die.

slaughter ['slɔːtər] vt (animal) schlachten; (fig: defeat) fertig|machen.

slave [sleɪv] n Sklave der (Sklavin die).

sled [sled] = **sledge**.

sledge [sledʒ] n Schlitten der.

sleep [sliːp] (pt & pp slept) ◆ n Schlaf der; (nap) Schläfchen das. ◆ vi schlafen. ◆ vt: **the house ~s six** in dem Haus können sechs Leute übernachten; **did you ~ well?** hast du gut geschlafen?; **I couldn't get to ~** ich konnte nicht einschlafen; **to go**

to ~ ein|schlafen; to ~ with sb mit jm schlafen.

sleeper ['sliːpər] n (train) Schlafwagenzug der; (sleeping car) Schlafwagen der; (Br: on railway track) Schwelle die; (Br: earring) Ohrstecker der.

sleeping bag ['sliːpɪŋ-] n Schlafsack der.

sleeping car ['sliːpɪŋ-] n Schlafwagen der.

sleeping pill ['sliːpɪŋ-] n Schlaftablette die.

sleeping policeman ['sliːpɪŋ-] n (Br) Geschwindigkeitsschwelle die.

sleepy ['sliːpɪ] adj schläfrig.

sleet [sliːt] ◆ n Schneeregen der. ◆ v impers: **it's ~ing** es rieselt Schneeregen.

sleeve [sliːv] n Ärmel der; (of record) Hülle die.

sleeveless ['sliːvlɪs] adj ärmellos.

slept [slept] pt & pp → **sleep**.

slice [slaɪs] ◆ n (of bread, meat) Scheibe die; (of cake, pizza) Stück das. ◆ vt (bread, meat) in Scheiben schneiden; (cake, vegetables) in Stücke schneiden.

sliced bread [ˌslaɪst-] n Schnittbrot das.

slide [slaɪd] (pt & pp slid [slɪd]) ◆ n (in playground) Rutsche die; (of photograph) Dia das; (Br: hair slide) Haarspange die. ◆ vi (slip) rutschen.

sliding door [ˌslaɪdɪŋ-] n Schiebetür die.

slight [slaɪt] adj (minor) leicht; **the ~est** der/die/das geringste; **not in the ~est** nicht im geringsten.

slightly ['slaɪtlɪ] adv leicht.

slim [slɪm] ◆ adj (person, waist) schlank; (book) schmal. ◆ vi ab|nehmen.

slimming ['slɪmɪŋ] n Abnehmen das.

sling [slɪŋ] (pt & pp slung) ◆ n (for arm) Schlinge die. ◆ vt (inf: throw) schmeißen.

slip [slɪp] ◆ *vi* rutschen. ◆ *n* (*mistake*) Ausrutscher *der*; (*of paper*) Zettel *der*; (*petticoat*) Unterrock *der*. ► **slip up** *vi* (*make a mistake*) einen Schnitzer machen.

slipper ['slɪpər] *n* Hausschuh *der*.

slippery ['slɪpərɪ] *adj* (*surface*) glatt; (*object*) schlüpfrig.

slip road *n* ([Br]: *onto motorway*) Auffahrt *die*; (*leaving motorway*) Ausfahrt *die*.

slit [slɪt] *n* Schlitz *der*.

slob [slɒb] *n* (*inf*) Schwein *das*.

slogan ['sləʊgən] *n* Slogan *der*.

slope [sləʊp] ◆ *n* (*incline*) Neigung *die*; (*hill*) Hang *der*; (*for skiing*) Piste *die*. ◆ *vi* sich neigen.

sloping ['sləʊpɪŋ] *adj* (*upwards*) ansteigend; (*downwards*) abfallend.

slot [slɒt] *n* (*for coin*) Schlitz *der*; (*groove*) Nut *die*.

slot machine *n* (*vending machine*) Automat *der*; (*for gambling*) Spielautomat *der*.

Slovakia [sləˈvækɪə] *n* Slowakei *die*.

slow [sləʊ] ◆ *adj* langsam; (*business*) flau. ◆ *adv* langsam; **to be ~** (*clock, watch*) nachgehen; **'slow'** (*sign on road*) 'langsam fahren'; **a ~ train** ein Nahverkehrszug. ► **slow down** *vt sep* verlangsamen. ◆ *vi* langsamer werden.

slowly ['sləʊlɪ] *adv* langsam.

slug [slʌg] *n* (*animal*) Nacktschnecke *die*.

slum [slʌm] *n* (*building*) Elendsquartier *das*. ► **slums** *npl* (*district*) Elendsviertel *das*.

slung [slʌŋ] *pt & pp* → **sling**.

slush [slʌʃ] *n* (*snow*) Schneematsch *der*.

sly [slaɪ] *adj* (*cunning*) schlau; (*deceitful*) verschlagen.

smack [smæk] ◆ *n* (*slap*) Schlag *der*; (*on bottom*) Klaps *der*. ◆ *vt* (*slap*) schlagen.

small [smɔːl] *adj* klein.

small change *n* Kleingeld *das*.

smallpox ['smɔːlpɒks] *n* Pocken *pl*.

smart [smɑːt] *adj* (*elegant*) elegant; (*clever*) clever; (*posh*) fein.

smart card *n* Chipkarte *die*.

smash [smæʃ] ◆ *n* (SPORT) Schmetterball *der*; (*inf: car crash*) Zusammenstoß *der*. ◆ *vt* (*plate*) zerschlagen; (*window*) ein|schlagen. ◆ *vi* (*plate, vase etc*) zerbrechen.

smashing ['smæʃɪŋ] *adj* (Br: *inf*) toll.

smear test ['smɪə-] *n* Abstrich *der*.

smell [smel] (*pt & pp* **-ed** OR **smelt**) ◆ *n* Geruch *der*; (*bad odour*) Gestank *der*. ◆ *vt* (*sniff at*) riechen an (+D); (*detect*) riechen. ◆ *vi* (*have odour*) riechen; (*have bad odour*) stinken; **to ~ of sthg** nach etw riechen.

smelly ['smelɪ] *adj* stinkend.

smelt [smelt] *pt & pp* → **smell**.

smile [smaɪl] ◆ *n* Lächeln *das*. ◆ *vi* lächeln.

smoke [sməʊk] ◆ *n* Rauch *der*. ◆ *vt & vi* rauchen; **to have a ~** eine rauchen.

smoked [sməʊkt] *adj* geräuchert.

smoked salmon *n* Räucherlachs *der*.

smoker ['sməʊkər] *n* Raucher *der* (-in *die*).

smoking ['sməʊkɪŋ] *n* Rauchen *das*; **'no ~'** 'Rauchen verboten'.

smoking area *n* Raucherzone *die*.

smoking compartment *n* Raucherabteil *das*.

smoky ['sməʊkɪ] *adj* (*room*) verräuchert.

smooth [smuːð] *adj* (*surface, road, mixture*) glatt; (*skin, wine, beer*) weich; (*flight, journey*) ruhig; (*takeoff, landing*) weich. ► **smooth down** *vt sep* glatt|streichen.

smother ['smʌðər] *vt* (*cover*) bedecken.

smudge [smʌdʒ] *n* Fleck *der*.

smuggle ['smʌgl] *vt* schmuggeln.

snack [snæk] *n* Imbiß *der*.

snack bar *n* Schnellimbiß *der*.

snail [sneɪl] *n* Schnecke *die*.

snake [sneɪk] n Schlange die.

snap [snæp] ◆ vt (break) zerbrechen. ◆ vi (break) brechen. ◆ n
(inf: photo) Schnappschuß der; (Br:
card game) Schnippschnapp das.

snare [sneəʳ] n (trap) Schlinge die.

snatch [snætʃ] vt (grab) schnappen;
(steal) klauen.

sneakers ['sniːkəz] npl (Am)
Turnschuhe pl.

sneeze [sniːz] ◆ n Niesen das. ◆ vi
niesen.

sniff [snɪf] ◆ vi (from cold, crying)
schniefen. ◆ vt (smell) schnuppern
an (+D).

snip [snɪp] vt schnippeln.

snob [snɒb] n Snob der.

snog [snɒg] vi (Br: inf) knutschen.

snooker ['snuːkəʳ] n Snooker das.

snooze [snuːz] n Nickerchen das.

snore [snɔːʳ] vi schnarchen.

snorkel ['snɔːkl] n Schnorchel der.

snout [snaʊt] n Schnauze die.

snow [snəʊ] ◆ n Schnee die. ◆ v
impers: it's ~ing es schneit.

snowball ['snəʊbɔːl] n Schneeball
der.

snowdrift ['snəʊdrɪft] n Schneewehe die.

snowflake ['snəʊfleɪk] n Schneeflocke die.

snowman ['snəʊmæn] (pl -men
[-men]) n Schneemann der.

snowplough ['snəʊplaʊ] n Schneepflug der.

snowstorm ['snəʊstɔːm] n Schneesturm der.

snug [snʌg] adj (place) gemütlich;
(person) behaglich.

so [səʊ] ◆ adv 1. (emphasizing degree)
so; it's ~ difficult (that ...) es ist so
schwierig (, daß ...). 2. (referring back)
also; ~ you knew already du hast es
also schon gewußt; I don't think ~ ich
glaube nicht; I'm afraid ~ leider ja; if
~ falls ja. 3. (also): ~ do I ich auch.
4. (in this way) so. 5. (expressing agreement): ~ there is ja, das stimmt. 6. (in
phrases): or ~ oder so, etwa; ~ as um;

~ that so daß. ◆ conj 1. (therefore)
deshalb; I'm away next week ~ I
won't be there ich bin nächste
Woche weg, also werde ich nicht
kommen. 2. (summarizing) also; ~
what have you been up to? na, was
treibst du so? 3. (in phrases): ~ what?
(inf) na und?; ~ there! (inf) das war's!

soak [səʊk] ◆ vt (leave in water)
ein|weichen; (make very wet) naß
machen. ◆ vi: to ~ through sthg etw
durchnässen. ▶ **soak up** vt sep
auf|saugen.

soaked [səʊkt] adj (very wet)
patschnaß.

soaking ['səʊkɪŋ] adj (very wet)
patschnaß.

soap [səʊp] n Seife die.

soap opera n Seifenoper die.

soap powder n Seifenpulver das.

sob [sɒb] ◆ n Schluchzer der. ◆ vi
schluchzen.

sober ['səʊbəʳ] adj (not drunk)
nüchtern.

soccer ['sɒkəʳ] n Fußball der.

sociable ['səʊʃəbl] adj gesellig.

social ['səʊʃl] adj (problem, conditions)
gesellschaftlich; (acquaintance, function) privat.

social club n Klub der.

socialist ['səʊʃəlɪst] ◆ adj sozialistisch. ◆ n Sozialist der (-in die).

social life n gesellschaftliches
Leben.

social security n (money) Sozialhilfe die.

social worker n Sozialarbeiter der
(-in die).

society [sə'saɪətɪ] n Gesellschaft die;
(organization, club) Verein der.

sociology [,səʊsɪ'ɒlədʒɪ] n Soziologie die.

sock [sɒk] n Socke die.

socket ['sɒkɪt] n (for plug)
Steckdose die; (for light bulb) Fassung
die.

sod [sɒd] n (Br: vulg) Sau die.

soda ['səʊdə] n (soda water) Soda das;
(Am: fizzy drink) Brause die.

soda water n Sodawasser das.

sofa ['səʊfə] n Sofa das.

sofa bed n Schlafcouch die.

soft [sɒft] adj weich; (touch, breeze) sanft; (not loud) leise.

soft cheese n Weichkäse der.

soft drink n alkoholfreies Getränk.

software ['sɒftweəʳ] n Software die.

soil [sɔɪl] n (earth) Erde die.

solarium [sə'leərɪəm] n Solarium das.

solar panel ['səʊlə-] n Sonnenkollektor der.

sold [səʊld] pt & pp → **sell**.

soldier ['səʊldʒəʳ] n Soldat der.

sold out adj ausverkauft.

sole [səʊl] ◆ adj (only) einzig; (exclusive) alleinig. ◆ n (of shoe, foot) Sohle die; (fish: pl inv) Seezunge die.

solemn ['sɒləm] adj (person) ernst; (occasion) feierlich.

solicitor [sə'lɪsɪtəʳ] n (Br) Rechtsanwalt der (-anwältin die).

solid ['sɒlɪd] adj (not liquid or gas) fest; (strong) stabil; (gold, silver, rock, oak) massiv.

solo ['səʊləʊ] (pl -s) n (MUS) Solo das; '~ m/cs' (traffic sign) 'Parken nur für Motorräder'.

soluble ['sɒljʊbl] adj löslich.

solution [sə'luːʃn] n Lösung die.

solve [sɒlv] vt lösen.

some [sʌm] ◆ adj 1. (certain amount of) etwas; ~ **meat** ein bißchen Fleisch; ~ **money** etwas Geld; **I had** difficulty getting here es war ziemlich schwierig für mich, hierher zu kommen; **do you want** ~ **more tea?** möchten Sie noch Tee? 2. (certain number of) einige; ~ **people** einige Leute; **I've known him for** ~ **years** ich kenne ihn schon seit einigen Jahren; **can I have** ~ **sweets?** kann ich Bonbons haben? 3. (not all) manche; ~ **jobs are better paid than others** manche Jobs sind besser bezahlt als andere. 4. (in imprecise statements) irgendein(-e); **she married**

~ **Italian (or other)** sie hat irgend so einen Italiener geheiratet. ◆ pron 1. (certain amount) etwas; **can I have** ~? kann ich etwas davon haben? 2. (certain number) einige; **can I have** ~? kann ich welche haben?; ~ **(of them) left early** einige (von ihnen) gingen vorher. ◆ adv (approximately) ungefähr; **there were** ~ **7,000 people there** es waren um die 7.000 Leute da.

somebody ['sʌmbədɪ] = **someone**.

somehow ['sʌmhaʊ] adv irgendwie.

someone ['sʌmwʌn] pron jemand; ~ **or other** irgend jemand.

someplace ['sʌmpleɪs] (Am) = **somewhere**.

somersault ['sʌməsɔːlt] n Purzelbaum der.

something ['sʌmθɪŋ] pron etwas; **it's really** ~ es ist ganz toll; **or** ~ (inf) oder so etwas; ~ **like** ungefähr; ~ **or other** irgend etwas.

sometime ['sʌmtaɪm] adv irgendwann.

sometimes ['sʌmtaɪmz] adv manchmal.

somewhere ['sʌmweəʳ] adv irgendwo; (go, travel) irgendwohin; (approximately) ungefähr.

son [sʌn] n Sohn der.

song [sɒŋ] n Lied das.

son-in-law n Schwiegersohn der.

soon [suːn] adv bald; (quickly) schnell; **too** ~ zu früh; **as** ~ **as** sobald; **as** ~ **as possible** so bald wie möglich; ~ **after** kurz danach; ~**er or later** früher oder später.

soot [sʊt] n Ruß der.

soothe [suːð] vt (pain, sunburn) lindern; (person, anger) beruhigen.

sophisticated [sə'fɪstɪkeɪtɪd] adj (chic) gepflegt; (complex) hochentwickelt.

sorbet ['sɔːbeɪ] n Sorbet das.

sore [sɔːʳ] ◆ adj (painful) schmerzhaft; (inflamed) wund; (Am: inf: angry) sauer. ◆ n wunde Stelle;

to have a ~ throat Halsschmerzen haben.

sorry ['sɒrɪ] adj (sad, upset) traurig; (in apologies): **I'm ~!** Entschuldigung; **I'm ~ I'm late** es tut mir leid, daß ich zu spät komme; **~?** (pardon) wie bitte?; **to feel ~ for sb** jn bemitleiden; **I'm ~ about yesterday** es tut mir leid wegen gestern.

sort [sɔːt] ◆ n (type) Sorte die. ◆ vt sortieren; **what ~ of car?** was für ein Auto?; **a ~ of** eine Art von; **~ of** irgendwie. ▶ **sort out** vt sep (classify) sortieren; (resolve) klären.

so-so adj & adv (inf) so lala.

soufflé ['suːfleɪ] n Soufflé das.

sought [sɔːt] pt & pp → **seek**.

soul [səʊl] n (spirit) Seele die; (soul music) Soul der.

sound [saʊnd] ◆ n Geräusch das; (volume) Ton der. ◆ vt (horn, bell) ertönen lassen. ◆ vi klingen. ◆ adj (structure) solide; (reliable) vernünftig; **to ~ like** (make a noise like) sich anlhören wie; (seem to be) sich anlhören.

soundproof ['saʊndpruːf] adj schalldicht.

soup [suːp] n Suppe die.

soup spoon n Suppenlöffel der.

sour ['saʊər] adj sauer; **to go ~** sauer werden.

source [sɔːs] n Quelle die; (cause) Ursache die.

sour cream n saure Sahne.

south [saʊθ] ◆ n Süden der. ◆ adj Süd-. ◆ adv (fly, walk) nach Süden; (be situated) im Süden; **in the ~ of England** in Südengland.

South Africa n Südafrika nt.

South America n Südamerika nt.

southbound ['saʊθbaʊnd] adj in Richtung Süden.

southeast [,saʊθ'iːst] n Südosten der.

southern ['sʌðən] adj südlich, Süd-.

South Pole n Südpol der.

southwards ['saʊθwədz] adv südwärts.

southwest [,saʊθ'west] n Südwesten der.

souvenir [,suːvə'nɪər] n Souvenir das, Andenken das.

Soviet Union [,səʊvɪət-] n: **the ~** die Sowjetunion.

sow¹ [səʊ] (pp **sown**) vt (seeds) säen.

sow² [saʊ] n (pig) Sau die.

soya ['sɔɪə] n Soja die.

soya bean n Sojabohne die.

soy sauce [,sɔɪ-] n Sojasoße die.

spa [spɑː] n Bad das.

space [speɪs] ◆ n Platz der; (in astronomy etc) Weltraum der; (period) Zeitraum der. ◆ vt in Abständen verteilen.

spaceship ['speɪsʃɪp] n Raumschiff das.

space shuttle n Raumtransporter der.

spacious ['speɪʃəs] adj geräumig.

spade [speɪd] n (tool) Spaten der. ▶ **spades** npl (in cards) Pik das.

spaghetti [spə'getɪ] n Spaghetti pl.

Spain [speɪn] n Spanien nt.

span [spæn] ◆ pt → **spin**. ◆ n (of time) Spanne die.

Spaniard ['spænjəd] n Spanier der (-in die).

spaniel ['spænjəl] n Spaniel der.

Spanish ['spænɪʃ] ◆ adj spanisch. ◆ n (language) Spanisch das.

spank [spæŋk] vt verhauen.

spanner ['spænər] n Schraubenschlüssel der.

spare [speər] ◆ adj (kept in reserve) zusätzlich, Extra-; (not in use) übrig. ◆ n (spare part) Ersatzteil das; (spare wheel) Ersatzreifen der. ◆ vt: **to ~ sb sthg** (time, money) jm etw geben; **with ten minutes to ~** mit noch zehn Minuten übrig.

spare part n Ersatzteil das.

spare ribs npl Spare Ribs pl.

spare room n Gästezimmer das.

spare time n Freizeit die.

spare wheel n Ersatzreifen der.

spark [spɑːk] n Funken der.

sparkling ['spɑːklɪŋ-] *adj* (*mineral water, soft drink*) sprudelnd.

sparkling wine *n* Schaumwein *der*.

spark plug *n* Zündkerze *die*.

sparrow ['spærəʊ] *n* Spatz *der*.

spat [spæt] *pt & pp* → **spit**.

speak [spiːk] (*pt* spoke, *pp* spoken) *vt & vi* sprechen; **who's ~ing?** (*on phone*) mit wem spreche ich?; **can I ~ to Sarah?** - **~ing!** (*on phone*) kann ich Sarah bitte sprechen? – Am Apparat!; **to ~ to sb about sthg** mit jm über etw (A) sprechen. ▶ **speak up** *vi* (*more loudly*) lauter sprechen.

speaker ['spiːkə^r] *n* (*person*) Redner *der* (-in *die*); (*loudspeaker, of stereo*) Lautsprecher *der*; **to be an English ~** Englisch sprechen.

spear [spɪə^r] *n* Speer *der*.

special ['speʃl] ◆ *adj* (*not ordinary*) besondere(-r)(-s); (*particular*) speziell. ◆ *n* (*dish*) Spezialität *die*; **'today's ~'** 'Tagesgericht'.

special delivery *n* (Br) Eilzustellung *die*.

special effects *npl* Special effects *pl*.

specialist ['speʃəlɪst] *n* (*doctor*) Facharzt *der* (-ärztin *die*).

speciality [ˌspeʃɪ'ælətɪ] *n* Spezialität *die*.

specialize ['speʃəlaɪz] *vi*: **to ~ (in)** sich spezialisieren (auf (+A).

specially ['speʃəlɪ] *adv* speziell.

special offer *n* Sonderangebot *das*.

special school *n* (Br) Sonderschule *die*.

specialty ['speʃltɪ] (Am) = **speciality**.

species ['spiːʃiːz] *n* Art *die*.

specific [spə'sɪfɪk] *adj* (*particular*) bestimmt; (*exact*) genau.

specification [ˌspesɪfɪ'keɪʃn] *n* (*of machine, building etc*) genaue Angaben *pl*.

specimen ['spesɪmən] *n* (MED) Probe *die*; (*example*) Exemplar *das*.

specs [speks] *npl* (*inf*) Brille *die*.

spectacle ['spektəkl] *n* (*sight*) Anblick *der*.

spectacles ['spektəklz] *npl* Brille *die*.

spectacular [spek'tækjʊlə^r] *adj* spektakulär.

spectator [spek'teɪtə^r] *n* Zuschauer *der* (-in *die*).

sped [sped] *pt & pp* → **speed**.

speech [spiːtʃ] *n* Sprache *die*; (*talk*) Rede *die*.

speech impediment [-ɪm-ˌpedɪmənt] *n* Sprachbehinderung *die*.

speed [spiːd] (*pt & pp* **-ed** OR **sped**) ◆ *n* Geschwindigkeit *die*; (*of film*) Lichtempfindlichkeit *die*; (*bicycle gear*) Gang *der*. ◆ *vi* (*move quickly*) rasen; (*drive too fast*) zu schnell fahren; **at ~** mit hoher Geschwindigkeit; **'reduce ~ now'** 'Geschwindigkeit senken'. ▶ **speed up** *vi* beschleunigen.

speedboat ['spiːdbəʊt] *n* Rennboot *das*.

speeding ['spiːdɪŋ] *n* Geschwindigkeitsüberschreitung *die*.

speed limit *n* Geschwindigkeitsbeschränkung *die*.

speedometer [spɪ'dɒmɪtə^r] *n* Tachometer *der*.

spell [spel] (Br *pt & pp* **-ed** OR **spelt**, Am *pt & pp* **-ed**) ◆ *vt* buchstabieren; (*subj: letters*) schreiben. ◆ *n* (*period*) Weile *die*; (*of weather*) Periode *die*; (*magic*) Zauberformel *die*.

spelling ['spelɪŋ] *n* (*correct order*) Schreibweise *die*; (*ability*) Rechtschreibung *die*.

spelt [spelt] *pt & pp* (Br) → **spell**.

spend [spend] (*pt & pp* spent [spent]) *vt* (*money*) ausgeben; (*time*) verbringen.

sphere [sfɪə^r] *n* (*round shape*) Kugel *die*.

spice [spaɪs] ◆ *n* Gewürz *das*. ◆ *vt* würzen.

spicy ['spaɪsɪ] *adj* pikant.

spider ['spaɪdə^r] *n* Spinne *die*.

spider's web *n* Spinnennetz *das*.

spike [spaɪk] n Spitze die.

spill [spɪl] (Br pt & pp **-ed** OR **spilt** [spɪlt], Am pt & pp **-ed**) ◆ vt verschütten. ◆ vi (liquid) überllaufen; (sugar, salt) verschüttet werden.

spin [spɪn] (pt **span** OR **spun**, pp **spun**) ◆ vt (wheel) drehen; (coin) werfen; (washing) schleudern. ◆ n (on ball) Drall der; **to go for a ~** (inf: in car) eine Spritztour machen.

spinach ['spɪnɪdʒ] n Spinat der.

spine [spaɪn] n Wirbelsäule die; (of book) Buchrücken der.

spinster ['spɪnstər] n ledige Frau.

spiral ['spaɪərəl] n Spirale die.

spiral staircase n Wendeltreppe die.

spire ['spaɪər] n Turmspitze die.

spirit ['spɪrɪt] n (soul) Geist der; (energy) Schwung der; (courage) Mut der; (mood) Stimmung die. ▸ **spirits** npl (Br: alcohol) Spirituosen pl.

spit [spɪt] (Br pt & pp **spat**, Am pt & pp **inv**) ◆ vi (person) spucken; (fire) zischen; (food) spritzen. ◆ n (saliva) Spucke die; (for cooking) Spieß der. ◆ v impers: **it's spitting** es tröpfelt.

spite [spaɪt]: **in spite of** prep trotz (+G).

spiteful ['spaɪtfʊl] adj boshaft.

splash [splæʃ] ◆ n (sound) Platschen das. ◆ vt spritzen.

splendid ['splendɪd] adj (beautiful) herrlich; (very good) großartig.

splint [splɪnt] n Schiene die.

splinter ['splɪntər] n Splitter der.

split [splɪt] (pt & pp **inv**) ◆ n (tear) Riß der; (crack) Spalt der. ◆ vt (tear) zerreißen; (wood) spalten; (stone) zerbrechen; (bill, cost, profits, work) teilen. ◆ vi (tear) reißen; (wood) splittern; (stone) brechen. ▸ **split up** vi (group, couple) sich trennen.

spoil [spɔɪl] (pt & pp **-ed** OR **spoilt**) vt (ruin) verderben; (child) verziehen.

spoke [spəʊk] ◆ pt → **speak**. ◆ n (of wheel) Speiche die.

spoken ['spəʊkn] pp → **speak**.

spokesman ['spəʊksmən] (pl **-men** [-mən]) n Sprecher der.

spokeswoman ['spəʊks,wʊmən] (pl **-women** [-,wɪmɪn]) n Sprecherin die.

sponge [spʌndʒ] n (for cleaning, washing) Schwamm der.

sponge bag n (Br) Kulturbeutel der.

sponge cake n Biskuitkuchen der.

sponsor ['spɒnsər] n (of event, TV programme) Sponsor der.

sponsored walk [,spɒnsəd-] n Wanderung mit gesponsorten Teilnehmern.

spontaneous [spɒn'teɪnjəs] adj spontan.

spoon [spuːn] n Löffel der.

spoonful ['spuːnfʊl] n Löffel der.

sport [spɔːt] n Sport der.

sports car [spɔːts-] n Sportwagen der.

sports centre [spɔːts-] n Sportzentrum das.

sports jacket [spɔːts-] n sportlicher Sakko.

sportsman ['spɔːtsmən] (pl **-men** [-mən]) n Sportler der.

sports shop [spɔːts-] n Sportgeschäft das.

sportswoman ['spɔːts,wʊmən] (pl **-women** [-,wɪmɪn]) n Sportlerin die.

spot [spɒt] ◆ n (stain) Fleck der; (dot) Punkt der; (of rain) Tropfen der; (on skin) Pickel der; (place) Stelle die. ◆ vt entdecken; **on the ~** (at once) auf der Stelle; (at the scene) an Ort und Stelle.

spotless ['spɒtlɪs] adj makellos sauber.

spotlight ['spɒtlaɪt] n Scheinwerfer der.

spotty ['spɒtɪ] adj pickelig.

spouse [spaʊs] n (fml) Gatte der (Gattin die).

spout [spaʊt] n Schnabel der.

sprain [spreɪn] vt verstauchen; **to ~ one's wrist** sich (D) das Handgelenk verstauchen.

sprang [spræŋ] pt → **spring**.

spray [spreɪ] ◆ n (of aerosol, perfume) Spray der; (droplets) Sprühnebel der; (from sea) Gischt die. ◆ vt (surface, wall) sprühen; (car, crops, paint, water) spritzen.

spread [spred] (pt & pp inv) ◆ vt (butter, jam, glue) streichen; (map, tablecloth, blanket) aus|breiten; (legs, fingers, arms) aus|strecken; (disease, news, rumour) verbreiten. ◆ vi (disease, news, rumour) sich verbreiten; (fire) sich aus|breiten. ◆ n (food) Aufstrich der. ▶ **spread out** vi (disperse) sich verteilen.

spring [sprɪŋ] (pt sprang, pp sprung) ◆ n (season) Frühling der; (coil) Feder die; (in ground) Quelle die. ◆ vi (leap) springen; **in (the) ~** im Frühling.

springboard ['sprɪŋbɔːd] n Sprungbrett das.

spring-cleaning [-'kliːnɪŋ] n Frühlingsputz der.

spring onion n Frühlingszwiebel die.

spring roll n Frühlingsrolle die.

sprinkle ['sprɪŋkl] vt (liquid) sprengen; (salt, sugar) streuen.

sprinkler ['sprɪŋklər] n Sprinkler der.

sprint [sprɪnt] ◆ n Sprint der. ◆ vi rennen; (SPORT) sprinten.

Sprinter® ['sprɪntər] n (Br: train) = Nahverkehrszug der.

sprout [spraʊt] n (vegetable) Rosenkohl der.

spruce [spruːs] n Fichte die.

sprung [sprʌŋ] ◆ pp → **spring**. ◆ adj (mattress) gefedert.

spud [spʌd] n (inf) Kartoffel die.

spun [spʌn] pt & pp → **spin**.

spur [spɜːr] n (for horse rider) Sporn der; **on the ~ of the moment** ganz spontan.

spurt [spɜːt] vi spritzen.

spy [spaɪ] n Spion der (-in die).

squall [skwɔːl] n Bö die.

squalor ['skwɒlər] n Schmutz der.

square [skweər] ◆ adj (in shape) quadratisch. ◆ n (shape) Quadrat das;

(in town) Platz der; (of chocolate) Stück das; (on chessboard) Feld das; **2 ~ metres** 2 Quadratmeter; **it's 2 metres ~** es ist 2 Meter im Quadrat; **we're (all) ~ now** (not owing money) jetzt sind wir quitt.

squash [skwɒʃ] ◆ n (game) Squash das; (Br: drink) Fruchtsaftgetränk das; (Am: vegetable) Kürbis der. ◆ vt zerquetschen.

squat [skwɒt] ◆ adj gedrungen. ◆ vi (crouch) hocken.

squeak [skwiːk] vi quietschen.

squeeze [skwiːz] vt (hand) drücken; (tube) aus|drücken; (orange) aus|pressen. ▶ **squeeze in** vi sich hinein|zwängen.

squid [skwɪd] n Tintenfisch der.

squint [skwɪnt] ◆ n Schielen das. ◆ vi blinzeln.

squirrel [Br 'skwɪrəl, Am 'skwɜːrəl] n Eichhörnchen das.

squirt [skwɜːt] vi spritzen.

St (abbr of Street) Str.; (abbr of Saint) St.

stab [stæb] vt stechen.

stable ['steɪbl] ◆ adj stabil. ◆ n Stall der.

stack [stæk] n (pile) Stapel der; **~s of money** (inf) haufenweise Geld.

stadium ['steɪdjəm] n Stadion das.

staff [stɑːf] n (workers) Personal das.

stage [steɪdʒ] n (phase) Phase die; (in theatre) Bühne die.

stagger ['stægər] ◆ vt (arrange in stages) staffeln. ◆ vi schwanken.

stagnant ['stægnənt] adj (water) stehend.

stain [steɪn] ◆ n Fleck der. ◆ vt beflecken.

stained glass [,steɪnd-] n farbiges Glas.

stainless steel ['steɪnlɪs-] n Edelstahl der.

staircase ['steəkeɪs] n Treppe die.

stairs [steəz] npl Treppe die.

stairwell ['steəwel] n Treppenhaus das.

stake [steɪk] n (share) Anteil der; (in gambling) Einsatz der; (post) Pfahl der;

to be at ~ auf dem Spiel stehen.

stale [steɪl] *adj* (*food*) trocken.

stalk [stɔːk] *n* Stiel *der*.

stall [stɔːl] ◆ *n* (*in market, at exhibition*) Stand *der*. ◆ *vi* (*car, engine*) ab|sterben. ▶ **stalls** *npl* (Br: *in theatre*) Parkett *das*.

stamina ['stæmɪnə] *n* Ausdauer *die*.

stammer ['stæmə^r] *vi* stottern.

stamp [stæmp] ◆ *n* (*for letter*) Briefmarke *die*; (*in passport, on document*) Stempel *der*. ◆ *vt* (*passport, document*) stempeln. ◆ *vi*: **to ~ on sthg** auf etw (A) treten; **to ~ one's foot** mit dem Fuß stampfen.

stamp-collecting [-kə,lektɪŋ] *n* Briefmarkensammeln *das*.

stamp machine *n* Briefmarkenautomat *der*.

stand [stænd] (*pt & pp* **stood**) ◆ *vi* stehen; (*get to one's feet*) auf|stehen. ◆ *vt* (*place*) stellen; (*put up with*) ertragen; (*withstand*) aus|halten. ◆ *n* (*stall*) Stand *der*; (*for umbrellas, coats, motorbike*) Ständer *der*; (*at sports stadium*) Tribüne *die*; **I can't ~ him** ich kann ihn nicht ausstehen; **to be ~ing** stehen; **to ~ sb a drink** jm ein Getränk spendieren; **'no ~ing'** (Am: AUT) 'Halten verboten'. ▶ **stand back** *vi* zurück|treten. ▶ **stand for** *vt fus* (*mean*) bedeuten; (*tolerate*) hin|nehmen. ▶ **stand in** *vi*: **to ~ in for sb** für jn ein|springen. ▶ **stand out** *vi* (*be conspicuous*) auf|fallen; (*be superior*) hervor|stechen. ▶ **stand up** *vi* (*be on feet*) stehen; (*get to one's feet*) auf|stehen. ◆ *vt sep* (*inf: boyfriend, girlfriend etc*) versetzen. ▶ **stand up for** *vt fus* ein|treten für.

standard ['stændəd] ◆ *adj* (*normal*) Standard-. ◆ *n* (*level*) Niveau *das*; (*point of comparison*) Maßstab *der*; **up to ~** der Norm entsprechend. ▶ **standards** *npl* (*principles*) Maßstäbe *pl*.

standard-class *adj* (Br: *on train*) zweiter Klasse.

standby ['stændbaɪ] *adj* (*ticket*) Standby-.

stank [stæŋk] *pt* → **stink**.

staple ['steɪpl] *n* (*for paper*) Heftklammer *die*.

stapler ['steɪplə^r] *n* Hefter *der*.

star [stɑː^r] ◆ *n* Stern *der*; (*famous person*) Star *der*. ◆ *vt* (*subj: film, play etc*): **the film ~s Cary Grant** in diesem Film spielt Cary Grant die Hauptrolle. ▶ **stars** *npl* (*horoscope*) Sterne *pl*.

starboard ['stɑːbəd] *adj* Steuerbord-.

starch [stɑːtʃ] *n* Stärke *die*.

stare [steə^r] *vi* starren; **to ~ at** an|starren.

starfish ['stɑːfɪʃ] (*pl inv*) *n* Seestern *der*.

starling ['stɑːlɪŋ] *n* Star *der*.

Stars and Stripes *n*: **the ~** das Sternenbanner.

start [stɑːt] ◆ *n* Anfang *der*, Beginn *der*; (SPORT) Start *der*. ◆ *vt* an|fangen, beginnen; (*car, engine*) an|lassen; (*business, club*) gründen. ◆ *vi* an|fangen, beginnen; (*car, engine*) an|springen; (*begin journey*) auf|brechen; **prices ~ at** OR **from £5** Preise ab 5 Pfund; **to ~ doing sthg** OR **to do sthg** beginnen, etw zu tun; **to ~ with** (*in the first place*) erstens; (*when ordering meal*) als Vorspeise. ▶ **start out** *vi* (*on journey*) auf|brechen; **to ~ out as sthg** ursprünglich etw sein. ▶ **start up** *vt sep* (*car, engine*) an|lassen; (*business*) gründen; (*shop*) eröffnen.

starter ['stɑːtə^r] *n* (Br: *of meal*) Vorspeise *die*; (*of car*) Anlasser *der*; **for ~s** (*in meal*) als Vorspeise.

starter motor *n* Anlasser *der*.

starting point ['stɑːtɪŋ-] *n* Ausgangspunkt *der*.

startle ['stɑːtl] *vt* erschrecken.

starvation [stɑːˈveɪʃn] *n* Verhungern *das*.

starve [stɑːv] *vi* (*have no food*) hungern; **I'm starving!** ich habe einen Mordshunger.

state [steɪt] ◆ *n* (*condition*) Zustand *der*; (*country, region*) Staat *der*. ◆ *vt* (*declare*) erklären; (*specify*) an|geben; **the State** der Staat; **the States** die Vereinigten Staaten.

statement ['steɪtmənt] *n* (*declaration*) Erklärung *die*; (*from bank*) Kontoauszug *der*.

state school *n* staatliche Schule.

statesman ['steɪtsmən] (*pl* **-men** [-mən]) *n* Staatsmann *der*.

static ['stætɪk] *n* (*on radio*, *TV*) atmosphärische Störungen *pl*.

station ['steɪʃn] *n* Bahnhof *der*; (*on radio*) Sender *der*.

stationary ['steɪʃnərɪ] *adj* stehend.

stationer's ['steɪʃnəz] *n* (*shop*) Schreibwarengeschäft *das*.

stationery ['steɪʃnərɪ] *n* Schreibwaren *pl*.

station wagon *n* (Am) Kombiwagen *der*.

statistics [stə'tɪstɪks] *npl* Statistik *die*.

statue ['stætʃuː] *n* Statue *die*.

Statue of Liberty *n*: **the ~** die Freiheitsstatue.

status ['steɪtəs] *n* Status *der*.

stay [steɪ] ◆ *n* (*time spent*) Aufenthalt *der*. ◆ *vi* (*remain*) bleiben; (*as guest*) übernachten; (Scot: *reside*) wohnen; **to ~ the night** übernachten. ▶ **stay away** *vi* weg|bleiben. ▶ **stay in** *vi* zu Hause bleiben. ▶ **stay out** *vi* (*from home*) weg|bleiben. ▶ **stay up** *vi* auf|bleiben.

STD code *n* Vorwahl *die*.

steady ['stedɪ] ◆ *adj* (*firm*, *stable*) stabil; (*hand*) ruhig; (*gradual*) stetig; (*job*) fest. ◆ *vt* fest|halten.

steak [steɪk] *n* Steak *das*; (*of fish*) Fischscheibe *die*.

steak and kidney pie *n* mit Rindfleisch und Nieren gefüllte Pastete.

steakhouse ['steɪkhaʊs, *pl* -haʊzɪz] *n* Steakhaus *das*.

steal [stiːl] (*pt* **stole**, *pp* **stolen**) *vt* stehlen; **to ~ sthg from sb** jm etw stehlen.

steam [stiːm] ◆ *n* Dampf *der*. ◆ *vt* (*food*) dünsten.

steamboat ['stiːmbəʊt] *n* Dampfschiff *das*.

steam engine *n* Dampflokomotive *die*.

steam iron *n* Dampfbügeleisen *das*.

steel [stiːl] ◆ *n* Stahl *der*. ◆ *adj* Stahl.

steep [stiːp] *adj* steil.

steeple ['stiːpl] *n* Kirchturm *der*.

steer ['stɪər] *vt* (*car*) lenken; (*boat*, *plane*) steuern.

steering ['stɪərɪŋ] *n* Lenkung *die*.

steering wheel *n* Lenkrad *das*.

stem [stem] *n* Stiel *der*.

step [step] ◆ *n* (*of staircase*, *ladder*) Stufe *die*; (*pace*) Schritt *der*; (*measure*) Maßnahme *die*; (*stage*) Schritt *der*. ◆ *vi*: **to ~ on sthg** auf etw (A) treten; **'mind the ~'** 'Vorsicht, Stufe'. ▶ **steps** *npl* (*stairs*) Treppe *die*. ▶ **step aside** *vi* (*move aside*) zur Seite treten. ▶ **step back** *vi* (*move back*) zurück|treten.

step aerobics *n* Step-Aerobic *das*.

stepbrother ['step,brʌðər] *n* Stiefbruder *der*.

stepdaughter ['step,dɔːtər] *n* Stieftochter *die*.

stepfather ['step,fɑːðər] *n* Stiefvater *der*.

stepladder ['step,lædər] *n* Trittleiter *die*.

stepmother ['step,mʌðər] *n* Stiefmutter *die*.

stepsister ['step,sɪstər] *n* Stiefschwester *die*.

stepson ['stepsʌn] *n* Stiefsohn *der*.

stereo ['sterɪəʊ] (*pl* -s) ◆ *adj* Stereo-. ◆ *n* (*hi-fi*) Stereoanlage *die*; (*stereo sound*) Stereo *das*.

sterile ['steraɪl] *adj* (*germ-free*) steril.

sterilize ['sterəlaɪz] *vt* (*container*, *milk*, *utensil*) sterilisieren.

sterling ['stɜːlɪŋ] ◆ *adj* (*pound*) Sterling-. ◆ *n* Sterling *der*.

sterling silver *n* Sterlingsilber *das*.

stern [stɜːn] ◆ *adj* (*strict*) streng. ◆ *n* (*of boat*) Heck *das*.

stew [stju:] *n* Eintopf *der.*

steward ['stjʊəd] *n* (*on plane, ship*) Steward *der;* (*at public event*) Ordner *der* (-in *die*).

stewardess ['stjʊədɪs] *n* Stewardess *die.*

stewed [stju:d] *adj:* ~ **fruit** Kompott *das.*

stick [stɪk] (*pt & pp* **stuck**) ◆ *n* (*of wood*) Stock *der;* (*for sport*) Schläger *der;* (*of chalk*) Stück *das;* (*of celery, cinammon*) Stange *die.* ◆ *vt* (*glue*) kleben; (*push, insert*) stecken; (*inf: put*) tun. ◆ *vi* kleben; (*jam*) klemmen. ▶ **stick out** *vi* (*protrude*) vorlstehen; (*be noticeable*) sich ablheben. ▶ **stick to** *vt fus* (*decision*) bleiben bei; (*promise*) halten. ▶ **stick up** *vt sep* (*poster, notice*) anlschlagen. ◆ *vi* hochlstehen. ▶ **stick up for** *vt fus* einltreten für.

sticker ['stɪkər] *n* Aufkleber *der.*

sticking plaster ['stɪkɪŋ-] *n* Heftpflaster *das.*

stick shift *n* (*Am: car*) Handschaltgetriebe *das.*

sticky ['stɪkɪ] *adj* klebrig; (*label, tape*) Klebe-; (*weather*) schwül.

stiff [stɪf] ◆ *adj* steif. ◆ *adv:* **to be bored** ~ (*inf*) sich zu Tode langweilen.

stile [staɪl] *n* Zauntritt *der.*

stiletto heels [stɪ'letəʊ-] *npl* (*shoes*) Stöckelschuhe *pl.*

still [stɪl] ◆ *adv* (*up to now*) noch; (*even now*) immer noch; (*despite that*) trotzdem. ◆ *adj* (*motionless*) bewegungslos; (*quiet, calm*) ruhig; (*not fizzy*) ohne Kohlensäure; **we've** ~ **got 10 minutes** wir haben noch 10 Minuten; ~ **more** noch mehr; **to stand** ~ stilllstehen.

Stilton ['stɪltn] *n* Stilton *der* (*britische, starke Blauschimmelkäse*).

stimulate ['stɪmjʊleɪt] *vt* anlregen.

sting [stɪŋ] (*pt & pp* **stung**) ◆ *vt* (*subj: bee, wasp*) stechen; (*subj: nettle*) brennen. ◆ *vi* (*skin, eyes*) brennen.

stingy ['stɪndʒɪ] *adj* (*inf*) geizig.

stink [stɪŋk] (*pt* **stank** OR **stunk**, *pp* **stunk**) *vi* stinken.

stipulate ['stɪpjʊleɪt] *vt* festllegen.

stir [stɜːr] *vt* umlrühren.

stir-fry ◆ *n* auf chinesische Art in einer Pfanne gebratenes Gemüse oder Fleisch. ◆ *vt* schnell braten.

stirrup ['stɪrəp] *n* Steigbügel *der.*

stitch [stɪtʃ] *n* (*in sewing*) Stich *der;* (*in knitting*) Masche *die;* **to have a** ~ (*stomach pain*) Seitenstechen haben. ▶ **stitches** *npl* (*for wound*) Stiche *pl.*

stock [stɒk] ◆ *n* (*of shop, business*) Warenbestand *der;* (*supply*) Vorrat *der;* (FIN) Aktienkapital *das;* (*in cooking*) Brühe *die.* ◆ *vt* (*have in stock*) auf Lager haben; **in** ~ vorrätig; **out of** ~ nicht vorrätig.

stock cube *n* Brühwürfel *der.*

Stock Exchange *n* Börse *die.*

stocking ['stɒkɪŋ] *n* Strumpf *der.*

stock market *n* Börse *die.*

stodgy ['stɒdʒɪ] *adj* (*food*) pappig.

stole [stəʊl] *pt* → **steal**.

stolen ['stəʊln] *pp* → **steal**.

stomach ['stʌmək] *n* (*organ*) Magen *der;* (*belly*) Bauch *der.*

stomachache ['stʌməkeɪk] *n* Bauchschmerzen *pl.*

stomach upset [-'ʌpset] *n* Magenverstimmung *die.*

stone [stəʊn] ◆ *n* Stein *der;* (*measurement: pl inv*) = 6,35kg; (*gem*) Edelstein *der.* ◆ *adj* Stein-.

stonewashed ['stəʊnwɒʃt] *adj* stonewashed.

stood [stʊd] *pt & pp* → **stand**.

stool [stu:l] *n* (*for sitting on*) Hocker *der.*

stop [stɒp] ◆ *n* (*for bus*) Haltestelle *die;* (*for train*) Station *die;* (*in journey*) Aufenthalt *der.* ◆ *vt* anlhalten; (*machine*) abllstellen; (*prevent*) verhindern. ◆ *vi* auflhören; (*vehicle*) halten; (*walker, machine, clock*) stehenlbleiben; (*on journey*) einen Halt machen; (*stay*) bleiben; **to** ~ **sb from doing sthg** jn daran hindern, etw zu tun; **to ~ sthg from happening** verhindern, daß etw geschieht; **to ~ doing sthg** aufhören, etw zu tun; **to put a ~ to sthg** etw ablstellen; **'stop'** (*road sign*) 'Stop'; **'stopping at ...'** (*train, bus*) 'Haltestellen ...'. ▸ **stop off** *vi* Zwischenstation machen.

stopover ['stɒp,əʊvə^r] *n* (*on flight*) Zwischenlandung *die*; (*on journey*) Zwischenaufenthalt *der*.

stopper ['stɒpə^r] *n* Stöpsel *der*.

stopwatch ['stɒpwɒtʃ] *n* Stoppuhr *die*.

storage ['stɔːrɪdʒ] *n* Lagerung *die*.

store [stɔː^r] ◆ *n* (*shop*) Laden *der*; (*department store*) Kaufhaus *das*; (*supply*) Vorrat *der*. ◆ *vt* lagern.

storehouse [ɪstɔːhaʊs, *pl* -haʊzɪz] *n* Lagerhaus *das*.

storeroom ['stɔːrʊm] *n* Lagerraum *der*.

storey ['stɔːrɪ] (*pl* **-s**) *n* (Br) Stockwerk *das*.

stork [stɔːk] *n* Storch *der*.

storm [stɔːm] *n* Sturm *der*.

stormy ['stɔːmɪ] *adj* stürmisch.

story ['stɔːrɪ] *n* Geschichte *die*; (Am) = **storey**.

stout [staʊt] ◆ *adj* (*fat*) beleibt. ◆ *n* (*drink*) Art britisches Dunkelbier.

stove [stəʊv] *n* (*for heating*) Ofen *der*; (*for cooking*) Herd *der*.

straight [streɪt] ◆ *adj* gerade; (*hair*) glatt; (*consecutive*) ununterbrochen; (*drink*) pur. ◆ *adv* (*in a straight line*) gerade; (*upright*) aufrecht; (*directly*) direkt; **~ ahead** geradeaus; **~ away** sofort.

straightforward [,streɪt'fɔːwəd] *adj* (*easy*) einfach.

strain [streɪn] ◆ *n* Belastung *die*; (*tension*) Spannung *die*; (*injury*) Zerrung *die*. ◆ *vt* (*muscle*) zerren; (*eyes*) überlanstrengen; (*food*) ablgießen; (*tea*) ablseihen.

strainer ['streɪnə^r] *n* Sieb *das*.

strait [streɪt] *n* Meerenge *die*.

strange [streɪndʒ] *adj* (*odd*) seltsam; (*unfamiliar*) fremd.

stranger ['streɪndʒə^r] *n* Fremde *der, die*.

strangle ['stræŋgl] *vt* erwürgen.

strap [stræp] *n* (*of bag, camera, shoe*) Riemen *der*; (*of dress*) Träger *der*; (*of watch*) Armband *das*.

strapless ['stræplɪs] *adj* trägerlos.

strategy ['strætɪdʒɪ] *n* Strategie *die*.

Stratford-upon-Avon [,strætfəd-əpɒn'eɪvn] *n* Stratford-upon-Avon.

straw [strɔː] *n* (*substance*) Stroh *das*; (*for drinking*) Strohhalm *der*.

strawberry ['strɔːbərɪ] *n* Erdbeere *die*.

stray [streɪ] ◆ *adj* (*animal*) streunend. ◆ *vi* streunen.

streak [striːk] *n* Streifen *der*; **lucky/unlucky ~** Glücks-/Pechsträhne *die*.

stream [striːm] *n* Strom *der*; (*small river*) Bach *der*.

street [striːt] *n* Straße *die*.

streetcar ['striːtkɑː^r] *n* (Am) Straßenbahn *die*.

street light *n* Straßenlampe *die*.

street plan *n* Stadtplan *der*.

strength [streŋθ] *n* Stärke *die*; (*of person, animal*) Kraft *die*; (*of structure*) Stabilität *die*.

strengthen ['streŋθn] *vt* (*structure*) verstärken; (*argument*) unterstützen.

stress [stres] ◆ *n* (*tension*) Stress *der*; (*on word, syllable*) Betonung *die*. ◆ *vt* betonen.

stretch [stretʃ] ◆ *n* (*of land*) Stück *das*; (*of water*) Teil *der*; (*of time*) Zeitraum *der*. ◆ *vt* (*rope, material*) spannen; (*body*) strecken; (*elastic, clothes*) dehnen. ◆ *vi* (*land, sea*) sich erstrecken; (*person, animal*) sich strecken; **to ~ one's legs** (*fig*) sich (D) die Beine vertreten. ▸ **stretch out** *vt sep* (*hand*) auslstrecken. ◆ *vi* (*lie down*) sich hinllegen.

stretcher ['stretʃə^r] *n* Tragbahre *die*.

strict [strɪkt] *adj* streng; (*exact*) genau.

strictly ['strɪktlɪ] *adv* streng; (*exclusively*) ausschließlich; **~ speaking** genau genommen.

stride [straɪd] n Schritt der.

strike [straɪk] (pt & pp **struck**) ◆ n (of employees) Streik der. ◆ vt (fml: hit) schlagen; (fml: collide with) treffen; (a match) an|zünden. ◆ vi (refuse to work) streiken; (happen suddenly) aus|-brechen; **the clock struck eight** es schlug acht Uhr.

striking ['straɪkɪŋ] adj auffallend.

string [strɪŋ] n Schnur die; (thinner) Bindfaden der; (of pearls, beads) Kette die; (of musical instrument, tennis racket) Saite die; (series) Reihe die; **a piece of ~** eine Schnur.

strip [strɪp] ◆ n Streifen der. ◆ vt (paint, wallpaper) entfernen. ◆ vi (undress) sich aus|ziehen.

stripe [straɪp] n Streifen der.

striped [straɪpt] adj gestreift.

strip-search vt Kleider zum Zweck einer Leibesvisitation ausziehen.

strip show n Strip-Show die.

stroke [strəʊk] ◆ n (MED) Schlaganfall der; (in tennis, golf) Schlag der; (swimming style) Stil der. ◆ vt streicheln; **a ~ of luck** ein Glücksfall.

stroll [strəʊl] n Spaziergang der.

stroller ['strəʊlər] n (Am: pushchair) Sportwagen der (für Kinder).

strong [strɒŋ] adj stark; (structure, bridge, chair) stabil; (possibility, subject) gut.

struck [strʌk] pt & pp → **strike**.

structure ['strʌktʃər] n Struktur die; (building) Bau der.

struggle ['strʌgl] ◆ n (great effort) Anstrengung die. ◆ vi (fight) kämpfen; **to ~ to do sthg** sich ab|mühen, etw zu tun.

stub [stʌb] n (of cigarette) Kippe die; (of cheque, ticket) Abschnitt der.

stubble ['stʌbl] n (on face) Stoppeln pl.

stubborn ['stʌbən] adj (person) stur.

stuck [stʌk] ◆ pt & pp → **stick**. ◆ adj (jammed) verklemmt; **to be ~** nicht weiter|können.

stud [stʌd] n (on boots) Stollen der;

(fastener) Niete die; (earring) Ohr-stecker der.

student ['stjuːdnt] n (at university, college) Student der (-in die); (at school) Schüler der (-in die).

student card n Studentenausweis der.

students' union [ˌstjuːdnts-] n Studentenvereinigung die.

studio ['stjuːdɪəʊ] (pl -s) n (for filming, broadcasting) Studio das; (of artist) Atelier das.

studio apartment (Am) = **studio flat**.

studio flat n (Br) Einzimmer-wohnung die.

study ['stʌdɪ] ◆ n (learning) Studium das; (piece of research) Studie die; (room) Arbeitszimmer das. ◆ vt (learn about) studieren; (examine) untersuchen. ◆ vi studieren.

stuff [stʌf] ◆ n (inf: substance) Stoff der; (things, possessions) Zeug das. ◆ vt stopfen.

stuffed [stʌft] adj (food) gefüllt; (inf: full up) voll; (dead animal) aus-gestopft.

stuffing ['stʌfɪŋ] n (food) Füllung die; (of pillow, cushion) Füllmaterial das.

stuffy ['stʌfɪ] adj (room, atmosphere) stickig.

stumble ['stʌmbl] vi stolpern.

stump [stʌmp] n Stumpf der.

stun [stʌn] vt (astound) fassungslos machen.

stung [stʌŋ] pt & pp → **sting**.

stunk [stʌŋk] pt & pp → **stink**.

stunning ['stʌnɪŋ] adj (very beautiful) hinreißend; (very surprising) sensa-tionell.

stupid ['stjuːpɪd] adj dumm.

sturdy ['stɜːdɪ] adj stabil.

stutter ['stʌtər] vi stottern.

sty [staɪ] n Schweinestall der.

style [staɪl] ◆ n Stil der. ◆ vt (hair) frisieren.

stylish ['staɪlɪʃ] adj elegant.

stylist ['staɪlɪst] n (hairdresser) Haarstilist der (-in die).

sub [sʌb] n (SPORT: inf) Ersatzspieler der (-in die); (Br: subscription) Abo das.

subdued [səb'djuːd] adj (person) still; (lighting, colour) gedämpft.

subject [n 'sʌbdʒekt, vb səb'dʒekt] ◆ n (topic) Thema das; (at school, university) Fach das; (GRAMM) Subjekt das; (fml: of country) Staatsbürger der (-in die). ◆ vt: **to ~ sb to sthg** jn etw (D) unterwerfen; **~ to availability** solange der Vorrat reicht; **~ to an additional charge** vorbehaltlich eines Aufschlages.

subjunctive [səb'dʒʌŋktɪv] n Konjunktiv der.

submarine [ˌsʌbmə'riːn] n Unterseeboot das.

submit [səb'mɪt] ◆ vt (present) vorllegen. ◆ vi (give in) sich fügen.

subordinate [sə'bɔːdɪnət] adj (GRAMM) untergeordnet.

subscribe [səb'skraɪb] vi: **to ~ to sthg** (to magazine, newspaper) etw abonnieren.

subscription [səb'skrɪpʃn] n Abonnement das.

subsequent ['sʌbsɪkwənt] adj später.

subside [səb'saɪd] vi (ground) sich senken; (noise, feeling) ablklingen.

substance ['sʌbstəns] n Stoff der.

substantial [səb'stænʃl] adj (large) erheblich.

substitute ['sʌbstɪtjuːt] n (replacement) Ersatz der; (SPORT) Ersatzspieler der (-in die).

subtitles ['sʌb,taɪtlz] npl Untertitel pl.

subtle ['sʌtl] adj (difference, change) fein; (person) feinfühlig; (plan) raffiniert.

subtract [səb'trækt] vt ablziehen.

subtraction [səb'trækʃn] n Subtraktion die.

suburb ['sʌbɜːb] n Vorort der; **the ~s** der Stadtrand.

subway ['sʌbweɪ] n (Br: for pedestrians) Unterführung die; (Am: underground railway) U-bahn die.

succeed [sək'siːd] ◆ vi (person) Erfolg haben; (plan) gelingen. ◆ vt (fml: follow) folgen (+D); **I ~ed in doing it** es ist mir gelungen.

success [sək'ses] n Erfolg der.

successful [sək'sesfʊl] adj erfolgreich.

succulent ['sʌkjʊlənt] adj saftig.

such [sʌtʃ] ◆ adj solche(-r)(-s). ◆ adv: **~ a lot** so viel; **it's ~ a lovely day** es ist so ein schöner Tag; **~ a thing should never have happened** so etwas hätte nie passieren dürfen; **~ people** solche Leute; **~ as** wie.

suck [sʌk] vt (teat) saugen; (sweet, thumb) lutschen.

sudden ['sʌdn] adj plötzlich; **all of a ~** plötzlich.

suddenly ['sʌdnlɪ] adv plötzlich.

sue [suː] vt verklagen.

suede [sweɪd] n Wildleder das.

suffer ['sʌfər] ◆ vt erleiden. ◆ vi leiden; **to ~ from** (illness) leiden an (+D).

suffering ['sʌfrɪŋ] n (mental) Leid das; (physical) Leiden das.

sufficient [sə'fɪʃnt] adj (fml) genug.

sufficiently [sə'fɪʃntlɪ] adv (fml) genug.

suffix ['sʌfɪks] n Nachsilbe die.

suffocate ['sʌfəkeɪt] vi ersticken.

sugar ['ʃʊgər] n Zucker der.

suggest [sə'dʒest] vt (propose) vorlschlagen; **to ~ doing sthg** vorlschlagen, etw zu tun.

suggestion [sə'dʒestʃn] n (proposal) Vorschlag der; (hint) Andeutung die.

suicide ['sʊɪsaɪd] n Selbstmord der; **to commit ~** Selbstmord begehen.

suit [suːt] ◆ n (man's clothes) Anzug der; (woman's clothes) Kostüm das; (in cards) Farbe die; (JUR) Prozeß der. ◆ vt (subj: clothes, colour, shoes) stehen (+D); (be convenient for) passen (+D); (be appropriate for) passen zu; **to be ~ed to** geeignet sein für; **pink doesn't ~ me** Rosa steht mir nicht; **does 10 o'clock ~ you?** paßt dir/Ihnen 10 Uhr?

suitable ['suːtəbl] adj geeignet; **to be ~ for** geeignet sein für.

suitcase ['suːtkeɪs] n Koffer der.

suite [swiːt] n (set of rooms) Suite die; (furniture) Garnitur die.

sulk [sʌlk] vi schmollen.

sultana [səl'tɑːnə] n (Br) Sultanine die.

sultry ['sʌltrɪ] adj (weather, climate) schwül.

sum [sʌm] n Summe die; (calculation) Rechnung die. ▶ **sum up** vt sep (summarize) zusammenlfassen.

summarize ['sʌmeraɪz] vt zusammenlfassen.

summary ['sʌmerɪ] n Zusammenfassung die.

summer ['sʌmeʳ] n Sommer der; **in (the) ~** im Sommer; **~ holidays** Sommerferien pl.

summertime ['sʌmetaɪm] n Sommer der.

summit ['sʌmɪt] n Gipfel der.

summon ['sʌmen] vt (send for) kommen lassen; (JUR) vorlladen.

sumptuous ['sʌmptʃʊes] adj luxuriös.

sun [sʌn] ◆ n Sonne die. ◆ vt: **to ~ o.s.** sich sonnen; **to catch the ~** viel Sonne ablbekommen; **in the ~** in der Sonne; **out of the ~** im Schatten.

Sun. (abbr of Sunday) So.

sunbathe ['sʌnbeɪð] vi sonnenbaden.

sunbed ['sʌnbed] n Sonnenbank die.

sun block n Sun-Block der.

sunburn ['sʌnbɜːn] n Sonnenbrand der.

sunburnt ['sʌnbɜːnt] adj: **to be ~** einen Sonnenbrand haben.

sundae ['sʌndeɪ] n Eisbecher der.

Sunday ['sʌndɪ] n Sonntag der, → Saturday.

Sunday school n Sonntagsschule die.

sundress ['sʌndres] n Strandkleid das.

sundries ['sʌndrɪz] npl (on bill) Verschiedenes.

sunflower ['sʌn,flaʊeʳ] n Sonnenblume die.

sunflower oil n Sonnenblumenöl das.

sung [sʌŋ] pt → **sing**.

sunglasses ['sʌn,glɑːsɪz] npl Sonnenbrille die.

sunhat ['sʌnhæt] n Sonnenhut der.

sunk [sʌŋk] pp → **sink**.

sunlight ['sʌnlaɪt] n Sonnenlicht das.

sun lounger [-,laʊndʒeʳ] n Liegestuhl der.

sunny ['sʌnɪ] adj sonnig.

sunrise ['sʌnraɪz] n Sonnenaufgang der.

sunroof ['sʌnruːf] n Schiebedach das.

sunset ['sʌnset] n Sonnenuntergang der.

sunshine ['sʌnʃaɪn] n Sonnenschein der; **in the ~** in der Sonne.

sunstroke ['sʌnstreʊk] n Sonnenstich der.

suntan ['sʌntæn] n Bräune die.

suntan cream n Sonnencreme die.

suntan lotion n Sonnenmilch die.

super ['suːpeʳ] ◆ adj (wonderful) prima. ◆ n (petrol) Super das.

superb [suːˈpɜːb] adj erstklassig.

superficial [,suːpeˈfɪʃl] adj (pej: person) oberflächlich; (wound) äußerlich.

superfluous [suːˈpɜːfluəs] adj überflüssig.

Superglue® ['suːpeɡluː] n Sekundenkleber der.

superior [suːˈpɪerɪeʳ] ◆ adj (in quality) überlegen; (in rank) höher. ◆ n Vorgesetzte der die.

supermarket ['suːpe,mɑːkɪt] n Supermarkt der.

supernatural [,suːpeˈnætʃrel] adj übernatürlich.

Super Saver® n (Br: rail ticket) reduzierte Fahrkarte, für die bestimmte Bedingungen gelten.

superstitious [ˌsuːpəˈstɪʃəs] adj abergläubisch.

superstore [ˈsuːpəstɔːr] n Verbrauchermarkt der.

supervise [ˈsuːpəvaɪz] vt beaufsichtigen.

supervisor [ˈsuːpəvaɪzər] n (of workers) Vorarbeiter der (-in die).

supper [ˈsʌpər] n Abendessen das.

supple [ˈsʌpl] adj (person) gelenkig; (material) geschmeidig.

supplement [n ˈsʌplɪmənt, vb ˈsʌplɪment] ♦ n (of magazine) Beilage die; (extra charge) Zuschlag der; (of diet) Zusatz der. ♦ vt ergänzen.

supplementary [ˌsʌplɪˈmentərɪ] adj zusätzlich, Zusatz-.

supply [səˈplaɪ] ♦ n (store) Vorrat der; (providing) Versorgung die. ♦ vt liefern; **to ~ sb with sthg** jn mit etw versorgen. ▶ **supplies** npl Vorräte pl.

support [səˈpɔːt] ♦ n (aid, encouragement) Unterstützung die; (object) Stütze die. ♦ vt unterstützen; (hold up) tragen; **to ~ a football team** ein Fan von einem Fußballverein sein.

supporter [səˈpɔːtər] n (SPORT) Fan der; (of cause, political party) Anhänger der (-in die).

suppose [səˈpəʊz] ♦ vt an|nehmen. ♦ conj = **supposing**; **I ~ so** vermutlich; **to be ~d to do sthg** etw tun sollen.

supposing [səˈpəʊzɪŋ] conj angenommen.

supreme [sʊˈpriːm] adj größte(-r) (-s).

surcharge [ˈsɜːtʃɑːdʒ] n Zuschlag der.

sure [ʃʊər] ♦ adj sicher. ♦ adv (inf: yes) klar; (Am: inf: certainly) wirklich; **to be ~ of o.s.** selbstsicher sein; **for ~** auf jeden Fall; **to make ~ that ...** sich vergewissern, daß ...

surely [ˈʃʊəlɪ] adv sicherlich.

surf [sɜːf] ♦ n Brandung die. ♦ vi surfen.

surface [ˈsɜːfɪs] n Oberfläche die.

surface area n Oberfläche die.

surface mail n Post auf dem Land-/Seeweg.

surfboard [ˈsɜːfbɔːd] n Surfbrett das.

surfing [ˈsɜːfɪŋ] n Surfen das; **to go ~** Surfen gehen.

surgeon [ˈsɜːdʒən] n Chirurg der (-in die).

surgery [ˈsɜːdʒərɪ] n (treatment) Chirurgie die; (Br: building) Praxis die; (Br: period) Sprechstunde die; **to have ~** operiert werden.

surname [ˈsɜːneɪm] n Nachname der.

surplus [ˈsɜːpləs] n Überschuß der.

surprise [səˈpraɪz] ♦ n Überraschung die. ♦ vt überraschen.

surprised [səˈpraɪzd] adj überrascht.

surprising [səˈpraɪzɪŋ] adj überraschend.

surrender [səˈrendər] ♦ vi kapitulieren. ♦ vt (fml: hand over) übergeben.

surround [səˈraʊnd] vt umgeben.

surrounding [səˈraʊndɪŋ] adj umliegend. ▶ **surroundings** npl Umgebung die.

survey [ˈsɜːveɪ] n (investigation) Untersuchung die; (poll) Umfrage die; (of land) Vermessung die; (Br: of house) Begutachtung die.

surveyor [səˈveɪər] n (Br: of houses) Gutachter der (-in die); (of land) Vermesser der (-in die).

survival [səˈvaɪvl] n Überleben das.

survive [səˈvaɪv] vt & vi überleben.

survivor [səˈvaɪvər] n Überlebende der die.

suspect [vb səˈspekt, n & adj ˈsʌspekt] ♦ vt (believe) vermuten; (mistrust) verdächtigen. ♦ n Verdächtige der die. ♦ adj verdächtig; **to ~ sb of sthg** jn einer Sache verdächtigen.

suspend [səˈspend] vt (delay) vorläufig ein|stellen; (from team, school, work) aus|schließen; (hang) auf|hängen.

suspender belt [sə'spendə-] *n*
Strumpfbandgürtel *der*.

suspenders [sə'spendəz] *npl* (Br: *for
stockings*) Strumpfbänder *pl*; (Am: *for
trousers*) Hosenträger *pl*.

suspense [sə'spens] *n* Spannung
die.

suspension [sə'spenʃn] *n* (*of vehicle*)
Federung *die*; (*from team*) Sperrung
die; (*from school, work*) Ausschluß *der*.

suspicion [sə'spiʃn] *n* (*mistrust*)
Mißtrauen *das*; (*idea*) Ahnung *die*;
(*trace*) Spur *die*.

suspicious [sə'spiʃəs] *adj* (*behaviour,
situation*) verdächtig; **to be ~ of sb/
sthg** jm/etw (D) mißtrauen.

swallow ['swɒləʊ] ♦ *n* (*bird*)
Schwalbe *die*. ♦ *vt & vi* schlucken.

swam [swæm] *pt* → **swim**.

swamp [swɒmp] *n* Sumpf *der*.

swan [swɒn] *n* Schwan *der*.

swap [swɒp] *vt* tauschen; (*ideas, sto-
ries*) ausltauschen; **to ~ sthg for sthg**
etw gegen etw einltauschen.

swarm [swɔːm] *n* (*of bees*) Schwarm
der.

swear [sweəʳ] (*pt* **swore**, *pp* **sworn**)
♦ *vi* (*use rude language*) fluchen;
(*promise*) schwören. ♦ *vt*: **to ~ to do
sthg** schwören, etw zu tun.

swearword ['sweəwɜːd] *n* Kraft-
ausdruck *der*.

sweat [swet] ♦ *n* Schweiß *der*. ♦ *vi*
schwitzen.

sweater ['swetəʳ] *n* Pullover *der*.

sweatshirt ['swetʃɜːt] *n* Sweatshirt
das.

swede [swiːd] *n* (Br) Kohlrübe *die*.

Swede [swiːd] *n* Schwede *der*
(Schwedin *die*).

Sweden ['swiːdn] *n* Schweden *nt*.

Swedish ['swiːdɪʃ] ♦ *adj*
schwedisch. ♦ *n* (*language*)
Schwedisch *das*. ♦ *npl*: **the ~** die
Schweden *pl*.

sweep [swiːp] (*pt & pp* **swept**) *vt*
(*with brush, broom*) kehren, fegen.

sweet [swiːt] ♦ *adj* (*food, drink, smell*)
süß; (*person, nature*) lieb. ♦ *n* (*br:*

candy) Bonbon *der or das*; (*dessert*)
Nachtisch *der*.

sweet-and-sour *adj* süßsauer.

sweet corn *n* Zuckermais *der*.

sweetener ['swiːtnəʳ] *n* (*for drink*)
Süßstoff *der*.

sweet potato *n* Batate *die*.

sweet shop *n* (*br*) Süßwaren-
geschäft *das*.

swell [swel] (*pp* **swollen**) *vi* anlschwellen.

swelling ['swelɪŋ] *n* Schwellung *die*.

swept [swept] *pt & pp* → **sweep**.

swerve [swɜːv] *vi* auslscheren.

swig [swɪg] *n* (*inf*) Schluck *der*.

swim [swɪm] (*pt* **swam**, *pp* **swum**)
♦ *vi* schwimmen. ♦ *n*: **to have a ~**
schwimmen; **to go for a ~** schwimmen gehen.

swimmer ['swɪməʳ] *n* Schwimmer
der (-in *die*).

swimming ['swɪmɪŋ] *n* Schwimmen *das*; **to go ~** schwimmen gehen.

swimming baths *npl* (Br)
Schwimmbad *das*.

swimming cap *n* Bademütze *die*.

swimming costume *n* (Br)
Badeanzug *der*.

swimming pool *n* Schwimmbecken *das*.

swimming trunks *npl* Badehose
die.

swimsuit ['swɪmsuːt] *n* Badeanzug
der.

swindle ['swɪndl] *n* Betrug *der*.

swing [swɪŋ] (*pt & pp* **swung**) ♦ *n*
(*for children*) Schaukel *die*. ♦ *vt & vi*
(*from side to side*) schwingen.

swipe [swaɪp] *vt* (*credit card etc*)
ablziehen.

Swiss [swɪs] ♦ *adj* schweizerisch.
♦ *n* (*person*) Schweizer *der* (-in *die*).
♦ *npl*: **the ~** die Schweizer *pl*.

Swiss cheese *n* Schweizer Käse *der*.

Swiss franc [-'fræŋk] *n*
(Schweizer) Franken *der*.

swiss roll *n* ≈ Biskuitrolle *die*.

switch [swɪtʃ] ♦ *n* (*for light, power,*

television) Schalter *der.* ◆ *vt* (*change*) ändern; (*exchange*) tauschen. ◆ *vi* wechseln. ► **switch off** *vt sep* (*light*) aus|schalten; (*radio, engine*) ab|schalten. ► **switch on** *vt sep* (*light, radio, engine*) ein|schalten.

switchboard ['swɪtʃbɔːd] *n* Telefonzentrale *die.*

Switzerland ['swɪtsələnd] *n* die Schweiz.

swivel ['swɪvl] *vi* sich drehen.

swollen ['swəʊln] ◆ *pp* → **swell**. ◆ *adj* (*ankle, arm etc*) geschwollen.

swop [swɒp] = **swap**.

sword [sɔːd] *n* Schwert *das.*

swordfish ['sɔːdfɪʃ] (*pl inv*) *n* Schwertfisch *der.*

swore [swɔːʳ] *pt* → **swear**.

sworn [swɔːn] *pp* → **swear**.

swum [swʌm] *pp* → **swim**.

swung [swʌŋ] *pt & pp* → **swing**.

syllable ['sɪləbl] *n* Silbe *die.*

syllabus ['sɪləbəs] *n* Lehrplan *der.*

symbol ['sɪmbl] *n* Symbol *das.*

sympathetic [ˌsɪmpə'θetɪk] *adj* (*understanding*) verständnisvoll.

sympathize ['sɪmpəθaɪz] *vi:* **to ~ (with sb)** (*feel sorry*) Mitleid haben (mit jm); (*understand*) Verständnis haben (für jn).

sympathy ['sɪmpəθɪ] *n* (*understanding*) Verständnis *das.*

symphony ['sɪmfənɪ] *n* Sinfonie *die.*

symptom ['sɪmptəm] *n* Symptom *das.*

synagogue ['sɪnəgɒg] *n* Synagoge *die.*

synthesizer ['sɪnθəsaɪzəʳ] *n* Synthesizer *der.*

synthetic [sɪn'θetɪk] *adj* synthetisch.

syringe [sɪ'rɪndʒ] *n* Spritze *die.*

syrup ['sɪrəp] *n* Sirup *der.*

system ['sɪstəm] *n* System *das;* (*hi-fi*) Anlage *die.*

T

ta [tɑː] *excl* (*Br: inf*) danke!

tab [tæb] *n* (*of cloth, paper etc*) Etikett *das;* (*bill*) Rechnung *die;* **put it on my ~** setzen Sie es auf meine Rechnung.

table ['teɪbl] *n* Tisch *der;* (*of figures etc*) Tabelle *die.*

tablecloth ['teɪblklɒθ] *n* Tischtuch *das.*

tablemat ['teɪblmæt] *n* Untersetzer *der.*

tablespoon ['teɪblspuːn] *n* Servierlöffel *der.*

tablet ['tæblɪt] *n* (*pill*) Tablette *die;* (*of soap*) Stück *das;* (*of chocolate*) Tafel *die.*

table tennis *n* Tischtennis *der.*

table wine *n* Tafelwein *der.*

tabloid ['tæblɔɪd] *n* Boulevardzeitung *die.*

tack [tæk] *n* (*nail*) kleiner Nagel.

tackle ['tækl] ◆ *n* (SPORT) Angriff *der;* (*for fishing*) Ausrüstung *die.* ◆ *vt* (SPORT) an|greifen; (*deal with*) an|gehen.

tacky ['tækɪ] *adj* (*inf*) geschmacklos.

taco ['tækəʊ] (*pl* **-s**) *n* mit Hackfleisch oder Bohnen gefüllter, sehr dünner knuspriger Maisfladen, mexikanische Spezialität.

tact [tækt] *n* Takt *der.*

tactful ['tæktfʊl] *adj* taktvoll.

tactics ['tæktɪks] *npl* Taktik *die.*

tag [tæg] *n* (*label*) Schild *das.*

tagliatelle [ˌtægljə'telɪ] *n* Bandnudeln *pl.*

tail [teɪl] *n* Schwanz *der.* ► **tails** *n* (*of coin*) Zahl *die.* ◆ *npl* (*formal dress*) Frack *der.*

tailgate ['teɪlgeɪt] *n* (*of car*) Heckklappe *die.*

tailor ['teɪləʳ] *n* Schneider *der* (**-in** *die*).

Taiwan [ˌtaɪˈwɑːn] *n* Taiwan *nt*.

take [teɪk] *vt* 1. (*gen*) nehmen; **to ~ the bus** den Bus nehmen. 2. (*carry*) mit|nehmen. 3. (*do, make*): **to ~ a bath/shower** ein Bad/eine Dusche nehmen; **to ~ an exam** eine Prüfung ab|legen; **to ~ a photo** ein Photo machen. 4. (*drive*) bringen. 5. (*require*) brauchen; **how long will it ~?** wie lange wird es dauern? 6. (*steal*): **to ~ sthg from sb** jm etw weg|nehmen. 7. (*size in clothes, shoes*) haben; **what size do you ~?** welche Größe hast du/haben Sie? 8. (*subtract*): **to ~ sthg from sthg** etw von etw ab|ziehen. 9. (*accept*) an|nehmen; **do you ~ traveller's cheques?** nehmen Sie Travellerschecks?; **to ~ sb's advice** js Rat folgen. 10. (*contain*) fassen. 11. (*react to*) auf|nehmen. 12. (*control, power*) übernehmen; **to ~ charge of** die Leitung übernehmen. 13. (*tolerate*) aus|halten, ertragen. 14. (*attitude, interest*) haben. 15. (*assume*): **I ~ it that ...** ich gehe davon aus, daß ... 16. (*temperature, pulse*) messen. 17. (*rent*) mieten. **► take apart** *vt sep* auseinander|nehmen. **► take away** *vt sep* (*remove*) weg|nehmen; (*subtract*) ab|ziehen. **► take back** *vt sep* (*return*) zurück|bringen; (*faulty goods, statement*) zurück|nehmen. **► take down** *vt sep* (*picture, curtains*) ab|nehmen. **► take in** *vt sep* (*include*) ein|schließen; (*understand*) verstehen; (*deceive*) herein|legen; (*clothes*) enger machen. **► take off** *vt sep* (*remove*) ab|nehmen; (*clothes*) aus|ziehen; (*as holiday*) sich (D) frei|nehmen. ◆ *vi* (*plane*) ab|heben. **► take out** *vt sep* (*from container, pocket*) heraus|nehmen; (*library book*) aus|leihen; (*loan*) auf|nehmen; (*insurance policy*) ab|schließen; (*go out with*) aus|führen. **► take over** *vi*: **to ~ over from sb** jn ab|lösen. **► take up** *vt sep* (*use up*) in Anspruch nehmen; (*trousers, skirt, dress*) kürzen; (*begin*): **to ~ up the clarinet** an|fangen, Klarinette zu spielen.

takeaway [ˈteɪkəˌweɪ] *n* (Br: *shop*) Restaurant *das* mit Straßenverkauf; (*food*) Essen *das* zum Mitnehmen.

taken [ˈteɪkn] *pp* → **take**.

takeoff [ˈteɪkɒf] *n* (*of plane*) Start *der*.

takeout [ˈteɪkaʊt] (Am) = **takeaway**.

takings [ˈteɪkɪŋz] *npl* Einnahmen *pl*.

talcum powder [ˈtælkəm-] *n* Körperpuder *der*.

tale [teɪl] *n* Geschichte *die*.

talent [ˈtælənt] *n* Talent *das*.

talk [tɔːk] ◆ *n* (*conversation*) Gespräch *das*; (*speech*) Vortrag *der*. ◆ *vi* reden, sprechen; **to ~ to sb (about sthg)** mit jm (über etw (A) sprechen; **to ~ with sb** mit jm reden. **► talks** *npl* Gespräche *pl*.

talkative [ˈtɔːkətɪv] *adj* gesprächig.

tall [tɔːl] *adj* groß; (*building, tree*) hoch; **how ~ are you?** wie groß bist du?; **I'm five and a half feet ~** ich bin 1,65 Meter groß.

tame [teɪm] *adj* (*animal*) zahm.

tampon [ˈtæmpɒn] *n* Tampon *der*.

tan [tæn] ◆ *n* (*suntan*) Bräune *die*. ◆ *vi* braun werden. ◆ *adj* (*colour*) gelbbraun.

tangerine [ˌtændʒəˈriːn] *n* Tangerine *die*.

tank [tæŋk] *n* (*container*) Tank *der*; (*vehicle*) Panzer *der*.

tanker [ˈtæŋkər] *n* (*truck*) Tankwagen *der*.

tanned [tænd] *adj* braungebrannt.

tap [tæp] ◆ *n* (*for water*) Hahn *der*. ◆ *vt* (*hit*) klopfen.

tape [teɪp] ◆ *n* (*cassette, video*) Kassette *die*; (*in cassette*) Tonband *das*; (*adhesive material*) Klebeband *das*; (*strip of material*) Band *das*. ◆ *vt* (*record*) auf|nehmen; (*stick*) kleben.

tape measure *n* Metermaß *das*.

tape recorder *n* Tonbandgerät *das*.

tapestry [ˈtæpɪstrɪ] *n* Wandteppich *der*.

tap water *n* Leitungswasser *das*.

tar [tɑːr] *n* Teer *der*.

target ['tɑːgɪt] n Ziel das; (board) Zielscheibe die.

tariff ['tærɪf] n (price list) Preisliste die; (Br: menu) Speisekarte die; (at customs) Zoll der.

tarmac ['tɑːmæk] n (at airport) Rollbahn die. ▶ **Tarmac®** n (on road) Makadam der.

tarpaulin [tɑːˈpɔːlɪn] n Plane die.

tart [tɑːt] n Törtchen das.

tartan ['tɑːtn] n (design) Schottenmuster das; (cloth) Schottenstoff der.

tartare sauce [ˌtɑːtə-] n Remouladensoße die.

task [tɑːsk] n Aufgabe die.

taste [teɪst] ◆ n Geschmack der. ◆ vt (sample) kosten; (detect) schmecken. ◆ vi: **to ~ of** sthg nach etw schmecken; **it ~s bad** es schmeckt schlecht; **it ~s good** es schmeckt gut; **to have a ~ of** sthg (food, drink) etw probieren; (fig: experience) etw kennenllernen.

tasteful ['teɪstfʊl] adj geschmackvoll.

tasteless ['teɪstlɪs] adj geschmacklos.

tasty ['teɪstɪ] adj lecker.

tattoo [təˈtuː] (pl -s) n (on skin) Tätowierung die; (military display) Zapfenstreich der.

taught [tɔːt] pt & pp → **teach**.

Taurus ['tɔːrəs] n Stier der.

taut [tɔːt] adj straff.

tax [tæks] ◆ n Steuer die. ◆ vt (goods, person) besteuern; (income) versteuern.

tax disc n (Br) Steuerplakette die.

tax-free adj steuerfrei.

taxi ['tæksɪ] ◆ n Taxi das. ◆ vi (plane) rollen.

taxi driver n Taxifahrer der (-in die).

taxi rank n (Br) Taxistand der.

taxi stand (Am) = **taxi rank**.

T-bone steak n T-bone-Steak das.

tea [tiː] n Tee der; (evening meal) Abendessen das.

tea bag n Teebeutel der.

teacake ['tiːkeɪk] n flaches Rosinenbrötchen, das getoastet und mit Butter gegessen wird.

teach [tiːtʃ] (pt & pp **taught**) vt & vi unterrichten; **to ~ sb** sthg, **to ~ sthg to sb** jm Unterricht in etw (D) geben; **to ~ sb (how) to do** sthg jm etw beilbringen.

teacher ['tiːtʃər] n Lehrer der (-in die).

teaching ['tiːtʃɪŋ] n (profession) Lehrberuf der; (of subject) Unterrichten das.

tea cloth = **tea towel**.

teacup ['tiːkʌp] n Teetasse die.

team [tiːm] n (SPORT) Mannschaft die; (group) Team das.

teapot ['tiːpɒt] n Teekanne die.

tear¹ [teər] (pt **tore**, pp **torn**) ◆ vt (rip) zerreißen. ◆ vi reißen; (move quickly) rasen. ◆ n Riß der. ▶ **tear up** vt sep zerreißen.

tear² [tɪər] n Träne die.

tearoom ['tiːrʊm] n Teestube die.

tease [tiːz] vt necken.

tea set n Teeservice das.

teaspoon ['tiːspuːn] n Teelöffel der.

teaspoonful ['tiːspuːnˌfʊl] n Teelöffel der.

teat [tiːt] n (of animal) Zitze die; (Br: of bottle) Sauger der.

teatime ['tiːtaɪm] n Abendessenszeit die.

tea towel n Geschirrtuch das.

technical ['teknɪkl] adj technisch; (point, reason) fachlich.

technical drawing n technische Zeichnung.

technicality [ˌteknɪˈkælətɪ] n (detail) technisches Detail.

technician [tekˈnɪʃn] n Techniker der (-in die).

technique [tekˈniːk] n (method) Methode die; (skill) Technik die.

technological [ˌteknəˈlɒdʒɪkl] adj technisch.

technology [tek'nɒlədʒɪ] *n* Technik *die*.

teddy (bear) ['tedɪ-] *n* Teddy *der*.

tedious ['tiːdjəs] *adj* langweilig.

tee [tiː] *n* Tee *das*.

teenager ['tiːnˌeɪdʒəʳ] *n* Teenager *der*.

teeth [tiːθ] *pl* → **tooth**.

teethe [tiːð] *vi*: **to be teething** zahnen.

teetotal [tiːˈtəʊtl] *adj* abstinent.

telegram ['telɪgræm] *n* Telegramm *das*.

telegraph ['telɪgrɑːf] ◆ *n* Telegraf *der*. ◆ *vt* telegrafieren.

telegraph pole *n* Telegrafenmast *der*.

telephone ['telɪfəʊn] ◆ *n* Telefon *das*. ◆ *vt & vi* anlrufen; **to be on the ~** (*talking*) telefonieren; (*connected*) ein Telefon haben.

telephone booth *n* Telefonzelle *die*.

telephone box *n* Telefonzelle *die*.

telephone call *n* Telefonanruf *der*.

telephone directory *n* Telefonbuch *das*.

telephone number *n* Telefonnummer *die*; **what's your ~?** wie ist deine/Ihre Telefonnummer?

telephonist [tɪˈlefənɪst] *n* (Br) Telefonist *der* (-in *die*).

telephoto lens [ˌtelɪˈfəʊtəʊ-] *n* Teleobjektiv *das*.

telescope ['telɪskəʊp] *n* Teleskop *das*.

television ['telɪˌvɪʒn] *n* Fernsehen *das*; (*set*) Fernseher *der*; **on (the) ~** (*broadcast*) im Fernsehen; **to watch ~** fernlsehen.

telex ['teleks] *n* Telex *das*.

tell [tel] (*pt & pp* **told**) ◆ *vt* (*inform*) sagen (+D); (*story, joke, lie*) erzählen; (*truth*) sagen; (*distinguish*) erkennen. ◆ *vi* (*know*) wissen; **can you ~ me the time?** kannst du mir sagen, wie spät es ist?; **to ~ sb sthg** jm etw sagen; **to ~ sb about sthg** jm etw erzählen; **to ~ sb how to do sthg** jm sagen, wie man etw tut; **to ~ sb to do sthg** jm sagen, etw zu tun. ► **tell off** *vt sep* schimpfen.

teller ['teləʳ] *n* (*in bank*) Kassierer *der* (-in *die*).

telly ['telɪ] *n* (Br: *inf*) Fernseher *der*.

temp [temp] ◆ *n* Zeitarbeitskraft *die*. ◆ *vi* Zeitarbeit machen.

temper ['tempəʳ] *n*: **to be in a ~** wütend sein; **to lose one's ~** wütend werden.

temperature ['temprətʃəʳ] *n* Temperatur *die*; (MED) Fieber *das*; **to have a ~** Fieber haben.

temple ['templ] *n* (*building*) Tempel *der*; (*of forehead*) Schläfe *die*.

temporary ['tempərərɪ] *adj* vorübergehend.

tempt [tempt] *vt* verleiten; **to be ~ed to do sthg** versucht sein, etw zu tun.

temptation [temp'teɪʃn] *n* Verlockung *die*.

tempting ['temptɪŋ] *adj* verlockend.

ten [ten] *num* zehn, → **six**.

tenant ['tenənt] *n* (*of house, flat*) Mieter *der* (-in *die*); (*of land*) Pächter *der* (-in *die*).

tend [tend] *vi*: **to ~ to do sthg** dazu neigen, etw zu tun.

tendency ['tendənsɪ] *n* (*trend*) Trend *der*; (*inclination*) Neigung *die*.

tender ['tendəʳ] ◆ *adj* (*affectionate*) zärtlich; (*sore*) empfindlich; (*meat*) zart. ◆ *vt* (*fml: pay*) anlbieten.

tendon ['tendən] *n* Sehne *die*.

tenement ['tenəmənt] *n* Mietshaus *das*.

tennis ['tenɪs] *n* Tennis *das*.

tennis ball *n* Tennisball *der*.

tennis court *n* Tennisplatz *der*.

tennis racket *n* Tennisschläger *der*.

tennis shoe *n* Tennisschuh *der*.

tenpin bowling ['tenpɪn-] *n* (Br) Bowling *das*.

tenpins ['tenpɪnz] (Am) = **tenpin bowling**.

tense [tens] ◆ *adj* angespannt; (*situa-*

tion) spannungsgeladen. ◆ *n* (GRAMM) Zeit *die*.

tension ['tenʃn] *n* (*of person*) Anspannung *die*; (*of situation*) Spannung *die*.

tent [tent] *n* Zelt *das*.

tenth [tenθ] *num* zehnte(-r)(-s), → **sixth**.

tent peg *n* Hering *der*.

tepid ['tepɪd] *adj* (*water*) lauwarm.

tequila [tɪ'kiːlə] *n* Tequila *der*.

term [tɜːm] *n* (*word, expression*) Ausdruck *der*; (*at school*) Halbjahr *das*; (*at university*) Semester *das*; **in the long ~** langfristig; **in the short ~** kurzfristig; **in ~s of** im Hinblick auf (+A); **in business ~s** geschäftlich. ▶ **terms** *npl* (*of contract*) Bedingungen *pl*; (*price*) Zahlungsbedingungen *pl*.

terminal ['tɜːmɪnl] ◆ *adj* (*illness*) unheilbar. ◆ *n* (*for buses*) Busbahnhof *der*; (*at airport, of computer*) Terminal *das*.

terminate ['tɜːmɪneɪt] *vi* (*train, bus*) enden.

terminus ['tɜːmɪnəs] *n* Endstation *die*.

terrace ['terəs] *n* (*patio*) Terrasse *die*; **the ~s** (*at football ground*) die Ränge.

terraced house ['terəst-] *n* (Br) Reihenhaus *das*.

terrible ['terəbl] *adj* schrecklich.

terribly ['terəblɪ] *adv* furchtbar.

terrier ['terɪər] *n* Terrier *der*.

terrific [tə'rɪfɪk] *adj* (*inf: very good*) toll; (*very great*) irrsinnig.

terrified ['terɪfaɪd] *adj* verängstigt.

territory ['terətrɪ] *n* (*political area*) Staatsgebiet *das*; (*terrain*) Gebiet *das*.

terror ['terər] *n* (*fear*) panische Angst.

terrorism ['terərɪzm] *n* Terrorismus *der*.

terrorist ['terərɪst] *n* Terrorist *der* (-in *die*).

terrorize ['terəraɪz] *vt* terrorisieren.

test [test] ◆ *n* Test *der*; (*at school*) Klassenarbeit *die*. ◆ *vt* (*check*) testen,

überprüfen; (*give exam to*) prüfen; (*dish, drink*) probieren.

testicles ['testɪklz] *npl* Hoden *pl*.

tetanus ['tetənəs] *n* Wundstarrkrampf *der*.

text [tekst] *n* Text *der*.

textbook ['tekstbʊk] *n* Lehrbuch *das*.

textile ['tekstaɪl] *n* Stoff *der*.

texture ['tekstʃər] *n* Beschaffenheit *die*; (*of fabric*) Struktur *die*.

Thai [taɪ] *adj* thailändisch.

Thailand ['taɪlænd] *n* Thailand *nt*.

Thames [temz] *n*: **the ~** die Themse.

than [*weak form* ðən, *strong form* ðæn] *prep & conj* als; **you're better ~ me** du bist besser als ich; **I'd rather stay in ~ go out** ich bleibe lieber zu Hause (, als auszugehen); **more ~ ten** mehr als zehn.

thank [θæŋk] *vt*: **to ~ sb (for sthg)** jm (für etw) danken. ▶ **thanks** *npl* Dank *der*. ◆ *excl* danke!; **~s to** dank (+D) or G; **many ~s!** vielen Dank!

Thanksgiving ['θæŋks,gɪvɪŋ] *n* amerikanisches Erntedankfest.

thank you *excl* danke (schön)!; **~ very much!** vielen Dank!; **no ~!** nein danke!

that [ðæt, *weak form of pron senses* 3, 4, 5 *& conj* ðət] (*pl* those) ◆ *adj* **1.** (*referring to thing, person mentioned*) der/die/das, die (*pl*), jene(-r)(-s), jene (*pl*); **~ film was good** der Film war gut; **those chocolates are delicious** die Pralinen da schmecken köstlich. **2.** (*referring to thing, person further away*) jene(-r) (-s), jene (*pl*); **I prefer ~ book** ich bevorzuge das Buch da; **I'll have ~ one** ich nehme das da. ◆ *pron* **1.** (*referring to thing, person mentioned*) das; **what's ~?** was ist das?; **~'s interesting** das ist interessant; **who's ~?** wer ist das?; **is ~ Lucy?** (*on telephone*) bist du das, Lucy?; (*pointing*) ist das Lucy?; **after ~** danach. **2.** (*referring to thing, person further away*) jene(-r)(-s), jene (*pl*); **I want those there** ich möchte die da. **3.** (*introducing relative clause: subject*) der/die/das, die (*pl*); **a shop ~ sells antiques** ein Geschäft, das Antiquitäten verkauft. **4.** (*introducing relative clause: object*) den/die/das, die (*pl*); **the film ~ I saw** den Film, den ich gesehen habe. **5.** (*introducing relative clause: after prep +D*) dem/der/dem, denen (*pl*); (*after prep +A*) den/die/das, die (*pl*); **the place ~ I'm looking for** der Ort, nach dem ich suche. ◆ *adv* so; **it wasn't ~ bad/good** es war nicht so schlecht/gut. ◆ *conj* daß; **tell him ~ I'm going to be late** sag ihm, daß ich später komme.

thatched [θætʃt] *adj* strohgedeckt.

that's [ðæts] = **that is**.

thaw [θɔː] ◆ *vi* (*snow, ice*) tauen. ◆ *vt* (*frozen food*) auftauen.

the [*weak form* ðə, *before vowel* ðɪ, *strong form* ðiː] *definite article* **1.** (*gen*) der/die/das, die (*pl*); **~ book** das Buch; **~ man** der Mann; **~ woman** die Frau; **~ girls** die Mädchen; **~ Wilsons** die Wilsons; **to play ~ piano** Klavier spielen. **2.** (*with an adjective to form a noun*): **~ British** die Briten; **~ impossible** das Unmögliche. **3.** (*in dates*) der; **~ twelfth (of May)** der Zwölfte (Mai); **~ forties** die Vierziger. **4.** (*in titles*) der/die; **Elizabeth ~ Second** Elizabeth die Zweite.

theater ['θɪətər] *n* (*Am: for plays, drama*) = **theatre**; (*for films*) Kino *das*.

theatre ['θɪətər] *n* (*Br*) Theater *das*.

theft [θeft] *n* Diebstahl *der*.

their [ðeər] *adj* ihr.

theirs [ðeəz] *pron* ihre(-r)(-s); **a friend of ~** ein Freund von ihnen.

them [*weak form* ðəm, *strong form* ðem] *pron* (*accusative*) sie; (*dative*) ihnen; **I know ~** ich kenne sie; **it's ~** sie sind es; **send it to ~** schicke es ihnen; **tell ~** sage ihnen; **he's worse than ~** er ist schlimmer als sie.

theme [θiːm] *n* Thema *das*.

theme park *n* Freizeitpark *der* (*mit themabezogenen Attraktionen*).

themselves [ðəm'selvz] *pron* (*reflexive*) sich; (*after prep*) sich (selbst); **they did it ~** sie machten es selbst.

then [ðen] *adv* dann; (*at time in past*) damals; **from ~ on** von da an; **until ~** bis dahin.

theory ['θɪərɪ] *n* Theorie *die*; **in ~** theoretisch.

therapist ['θerəpɪst] *n* Therapeut *der* (**-in** *die*).

therapy ['θerəpɪ] *n* Therapie *die*.

there [ðeər] ◆ *adv* (*existing, present*) da; (*at, in that place*) dort; (*to that place*) dorthin. ◆ *pron*: **~ is** da ist, es gibt; **~ are** da sind, es gibt; **is Bob ~, please?** (*on phone*) ist Bob da?; **over ~** da drüben; **~ you are** (*when giving*) bitte schön.

thereabouts [,ðeərə'bauts] *adv*: **or ~** so ungefähr.

therefore ['ðeəfɔːr] *adv* deshalb.

there's [ðeəz] = **there is**.

thermal underwear [,θɜːml-] *n* Thermounterwäsche *die*.

thermometer [θə'mɒmɪtər] *n* Thermometer *das*.

Thermos (flask)® ['θɜːməs-] *n* Thermosflasche® *die*.

thermostat ['θɜːməstæt] *n* Thermostat *der*.

these [ðiːz] *pl* → **this**.

they [ðeɪ] *pron* sie; (*people in general*) man.

thick [θɪk] *adj* dick; (*fog, hair*) dicht; (*inf: stupid*) dumm; **it's 1 metre ~** es ist 1 Meter dick.

thicken ['θɪkn] ◆ *vt* (*sauce, soup*) eindicken. ◆ *vi* (*mist, fog*) dichter werden.

thickness ['θɪknɪs] *n* Dicke *die*.

thief [θiːf] (*pl* **thieves** [θiːvz]) *n* Dieb *der* (**-in** *die*).

thigh [θaɪ] *n* Oberschenkel *der*.

thimble ['θɪmbl] *n* Fingerhut *der*.

thin [θɪn] *adj* dünn.

thing [θɪŋ] *n* (*object*) Ding *das*; (*event, action, subject*) Sache *die*; **the ~ is** die Sache ist die, daß ...; **for one ~** erstens. ▶ **things** *npl* (*clothes, posses-*

sions) Sachen *pl*; **how are ~s?** (*inf*) wie geht's?

thingummyjig ['θɪŋəmɪdʒɪg] *n* (*inf*) Dingsbums *der/die/das*.

think [θɪŋk] (*pt & pp* **thought**) ◆ *vt* denken; (*believe*) meinen. ◆ *vi* (*reflect*) nach|denken; **to ~ about** (*have in mind*) nach|denken über (+A); (*consider*) denken an (+A); **to ~ of** denken an (+A); (*invent*) sich (D) aus|denken; (*remember*) sich erinnern an (+A); **what do you ~ of it?** was hältst du davon?; **to ~ of doing sthg** daran denken, etw zu tun; **I ~ so** ich glaube schon; **I don't ~ so** ich glaube nicht; **do you ~ you could ...?** meinst du, du könntest ...?; **to ~ highly of sb** jn hoch ein|schätzen. ▶ **think over** *vt sep* nach|denken über (+A). ▶ **think up** *vt sep* aus|denken.

third [θɜ:d] *num* dritte(-r)(-s), → **sixth**.

third party insurance *n* Haftpflichtversicherung *die*.

Third World *n*: **the ~** die dritte Welt.

thirst [θɜ:st] *n* Durst *der*.

thirsty ['θɜ:stɪ] *adj* durstig.

thirteen [‚θɜ:'ti:n] *num* dreizehn, → **six**.

thirteenth [‚θɜ:'ti:nθ] *num* dreizehnte(-r)(-s), → **sixth**.

thirtieth ['θɜ:tɪəθ] *num* dreißigste(-r)(-s), → **sixth**.

thirty ['θɜ:tɪ] *num* dreißig, → **six**.

this [ðɪs] (*pl* **these**) ◆ *adj* diese(-r)(-s), diese (*pl*); **I prefer ~ book** ich bevorzuge dieses Buch; **these chocolates are delicious** diese Pralinen schmecken köstlich; **~ morning** heute morgen; **~ week** diese Woche; **I'll have ~ one** ich nehme dieses; **there was ~ man ...** da war dieser Mann ... ◆ *pron* **1.** (*referring to thing, person mentioned*) das; **~ is for you** das ist für dich; **what are these?** was ist das?; **~ is David Gregory** (*introducing someone*)

das ist David Gregory; (*on telephone*) hier ist David Gregory. **2.** (*referring to thing, person nearer*) diese(-r)(-s), diese (*pl*); **I want these here** ich möchte diese hier. ◆ *adv* so; **it was ~ big** es war so groß.

thistle ['θɪsl] *n* Distel *die*.

thorn [θɔ:n] *n* Dorn *der*.

thorough ['θʌrə] *adj* gründlich.

thoroughly ['θʌrəlɪ] *adv* (*completely*) völlig.

those [ðəʊz] *pl* → **that**.

though [ðəʊ] ◆ *conj* obwohl. ◆ *adv* doch; **even ~** auch wenn.

thought [θɔ:t] ◆ *pt & pp* → **think**. ◆ *n* (*idea*) Gedanke *der*; (*thinking*) Überlegung *die*. ▶ **thoughts** *npl* (*opinion*) Gedanken *pl*.

thoughtful ['θɔ:tfʊl] *adj* (*serious*) nachdenklich; (*considerate*) rücksichtsvoll.

thoughtless ['θɔ:tlɪs] *adj* gedankenlos.

thousand ['θaʊznd] *num* tausend; **a** OR **one ~** eintausend; **~s of** Tausende von, → **six**.

thrash [θræʃ] *vt* (*inf: defeat*) vernichtend schlagen.

thread [θred] ◆ *n* (*of cotton etc*) Faden *der*. ◆ *vt* (*needle*) ein|fädeln.

threadbare ['θredbeər] *adj* abgenutzt.

threat [θret] *n* Drohung *die*; (*possibility*) Gefahr *die*.

threaten ['θretn] *vt* bedrohen; **to ~ to do sthg** drohen, etw zu tun.

threatening ['θretnɪŋ] *adj* drohend.

three [θri:] *num* drei, → **six**.

three-D *adj* drei-D-.

three-piece suite *n* Polstergarnitur *die*.

three-quarters [-'kwɔ:təz] *n* drei Viertel *pl*; **~ of an hour** eine Dreiviertelstunde.

threshold ['θreʃhəʊld] *n* (*fml*) Schwelle *die*.

threw [θru:] *pt* → **throw**.

thrifty ['θrɪftɪ] *adj* sparsam.

thrilled [θrɪld] *adj* begeistert.

thriller ['θrɪlər] n Thriller der.

thrive [θraɪv] vi (plant, animal) gedeihen; (person) auf|blühen; (business, tourism) florieren.

throat [θrəʊt] n Hals der.

throb [θrɒb] vi (head, pain) pochen; (noise, engine) dröhnen.

throne [θrəʊn] n Thron der.

throttle ['θrɒtl] n (of motorbike) Gasgriff der.

through [θruː] ◆ prep durch; (during) während (+G). ◆ adv durch. ◆ adj: to be ~ (with sthg) (finished) (mit etw) fertig sein; you're ~ (on phone) Sie sind durch; Monday ~ Thursday (Am) Montag bis Donnerstag; to let sb ~ jn durch|lassen; ~ traffic Durchgangsverkehr der; a ~ train ein durchgehender Zug; 'no ~ road' (Br) 'Keine Durchfahrt'.

throughout [θruː'aʊt] ◆ adv (all the time) die ganze Zeit; (everywhere) überall. ◆ prep: ~ the day/morning den ganzen Tag/Morgen über; ~ the year das ganze Jahr hindurch; ~ the country im ganzen Land.

throw [θrəʊ] (pt threw, pp thrown [θrəʊn]) vt werfen; (a switch) betätigen; to ~ the dice würfeln; to ~ sthg in the bin etw in den Mülleimer werfen. ▶ **throw away** vt sep weg|werfen. ▶ **throw out** vt sep (get rid of) weg|werfen; (person) hinaus|werfen. ▶ **throw up** vi (inf: vomit) sich übergeben.

thru [θruː] (Am) = **through**.

thrush [θrʌʃ] n (bird) Drossel die.

thud [θʌd] n dumpfes Geräusch.

thug [θʌg] n Schläger der.

thumb [θʌm] ◆ n Daumen der. ◆ vt: to ~ a lift trampen.

thumbtack ['θʌmtæk] n (Am) Reißzwecke die.

thump [θʌmp] ◆ n (punch) Schlag der; (sound) dumpfer Schlag. ◆ vt schlagen.

thunder ['θʌndər] n Donner der.

thunderstorm ['θʌndəstɔːm] n Gewitter das.

Thurs. (abbr of Thursday) Do.

Thursday ['θɜːzdɪ] n Donnerstag der, → **Saturday**.

thyme [taɪm] n Thymian der.

tick [tɪk] ◆ n (written mark) Haken der; (insect) Zecke die. ◆ vt ab|haken. ◆ vi (clock, watch) ticken. ▶ **tick off** vt sep (mark off) ab|haken.

ticket ['tɪkɪt] n (for cinema, theatre, match) Eintrittskarte die; (for plane) Flugschein der, Ticket das; (for bus, tube) Fahrschein der; (for train) Fahrkarte die; (for car park) Parkschein der; (label) Etikett das; (for lottery) Los das; (for speeding, parking) Strafzettel der.

ticket collector n (at barrier) Fahrkartenkontrolleur der (-in die).

ticket inspector n (on train) Schaffner der (-in die).

ticket machine n Fahrscheinautomat der.

ticket office n (in cinema, theatre) Kasse die; (in station) Fahrkartenschalter der.

tickle ['tɪkl] vt & vi kitzeln.

ticklish ['tɪklɪʃ] adj kitzlig.

tick-tack-toe n (Am) Spiel, bei dem Dreierreihen von Kreisen und Kreuzen zu erzielen sind.

tide [taɪd] n (of sea) Gezeiten pl.

tidy ['taɪdɪ] adj ordentlich. ▶ **tidy up** vt sep auf|räumen.

tie [taɪ] (pt & pp tied, cont tying) ◆ n (around neck) Krawatte die; (draw) Unentschieden das; (Am: on railway track) Schwelle die. ◆ vt binden; (knot) machen. ◆ vi (game) unentschieden spielen; (competition) gleich stehen. ▶ **tie up** vt sep (fasten) fest|binden; (parcel) verschnüren; (laces) binden; (delay) auf|halten.

tiepin ['taɪpɪn] n Krawattennadel die.

tier [tɪər] n (of seats) Rang der.

tiger ['taɪgər] n Tiger der.

tight [taɪt] ◆ adj (drawer, tap) fest; (nut, knot) fest angezogen; (clothes, shoes, bend) eng; (rope, material) straff;

(*schedule*) knapp; (*chest*) beengt; (*inf: drunk*) blau. ◆ *adv* (*hold*) fest.

tighten ['taɪtn] *vt* (*nut, knot*) fest anlziehen; (*rope*) straffen.

tightrope ['taɪtrəʊp] *n* Hochseil *das.*

tights [taɪts] *npl* Strumpfhose *die;* **a pair of ~** eine Strumpfhose.

tile ['taɪl] *n* (*for roof*) Ziegel *der;* (*for floor*) Fliese *die;* (*for wall*) Kachel *die.*

till [tɪl] ◆ *n* (*for money*) Kasse *die.* ◆ *prep & conj* bis.

tiller ['tɪlər] *n* Ruderpinne *die.*

tilt [tɪlt] *vt & vi* kippen.

timber ['tɪmbər] *n* (*wood*) Holz *das;* (*of roof*) Balken *der.*

time [taɪm] ◆ *n* Zeit *die;* (*occasion*) Mal *das.* ◆ *vt* (*measure*) stoppen; (*arrange*) zeitlich ablstimmen; **to be well ~d** gut abgepaßt sein; **I haven't got the ~** mir fehlt die Zeit; **it's ~ to go** es ist Zeit zu gehen; **what's the ~?** wie spät ist es?, wieviel Uhr ist es?; **two at a ~** zwei auf einmal; **two ~s two** zwei mal zwei; **five ~s as much** fünf mal so viel; **three ~s a week** dreimal die Woche; **in a month's ~** in einem Monat; **to have a good ~** sich amüsieren; **all the ~** die ganze Zeit; **every ~** jedesmal; **from ~ to ~** von Zeit zu Zeit; **for the ~ being** vorläufig; **in ~** (*arrive*) rechtzeitig; **in good ~** früh; **last ~** letztes Mal; **most of the ~** meistens; **on ~** pünktlich; **some of the ~** manchmal; **this ~** diesmal.

time difference *n* Zeitunterschied *der.*

time limit *n* Frist *die.*

timer ['taɪmər] *n* (*machine*) Schaltuhr *die.*

time share *n* Ferienwohnung, an der man einen Besitzanteil hat.

timetable ['taɪm,teɪbl] *n* (*of trains, buses, boats etc*) Fahrplan *der;* (SCH) Stundenplan *der;* (*of events*) Programm *das.*

time zone *n* Zeitzone *die.*

timid ['tɪmɪd] *adj* scheu.

tin [tɪn] ◆ *n* (*metal*) Blech *das;* (*container*) Dose *die.* ◆ *adj* Blech-.

tinfoil ['tɪnfɔɪl] *n* Alufolie *die.*

tinned food [tɪnd-] *n* (Br) Konserven *pl.*

tin opener [-,əʊpnər] *n* (Br) Dosenöffner *der.*

tinsel ['tɪnsl] *n* Lametta *das.*

tint [tɪnt] *n* (*colour*) Ton *der.*

tinted glass [,tɪntɪd-] *n* getöntes Glas.

tiny ['taɪnɪ] *adj* winzig.

tip [tɪp] ◆ *n* (*point, end*) Spitze *die;* (*of cigarette*) Filter *der;* (*to waiter, taxi driver etc*) Trinkgeld *das;* (*piece of advice*) Tip *der;* (*rubbish dump*) Müllhalde *die.* ◆ *vt* (*waiter, taxi driver etc*) Trinkgeld geben (+D); (*tilt*) kippen; (*pour*) schütten. ▶ **tip over** *vt sep & vi* umlkippen.

tire ['taɪər] ◆ *vi* ermüden. ◆ *n* (Am) = **tyre.**

tired ['taɪəd] *adj* müde; **to be ~ of sthg** (*fed up with*) etw satt haben.

tired out *adj* müde.

tiring ['taɪərɪŋ] *adj* ermüdend.

tissue ['tɪʃuː] *n* (*handkerchief*) Taschentuch *das.*

tissue paper *n* Seidenpapier *das.*

tit [tɪt] *n* (*vulg: breast*) Titte *die.*

title ['taɪtl] *n* Titel *der.*

T-junction *n* Einmündung *die* (*in eine Vorfahrtsstraße*).

to [*unstressed before consonant* tə, *unstressed before vowel* tʊ, *stressed* tuː] ◆ *prep* **1.** (*indicating direction*) nach; **to go ~ France** nach Frankreich fahren; **to go ~ school** in die Schule gehen; **to go ~ work** zur Arbeit gehen. **2.** (*indicating position*): **~ one side** auf der einen Seite; **~ the left/right** (*move*) nach links/rechts. **3.** (*expressing indirect object*): **to give sthg ~ sb** jm etw geben; **to listen ~ the radio** Radio hören; **we added milk ~ the mixture** wir fügten Milch zu der Mischung hinzu. **4.** (*indicating reaction, effect*) zu; **~ my surprise** zu meiner Überraschung. **5.** (*until*) bis; **to count ~ ten** bis zehn zählen; **we work from 9 ~ 5** wir arbeiten von 9 bis 5. **6.** (*indicat-*

ing change of state): **to turn ~ sthg** zu etw werden; **it could lead ~ trouble** das könnte Ärger geben. **7.** (*Br: in expressions of time*) vor; **it's ten ~ three** es ist zehn vor drei. **8.** (*in ratios, rates*): **10 kilometres ~ the litre** 10 Kilometer pro Liter. **9.** (*of, for*): **the key ~ the car** der Schlüssel für das Auto; **a letter ~ my daughter** ein Brief an meine Tochter. **10.** (*indicating attitude*) zu; **to be rude ~ sb** frech zu jm sein. ◆ *with infinitive* **1.** (*forming simple infinitive*): **~ laugh** lachen; **~ walk** gehen. **2.** (*following another verb*): **to begin ~ do sthg** anfangen, etw zu tun; **to want ~ do sthg** etw tun wollen. **3.** (*following an adjective*) zu; **difficult ~ do** schwer zu tun; **ready ~ go** bereit zu gehen. **4.** (*indicating purpose*) um zu; **we came here ~ look at the castle** wir sind hierher gekommen, um das Schloß anzuschauen.

toad [təʊd] *n* Kröte *die*.

toadstool ['təʊdstuːl] *n* Giftpilz *der*.

toast [təʊst] ◆ *n* Toast *der*. ◆ *vt* (*bread*) toasten; **a piece** OR **slice of ~** eine Scheibe Toast.

toasted sandwich ['təʊstɪd-] *n* getoastetes Sandwich.

toaster ['təʊstər] *n* Toaster *der*.

toastie ['təʊstɪ] = **toasted sandwich**.

tobacco [tə'bækəʊ] *n* Tabak *der*.

tobacconist's [tə'bækənɪsts] *n* Tabakladen *der*.

toboggan [tə'bɒgən] *n* Schlitten *der*.

today [tə'deɪ] *n* & *adv* heute.

toddler ['tɒdlər] *n* Kleinkind *das*.

toe [təʊ] *n* Zeh *der*.

toe clip *n* Rennhaken *der*.

toenail ['təʊneɪl] *n* Zehennagel *der*.

toffee ['tɒfɪ] *n* (*sweet*) Karamelbonbon *der*; (*substance*) Karamel *der*.

together [tə'geðər] *adv* zusammen; (*at the same time*) gleichzeitig; **~ with** zusammen mit.

toilet ['tɔɪlɪt] *n* Toilette *die*; **to go to** the **~** auf die Toilette gehen; **where's** the **~?** wo ist die Toilette?

toilet bag *n* Kulturbeutel *der*.

toilet paper *n* Toilettenpapier *das*.

toiletries ['tɔɪlɪtrɪz] *npl* Toilettenartikel *pl*.

toilet roll *n* Rolle *die* Toilettenpapier.

toilet water *n* Eau de Toilette *das*.

token ['təʊkn] *n* (*metal disc*) Marke *die*.

told [təʊld] *pt* & *pp* → **tell**.

tolerable ['tɒlərəbl] *adj* leidlich.

tolerant ['tɒlərənt] *adj* tolerant.

tolerate ['tɒləreɪt] *vt* (*put up with*) ertragen; (*permit*) dulden.

toll [təʊl] *n* (*for road, bridge*) Gebühr *die*, Maut *die* (Österr).

tollbooth ['təʊlbuːθ] *n* Kabine, an der Straßengebühr gezahlt wird.

toll-free *adj* (Am) gebührenfrei.

tomato [Br tə'mɑːtəʊ, Am tə'meɪtəʊ] (*pl* -**es**) *n* Tomate *die*.

tomato juice *n* Tomatensaft *der*.

tomato ketchup *n* Tomatenketchup *der*.

tomato puree *n* Tomatenmark *das*.

tomato sauce *n* Tomatensoße *die*.

tomb [tuːm] *n* Grab *das*.

tomorrow [tə'mɒrəʊ] *n* & *adv* morgen; **the day after ~** übermorgen; **~ afternoon** morgen nachmittag; **~ morning** morgen früh; **~ night** morgen abend.

ton [tʌn] *n* (*in UK*) = 1.016 kg, Tonne *die*; (*in US*) = 907 kg, Tonne *die*; (*metric tonne*) Tonne *die*; **~s of** (*inf*) haufenweise.

tone [təʊn] *n* Ton *der*.

tongs [tɒŋz] *npl* (*for hair*) Lockenstab *der*; (*for sugar*) Zuckerzange *die*.

tongue [tʌŋ] *n* Zunge *die*.

tonic ['tɒnɪk] *n* (*tonic water*) Tonic *das*; (*medicine*) Tonikum *das*.

tonic water *n* Tonic *das*.

tonight [tə'naɪt] *n* & *adv* heute

abend; (*later*) heute nacht.

tonne [tʌn] *n* Tonne *die*.

tonsillitis [ˌtɒnsɪˈlaɪtɪs] *n* Mandel-entzündung *die*.

too [tuː] *adv* zu; (*also*) auch; **it's not ~ good** es ist nicht besonders gut; **it's ~ late to go out** es ist zu spät zum Ausgehen; **~ many** zu viele; **~ much** zuviel.

took [tʊk] *pt* → **take**.

tool [tuːl] *n* Werkzeug *das*.

tool kit *n* Werkzeug *das*.

tooth [tuːθ] (*pl* **teeth**) *n* Zahn *der*.

toothache [ˈtuːθeɪk] *n* Zahn-schmerzen *pl*.

toothbrush [ˈtuːθbrʌʃ] *n* Zahn-bürste *die*.

toothpaste [ˈtuːθpeɪst] *n* Zahn-pasta *die*.

toothpick [ˈtuːθpɪk] *n* Zahnstocher *der*.

top [tɒp] ♦ *adj* (*highest*) oberste(-r) (-s); (*best, most important*) beste(-r) (-s). ♦ *n* (*of hill, tree*) Spitze *die*; (*of table*) Platte *die*; (*of class, league*) Erste *der die*; (*of bottle, jar*) Deckel *der*; (*of pen, tube*) Kappe *die*; (*garment*) Oberteil *das*; (*of street, road*) Ende *das*; **at the ~ (of)** oben (auf (+A)); **on ~ of** (*on highest part of*) oben auf (+A); **on ~ of that** obendrein; **at ~ speed** mit Höchstgeschwindigkeit; **~ gear** höchster Gang. ► **top up** *vt sep* (*glass*) nachlfüllen. ♦ *vi* (*with petrol*) vollltanken.

top floor *n* oberstes Stockwerk.

topic [ˈtɒpɪk] *n* Thema *das*.

topical [ˈtɒpɪkl] *adj* aktuell.

topless [ˈtɒplɪs] *adj* oben ohne.

topped [tɒpt] *adj*: **~ with** (*food*) mit.

topping [ˈtɒpɪŋ] *n* Soße oder Garnierung zu einem Gericht.

torch [tɔːtʃ] *n* (Br: *electric light*) Taschenlampe *die*.

tore [tɔːr] *pt* → **tear¹**.

torment [tɔːˈment] *vt* (*annoy*) pla-gen.

torn [tɔːn] ♦ *pp* → **tear¹**. ♦ *adj* (*ripped*) zerrissen.

tornado [tɔːˈneɪdəʊ] (*pl* **-es** OR **-s**) *n* Wirbelsturm *der*.

torrential rain [təˈrenʃl-] *n* strö-mender Regen.

tortoise [ˈtɔːtəs] *n* Schildkröte *die*.

tortoiseshell [ˈtɔːtəʃel] *n* Schild-patt *das*.

torture [ˈtɔːtʃər] ♦ *n* (*punishment*) Folter *die*. ♦ *vt* (*punish*) foltern.

Tory [ˈtɔːrɪ] *n* Tory *der*.

toss [tɒs] *vt* (*throw*) werfen; (*salad*) mischen; (*pancake*) wenden; **to ~ a coin** mit einer Münze losen.

total [ˈtəʊtl] ♦ *adj* (*number, amount*) gesamt; (*complete*) völlig. ♦ *n* Gesamtzahl *die*; (*sum*) Gesamt-summe *die*; **in ~** insgesamt.

touch [tʌtʃ] ♦ *n* Berührung *die*; (*sense of touch*) Tastsinn *der*; (*small amount*) Spur *die*; (*detail*) Detail *das*. ♦ *vt* berühren. ♦ *vi* sich berühren; **to get in ~ (with sb)** sich (mit jm) in Verbindung setzen; **to keep in ~ (with sb)** (mit jm) in Kontakt bleiben. ► **touch down** *vi* (*plane*) auflsetzen.

touching [ˈtʌtʃɪŋ] *adj* (*moving*) rührend.

tough [tʌf] *adj* (*resilient*) wider-standsfähig; (*meat*) zäh; (*difficult*) schwierig; (*harsh, strict*) hart.

tour [tʊər] ♦ *n* (*journey*) Tour *die*; (*of city, castle etc*) Besichtigung *die*; (*of pop group, theatre company*) Tournee *die*. ♦ *vt* reisen durch; **on ~** auf Tournee.

tourism [ˈtʊərɪzm] *n* Tourismus *der*.

tourist [ˈtʊərɪst] *n* Tourist *der* (-in *die*).

tourist class *n* Touristclass *die*.

tourist information office *n* Fremdenverkehrsbüro *das*.

tournament [ˈtɔːnəmənt] *n* Turnier *das*.

tour operator *n* Reiseveran-stalter *der*.

tout [taʊt] *n* Schwarzhändler *der*.

tow [təʊ] *vt* ablschleppen.

toward [təˈwɔːd] (*Am*) = **towards**.

towards [təˈwɔːdz] *prep* (Br: *in the*

direction of) zu; (*facing*) nach; (*with regard to*) gegenüber (+D); (*with time*) gegen; (*to help pay for*) für; **to run ~ sb** auf jn zullaufen; **to sit ~ the front/ back** vorne/hinten sitzen.

towaway zone ['təʊəwei-] *n* (Am) Abschleppzone *die*.

towel ['taʊəl] *n* Handtuch *das*.

toweling ['taʊəlɪŋ] (Am) = **towelling**.

towelling ['taʊəlɪŋ] *n* (Br) Frottee *das*.

towel rail *n* Handtuchhalter *der*.

tower ['taʊər] *n* Turm *der*.

tower block *n* (Br) Hochhaus *das*.

Tower Bridge *n* Zwillingszugbrücke über die Themse, in der Nähe des Londoner Tower.

Tower of London *n*: **the ~** der Londoner Tower.

town [taʊn] *n* Stadt *die*.

town centre *n* Stadtzentrum *das*.

town hall *n* Rathaus *das*.

towpath ['taʊpɑːθ, *pl* -pɑːðz] *n* Treidelpfad *der*.

towrope ['təʊrəʊp] *n* Abschleppseil *das*.

tow truck *n* (Am) Abschleppwagen *der*.

toxic ['tɒksɪk] *adj* giftig.

toy [tɔɪ] *n* Spielzeug *das*.

toy shop *n* Spielwarengeschäft *das*.

trace [treɪs] ◆ *n* Spur *die*. ◆ *vt* (*find*) finden.

tracing paper ['treɪsɪŋ-] *n* Pauspapier *das*.

track [træk] *n* (*path*) Weg *der*; (*of railway*) Gleis *das*; (SPORT) Bahn *die*; (*song*) Stück *das*. ▶ **track down** *vt sep* ausfindig machen.

tracksuit ['træksuːt] *n* Trainingsanzug *der*.

tractor ['træktər] *n* Traktor *der*.

trade [treɪd] ◆ *n* (COMM) Handel *der*; (*job*) Handwerk *das*. ◆ *vt* (*exchange*) tauschen. ◆ *vi* (COMM) handeln; **the book ~** das Buchwesen.

trade-in *n* (*action*) Inzahlungnahme *die*.

trademark ['treɪdmɑːk] *n* Warenzeichen *das*.

trader ['treɪdər] *n* Händler *der* (-in *die*).

tradesman ['treɪdzmən] (*pl* -men [-mən]) *n* (*deliveryman*) Lieferant *der*; (*shopkeeper*) Einzelhändler *der*.

trade union *n* Gewerkschaft *die*.

tradition [trə'dɪʃn] *n* Tradition *die*.

traditional [trə'dɪʃənl] *adj* traditionell.

traffic ['træfɪk] (*pt* & *pp* -ked) ◆ *n* (*cars etc*) Verkehr *der*. ◆ *vi*: **to ~ in** handeln mit.

traffic circle *n* (Am) Kreisverkehr *der*.

traffic island *n* Verkehrsinsel *die*.

traffic jam *n* Stau *der*.

traffic lights *npl* Ampel *die*.

traffic warden *n* (Br) = Hilfspolizist *der* (Politesse *die*).

tragedy ['trædʒədi] *n* Tragödie *die*.

tragic ['trædʒɪk] *adj* tragisch.

trail [treɪl] ◆ *n* (*path*) Weg *der*; (*marks*) Spur *die*. ◆ *vi* (*be losing*) zurückl liegen.

trailer ['treɪlər] *n* (*for boat, luggage*) Anhänger *der*; (Am: *caravan*) Wohnwagen *der*; (*for film, programme*) Vorschau *die*.

train [treɪn] ◆ *n* (*on railway*) Zug *der*. ◆ *vt* (*teach*) ausl bilden. ◆ *vi* trainieren; **by ~** mit dem Zug.

train driver *n* Zugführer *der* (-in *die*).

trainee [treɪ'niː] *n* Auszubildende *der die*; (*in management*) Trainee *der die*.

trainer ['treɪnər] *n* (*of athlete etc*) Trainer *der* (-in *die*). ▶ **trainers** *npl* (Br: *shoes*) Trainingsschuhe *pl*.

training ['treɪnɪŋ] *n* (*instruction*) Ausbildung *die*; (*exercises*) Training *das*.

training shoes *npl* (Br) Trainingsschuhe *pl*.

tram [træm] *n* (Br) Straßenbahn *die*.

tramp [træmp] n Tramp der.

trampoline ['træmpəli:n] n Trampolin das.

trance [trɑ:ns] n Trance die.

tranquilizer ['træŋkwɪlaɪzər] (Am) = **tranquillizer**.

tranquillizer ['træŋkwɪlaɪzər] n (Br) Beruhigungsmittel das.

transaction [træn'zækʃn] n Geschäft das.

transatlantic [,trænzət'læntɪk] adj transatlantisch.

transfer [n 'trænsfɜ:r, vb træns'fɜ:r] ◆ n (of money) Überweisung die; (of power) Übertragung die; (SPORT) Transfer der; (picture) Abziehbild das; (Am: ticket) Fahrkarte mit Umsteigeerlaubnis. ◆ vt übertragen; (money) überweisen. ◆ vi (change bus, plane etc) um|steigen; '~s' (in airport) 'Transitpassagiere'.

transfer desk n (in airport) Transitschalter der.

transform [træns'fɔ:m] vt verändern.

transfusion [træns'fju:ʒn] n Transfusion die.

transistor radio [træn'zɪstə-] n Transistorradio das.

transit ['trænzɪt]: **in transit** adv im Transit.

transitive ['trænzɪtɪv] adj transitiv.

transit lounge n Transit Lounge die.

translate [træns'leɪt] vt übersetzen.

translation [træns'leɪʃn] n Übersetzung die.

translator [træns'leɪtər] n Übersetzer der (-in die).

transmission [trænz'mɪʃn] n Übertragung die.

transmit [trænz'mɪt] vt übertragen.

transparent [træns'pærənt] adj (see-through) durchsichtig.

transplant ['trænsplɑ:nt] n Transplantation die.

transport [n 'trænspɔ:t, vb træn'spɔ:t] ◆ n (cars, trains, planes etc) Verkehrsmittel pl; (moving) Transport der, Beförderung die. ◆ vt transportieren, befördern.

transportation [,trænspɔ:'teɪʃn] n (Am) (cars, trains, planes etc) Verkehrsmittel pl; (moving) Transport der, Beförderung die.

trap [træp] ◆ n Falle die. ◆ vt: **to be trapped** (stuck) fest|sitzen.

trapdoor [,træp'dɔ:r] n Falltür die.

trash [træʃ] n (Am: waste material) Müll der.

trashcan ['træʃkæn] n (Am) Mülleimer der.

trauma ['trɔ:mə] n Trauma das.

traumatic [trɔ:'mætɪk] adj traumatisch.

travel ['trævl] ◆ n Reisen das. ◆ vt (distance) fahren. ◆ vi reisen; (in vehicle) fahren.

travel agency n Reisebüro das.

travel agent n Reisebürokaufmann der (-kauffrau die); **~'s** (shop) Reisebüro das.

Travelcard ['trævlkɑ:d] n (Br) Zeitkarte die.

travel centre n (in railway, bus station) Reiseinformation die.

traveler ['trævlər] (Am) = **traveller**.

travel insurance n Reiseversicherung die.

traveller ['trævlər] n (Br) Reisende der die.

traveller's cheque n Reisescheck der.

travelsick ['trævəlsɪk] adj reisekrank.

trawler ['trɔ:lər] n Trawler der.

tray [treɪ] n Tablett das.

treacherous ['tretʃərəs] adj (person) verräterisch; (roads, conditions) gefährlich.

treacle ['tri:kl] n (Br) Sirup der.

tread [tred] (pt **trod**, pp **trodden**) ◆ n (of tyre) Profil das. ◆ vi: **to ~ on sthg** auf etw (A) treten.

treasure ['treʒər] n Schatz der.

treat [tri:t] ◆ vt behandeln. ◆ n (special thing) Freude die; **to ~ sb to**

sthg jm etw spendieren.

treatment ['tri:tmənt] n Behandlung die.

treble ['trebl] adj dreifach; ~ **the amount** dreimal soviel.

tree [tri:] n Baum der.

trek [trek] n Wanderung die.

tremble ['trembl] vi zittern.

tremendous [trɪ'mendəs] adj enorm; (inf: very good) toll.

trench [trentʃ] n Graben der.

trend [trend] n (tendency) Tendenz die; (fashion) Trend der.

trendy ['trendɪ] adj (inf) trendy.

trespasser ['trespəsər] n Unbefugte der die; '~s will be prosecuted' 'Betreten verboten'.

trial ['traɪəl] n (JUR) Prozeß der; (test) Test der; **a ~ period** eine Probezeit.

triangle ['traɪæŋgl] n Dreieck das.

triangular [traɪ'æŋgjʊlər] adj dreieckig.

tribe [traɪb] n Stamm der.

tributary ['trɪbjʊtrɪ] n Nebenfluß der.

trick [trɪk] ◆ n Trick der. ◆ vt überlisten; **to play a ~ on sb** jm einen Streich spielen.

trickle ['trɪkl] vi (liquid) tropfen.

tricky ['trɪkɪ] adj knifflig.

tricycle ['traɪsɪkl] n Dreirad das.

trifle ['traɪfl] n (dessert) Nachtisch aus mit Sherry getränktem Biskuit, Früchten, Vanillecreme und Sahne in Schichten.

trigger ['trɪgər] n Abzug der.

trim [trɪm] ◆ n (haircut) Nachschneiden das. ◆ vt (hair, beard, hedge) nach|schneiden.

trinket ['trɪŋkɪt] n Schnickschnack der.

trio ['tri:əʊ] (pl -s) n Trio das.

trip [trɪp] ◆ n (voyage) Reise die; (short) Ausflug der. ◆ vi stolpern.
▶ **trip up** vi stolpern.

triple ['trɪpl] adj dreifach.

tripod ['traɪpɒd] n Stativ das.

triumph ['traɪəmf] n Triumph der.

trivial ['trɪvɪəl] adj (pej) trivial.

trod [trɒd] pt → **tread**.

trodden ['trɒdn] pp → **tread**.

trolley ['trɒlɪ] (pl -s) n (Br: at airport etc) Gepäckwagen der; (Br: in supermarket) Einkaufswagen der; (Br: for food, drinks) Wagen der; (Am: tram) Straßenbahn die.

trombone [trɒm'bəʊn] n Posaune die.

troops [tru:ps] npl Truppen pl.

trophy ['trəʊfɪ] n Trophäe die.

tropical ['trɒpɪkl] adj tropisch; ~ **fruit** Südfrucht die.

trot [trɒt] ◆ vi (horse) traben. ◆ n: **on the ~** (inf) hintereinander.

trouble ['trʌbl] ◆ n (problems) Ärger der; (difficulty) Schwierigkeiten pl; (inconvenience) Mühe die; (pain, illness) Beschwerden pl. ◆ vt (worry) beunruhigen; (bother) stören; **to be in ~** (having problems) in Schwierigkeiten sein; (with police, parents) Ärger haben; **to get into ~** Ärger bekommen; **to take the ~ to do sthg** sich die Mühe machen, etw zu tun; **it's no ~** das macht keine Umstände.

trough [trɒf] n (for animals) Trog der.

trouser press ['traʊzə-] n Hosenspanner der.

trousers ['traʊzəz] npl Hose die; **a pair of ~** eine Hose.

trout [traʊt] (pl inv) n Forelle die.

trowel ['traʊəl] n (for gardening) Schaufel die.

truant ['tru:ənt] n: **to play ~** die Schule schwänzen.

truce [tru:s] n Waffenstillstand der.

truck [trʌk] n Lastwagen der, LKW der.

true [tru:] adj (not false, actual) wahr; (genuine, sincere) echt.

truly ['tru:lɪ] adv: **yours ~** mit freundlichen Grüßen.

trumpet ['trʌmpɪt] n Trompete die.

trumps [trʌmps] npl Trumpf der.

truncheon ['trʌntʃən] n Schlagstock der.

trunk [trʌŋk] n (of tree) Stamm der; (Am: of car) Kofferraum der; (case, box)

Truhe die; (of elephant) Rüssel der.

trunk call n (Br) Ferngespräch das.

trunk road n (Br) Landstraße die.

trunks [trʌŋks] npl (for swimming) Badehose die.

trust [trʌst] ◆ n (confidence) Vertrauen das. ◆ vt vertrauen (+D); (fml: hope) hoffen.

trustworthy ['trʌst,wɜːðɪ] adj vertrauenswürdig.

truth [truːθ] n Wahrheit die.

truthful ['truːθful] adj (statement, account) wahr; (person) ehrlich.

try [traɪ] ◆ n (attempt) Versuch der. ◆ vi versuchen; (make effort) sich bemühen. ◆ vt versuchen; (food) probieren; (JUR): **to ~ sb** jn vor Gericht bringen; **to ~ to do sthg** versuchen, etw zu tun. ► **try on** vt sep (clothes) an|probieren. ► **try out** vt sep aus|probieren.

T-shirt n T-Shirt das.

tub [tʌb] n (of margarine etc) Becher der; (inf: bath) Wanne die.

tube [tjuːb] n (container) Tube die; (Br: inf: underground) U-Bahn die; (pipe) Rohr das; **by ~** mit der U-Bahn.

tube station n (Br: inf) U-Bahnhaltestelle die.

tuck [tʌk]: **tuck in** ◆ vt sep (shirt) hinein|stecken; (child, person) zu|decken. ◆ vi (inf) rein|hauen.

tuck shop n (Br) = Süßwarenladen der (in einer Schule).

Tudor ['tjuːdəʳ] adj (architecture) Tudor- (16. Jahrhundert).

Tues. (abbr of Tuesday) Di.

Tuesday ['tjuːzdɪ] n Dienstag der, → **Saturday**.

tuft [tʌft] n (of hair, grass) Büschel das.

tug [tʌg] ◆ vt ziehen. ◆ n (boat) Schlepper der.

tuition [tjuːˈɪʃn] n Unterricht der.

tulip ['tjuːlɪp] n Tulpe die.

tumble-dryer ['tʌmbldraɪəʳ] n Wäschetrockner der.

tumbler ['tʌmbləʳ] n (glass) Glas das.

tummy ['tʌmɪ] n (inf) Bauch der.

tummy upset n (inf) Bauchschmerzen pl.

tumor ['tuːmər] (Am) = **tumour**.

tumour ['tjuːməʳ] n (Br) Tumor der.

tuna (fish) [Br 'tjuːnə-, Am 'tuːnə-] n Thunfisch der.

tuna melt n (Am) mit Thunfisch und Käse überbackener Toast.

tune [tjuːn] ◆ n Melodie die. ◆ vt (radio, TV, engine) ein|stellen; (instrument) stimmen; **in ~** (instrument) richtig gestimmt; **out of ~** (instrument) verstimmt; **to sing in/out of ~** richtig/falsch singen.

tunic ['tjuːnɪk] n (SCH) Trägerkleid das.

Tunisia [tjuːˈnɪzɪə] n Tunesien nt.

tunnel ['tʌnl] n Tunnel der.

turban ['tɜːbən] n Turban der.

turbo ['tɜːbəʊ] (pl -s) n Turbo der.

turbulence ['tɜːbjʊləns] n (when flying) Turbulenz die.

turf [tɜːf] n (grass) Rasen der.

Turk [tɜːk] n Türke der (Türkin die).

turkey ['tɜːkɪ] (pl -s) n Truthahn der, Pute die.

Turkey ['tɜːkɪ] n Türkei die.

Turkish ['tɜːkɪʃ] ◆ adj türkisch. ◆ n (language) Türkisch das. ◆ npl: **the ~** die Türken pl.

Turkish delight n Rachatlukum das.

turn [tɜːn] ◆ n (in road) Abzweigung die; (of knob, key, switch) Drehung die. ◆ vi (person) sich wenden; (turn round) sich um|drehen; (car) ab|biegen; (rotate) sich drehen; (milk) sauer werden. ◆ vt (head, car) wenden; (table, chair, knob, key) drehen; (page) um|blättern; (a switch) stellen; (become) werden; **to ~ sthg black** etw schwarz machen; **to ~ into sthg** (become) sich in etw (A) verwandeln; **to ~ sthg into sthg** etw in etw (A) verwandeln; **to ~ left/right** links/rechts ab|biegen; **to ~ the corner** um die Ecke biegen; **it's your ~** du bist an der Reihe; **at the ~ of the century** um die Jahrhundertwende; **to take it**

in ~s to do sthg sich ab|wechseln, etw zu tun; to ~ sthg inside out etw um|kehren. ▶ **turn back** vt sep (person, car) zurück|weisen. ◆ vi um|kehren. ▶ **turn down** vt sep (heating) herunter|stellen; (radio) leiser stellen; (offer, request) ab|lehnen. ▶ **turn off** vt sep (engine, water, gas) ab|stellen; (light, TV) aus|schalten; (tap) zu|drehen. ◆ vi (leave road) ab|fahren. ▶ **turn on** vt sep (light, TV) ein|schalten; (engine, water, gas, tap) an|stellen. ▶ **turn out** vt sep (light) aus|machen. ◆ vi (come, attend) erscheinen. ◆ vt fus: to ~ out well/badly gut/schlecht aus|gehen; to ~ out to be sthg sich als etw heraus|stellen. ▶ **turn over** vt sep (page) um|blättern; (card, omelette) um|drehen. ◆ vi (in bed) sich um|drehen; (Br: change channels) um|stellen. ▶ **turn round** vt sep (car, table etc) um|drehen. ◆ vi (person) sich um|drehen. ▶ **turn up** vt sep (heating) auf|drehen; (radio, volume) lauter stellen. ◆ vi (come, attend) erscheinen.

turning ['tɜːnɪŋ] n (off road) Abzweigung die.

turnip ['tɜːnɪp] n weiße Rübe.

turn-up n (Br: on trousers) Aufschlag der.

turps [tɜːps] n (Br: inf) Terpentin das.

turquoise ['tɜːkwɔɪz] adj türkis.

turtle ['tɜːtl] n Schildkröte die.

turtleneck ['tɜːtlnek] n Rollkragenpullover der.

tutor ['tjuːtər] n (private teacher) Privatlehrer der.

tuxedo [tʌk'siːdəʊ] (pl -s) n (Am) Smoking der.

TV n Fernsehen das; (television set) Fernseher der; on ~ im Fernsehen.

tweed [twiːd] n Tweed der.

tweezers ['twiːzəz] npl Pinzette die.

twelfth [twelfθ] num zwölfte(-r) (-s), → sixth.

twelve [twelv] num zwölf, → six.

twentieth ['twentɪəθ] num zwanzigste(-r)(-s); the ~ century das zwanzigste Jahrhundert, → sixth.

twenty ['twentɪ] num zwanzig, → six.

twice [twaɪs] adv zweimal; it's ~ as good das ist doppelt so gut.

twig [twɪg] n Zweig der.

twilight ['twaɪlaɪt] n Dämmerung die.

twin [twɪn] n Zwilling der.

twin beds npl zwei Einzelbetten pl.

twine [twaɪn] n Bindfaden der.

twin room n Zweibettzimmer das.

twist [twɪst] vt drehen; to ~ one's ankle sich (D) den Fuß verrenken.

twisting ['twɪstɪŋ] adj (road, river) sich windend.

two [tuː] num zwei, → six.

two-piece adj (swimsuit, suit) zweiteilig.

type [taɪp] ◆ n (kind) Art die. ◆ vt & vi tippen.

typewriter ['taɪp‚raɪtər] n Schreibmaschine die.

typhoid ['taɪfɔɪd] n Typhus der.

typical ['tɪpɪkl] adj typisch.

typist ['taɪpɪst] n Schreibkraft die.

tyre ['taɪər] n (Br) Reifen der.

Tyrol [tɪ'rəʊl] n: the ~ Tirol nt.

U

U adj (Br: film) jugendfrei.

UFO n (abbr of unidentified flying object) Ufo das.

ugly ['ʌglɪ] adj (unattractive) häßlich.

UHT adj (abbr of ultra heat treated): ~ milk H-Milch die.

UK n: the ~ das Vereinigte Königreich.

ulcer [ˈʌlsər] n Geschwür das.

ultimate [ˈʌltɪmət] adj (final) endgültig; (best, greatest) größte(-r) (-s).

ultraviolet [ˌʌltrəˈvaɪələt] adj ultraviolett.

umbrella [ʌmˈbrelə] n Regenschirm der.

umpire [ˈʌmpaɪər] n Schiedsrichter der.

UN n (abbr of United Nations): **the ~** die UNO.

unable [ʌnˈeɪbl] adj: **to be ~ to do sthg** etw nicht tun können.

unacceptable [ˌʌnəkˈseptəbl] adj unannehmbar.

unaccustomed [ˌʌnəˈkʌstəmd] adj: **to be ~ to sthg** an etw (A) nicht gewöhnt sein.

unanimous [juːˈnænɪməs] adj einstimmig.

unattended [ˌʌnəˈtendɪd] adj (baggage) unbeaufsichtigt.

unattractive [ˌʌnəˈtræktɪv] adj unattraktiv.

unauthorized [ʌnˈɔːθəraɪzd] adj unbefugt.

unavailable [ˌʌnəˈveɪləbl] adj nicht erhältlich.

unavoidable [ˌʌnəˈvɔɪdəbl] adj unvermeidlich.

unaware [ˌʌnəˈweər] adj: **to be ~ of sthg** sich (D) einer Sache (G) nicht bewußt sein.

unbearable [ʌnˈbeərəbl] adj unerträglich.

unbelievable [ˌʌnbɪˈliːvəbl] adj unglaublich.

unbutton [ʌnˈbʌtn] vt aufknöpfen.

uncertain [ʌnˈsɜːtn] adj unsicher.

uncertainty [ʌnˈsɜːtntɪ] n Unsicherheit die.

uncle [ˈʌŋkl] n Onkel der.

unclean [ˌʌnˈkliːn] adj unsauber.

unclear [ˌʌnˈklɪər] adj unklar.

uncomfortable [ˌʌnˈkʌmftəbl] adj (chair, bed) unbequem; **to feel ~** (person) sich nicht wohl fühlen.

uncommon [ʌnˈkɒmən] adj (rare) ungewöhnlich.

unconscious [ʌnˈkɒnʃəs] adj (after accident) bewußtlos; (unaware) unbewußt; **to be ~ of sthg** sich (D) einer Sache (G) nicht bewußt sein.

unconvincing [ˌʌnkənˈvɪnsɪŋ] adj nicht überzeugend.

uncooperative [ˌʌnkəʊˈɒpərətɪv] adj nicht entgegenkommend.

uncork [ʌnˈkɔːk] vt entkorken.

uncouth [ʌnˈkuːθ] adj ungehobelt.

uncover [ʌnˈkʌvər] vt (discover) entdecken; (car, swimming pool etc) ab|decken.

under [ˈʌndər] prep unter (+A,D); (according to) nach; **children ~ ten** Kinder unter zehn; **the circumstances** unter diesen Umständen; **to be ~ pressure** unter Druck sein.

underage [ˌʌndərˈeɪdʒ] adj minderjährig.

undercarriage [ˈʌndəˌkærɪdʒ] n Fahrwerk das.

underdone [ˌʌndəˈdʌn] adj (food) nicht gar; (rare) nicht durchgebraten.

underestimate [ˌʌndərˈestɪmeɪt] vt unterschätzen.

underexposed [ˌʌndərɪkˈspəʊzd] adj (photograph) unterbelichtet.

undergo [ˌʌndəˈgəʊ] (pt **-went**, pp **-gone**) vt sich unterziehen (+D).

undergraduate [ˌʌndəˈgrædjʊət] n Student der (-in die).

underground [ˈʌndəgraʊnd] ◆ adj unterirdisch; (secret) Untergrund-. ◆ n (Br: railway) U-Bahn die.

undergrowth [ˈʌndəgrəʊθ] n Gestrüpp das.

underline [ˌʌndəˈlaɪn] vt unterstreichen.

underneath [ˌʌndəˈniːθ] ◆ prep unter (+A,D). ◆ adv darunter. ◆ n Unterseite die.

underpants [ˈʌndəpænts] npl Unterhose die.

underpass [ˈʌndəpɑːs] n Unterführung die.

undershirt [ˈʌndəʃɜːt] *n* (Am) Unterhemd *das*.

underskirt [ˈʌndəskɜːt] *n* Unterrock *der*.

understand [ˌʌndəˈstænd] (*pt & pp* -stood) *vt & vi* verstehen; **I don't ~** ich verstehe das nicht; **to make o.s. understood** sich verständlich machen; **I ~ that ...** (*believe*) ich habe gehört, daß ...

understanding [ˌʌndəˈstændɪŋ] ◆ *adj* verständnisvoll. ◆ *n* (*agreement*) Vereinbarung *die*; (*knowledge*) Kenntnis *die*; (*interpretation*) Annahme *die*; (*sympathy*) Verständnis *das*.

understatement [ˌʌndəˈsteɪtmənt] *n*: **that's an ~** das ist untertrieben.

understood [ˌʌndəˈstʊd] *pt & pp* → **understand**.

undertake [ˌʌndəˈteɪk] (*pt* -took, *pp* -taken) *vt* (*job, task*) übernehmen; **to ~ to do sthg** sich verpflichten, etw zu tun.

undertaker [ˈʌndəˌteɪkər] *n* (*firm*) Bestattungsinstitut *das*; (*person*) Leichenbestatter *der*.

undertaking [ˌʌndəˈteɪkɪŋ] *n* (*promise*) Versprechen *das*; (*task*) Unternehmen *das*.

undertook [ˌʌndəˈtʊk] *pt* → **undertake**.

underwater [ˌʌndəˈwɔːtər] ◆ *adj* Unterwasser-. ◆ *adv* unter Wasser.

underwear [ˈʌndəweər] *n* Unterwäsche *die*.

underwent [ˌʌndəˈwent] *pt* → **undergo**.

undesirable [ˌʌndɪˈzaɪərəbl] *adj* unerwünscht.

undo [ʌnˈduː] (*pt* -did, *pp* -done) *vt* auflmachen; (*tie*) lösen.

undone [ˌʌnˈdʌn] *adj* (*coat, shirt, shoelaces*) offen.

undress [ʌnˈdres] ◆ *vi* sich auslziehen. ◆ *vt* auslziehen.

undressed [ʌnˈdrest] *adj* ausgezogen; **to get ~** sich auslziehen.

uneasy [ʌnˈiːzɪ] *adj* unbehaglich.

uneducated [ˌʌnˈedjʊkeɪtɪd] *adj* ungebildet.

unemployed [ˌʌnɪmˈplɔɪd] ◆ *adj* arbeitslos. ◆ *npl*: **the ~** die Arbeitslosen *pl*.

unemployment [ˌʌnɪmˈplɔɪmənt] *n* Arbeitslosigkeit *die*.

unemployment benefit *n* Arbeitslosenunterstützung *die*.

unequal [ʌnˈiːkwəl] *adj* ungleich.

uneven [ʌnˈiːvn] *adj* (*surface*) uneben; (*speed, beat*) ungleichmäßig; (*share, competition, race*) ungleich.

uneventful [ˌʌnɪˈventfʊl] *adj* ereignislos.

unexpected [ˌʌnɪkˈspektɪd] *adj* unerwartet.

unexpectedly [ˌʌnɪkˈspektɪdlɪ] *adv* unerwartet.

unfair [ʌnˈfeər] *adj* ungerecht.

unfairly [ʌnˈfeəlɪ] *adv* ungerecht.

unfaithful [ʌnˈfeɪθfʊl] *adj* untreu.

unfamiliar [ˌʌnfəˈmɪljər] *adj* ungewohnt; **to be ~ with sthg** sich mit etw nicht auslkennen.

unfashionable [ˌʌnˈfæʃnəbl] *adj* unmodern.

unfasten [ʌnˈfɑːsn] *vt* auflmachen.

unfavourable [ʌnˈfeɪvrəbl] *adj* ungünstig.

unfinished [ʌnˈfɪnɪʃt] *adj* unvollendet; (*work*) unerledigt.

unfit [ʌnˈfɪt] *adj* (*not healthy*) nicht fit; **to be ~ for sthg** für etw ungeeignet sein; **to be ~ for work** arbeitsunfähig sein.

unfold [ʌnˈfəʊld] *vt* (*map, sheet*) auseinanderlfalten.

unforgettable [ˌʌnfəˈgetəbl] *adj* unvergeßlich.

unforgivable [ˌʌnfəˈgɪvəbl] *adj* unverzeihlich.

unfortunate [ʌnˈfɔːtʃnət] *adj* bedauerlich.

unfortunately [ʌnˈfɔːtʃnətlɪ] *adv* leider.

unfriendly [ʌnˈfrendlɪ] *adj* unfreundlich.

unfurnished [ˌʌnˈfɜːnɪʃt] adj unmöbliert.

ungrateful [ʌnˈɡreɪtfʊl] adj undankbar.

unhappy [ʌnˈhæpɪ] adj (sad) unglücklich; (not pleased) unzufrieden; **to be ~ about sthg** mit etw unzufrieden sein.

unharmed [ʌnˈhɑːmd] adj unverletzt.

unhealthy [ʌnˈhelθɪ] adj ungesund.

unhelpful [ˌʌnˈhelpfʊl] adj: **to be ~** (person) nicht hilfsbereit sein; (information) nicht hilfreich sein.

unhurt [ˌʌnˈhɜːt] adj unverletzt.

unhygienic [ˌʌnhaɪˈdʒiːnɪk] adj unhygienisch.

unification [ˌjuːnɪfɪˈkeɪʃn] n Vereinigung die.

uniform [ˈjuːnɪfɔːm] n Uniform die.

unimportant [ˌʌnɪmˈpɔːtənt] adj unwichtig.

unintelligent [ˌʌnɪnˈtelɪdʒənt] adj nicht intelligent.

unintentional [ˌʌnɪnˈtenʃənl] adj unbeabsichtigt.

uninterested [ˌʌnˈɪntrəstɪd] adj uninteressiert.

uninteresting [ˌʌnˈɪntrestɪŋ] adj uninteressant.

union [ˈjuːnjən] n (of workers) Gewerkschaft die.

Union Jack n: **the ~** der Union Jack (die britische Fahne).

unique [juːˈniːk] adj einmalig; **to be ~ to** beschränkt sein auf (+A).

unisex [ˈjuːnɪseks] adj Unisex-.

unit [ˈjuːnɪt] n Einheit die; (department) Abteilung die; (piece of furniture) Element das; (machine) Anlage die.

unite [juːˈnaɪt] ◆ vt vereinigen. ◆ vi sich zusammenlschließen.

United Kingdom [juːˈnaɪtɪd-] n: **the ~** das Vereinigte Königreich.

United Nations [juːˈnaɪtɪd-] npl: **the ~** die Vereinten Nationen pl.

United States (of America) [juːˈnaɪtɪd-] npl: **the ~** die Vereinigten Staaten pl (von Amerika).

unity [ˈjuːnətɪ] n Einigkeit die.

universal [ˌjuːnɪˈvɜːsl] adj allgemein.

universe [ˈjuːnɪvɜːs] n Universum das.

university [ˌjuːnɪˈvɜːsətɪ] n Universität die.

unjust [ˌʌnˈdʒʌst] adj ungerecht.

unkind [ʌnˈkaɪnd] adj (person) unfreundlich; (remark) häßlich.

unknown [ˌʌnˈnəʊn] adj unbekannt.

unleaded (petrol) [ˌʌnˈledɪd-] n Bleifrei das.

unless [ənˈles] conj es sei denn.

unlike [ˌʌnˈlaɪk] prep (different to) nicht ähnlich (+D); (in contrast to) im Gegensatz zu; **it's ~ him** es ist nicht typisch für ihn.

unlikely [ʌnˈlaɪklɪ] adj (not probable) unwahrscheinlich; **to be ~ to do sthg** etw wahrscheinlich nicht tun.

unlimited [ʌnˈlɪmɪtɪd] adj unbegrenzt; **~ mileage** unbegrenzte Meilenzahl.

unlisted [ʌnˈlɪstɪd] adj (Am: phone number): **to be ~** nicht im Telefonbuch stehen.

unload [ˌʌnˈləʊd] vt entladen.

unlock [ˌʌnˈlɒk] vt auflschließen.

unlucky [ʌnˈlʌkɪ] adj unglücklich.

unmarried [ˌʌnˈmærɪd] adj unverheiratet.

unnatural [ʌnˈnætʃrəl] adj unnatürlich.

unnecessary [ʌnˈnesəsərɪ] adj unnötig.

unobtainable [ˌʌnəbˈteɪnəbl] adj (product) nicht erhältlich; (phone number) nicht erreichbar.

unoccupied [ˌʌnˈɒkjʊpaɪd] adj (place, seat) frei.

unofficial [ˌʌnəˈfɪʃl] adj inoffiziell.

unpack [ˌʌnˈpæk] vt & vi auslpacken.

unpleasant [ʌnˈpleznt] adj unangenehm.

unplug [ʌnˈplʌɡ] vt den Stecker

herauslziehen von.

unpopular [ˌʌnˈpɒpjʊləʳ] *adj* unbeliebt.

unpredictable [ˌʌnprɪˈdɪktəbl] *adj* unberechenbar.

unprepared [ˌʌnprɪˈpeəd] *adj* unvorbereitet.

unprotected [ˌʌnprəˈtektɪd] *adj* ungeschützt.

unqualified [ˌʌnˈkwɒlɪfaɪd] *adj* (*person*) unqualifiziert.

unreal [ˌʌnˈrɪəl] *adj* unwirklich.

unreasonable [ʌnˈriːznəbl] *adj* unangemessen.

unrecognizable [ˌʌnrekəgˈnaɪzəbl] *adj* unkenntlich.

unreliable [ˌʌnrɪˈlaɪəbl] *adj* unzuverlässig.

unrest [ˌʌnˈrest] *n* Unruhen *pl*.

unroll [ˌʌnˈrəʊl] *vt* auflrollen.

unsafe [ˌʌnˈseɪf] *adj* unsicher.

unsatisfactory [ˌʌnsætɪsˈfæktərɪ] *adj* unbefriedigend.

unscrew [ˌʌnˈskruː] *vt* (*lid, top*) ablschrauben.

unsightly [ʌnˈsaɪtlɪ] *adj* unansehnlich.

unskilled [ʌnˈskɪld] *adj* (*worker*) ungelernt.

unsociable [ʌnˈsəʊʃəbl] *adj* ungesellig.

unsound [ˌʌnˈsaʊnd] *adj* (*building, structure*) nicht sicher; (*argument, method*) nicht stichhaltig.

unspoiled [ˌʌnˈspɔɪlt] *adj* (*place, beach*) unberührt.

unsteady [ˌʌnˈstedɪ] *adj* (*pile, person*) wackelig; (*structure*) unsicher; (*hand*) zitterig.

unstuck [ˌʌnˈstʌk] *adj*: **to come ~** (*label, poster etc*) sich lösen.

unsuccessful [ˌʌnsəkˈsesfʊl] *adj* erfolglos.

unsuitable [ˌʌnˈsuːtəbl] *adj* unpassend.

unsure [ˌʌnˈʃɔːʳ] *adj*: **to be ~ of sthg** sich (D) einer Sache (G) nicht sicher sein; **to be ~ about sb** sich (D) über jn nicht im klaren sein.

unsweetened [ʌnˈswiːtnd] *adj* ungesüßt.

untidy [ʌnˈtaɪdɪ] *adj* unordentlich.

untie [ˌʌnˈtaɪ] (*cont* **untying** [ˌʌnˈtaɪɪŋ]) *vt* (*person*) loslbinden; (*knot*) auflbinden.

until [ənˈtɪl] *prep & conj* bis; **~ the evening/end** bis zum Abend/Ende; **not ~** erst.

untrue [ˌʌnˈtruː] *adj* (*false*) unwahr; **to be ~** nicht wahr sein.

untrustworthy [ˌʌnˈtrʌstˌwɜːðɪ] *adj* nicht vertrauenswürdig.

unusual [ʌnˈjuːʒl] *adj* ungewöhnlich.

unusually [ʌnˈjuːʒəlɪ] *adv* ungewöhnlich.

unwell [ˌʌnˈwel] *adj* unwohl; **to feel ~** sich nicht wohl fühlen.

unwilling [ˌʌnˈwɪlɪŋ] *adj*: **to be ~ to do sthg** etw nicht tun wollen.

unwind [ˌʌnˈwaɪnd] (*pt & pp* **unwound** [ˌʌnwaʊnd]) ◆ *vt* ablwickeln. ◆ *vi* (*relax*) sich entspannen.

unwrap [ˌʌnˈræp] *vt* auslpacken.

unzip [ˌʌnˈzɪp] *vt*: **to ~ sthg** den Reißverschluß von etw auflmachen.

up [ʌp] ◆ *adv* **1.** (*towards higher position, level*) hoch; **we walked ~ to the top** wir sind zum Gipfel hoch gelaufen; **to pick sthg ~** etw auflheben; **prices are going ~** die Preise steigen. **2.** (*in higher position*) oben; **she's ~ in her bedroom** sie ist oben in ihrem Zimmer; **~ there** da oben. **3.** (*into upright position*): **to stand ~** auflstehen; **to sit ~** (*from lying position*) sich auflsetzen; (*sit straight*) sich gerade hinlsetzen. **4.** (*northwards*): **I'm coming ~ to Edinburgh** ich komme hoch nach Edinburgh. **5.** (*in phrases*): **to walk/jump ~ and down** auf und ab gehen/springen; **~ to six weeks/ten people** bis zu sechs Wochen/zehn Personen; **are you ~ to travelling?** bist du reisefähig?; **what are you ~ to?** was treibst du so?; **it's ~ to you** das liegt ganz bei dir; **~ until ten o'clock** bis um zehn Uhr. ◆ *prep* **1.** (*towards* *higher position*): **to walk ~ a hill** einen Hügel hinauf|gehen; **I went ~ the stairs** ich ging die Treppe hinauf. **2.** (*in higher position*): **~ a hill** oben auf einem Hügel. **3.** (*at end of*): **they live ~ the road from us** sie wohnen weiter oben in der gleichen Straße wie wir. ◆ *adj* **1.** (*out of bed*) auf; **I was ~ at six today** ich war heute um sechs auf. **2.** (*at an end*) um, zu Ende; **time's ~** die Zeit ist um. **3.** (*rising*): **the ~ escalator** die Rolltreppe nach oben. ◆ *n*: **~s and downs** Höhen und Tiefen.

update [ˌʌpˈdeɪt] *vt* auf den neusten Stand bringen.

uphill [ˌʌpˈhɪl] *adv* bergauf.

upholstery [ʌpˈhəʊlstərɪ] *n* Polsterung *die*.

upkeep [ˈʌpkiːp] *n* Instandhaltung *die*.

up-market *adj* anspruchsvoll.

upon [əˈpɒn] *prep* (*fml: on*) auf (+A,D); **~ hearing the news, we ...** als wir die Nachricht hörten ...

upper [ˈʌpər] ◆ *adj* obere(-r)(-s). ◆ *n* (*of shoe*) Obermaterial *das*.

upper class *n* Oberschicht *die*.

uppermost [ˈʌpəməʊst] *adj* (*highest*) oberste(-r)(-s).

upper sixth *n* (Br: SCH) ≃ dreizehnte Klasse.

upright [ˈʌpraɪt] *adj & adv* aufrecht.

upset [ʌpˈset] (*pt & pp inv*) ◆ *adj* (*distressed*) bestürzt. ◆ *vt* (*distress*) erschüttern; (*plans*) durcheinander|bringen; (*knock over*) um|stoßen; **to have an ~ stomach** sich (D) den Magen verdorben haben; **to be ~ about sthg** über etw (A) bestürzt sein; **to get ~ about sthg** sich über etw (A) aufregen.

upside down [ˌʌpsaɪd-] ◆ *adj* auf dem Kopf stehend. ◆ *adv* verkehrt herum.

upstairs [ˌʌpˈsteəz] ◆ *adj* im Obergeschoß. ◆ *adv* (*on a higher floor*) oben; **to go ~** nach oben gehen.

up-to-date *adj* (*modern*) modern; (*well-informed*) aktuell.

upwards [ˈʌpwədz] *adv* nach oben; **~ of 100 people** mehr als 100 Leute.

urban [ˈɜːbən] *adj* städtisch, Stadt-.

urban clearway [-ˈklɪəweɪ] *n* (Br) ≃ Stadtautobahn *die*.

Urdu [ˈʊəduː] *n* Urdu *das*.

urge [ɜːdʒ] *vt*: **to ~ sb to do sthg** jn drängen, etw zu tun.

urgent [ˈɜːdʒənt] *adj* dringend.

urgently [ˈɜːdʒəntlɪ] *adv* dringend.

urinal [ˌjʊəˈraɪnl] *n* (*fml*) (*place*) Pissoir *das*; (*bowl*) Urinal *das*.

urinate [ˈjʊərɪneɪt] *vi* (*fml*) urinieren.

urine [ˈjʊərɪn] *n* Urin *der*.

us [ʌs] *pron* uns; **they know ~** sie kennen uns; **it's ~** wir sind's; **send it to ~** schicke es uns; **tell ~** sage uns; **they're worse than ~** sie sind schlimmer als wir.

US *n* (*abbr of United States*): **the ~** die USA *pl*.

USA *n* (*abbr of United States of America*): **the ~** die USA *pl*.

usable [ˈjuːzəbl] *adj* brauchbar.

use [*n* juːs, *vb* juːz] ◆ *n* (*using*) Benutzung *die*; (*purpose*) Verwendung *die*. ◆ *vt* benutzen, verwenden; (*exploit*) aus|nutzen; (*run on*) brauchen; **to be of ~** nützlich sein; **to have the ~ of sthg** etw benutzen können; **to make ~ of sthg** Gebrauch machen von etw; (*opportunity*) etw aus|nutzen; **'out of ~'** 'außer Betrieb'; **to be in ~** in Gebrauch sein; **it's no ~** es hat keinen Zweck; **what's the ~?** wozu?; **to ~ sthg as sthg** etw als etw gebrauchen; **'~ before ...'** (*food, drink*) 'mindestens haltbar bis ...'▶ **use up** *vt sep* verbrauchen.

used [*adj* juːzd, *aux vb* juːst] ◆ *adj* (*towel, glass etc*) benutzt; (*car*) Gebraucht-. ◆ *aux vb*: **I ~ to live here** ich habe früher hier in der Nähe gewohnt; **I ~ to go there every day** ich bin früher jeden Tag dorthin gegangen; **to be ~ to sthg** an etw (A) gewöhnt sein; **to get ~ to sthg** sich an etw (A) gewöhnen.

useful ['juːsfʊl] *adj* nützlich.

useless ['juːslɪs] *adj* (*not useful*) nutzlos; (*pointless*) zwecklos; (*inf: very bad*): **to be** ~ zu nichts zu gebrauchen sein.

user ['juːzər] *n* Benutzer der (-in die).

usher ['ʌʃər] *n* (*at cinema, theatre*) Platzanweiser der.

usherette [,ʌʃə'ret] *n* Platzanweiserin die.

USSR *n*: **the (former)** ~ die (ehemalige) UdSSR.

usual ['juːʒəl] *adj* üblich; **as** ~ wie gewöhnlich.

usually ['juːʒəlɪ] *adv* normalerweise.

utensil [juː'tensl] *n* Gerät das.

utilize ['juːtəlaɪz] *vt* (*fml*) nutzen.

utmost ['ʌtməʊst] ◆ *adj* äußerste(-r) (-s). ◆ *n*: **to do one's** ~ sein möglichstes tun.

utter ['ʌtər] ◆ *adj* völlig. ◆ *vt* von sich geben.

utterly ['ʌtəlɪ] *adv* völlig.

U-turn *n* (*in vehicle*) Wenden das.

vacancy ['veɪkənsɪ] *n* (*job*) freie Stelle; **'vacancies'** 'Zimmer frei'; **'no vacancies'** 'belegt'.

vacant ['veɪkənt] *adj* (*room, seat*) frei; **'vacant'** (*toilet*) 'frei'.

vacate [və'keɪt] *vt* (*fml: room, house*) räumen.

vacation [və'keɪʃn] ◆ *n* (*Am: holiday*) Urlaub der. ◆ *vi* (*Am*) Urlaub machen; **to go on** ~ in Urlaub gehen.

vacationer [və'keɪʃənər] *n* (*Am*) Urlauber der (-in die).

vaccination [,væksɪ'neɪʃn] *n* Impfung die.

vaccine [Br 'væksiːn, Am væk'siːn] *n* Impfstoff der.

vacuum ['vækjʊəm] *vt* staublsaugen.

vacuum cleaner *n* Staubsauger der.

vague [veɪg] *adj* vage; (*shape, outline*) verschwommen; (*person*) geistesabwesend.

vain [veɪn] *adj* (*pej: conceited*) eitel; **in** ~ vergeblich.

Valentine card ['væləntaɪn-] *n* Karte die zum Valentinstag.

Valentine's Day ['væləntaɪnz-] *n* Valentinstag der.

valet ['væleɪ, 'vælɪt] *n* (*in hotel*) für den Reinigungsservice der Gäste zusiändiger Hotelangestellter.

valet service *n* (*in hotel, for car*) Reinigungsservice der.

valid ['vælɪd] *adj* (*ticket, passport*) gültig.

validate ['vælɪdeɪt] *vt* (*ticket*) bestätigen.

Valium® ['vælɪəm] *n* Valium das.

valley ['vælɪ] *n* Tal das.

valuable ['væljʊəbl] *adj* wertvoll. ► **valuables** *npl* Wertsachen *pl*.

value ['væljuː] *n* (*financial*) Wert der; (*usefulness*) Nutzen der; **a** ~ **pack** ≈ ein Sonderangebot; **to be good** ~ **(for money)** (das Geld) wert sein. ► **values** *npl* (*principles*) Werte *pl*.

valve [vælv] *n* Ventil das.

van [væn] *n* Lieferwagen der.

vandal ['vændl] *n* Rowdy der.

vandalize ['vændəlaɪz] *vt* mutwillig zerstören.

vanilla [və'nɪlə] *n* Vanille die.

vanish ['vænɪʃ] *vi* verschwinden.

vapor ['veɪpər] (*Am*) = **vapour**.

vapour ['veɪpər] *n* (*Br*) Dampf der.

variable ['veərɪəbl] *adj* unbeständig.

varicose veins ['værɪkəʊs-] *npl* Krampfadern *pl*.

varied ['veərɪd] *adj* unterschiedlich.

variety [və'raɪətɪ] *n* (*collection*)

Vielfalt die; (of products) Auswahl die; (type) Sorte die.

various ['veərɪəs] adj verschiedene(-r)(-s).

varnish ['vɑːnɪʃ] ◆ n (for wood) Lack der. ◆ vt (wood) lackieren.

vary ['veərɪ] vi & vt ändern; **to ~ from sthg to sthg** zwischen etw (D) und etw (D) schwanken; **'prices ~'** = 'unterschiedliche Preise'.

vase [Br vɑːz, Am veɪz] n Vase die.

Vaseline® ['væsəliːn] n Vaseline die.

vast [vɑːst] adj riesig.

vat [væt] n Bottich der.

VAT [væt, viːeɪ'tiː] n (abbr of value added tax) MwSt.

vault [vɔːlt] n (in bank) Tresorraum der; (in church) Gewölbe das.

VCR n (abbr of video cassette recorder) Videorekorder der.

VDU n (abbr of visual display unit) Bildschirmgerät das.

veal [viːl] n Kalbfleisch das.

veg [vedʒ] abbr = **vegetable**.

vegan ['viːgən] ◆ adj streng vegetarisch. ◆ n Veganer der (-in die).

vegetable ['vedʒtəbl] n Gemüse das.

vegetable oil n Pflanzenöl das.

vegetarian [,vedʒɪ'teərɪən] ◆ adj vegetarisch. ◆ n Vegetarier der (-in die).

vegetation [,vedʒɪ'teɪʃn] n Vegetation die.

vehicle ['viːəkl] n Fahrzeug das.

veil [veɪl] n Schleier der.

vein [veɪn] n Vene die.

Velcro® ['velkrəʊ] n Klettverschluß® der.

velvet ['velvɪt] n Samt der.

vending machine ['vendɪŋ-] n Automat der.

venetian blind [vɪ,niːʃn-] n Jalousie die.

venison ['venɪzn] n Wild das.

vent [vent] n (for air, smoke etc) Abzug der.

ventilation [,ventɪ'leɪʃn] n Belüftung die.

ventilator ['ventɪleɪtər] n (fan) Ventilator der.

venture ['ventʃər] ◆ n Unternehmung die. ◆ vi (go) sich wagen.

venue ['venjuː] n Veranstaltungsort der.

veranda [və'rændə] n Veranda die.

verb [vɜːb] n Verb das.

verdict ['vɜːdɪkt] n Urteil das.

verge [vɜːdʒ] n (of lawn, path) Rand der; (of road) Bankette die; **'soft ~s'** 'Bankette nicht befahrbar!'

verify ['verɪfaɪ] vt überprüfen.

vermin ['vɜːmɪn] n Ungeziefer das.

vermouth ['vɜːməθ] n Wermut der.

versa → **vice versa**.

versatile ['vɜːsətaɪl] adj (person) flexibel; (machine, food) vielseitig.

verse [vɜːs] n (of song, poem) Vers der; (poetry) Lyrik die.

version ['vɜːʃn] n Version die; (of book, film, play) Fassung die.

versus ['vɜːsəs] prep gegen.

vertical ['vɜːtɪkl] adj senkrecht.

vertigo ['vɜːtɪgəʊ] n Schwindel der.

very ['verɪ] ◆ adv sehr. ◆ adj genau; **~ much** sehr; **not ~** nicht sehr; **my ~ own room** mein eigenes Zimmer; **the ~ person** genau derjenige/diejenige.

vessel ['vesl] n (fml: ship) Schiff das.

vest [vest] n (Br: underwear) Unterhemd das; (Am: waistcoat) Weste die.

vet [vet] n (Br) Tierarzt der (-ärztin die).

veteran ['vetrən] n (of war) Veteran der.

veterinarian [,vetərɪ'neərɪən] (Am) = **vet**.

veterinary surgeon ['vetərɪnrɪ-] (Br: fml) = **vet**.

VHF n (abbr of very high frequency) UKW.

VHS n (abbr of video home system) VHS.

via ['vaɪə] prep (place) über (+A); (by means of) durch.

viaduct ['vaɪədʌkt] *n* Viadukt *der.*

vibrate [vaɪ'breɪt] *vi* vibrieren.

vibration [vaɪ'breɪʃn] *n* Vibration *die.*

vicar ['vɪkər] *n* Pfarrer *der.*

vicarage ['vɪkərɪdʒ] *n* Pfarrhaus *das.*

vice [vaɪs] *n* (*fault*) Laster *das.*

vice-president *n* Vizepräsident *der* (-in *die*).

vice versa [,vaɪsɪ'vɜːsə] *adv* umgekehrt.

vicinity [vɪ'sɪnətɪ] *n*: **in the ~** in der Nähe.

vicious ['vɪʃəs] *adj* (*attack, animal*) bösartig; (*comment*) boshaft.

victim ['vɪktɪm] *n* Opfer *das.*

Victorian [vɪk'tɔːrɪən] *adj* viktorianisch (*zweite Hälfte des 19. Jahrhunderts*).

victory ['vɪktərɪ] *n* Sieg *der.*

video ['vɪdɪəʊ] (*pl* -s) ◆ *n* (*recording, tape*) Video *das*; (*video recorder*) Videorecorder *der.* ◆ *vt* (*using video recorder*) auflnehmen; (*using camera*) (mit einer Videokamera) filmen; **on ~** auf Video.

video camera *n* Videokamera *die.*

video game *n* Videospiel *das.*

video recorder *n* Videorecorder *der.*

video shop *n* Videoverleih *der.*

videotape ['vɪdɪəʊteɪp] *n* Videokassette *die.*

Vienna ['vɪenə] *n* Wien *nt.*

Vietnam [Br ,vjet'næm, Am ,vjet-'nɑːm] *n* Vietnam *nt.*

view [vjuː] ◆ *n* (*scene*) Aussicht *die*; (*line of sight*) Sicht *die*; (*opinion*) Ansicht *die*; (*attitude*) Betrachtung *die.* ◆ *vt* (*look at*) betrachten; **in my ~** meiner Ansicht nach; **in ~ of** (*considering*) angesichts (+G); **to come into ~** in Sicht kommen.

viewer ['vjuːər] *n* (*of TV*) Zuschauer *der* (-in *die*).

viewfinder ['vjuː,faɪndər] *n* Sucher *der.*

viewpoint ['vjuːpɔɪnt] *n* (*opinion*) Standpunkt *der*; (*place*) Aussichtspunkt *der.*

vigilant ['vɪdʒɪlənt] *adj* (*fml*) wachsam.

villa ['vɪlə] *n* Villa *die.*

village ['vɪlɪdʒ] *n* Dorf *das.*

villager ['vɪlɪdʒər] *n* Dorfbewohner *der* (-in *die*).

villain ['vɪlən] *n* (*of book, film*) Bösewicht *der*; (*criminal*) Verbrecher *der.*

vinaigrette [,vɪnɪ'gret] *n* Vinaigrette *die.*

vine [vaɪn] *n* (*grapevine*) Rebe *die*; (*climbing plant*) Kletterpflanze *die.*

vinegar ['vɪnɪgər] *n* Essig *der.*

vineyard ['vɪnjəd] *n* Weinberg *der.*

vintage ['vɪntɪdʒ] ◆ *adj* (*wine*) erlesen. ◆ *n* (*year*) Jahrgang *der.*

vinyl ['vaɪnɪl] *n* PVC *das.*

viola [vɪ'əʊlə] *n* Bratsche *die.*

violence ['vaɪələns] *n* (*violent behaviour*) Gewalt *die.*

violent ['vaɪələnt] *adj* (*person, behaviour*) gewalttätig; (*storm, row*) heftig.

violet ['vaɪələt] ◆ *adj* violett. ◆ *n* (*flower*) Veilchen *das.*

violin [,vaɪə'lɪn] *n* Geige *die.*

VIP *n* (*abbr of very important person*) Prominente *der die.*

virgin ['vɜːdʒɪn] *n* Jungfrau *die.*

Virgo ['vɜːgəʊ] (*pl* -s) *n* Jungfrau *die.*

virtually ['vɜːtʃʊəlɪ] *adv* praktisch.

virtual reality ['vɜːtʃʊəl-] *n* virtuelle Realität.

virus ['vaɪrəs] *n* Virus *das.*

visa ['viːzə] *n* Visum *das.*

viscose ['vɪskəʊs] *n* Viskose *die.*

visibility [,vɪzɪ'bɪlətɪ] *n* Sicht *die.*

visible ['vɪzəbl] *adj* (*that can be seen*) sichtbar; (*noticeable*) offensichtlich.

visit ['vɪzɪt] ◆ *vt* besuchen. ◆ *n* Besuch *der.*

visiting hours ['vɪzɪtɪŋ-] *npl* Besuchszeit *die.*

visitor ['vɪzɪtər] *n* Besucher *der* (-in *die*).

visitor centre *n* (*at tourist attraction*)

Touristeninformation *die.*
visitors' book *n* Gästebuch *das.*
visitor's passport *n* (Br)
Reisepaß *der.*
visor ['vaɪzər] *n* (of hat) Schirm *der;*
(of helmet) Visier *das.*
vital ['vaɪtl] *adj* (essential) wesentlich.
vitamin [Br 'vɪtəmɪn, Am 'vaɪtəmɪn]
n Vitamin *das.*
vivid ['vɪvɪd] *adj* (colour) leuchtend;
(description, memory) lebhaft.
V-neck *n* (design) V-Ausschnitt *der.*
vocabulary [və'kæbjʊləri] *n*
Wortschatz *der.*
vocational [vəʊ'keɪʃənl] *adj* Berufs-.
vodka ['vɒdkə] *n* Wodka *der.*
voice [vɔɪs] *n* Stimme *die.*
voice mail *n* Voice mail *die;* **to
send/receive ~** eine Voice mail hin-
ter|lassen/erhalten.
volcano [vɒl'keɪnəʊ] (*pl* -es OR -s) *n*
Vulkan *der.*
volleyball ['vɒlɪbɔːl] *n* Volleyball
der.
volt [vəʊlt] *n* Volt *das.*
voltage ['vəʊltɪdʒ] *n* Spannung *die.*
volume ['vɒljuːm] *n* (sound level)
Lautstärke *die;* (space occupied)
Rauminhalt *der;* (amount) Menge *die;*
(book) Band *der.*
voluntary ['vɒləntri] *adj* freiwillig;
(work) ehrenamtlich.
volunteer [ˌvɒlən'tɪər] ◆ *n*
Freiwillige *der, die.* ◆ *vt:* **to ~ to do sthg**
sich an|bieten, etw zu tun.
vomit ['vɒmɪt] ◆ *n* Erbrochene *das.*
◆ *vi* sich übergeben.
vote [vəʊt] ◆ *n* (choice) Stimme *die;*
(process) Abstimmung *die;* (number of
votes) Stimmen *pl.* ◆ *vi:* **to ~ (for)**
wählen.
voter ['vəʊtər] *n* Wähler *der* (-in *die*).
voucher ['vaʊtʃər] *n* Gutschein *der.*
vowel ['vaʊəl] *n* Vokal *der.*
voyage ['vɔɪɪdʒ] *n* Reise *die.*
vulgar ['vʌlɡər] *adj* (rude) vulgär; (in
bad taste) ordinär.
vulture ['vʌltʃər] *n* Geier *der*

W (abbr of west) W.
wad [wɒd] *n* (of paper, banknotes)
Bündel *das;* (of cotton) Bausch *der.*
waddle ['wɒdl] *vi* watscheln.
wade [weɪd] *vi* waten.
wading pool ['weɪdɪŋ-] *n* (Am)
Planschbecken *das.*
wafer ['weɪfər] *n* (biscuit) Waffel
die.
waffle ['wɒfl] ◆ *n* (pancake) Waffel
die. ◆ *vi* (inf) schwafeln.
wag [wæɡ] *vt* wedeln mit.
wage [weɪdʒ] *n* Lohn *der.* ▶ **wages**
npl Lohn *der.*
wagon ['wæɡən] *n* (vehicle) Wagen
der; (Br: of train) Waggon *der.*
waist [weɪst] *n* Taille *die.*
waistcoat ['weɪskəʊt] *n* Weste
die.
wait [weɪt] ◆ *n* Wartezeit *die.* ◆ *vi*
warten; **I can't ~!** ich kann es nicht
erwarten! ▶ **wait for** *vt fus* warten
auf (+A); **to ~ for sb to do sthg** darauf
warten, daß jd etw tut.
waiter ['weɪtər] *n* Kellner *der;* **~!**
Herr Ober!
waiting room ['weɪtɪŋ-] *n* Warte-
raum *der;* (at doctor's) Wartezimmer
das.
waitress ['weɪtrɪs] *n* Bedienung
die.
wake [weɪk] (*pt* **woke**, *pp* **woken**)
◆ *vt* wecken. ◆ *vi* auflwachen.
▶ **wake up** *vt sep* auflwecken. ◆ *vi*
(wake) auflwachen.
Waldorf salad ['wɔːldɔːf-] *n*
Waldorfsalat *der.*
Wales [weɪlz] *n* Wales *nt.*
walk [wɔːk] ◆ *n* Spaziergang *der;*
(hike) Wanderung *die;* (path) Fußweg
der. ◆ *vi* zu Fuß gehen; (as hobby)
wandern. ◆ *vt* (distance) gehen; (dog)

Gassi gehen mit; **to go for a ~** spazieren|gehen; **it's a short ~** es ist ein kurzes Stück zu Fuß; **to take the dog for a ~** mit dem Hund Gassi gehen; 'walk' (Am) 'gehen', 'don't ~' (Am) 'warten'. ▶ **walk away** vi weglgehen. ▶ **walk in** vi rein|kommen/rein|gehen. ▶ **walk out** vi gehen.

walker ['wɔːkəʳ] n Spaziergänger der (-in die); (hiker) Wanderer der (Wanderin die).

walking boots ['wɔːkɪŋ-] npl Wanderschuhe pl.

walking stick ['wɔːkɪŋ-] n Spazierstock der.

Walkman® ['wɔːkmən] n Walkman der.

wall [wɔːl] n (inside) Wand die; (outside) Mauer die.

wallet ['wɒlɪt] n Brieftasche die.

wallpaper ['wɔːl,peɪpəʳ] n Tapete die.

wally ['wɒlɪ] n (Br: inf) Trottel der.

walnut ['wɔːlnʌt] n (nut) Walnuß die.

waltz [wɔːls] n Walzer der.

wander ['wɒndəʳ] vi herum|wandern.

want [wɒnt] vt wollen; (need) brauchen; **to ~ to do sthg** etw tun wollen; **to ~ sb to do sthg** wollen, daß jd etw tut.

war [wɔːʳ] n Krieg der.

ward [wɔːd] n (in hospital) Station die.

warden ['wɔːdn] n (of park) Aufseher der (-in die); (of youth hostel) Herbergsvater der (-mutter die).

wardrobe ['wɔːdrəʊb] n Kleiderschrank der.

warehouse ['weəhaʊs, pl -haʊzɪz] n Lagerhalle die.

warm [wɔːm] ◆ adj warm. ◆ vt wärmen. ▶ **warm up** vt sep auf|wärmen. ◆ vi (get warmer) wärmer werden; (do exercises) sich auf|wärmen; (machine, engine) warm|laufen.

war memorial n Kriegerdenkmal das.

warmth [wɔːmθ] n (heat) Wärme die.

warn [wɔːn] vt warnen; **to ~ sb about sthg** jn vor etw warnen; **to ~ sb not to do sthg** jn davor warnen, etw zu tun.

warning ['wɔːnɪŋ] n (of danger) Warnung die; (advance notice) Vorwarnung die.

warranty ['wɒrəntɪ] n (fml) Garantie die.

warship ['wɔːʃɪp] n Kriegsschiff das.

wart [wɔːt] n Warze die.

was [wɒz] pt → **be**.

wash [wɒʃ] ◆ vt waschen; (dishes) ablwaschen. ◆ vi sich waschen. ◆ n: **to give sthg a ~** etw waschen; **to have a ~** sich waschen; **to ~ one's hands** sich (D) die Hände waschen. ▶ **wash up** vi (Br: do washing-up) ablwaschen; (Am: clean oneself) sich waschen.

washable ['wɒʃəbl] adj waschbar.

washbasin ['wɒʃ,beɪsn] n Waschbecken das.

washbowl ['wɒʃbəʊl] n (Am) Waschbecken das.

washer ['wɒʃəʳ] n (ring) Dichtungsring der.

washing ['wɒʃɪŋ] n (activity) Waschen das; (clothes) Wäsche die.

washing line n Wäscheleine die.

washing machine n Waschmaschine die.

washing powder n Waschpulver das.

washing-up n (Br): **to do the ~** ablwaschen.

washing-up bowl n (Br) Abwaschschüssel die.

washing-up liquid n (Br) Geschirrspülmittel das.

washroom ['wɒʃrʊm] n (Am) Toilette die.

wasn't [wɒznt] = **was not**.

wasp [wɒsp] n Wespe die.

waste [weɪst] ◆ n (rubbish) Abfall der. ◆ vt verschwenden; **a ~ of money** eine Geldverschwendung; **a ~ of time** eine Zeitverschwendung.

wastebin ['weɪstbɪn] n Abfalleimer der.

waste ground n Ödland das.

wastepaper basket [ˌweɪst-'peɪpə-] n Papierkorb der.

watch [wɒtʃ] ◆ n (wristwatch) (Armband)uhr die. ◆ vt beobachten; (film) sich (D) anlsehen; (be careful with) achten auf (+A); **to ~ television** fernlsehen. ▶ **watch out** vi (be careful) **to ~ out for** (look for) Ausschau halten nach.

watchstrap ['wɒtʃstræp] n Uhrband das.

water ['wɔːtər] ◆ n Wasser das. ◆ vt (plants, garden) gießen. ◆ vi (eyes) tränen; **my mouth was ~ing** mir lief das Wasser im Mund zusammen.

water bottle n Wasserflasche die.

watercolour ['wɔːtəˌkʌlər] n (picture) Aquarell das.

watercress ['wɔːtəkres] n Brunnenkresse die.

waterfall ['wɔːtəfɔːl] n Wasserfall der.

watering can ['wɔːtərɪŋ-] n Gießkanne die.

watermelon ['wɔːtəˌmelən] n Wassermelone die.

waterproof ['wɔːtəpruːf] adj wasserdicht.

water purification tablets [-pjʊərɪfɪ'keɪʃn-] npl wasseraufbereitende Tabletten pl.

water skiing n Wasserskilaufen das.

watersports ['wɔːtəspɔːts] npl Wassersport der.

water tank n Wassertank der.

watertight ['wɔːtətaɪt] adj wasserdicht.

watt [wɒt] n Watt das; **a 60- ~ bulb** eine 60-Watt Glühbirne.

wave [weɪv] ◆ n Welle die. ◆ vt (hand) winken mit; (flag) schwenken. ◆ vi (move hand) winken.

wavelength ['weɪvleŋθ] n Wellenlänge die.

wavy ['weɪvɪ] adj (hair) gewellt.

wax [wæks] n Wachs das; (in ears) Schmalz das.

way [weɪ] n (manner) Art die; (method) Art und Weise die; (route, distance) Weg der; (direction) Richtung die; **which ~ is the station?** wie kommt man zum Bahnhof?; **the town is out of our ~** die Stadt liegt nicht auf unserem Weg; **to be in the ~** im Weg sein; **to be on the ~** auf dem Weg sein; **to get out of the ~** aus dem Weg gehen; **to get under ~** in Gang kommen; **a long ~** ein weiter Weg; **a long ~ away** weit entfernt; **to lose one's ~** sich verlaufen; (in car) sich verfahren; **on the ~ back** auf dem Rückweg; **on the ~ there** auf dem Hinweg; **that ~** (like that) so; (in that direction) dort entlang; **this ~** (like this) so; (in this direction) hier entlang; **'give ~'** 'Vorfahrt beachten'; **'~ in'** 'Eingang'; **'~ out'** 'Ausgang'; **no ~!** (inf) auf keinen Fall!

WC n (abbr of water closet) WC das.

we [wiː] pron wir.

weak [wiːk] adj schwach; (drink, soup) dünn.

weaken ['wiːkn] vt schwächen.

weakness ['wiːknɪs] n Schwäche die.

wealth [welθ] n Reichtum der.

wealthy ['welθɪ] adj reich.

weapon ['wepən] n Waffe die.

wear [weər] (pt wore, pp worn) ◆ vt tragen. ◆ n (clothes) Kleidung die; **~ and tear** Verschleiß der. ▶ **wear off** vi nachllassen. ▶ **wear out** vi sich ablnutzen.

weary ['wɪərɪ] adj müde.

weasel ['wiːzl] n Wiesel das.

weather ['weðər] n Wetter das; **what's the ~ like?** wie ist das Wetter?; **to be under the ~** (inf) nicht auf dem Posten sein.

weather forecast n Wettervorhersage die.

weather forecaster [-fɔːkɑːstər] n Meteorologe der (Meteorologin die).

weather report n Wetterbericht der.

weather vane [-veɪn] n Wetterfahne die.

weave [wi:v] (pt **wove**, pp **woven**) vt (material) weben; (basket) flechten.

web [web] n (of spider) Netz das.

Web site n Web-Seite die.

Wed. (abbr of Wednesday) Mi.

wedding ['wedɪŋ] n Hochzeit die.

wedding anniversary n Hochzeitstag der.

wedding cake n Hochzeitskuchen der.

wedding dress n Hochzeitskleid das.

wedding ring n Ehering der.

wedding reception n Hochzeitsfeier die.

wedge [wedʒ] n (of cake) Stück das; (of wood etc) Keil der.

Wednesday ['wenzdɪ] n Mittwoch der, → **Saturday**.

wee [wi:] ◆ adj (Scot) klein. ◆ n (inf) Pipi das.

weed [wi:d] n Unkraut das.

week [wi:k] n Woche die; **a ~ today** heute in einer Woche; **in a ~'s time** in einer Woche.

weekday ['wi:kdeɪ] n Wochentag der.

weekend [,wi:k'end] n Wochenende die.

weekly ['wi:klɪ] ◆ adj & adv wöchentlich. ◆ n Wochenzeitschrift die.

weep [wi:p] (pt & pp **wept**) vi weinen.

weigh [weɪ] vt wiegen; **how much does it ~?** wieviel wiegt es?

weight [weɪt] n Gewicht das; **to lose ~** ablnehmen; **to put on ~** zulnehmen. ▶ **weights** npl (for weight training) Hanteln pl.

weightlifting ['weɪt,lɪftɪŋ] n Gewichtheben das.

weight training n Hanteltraining das.

weir [wɪəʳ] n Wehr das.

weird [wɪəd] adj sonderbar.

welcome ['welkəm] ◆ adj willkommen. ◆ n Willkommen das. ◆ vt begrüßen. ◆ excl willkommen!; **to make sb feel ~** jn herzlich auflnehmen; **you're ~!** bitte, gern geschehen!; **to be ~ to do sthg** etw gerne tun können; **you're ~ to stay** Sie sind bei uns herzlich willkommen.

weld [weld] vt schweißen.

welfare ['welfeəʳ] n Wohl das; (Am: money) Sozialhilfe die.

well [wel] (compar **better**, superl **best**) ◆ adj (healthy) gesund. ◆ adv gut. ◆ n (for water) Brunnen der; **to get ~** gesund werden; **get ~ soon!** gute Besserung!; **to go ~** gutlgehen; **~ done!** gut gemacht!; **it may ~ happen** es kann durchaus passieren; **it's ~ worth it** es lohnt sich unbedingt; **as ~** (in addition) auch; **as ~ as** (in addition to) sowohl … als auch.

we'll [wi:l] = **we shall, we will**.

well-behaved [-bɪ'heɪvd] adj artig.

well-built adj: **to be ~** gut gebaut sein.

well-done adj (meat) gut durchgebraten.

well-dressed [-'drest] adj gutgekleidet.

wellington (boot) ['welɪŋtən-] n Gummistiefel der.

well-known adj bekannt.

well-off adj (rich) wohlhabend.

well-paid adj gutbezahlt.

welly ['welɪ] n (Br: inf) Gummistiefel der.

Welsh [welʃ] ◆ adj walisisch. ◆ n (language) Walisisch das. ◆ npl: **the ~** die Waliser pl.

Welshman ['welʃmən] (pl **-men** [-mən]) n Waliser der.

Welsh rarebit [-'reəbɪt] n Toast mit geschmolzenem Käse.

Welshwoman ['welʃ,wumən] (pl **-women** [-,wɪmɪn]) n Waliserin die.

went [went] pt → **go**.

wept [wept] *pt & pp* → **weep**.

were [wɜ:r] *pt* → **be**.

we're [wɪər] = **we are**.

weren't [wɜ:nt] = **were not**.

west [west] ◆ *n* Westen *der*. ◆ *adj* West-, westlich. ◆ *adv* (*fly, walk, be situated*) nach Westen; **in the ~ of England** im Westen Englands.

westbound ['westbaund] *adj* in Richtung Westen.

West Country *n*: **the ~** *der Südwesten Englands, mit den Grafschaften Cornwall, Devon und Somerset*.

West End *n*: **the ~** (*of London*) *Londoner Viertel mit Theatern und großen Kaufhäusern*.

western ['westən] ◆ *adj* westlich. ◆ *n* (*film*) Western *der*.

West Germany *n* Westdeutschland *nt*.

West Indies [-'ɪndi:z] *npl* Westindische Inseln *pl*.

Westminster ['westmɪnstər] *n* Westminster *nt* (*Sitz des britischen Parlaments*).

Westminster Abbey *n* die Abtei von Westminster.

westwards ['westwədz] *adv* westwärts.

wet [wet] (*pt & pp inv* OR **-ted**) ◆ *adj* naß; (*rainy*) regnerisch. ◆ *vt* naß machen; **to get ~** naß werden; '**~ paint**' 'frisch gestrichen'.

wet suit *n* Tauchanzug *der*; (*for surfing*) Surfanzug *der*.

we've [wi:v] = **we have**.

whale [weɪl] *n* Wal *der*.

wharf [wɔ:f] (*pl* **-s** OR **wharves** [wɔ:vz]) *n* Kai *der*.

what [wɒt] ◆ *adj* **1.** (*in questions*) welche(-r)(-s); **~ colour is it?** welche Farbe hat es?; **he asked me ~ colour it was** er fragte mich, welche Farbe es hatte. **2.** (*in exclamations*) was für; **~ a surprise!** was für eine Überraschung!; **~ a beautiful day!** was für ein schöner Tag! ◆ *pron* **1.** (*in questions*) was; **~ is going on?** was ist los?; **~ are they doing?** was tun sie da?; **~'s**

your name? wie heißt du?; **she asked me ~ happened** sie fragte mich, was passiert war; **~ is it for?** wofür ist das? **2.** (*introducing relative clause*) was; **I didn't see ~ happened** ich habe nicht gesehen, was passiert ist; **you can't have ~ you want** du kannst nicht das haben, was du willst. **3.** (*in phrases*): **~ for?** wozu?; **~ about going out for a meal?** wie wäre es mit Essen gehen? ◆ *excl* was!

whatever [wɒt'evər] *pron*: **take ~ you want** nimm, was du willst; **~ I do, I'll lose** was ich auch tue, ich verliere; **~ that may be** was auch immer das sein mag.

wheat [wi:t] *n* Weizen *der*.

wheel [wi:l] *n* Rad *das*; (*steering wheel*) Lenkrad *das*.

wheelbarrow ['wi:l,bærəu] *n* Schubkarre *die*.

wheelchair ['wi:l,tʃeər] *n* Rollstuhl *der*.

wheelclamp [,wi:l'klæmp] *n* Parkkralle *die*.

wheezy ['wi:zɪ] *adj* keuchend.

when [wen] ◆ *adv* (*in questions*) wann. ◆ *conj* (*specifying time*) wenn; (*in the past*) als; (*although, seeing as*) wo ... doch.

whenever [wen'evər] *conj* (immer)wenn; **~ you like** wann immer du willst.

where [weər] *adv & conj* wo; **~ do you come from?** woher kommst du?; **~ are you going?** wohin gehst du?

whereabouts ['weərəbauts] ◆ *adv* wo. ◆ *npl* Aufenthaltsort *der*.

whereas [weər'æz] *conj* während.

wherever [weər'evər] *conj* wo immer; (*from any place*) woher auch immer; (*to any place*) wohin auch immer; (*everywhere*) überall wo; **~ that may be** wo immer das sein mag.

whether ['weðər] *conj* ob.

which [wɪtʃ] ◆ *adj* (*in questions*) welche(-r)(-s); **~ room do you want?** welches Zimmer willst du?; **~ one?** welches?; **she asked me ~ room I**

wanted sie fragte mich, welches Zimmer ich wollte. ◆ *pron* 1. (*in questions: subject*) welche(-r)(-s); ~ **is the cheapest?** welches ist das billigste?; **he asked me ~ was the best** er fragte mich, welcher der Beste war. 2. (*in questions: object*) welche(-n)(-s); ~ **do you prefer?** welches gefällt dir besser?; **he asked me ~ I preferred** er fragte mich, welchen ich bevorzugte. 3. (*in questions: after prep* +A) welche(-n) (-s); ~ **should I put the vase on?** auf welchen soll ich die Vase stellen? 4. (*in questions: after prep* +D) welcher/welchem/welchem; **he asked me ~ I was talking about** er fragte mich, von welchem ich gesprochen hatte. 5. (*introducing relative clause: subject*) der/die/das, die (*pl*); **the house ~ is on the corner** das Haus, das an der Ecke steht. 6. (*introducing relative clause: object, after prep* +A) den/die/das, die (*pl*); **the television ~ I bought** der Fernseher, den ich gekauft habe. 7. (*introducing relative clause: after prep* +D) dem/der/dem, denen (*pl*); **the settee on ~ I'm sitting** das Sofa, auf dem ich sitze. 8. (*referring back*) was; **he's late, ~ annoys me** er ist spät dran, was mich ärgert; **he's always late, ~ I don't like** er verspätet sich immer, was ich nicht leiden kann.

whichever [wɪtʃ'evəʳ] ◆ *adj* (*any*) welche(-r)(-s); (*no matter which*) egal welche. ◆ *pron* welche(-r)(-s).

while [waɪl] ◆ *conj* während; (*although*) obgleich. ◆ *n*: **a ~** eine Weile; **for a ~** eine Weile; **in a ~** bald; **a short ~ ago** vor kurzem.

whim [wɪm] *n* Laune *die*.

whine [waɪn] *vi* (*make noise*) winseln; (*complain*) jammern.

whip [wɪp] ◆ *n* Peitsche *die*. ◆ *vt* peitschen.

whipped cream [wɪpt-] *n* Schlagsahne *die*, Schlagobers *das* (*Österr*).

whirlpool ['wɜːlpuːl] *n* (*Jacuzzi*) Whirlpool *der*.

whisk [wɪsk] ◆ *n* (*utensil*) Quirl *der*. ◆ *vt* (*eggs, cream*) schlagen.

whiskers ['wɪskəz] *npl* (*of person*) Backenbart *der*; (*of animal*) Schnurrhaar *das*.

whiskey ['wɪskɪ] (*pl* **-s**) *n* Whiskey *der*.

whisky ['wɪskɪ] *n* Whisky *der*.

whisper ['wɪspəʳ] *vt* & *vi* flüstern.

whistle ['wɪsl] ◆ *n* (*instrument*) Pfeife *die*; (*sound*) Pfiff *der*. ◆ *vi* pfeifen.

white [waɪt] ◆ *adj* weiß; (*coffee, tea*) mit Milch. ◆ *n* (*colour*) Weiß *das*; (*of egg*) Eiweiß *das*; (*person*) Weiße *der die*.

white bread *n* Weißbrot *das*.

White House *n*: **the ~** das Weiße Haus (*Amtssitz des US-Präsidenten*).

white sauce *n* Béchamelsoße *die*.

white spirit *n* Terpentinersatz *der*.

whitewash ['waɪtwɒʃ] *vt* tünchen.

white wine *n* Weißwein *der*.

whiting ['waɪtɪŋ] (*pl inv*) *n* Wittling *der*.

Whitsun ['wɪtsn] *n* Pfingsten *das*.

who [huː] *pron* (*in questions*) wer; (*accusative*) wen; (*dative*) wem; (*in relative clauses*) der/die/das, die (*pl*).

whoever [huː'evəʳ] *pron* (*whichever person*) wer immer; ~ **it is** wer es auch ist.

whole [həʊl] ◆ *adj* ganz. ◆ *n*: **the ~ of the money** das ganze Geld; **on the ~** im großen und ganzen.

wholefoods ['həʊfuːdz] *npl* Vollwertkost *die*.

wholemeal bread ['həʊlmiːl-] *n* (*Br*) Vollkornbrot *das*.

wholesale ['həʊlseɪl] *adv* (COMM) en gros.

wholewheat bread ['həʊl,wiːt-] (*Am*) = **wholemeal bread**.

whom [huːm] *pron* (*fml: in questions*) wen; (*dative*) wem; (*in relative clauses*) den/die/das, die (*pl*); (*dative*) dem/der/dem, denen (*pl*); **to ~** (*in questions*) wem; (*in relative clauses*) dem/der/dem, denen (*pl*).

whooping cough ['hu:pɪŋ-] *n*
Keuchhusten *der*.

whose [hu:z] ◆ *adj* (*in questions*)
wessen; (*in relative clauses*) dessen/
deren/dessen, deren (*pl*). ◆ *pron* (*in
questions*) wessen; **~ jumper is this?**
wessen Pullover ist das?; **the
woman ~ daughter I know** die Frau,
deren Tochter ich kenne; **~ is this?**
wem gehört das?

why [waɪ] *adv & conj* warum; **~ not?**
warum nicht?

wick [wɪk] *n* (*of candle, lighter*) Docht
der.

wicked ['wɪkɪd] *adj* (*evil*) böse,
schlecht; (*mischievous*) schelmisch.

wicker ['wɪkə*r*] *adj* Korb-.

wide [waɪd] ◆ *adj* breit; (*opening*)
weit; (*range, difference, gap*) groß.
◆ *adv*: **to open sthg ~** etw weit öffnen; **how ~ is the road?** wie breit ist
die Straße?; **it's 12 metres ~** er/sie/es
ist 12 Meter breit; **~ open** weit offen.

widely ['waɪdlɪ] *adv* weit.

widen ['waɪdn] ◆ *vt* verbreitern.
◆ *vi* (*gap, difference*) größer werden.

widespread ['waɪdspred] *adj*
weitverbreitet.

widow ['wɪdəʊ] *n* Witwe *die*.

widower ['wɪdəʊə*r*] *n* Witwer *der*.

width [wɪdθ] *n* Breite *die*.

wife [waɪf] (*pl* **wives**) *n* Ehefrau *die*.

wig [wɪg] *n* Perücke *die*.

wild [waɪld] *adj* wild; (*crazy*) verrückt; **to be ~ about** (*inf*) verrückt
sein auf (+A).

wild flower *n* wilde Blume.

wildlife ['waɪldlaɪf] *n* Tierwelt *die*.

will¹ [wɪl] *aux vb* **1.** (*expressing future
tense*) werden; **I ~ see you next week**
wir sehen uns nächste Woche; **~ you
be here next Friday?** wirst du nächsten Freitag hier sein?; **yes I ~** ja,
werde ich; **no I won't** nein, werde ich
nicht. **2.** (*expressing willingness*)
wollen, werden; **I won't do it** ich
werde das nicht tun; **no one ~ do it**
niemand will das machen.
3. (*expressing polite question*): **~ you**

have some more tea? möchten Sie
noch mehr Tee? **4.** (*in commands,
requests*): **~ you please be quiet!** sei
bitte ruhig!; **close that window, ~
you?** mach doch das Fenster zu,
bitte.

will² [wɪl] *n* (*document*) Testament
das; **against his ~** gegen seinen
Willen.

willing ['wɪlɪŋ] *adj*: **to be ~ (to do
sthg)** bereit sein (, etw zu tun).

willingly ['wɪlɪŋlɪ] *adv* bereitwillig,
gern.

willow ['wɪləʊ] *n* Weide *die*.

win [wɪn] (*pt & pp* **won**) ◆ *n* Sieg *der*.
◆ *vt* gewinnen. ◆ *vi* gewinnen; (*in
battle*) siegen; (*be ahead*) in Führung
liegen.

wind¹ [wɪnd] *n* Wind *der*; (*in stomach*)
Blähungen *pl*.

wind² [waɪnd] (*pt & pp* **wound**) ◆ *vi*
(*road, river*) sich winden. ◆ *vt*: **to ~
sthg round sthg** etw um etw wickeln.
▶ **wind up** *vt sep* (*Br: inf: annoy*) är-
gern; (*car window*) hoch|kurbeln;
(*clock, watch*) auf|ziehen.

windbreak ['wɪndbreɪk] *n* Wind-
schutz *der*.

windmill ['wɪndmɪl] *n* Windmühle
die.

window ['wɪndəʊ] *n* Fenster *das*.

window box *n* Blumenkasten *der*.

window cleaner *n* Fensterputzer
der (-in *die*).

windowpane ['wɪndəʊ,peɪn] *n*
Fensterscheibe *die*.

window seat *n* Fensterplatz *der*.

window-shopping *n* Schaufensterbummel *der*.

windowsill ['wɪndəʊsɪl] *n* Fen-
stersims *das*.

windscreen ['wɪndskri:n] *n* (*Br*)
Windschutzscheibe *die*.

windscreen wipers *npl* (*Br*)
Scheibenwischer *pl*.

windshield ['wɪndʃi:ld] (*Am*) =
windscreen.

Windsor Castle ['wɪnzə-] *n* Schloß
Windsor.

windsurfing ['wɪnd,sɜːfɪŋ] n Windsurfen das; **to go ~** windsurfen gehen.

windy ['wɪndɪ] adj windig.

wine [waɪn] n Wein der.

wine bar n (Br) Weinstube die.

wineglass ['waɪnglɑːs] n Weinglas das.

wine list n Weinkarte die.

wine tasting [-'teɪstɪŋ] n Weinprobe die.

wine waiter n Weinkellner der.

wing [wɪŋ] n Flügel der; (of plane) Tragfläche die; (Br: of car) Kotflügel der. ▶ **wings** npl: **the ~s** (in theatre) die Kulissen.

wink [wɪŋk] vi zwinkern.

winner ['wɪnər] n Gewinner der (-in die); (SPORT) Sieger der (-in die).

winning ['wɪnɪŋ] adj (person, team) siegreich; (ticket, number) Gewinn-.

winter ['wɪntər] n Winter der; **in (the) ~** im Winter.

wintertime ['wɪntətaɪm] n Winterzeit die.

wipe [waɪp] vt ablwischen; (floor) auflwischen; **to ~ one's feet** sich (D) die Füße abltreten; **to ~ one's hands** sich (D) die Hände ablwischen. ▶ **wipe up** vt sep (liquid, dirt) auflwischen. ◆ vi (dry the dishes) abltrocknen.

wiper ['waɪpər] n (AUT) Scheibenwischer der.

wire ['waɪər] ◆ n Draht der; (electrical wire) Kabel das. ◆ vt (plug) anlschließen.

wireless ['waɪəlɪs] n Radio das.

wiring ['waɪərɪŋ] n Leitungen pl.

wisdom tooth ['wɪzdəm-] n Weisheitszahn der.

wise [waɪz] adj weise.

wish [wɪʃ] ◆ n Wunsch der. ◆ vt wünschen; **best ~es** alles Gute; **to ~ for sthg** sich (D) etw wünschen; **to ~ to do sthg** (fml) etw zu tun wünschen; **to ~ sb luck/happy birthday** jm Glück/alles Gute zum Geburtstag wünschen; **if you ~** (fml) wenn Sie es wünschen.

witch [wɪtʃ] n Hexe die.

with [wɪð] prep **1.** (gen) mit; **come ~ me** komm mit mir; **a man ~ a beard** ein Mann mit Bart; **a room ~ a bathroom** ein Zimmer mit Bad; **he hit me ~ a stick** er hat mich mit einem Stock geschlagen; **be careful ~ that!** sei vorsichtig damit!; **to argue ~ sb** mit jm streiten; **topped ~ cream** mit Sahne. **2.** (at house of) bei; **we stayed ~ friends** wir haben bei Freunden übernachtet. **3.** (indicating emotion) vor (+ D); **to tremble ~ fear** vor Angst zittern.

withdraw [wɪð'drɔː] (pt -drew, pp -drawn) ◆ vt (take out) herauslnehmen; (money) ablheben. ◆ vi (from race, contest) zurücklziehen.

withdrawal [wɪð'drɔːəl] n (from bank account) Abhebung die.

withdrawn [wɪð'drɔːn] pp → **withdraw**.

withdrew [wɪð'druː] pt → **withdraw**.

wither ['wɪðər] vi verwelken.

within [wɪ'ðɪn] ◆ prep innerhalb (+G). ◆ adv innen; **~ walking distance** zu Fuß erreichbar; **~ the next week** innerhalb der nächsten Woche; **~ 10 miles** im Umkreis von 10 Meilen.

without [wɪð'aʊt] prep ohne; **~ doing sthg** ohne etw zu tun.

withstand [wɪð'stænd] (pt & pp -stood) vt standlhalten (+D).

witness ['wɪtnɪs] ◆ n Zeuge der (Zeugin die). ◆ vt (see) Zeuge sein (+G).

witty ['wɪtɪ] adj geistreich.

wives [waɪvz] pl → **wife**.

wobbly ['wɒblɪ] adj wackelig.

wok [wɒk] n Wok der.

woke [wəʊk] pt → **wake**.

woken ['wəʊkn] pp → **wake**.

wolf [wʊlf] (pl **wolves** [wʊlvz]) n Wolf der.

woman ['wʊmən] (pl **women**) n Frau die.

womb [wuːm] n Gebärmutter die.

women ['wɪmɪn] pl → **woman**.

won [wʌn] pt & pp → **win**.

wonder ['wʌndər] ♦ vi (ask oneself) sich fragen. ♦ n (amazement) Staunen das, Verwunderung die; **I ~ if I could ask you a favour?** könnte ich Sie/dich vielleicht um einen Gefallen bitten?

wonderful ['wʌndəful] adj wunderbar.

won't [wəunt] = **will not**.

wood [wud] n Holz das; (small forest) Wald der.

wooden ['wudn] adj Holz-, hölzern.

woodland ['wudlənd] n Waldung die.

woodpecker ['wud,pekər] n Specht der.

woodwork ['wudwɜːk] n (SCH) Werkunterricht der.

wool [wul] n Wolle die.

woolen ['wulən] (Am) = **woollen**.

woollen ['wulən] adj (Br) Woll-.

woolly ['wulɪ] adj wollen.

wooly ['wulɪ] (Am) = **woolly**.

Worcester sauce ['wustə-] n Worcestersoße die.

word [wɜːd] n Wort das; **in other ~s** mit anderen Worten; **to have a ~ with sb** mit jm sprechen.

wording ['wɜːdɪŋ] n Wortlaut der.

word processing [-'prəusesɪŋ] n Textverarbeitung die.

word processor [-'prəusesər] n Textverarbeitungssystem das.

wore [wɔːr] pt → **wear**.

work [wɜːk] ♦ n Arbeit die; (painting, novel etc) Werk das. ♦ vi arbeiten; (operate) funktionieren; (have desired effect) klappen; (take effect) wirken. ♦ vt (machine, controls) bedienen; **out of ~** arbeitslos; **to be at ~** (at workplace) in der Arbeit sein; (working) arbeiten; **to be off ~** nicht arbeiten; **the ~s** (inf: everything) alles; **how does it ~?** wie funktioniert das?, wie geht das?; **it's not ~ing** es funktioniert nicht, es geht nicht. ▶ **work out** vt sep (price, total) auslrechnen; (solution) herauslfinden; (method, plan) auslarbeiten. ♦ vi (result) laufen; (be successful) klappen; (do exercise) trainieren; **it ~s out at £20 each** (bill, total) es kommt für jeden auf 20 Pfund.

worker ['wɜːkər] n Arbeiter der (-in die).

working class ['wɜːkɪŋ-] n: **the ~** die Arbeiterklasse.

working hours ['wɜːkɪŋ-] npl Arbeitszeit die.

workman ['wɜːkmən] (pl -men [-mən]) n Handwerker der.

work of art n Kunstwerk das.

workout ['wɜːkaut] n Fitneßtraining das.

work permit n Arbeitserlaubnis die.

workplace ['wɜːkpleɪs] n Arbeitsplatz der.

workshop ['wɜːkʃɒp] n (for repairs) Werkstatt die.

work surface n Arbeitsfläche die.

world [wɜːld] ♦ n Welt die. ♦ adj Welt-.

worldwide [,wɜːld'waɪd] adv weltweit.

World Wide Web n: **the ~** das World Wide Web.

worm [wɜːm] n Wurm der.

worn [wɔːn] ♦ pp → **wear**. ♦ adj (clothes) abgetragen; (carpet) abgenutzt.

worn-out adj (clothes, shoes etc) abgetragen; (tired) erschöpft.

worried ['wʌrɪd] adj besorgt.

worry ['wʌrɪ] ♦ n Sorge die. ♦ vt beunruhigen. ♦ vi: **to ~ (about)** sich (D) Sorgen machen (über (+A).

worrying ['wʌrɪɪŋ] adj beunruhigend.

worse [wɜːs] adj & adv schlechter, schlimmer; **to get ~** schlechter werden; **he's getting ~** (more ill) es geht ihm schlechter; **to be ~ off** (in worse position) schlechter dran sein; (poorer) schlechter dalstehen.

worsen ['wɜːsn] vi sich verschlechtern.

worship ['wɜːʃɪp] ◆ n (church service) Gottesdienst der. ◆ vt (god) preisen; (fig: person) anbeten.

worst [wɜːst] ◆ adj schlechteste(-r) (-s), schlimmste(-r)(-s). ◆ adv am schlechtesten, am schlimmsten. ◆ n: **the ~** der/die/das Schlechteste, der/die/das Schlimmste.

worth [wɜːθ] prep: **how much is it ~?** wieviel ist das wert?; **it's ~ £50** es ist 50 Pfund wert; **it's ~ seeing** es ist sehenswert; **it's not ~ it** es lohnt sich nicht; **£50 ~ of traveller's cheques** Reiseschecks im Wert von 50 Pfund.

worthless ['wɜːθlɪs] adj wertlos.

worthwhile [ˌwɜːθ'waɪl] adj lohnenswert.

worthy ['wɜːðɪ] adj (winner, cause) würdig; **to be ~ of sthg** etw verdienen.

would [wʊd] aux vb 1. (in reported speech): **she said she ~ come** sie sagte, sie würde kommen. 2. (indicating condition): **what ~ you do?** was würdest du tun?; **what ~ you have done?** was hättest du getan?; **I ~ be most grateful** ich wäre äußerst dankbar. 3. (indicating willingness): **she ~n't go** sie wollte einfach nicht gehen; **he ~ do anything for her** er würde alles für sie tun. 4. (in polite questions): **~ you like a drink?** möchtest du etwas trinken?; **~ you mind closing the window?** könntest du das Fenster zu machen? 5. (indicating inevitability): **he ~ say that** er mußte das sagen. 6. (giving advice): **I ~ report it if I were you** ich würde es melden, wenn ich du wäre. 7. (expressing opinions): **I ~ prefer coffee** ich hätte lieber Kaffee; **I ~ prefer to go by bus** ich würde lieber mit dem Bus fahren; **I ~ have thought (that)** ... ich hätte gedacht, (daß) ...

wound[1] [wuːnd] ◆ n Wunde die. ◆ vt verwunden.

wound[2] [waʊnd] pt & pp → **wind**[2].

wove [wəʊv] pt → **weave**.

woven ['wəʊvn] pp → **weave**.

wrap [ræp] vt (package) einwickeln; **to ~ sthg round sthg** etw um etw wickeln. ► **wrap up** vt sep (package) einwickeln. ◆ vi (dress warmly) sich warm einpacken.

wrapper ['ræpəʳ] n Hülle die; (for sweets) Bonbonpapier das.

wrapping ['ræpɪŋ] n (material) Verpackung die.

wrapping paper n Geschenkpapier das.

wreath [riːθ] n Kranz der.

wreck [rek] ◆ n Wrack das. ◆ vt (destroy) kaputtmachen; (spoil) ruinieren; **to be ~ed** (ship) schiffbrüchig sein.

wreckage ['rekɪdʒ] n Trümmer pl.

wrench [rentʃ] n (Br: monkey wrench) Engländer der; (Am: spanner) Schraubenschlüssel der.

wrestler ['resləʳ] n Ringer der (-in die).

wrestling ['reslɪŋ] n Ringen das.

wretched ['retʃɪd] adj (miserable) unglücklich; (very bad) erbärmlich.

wring [rɪŋ] (pt & pp **wrung**) vt (clothes, cloth) auswringen.

wrinkle ['rɪŋkl] n Falte die.

wrist [rɪst] n Handgelenk das.

wristwatch ['rɪstwɒtʃ] n Armbanduhr die.

write [raɪt] (pt **wrote**, pp **written**) ◆ vt schreiben; (Am: send letter to) schreiben (+D). ◆ vi schreiben; **to ~ to sb** (Br) jm schreiben. ► **write back** vi zurückschreiben. ► **write down** vt sep aufschreiben. ► **write off** vt sep (Br: inf: car) zu Schrott fahren. ◆ vi: **to ~ off for sthg** etw bestellen. ► **write out** vt sep (list) aufstellen; (essay) ins reine schreiben; (cheque, receipt) ausstellen.

write-off n (vehicle) Totalschaden der.

writer ['raɪtəʳ] n (author) Schriftsteller der (-in die).

writing ['raɪtɪŋ] n (handwriting) Schrift die; (activity, words) Schreiben das.

writing desk n Schreibtisch der.

writing pad n Schreibblock der.

writing paper n Schreibpapier das.

written ['rɪtn] ◆ pp → **write**. ◆ adj (exam, notice) schriftlich.

wrong [rɒŋ] ◆ adj falsch; (bad, immoral) unrecht. ◆ adv falsch; **what's ~?** was ist los?; **something's ~ with the car** mit dem Auto stimmt etwas nicht; **to be in the ~** im Unrecht sein; **to get sthg ~** etw falsch machen; **to go ~** (machine) kaputt|gehen; '**~ way'** (Am) Schild, das anzeigt, daß man nicht in eine Straße einbiegen darf.

wrongly ['rɒŋlɪ] adv fälschlicherweise.

wrong number n: you've got the ~ Sie sind falsch verbunden.

wrote [rəʊt] pt → **write**.

wrought iron [rɔːt-] n Schmiedeeisen das.

wrung [rʌŋ] pt & pp → **wring**.

xing (Am: abbr of crossing): '**ped ~'** Schild für einen Fußgängerüberweg.

XL (abbr of extra-large) XL.

Xmas ['eksməs] n (inf) Weihnachten das.

X-ray ◆ n (picture) Röntgenbild das. ◆ vt röntgen; **to have an ~** sich röntgen lassen.

yacht [jɒt] n (for pleasure) Jacht die; (for racing) Segelboot das.

yard [jɑːd] n (unit of measurement) = 91,44 cm, Yard das; (enclosed area) Hof der; (Am: behind house) Hinterhof der.

yard sale n (Am) Verkauf von gebrauchten Gegenständen vor einem Haus.

yarn [jɑːn] n (thread) Garn das.

yawn [jɔːn] vi (person) gähnen.

yd abbr = **yard**.

yeah [jeə] adv (inf) ja.

year [jɪəʳ] n Jahr das; (at school, of wine) Jahrgang der; **next ~** nächstes Jahr; **this ~** dieses Jahr; **I'm 15 ~s old** ich bin 15 Jahre alt; **I haven't seen her for ~s** (inf) ich hab' sie seit Jahren nicht mehr gesehen; **which ~ are you in?** (at school) in welche Klasse gehst du?

yearly ['jɪəlɪ] adj jährlich; (every year) Jahres-.

yeast [jiːst] n Hefe die.

yell [jel] vi schreien.

yellow ['jeləʊ] ◆ adj gelb. ◆ n Gelb das.

yellow lines npl gelbe Linie am Straßenrand, die Parkverbot anzeigt.

Yellow Pages® n: **the ~** die gelben Seiten pl.

yes [jes] adv ja; (contradicting) doch.

yesterday ['jestədɪ] ◆ n Gestern das. ◆ adv gestern; **the day before ~** vorgestern; **~ afternoon** gestern nachmittag; **~ morning** gestern morgen.

yet [jet] ◆ adv noch; (in questions) schon. ◆ conj doch; **not ~** noch nicht; **I've ~ to do it** ich muß es noch tun; **~ again** schon wieder; **~ another delay** noch eine Verspätung; **are you ready ~?** bist du schon fertig?

yew [juː] n Eibe die.

yield [jiːld] ◆ vt (profit, interest) ab|werfen. ◆ vi (break, give way) nach|geben; '**yield'** (Am: AUT) 'Vorfahrt beachten'.

YMCA n CVJM.

yob [jɒb] n (Br: inf) Rowdy der.

yoga ['jəʊgə] n Yoga der.

yoghurt ['jɒgət] n Joghurt der.

yolk [jəʊk] n Dotter der, Eigelb das.

York Minster [jɔːkˈmɪnstəʳ] n die

Kathedrale von York.

Yorkshire pudding ['jɔːkʃə-] *n* *souffléartige kleine Pfannkuchen, die zu Roastbeef gegessen werden.*

you [juː] *pron* **1.** (*subject: singular*) du; (*plural*) ihr; (*polite form*) Sie; **~ Germans** ihr Deutschen. **2.** (*direct object, after prep +A: singular*) dich; (*plural*) euch; (*polite form*) Sie; **I hate ~!** ich hasse dich/Sie/euch!; **I did it for ~** ich habe es für dich/Sie/euch getan. **3.** (*indirect object, after prep +D: singular*) dir; (*plural*) euch; (*polite form*) Ihnen; **I told ~** ich habe es dir/Ihnen/euch gesagt; **after ~!** nach Ihnen! **4.** (*indefinite use: subject*) man; (*object*) einen; **~ never know** man kann nie wissen.

young [jʌŋ] ♦ *adj* jung. ♦ *npl*: **the ~** die Jugend.

younger ['jʌŋgər] *adj* jüngere(-r) (-s).

youngest ['jʌŋgəst] *adj* jüngste(-r) (-s).

youngster ['jʌŋstər] *n* Jugendliche *der die*; (*child*) Kleine *der die*.

your [jɔːr] *adj* **1.** (*singular subject*) dein/deine, deine (*pl*); (*plural subject*) euer/eure, eure (*pl*); (*polite form*) Ihr/Ihre, Ihre (*pl*); **~ dog** dein/euer/Ihr Hund; **~ house** dein/euer/Ihr Haus; **~ children** deine/eure/Ihre Kinder. **2.** (*indefinite subject*): **it's good for ~ teeth** es ist gut für die Zähne.

yours [jɔːz] *pron* (*singular subject*) dein/deine/deines, deine (*pl*); (*plural subject*) euer/eure/eures, eure (*pl*); (*polite form*) Ihr/Ihre/Ihres, Ihre (*pl*); **a friend of ~** ein Freund von dir.

yourself [jɔːˈself] (*pl* **-selves**) *pron* (*reflexive, after prep +A: singular*) dich; (*reflexive, after prep +D: singular*) dir; (*plural*) euch; (*polite form*) sich; **did you do it ~?** hast du/haben Sie das selbst gemacht?; **did you do it**

yourselves? habt ihr das selbst gemacht?

youth [juːθ] *n* Jugend *die*; (*young man*) Jugendliche *der*.

youth club *n* Jugendklub *der*.

youth hostel *n* Jugendherberge *die*.

Yugoslavia [ˌjuːgəˈslɑːvɪə] *n* Jugoslawien *nt*.

yuppie ['jʌpɪ] *n* Yuppie *der*.

YWCA *n* CVJF.

Z

zebra [*Br* 'zebrə, *Am* 'ziːbrə] *n* Zebra *das*.

zebra crossing *n* (*Br*) Zebrastreifen *der*.

zero ['zɪərəʊ] (*pl* **-es**) *n* Null *die*; **five degrees below ~** fünf Grad unter Null.

zest [zest] *n* (*of lemon, orange*) Schale *die*.

zigzag ['zɪgzæg] *vi* im Zickzack laufen.

zinc [zɪŋk] *n* Zink *das*.

zip [zɪp] ♦ *n* (*Br*) Reißverschluß *der*. ♦ *vt* den Reißverschluß zulziehen an (+D). ► **zip up** *vt sep* den Reißverschluß zulziehen an (+D).

zip code *n* (*Am*) Postleitzahl *die*.

zipper ['zɪpər] *n* (*Am*) Reißverschluß *der*.

zit [zɪt] *n* (*inf*) Pickel *der*.

zodiac ['zəʊdɪæk] *n* Tierkreis *der*.

zone [zəʊn] *n* Zone *die*.

zoo [zuː] (*pl* **-s**) *n* Zoo *der*.

zoom (lens) [zuːm-] *n* Zoom *das*.

zucchini [zuːˈkiːnɪ] (*pl inv*) *n* (*Am*) Zucchini *die*.